THE *ALS* GUIDE TO AUSTRALIAN WRITERS

Martin Duwell is a Senior Lecturer in the English Department of the University of Queensland where he has taught Australian Literature, Rhetoric and Old Icelandic. He was, for many years, the owner and editor of the poetry publisher Makar Press, and has written extensively on Australian poetry. He has been assistant editor of *A.L.S.* since 1982.

Marianne Ehrhardt has recently retired as a Senior Librarian at the University of Queensland. She previously worked in various English public libraries. She was a compiler and joint compiler of the *A.L.S.* Annual Bibliography for more than ten years, from volumes 5-12, and is the author of several other bibliographies.

Carol Hetherington is currently a Research Assistant in the Department of English at the University of Queensland. She has been associated with the compilation of the *A.L.S.* Annual Bibliography since 1987 (as well as in 1973-4). Carol Hetherington has worked as a librarian in the Fryer Library, and was co-editor of its Hayes Collection catalogue.

UQP STUDIES IN AUSTRALIAN LITERATURE

General Editor: Anthony J. Hassall
                     James Cook University of North Queensland

Advisory Editors: Bruce Bennett
                     Australian Defence Force Academy

                     Jennifer Strauss
                     Monash University

Also in this series:

Adam Shoemaker, *Black Words, White Page: Aboriginal Literature 1929-1988*

J.J. Healy, *Literature and the Aborigine in Australia*

David Brooks and Brenda Walker (eds), *Poetry and Gender: Statements and Essays in Australian Women's Poetry and Poetics*

Anthony J. Hassall, *Strange Country: A Study of Randolph Stow*

Cliff Hanna, *The Folly of Spring: A Study of John Shaw Neilson's Poetry*

Philip Neilsen, *Imagined Lives: A Study of David Malouf*

Livio Dobrez, *Parnassus Mad Ward: Michael Dransfield and the New Australian Poetry*

Shirley Walker, *Flame and Shadow: A Study of Judith Wright's Poetry*

Julian Croft, *The Life and Opinions of Tom Collins: A Study of the Works of Joseph Furphy*

Carole Ferrier (ed.), *Gender, Politics and Fiction: Twentieth Century Australian Women's Novels*

Elaine Barry, *Fabricating the Self: The Fictions of Jessica Anderson*

Jennifer Strauss, *Boundary Conditions: The Poetry of Gwen Harwood*

Martin Duwell and Laurie Hergenhan (eds), *The ALS Guide to Australian Writers: A Bibliography 1963-1990*

Laurie Hergenhan, *Unnatural Lives: Studies in Australian Convict Fiction*

Ken Gelder, *Atomic Fiction: The Novels of David Ireland*

Paul Salzman, *Helplessly Tangled in Female Arms and Legs: Elizabeth Jolley's Fictions*

Anthony J. Hassall, *Dancing on Hot Macadam*

Michael Ackland, *That Shining Band: A Study of Australian Colonial Verse Tradition*

Ken Stewart (ed.), *The 1890s: Australian Literature and Literary Culture*

In preparation:

Philip Mead (ed.), *Kenneth Slessor: Critical Essays*

David Brooks (ed.), *A.D. Hope: Critical Essays*

Fiona Giles, *Nineteenth Century Australian Women's Romance*

Annette Stewart, *Barbara Hanrahan*

Catherine Pratt, *Henry Handel Richardson*

Bruce Bennett, *Australian Short Fiction*

Dennis Haskell, *Bruce Dawe*

Margaret Harris (ed.), *Christina Stead*

THE *ALS* GUIDE TO AUSTRALIAN WRITERS

A BIBLIOGRAPHY 1963–1995

SECOND EDITION
Edited by
Martin Duwell
Marianne Ehrhardt
Carol Hetherington

University of Queensland Press

First published 1992 by University of Queensland Press
Box 42, St Lucia, Queensland 4067 Australia
Second edition 1997

The typeset text for this book was supplied by the editors in camera-ready form.
Printed in Australia by McPherson's Printing Group.

Distributed in the USA and Canada by
International Specialized Book Services, Inc.,
5804 N.E. Hassalo Street, Portland, Oregon 97213–3640

Cataloguing in Publication Data
National Library of Australia

The ALS guide to Australian writers : a bibliography 1963–1995.
2nd ed.

1. Australian literature — Bio-bibliography — Dictionaries.
2. Authors, Australian — 20th century — Biography —
Dictionaries. I. Duwell, Martin, 1948–   . II. Ehrhardt,
Marianne. III. Hetherington, Carol, 1945–   . IV. Title:
Australian literary studies guide to Australian writers.
(Series : Studies in Australian literature (St. Lucia,
Qld.)).

A820.9003

ISBN 0 7022 2969 5

Contents

Introduction   *vii*
Introduction to the second edition   *xi*
Acknowledgments   *xiii*
Abbreviations   *xiv*

A   Abdullah — Auchterlonie   *1*
B   Bail — Buzo   *13*
C   Cambridge — Cusack   *45*
D   D'Alpuget — Dyson   *74*
E   Eldershaw — Ewers   *98*
F   Facey — Furphy   *103*
G   Garner — Gunn   *120*
H   Hackston — Huxley   *137*
I   Idriess — Ireland   *190*
J   James — Jury   *194*
K   Kalamaras — Koch   *208*
L   Lambert — Lurie   *229*
M   McAuley — Murray   *258*
N   Neild — Nowra   *314*
O   Oakley — Pi O.   *320*
P   Page — Prichard   *327*
R   Richardson — Rudd   *355*
S   Sacchi — Stow   *370*
T   Taylor — Turner   *414*
U   Unaipon — Upfield   *426*
V   Vidal   *427*
W   Walch — Wrightson   *428*
Z   Zwicky   *488*

Introduction

This *Guide* cumulates, in the sense of collecting and integrating under individual authors, material from the series of 'Annual Bibliographies of Studies in Australian Literature', compiled by various people and published in *Australian Literary Studies* between 1964 and 1991. In this way information built up over many years is now made readily accessible. It has also been revised, and corrections and additions have been made. The material relating to each author has been arranged under the headings (where appropriate) of 'collections', 'fiction', 'drama', 'poetry', 'non-fiction' and 'critical material' (bibliographies, where available, appear at the beginning of this section).

The *A.L.S.* Annual Bibliography, though necessarily selective, is the most comprehensive printed guide to commentary about contemporary Australian writers. It contains critical, biographical, historical, bibliographical material, and includes articles, reviews and interviews. As well as listing commentary on selected Australian authors, this *Guide* - like the Annual Bibliography on which it is based - offers a listing, along with selected reviews, of the primary works of those authors published between 1963 and 1990. Hence the cumulation is the most comprehensive listing of its kind for the period 1963-1990, a period which has seen both the rise of academic study of Australian literature and a proliferation of non-academic commentaries. Both these developments are linked with the more widespread recognition of both the extent and the value of Australian literature and culture. This recognition owes a great deal to such institutional changes as the expansion of Universities and the work of the Literature Board of the Australia Council (growing out of the Commonwealth Literature Fund) and to an increased readership which in turn contributed to more publications.

The general and basis for this *Guide*'s selection of authors is that they should have attracted substantial critical discussion, for this is primarily a bibliography of commentary about writers, and it was originally devised as such in order to fill a need: to facilitate the study of Australian literature. The selection criterion has always been interpreted as generously as possible, the aim being to add as many emerging writers as space permits. The *Guide*, then, reflects changing critical values and tastes rather than imposing them. Hence it does not aim at finality or 'completeness'; rather it is part of an on-going process, like the Annual Bibliographies on which it is based. New material, some of it retrospective, is added as it becomes available, if not always as soon as we would like. In this way 'new' authors and overlooked material are added. We hope that future cumulations will follow on from this one.

Other literary bibliographies are largely complementary to this one. For instance, the annual *Australian National Bibliography* aims at a complete listing of books only (not articles etc) by and about Australian authors; *AustLit* (published by the Australian Defence Force Academy) is, on the other hand, a database which aims to list all material - articles, reviews, newspaper profiles, etc. - on all authors. Unlike the similarly orientated Fryer Library card index, *AustLit* does not organise the material into sections such as reviews, interviews and so on.

The nature of this *Guide* is better understood in the context of the origins of the Annual *A.L.S.* Bibliographies on which it is based. In the early 1960s if one wanted to write about Australian authors there was no way of checking with any completeness what - if anything - had already been written about them. The two main historical bibliographies, those by Morris Miller and by Miller Macartney were concerned with primary works and extended only (in the latter) to 1950. There was a need, then, both for retrospective bibliographies of critical commentary, such as the selective one in the Appendix to Geoffrey Dutton's *Australian Literature* (1963 revised 1976), for full bibliographies of individual authors, and for the kind of annual listing on which the more established studies of established literatures relied, the most formidable being the annual *PMLA* bibliography which served English, American and other literatures. The decision to adapt the latter as a model may in retrospect seem an ambitious one for Australian literary studies, but at the time it seemed necessary and possible, partly because the output of critical studies, as of primary works in the Australian field, was not nearly as large as it became by the end of the 1960s as a result of various 'new impulses'. It was really a case of making a decision - and an act of faith - without realizing the full consequences of maintaining an expanding annual bibliography.

This expansion, which still involved keeping the bibliography within certain limits, given its journal-based publication, meant that modifications have had to be made along the way. From the beginning, important editions (those with introductions and other editorial material) of past and contemporary writers, along with reviews of these were considered an important part of the bibliography. But as more and more contemporary authors were added, so the number of primary works listed and of reviews increased substantially. This was a departure from the *Modern Languages Association* and other academic bibliographies, with their exclusive emphasis on critical books and articles. In the early years, reviews of performances of plays were included but these were eventually dropped and the early instances have been removed entirely from this cumulation. Also in the early years, newspaper material was not included. When it was, later on, it became necessary to limit such material and of reviews to a few main sources. More recently newspaper profiles and feature articles have had to be omitted. Overseas articles - especially from non-English-speaking countries - have always been difficult to trace. Gradually, partly through personal contact with scholars abroad, we have been able to include more, though coverage in this area remains incomplete. Recently, since relevant publications in North America are listed in an annual bibliography in *Antipodes*, they have not been re-listed in the *A.L.S.*

Annual Bibliographies, except for those in *Ariel* and *World Literatures Written in English*. Such modifications have inevitably entailed some fluctuations over the years, though these have affected the shorter ancillary material (e.g. reviews) rather than the main material - critical articles - of the bibliographies. These fluctuations have become part of the geological layers of the bibliography, rather than modifications that we were able to iron out into perfect consistency in this cumulation. So this is reflected in the *Guide*. However the basic aims of the compilation have not altered: and its comprehensiveness within its guidelines has been maintained as far as possible.

One of the main modifications undertaken has involved the addition from time to time of retrospective material. When contemporary authors are first added to the listing because of the degree of critical attention devoted to them, their previous works, (post-1963) along with reviews of them have also been added. The present cumulation has continued this process by adding authors not included in previous listings. There is a difference, however, between contemporary authors and those of the past (those who had ceased writing before 1963). When substantial articles on a past author, or an edition of his or her work, is published, these have been added to the bibliography, but there has been no retrospective listing of his or her works, as a whole, as with contemporaries. This is partly an attempt to stem the flood, partly because such listings of some authors are available in existing bibliographies.

The *Guide* does not reprint the General section of the *A.L.S.* bibliography. The compilers felt that there was little point in cumulating such a large amount of material which for convenience of compilation is organized not by subject but by authors' surnames. Indeed the need for a comprehensive bibliography of general items organized under subject headings is one that remains to be addressed quite apart from the *A.L.S.* project. The General sections of the Annual Bibliography provide an invaluable resource for such an undertaking and in the meantime will repay careful consultation by those interested in special topics rather than individual authors. The General section is particularly useful to those involved in the expanding field of Australian studies. Indeed for some years now items have been added for their relevance to this area rather than to strictly 'literary' studies.

Something remains to be said about the dedicated work done over the years by those numerous and indispensable compilers of the *A.L.S.* Annual Bibliographies. In the first instance, in the 1964 listing, Brian Kiernan undertook this work by invitation and single-handed. The next few listings were similarly compiled by the voluntary effort of individuals. Just as this was proving too much of a burden, new opportunities arose. Spencer Routh, then Reference Librarian at the University of Queensland, pointed out that material could be more readily selected by drawing upon the comprehensive and up-to-date card index of the Fryer Library. Mr Routh kindly offered to arrange this, in consultation with the Fryer Librarian at that time, Ms Nancy Bonnin, and with the help of the librarians, notably Ms Marianne Ehrhardt, who has contributed the most frequently to the compilation (as well as to this cumulation). The arrangement has been encouraged by the present Fryer Librarian, Ms Margaret O'Hagan. However, in

recent years, more independent research work has fallen to the compilers of the
A.L.S. bibliography. This added burden has been partly offset because two *A.L.S.*
research assistants, Ms Carol Hetherington and Dr Irmtraud Petersen have
regularly undertaken the work using sources in addition to the Fryer Index.
Recently material from *AustLit* has also kindly been made available for the
updating required in this *Guide*. We wish to thank the individuals and institutions
involved in the above assistance; the many annual compilers who have agreed to
have their listings reprinted here; the Literature Board of the Australia Council
which has granted *A.L.S.* its main financial assistance over the years; and the
English Department, University of Queensland. The University of Queensland
also provided a special grant which helped to make this cumulation possible.
More recently the following have contributed funding to tide the Annual
Bibliography over difficult times: the Association for the Study of Australian
Literature, the National Centre for Australian Studies (Monash University), the
Australian Centre (Melbourne University) and the Australian Academy of the
Humanities.

Martin Duwell
Laurie Hergenhan

Introduction to second edition

This new edition of the *A.L.S. Guide to Australian Writers* continues the process of cumulation by adding to the original bibliography the five Annual Bibliographies of Australian Literature published in *A.L.S.* between 1992 and 1996, bringing the entries of the *Guide* up to date as far as 1995. These bibliographies were compiled by Dr Irmtraud Petersson and Ms Carol Hetherington under the continuing supervision of Professor Laurie Hergenhan. Some errors in the original database, brought to our attention, have been corrected and this edition differs from the first in that a substantial amount of the retrospective material for new authors, appears here for the first time, having not been included in the annual bibliographies.

The bibliography has continued its process of evolution and fine-tuning, noted in the introduction to the first edition. Noteworthy has been a radical alteration in style of documentation. We have not tried either to re-style the first cumulation to match the style of current Annual Bibliographies or to convert these to the style originally used. It has been our judgement that the user will find the different styles equally intelligible.

Martin Duwell

Acknowledgments

Our gratitude is recorded to those people who compiled the individual issues of the Annual Bibliography: Brian Kiernan, Annette Stewart, Geoffrey Hiller, Axel Kruse, Ken Stewart, Maria McGinity, Spencer Routh, L.M. Burns, Marianne Ehrhardt, Carolyn Foley, Carol Hetherington, Nancy Bonnin, Margaret Brennan, Margaret Waugh and Irmtraud Petersson.

We would also like to thank Jeanette Champ and Karen Wilkins who entered most of the individual bibliographies and Vic Lloyd who proofread this stage of the process. Special thanks are also due to Barry Maher who prepared the computer programme which did the cumulating and also supervised this stage, and to Richard Scullard for invaluable help in preparing the cumulated version for publication.

The preparation of this second edition is, perhaps, also a fitting moment to acknowledge the continuing supervisory role played by Professor Laurie Hergenhan, the founder and guiding force behind the thirty-three annual bibliographies cumulated here.

Abbreviations

The following abbreviations are used throughout the bibliography:

ABR	*Australian Book Review*
A.L.S.	*Australian Literary Studies*
A.& R.	Angus and Robertson
M.U.P.	Melbourne University Press
O.U.P.	Oxford University Press
S.M.H.	*Sydney Morning Herald*
T.L.S.	*Times Literary Supplement*
U.Q.P.	University of Queensland Press
WLWE	*World Literature Written in English*

ABDULLAH, MENA

Fiction

With Ray Mathew. *The Time of the Peacock*. (Sydney: A.& R., 1965). Reprinted with introduction by Thomas Shapcott (Pymble, NSW: Collins/A.& R., 1992). Reviewed by H. Horton, *Imago* 5.1, 1993: 93-94.

Critical Material

Brydon, Diana. 'Discovering "Ethnicity": Joy Kogawa's *Obasan* and Mena Abdullah's *Time of the Peacock*'. In *Australian/Canadian Literatures in English: Comparative Perspectives*, edited by Russell McDougall and Gillian Whitlock (North Ryde, N.S.W.: Methuen Australia, 1987), 94-110.

Gooneratne, Yasmine. 'Mena Abdullah, Australian Writer'. In *Striking Chords: Multicultural Literary Interpretations*, edited by Sneja Gunew and Kateryna O. Longley (North Sydney: Allen & Unwin, 1992), 115-24.

Malak, Amin. '"The World Is Your People": *The Time of the Peacock* and the Evolution of an Australian Identity'. *Kunapipi* 16.2, 1994, 43-47.

Ryan, J.S. 'Between Two Worlds: The Short Stories of Mena Abdullah'. *Literary Criterion* (Mysore), VI, No. 4, 1966, 73-7.

ADAMS, FRANCIS

Fiction

John Webb's End; or Strong as Death. Edited and introduced by Meg Tasker. Australian Books on Demand 12. (Canberra: Mulini Press, 1995).

Critical Material

Arinshtein, Leonid M. 'A Francis William Lauderdale Adams Unknown Poem'. *Victorian Poetry*, VII, 1969, 55-56.

Britain, I.M. 'Francis Adams: The Arnoldian as Socialist'. *Historical Studies*, XV, 1972, 401 23.

Jarvis, Doug. 'Francis Adams: Australia's Champion of Realism'. *New Literature Review*, No. 12, 1983, 25-35.

Jones, Edgar. 'Francis Adams, 1862-1893: A Forgotten Child of his Age'. *Essays and Studies*, N.S., XX, 1967, 76-103.

Turnbull, Clive. 'These Tears of Fire: The Story of Francis Adams'. In his *Australian Lives*. (Melbourne: F.W. Cheshire, 1965), 97-125.

ADAMS, GLENDA

Fiction

Dancing on Coral. (North Ryde, N.S.W.: A.& R.; New York: Viking; Ringwood, Vic.: Penguin, 1987).

Reviewed by D. Anderson, *Times on Sunday*, 30 August, 1987, 33; J. Chimonyo,

Age Saturday Extra, 15 August, 1987, 14; D. Johnson, *S.M.H.*, 29 August, 1987, 49; E. Jolley, *ABR*, No. 96, 1987, 5-6; S. McKernan, *Bulletin*, 8 September, 1987, 88; G. Oldham, *Antioch Review*, 46.3, 1988, 395; T.A. White, *Fremantle Arts Review*, 2, No. 12, 1987, 14.

Games of the Strong. (North Ryde, N.S.W.: A.& R., 1988; New York: Cane Hill Press, 1989). First published Sydney: A.& R, 1982.
Reviewed by B. Birskys, *Woman Writer*, 5, No. 17, 1989, 4-5; V. Brady, *Island Magazine*, No. 13, 1982, 52-54; R. Creswell, *S.M.H.*, 6 March, 1982, 45; C. Lansbury, *New York Times Book Review*, 30 July, 1989, 9; P. Lewis, *Stand*, 5, No. 2, 1984, 64-70; M. Lord, *ABR*, No. 45, 1982, 39; M. Macleod, *Span*, No. 14, 1982, 20-24 and *Kunapipi*, 5, No. 1, 1983, 101-105; G. Manning, *Meanjin*, 41, 1982, 486-92; E. Riddell, *Bulletin*, 11 May, 1982, 79; M. Smith, *Weekend Australian*, 17-18 July, 1982, Weekend 10.

The Hottest Night of the Century: Short Stories. (North Ryde, N.S.W.: A.& R., 1988). First published Sydney: A.& R., 1979.
Reviewed by K. Gelder, *CRNLE Reviews Journal*, No. 2, 1980, 6-9; C. Gillam, *Westerly*, 25, No. 1, 1980, 107-109; K.H., *Womanspeak*, 5, No. 2, 1980, 27; C. Lansbury, *New York Times Book Review*, 30 July, 1989, 9; R. Lucas, *S.M.H.*, 8 October, 1988, 78; M. Macleod, *S.M.H.*, 15 December, 1979, 18 and *Kunapipi*, 2, No. 1, 1980, 135-39; T. Malkovic, *Artlook*, 6, No. 9, 1980, 64-5; S. Morell, *Quadrant*, 23, No. 12, 1979, 70-71; E. Riddell, *S.M.H.*, 15 September, 1979, 17; M. Smith, *ABR*, No. 19, 1980, 23-24; E. Webby, *Meanjin*, 40, 1981, 200-208.

Longleg. (North Ryde, N.S.W.: Collins/A.& R., 1990; New York: Cane Hill, 1992).
Reviewed by C. Bird, *Age*, 15 September, 1990, Saturday Extra 11; J. Crowley, *New York Times Book Review*, 13 September, 1992, 13; K. England, *ABR*, No. 124, 1990, 10-11; D. English, *Weekend Australian*, 15-16 September, 1990, Review 7; N. Hasluck, *Voices*, 1.1, 1991, 90-94; L. Kramer, *Quadrant*, 34, No. 12, 1990, 68-69; A.P. Riemer, *S.M.H.*, 24 August, 1990, 73.

Non-Fiction

'Calling up the Spirits: Some Thoughts on the Writing Process'. *Island*, 47, 1991, 26-29.
'Fun in the Bath House'. *Southerly*, 49, No. 3, 1989, 316-28. Autobiographical paper on the process of writing. Herbert Blaiklock Memorial Lecture, University of Sydney, 1988.

Critical Material

Baker, Candida. 'Glenda Adams'. In her *Yacker 3* (Sydney: Picador, 1989), 12-41.
Brooks, Karen. 'Odysseus Unbound/ Singing with Sirens: Liminality and Stasis in Glenda Adams' *Dancing on Coral*'. *New Literatures Review*, 28/29, 1994-95, 55-64.
Dutkiewicz, Adam. 'Interview'. *Words & Visions*, 2, No. 3, 1988, 16-21.
Hutchinson, Jan. 'Interview with Glenda Adams'. *Fine Line*, No. 4, 1988, 46-52.
Pybus, Cassandra. 'Fiddling with Words'. Interview. *Island*, 47, 1991, 20-25.

ADAMSON, BARTLETT

Critical Material

Fox, Len. *Bartlett Adamson*. (Sydney: The Fellowship of Australian Writers, 1963). Paper given to commemorate Adamson's death.

ADAMSON, ROBERT

Fiction

With Bruce Hanford. *Zimmer's Essay*. (Sydney: Wild and Woolley, 1974).
Reviewed by J. Dawson, *Canberra Times*, 1 November, 1974, 16; D. D6ouglas, *Union Recorder*, LIV, 1974, 260; D. Freney, *Tribune*, 15 October, 1974, 10; D. Gilbey, *Southerly*, XXXVII, 1977, 461-64; W. Green, *Westerly*, No. 4, 1974, 74-75;

C. Harrison-Ford, *Australian*, 21 September, 1974, 43 and *Stand*, XVI, No. 3, 1975, 41; R.D. Jones, *Makar*, XI, No. 1, 1975, 45-46; R. McConchie, *Overland*, No. 60, 1975, 83-85; S. Walsh, *S.M.H.*, 11 January, 1975, 15; E. Whitton, *National Times*, 7-12 October, 1974 22-23.

Poetry

Canticles on the Skin. (Sydney: Illumination Press, 1970).
Reviewed by R. Dunlop, *Poetry Australia*, No. 38, 1971, 61-64; K.L. Goodwin, *Meanjin*, XXX, 1971, 365; R. Hall, *Australian*, 24 October, 1970, 23; C. Harrison-Ford, *Union Recorder*, L, No. 26, 1970, 8-9; P. Roberts, *S.M.H.*, 5 December, 1970, 26; K. Slessor, *Sydney Telegraph*, 15 August, 1970, 13; T. Thorne, *Poetry Magazine*, No. 18, 1970, 35.

The Clean Dark. (Sydney: Paper Bark Press, 1989).
Reviewed by H. Cam, *S.M.H.*, 23 September, 1989, 81; P. Craven, *ABR*, No. 116, 1989, 36-37; R. Darling, *Antipodes* 4.1, 1990, 68; M. Duwell, *Weekend Australian*, 6-7 January, 1990, Weekend 6; D. Reiter, *Age Monthly Review*, 9, No. 10, 1990, 8-9; N.C. Roper, *Westerly*, 35, No. 1, 1990, 81-82; G.K. Smith, *Age*, 6 January, 1990, Saturday Extra 7; W. Tonetto, *Southerly*, 50, No. 2, 1990, 255-61; J. Tranter, *Editions*, No. 4, 1989, 31.

Cross the Border. (Sydney: New Poetry for the Poetry Society of Australia, 1977).
Reviewed by M. Dugan, *Age*, 14 December, 1977, 18; R.D. Jones, *National Times*, 14 October, 1978, 40; F. Kellaway, *Overland*, No. 69, 1978, 71; T. Shapcott, *Weekend Australian Magazine*, 10-11 September, 1977, 12.

The Law at Heart's Desire. (Sydney: Prism, 1982).
Reviewed by G. Catalano, *Meanjin*, XLII, 1983, 259-60; M. Duwell, *Weekend Australian*, 28-29 May, 1983, Weekend Australian Magazine 14; F. Kellaway, *Overland*, No. 911, 1983, 56-57; S. McKernan, *Canberra Times*, 21 May, 1983, 12; T. Shapcott, *Age Saturday Extra*, 14 May, 1983, 11.

The Rumour. (Sydney: New Poetry, 1971). Prism Poets, 3.
Reviewed by K.L. Goodwin, *Meanjin*, XXXI, 1972, 500, 508; C. Harrison-Ford, *New Poetry*, XX, No. 1-2, 1972, 51-54; P. Law, *Poetry Australia*, No. 47, 1973, 78-79; D. Malouf, *Australian*, 12 February, 1972, 15.

Selected Poems (Sydney: A.& R., 1978).
Reviewed by R. Gray, *S.M.H.*, 22 July, 1978, 18.

Selected Poems 1970-1989. (St. Lucia: U.Q.P., 1990).
Reviewed by D. Hewett, *Scripsi*, 7.1, 1991, 247-58; B. Josephi, *Voices*, 1.3, 1991, 104-07.

Swamp Riddles. (Sydney: Island Press, 1974).
Reviewed by R. Dobson, *Age*, 14 December, 1974, 17; D. Douglas, *Union Recorder*, LIV, 1974, 168; D. Hewett, *Australian*, 4 January, 1975, 19; M. Johnston, *S.M.H.*, 21 September, 1974, 13; R.D. Jones, *Makar*, XI, No. 3, 1975, 46-47; A. Taylor, *Poetry Australia*, No. 58, 1976, 72-73; J. Tranter, *New Poetry*, XX, No. 4, 1974, 52-58.

Theatre I-XIX (Sydney: Pluralist Press, 1976).
Reviewed by R. Gray, *S.M.H.*, 19 June, 1976, 17.

Waving to Hart Crane. (Sydney: A.& R.: 1994).
Reviewed by M. Duwell, *Weekend Australian*, 24-25 June, 1995, Review 7; K. Hart, *Age*, 4 Feb., 1995, Saturday Extra 9; M. Griffin, *ABR*, 166, 1994: 52-53; J. Jones, *Southerly*, 55.2, 1995, 191-200; D. Leadbetter, *Overland*, 141, 1995, 63-64; M. Wiley, *Antipodes*, 9.1, 1995, 55-56.

Where I Come From. (Sydney: Big-Smoke Books, 1979).
Reviewed by D. Brooks, *New Poetry*, XXVII, No. 3, 1979, 44-49; D. Haskell, *Southerly*, XL, 1980, 226-40; G. Page, *National Times*, 20 October, 1979, 34; J.

Rodriguez, *Luna*, IV, No. 2, 1979, 30-31; J. Tranter, *Age*, 5 January, 1980, 19.

Non-Fiction

Wards of State: An Autobiographical Novella. (North Ryde, NSW: A.& R., 1992).
Reviewed by G. Catalano, *Age*, 28 March, 1992, Saturday Extra 10; A. Croggan, *Voices*, 2.2, 1992, 103-07; R. Dingli, *Northern Perspective*, 16.2, 1993: 136-37; I. Indyk, *Weekend Australian*, 26-27 February: Review 5; A. Inglis, *Modern Times*, April, 1992, 31-32; M.R. Liverani, *Weekend Australian*, 28-29 March, 1992, Review 6; B. Roberts, *ABR*, 139, 1992, 8-9.

'Scrapbooks of Dreaming'. *Outrider*, 5, No. 1, 1988, x-xii.

'The Shadow of Doubt and "Derivations" in Australian Poetry'. *Meanjin*, 49, 1990, 537-548.

Critical Material

Brooks, David. 'Feral Symbolists: Robert Adamson, John Tranter, and the Response to Rimbaud'. *A.L.S.*, 16. No. 3, 1994, 280-88.

Duwell, Martin. 'Homages and Invocations: The Early Poetry of Robert Adamson'. *A.L.S.*, 14, No. 2, 1989, 229-38.

Harris, Robert. 'Robert Adamson's Reckoning'. *Overland*, No. 121, 1990, 57-62.

Haskell, Dennis. 'Getting Further Away: The Poetry of Robert Adamson'. *Southerly*, XXXVIII, 1978, 60-71.

---. 'Thoughts on Some Recent Poetry'. *A.L.S.*, VIII, 1977, 136-48.

Hogue, Derry. 'Safe-blower to Poet: Derry Hogue Interviews a Young, Talented and Unusual Australian Poet'. *Australian*, 11 July, 1973, 12.

Malouf, David. 'Some Volumes of Selected Poems of the 1970s, II'. *A.L.S.*, X, 1982, 309-10.

Page, Geoff. 'Robert Adamson'. In his *A Reader's Guide to Contemporary Australian Poetry* (St. Lucia: U.Q.P., 1995), 11-13.

Sharkey, Michael. 'Robert Adamson and the Persistence of Mallarme: An Interview with Michael Sharkey'. *Southerly*, XLV, No. 3, 1985, 308-320.

Smith, Martin. 'Personality'. *Campaign*, No. 24, 1977, 9. Interview.

Tranter, John. 'The Truth I Know'. *Makar*, XIV, No. 1, 4-13. Interview.

Wilding, Michael. '"My Name is Rickeybockey": The Poetry of Robert Adamson and the Spirit of Henry Kendall'. *Southerly*, XLVI, No. 1, 1986, 25-43.

---. 'The Poetry of Robert Adamson'. *Commonwealth Review* 3.2, 1991-92, 179-91. Reprinted in *Australian Literature Today*, edited by R. K. Dhawan and David Kerr (New York: Indian Society for Commonwealth Studies/Advent Press, 1993), 179-91.

Wynhausen, Elizabeth. 'Thriving on the System'. *Australian*, 21 September, 1974, 40.

ADAMSON, WALTER

Fiction

Australia of All Places. (Richmond, Vic.: Hodja Publications, 1984).
Reviewed by J. Waten, *Age*, 28 July, 1984, 15.

The Institution. Translated by Sonja Delander. (Melbourne: Outback, 1976).
Reviewed by K. Ahearne, *ABR*, No. 83, 1986, 24; T. Forshaw, *Weekend Australian*, 17-18 June, 1986, Weekend 17; C. Harrison-Ford, *Meanjin*, 36, No. 2, 1977, 246-52.

The Man with the Suitcase: Selected Stories. (Ferntree Gully, Vic.: Houghton Mifflin, Aust., 1989).
Reviewed by D. Davison, *Weekend Australian*, 5-6 August, 1989, Weekend 6; J. Hanrahan, *ABR*, No. 112, 1989, 8; P. Hawker, *Herald*, 9 June, 1989, 9; W. Tonetto, *Age*, 29 July, 1989, 8.

Poetry

Adamson's Three Legged World. Cheltenham, Vic.: Abalone Press, 1985).

Reviewed by J. Irving, *ABR*, No. 73, 1985, 28-9; J. Strauss, *Overland*, No. 101, 1985, 91-2.

Critical Material

Delander, Sonja. 'Interview with Walter Adamson'. *Outrider*, 3, No. 2, 1986, 3-8.

Jurgensen, Manfred. 'Inmate and Outsider: The Migrant Writer Walter Adamson'. *Outrider*, 3, No. 2, 1986, 9-17.

AFFORD, MAX

Drama

Mischief in the Air: Radio and Stage Plays. (St Lucia: U.Q.P., 1974). Includes 'Foreword' by Alrene Sykes and 'Introduction: Max Afford, Playwright', by Leslie Rees.

Reviewed by M. Armitage, *Advertiser*, 15 February, 1975, 20.

ALDRIDGE, JAMES

Fiction

My Brother Tom. (London: Hamilton, 1966).

Reviewed by M.T. McIntyre, *ABR*, No. 6, 1967, 55; D.H. Brick, *Australian*, 24 December, 1966, 9; T. Healy, *Age*, 11 March, 1967, 23; M. Vintner, *S.M.H.*, 6 May, 1967, 17.

The True Story of Lilli Stubeck. (Melbourne: Hyland House, 1984).

Reviewed by L. Clancy, *ABR*, No. 68, 1985, 25; W. Noonan, *Australian Weekend Magazine*, 22-23 December, 1984, 11.

The True Story of Spit MacPhee. (Ringwood: Penguin, 1986).

Reviewed by W. McVitty, *Australian Weekend Magazine*, 23-24 August, 1986, 15; G. Turner, *Age*, 7 June, 1986, 11.

Critical Material

Juers, Evelyn. 'The Heroic Ordinary: The Novels of James Aldridge'. *Age Monthly Review*, February, 1987, 7-8.

Stone, Michael. 'Spit McPhee: Australia's Tom Sawyer'. *Orana*, 26.4, 1990, 179-186.

AMANATIDES, DINA

Critical Material

Kanarakis, George. 'The Greek Literary Presence in Australia". *New Literatures Review*, 15, 1988, 1-10.

Nickas, Helen. *Migrant Daughters: The Female Voice in Greek-Australian Prose Fiction.* (Melbourne: Owl Publishing, 1992), 20-48, 189-204.

ANDERSON, ETHEL

Fiction

At Parramatta. With an afterword by Paul Salzman. (Ringwood, Vic.: Penguin, 1985). First published Melbourne: Cheshire, 1956.

Reviewed by B. Abbyad, *Tribune*, No. 2404, 1985, 11; L. Forsyth, *ABR*, No. 74, 1985, 36-37; K. Goldsworthy, *Age Saturday Extra*, 20 July, 1985, 13; P. Goldsworthy, *S.M.H.*, 29 June, 1985, 42.

The Best of Ethel Anderson. Chosen by John Douglas Pringle. (Sydney: A.& R., 1973). Spine has title: *Tales of Parramatta and India: The Best of Ethel Anderson.*

Reviewed by M. Eldridge, *Canberra Times*, 22 February, 1974, 16; T. Forshaw, *Australian*, 3 November, 1973, 45; H. Frizell, *S.M.H.*, 1 December, 1973, 13.

Critical Material

Foott, Bethia. *Ethel and the Governors' General: A Biography of Ethel Anderson*

(1883-1958) and Brigadier-General A.T. Anderson (1868-1949). (Paddington, NSW: Rainforest Publishing, 1992). Reviewed by V. Farrer, *ABR*, 141, 1992, 52-53; C. Franklin, *Southerly*, 52.4, 1992, 177-82.Jefferis, Barbara. 'A Legendary Deaf Ear'. *Hemisphere*, XIX, No. 4, 1975, 9-14.

Franklin, Carol. 'An Australian Eclogue Book: Ethel Anderson's "Squatter's Luck"'. *Southerly*, 52.1, 1992, 33-47.

Jones, Dorothy. 'Edgy Laughter: Women and Australian Humour'. *A.L.S.*, 16.2, 1993: 161-67. Includes discussion of work by Anderson.

---. 'Living in the Country: A Woman's Reading'. *Australian-Canadian Studies*, 10.2, 1992: 87-98. Includes discussion of work by Anderson.

Pringle, John Douglas. 'Ethel Anderson'. In his *On Second Thoughts: Australian Essays*, (Sydney: A.& R., 1971), 104-16.

Smith, Angela. 'Is Phallocentricity a Sin? or a Peccadillo? Comedy and Gender in Ethel Anderson's *At Parramatta* and Patrick White's *Voss*'. In *European Perspectives: Contemporary Essays on Australian Literature,* edited by Giovanna Capone (*A.L.S.*, 15.2 (special issue)/ St. Lucia: U.Q.P., 1991), 149-61.

ANDERSON, JESSICA

Fiction

The Commandant. (London: Macmillan, 1975, Ringwood, Vic.: Penguin, 1981). Reviewed by D. Gallagher, *Southerly*, XXXVIII, 1978, 477; H. Hewitt, *Canberra Times*, 27 June, 1982, 8.

The Impersonators. (South Melbourne: Macmillan, 1980). Reviewed by L. Clancy, *Overland*, No. 84, 1981, 26-30; R. Creswell, *ABR*, No. 28, 1981, 14; C. Ray, *Spectator*, CCXXV, 1970, 189.

The Last Man's Head. (Ringwood, Vic.: Penguin, 1987). First published London: Macmillan, 1970. Reviewed by S. Knight, *ABR*, No. 96, 1987, 8-10; esp. 8-9.

One of the Wattle Birds. (Ringwood, Vic.: Penguin, 1994). Reviewed by J. Croft, *Weekend Australian*, 9-10 July, 1994, Review 7; H. Elliot, *S.M.H.*, 23 July, 1994, Spectrum 9A; R. Lucas, *Bulletin*, 5 July, 1994, 89; J. Maiden, *Overland* 138, 1995, 168-70; W. Ommundsen, *Editions*, 21, 1994, 7-8; A. Peek, *ABR*, 162, 1994, 14-15; R. Sorensen, *Age*, 23 July, 1994, Saturday Extra 7.

The Only Daughter. (New York: Viking, 1985). Reviewed by C. Rooke, *Malahat Review*, No. 72, 1985, 140-41; R. Stevenson, *T.L.S.*, 19 June, 1987, 668; R. Willbanks, *World Literature Today*, LXI, No. 2, 1987, 346-347; H. Wolitzer, *New York Times Book Review*, 24 March, 1985, 12.

An Ordinary Lunacy. (London: Macmillan, 1963). Reviewed by A. Davies, *Nation*, 2 November, 1963, 22-23; H.P. Heseltine, *Meanjin*, XXII, 1963, 422-23; D. Jones, *Span*, No. 26, 1988, 107-109.

Stories From the Warm Zone and Sydney Stories. (Ringwood, Vic.: Penguin, 1987). Reviewed by J. Colmer, *Weekend Australian. Weekend Magazine*, 4-5 July, 1987, 14; A.M. Conway, *T.L.S.*, 26 February-3 March, 1988, 215; H. Daniel, *Age Saturday Extra*, 20 June, 1987, 16; D. Durrent, *London Magazine*, 29, Nos. 3-4, 1989, 130; P. Jacobs, *Fremantle Arts Review*, II, No. 10, 1987, 14-15; D. Johnson, *S.M.H.*, 13 June, 1987, 49; H. Pakula, *New York Times Book Review*, 29 November, 1987, 7; C. Peake, *Times on Sunday*, 31 May, 1987, 32; G. Raines, *Australian Studies*, No. 3, 1989, 81-88; P. Salzman, *ABR*, No. 92, 1987, 8-9; R. Willbanks, *Antipodes*, II, No. 1, 1988, 50.

Taking Shelter. (Ringwood, Vic.: Viking, 1989). Reviewed by R. Blair, *Island Magazine*, Nos. 43-44, 1990, 84-6; H. Dakin, *Southerly*, 50, No. 4, 1990, 529-32; T. Glyde, *T.L.S.*, 14-20 September, 1990, 980; J. Grant, *ABR*, No. 120, 1990, 3-4; K. Jennings, *S.M.H.*, 21 April, 1990, 72; T.

Lewis, *Northern Perspective*, 14.1, 1991, 113; D. Myers, *Imago*, 3.1, 1991, 81-83; D. Myers, *LiNQ*, 18.1, 1991, 151-53; C. Peake, *Weekend Australian*, 21-22 April, 1990, Weekend 6; P. Pierce, *Bulletin*, 19 June, 1990, 142-3; R. Sorensen, *Age*, 21 April, 1990, Saturday Extra 10; J. Wilcox, *New York Times Book Review*, 11 March, 1990, 12-13; R. Willbanks, *Antipodes*, 4.2, 1990, 137-38.

Tirra Lirra by the River. (South Melbourne: Macmillan, 1978).
Reviewed by J. Bedford, *National Times*, 9 September, 1978, 41; D. Bird, *Westerly*, XXV, No. 4, 1980, 78-80; C. Hanna, *Southerly*, XL, 1980, 361-63; C. Rooke, *Malahat Review* (Canada), No. 68, 1984, 143.

    Critical Material
Baker, Candida. 'Drawing on Buried Memories'. *Australian Society*, VI, No. 7, 1987, 37-38, 58.
---. 'Jessica Anderson'. In her *Yacker 2: Australian Writers Talk About Their Work* (Sydney: Picador, 1987), 14-27.
Barry, Elaine. 'The Expatriate Vision of Jessica Anderson'. *Meridian*, III, No. 1, 1984, 3-11.
---. *Fabricating the Self: The Fictions of Jessica Anderson*. (St Lucia: U.Q.P., 1992). Reviewed by S. Lever, *A.L.S.*, 16.2, 1993: 229-33; S.K. Martin, *ABR*, 145, 1992, 50-51; N. Potter, *Antipodes*, 6.2, 1992: 162-63.
Blair, Ruth. 'Jessica Anderson's Mysteries'. *Island Magazine*, No. 31, 1987, 10-15.
Ellison, Jennifer. 'Jessica Anderson'. In her *Rooms of Their Own* (Ringwood, Vic.: Penguin, 1986), 28-49
Ferrier, Elizabeth. 'Mapping the Local in the Unreal City'. *Island Magazine*, No. 41, 1989, 65-69. Discusses work by Anderson.
---. 'The Return of the Repressed: The "Empire" of the Local and Jessica Anderson's *Tirra Lirra by the River*'. In *Re-Siting Queen's English: Text and Tradition in Post-Colonial Literatures*, edited by Gillian Whitlock and Helen Tiffin (Amsterdam/Atlanta: Rodopi, 1992), 157-68.
Frizell, Helen. 'From Short Story to Prize-winning Novel'. *S.M.H.*, 3 May, 1979, 6.
Gallagher, Donat. 'A Rare Passion for Justice: Jessica Anderson's *The Last Man's Head*'. *Quadrant*, XXXII, No. 7, 1988, 9-13.
Garlick, Barbara. 'Of Rinos and Caryatids: The Dialogic Imperative in Jessica Anderson'. *Journal of Narrative Technique* 21.1, 1991: 72-82.
Grenville, Kate, and Sue Woolfe. *Making Stories: How Ten Australian Novels Were Written*. (St Leonards, NSW: Allen & Unwin, 1993). Includes contribution on Jessica Anderson, *The Commandant*.
Haynes, Roslynn. 'Art as Reflection in Jessica Anderson's *Tirra Lirra by the River*'. *A.L.S.*, XII, No. 3, 1986, 316-23.
Jones, Dorothy. 'Edgy Laughter: Women and Australian Humour'. *A.L.S.*, 16.2, 1993: 161-67.
---. 'Fabricating Texts of Empire'. *Kunapipi*, 16.3, 1995, 1-16. Includes discussion of *Tirra Lirra by the River*.
McGrath, Sandra. 'Private Voice, Public Eye'. *Weekend Australian Magazine*, 12-13 May, 1979, 4.
Roff, Sue. 'Rites of Passage: Six Australian Authors in Search of the Same Character'. *Australian Society*, III, No. 9, 1984, 33-34.
Sykes, Alrene. 'Jessica Anderson: Arrivals and Places'. *Southerly*, XLVI, No. 1, 1986, 57-71.
Willbanks, Ray. 'A Conversation with Jessica Anderson'. *Antipodes*, II, No. 1, 1988, 49-51.
---. 'Jessica Anderson'. In his *Speaking Volumes: Australian Writers and Their Work* (Ringwood, Vic.: Penguin, 1991).

ANDREONI, GIOVANNI

Critical Material

Fochi, Anna. 'Giovanni Andreoni: An Italian Writer in Australia'. *Westerly*, XXVIII, No. 2, 1983, 45-53.

ARCHIBALD, J.F.

Critical Material

'The Fiery Idealist, John Feltham Archibald, 1886-1903'. *Bulletin*, 29 January, 1980, 244.

Lawson, Sylvia. *The Archibald Paradox: A Strange Case of Authorship*. (Ringwood, Vic.: Allen Lane, 1983). Reviewed by D. Adams, *Overland*, No. 94-5, 1984, 79-81; P. Botsman, *Courier-Mail*, 17 December, 1983, 24; J. Croft, *Labour History* (Canberra), No. 48, 1985, 101-102; M. Davie, *T.L.S.*, 1-7 January, 1987, 20; M. Dunlevy, *Canberra Times*, 29 October, 1983, 20; K. Goodwin, *Australian Journal of Politics and History*, XXXIV, No. 2, 1988, 283; D. Green, *Meanjin*, XLIV, No. 2, 1985, 193-208; R. Hall, *S.M.H.*, 12 November, 1983, 41; P. Law, *National Times*, 11-17 November, 1983, 29; W.M. Maidment, *A.L.S.*, XII, No. 1, 1985, 137-141; B. Matthews, *ABR*, No. 61, 1984, 16-18; N. McLachlan, *Age Saturday Extra*, 5 November, 1983, 14; H. McQueen, *Australian Society*, III, No. 4, 1984, 42-44; P. Morgan, *Quadrant*, XXVIII, Nos. 7-8, 1984, 96-98; C. Semmler, *Weekend Australian Magazine*, 12-13 November, 1983, 16; J. Walter, *Meanjin*, XLV, No. 4, 1986, 479-87; J.A. Weigel, *Antipodes*, II, No. 1, 1988, 47; P. Williams, *Arena*, No. 73, 1985, 163-174. See also Paul Carter, 'Infamies', *Age Monthly Review*, IV, No. 3, 1984, 16 and Stephen Murray-Smith, 'The Knives of Leavis', *Age Monthly Review*, No. 4, 1984, 2 & 23.

---. *Archibald*. (Melbourne: O.U.P., 1971). Great Australians. Reviewed by R. Campbell, *Daily Telegraph*, 27 March, 1971, 52.

---. 'Jules Francois Archibald and the Sydney *Bulletin*, 1880-1902'. *Commonwealth* (Paris), VI, No. 2, 1984, 19-21.

---. 'Silencing the New(s)'. *Age Monthly Review*, IV, No. 5, 1984, 13-14.

Stewart, Douglas. 'J.F. Archibald's Paper'. In his *Writers of the Bulletin*. (Sydney: Australian Broadcasting Corporation, 1977), 9-22.

ASTLEY, THEA

Fiction

The Acolyte. (Sydney: A.& R., 1972).

Reviewed by M. Eldridge, *Canberra Times*, 14 October, 1972, 10; D. Gilbey, *Southerly*, XXXIII, 1973, 83-85; C. Grimm, *Australian*, 14 October, 1972, 35; N. Keesing, *S.M.H.*, 16 September, 1972, 21; F. King, *Bulletin*, 23 September, 1972, 54-55 (see also letter to the editor by Thea Astley, *Bulletin*, 7 October, 1972, 4); W.A. Murray, *ABR*, XI, 1973, 72; V. Osborne, *Sunday Telegraph*, 24 September, 1972, 29.

Beachmasters. (Ringwood, Vic.: Penguin, 1985).

Reviewed by L. Clancy, *Age Saturday Extra*, 16 March, 1985, 13; S. Dawson, *T.L.S.*, No. 4, 1985, 311, 1295; G. Dutton, *Bulletin*, 28 May, 1985, 92, 94; K. England, *Advertiser Saturday Review*, 9 March, 1985, 7; K. Goodwin, *Courier-Mail*, 11 May, 1985, 28; S. McKernan, *Caerra Times*, 6 April, 1985, 17; A. Mitchell, *Weekend Australian Magazine*, 16-17 March, 1985, 11; N. Phelan, *S.M.H.*, 9 March, 1985, 41; S. Walker, *ABR*, No. 72, 1985, 17-20; P. Wolfe, *Newsletter of the A.A.A.L.S.*, I, No. 2, 1985, 5; V. Young, *New York Times Book Review*, 22 June, 1986, 12.

A Boatload of Home Folk. (Sydney: A.& R., 1968).

Reviewed by L.J. Clancy, *Meanjin*, XXVIII, 1969, 416-18; T. Forshaw, *Nation*, 26

October, 1968, 22; N. Keesing, *Bulletin*, 5 October, 1968, 81; L.V. Kepert, *S.M.H.*, 14 September, 1968, 20; L. Mason, *Canberra Times*, 7 September, 1968, 14; P. Mathers, *Age*, 21 September, 1968, 14; J. McLaren, *Overland*, No. 40, 1968, 40; W.S. Ramson, *Australian*, 5 October, 1968, 10; P. Rappolt, *Advertiser*, 14 September, 1968, 24; K. Rushbrooke, *Realist*, No. 32, 1969, 74-75; J.S. Ryan, *ABR*, VII, 1968, 216; M. Wilding, *Southerly*, XXX, 1970, 72-73.

Coda. (Port Melbourne: Heinemann; New York: Putnam's, 1994).
Reviewed by M. Cosic, *S.M.H.*, 26 February, 1994, Spectrum 11A; B. Lowry, *New York Times Book Review*, 2 October, 1994, 12; R. Lucas, *Bulletin*, 15 March, 1994, 109; S. Milnes, *Antipodes*, 9.1, 1995, 41-42; C. O'Farrell, *ABR*, 158, 1994, 5-6; A. Riemer, *Age*, 5 February, 1994, Saturday Extra 7; J. Scheckter, *World Literature Today*, 69.3, 1995, 641.

Hunting the Wild Pineapple and Other Related Stories. (Melbourne: Nelson (Australia), 1979; New York: Putnam, 1990).
Reviewed by C. Bliss, *World Literature Today*, 66.1, 1992, 202; S. Curry, *Antipodes*, 5.1, 1991, 65; H. Frizell, *S.M.H.*, 22 September, 1979, 17; S. Hall, *24 Hours*, IV, No. 12, 1980, 65; V. Ikin, *CRNLE Reviews Journal*, No. 2, 1982, 5-10; N. Jillet, *Age*, 24 November, 1979, 27; S. McInerney, *S.M.H.*, 15 August, 1981, 45; E. Perkins, *Quadrant*, XXIV, No. 4, 1980, 68-69; G. Savage, *ABR*, No. 24, 1980, 7; C. Talbot, *Weekend Australian Magazine*, 17-18 November, 1979, 15; E. Webby, *Meanjin*, XXXIX, 1980, 129-30; H. Wolitzer, *New York Times Book Review*, 23 December, 1990, 6.

It's Raining in Mango: Pictures From the Family Album. (New York: G.P. Putnam's Sons, 1987; Ringwood, Vic.: Viking, 1988). Reviewed by K. Ahearne, *Age Saturday Extra*, 23 April, 1988, 13; I. Baranay, *ABR*, No. 100, 1988, 12; P. Brady, *Antipodes*, I, No. 2, 1987, 114; R. Brown, *New York Times Book Review*, 22 November, 1987, 14; J. Maiden, *Age Monthly Review*, VIII, No. 9, 1988, 33; S. McKernan, *Bulletin*, 21 June, 1988, 119; W. Noonan, *Weekend Australian*, 4 June, 1988, Weekend 16; E. Webby, *S.M.H.*, 25 June, 1988, 76.

An Item from the Late News. (St Lucia: U.Q.P., 1982).
Reviewed by M. Brakmanis, *Ash Magazine*, No. 12, 1983, 32-33; C. Campbell and E. Perkins, *LiNQ*, X, No. 4, 1982-3, 66-68; L. Clancy, *ABR*, No. 48, 1983, 27; G. Dutton, *Bulletin*, 30 November, 1982, 87-88; H. Garner, *National Times*, 17-23 October, 1982, 22; K. Goodwin, *Courier-Mail*, 6 November, 1982, 26; A. Hildyard, *Island Magazine*, Nos. 18-19, 1984, 40-44; G. Houghton, *WLWE.*, *XXII*, 1983, 223-25; B. Matthews, *Age Saturday Extra*, 15 January, 1983, 8; R. McMaster, *S.M.H.*, 9 October, 1982, 37; K. Roberts, *Overland*, No. 91, 1983, 63-64.

A Kindness Cup. (Melbourne: Thomas Nelson (Australia), 1974).
Reviewed by R.F. Brissenden, *Australian*, 15 February, 1975, 27; H. Frizell, *S.M.H.*, 9 November, 1974, 15; D. Gilbey, *Southerly*, XXXVI, 1976, 442-44; R. Nicholls, *Age*, 1 March, 1975, 15; R. O'Grady, *Advertiser*, 1 February, 1975, 20; M. Pettigrove, *Canberra Times*, 31 January, 1975, 9; J. Tittensor, *Nation Review*, 6-12 December, 1974, 231.

Reaching Tin River. (Port Melbourne: Heinemann; New York: G. P. Putnam's, 1990).
Reviewed by L. Clancy, *ABR*, No. 118, 1990, 10-11; H. Daniel, *Age*, 10 March, 1990, Saturday Extra 8; D. Davison, *Weekend Australian*, 14-15 April, 1990, Weekend 5; S. Dowrick, *Australian Society*, 9, No. 4, 1990, 49; P. Pierce, *Bulletin*, 1 May, 1990, 103-4; R. Ross, *Antipodes* 4.1, 1990, 66; L. Shrubb, *Quadrant*, 35.5, 1991, 73-76; R. Sorensen, *CRNLE Reviews Journal*, No.1, 1990, 48-54; A. Stretton, *S.M.H.*, 3 March, 1990, 81.

The Slow Natives. (Sydney: A.& R., 1965).
Reviewed by A. Ashworth, *Southerly*, XXVI, No. 1, 1966, 62-6; C. Black,

Australian, 8 January, 1966, 11; J.K. Ewers, *W.A. Teachers' Journal*, LVI, 1966, 84; N. Jillet, *Age*, 6 November, 1965, 21; L.V. Kepert, *S.M.H.*, 16 October, 1965, 18; *T.L.S.*, 10 February, 1966, 97.

Vanishing Points. (Port Melbourne: Heinemann; New York: Putnam's, 1992). Reviewed by C. Bliss, *World Literature Today*, 67. No.3, 1993, 665; J. Burke, *Overland*, 129, 1992, 80-82; M. Ennesmarvin, *Studies in Short Fiction*, 30, No.4, 1993, 615; L. Frost, *Age*, 29 August, 1992, Saturday Extra 10; H. Grützner, *Editions*, 14, 1992, 23; M. Halligan, *Weekend Australian*, 10-11 October, 1992, Review 6; S. Hughes, *Modern Times*, September, 1992, 32-33; N. Krauth, *ABR*, 144, 1992, 5-7; M. Maclean, *ABR*, 144, 1992, 8-9; P. Pierce, *Bulletin* 17 November, 1992, 91; R. Ross, *Antipodes*, 6.2, 1992, 150; R. Sorensen, *S.M.H.*, 22 August, 1992, 44. See also *ABR*, 144, 1992, Interview by R. Sorensen, 9-11; articles by H. Heseltine, 12-14, and E. Perkins, 14-16..

Non-Fiction

'Being a Queenslander: A Form of Literary and Geographical Conceit'. (Surry Hills, N.S.W.: Wentworth Press, 1978). Sixth Herbert Blaiklock Memorial Lecture. Also published *Southerly*, 36, 1976, 252-64.

'The Idiot Question (Australian Writers in Profile, 7)'. *Southerly*, XXX, 1970, 3-8.

'Writing in North Queensland'. *LiNQ*, IX, No. 1, 1981, 2-10.

Critical Material

Smith, Ross and Frost, Cheryl. 'Thea Astley: A Bibliography'. *LiNQ*, X, No. 4, 1982-3, 87-105.

'Well, We've Heard of Sleeping on It', *S.M.H.*, 23 September, 1968, 6. Interview.

Brady, Veronica. '"In a Critical Condition": Two Responses to John Docker: II'. *Westerly*, XXX, No. 2, 1985, 83-87. Refers to Astley's *An Item from the Late News* to refute an argument of Docker's.

Baker, Candida. 'Thea Astley'. In her *Yacker: Australian Writers Talk About Their Work* (Sydney: Picador, 1986), 28-53.

Burns, Robert. 'The Underdog-Outsider: The Achievement of Mathers' *Trap*'. *Meanjin*, XXXIX, 1970, 95-105. Discusses *Trap* in relation to *The Slow Natives* and other recent novels.

Burrows, J.F. 'Chalk and Cheese'. *Southerly*, XXIII, No. 4, 1963, 276-80. Review of *The Well-Dressed Explorer*, and George Turner's *The Cupboard under the Stairs*.

Clancy Laurie. 'The Fiction of Thea Astley'. *Meridian*, V, No. 1, 1986, 43-52.

Couper, J.M. 'The Novels of Thea Astley'. *Meanjin*, XXVI, 1967, 332-338.

Drewe, Robert. 'Profile of a Prize Novelist'. *Age*, 28 May, 1966, 22.

Ellison, Jennifer. 'Thea Astley'. In her *Rooms of Their Own* (Ringwood, Vic.: Penguin, 1986), 50-69.

Frizell, Helen. 'To Battle over Papers'. *S.M.H.*, 26 March, 1980, 7.

Fuller, Peter. 'To the Islands with Thea Astley'. *Canberra Times*, 9 March, 1985, 17.

Goldsworthy, Kerryn. 'Thea Astley's Writing: Magnetic North'. *Meanjin*, XLII, 1983, 478-85.

---. 'Voices in Time: *A Kindness Cup* and *Miss Peabody's Inheritance*'. *A.L.S.*, No. 4, 1986, 471-81.

Goodwin, Ken. 'Revolution as Bodily Fiction: Thea Astley and Margaret Atwood'. *Antipodes*, 4.2, 1990, 109-14.

Hall, Sandra. 'Why Write Novels?'. *Bulletin*, 26 October, 1968, 52-54, esp. 54.

Haynes, Roslynn D. 'Shelter From the Holocaust: Thea Astley's *An Item from the Late News*'. *Southerly*, 48, No. 2, 1988, 138-51.

Headon, David. 'Interview with Australian Novelist, Thea Astley'. *Northern Perspective*, VII, No. 1, 1984, 19-22.

Johnson, Sue. 'The Passions of Thea Astley'. *National Times*, 7-13 October, 1983, 33.

Jones, Margaret. 'Third Award Win: Authoress of *The Acolyte*'. *S.M.H.*, 11 April,

1973, 2.

Kirkby, Joan. '"The Vertigris of Glory": The Lure of Abjection in Thea Astley's *The Acolyte*'. *Kunapipi*, 1, No. 1, 1994, 27-43.

Lindsay, Elaine. 'Reading Thea Astley: From Catholicism to Post-Christian Feminism'. *Antipodes*, 9.2, 1995, 119-22.

Livingstone, Tess. 'Thea Astley: Tea, Quips and Education Trendies'. *Courier-Mail*, 6 August, 1983, 22. Interview.

Matthews, Brian. 'Life in the Eye of the Hurricane: The Novels of Thea Astley'. *Southern Review*, XI, 1973, 148-73.

---. 'Thea Astley: "Before Feminism ... After Feminism"'. In his *Romantics and Mavericks: The Australian Short Story*. (Townsville, Qld.: James Cook University of North Queensland, 1987), 16-22. The Colin Roderick Lectures; 1986. Monograph/Foundation for Australian Literary Studies, No. 14.2.

Milnes, Stephen. 'The Negative Determinations of Literary Criticism - Thea Astley and Writing as a Man'. *Antipodes*, 8, No. 2, 1994, 105-09.

Nash, Ellen. 'Thea Astley, the Novelist Next Door'. *Cleo*, No. 44, 1976, 25-27.

Nicklin, Lenore. 'Thea Astley: Writing in the Rainforest'. *S.M.H.*, 13 October, 1979, 14.

Oost, Victor. 'Culture and Literature - Heterosexual Relations in Four Australian Short Stories'. *Antipodes*, 8, No. 1, 1994, 25-30. Includes discussion of stories by Astley.

Perkins, Elizabeth. 'Hacking at Tropical Undergrowth: Exploration in Thea Astley's North Queensland'. *Outrider* [10.1&2, 1993]: 377-86.

---. 'A Life of its Own: A Deconstructive Reading of Astley's *A Kindness Cup*'. *Hecate*, XI, No. 1, 1985, 11-18.

Ross, Robert L. 'An Interview with Thea Astley'. *WLWE*, XXVI, No. 2, 1986, 264-268.

---. 'Mavis Gallant and Thea Astley on Home Truths, Home Folk'. *Ariel*, XIX, No. 1, 1988, 83-89.

---. 'Reaching toward "The Center": Thea Astley's *Coda*'. *The World and I*, 10.2, 1995, 316-21.

---. 'The Shape of Language in Thea Astley's Work'. *WLWE*, XXVIII, No. 2, 1988, 260-265.

---. 'Thea Astley: Writing the Parish and Extending the Metaphor'. In his (ed.) *International Literature in English: Essays on the Major Writers* (New York: Garland, 1991), 593-602.

Sharrad, Paul. 'The Well-Dressed Pacific Explorer, Thea Astley's *The Beachmasters*: A Study in Displacement'. *Ariel*, 21, No. 4, 1990, 101-17.

Smith, Graeme Kinross. 'Thea Astley'. *Kunapipi*, IV, No. 1, 1982, 20-37.

Smith, Margaret. 'Pioneer's Lament'. *Weekend Australian Magazine*, 8-9 August, 1981, 16.

Tareka, Nicola Jane. *The Legend of the Leap: A Background to the Legend in Thea Astley's 'A Kindness Cup'*. (Townsville, Qld.: James Cook University, 1986). Monograph/Foundation for Australian Literary Studies, No. 13.

Willbanks, Ray. 'Thea Astley'. In his *Speaking Volumes: Australian Writers and Their Work* (Ringwood, Vic.: Penguin, 1991).

ATKINSON, LOUISA

Fiction

Cowanda: The Veteran's Grant. Edited and introduced by Elizabeth Lawson. Aust. Books on Demand 11. (Canberra: Mulini Press, 1995). First published 1859. Reviewed by *Margin*, 35, 1995, 38.

Myra. (Cook, N.S.W.: Mulini Press, 1989). First serialised in *Sydney Mail* 1864. Reviewed by D. Leadbetter, *ABR*, No. 117, 1989/90, 32.

Debatable Ground (or The Carlillawarra Claimants). (Canberra: Mulini Press, 1992). Introduction by Victor Crittenden. First published as a serial in the *Sydney Mail* from March 1, 1861.
Reviewed by L. Clancy, *Weekend Australian*, 20-21 March, 1993: Review 6.

Critical Material

Clarke, Patricia. *Pioneer Writer: The Life of Louisa Atkinson: Novelist, Journalist, Naturalist*. (Sydney: Allen & Unwin, 1990). Reviewed by F.D. Glass, *Journal of Australian Studies*, 29, 1991, 83; K. Lamb, *Weekend Australian*, 5-6 January 1991, Review 5; E. Morrison, *Australian Historical Studies*, 24.97, 1991, 467-69; S. Stackhouse, *S.M.H.* 12 January, 1991, 35; S. Walker, *A.L.S.*, 15.3, 1992, 238-411.
Crittenden, Victor. 'Louisa Atkinson as Short Story Writer'. *Margin*, 36, 1995, 21-26.
Lawson, Elizabeth. *Louisa Atkinson: The Distant Sound of Native Voices*. Occasional Paper 15 (Canberrra: English Department, University College, Australian Defence Force Academy, 1989). Reviewed by E. Morrison, *Southerly*, 50, No. 3, 1990, 394-95.
---. 'Louisa Atkinson: Naturalist and Novelist'. In *A Bright and Fiery Troop: Australian Women Writers of the Nineteenth Century*, edited by Debra Adelaide (Ringwood: Penguin, 1988), 69-83.
---. 'Louisa Atkinson: Writings on Aboriginal Land Ownership'. *Margin*, No. 21, 1989, 15-20.
White, Graham. 'Louisa Atkinson: Celebrant of the Colonial Landscape'. *Southerly*, 51.1, 1991, 113-26.

AUCHTERLONIE, DOROTHY

Also published as Dorothy Green.

Poetry

The Dolphin. (Canberra: Australian National University Press, 1967).
Reviewed by B. Beaver, *S.M.H.*, 10 February, 1968, 19; R. Hall, *Australian*, 10 August, 1968, 13; M. Irvin, *Poetry Magazine*, No. 4, 1968, 33-34; A. King, *Meanjin*, XXVII, 1968, 173; S.E. Lee, *Southerly*, XXVIII, 1968, 150-51; R. Ward, *ABR*, VII, 1968, 93.

Something to Someone. (Canberra: Brindabella Press, 1983).
Reviewed by B. Beaver, *Weekend Australian Magazine*, 24-25 November, 1984, 16; J. Rodriguez, *S.M.H.*, 22 September, 1984, 44.

Critical Material

Campbell, Richard. 'Dorothy Green 1915-1991'. *LiNQ*, 18.2, 1992, 111-17.
Dowse, Sara. 'In the Nature of a Prophet: Sara Dowse Profiles Dorothy Green'. *Australian Society*, 9, No. 2, 1990, 18-21.
Headon, David. 'Love and Thunder'. *Overland*, 123, 1991, 78-80. Obituary.
Perkins, Elizabeth. 'Gender and Identity in the Poetry of Margaret Diesendorf and Dorothy Auchterlonie'. In *Poetry and Gender: Statements and Essays in Australian Women's Poetry and Poetics*, edited by David Brooks and Brenda Walker (St Lucia: U.Q.P., 1989), 129-44.
---. 'The Work of Dorothy Green'. *Southerly*, 50, No. 3, 1990, 279-93. This issue of *Southerly* is a special issue in honour of Green.

B

BAIL, MURRAY

Fiction

Contemporary Portraits and Other Stories. (St Lucia: U.Q.P., 1975). Paperback Prose, 10. Republished as *The Drover's Wife*. (London: Faber, 1986).
Reviewed by G. Hutchinson, *Makar*, XI, No. 3, 1976, 42-51; B. Kiernan, *National Times*, 2-7 August, 1976, 36-37; L.R. Lippard, *Quadrant*, XX, No. 1, 1976, 62-63; J. Mellors, *Listener*, XCVI, 1976, 854; R. Stevenson, *T.L.S.*, 19 June, 1987, 668; J. Sutherland, *T.L.S.*, 9 April, 1976, 445.

Holden's Performance. (Ringwood, Vic.: Viking, 1987).
Reviewed by G. Catalano, *Quadrant*, XXXI, No. 9, 1987, 75-76; P. Corris, *S.M.H.*, 23 May, 1987, 48; P. Craven, *Age Saturday Extra*, 16 May, 1987, 15; J. Davidson, *Times on Sunday*, 17 May, 1987, 34; B. Edwards, *Mattoid*, No. 30, 1988, 105-108; N. Jose, *Island Magazine*, No. 33, 1987, 3-7; R. Lucas, *S.M.H.*, 19 March, 1988, 74; G. Murnane, *ABR*, No. 92, 1987, 4-6; P. Nelson, *Weekend Australian. Weekend Magazine*, 30 April-1 May, 1988, 14; R. Willbanks, *Antipodes*, I, No. 2, 1987, 115; G. Windsor, *Bulletin*, 2 June, 1987, 79-80.

Homesickness. (South Melbourne: Macmillan, 1980).
Reviewed by D. Anderson, *Westerly*, XXV, No. 4, 1980, 94-96; G. Baxter, *Weekend Australian Magazine*, 11-12 October, 1980, 16; H. Daniel, *Age*, 11 October, 1980, 30; S. Edgar, *Canberra Times*, 11 October, 1980, 23; M. Field, *National Times*, 12-18 October, 1980, 62; K. Gelder, *CRNLE Reviews Journal*, No. 2, 1981, 13-15; A. Gould, *ABR*, No. 25, 1980, 25-26; R. Hall, *S.M.H.*, 20 September, 1980, 20; V. Laughton, *Ash Magazine*, No. 6, 1981, 33; P. Lewis, *T.L.S.*, 19 September, 1980, 1044; J. Naughton, *Listener*, CIV, 1980, 313; E. Perkins, *Quadrant*, XXV, No. 4, 1981, 66-68; P. Pierce, *Meanjin*, XL, 1981, 107-08; E. Riddell, *Bulletin*, 9 September, 1980, 72, 75; T. Shapcott, *Courier-Mail*, 11 October, 1980, 22; C. Treloar, *Advertiser*, 11 October, 1980, 23.

Non-Fiction

Longhand: A Writer's Notebook. (Ringwood: Vic.: McPhee Gribble, 1989).
Reviewed by D. Anderson, *Editions*, 1, No.5, 1989-90, 10; P. Craven, *Age Saturday Extra*, 28 October, 1989, 10; J. Davidson, *Weekend Australian*, 23-24 December, 1989, 6; P. Pierce, *Bulletin*, 7 November, 126-27.

[Statement in reply to a questionnaire on his fiction]. *A.L.S.*, VIII, 1977, 188.

Critical Material

'Portrait of Murray Bail: An Interview'. *Going Down Swinging*, No. 2, 1981.
'The Novelist of Long Distance'. *Weekend Australian Magazine*, 11-12 October, 1980, 16.
Ahearne, Kate, Lysenko, Myron and Brophy, Kevin. 'An Interview with Murray

Bail'. *Aspect*, No. 21, 1981, 55-59.

Ahearne, Kate. 'Games Murray Bail Plays'. *Going Down Swinging*, No. 2, 1981, 48-56.

Arens, Werner. 'The Ironical Fate of "The Drover's Wife": Four Versions from Henry Lawson (1892) to Barbara Jefferis (1980)'. In *The Story Must Be Told: Short Narrative Prose in the New English Literatures*, edited by Peter O. Stummer (Wurzburg: Konigshausen und Neumann, 1986); 119-133.

Bowering, George. 'Wiebe and Bail: Re Making the Story'. In *Postcolonial Fictions*, edited by Michèle Drouart, special issue in two volumes incl. SPACLALS Conference Proceedings. *SPAN* 36, 1993, 668-75.

Casey, Constance. 'Down Under, Out Back and Over There'. [Washington Post] *Book World*, 4 October, 1981, 14-15.

Chisholm, Anne. 'The Blue-Biro World of Murray Bail'. *National Times*, 15-21 February, 1981, 41-42.

Clunies-Ross, Bruce A. 'Laszlo's Testament; or, Structuring the Past and Sketching the Present in Contemporary Short Fiction, mainly Australian'. *Kunapipi*, I, No. 2, 1979, 110-23.

Daniel, Helen. *Liars: Australian New Novelists*. (Ringwood, Vic.: Penguin, 1988), 191-224.

Davidson, Jim. 'Interview - Murray Bail'. *Meanjin*, XLI, 1982, 264-76. Reprinted in his *Sideways From the Page: The Meanjin Interviews* (Melbourne: Fontana/Collins, 1983), 373-390.

Dixon, Robert. '"The Great Australian Emptiness" Revisited: Murray Bail's *Holden's Performance*'. *A.L.S.*, 15.1, 1991, 26-37.

Frizell, Helen. 'Award-Winning Novel Took Three Years'. *S.M.H.*, 11 October, 1980, 25. On the National Book Council award see also p 3 and *ABR*, No. 25, 1980, 24.

Grealy, Michael. 'The Greying of Murray Bail'. *Advertiser*, 25 October, 1980, 21. Interview.

Hardy, Oliver. 'The Man who Warms to his Craft'. *Courier-Mail*, 11 October, 1980, 23.

Herk, Aritha van. 'Post-Modernism: Homesick for Homesickness' (includes discussion of *Homesickness*). In *The Commonwealth Novel Since 1960* edited by Bruce King (Houndmills, Basingstoke, Hampshire and London: Macmillan, 1991), 216-30.

Huggan, Graham. 'Some Recent Australian Fictions in the Age of Tourism: Murray Bail, Inez Baranay, Gerard Lee'. *A.L.S.*, 16.2, 1993, 168-78.

Ommundsen, Wenche. 'The World, the Text, and the Tourist: Murray Bail's *Homesickness* as Guide to the Real'. *Journal of Narrative Technique*, 21.1, 1991, 1-13.

Pons, Xavier. 'Australia Takes on the World: Identity and Representation in Murray Bail's *Homesickness*'. *Commonwealth*, 14.1, 1991, 1-8.

Sayers, Stuart. 'A Search for Something Else'. *Age*, 9 August, 1980, 26.

Spinks, Lee. 'Texts and Counter-Texts: The Allegorical Art of Murray Bail'. *SPAN*, 39, 1994, 1-14.

Stewart, Annette. 'Art and the Australian Artist: In White, Malouf, Murnane and Bail'. *Quadrant*, XXXI, No. 8, 1987, 52-59.

---. 'Recent Australian Fiction'. *WLWE*, 1983, 212-23.

Thomas, Glen. 'Patrick White and Murray Bail: Appropriations of "The Prodigal Son"'. *A.L.S.*, 15.1, 1991, 81-86.

Vauthier, Simone. 'Images Visuelles, Images Verbales: "The Drover's Wife" de Murray Bail'. In *La Nouvelle de Langue Anglaise. The Short Story* (Paris: Service des Publications de la Sorbonne Nouvelle, 1988), 137-145.

BALODIS, JANIS

Drama
Too Young for Ghosts. (Sydney: Currency Press, 1991).
Reviewed by A. Cromwell, *Antipodes*, 7.1, 1993, 70-72; P. Nelson, *Weekend Australian*, 9-10 May, 1992, Review 6.
Wet and Dry. (Sydney: Currency Press, 1991).
Reviewed by A. Cromwell, *Antipodes*, 7.1, 1993, 70-72; G. Milne, *Australasian Drama Studies* 21, 1992, 176-79.

Critical Material
Gilbert, Helen. 'Ghosts in a Landscape: Louis Nowra's *Inside the Island* and Janis Balodis' *Too Young for Ghosts'*. *Southern Review*, 27.4, 1994, 432-47.
Kelly, Veronica. 'Falling between Stools: The Theatre of Janis Balodis'. *Ariel*, 23.1, 1992, 113-32.
---. '"Projecting the Inner World onto an Existing Landscape": an Interview'. *Australasian Drama Studies*, 17, 1990: 4-39.
McNaughton, Howard. 'The Speaking Abject: The Impossible Possible World of Realized Empire'. Includes discussion of *Too Young for Ghosts*. In *De-scribing Empire: Post-colonialism and Textuality*, edited by Chris Tiffin and Alan Lawson (London and New York: Routledge, 1994), 218-29.

BANFIELD, E.J.

Critical Material
Heseltine, H.P. 'The Confessions of a Beachcomber'. *LiNQ*, IX, No. 1, 1981, 35-52.
McGregor, Adrian. 'In Search of E.J. Banfield'. *Courier-Mail*, 24 September, 1983, 27.
Noonan, Michael. *A Different Drummer: The Story of E.J. Banfield, the Beachcomber of Dunk Island*. (St Lucia: U.Q.P., 1983). Reviewed by J. Ackland, *Luna*, No. 18, 1984, 36-39; G. Dutton, *Age Saturday Extra*, 17 December, 1983, 13; S. Murray, *Canberra Times*, 28 January, 1984, 18; M. O'Connor, *ABR*, No. 59, 1984, 7-9; E. Riddell, *Bulletin*, 20 December, 1983, 62, 64 & 67; J. Rowbotham, *Courier-Mail*, 15 October, 1983, 21; O. Ruhen, *Weekend Australian Magazine*, 26-27 November, 1983, 14.

BARANAY, INEZ

Fiction
Between Careers. (Sydney, NSW: Collins/Imprint, 1989).
Reviewed by V. Brady, *ABR*, 112, 1989, 4-6; R. O'Grady, *Age*, 24 June, 1989, Saturday Extra 9; D. Davison, *Weekend Australian*, 5-6 August, 1989, 6; M. McClusky, *Independent Monthly*, August 1989, 37.

The Edge of Bali. (Pymble, NSW: Imprint, 1992).
Reviewed by G.Carey, *ABR*, 145, 1992, 20-21; J. Chimonyo, *Age*, 12 December, 1992, Saturday Extra 10; S. Kelen, *S.M.H.*, 17 October, 1992, 44; L. Trainor, *Weekend Australian*, 17-18 October, 1992, Review 7.

Pagan. (North Ryde, NSW: A.& R., 1990).
Reviewed by L. Davison, *ABR*, 120, 1990, 5-6; M. de Kretser, *S.M.H.*, 5 May, 1990, 73; D. Emmerson, *Weekend Australian*, 19- 20 May, 1990, Weekend 5; J.Hanrahan, *Age*, 28 April, 1990, Saturday Extra 9; J. Maddocks, *Editions*, 2.5, 1991, 12.

The Saddest Pleasure. (Sydney: Collins Imprint, 1989).
Reviewed by J. Chimonyo, *Age*, 17 February, 1990, Saturday Extra 11; S. Lovell, *Imago* 2.1, 1990, 87.

Non-Fiction
Rascal Rain: A Year in Papua New Guinea. (Pymble, NSW: A.& R., 1994).
Reviewed by M. Challinger, *ABR*, 160, 1994, 42-43; J. C. Grayson, *Weekend Australian*, 18-19 June , 1994, Review 6; J.Hanrahan, *Age*, 11 June, 1994, Saturday Extra 8; B. Lambert, *Australian Multicultural Book Review*, 2.3, 1994, 57-59; S. M. Stewart, *Overland*, 137, 1994, 86.

Critical Material
Bartlett, Alison. 'No End to Romance? Sexual Economies in Inez Baranay's *Between Careers'*. *LiNQ*, 22.2, 1995, 29-40.
---. 'Trucking in and out of Universities: An Interview between Inez Baranay and Alison Bartlett'. *LiNQ*, 22.2, 1995, 20-28.
Huggan, Graham. ' Some Recent Australian Fictions in the Age of Tourism: Murray Bail, Inez Baranay, Gerard Lee'. *A.L.S.*, 16.2, 1993, 168-78.
Whitlock, Gillian. 'Graftworks: Australian Women's Writing 1970-90'. In *Gender, Politics and Fiction: Twentieth Century Australian Women's Novels*, edited by Carole Ferrier (St. Lucia: U.Q.P., 1992), 236-258.

BARNARD, MARJORIE

Collection
M. Barnard Eldershaw: 'Plaque with Laurel', Essays Reviews & Correspondence. Edited by Maryanne Dever. (St Lucia: U.Q.P., 1995).
Reviewed by F. Capp, *Age*, 18 Feb., 1995, Saturday Extra 8; I. Saunders, *Westerly*, 40.2, 1995, 88-90; G. Thomas, *Social Alternatives*, 14.4, 1995, 56-57.

Fiction
But Not For Love: Stories of Marjorie Barnard and M. Barnard Eldershaw. Introduction by Robert Darby. (Sydney: Allen and Unwin, 1988).
The Persimmon Tree and Other Stories. (London: Virago, 1985).
Reviewed by L. Clancy, *ABR*, No. 82, 1986, 28; J. Mellors, *Listener*, 9 January, 1986, 29.

Non-Fiction
As Good as a Yarn with You: Letters between Miles Franklin, Katharine Susannah Prichard, Jean Devanny, Marjorie Barnard, Flora Eldershaw and Eleanor Dark. Edited by Carole Ferrier (Cambridge: Cambridge UP, 1992).
Reviewed by N. Albinski, *Antipodes*, 7.2, 1993, 161; F. Capp, *Age*, 22 August, 1992, Saturday Extra 9; K. Holmes, *Australian Women's Book Review*, 5.3, 1993, 10; A. Inglis, *Editions*, 14: 9-10, 1992; S. Lever, *Overland*, 129, 1992, 86-87; M. Lord, *Weekend Australian*, 8-9 August, 1992, Review 7; S. Martin, *Hecate*, 18.2, 1992, 126-37; E. Morrison, *Australian Historical Studies*, 101, 1993, 657-59; J. Roe, *Australian Feminist Studies*, 17, 1993, 245-46; S. Sheridan, *Modern Times*, August, 1992, 34-35; L. Sussex, *ABR*, 145, 1992, 48-49.

Miles Franklin: The Story of a Famous Australian. (St. Lucia: U.Q.P., 1988). With a new introduction by Jill Roe. First published Boston: Twayne; Melbourne: Hill of Content, 1967.
Reviewed by F. Davis, *Fremantle Arts Review*, 4, No. 5 (1989), 14; R. Gostand, *Social Alternatives*, 8, No. 2 (1989), 73-74.

'How *Tomorrow and Tomorrow* Came to be Written'. *Meanjin*, XXIX, 1970, 328-39.

Critical Material
Baker, Candida. 'Marjorie Barnard'. In her *Yacker 2: Australian Writers Talk About Their Work* (Sydney: Picador, 1987), 28-41.
Buckridge, Patrick. '"Greatness" and Australian Literature in the 1930s and 1940s: Novels by Dark and Barnard Eldershaw'. *A.L.S.*, 17.1, 1995, 29-37.

Darby, Robert. 'An Unfinished and Unpublished Story by Marjorie Barnard'. Includes story and textual note. *Notes & Furphies*, No. 21, 1988, 2-6.
Dever, Maryanne. '"Conventional Women of Ability": M. Barnard Eldershaw and the question of cultural authority'. In *Wallflowers and Witches: Women and Culture in Australia 1910-1945*, edited by Maryanne Dever (St Lucia: U.Q.P., 1994), 133-46.
---. '"No Time is Inopportune for a Protest": Aspects of the Political Activities of Marjorie Barnard and Flora Eldershaw'. *Hecate*, 17.2, 1991, 9-21.
Fairbairns, Zoe. 'Marjorie Barnard: Talking with Zoe Fairbairns'. In *Writing Lives: Conversations Between Women Writers*, edited by Mary Chamberlain (London: Virago, 1988), 37-44.
Ferrier, Carole. 'Women of Letters and the Uses of Memory'. In *Wallflowers and Witches: Women and Culture in Australia 1910-1945*, edited by Maryanne Dever (St Lucia: U.Q.P., 1994), 73-90. Includes discussion of Barnard and others.
Giuffre, Giulia. 'Marjorie Barnard'. In her *A Writing Life: Interviews with Australian Women Writers*. (Sydney: Allen and Unwin, 1990), 131-49.
Hickey, Bernard. 'Marjorie Barnard: "Pools Left Clear"'. In *Saggi e ricerche sulle culture extraeuropee*, edited by G. Bellini, C. Gorlier, and S. Zoppi (Rome: Bulzoni, 1986), 39-51. Africa, America, Asia, Australia, 2.
Keesing, Nancy. 'Everything is Not Enough; an Interview with Marjorie Barnard'. *Overland*, No. 67, 1977, 49-53.
McInerney, Sally. 'Recognition for a Writer who Wanted to Change Things Despite the Censor'. *S.M.H.*, 19 November, 1983, 43.
Phillips, Valmai. 'Obituary - Marjorie Faith Barnard (1898-1987)'. *Newsletter of the Royal Australian Historical Society and Affiliated Societies*, XL,4, 1987. Other obituaries appeared in *Quadrant*, XXI, No. 7, 1987, 9; *S.M.H.*, 9 May, 1987, 6; *Womanspeak*, X, No. 5, 1987, 25 and elsewhere.
Williamson, Kristin. 'The Remarkable Marjorie Barnard'. *National Times*, 19-25 August, 1983, 32.

BARTON, CHARLOTTE

Critical Material
Muir, Marcie. *Charlotte Barton: Australia's First Children's Author*. (Sydney: Wentworth Books, 1980). Reviewed by H. Frizell, *S.M.H.*, 1 November, 1980, 21.

BAYLEBRIDGE, WILLIAM

Poetry
Salvage: Collected Works of William Baylebridge. Vol. IV. (Sydney: A.& R., 1964).
Reviewed by G. Cross, *S.M.H.*, 21 August, 1965, 16; J. McAuley, *Bulletin*, 7 August, 1965, 16.
The Growth of Love. Edited with an introduction by P.R. Stephensen. (Sydney: A.& R., 1963). Vol. III of Memorial Edition of Baylebridge's works.

Critical Material
Claremont, Robyn. 'William Baylebridge: Man's Voice Proclaiming Man'. *A.L.S.*, I, No. 3, 1964, 155-69.
Lindsay, Jack. 'Zarathustran Walkabout'. *T.L.S.*, 9 April, 1976, 423.
Macainsh, Noel. 'Baylebridge, Nietzsche, Shaw: Some Observations on the "New Nationalism"'. *A.L.S.*, VII, 1975, 141-59. Reprinted in his *The Pathos of Distance* (Bern, New York, Paris: Peter Lang, 1992), 157-178.
---. 'William Baylebridge and *The Daily Mail*'. *Southerly*, XXXV, 1975, 260-69.

BAYNTON, BARBARA

Collection

Barbara Baynton; edited by Sally Krimmer and Alan Lawson. (St Lucia: U.Q.P., 1980). Portable Australian Authors.
Reviewed by M. Eldridge, *Canberra Times*, 29 November, 1980, 18; J. McLaren, *ABR*, No. 23, 1980, 6; K. Stewart, *A.L.S.*, X, 1982, 541-43; G. Windsor, *Quadrant*, XXV, No. 3, 1981, 69-70.

Fiction

Bush Studies. (Sydney: A.& R., 1965). Contains also the following: Gullett, H.B. 'Memoir of Barbara Baynton'. 1-27; Phillips, A.A. 'Barbara Baynton's Stories'. 27-45.
Reviewed by M. Dunlevy, *Canberra Times*, 26 March, 1966, 13; B. Elliott, *ABR*, V, 1966, 134; G. Johnston, *Australian*, 7 May, 1966, 9; J. Lindsay, *Meanjin*, XXV, 1966, 345-8; K. Tennant, *S.M.H.*, 19 March, 1966, 15; *T.L.S.*, 9 June, 1966, 520.

Bush Studies. (Pymble, NSW: A.& R., 1993). Introduction by Elizabeth Webby. Memoir H.B. Gullett.

Critical Material

Krimmer, Sally. 'New Light on Barbara Baynton'. *A.L.S.*, VII, 1976, 425-30; Bibliography, 430-33.

Astley, Thea. 'The Teeth Father Naked at Last: The Short Stories of Barbara Baynton'. In her *Three Australian Writers*. (Townsville: Townsville Foundation for Australian Literary Studies, 1979), 12-22.

Barnes, John. 'Australian Books in Print: Filling Some Gaps'. *Westerly*, No. 2, 1967, 60-63.

Colmer, John. 'Multiple Perspectives in Barbara Baynton's Short Stories'. In *The Story Must Be Told: Short Narrative Prose in the New English Literatures*, edited by Peter O. Stummer (Wurzburg: Konigshausen und Neumann, 1986), 108-118.

Craig, Caroline. 'Colonial Women Writers: Barbara Baynton (1857-1929)'. *Refractory Girl*, No. 17, 1979, 33-34.

Franklin, C. 'Furphy 4: "To My Country": Brereton Not Baynton!' *Notes & Furphies*, 26, 1991, 17-18.

Frost, Lucy. 'Barbara Baynton: An Affinity with Pain'. In *Who is She?*, edited by Shirley Walker (St Lucia: U.Q.P., 1983), 56-70.

Hackforth-Jones, Penne. *Barbara Baynton: Between Two Worlds*. (Ringwood, Vic.: Penguin, 1989). Reviewed by K. Ahearne, *Age Saturday Extra*, 4 March, 1989, 10; J. Clark and B. Brooks, *S.M.H.*, 4 March, 1989, 88; F.B. Cogan, *Antipodes*, 3.2, 1989, 153; S. Sheridan, *A.L.S.*, 14, No. 1, 1989, 118-22; K. Stewart, *Weekend Australian*, 25-26 February, 1989, Weekend 9; J. Stone, *Biblionews and Australian Notes and Queries*, 14, No.2, 1989, 57-59.

Iseman, Kay. 'Barbara Baynton: Woman as "The Chosen Vessel"'. *A.L.S.*, XI, 1983, 25-37.

Kirkby, Joan. 'Barbara Baynton: An Australian Jocasta'. *Westerly*, 34, No.4, 1989, 114-24.

Lindsay, Jack. 'Barbara Baynton: A Master of Naturalism'. In his *Decay and Renewal* (Sydney: Wild & Woolley, 1976), 262-66.

Matthews, Brian. 'Disguises and Persecutions: Miles Franklin, Louisa Lawson, Barbara Baynton'. In his *Romantics and Mavericks: The Australian Short Story*. (Townsville, Qld.: James Cook University of North Queensland, 1987), 4-15. The Colin Roderick Lectures; 1986. Monograph/Foundation for Australian Literary Studies No. 4.

Moore, Rosemary. 'The Enigma of Woman: Barbara Baynton's *Human Toll*'. *Australian Feminist Studies*, 12, 1990, 83-93.

---. 'Envisioning Female Sexuality in Barbara Baynton's *Human Toll*'. In *The Time to Write: Australian Women Writers 1890-1930*, edited by Kay Ferres (Ringwood, Vic.: Penguin, 1993), 218-37.
---. '"Squeaker's Mate": A Bushwoman's Tale'. *Australian Feminist Studies*, No. 3, 1986, 26-44.
Niall, Brenda. 'The Houses Barbara Baynton Built'. *This Australia*, I, No. 4, 1982, 37-42.
Palmer, Vance. *Intimate Portraits*, ed. H.P. Heseltine. (Melbourne: Cheshire, 1969), 83-87.
Phillips, A.A. 'Barbara Baynton and the Dissidence of the Nineties'. In *An Overland Muster*, edited by S. Murray-Smith (Brisbane: Jacaranda Press, 1965), 178-90. First published *Overland*, No. 22, 1961, 15-20.
Ryan, J.S. 'Barbara Baynton in the Upper Hunter'. *Armidale & District Historical Society. Journal & Proceedings*, No. 21, 1978, 79.
Schaffer, Kay. 'Barbara Baynton: A Dissident Voice From the Bush'. In her *Women and the Bush: Forces of Desire in the Australian Cultural Tradition* (Melbourne: Cambridge University Press, 1988), 148-70.
Sheridan, Susan. 'Gender and Genre in Barbara Baynton's *Human Toll*'. *A.L.S.*, 14, No.1 (1989), 66-77.
Walker, Shirley. 'Barbara Baynton's *Human Toll*: A Modernist Text?'. *Southerly*, 49, No.2, 1989, 131-48.
Webby, Elizabeth. 'Barbara Baynton's Revisions to "Squeaker's Mate"'. *Southerly*, XLIV, 1984, 455-68.

BEAVER, BRUCE

Fiction
You Can't Come Back. (Adelaide: Rigby, 1966).
Reviewed by E. Castle, *Overland*, No. 35, 1966, 56-7; S. Edgar, *Canberra Times*, 22 October, 1966, 12; M. Eldridge, *Canberra Times*, 6 April, 1985, 16; L.V. Kepert, *S.M.H.*, 3 September, 1966, 18; D. Whitelock, *ABR*, V, 1966, 234 and *Southerly*, XXVI, 1966, 281-2; R.M. Wilding, *Bulletin*, 17 September, 1966, 59.

Poetry
Anima and Other Poems. (St Lucia: U.Q.P., 1994).
Reviewed by J. Boe, *Antipodes*, 8.2, 1994, 156; H. Cam, *S.M.H.*, 23 July, 1994, Spectrum 11A; L. Cataldi, *Overland*, 140, 1995, 82-83; M. Duwell, *Weekend Australian*, 26-27 November, 1994, Review 4; J. Malone, *Redoubt*, 19, 1994, 120-21; S. Patton, *ABR*, 161, 1994, 45-46 (see also interview by R. Sorensen 46-48); N. Rowe, *Voices* 4.4, 1994-95, 109-16.

As It Was... (St Lucia: U.Q.P., 1979).
Reviewed by V. Brady, *ABR*, No. 13, 1979, 5-7; A. Burke, *Westerly*, XXV, No. 2, 1980, 124-27; D. Haskell, *Southerly*, XL, 1980, 226-40; M. Hulse, *PN Review*, XIII, No. 1, 1986, 72; R. Macklin, *Bulletin*, 19 June, 1979, 81-82, rptd. 26 June, 1979, 68; S. Morrell, *24 Hours*, IV, No. 9, 1979, 67; G. Page, *National Times*, 20 October, 1979, 34; G. Rowlands, *Overland*, No. 96, 1984, 68-69.

Bruce Beaver Reads from His Own Work. (St Lucia: U.Q.P., 1972). Poets on record, 7. Record and booklet. Booklet includes notes by the author and selected bibliography.
Reviewed by M. Duwell, *Makar*, VIII, No. 2, 1972, 47-48.

Charmed Lives. (St. Lucia: U.Q.P., 1988).
Reviewed by D. Porter, *Weekend Australian* 31 December-1 January, Weekend 5; C. Wallace-Crabbe, *Age Saturday Extra* 28 January, 13.

Death's Directives. (Sydney: Prism Books, 1978).
Reviewed by B. Giles, *ABR*, No. 14, 1979, 12; R. Harris, *New Poetry*, XXVII,

No. 1, 1979, 73-74; C. Pollnitz, *Southerly*, XXXIX, 1979, 476-78.

Lauds and Plaints: Poems, 1968-1972. (Sydney: South Head Press, 1974).
Reviewed by J.B. Beston, *S.M.H.*, 20 July, 1974, 16 and *Westerly*, No. 3, 1974,
71-74; R.M. Beston, *Hemisphere*, XVIII, No. 12, 1974, 40; B. Breen, *Twentieth
Century*, XXIX, No. 1, 1975, 58-62; J. Jenkins, *Etymspheres*, Series I, No. 2,
1975, 43-48; M. Jurgensen, *Makar*, X, No. 2, 1974, 42-44; S.E. Lee, *Southerly*,
XXXV, 1975, 295-98; T. Shapcott, *Australian*, 15 June, 1974, Weekend section,
6.

Letters to Live Poets. (Sydney: South Head Press, 1969).
Reviewed by R. Hall, *Australian*, 28 March, 1970, 14; C. Harrison-Ford, *Poetry
Magazine*, XVIII, No. 5, 1970, 41-43; M. Irvin, *Twentieth Century*, XXIV, 1970,
373-75; G. Lehmann, *Bulletin*, 30 May, 1970, 50-51; A. Riddell, *S.M.H.*, 7
November, 1970, 23; T.W. Shapcott, *ABR*, IX, 1970, 93; R.A. Simpson, *Age*, 28
March, 1970, 15; J. Tulip, *Southerly*, XXX, 1970, 154-57; *T.L.S.*, 23 July, 1970,
832.

New and Selected Poems 1960-1990. (St. Lucia: U.Q.P., 1991).
Reviewed by R. Darling, *Antipodes*, 7.1, 1993, 59-60; M. Duwell, *Weekend
Australian*, 31 August-1 September, 1991, Review 4; C. Harrison-Ford, *Voices*,
1.3, 1991, 92-96; M. Johnson, *World Literature Today*, 66.3, 1992, 577; L.
Norfolk, *T.L.S.*, 5 July, 1991, 21-22; P. Porter, *Island*, 51, 1992, 40-43; P.
Washington, *CRNLE Reviews Journal*, 1, 1992, 86-89.

Odes and Days. (Sydney: South Head Press, 1975).
Reviewed by J.B. Beston, *Westerly*, No. 2, 1975, 68-70 and *S.M.H.* 28 June,
1975, 16; R.D. FitzGerald, *Meanjin*, XXXV, 1976, 197-202; K.L. Goodwin,
Makar, XI, No. 2, 1975, 44-47; W.H. New, *Poetry Australia*, No. 64, 1977,
66-67; A. Summers, *Advertiser*, 17 January, 1976, 20; J. Tulip, *Australian*, 23
August, 1975, 30.

Open at Random. (Sydney: South Head Press, 1967).
Reviewed by D. Anderson, *Southerly*, XXIX, 1969, 71-72; B.A. Breen, *Twentieth
Century*, XXIII, 1968, 179-81; R. Dunlop, *Poetry Australia*, No. 24, 1968, 36-37;
R. Hall, *Australian*, 14 December, 1968, 19; F. Haynes, *Critic* (Perth), IX, 1969,
73-74; M. Irvin, *S.M.H.*, 7 September, 1968, 24; E. Jones, *Nation*, 23 November,
1968, 22; G. Lehmann, *Bulletin*, 12 October, 1968, 80; M. Richards, *Meanjin*,
XXVIII, 1969, 275; R. Ward, *ABR*, VII, 1968, 206.

Seawall and Shoreline. (Sydney: South Head Press, 1964).
Reviewed by R. Dunlop, *Poetry Australia*, No. 1, 1965, 23-5; E. Jones,
Australian, 13 March, 1965, 11; S.E. Lee, *Southerly*, XXV, 1965, 133-4; T.W.
Shapcott, *ABR*, IV, 1965, 69; T. Sturm, *Landfall*, XIX, 1966, 393-5.

Selected Poems. (Sydney: A.& R., 1979).
Reviewed by V. Brady, *ABR*, No. 13, 1979, 5-7; K. Goodwin, *Weekend
Australian Magazine*, 1-2 September, 1979, 10; A. Gould, *Tasmanian Review*, No.
5, 1980, 43-44; R. Gray, *S.M.H.*, 3 November, 1979, 20; D. Haskell, *Southerly*,
XL, 1980, 226-40; G. Page, *National Times*, 20 October, 1979, 34.

   Non-Fiction
Headlands. (St Lucia: U.Q.P., 1986).
Reviewed by J. Colmer, *Weekend Australian Magazine*, 8-9 March, 1986, 15; A.
Gould, *Quadrant*, XXX, No. 10, 1986, 69-74; B. Hill, *ABR*, No. 80, 1986,
10-11; J. Rodriguez, *S.M.H.*, 14 March, 1987, 47 and *Scope*, XXXI, No. 2,
1986, 8; V. Sen, *Canberra Times*, 31 May, 1986, B3.

'Work notes for a New Book and Beyond'. *Meanjin*, 48, No. 2, 1989, 340-43.

   Critical Material
Beston, John and Beston, Rose Marie. 'The *Livres Composes* of Bruce Beaver:

Letters to Live Poets and *Lauds and Plaints*'. *WLWE*, XIV, 1975, 207-20.

Beston, John. 'An Interview with Bruce Beaver'. *WLWE*, XIV, 1975, 231-36.

Clarke, Simon. 'Full-time Occupation of Being a Poet'. *Age Saturday Extra*, 1 January, 1983, 5.

Bourke, Lawrence. 'To a Live Poet: Bruce Beaver'. *Southerly*, 52.3, 1992, 161-67.

Davies, Mark. 'Bruce Beaver: A Short Appreciation'. *Northern Perspective*, 13, No.2, 12-15.

Dingemans, Andre. 'Interviews with Bruce Beaver - 1978 and 1987'. *Fine Line*, No. 2, 1987, 3-14.

Duwell, Martin. '"Having Been Someone Like Myself": The Early Poetry of Bruce Beaver'. *Southerly*, 55.1, 1995, 23-39.

FitzGerald, Robert D. 'Bruce Beaver's Poetry'. *Meanjin*, XXVIII, 1969, 407-12.

Josephi, Beate. 'The Poetry of Bruce Beaver'. *Quadrant*, XXIII, No. 9, 1979, 55-60.

Krause, Tom. 'Prize-winner is Eager to Get on with Writing'. *Weekend Australian*, 20-21 November, 1982, 14. Interview.

Krausmann, Rudi. 'Bruce Beaver, Interview'. *Aspect*, II, No. 2, 1976, 29-33.

McCauley, Shane. 'Confessional Poetry'. *Artlook*, VI, No. 6, 1980, 55-56.

McLaren, John. 'Discontinuous Autobiography: Some Work of Alan Marshall and Bruce Beaver'. In *Autobiographical and Biographical Writing in the Commonwealth*, edited by Doireann MacDermott (Sadabell, Barcelona: Editorial AUSA, 1984), 147-151.

Page, Geoff. 'Bruce Beaver'. In his *A Reader's Guide To Contemporary Australian Poetry* (St. Lucia: U.Q.P., 1995), 17-21.

Porter, Dorothy. 'Charmed Beaver'. *Southerly*, 55.1, 1995, 21-22.

Powell, Craig. 'Gift-bearing Hands: The Poetry of Bruce Beaver'. *Quadrant*, XII, No. 5, 13-18.

Shapcott, Thomas. 'Bruce Beaver, an Interview with Thomas Shapcott'. *Quadrant*, XX, No. 4, 1976, 43-49.

Stasko, Nicolette. 'The Love Poetry of Bruce Beaver'. *Southerly*, 55.1, 1995, 40-52.

Tulip, James. 'The Australian-American Connexion'. *Poetry Australia*, No. 32, 1970, 48-49.

BECKE, LOUIS

Fiction

South Sea Supercargo. Edited by A. Grove Day. (Brisbane: Jacaranda, 1967).
Reviewed by M. Dunlevy, *Canberra Times*, 4 May, 1968, 13; T. Keneally, *Australian*, 2 March, 1968, 11; E. Perkins, *A.L.S.*, III, 1968, 235-38; C. Semmler, *ABR*, VII, 1968, 61; C. Tolchard, *S.M.H.*, 2 March, 1968, 19.

Critical Material

Day, A. Grove. 'By Reef and Tide: Louis Becke's Literary Reputation'. *Australian Letters*, VI, No. 1, 1963-4, 17-26.

---. *Louis Becke*. (New York: Twayne; Melbourne: Hill of Content, 1966). TWAS 9. Reviewed by M. Dunlevy, *Canberra Times*, 18 November, 1967, 11; J. Higgins, *Western Humanities Review*, XXII, 1968, 176-79; T. Keneally, *Australian*, 2 March, 1968, 11; H.E. Maude, *Journal of Pacific History*, II, 1967, 225-27; E. Perkins, *A.L.S.*, III, 1968, 235-38; C. Semmler, *ABR*, VII, 1968, 61; C. Tolchard, *S.M.H.*, 25 November, 1967, 20; B. Wannan, *Age*, 23 December, 1967, 23.

---. 'Louis Becke's First Appearance in Print'. *Biblionews*, I, No. 1, 1966, 19.

Dixon, Robert. *Writing the Colonial Adventure: Race, Gender and Nation in Anglo-Australian Popular Fiction, 1875-1914*. (Melbourne: Cambridge UP, 1995).

Earnshaw, John. 'South Seas Fact and Fiction'. *Biblionews*, I, No. 2, 1966, 21-2.
Gilbert, Mark. 'Literary Buccaneering: Boldrewood, Becke and *The Bulletin*'. *Adelaide A.L.S. Working Papers*, II, No. 2, 1977, 24-35.

BEDFORD, JEAN

Fiction

With Rosemary Cresswell. *Colouring In: A Book of Ideologically Unsound Love Stories*. (Fitzroy, Vic.: McPhee Gribble in association with Penguin, 1986).
Reviewed by D.J. Eszenyi and K. Goldsworthy, *ABR*, No. 83, 1986, 16-18; T. Forshaw, *Weekend Australian Magazine*, 7-8 June, 1986, 17; P. Hawker, *National Times*, 13-19 June, 1986, 33; V. Sen, *Canberra Times*, 26 July, 1986, B2; E. Webby, *S.M.H.*, 28 June, 1986, 48.

Country Girl Again and Other Stories. (Fitzroy, Vic.: McPhee Gribble; Ringwood, Vic.: Penguin, 1985). First published as *Country Girl Again* (Carlton South, Vic.: Sisters Publishing, 1979).
Reviewed by D. Anderson, *National Times*, 15-21 February, 1985, 33; D.R. Burns, *ABR*, No. 19, April, 1980, 20-21; L. Clancy, *Age Saturday Extra*, 6 April, 1985, 10; F. Davis, *Fremantle Arts Centre Broadsheet*: Books, IV, No. 3, 1985, 2-3; V. Fraser, *National Times*, 1 December, 1979, 55; R. Gostand and S. Cassidy, *Social Alternatives*, V, No. 4, 1986, 56-57; J. Neville, *S.M.H.*, 1 December, 1979, 18; M. Smith, *Weekend Australian Magazine*, 1-2 March, 1980, 15; R. Stone, *S.M.H.*, 13 April, 1985, 40; K. Tennant, *Overland*, No. 99, 1985, 73; S. Walker, *ABR*, No. 70, 1985, 20-21.

If with a Beating Heart. (Melbourne: McPhee Gribble, 1993).
Reviewed by P. Craven, *Age*, 13 November, 1993, Saturday Extra 8; J. Murray-Smith, *Weekend Australian*, 27-28 November, 1993, Review 6; R. N. Myatt, *Northern Perspective*, 17.1, 1994, 82-83; H.L.E. Neilson, *ABR*, 157, 1993/1994, 5-6.

A Lease of Summer. (Ringwood, Vic.: McPhee Gribble, 1990).
Reviewed by C. Bird, *Age*, 25 August, 1990, Saturday Extra 9; D. Emmerson, *ABR*, No. 124, 1990, 19-20; P. Pierce, *Bulletin*, 27 November, 1990, 135; A. P. Riemer, *S.M.H.*, 25 August, 1990, 73.

Love Child. (Ringwood, Vic.: Penguin, 1986).
Reviewed by K. Ahearne, *ABR*, No. 84, 1986, 16-17; S. Dowse, *National Times on Sunday*, 10 August, 1986, 34; T. Forshaw, *Weekend Australian Magazine*, 16-17 August, 1986, 16; T. Glad, *Social Alternatives*, VI, No. 4, 1987, 68-69; esp. 68; B. Matthews, *Overland*, No. 106, 1987, 80-82; C. Pybus, *Island Magazine*, No. 32, 1987, 62; V. Sen, *Canberra Times*, 1 November, 1986, B2; R. Stone, *S.M.H.*, 9 August, 1986, 45.

Signs of Murder. (Sydney: A.& R., 1994).
Reviewed by G. Blundell, *Weekend Australian*, 10-11 December, 1994, Review 6; J.R. Carroll, *ABR* 166: 63-64, 1994.

Sister Kate: A Novel. (Ringwood, Vic.: Penguin, 1982).
Reviewed by S. Hall, *Bulletin*, 28 September, 1982, 102; A. Hildyard, *Island Magazine*, Nos. 18-19, 1984, 40-44; B. Jefferis, *National Times*, 5 September, 1982, 22; F. McInherny, *ABR*, No. 46, 1982, 26; L. Maurer, *CRNLE Reviews Journal*, No. 1, 1983, 19-20.

To Make a Killing. (Pymble, NSW: A.& R., 1992).
Reviewed by G. Blundell, *Weekend Australian*, 8-9 August, 1992, Review 6; J. Carroll, *ABR*, 142, 1992, 57-58; S. Coupe, *S.M.H.*, 15 August, 1992, 43.

Worse Than Death. (North Ryde, NSW: A.& R., 1991).
Reviewed by R. Hood, *Scarp*, 18, 1991, 62-65; J. Stephens, *ABR*, 128, 1991, 15.

Non-Fiction
'Fiction: A Way of Avoiding Libel'. In *The View from Tinsel Town*, edited by Tom Thompson (Ringwood, Vic.: Southerly/Penguin, 1985), 47-48.

Critical Material
Bartlett, Alison. 'Other Stories: The Representation of History in Recent Fiction by Australian Women Writers'. *Southerly*, 53.1, 1993, 165-80. Discusses *Sister Kate*.
Ellison, Jennifer. 'Jean Bedford'. In her *Rooms of Their Own* (Ringwood, Vic.: Penguin, 1986), 70-89.

BEDFORD, RANDOLPH

Non-Fiction
Naught to Thirty-Three (Carlton: M.U.P., 1976). Foreword by Geoffrey Blainey. First published Sydney: Currawong, 1944.
Reviewed by L. Cantrell, *A.L.S.*, VIII, 1978, 378-82.

Critical Material
Smith, Ross and Frost, Cheryl. 'Randolph Bedford (1868-1941): A Bibliography'. *LiNQ*, X, No. 4, 1982/83, 106-64.

Cooper, Roslyn Pesman. 'Randolph Bedford in Italy'. *Overland*, No. 120, 1990, 12-15.
Lindsay, Norman. 'Randolph Bedford'. In his *Bohemians of the Bulletin*. (Sydney: ABR, 1965), 101-14.
Palmer, Vance. *Intimate Portraits*, ed. H.P. Heseltine. (Melbourne: Cheshire, 1969), 98-102.
---. 'Randolph Bedford'. *Overland*, No. 26, 1963, 21-2.

BERGNER, HERZ

Critical Material
'Racial Alienation: Common Theme in Contemporary Jewish Literature: Sydney Paper on Jewish Writers'. *Australian Jewish News*, 31 December, 1971, 14. Report of a paper by M.J. Haddock.
Sayers, Stuart. 'Surgeons between Covers'. *Age*, 7 February, 1970, 12.
Waten, Judah. 'In Other Tongues'. *Nation*, 27 June, 1970, 22-23.

BEYNON, RICHARD

Drama
Summer Shadows. (Sydney: Currency Press in association with the Spoleto Melbourne Festival of Three Worlds, 1986).
Reviewed by A. Roper, *English in Australia*, No. 80, 1987, 53-55.

Critical Material
Davison, P.H. 'Three Australian Plays: National Myths under Criticism'. *Southerly*, XXIII, No. 2, 1963, 110-27. Considers *The Shifting Heart*.
Dente Baschiera, Carla. *'The Shifting Heart': Il Dramma Dei Migranti Italiani in Australia*. (Pisa Italy: ETS, 1984). Quaderni di Letteratura Anglo-Americana Series.
Jones, Margaret. 'Beynon Writes again - after 27 Years'. *Age*, 1 August, 1983, 12.

BJELKE-PETERSEN, MARIE

Critical Material
Alexander, Alison. *A Mortal Flame: Marie Bjelke Petersen, Australian Romance Writer*. (Hobart: Blubber Head Press, 1994). Reviewed by E. Dean, *Island*, 60-61,

1994, 148, 150; M. Jones, *S.M.H.*, 13 August, 1994, Spectrum 9A.
Smith, Ross. 'A Forgotten Novel of North Queensland: Marie Bjelke-Petersen's *Jungle Night*'. *LiNQ*, 16, No.1, 1988, 89-99.

BLACKHAM, H.H.

Critical Material
Depasquale, Paul. 'H.H. Blackham: Irish Poet in Exile'. *South Australiana*, IX, 1970, 74-89.

BLAIR, RON

Drama
The Christian Brothers. (Sydney: Currency Press, 1976). Bound with Barry Oakley. *A Lesson in English*.

Marx. (Sydney: Currency Press, 1983).
Reviewed by H. Hewitt, *Canberra Times*, 21 May, 1983, 13; E. Perkins, *LiNQ*, XI, No. 1, 1983, 89-100.

'Christopher Brennan: A TV Drama'. *Quadrant*, XXI, No. 6, 1977, 20-27. Playscript.
'Mad, Bad and Dangerous to Know'. *Quadrant*, XX, No. 10, 1976, 15-21.
'Marx'. *Theatre Australia*, II, No. 12, 1978, 34-39, and III, No. 1, 1978, 35-43.

Non-Fiction
'Understanding the Past'. *Australasian Drama Studies*, No. 9, 1986, 21-34.

Critical Material
Baker, Tony. 'Spotlight'. *Theatre Australia*, II, No. 6, 1977, 59-60. Interview.
Brady, Veronica. *Playing Catholic: Essays on Four Catholic Plays*. (Sydney: Currency Press, 1991). Discusses *The Christian Brothers*.
Elias, Sophie. 'An Interview with Ron Blair 6th August, 1979'. *Commonwealth* (Toulouse), IV, 1979-1980, 139-45.
Griffiths, Gareth. 'Experiments with Form in Recent Australian Drama'. *Kunapipi*, II, No. 1, 1980, 82-83.
James, Pip. 'A Playwright's Lament for the 'Loo'. *Weekend Australian Magazine*, 10-11 October, 1981, 18.
Johnson, Chris. 'Ron Blair's *The Christian Brothers* in Performance'. *WLWE*, XXI, 1982, 283-87.
Rutherford, Anna. '"A Vision or a Waking Dream?": Ron Blair's *The Christian Brothers*'. *Kunapipi*, II, No. 2, 1980, 23-31.

BLIGHT, JOHN

Poetry
A Beachcomber's Diary. (Sydney: A.& R., 1963).
Reviewed by J.M. Couper, *Poetry Magazine*, No. 2, 1964, 34; P. Jeffery, *Westerly*, No. 4, 1964, 55-9; S.E. Lee, *Southerly*, XXIV, No. 3, 1964, 133-4.

Hart: Poems. (Melbourne: Thomas Nelson (Australia), 1975).
Reviewed by P. Porter, *Australian*, 1 November, 1975, 41; R.A. Simpson, *Age*, 20 September, 1975, 16; D. Stewart, *S.M.H.*, 18 October, 1975, 18; R. Tamplin, *T.L.S.*, 9 April, 1976, 443.

Holiday Sea Sonnets. (St. Lucia: U.Q.P., 1985).
Reviewed by B. Beaver, *Weekend Australian Magazine*, 20-21 July, 1985, 16; G. Catalano, *Age Saturday Extra*, 29 June, 1985, 16; M. Haig, *Quadrant*, XXIX, No. 8, 1985, 86-89; M. Hulse, *PN Review*, XIII, No. 1, 1986, 72; G. Page, *ABR*, No. 75, 1985, 31-33; E. Perkins, *Outrider*, III, No. 2, 186-92; K. Purnell, *Luna*, No. 21, 1985, 35-36; J. Rodriguez, *S.M.H.*, 25 May, 1985, 41.

My Beachcombing Days: Ninety Sea Sonnets. (Sydney: A.& R., 1968).
Reviewed by B. Beaver, *S.M.H.*, 24 August, 1968, 23; G. Dutton, *ABR*, VII, 1968, 162; K. England, *Advertiser*, 20 July, 1968, 20; E. Jones, *Nation*, 3 August, 1968, 21-22; S.E. Lee, *Southerly*, XXVIII, 1968, 305-06; G. Lehmann, *Bulletin*, 8 March, 1969, 70-71 (see also letters to the editor by I.B. Smith, *Bulletin*, 22 March, 1969, 86, and J. Blight, 5 April, 1969, 70); R. Mills, *Makar*, IV, No. 4, 1968, 40-43; G. Page, *Canberra Times*, 4 January, 1969, 11; M. Richards, *Meanjin*, XXVIII, 1969, 269-70.

The New City Poems. (Sydney: A.& R., 1980).
Reviewed by G. Burns, *ABR*, No. 34, 1981, 9-10; G. Catalano, *Meanjin*, XL, 1981, 119-20; M. Duwell, *Weekend Australian Magazine*, 20-21 December, 1980, 14.

Pageantry for a Lost Empire. (Melbourne: Nelson, 1978).
Reviewed by B. Beaver, *Age*, 17 June, 1978, 21 and *New Poetry*, No. 26, 1978, 29-31; G. Dutton, *Bulletin*, 25 July, 1978, 62; P. Edmonds, *ABR*, No. 3, 1978, 19; E. Lindsay, *24 Hours*, III, No. 9, 1978, 68.

Selected Poems 1939-1975. (Melbourne: Thomas Nelson (Australia), 1976).
Reviewed by B. Giles, *Luna*, No. 3, 1976, 50-51; J. Griffin, *Advertiser*, 30 October, 1976, 20; M. Macleod, *S.M.H.*, 16 October, 1976, 17; P. Neilsen, *Age*, 23 October, 1976, 17; T. Shapcott, *Australian*, 1 January, 1977, 18.

Selected Poems 1939-1990. Selected and introduced by Martin Duwell. (St Lucia: U.Q.P., 1992).
Reviewed by L. Cataldi, *CRNLE Reviews Journal*, 2, 1993, 78-85; M. Sariban, *Outrider* [10.1&2], 1993, 192-95.

   Non-Fiction
'Soaring with the Culture Vultures'. *Educational Magazine*, XXXVI, No. 3, 1979, 33-35.
   Critical Material
'A Prolific Writer'. *S.M.H.*, 16 October, 1976, 17.
'Brisbane Poet Wins Award'. *Courier-Mail*, 22 November, 1976, 9. Patrick White Prize.
Aiton, Douglas. 'John Blight Figures with Words'. *Age*, 16 October, 1976, 18.
Beaver, Bruce. 'Two Views of the Poetry of John Blight: I'. *Southerly*, XXXVI, 1976, 50-56.
Malouf, David. 'Some Volumes of Selected Poems of the 1970s'. *A.L.S.*, X, 1981, 13-21.
---. 'Two views of the Poetry of John Blight: II'. *Southerly*, XXXVI, 1976, 56-70.
Mishinski, Judy. 'Poetry was his Refuge from Ledger'. *Sunday Mail* (Brisbane), 2 June, 1985, 11.
Page, Geoff. 'John Blight'. In his *A Reader's Guide To Contemporary Australian Poetry* (St. Lucia: U.Q.P., 1995), 24-27.
Rowbotham, David. 'Once there Was a Swagman Poet...'. *Courier-Mail*, 30 July, 1983, 22.
Wright, Judith. 'Poets of the 'Forties and 'Fifties'. In her *Preoccupations in Australian Poetry*. (Melbourne: O.U.P., 1965), 193-210.

BOAKE, BARCROFT

   Critical Material
Burke, Keast, and Fielder, Watty. 'The First Published Poem by Barcroft Boake'. *Biblionews*, XVI, No. 5, 1963.
Semmler, Clement. *Barcroft Boake*. (Melbourne: Lansdowne Press, 1965). Reviewed by A. Brissenden, *ABR*, V, 1966, 63; D. Douglas, *A.L.S.*, II, 1966, 226; R. McCuaig, *Canberra Times*, 29 January, 1966, 11.

---. 'A.G. Stephens as Editor of Barcroft Boake's Poems'. *A.L.S.*, III, 228-30.
---. 'Brunton Stephens as Literary Critic'. *A.L.S.*, II, 1965, 92-102.
Stephens, Alison. 'A.G. Stephens as Editor of Barcroft Boake's Poems: A Comment'. *A.L.S.*, IV, 1969, 80-83. Discusses Clement Semmler, 'A.G. Stephens as Editor of Barcroft Boake's Poems', *A.L.S.*, III, 1968, 228-3.
Wright, Judith. 'Adam Lindsay Gordon and Barcroft Boake'. In her *Preoccupations in Australian Poetry*. (Melbourne: O.U.P., 1965), 57-67.

BOLDREWOOD, ROLF

Collection
Rolf Boldrewood. Edited with an introduction by Alan Brissenden. (St Lucia, U.Q.P., 1979).

Fiction
The Miner's Right: A Tale of the Australian Goldfields. With an introduction by R.G. Geering. Facsimile edition. (Sydney: Sydney University Press, 1973). Australian Literary Reprints. First published London: Macmillan, 1890.
Reviewed by M. Dunlevy, *Canberra Times*, 18 August, 1973, 13; O. Ruhen, *Australian*, 29 August, 1973, 14; M. Wilding, *Southerly*, XXXV, 1975, 99-102.

Non-Fiction
Australian Grazier's Guide. Edited by J.S. Ryan. (Armidale: CALLS, U of New England, 1994).
Reviewed in *Margin*, 35, 1995, 31.

Old Melbourne Memories. With an introduction and editorial commentary by C.E. Sayers. (Melbourne: Heinemann, 1969). Slightly abridged from the first edition, Melbourne: George Robertson, 1884.
Reviewed by 'Batman', *Bulletin*, 6 December, 1969, 57; D. Denholm, *Overland*, No. 45, 1970, 43-44. C. Turnbull, *Age*, 1 November, 1969, 16; L. Ward, *Canberra Times*, 25 October, 1969, 17.

Critical Material
Brady, Veronica. 'The Impulse to Order: *Robbery under Arms*'. *AULLA 19th Congress. Papers and Proceedings*, 1978, 43-51.
Brissenden, Alan. *Rolf Boldrewood*. (Melbourne: O.U.P., 1973). Australian Writers and Their Work. Reviewed by M. Dunlevy, *Canberra Times*, 16 June, 1973, 10; A. Mitchell, *A.L.S.*, VI, 1974, 332-36; J. Waten, *Age*, 21 April, 1973, 13.
---. '*Robbery under Arms*: A Continuing Success'. In *The Australian Experience: Critical Essays on Australian Novels*, edited by W.S. Ramson (Canberra: Australian National University Press, 1974), 38-60.
Compton, Margaret E. '"A Kangaroo Drive": Introductory Note'. *Armidale & District Historical Society. Journal & Proceedings*, No. 18, 1975, 28-29.
Crittenden, Victor. 'A Passion for Gardening: Mrs Boldrewood's Gardening Book'. *Margin*, 34, 1994, 35-38.
Dixon, Robert. 'Rolf Boldrewood's *War to the Knife*: Narrative Form and Ideology in the Historical Novel'. *A.L.S.*, XIII, No. 3, 1986, 324-34.
---. *Writing the Colonial Adventure: Race, Gender and Nation in Anglo-Australian Popular Fiction, 1875-1914*. (Melbourne: Cambridge UP, 1995).
Dowsley, G. '*Robbery under Arms*: A Re-assessment'. *Tasmanian Journal of Education*, II, 1968, 73-77.
Earnshaw, John. 'South Seas Fact and Fiction'. *Biblionews*, I, No. 2, 1966, 21-2.
Elliott, Brian. 'The Composition of *Geoffry Hamlyn*: The Legend and the Facts'. *A.L.S.*, III, 1968, 271-89. Discusses Boldrewood as a source of information.
Gilbert, Mark. 'Literary Buccaneering: Boldrewood, Becke and *The Bulletin*'. *Adelaide A.L.S. Working Papers*, II, No. 2, 1977, 23-35.

Hamer, Clive. 'Boldrewood Reassessed'. *Southerly*, XXVI, 1966, 263-78.

Kettler, Ned. 'My Colonial Oath'. *Realist*, No. 31, 1968, 6-11.

McCarthy, P.H. *Starlight: The Man and the Myth*. (Melbourne: Hawthorn Press, 1972).

McLaren, John. 'Rolf Boldrewood and the Mythologisation of Australia'. *Meanjin*, XXXVII, 1978, 251-56.

Middleton, Delys E.J. 'Villain or Hero? The Bushranger in *Ralph Rashleigh*, *Robbery under Arms*, and *The Hero of Too*'. *Armidale and District Historical Society Journal and Proceedings*, No. 13, 1970, 27-36.

Mitchell, Bruce. 'On the Trail of "Terrible Hollow"'. *Notes & Furphies*, No. 10, 1983, 15-16.

Moore, T. Inglis. *Rolf Boldrewood*. (Melbourne: O.U.P., 1968). Great Australians Series.

Nedeljkovic, Maryvonne. 'Reve et Realites; les Debuts de la Litterature d'Immigres en Australie; Rolf Boldrewood et les Problemes d'Adaptation: *(Robbery Under Arms, 1888*, et *The Squatter's Dream, 1890)*'. *Commonwealth* (Rodez) I, 1974-1975, 79-93.

Pierce, Peter. '"Weary With Travelling Through Realms of Air..." Romantic Fiction of 'Boldrewood', Haggard, Wells and Praed'. *Westerly*, XXXII, No. 2, 1987, 79-90.

Roberts, Alan. 'A Forgotten Boldrewood Book'. *Biblionews and Australian Notes & Queries*, second series V, No. 2, 1971, 13-16.

Rosenberg, Jerome H. 'Cultural Symbolism in *Robbery under Arms*'. WLWE, XVII, 1978, 488-504.

---. 'Narrative Perspective and Cultural History in *Robbery Under Arms*'. *A.L.S.*, VI, 1973, 11-23.

Ryan, John. 'A Minor Case of Boldrewood Editing'. *Biblionews and Australian Notes & Queries*, 20.1, 1995, 13-16.

---. '*Robbery Under Arms* and "The Appearance of Being Built Up From A Factual Article"'. *Biblionews and Australian Notes & Queries*, 17.4, 1992, 101-10.

---. 'Rolf Boldrewood in Armidale'. *Armidale and District Historical Society Journal and Proceedings*, No. 12, 1970, 87-96.

---. 'Rolf Boldrewood and his Australian Model for Closer Colonization of North Africa'. *Margin*, 26, 1991, 10-16.

---. 'A Walter Scott Model for the Structure of *Robbery Under Arms*'. *Notes and Furphies*, No. 22, 1989, 7-9.

S[tewart], K.A. 'Terrible Hollow'. *Notes & Furphies*, No. 10, 1983, 14-15.

Stewart, Ken. 'In Pursuit of "Terrible Hollow"'. *Notes & Furphies*, No. 9, 1982, 4-5.

Turner, Graeme. 'Ripping Yarns, Ideology, and *Robbery Under Arms*'. *A.L.S.*, 14, No. 2, 1989, 239-50.

Walker, R.B. 'Another Look at the Lambing Flat Riots, 1860-1861'. *Journal of the Royal Australian Historical Society*, LVI, 1970, 193-25.

---. 'History and Fiction in Rolf Boldrewood's *The Miner's Right*'. *A.L.S.*, III, 1967, 28 40.

---. 'The Historical Basis of *Robbery Under Arms*'. *A.L.S.*, II, No. 1, 1965, 3-14.

Wilkes, G.A. 'Kingsley and Boldrewood'. *Southerly*, XXXII, 1972, 232-33. Identifies characters in *Babes in the Bush*.

Wright, P.A. 'The Kangaroo Problem over the Last Hundred Years'. *Armidale and District Historical Society. Journal & Proceedings*, No. 18, 1975, 42-47.

BONWICK, JAMES

Critical Material

Featherstone, Guy. 'James Bonwick. III. A Checklist of his Articles and

Contributions'. *La Trobe Library Journal*, V, No. 18, 1976, 34-35.
Blake, L.J. 'James Bonwick'. *Educational Magazine*, XXI, 1964, 350-56.

BOSWELL, ANNABELLA

Non-Fiction
Annabella Boswell's Journal. Edited and with an Introduction by Morton Herman.
(Sydney: A.& R., 1965).
Reviewed by N. Keesing, *Southerly*, XXV, 1965, 209-12; J. Lindsay, *ABR*, IV,
1965, 160.

*Annabella Boswell's Other Journal 1848-1851, Called 'Further Recollections of my
Early Days in Australia'*. (Canberra: Mulini Press, 1992). Australian Books on
Demand 1.
Reviewed by L. Clancy, *Weekend Australian*, 20-21 March, 1993: Review 6.

BOYD, MARTIN

Fiction
The Cardboard Crown (first published 1952); *A Difficult Young Man* (first
published 1955); *Outbreak of Love* (first published 1957); *When Blackbirds Sing*
(first published 1962). All reprinted Melbourne: Lansdowne, 1971; reprinted with
prefaces by Dorothy Green, 1984.
Reviewed by M. Dunlevy, *Canberra Times*, 27 March, 1971, 14; B. Kiernan,
Australian, 26 June, 1971, 22; E. Martin, *Sunday Review*, 25 April, 1971, 828; I.
Mudie, *S.M.H.*, 10 April, 1971, 17; J. Waten, *Age*, 20 March, 1971, 13.

A Difficult Young Man. (Melbourne: Lansdowne Press, 1965). First published
1955.
Reviewed by D. Green, *Canberra Times*, 13 November, 1965, 13.

Lucinda Brayford. (Melbourne: Lansdowne Press, 1969). Republished with an
introduction by Dorothy Green (Ringwood, Vic.: Penguin, 1985). First published
London: Cresset Press, 1946.
Reviewed by L. Clancy, *ABR*, No. 74, 1985, 35-36; W.S. Ramson, *Canberra
Times*, 27 June, 1970, 12.

Nuns in Jeopardy. (Ringwood, Vic.: Penguin, 1985). First published 1940.
Reviewed by L. Clancy, *ABR*, No. 79, 1986, 22.

Such Pleasure. With an introduction by Brenda Niall. (Ringwood, Vic.: Penguin,
1985). First published London: Cresset Press, 1949.
Reviewed by L. Clancy, *ABR*, No. 74, 1985, 35-36.

The Tea-Time of Love: The Clarification of Miss Stilby. (London: Bles, 1969).
Reviewed by L. Cantrell, *Meanjin*, XXX, 1971, 133; J. Hemmings, *Listener*, 8
May, 1969, 656.

When Blackbirds Sing. Introduction by Dorothy Green. (Ringwood, Vic.: Penguin,
1993). First published 1962.

Non-Fiction
Day of My Delight. (Melbourne: Lansdowne, 1965).
Reviewed by K. Cantrell, *Southerly*, XXVIII, 1968, 141-44; D. Davis, *Australian*,
18 December, 1965, 9; M. Dunlevy, *Canberra Times*, 5 February, 1966, 13; M.
MacCallum, *Nation*, 8 January, 1966, 23-4; J. McAuley, *S.M.H.*, 18 December,
1965, 16; S. Murray-Smith, *ABR*, V, 1966, 59; C. Osborne, *Bulletin*, 29 January,
1966, 31; J.E.S., *Biblionews*, I, No. 2, 1966, 29-30; M. Sayle, *Sunday Times*
(London), 29 May, 1966 and *T.L.S.*, 30 June, 1966, 570.

'De Gustibus'. *Overland*, No. 50-51, 1972, 5-9.
'Dubious Cartography'. *Meanjin*, XXIII, No. 1, 1964, 5-13. Deals with criticism
of his own work, particularly that by Kathleen Fitzpatrick in *Martin Boyd*,

Australian Writers and their Work series (Melbourne: Lansdowne Press, 1963). 'Preoccupations and Intentions (Australian Writers in Profile: 1)'. *Southerly*, XXVIII, 1968, 83-90.

Critical Material

Nase, Pamela. 'Martin Boyd: A Checklist'. *A.L.S.*, V, 1972, 404-14.

Niall, Brenda. *Martin Boyd* (Melbourne: O.U.P., 1978). Australian Bibliographies. Reviewed by A. Lawson, *A.L.S.*, IX, 1979, 257-59; E. Perkins, *LiNQ*, VI, No. 2, 1978, 85.

'Mr. Martin Boyd'. *Times*, 10 June, 1972, 14.

'Novelist Martin Boyd Dies, 79'. *Canberra Times*, 7 June, 1972, 15. Similar reports in *S.M.H.*, 6 June, 1972, 10.

Boyd, David. 'An Open House'. *Bulletin*, 23-30 December, 1980, 140-46.

Bradley, Anthony. 'The Structure of Ideas Underlying Martin Boyd's Fiction'. *Meanjin*, XXVIII, 1969, 177-83.

Davidson, Frank. 'Australia's Challenge to Martin Boyd'. *Span*, No. 24, 1987, 96-106.

Dobrez, Patricia. 'Guzzling without Grace'. *Bulletin*, 23-30 December, 1980, 147-50. T.V. serial of *Lucinda Brayford*.

---. 'Martin Boyd on Love: The Human Form Divine'. *Quadrant*, XXVI, No. 11, 1982, 27-31.

---. 'Martin Boyd's Aestheticism: A Late Victorian Legacy'. Australian Victorian Studies Association. *Brisbane Conference Papers 1978* (St Lucia: A.V.S.A., 1980), 29-39.

Dolin, Kieran. '*Mater Dolorosa*: War and Motherhood in *Lucinda Brayford*'. *Westerly*, 34, No. 4, 1989, 51-7.

---. 'The Significance of *Outbreak of Love* in the Langton Tetralogy'. *Southerly*, 50, No.2, 1989, 192-204.

Dutton, Geoffrey. 'Gentlemen vs. Lairs'. *Quadrant*, IX, No. 1, 1965, 14-20.

Fitzpatrick, Kathleen. *Martin Boyd*. (Melbourne: Lansdowne Press, 1963). Australian Writers and their Work series.

---. 'A Commentary'. *Meanjin*, XXIII, 14-17. A reply to Boyd's article, 'Dubious Cartography', *Meanjin*, XXIII, No. 1, 1964, 5-13.

French, A.L. 'Martin Boyd: An Appraisal'. *Southerly*, XXVI, 1966, 219-234.

Gould, Warwick. 'The Family Face: Martin Boyd's Art of Memoir'. *A.L.S.*, VII, 1976, 269-78.

Green, Dorothy. '"The Fragrance of Souls": A Study of *Lucinda Brayford*'. *Southerly*, XXVIII, 1968, 110-26.

---. 'From Yarra Glen to Rome: Martin Boyd, 1893-1972'. *Meanjin*, XXXI, 1972, 245-58.

---. 'Martin Boyd'. In *The Literature of Australia*, edited by Geoffrey Dutton, revised edition (Ringwood, Vic.: Penguin, 1976), 509-27.

Hamilton, K.G. 'Two Difficult Young Men: Martin Boyd's *A Difficult Young Man* and Christina Stead's *The People with the Dogs*' In *Studies In the Recent Australian Novel*, edited by K.G. Hamilton (St Lucia: U.Q.P., 1978), 141-67.

Herring, Thelma. 'Martin Boyd and the Critics: A Rejoinder to A.L. French'. *Southerly*, XXVIII, 1968, 127-40. Discusses 'Martin Boyd: An Appraisal'. *Southerly*, XXVI, 1966, 219-34.

Johnston, Grahame. 'A Tribute to Martin Boyd'. *Canberra Times*, 13 June, 1972, 17.

Jose, Nicholas. 'The Dream of Europe: *For Love Alone, The Aunt's Story* and *The Cardboard Crown*'. *Meridian*, VI, No. 2, 1987, 113-125; esp. 121-124.

Kramer, Leonie. 'Martin Boyd'. *Australian Quarterly*, XXX, 1963, 32-8.

---. 'The Seriousness of Martin Boyd'. *Southerly*, XXVIII, 1968, 91-109.

Long, Nonie. 'John Mills, Emma and the a Becketts'. *Overland*, No. 114, 1989,

15-18.
McFarlane, Brian. *Martin Boyd's Langton Novels*. (Port Melbourne: Edward Arnold (Australia), 1980). Studies in Australian Literature. Reviewed by J. Croft, *A.L.S.*, X, 1982, 400-01; H. Elliott, *ABR*, No. 48, 1983, 34; D. Green, *CRNLE Reviews Journal*, No. 1, 1981, 82-83.
---. 'Martin Boyd's Langton Sequence'. *Southerly*, XXXV, 1975, 69-87.
McKernan, Susan. 'Much Else in Boyd: The Relationship Between Martin Boyd's Non-Fiction Work and his Later Novels'. *Southerly*, XXXVIII, 1978, 309-30.
McLaren, John. 'Gentlefolk Errant: The Family Writings of Martin Boyd'. *A.L.S.*, V, 1972, 339-51.
Mitchell, Adrian. 'Martin Boyd: The True Amateur of Life'. *Issue*, III, No. 10, 1973, 23-25.
Moon, Kenneth. 'Pulp Writing and Coincidence in Martin Boyd's *Lucinda Brayford*'. *Southerly*, XXXVIII, 1978, 183-93.
Nase, Pamela. 'Martin Boyd's Langton Novels: Praising Superior People'. In *The Australian Experience: Critical Essays on Australian Novels*, edited by W.S. Ramson (Canberra: Australian National University Press, 1974), 229-48.
Neate, Anthony. 'An Australian Novel in Form V'. *Teaching of English*, No. 9, 1966, 33-8. Discusses *A Difficult Young Man*.
Niall, Brenda. *Martin Boyd*. (Melbourne: O.U.P., 1974). Australian Writers and Their Work. Reviewed by C. Hadgraft, *A.L.S.*, VI, 1974, 437-38.
---. *Martin Boyd: A Life*. (Carlton, Vic.: M.U.P., 1989). Reviewed by M. Clark, *S.M.H.*, 19 November, 1988, 90; W. Crocker, *Overland*, No. 114, 1989, 9-14 (review Article); T. Davidson, *Fremantle Arts Review*, 4, No. 3, 1989, 14-15; K. Dolin, *Westerly*, 34, No. 1, 1989, 85-6; M. Harris, *Antipodes*, 3.2, 1989, 156; W. R. Johnston, *Australian Journal of Politics and History*, 35, No. 2, 1989, 291; B. McFarlane, *ABR*, No. 106, 1988, 29-30; S. McKernan, *Southerly*, 49, No. 3, 1989, 531-33; C. Munro, *A.L.S.*, 14, No. 1, 1989, 138-42; C. Peake, *Weekend Australian*, 3-4 December, 1988, Weekend 11; B. Reid, *Age Saturday Extra*, 25 February, 1989, 13 and *Age Monthly Review*, 9, No. 5, 1989, 7-8; J. Roe, *Australian Historical Studies*, 24, No.94, 1990, 152-53.
---. 'Martin Boyd as "Walter Beckett"'. *A.L.S.*, VIII, 1978, 369-71.
---. 'Second Thoughts on the Langton Novels: Martin Boyd's Revisions'. *A.L.S.*, VII, 1976, 321-24.
---. 'The Double Alienation of Martin Boyd'. *Twentieth Century*, XVII, 1963, 197-206. Reply by Boyd, XVIII, 1963, 73-4; reply by Niall 74-5.
---. 'The World of Martin Boyd'. *Hemisphere*, XVI, No. 9, 1972, 23-25.
---. 'Three Versions of *The Montforts*'. *Bibliographical Society of Australia and New Zealand. Bulletin*, III, No. 4, 1978, 153-57.
O'Grady, Desmond. 'Those Marvellous Blue Skies: Martin Boyd's Seventeen Years in Rome'. *Overland*, No. 56, 1973, 26-30.
---. 'Writer between two worlds'. *Age*, 20 November, 1965, 21.
O'Neill, Terence. 'Literary Cousins: Nuns in Jeopardy'. *A.L.S.*, X, 1982, 375-78.
---. 'Martin Boyd Memorial Plaque, Little Evensden, Cambridge, England'. *Notes & Furphies*, No. 21, 1988, 12.
---. 'Martin Boyd's Missing Novels: A Partial Solution'. *A.L.S.*, VIII, 1978, 366-68.
Philipp, Franz. *Arthur Boyd*. (London: Thames & Hudson, 1967), 19-26, 52-56.
Ramson, W.S. '*Lucinda Brayford*: A Form of Music'. In *The Australian Experience: Critical Essays on Australian Novels*, edited by W.S. Ramson (Canberra: Australian National University Press, 1974), 209-28.
Riddell, Elizabeth. 'Martin Boyd: Expatriate in Self-Exile'. *Australian*, 7 June, 1972, 11. See also her correction in *Australian*, 15 June, 1972, 6.
Riemer, A.P. 'This World, the Next, and Australia - the Emergence of a Literary

Commonplace'. *Southerly*, XLIV, 1984, 251-70.
Ruskin, Pamela. 'Those Brilliant Boyds'. *Walkabout*, XXXV, No. 2, 1969, 20-23.
Shadwick, Alan. 'Mr. Martin Boyd'. *Times*, 14 June, 1972, 18.
Smith, Graeme Kinross. 'Martin Boyd'. *Westerly*, No. 2, 1975, 33-37.
St Pierre, Paul M. 'Martin Boyd: The Last Years'. *Southerly*, XLIV, 1984, 441-53.
Stewart, Annette. 'The Search for the Perfect Human Type: Women in Martin Boyd's Fiction'. In *Who is She?*, edited by Shirley Walker (St Lucia: U.Q.P., 1983), 118-35.
Tausky, Thomas E. 'Orpheus in the Underworld: Music in the Novels of Robertson Davies and Martin Boyd'. *Antipodes*, 5.1, 1991, 5-14.
Tennant, Kylie. 'Most Glorious Animals'. *S.M.H.*, 10 June, 1972, 18.
Wallace, F. 'The Craft of Martin Boyd'. *Twentieth Century*, XXIV, 1970, 336-42.

BRADY, E.J.

Critical Material
Semmler, Clement. 'Two Australian Balladists: W.H. Ogilvie and E.J. Brady'. *Antipodes*, II, No. 1, 1988, 33-38.
Webb, John. 'Poets versus Critics'. *A.L.S.*, V, 1972, 312-16.

BRAND, MONA

Critical Material
Tilley, Christine M. 'Mona Brand: A Checklist, 1935-1980'. *A.L.S.*, X, 1981, 117-27.
Australian Feminist Studies 21, 1995. Special Issue: Third International Women Playwrights Conference. 3-172. Includes conversation with Mona Brand and other Australian playwrights.
Poole, Gaye. 'A Very Humanitarian Type of Socialism: an Interview with Mona Brand'. *Australasian Drama Studies*, 21, 1992, 3-22.

BRENNAN, CHRISTOPHER

Collection
Christopher Brennan. Edited with an introduction and notes by Terry Sturm. (St Lucia: U.Q.P., 1984). Portable Australian Authors.
Reviewed by A. Clark, *A.L.S.*, XII, No. 1, 1985, 143-147; L. Ferrier, *CRNLE Reviews Journal*, No. 2, 1985, 77-79; P. Lugg, *Canberra Times*, 2 March, 1985, 18; T. Malone, *ABR*, No. 73, 1985, 31-32; R. Morse, *PN Review*, XIII, No. 5, 1987, 93-94; J.J. O'Carroll, *AUMLA: Journal of the Australasian Universities Language and Literature Association*, No. 65, 1986, 119-122.

Poetry
Christopher Brennan: Selected Poems. (Sydney: A.& R., 1966). Australian Poets Series. Edited and with an Introduction by A.R. Chisholm.
Reviewed by J.M. Allen, *Poetry Magazine*, No. 4, 1966, 27; R. McCuaig, *Canberra Times*, 18 June, 1966, 11; V. Smith, *Bulletin*, 6 August, 1966, 46.

Musicopoematographoscope and Pocket Musicopoematographoscope: Prose-Verse-Poster-Algebraic-Symbolico-Riddle. With an introduction by Axel Clark. (Sydney: Hale & Iremonger, 1981).
Reviewed by L.J. Austin, *Quadrant*, XXVI, No. 4, 1982, 51-53; P. Hasluck, *Westerly*, XXVII, No. 2, 1982, 96-98; J. Stone, *Biblionews and Australian Notes & Queries*, VII, No. 2, 1982, 45-46; J. Tranter, *S.M.H.*, 9 January, 1982, 40.

Poems [1913]. With an introduction by G.A. Wilkes. Facsimile edition. (Sydney: Sydney University Press, 1972). Australian Literary Reprints. First published

Sydney: Philip, 1913.
Reviewed by A.R. Chisholm, *Age*, 10 February, 1973, 15; G. Jones, *Westerly*, No. 1, 1973, 73-74; S.E. Lee, *Southerly*, XXXIII, 1973, 335-36; T. Sturm, *New Poetry*, XXI, No. 3, 1973, 66-67.
Poems 1913. Introduced by Robert Adamson. (Pymble, NSW: A.& R., 1992).
Reviewed by G. Dutton, *ABR*, 143, 1992, 49-51; A. Gould, *Quadrant*, 37.10, 1992, 81-83.
Selected Poems. Chosen with an introduction by G.A. Wilkes (Sydney: A.& R., 1973).

Non-Fiction

The Prose of Christopher Brennan; edited by A.R. Chisholm and J.J. Quinn. (Sydney: A.& R., 1962).
Reviewed by N. Braham, *Twentieth Century*, XVII, 1963, 215-24; A. Denat, *A.L.S.*, I, No. 2, 1963, 141-2; W. Kirsop, *Southerly*, XXIII, No. 3, 1963, 203-10; L. Kramer, *ABR*, II, 1963, 56; J. McAuley, *Bulletin*, 2 March, 1963, 36; G.A. Wilkes, *Meanjin*, XXII, No. 1, 1963, 80-4.

Critical Material

Chaplin, Harry F. *A Brennan Collection: An Annotated Catalogue of First Editions, Inscribed Copies, Manuscripts and Associated Items*. (Sydney: Wentworth Press, 1966).

Adamson, Robert. 'Christopher Brennan: The Man and the Poet'. In *Australian Literature Today*, edited by R.K. Dhawan and David Kerr (New York: Indian Society for Commonwealth Studies/ Advent P, 1993), 148-57.

Ailwood Keel, G.D. '*The Sydney University Review* (1881-3)'. *Southerly*, XXXVII, 1977, 427-40.

Andraud, R. 'Christopher Brennan (1870-1932)'. *Southerly*, XL, 1980, 102-08. Obituary, first published, in French, in the *Revue Anglo-Americaine*, December, 1934.

Austin, L.J. 'Mallarme to Brennan: The Missing letters'. *Quadrant*, XXI, No. 11, 1977, 36.

---. 'New Light on Brennan and Mallarme'. In *Studies in Honour of A.R. Chisholm*, edited by Wallace Kirsop (Melbourne: Hawthorn Press for Monash University, 1970). 16-24.

Bavinton, Anne. 'The Darkness of Brennan's "Lilith"'. *Meanjin*, XXIII, No. 1, 1964, 63-9.

Buckley, Vincent. 'Imagination's Home'. *Quadrant*, XXIII, No. 3, 1979, 24-29.

Campion, Edmund. 'Christopher Brennan at Riverview'. *Quadrant*, XXII, No. 1, 1978, 26-29.

Castle, Edgar. 'A Voice from the Deep'. *Symposium* (Perth), I, No. 2, 1978, 39-41.

---. 'Towards the Source of "The Wanderer"'. *A.L.S.*, IX, 1979, 234-36.

Chisholm, A.R. *The Familiar Presence*. (Melbourne: M.U.P., 1966), passim.

---. *A Study of Christopher Brennan's The Forest of Night*. (Carlton: M.U.P., 1970). Reviewed by A. Frost, *Meanjin*, XXIX, 1970, 516-22; *Poetry Magazine*, XVIII, No. 5, 1970, 46. T. Sturm, *A.L.S.*, V, 1971, 214-17; G.A. Wilkes, *Southerly*, XXXI, 1971, 155-60.

---. 'Brennan, Peterley, and Pennington'. *Meanjin*, XXXI, 1972, 497-98.

---. 'Brennan, the Sea and the Seasons: Notes on *Towards the Source*'. *Meanjin*, XXV, 1966, 192-5.

---. 'Christopher Brennan and the Idea of Eden'. *Meanjin*, XXVI, 1967, 153-160.

---. 'Christopher Brennan, Poet and Scholar: A Centenary Assessment'. *Meanjin*, XXIX, 1970, 277-80.

---. 'A Note on Brennan's German'. Quadrant, XXI, No. 11, 1977, 36.

---. 'Some Addenda for Brennan's Biography'. *Meanjin*, XXIX, 1970, 511-15. Largely a reproduction of reminiscences by Philip Brennan.

Clark, Axel, Fletcher, John, and Marsden, Robin (eds.). *Between Two Worlds*. (Sydney: Wentworth Press, 1979). Especially the essays by Vincent Buckley (rptd. from *Quadrant*, XXIII, No. 3, 1979, 24-9), Fay Zwicky, 'Gallic Sanction', 90-100 (rptd. from *Westerly*, No. 3, 1978, 77-85), and A.D. Hope, 'Brennan's Lilith', 101-10.

Clark, Axel. *Christopher Brennan, A Critical Biography*. (Carlton: M.U.P., 1980). Reviewed by E. Campion, *Bulletin*, 29 July, 1980, 68; D. Carter, *Helix*, No. 7-8, 1981, 185-87; D. English, *ABR*, No. 25, 1980, 27-28; A. Frost, *Historical Studies*, XIX, 1981, 489-90; K. Goodwin, *Courier-Mail*, 26 July, 1980, 25; D. Green, *Meanjin*, XL, 1981, 93-105; R. Hall, *S.M.H.*, 19 July, 1980, 20; V. Ikin, *Westerly*, XXV, No. 4, 1980, 80-82; C. James, *London Review of Books*, IV, No. 13, 1982, 6-8; B. Matthews, *Overland*, No. 84, 1981, 66-69; C. Pearson, *Advertiser*, 8 November, 1980, 24; B. Plews, *CRNLE Reviews Journal*, No. 2, 1980, 27-30; E. Riddell, *National Times*, 10-16 August, 1980, 43; A.M. Stewart, *Tasmanian Historical Research Association Papers and Proceedings*, XXVIII, No. 1, 1981, 43-47; T. Sturm, *A.L.S.*, X, 1982, 402-05; C. Wallace-Crabbe, *Age*, 16 August, 1980, 29; P. Ward, *Weekend Australian Magazine*, 13-14 September, 1980, 1; G. Windsor, *Quadrant*, XXV, No. 5, 1981, 32-34. See also *ABR*, No. 25, 1980, 24.

---. 'Brennan's Aeschylus'. *Quadrant*, XXI, No. 11, 1977, 43-46.

---. 'The Childhood of Christopher Brennan'. *Quadrant*, XXIII, No. 4, 1979, 54-58.

---. '*Hermes* and Christopher Brennan'. *Southerly*, XXXVII, 1977, 407-20.

---. 'The Wanderer of Many Years'. *Hemisphere*, XXV, 1981, 237-41.

Coll, S. 'C.B. In a Girls' School'. *Biblionews*, I, No. 2, 1966, 13-15.

Croft, Julian. *The Federal and National Impulse in Australian Literature, 1890-1958*. (Townsville: Foundation for Australian Literary Studies, 1989) Monograph 18. The Colin Roderick Lectures, 1988. Includes paper on Brennan.

Denat, A. 'Christopher Brennan: Comparatiste Australien'. *Revue de Literature Comparee*, July-September, 1964, 431-9.

Dobrez, L.A.C. 'Christopher Brennan. The Wanderer'. In *Australian Poems in Perspective*, edited by P.K. Elkin (St Lucia: U.Q.P., 1978), 11-36.

Docker, John. 'The "Eternal Hermit": Christopher Brennan'. In his *Australian Cultural Elites: Intellectual Traditions in Sydney and Melbourne*. (Sydney: A.& R., 1974), 3-21.

Douglas, Dennis. 'Brennan's Philosophical Interests and the "Characteristic Weaknesses" of his Verse'. *Meanjin*, XXXV, 1976, 188-95.

Dunlevy, Maurice. 'A Duckbilled Platypus'. *Canberra Times*, 24 October, 1970, 12.

Fletcher, John. 'Robert Schachner (1875-1912) and Australia'. *Biblionews and Australian Notes & Queries*, IX, No. 2, 1984, 45-53.

French, A.L. 'The Verse of C.J. Brennan'. *Southerly*, XXIV, No. 1, 1964, 6-18; see letter of comment by 'Author of *The Frogs*' in *ABR*, III, 1964, 258.

Frost, Alan. 'Brennan's "Grand Oeuvre"'. *Makar*, No. 18, 1964, 18-23.

Gollan, Myfanwy. 'Starting a Conversation'. *Bulletin Literary Supplement*, 30 June, 1981, 24-27.

Green, Dorothy. 'Towards the Source'. *Southerly*, XXXVII, 1977, 363-81.

Heseltine, H.P. '"Cyrus Brown of Sydney Town": Christopher Brennan and Dowell O'Reilly'. In *Bards, Bohemians, and Bookmen*, edited by Leon Cantrell (St Lucia: U.Q.P., 1976), 136-52.

---. 'The Australian Nineties: An Experiment in Critical Method'. *The Teaching of English*, No. 6, 1965, 17-32.

Kerr, Margaret. 'The Dismissal of Chris Brennan from the University of Sydney'. *A.L.S.*, VII, 1976, 413-15.

Kirsop, Wallace. '"The Greatest Renewal, the Greatest Revelation": Brennan's Commentary on Mallarme'. *Meanjin*, XXIX, 1970, 303-11.

Kirsten (Turnbull), Marcia. 'Chris Brennan: A Student Remembers'. *Southerly*, XXXI, 1971, 222-24.

Macainsh, Noel. 'Brennan and Berlin: Some Circumstances'. *Southerly*, 49, No. 1, 1989, 83-95. Reprinted in his *The Pathos of Distance* (Bern, New York: Peter Lang, 1992), 63-74.

---. 'Brennan and Music'. *Southerly*, XLVII, No. 1, 1987, 100-112. Reprinted in his *The Pathos of Distance* (Bern, New York: Peter Lang, 1992), 75-87.

---. 'Brennan and Nietzsche'. *Southerly*, XXVI, 1966, 259-61.

---. 'Brennan und Novalis: Einige Bemerkungen zu Brennans "Prelude"'. *LiNQ*, III, No. 2, 19-29.

---. 'Brennan on Nietzche' [sic]. *LiNQ*, III, Nos. 3 & 4, 1974, 20-23.

---. 'Brennan's "Wanderer" - Some Remarks on Scansion'. *LiNQ*, III, Nos. 3 & 4, 1974, 16-19.

---. 'Christopher Brennan and "Die Romantik"'. *Southerly*, XXIII, No. 3, 1964, 150-63. Reprinted in his *The Pathos of Distance* (Bern, New York: Peter Lang, 1992), 27-40.

---. 'Christopher Brennan's Poetic'. *Southerly*, XLIV, 1984, 306-28. Reprinted in his *The Pathos of Distance* (Bern, New York: Peter Lang, 1992), 41-62.

---. 'Christopher Brennan's "Wanderer"'. *Quadrant*, XXII, No. 2, 1978, 54-59. Reprinted in his *The Pathos of Distance* (Bern, New York: Peter Lang, 1992), 13-26.

---. 'Romance and Tale: A Duadic Principle in Brennan's *Poems 1913*'. *AUMLA*, 83, 1995, 55-67.

---. 'Steps into the Forest: Christopher Brennan's Fatal Attraction'. *AUMLA*, 1989, 229-51. Reprinted in his *The Pathos of Distance* (Bern, New York: Peter Lang, 1992), 88-108.

---. 'Structure and Theme in Brennan's "The Wanderer". *LiNQ*, III, Nos. 3 & 4, 1974, 24-33.

---. 'The Transposed World - Aestheticism and Christopher Brennan'. *Southerly*, XLII, 1982, 56-69.

Marsden, Robin B. 'New Light on Brennan'. *Southerly*, XXXI, 1971, 119-35. Unpublished poems and other material from the Peden family collection.

---. 'Two Unpublished Poems of C.J. Brennan'. *Southerly*, XXXIII, 1973, 180-84.

---. 'Christopher Brennan's Berlin Years 1892-1894'. *Quadrant*, XXI, No. 11, 1977, 37-42.

Martin, David. 'Neither So Great Nor So Small'. In *An Overland Muster*, edited by S. Murray-Smith (Brisbane: Jacaranda Press, 1965), 156-61. First published *Overland*, No. 19, 1960-1, 49-50.

Matthews, John. '"Redeem the Time": Imaginative Synthesis in the Poetry of Duncan Campbell Scott and Christopher Brennan'. In *Australian/Canadian Literatures in English: Comparative Perspectives*, edited by Russell McDougall and Gillian Whitlock (North Ryde, N.S.W.: Methuen Australia, 1987), 187-204.

McAuley, James. *C.J. Brennan*. (Melbourne: Lansdowne Press, 1963). Australian Writers and their Work series.

---. *Christopher Brennan*. (Melbourne: O.U.P., 1973). Australian Writers and Their Work. Reviewed by K.L. Goodwin, *Notes & Queries*, n.s. XXIII, No. I, 1976, 42-43; M. Thorpe, *English Studies*, LV, 1974, 550.

---. 'The Erotic Theme in Brennan'. *Quadrant*, XII, No. 6, 1968, 8-15.

McSwain, Ken. 'The Hidden Structure: An Approach to Brennan's *Poems* (1913)'. *Southerly*, XL, 1980, 78-100.

Merewether, Mary A. 'Brennan and Yeats: An Historical Survey'. *Southerly*, XXXVII, 1977, 389-406.

---. '*The Burden of Tyre* and Brennan's *Poems (1913)*'. *Southerly*, XXX, 1970, 267-84.

Muner, Mario. 'Christopher Brennan: His Personality and the Unity of His Poetry'. *Meanjin*, XXX, 1971, 63-69.

Pascoe, Bruce. 'Christopher Brennan: The Spiritual Search as Mankind's Destiny'. *Canberra Times*, 30 October, 1982, 11.

Pennington, Richard. *Christopher Brennan: Some Recollections*, with a foreword by G.A. Wilkes. (Sydney: A.& R., 1970). Reviewed by A.R. Chisholm, *Age*, 2 May, 1970, 14 and in *Meanjin*, XXIX, 1970, 245-49; C. Harrison-Ford, *Union Recorder*, L, No. 13, 1970, 6; N. Keesing, *Bulletin*, 23 May, 1970, 55; D. Rowbotham, *Courier-Mail*, 9 May, 1970, 15; C. Semmler, *ABR*, IX, 1970, 211-12; K. Slessor, *Daily Telegraph* (Sydney), 23 May, 1970, 21.

Reader, Hazel. 'In Memory of a Giant'. *Australian*, 31 October, 1970, 19.

Rhodes, Winston H. 'Christopher Brennan'. *Landfall*, XVIII, 1964, 338-48.

Riem, Antonella. 'The "Larger" and "Sadder" Mysteries of Life in the Poetry of Christopher Brennan and John Shaw Neilson'. In her *The Labyrinths of Self: A Collection of Essays on Australian and Caribbean Literature*. (Leichhardt, N.S.W.: FILEF. Italo-Australian Publications, 1987), 111-123.

Singh, P. Sanajaoba. 'Nineteenth Century Australian Poetry and Christopher Brennan'. *Journal of Australian Literature*, 1, No. 1, 1990, 79-84.

Smith, Martin. 'Christopher Brennan: A Man of Words'. *Campaign*, No. 29, 1977, 15.

Smith, Sybille. 'Brennan's Stature as Critic'. *Quadrant*, VII, No. 1, 1963, 65-70.

Smith, Vivian. 'Christopher Brennan and Arthur Symons'. *Southerly*, XXVII, 1967, 219-222.

Stephens, A.G. 'Chris Brennan'. In *The Writer in Australia*, edited by John Barnes (Melbourne: O.U.P., 1969), 131-57. This essay first published 1933.

Stewart, Annette. 'Christopher Brennan: The Disunity of *Poems 1913*'. *Meanjin*, XXIX, 1970, 281-302.

Sturm, T.L. 'The Social Context of Brennan's Thought'. *Southerly*, XXVIII, 1968, 250-71.

---. 'The Structure of Brennan's *The Wanderer*'. In *Bards, Bohemians, and Bookmen*, edited by Leon Cantrell (St Lucia: U.Q.P., 1976), 114-35.

Taylor, Andrew. 'Christopher Brennan's Double Exile'. In his *Reading Australian Poetry* (St Lucia: U.Q.P., 1987), 36-52.

Tulip, James. 'The Vision and Place of Christopher Brennan'. *St. Mark's Review*, No. 91, 1977, 30-38.

Walker, Shirley. 'The Boer War: Paterson, Abbott, Brennan, Miles Franklin and Morant'. *A.L.S.*, XII, No. 2, 1985, 207-222.

Wilkes, G.A. 'Brennan's *The Wanderer*: A Progressive Romanticism?' *Southerly*, XXX, 1970, 252-63.

---. 'Christopher Brennan'. In *The Literature of Australia*, edited by Geoffrey Dutton (Adelaide: Penguin Books, 1964), 306-17.

---. 'Interpreting Brennan's Poetry; or, "The I of My Verses is not Necessarily ME"'. *Southerly*, XXXVII, 1977, 421-26.

Wolf, Volker. 'Christopher Brennan and Europe - A German Version of Brennan's "We Sat Entwined ..."'. *LiNQ*, VII, Nos. 2 & 3, 1979, 92-96.

Wright, Judith. 'Christopher Brennan'. In her *Preoccupations in Australian Poetry* (Melbourne: O.U.P., 1965), 80-97.

---. 'Christopher Brennan'. *Southerly*, XXX, 1970, 243-51.

Zwicky, Fay 'Gallic Sanction: Kiss of Death, Another Look at Brennan's Reputation'. *Westerly*, No. 3, 1978, 77-85.

BRERETON, JOHN LE GAY

Critical Material

Mitchell Library. *Guide to the Papers of John Le Gay Brereton in the Mitchell Library, State Library of N.S.W.*. (Sydney: Library Council of New South Wales, 1981). Reviewed by K. J. Henderson, *Archives and Manuscripts*, X, 1982, 170-71.

Fletcher, John. 'Robert Schachner (1875-1912) and Australia'. *Biblionews and Australian Notes & Queries*, IX, No. 2, 1984, 45-53.

'John Le Gay Brereton, The University, and Australian Literature'. *Notes & Furphies*, 31, 1993, 3-7 (see also Vera Newson, 'A Little Oral History'. *Notes & Furphies*, 31, 1993, 8).

Franklin, C. 'Furphy 4: "To My Country": Brereton Not Baynton!' *Notes & Furphies*, 26, 1991, 17-18.

Heseltine, H. *John Le Gay Brereton*. (Melbourne: Lansdowne Press, 1965).

---. 'Brereton, the Bulletin and A.G. Stephens'. *A.L.S.*, No. 1, 1963, 16-31.

Mackaness, George. 'John Le Gay Brereton'. *Bibliomania: An Australian Book Collector's Essays* (Sydney: A.& R., 1965), 164-71.

Smee, Roy A. 'The Lost Letters of J. Le Gay Brereton'. *Notes and Furphies*, No. 17, 1986, 15-17.

Smith, Martin. 'Martin Smith Tells the Story of John Le Gay Brereton'. *Campaign*, No. 24, 1977, 17.

BRISSENDEN, R.F

Fiction

Poor Boy. (Sydney: Allen and Unwin, 1987).

Reviewed by K. Ahearne, *Australian Society*, VI, No. 11, 1987, 44-45; D. Anderson, *Times on Sunday*, 25 October, 1987, 33; R. Beecham, *Age Saturday Extra*, 14 November, 1987, 16; D. Colmer, *Weekend Australian*, 7-8 November, 1987, 19; M.J. Tolley, *Quadrant*, XXXII, Nos. 1&2, 1988, 113-114.

Wildcat. (Sydney: Allen & Unwin, 1991).

Reviewed by J. Bedford, *Voices*, 1.3, 1991, 97-100; J. Carroll, *ABR*, 129, 1991, 20; R. Hood, *Scarp*, 18, 1991, 62-65; S. Knight, *S.M.H.*, 18 May, 1991, 49; P. Pierce, *Age*, 20 April, 1991, Saturday Extra 6; P. Rolfe, *Bulletin*, 14 May, 1991, 117.

Poetry

Building a Terrace. (Canberra: A.N.U. Press, 1975).

Reviewed by G. Dutton, *Nation Review*, 9-15 January, 1976, 334-35; R. Gray, *S.M.H.*, 29 November, 1975, 17; E. Jones, *Age*, 7 August, 1976, 23; G. Page, *Canberra Times*, 9 January, 1976, 6; W. Walsh, *T.L.S.*, 9 April, 1976, 443.

Elegies. (Deakin: Brindabella Press, 1975).

Reviewed by G. Page, *Canberra Times*, 2 May, 1975, 10.

Sacred Sites. (Canberra: Phoenix Review/Bistro Editions, 1990).

Reviewed by A. Choate, *Westerly*, 36.2, 1991, 85-86; M. Duwell, *Weekend Australian*, 13-14 April, 1991, Review 6; C. Harrison-Ford, *Voices*, 1.3, 1991, 92-96.

Suddenly Evening: The Selected Poems of R.F. Brissenden. Edited and introduced by David Brooks. (Ringwood, Vic.: McPhee Gribble, 1993).

Reviewed by B. Giles, *ABR* 149, 1993, 49; K. Hart, *Age* 20 March, 1993, Saturday Extra 8; K. Hart, *Voices*, 3.2, 1993, 106-09.

The Whale in Darkness. (Canberra: A.N.U. Press, 1980).

Reviewed by G. Dutton, *Bulletin*, 6 May, 1980, 85-86; R. Elliott, *Canberra Times*, 24 May, 1980, 14; R. Gray, *S.M.H.*, 15 May, 1980, 16; J. McLaren,

Overland, No. 81, 1980, 69-70 and *ABR*, No. 20, 1980, 19; G. Page, *National Times*, 4-10 May, 1980, 46; K. Tennant, *Hemisphere*, XXV, 1981, 282; L. Trainor, *Canberra Times*, 17 May, 1980, 15.

Critical Material

Brooks, David. 'Aphrodite, Heraclitus and the Mirror of History'. *Quadrant*, XXV, No. 3, 1981, 49-52.
Hart, Kevin. 'Art and the Academy'. *Makar*, XII, No. 2, 1976, 33-39. Interview.
Page, Geoff. 'R.F. Brissenden'. In his *A Reader's Guide To Contemporary Australian Poetry* (St. Lucia: U.Q.P., 1995), 30-31.

BROOKS, DAVID

Fiction

The Book of Sei and Other Stories. (Sydney: Hale & Iremonger, 1985; London: Faber, 1988).
Reviewed by D. Anderson, *National Times*, 4-10 April, 1986, 32; K. Brophy, *Age Monthly Review*, 6, No. 4, 1986, 6-7; K. Gelder, *ABR*, No. 81, 1986, 4-6; I. Indyk, *S.M.H.*, 14 June, 1986, 46; A. Stokes, *Weekend Australian*, 5-6 July, 1986, Weekend 15; A. Vaux, *T.L.S.*, 13-19 May, 1988, 534.

The House of Balthus. (St Leonards, NSW: Allen & Unwin, 1995).
Reviewed by D. Anderson, *ABR*, 175, 1995, 24-25; O. Richardson, *Weekend Australian*, 4-5 Nov., 1995, Review 9.

Sheep and the Diva. (Fitzroy, Vic.: McPhee Gribble, 1990).
Reviewed by H. Daniel, *Overland*, No. 120, 1990, 87-89; C. Ferrall, *ABR*, No. 121, 1990, 13; S. Hall, *Bulletin*, 5 June, 1990, 118; L. Jacobs, *CRNLE Reviews Journal*, 2, No. 2, 1990, 75-80; B. Matthews, *Age Saturday Extra*, 26 May, 1990, 8; A.P. Riemer, *S.M.H.*, 2 June, 1990, 78; I. Salusinszky, *Weekend Australian*, 23-24 June, 1990, Weekend 9; T. Tate, *Westerly*, 36.1, 1991, 87-88.

Poetry

The Cold Front. (Sydney: Hale & Iremonger, 1983).
Reviewed by J. Hawke, *Aspect*, No. 31, 1984, 69-70; M. Jones, *Meanjin*, 42, 1983, 260-62; J. Maiden, *S.M.H.*, 13 August, 1983, 38; C. Powell, *Poetry Australia*, No. 92, 1984, 77-80; M. Radzner, *ABR*, No. 56, 1983, 30-1; M. Richards, *Island Magazine*, Nos. 18-19, 1984, 52-57.

Critical Material

Catalano, Gary. 'Poised upon a Border: The Writing of David Brooks'. *Imago*, 6.1, 1994, 65-68.
Gelder, Ken. 'Postmodernism's "Lost Objects": Desire in the Recent Fiction of Murnane, Brooks, Henshaw and Jones'. *Island Magazine*, No. 41, 1989, 49-53.
Perkins, Elizabeth. 'Metaphor and Meaning in David Brooks' *The Cold Front* and Andrew Lansdown's *Windfalls*'. *LiNQ*, 14, No. 2, 1986, 35-47.

BROWN, ELIZA

Non-Fiction

A Faithful Picture: The Letters of Eliza and Thomas Brown at York in the Swan River Colony 1841-1852. Edited by Peter Cowan, introduced by Alexandra Hasluck. (Fremantle, WA: Fremantle Arts Centre P, 1977).

Critical Material

Bird, Delys. 'The Self and the Magic Lantern: Gender and Subjectivity in Australian Colonial Women's Writing', *A.L.S.*, 15.3, 1992, 123-30.
---. 'Women in the Wilderness: Gender, Landscape and Eliza Brown's Letters and Journal'. *Westerly*, 36.4, 1991, 33-38.
Hay, John A. 'Deconstructing Utopia: The Blind Metaphors of Colonial Painters

and Diarists'. In *The Writer's Sense of the Past*, edited by Kirpal Singh (Singapore: Singapore UP, 1987), 133-51.

BRUCE, MARY GRANT

Fiction
The Peculiar Honeymoon and Other Writings. Edited by Prue McKay. (Melbourne: McPhee-Gribble, 1986).
Reviewed by W. McVitty, *Weekend Australian Magazine*, 7-8 March, 1987, 15; G. Murnane, *Fine Line*, No. 1, 1987, 28-30; L. Wevers, *Australian Studies*, 6, 1994, 99-102.

Critical Material
Alexander, Alison. *Billabong's Author: The Life of Mary Grant Bruce*. (Sydney: A.& R., 1979). Reviewed by D. Duke, *ABR*, No. 18, 1980, 23; R. Elliott, *Canberra Times*, 30 December, 1979, 8; K. England, *Advertiser*, 6 October, 1979, 22; C. Fleming, *CRNLE Reviews Journal*, No. 2, 1980, 59-62; P. Grimshaw, *Overland*, No. 80, 1980, 58-60; S. Hall, *24 Hours*, IV, No. 10, 1979, 72-73; W. McVitty, *Age*, 24 November, 1979, 27; E. Riddell, *Bulletin*, 13 November, 1979, 93-94; J. Rodriguez, *A.L.S.*, IX, 1980, 413-16; V.A. Salisbury, *Tasmanian Historical Research Association. Papers and Proceedings*, XXVII, 1980, 79-80; R. Stow, *T.L.S.*, 28 March, 1980, 374; V. Wallace-Crabbe, *National Times*, 3 November, 1979, 56.
Niall, Brenda. *Seven Little Billabongs: The World of Ethel Turner and Mary Grant Bruce*. (Carlton: M.U.P., 1979). Reviewed by R. Elliott, *Canberra Times*, 30 December, 1979, 8; C. Fleming, *CRNLE Reviews Journal*, No. 2, 1980, 59-62; P. Grimshaw, *Overland*, No. 80, 1980, 58-60; H. King, *Journal of the Royal Australian Historical Society*, LXVII, No. 1, 1981, 75-76; W. McVitty, *Age*, 23 February, 1980, 26; J. Pausacker, *ABR*, No. 17, 1979, 12-13; E. Riddell, *Bulletin*, 13 November, 1979, 93-94; J. Rodriguez, *A.L.S.*, IX, 1980, 413-16; M. Saxby, *S.M.H.*, 26 January, 1980, 16.
---. 'Mythmakers of Australian Childhood'. *This Australia*, No. 1, 1981/82, 64-72.

BUCKLEY, VINCENT

Poetry
Arcady and Other Places. (Melbourne: M.U.P., 1966).
Reviewed by W.T. Andrews, *Westerly*, No. 3, 1967, 61-62; B. Beaver, *S.M.H.*, 10 December, 1966, 16; R.F. Brissenden, *Australian*, 26 November, 1966, 11; D. Douglas, *Age*, 3 December, 1966, 23; R. Dunlop, *Poetry Australia*, No. 14, 1967, 48; R. Hall, *Bulletin*, 7 January, 1967, 29; H.P. Heseltine, *Poetry Magazine*, No. 3, 1967, 25-28; M. Jurgensen, *Twentieth Century*, XXI, 1967, 372-375; S.E. Lee, *Southerly*, XXVII, 1967, 60-61; B. McPherson, *Canberra Times*, 1 April, 1967, 9; T.W. Shapcott, *ABR*, VI, 1966, 33; A. Taylor, *Overland*, No. 36, 1967, 43-44.
Golden Builders and Other Poems. (Sydney: A.& R., 1976).
Reviewed by A. Gould, *Poetry Australia*, No. 64, 1977, 68-73; E. Lindsay, *Australian*, 19 February, 1977, 29; J. Rodriguez, *Age*, 20 August, 1977, 23; C. Wallace-Crabbe, *T.L.S.*, 9 June, 1978, 643. 'Golden Builders' was originally published in *Poetry Australia*, No. 42, 1972, 35-57, and was reviewed by V. Brady, *Westerly*, No. 2, 1973, 68-76 (review article); D. Malouf, *Australian*, 29 April, 1972, 20; J. O'Hara, *Review*, 27 May-2 June, 1972, 903; J.H. Wright, *Westerly*, No. 3, 1973, 48-53 (Review Article).
Last Poems. (Ringwood, Vic.: McPhee Gribble/Penguin, 1991).
Reviewed by L. Bourke, *Southerly*, 51.4, 1991, 142-51; D. Coad, *World Literature Today*, 67.3, 1993, 666-67; M. Duwell, *Weekend Australian*, 3-4 August, 1991, Review 4; B. Giles, *ABR*, 131, 1991, 41-42; A. Riemer, *S.M.H.*, 6

April, 1991, 42; T. Shapcott, *Age*, 13 April, 1991, Saturday Extra 7.

Late-Winter Child. (Melbourne: O.U.P., 1979).
Reviewed by G. Bitcon, *Southerly*, XLI, 1981, 474-75; G. Burns, *Age*, 13 September, 1980, 27; G. Catalano, *Meanjin*, XXXIX, 1980, 355-58; M. Crennan, *ABR*, No. 24, 1980, 13; H. Lomas, *London Magazine*, N.S. XX, Nos. 8-9, 1980, 131-32; J. Ohmart, *Canberra Times*, 11 October, 1980, 22; G. Rowlands, *Overland*, No. 82, 1980, 70-71; J. Tulip, *Quadrant*, XXV, No. 5, 1981, 74-75.

The Pattern. (Melbourne: O.U.P., 1979).
Reviewed by G. Bitcon, *Southerly*, XLI, 1981, 476-77; G. Burns, *Age*, 13 September, 1980, 27; G. Catalano, *Meanjin*, XXXIX, 1980, 355-58; M. Crennan, *ABR*, No. 24, 1980, 13; H. Lomas, *London Magazine*, N.S. XX, Nos. 8-9, 1980, 131-32; J. Ohmart, *Canberra Times*, 11 October, 1980, 22; G. Rowlands, *Overland*, No. 82, 1980, 70-71; J. Tulip, *Quadrant*, XXV, No. 5, 1981, 74-75; G. Windsor, *Age Monthly Review*, II, No. 3, 1982, 9-10.

Selected Poems. (Sydney: A.& R., 1981).
Reviewed by G. Page, *Quadrant*, XXVI, No. 8, 1982, 75; J. Rodriguez, *Age Saturday Extra*, 19 March, 1983, 10; P. Steele, *ABR*, No. 46, 1982, 22-23.

Non-Fiction

Cutting Green Hay: Friendships, Movements and Cultural Conflicts in Australia's Great Decades. (Ringwood, Vic.: Penguin, 1983).
Reviewed by V. Brady, *Australian Journal of Cultural Studies*, I, No. 2, 205-11; T. Coady, *Meanjin*, XLII, 349-57, see also J. Brett, 'Where Were the Women?' 367-68; M. Costigan, *Weekend Australian Magazine*, 4-5 June, 16; H. Dow, *Overland*, No. 92, 55-57; E. Duyker, *Institute for Modern Biography Newsletter*, III, No. 4, 10-11; R. Hall, *National Times*, 17-23 June, 34; J. Hanrahan, *Age Saturday Extra*, 4 June, 12; B. Matthews, *ABR*, No. 53, 2-4; J.D. Pringle, *S.M.H.*, 11 June, 42; P. Steele, *Scripsi*, II, Nos. 2-3, 133-39.

Memory Ireland: Insights Into the Contemporary Irish Condition. (Ringwood, Vic.: Penguin, 1985).
Reviewed by M. Gollan, *S.M.H.*, 23 March, 1985, 40; S. Leonard, *Courier-Mail*, 18 May, 1985, 31; M.R. Liverani, *Weekend Australian Magazine*, 16-17 March, 1985, 11; O. MacDonagh, *Age Saturday Extra*, 30 March, 1985, 15; D.J. O'Hearn, *ABR*, No. 70, 1985, 6-7; A. Roberts, *Advertiser*, 27 April, 1985, 7; G. Windsor, *Bulletin*, 16 April, 1985, 78.

Poetry and the Sacred. (London: Chatto & Windus, 1968).
B. Beaver, *S.M.H.*, 9 August, 1969, 17; M.J. Crennan, *Quadrant*, XIII, No. 7 (retrospectively renumbered as XIV, No. 1), 1970, 77-80; J. Docker, *Nation*, 23 August, 1969, 20-21 (see also letter to the editor by P. McCaughey, *Nation*, 6 September, 1969, 15); D. Donoghue, *Listener*, LXXXII, 1969, 86-87; P. Morgan, *Bulletin*, 2 August, 1969, 48-49; A. Ridler, *Review of English Studies*, N.S. XX, 1969, 522-24; J. S[ankey], *Twentieth Century* (London), CLXXVI, No. 1039, CLXXVII, No. 1040 (double issue), 1968/69, 91; C. Semmler, *ABR*, VIII, 1969, 63-64; P. Steele, *Age*, 27 September, 1969, 15.

'Ease of American Language'. In *The American Model: Influence and Independence in Australian Poetry*, edited by Joan Kirkby (Sydney: Hale & Iremonger, 1982), 137-159. Contains autobiographical material.
'The Image of Man in Australian Poetry'. In *The Writer in Australia*, edited by John Barnes (Melbourne: O.U.P., 1969), 273-96. This essay published in his *Essays in Poetry* (1957).
'Poetry in a Pop Culture World'. *Quadrant*, XV, No. 4, 1971, 36-43.
'Self Portrait'. *ABR*, No. 85, 1986, 10-11.
'What Do Catholics Believe?' *Bulletin*, 14 March, 1970, 41. Contribution to a symposium.

Critical Material
'Vincent Buckley's "Stroke": A Discussion' [by members of a Monash University seminar]. *A.L.S.*, IV, 1969, 139-47.
Booth, Elizabeth. 'Vincent Buckley, an Interview'. *Quadrant*, XX, No. 8, 1976, 27-32.
Buckley, Brian. 'Vincent Buckley's Melbourne'. *Quadrant*, XXVII, No. 8, 1983, 35-38.
Carter, David. 'The Death of Satan and the Persistence of Romanticism'. *Literary Criterion* (Mysore), V, Nos. 3-4, 1980, 65-69.
Colmer, John. 'The Quest for Roots: Vincent Buckley and Sally Morgan'. In his *Australian Autobiography: A Personal Quest.* (Melbourne: O.U.P., 1989), 98-116.
Cross, Gustav. 'Australian Poetry in the 'Sixties'. *Poetry Australia*, No. 5, 1965, 33-8.
Davidson, Jim. 'Vincent Buckley'. *Meanjin*, 38, 1979, 443-458. Interview. Reprinted in his *Sideways from the Page* (Melbourne: Fontana, 1983), 209-229.
Duggan, Tom. 'Oz, Through Green Glasses'. *Age Saturday Extra*, 28 May, 1983, 2.
Green, Dorothy. 'Historical Myopia'. *Age Monthly Review*, II, No. 4, 1982, 14.
Kavanagh, Paul and Peter Kuch. 'Scored for the Voice: An Interview with Vincent Buckley'. *Southerly*, 47, No. 3, 1987, 249-66. Reprinted in their *Conversations: Interviews with Australian Writers* (North Ryde, NSW: Collins/A.& R, 1991).
Krause, Tom. 'Thoughts on a Life of Rhyme and Reason'. *Weekend Australian Magazine*, 4-5 June, 1983, 14.
O'Shea, Helen. 'A Poet's Place'. *Mattoid*, No. 19, 1984, 31-33.
O'Sullivan, Vincent. 'Singing Mastery: The Poetics of Vincent Buckley'. *Westerly* 34, No. 2, 1989, 50-57.
Page, Geoff. 'Vincent Buckley'. In his *A Reader's Guide To Contemporary Australian Poetry* (St. Lucia: U.Q.P., 1995), 32-35.
Rosenbloom, Henry. 'An Interview with Vincent Buckley'. *Meanjin*, XXVIII, 1969, 317-25.
Rowe, Noel. 'Believing More and Less: The Later Poetry of Vincent Buckley'. *Meridian*, 10.1, 1991, 4-18.
Sayers, Stuart. 'Dublin Prize to Vincent Buckley'. *Age*, 3 December, 1977, 26.
Steele, Peter. 'Vincent Buckley as Critic'. *Meanjin*, XXVIII, 1969, 309-16.
---. 'Vincent Buckley: Tracing Personality'. *Quadrant*, 35.7-8, 1991, 32-43. Reprinted in *Australian Literature Today*, edited by R.K. Dhawan and David Kerr (New York: Indian Society for Commonwealth Studies/ Advent P, 1993), 158-78.
Taylor, Andrew. 'Irrationality Individuality Drug Poetry Romanticism - Where We are Today'. *Meanjin*, XXXI, 1972, 373-84.
Thomson, A.K. 'The Poetry of Vincent Buckley: An Essay in Interpretation'. *Meanjin*, XXVIII, 1969, 293-308.
Thornton-Smith, C.B. 'Catholic Revolutionaries: A Reply to Patrick O'Brien'. *Quadrant*, XVI, No. 2, 1972, 63-65.
Wallace-Crabbe, Chris. 'Vincent Buckley: The Poetry of Presence'. *Overland*, No.114, 1989, 31-34. See also *Journal of Popular Culture*, 23, No. 2, 1989, 81-91.

BUCKMASTER, CHARLES

Poetry
Charles Buckmaster: Collected Poems. ed. Simon Macdonald. (St. Lucia: U.Q.P., 1989).
Reviewed by A. Burke, *Phoenix Review*, 7 & 8, 1992, 156-58; H. Cam, *S.M.H.*, 29 July, 1989, 78; M. Duwell, *Weekend Australian*, 16-17 December, 1989, Weekend 8; J. Forbes, *Editions*, No. 1, 1989, 12; K. Hart, *ABR*, No. 113, 1989,

24; J. Rodriguez, *Overland*, No. 117, 1990, 84-86; J. Strauss, *Age Saturday Extra*, 28 October, 1989, 9.

Deep Blue and Green. (Heidelberg, Vic.: Cross Currents, 1970).
Reviewed by C. Harrison-Ford, *Poetry Magazine*, No. 18, 1970, 42.

The Lost Forest. (Sydney: New Poetry, 1971).
Reviewed by P. Roberts, *S.M.H.*, 29 April, 1972, 16.

Critical Material
Afterman, Allen. 'The Poetry of Michael Dransfield and Charles Buckmaster'. *Meanjin*, XXXII, 1973, 478-81.
Dugan, Michael. 'Charles Buckmaster: A Memoir'. *Overland*, No. 119, 1990, 67-73.

BURKE, JAMES LESTER

Non-Fiction
A Burglar's Life; or, The Stirring Adventures of the Great English Burglar, Mark Jeffrey: A Thrilling History of the Dark Days of Convictism in Australia. Edited with an introduction by W. and J.E. Hiener. (Sydney: A.& R., 1968). First published Launceston: *Examiner* and *Tasmanian* Offices, 1893. Editors suggest James Lester Burke as the probable author.
Reviewed by L.T. Hergenhan, *A.L.S.*, IV, 1969, 200.

Critical Material
Butterss, Philip. 'James Lester Burke, Martin Cash and Frank the Poet'. *A.L.S.*, 15.3, 1992, 22-25.
Hiener, W. and J.E. 'James Lester Burke, Author of *Martin Cash*'. *A.L.S.*, II, No. 1, 1965, 63-6.

BURKE, JANINE

Fiction
A Company of Images. (Richmond, Vic.: Greenhouse, 1989).
Reviewed by H. Daniel, *Overland*, No. 116, 1989, 94-6; D. Davison, *Weekend Australian*, 22-23 April, 1989, Weekend 9; M. Denholm, *Blast*, No. 9, 1989, 26; S. McKernan, *Bulletin*, 27 June, 1989, 120-1; J. Mendelssohn, *S.M.H.*, 18 March, 1989, 86; R. Sorenson, *Age*, 25 March, 1989, Saturday Extra 9; B. Walker, *ABR*, No. 110, 1989, 34-5.

Lullaby. (Sydney: Picador, 1994).
Reviewed by H. Daniel, *S.M.H.*, 14 May, 1994, Spectrum 9A; D. Davison, *Weekend Australian*, 11-12 June, 1994, Review 6; H. Demidenko, *AWBR*, 7.1, 1995, 31; C. Keneally, *ABR*, 160, 1994: 8-9 (see also interview with Burke, 9-12); A. Riemer, *Age*, 9 July, 1994, Saturday Extra 9; M. Shmith, *Age*, 18 June, 1994, Saturday Extra 8.

Second Sight. (Richmond, Vic.: Greenhouse, 1986).
Reviewed by K. Ahearne, *Overland*, No. 106, 1987, 76-78; D. Bird, *ABR*, No. 87, 1986-7, 27-8; T. Forshaw, *Weekend Australian*, 24-25 January, 1987, Weekend 15; L. Forsyth, *Age*, 15 November, 1986, Saturday Extra 16; S. McKernan, *Bulletin*, 20 January, 1987, 47-8; C. Pybus, *Island Magazine*, No. 32, 1987, 61-2; T. Scanlon, *Northern Perspective*, 10, No. 1, 1987, 75; N. Stasko, *Phoenix Review*, No. 1, 1986-7, 123-27.

Speaking. (Richmond, Vic.: Greenhouse, 1984).
Reviewed by S. Dowse, *Island Magazine*, No. 23, 1985, 59-60; J. Hanrahan, *ABR*, No. 83, 1986, 15-16; R. Macklin, *Weekend Australian*, 19-20 January, 1985, Weekend 11; N. Phelan, *S.M.H.*, 23 March, 1985, 41; E. Perkins, *CRNLE Reviews Journal*, No. 2, 1985, 4-11.

Non-Fiction

'In the Light of Contradictions: Second Sight in Tuscany'. *Island Magazine*, No. 39, 1989, 63-7.

Critical Material

Bartlett, Alison. 'Other Stories: The Representation of History in Recent Fiction by Australian Women Writers'. *Southerly*, 53.1, 1993, 165-80. Discusses *Second Sight*.

Salzmann, Paul. 'Talking/Listening: Anecdotal Style in Recent Australian Women's Fiction'. *Southerly*, 49, No. 4, 1989, 539-53.

BURN, DAVID

Drama

The Bushrangers. Edited by W. and J.E. Hiener. (South Yarra, Vic.: Heinemann Educational Australia, 1971). Australian Theatre Workshop. First produced 1829.

Reviewed by K. Brisbane, *Australian*, 28 August, 1971, 17; A. Brissenden, *Advertiser*, 24 July, 1971, 20; J. Gibson, *Canberra Times*, 16 October, 1971, 15; L. Radic, *Age*, 28 August, 1971, 15.

Critical Material

Hanger, Eunice. 'David Burn in Sydney, 1844-1845'. *Southerly*, XXIV, No. 4, 1964, 232-41.

Oppenheim, Helen. 'Coppin - How Great? Alex Bagot's *Father of the Australian Theatre*'. *A.L.S.*, III, 1967, 132-34.

BUZO, ALEXANDER

Fiction

Prue Flies North. (Port Melbourne: Mandarin, 1991).

Reviewed by P. Bryan, *ABR*, 135, 1991, 50-51; D. Davison, *Weekend Australian*, 26-27 October, 1991: Review 6; R. Fitzgerald, *Age*, 9 November, 1991, Saturday Extra 7.

The Search for Harry Allway. (North Ryde, N.S.W.: A.& R., 1985).

Reviewed by H. Daniel, *Age Saturday Extra*, 21 September, 1985, 13; K. England, *Advertiser Saturday Review*, 2 November, 1985, 22; F. Giles, *Overland*, No. 102, 1986, 79-80; K. Harle, *ABR*, No. 77, 1985, 39-40; S. McKernan, *Bulletin*, 22 October, 1985, 116.

Drama

Big River [and] *The Marginal Farm*. (Sydney: Currency Press, 1985).

Reviewed by B. Jefferis, *Weekend Australian*, 15-16 June, 1985, 14; H. McNaughton, *CRNLE Reviews Journal*, No. 2, 1985, 55-57; E. Perkins, *Australasian Drama Studies*, No. 7, 1985, 135-138.

Coralie Lansdowne Says No. Preface by Ken Horler (Sydney: Currency Press, London: Eyre Methuen, 1974). Currency Methuen Plays, Series 3.

'The Front Room Boys'. In *Plays*, edited by Graeme Blundell (Ringwood, Vic., Harmondsworth, Middlesex: Penguin, 1970).

Reviewed by T. Sturm, *Bulletin*, 9 January, 1971, 37-38.

Macquarie. Introduced by Katharine Brisbane; preface by Manning Clark. (Sydney: Currency Press, 1971). Currency Playtexts series, 1.

Reviewed by H. Hewitt, *Canberra Times*, 15 April, 1972, 15; A. Kruse, *Southerly*, XXXIII, 1973, 245; R. Wissler, *Makar*, IX, No. 1, 1973, 45-48.

Makassar Reef. (Sydney: Currency Press, 1979).

Reviewed by J. McCallum, *Theatre Australia*, IV, No. 8, 1980, 59; F. de Groen, *CRNLE Reviews Journal* (Adelaide), No. 1, 1980, 102-09.

Martello Towers. (Sydney: Currency Press; London: Eyre Methuen, 1976).
Reviewed by F. de Groen, *CRNLE Reviews Journal*, No. 1, 1980, 102-09.

'Norm and Ahmed'. A *Komos* Playscript. Supplement to *Komos*, II, No. 2, 1969.

Norm and Ahmed; Rooted; The Roy Murphy Show: Three Plays. Introduced by Katharine Brisbane (Sydney: Currency Press; London: Eyre Methuen, 1973).
Reviewed by R. Cavan, *Plays and Players*, XXII, No. 2, 1974, 43; R. Craig, *Drama*, No. 114, 1974, 73-74; H. Hewitt, *Canberra Times*, 22 February, 1974, 17; K. Jamieson, *Makar*, X, No. 1, 1974, 46-50; L. Radic, *Age*, 16 February, 1974, 14.

Norm and Ahmed and Other Plays. (Sydney, Currency Press, 1993). New Introduction. First published 1977.

Non-Fiction

'Alex Buzo on *Young Person's Guide to the Theatre*'. In *Writers in Action: The Writer's Choice Evenings*, edited by Gerry Turcotte (Sydney: Currency Press, 1990), 139-60.

Glancing Blows: Life and Language in Australia. (Ringwood, Vic.: Penguin, 1987).
Reviewed by S. Knight, *ABR*, No. 95, 1987, 20-21; R. Lucas, *S.M.H.*, 20 June, 1987, 49.

'My Survival As An Indigine', in Thompson, Tom (ed.). *The View from Tinsel Town*. (Ringwood, Vic.: Southerly/Penguin, 1985), 27-34. See also 'My Survival as an Indigine'. *National Times*, 24-30 January, 1986, 13.

Critical Material

'Playwright Gets Live-In Grant'. *Age*, 19 April, 1972, 2.
'Front Room Boys in the Royal Court'. *Australian*, 13 May, 1971, 2.
'London Success for Buzo'. *Sunday Australian*, 17 October, 1971, 26.
'Mr. Brown Goes to Washington'. *Theatre-Australia*, III, No. 11, 1979, 43-44. Experiences in the U.S.A.
'Taking Success Calmly'. *Australian*, 15 February, 1972, 9.
'The Waffle of Empty Pseuds'. *National Times*, 24-29 May, 1976, 26-27.
Arnold, Roslyn. 'Aggressive Vernacular: Williamson, Buzo and the Australian Tradition'. *Southerly*, XXXV, 1975, 385-96.
Baxendale, J.G. and Ryan, J. 'Armidale's Playwright - Alexander Buzo'. *Armidale and District Historical Society. Journal and Proceedings*, No. 17, 1974, 86-93.
Blanch, Kirsten. 'Organised Niceness'. *Theatre Australia*, II, No. 11, 1978, 16-17.
Dente, Carla. 'Performing Stereotypes in Conflict: *Norm and Ahmed* by Alexander Buzo'. In *A Passage to Somewhere Else*, edited by Doireann MacDermott and Susan Ballyn, Proceedings of the Commonwealth Conference held in the University of Barcelona 30 September - 2 October, 1987 (Barcelona: Promociones y Publicaciones Universitarias, 1988), 31-40.
Duigan, Virginia. 'From Comic Strips to Comparison with Brecht: With a Film Coming, 1973 Should be Good to Alex Buzo'. *National Times*, 29 January-3 February, 1973, 16.
Dutton, Geoffrey and Harris, Max (eds.). *Australia's Censorship Crisis*. (Melbourne: Sun Books, 1970), 217-24.
Fitzpatrick, Peter. 'Alexander Buzo'. In his *After 'The Doll'*. (Melbourne: Edward Arnold, 1979), 98-111.
Forster, Deborah. 'Buzo Fusses to Get it Right, to the Last Detail'. *Age*, 1 March, 1980, 24.
Griffiths, Gareth. 'Experiments with Form in Recent Australian Drama'. *Kunapipi*, II, No. 1, 1980, 76-77.
Hall, Sandra. 'How Permissive Would They Get?' *Bulletin*, 9 August, 1969, 43-45.

Hogan, Christine. 'The Precise Mr. Buzo'. *S.M.H.*, 25 January, 1979, 10.

Jobson, Sandra. 'Now It's a Seven-Letter Word'. *S.M.H.*, 8 November, 1969, 14.

Jones, Margaret. 'Buzo's Back with a Burst'. *S.M.H.*, 29 April, 1972, 7.

McCallum, John (ed.). *Buzo*. (North Ryde, N.S.W.: Methuen Australia, 1987). Reviewed by E. Perkins, *Australasian Drama Studies*, No. 14, 1989, 157-61.

---. 'Coping with Hydrophobia: Alexander Buzo's Moral World'. *Meanjin*, XXXIX, 1980, 60-69.

McDonald, Willa. 'The Passage of Buzo: From Satire to Irony'. *Bulletin*, 22 January, 1985, 44-45.

McKay, Andrew. 'Travelling even Further North'. *Weekend Australian Magazine*, 8-9 March, 1980, 14.

[O'Brien, Dennis] 'Thank You Censor'. *Bulletin*, 19 July, 1969, 45-46.

Peake, Catherine. 'A Different Buzo - For and Against'. *National Times*, 13-19 April, 1980, 46.

Radic, Leonard. 'Alex Buzo: First of a New Breed'. *Age*, 27 May, 1972, 16.

---. 'The Gamble Paid Off for Alexander Buzo'. *Age*, 24 November, 1973, 14.

---. 'Poised to Break the Audience Barrier'. *Age*, 29 May, 1971, 16.

Robinson, Ian. 'Amateur Societies Will Love It'. *National Times*, 24-29 May, 1976, 26-27.

Ryan, J.S. 'Alexander Buzo's *Macquarie*'. *Armidale and District Historical Society. Journal and Proceedings*, No. 17, 1974, 94-107.

---. 'Alex Buzo and the Mythologizing of Rural 1960s Innocents in New South Wales'. *Margin*, 34, 1994, 31-34.

Sirmai, Geoffrey. 'An Interview with Alex Buzo'. *Southerly*, XLVI, No. 1, 1986, 80-91.

Sturm, Terry. *Alexander Buzo's Rooted/Norm and Ahmed: A Critical Introduction*. (Sydney: Currency Press, 1980). Reviewed by G.D., *English in Australia*, No. 65, 1983, 65-66.

Sturm, T.L. 'Alexander Buzo: An Imagist with a Personal Style of Surrealism'. *Southerly*, XXXV, 1975, 343-58.

Sykes, Alrene. 'Australian Bards and British Reviewers'. *A.L.S.*, VII, 1975, 39-49.

Tompkins, Joanne. 'Re-Orienting Australasian Drama: Staging Theatrical Irony', *Ariel*, 25.4, 1994, 117-33. Includes discussion of *Norm and Ahmed*.

Verburgt, Ron. 'Middle Class Dissenter: an Interview with Alexander Buzo'. *Australasian Drama Studies*, 22, 1993, 33-52.

Zachariah, Richard. 'Buzo: One Step Further'. *Sunday Australian*, 4 June, 1972, 21.

CAMBRIDGE, ADA

Fiction

A Marked Man. Introduced by Debra Adelaide. (London: Pandora, 1987). First published London: Heinemann, 1890.
Reviewed by S. McKernan, *Times on Sunday*, 23 August, 1987, 33; P. Pierce, *Age Saturday Extra*, 5 September, 1987, 13; H. Thomson, *ABR*, No. 91, 1987, 6-7.

Sisters. Introduction by Nancy Cato. (Ringwood, Vic.: Penguin, 1989). First published London: Hutchinson, 1904.
Reviewed by M. Arkin, *Antipodes*, 5.2, 1991, 61; C. Burns, *ABR*, No. 118, 1990, 30-31; S. Thomas, *Meridian*, 10.1, 1991, 70-72.

The Three Miss Kings. With a new introduction by Audrey Tate. (London: Virago, 1987). First published London: Heinemann; Melbourne: Melville, Mullen and Slade, 1891.
Reviewed by S. McKernan, *Times on Sunday*, 23 August, 1987, 33; H. Thomson, *ABR*, No. 95, 1987, 15-16.

A Woman's Friendship. Edited by Elizabeth Morrison. (Kensington, N.S.W.: New South Wales University Press, 1988). Originally serialised in *The Age*, 31 August, 1889-26 October, 1889.
Reviewed by M. Arkin, *Antipodes*, 5.2, 1991, 162-63; C. Burns, *ABR*, No. 118, 1990, 30-31; L. Clancy, *Weekend Australian*, 18-19 August, 1990, Review 5; H. Love, *Bibliographical Society of Australia and New Zealand Bulletin*, 12, No. 1, 1988 (issued, 1990), 42-44; K. Stewart, *A.L.S.*, 14, No. 4, 1990, 525-29; S. Thomas, *Meridian*, 8, No. 2, 1989, 184-187; L. Wakeling and M. Bradstock, *Southerly*, 50, No. 1, 1990, 115-22.

Poetry

Unspoken Thoughts. Edited by Patricia Barton. (Campbell, A.C.T.: English Department, University College, Australian Defence Force Academy, 1988). Occasional paper, No. 10. First published London: Kegan Paul, Trench & Co., 1887.
Reviewed by S. Thomas, *Meridian*, 8, No. 2, 1989, 184-87; L. Wakeling and M. Bradstock, *Southerly*, 50, No. 1, 1990, 115-22.

Non-Fiction

Thirty Years in Australia. Introduction by Louise Wakeling and Margaret Bradstock. (Kensington, N.S.W.: New South Wales University Press, 1989). First published London: Methuen, 1903.
Reviewed by M. Ackland, *Bibliographical Society of Australia and New Zealand Bulletin*, 16.3, 1992, 125-34; L. Clancy, *Weekend Australian*, 18-19 August, 1990, Review 5; E. Morrison, *ABR*, No. 126, 1990, 37; S. Walker, *A.L.S.*, 15.3, 1992, 238-41.

Critical Material

Barton, Patricia. 'Ada Cambridge: Creative Roles, Fact and Fiction'. In *Role Playing, Creativity, Therapy*. Papers from a Joint Seminar of the English Department, University College, Australian Defence Force Academy, Canberra, and the School of Psychiatry, University of New South Wales (Canberra: English Department, University College, Australian Defence Force Academy, 1987), 33-46. Occasional Paper, No. 7.

---. 'Ada Cambridge: Writing For Her Life'. In *A Bright and Fiery Troop: Australian Women Writers of the Nineteenth Century*, edited by Debra Adelaide (Ringwood: Penguin, 1988), 133-50.

---. 'Re-opening the Case of Ada Cambridge'. *A.L.S.*, XIII, No. 2, 1987, 201-109.

Bradstock, Margaret and Louise Wakeling. 'Ada Cambridge and the First *Thirty Years*'. *A.L.S.*, 14, No. 3, 1990, 387-90.

Bradstock, Margaret. 'Gaunt and Cambridge: The Warrnambool Connection', *Bibliographical Society of Australia and New Zealand Bulletin*, 16.4, 1992, 155-57.

---. 'New Light on Ada Cambridge'. *A.L.S.*, 14, No. 1, 1989, 107-13.

Bradstock, Margaret, and Louise Wakeling. *Rattling the Orthodoxies: A Life of Ada Cambridge*. (Ringwood, Vic.: Penguin. 1991). Reviewed by M. Ackland, *Bibliographical Society of Australia and New Zealand Bulletin*, 16.3, 1992, 125-34; M. Arkin, *Antipodes*, 5.2, 1991, 162-63; L. Clancy, *Age*, 30 November, 1991, Saturday Extra 8; G. Dutton, *Bulletin*, 16 April, 1991, 122; C. Keneally, *Weekend Australian*, 4-5 May, 1991, Review 4; M. de Kretser, *S.M.H.*, 30 March, 1991, 29; J. MacBean, *Australian Women's Book Review*, 3.3, 1991, 15-16; S. McKernan, *Overland*, 124, 1991, 73-76; E. Morrison, *Australian Historical Studies*, 24.97, 1991, 467-69; M. Sharkey, *ABR*, 130, 1991, 16-17; L. Sussex, *CRNLE Reviews Journal*, 1, 1991, 27-29; S. Walker, *A.L.S.*, 15.3, 1992, 238-41.

Bradstock, Margaret. 'Unspoken Thoughts: A Reassessment of Ada Cambridge'. *A.L.S.*, 14, No. 1, 1989, 51-65.

[Craig, Caroline]. 'Colonial Women Writers: Ada Cambridge (1844-1926)'. *Refractory Girl*, No.17, 1979, 31-32.

Dingley, R.J. 'Ada Cambridge, G.F. Cross, and the "Modern Pulpit"'. *A.L.S.*, 15.3, 1992, 217-20.

Higgins, Susan. '"That Singular Anomaly, the Lady Novelist" in 1888'. *Australia 1888 Bulletin*, No. 7, 1981, 68-73.

McPherson, Bernice. 'A Colonial Feminine Ideal: Femininity and Representation'. *Journal of Australian Studies*, 42, 1994, 5-17. Includes discussion of Cambridge.

Morrison, Elizabeth. 'Editing a Newspaper Novel for the Colonial Texts Series: *A Woman's Friendship*'. In *Editing in Australia*, edited by Paul Eggert (Canberra: English Department, University College, A.D.F.A., 1990) Occasional Paper 17.

---. 'Newspaper Publication of Novels of Ada Cambridge'. *A.L.S.*, XII, No. 4, 1986, 530-31.

Roe, Jill. '"The Scope of Women's Thought is Necessarily Less": The Case of Ada Cambridge'. *A.L.S.*, V, 1972, 388-403.

Sheridan, Susan. 'Ada Cambridge and the Female Literary Tradition'. In *Nellie Melba, Ginger Meggs and Friends: Essays in Australian Cultural History*, edited by Susan Dermody, John Docker, Drusilla Modjeska (Malmsbury, Vic.: Kibble Books, 1982), 162-75.

Shillingsburg, Peter L. 'The Meanings of a Scholarly Edition'. *Bibliographical Society of Australia and New Zealand Bulletin*, 13, No. 2, 1989 (issued 1990), 41-49. Includes discussion of E. Morrison's edition of Cambridge's *A Woman's Friendship*.

Tate, Audrey. *Ada Cambridge: Her Life and Work 1844-1926*. (Carlton, Vic.: MUP, 1991). Reviewed by M. Ackland, *Bibliographical Society of Australia and New Zealand Bulletin*, 16.3, 1992, 125-34; P. Barton, *ABR*, 132, 1991, 12-13; L. Clancy, *Age*, 30 November, 1991, Saturday Extra 8; G. Dutton, *Bulletin*, 16 April, 1991,

122; C. Keneally, *Weekend Australian*, 4-5 May, 1991, Review 4; M. de Kretser, *S.M.H.*, 30 March, 1991, 29; J. MacBean, *Australian Women's Book Review*, 3.3, 1991, 15-16; S. McKernan, *Overland*, 124, 1991, 73-76; S. Martin, *Journal of Australian Studies*, 34, 1992, 92-93; E. Morrison, *Australian Historical Studies*, 24.97, 1991, 467-69; S. Walker, *A.L.S.*, 15.3, 1992, 238-41.

Thomas, Sue. 'Ada Cambridge's *Unspoken Thoughts*'. *Notes & Furphies*, No. 18, 1987, 9-10.

Wakeling, Louise. '"Rattling the Orthodoxies": A View of Ada Cambridge's *A Marked Man*'. *Southerly*, 49, No. 4, 1989, 609-23.

---. 'The Source of Ada Cambridge's "The Camp"'. *A.L.S.*, 14, No. 1, 1989, 113-17.

Zinkhan, Elaine. 'Ada Cambridge: *A Marked Man*, the *Manchester Weekly Times Supplement*, and Late-Nineteenth-Century Fiction Publication'. *Bibliographical Society of Australia and New Zealand Bulletin*, 17.4, 1993, 155-79.

---. 'Ada Cambridge: A Poetry Manuscript and Holograph Inscriptions in America, Formerly Part of the James Carleton Young Collection'. *Bibliographical Society of Australia and New Zealand Bulletin*, 14.4, 1990, 121-40.

CAMPBELL, DAVID

Fiction

Evening Under Lamplight: Selected Stories of David Campbell. With a foreword by David Malouf. (St Lucia: U.Q.P., 1987). Also published as *Flame and Shadow* (St Lucia: UQ.P., 1976).

Flame and Shadow: Selected Stories. (St Lucia: U.Q.P., 1976). Reviewed by L. Cataldi, *Nation Review*, 2-8 June, 1977, 20; P. Corris, *Australian*, 1 January, 1977, 18; R. Creswell, *24 Hours*, II, No. 3, 1977, 48; B. Elliott, *Advertiser*, 19 February, 1977, 21. First published Sydney: A.& R., 1959.

Poetry

The Branch of Dodona and Other Poems, 1969-1970. (Sydney: A.& R., 1970). Reviewed by S.E. Lee, *Southerly*, XXXI, 1971, 228-29; P.Roberts, *S.M.H.*, 17 July, 1971, 24; T.W. Shapcott, *ABR*, X, 1970/71, 44; K. Slessor, *Daily Telegraph*, (Sydney), 19 December, 1970, 45; J. Tulip, *Bulletin*, 14 August, 1971, 48.

Collected Poems. Edited by Leonie Kramer (North Ryde, N.S.W.: A.& R., 1989). Reviewed by R. F. Brissenden, *Weekend Australian*, 23-24 December, 1989, Weekend 7; I. Indyk, *S.M.H.*, 25 November, 1989, 88.

Deaths and Pretty Cousins. (Canberra: Australian National University Press, 1975). Reviewed by R. Gray, *S.M.H.*, 8 November, 1975, 15; L. Murray, *National Times*, 12-17 April, 1976, 23-24; G. Page, *Canberra Times*, 9 January, 1976, 6; P. Porter, *T.L.S.*, 9 April, 1976, 431; T. Shapcott, *Australian*, 11 October, 1975, 41; C. Wallace-Crabbe, *Age*, 22 May, 1976, 22.

Devil's Rock and Other Poems, 1970-1972. (Sydney: A.& R., 1974). Reviewed by R. Adamson, *Australian*, 22 March, 1975, 41; B. Beaver, *Poetry Australia*, No. 57, 1975, 68-69; R. Pulvers, *Canberra Times*, 4 April, 1975, 10.

The History of Australia. Drawings by Keith Looby, songs and poems by David Campbell. (Sydney: Macleay Museum, 1976). Contains 'Looby Songs' and 'Ku-Ring-Gai Rock Carvings'. Reviewed by G. Page, *Canberra Times*, 12 February, 1977, 15.

The Man in the Honeysuckle. (Sydney: A.& R., 1979). Reviewed by P. Fowell, *24 Hours*, V, No. 1, 1980, 54; P. Martin, *ABR*, No. 19, 1980, 15; G. Page, *National Times*, 12 January, 1980, 29; R.A. Simpson, *Age*, 5 April, 1980, 18; D. Stewart, *S.M.H.*, 1 December, 1979, 18; M. Thwaites, *Canberra Times*, 19 January, 1980, 15.

Selected Poems, 1942-1968. (Sydney: A.& R., 1968).
Reviewed by D. Anderson, *Southerly*, XXIX, 1969, 73-74; B. Beaver, *S.M.H.*, 7 December, 1968, 20; R. Dunlop, *Poetry Australia*, No. 26, 1969, 39-40; D. Green, *Canberra Times*, 9 November, 1968, 14; R. Hall, *Australian*, 15 March, 1969, 18; N. Keesing, *Poetry Magazine*, No. 1, 1969, 7-9; F. Kellaway, *Overland*, No. 40, 1968, 36; G. Lehmann, *Bulletin*, 14 December, 1968, 80-81; J.S.M., *Realist*, No. 34, 1969, 74-76; P. Porter, *London Magazine*, N.S., IX, Nos. 4-5, 1969, 200; M. Richards, *Meanjin*, XXVIII, 1969, 272-73; R. Ward, *ABR*, VIII, 1968, 44.
Starting from Central Station: A Sequence of Poems. (Canberra: Brindabella Press, 1973).
Reviewed by R.A. Simpson, *Age*, 28 September, 1974, 17.
Words with a Black Orpington. (Sydney: A.& R., 1978).
Reviewed by V. Brady, *Makar*, XIV, No. 3, 1980, 56-60; A. Gould, *Nation Review*, 4 May, 1978, 15; R. Hall, *Weekend Australian Magazine*, 4-5 March, 1978, 8; [S.E. Lee], *Southerly*, XXXIX, 1979, 439-42; E. Lindsay, *Quadrant*, XXIII, No. 3, 1979, 70; N. Macainsh, *ABR*, No. 4, 1978, 10; J. Rodriguez, *S.M.H.*, 8 July, 1978, 19; T. Shapcott, *Age*, 1 July, 1978, 23; J. Tranter, *24 Hours*, III, No. 6, 1978, 70-71.

    Critical Material
'Mr David Campbell'. *Canberra Times*, 31 July, 1979, 8.
'The Poet of the Monaro'. *S.M.H.*, 12 January, 1976, 7.
Poetry Australia. No. 80, 1981, commemorative issue, ed. Leonie Kramer, contains: Manifold, John, 'John Manifold to Judy Campbell', extracts from letters, 9-11; Shaw, Roderick, 'A Conversation with David Campbell', 26-32; Gullett, Joe, 'Do you Know Dave Campbell?' 49-55; Stewart, Douglas, 'Debts of Gratitude', 57-61; Hope, A. D., 'Variations on a Theme - David Campbell's Translations', 62-65; Gould, Alan, 'David Campbell and the Younger Poets in Canberra 1972-9', 66-69. Reviewed by G. Dutton, *Bulletin*, 19 January, 1982, 76; G. Lehmann, *S.M.H.*, 30 January, 1982, 41.
Allsopp, Michael. 'David Campbell: Poet of the Monaro'. *London Magazine*, N.S. XX, Nos. 8-9, 1980, 132-35.
Brissenden, R.F. 'Remembering David Campbell'. *Quadrant*, XXIV, Nos. 1-2, 1980, 16-20.
---. '"Speak with the Sun": Energy, Light and Love in the Poetry of David Campbell'. In *Australian Papers: Yugoslavia, Europe and Australia*, edited by Mirko Jurak (Ljubljana: Edvard Cardelj University, 1983), 203-15.
Clark, Manning. *David Campbell 1915-1979, Words Spoken at his Funeral.* (Canberra: Brindabella Press, 1979).
Dobson, Rosemary. 'Imitations and Versions of Russian Poetry: The Record of an Experiment'. *A.L.S.*, XI, 1983, 94-99. Discusses *Moscow Trefoil: Seven Russian Poets.*
---. 'A Rare Poet of his Time'. *Age*, 4 August, 1979, 24. See also K. Haley, 31 July, 1979, 3.
Dunlevy, Maurice. 'Three David Campbells'. *Canberra Times*, 21 November, 1970, 12.
Dutton, Geoffrey. 'Poetry, Life Won't be the Same'. *Bulletin*, 14 August, 1979, 72, 75.
Gooneratne, Yasmine. 'It's Droughty in the Morning'. *Hemisphere*, XIX, No. 11, 1975, 36-38.
Hart, Kevin. 'New Directions: An Interview with David Campbell'. *Makar*, XI, No. 1, 1975, 4-10.
Heseltine, Harry (ed.). *A Tribute to David Campbell: A Collection of Essays.* (Kensington, N.S.W.: University of New South Wales Press, 1987). Reviewed by D. Brooks, *Weekend Australian. Weekend Magazine*, 25-26 April, 1987, 14; G. Burns, *Age Saturday Extra*, 16 May, 1987, 14; K. Hart, *ABR*, No. 91, 1987, 25-26; J.

Tulip, *A.LS.*, XIII, No. 2, 1987, 246-250.
Hines, Barbara. 'Rocking Chair Portrait of a Poet Farmer. *Canberra Times*, 9 July, 1969, 17. Interview.
Kinross Smith, Graeme. 'David Campbell: A Profile'. *Westerly*, No. 3, 1973, 31-38.
Kramer, Leonie. 'An Appreciation'. *S.M.H.*, 31 July, 1979, 8.
---. 'David Campbell and the Natural Tongue'. *Quadrant*, XIII, No. 3, 1969, 13-17.
---. 'The Surreal Landscape of David Campbell'. *Southerly*, XLI, 1981, 3-16.
Larkin, John. 'David Campbell: Hands of a Farmer, Mind of a Poet'. *Age*, 28 May, 1970, 2.
Malouf, David. 'Some Volumes of Selected Poems of the 1970s'. *A.L.S.*, X, 1981, 13-21.
McDonald, Roger. 'David Campbell'. *Notes & Furphies*, No. 4, 1980, 1.
McKernan, Susan. 'The Writer in Crisis: Judith Wright and David Campbell'. In her *A Question of Commitment: Australian Literature in the Twenty Years after the War*. (Sydney: Allen and Unwin, 1989). 141-65.
Mitchell, Elyne. 'Where the Ice-Trees Burn'. *Canberra Times*, 1 September, 1979, 13.
Page, Geoff. 'David Campbell'. In his *A Reader's Guide To Contemporary Australian Poetry* (St. Lucia: U.Q.P., 1995), 39-41.
---. 'David Campbell: The Last Ten Years'. *ABR*, No. 15, 1979, 21-23.
Robinson, Dennis. 'David Campbell's Poetic Mind'. *A.L.S.*, XI, 1984, 480-92.
Smith, Vivian. 'Experiment and Renewal: A Missing Link in Modern Australian Poetry'. *Southerly*, XLVII, No. 1, 1987, 3-18; esp. 7-18.
---. 'The Poetry of David Campbell'. *Southerly*, XXV, No. 3, 1965, 193-8.
Taylor, Andrew. 'Poets, Urban and Rural'. *Advertiser*, 22 August, 1978, 22.
Tonetto, Walter. 'Of Wings that Beat in the Ovoid of Memory'. In *Australian Writing Now*, edited by Manfred Jurgensen and Robert Adamson (Ringwood, Vic.: Penguin, 1988), 211-232. On David Campbell and Michael Dransfield.
Wallace-Crabbe, Robin. 'David Campbell, an Appreciation'. *Overland*, No. 79, 1980, 55-59.
Ward, Peter. 'The Man from Monaro'. *Weekend Australian Magazine*, 4-5 August, 1979, 2. See also *Advertiser*, 1 August, 1979, 30; *Australian*, 31 July, 1979, 2.

CAMPBELL, MARION

Fiction
Lines of Flight. (Fremantle, W.A.: Fremantle Arts Centre Press, 1985).
Reviewed by I. Baranay, *S.M.H.*, 16 November, 1985, 46; K.H., *Womanspeak*, 9, No. 5, 1986, 28 and 10, No. 1, 1986, 22; S. McKernan, *Bulletin*, 12 November, 1985, 140; S. Moore, *ABR*, No. 77, 1985-6, 32-4; S. Muecke, *Age Monthly Review*, 5, No. 9, 1986, 10-11; W. Noonan, *Weekend Australian*, 16-17 November, 1985, 16; C. Pybus, *Island Magazine*, No. 28, 1986, 60-2; B. Walker, *Phoenix Review*, No. 1, 1986-7, 111-13.

Not Being Miriam. (Fremantle, W.A.: Fremantle Arts Centre Press, 1988).
Reviewed by D. Bird, *ABR*, No. 107, 1988, 32-4; H. Elliott, *Age*, 5 November, 1988, Saturday Extra 13; D. English, *Weekend Australian*, 24-25 December, 1988, Weekend 6; I. Indyk, *Southerly*, 49, No. 1, 1989, 127; R. Lucas, *Australian Feminist Studies*, No. 10, 1989, 131-5; S. McKernan, *Bulletin*, 18 October, 1988, 117-8; D. Matthews, *Overland*, No. 114, 1989, 95-6; J. Mead, *Island Magazine*, No. 39, 1989, 86-90; I Salusinszky, *Age Monthly Review*, 9, No. 6, 1989, 23; P. Tandy, *Westerly*, 33, No. 4, 1988, 92-4; K. Veitch, *S.M.H.*, 3 December, 1988, 86.

Critical Material
Gillett, Sue. 'Away from the Gaze, Into the Maze: Marion Campbell's *Not Being Miriam*'. *Southerly*, 54.2, 1994, 47-57.
Keane, Colleen. 'Post-Humanism, Plurality and *Not Being Miriam*'. *Meridian*, 13.1,

1994, 27-37.
Liddelow, Eden. 'Home Is Where the Art Is: Beverley Farmer and Marion Campbell'. *Scripsi*, 4, No. 2, 1986, 281-94.
Midalia, Susan. 'Return to Oz, or "Something Tells Me We're Not in France Anymore": Female Identity in Marion Campbell's *Lines of Flight*'. *WLWE*, 33.2&34.1, 1993-94, 75-89.
Spence, Valerie. 'Representations of Subjectivity in *Not Being Miriam*'. *SPAN*, 37, 1993, 33-47.

CAMPBELL, THOMAS

Critical Material
Castle, Edgar. 'Kangaroo with Flowers'. *Southern Review*, I, No. 2, 1964, 24-9. Discusses Campbell's 'Departure of Emigrants'.

CAMPION, SARAH

Fiction
Mo Burdekin. Introduction by Elisabeth Lawson. (Ringwood, Vic.: Penguin, 1990). First published London: Davies, 1941.
Reviewed by M. Arkin, *Antipodes*, 5.2, 1991, 61; C. Burns, *Australian Women's Book Review*, 2, No. 2, 1990, 28-29. L. Clancy, *Weekend Australian*, 12-13 May, 1990, Weekend 8; F.D. Glass, *Journal of Australian Studies*, No. 27, 1990, 102; E. Morrison, *ABR*, No. 120, 33-34.

Critical Material
Lawson, Elizabeth. 'Lucy's Gold, *The Pommy Cow*, in Herbertland: Sarah Campion's "Mo Burdekin" Novels'. *LiNQ*, XV, No. 2, 1987, 71-79.
Store, R. 'North Queensland's Literature. Part I'. *Islands Review* (Townsville), I, No. 3, 1968, 9-13.

CAPPIELLO, ROSA

Fiction
Oh Lucky Country. (St Lucia: U.Q.P., 1984). Translation of *Paese Fortunato* (Milan: Feltrinelli, 1981).
Reviewed by H. Garner, *Helix*, Nos. 21, 22, 1985, 110-111; C. Gerrish, *Womanspeak*, IX, No. 2, 1985, 28; J. Gioscio, *LiNQ*, XIII, No. 1, 1985, 70-74; M. Harrison, *Age Monthly Review*, V, No. 1, 1985, 16-19; M. Jurgensen, *Outrider*, II, No. 1, 1985, 245-246; R. Macklin, *Weekend Australian Magazine*, 12-13 January, 1985, 12; D. Myers, *Age Saturday Extra*, 26 January, 1985, 11; R. Pascoe, *ABR*, No. 68, 1985, 35; A. Stretton, *S.M.H.*, 12 January, 1985, 36.

Non-Fiction
'Why I Write What I Write'. *Australian Society*, VI, No. 1, 1987, 25-26.

Critical Material
Gunew, Sneja. 'The Grotesque Migrant Body: Rosa Capiello's *Oh Lucky Country*' in her *Framing Marginality: Multicultural Literary Studies* (Carlton, Vic.: MUP, 1994), 93-110.
---. 'Rosa Cappiello's *Oh Lucky Country*: Multi-cultural Reading Strategies'. *Meanjin*, XLIV, No. 4, 1985, 517-528.
Harrison, M. 'Between the Peaks'. *Look & Listen*, I, No. 6, 1985, 85.
Pertosi, Giampaolo. 'The Impact of a Migrant's Anger'. *Bulletin*, 21 February, 1984, 58-59.
Rando, Gaetano. 'Italo-Australian Fiction'. *Meanjin*, XLIII, No. 3, 1984, 341-349.
Rizzo, Santina. 'Interview with Rosa Cappiello'. *New Literatures Review*, 24, 1992: 117-22.

CARBONI, RAFFAELLO
Critical Material
Gorlier, Claudio. 'Hero and Comedian: Some Afterthoughts on Raffaello Carboni'.
In *Australia and Italy: Contributions to Intellectual Life*, edited by Giovanna Capone
(Ravenna: Longo Editore/Universita di Bologna: 1989.

CAREW, ELSIE
Critical Material
Keesing, Nancy. *Elsie Carew: Australian Primitive Poet.* (Sydney: Wentworth Press,
1965). Reviewed by V. Smith, *Bulletin*, 22 May, 1965, 58.
---. 'Australian Primitive Poets'. *Opinion*, IX, No. 1, 1965, 22-34.

CAREY, PETER
Fiction
The Big Bazoohley. (St Lucia: U.Q.P., 1995).
Reviewed by N. Krauth, *ABR*, 175, 1995, 57-58.

Bliss. (St Lucia: U.Q.P.; London: Faber, 1981).
Reviewed by R. Barnes, *National Times*, 11-17 October, 1981, 42; G. Burns, *ABR*,
No. 41, 1982, 27-29; J. Cooke, *New Statesman*, 20 November, 1981, 22; D.
Durrant, *London Magazine*, N.S. XXI, No. 11, 1982, 97-98; K. Gelder, *CRNLE
Reviews Journal*, No. 1, 1983, 46-48; S. Hall, *Bulletin*, 24 September, 1985, 156;
J. Jenkins, *Artlook*, IX, No. 5, 1983, 49; N. Jillett, *Age*, 19 September, 1985, 14;
F. Kermode, *London Review of Books*, III, Nos. 22-23, 1981, 17; F. King, *Spectator*,
12 December, 1981, 21; M. MacDonald, *Courier-Mail*, 2 November, 1985, 9; D.
Macdonald, *Canberra Times*, 23 October, 1985, 31; S. McKernan, *Overland*, No. 88,
1982, 57-58; P. Neilsen, *Image*, V, No. 1, 1982, 21-22; J. Neville, *S.M.H.*, 10
October, 1981, 44; P. Pierce, *Meanjin*, XL, 1981, 522-28; E. Riddell, *Bulletin*, 6
October, 1981, 68; M. Roberts, *Going Down Swinging*, No. 5, 1982, 69-72; J. Ryle,
T.L.S., 20 November, 1981, 1350; M. Smith, *Weekend Australian Magazine*, 7-8
November, 1981, 12; A.M. Stewart, *Quadrant*, XXVI, No. 6, 1982, 87-88; J.
Tranter, *Age*, 3 October, 1981, 27; E. Williams, *Weekend Australian Magazine*,
14-15 September, 1985, 13.

Collected Stories. (St Lucia: U.Q.P., 1994; London: Faber, 1995).
Reviewed by L. Sage, *T.L.S.*, 18 Aug., 1995, 19.

Exotic Pleasures. (London: Pan, 1981). Paperback edition of *The Fat Man in History*
in the form published by Faber, 1980.
Reviewed by F. Kermode, *London Review of Books*, III, Nos. 22-23, 1981, 17.

The Fat Man in History. (St Lucia: U.Q.P., 1974).
Reviewed by R. Adamson, *Australian*, 21 September, 1974, 43; D. Gilbey, *Southerly*,
XXXVII, 1977, 467-71; W. Green, *Westerly*, No. 4, 1975, 73-76; C. Harrison-Ford,
Stand, XVI, No. 3, 1975, 43-44; B. Kiernan, *Meanjin*, XXXIV, 1975, 39 and
National Times, 2-7 August, 1976, 36-37; M. Lurie, *Nation Review*, 29 November-5
December, 1974, 204; N.J. MacLeod, *Makar*, X, No. 3, 1975, 41-43; R.
McConchie, *Overland*, No. 60, 1975, 83-85; G. Page, *Canberra Times*, 7 February,
1975, 9; D. Stewart, *S.M.H.*, 19 October, 1974, 13; J. Sutherland, *T.L.S.*, 9 April,
1976, 445; D. Vines, *Blacksmith*, No. 2, 1975, 54.

The Fat Man in History. (London: Faber, 1980). Stories selected from the U.Q.P.
volumes *The Fat Man in History* and *War Crimes*.
Reviewed by P. Lewis, *T.L.S.*, 31 October, 1980, 1240; J. Mellors, *London
Magazine*, N.S. XX, Nos. 8-9, 1980, 116-17; P. Thompson, *New Statesman*, 24
October, 1980, 26; P. van Schaik, *UNISA English Studies*, XIX, No. 2, 1981, 53.

Illywhacker. (London: Faber and Faber; New York: Harper & Row; St. Lucia:

U.Q.P., 1985).
Reviewed by L. Clancy, *ABR*, No. 73, 1985, 14-15; H. Daniel, *Southerly*, XLVI, No. 2, 1986, 156-67; G. Dutton, *Bulletin*, 16 July, 1985, 90; M. Duwell, *Overland*, No. 101, 1985, 92-94; K. England, *Advertiser Saturday Review*, 6 July, 1985, 7; P. Goldsworthy, *Island Magazine*, No. 24, 1985, 56-57; M. Halligan, *Canberra Times*, 24 August, 1985, B2; J. Hanrahan, *Age Saturday Extra*, 6 July, 1985, 14; H. Herbert, *National Times*, 26 April-2 May, 1985, 31; A. Hislop, *T.L.S.*, 3 May, 1985, 492; V. Ikin, *Phoenix Review*, No. 1, 1986/87, 125-127; H. Jacobson, *New York Times Book Review*, 17 November, 1985, 15; L.R. Leavis and J.M. Blom, *English Studies*, LXVII, No. 5, 1986, 437; P. Lewis, *London Magazine*, XXV, Nos. 1-2, 1985, 148-152; R. Lewis, *New Statesman*, 19 April, 1985, 32-34; O. Masters, *Fremantle Arts Review*, I, No. 1, 1986, 12-13; J. Mellors, *Listener*, 25 April, 1985, 27; A. Mitchell, *Weekend Australian Magazine*, 6-7 July, 1985, 15; A. Mitchell, *The New Yorker*, 11 November, 1985, 154, 156; A.A. Phillips, *Age Monthly Review*, V, No. 4, 1985, 3-4; P. Pierce, *National Times*, 5-11 July, 1985, 30; D. Profumo, *Books & Bookmen*, No. 355, 1985, 35; S. Roff, *Newsletter of the A.A.A.L.S.*, II, No. 1, 1988, 10; C. Semmler, *Courier-Mail*, 27 July, 1985, 31; P. Smelt, *British Book News*, May, 1985, 300; N. Spice, *London Review of Books*, VII, No. 7, 1985, 20-21; A. Stewart, *Quadrant*, XXIX, No. 12, 1985, 86-87; E. Webby, *S.M.H.*, 13 July, 1985, 47.

Oscar and Lucinda. (London: Faber and Faber; St Lucia: U.Q.P., 1988).
Reviewed by D. Anderson, *S.M.H.*, 20 February, 1988, 71; G. Dyer, *New Statesman*, 1 April, 1988, 28; R. Edmond, *Australian Studies*, No. 3, 1989, 88-95; S. Faulks, *Age Saturday Extra*, 29 October, 1988, 5; M. Harris, *Southerly*, 49, No. 1, 1989, 109-13; H. Jacobson, *Weekend Australian. Weekend Magazine*, 20-21 February, 1988, 13; M.R. Liverani, *Overland*, No. 110, 1988, 70-72; R. Moran, *Fremantle Arts Review*, III, No. 8, 1988, 15; G. Nicholls, *Lot's Wife*, No. 4, 1988, 12; W. Ommundsen, *Different Perspectives* (Supplement to *Mattoid*, No. 30), 1988, 73-76; P. Pierce, *Age Saturday Extra*, 20 February, 1988, 11; N.J.Richey, *World Literature Today*, 63.3, 1989, 534-35; E. Riddell, *ABR*, No. 98, 1988, 14-15; M. Roberts, *Times on Sunday*, 14 February, 1988, 32; M. da Silva, *Outrider*, 6, No. 2, 1989, 148-59; C. K. Stead, *Scripsi*, 5, No. 2, 1989, 3-8; A. Stewart, *Quadrant*, XXXII, No. 12, 1988, 66-67; M. Trefely-Deutch, *Phoenix Review*, No.3, 1988, 99-101; T. Wilhelmus, *Hudson Review*, 41.3, 1988, 548-56; G. Windsor, *Bulletin*, 23 February, 1988, 69-70.

The Tax Inspector. (St. Lucia: U.Q.P.; London: Faber, 1991).
Reviewed by V. Brady, *Overland*, 125, 1991, 80-83; A. Burke, *Editions*, 12, 1991, 22-23; L. Clancy, *Australian Society*, 10.8, 1991, 38-39; J. Coe, *London Review of Books*, 13.17, 1991, 12; J. Craig, *Southerly*, 52.1, 1992, 152-56; H. Daniel, *Age*, 27 July, 1991, Saturday Extra 9; R. Dixon, *LiNQ*, 18.2, 1991, 133-41; P.K. Elkin, *Northern Perspective*, 16.1, 1993: 117-18; C. Floyd, *SPAN*, 33, 1992, 177-81; D. Giese, *Weekend Australian*, 27-28 July, 1991, Review 4; P. Hawker, *ABR*, 133, 1991, 15-17; E. Liddelow, *Scripsi*, 7.2, 1991, 93-100; N. Mansfield, *CRNLE Reviews Journal*, 1, 1992, 76-78; *New York Times Book Review*, 28 February, 1993, 32; P. Pierce, *Bulletin*, 13 August, 1991, 112; A.P. Riemer, *S.M.H.*, 3 August, 1991, 43; R. Ross, *Antipodes*, 6.1, 1992, 87; E. White, *T.L.S.*, 30 August, 1991, 21.

The Unusual Life of Tristan Smith. (St Lucia: U.Q.P., 1994).
Reviewed by D. Callahan, *Antipodes*, 9.2, 1995, 145-46; H. Daniel, *Age*, 20 August, 1994, Saturday Extra 7; J. Doyle, *Voices*, 5.4, 1995-96, 123-26; N. Hasluck, *Quadrant*, 39.1-2, 1995, 102-04; E. Korn, *T.L.S.*, 2 September, 1994, 10; M. Maclean, *ABR*, 164, 1994, 8-10; B. Pascoe, *Eureka Street*, 4.10, 1994, 34-35; P. Pierce, *Bulletin*, 30 August, 1994, 88-89; A. Riemer, *S.M.H.*, 20 August, 1994, Spectrum 9A; G. Turcotte, *Weekend Australian*, 20-21 August, 1994, Review 7.

War Crimes. (St Lucia: U.Q.P., 1979).
Reviewed by D.R. Burns, *ABR*, No. 19, 1980, 20-21; G. Dutton, *Bulletin*, 4 December, 1979, 66-67; M. Fabre, *CRNLE Reviews Journal*, No. 1, 1980, 72-76; M. Halligan, *Canberra Times*, 22 December, 1979, 13; K. Hughes, *Weekend Australian Magazine*, 1-2 December, 1979, 12; J. Legasse, *Westerly*, XXV, No. 2, 1980, 122-24; P. Neilsen, *Image*, III, No. 4, 1979, 52-53; J. Neville, *S.M.H.*, 13 October, 1979, 20; J. Paris, *Campaign*, No. 48, 1979, 31; P. Pierce, *National Times*, 10 November, 1979, 46; E. Riddell, *24 Hours*, IV, No. 11, 1979, 79; J. Tittensor, *Age*, 19 January, 1980, 26 (see also L. Radic, *Age*, 31 January, 1980, 10 and J. Tittensor, *Age*, 5 February, 1980, 10); E. Webby, *Meanjin*, XXXIX, 1980, 131-32.

Non-Fiction

A Letter to Our Son. (St Lucia: U.Q.P., 1994).

'Peter Carey on *Oscar and Lucinda*'. In *Writers in Action: The Writer's Choice Evenings*, edited by Gerry Turcotte (Sydney: Currency Press, 1990), 1-23.

Critical Material

'An Interview with Peter Carey'. *Going Down Swinging*, No. 1, 1980, 43-55.

Adam, Ian. 'Breaking the Chain: Anti-Saussurean Resistance in Birney, Carey and C. S. Pierce'. *WLWE*, 29, No. 2, 1989, 11-22. Reprinted in *Past the Last Post: Theorizing Post-Colonialism and Postmodernism*, edited by Ian Adams and Helen Tiffin (Hemel Hampstead: Harvester Wheatsheaf, 1991),79-93.

Ahearne, Kate. 'Kate Ahearne in Conversation with Peter Carey'. *ABR*, No. 99, 1988, 14-15.

---. 'Peter Carey and Short Fiction in Australia'. *Going Down Swinging* (Melbourne), No. 1, 1980, 7-17.

Baker, Candida. 'Peter Carey'. In her *Yacker: Australian Writers Talk About Their Work* (Sydney: Picador, 1986), 54-77.

Bisutti, Francesca. 'The Factory of Invention: Peter Carey's Real Fictions'. In *Saggi e ricerche sulle culture extraeuropee*, edited by G. Bellini, C. Gorlier, and S. Zoppi (Rome: Bulzoni, 1986), 61-68. Africa, America, Asia, Australia, 2.

Blaber, Ronald and Marvin Gilman. *Roguery: The Picaresque Tradition in Australian, Canadian and Indian Fiction*. (Springwood, N.S.W.: Butterfly , 1990). Contains readings from Carey's work.

Bliss, Carolyn. 'The Revisionary Lover: Misprision of the Past in Peter Carey'. *Australian & New Zealand Studies in Canada*, 6, 1991: 45-54.

---. 'Time and Timelessness in Peter Carey's Fiction: The Best of Both Worlds'. *Antipodes*, 9.2, 1995, 97-105.

Bode, Barbara. 'Angels and Devils: Child Sexual Abuse in Peter Carey's *The Tax Inspector*'. *Antipodes*, 9.2, 1995, 107-10.

Brown, Ruth. 'English Heritage and Australian Culture: The Church and Literature of England in *Oscar and Lucinda*'. *A.L.S.*, 17.2, 1995, 135-40.

Burns, D.R. 'Feasibility through Fictional Ploys: Peter Carey's Accord with Stephen Potter'. *Overland*, 137, 1994, 39-44.

Callahan, David. 'Peter Carey's *Oscar and Lucinda* and the Subversion of Subversion'. *Australian Studies*, No. 4, 1990, 20-26.

---. 'Whose History is the Fat Man's?: Peter Carey's *The Fat Man in History*'. *SPAN*, 40, 1995, 34-53.

Clunies Ross, Bruce A. 'Laszlo's Testament; or, Structuring the Past and Sketching the Present in Contemporary Short Fiction, mainly Australian'. *Kunapipi*, I, No. 2, 1979, 110-23.

Daniel, Helen. *Liars: Australian New Novelists*. (Ringwood, Vic.: Penguin, 1988), 145-184.

---. 'Peter Carey: The Rivalries of the Fictions'. In *International Literature in English: Essays on the Major Writers*, edited by Robert Ross (New York: Garland,

1991), 405-15.

Dare, Tim. 'He Bit, Chewed and Found Bliss'. *S.M.H.*, 27 May, 1982, 3.

Dessaix, Robert. 'An Interview with Peter Carey'. *ABR*, 167, 1994, 18-20.

Dixon, Robert. 'Closing the Can of Worms: Enactments of Justice in *Bleak House*, *The Mystery of a Hansom Cab* and *The Tax Inspector*'. *Westerly*, 37.4, 1992, 37-45.

Dovey, Teresa. 'An Infinite Onion: Narrative Structure in Peter Carey's Fiction'. *A.L.S.*, XI, 1983, 195-204.

Edwards, Brian. 'Deceptive Constructions: the Art of Building in Peter Carey's *Illywhacker*'. *Australian and New Zealand Studies in Canada*, 4, 1990, 39-56.

Fuller, Peter. 'Carey Gives the Lie to Some Old Lies'. *Canberra Times*, 21 August, 1985, 27.

Fletcher, M.D. 'Peter Carey's Post-Colonial Australia I: *Illywhacker*: Lies, Dependence, and Political History'. In *Australian Political Ideas*, edited by Geoff Stokes (Kensington, NSW: U of New South Wales Press, 1994), 134-42.

---. 'Peter Carey's Post-Colonial Australia II: *Oscar and Lucinda*: Misunderstanding, Victimisation, and Political History'. In *Australian Political Ideas*, edited by Geoff Stokes (Kensington, NSW: U of New South Wales Press, 1994), 143-51.

---. 'Post-Colonial Peter Carey'. *SPAN*, 32, 1991, 12-23.

---. 'The Theme of Entrapment in Peter Carey's Fiction'. *Commonwealth Review* 3.2, 1991-2, 74-79. Reprinted in *Australian Literature Today*, edited by R. K. Dhawan and David Kerr (New York: Indian Society for Commonwealth Studies/Advent Press, 1993), 74-79.

Fuery, Patrick. 'Prisoners and Spiders Surrounded by Signs: Postmodernism and the Postcolonial Gaze in Contemporary Australian Culture'. In *Recasting the World: Writing after Colonialism*, edited by Jonathan White (Baltimore: Johns Hopkins UP, 1993), 190-207. Includes discussion of work by Carey.

Gelder, Kenneth. 'History, Politics and the (Post) modern: Receiving Australian Fiction'. *Meanjin*, XLVII, No. 3, 1988, 551-559. Discusses the work of Gerald Murnane, Alan Wearne and Peter Carey.

Glover, Richard. 'Peter Carey: from Advertising to Tall Stories'. *Age Saturday Extra*, 6 July, 1985, 3.

Grenville, Kate, and Sue Woolfe. *Making Stories: How Ten Australian Novels Were Written*. (St Leonards, NSW: Allen & Unwin, 1993). Includes contribution on *Oscar and Lucinda*.

Harvey, Oliver. 'Carey Makes a Novel Switch'. *Courier-Mail*, 16 October, 1982, 28. Interview.

Hassall, Anthony J. *Dancing on Hot Macadam: Peter Carey's Fiction*. (St Lucia: U.Q.P., 1994). Reviewed by P. Bond, *Antipodes*, 8.2, 1994, 160-61; J. Croft, *Weekend Australian*, 4-5 June, 1994, Review 7; V. Ikin, *S.M.H.*, 26 February, 1994, Spectrum 9A; B. Kiernan, *A.L.S.*, 17.2, 1995, 198-202; B.M., *T.L.S.*, 8 April, 1994, 32; A. Riemer, *ABR*, 168, 1995, 44-45; S. St Vincent Welch, *Editions*, 22, 1995, 24.

---. 'Telling Lies and Stories: Peter Carey's *Bliss*'. *Modern Fiction Studies*, 35.4, 1989, 637-55.

Hawley, Janet. 'How an Ad Man found Bliss'. *Age*, 26 September, 1981, 26.

Herman, Luc. 'Canonizing Australia: The Case of Peter Carey'. In *Shades of Empire in Colonial and Post-Colonial Literatures*, edited by C.C. Barfoot and Theo D'haen (Amsterdam/Atlanta, Ga.: Rodopi, 1993), 109-115.

Holst Petersen, Kirsten. 'Gambling on Reality: A Reading of Peter Carey's *Oscar and Lucinda*'. In *European Perspectives: Contemporary Essays on Australian Literature*, edited by Giovanna Capone (*A.L.S.*, 15.2 (special issue)/ St. Lucia: U.Q.P., 1991), 107-16.

Ifeka, Helena. 'Peter Carey: Interview'. *Hermes*, 1992, 15-23.

Ikin, Van. 'Answers to Seventeen Questions: An Interview with Peter Carey'. *Science Fiction* (Sydney), I, No. 1, 1977, 30-39.

---. 'Peter Carey: the Stories'. *Science Fiction* (Sydney), I, No. 1, 1977, 19-29.

Huggan, Graham. 'Is the (Günter) Grass Greener on the Other Side? Oskar and Lucinde in the New World'. *WLWE*, 30.1, 1990: 1-10.

Jach, Antoni. 'An Interview with Peter Carey'. *Mattoid*, 31, 1988, 24-36.

Jardine, Cassandra. 'Apocalypse Free ... With every Fifth Packet'. *New Fiction* (London), No. 26, 1980, 4-5. Interview.

Kane, Paul. 'Postcolonial/Postmodern: Australian Literature and Peter Carey'. *World Literature Today*, 67.3, 1993, 519-22.

Lamb, Karen. *Peter Carey: The Genesis of Fame*. (Pymble, NSW: Collins A.& R, 1992). Reviewed by S. Lever, *A.L.S.*, 16.2, 1993: 229-33.

Lawson, Valerie. 'Peter Carey: Advertising Doesn't Hurt him a Scrap'. *S.M.H.*, 5 September, 1981, 47.

Maddocks, John. 'Bizarre Realities: An Interview with Peter Carey'. *Southerly*, XLI, 1981, 27-40.

Manning, Greg. 'Reading Lesson: "The Fat Man in History", Teaching and Deconstructive Practice'. *Span*, XXI, 1985, 38-55.

McCluskey, Phil. 'The Handsomest Drowned Man in the Outback: Contextualizing a Structural Magic Realism'. In *Postcolonial Fictions* edited by Michèle Drouart, special issue in two volumes incl. SPACLALS Conference Proceedings. *SPAN* 36, 1993, 88-94. Discusses *Illywhacker*.

Morton-Evans, Michael. 'Carey Reaches a Blissful Peak in his Literary Career'. *Australian*, 26 July, 1984, 8.

Munro, Craig. 'Building the Fabulist Extensions'. *Makar*, XII, No. 1, 1976, 3-12. Interview. An excerpt also published in *A.L.S.*, VIII, 1977, 182-87.

Neilsen, Philip. 'Excerpt From Interview: Tell Me What Colour You Think the Sky Is'. *A.L.S.*, X, No. 2, 1981, 191-3

Omundsen, Wenche. 'Narrative Navel-Gazing, or, How to Recognise a Metafiction When You See One'. *Southern Review*, 22, No. 3, 1989, 264-74. Includes a discussion of *Oscar and Lucinda*.

Riem Natale, Antonella. 'Harry Joy's Children: The Art of Story Telling in Peter Carey's *Bliss*'. *A.L.S.* 16.3, 1994, 341-47.

Ross, Robert. '"It Cannot *Not* Be There": Borges and Australia's Peter Carey'. In *Borges and His Successors: The Borgesian Impact on Literature and the Arts*, edited by Edna Aizenberg (Columbia, Miss.: Uni of Missouri Press, 1989), 44-58.

Ryan, Sue. 'Metafiction in *Illywhacker*: Peter Carey's Renovated Picaresque Novel'. *Commonwealth*, 14.1, 1991, 33-40.

Ryan-Fazilleau, Suzan. 'One-Upmanship in Peter Carey's Short Stories'. *Journal of the Short Story in English*, 16, 1991, 51-63.

Sayers, Stuart. 'In Pursuit of Logic'. *Age*, 28 September, 1974, 16.

---. 'A Particular Bent for the Bizarre'. *Age*, 27 October, 1979, 26.

Schmidt-Haberkamp, Barbara. 'Wider den Pauschaltourismus der Literatur: Peter Careys australisches Panoptikum *Illywhacker*'. *Arbeiten aus Anglistik und Amerikanistik*, 17.1, 1992, 71-82.

Sharrad, Paul. 'Responding to the Challenge: Peter Carey and the Reinvention of Australia'. *Span*, No. 25, 1987, 37-46.

Sorensen, Rosemary. 'Reputations Made and Unmade: Rosemary Sorensen Talks to Evan Green, Alex Miller and Peter Carey'. *ABR*, 134, 1991, 10-11.

Stewart, Annette M. 'Recent Australian Fiction'. *WLWE*, XXII, 1983, 212-23.

Tate, Trudi. 'Unravelling the Feminine: Peter Carey's "Peeling". *Meanjin*, XLVI, No. 3, 1987, 394-399.

Tausky, Thomas E. 'Getting the Corner Right: An Interview with Peter Carey'. *Australian and New Zealand Studies in Canada*, No. 4, 1990, 27-38.

Thwaites, Tony. 'More Tramps at Home: Seeing Australia First'. *Meanjin*, XLVI, No. 3, 1987, 400-409.

Toomey, Philippa. 'Peter Carey's Refreshment'. *Times*, 27 October, 1980, 6; reprinted as 'Fictional Future from Bits, Pieces'. *Canberra Times*, 9 November, 1980, 8. Interview.
Turner, Graeme. 'American Dreaming: The Fictions of Peter Carey'. *A.L.S.*, XII, No. 4, 1986, 431-41.
---. 'Nationalising the Author: The Celebrity of Peter Carey'. *A.L.S.*, 16.2, 1993: 131-39.
Wachtel, Eleanor. '"We Really Can Make Ourselves Up": An Interview with Peter Carey'. *Australian & New Zealand Studies in Canada*, 9, 1993: 103-05.
Willbanks, Ray. 'Peter Carey'. In his *Speaking Volumes: Australian Writers and Their Work* (Ringwood, Vic.: Penguin, 1991).

CASEY, GAVIN

Fiction
Short-Shift Saturday and Other Stories. (Sydney: A.& R., 1974). A.& R. Classics. Originally published in 1942 as *It's Harder for Girls* (Sydney: A.& R., 1942). Includes John Barnes, 'Gavin Casey: The View from Kalgoorlie', a revision of an article from *Meanjin*, 1964.
View from Kalgoorlie. (Perth: Landfall Press, 1969). Selected short stories by Gavin Casey, Wally Wynne, and Ted Mayman, with a biographical introduction by Ted Mayman.

Non-Fiction
With Ted Mayman. *The Mile that Midas Touched*. (Adelaide: Rigby, 1964).
Reviewed by M.H. Ellis, *Bulletin*, 5 December, 1964, 55; H.A. Lindsay, *ABR*, III, 1964, 211.
'Means and Ends in Writing'. *A.L.S.*, IX, 1979, 225-31.

Critical Material
Barnes, John. 'Gavin Casey: The View from Kalgoorlie'. *Meanjin*, XXIII, No. 4, 1964, 341-7.
Casey-Congdon, Dorothy. *Casey's Wife*. (Perth: Artlook Books, 1982). Reviewed by B. Hunter, *Courier-Mail*, 12 March, 1983, 26; J. Waten, *Age Saturday Extra*, 5 March, 1983, 10.
Drake-Brockman, Henrietta. 'Gavin Casey'. *Westerly*, No. 4, 1964, 7-10.
Dunlevy, Maurice. 'Novelist Not Impressed by Canberra's Winter Sunshine'. *Canberra Times*, 12 July, 1974, 10.
Hewett, Dorothy. 'Literary Obituary'. *The Critic*, No. 7, 1964, 62-63. Compares Casey to Henry Lawson.
Kemeny, P. 'Gavin Casey and the Australian Common Man'. *Australian Quarterly*, XXXVIII, No. 3, 1966, 88-92.
Mayman, Ted. 'Gavin Casey's World'. *A.L.S.*, IX, 1979, 231-34. Expanded from *Artlook*, II, No. 11, 1976, 19-21.
Vickers, F.B. 'Gavin Casey - The Man I Knew'. *Overland*, No. 30, 1964, 25.

CASTRO, BRIAN

Fiction
After China. (Sydney: Allen & Unwin, 1992).
Reviewed by C. Bennett, *CRNLE Reviews Journal*, 2, 1992, 26-28; J. Chimonyo, *Age*, 29 August, 1992, Saturday Extra 10; D. Coad, *World Literature Today*, 67.3, 1993, 667; H. Daniel and D. Gilbert, *ABR*, 142, 1992, 4-7; J. Grixti, *Imago*, 5.2, 1993, 92-94; P. Pierce, *Bulletin*, 28 July, 1992, 91; M. Sharkey, *Weekend Australian*, 22-23 August, 1992, Review 7R; Sorensen, *Meanjin*, 25.4, 1993: 778-83.
Birds of Passage. (Sydney: Allen and Unwin, 1983).
Reviewed by G. Burns, *ABR*, No. 60, 1984, 17-18; L. Clancy, *ABR*, No. 68, 1985,

35-36; N. Creech, *Weekend Australian*, 20-21 August, 1983, Weekend 15; A. Gould, *Age*, 17 September, 1983, Saturday Extra 15;G. Higginson, *Muse*, No. 29, 1983, 18. F. Kellaway, *Overland*, No.93, 1983, 65-66; N. Rose, *Age Monthly Review*, 3, No. 9, 1984, 20; V. Wright, *Weekend Australian*, 8-9 September, 1984, Weekend 14.

Double-Wolf. (North Sydney: Allen & Unwin, 1991).
Reviewed by Reviewed by M.J. Campbell, *Overland*, 125, 1991, 87-88; H. Daniel, *Age*, 22 June, 1991, Saturday Extra 8; J. Grixti, *Imago*, 5.2, 1993: 92-94; N. Jose, *Voices*, 1.4, 1991, 97-99; R. Kosky, *Editions*, 12, 1991, 24-25; J. McLaren, *ABR*, 132, 1991, 38-40; P. Pierce, *S.M.H.*, 6 July, 1991, 41; I. Salusinszky, *Weekend Australian*, 10-11 August, 1991, Review 4.

Drift. (Port Melbourne: Heinemann, 1994).
Reviewed by D. Coad, *World Literature Today*, 69.3, 1995, 641-42; M. Condon, *Weekend Australian*, 16-17 July, 1994, Review 6; K. England, *ABR*, 162, 1994, 10-13; J. Hanrahan, *Age*, 20 August, 1994, Saturday Extra 8; M. McGirr, *Eureka Street*, 4.8, 1994, 41-42; P. Pierce, *Bulletin*, 16 August, 1994, 104-05; A. Riemer, *S.M.H.*, 2 July, 1994, Spectrum 9A.

Pomeroy. (Sydney: Allen and Unwin, 1990).
Reviewed by R. F. Brissenden, *Editions*, No. 8-9, 1990, 7-8; M. Halligan, *Weekend Australian*, 26-27 May, 1990, Review 5; C. Keneally, *ABR*, No. 118, 1990, 15-16.

Non-Fiction
'Heterotopias: Writing and Location'. *A.L.S.*, 17.2, 1995, 178-82. Paper delivered at the Australian Studies Conference at Guangzhou, Zhongshan University, 1994.
'Lesions'. *Meanjin*, 54.1, 1995, 59-68. Includes discussion of his attitude to writing and literature.
'The Private & the Public: A Meditation on Noise'. (With an excerpt from *Double-Wolf*). *Island* 47, 1991, 14-19.

Critical Material
Daniel, Helen. 'Outside the Prison of Logic'. Interview. *Island*, 59, 1994, 20-29.
O'Loghlin, Libby. 'Talking to Writers: Brian Castro'. *Redoubt*, 21, 1995, 112-15. Interview.
Ouyang Yu. 'Brian Castro: The Other Representing the Other'. *Literary Criterion*, 30.1&2, 1995, 30-48.
Pierce, Peter. '"Things Are Cast Adrift": Brian Castro's Fiction'. *A.L.S.*, 17.2, 1995, 149-56.
Pons, Xavier. 'Alienness and Alienation in Brian Castro's *Birds of Passage*'. In *A Passage to Somewhere Else*, edited by Doireann MacDermott and Susan Ballyn (Barcelona: Promocions y Publicacions Universitarias, 1988), 129-134.
---. 'Impossible Coincidences: Narrative Strategy in Brian Castro's *Birds of Passage*'. *A.L.S.*, 14, No. 4, 464-75.
Sorensen, Rosemary. 'Yearning for Diversion: An Interview with Brian Castro'. *ABR*, 142, 1992, 8-9.
Tacey, David. 'Freud, Fiction & the Australian Mind'. *Island*, 49, 1991, 8-13.

CATALDI, LEE

Poetry
Invitation to a Marxist Lesbian Party. (Sydney: Wild & Woolley, 1978).
Reviewed by E.M. Bradstock, *Campaign*, 49, 1979; K. Goodwin, *Weekend Australian Magazine*, 17-18 March, 1979: 11; H. Juricek, *Womanspeak*, 5.2, 1980, 30; C. Pollnitz, *Southerly*, 39, 1979, 462-78; J. Rodriguez, *ABR*, 10, 1979, 18-19; G. Rowlands, *Overland*, 76, 1979, 112-14; J. Strauss, *Luna*, 4.1, 1979, 31-33; T. Thorne, *New Poetry*, 27.2, 1979, 80-82.

The Women Who Live on the Ground: Poems 1978-1988. (Ringwood, Vic.: Penguin, 1990).

Reviewed by M. Duwell, *Weekend Australian Magazine*, 9-10 June, 1990, Review 8; P. Mead, *Age*, 30 June, 1990, Saturday Extra 9; A. Wallace, *Southerly*, 50.4, 1990, 524-28; L. McCredden, *Editions*, 12, 1991, 24; A. Glad, *Social Alternatives*, 9.2, 1990, 60.

Critical Material

Rowe, Noel. 'The Crossroads of Language: The Poetry of Lee Cataldi'. In his *Modern Australian Poets* (Sydney: Sydney UP in association with O.U.P., 1994), 47-58.

Spurr, Barry. *The Poetry of Lee Cataldi*. (Newtown, NSW: B. Spurr, 1994).

CATO, NANCY

Fiction

All the Rivers Run. (London: New English Library, 1978). First published London: Heinemann, 1958.
Reviewed by B. D'Alpuget, *24 Hours*, III, No. 12, 1979, 62; A. Gould, *Canberra Times*, 9 December, 1978, 22; N. Jillett, *Age*, 14 October, 1978, 27; N. Keesing, *S.M.H.*, 23 September, 1978, 17; D. Pryor, *Age Saturday Extra*, 15 October, 1983, 15; E. Riddell, *National Times*, 30 September, 1978, 37; P. Ruskin, *ABR*, No. 7, 1979, 6-7; P. Ward, *Weekend Australian Magazine*, 23-24 September, 1978, 8.

Brown Sugar. (London: Heinemann, 1974).
Reviewed by T. Forshaw, *Australian*, 18 January, 1975, 29; E. Kynaston, *Overland*, No. 63, 1976, 56-59; M. Pettigrove, *Canberra Times*, 31 January, 1975, 9; *T.L.S*, 8 November, 1974, 1249.

A Distant Island. (London: Hodder & Stoughton, 1988).
Reviewed by D. Johnson, *S.M.H.*, 8 October, 1988, 79; M. McClusky, *Weekend Australian* 19-20 November, 1988, Weekend 9.

Forefathers. (London: New English Library, 1983).
Reviewed by G. Dutton, *Bulletin*, 10 May, 1983, 75; T. Livingstone, *Courier-Mail*, 5 November, 1983, 30; V. Wright, *Weekend Australian Magazine*, 21-22 April, 1984, 18.

The Heart of the Continent. (Sevenoaks, U.K.: New English Library, 1989).
Reviewed by D. Johnson, *S.M.H.*, 6 January, 1990, 35; D. Leadbetter, *ABR*, No. 118, 1990, 42; M. R. Liverani, *Weekend Australian*, 17-18 February, 1990, Weekend 5.

The Lady Lost in Time. (Sydney: Collins, 1986).
Reviewed by D. Rowbotham, *Courier-Mail: The Great Weekend*, 17 May, 1986, 6; P. Salzman, *ABR*, No. 96, 1987, 30.

Marigold. (Sevenoaks: New English Library / Hodder & Stoughton, 1992).
Reviewed by L. Kirby, *ABR*, 144, 1992, 52; G. Windsor, *Weekend Australian*, 26-27 September, 1992, Review 4.

Northwest by South. (London: Heinemann, 1964).
Reviewed by J. Graham, *Canberra Times*, 2 October, 1965; D. Douglas, *Age*, 20 November, 1965; M.I. Birch, *Australian Book Review*, October, 1965.

Non-Fiction

Mister Maloga: Daniel Matthews and his River Murray Mission. (St Lucia: U.Q.P., 1976). Revised version 1993.

The Noosa Story (Brisbane: Jacaranda, 1979).

Critical Material

Frizell, Helen. 'The Perseverance of Nancy Cato'. *S.M.H.*, 30 September, 1978, 13.
Giuffre, Giulia. 'Nancy Cato'. In her *A Writing Life: Interviews with Australian Women Writers*. (Sydney: Allen and Unwin, 1990), 151-167.

Hillary, Gay. 'The "Mad Poet" of Hope Valley'. *Canberra Times*, 23 February, 1968, 3.
Sayers, Stuart. 'Three Novels Renewed as One'. *Age*, 7 October, 1978, 26.

CHABRILLAN, CELESTE DE

Fiction
The Gold Robbers. Translated from the French by Lucy and Caroline Moorehead with preface by A.R. Chisholm. (Melbourne: Sun Books, 1970). First published as *Les Voleurs d'or*, Paris: Levy Freres, 1857.

Critical Material
Chisholm, A.R. 'Celeste de Chabrillan and the Gold Rush'. *Meanjin*, XXVIII, 1969, 197-201.
McLean, Jeanne. 'Céleste de Chabrillan'. *Margin*, 26, 1991, 1-9.

CHRISTESEN, C.B.

Collection
The Hand of Memory: Selected Stories and Verse. (Melbourne: Meanjin Press, 1970).
Reviewed by P. Bladen, *Expression*, X, No. 3, 1971, 91-93; M. Dunlevy, *Canberra Times*, 24 April, 1971, 12; C. Hadgraft, *Meanjin*, XXXI, 1972, 233-34; C. Harrison-Ford, *Bulletin*, 12 June, 1971, 46-47; H.P. Heseltine, *Overland*, No. 48, 1971, 46-47; C. Semmler, *Hemisphere*, XVI, No. 7, 1972, 37-38; J. Waten, *Age*, 24 April, 1971, 16 and *S.M.H.*, 26 June, 1971, 21; R.B.J. Wilson, *Meanjin*, XXXI, 1972, 221.

Fiction
The Troubled Eyes of Women. (St. Lucia: U.Q.P., 1990). Includes stories from *The Hand of Memory*.
Reviewed by M. Clark, *Overland*, No. 118, 1990, 72-73; A. Moy, *Imago*, 2, No. 1, 1990, 90-91; L. Trainor, *Weekend Australian*, 10-11 February, 1990, Weekend 10.

Non-Fiction
'Autobituary'. *Overland*, No. 48, 1971, 16-19.

Critical Material
Heseltine, H.P. 'One Hundred Not Out'. *Meanjin*, XXIV, 1965, 132-9.
Kiernan, Brian. '*Meanjin* Man'. *Australian*, 14 August, 1971, 17.
Muner, Mario. 'Nature in the Poetry of C.B. Christesen: an Italian View'. Translated from the Italian by A.R. Chisholm. *Meanjin*, XXXIV, 1975, 8-12.

CHUBB, C.F.

Critical Material
Annand, Peter. 'Chubb's Ode: An Historical Note'. *Makar*, VII, No. 4, 1971, 12-13.
Clarke, C.G. Drury. 'The Chubbs: Separation and Since'. *Royal Historical Society of Queensland Journal Year-Book of Proceedings*, VIII, 1967/68, 460-78.

CLARKE, MARCUS

Collection
A Marcus Clarke Reader. Edited with an introduction by Bill Wannan. (Melbourne: Lansdowne Press, 1963). Discusses stories and essays of Clarke.
Reviewed by K.J.B., *Education Gazette*, LVIII, 1964, 458; B. Elliott, *ABR*, III, 1964, 81.

Marcus Clarke. Selected and edited with an introduction and bibliography by Michael Wilding. (St Lucia: U.Q.P., 1976). Portable Australian Authors.
Reviewed by L.S. Fallis, *World Literature Today*, LI, No. 3, 1977, 398; J. Maddocks, *Quadrant*, No. 7, 1977, 75-76.

Fiction

For the Term of His Natural Life. Introduction by George Ivan Smith (Sydney: A.& R., 1969). Pacific Books. First published as a separate work Melbourne: George Robertson, 1874.
Reviewed by J. Poole, *Historical Studies*, XV, 1972, 307-10.

For the Term of his Natural Life With an introduction by F.H. Mares. (Penrith, N.S.W.: Discovery Press, 1968). First published as a separate work Melbourne: George Robertson, 1874.

For the Term of his Natural Life. Condensed illustrated edition. (Sydney: A.& R., 1982).
Reviewed by M. Thomas, *Canberra Times*, 11 June, 1983, 16.

For the Term of his Natural Life. Introduction by Laurie Hergenhan. (Pymble, NSW: Collins A.& R., 1992).

His Natural Life. Edited with an introduction by Stephen Murray-Smith. (Harmondsworth, Middlesex: Penguin Books, 1970). Edition of the original serial publication, 1870-72.
Reviewed by L.T. Hergenhan, *Meanjin*, XXXI, 1972, 101-06 and *A.L.S.*, V, 1971, 223-24; J. Poole, *Historical Studies*, XV, 1972, 307-10 and *Overland*, No. 47, 1971, 50-51.

Marcus Clarke: Stories. With an introduction by Michael Wilding. (Sydney: Hale and Iremonger, 1983). First published Melbourne: Ferguson & Mitchell, 1890.
Reviewed by D. Grant, *ABR*, No. 67, 1984-85, 29-30.

Old Tales of a Young Country. With an introduction by Joan Poole. Facsimile edition (Sydney: Sydney University Press, 1972). First published Melbourne: Mason, Firth & McCutcheon, 1871.
Reviewed by A.R. Chisholm, *Age*, 10 February, 1973, 15; M. Wilding, *Southerly*, XXXIII, 1973, 394-408; M. Williams, *S.M.H.*, 26 May, 1973, 23.

Drama

A Daughter of Eve, or A Lesson in Love: A Comedy in Two Acts (1880). (Clayton, Vic.: English Dept., Monash University, 1986). Monash Nineteenth Century Drama Series.

Goody Two Shoes. Edited by Dennis Davidson. (Clayton, Vic.; English Dept., Monash University, 1993). Monash Nineteenth Century Drama Series, 12. First published Melbourne: Robert Bell [1870?].

Reverses: A Comedy Drama. Edited by Dennis Davison. (Melbourne: Monash University English Department, 1981). Monash Nineteenth-Century Drama Series, No. 5.

Non-Fiction

A Colonial City: High and Low Life: Selected Journalism. Edited by L.T. Hergenhan. (St Lucia: U.Q.P., 1972).
Reviewed by L. Cantrell, *Makar*, VIII, No. 2, 1972, 14-16; B. Dyster, *Journal of the Royal Australian Historical Society*, LXI, 1975, 287-88; B. Elliott, *Advertiser*, 1 July, 1972, 18; D. Green, *Hemisphere*, XVI, No. 10, 1972, 39-40; *National Times*, 9-14 October, 1972, 23; S. Jackman, *Australian Economic History Review*, XIII, 1973, 193-95; C. Pearl, *S.M.H.*, 29 June, 1972, 21; S. Murray-Smith, *A.L.S.*, VI, 1973, 104-05; G. Serle, *Historical Studies*, XV, 1973, 801-803; K. Smithyman, *Journal of Commonwealth Literature*, XI, 1976, 81-82; D. Stewart, *Sunday Telegraph*, 20 August, 1972, 26; C. Turnbull, *Age*, 26 August, 1972, 16; *Westerly*, No. 4, 1972, 69-70; M. Wilding, *Southerly*, XXXIII, 1973, 441-50.
See also G. Davison, *Historical Studies*, XVI, 1974, 292-305.

'Preface to Gordon's *Poems*'. In *The Writer in Australia*, edited by John Barnes (Melbourne; O.U.P., 1969), 33-37. This preface first published 1876.

Critical Material

McLaren, Ian F. *Marcus Clarke: An Annotated Bibliography*. (Melbourne: Library Council of Victoria, 1982). Reviewed by L. Hergenhan, *A.L.S.*, XI, 1984, 562-64; I. Laurenson, *Bulletin of the Bibliographical Soc. of Australia and New Zealand*, VII, No. 1, 64-66; A. Lawson, *Australian Historical Bibliography*, No. 9, 1984, 66-67; C. Tiffin, *ABR*, No. 53, 1983, 28-29; H.N. Warren, *Royal Historical Society of Victoria Journal*, LIV, No. 4, 1983, 60-61; M. Wilding, *Southerly*, XLIII, 1983, 358-59.

Simmons, Samuel Rowe. *Marcus Clarke: An Annotated Checklist 1863-1972*. Edited with additions by L.T. Hergenhan. (Sydney: Wentworth Press, 1975). Studies in Australian bibliography, No. 22. Reviewed by I. McLaren, *Age*, 21 May, 1977, 17; J. Poole, *Biblionews and Australian Notes & Queries*, Series 3, II, No. 1, 1977, 11-13; M. Wilding, *A.L.S.*, VIII, 1977, 96-103.

Margin, No. 7, 1981: Marcus Clarke Commemorative Issue. Contains three contributions by Ian F. McLaren, on the Centenary, on the film of *His Natural Life*, and on a letter by Clarke; a play by Clarke and one about him; and other items of Clarkeana.

Abbott-Young, Wendy. 'Marcus Clarke: Some Notes and Queries'. *Margin*, No. 10, 1983, 11-22.

Abraham, Lyndy. 'The Australian Crucible: Alchemy in Marcus Clarke's *His Natural Life*'. *A.L.S.*, 15.1, 1991, 38-55.

Albinski, Nan Bowman. 'Marcus Clarke's First Australian Publication'. *Margin*, No. 21, 1989, 1-10.

Albion, Douglas. 'Illustrations from Marcus Clarke's *The Term of His Natural Life*'. *Literature and Aesthetics*, 1, 1991, 97-99.

Barry, John Vincent. *The Life and Death of John Price*. (Melbourne: M.U.P., 1964), passim. Discusses the use of historical characters and incidents in *His Natural Life*.

Bland, Patricia. 'Marcus Clarke: The Affinity of his Journalism with the Novel *His Natural Life*'. *Adelaide A.L.S. Working Papers*, I, No. 2, 1975, 32-41.

Boehm, Harold J. '*His Natural Life* and Its Sources'. *A.L.S.*, V, 1971, 42-64.

---. 'The Pattern of *His Natural Life*: Conflict, Imagery, and Theme as Elements of Structure'. *Journal of Commonwealth Literature*, VII, 1972, 57-17.

Burrows, J.F. '*His Natural Life* and the Capacities of Melodrama'. *Southerly*, XXXIV, 1974, 280-301.

Colmer, John. '*For the Term of His Natural Life*: A Colonial Classic Revisited'. *Yearbook of English Studies*, XIII, 1983, 133-44.

Davison, Dennis. 'Marcus Clarke's Unwritten Play'. *Margin*, 27, 1992, 20-22.

---. 'The Varied and Lively Writing of Marcus Clarke'. *Age*, 1 August, 1981.

Denholm, Decie. 'Port Arthur: The Men and the Myth'. *Historical Studies*, XIV, 1970, 406-23, esp. 421-23.

---. 'The Sources of *His Natural Life*'. *A.L.S.*, IV, 1969, 174-78.

Edwards, P.D. 'Charles Reade, Wilkie Collins and Marcus Clarke'. *A.L.S.*, IX, 1984, 400-04.

---. 'The English Publication of *His Natural Life*'. *A.L.S.*, X, 1982, 520-26.

Elliott, Brian. *Marcus Clarke*. (Melbourne: O.U.P., 1969). Great Australians.

Goodenough, Warwick. 'For the Term of His Natural Life'. *Opinion*, X, 1966, 31-40.

Hamer, Clive. 'Marcus Clarke: His Minor Novels and a Checklist'. *Biblionews*, I, No. 1, 1966, 4-11. See also *Biblionews*, I, No. 2, 1966, 26 and *Biblionews*, No. 4, 1966, 29.

Hergenhan, L.T. 'The Contemporary Reception of *His Natural Life*'. *Southerly*, XXXI, 1971, 50-63.

---. 'The Corruption of Rufus Dawes'. *Southerly*, XXIX, 1969, 211-21.

---. 'English Publication of Australian Novels in the Nineteenth Century: The Case of *His Natural Life*'. In *Bards, Bohemians, and Bookmen*, edited by Leon Cantrell (St Lucia: U.Q.P., 1976), 56-71.

---. 'Marcus Clarke and the Australian Landscape'. *Quadrant*, XIII, No. 4, 1969, 31-41.

---. '"Poet of our Desolation": Marcus Clarke's *His Natural Life*'. In his *Unnatural Lives*. (St Lucia: U.Q.P., 1983), 47-61.

---. 'The Redemptive Theme in *His Natural Life*'. *A.L.S.*, II, No. 1, 1965, 32-49.

Horner, J.C. 'The Themes of Four Convict Novels'. *Tasmanian Historical Research Association, Papers and Proceedings*, XV, 1967, 18-32.

Irvin, Eric. 'Marcus Clarke and the Theatre'. *A.L.S.*, VII, 1975, 3-14.

Jordens, A.M. 'Marcus Clarke's Library'. *A.L.S.*, VII, 1976, 399-412.

Kelly, Veronica. *Annotated Checklist of Comments on the Performances and Banning of Marcus Clarke's 'The Happy Land', in Melbourne and Sydney*. (Clayton, Vic.: English Dept., Monash University, 1985). Monash Bibliographical Series, 2.

---. 'The Banning of Marcus Clarke's "The Happy Land": Stage, Press and Parliament'. *Australasian Drama Studies*, II, No. 1, 1983, 70-111.

Kingston, Claude. '1907 Film Epic Was Kind to Me'. *Age*, 14 May, 1966, 22.

Maddocks, John. 'Bohemia and Brutal Times'. *Hemisphere*, XXIII, 1979, 300-05.

Mares, F.H. 'Henry Kingsley, Marcus Clarke and Rolf Boldrewood'. In *The Literature of Australia*, edited by Geoffrey Dutton (Adelaide: Penguin Books, 1964), 247-58.

McDonald, Avis. 'Marcus Clarke: Books and Drama in North America'. *Margin*, No. 8, 1982, 13.

---. 'Marcus Clarke, Centenary Commemoration'. *Notes & Furphies*, No. 7, 1981, 8-9.

---. '"Men in Fetters . . . a Picture of Man's Stage"'. *WLWE*, XXIII, 1984, 74-81.

---. 'Richard Bentley and the Publication of *His Natural Life*'. *Bibliographical Society of Australia and New Zealand. Bulletin*, VI, No. 1, 1982, 3-21.

---. 'Rufus Dawes and Changing Narrative Perspectives in *His Natural Life*'. *A.L.S.*, XII, No. 3, 1986, 347-58.

McLean, Margaret. 'Frederick Hugh Thomas and Marcus Clarke'. *Margin*, 24, 1991, 14-16. Note mentioning a possible background to *His Natural Life*.

McVilly, David. 'Personalities from the Past: Marcus Clarke Librarian'. *Australian Library Journal*, XXIV, 1975, 70-71.

Meehan, Michael. 'The Art of Guttling: Marcus Clarke and Australian Gastronomy'. *Meanjin*, 49, No. 2, 241-51.

Nesbitt, Bruce. 'Marcus Clarke, "Damned Scamp"'. *A.L.S.*, V, 1971, 93-98.

Patane, Leonardo R. 'La letteratura dei "Convicts" e l'opera di Marcus Clarke'. *Narrativa*, VIII, 1963, 78-91.

Pitt, Joyce. 'Marcus Clarke and *The Critic in Church*'. *Margin*, No. 22, 1989, 12.

Poole, Joan E. 'The Buncle Correspondence'. *Biblionews and Australian Notes & Queries*, Second series, III, No. 2, 1969, 21.

---. '"Damned Scamp": Marcus Clarke or James Erskine Calder'. *A.L.S.*, VI, 1974, 423-28.

---. 'Marcus Clarke: "Christianity is Dead"'. *A.L.S.*, VI, 1973, 128-42.

---. 'Marcus Clarke's Contributions to "Under the Verandah"'. *Southerly*, XXXI, 1971, 220-21.

---. 'Marcus Clarke and His Sources'. *Opinion*, X, No. 3, 1966, 38-42.

---. 'Maurice Frere's Wife: Marcus Clarke's Revision of *His Natural Life*'. *A.L.S.*, IV, 1970, 383-94.

Poole, Joan E., and Wilding, Michael. 'Marcus Clarke's Contributions to *Notes and Queries*'. *A.L.S.*, VI, 1973, 186-89.

Quartermaine, Peter. 'Two Australian Films: Images and Contexts - *For the Term of his Natural Life* (1927) and *Don's Party* (1976)'. *Commonwealth* (Paris), VI, No. 2,

1984, 104-12.
Riem, Antonella. 'Kirkland's Flogging in Marcus Clarke's *For the Term of His Natural Life*'. In her *The Labyrinths of Self: A Collection of Essays on Australian and Caribbean Literature*. (Leichhardt, N.S.W.: FILEF. Italo-Australian Publications, 1987), 153-160.
Robertson, Robert T. 'Form into Shape: *His Natural Life* and *Capricornia* in a Commonwealth Context'. In *Commonwealth Literature and the Modern World*, edited by Hena Maes-Jelinek (Brussels: Didier, 1975), 137-46.
Robson, L.L. 'The Historical Basis of *For the Term of his Natural Life*'. *A.L.S.*, I, No. 2, 1963, 104-21.
Runcie, Catherine. 'Rufus Dawes: His Natural and His Spiritual Life'. *Southerly*, XLV, No. 1, 1985, 62-80.
Ryan, S.J. 'Illegitimates Both: George Rex and John Rex in Legend and Story'. *Margin*, No. 15, 1985, 4-8.
Scheckter, John. 'The Lost Child in Australian Fiction'. *Modern Fiction Studies*, XXVII, No. 1, 1981, 61-72.
Shillinglaw, J.J. 'Review of *His Natural Life*'. [rptd. from *Herald* (Melbourne), May 9 1874]. *La Trobe Library Journal*, VI, No. 23, 1979, 55-57.
Sprod, Dan. *Alexander Pearce of Macquarie Harbour* (Hobart: Cat and Fiddle Press, 1978). Reviewed by T. Bowden, *24 Hours*, III, No. 8, 1978, 61-63; D. Boyce, *National Times*, 22 July, 1978, 29; P. Thompson, *S.M.H.*, 29 July, 1978, 19.
Stewart, Annette. 'The Design of *For the Term of His Natural Life*'. *A.L.S.*, VI, 1974, 394-403.
Stewart, Ken. 'Marcus Clarke's Character - And Handwriting'. *Notes & Furphies*, No. 14, 1985, 3-4.
Stuart, Lurline. 'J.J. Shillinglaw's Annotations on *His Natural Life*'. *La Trobe Library Journal*, VI, No. 23, 1979, 45-53.
---. 'Marcus Clarke: *Long Odds* and the 1873 Melbourne Cup'. *A.L.S.*, VI, 1974, 422-23.
Sussex, Lucy. 'The Earliest Australian Detective Story'. *Margin*, No. 22, 1989, 30-1.
Tinkler, John F. 'Canadian Cultural Norms & Australian Social Rules: Susanna Moodie's "Roughing it in the Bush" and Marcus Clarke's "His Natural Life"'. *Canadian Literature*, (Vancouver), No. 94, 1982, 10-22.
Tregenza, John. *Professor of Democracy: The Life of Charles Henry Pearson, 1830-1894, Oxford Don and Australian Radical*. (Melbourne: M.U.P., 1968), 163-65. Mentions work of Marcus Clarke on a board of enquiry into the Jika Reformatory, 1878.
Whitlock, Gillian. '"The Carcereal Archipelago": Marcus Clarke's *His Natural Life* and John Richardson's *Wacousta*'. In *Australian/Canadian Literature in English: Comparative Perspectives*, edited by Russell McDougall and Gillian Whitlock (North Ryde, N.S.W.: Methuen Australia, 1987), 49-67.
Wilding, Michael. *Marcus Clarke*. (Melbourne: O.U.P., 1977). Australian Writers and Their Work. Reviewed by C.M.H. Clark, *Nation Review*, 1-7 December, 1977, 18; L.T. Hergenhan, *A.L.S.*, VIII, 1978, 521-22.
---. 'Marcus Clarke: Australia's First Drug Writings'. *The Australasian Weed*, II, 1977, 14-18.
---. 'Marcus Clarke - Bohemian'. *Hemisphere*, XXVI, 1981, 148-51.
---. 'Marcus Clarke: *His Natural Life*'. In *The Australian Exerience: Critical Essays on Australian Novels*, edited by W.S. Ramson (Canberra: Australian National University Press, 1974), 19-37.
---. 'Marcus Clarke's *Chidiock Tichbourne*'. *A.L.S.*, VI, 381-93.
---. 'The Short Stories of Marcus Clarke'. In *Bards, Bohemians, and Bookmen*, edited by Leon Cantrell (St Lucia: U.Q.P., 1976), 72-97.
---. '"Weird Melancholy": Inner and Outer Landscapes in Marcus Clarke's Stories'.

In *Mapped But Not Known: The Australian Landscape of the Imagination*, edited by P.R. Eaden and F.H. Mares (Netley, S.A.: Wakefield Press, 1986), 128-145.

CLIFT, CHARMIAN

Fiction

With George Johnston. *High Valley*. Afterword by Nadia Wheatley. (North Ryde, N.S.W.: A.& R., 1990). First published Sydney: A.& R., 1949.
Reviewed by V. Sen, *Canberra Times*, 10 June, 1990, 18; P. Nelson, *Weekend Australian*, 23-24 June, 1990, Review 10.

Honour's Mimic. (Sydney: Collins, 1989). First published London: Hutchinson, 1964.
Reviewed by P. Nelson, *Weekend Australian*, 25-26 March, 1989, 7; C. Keneally, *The Adelaide Review*, No. 66, 1989, 25 and *The Sydney Review*, No. 15, 1989, 19-20; R. Wighton, *Weekend Australian*, 11-12 July, 1992, Review 6.

With George Johnston. *The Sponge Divers*. (North Ryde, NSW: A.& R/Imprint, 1992). First published London: Collins, 1955.
Reviewed by R. Wighton, *Weekend Australian*, 11-12 July, 1992, Review 6.

With George Johnston. *Strong Man from Piraeus and Other Stories*. Chosen and introduced by Garry Kinnane. (Melbourne: Thomas Nelson, 1984).
Reviewed by C. Castan, *Social Alternatives*, V, No. 4, 1986, 58; P. Corris, *National Times*, 6-12 April, 1984, 33; H. Daniel, *Age Saturday Extra*, 19 May, 1984, 17; B. Farmer, *ABR*, No. 62, 1984, 15-16; K. Gelder, *CRNLE Reviews Journal*, No. 2, 1985, 43-46; M. Halligan, *Canberra Times*, 23 June, 1984, 16; B. Little, *Weekend Australia*, 28-29 April, 1984, 13; R. Lucas, *S.M.H.*, 28 April, 1984, 40; P. Rolfe, *Bulletin*, 8 May, 1984, 82-83.

Walk to the Paradise Gardens. Introduced by Nadia Wheatley. (Sydney: Collins, 1989). First published London: Hutchinson, 1960.
Reviewed by G. Clark, *Courier Mail*, 2 December, 1989, 6; V. Sen, *Canberra Times*, 8 July, 1990, 18.

Non-Fiction

Being Alone with Oneself. Edited and introduced by Nadia Wheatley. (North Ryde, NSW: Collins/A.& R., 1991).
Reviewed by F. Capp, *Island*, 48, 1991, 62-63; P. Nelson, *Weekend Australian*, 25-26 May, 1991, Review 5; J.S. Smark, *ABR*, 132, 1991, 147.

Images in Aspic. With an introduction by Margaret McClusky (Sydney: Collins, 1989). First published Sydney: Horwitz, 1965.
Reviewed by R. Wighton, *Weekend Australian*, 11-12 July, 1992, Review 6.

Mermaid Singing. (North Ryde, NSW: A.& R, 1989). First published London: Michael Joseph, 1956.
Reviewed by R. Wighton, *Weekend Australian*, 11-12 July, 1992, Review 6.

Peel Me a Lotus. (Sydney: Collins, 1969; 1988). First published London: Hutchinson, 1959.
Reviewed by M. McClusky, *ABR*, No. 105, 1988, 37-8; R. Wighton, *Weekend Australian*, 11-12 July, 1992, Review 6.

Trouble in Lotus Land. Edited and introduced by Nadia Wheatley. (North Ryde, N.S.W.: A.& R., 1990).
Reviewed by T. White, *ABR*, No. 127, 1990, 7-8; S. Vincent, *Independent Monthly*, 2, No. 6, 1990-91, 46-7.

The World of Charmian Clift. Introduction by George Johnston. (Sydney: Ure Smith, 1970). Reprinted with additional introduction by Martin Johnston, Sydney: Collins, 1983. Reprinted with introduction by Rodney Hall, Ringwood: Penguin, 1989.
Reviewed by J. Battersby, *ABR*, IX, 1970, 157-8; S. Edgar, *Canberra Times*, 2 May, 1970, 13; B. Farmer, *ABR*, No. 62, 1984, 15-16; M. Halligan, *Canberra Times*, 29

October, 1989, 24; S. Lawson, *Australian*, 28 March, 1970, 14; R. Lucas, *S.M.H.*, 8 July, 1989, 77.

'My Husband George'. *Pol*, No. 9, 1969, 83-85.

  Critical Material
Chick, Suzanne. *Searching for Charmian*. Sydney: Macmillan, 1994). Reviewed by P. Coleman, *Weekend Australian*, 5-6 March, 1994, Review 7; H. Elliott, *ABR*, 160, 1994, 35-36; D. Falconer, *Voices*, 4.3, 1994, 116-21; J. Hanrahan, *Age*, 19 March, 1994, Saturday Extra 8; J.D. Pringle, *S.M.H.*, 5 March, 1994, Spectrum 10A; C. Semmler, *Quadrant*, 38.7-8, 1994, 116-18.
Elliott, Helen. 'Something Charming'. *ABR*, 142, 1992, 14-16.
Foster, David. 'Charmian Clift' in his (ed.) *Self Portraits*, (Canberra: National Library of Australia, 1991). Transcription of interview.
Kinnane, Garry. *George Johnston: A Biography*. (Melbourne: Nelson, 1986).
Knuckey, Marie. 'In Search of Charmian's Island'. *S.M.H.*, 1 June, 1972, Look! section, 10.
Mellick, Stan. 'The New and the Old: Responses to Translocation'. *Commonwealth*, 6, No. 2, 1984, 29-34.
Tolchard, Clifford. 'My Husband George: My Wife Charmian: The Johnston-Clift Partnership'. *Walkabout*, XXXV, No. 1, 1969, 26-29.

COLLINS, BETTY

  Fiction
The Copper Crucible. (Brisbane: Jacaranda, 1966).
Reviewed by H. Batman, *ABR*, 5, No. 7, 1966, 135; G.W. Ford, *Realist*, No. 24, 1966, 27; F. Stevens, *Australian*, 9 April, 1966; F. Wells, *S.M.H.*, 9 April, 1966, 13.

The Second Step. (Sydney: Australasian Book Society, 1972).
Reviewed by E. Capocci, *Tribune*, 8-14 May, 1973, 8; A.R. Chisholm, *Age*, 20 January, 1973, 18; V. Ikin, *Union Recorder*, 2 August, 1973, 254; M.J., *Tribune*, 13-19 February, 1973, 10; S. Kiernan, *S.M.H.*, 24 June, 1973, 24.

  Critical Material
Syson, Ian. 'In Search of Betty Collins'. *Hecate*, 15, No. 2, 1989, 51-7.
---. '"The Problem With Finding the Time": Working Class Women's Writing in Australia'. *Hecate*, 19.2, 1993, 65-84. Includes discussion of Collins
---. 'Towards a Poetics of Working Class Writing'. *Southern Review* (Adelaide), 26.1, 1993, 86-100.

CONWAY, JILL KER

  Non-Fiction
The Road from Coorain. (Richmond, Vic.: Heinemann: New York: Alfred Knopf, 1989).
Reviewed by K. Ahearne, *Age*, 16 September, 1989, Saturday Extra, 9; N. Albinski, *Antipodes*, 5.2, 1991, 121-23; E. Campion, *Bulletin*, 15 August 1989, 146; M. Halligan, *Weekend Australian*, 16-17 September, 1989, Review 9; J. Kitson, *ABR*, 115, 1989, 11; V. Klinkenborg, *New York Times Book Review*, 7 May, 1989, 3; S. A. Levinson, *S.M.H.*, 6 May, 1989, 89; Macintyre, *London Review of Books*, 11.18, 1989, 12-13; A.P. Riemer, *S.M.H.*, 6 May, 1989, 89; P. Shrubb, *Quadrant*, 34.7-8, 1990, 64-68; H. Smith, *Australian Studies*, 6, 1992, 140-42; S. Wyndham, *Weekend Australian*, 15-16 December, 1990, Review 7.

True North: A Memoir. (London/Milsons Point, N.S.W.: Hutchinson, 1994).
Reviewed by R. Bittoun, *S.M.H.*, 13 August, 1994, Spectrum 11A; C. Brightman, *New York Times Book Review*, 21 August, 1994, 11-12; L. Frost, *Age*, 17 September, 1994, Saturday Extra, 8; D. Giese, *ABR*, 165, 1994, 44-45; J.Haines, *Eureka Street*,

4.7, September, 44-45; V. Senn, *Voices*, 5.1, 1995, 104-07; L. Slattery, *Weekend Australian*, 17-18 September, 1994, Review 6.

Critical Material
McCooey, David. 'Parents, Crisis and Education: Jill Ker Conway's *The Road from Coorain*'. *Australian & New Zealand Studies in Canada*, 11, 1994, 91-102.

COOPER, CHARLES

Critical Material
Ouyang Yu. 'Charles Cooper and the Representation of the Chinese in Australian Fictions'. *Westerly*, 38.4, 1993, 65-73.

COPPIN, GEORGE S.

Critical Material
Oppenheim, Helen. 'Coppin - How Great? Alex Bagot's *Father of the Australian Theatre*'. *A.L.S.*, III, 1967, 126-137.

CORRIS, PETER

Fiction
Aftershock. (Sydney: Transworld/Bantam, 1991).
Reviewed by L. Clancy, *Age*, 5 October, 1991, Saturday Extra 10.

The Azanian Action. (North Ryde, NSW: A.& R., 1991).
Reviewed by P. Bryan, *ABR*, 134, 1991, 52-53; L. Clancy, *Age*, 5 October, 1991, Saturday Extra 10.

The Baltic Business: A Novel. (Ringwood, Vic.: Penguin, 1988).
Reviewed by A. Enstice, *Lot's Wife*, XXVIII, No. 2, 1988, 14; P. Pierce, *Age Saturday Extra*, 6 February, 1988, 13; R. Tanter, *ABR*, No. 99, 1988, 32-33.

'Beverly Hills' Browning. (Ringwood, Vic.: Penguin, 1987).
Reviewed by L.V. Kepert, *S.M.H.*, 5 December, 1987, 76; R. Tanter, *ABR*, No. 99, 1988, 32-33.

Beware of the Dog. (Sydney: Bantam, 1992).
Reviewed by J. Carroll, *ABR*, 140, 1992, 67-68; S. Coupe, *S.M.H.*, 4 April, 1992, 43; R. Hood, *Scarp*, 20, 1992, 68.

The Big Drop, and Other Cliff Hardy Stories. (Sydney: George Allen & Unwin, 1985).
Reviewed by D. Colmer, *Weekend Australian Magazine*, 7-8 December, 1985, 19; R. Kenny, *ABR*, No. 81, 1986, 24-25; M. Thomas, *Canberra Times*, 9 November, 1985, B4.

'Box Office' Browning. (Ringwood, Vic.: Viking, 1987).
Reviewed by D. Colmer, *Australian Weekend Magazine*, 4-5 April, 1987, 16; H. Daniel, *Age Saturday Extra*, 28 March, 1987, 11; L.V. Kepert, *S.M.H.*, 4 April, 1987, 47.

The Brothers Craft. Sydney: Bantam, 1992).
Reviewed by S. Coupe, *S.M.H.*, 13 February, 1993, 46; G. Windsor, *Weekend Australian*, 6-7 February, 1993, Review 5.

Browning Battles On. (Pymble, NSW: A.& R., 1993).
Reviewed by S. Coupe, *S.M.H.*, 13 February, 1993, 46.

Browning in Buckskin. (Ringwood, Vic.: Penguin, 1991).
Reviewed by P. Rolfe, *Bulletin*, 14 May, 1991, 117.

Browning P.I. (Sydney: A.& R., 1992)
Reviewed by J. Carroll, *ABR*, 139, 1992, 48-49; B. Molloy, *Imago*, 4.2, 1992, 103-04.

Browning Without a Cause. (Potts Point, NSW: ETT Imprint, 1995).
Reviewed by J.R. Carroll, *ABR*, 176, 1995, 70; S. Coupe, *S.M.H.*, 7 Oct., 1995, Spectrum 13A.

Burn and Other Stories. (Sydney: Bantam, 1993).
Reviewed by S. Coupe, *S.M.H.* 13 February, 1993, 46; J. Stephens, *ABR*, 148, 1993, 51-52.

A Cliff Hardy Collection. (Sydney: Pan, 1985). Contents: *The Dying Trade.* First published Sydney: McGraw-Hill, 1980; *The Marvellous Boy.* First published Sydney: Pan, 1982; *White Meat.* First published Sydney: Pan, 1981.

The Cliff Hardy Omnibus. (Sydney: Unwin Paperbacks, 1988). Contents: *The Empty Beach*, first published Sydney: Allen & Unwin, 1983; *Make Me Rich* first published Sydney: Unwin Paperbacks, 1986; *The Greenwich Apartments* first published Sydney: Unwin Paperbacks, 1986.

Cross Off. (Sydney: Pan Macmillan, 1993).
Reviewed by G. Blundell, *Weekend Australian*, 23-24 October, 1994, Review 7.

Deal Me Out: A Cliff Hardy Novel. (Sydney: Allen & Unwin, 1986).
Reviewed by P. Hawker, *ABR*, No. 86, 1986, 28-29; S. Knight, *S.M.H.*, 26 April, 1986, 43; P. Pierce, *National Times*, 16-22 May, 1986, 35; M. Thomas, *Canberra Times*, 17 May, 1986, B4.

The Empty Beach. (Sydney: George Allen & Unwin, 1983).
Reviewed by D. Anderson, *S.M.H.*, 25 June, 1983, 37; R.F. Brissenden, *National Times*, 17-23 June, 1983, 33; N. Callendar, *New York Times Book Review*, 3 May, 1987, 46; R. Davie, *Age*, 9 July, 1983, 11; M. Thomas, *Canberra Times*, 18 June, 1983, 15.

Get Even. (Chippendale, NSW: Pan Macmillan, 1994).
Reviewed by G. Blundell, *Weekend Australian*, 10-11 December, 1994, Review 6; J. Carroll, *ABR*, 1994, 62: 59-60.

The Greenwich Apartments: A Cliff Hardy Novel. (Sydney: Unwin Paperbacks, 1986).
Reviewed by P. Rolfe, *Bulletin*, 6 January, 1987, 76; M. Thomas, *Canberra Times*, 8 November, 1986, B2; B. Tivey, *Weekend Australian. Weekend Magazine*, 13-14 December, 1986, 16.

The Gulliver Fortune. (Sydney: Bantam Books, 1989).
Reviewed by D. J. Eszenyi, *ABR*, No. 116, 1989, 24; S. Knight, *S.M.H.*, 7 October, 1989, 82; B. Matthews, *Weekend Australian*, 7-8 October, 1989, Weekend 8; P. Rolfe, *Bulletin*, 31 October, 1989, 116.

Heroin Annie and Other Cliff Hardy Stories. (Sydney: George Allen & Unwin, 1984).
Reviewed by R.F. Brissenden, *Weekend Australian Magazine*, 17-18 March, 1984, 13; P. Cook, *National Times*, 16-22 March, 1984, 31; J. Hanrahan, *ABR*, No. 60, 1984, 15-16; S. Knight, *S.M.H.*, 31 March, 1984, 41; C. Pearson, *Advertiser*, 3 March, 1984, 34; M. Thomas, *Canberra Times*, 24 March, 1984, 22; G. Turner, *Age Saturday Extra*, 3 March, 1984, 17.

The January Zone. (Sydney: Unwin Paperbacks, 1987).
Reviewed by K. Ahearne, *Australian Society*, VI, No. 11, 1987, 44-45; D. Anderson, *Times on Sunday*, 25 October, 1987, 33; R. Davie, *Age Saturday Extra*, 12 September, 1987, 14; S. Knight, *ABR*, No. 96, 1987, 8-10, esp. 9; R. Pearson, *Weekend Australian. Weekend Magazine*, 10-11 October, 1987, 14; J. Shaw, *S.M.H.*, 19 September, 1987, 46.

The Japanese Job. (Pymble, NSW: A.& R., 1992).
Reviewed by G. Blundell, *Weekend Australian*, 21-22 November, 1992, Review 7; J. Carroll, *ABR*, 144, 1992, 67-68.

The Kimberley Killing. (Ringwood, Vic.: Penguin, 1989).

Reviewed by K. Green, *Fremantle Arts Review*, 4, No. 4, 1989, 15; S. Knight, *S.M.H.*, 18 February, 1989, 86; R. Wallace-Crabbe, *Weekend Australian* , 11-12, March, 1989, Weekend 11.

Make Me Rich. (Sydney: Unwin Paperbacks, 1986).
Reviewed by R.F. Brissenden, *Age Monthly Review*, V, No. 10, 1986, 17-18; D. Colmer, *Weekend Australian Magazine*, 18-19 May, 1985, 13; R. Davie, *Age Saturday Extra*, 20 April, 1985, 14; K. England, *Advertiser*, 27 April, 1985, 7; S. Knight, *S.M.H.*, 4 May, 1985, 45; J. Popple, *Canberra Times*, 18 May, 1985, 14.

Man in the Shadows: A Novel and Six Stories. (Sydney: Unwin Paperbacks, 1988).
Reviewed by S. Knight, *S.M.H.*, 20 August, 1988, 79.

Matrimonial Causes. (Sydney: Bantam, 1993; New York: Dell, 1994).
Reviewed by J. Carroll, *ABR*, 156, 1993, 61-62; J. Paznik-Bondarin, *Antipodes*, 9.2, 1995, 149-50.

Naismith's Dominion. Sydney: Bantam, 1990).
Reviewed by M. Halligan, *Weekend Australian*, 15-16 December 1990, Review 5.

O'Fear . (Sydney: Bantam, 1989).
Reviewed by R. F. Brissenden, *Weekend Australian*, 3-4 March, 1990, Weekend 6; B. Turner, *S.M.H.* , 20 January, 1990, 71.

Pokerface. (Ringwood, Vic.: Penguin, 1985).
Reviewed by D. Colmer, *Weekend Australian Magazine*, 7-8 December, 1985, 19; R. Kenny, *ABR*, No. 81, 1986, 24-25; M. Thomas, *Canberra Times*, 9 November, 1985, B4.

Set-up. (Sydney: Pan Macmillan, 1992).
Reviewed by G. Blundell, *Weekend Australian*, 21-22 November, 1992, Review 7; S. Coupe, *S.M.H.*, 15 August, 1992, 43.

The Time Trap. (Pymble, NSW: A.& R., 1994).
Reviewed by J. Carroll, *ABR*, 158, 1994, 52-53.

Wet Graves. (Sydney; New York; London: Bantam Books, 1991).
Reviewed by R. Hood, *Scarp*, 18, 1991, 62-65; S. Knight, *S.M.H.* 6 April, 1991, 41; T. Smith, *ABR*, 129, 1991, 21.

Wimmera Gold. (Sydney: Bantam, 1994).
Reviewed by J.R. Carroll, *ABR*, 164, 1994, 62-63.

The Winning Side. (Sydney: George Allen & Unwin, 1984).
Reviewed by H. Daniel, *Age Saturday Extra*, 8 December, 1984, 19; G. Kelly, *ABR*, No. 77, 1985, 34-35; M. Thomas, *Canberra Times*, 29 December, 1984, 12.

Non-Fiction

'Detective City'. In *The View from Tinsel Town*, edited by Tom Thompson (Ringwood, Vic.: Southerly/Penguin, 1985), 106-110.
'Detective City'. *National Times*, 10-16 January, 1986, 11.
'Ray Crawley and *The Kimberley Killing*'. *SPAN*, 31, 1991, 1-18. Transcript of a talk given in the *Writer's Choice* series, U of Sydney.

Critical Material

Baker, Candida. 'Peter Corris'. In her *Yacker 3* (Sydney: Picador, 1989), 42-64.
Bath, Rob. 'Once More Down These Mean Streets'. *Ash Magazine*, No. 11, 1982, 13-15.
Knight, Stephen. 'Real Pulp at Last: Peter Corris's Thrillers'. *Meanjin*, XLV, No. 4, 1986, 446-52.
---. 'The Case of the Missing Genre: In Search of Australian Crime Fiction'. *Southerly*, XLVIII, No. 3, 1988, 235-249.
Langer, Beryl. 'The Real Thing: Cliff Hardy and CocaCola-nisation'. *SPAN*, 31, 1991, 29-44.

Sorenson, Rosemary. 'Down a Curious Track with Corris: Peter Corris Talks About His New Historical Novel and How to Make the Most of a Genre'. *ABR*, No. 116, 1989, 25. Interview.
Thomas, Nicholas. 'Fear and Loathing in the Postcolonial Pacific'. *Meanjin*, 51.2, 1992, 265-76.
Tolley, Michael J. 'Peter Corris: From Hardy to Browning'. *Quadrant*, XXXI, No. 12, 1987, 63-65.

COTTRELL, DOROTHY

Critical Material

Ross, Barbara. 'Dorothy Cottrell's Grey Country: Extracts from *Wheelrhyme*'. *Coppertales*, 2, 1995, 7-16.
---. 'Drawn by "Dossie"'. With an excerpt from Cottrell's unpubl. novel *Wheelrhyme*. *Voices* 1.4, 1991-92, 21-36.

COUANI, ANNA

Collection

With Peter Lyssiotis. *The Harbour Breathes*. (Glebe, NSW: Sea Cruise; East Burwood, Vic.: Masterthief, 1989).
Reviewed by K. Brophy, *Going Down Swinging*, 10-11, 1990, 254-55; J. Duke, *Overland*, 118, 1990, 85-86; P. Edmonds, *Arena*, 94, 1991, 185-87; E. Hatzimanolis, *Antithesis*, 4.1, 1990, 181-86; I. Indyk, *S.M.H.* 20 January, 1990, 71; S. McQuire, *Age Monthly Review*, 9.6, 1989, 16-19; J. Strauss, *Australian Women's Book Review*, 2.3, 1990, 31-32; B. Walker, *Phoenix Review*, 7 & 8, 1992, 158-61.

Fiction

Italy. (Clifton Hill, Vic.: Rigmarole, 1977).
Reviewed by K. Brophy, *Going Down Swinging*, 1, 1980, 71-72; G. Catalano, *Luna*, 3.2, 1979, 32-35; C. Harrison Ford, *S.M.H.*, 19 August, 1978, 19; J. Maiden, *Australian Small Press Review*, 6, 1978, 32-33; R. Sellick, *SPAN*, 7, 1978, 60-61; *Imprint*, 2.1, 1978, 43.

Italy, and The Train. (Clifton Hill, Vic.: Rigmarole, 1985).
Reviewed by K. Ahearne, *Age*, 20 April, 1985, Saturday Extra 15; F. Capp, *ABR*, 71, 1985, 39.

With Barbara Brooks. *Leaving Queensland, and The Train*. (Glebe, NSW: Sea Cruise Books, 1983).
Reviewed by C. Gerrish, *Womanspeak*, 8.1, 1983, 27; K. Petersen-Schaefer, *ABR*, 56, 1983, 29; L. Rydzynski, *Aspect*, 28, 1983, 66-68; L. Stokes, *Compass*, 5.3, 1985, 17.

Were All Women Sex Mad? and Other Stories. (Melbourne: Rigmarole Books, 1982).
Reviewed by S. Cunningham, *Idiom*, 20.1, 1985, 27-28; A. Hildyard, *Island*, Magazine 18/19, 1984, 40-44; A. Kefala, *Aspect*, 25, 1982, 73-78; J. Maiden, *S.M.H.*, 12 June, 1982, 37-42; M. Smith, *ABR*, 50, 1983, 24-25; E. Webby, *Meanjin*, 42.1, 1983, 34-41.

Non-Fiction

'Authors Statements: Anna Couani'. *A.L.S.*, 10.2, 1991, 194-95.
'Statement'. In *Poetry and Gender: Statements and Essays in Australian Women's Poetry and Poetics* edited by David Brooks and Brenda Walker (St Lucia: U.Q.P., 1989), 30-31.

Critical Material

Gunew, Sneja. 'Homeland, Nostalgia, the Uncanny: The Work of Anna Couani'. In her *Framing Marginality: Multicultural Literary Studies* (Carlton, Vic.: MUP, 1994), 111-31.

Hatzimanolis, Efi. 'Ethnicity, in Other Words: Anna Couani's Writing'. *Southerly*, 55.3, 1995, 91-99.
Kirkby, Joan. 'A Woman is Watching Things: The Work of Anna Couani'. *Meanjin*, 42.4, 1983, 491-503.
Lysenko, Myron, and Kevin Brophy. 'Interview: Anna Couani'. *Going Down Swinging*, 5, 1982, 30-36.

COUVREUR, J.C. (TASMA)

Fiction

A Sydney Sovereign. Edited and introduced by Michael Ackland. (Pymble, NSW: A.& R., 1993). First published Truebner, 1889.
Reviewed by H. Horton, *Imago*, 6.1, 1994, 103-04; S. Hughes, *S.M.H.*, 24 July, 1993, 45; S.K. Martin, *Southerly*, 54.2, 1994, 169-73; E. Morrison, *ABR*, 155, 1993, 22-23.

Uncle Piper of Piper's Hill. Edited by Cecil Hadgraft and Ray Beilby. (Melbourne: Nelson Australia, 1969). First published London: Trubner, 1889.
Reviewed by L. Kramer, *Journal of the Royal Australian Historical Society*, LV, 1969, 402-04.

Uncle Piper of Piper's Hill. Introduction by Margaret Harris. (London: Pandora, 1987). First published London, Trubner, 1889.
Reviewed by M. McClusky, *ABR*, No. 104, 1988, 30-32.

Critical Material

Clarke, Patricia. *Tasma: The Life of Jessie Couvreur.* (St Leonards, NSW: Allen & Unwin, 1994). Reviewed by M. Ackland, *A.L.S.*, 17.2, 1995, 204-07; J. Hooton, *ABR*, 160, 1994, 31-32; J. Mead, *Journal of Australian Studies*, 46, 1995, 95; J. Roe, *Journal of the Royal Australian Historical Society*, 81.1, 1995, 110-12.
Giles, Fiona. '"The Softest Disorder": Representing Cultural Indeterminacy'. In *Describing Empire: Post-colonialism and Textuality* edited by Chris Tiffin and Alan Lawson, (London and New York: Routledge, 1994), 141-51. Discusses *The Penance of Portia James.*
Harris, Margaret. 'The Writing of Tasma, the Work of Jesse Couvreur'. In *A Bright and Fiery Troop: Australian Women Writers of the Nineteenth Century*, edited by Debra Adelaide (Ringwood: Penguin, 1988), 165-182.
Higgins, Susan. '"That Singular Anomaly, the Lady Novelist" in 1888'. *Australia 1888 Bulletin*, No. 7, 1981, 68-73.
Martin, Susan. 'Why Do All these Women Have Moustaches? Gender, Boundary and Frontier in *Such is Life* and "Monsieur Caloche"'. *Southern Review*, 25.1, 1992, 68-77.
Sussex, Lucy. 'Tasma's First Publication'. *A.L.S.*, 15.3, 1992, 225-27.

COWAN, PETER

Fiction

The Colour of the Sky. (Fremantle: Fremantle Arts Centre Press, 1986).
Reviewed by J. Barnes, *Age Saturday Extra*, 25 October, 1986, 15; T. Forshaw, *Weekend Australian Magazine*, 29-30 March, 1986, 12; S. McKernan, *Bulletin*, 10 June, 1986, 107, 109; P. Salzman, *ABR*, No. 85, 1986, 29-30.

The Empty Street. (Sydney: A.& R., 1965).
Reviewed by *T.L.S.*, 6 January, 1966, 6; J. Graham, *Canberra Times*, 4 September, 1965, 11; D. Hewett, *The Critic* (Perth), VI, 87-9; N. Keesing, *ABR*, IV, 1965, 207; J. McLaren, *Overland*, No. 33, 1966, 44-5; E. Morgan, *New Statesman*, 21 January, 1966, 96; K. Tennant, *S.M.H.*, 21 August, 1965, 16; G.A. Wilkes, *Southerly*, XXV, No. 3, 1965, 214.

The Hills of Apollo Bay. (Fremantle, W.A.: Fremantle Arts Centre Press, 1989).

Reviewed by J. Barnes, *Overland*, No. 116, 1989, 85-86; K. Cummings, *S.M.H.*, 8 April, 1989, 88; R. Jolly, *Southerly*, 49, No. 4, 1989, 667-71; J. Lewis, *Westerly*, 34, No. 3, 1989, 88-90; M. Missen, *Age Saturday Extra*, 18 March, 1989, 10; A. Peek, *ABR*, No. 110, 1989, 31-32; S. Pritchard, *Age Monthly Review*, 9, No. 4, 1989, 22-23.

Mobiles. (Fremantle: Fremantle Arts Centre Press, 1979).
Reviewed by N. Keesing, *Age*, 2 February, 1980, 26; S. Morrell, *Quadrant*, XXIII, No. 12, 1979, 70-71; T. Shapcott, *ABR*, No. 18, 1980, 18; B. Williams, *Westerly*, XXV, No. 2, 1980, 104-07.

Seed. (Sydney: A.& R., 1966).
Reviewed by E. Castle, *Overland*, No. 35, 1966, 56-7; J.K. Ewers, *W.A. Teachers' Journal*, LVI, 1966, 375; D. Green, *Meanjin*, XXV, 1966, 480-4; I. Hamilton, *New Statesman*, 16 December, 1966, 911; N. Jillett, *Age*, 20 August, 1966, 25; N. Keesing, *ABR*, V, 1966, 236 and *Bulletin*, 10 September, 1966, 45-6; H.G. Kippax, *S.M.H.*, 27 August, 1966, 20; V. Smith, *Australian*, 8 October, 1966, 10; L. Ward, *Canberra Times*, 10 September, 1966, 10; D. Whitelock, *Southerly*, XXVI, 1966, 283-4.

Summer. (Sydney: A.& R., 1964).
Reviewed by D. Ashley, *Westerly*, No. 1, 1965, 68-70; H.P. Heseltine, *Meanjin*, XXIII, No. 2, 1964, 220-2; T.A. Hungerford, *The Critic* (Perth), No. 6, 1964, 55; F.H. Mares, *Southerly*, XXIV, No. 4, 1964, 247-8; J. McLaren, *Overland*, No. 30, 1964, 55; C. Wallace-Crabbe, *Bulletin*, 25 July, 1964, 54.

The Tenants. (South Fremantle, WA: Fremantle Arts Centre Press, 1994).
Reviewed by R. Bittoun, *S.M.H.*, 16 April, 1994, Spectrum 9A; L. Davison, *ABR*, 158, 1994, 12-13 (see also interview by M.Luke, 13-14); L. Trainor, *Weekend Australian*, 12-13 March, 1994, Review 6; P. Wolfe, *Antipodes*, 9.1, 1995, 45.

The Tins and Other Stories. (St Lucia: U.Q.P., 1973). Paperback Prose, 4.
Reviewed by G. Engwerder, *Overland*, No. 60, 1975, 87-88; T. Forshaw, *S.M.H.*, 4 August, 1973, 20; M. Lange, *Makar*, IX, No. 2, 1973, 48-50; L. Sandercock, *Nation Review*, 31 August-6 September, 1973, 1462; E. Scott, *Quadrant*, XXII, No. 6, 1978, 79; B. Williams, *Westerly*, No. 3, 1973, 39-41.

Voices. (Fremantle, W.A.: Fremantle Arts Centre Press, 1988).
Reviewed by M. Flanagan, *Overland*, No. 112, 1988, 77-78; T. Lintermans, *Age Saturday Extra*, 2 July, 1988, 14.

A Window in Mrs X's Place: Selected Stories. (Ringwood, Vic.: Penguin, 1986).
Reviewed by K. Gelder, *ABR*, No. 81, 1986, 4-6; B. Jefferis, *Weekend Australian Magazine*, 10-11 May, 1986, 15; C. McGregor, *Westerly*, XXXI, No. 2, 1986, 81-83; S. McKernan, *Bulletin*, 10 June, 1986, 107, 109.

Non-Fiction

'The Novel in the Nineteen Thirties - A Western Australian View'. *Westerly*, XXXI, No. 4, 1986, 22-29.
'Writers and Their Audiences'. *Fremantle Arts Review*, II, No. 7, 1987, 10-11.

Critical Material

Barnes, John. 'New Tracks to Travel: The Stories of White, Porter and Cowan'. *Meanjin*, XXV, 1966, 154-70.
Bennett, Bruce. 'Of Books and Covers: Peter Cowan'. *Fremantle Arts Review*, III, No. 8, 1988, 10-12 and *Overland*, No. 114, 1989, 58-62.
Bennett, Bruce, and Susan Miller, eds. *Peter Cowan: New Critical Essays*. (Nedlands, WA: U of Western Australia P in assoc. with The Centre for Studies in Australian Literature, 1992). Reviewed by N. Birns, *Antipodes*, 8.2, 1994, 158; O. Yu, *ABR*, 144, 1992, 53.
Bennett, Bruce. 'Regionalism in Peter Cowan's Short Fiction'. *WLWE*, XVIII, 1979,

336-44.
Johnston, Grahame. 'A Joyless World: The Fiction of Peter Cowan'. *Westerly*, No. 1, 1967, 67-69.
Jolley, Elizabeth. 'Silence and Spaces'. *Overland*, No. 108, 1987, 59-64.
Lewis, Julie. 'The Modernist Impulse: Peter Cowan's Early Fiction'. *Overland*, 131,1993, 58-64.
Lipscombe, Don. 'Paradox of Peter Cowan'. *Bulletin*, 10 September, 1966, 36.

CROFT, JULIAN

Fiction
Their Solitary Way. (Sydney: A.& R., 1985).
Reviewed by H. Daniel, *Age*, 16 November, 1985, 12; L. Forsyth, *ABR*, 79, 1986, 11-12; S. Hosking, *Overland*, 103, 1986, 67-69.

Poetry
Breakfasts in Shanghai. (Sydney: A.& R., 1984).
Reviewed by B. Beaver, *Weekend Australian Magazine*, 25-26 August, 1984, 15; G. Dutton, *Bulletin*, 2 October, 1984, 80-81; J. Rodriguez, *S.M.H.*, 2 March, 1985, 42; G. Page, *Quadrant*, 29.4, 1985, 71-5; F.G. Kellaway, *Overland*, 99, 1985, 70-2; D. Tofts, *ABR*, 66, 1984, 30-1; C. Vleeskens, *CRNLE Reviews Journal*, 2, 1982, 44-5.
Confessions of a Corinthian: Poems. (North Ryde, NSW: Collins/A.& R., 1991).
Reviewed by M. Duwell, *Weekend Australian*, 23-24 November, 1991, Review 7;D. Fahey, *Southerly*, 52.1, 1992, 140-48; P. Mead, *Australian Society*, 10.8, 1991, 40-42; P. Nelson, *Quadrant*, 36.3, 1992, 84-85; R. Pretty, *ABR*, 132, 1991, 44-45.
Loose Federation. (Armidale, NSW: Kardoorair P, 1979). With Michael Sharkey.

Critical Material
Perkins, Elizabeth. 'Characters in Search of History: Five Contemporary Australian Novels'. In *Australian Writing Now* edited by Manfred Jurgensen and Robert Adamson (Ringwood, Vic.: Outrider/Penguin, 1988), 58-71.
Spence, Nigel. 'Julian Croft and the Problem of an Australian Diction'. *Westerly*, 38.3, 1993, 17-26.

CROSS, ZORA

Critical Material
Saunders, Julia. 'A Writer's Friends & Associates: Notes From Correspondence in the Zora Cross Papers'. *Hecate*, 16, Nos. 1-2, 1989, 90-96.
Sharkey, Michael. 'David McKee Wright's Roman Novel'. *Southerly*, 51.1, 1991, 71-87.
---. 'Zora Cross's Entry into Australian Literature'. *Hecate*, 16, Nos. 1-2, 1989, 65-89.
---. 'Zora, Dave and Henry: Some Recollections of Henry Lawson by Zora Cross'. *Overland*, No. 117, 1989, 67-72.

CUSACK, DYMPHNA

Fiction
Black Lightning. (London: Heinemann, 1964).
Reviewed by A.R. Chisholm, *Age*, 30 January, 1965, 40; M. Jones, *S.M.H.*, 16 January, 1965, 15.
A Bough in Hell. (London: Heinemann,1971).
Reviewed by S. Despoja, *Advertiser*, 15 January, 1972, 30; W.L. Marshall, *Sunday Australian*, 26 March, 1972, 27; D. Martin, *S.M.H.*, 26 February, 1972, 22.
With Florence James. *Come in Spinner*. Complete and unabridged version, introduced by F. James. (Sydney: A.& R., 1989). First published Melbourne: Heinemann, 1951.

Reviewed by C. Bird, *ABR*, No. 111, 1989, 34; K. Goldsworthy, *Weekend Australian*, 27-28 May, 1989, Weekend 9; H. Rowley, *Age Saturday Extra*, 3 June, 1989, 10.

Jungfrau. Introduction by Florence James (Ringwood, Vic.: Penguin, 1989). First published Sydney: Bulletin, 1936.
Reviewed by M. Dever, *Editions*, 1, 1989, 20.

With Miles Franklin. *Pioneers on Parade: A Novel*. (North Ryde, N.S.W.: A.& R., 1939). First published Sydney: A.& R., 1939.
Reviewed by G. Flynn, *Weekend Australian*, 19-20 November, 1988, Weekend 9; J. Roe, *Australian Society*, 7, No. 12, 1988/89, 40-41.

   Non-Fiction
A Window in the Dark. Introduced and edited by Debra Adelaide. (Canberra: National Library of Australia, 1991).
Reviewed by L. Clancy, *Age*, 21 March, 1992, Saturday Extra 9; R. Darby, *Blast* 18, 1992, 38-39; H. McQueen, *Australian Society*, 11.1&2, 1992, 43-44; M. Whitlam, *Voices*, 2.1, 1992, 88-90.
'From an Autobiography that I shall never Write'. *Hecate*, VI, No. 2, 1980, 84-87.

   Critical Material
Tattersall, Edith M. 'Preliminary Checklist of Works by Ellen Dymphna Cusack'. *Armidale & District Historical Society. Journal & Proceedings*, No. 18, 1975, 49-60.
'Caddie's Heirs'. *S.M.H.*, 9 March, 1973, 6. Letter to the editor.
'Dymphna Cusack'. *Notes & Furphies*, No. 8, 1982, 7.
'The Grand Old Lady of Aust Literature'. *S.M.H.*, 25 September, 1975, 10.
Baker, Catherine A.W. 'Dymphna Cusack: A Biographical Note'. *Armidale and District Historical Society Journal and Proceedings*, No. 15, 1971/72, 77-79.
Bertrand, Ina. 'Come in Spinner': Two Views of the Forties'. *Journal of Australian Studies*, 41, 1994, 12-23. Compares the TV mini-series and the novel.
Cottle, Drew. 'Dymphna Cusack, a Farewell, 1902-1981'. *Independent Australian*, IV, No. 3, 1981, 2 & 5.
Darby, Robert. 'Writing in a Half Free Country'. *Independent Australian*, III, No. 4, 1979, 3-6.
de Groen, Frances. 'Dymphna Cusack's *Comets Soon Pass*: The Genius and the Potato Wife'. In *Wallflowers and Witches: Women and Culture in Australia 1910-1945*, edited by Maryanne Dever (St Lucia: U.Q.P., 1994), 91-104.
Dunlevy, Maurice. 'Book of "Barnyard Morals" was Spinner for Author'. *Canberra Times*, 17 October, 1975, 18.
Freehill, Norman, with Dymphna Cusack. *Dymphna Cusack*. (Melbourne: Thomas Nelson (Australia), 1975. Reviewed by G. Jamison, *Age*, 25 October, 1975, 21.
Gamble, Fred. 'Dymphna Cusack 1902-1981'. *Muse*, No. 13, 18 December, 1981-18 February, 1982, 22.
James, Florence and Marilla North. '*Come In Spinner*: An Addendum'. *Meanjin*, 49, No. 1, 1989, 178-88.
Knuckey, Marie. 'Look! Come in Dymphna'. *S.M.H.*, 21 August, 1980, 14.
Lloyd, Vic. 'Dymphna Cusack's *Morning Sacrifice*'. *Australasian Drama Studies*, No. 10, 1987, 67-77.
Molloy, Bruce. 'Interview with Dymphna Cusack'. *Imago*, 1, No. 2, 1989, 42-52. Interview took place 25 July 1973.
Stirling, Monica. 'Dymphna Cusack: A Profile'. *Meanjin*, XXIV, No. 3, 1965, 317-24.
Wills, Nancy. 'Dymphna Cusack: Writer of Conviction'. *Tribune*, 11 November, 1981, 13. Obituary. Her death was also noted in *Artforce*, No. 37, 1981, 2; *Artlook*, VII, No. 12, 1981, 9; *Canberra Times*, 21 October, 1981, 33; *Courier-Mail*, 20 October, 1981, 16.

D'ALPUGET, BLANCHE

Fiction

Monkeys in the Dark. (Sydney: Aurora Press, 1980).
Reviewed by D. Armstrong, *Bulletin*, 5 August, 1980, 59; J. Bedford, *National Times*, 3-9 August, 1980, 31; H. Daniel, *Age*, 25 October, 1980, 29; A. Gould, *ABR*, No. 25, 1980, 25-6; C. Koch, *S.M.H.*, 24 May, 1980, 20; P. Pierce, *Meanjin*, 40, No. 4, 1981, 522-8; P. Sharrad, *CRNLE Reviews Journal*, No. 1, 1981, 1-3.

Turtle Beach. (Ringwood: Penguin, 1980; New York: Simon & Schuster, 1983).
Reviewed by J. Bedford, *National Times*, 1-7 March, 1981, 48; G. Dutton, *Bulletin*, 12 May, 1981, 89; K. Goldsworthy, *Meanjin*, 44, No. 4, 1985, 506-15, esp. 512; N. Jillett, *Age*, 7 March, 1981, 27; F. McInherny, *ABR*, No. 30, 1981, 5; P. Pierce, *Menjin*, 40, No. 4, 522-8, 1981; D. Smith, *Nation*, 237, 1983, 544-5; L. Strahan, *Helix*, Nos 9-10, 1981, 28-35.

White Eye. (Ringwood, Vic.: Viking, 1993).
Reviewed by J. Chimonyo, *Age*, 6 November, 1993, Saturday Extra 9; H. Daniel, *S.M.H.*, 6 November, 1993, Spectrum 11A; C. Keneally, *ABR*, 157, 1993/1994, 8-9; R. Lucas, *Bulletin*, 16 November, 1993, 104-05; G. Turcotte, *Weekend Australian*, 6-7 November, 1993, Review 9; P. Wolfe, *Antipodes*, 9.2, 1995, 147-48.

Winter in Jerusalem. (Richmond, Vic.: Heinemann; London: Secker and Warburg, 1986).
Reviewed by D. Anderson, *National Times*, 1-7 August, 1986, 35; A. Boston, *T.L.S.*, 10 October, 1986, 1130; G. Coger, *Antipodes*, I, No. 1, 1987, 54; P. Goldsworthy, *ABR*, No. 85, 1986, 7-8; M. Hulse, *PN Review*, XIII, No. 5, 1987, 80-81; B. Jefferis, *Weekend Australian Magazine*, 9-10 August, 1986, 15; T. Koch, *Courier-Mail: The Great Weekend*, 27 September, 1986, 7; S. Lipski, *Age Saturday Extra*, 30 August, 1986, 12; P. Pierce, *S.M.H.*, 2 August, 1986, 45; R. Samuel, *New York Times Book Review*, 8 June, 1986, 15 and 17; M. Thomas, *Canberra Times*, 2 August, 1986, B2; A. Ward, *British Book News*, February, 1987, 94.

Non-Fiction

'Jakarta, Jerusalem and the Caves'. *Island Magazine*, Nos. 34-35, 1988, 71-76.

Critical Material

Baker, Candida. 'Blanche d'Alpuget'. In her *Yacker: Australian Writers Talk About Their Work* (Sydney: Picador, 1986), 78-103.
Docker, John. 'Blanche D'Alpuget's *Robert J. Hawke* and *Winter In Jerusalem*'.

Hecate, XIII, No. 1, 1987, 51-65.
Ellison, Jennifer. 'Blanche d'Alpuget'. In her *Rooms of Their Own* (Ringwood, Vic.: Penguin, 1986), 8-27.
Little, Graham. 'Blanche D'Alpuget' in his *Speaking for Myself* (Melbourne: McPhee Gribble, 1989), 157-69.
Maack, Annegret. '"Can We Ever Understand Alien Cultures?": Christopher Koch and Blanche D'Alpuget'. In *Australien Zwischen Europa und Asien*, edited by Gerhard Stilz and Rudolf Bader (Bern: Peter Lang, 1993), 123-33.
McKeogh, Sean. 'Desani and D'Alpuget: Representing Other Cultures'. *New Literatures Review*, No. 16, 1988, 31-37.
Riem, Antonella. 'The Conflict Between Two Differing Consciences: Blanche D'Alpuget's *Turtle Beach*'. In her *The Labyrinths of Self: A Collection of Essays on Australian and Caribbean Literature*. (Leichhardt, N.S.W.: FILEF. Italo-Australian Publications, 1987), 169-179. Also published in *Literary Criterion*, 30.1&2, 1995, 105-12.
Strauss, Jennifer. '"Everyone is in Politics": Margaret Atwood's *Bodily Harm* and Blanche D'Alpuget's *Turtle Beach*. I. Being There, Being Here', and Tiffin Helen, '"Everyone is in Politics": Margaret Atwood's *Bodily Harm* and Blanche D'Alpuget's *Turtle Beach*. II. Voice and Form'. In *Australian/Canadian Literatures in English: Comparative Perspectives*, edited by Russell McDougall and Gillian Whitlock (North Ryde, N.S.W.: Methuen Australia, 1987), 111-132.

DALEY, VICTOR

Poetry
Victor Daley. Edited with an introduction by H.J. Oliver. (Sydney: A.& R., 1963).
Critical Material
Lindsay, Norman. 'Victor Daley'. *Bohemians of the Bulletin* (Sydney: A.& R., 1965), 41-47.

DARK, ELEANOR

Fiction
Lantana Lane. (London: Virago, 1986). First published London: Collins, 1959.
Reviewed by H. Garner, *Australian Society*, V, No. 8, 1986, 33-34, 38.

The Little Company. With a new introduction by Drusilla Modjeska. (London: Virago, 1985). First published Sydney: Collins, 1945.

No Barrier. Introduction by Barbara Brooks. (North Ryde, NSW: A.& R., 1991). First published London: Collins, 1953.

Return to Coolami, 1936. Introduction by Barbara Brooks and Judith Clark. (North Ryde, NSW: A.& R., 1991). First published 1936.

Storm of Time. Introduction by Barbara Brooks with Judith Clark. (North Ryde, NSW: A.& R, 1991). First published London: Collins, 1948.

The Timeless Land. With introduction by Humphrey McQueen. (North Ryde, N.S.W.: A.& R., 1990). First published London: Collins, 1941.

Waterway. (Sydney: A.& R., 1979). First published Sydney: Johnston, 1938.
Reviewed by L. Clancy, *Weekend Australian*, 20-21 October, 1990, Review 5; E. Perkins, *Quadrant*, XXIII, No. 9, 1979, 70-71 and *CRNLE Reviews Journal*, No. 2, 1979, 30-34.

Non-Fiction
As Good as a Yarn with You: Letters between Miles Franklin, Katharine Susannah Prichard, Jean Devanny, Marjorie Barnard, Flora Eldershaw and Eleanor Dark. Edited by Carole Ferrier. (Cambridge: Cambridge UP, 1992). For reviews see Barnard, Marjorie.

Critical Material

Anderson, Hugh. 'Eleanor Dark: A *Bulletin* Checklist'. *Biblionews* and *Australian Notes & Queries*, Second series, III, No. 2, 1969, 2.

'Eleanor Dark Dies'. *Canberra Times*, 17 September, 1985, 13. For other obituaries see *Age*, 17 September, 1985, 6; *Courier-Mail*, 17 September, 1985, 30; *Notes & Furphies*, No. 15,1985, 10.

Buckridge, Patrick. '"Greatness" and Australian Literature in the 1930s and 1940s: Novels by Dark and Barnard Eldershaw'. *A.L.S.*, 17.1, 1995, 29-37.

Day, A. Grove. *Eleanor Dark*. (Boston: Twayne, 1976). Twayne's World Author Series 382. Reviewed by D. Cusack, *S.M.H.*, 25 June, 1977, 16; L.S. Fallis, *World Literature Today*, LI, No. 3, 1977, 503; C. Hadgraft, *A.L.S.*, IX, 1980, 561-64.

Doecke, Brenton. 'Challenging History Making: Realism, Revolution and Utopia in *The Timeless Land*'. *A.L.S.*, 17.1, 1995, 49-57.

Ferrier, Carole. 'Women of Letters and the Uses of Memory'. In *Wallflowers and Witches: Women and Culture in Australia 1910-1945*, edited by Maryanne Dever (St Lucia: U.Q.P., 1994), 73-90.

Giuffre, Giulia.'Eleanor Dark'. Interview with Dr. Eric Dark. *Southerly*, XLVII, No. 1, 1987, 83-93. Reprinted, expanded, in her *A Writing Life: Interviews with Australian Women Writers*. (Sydney: Allen and Unwin, 1990).

Hergenhan, Laurie. '"The Precarious Present" and the Future; Eleanor Dark's *The Timeless Land*. In his *Unnatural Lives* (St Lucia: U.Q.P., 1983), 108-121.

Lockwood, Betty. 'And Then, There Were Women'. *Womanspeak*, II, No. 4, 1976, 20-21.

McQueen, Humphrey. 'The Novels of Eleanor Dark'. *Hemisphere*, XVII, No. 1, 1973, 38-41. Republished as 'The Thinker from The Bush: Eleanor Dark', in his *Gallipoli to Petrov* (Sydney: Allen & Unwin, 1984), 88-93.

Modjeska, D. 'Dialogue with Dark'. *Age Monthly Review*, V, No. 11, 1986, 3-6.

---. 'Eleanor Dark: Retrospective'. *Refractory Girl*, No. 29, 1986, 38-39.

O'Reilly, Helen. 'The Timeless Eleanor Dark'. *Outrider*, 6, No. 1, 1989, 43-47.

Tennant, Kylie. 'A Little Company against the Bulldozer Mentality: Eleanor Dark Interviewed by Kylie Tennant'. *S.M.H.*, Look! Section, 15 February, 1974, 3.

Thomson, A.K. *Understanding the Novel: The Timeless Land*. (Brisbane: Jacaranda Press, 1966).

DARRELL, GEORGE

Drama

The Sunny South. Edited by Margaret Williams. With an historical note by Geoffrey Serle (Sydney: Currency Press; London: Eyre Methuen, 1975).

Critical Material

Irvin, Eric. *Gentleman George, King of Melodrama: The Theatrical Life and Times of George Darrell, 1841-1921*. (St Lucia: U.Q.P., 1980). Reviewed by R. Dobson, *Age*, 13 December, 1980, 27; A. Hughes, *Nineteenth Century Theatre Review*, X, 1982, 122-23; H. G. Kippax, *S.M.H.*, 3 January, 1981, 38; J. McCallum, *Theatre Australia*, V, No. 11, 1981, 60; B. Oakley, *National Times*, 12-18 October, 1980, 64; E. Perkins, *LiNQ*, VIII, No. 2, 1980, 100-102; J. Rickard, *Journal of Australian Studies*, No. 8, 1981, 99-101.

---. 'George Darrell, an Ambitious Dramatist'. *Quadrant*, XX, No. 5, 1976, 39-45.

DARVILLE ['DEMIDENKO'], HELEN.

Fiction

The Hand that Signed the Paper. (St Leonards, NSW: Allen & Unwin, 1994). First published under name of Demidenko, later reprints under Darville.

Reviewed by H. Bowers, *Imago*, 7.1, 1995, 91-92; P. Christoff, *Arena Magazine*, 18,

1995, 44-48; M. Cosic, *S.M.H.*, 20 Aug., 1994: Spectrum 9A; L. Forsyth, *Overland*, 141, 1995, 31-32; C. Harboe-Ree, *ABR*, 165, 1994, 20-21 (see also interview with Demidenko, 21); A. Hay, *Independent Monthly*, Oct., 1994, 78-79; J. Hughes, *Meanjin*, 53.4, 1994, 765-67; R. Lucas, *Bulletin*, 25 Oct., 1994, 96-97; S. Mitchell, *Weekend Australian*, 12-13 Nov., 1994, 48; A. Riemer, *Age*, 24 Sept., 1994, Saturday Extra 9; C. Stein, *Australian Multicultural Book Review*, 3.3, 1995, 42-46; M. Teichmann, *Eureka Street*, 5.6, 1995, 34-35.

Critical Material

'Forum on the Demidenko Controversy'. Comments on the Miles Fanklin Award. *ABR*, 173, 1995, 14-20. See also 'Letters', *ABR*, 174, 1995, 3-6; *ABR*, 175, 1995, 3.

Forsyth, L. '"While Out Boating One Sunday Afternoon..." or "Hindsight is 20/20"'. *Notes & Furphies*, 35, 1995, 5.

Fraser, Morag. 'The Begetting of Violence'. *Meanjin*, 54.3, 1995, 419-29.

Gaita, Raimond. 'Literary and Public Honours'. *Quadrant*, 39.9, 1995, 32-36.

Hyde, Jane. 'On Not Being Ethnic: Anglo-Australia and the Lesson of Helen Darville-Demidenko'. *Quadrant*, 39.11, 1995, 49-52.

Kirkpatrick, Peter. 'The Jackboot Doesn't Fit: Moral Authoritarianism and The Hand that Signed the Paper'. *Southerly*, 55.4, 1995, 155-65.

Laster, Kathy. 'Crime and Punishment'. *Meanjin*, 54.4, 1995, 626-39.

Levy, Bronwen. 'Third Time Lucky, or After the Wash-up'. *Imago*, 7.3: 108-17. Discusses the public debate about H. Garner's *The First Stone* and H. Demidenko's *The Hand that Signed the Paper*.

Liberman, Serge. 'On Helen Demidenko's *The Hand that Signed the Paper*'. *Southerly*, 55.3, 1995, 161-74.

Liebmann, Steve. 'Keneally on Demidenko'. Interview. *Notes & Furphies*, 35, 1995, 4-5. See also Letter to the Editor by Debra Adelaide, 1-2; 'ALS Gold Medal Winner: Helen Demidenko. Judges Response' 3.

McLaren, John. 'Truth in Fiction'. *Overland*, 141, 1995, 29-30.

Manne, Robert. 'The Strange Case of Helen Demidenko'. *Quadrant*, 39.9, 1995, 21-28.

Neumann, Anne Waldron. 'The Ethics of Fiction's Reception'. *Quadrant*, 39.11, 1995, 53-56.

---. The Rationalizing of Violence, the Inciting of Violence'. *Meanjin*, 54.4, 1995, 613-25.

Schaffer, William. 'The Book that Evaded the Question'. *Southerly*, 55.3, 1995, 175-84.

Weis, Bob. 'Response'. *Overland*, 141, 1995, 33-39. Personal response to Darville's novel.

DAVIS, A.H.

See Rudd, Steele.

DAVIS, JACK

Drama

The Dreamers. (Sydney: Currency Press, 1986).
Reviewed by M. Narogin, *Australasian Drama Studies*, Nos. 15-16, 1989/90, 187-89.

Honey Spot. Illustrated by Ellen Jose. (Sydney: Currency Press, 1987 [i.e. 1988]).
Reviewed by W. Michaels, *English in Australia*, No. 88, 1989, 40; M. Narogin, *Australasian Drama Studies*, Nos. 15-16, 1989/90, 187-89.

Kullark: and The Dreamers. Introduction by H.C. Coombs, with an account of the Nyoongah people by R.M. Berndt (Sydney: Currency Press, 1982).
Reviewed by B. Marshall-Stoneking, *Weekend Australian Magazine*, 20-21 August,

1983, 14; J. McCallum, *S.M.H.*, 29 January, 1983, 32; C. O'Brien, *Australasian Drama Studies*, II No. 1, 1983, 125-126; E. Perkins, *LiNQ*, XI, No. 1, 1983, 89-100.
No Sugar. (Sydney: Currency Press, 1986).
Reviewed by M. Narogin, *Australasian Drama Studies*, Nos. 15-16, 1989/90, 187-89.

   Poetry
Black Life: Poems. (St. Lucia: U.Q.P., 1992).
Reviewed by M. Flanagan, *Age*, 27 June, 1992, Saturday Extra 7; A. Shoemaker, *Weekend Australian*, 2-3 May, 1992, Review 6; L. Sutton, *CRNLE Reviews Journal*, 2, 1992, 53-59; J.P. Turner, *Antipodes*, 7.1, 1993, 74; C. Ward, *SPAN*, 33, 1992, 168-69.

John Pat and Other Poems. (Melbourne: Dent, 1988).
Reviewed by H. Cam, *S.M.H.*, 10 December, 1988, 82; L. Dale, *Westerly*, 35, No. 1, 1990, 82-84; B. Hill, *Age Saturday Extra*, 14 January, 1989, 13; M. O'Connor, *Weekend Australian*, 26-27 November, 1988, Weekend 7.

   Non-Fiction
A Boy's Life. (Broome, WA: Magabala Books, 1991). Autobiographical.
'Jack Davis on *Barungin*'. In *Writers in Action: The Writer's Choice Evenings*, edited by Gerry Turcotte (Sydney: Currency Press, 1990), 179-202.

   Critical Material
Balme, Christopher B. 'The Aboriginal Theatre of Jack Davis: Prolegomena to a Theory of Syncretic Theatre'. In *Crisis and Creativity in the New Literatures in English* Cross Cultures 1, edited by Geoffrey V. Davis and Hena Maes-Jelinek (Amsterdam; Atlanta, Ga.: Rodopi, 1990), 401-17.
Beston, John. 'The Aboriginal Poets in English: Kath Walker, Jack Davis and Kevin Gilbert'. *Meanjin*, 36, No. 4, 1977, 446-62.
Cato, Nancy. 'An Australian Voice is Heard in Canada'. *This Australia*, VI, No. 1, 1987, 88-89.
Chesson, Keith. *Jack Davis: A Life Story*. (Melbourne: Dent, 1988). Reviewed by L. Dale, *Westerly*, 35, No. 1, 1990, 82-4; B. Hill, *Age Saturday Extra*, 14 January, 1989, 13; A Shoemaker, *Australian Aboriginal Studies*, No. 1, 1990, 61-63.
Dibble, Brian, and Margaret Macintyre. 'Hybridity in Jack Davis' *No Sugar*'. *Westerly*, 37.4, 1992, 93-98.
Dibble, Brian, and Margaret MacIntyre. 'Looking at Them Looking at Us: Jack Davis's *No Sugar*'. In *Australia in the World: Perceptions and Possibilities*, edited by Don Grant and Graham Seal (Perth: Black Swan P; Curtin U of Technology, 1994), 40-44.
Gilbert, Helen. 'De-scribing Orality'. In *De-scribing Empire: Post-colonialism and Textuality*, edited by Chris Tiffin and Alan Lawson (London and New York: Routledge, 1994), 98-111.
---. 'Historical Re-presentation: Performance and Counter-discourse in Jack Davis's Plays'. *New Literatures Review*, 19, 1990, 91-101.
Langsam, David. 'Jack Davis and Marli Biyol in London'. *Australian Society*, VII, No. 8, 1988, 41-42. Interview and comment on reception of *No Sugar* in England.
Lloyd, Tim. 'At Last - They Can't Ignore Jack'. *Advertiser Saturday Review*, 30 March, 1985, 5.
McDonald, Roger. *Gone Bush* (Sydney: Bantam, 1990), 147-60. Talk with Davis.
O'Brien, Patrick. 'Jack Davis and "The Dreamers"'. *Artlook*, August, 1983, 42-44.
Mitchell, Tony. 'Colonial Discourse and the National Imaginary'. *Canadian Theatre Review*, 74, 1993, 18-21.
Olb, Suzanne. 'The White Problem: Jack Davis' Confronting Realism'. *New Theatre Australia*, 6, 1988, 4-7.
Page, Geoff. 'Jack Davis'. In his *A Reader's Guide To Contemporary Australian Poetry* (St. Lucia: U.Q.P., 1995), 46-48.

Radic, Leonard. 'Davis's Exercise in Conscience-Raising'. *Age*, 27 February, 1985, 14.

Riemenschneider, Dieter. 'Intercultural Exchange between Ethnic Minority and English Language Majority: The Writing of Jack Davis and Witi Ihimaera'. In *Imagination and the Creative Impulse in the New Literatures in English*, edited by M-T Bindella and G.V. Davis, Cross/Cultures 9 (Amsterdam; Atlanta: Rodopi, 1993), 271-80.

Shoemaker, Adam. 'An Interview with Jack Davis'. *Westerly*, No. 4, 1982, 111-116.

---. '"Fiction or Assumed Fiction": The Short Stories of Colin Johnson, Jack Davis and Archie Weller'. In *Connections: Essays on Black Literatures*, edited by Emmanuel Nelson (Canberra: Aboriginal Studies, 1988), 53-59.

Turcotte, Gerry, ed. *Jack Davis: The Maker of History*. (Pymble, NSW: Collins/A.& R. School Texts, 1993).

Webby, Elizabeth. *Modern Australian Plays*. Revised edition of Horizon Studies in Literature, originally published 1990 (South Melbourne: Sydney UP/O.U.P., 1992). Discusses *The First Born*.

DAVISON, FRANK DALBY

Fiction

Dusty; Man-shy. Afterword by H.P. Heseltine. (Sydney: Reader's Digest, 1992). Originally published Sydney: A.& R., 1931; 1946.

The Road to Yesterday. (Sydney: A.& R., 1964).
Reviewed by J. Barnes, *Meanjin*, XXIII, No. 3, 1964, 323-5; J. McLaren, *Overland*, No. 44, 1970, 52-53.

The Wells of Beersheba and Other Stories. (North Ryde, N.S.W.: A.& R., 1985). First published Sydney, A.& R., 1933.
Reviewed by L. Clancy, *Age Saturday Extra*, 2 August, 1986, 16; R. Darby, *Overland*, No. 109, 1987, 60-64.

The White Thorntree. (Sydney: Ure Smith, 1968). Reprinted in 2v. in 1970.
Reviewed by J. Barnes, *Westerly*, No. 1, 1971, 62-64; A. Brissenden, *Advertiser*, 23 May, 1970, 22; R. Burns, *Nation*, 25 July, 1970, 20-22; M. Dunlevy, *Canberra Times*, 2 May, 1970, 12 and 3 October, 12; B. Kiernan, *Australian*, 13 June, 1970, 19; J. Morrison, *Age*, 23 November, 1968, 13 and *Age*, 9 May, 1970, 16; M. Vintner, *S.M.H.*, 11 January, 1969, 19; O. Webster, *Overland*, No. 40, 1968, 34-35 and *Bulletin*, 2 May, 1970, 54-55, and 10 October, 1970, 53-55; D. Whitelock, *ABR*, VIII, 1968, 39; G.A. Wilkes, *Southerly*, XXIX, 1969, 153-56. See also Stuart Sayers, *Age*, 25 April, 1970, 15.

Non-Fiction

'Among the Sundries'. *Overland*, No. 100, 1985, 57-58.

'Testimony of a Veteran (Australian Writers in Profile, 5)'. *Southerly*, XXIX, 1969, 83-92.

Critical Material

Barnes, John. 'Frank Dalby Davison'. *Westerly*, No. 3, 1967, 16-20.

Dow, Hume. *Frank Dalby Davison*. (Melbourne: O.U.P., 1971). Australian Writers and Their Work. Reviewed by L. Kramer, *A.L.S.*, V, 1972, 433-37; W. Walsh, *Notes and Queries*, n.s. XXII, 1975, 219; J. Waten, *Age*, 23 September, 1972, 15 and *S.M.H.*, 1 July, 1972, 20.

Green, Dorothy. 'Love and the Thirteenth Chapter of [I] Corinthians'. *Bulletin*, 21-28 December, 1982, 188-95.

Hadgraft, Cecil. 'Indulgence: David Martin's *The Hero of Too*, Frank Dalby Davison's *The White Thorntree*, Dal Stivens's *A Horse of Air*, David Malouf's *Johnno*, and Frank Hardy's *But the Dead are Many*'. In *Studies in the Recent Australian Novel*, edited by K.G. Hamilton (St Lucia: U.Q.P., 1978), 194-224.

Heseltine, H.P. 'The Fellowship of All Flesh: The Fiction of Frank Dalby Davison'. *Meanjin*, XXVII, 1968, 275-90.

Kiernan, Brian. 'Frank Dalby Davison, Author of *Man-Shy*, Dies at 77'. *Australian*, 25 May, 1970, 3. See also *S.M.H.*, 25 May, 1970, 4.

Morrison, John. *The Happy Warrior*. (Fairfield, Vic.: Pascoe Publishing, 1987), 55-61.

---. 'Frank Davison'. *Overland*, No. 65, 1976, 23-25.

Phillips, Arthur. 'Frank Dalby Davison, M.B.E., 1893-1970'. *Meanjin*, XXIX, 1970, 252-52.

Rorabacher, Louise E. *Frank Dalby Davison*. (Boston: Twayne, 1979). Twayne's World Authors Series. Reviewed by D. Green, *Age*, 31 May, 1980, 24; C. Hadgraft, *A.L.S.*, IX, 1980, 561-64.

Sayers, Stuart. 'Four Hours with Farmer Frank'. *Age*, 30 August, 10. Report of the production of a TV study of Frank Dalby Davison.

---. 'Writers and Readers'. *Age*, 9 November, 1968, 12. On the writing and publication of *The White Thorntree*.

Smith, Graeme Kinross. 'Frank Dalby Davison'. *Westerly*, No. 4, 1974, 45-49.

Waten, Judah. 'Writer Returns to Fold with Mammoth Work'. *S.M.H.*, 9 November, 1968, 23.

Webster, Owen. *The Outward Journey*. (Canberra: A.N.U. Press, 1978). Reviewed by J. Barnes, *Overland*, No. 75, 1979, 50-52.

H. Dow, *ABR*, No. 10, 1979, 6-7; B. Elliott, *Advertiser*, 14 April, 1979, 17; V. Ikin, *Quadrant*, XXIII, No. 10, 1979, 72; A.A. Phillips, *Meanjin*, XXXVIII, 1979, 253-57; C. Semmler, *24 Hours*, IV, No. 3, 1979, 61-62; J. Waten, *Age*, 18 November, 1978, 25.

---. 'Five Hundred Copies by an Old Man'. *Nation Review*, 18-24 May, 1973, 965. Refers to *The White Thorntree*.

---. 'Frank Dalby Davison'. *Overland*, No. 44, 1970, 35-37.

---. 'Frank Davison's Magnum Opus Has a Soft Sell-out'. *Bulletin*, 5 July, 1969, 43-44.

DAVITT, ELLEN

Fiction

Force and Fraud: A Tale of the Bush. Introduction by Lucy Sussex. Australian Books on Demand 6. (Canberra: Mulini Press, 1993). Originally published in *Australian Journal*, 1865.

Reviewed by S. Coupe, *S.M.H.*, 24 July, 1993, 45; J. Davies, *ABR*, 154, 1993, 46.

Critical Material

Sussex, Lucy. 'An Early Australian Murder Mystery Novel: Ellen Davitt and *Force and Fraud*'. *Margin*, 25, 1991, 7-9.

---.'*Force and Fraud* by Ellen Davitt: Australia's First Crime Novel'. *Mean Streets: A Quarterly Journal of Crime, Mystery and Detection*, 9, 1993, 42-45.

DAWE, BRUCE

Fiction

Over Here, Harv. (Ringwood, Vic: Penguin, 1983). Reprinted as a Puffin book, 1984.

Reviewed by L. Clancy, *Age Saturday Extra*, 15 October, 1983, 14; R.E. Jones, *True North Down Under* (Lantzville, British Columbia), No. 2, 1984, 105-107; J. Hanrahan, *ABR*, No. 55, 1983, 4-5; D. Rowbotham, *Courier-Mail*, 12 November, 1983, 30; V. Sen, *Canberra Times*, 5 November, 1983, 17.

Poetry

Beyond the Sub-divisions. (Melbourne: Cheshire, 1969).

Reviewed by R. Dunlop, *Poetry Australia*, No. 32, 1970, 52-53; C. Harrison-Ford, *Poetry Magazine*, XVIII, No. 2, 1970, 40-42; F. Kellaway, *Overland*, No. 46, 1970/71, 39; G. Lehmann, *Bulletin*, 2 May, 1970, 56; G. Page, *Canberra Times*, 10 January, 1970, 17; A. Riddell, *S.M.H.*, 7 November, 1970, 23; R.A. Simpson, *Age*, 24 January, 1970, 11; J. Tulip, *Southerly*, XXX, 1970, 151-53; P. Ward, *ABR*, IX, 1970, 127-28.

Bruce Dawe Reads from His Own Work. (St Lucia: U.Q.P., 1971). Poets on Record, 5. Record and booklet. Booklet includes notes by the author and selected bibliography.
Reviewed by P. Annand, *Makar*, VII, No. 4, 1971, 42-43; A.C. Lyons, *Twentieth Century*, XXVI, 1971, 183; D. Malouf, *Australian*, 18 December, 1971, 16; P. Roberts, *S.M.H.*, 29 April, 1972, 16.

Condolences of the Season: Selected Poems. (Melbourne: Cheshire, 1971). Reviewed by G. Curtis, *Makar*, VII, No. 3, 1971, 44-46; R. Dunlop, *Poetry Australia*, No. 43, 1972, 62-63; C. Harrison-Ford, *Nation*, 27 November, 1971, 22-23; E. Kynaston, *Review*, 26 February-3 March, 1972, 530; I. Mudie, *Issue*, I, No. 3, 1971, 30; G. Page, *Canberra Times*, 25 March, 1972, 12; P. Roberts, *S.M.H.*, 20 May, 1972, 12; R.A. Simpson, *Age*, 20 November, 1971, 11; J. Tulip, *Southerly*, XXXIII, 1973, 231-33.

An Eye for a Tooth. (Melbourne: Cheshire, 1968).
Reviewed by B. Beaver, *S.M.H.*, 27 April, 1968, 17; R. Burns, *Poetry Magazine*, No. 6, 1968, 38-41; L.J. Clancy, *Overland*, No. 39, 1968, 50; D. Douglas, *Age*, 16 March, 1968, 13; R. Dunlop, *Poetry Australia*, No. 24, 1968, 37; D. Green, *Canberra Times*, 27 April, 1968, 10; R. Hall, *Australian*, 14 September, 1968, 12; M. Irvin, *Bulletin*, 23 March, 1968, 76; E. Jones, *Nation*, 22 February, 1969, 22; S.E. Lee, *Southerly*, XXVIII, 1968, 146-47; E. Marsh, *Westerly*, No. 3, 1968, 56-57; J. McAuley, *Twentieth Century*, XXIII, 1968, 84-85; T. Shapcott, *ABR*, VII, 1968, 106-07.

Heat-Wave. (Bulleen, Vic.: Sweeney Reed, 1970).
Reviewed by R.A. Simpson, *Age*, 14 November, 1970, 18.

Just a Dugong at Twilight. Mainly light verse; illustrations by Collette. (Melbourne: Cheshire, 1975).
Reviewed by A. Gould, *Nation Review*, 2-8 April, 1976, 621.

Mortal Instruments: Poems 1990-1995. (Melbourne: Longman, 1995).
Reviewed by H. Cam, *S.M.H.*, 30 Sept., 1995, Spectrum 14A; A. Gould, *ABR*, 176, 1995, 52-53; K. Hart, *Age*, 18 Nov., 1995, Saturday Extra 8.

A Need of Similar Name. (Melbourne: Cheshire, 1965).
Reviewed by D. Douglas, *Age*, 16 July, 1966, 23; F. Haynes, *Westerly*, No. 3, 1966, 90-4; M. Jurgensen, *Twentieth Century*, XXI, 1966, 86-7; S.E. Lee, *Southerly*, XXVI, 1966, 130-1; D. Rowbotham, *Poetry Australia*, No. 10, 1966, 34-7; V. Smith, *Bulletin*, 19 March, 1966, 48; A. Taylor, *Overland*, No. 35, 1966, 55-6; J. Wright, *Poetry Magazine*, No. 4, 1967, 28-29.

Sometimes Gladness: Collected Poems 1954-1978. (Melbourne: Longman Cheshire, 1978).
Reviewed by B. Beaver, *Age*, 16 December, 1978, 27; V. Brady, *ABR*, No. 11, 1979, 19; D. Dodwell, *Helix*, Nos. 9 & 10 Supplement 'Fresh Flounder', 1981, 10-12; G. Dutton, *Bulletin*, 16 January, 1979, 66-67; K. Goodwin, *Weekend Australian Magazine*, 10-11 February, 1979, 8; E. Jones, *National Times*, 10 February, 1979, 31; M. Macleod, *Meanjin*, XXXIX, 1980, 103-11; L. Murray, *S.M.H.*, 3 February, 1979, 19; G. Page, *Quadrant*, XXIV, No. 4, 1980, 53-55; T Shapcott, *24 Hours*, IV, No. 1, 1979, 49.

Sometimes Gladness: Collected Poems 1954-1982. 2nd ed. (Melbourne: Longman

Cheshire, 1983). First edition published Melbourne: Longman, Cheshire, 1978.
Reviewed by V. O'Sullivan, *Westerly*, XXX, No. 1, 1985, 87-89.
Sometimes Gladness: Collected Poems 1954-1987. 3rd ed. (Melbourne: Longman Cheshire, 1988). First edition published Melbourne: Longman, Cheshire, 1978.
Reviewed by R. Fitzgerald, *Weekend Australian*, 26-27 November, 1988, Weekend 10.
This Side of Silence: Poems 1987-1990. (Melbourne: Longman Cheshire, 1990).
Reviewed by D. Gilbey, *ABR*, 128, 1991, 35-36; I. Salusinszky, *Weekend Australian*, 2-3 March, 1991, Review 5; J. Strauss, *Age*, 13 April, 1991, Saturday Extra 7.
Towards Sunrise: Poems 1979-1986. (Melbourne: Longman Cheshire, 1986).
Reviewed by P. Lugg, *Canberra Times*, 8 November, 1986, B3; J. Rodriguez, *S.M.H.*, 14 March, 1987, 47.

Non-Fiction

'A Good Innings on a Sticky Wicket'. *ABR*, No. 55, 1983, 6-8. Self-portraits 4.
Essays and Opinions. Edited by Ken Goodwin. (Melbourne: Longman Cheshire, 1990). Includes articles, talks, interviews, critical articles and bibliography.
Reviewed by I. Salusinszky, *Weekend Australian*, 2-3 March, 1991, Review 5.
'Public Voices and Private Feeling'. In *The American Model: Influence and Independence in Australian Poetry*, edited by Joan Kirkby (Sydney: Hale & Iremonger, 1982), 160-172.
The Writer and the Community. (Toowoomba, Qld: University College of Southern Queensland, 1990).

Critical Material

'Bruce Dawe'. *Southerly*, XXXIX, 1979, 235-44. Australian Poets in Profile, 1.
Astley, Thea. 'The Shock of the Expected: Bruce Dawe's *Condolences of the Season*'. In her *Three Australian Writers*. (Townsville: Townsville Foundation for Literary Studies, 1979), 1-11.
Bennett, Bruce and Brian Dibble. 'An Interview with Bruce Dawe'. *Westerly*, XXIV, No. 4, 1979, 63-68.
Brock, Paul. 'A View of Bruce Dawe's Poetry'. *Southerly*, XLII, 1982, 226-37.
Carter, David. 'The Death of Satan and the Persistence of Romanticism'. *Literary Criterion*, XV, Nos. 3-4, 1980, 72-77.
Collins, Martin. 'Here's a Poet with a Few Honest Thoughts on Sweat'. *Australian*, 11 March, 1967, 26.
Curtis, Graeme. 'Some Aspects of Bruce Dawe's Poetry'. *Makar*, VI, No. 4, 1970, 4-10.
Dennett, Susan. 'A Conversation with Bruce Dawe'. *Idiom*, 23, No. 2, 1988, 11-13.
Garner, Mark, and Newsome, Bernard. 'Hangmen and Associations: The Final Analysis'. *English in Australia*, No. 48, 1979, 18-28.
Goodwin, Ken. *Adjacent Worlds: A Literary Life of Bruce Dawe*. (Melbourne: Longman Cheshire, 1988). Reviewed by R. Fitzgerald, *Weekend Australian*, 26-27 November, 1989, Weekend 10.
Hainsworth, John. 'Bruce Dawe. "First Corinthians at the Crossroads". "A Victorian Hangman Tells his Love"'. In *Australian Poems in Perspective*, edited by P.K. Elkin (St Lucia: U.Q.P., 1978), 203-13.
---. 'Paradoxes of Bruce Dawe's Poetry'. *Southerly*, XXXVI, 1976, 186-93.
Hansen, I.V. *Bruce Dawe: The Man Down the Street: Some Study Material*. (Melbourne: Victorian Association for the Teaching of English, 1972).
Headon, David. 'Interview with Australian Poet, Bruce Dawe'. *Northern Perspective* (Darwin), VII, No. 2, 1985, 34-37.
Hetherington, John. 'Bruce Dawe, Poet'. *Age*, 11 March, 1967, 24.
Jackson, Neil. 'Impressions of Bruce Dawe: May 1978'. *Opinion*, VIII, No. 2, 1979, 28-29.

Josephi, Beate. 'Suburbia'. *Advertiser*, 1 April, 1980, 25.

Kavanagh, Paul and Peter Kuch. 'The Fire i' the Flint'. *Southerly*, XLIII, 1983, 3-19.

Interview. Reprinted in their *Conversations: Interviews with Australian Writers* (North Ryde, NSW: Collins/A.& R, 1991), 28-51.

Kuch, Peter. *Bruce Dawe*. (Melbourne: O.U.P., 1995).

Law, Pamela. 'Raining down Meaning: The Poetry of Bruce Dawe'. *Southerly*, XXXIX, 1979, 192-203.

Lee, Chris. 'Speaking for the People: Bruce Dawe and the Role of the Poet in Australian Culture'. *Bulletin of Otemon Gakuin University English Literature Association*, 4, 1995, 69-76.

Macleod, Mark. 'Bruce Dawe and the Americans'. *A.L.S.*, IX, 1979, 143-55.

---. 'Bruce Dawe and Frank Sargeson: Speaking in Other Voices'. *A.L.S.*, XI, 1983, 3-13.

---. '"We had not Heard Ourselves so Accurately Before"'. *S.M.H.*, 22 November, 1980, 20.

Martin, Philip. 'In the Matter of Law v. Dawe: Case for the Defence'. *Southerly*, XXXIX, 1979, 355-63.

---. 'Public Yet Personal: Bruce Dawe's Poetry'. *Meanjin*, XXV, 1966, 290-4.

McGregor, Craig (ed.). *In the Making*. (Melbourne: Nelson Australia, 1969), 30-37. Includes a fairly long autobiographical statement by Dawe. Abridged reprint 'Creators: The Australian Influence', in *Walkabout*, XXXVI, No. 12. 1970, 41-48.

---. 'Australia's Most Popular Poet'. *National Times*, 29 August-4 September, 1982, 19 & 21.

Mishra, Vijay. 'The Formulaic Text: The Poetry of Bruce Dawe'. *English in Australia*, No. 82, 1987, 37-46.

O'Connor, Terry. 'No Frills for Australia's Poetry Salesman'. *Courier-Mail*, 25 November, 1980, 5.

Page, Geoff. 'Bruce Dawe'. In his *A Reader's Guide To Contemporary Australian Poetry* (St. Lucia: U.Q.P., 1995), 48-52.

Rowe, Noel. *Modern Australian Poets*. (Sydney: Sydney UP in assoc. with O.U.P., 1994). Includes discussion of the poetry of Dawe.

---. 'Reticent Desire: The Poetry of Bruce Dawe'. *Outrider*, 9.1, 1992, 83-97.

Rowlands, Graham. 'Sometimes Gladness: Bruce Dawe's Poetry'. *Overland*, No. 92, 1983, 9-14.

Sayers, Stuart. 'Poet's Progress from Llewellyn Rhys to Bruce Dawe'. *Age*, 22 November, 1980, 29. For other comment on the Patrick White award see *Courier-Mail*, 22 November, 1980, 18, *S.M.H.*, 22 November, 1980, 2, *Weekend Australian*, 22-23 November, 1980, 2.

Shaw, Basil John. *Times and Seasons: An Introduction to Bruce Dawe*. Illustrations by Brian Dean (Melbourne: Cheshire, 1974). Reviewed by S.E. Lee, *Southerly*, XXXV, 1975, 312.

Smith, Graeme Kinross. 'The Singer of Concerns'. *Overland*, No. 108, 1987, 38-48.

Spurr, Barry. *The Poetry of Bruce Dawe*. (Glebe, NSW: Pascal Press, 1995).

Steele, Peter. 'Haunting Presences: Four Gestures of the Imagination'. *Quadrant*, 37.3, 1993, 47-54. Discusses 'A Week's Grace'.

Talty, Jack. 'Bruce Dawe. *Sometimes Gladness*'. *Courier-Mail*, 23 October, 1984, 15.

Wallace-Crabbe, Chris. 'Bruce Dawe's Inventiveness'. *Meanjin*, XXXV, 1976, 94-101.

Wallis, John. 'Bruce Dawe: Poetry and Politics'. *Checkpoint* (Melbourne), No. 6, 1970, 12-15.

Wright, John M. 'Bruce Dawe's Poetry'. *Westerly*, No. 1, 1974, 36-44.

Yeabsley, C. D. 'Interview with Bruce Dawe'. *Westerly*, 35, No. 1, 1990, 73-76.

DE BOISSIERE, RALPH

Fiction
Crown Jewel. (London: Allison & Busby, Picador, 1981). First published Melbourne: Australasian Book Society, 1952.
Reviewed by L. James, *Journal of Commonwealth Literature*, XVII, No. 1, 1982, 13-15; T. Krause, *Weekend Australian Magazine*, 8-9 August, 1981, 16; J. Mellors, *Listener*, CV, 1981, 787; C. Moorehead, *Spectator*, 18 July, 1981, 21-22.

Non-Fiction
'On Writing a Novel'. *Journal of Commonwealth Literature*, XVII, No. 1, 1982, 1-12.

Critical Material
Birbalsingh, F.M. 'The Novels of Ralph De Boissiere'. *Journal of Commonwealth Literature*, No. 9, 1970, 104-08.
Gardiner, Allan. 'Comrades in Words: Ralph de Boissiere Interviewed by Allan Gardiner', *Kunapipi*, 15.1, 1993, 33-41.
Nelson, Penelope. 'Ralph de Boissiere: A Novelist of Two Hemispheres'. *Margin*, 25, 1991, 4-6.
Ramchand, Ken. 'Interview with Ralph de Boissiere: Back to *Kangaroos*'. *CRNLE Reviews Journal*, 1, 1993, 7-32.
Sayers, Stuart. 'Better Late than Never'. *Age*, 8 August, 1981, 26. Reprint of *Crown Jewel*.

DE BOOS, CHARLES

Fiction
Mark Brown's Wife: A Tale of the Gold-fields. Introduction by Victor Crittenden. Australian Books on Demand 4. (Canberra: Mulini Press, 1992). Originally published in *Sydney Mail*, 1871.
Reviewed by L. Clancy, *Weekend Australian* 20-21 March, 1993, Review 6.

Critical Material
Hamer, Clive. 'The Surrender to Truth in the Early Australian Novel'. *A.L.S.*, II, No. 2, 1965, 103-16.
Healy, J.J. 'The Treatment of the Aborigine in Early Australian Fiction, 1840-70'. *A.L.S.*, V, 1972, 233-53.

DE GROEN, ALMA

Drama
The Girl Who Saw Everything. (Sydney: Currency Press, 1993).
Reviewed by E. Perkins, *Australasian Drama Studies* 24, 1994, 197-200.

Going Home and Other Plays. (Sydney: Currency Press, 1977). Includes 'The Joss Adams Show' and 'Perfectly All Right'.
Reviewed by H. Van Der Poorten, *Theatre Australia*, II, No. 3, 1977, 62.

The Rivers of China. (Sydney: Currency Press, 1988). Reviewed by M. Lord, *Australian Society*, VII, No. 10, 1988, 49-51.
Vocations. Going Home. (Paddington, N.S.W.: Currency Press, 1984).
Reviewed by C. Hunt, *English in Australia*, No. 69, 1984, 47-48; T. Thompson, *National Times*, 9-15 March, 1984, 34

Critical Material
Gilbert, Helen. 'The Catherine Wheel: Travel, Exile and the (Post) Colonial Woman'. *Southerly*, 53.2, 1993, 58-77. Discusses *The Rivers of China*.
---. '"Walking Around in Other Times": An Interview with Alma De Groen'. *Australasian Drama Studies*, Nos. 15-16, 1989/1990, 11-20.
Hall, Jeni-Rose. 'Language as an Instrument of Transformation in de Groen's *The*

Rivers of China'. LiNQ 20.1, 1993, 26-35.
Perkins, Elizabeth. 'Alma De Groen: An Interview'. *LiNQ*, XIV, No. 3, 1986, 7-14.
---. 'Form and Transformation in the Plays of Alma De Groen'. *Australasian Drama Studies*, No. 11, 1987, 5-21.
---. *The Plays of Alma De Groen*. (Amsterdam; Atlanta, GA: Rodopi, 1994). Reviewed by J. Tompkins, *SPAN*, 40, 1995, 111-13.
Pickett, Carolyn. 'Reality, Realism and a Place to Write in Alma de Groen's *Vocations'. Australasian Drama Studies*, 22, 1993, 63-72.
Wearne, Heather M. 'Discourses of Disruption and Alma de Groen's *The Rivers of China'. Australasian Drama Studies*, 21, 1992, 61-73.

DEMIDENKO, HELEN

see Darville [Demidenko], Helen.

DENIEHY, DANIEL

Critical Material

Glass, F. Devlin. 'Daniel Deniehy: A Checklist of Writings and Speeches'. *A.L.S.*, IX, 1980, 388-98.
Glass, F. Devlin. '"Botany Bay Litterateur": D.H. Deniehy's Literary Criticism'. *A.L.S.*, IX, 1979, 214-24.
---. 'D.H. Deniehy as a Critic of Colonial Literature'. *A.L.S.*, IX, 1980, 328-36.
---. '"Two and a Half Tons of Books": Daniel Henry Deniehy's Library'. *Australian Academic and Research Libraries*, VII, No. 1, 1976, 37-52.
Jordens, Ann-Mari. *The Stenhouse Circle: Literary Life in Mid-Nineteenth Century Sydney*. (Carlton: M.U.P., 1979).
Pearl, Cyril. *Brilliant Dan Deniehy: A Forgotten Genius*. (Melbourne: Nelson (Australia), 1972). Reviewed by R.T. Foster, *Sun-Herald*, 19 November, 1972, 69; P.P. McGuinness, *S.M.H.*, 2 December, 1972, 29; J. Waten, *Age*, 16 December, 1972, 13.

DENNIS, C.J.

Collection

The C.J. Dennis Collection: From His 'Forgotten' Writings; edited by Garrie Hutchinson. (Melbourne: Lothian, 1987).
Reviewed by R. Lucas, *S.M.H.*, 3 September, 1988, 81; B. Millington, *Age Saturday Extra*, 27 August, 1988, 14.

Poetry

The Glugs of Gosh. (Sydney: A.& R., 1975, reprinted 1980). First published Sydney: A.& R., 1917.
Reviewed by R. Elliott, *Canberra Times*, 15 November, 1980, 17; K. Goodwin, *Weekend Australian Magazine*, 12-13 July, 1980, 16; W. McVitty, *Nation Review*, 21-27 March, 1975, 614.
The Sentimental Bloke. First published North Ryde, N.S.W.: A.& R., 1915. Film version discussed in *Newsletter (National Film and Sound Archives)*, No. 7, 1987, 5.
The Sentimental Bloke. Book by Nancy Brown and Lloyd Thomson, lyrics by Nancy Brown, Albert Arlen, Lloyd Thomson and C.J. Dennis, music by Albert Arlen. First published Sydney: A.& R., 1977.

Critical Material

McLaren, Ian. *C.J. Dennis: A Comprehensive Bibliography*. (Adelaide: Libraries Board of South Australia, 1979). Reviewed by J. Arnold, *Age*, 30 June, 1979, 29; B. Elliott, *Advertiser*, 19 May, 1979, 21. See also '30-year Study of C.J. Dennis'. *Advertiser*, 20 April, 1979, 13.
---. *C.J. Dennis: A Chronological Checklist of his Contributions to Journals*

(Adelaide: Libraries Board of South Australia, 1976). Reviewed by A. Lawson, *A.L.S.*, VIII, 1978, 382-87.

---. *C.J. Dennis in the Herald and Weekly Times*. (East Malvern, Vic.: Dalriada Press, 1981). Reviewed by D.J. Jones, *Incite*, II, No. 13, 1981, 3.

'C.J. Dennis Centenary'. *Philatelic Bulletin* (Australia Post) XXIV, No. 3, 1977, 66-69.

'Cover Story: "The Sentimental Bloke" to Talk with an Oxford Bleat!' *Notes & Furphies*, No. 13, 1984, 5-6. Proposed film; includes a para by Kenneth Slessor. Reprinted from *Smith's Weekly*, 30 May, 1981.

Borchardt, D.H. 'C.J. Dennis and his Work; A Review of Ian McLaren's Bibliographies'. *Australian Academic & Research Libraries*, XII, 1981, 204-06.

Channell, Ian. 'An Australian Masterpiece'. *Quadrant*, IX, No. 4, 1965, 50-2. Discusses Raymond Longford's film, *The Sentimental Bloke* (1918).

Chisholm, Alec J. *C.J. Dennis, his Remarkable Career*. (Sydney: A.& R., 1976). Arkon. Reprint of *The Making of a Sentimental Bloke*, published by Georgian House, 1946.

Chisholm, Alec. *The Life and Times of C.J. Dennis*. (Sydney: A.& R., 1982). Reviewed by G. Hutton, *Age Saturday Extra*, 24 December, 1982, 7.

Dermody, Susan. 'Two Remakes: Ideologies of Film Production 1919-1932'. In *Nellie Melba: Ginger Meggs and Friends: Essays in Australian Cultural History*, edited by Susan Dermody, John Docker and Drusilla Modjeska (Malmsbury, Vic: Kibble Books, 1982), 33-59.

Dutton, Geoffrey. 'Gentlemen vs. Lairs'. *Quadrant*, IX, No. 1, 1965, 14-20.

Elliott, Brian. 'C.J. Dennis and the Sentimental Bloke'. *Southerly*, XXXVII, 1977, 243-65.

Green, O.S. 'C.J. Dennis; People's Poet'. *Educational Magazine*, XXXIII, No. 4, 1977, 41-45.

Herron, S.G. 'C.J. Dennis'. *Anapress* (Melbourne), No. 2, 1964, 12-13.

Hetherington, John. 'A Sentimental Bloke Named Hal Gye'. *Age*, 24 September, 1966, 22. Discusses Dennis' illustrator.

Hutchinson, Garrie. 'Happy Birthday, Den'. *Age*, 4 September, 1984, 23.

Inglis, K.S. 'The Anzac Tradition'. *Meanjin*, XXIV, 1965, 25-54.

Keesing, Nancy. '"The Bloke's" American Cousins'. *S.M.H.*, 12 June, 1976, 14.

'Lee, Mariel' (Mary L. Lane). 'Creator of *The Sentimental Bloke*: C.J. Dennis'. *Expression*, X, No. 4, 1971, 33-38.

Lindsay, Elaine. 'The Bloke and His Mates'. *Australian*, 22 January, 1977, 19.

Macdougall, Jim. 'In the City of Doreens'. *Quadrant*, XX, No. 11, 1976, 60-61.

McLaren, Ian. 'C.J. Dennis and the Roberts Family'. *Biblionews and Australian Notes & Queries*, IV, Nos. 3-4, 1970, 15-17.

McQueen, Humphrey. '"We are not Safe, Clarence; We are not Safe": Sentimental Thoughts on "A Moody Bloke"'. *Meanjin*, XXXVI, 1977, 343-53. Republished as 'Sentimental Thoughts of "A Moody Bloke": C.J. Dennis', in his *Gallipoli to Petrov*. (Sydney: Allen & Unwin, 1984), 23-24.

Moffitt, Ian. 'Laureate of the Larrikin'. *Australian*, 9 August, 1975, 25.

Porteous, Alexander. '*The Sentimental Bloke* and his Critics'. *A.L.S.*, I, No.4, 1964, 260-73.

Reines, Rosalind. 'The Sentimental Bloke Returns to the Stage'. *S.M.H.*, 26 March, 1983, 40.

Sayers, Stuart. 'The Idylls of Toolangi'. *Age*, 10 April, 1971. Biographical article, with some previously unpublished poems. The same article, with the poem 'The Corpse That Won't Lie Still' abridged, appeared as 'Play Days of a Sentimental Bloke'. *S.M.H.*, 10 April, 1971, 14.

Watts, Barry (ed.). *The World of the Sentimental Bloke*. (Sydney: A.& R., 1976). Reviewed by I. McLaren, *Age*, 18 December, 1976, 19; H. McQueen, *Nation*

Review, 3-9 February, 1977, 381; S. Shayle, *24 Hours*, II, No. 3, 1977, 56.
Watts, Barry. 'The Blanky Australaise'. *Age*, 28 August, 1976, 17.

DEVANEY, JAMES
Critical Material
Taylor, Cheryl and Smith, Ross. 'James Martin Devaney (1890-1976) (Pseudonym Fabian): A Bibliography'. *LiNQ*, XII, Nos. 1-3, 1984, 83-109.
'Well Known Writer Dies, 86'. *Sunday Mail* (Brisbane), 15 August, 1976, 3; see also *S.M.H.*, 17 August, 1976, 13.
Hadgraft, Cecil. 'A Tribute to James Devaney'. *Meanjin*, XXIV, 1965, 215-21.
Rowbotham, David. 'Modest Author Will be 80'. *Courier-Mail*, 3 April, 1970, 9.

DEVANNY, JEAN
Fiction
The Butcher Shop. Introduced by Heather Roberts (Auckland: Auckland University Press; London: O.U.P., 1982). First published London: Duckworth, 1926.
Reviewed by K. Cochrane, *CRNLE Reviews Journal*, No. 2, 1983, 49-50; C. Ferrier, *Hecate*, IX, 1983, 160-66; A. MacDonald, *Weekend Australian Magazine*, 5-6 June, 1982, 11; J.D. McLaren, *ABR*, No. 43, 1982, 31.
Cindie: A Chronicle of the Canefields. (London: Virago Press, 1986).First published London: Robert Hale, 1949.
Reviewed by V. Brady, *Australian Society*, VI, No. 6, 1987, 43-45 and *Womanspeak*, No. 4, 1987, 28.
Paradise Flow. Edited and introduced by Carole Ferrier (St Lucia: Hecate Press, 1985).
Reviewed by D. Carter, *Age Saturday Extra*, 23 August, 1986, 12; K. H., *Womanspeak*, X, No. 2, 1986, 26; C. Taylor, *LiNQ*, XV, No. 2, 1987, 94-95.
Sugar Heaven. With an introduction by Carole Ferrier (Melbourne: Redback Press, 1982). First published Sydney: Modern Publishers, 1936.
Reviewed by H. Daniel, *Age Saturday Extra*, 20 November, 1982, 13; C. Ferrier, *Hecate*, XI, No. 1, 1985, 19-25; J. Stone, *Chain Reaction*, No. 31, 1983, 35-36.
Non-Fiction
As Good as a Yarn with You: Letters between Miles Franklin, Katharine Susannah Prichard, Jean Devanny, Marjorie Barnard, Flora Eldershaw and Eleanor Dark. Edited by Carole Ferrier. (Cambridge: Cambridge UP, 1992). For reviews see Barnard, Marjorie.
Point of Departure: The Autobiography of Jean Devanny. Edited by Carole Ferrier. (St Lucia: U.Q.P., 1986).
Reviewed by E. Harrison, *Socialist Action*, No. 15, 1986, 19; R. Pascoe, *Weekend Australian. Weekend Magazine*, 31 January-1 February, 1987, 15; J. Roe, *A.L.S.*, XIII, No. 2, 1987, 242-245; S. Roff, *Antipodes*, II, No. 1, 1988, 72; H. Rowley, *Age Saturday Extra*, 17 January, 1987, 13; E. Ryan, *Australian Feminist Studies*, 4, 1987, 189-93; J. Sendy, *Overland*, No. 107, 1987, 77-80; C. Taylor, *LiNQ*, XV, No. 2, 1987, 91-93; J. Walter, *ABR*, No. 89, 1987, 20-21; J. Wells, *Hecate*, XIII, No. 1, 1987, 129-131.
Critical Material
Ferrier, Carole. 'Jean Devanny: A Bibliography'. *Hecate*, XIII, No. 1, 1987, 138-171.
Brown, Kay. 'Kay Brown Remembers Jean Devanny'. *Hecate*, XIII, No. 1, 1987, 132-137.
Capp, Fiona. *Writers Defiled: Security Surveillance of Australian Authors and Intellectuals 1920-1960*. (Ringwood, Vic.: McPhee Gribble, 1993). Includes

discussion of Jean Devanny.

da Rimini, Francesca and Pierce, Julianne. 'Creating Feeling'. *Artlink*, VIII, No. 4, 1987, 38. Discusses film of *Point of Departure*.

Ferres, Kay. 'Written on the Body: Jean Devanny, Sexuality and Censorship'. *Hecate*, 20.1, 1993, 123-34.

Ferrier, Carole. 'Women of Letters and the Uses of Memory'. In *Wallflowers and Witches: Women and Culture in Australia 1910-1945*, edited by Maryanne Dever (St Lucia: U.Q.P., 1994), 73-90.

---. 'Constructing and Deconstructing Jean Devanny'. In *Writing Lives: Feminist Biography and Autobiography*, edited by Susan Magarey, Caroline Guerin, and Paula Hamilton (Adelaide: Australian Feminist Studies, Research Centre for Women's Studies U of Adelaide, 1992/*Australian Feminist Studies* 16, 1992, special issue), 145-57.

---. 'Jean Devanny, Katharine Susannah Prichard, and the "Really Proletarian Novel"'. In *Gender, Politics and Fiction: Twentieth Century Women's Novels*, edited by Carole Ferrier (St Lucia: U.Q.P., 1985), 101-17.

---. 'Jean Devanny's New Zealand Novels'. *Hecate*, VI, No. 1, 1980, 37-47.

---. 'Jean Devanny's Queensland Novels'. *LiNQ*, VIII, No. 3, 1980, 20-30.

---. 'Politics & Sexuality'. *Sixty Years of Struggle*, No. 2, 1981, 27-32. Biographical.

---. 'Re-Presenting Jean Devanny'. *Hecate*, XIII, No. 2, 1988, 145-148.

---. '*Sugar Heaven* and the Reception of Working Class Texts'. *Hecate*, XI, No. 1, 1985, 19-25.

Klaus, H. Gustav. 'Devanny in Germany'. *Hecate*, XIV, No. 2, 1988, 73-78.

Levy, Bronwen. Letter to the editor. *ABR* No. 95, 1987, 36-37.

Store, Ronald E. and Anderson, Richard. 'Jean Devanny: A Biographical and Bibliographical Note'. *Australian Academic and Research Libraries*, I, 1970, 66-72.

Tóth, Agnes. 'A Bush Cinderella: *Cindy* by Jean Devanny'. *Hungarian Studies in English*, 22, 1992, 113-17.

DICKENS, CHARLES

Critical Material

Lansbury, Coral. 'Charles Dickens and his Australia'. *Journal of the Royal Australian Historical Society*, LII, 1966, 115-28. Discusses the reception of Dickens' novels in Australia, their serialization in Australian journals, Australian productions of his plays, and his treatment of Australia in his novels.

DIESENDORF, MARGARET

Poetry

Holding the Golden Apple. (Brisbane: Phoenix Publications, 1991).

Reviewed by H. Cam, *S.M.H.*, 21 September, 1991, 42; J. Davies, *Southerly*, 53.1, 1993, 202-10; C. Gaffney, *Northern Perspective*, 15.2, 98-99; S. Gardner, *Imago*, 4.3, 1992, 92-93; B. Giles, *Age*, 14 December, 1991, Saturday Extra 7 and *Redoubt*, 13, 1992, 81-85; A. Nugent, *Blast*, 17, 1991, 44-45; E. Perkins, *SPAN*, 32, 1991, 164-69 and *LiNQ*, 18.2, 1991, 164-69.

Light. (Sydney: Edwards & Shaw, 1981).

Reviewed by S. Amanuddin, *World Literature Today*, 56, 1982, 402; J. Blight, *Outrider*, 1.2, 1984, 230-31; M. Duwell, *Australian*, 31 July-1 August, 1982, 10; G. Harwood, *Luna*, 14, 1982, 32-35; A. Kefala, *Aspect*, 25, 1982, 73-78; P. Kerr, *ABR*, 47, 1982/83, 40; G. Page, *Quadrant*, 26.8, 1982, 75-77.

Critical Material

Munro, P. 'Obituary'. *ABR*, 152, 1993, 58-59.

Perkins, Elizabeth. 'Gender and Identity in the Poetry of Margaret Diesendorf and Dorothy Auchterlonie'. In *Poetry and Gender*, edited by David Brooks and Brenda

Walker (St Lucia: U.Q.P., 1989), 129-44.
Tonetto, Walter. 'Margaret Diesendorf: Lyric Possibilities from Another Age'. *Outrider*, 90, 1990, 250-57.

DOBSON, ROSEMARY

Fiction
Summer Press. (St Lucia: U.Q.P., 1987).
Reviewed by L. Hanrahan, *Times on Sunday*, 8 November, 1987, 32; A. Nieuwenhuizen, *Age Saturday Extra*, 10 October, 1987, 14.

Poetry
Cock Crow. (Sydney: A.& R., 1965).
Reviewed by G. Cross, *S.M.H.*, 27 November, 1965, 20; R. Dunlop, *Poetry Australia*, No. 7, 1964, 39-45; B. Elliott, *ABR*, IV, 1965, 232; R. D. FitzGerald, *Southerly*, XXVI, 1966, 132-7; F. Haynes, *Westerly*, No. 3, 1966, 90-4; L. Kramer, *Poetry Magazine*, No. 2, 1968, 3-7; J. McAuley, *Twentieth Century*, XX, 1965, 185-6; B. Nesbitt, *Australian*, 20 November, 1965, 11; V. Smith, *Bulletin*, 25 September, 1965, 53-4; A. Taylor, *Overland*, No. 35, 1966, 55.

Collected Poems. (North Ryde, NSW: A.& R., 1991)
Reviewed by B. Giles, *Redoubt*, 13, 1992, 81-85; D. Fahey, *ABR*, 135, 1991,-37-38; V. Muller, *Imago*, 4.2, 1992, 100-01; J. Owen, *Quadrant*, 35.12, 1991, 86-88; W. Senn, *Westerly*, 37.1, 1992, 93-94.

Greek Coins: A Sequence of Poems. (Canberra: Brindabella Press, 1977).
Reviewed by H. Frizell, *S.M.H.*, 21 January, 1978, 19; R.A. Simpson, *Age*, 11 February, 1978, 23.

L'Enfant au Cacatoes. Trad. par Louis Dautheuil et Margaret Diesendorf. (Paris: Seghers, 1967). Collection Autour du Monde, 94. Translated principally from *Child with a Cockatoo* (1955), but also including poems from *The Ship of Ice* (1948) and *In a Convex Mirror* (1944).
Reviewed by B.A. Breen, *Twentieth Century*, XXV, 1971, 279-80; M. Denat, *ABR*, VII, 1968, 89.

Over the Frontier. (Sydney: A.& R., 1978).
Reviewed by A. Gould, *Nation Review*, 14-18 July, 1978, 19; R. Hall, *Weekend Australian Magazine*, 4-5 March, 1978, 8; E. Lindsay, *24 Hours*, III, No. 7, 1978, 64; N. Macainsh, *ABR*, No. 4, 1978, 9-10; J. Rodriguez, *S.M.H.*, 8 July, 1978, 19; T. Shapcott, *Age*, 1 July, 1978, 23.

Rosemary Dobson Reads from Her Own Work. (St Lucia: U.Q.P., 1970). Poets on Record, 2. Record and booklet. Booklet includes notes by Rosemary Dobson and selected bibliography.
Reviewed by M. Duwell, *Makar*, VII, No. 1, 1971, 43-45; S.E. Lee, *Southerly*, XXXI, 1971, 238-39; A C. Lyons, *Twentieth Century*, XXVI, 1971, 181-83; G. Page, *Canberra Times*, 27 March, 1971, 15; J.D. Pringle, *S.M.H.*, 3 April, 1971, 24; R.A. Simpson, *Age*, 27 February, 1971, 17; K. Slessor, *Daily Telegraph* (Sydney), 2 January, 1971, 10; J. Tulip, *Bulletin*, 6 March, 1971, 46.

Rosemary Dobson. With an introduction by the author. (Sydney: A.& R., 1963). Australian Poets series.

Selected Poems. (Sydney: A.& R., 1980).
Reviewed by B. Giles, *ABR*, No. 20, 1980, 15; E.L. Mash, *Westerly*, XXV, No. 3, 1980, 103-06.

The Three Fates and Other Poems. (Sydney: Hale & Iremonger, 1984).
Reviewed by B. Beaver, *Weekend Australian Magazine*, 15-16 September, 1984, 15; P. Carter, *Meanjin*, XLIV, No. 1, 1985, 48-58; T. Harrington, *Mattoid*, XXXVI,

No. 3, 1986, 86-89; E. Lawson, *Phoenix Review*, No. 1, 1986/1987, 119-121; P. Martin, *ABR*, No. 66, 1984, 14-15; S. McKernan, *Canberra Times*, 29 December, 1984, 12; R. Morse, *PN Review*, XII, No. 3, 1985, 64-65; G. Page, *Quadrant*, XXIX, No. 4, 1985, 71-75; M. Richards, *Island Magazine*, No. 22, 1985, 53-55; E. Riddell, *Overland*, No. 98, 1985, 53-55; J. Rodriguez, *S.M.H.*, 22 September, 1984, 44; J. Tulip, *Southerly*, XLV, No. 1, 1985, 45-53.

Non-Fiction

Focus on Ray Crooke. (St Lucia: U.Q.P., 1971). Artists in Queensland.

'Australian Poets in Profile: 2'. *Southerly*, XL, 1980, 3-10.

'Imitations and Versions of Russian Poetry: The Record of an Experiment'. *A.L.S.*, XI, 1983, 94-99. Discusses *Moscow Trefoil: Seven Russian Poets*.

'Over My Shoulder'. *Island Magazine*, 39, 1989, 55-59. Paper presented at the Salamanca Writers Weekend on the theme of 'The Uses of the Past'.

'Poetry and Painting: A Personal View'. *Quadrant*, XXI, No. 11, 1977, 68-72.

'A World of Difference: Australian Poetry and Painting in the 1940s'. *Southerly*, XXXIII, 1973, 365-83. Partly autobiographical.

Critical Material

Ayres, Marie-Louise. '"The Folds of Unseen Linen": The Fabric of Rosemary Dobson's Poetry'. *A.L.S.*, 17.1, 1995, 3-9.

Brady, Veronica. 'Over the Frontier: The Poetry of Rosemary Dobson'. In *Poetry and Gender: Statements and Essays in Australian Women's Poetry and Poetics*, edited by David Brooks and Brenda Walker (St. Lucia: U.Q.P., 1989), 105-127.

Burrows, J.F. 'Rosemary Dobson's Sense of the Past'. *Southerly*, XXX, 163-76.

Catalano, Gary. 'The Figure in the Doorway: On the Poetry of Rosemary Dobson'. *Quadrant*, 37.10, 1993, 28-32.

Dunlevy, Maurice. 'A Poet Divided in Purpose'. *Canberra Times*, 4 March, 1972, 10.

Giles, Barbara. 'Austerity and Light: A Tribute to Rosemary Dobson'. *Southerly*, 52.3, 1992, 41-44.

Glasgow, Liz. 'Patrick White Prize to Dobson'. *Weekend Australian*, 17-18 November, 1984, 21. Prize also reported in *S.M.H.*, 17 November, 1984, 40.

Heales, Robyn S. 'Art Builds on Art: Rosemary Dobson and Thea Proctor'. *A.L.S.*, VII, 1975, 64-71.

Hope, A.D. 'Rosemary Dobson: A Portrait in a Mirror'. *Quadrant*, XIV, No. 4, 1972, 10-14.

Kavanagh, Paul and Peter Kuch. 'Precisions, Discriminations and Humilities'. *Southerly*, XLIII, 1983, 363-76. Interview. Reprinted in their *Conversations: Interviews with Australian Writers*. (North Ryde, NSW: Collins/A.& R, 1991), 52-72.

Kobulniczky, Susan. 'Profile of Rosemary Dobson'. *Artlook*, III, No. 3, 1977, 30.

Lee, Stuart. 'Rosemary Dobson'. *Quadrant*, IX, No. 4, 1965, 56-62.

Malouf, David. 'Some Volumes of Selected Poems of the 1970's'. *A.L.S.*, X, 1981, 13-21.

McAuley, James. 'The Poetry of Rosemary Dobson'. *A.L.S.*, VI, 1973, 3-10.

McCooey, David. 'Looking into the Landscape: The Elegiac Art of Rosemary Dobson'. *Westerly*, 40.2, 1995, 15-25.

Mitchell, Adrian. 'A Frame of Reference: Rosemary Dobson's Grace Notes for Humanity'. *A.L.S.*, X, 1981, 3-12.

Page, Geoff. 'Rosemary Dobson'. In his *A Reader's Guide To Contemporary Australian Poetry* (St. Lucia: U.Q.P., 1995), 55-57.

Reid, Owen. 'Rosemary Dobson'. *Tasmanian Education*, XVI, 1964, 129-32.

Rowe, Noel. *Modern Australian Poets*. (Sydney: Sydney UP in association with O.U.P., 1994). Includes discussion of the poetry of Dobson.

Sayers, Stuart. 'Poet Ponders until the Time Is Ripe'. *Age Saturday Extra*, 8 September, 1984, 18. Interview.

Senn, Werner. 'Speaking the Silence: Contemporary Poems on Paintings'. *Word and Image*, 5, No. 2, 1989, 181-97.
Smith, Graeme Kinross. 'The Intricate, Devised Hearing of Sight: A Profile of Rosemary Dobson'. *Westerly*, No. 3, 1974, 55-63.
Strauss, Jennifer. 'The Poetry of Dobson, Harwood & Wright: "within the bounds of feminine sensibility?"'. *Meanjin*, XXXVIII, 1979, 334-49. Republished in *Still the Frame Holds: Essays on Women Poets and Writers*, edited by Sheila Roberts and Yvonne Pacheco Tevis (San Bernadino, CA: Borgo Press, 1993), 79-99.
Thompson, John. 'Poetry in Australia: Rosemary Dobson'. *Southerly*, XXVIII, 203-14. Transcript of an interview telecast in 1965.
Westcott, Pat. 'An Angel Tips Her Halo: Rosemary Dobson's Place Among our Poets'. *Bulletin*, 11 January, 1964, 16-17.

DRAKE-BROCKMAN, HENRIETTA
Critical Material
Barnes, John. 'Henrietta Drake-Brockman'. *Westerly*, No. 2, 1968, 71.
Durack, Mary. 'Henrietta as I Knew Her'. *Overland*, No. 39, 1968, 46-47.
Ewers, John K. 'Henrietta - and the Fellowship of Australian Writers'. *Westerly*, No. 2, 1968, 75-78.
Hasluck, Alexandra. 'Henrietta Drake-Brockman'. *Meanjin*, XXVII, 1968, 233-37. Reprinted with some revisions in her *Of Ladies Dead: Stories not in the Modern Manner.* (Sydney: A.& R., 1970), 139-44.
---. 'Henrietta as Historian'. *Westerly*, No. 2, 1968, 72-74.

DRANSFIELD, MICHAEL
Poetry
Drug Poems. (Melbourne: Sun Books, 1972).
Reviewed by D. Anderson, *Bulletin*, 25 March, 1972, 49; O. Briansmith, *Segment*, 1, 1972, 59-60; M. Dugan, *Age*, 1 April, 1972, 12; C. Harrison-Ford, *Nation*, 13 May, 1972, 21-22; I. McKay, *Makar*, 8.1, 1972, 30-32; P. Roberts, *S.M.H.*, 20 May, 1972, 12; R.A. Simpson, *Age*, 9 September, 1972, 15; A. Taylor, *Advertiser*, 11 March, 1972, 20.

The Inspector of Tides. (St Lucia: U.Q.P., 1972). Paperback Poets, 8.
Reviewed by K. England, *Advertiser*, 22 July, 1972, 18; C. Harrison-Ford, *Nation*, 13 May, 1972, 21-22; M. Johnston, *Sunday Telegraph*, 25 June, 1972; F.G. Kellaway, *Overland*, 53, 1972, 62; S.E. Lee, *Southerly*, XXXII, 1972, 302-3; 308-10; A.C. Lyons, *Twentieth Century*, 27, 1972, 91-92; I. McKay, *Makar*, 8.1, 1972, 30-32; D. Malouf, *Australian*, 12 August, 1972, 17; P. Roberts, *S.M.H.*, 20 May, 1972, 12; T. Shapcott, *ABR*, 11, 1972, 249; *T.L.S.*, 12 October, 1973, 1216; J. Tulip, *Bulletin*, 1 July, 1972, 49.

Memoirs of a Velvet Urinal. (Adelaide: Maximus Books, 1975).
Reviewed by M. Dunlevy, *Canberra Times*, 30 May, 1975, 10; K.L. Goodwin, *Makar*, XI, No. 2, 1975, 51-52; S. E. Lee, *Southerly*, 36.3, 1976, 331-59.

Michael Dransfield: Collected Poems. Edited by Rodney Hall. (St Lucia: U.Q.P., 1987).
Reviewed by P.Dobrez, *Age Saturday Extra*, 17 October, 1987, 13; J. Forbes, *Scripsi*, V, No. 1, 1988, 215-221; K. Hart, *Overland*, No. 112, 1988, 86-87; D. Haskell, *Fremantle Arts Review*, III, No. 3, 1988, 14; M. Roberts, *Southerly*, XLVIII, No. 4, 1988, 481-486; J. Tranter, *Weekend Australian. Weekend Magazine*, 21-22 November, 1987, 16; V. Wright, *Weekend Australian. Weekend Magazine*, 31 October-1 November, 1987, 22.

The Second Month of Spring. Collected and edited by Rodney Hall. (St Lucia: U.Q.P., 1980).

Reviewed by G. Dutton, *Bulletin*, 6 May, 1980, 85-86; G. Rowlands, *Overland*, No. 82, 1980, 65-66.

Streets of the Long Voyage. (St Lucia: U.Q.P., 1970).
Reviewed by B.A. Breen, *Twentieth Century*, 25, 1971, 280-82; K. Goodwin, *Meanjin Quarterly*, 30, 1971, 367; D. Hewett, *Westerly*, 4, 1971, 55-59; F.G. Kellaway, *Overland*, 53, 1972, 62; S. Lawson, *Australian*, 23 May, 1970, 19; G. Page, *Canberra Times*, 16 May, 1970, 13; P. Roberts, *S.M.H.*, 1 August, 1970, 24; Graham Rowlands, *Makar*, VI, No. 1, 1970, 17-20; T. Shapcott, *ABR*, 9, 1970, 255-56, 277-79; R.A. Simpson, *Age*, 15 August, 1970, 17; J. Tulip, *Southerly*, 31, 1971, 76-77.

Voyage into Solitude. Collected and edited by Rodney Hall. (St Lucia: U.Q.P., 1978). Reviewed by G. Dutton, *Bulletin*, 26 June, 1979, 66; B. Pascoe, *ABR*, No. 12, 1979, 13-14; G. Rowlands, *Helix*, No. 4, 1979, 80-82; J. Tulip, *Age*, 1 September, 1979, 24.

Critical Material

'The Poet Who Dared to be Different'. *S.M.H.*, 10 May, 1973, 3.

Afterman, Allen. 'The Poetry of Michael Dransfield and Charles Buckmaster'. *Meanjin*, XXXII, 1973, 478-81.

Burton, Barry. 'The Poetry of Michael Dransfield'. *Adelaide A.L.S. Working Papers*, II, No. 1, 1976, 3-44.

Dobrez, Livio. 'Damages'. *Helix*, No. 16, 1983, 47-57.

---. *Parnassus Mad Ward: Michael Dransfield and the New Australian Poetry*. (St. Lucia: U.Q.P., 1990). Reviewed by A. Burke, *Westerly*, 36.2, 1991, 93-94; R. Darling, *Antipodes*, 5.1, 1991, 72; M. Duwell, *A.L.S.*, 15.1, 1991, 94-96; J. Grant, *Weekend Australian*, 19-20 January, 1991, Review 6; C. Keneally, *Overland*, 122, 1991, 86-88; E. Travers, *Scripsi*, 7.1, 1991, 293-300.

Dransfield, Frances. 'Death of a Poet'. *S.M.H.*, 25 June, 1973, 6. Letter to the editor.

Dutton, Geoffrey. 'Such a Drag It Is, Being Dead'. *Nation Review*, 11-17 May, 1973, 912.

Hewett, Dorothy. 'The Voyage out from Xanadu'. *New Poetry*, XXVII, No. 1, 1979, 4-11.

McCauley, Shane. 'Confessional Poetry'. *Artlook*, VI, No. 6, 1980, 55-56.

Mora, Mirka. 'Mirka Mora, Conversation with Rudi Krausmann'. *Aspect*, II, No. 2, 1976, 5-8.

Page, Geoff. 'Michael Dransfield'. In his *A Reader's Guide To Contemporary Australian Poetry* (St. Lucia: U.Q.P., 1995), 58-60.

---. 'Michael Dransfield. "Minstrel". "Portrait of the Artist as an Old Man". "Bums' Rush". "I Tell Myself I'm through with Love"'. In *Australian Poems in Perspective*, edited by P.K. Elkin (St Lucia: U.Q.P., 1978), 215-31.

---. 'Michael Dransfield: The Poetry not the Myth'. *Quadrant*, XXI, No. 4, 1977, 66-69.

Tonetto, Walter. 'Of Wings that Beat in the Ovoid of Memory'. In *Australian Writing Now*, edited by Robert Adamson and Manfred Jurgensen (Ringwood, Vic.: Penguin, 1988), 211-232. Review Article.

DREWE, ROBERT

Fiction

The Bay of Contented Men. (Sydney: Picador, 1989).
Reviewed by D. Anderson, *Age Monthly Review*, 10, No. 1, 1990, 3-6; M Anthony, *Westerly*, 35, No. 2, 1990, 84-86; H. Daniel, *S.M.H.*, 18 November, 1989, 89; K. England, *ABR*, No. 116, 1989, 14-15; T. Kelly, *Weekend Australian*, 9-10 December, 1989, Weekend 8; J. MacGregor, *Age Saturday Extra*, 30 December, 1989, 6; D.

Montrose, *T.L.S.*, 6 September, 1991, 21; P. Pierce, *Bulletin*, 9 January, 1990, 80-81.

The Bodysurfers. (Darlinghurst: James Fraser, 1983).
Reviewed by J. Bedford, *National Times*, 28 October-3 November, 1983, 28; L. Clancy, *ABR*, No. 57, 1983, 19-20; J. Crace, *T.L.S.*., 24 August, 1984, 935; K. England, *Advertiser*, 24 December, 1983, 25; A. Mitchell, *Weekend Australian Magazine*, 29-30 October, 1983, 14; C.K. Stead, *S.M.H.*, 17 December, 1983, 36; J. Webb, *Westerly*, XXIX, No. 2, 1984, 107-09.

A Cry in the Jungle Bar. (Sydney: Collins, 1979).
Reviewed by M. Anthony, *Westerly*, XXV, No. 1, 1980, 110-12; B. Beresford, *Quadrant*, XXIII, No. 12, 1979, 69-70; T. Bowden, *National Times*, 18 August, 1979, 51; V. Brady, *Westerly*, XXV, No. 2, 1980, 61-75; L. Clancy, *Overland*, No. 80, 1980, 52-53; M. Eldridge, *Canberra Times*, 27 September, 1980, 15; N. Jillett, *Age*, 11 August, 1979, 23; K. Lane, *24 Hours*, IV, No. 10, 1979, 70; P. McNamara, *Australian Weekend Magazine*, 18-19 August, 1979, 10; J. Miles, *Advertiser*, 11 August, 1979, 27; J. Modder, *Courier-Mail*, 11 August, 1979, 19; E. Riddell, *Bulletin*, 4 September, 1979, 80, 83; M. Smith, *ABR*, No. 19, 1980, 23-24; L. Strahan, *Helix*, Nos. 9 & 10 Supplement 'Fresh Flounder, 1981, 28-35; M. Williams, *S.M.H.*, 11 August, 1979, 17; D. Wilson, *T.L.S.*, 11 April, 1980, 416.

Fortune. (Sydney: Pan Books, 1986).
Reviewed by V. Brady, *Westerly*, XXXIII, No. 1, 1988, 86-89; B. Edwards, *Mattoid*, No. 28, 1987, 111-113; B. Hunter, *Courier-Mail: The Great Weekend*, 1 November, 1986, 6; R. Jones, *Age Saturday Extra*, 22 November, 1986, 12; S. McKernan, *Bulletin*, 6 January, 1987, 787-79; P. Pierce, *S.M.H.*, 8 November, 1986, 49; M. Thomas, *Canberra Times*, 13 December, 1986, B3; B. Walker, *Westerly*, XXXII, No. 2, 1987, 105-107; P. Wolfe, *Antipodes*, II, No. 1, 1988, 63.

Our Sunshine. (Sydney: Pan Macmillan/ Picador, 1991).
Reviewed by B. Edwards, *Mattoid*, 41, 1991, 162-65; K. Goldsworthy, *Editions*, 13, 1992, 10-11; T. Lane, *ABR*, 137, 1991, 15; P. Pierce, *Bulletin*, 26 November, 1991, 116; A.P. Riemer, *S.M.H.*, 23 November, 1991, 48; T. Shapcott, *Age*, 16 November, 1991, Saturday Extra 7; D. Tacey, *Island*, 53, 1992, 58-62; R. Willbanks, *Antipodes*, 7.2, 1993, 151-52; M. Wilding, *Weekend Australian*, 23-24 November, 1991, Review 7.

The Savage Crows. (Sydney: Collins, 1976).
Reviewed by B. Beaver, *ABR*, No. 1, 1978, 33-34; V. Brady, *Westerly*, No. 1, 1977, 102-03; D.R. Burns, *Nation Review*, 19-25 November, 1976, 117; M. Clark, *Bulletin*, 16 October, 1976, 58; R. Dinnage, *New Statesman*, 26 August, 1977, 280; D. Green, *National Times*, 12-17 September, 1977, 19-20; R. Hall, *Australian*, 23 October, 1976, 33; C.J. Hanna, *Southerly*, XXXVII, 1977, 113-15; C. Semmler, *Hemisphere*, XXI, No. 7, 1977, 29; D. Stewart, *S.M.H.*, 16 October, 1976, 19.

Non-Fiction
'A Cry in the Jungle Bar: Australians in Asia'. *Meridian*, V, No. 2, 1986, 133-39.
'From Gossip to Myth'. *Island*, 51, 1992, 10-13.
Sant, Andrew, ed. *Toads: Australian Writers: Other Work, Other Lives*, edited by Andrew Sant (Sydney: Allen & Unwin, 1992). Collection of autobiographical essays on writing and money. Includes Drewe.

Critical Material
Baker, Candida. 'Robert Drewe'. In her *Yacker 3* (Sydney: Picador, 1989), 66-98.
Bennett, Bruce. 'Literature and Journalism: The Fiction of Robert Drewe'. *Ariel*, 20, No. 3, 3-16.
Brown, Jodie. 'Mudrooroo's *Doctor Wooreddy's Prescription for Enduring the End of the World* and Robert Drewe's *The Savage Crows*'. *Westerly*, 38.3, 1993, 71-78.

Edelson, Phyllis Fahrie. 'The Role of History In Three Contemporary Australian Novels' [By Drewe, Winton and Krauth]. *Journal of Popular Culture*, 23, No. 2, 1989, 63-71.

Hawley, Janet. 'Humor amid the Complexities of a Rising Author'. *Age*, 25 August, 1979, 25.

Johnstone, Richard. 'Unexplored Country'. *London Magazine*, N.S. XX, Nos. 8-9, 1980, 63-70.

Neville, Jill. 'The Insider's View'. *National Times*, 20 October, 1979, 33.

Pércopo, Maureen Lynch. 'Mostri Bianchi: La Colonizzazione della Terra Australis Incognita'. In *Metamorfosi, Mostri, Labirinti*, edited by G. Cerina, M. Domenichelli, P. Tucci, M. Virdis (Rome: Bulzoni, 1991), 379-97. Discusses *The Savage Crows* and Colin Johnson's *Dr Wooreddy*.

---. 'Shipwreck in the Southland: The Fictional (Mis)Fortunes of the *Fortuyn*'. In *Naufragi*, edited by Laura Sannia Nowé and Maurizio Virdis (Rome: Bulzoni, 1993), 631-59.

---. 'Terra Australis Incognita: Robert Drewe's *The Savage Crows*: Reflections on the Language of Guilt in "Events at the Anglo-Australian Guano Company"'. *Annali della Facolta di Magistero dell' Universita di Cagliari* (Italy). Nuova serie, Vol. XI, 1987.

Stow, Randolph. 'Transfigured Histories: Recent Novels of Patrick White and Robert Drewe'. *A.L.S.*, IX, 1979, 26-38.

Thieme, John. 'Robert Drewe's Australias - with particular reference to *The Bodysurfers*'. In *The Making of Pluralist Australia 1950-1990* (Selected papers from Inaugural EASA Conference 1991) edited by Werner Senn and Giovanna Capone (Bern: Peter Lang. 1992).

Toorn, Penny van. 'Bakhtin and the Novel as Empire: Textual Politics in Robert Drewe's *The Savage Crows* and Rudy Wiebe's *The Temptations of Big Bear*'. *JCL*, 27.1, 1992, 96-109.

Willbanks, Ray. 'Robert Drewe'. In his *Speaking Volumes: Australian Writers and Their Work* (Ringwood, Vic.: Penguin, 1991).

DUGGAN, LAURIE

Poetry

Adventures In Paradise. (Darlington, N.S.W.: Magic Sam Books, 1982).
Reviewed by M. Duwell, *Weekend Australian*, 22-23 January, 1983, Weekend 9; J. Forbes, *Scripsi*, 1, Nos. 3-4, 1982, 104-7.

The Ash Range. (Sydney: Picador, 1987).
Reviewed by D. Brooks, *Weekend Australian*, 20-21 February, 1988, Weekend 13; V. Buckley, *Times On Sunday*, 24 May, 1987, 33; P. Carter, *Overland*, No.109, 1987, 67-69; C. Eagle, *Age Saturday Extra*, 23 May, 1987, 12; P. Goldsworthy, *ABR*, No. 92, 1987, 19-20; S. McKernan, *Bulletin*, 7 July, 1987, 78, 80; P. Mead, *Scripsi*, 4, No. 4, 1987, 23-40; M. Roberts, *Phoenix Review* 3, 1988, 106-107.

Blue Notes. (Sydney: Pan Picador, 1990).
Reviewed by K. Bolton, *Overland*, No. 121, 1990, 91-93; L. Jacobs, *ABR*, No. 127, 1990, 27-28; G. O'Brien, *Scripsi*, 6, No. 3, 1990, 185-193; T. Shapcott, *Age*, 22 September, 1990, Saturday Extra 7; C. Wallace-Crabbe, *Westerly*, 36.2, 1991, 89-91.

East. (Melbourne: Rigmarole of the Hours, 1977).
Reviewed by J. Grant, *Poetry Australia*, No. 67, 1978, 70-74; C. Harrison-Ford, *S.M.H.*, 7 January, 1978, 17; T. Thompson, *Australasian Small Press Review*, Nos. 7-8, 1979, 47-49.

The Epigrams of Martial. (Melbourne: Scripsi, 1989).
Reviewed by H. Cam, *S.M.H.*, 24 June, 1989, 84.

The Great Divide. (Sydney: Hale & Iremonger, 1985).
Reviewed by B. Beaver, *Weekend Australian*, 31 August - 1 September, 1985,

Weekend 15.

Under The Weather. (Sydney: Wild and Woolley, 1978).
Reviewed by K. Goodwin, *Weekend Australian,* 9-10 June, 1979, Weekend 11; M. Harrison, *S.M.H.,* 1 September, 1979, 18; K. Lilley, *New Poetry,* 26, No. 4, 1978/1979, 57; C. Pollnitz, *Southerly,* 39, 1979, 462-78, esp. 471; J. Rodriguez, *ABR,* No. 10, 1979, 18-19.

Non-Fiction
'Living Poetry'. *Meanjin,* 53.2, 1994, 267-82. Extracts from his diary.

Critical Material
Bourke, Lawrence. *'The Ash Range,* Landscape and Identity'. *Westerly,* 38.1, 1993, 17-24.
Duwell, Martin. 'Interview with Laurie Duggan'. In his *A Possible Contemporary Poetry* (St Lucia: Makar, 1982), 85-91.
Harrison-Ford, Carl. *'The Great Divide'. Scripsi,* 3, Nos. 2-3, 1985, 245-53. Review article.
Page, Geoff. 'Laurie Duggan'. In his *A Reader's Guide To Contemporary Australian Poetry* (St. Lucia: U.Q.P., 1995), 61-62.

DUNN, MAX
Critical Material
Cook, C.O. Leigh. 'The Masks of Max Dunn'. *Westerly,* Nos. 3-4, 1965, 57-66.
Simpson, R.A. 'Max Dunn - A Man and his Poetry'. *Quadrant,* VIII, No. 4, 1964, 48-53.

DURACK, MARY
Critical Material
Bennett, Jack. 'A Conversation with Mary Durack'. *Antipodes,* 3.1, 1989, 43-46.
Forrest, Peter. 'Dame Mary Durack: An Appreciation'. *Northern Perspective,* 18.1, 1995, 1-5. Obituary.
Giblett, Rod. 'Kings in Kimberley Watercourses: Sadism and Pastoralism'. In *Postcolonial Fictions,* edited by Michèle Drouart (Special issue in two volumes incl. SPACLALS Conference Proccedings, *SPAN,* 36, 1993), 541-59.
Hickey, Bernard. '"Looking at Country": Dame Mary Durack's *Kings in Grass Castles'.* In *Percorsi immaginati: Viaggio, metafora e modello in scrittori anglofoni d'Africa, Asia, America, Australia,* edited by Giovanna Capone (Bologna: CLUEB (Cooperativa Libraria Universitaria Editrice Bologna), 1993), 75-87.
Puchy-Palmos, Alison. 'Dame Mary Durack 1913-1994'. *Westerly,* 40.1, 1995, 5-6. Obituary.

DUTTON GEOFFREY
Fiction
Andy. (London, Sydney: Collins, 1968).
Reviewed by E. Bray, *Canberra Times,* 26 October, 1968, 12; G. Hutton, *Age,* 28 September, 1968, 13; N. Keesing, *Bulletin,* 19 October, 1968 (see also letters to the editor in *Bulletin,* 9 November, 1968, 86, and 21 December, 1968, 62); B. Kiernan, *Australian,* 12 October, 1968, 12; J.S. Ryan, *ABR,* VII, 1968, 216-17; M. Vintner, *S.M.H.,* 12 October, 1968, 24.

The Eye Opener. (St Lucia: U.Q.P., 1982).
Reviewed by V. Brady, *Island Magazine,* No. 13, 1982, 54; R. Elliott, *Canberra Times,* 27 March, 1982, 13; B. Jefferis, *S.M.H.,* 6 March, 1982, 45; J. Waten, *Age Saturday Extra,* 6 March, 1982, 14.

Flying Low. (St. Lucia: U.Q.P., 1992)

Reviewed by D. Davison, *Weekend Australian*, 21-22 March, 1992, Review 7; F. James, *S.M.H.*, 28 March, 1992, 47; K. Goodwin, *Outrider*, [10.1&2], 1993, 218-20; T. Shapcott, *Age*, 8 February, 1992, Saturday Extra 8; G. Watt, *Antipodes*, 7.2, 1993, 158.

Queen Emma of the South Seas: A Novel. (South Melbourne: Sun Books, 1988). Previously published South Melbourne: Macmillan, 1976.
Reviewed by R. Lucas, *S.M.H.*, 12 November, 1988, 90.

Tamara. (London, Sydney: Collins, 1970, i.e. 1969).
Reviewed by A.R. Chisholm, *Age*, 15 November, 1969, 14; J. Frow, *Canberra Times*, 3 January, 1970, 14; S. Hall, *Bulletin*, 22 November, 1969, 66; D. Whitelock, *ABR*, IX, 1969/70, 55. See also Stuart Sayers, *Age*, 22 November, 1969, 12.

The Wedge-Tailed Eagle. (South Melbourne: Macmillan, 1980).
Reviewed by L. Clancy, *Age Saturday Extra*, 10 March, 1984, 15.

Poetry
A Body of Words. (Sydney: Edwards & Shaw, 1977).
Reviewed by A. Gould, *Nation Review*, 22-28 December, 1977, 17; J. Griffin, *Advertiser*, 3 December, 1977, 28; F. Kellaway, *Overland*, No. 72, 1978, 53-54; [S.E. Lee], *Southerly*, XXXIX, 1979, 446-48;E. Lindsay, *Weekend Australian Magazine*, 31 December, 1977-1 January, 1978, 7; G. Page, *Canberra Times*, 25 February, 1978, 13; J. Rodriguez, *ABR*, No. 2, 1978, 33.

Findings and Keepings: Selected Poems 1939-1969. (Adelaide: Australian Letters, 1970).
Reviewed by R.F. Brissenden, *Canberra Times*, 26 September, 1970, 13; K. England, *Advertiser*, 18 April, 1970, 18; R. Hall, *Australian*, 6 June, 1970, 19; S.E. Lee, *Southerly*, XXXI, 1971, 235-37; G. Lehmann, *Bulletin*, 28 March, 1970, 57; P. Roberts, *S.M.H.*, 13 June, 1970, 22; T.W. Shapcott, *ABR*, IX, 1970, 185-86; R.A. Simpson, *Age*, 28 March, 1970, 15.

New Poems to 1972. (Adelaide: Australian Letters, 1972).
Reviewed by K. England, *Advertiser*, 24 June, 1972, 16; E. Kynaston, *Review*, 8-14 April, 1972, 702.

New and Selected Poems. (Pymble, NSW: A.& R., 1993).
Reviewed by K. Brophy, *ABR*, 157, 1993/1994, 48-49; H. Cam, *S.M.H.*, 20 November, 1993, Spectrum 13A; N. Jose, *Voices*, 3.4, 1993, 100-02; D. Haskell, *Westerly*, 40.4, 1995, 99-101; T. Shapcott, *Overland*, 137, 1994, 62-64.

Poems Soft and Loud. (Melbourne: Cheshire, 1967).
Reviewed by B. Beaver, *S.M.H.*, 10 February, 1968, 19; L.J. Clancy, *Overland*, No. 39, 1968, 49-51; J.M. Couper, *Poetry Magazine*, No. 3, 1968, 30-32; H. Hewitt, *Canberra Times*, 15 June, 1968, 14; M. Irvin, *Bulletin*, 27 January, 1968, 52; E. Jones, *Nation*, 22 February, 1969, 22; S.E. Lee, *Southerly*, XXVIII, 1968, 149-50; E. Marsh, *Westerly*, No. 3, 1968, 56; T. Shapcott, *ABR*, VII, 1968, 85.

Selective Affinities. (North Ryde, N.S.W.: A.& R., 1985).
Reviewed by B. Beaver, *Weekend Australian Magazine*, 12-13 October, 1985, 31; S. Edgar, *Island Magazine*, Nos. 25-26, 1986, 118-20; G. Page, *ABR*, No. 75, 1985, 31-33; K. Russell, *Quadrant*, XXX, Nos. 1-2, 1986, 128-30.

Non-Fiction
Out in the Open: An Autobiography. (St Lucia: U.Q.P., 1994).
Reviewed by D. Andersen, *S.M.H.*, 1 October, 1994, Spectrum 13A; E. Campion, *Bulletin*, 11 October, 1994, 95; R. Drewe, *T.L.S.*, 4 Aug., 1995, 24; J. Griffin, *Weekend Australian*, 15-16 October, 1994, Review 6; D. Haskell, *Westerly*, 40.4, 1995, 99-101; J. Lewis, *ABR*, 165, 1994, 47-48; A. Riemer, *Independent Monthly*, (November), 1994, 72-74; R. Ross, *Antipodes*, 9.2, 1995, 172; C. Semmler, *Quadrant*, 39.1-2, 1995, 107-09; B. Williams, *Eureka Street*, 4.10, 1994, 30-32.

'A Scattered Childhood'. *Voices*, 3.4, 1993, 5-19. Extracts *Out in the Open*.

Critical Material

Fitzgerald, Ross. 'Beware of Being an Editor'. *The Australian Author*, IX, No. 2, 1987, 17-18. Letter to the editor.

Foster, David. 'Aggression in Sleepy Hollow'. *ABR*, No. 65, 1984, 9-10.

Hall, Sandra. 'Why Write Novels?' *Bulletin*, 26 October, 1968, 52-54.

Hergenhan, Laurie. 'Open Access? Geoffrey Dutton's *Out in the Open* and Contemporary Autobiography'. *Imago*, 7.3, 1995, 54-65. Review article.

Jones, M. 'Can You Pick the Pornography?'. *S.M.H.*, 1 November, 1969, 16.

Keesing, Nancy. 'Geoffrey Dutton: Nancy Keesing Protests'. *The Australian Author*, IX, No. 2, 1987, 18. Letter to the editor.

McDonald, Roger. *Gone Bush*. (Sydney: Bantam, 1990). Includes talk with Dutton.

Page, Geoff. 'Geoffrey Dutton'. In his *A Reader's Guide To Contemporary Australian Poetry* (St. Lucia: U.Q.P., 1995), 63-65.

Pullan, Robert. '"You've had a rough passage - I'm sorry" Geoffrey Dutton'. *The Australian Author*, IX, No. 1, 1987, 9-10.

DYSON, EDWARD

Fiction

The Golden Shanty: Short Stories. Introduction by Norman Lindsay. (Sydney: A.& R., 1963).

Critical Material

Lindsay, Norman. 'Ted Dyson'. *Bohemians of the Bulletin* (Sydney: A.& R., 1965), 153-60.

Palmer, Vance. *Intimate Portraits*. Edited by H.P. Heseltine. (Melbourne: Cheshire, 1969), 103-07.

Ryan, J.S. 'The Authentic Early Depiction of Donahs and Larrikins by Edward G. Dyson'. *Margin*, No. 21, 1989, 21-31.

E

Evergreen. Drama Series. 19( ) ( ); ( ) ( ); ( ) AUSTIN, WILLIAM. (2)
O'NEILL, J. Miner.
Encyclopaedia. Prose. 'Meeting of the Committees'. Meanjin, 8( ), ( ) No. 2, (
[ ] ( ), 127, Letter, to ( )
John Sherry Prose. 'The Short Story Review'. Meanjin, III, No. 2, 1993, 5-8.
Paul. Short story. 'Window to the World'. Southerly, 59 ( ) ( ), 1967 ( ) ( ).
Kendall, ( ) ( ) ( ), Walter Scott. 'Dandory'. Sydney University Press, ( ) ( ) ( ) 1969
'Encyclopaedia' ( ) Prose. Mantine ( ) ( ). Now also ( ) ( )
Archer, P. J. ( ). 'Smith'. Durham University Review. Page ( ) ( ) 91 ( ) and ( ) ( )
No. ( ). ( ) ( ) 78 ( ). ( ) ( ) 11 and Bye ( ) ( ) ( ).
McDonald, Roger. Prose. 'Letter'. Quadrant, ( ) ( ). Fortune [ ] ( ) ( ) collection
'Encyclopaedia'. Modify. Critic. ( ) A Review, ( ) ( ) [ ] V No. ( ) Source: ( ) Survey.
Review. ( ) ( ), III, ( ) 1968, ( ) ( )
Cardford, Rooth. 'Window, hard', Lady: criticism. 'I'm sorry'. Geoffrey Dutton. Scor
Australian Author, IX, No. 2( ) ( ) ( )3 ( ), ( ) ( ) ( )

ELDERSHAW, FLORA

See also Eldershaw, M. Barnard

Non-Fiction

As Good as a Yarn with You: Letters between Miles Franklin, Katharine Susannah Prichard, Jean Devanny, Marjorie Barnard, Flora Eldershaw and Eleanor Dark. Edited by Carole Ferrier. (Cambridge: Cambridge UP, 1992). For reviews see Barnard, Marjorie.

The Peaceful Army. (Ringwood, Vic.: Penguin, 1988). New edition with a foreword by Dale Spender. First published Sydney: The Women's Executive Committee and Advisory Council of Australia's 150th Anniversary Celebrations, 1938.
Reviewed by M. Dever, *Hecate*, XIV, No. 2, 1988, 91-94.

Critical Material

Dever, Maryanne. 'The Case for Flora Eldershaw'. *Hecate*, 15, No. 2, 1989, 38-48.
---. '"No Time is Inopportune for a Protest": Aspects of the Political Activities of Marjorie Barnard and Flora Eldershaw'. *Hecate*, 17.2, 1991, 9-21.
Ferrier, Carole. 'Women of Letters and the Uses of Memory'. In *Wallflowers and Witches: Women and Culture in Australia 1910-1945*, edited by Maryanne Dever (St Lucia: U.Q.P., 1994), 73-90.
Saunders, Ian. 'The Texts of *Tomorrow and Tomorrow and Tomorrow*: Author, Agent, History'. *Southern Review*, 26.2, 1993, 239-61.

ELDERSHAW, M. BARNARD

See also Eldershaw, Flora; Barnard, Marjorie.

Collection

M. Barnard Eldershaw: 'Plaque with Laurel', Essays Reviews & Correspondence. Edited by Maryanne Dever. (St Lucia: U.Q.P., 1995).
Reviewed by F. Capp, *Age*, 18 Feb., 1995, Saturday Extra 8; I. Saunders, *Westerly*, 40.2, 1995, 88-90; G. Thomas, *Social Alternatives*, 14.4, 1995, 56-57.

Fiction

But Not For Love: Stories of Marjorie Barnard and M. Barnard Eldershaw. Introduction by Robert Darby. (Sydney: Allen and Unwin, 1988).
Reviewed by C. Burns, *ABR*, No. 115, 1989, 5-6; F. Capp. *Saturday Age Extra*, 1 April, 1989, 11; M. Dever, *Editions*, 2, 1989, 14; B. Farmer, *Overland*, No. 115,

1989, 95-96; K. Goldsworthy, *Weekend Australian*, 29-30 April, 1989, Weekend 10.

Tomorrow and Tomorrow and Tomorrow. With a new introduction by Anne Chisholm. (London: Virago, 1983; Garden City, N.Y.: Dial Press, 1984). Abridged version published as *Tomorrow and Tomorrow* (Melbourne: Georgian House, 1947). Reviewed by B. Jefferis, *Weekend Australian Magazine*, 10-11 September, 1983, 14; B. Josephi, *CRNLE Reviews Journal*, No. 2, 1984, 59-63; Y. Rousseau, *Age Saturday Extra*, 27 August, 1983, 10; C. Steele, *Canberra Times*, 22 October, 1983, 16.

 Critical Material

Buckridge, Patrick. '"Greatness" and Australian Literature in the 1930s and 1940s: Novels by Dark and Barnard Eldershaw'. *A.L.S.*, 17.1, 1995, 29-37.

Burns, Robert. 'Flux and Fixity: M. Barnard Eldershaw's *Tomorrow and Tomorrow*'. *Meanjin*, XXIX, 1970, 320-27.

Cadzow, Jane. 'The World of Literature Catches up with Tomorrow'. *Weekend Australian*, 19-20 November, 1983, 6.

Carter, David. '"Current History Looks Apocalyptic": Barnard Eldershaw, Utopia and the Literary Intellectual, 1930s-1940s'. *A.L.S.*, 14, No. 2, 1989, 174-87.

Dever, Maryanne. '"Conventional Women of Ability": M. Barnard Eldershaw and the Question of Cultural Authority'. In *Wallflowers and Witches: Women and Culture in Australia 1910-1945*, edited by Maryanne Dever (St Lucia: U.Q.P.,), 133-46.

McQueen, Humphrey. 'Memory and Imagination', *Social Alternatives*, 8, No. 3, 1989, 20-22.

Roe, Jill. 'The Historical Imagination and its Enemies: M. Barnard Eldershaw's *Tomorrow and Tomorrow and Tomorrow*'. *Meanjin*, XLIII, 1984, 241-52.

Rorabacher, Louise E. *Marjorie Barnard and M. Barnard Eldershaw* (New York: Twayne Publishers, 1973). Twayne's World Authors series, 257. Reviewed by H.P. Heseltine, *A.L.S.*, VI, 1974, 444-45.

ELLIOTT, SUMNER LOCKE

 Fiction

About Tilly Beamis. (London: Pan Books, 1985).
Reviewed by L. Clancy, *ABR*, No. 79, 1986, 12; H. Falkner, *Weekend Australian Magazine*, 25-26 January, 1986, 12; I. Indyk, *S.M.H.*, 8 March, 1986, 47.

Edens Lost. (New York: Harper & Row, 1969).
Reviewed by G. Davenport, *New York Times Book Review*, 28 September, 1969, 56-57.

Fairyland. (New York: Harper & Row, 1990; Sydney: Pan, 1991).
Reviewed by C. Bram, *New York Times Book Review*, 20 May, 1990, 30; A. Wearne, *Age*, 21 September, 1991, Saturday Extra 9; R. Willbanks, *World Literature Today*, 65.2, 1991, 361.

Going. (South Melbourne: Macmillan; New York: Harper & Row, 1975).
Reviewed by A. Broyard, *New York Times*, 5 February, 1975, 35; V. Ikin, *Science Fiction* (Sydney), I, No. 1 1977, 82-86; T. LeClair, *New York Times Book Review*, 9 February, 1975, 6; M. Pettigrove, *Canberra Times*, 28 August, 1975, 8; K. Tennant, *S.M.H.*, 29 March, 1975, 13; G. Turner, *Age*, 12 April, 1975, 17.

The Man Who Got Away. (New York: Harper, 1972).
Reviewed by S. Blackburn, *New York Times Book Review*, 15 October, 1972, 2; D. Hinch, *National Times*, 30 October-4 November, 1972, 37; O. Ruhen, *Age*, 23 March, 1974, 12.

Radio Days. (Pymble, NSW: A.& R, 1993).
Reviewed by L. Bowman, *Imago*, 6.1, 1994, 97-98.

Signs of Life: A Novel. (New Haven, CT: Ticknor & Fields, 1981).
Reviewed by B. Oakley, *S.M.H.*, 17 October, 1981, 48; L. Ricou, *Queen's*

Quarterly, XC, 1983, 532-36.
Some Doves and Pythons. (London: Gollancz, 1966).
Reviewed by N. Jillett, *Age*, 12 November, 1966, 24.
Waiting for Childhood. (Sydney: Pan, 1988). Previously published New York: Harper & Row, 1987.
Reviewed by D. Johnson *S.M.H.*, 24 December, 1988, 35; R. Sorensen, *Age Saturday Extra*, 4 February, 1989, 14; J.A. Weigel, *Antipodes*, I, No. 2, 1987, 114; *New Yorker*, 19 October, 1987, 119-120.
Water Under the Bridge. (Melbourne: Macmillan; New York: Simon & Schuster, 1977).
Reviewed by P. Corris, *Weekend Australian Magazine*, 4-5 March, 1978, 9; M. Halligan, *Canberra Times*, 15 July, 1978, 12; C. Hanna, *Southerly*, XL, 1980, 360-61; N. Jillett, *Age*, 18 February, 1978, 23; N. Keesing, *S.M.H.*, 18 February, 1978, 17; K. Kellaway, *ABR*, No. 1, 1978, 23-25; D. O'Grady, *Overland*, No. 75, 1979, 59; P. Pierce, *Meanjin*, XXXVII, 1978, 393-401; A. Roberts, *Advertiser*, 4 March, 1978, 25; D. Rowbotham, *Courier-Mail*, 18 February, 1978, 19; R. Stow, *T.L.S.*, 4 August, 1978, 897; J. Tranter, *National Times*, 6-11 March, 1978, 32; A. Tyler, *New York Times Book Review*, 28 August, 1977, 7.

Non-Fiction

'Pleasing Yourself'. Interview by Kate Jennings. *Island*, 48, 1991, 24-29.
'You Must Like Your Work'. *Southerly*, XXXV, 1975, 107-10. Australian writers in profile: 12.

Critical Material

See newspaper reports on Locke Elliott's visit to Australia and interviews, *Australian*, 11 February, 1974, 12; *S.M.H.*, 23 March, 1974, 17; *Age*, 23 March, 1974, 14; *S.M.H.*, 1 April, 1974, 7.
'Literary Win for Elliott'. *Courier-Mail*, 19 November, 1977, 68. Patrick White Literary Award.
Arnold, Roslyn. *Sumner Locke Elliott's Rusty Bugles: A Critical Introduction*. (Sydney: Currency Press, 1983). Reviewed by G.D., *English in Australia*, No. 65, 1983, 65-66.
Baker, Candida. 'Sumner Locke Elliott'. In her *Yacker 2: Australian Writers Talk About Their Work* (Sydney: Picador, 1987), 42-70.
Fitton, Doris. 'My Aim - The Greatest Plays'. *S.M.H.*, 5 June, 1971, 19.
---. 'Not without Dust and Heat'. *S.M.H.*, 12 June, 1971, 19.
Hersey, April. 'After the Golden Age'. *Bulletin*, 7 October, 1967, 73.
Hunter, James. 'Success: Being Able to Afford to Say "No"'. *Age*, 5 November, 1977, 23.
Krause, Tom. 'Rusty but Untarnished'. *Weekend Australian Magazine*, 31 October-1 November, 1981, 15. T.V. production of *Rusty Bugles*.
Packer, Clyde. 'An Interview with Sumner Locke Elliott'. *Quadrant*, XXVIII, No. 11, 1984, 19-23.
Palmer, Jenny. 'PS: We Hear You'. *Bulletin*, 27 December-3 January, 1984, 148-51. Interview.
Ward, Peter. 'Literary View (Interview with Locke Elliott)'. *Weekend Australian Magazine*, 4-5 March, 1978, 9.
Wynhausen, Elisabeth. 'The Man who Got Away'. *National Times*, 27 June-3 July, 1982, 19.

ELLIS, HAVELOCK

Fiction

Kanga Creek. Introduction by John Heuzenroeder. (Melbourne: Thomas Nelson (Australia), 1970). First published 1922.

Critical Material

Dutton, Geoffrey. *Kanga Creek: Havelock Ellis in Australia*. (Woollahra, N.S.W.: Picador, 1989). Reviewed by G. Burns, *Age Saturday Extra*, 1 April, 1989, 9; L. Clancy, *Weekend Australian*, 22-23 April, 1989, Weekend 10; M. Clark, *S.M.H.*, 4 March, 1989, 88; J. Davidson, *Australian Society*, 8, No. 4, 1989, 44-45; B. Dunbar, *Southerly*, 50, No. 2, 1990, 264-67. H. Rowley, *ABR*, N0. 110, 1989, 26-27.
Heuzenroeder, John. 'Havelock Ellis's Australian Idyll'. *A.L.S.*, III, 1967, 3-17.

ENRIGHT, NICK

Drama

Daylight Saving. (Sydney: Currency Press, 1990).
Reviewed by P. Fitzpatrick, *Australasian Drama Studies*, 19, 1991, 115-17; J. Rose, *Voices*, 3.3, 1993, 108-12.

Don Juan. (Paddington, N.S.W.: Currency Press/State Theatre Company of South Australia, 1984). Translation of Moliere's play.
Reviewed by J. Rose, *Voices*, 3.3, 1993, 108-12.

Good Works. (Sydney: Currency Press, 1995).
Reviewed by L. Nowra, *ABR*, 174, 1995, 20-21.

Mongrels. (Paddington, N.S.W.: Currency Press, 1994).
Reviewed by N. Fletcher, *Australasian Drama Studies*, 27, 1995, 156-61; G. Milne, *Eureka Street*, 4.10, 1994, 41-42; S. Sejavka, *ABR*, 167, 1994-95, 65-66.

On the Wallaby. (Sydney: Currency Press, 1982).
Reviewed by M. Blaylock and H. Hardwick, *Australasian Drama Studies*, 1.2, 1983, 157-59; A. Jetnikoff, *LiNQ*, 11.1, 1983, 80-87; M. Lord, *ABR*, 50, 1983, 28M.

A Property of the Clan. (Paddington, N.S.W.: Currency Press, 1994).
Reviewed by N. Fletcher, *Australasian Drama Studies*, 26, 1995, 200-04; G. Milne, *Eureka Street*, 4.10, 1994, 41-42.

St. James Infirmary. (Padington, N.S.W.: Currency Press, 1993).
Reviewed by N. Fletcher, *Australasian Drama Studies*, 26, 1995, 200-04; J. Rose, *Voices*, 3.3, 1993, 108-12.

Poetry

Carnival of the Animals: Verse to Accompany the Zoolological Fantasia of Camille Saint-Saens. (Crows Nest, N.S.W.: ABC Enterprises, 1990).
Reviewed by J. Rose, *Voices*, 3.3, 1993, 108-12.

Critical Material

Kelly, Veronica. 'Enright's *Mongrels* as Intervention in the Canon of Contemporary Australian Drama'. *Southerly*, 54.2, 1994, 5-22.
---. '"A Form of Music": An Interview with Nick Enright'. *Australasian Drama Studies*, 24, 1994, 58-76.
Milne, Geoffrey. 'Have Faith in Good Works: Geoffrey Milne Reviews the Work of Playwright Nick Enright'. *Eureka Street*, 5.6, 1995, 45-46.

ESSON, LOUIS

Collection

Ballades of Old Bohemia: An Anthology of Louis Esson. Edited by Hugh Anderson. (Ascot Vale: Red Rooster Press, 1980). Reviewed by M. Lord, *ABR*, No. 25, 1980, 37; J. McCallum, *Theatre Australia*, V, No. 10, 1981, 52; L. Radic, *Age*, 4 October, 1980, 32; D. Walker, *Labour History*, No. 44, 1983, 137-38.

Drama

The Time is Not Yet Ripe. Edited by Philip Parsons. (Sydney: Currency Press, 1973). The National Theatre. First published Melbourne: Fraser and Jenkinson, 1912.

Reviewed by S. Edgar, *Canberra Times*, 24 May, 1974, 8.

The Woman Tamer. With Buzo, *Norm and Ahmed*. (Sydney: Currency Press, 1976). First published in his *Three Short Plays*, Melbourne: Fraser and Jenkinson, 1911. Reviewed by H. van der Poorten, *Theatre-Australia*, I, No. 8, 1977, 56.

   Non-Fiction

'Letters from London, 1920-1921'. In *The Writer in Australia*, edited by John Barnes (Melbourne: O.U.P., 1969), 191-99.

   Critical Material

Fitzpatrick, Peter. *Pioneer Players: The Lives of Louis and Hilda Esson*. (Cambridge: Cambridge UP., 1995). Reviewed by J. McCallum, *Weekend Australian*, 25-26 Nov., 1995, Review 9; H. McQueen, *Independent*, Dec., 1995/Jan., 1996, 84-86.

Hainsworth, J.D. 'Some Louis Esson Manuscripts'. *Southerly*, XLIII, 1983, 347-57. Play scripts.

Healey, Ken. 'Esson Play in Same Week as Conference Offers Retrospective Look'. *Canberra Times*, 9 May, 1980, 10.

---. 'Louis Esson Play for Rep's Festival'. *Canberra Times*, 13 June, 1980, 12.

Ikin, Van. *'The Time is not yet Ripe* and Contemporary Attitudes to Politics'. *A.L.S.*, VIII, 1978, 296-306.

McCallum, John. 'Irish Memories and Australian Hopes: William Butler Yeats and Louis Esson'. *Westerly*, 34, N0. 2, 1989, 33-40.

---. 'Something With a Cow In It'. *Overland*, No. 108, 1987, 6-13.

Makeham, Paul. 'Framing the landscape: Prichard's *Pioneers* and Esson's *The Drovers*'. *Australasian Drama Studies*, 23, 1993, 121-34.

Walker, David. 'A Bohemian's Progress: Louis Esson in Melbourne, 1904-1914'. *Meanjin*, XXXI, 1972, 417-26. Expanded and reprinted as 'Bushed: Louis Esson in Melbourne and Paris, 1904-1914' in his *Dream and Disillusion: A Search for Australian Cultural Identity*. (Canberra: A.N.U. Press, 1976), 11-30.

Webby, Elizabeth. *Modern Australian Plays*. Horizon Studies in Literature. (Sydney: Sydney UP in association with O.U.P., 1990). Includes discussion of *The Time Is Not Yet Ripe*.

EVANS, GEORGE ESSEX

   Critical Material

Kelly, Veronica. 'George Essex Evans the Playwright'. *Margin*, No. 19, 1987, 1-6.

Fitzgerald, Ross. 'George Essex Evans, 1863-1909, Poet of Toowoomba'. *Imago*, 1, No. 2, 1989, 53-56.

Tiffin, Chris. 'Metaphor and Emblem: George Essex Evans's Public Poetry'. *Literary Criterion*, 26.4, 1991, 61-74.

EWERS, J.K.

   Non-Fiction

Companion to 'Who Rides On the River' (Sydney: A.& R., 1965).

   Critical Material

Bibby, Peter (ed.) *The Ultimate Honesty: Recollections of John K. Ewers, 1904-1978, with some Glimpses Culled from his Works*. (Perth: Fellowship of Australian Writers (W.A. Branch), 1982). Reviewed by G. Phillips, *ABR*, No. 52, 1985, 27-28.

Glaskin, G.M. 'So long, Keith Ewers'. *Australian Author*, X, No. 3, 1978, 30-33.

FACEY, A.B.

Non-Fiction

A Fortunate Life. (Fremantle: Fremantle Arts Centre Press; Ringwood, Vic.: Penguin, 1981). Reviewed by P. Botsman, *S.M.H.*, 12 September, 1981, 43; D. Collin, *Westerly*, XXVII, No. 1, 1982, 109-113; K. Eikins, *English in Australia*, No. 61, 1982, 76; T. Forshaw, *Age*, 29 August, 1981, 30; J.B. Hirst, *Historical Studies*, No. 78, 1982, 112-114; V. Horn, *ABR*, No. 39, 1982, 33; A. Jach, *National Times*, 6-12 July, 1984, 33; S. Macintyre, *Studies in Western Australian History*, No. 5, 1982, 79-85, esp. 79-81; M. Macleod, *Span*, No. 14, 1982, 20-24, esp. 23 and *Kunapipi*, IV, No. 1, 1982, 144-148, esp. 144; I. Morice, *Island Magazine*, Nos. 9-10, 1982, 92-93; *Overland*, No. 84, 1981, 72; M. Power, *Institute for Modern Biography Newsletter*, III, No. 1, 1982, 30-32; E. Riddell, *Bulletin*, 1 September, 1981, 94; C. Semmler, *Bulletin*, 11 March, 1986, 92; P. Shrubb, *Quadrant*, XXV, No. 11, 1981, 39-42; M. Wilding, *London Review of Books*, VIII, No. 8, 1986, 18.

Critical Material

Amadio, Nadine. 'The Sorcerer From the West'. *Arts National*, III, No. 1, 1985, 80-83, 115, esp. 83, 115.

Bliss, Carolyn. 'The Mythology of Family: Three Texts of Popular Australian Culture'. *New Literatures Review*, No. 18, 1989, 60-72. Includes discussion of *A Fortunate Life*.

Capper, Wendy. 'Facey's *A Fortunate Life* and Traditional Oral Narratives'. *A.L.S.*, XIII, No. 3, 1988, 266-281.

Colmer, John. 'Australian Autobiography: Flawed and Fortunate Lives'. *Meridian*, III, No. 2, 1984, 135-141; esp. 140.

---. 'Flawed and Fortunate Lives: Patrick White and A.B. Facey'. In his *Australian Autobiography: A Personal Quest* (Melbourne: O.U.P., 1989), 86-97.

Dibble, Brian. 'So Far, A Fortunate Life...'. *ABR*, No. 74, 1985, 20-22; esp. 22.

Hirst, John. 'What Grandma Taught'. *Overland*, 124, 1991, 5-11. Chapter from his *The World of Albert Facey* (North Sydney: History Institute of Victoria / Allen & Unwin, 1992).

---. *The World of Albert Facey* (North Sydney: History Institute of Victoria / Allen & Unwin, 1992). Reviewed by G. Bolton, *AJPH*, 39.1, 1993, 98-99; P. Cochrane, *Australian Historical Studies*, 25.100, 1993, 485-86; P. Deery, *Journal of Australian Studies*, 38, 1993, 81.

Indyk, Ivor. 'A.B. Facey's Australian Autobiography'. *A.L.S.*, XIII, No. 1, 1987, 29-39.

MacDermott, Doireann. 'The Autobiography of an Unknown Australian: Albert Facey's A Fortunate Life'. *Proceedings of the EACLALS Conference*, 10-13 April, 1985.

Mitchell, Adrian. '"The Western Art of Makeshift", A.B. Facey and M. Allerdale Grainger'. In *Australian/Canadian Literatures in English: Comparative Perspectives*, edited by Russell McDougall and Gillian Whitlock (North Ryde, N.S.W.: Methuen Australia, 1987), 33-48.

Newman, Joan. 'Facey's Folkloric History'. *Australian Folklore*, No. 4, 1990, 3-11.

---. 'Reader-Response to Transcribed Oral Narrative: *A Fortunate Life* and *My Place*'. *Southerly*, XLVIII, No. 4, 1988, 376-388.

Stodart, Eleanor. 'Are Writers of Non-Fiction Really "Authors" At All?' *The Australian Author*, XVI, No. 3, 1984, 7.

Wearne, Heather. 'The "Fortunate" and the "Imagined": Landscape, Myth and Created Self in A.B. Facey and David Malouf'. In *The Making of Pluralist Australia 1950-1990*, selected papers from the inaugural EASA Conference 1991, (Bern: Peter Lang, 1992).

FARMER, BEVERLEY

Collection

A Body of Water: A Year's Notebook. (St Lucia: U.Q.P., 1990).
Reviewed by G. Bouras, *Island*, 46, 1991, 60-65; C. Clutterback, *Southerly*, 51.1, 1991, 159-65; M. Collins, *Australian Women's Book Review*, 2, No. 2, 1990, 24-25; M. Denholm, *Overland*, No. 119, 1990, 91-92; S. Dowse, *Westerly*, 36.1, 1991, 90-92G; Dutton, *ABR*, No. 119, 1990, 11; D. English, *Weekend Australian*, 14-15 April, 1990, Weekend 6; T. Glyde, *T.L.S.*, 14-20 September, 1990, 980; L. Jacobs, *CRNLE Reviews Journal*, No. 1, 1990, 55-60; N. Lee-Jones, *Antipodes*, 5.2, 1991, 150; R. Sorenson, *Age*, 24 February, 1990, Saturday Extra 8; K. Veitch, *S.M.H.*, 10 February, 1990, 75.

Fiction

Alone. (Fitzroy, Vic.: McPhee Gribble; Ringwood, Vic.: Penguin, 1980).
Reviewed by E. Liddelow, *Scripsi*, IV, No. 2, 1986, 281-94.

Home Time. (Vic.: McPhee Gribble; Ringwood, Vic.: Penguin Books, 1985).
Reviewed by K. Ahearne, *ABR*, No. 75, 1985, 12-14; H. Daniel, *Age Saturday Extra*, 14 September, 1985, 15; K. England, *Advertiser*, 14 September, 1985, 7; R. Gostand and S. Cassidy, *Social Alternatives*, V, No. 4, 1986, 56-57; M. Halligan, *Canberra Times*, 9 November, 1985, B2; L. Jacobs, *CRNLE Reviews Journal*, No. 2, 1985, 39-42; E. Liddelow, *Scripsi*, IV, No. 2, 1986, 281-94; R. Lucas, *S.M.H.*, 28 September, 1985, 46; R. Weinreich, *New York Times Book Review*, 18 May, 1986, 24; G. Windsor, *Bulletin*, 15 October, 1985, 91.

The House in the Light. (St Lucia: U.Q.P., 1995).
Reviewed by M. Condon, *Weekend Australian*, 13-14 May, 1995, Review 8; D. Bird, *ABR*, 170, 1995, 47-48; D. Falconer, *Age*, 15 April, 1995, Saturday Extra 9; H. Horton, *Imago*, 7.3, 1995, 138-39; J. Maiden, *Overland*, 141, 1995, 82-84.

Milk. (Fitzroy, Vic.: McPhee Gribble; Ringwood, Vic.: Penguin, 1983).
Reviewed by I. Baranay, *S.M.H.*, 10 December, 1983, 38; J. Bedford, *National Times*, 2-8 December, 1983, 24; G. Burns, *Island Magazine*, No. 22, 1985, 38-40; G. Dutton, *Bulletin*, 17 January, 1984, 60; T. Forshaw, *Quadrant*, XXVIII, No. 9, 1984, 81-84; N. Keesing, *Weekend Australian Magazine*, 14-15 June, 1984, 12; E. Liddelow, *Scripsi*, IV, No. 2, 1986, 281-94; S. McKernan, *Canberra Times*, 21 January, 1984, 18; J. Webb, *Westerly*, No. 2, 1984, 107-108.

The Seal Woman. (St Lucia: U.Q.P., 1992).
Reviewed by M. Arkin, *Antipodes*, 7.1, 1993, 73; C. Blanche, *Quadrant*, 37.3, 1993, 84-86; K. Cummings, *Australian Women's Book Review*, 5.1, 1993, 6-7; L. Jacobs, *ABR*, 144, 1992, 17-19; K. Lamb, *Age*, 29 August, 1992, Saturday Extra 9; A. Nettelbeck, *CRNLE Reviews Journal*, 2, 1993, 97-98; M. Sharkey, *Weekend Australian*, 19-20 September, 1992, Review 7; N. Stasko, *Southerly*, 53.4, 1993, 174-82; A. Wearne, *S.M.H.*, 19 September, 1992, 44.

Non-Fiction
'New Directions via *A Body of Water*'. *A.L.S.*, 17.2, 1995, 175-78. Paper given at the Australian Studies Centre, University of Queensland, 1994.
'Preoccupations'. *A.L.S.*, 14, No. 3, 1990, 390-92.

Critical Material
Ahearne, Kate. 'Exploring Life's Lonely Struggle'. *National Times*, 9-15 December, 1983, 29.
Ellison, Jennifer. 'Beverley Farmer'. In her *Rooms of Their Own* (Ringwood, Vic.: Penguin, 1986), 110-131.
Jacobs, Lyn. 'The Fiction of Beverley Farmer'. *A.L.S.*, 14, No. 3, 1990, 325-35.
Liddelow, Eden. 'Home Is Where the Art Is: Beverley Farmer and Marion Campbell'. *Scripsi*, 4, No. 2, 1986, 281-94.
Ommundsen, Wenche. 'An Interview with Beverley Farmer'. *Mattoid*, No. 31, 1988, 110-121.
Pons, Xavier. 'Dramatising the Self: Beverley Farmer's Fiction'. *A.L.S.*, 17.2, 1995, 141-48.
Pybus, Cassandra. 'Loss and Reassurance: Beverley Farmer's Fiction'. *Island Magazine*, Nos. 25-26, 1986, 36-38.
Riem, Antonella. 'Isolation in Olga Masters's *The Home Girls* and Beverley Farmer's *Milk*'. In her *The Labyrinths of Self: A Collection of Essays on Australian and Caribbean Literature*. (Leichhardt, N.S.W.: FILEF. Italo-Australian Publications, 1987), 141-151.
Whitlock, Fiona. 'Beverley Opens Up Yet Another Literary Chapter'. *Australian*, 20 September, 1985, 15.
Willbanks, Ray. 'Beverley Farmer'. In his *Speaking Volumes: Australian Writers and Their Work* (Ringwood, Vic.: Penguin, 1991).

FARRELL, JOHN

Critical Material
Tearle, Sheila E., and Dowd, B.T. 'John Farrell: Poet, Patriot, and Journalist'. *Journal of the Royal Australian Historical Society*, LVII, 1971, 143-59.

FAUCHERY, ANTOINE

Non-Fiction
Letter from a Miner in Australia. (Melbourne: Georgian House, 1965). Translated by A.R. Chisholm. Prefaces by Theodore de Banville, Jack Cato, A.R. Chisholm.

FIELD, BARRON

Critical Material
Allars, K.G. 'Barron Field: His Association with New South Wales'. *Journal of the Royal Australian Historical Society*, LIII, 1967, 173-95.
Currey, C.H. *Sir Francis Forbes: The First Chief Justice of the Supreme Court of New South Wales*. (Sydney: A.& R., 1968).
Mackaness, George. 'Barron Field'. *Bibliomania: An Australian Book Collector's Essays* (Sydney: A.& R., 1965), 182-7.

FINN, EDMUND (GARRYOWEN)

Non-Fiction
Garryowen's Melbourne: A Selection from the Chronicles of Early Melbourne, 1835-1852. Edited by Margaret Weidenhofer. (Melbourne: Nelson Australia, 1967).
Critical Material
Grant, E. 'Owen's Garden'. *Walkabout*, XXXIII, No. 3, 1967, 5.
Smith, Laura. 'Halfpenny's History'. *Walkabout*, XXXIII, No. 3, 1967, 5.
Weidenhofer, Margaret. 'Garryowen, Chronicler of Early Melbourne'. *Walkabout*, XXXII, No. 11, 1966, 27-9.

FITZGERALD, R. D.

Collection
Robert D. FitzGerald. Edited with an introduction by Julian Croft. (St Lucia: U.Q.P., 1987). Reviewed by L. McCredden, *Meridian*, VI, No. 2, 1987, 191-192; J. Tulip, *A.L.S.*, XIII, No. 2, 1987, 246-248.
Poetry
Forty Years' Poems. (Sydney: A.& R., 1965).
Reviewed by R. Burns, *Nation*, 16 October, 1965, 21-2; R. Dunlop, *Poetry Australia*, No. 7, 1965, 39-43; B. Elliott, *ABR*, IV, 1965, 178; F. Haynes, *Westerly*, No. 3, 1966, 90-4; G. Johnston, *Australian*, 25 September, 1965, 11; J. McAuley, *S.M.H.*, 7 August, 1965, 13; R. McCuaig, *Canberra Times*, 24 July, 1965, 10; A.A. Phillips, *Meanjin*, XXIV, 1965, 368-9; V. Smith, *Bulletin*, 28 August, 1965, 52-3; J. Thompson, *Poetry Magazine*, No. 5, 1965, 28-30.
Product, Later Verses. (Sydney: A.& R., 1977).
Reviewed by R. Dobson, *Overland*, No. 81, 1980, 40-41; R. Hall, *Weekend Australian Magazine*, 4-5 March, 1978, 8; H.P.Heseltine, *Meanjin*, XXXVIII, 1979, 120-22; [S.E. Lee], *Southerly*, XXXIX, 1979, 433-36; N. Macainsh, *ABR*, No. 4, 1978, 10; T. Shapcott, *Age*, 1 July, 1978, 23; D. Stewart, *S.M.H.*, 3 June, 1978, 17; J. Tranter, *24 Hours*, III, No. 6, 1978, 70-71.
R.D. FitzGerald; with an introduction by the author. (Sydney: A.& R., 1963). Australian Poets series.
R.D. FitzGerald Reads from His Own Work. (St Lucia: U.Q.P., 1971). Poets on Record, 4. Record and booklet.
Reviewed by P. Annand, *Makar*, VII, No. 4, 1971, 42-43; A.C. Lyons, *Twentieth Century*, XXVI, 1971, 183; D. Malouf, *Australian*, 18 December, 1971, 16; P. Roberts, *S.M.H.*, 29 April, 1972, 16; R.A. Simpson, *Age*, 8 January, 1972, 11.
Non-Fiction
'Narrative Poetry'. *Southerly*, XXVI, 1966, 11-24. C.L.F. lecture.
'Nationalism and Internationalism'. *Southerly*, XXVII, 1967, 260-265. Speech at Annual Dinner of the English Association, 1966.
'A Pilgrimage in the Sud-Ouest'. *Meanjin*, XXV, 1966, 179-89.
'Places of Origin'. *Overland*, No. 33, 1966, 19-23.
'A Poet on Poetry'. *Australian*, 10 September, 1969, 12-13.
'Verse and Worse'. *Southerly*, XXXIII, 1973, 156-66.
Critical Material
Anderson, Hugh. 'A Checklist of the Poems of Robert D. FitzGerald, 1917-1965'. *A.L.S.*, IV, 1970, 280-86.
Van Wageningen, J., and O'Brien, P. *R.D. FitzGerald: A Bibliography*. (Adelaide: Libraries Board of South Australia, 1970). Bibliographies of Australian Writers.
State Library of South Australia. 'Bibliographies of Australian Writers: Supplements'. *Index of Australian Book Reviews*, VI, No. 4, 1970, 305-06; VII, 1971, 287-288; VIII, 1972, 235-239; IX, 1973, 137-40; X, 1974, 151-55; XI, 1975, 203-4.

Brett, Innes. 'R.D. FitzGerald: Valediction 28 May, 1987'. *Southerly*, XLVII, No. 3, 1987, 237-238. Other obituaries appeared in *Meanjin*, XLVI, No. 3, 1987, 283-286; *Southerly*, XLVII, No. 3, 1987, 235-237; *Overland*, No. 108, 1987, 56-57.

Cantrell, K.M. 'Some Elusive Passages in *Essay on Memory*: A Reading Based on a Discussion with R.D. FitzGerald'. *Southerly*, XXX, 1970, 44-52.

Croft, Julian. *The Federal and National Impulse in Australian Literature, 1890-1958*. The Colin Roderick Lectures, Monograph 18 (Townsville, Qld.: Foundation for Australian Literary Studies, 1988). Includes paper on FitzGerald.

---. 'R.D. FitzGerald "The Wind at your Door"'. In *Australian Poems in Perspective*, edited by P.K. Elkin (St Lucia: U.Q.P., 1978), 89-99.

---. 'R.D. FitzGerald's "The Face of the Waters"'. *A.L.S.*, IX, 1979, 71-76.

---. 'R.D. FitzGerald (Valediction)'. *Notes and Furphies*, No. 18, 1987, 3-4. Obituary.

Cross, Gustav. 'Australian Poetry in the 'Sixties'. *Poetry Australia*, No. 5, 1965, 33-8.

Day, A. Grove. 'R.D. FitzGerald and Fiji'. *Meanjin*, XXIV, 1965, 277-86.

---. *Robert D. FitzGerald*. (New York: Twayne Publishers, 1974). Twayne's World Authors series, 286. Reviewed by T.I. Moore, *Meanjin*, XXXIV, 1975, 104-05; C.M. Tiffin, *A.L.S.*, VII, 1975, 99-101.

Harris, Max. 'Cheers for Men of Conscience'. *Australian*, 25 October, 1969, 21.

Hawley, Janet. 'A Medal in the Mailbox'. *Australian*, 4 June, 1974, 10.

Keesing, Nancy. 'Robert D. FitzGerald'. *Overland*, No. 25, 1963, 31-2. Biographical.

Kramer, Leonie. 'R.D. FitzGerald - Philosopher or Poet?' *Overland*, No. 33, 1966, 15-18.

Lloyd, John. 'R.D. FitzGerald: Motif in Later Lyrical Development'. *Makar*, No. 20, 1964, 26-35.

Mares, F.H. 'The Poetry of Robert FitzGerald'. *Southerly*, XXVI, 1966, 3-10.

McGregor, Craig. 'A Kind of Life's Work'. *S.M.H.*, 7 August, 1965, 13. An interview.

Mezger, Ross. 'The Poetic Narrative of R.D. FitzGerald's *Between Two Tides*'. *A.L.S.*, VIII, 1978, 457-70.

Petersen, D. 'Man the Seeker: Robert FitzGerald and Jemesa Asesela. A General Introduction to One of FitzGerald's Fijian Sources'. *LiNQ*, IV, Nos. 3 & 4, 1975, 13-17.

Phillips, A.A. 'R.D. FitzGerald'. In his *Responses: Selected Writings* (Kew, Vic.: Australian International Press & Publications, 1979), 131-33. Review of *Forty Years' Poems*, first published *Meanjin*, XXIV, 1965, 368-69.

---. 'The Unresented Critic'. *Bulletin*, 6 July, 1982, 73-74.

Ryan, J.S. 'Some Convict Sources in Keneally and FitzGerald'. *A.L.S.*, IX, 1980, 385-87.

Smith, Graeme Kinross. 'R.D. FitzGerald - a Profile'. *A.L.S.*, VII, 1976, 316-20.

Stewart, Douglas. 'Robert D. FitzGerald, A Background to his Poetry'. In *The Literature of Australia*, edited by Geoffrey Dutton (Adelaide: Penguin Books, 1964), 332-41.

Sturm, Terry. 'The Poetry of R.D. FitzGerald'. *Landfall*, XX, 1966, 162-7.

---. 'R.D. FitzGerald's Poetry and A.N. Whitehead'. *Southerly*, XXIX, 1969, 288-304. See note in *Southerly*, XXX, 1970, 80.

Thompson, John. 'Poetry in Australia: R.D. FitzGerald'. *Southerly*, XXVII, 1967, 233-242. Transcript of an interview telecast in 1965.

Vallis, Val. 'R.D. FitzGerald - A Critical Tribute'. In his *Heart Reasons, These . . .: Commentaries on Five Australian Poets* The Colin Roderick Lectures, Monograph 16 (Townsville, Qld.: Foundation for Australian Literary Studies, 1988). 27-49.

Wilkes, G.A. *R.D. FitzGerald*. (Melbourne: O.U.P., 1981). Australian Writers and

their Work. Reviewed by J.D. McLaren, *ABR*, No. 39, 1982, 32.
---. 'The Poetry of R.D. FitzGerald'. *Southerly*, XXVII, 1967, 243-258.
Wright, Judith. 'R.D. FitzGerald'. In her *Preoccupations in Australian Poetry*. (Melbourne: O.U.P., 1965), 154-69; and passim.

FORBES, JOHN

Poetry
New and Selected Poems. (North Ryde, NSW: A.& R., 1991).
Reviewed by L. Bourke, *Voices*, 2.3, 1992, 104-07; H. Cam, *S.M.H.*, 13 June, 1992, 43; M. Duwell, *Scripsi*, 8.1, 1992, 257-63; T. Shapcott, *Age*, 9 May, 1992, Saturday Extra 10.
Stalin's Holidays. (Glebe, N.S.W.: Transit Poetry, 1980).
Reviewed by G. Bitcon, *Southerly*, XLI, 1981, 472-73; G. Catalano, *Meanjin*, XL, 1981, 350-53; M. Duwell, *Weekend Australian Magazine*, 4-5 April, 1981, 11; M. Heyward, *Scripsi*, (Melbourne) I, No. 1, 1981, 40-42; G. Page, *National Times*, 7-13 June, 1981, 62; G. Rowlands, *Overland*, No. 86, 1981, 62-63; T. Shapcott, *Age*, 23 May, 1981, 30; R.A. Simpson, *ABR*, No. 30, 1981, 14.
The Stunned Mullet and Other Poems. (Sydney: Hale & Iremonger, 1988).
Reviewed by L. Bourke, *Poetry Australia*, No. 118, 1989, 29-40; K. Brophy, *Arena*, No. 86, 1989, 169-74; T. Code, *Different Perspectives* (Supplement to *Mattoid*, No. 30), 1988, 77-97; P. Craven, *Weekend Australian*, 17-18 September, 1988, Weekend 10; K. Hart, *Overland*, No. 113, 1988, 95-96; P. Kirkpatrick, *Antithesis*, 4, No. 1, 1990, 189-94; J. Strauss, *Age Saturday Extra*, 28 May, 1988, 14; C. Wallace-Crabbe, *Scripsi*, 5, No. 2, 1989, 193-96.
Tropical Skiing. (Sydney: A.& R., 1977). Poets of the Month.
Reviewed by V. Ikin, *Quadrant*, XXI, No. 9, 1977, 78-79; P. Law, *Poetry Australia*, No. 65, 1977, 78; C. Pollnitz, *Southerly*, XXXVI, 1976, 467; R.A. Simpson, *Age*, 29 May, 1976, 21.

Non-Fiction
[Statement in reply to a questionnaire on his poetry]. *A.L.S.*, VIII, 1977, 156-57.

Critical Material
Code, Trevor. 'Speaking with John Forbes, August, 1989'. *Mattoid*, No. 34, 1989, 108-29.
Duwell, Martin. 'John Forbes'. In his *A Possible Contemporary Poetry* (St Lucia: Makar, 1982). Interview.
Haskell, Dennis. 'Thoughts on Some Recent Poetry'. *A.L.S.*, VIII, 1977, 136-48.
Jenkins, John. 'John Forbes'. *Helix*, Nos. 5-6, 1980, 96-104.
Page, Geoff. 'John Forbes'. In his *A Reader's Guide To Contemporary Australian Poetry* (St. Lucia: U.Q.P., 1995), 69-71.
Sant, Andrew, ed. *Toads: Australian Writers: Other Work, Other Lives*, edited by Andrew Sant (Sydney: Allen & Unwin, 1992). Collection of autobiographical essays on writing and money. Includes Forbes.
Strauss, Jennifer. *Stop Laughing! I'm Being Serious: Three Studies in Seriousness and Wit in Contemporary Australian Poetry* The Colin Roderick Lectures, Monograph 21 (Townsville, Qld.: Foundation for Australian Literary Studies, 1990). Discusses Forbes.
Trigg, Stephanie. 'Does This Really Go With That?' *Island Magazine*, No. 36, 1988, 22-29. On recent Australian poetry.

FORBES, WILLIAM ANDERSON

Critical Material
McDonald, Lorna L. '"Oh, Vaunted Queensland!": A Literary Interpretation, 1862-69'. *A.L.S.*, VI, 1973, 177-86.

FORREST, DAVID (DAVID DENHOLM)

Non-Fiction

'The Split-Level Culture'. In *Literary Australia*, edited by Clement Semmler and Derek Whitelock (Melbourne: Cheshire, 1966), 34-50. Includes comment about his writing.

Critical Material

Hosking, Rick. 'The Usable Past: Australian War Fiction of the 1950s'. *A.L.S.*, XII, No. 2, 1985, 234-247.

Semmler, Clement. 'David Forrest: A Voice for Youth and Irony'. *Australian Quarterly*, XXXVIII, 1966, 45-54.

Watson, Betty L. 'The Australian Image: Social Realism, Send-Up and Satire'. *English in Australia*, No. 18, 1971, 11-21.

FORTUNE, MARY

Non-Fiction

The Fortunes of Mary Fortune. Edited with introduction by Lucy Sussex (Ringwood, Vic.: Penguin, 1989).

Reviewed by C. Bird, *Australian Women's Book Review*, 1, No. 2, 1989, 29; P. Butterss, *Antithesis*, 4, No. 1, 1990, 176-78; D. Davison, *Margin*, No. 22, 1989, 29; M. Luke, *ABR*, No. 115, 1989, 42; R. Lucas, *S.M.H.*, 14 October, 1989, 81; A. Rawlins, *Weekend Australian*, 28-29 October, 1989, Weekend 8 and *Overland*, No. 117, 1990, 92-94; K. Stewart, *A.L.S.*, 14, No.4, 1990, 525-29.

Critical Material

Sussex, Lucy. 'Cherchez la femme: Finding Mrs Fortune'. *Hecate*, 14, No. 2, 1988, 56-65.

Sussex, Lucy, and Mary Lord. 'Mary Fortune and the First Detective Story'. *Overland*, 125, 1991, 47. Letters relating to the publication date of Fortune's short story 'The Dead Witness'.

Sussex, Lucy. 'Shrouded in Mystery: Waif Wander (Mary Fortune)'. In *A Bright and Fiery Troop: Australian Women Writers of the Nineteenth Century*, edited by Debra Adelaide (Ringwood: Penguin, 1988), 117-131.

FOSTER, DAVID

Fiction

The Adventures of Christian Rosy Cross. (Ringwood, Vic.: Penguin, 1986).

Reviewed by J. Cotter, *ABR*, No. 86, 1986, 7-8; H. Daniel, *Age Saturday Extra*, 23 August, 1986, 12; V. Foster, *Phoenix Review*, No. 2, 1987/88, 114-117; T. Glad, *Social Alternatives*, VI, No. 4, 1987, 68-69; esp. 69; J. Hanrahan, *National Times on Sunday*, 7 September, 1986, 38; D. Matthews, *Overland*, No. 106, 1987, 80-82; H. McQueen, *S.M.H.*, 30 August, 1986, 42; C. Pybus, *Island Magazine*, No. 32, 1987, 63-64; M. Thomas, *Canberra Times*, 29 November, 1986, B3.

Dog Rock: A Postal Pastoral. (Ringwood, Vic.: Penguin, 1985).

Reviewed by D. Anderson, *National Times*, 4-10 January, 1985, 34; I. Baranay, *S.M.H.*, 26 January, 1985, 36; H. Daniel, *Age Saturday Extra*, 26 January, 1985, 12; G. Dutton, *Bulletin*, 26 February, 1985, 84-85; K. England, *Advertiser*, 23 March, 1985, 6; K. Goldsworthy, *ABR*, No. 71, 1985, 20; J. Lewis, *Fremantle Arts Centre Broadsheet: Books*, IV, No. 2, 1985, 4; S. McKernan, *Age Monthly Review*, IV, No. 11, 1985, 3-4; V. Sen, *Canberra Times*, 9 March, 1985, 20.

With David Lyall. *The Empathy Experiment*. (Sydney: Wild & Woolley, 1977).

Reviewed by D. Broderick, *24 Hours*, 3, No. 1, 1978, 62; E. Lindsay, *Australian*, 22 April, 1978, 9; W. Noonan, *S.M.H.*, 12 August, 1978, 19; G. Turner, *Age*, 1 April, 1978, 24.

Escape to Reality. (Melbourne: Macmillan, 1977).
Reviewed by W. Blaxland, *S.M.H.*, 14 January, 1978, 17; P. Corris, *Weekend Australian Magazine*, 5-6 November, 1977, 12.

Hitting the Wall: Two Novellas. (Ringwood, Vic.: Penguin, 1989).
Reviewed by B. Birskys, *Span*, No. 29, 1989, 115-16; R.F. Brissenden, *Weekend Australian*, 11-12 March, 1989, Weekend 10; K. Goldsworthy, *Age Saturday Extra*, 4 March, 1989, 11; C. Mann, *Antipodes*, 4.1, 1990, 66; M. Roberts, *ABR*, No. 109, 1989, 34-35; W. Tonetto, *Mattoid*, No. 36, 1990, 155-67.

Mates of Mars. (Ringwood, Vic.: Penguin, 1991).
Reviewed by H. Daniel, *Age*, 10 August, 1991, Saturday Extra 8; T. Dowling, Weekend Australian, 17-18 August, 1991, Review 5; A.M. Hertzberg, *Overland*, 125, 1991, 95-96; A. Peek, *ABR*, 133, 1991, 12-13; R. Sorensen, *S.M.H.*, 3 August, 1991, 42.

Moonlite. (Sth. Melbourne: Macmillan, 1980).
Reviewed by R. Barnes, *National Times*, 24-30 May, 1981, 52; M. Clark, *Bulletin*, 23 June, 1981, 87,89; H. Daniel, *Age*, 13 June, 1981, 25; N. Keesing, *S.M.H.*, 6 June, 1981, 46; S. McKernan, *Age Monthly Review*, 4, No. 11, 1985, 3-4.

North South West. (Sth. Melbourne: Macmillan, 1973).
Reviewed by R. Nicholls, *Age*, 2 February, 1974, 12; D. Swain, *Canberra Times*, 21 December, 1973, 9; K. Tennant, *S.M.H.*, 5 January, 1974, 16.

The Pale Blue Crochet Coathanger Cover. (Ringwood, Vic.: Penguin, 1988).
Reviewed by H. Daniel, *Age Saturday Extra*, 30 July, 1988, 14; D.F. Porter, *Weekend Australian*, 30-31, July, 1988, Weekend 15; A. Peek *Antipodes*, 3.1, 1989, 62; D.P. Reiter, *Redoubt*, No. 4, 1988, 68-70; A.P. Riemer, *S.M.H.*, 30 July, 1988, 77.

Plumbum. (Ringwood, Vic.: Penguin, 1983).
Reviewed by L. Clancy, *Age Saturday Extra*, 28 January, 1984, 13; H. Daniel, *ABR*, No. 60, 1984, 18-19; G. Dutton, *Bulletin*, 20 December, 1983, 62; T. Forshaw, *Quadrant*, 28, No. 6, 1984, 86-7; S. Knight, *S.M.H.*, 14 April, 1984, 41; S. McKernan, *Age Monthly Review*, 4, No. 11, 1985, 3-4; H. Thomas, *National Times*, 23-29 December, 1983, 29.

The Pure Land. (Melbourne: Macmillan, 1974).
Reviewed by S. Edgar, *Canberra Times*, 7 March, 1975, 10; C. Harrison-Ford, *Australian*, 16 November, 1974, 37; J. Tittensor, *Nation Review*, 11-17 October, 1974, 1653.

Testostero. (Ringwood, Vic.: Penguin, 1987).
Reviewed by A. Cromwell, *Antipodes*, II, No. 1, 1988, 60; H. Daniel, *Age Saturday Extra*, 14 February, 1987, 16; V. Foster, *Phoenix Review*, No. 2, 1987/88, 114-117; D. Hewett, *Overland*, No. 108, 1987, 83-86; esp. 84-85; M. Johnston, *Times on Sunday*, 8 February, 1987, 27; S. McKernan, *ABR*, No. 89, 1987, 23-24; A. Mitchell, *Weekend Australian. Weekend Magazine*, 28 February-1 March, 1987, 15.

Poetry
The Fleeing Atalanta. (Adelaide: Maximus Books, 1975).
Reviewed by S.E. Lee, *Southerly*, 36, 1976, 331-56; T. Thorne, *Australian*, 14 February, 1976, 32.

Non-Fiction
'The Reader-Writer Feedback Cycle'. *Island*, 46, 1991, 30-34.

Critical Material
Baker, Candida. 'David Foster'. In her *Yacker: Australian Writers Talk About Their Work* (Sydney: Picador, 1986), 104-126.
Broinowski, Alison. 'Foster At Forty Plus'. *Australian Literary Quarterly*, 6-7 June, 1987, 10.

Burns, D.R. 'The Coming of the "Contained Account": *Moonlite*, David Foster's Landmark Novel'. *Overland*, 129, 1992, 62-67.

Daniel, Helen. *Liars: Australian New Novelists*. (Ringwood, Vic.: Penguin, 1988), 77-104.

Gelder, Kenneth. 'The "Self-Contradictory" Fiction of David Foster'. In *Aspects of Australian Fiction: Essays Presented to John Colmer*, edited by Alan Brissenden (Nedlands, WA.: University of Western Australia Press, 1990), 149-59.

Keesing, Nancy. 'Attitudes to Science in Australia'. *Quadrant*, XXXII, No. 4, 1988, 3. Letter discussing article by Noel Macainsh, specifically mentioning David Foster.

Minogue, Dennis. 'Literature Called to the Man in Science'. *Age*, 23 November, 1974, 2.

Riemer, A.P. 'Bare-Breech'd Brethren: The Novels of David Foster'. *Southerly*, XLVII, No. 2, 1987, 126-144.

Sant, Andrew, ed. *Toads: Australian Writers: Other Work, Other Lives*, edited by Andrew Sant (Sydney: Allen & Unwin, 1992). Collection of autobiographical essays on writing and money. Includes Foster.

Shaw, Narelle. 'Boundary Crossing: The Novels of David Foster'. *A.L.S.*, 16.1, 1993, 38-49.

---. 'The Fellowship of Light and Darkness: David Foster's *Moonlite*'. *Westerly*, 37.3, 1992, 55-63.

---. 'Nothing is Random: David Foster's *Plumbum*'. *Southerly*, 50, No. 1, 1990, 80-92.

---. 'The Passion of D'Arcy D'Oliveres: David Foster's "Dog Rock" Novels'. *Antipodes*, 4.1, 1990, 29-34.

---. '*Testostero*: David Foster's Comic Novel'. *Journal of Commonwealth Literature*, 26.1, 1991, 65-78.

Travers, E.A. 'On the Philosophical: An Interview with David Foster'. *Westerly*, 37.1, 1992, 71-78.

FRANKLIN, MILES

Fiction

Bring the Monkey. With an introduction by Bronwen Levy. (London: Pandora, 1987). First published Sydney: Endeavour Press, 1933.

Reviewed by R. Davie, *Age Saturday Extra*, 2 March, 1985, 15; K. England, *Advertiser*, 9 February, 1985, 37; B. Tivey, *Weekend Australian Magazine*, 16-17 February, 1985, 11.

My Brilliant Career. (Sydney: A.& R., 1965, 1978; London: Virago, 1981; New York: St Martin's Press, 1981). First published Edinburgh: Blackwood, 1901.

Reviewed by V. Coleman, *Quadrant*, XXIII, No. 10, 1979, 67-69; M. Dunlevy, *Canberra Times*, 26 March, 1966, 13; B. Elliott, *ABR*, V, 1966, 134; G. Johnston, *Australian*, 7 May, 1966, 9; H. MacGregor, *Books and Bookmen*, XI, No. 12, 1966, 32; C. Moorehead, *Spectator*, 20 June, 1981, 24-25; A.A. Phillips, *Age*, 13 August, 1966, 24; P. Rose, *New York Times Book Review*, 4 January, 1981, 8, 21. See also letter from P. Rose, 15 February, 1981, 37.

My Brilliant Career and My Career Goes Bung. Introduction by Elizabeth Webby. (North Ryde, N.S.W.: A.& R., 1990).

Reviewed by L. Clancy, *Weekend Australian*, 20-21 October, 1990, Review 5.

My Career Goes Bung: Purporting to be the Autobiography of Sybylla Penelope Melvyn. (London: Virago, 1981). First published Melbourne: Georgian House, 1946.

Reviewed by J. Campbell, *New Statesman*, 15 May, 1981, 21; C. Moorehead, *Spectator*, 20 June, 1981, 24-25.

On Dearborn Street. With an introduction by Roy Duncan. (St Lucia: U.Q.P., 1981).

Reviewed by J. Abbott, *Age*, 5 December, 1981, 27; H. Brown, *Canberra Times*, 27

February, 1982, 15; A. Clark, *ABR*, No. 40, 1982, 9-10; D. Kirkby, *A.L.S.*, X, 1982, 409-10; A.A. Phillips, *Age Saturday Extra*, 4 September, 1982, 15; J. Roe, *National Times*, 8-14 November, 1981, 59.

With Dymphna Cusack. *Pioneers on Parade: A Novel*. (North Ryde, NSW: A.& R., 1988). First published Sydney: A.& R., 1939.
Reviewed by G. Flynn, *Weekend Australian*, 19-20 November, 1988, Weekend 9; J. Roe, *Australian Society*, 7, No. 12, 1988/89, 40-41.

Some Everyday Folk and Dawn. With a new introduction by Jill Roe. (London: Virago Press, 1988). First published Edinburgh: Blackwood, 1909.

Up the Country: 'Brent of Bin Bin'. (Sydney: A.& R., 1966). First published Edinburgh: Blackwood, 1928.
Reviewed by L.J. Clancy, *Australian*, 9 July, 1966, 10.

Up the Country: A Saga of Pioneering Days. (Sydney: A.& R., 1984). First published Edinburgh: Blackwood, 1928: Australian edition with author's note A.& R., 1951. This edition edited (anonymously) from a manuscript held by Berkelouw.
Reviewed by L. Clancy, *ABR*, No. 69, 1985, 29-30; B. Jefferis, *Weekend Australian Magazine*, 29-30 September, 1984, 15; D. Myers, *Age Saturday Extra*, 22 September, 1984, 17.

Non-Fiction

As Good as a Yarn with You: Letters between Miles Franklin, Katharine Susannah Prichard, Jean Devanny, Marjorie Barnard, Flora Eldershaw and Eleanor Dark. Edited by Carole Ferrier. (Cambridge: Cambridge UP, 1992). For reviews see Barnard, Marjorie.

Childhood at Brindabella, My First Ten Years. (Sydney: A.& R., 1974). A.& R. Classics. First published Sydney: A.& R., 1963.
Reviewed by V. Coleman, *Quadrant*, XXIII, No. 10, 1979, 67-69.

My Congenials: Miles Franklin & Friends in Letters. Edited by Jill Roe. 2 vols. (Pymble, NSW: State Library of New South Wales in assoc. with Collins A.& R.
Reviewed by C. Ferrier, *Weekend Australian*, 30-31 October, 1993, Review 7; S. Lever, *A.L.S.*, 17.1, 1995, 104-05; R. Lucas, *Bulletin*, 12 October, 1993, 113; E. Webby, *S.M.H.*, 2 October: Spectrum 11A.

Critical Material

Guide to the Papers and Books of Miles Franklin in the Mitchell Library, State Library of N.S.W. (Sydney: Library Council of N.S.W., 1980). Mitchell Library Manuscripts Guides, No. 3. Reviewed by V. Coleman, *Quadrant*, XXIV, No. 10, 1980, 69.

Barnard, Marjorie. *Miles Franklin*. (Melbourne: Hill of Content; New York: Twayne, 1967). Reviewed by G. Johnston, *Nation*, 20 January, 1968, 21; N. Keesing, *Bulletin*, 9 December, 1967, 80; S. Murray-Smith, *ABR*, VII, 1968, 71; W. Stone, *A.L.S.*, IV, 1969, 88-90; K. Tennant, *S.M.H.*, 2 December, 1967, 21.
Barnes, John. 'Australian Books in Print: Filling Some Gaps'. *Westerly*, No. 2, 1967, 60-63.
---. 'Joseph Furphy and Miles Franklin'. *Overland*, No. 119, 1990, 78-86.
Beasley, Jack. *Journal of an Era: Notes from the Red Letter Days*. (Earlwood, N.S.W.: Wedgetail Press, 1988), 97-100.
Bertrand, Ina. '"Woman's Voice": The Autobiographical Form in Three Australian Filmed Novels'. *Literature/Film Quarterly*, 21.2, 1993, 130-37. Discusses works by Franklin, Garner, and Gunn.
Bird, Delys. 'Towards an Aesthetics of Australian Women's Fiction: *My Brilliant Career* and *The Getting of Wisdom*'. *A.L.S.*, XI, 1983, 171-81.
Bright, Anne. 'A letter from Brent of Bin Bin'. *South Australiana*, IV, 1965, 16-20.
Clancy, Jack. 'Bringing Franklin up to date: The Film of *My Brilliant Career*'.

A.L.S., IX, 1980, 363-67.

Coleman, Verna. *Miles Franklin in America: Her Unknown (Brilliant) Career.* (Sydney: A.& R., 1981). Reviewed by M. Barnard, *Quadrant*, XXVI, No. 3, 1982, 89-90; J. Breen, *New Statesman*, 12 March, 1982, 19-20; M. Dunlevy, *Canberra Times*, 20 February, 1982, 12; B. Faust, *ABR*, No. 40, 1982, 8-9; D. Kirkby, *A.L.S.*, X, 1982, 548; J. Kitson, *Age*, 19 February, 1982, 16; D. McCulloch, *Advertiser*, 6 March, 1982, 26; E. Riddell, *Bulletin*, 26 January, 1982, 90; C. Semmler, *Courier-Mail*, 6 February, 1982, 24.

Cvetkovski, Vladimir. 'Miles Franklin's Journey to Macedonia'. In *A Passage to Somewhere Else*, Proceedings of the Commonwealth Conference held in the University of Barcelona, 30 September-2 October, 1987, edited by Doireann MacDermott and Susan Ballyn (Barcelona: Promociones y Publicaciones Universitarias, 1988), 25-30.

Duncan, Roy. 'Miles Franklin - An Unpublished Teenage Novel'. *A.L.S.*, VIII, 1977, 91-93.

Dutton, Geoffrey. 'Gentlemen vs. Lairs'. *Quadrant*, IX, No. 1, 1965, 14-20.

Frizell, Helen. 'Miles Franklin: The Track from Brindabella'. *S.M.H.*, 28 April, 1979, 12. See also 21 April, 1979, 19, 5 May, 1979, 19.

Gardner, Susan. '"My Brilliant Career": Portrait of the Artist as a Wild Colonial Girl'. In *Gender, Politics and Fiction: Twentieth Century Women's Novels*, edited by Carole Ferrier (St Lucia: U.Q.P., 1985), 22-43.

Gilchrist, Hugh. 'Miles Franklin in Macedonia'. *Quadrant*, XXVI, No. 8, 1982, 54-57.

Gingell, Susan. 'Delineating the Differences: An Approach to Miles Franklin's *My Brilliant Career*'. *Australian and New Zealand Studies in Canada*, No. 3, 1990, 43-55.

Heseltine, H.P. 'C. Hartley Grattan in Australia: Some Correspondence, 1937-38'. *Meanjin*, XXIX, 1970, 356-64.

Hickey, Bernard. 'On Re-Reading Miles Franklin'. In *Australian Papers: Yugoslavia, Europe and Australia*, edited by Mirko Jurak (Ljubljana: Edvard Cardelj University, 1983), 153-57.

Hooton, Joy. 'Miles Franklin's Childhood at Brindabella'. *Meanjin*, XLVI, No. 1, 1987, 58-66.

Kent, Valerie. 'Alias Miles Franklin'. In *Gender, Politics and Fiction: Twentieth Century Women's Novels*, edited by Carole Ferrier (St Lucia, U.Q.P., 1985), 44-58.

Kirkby, Dianne. 'Miles Franklin on Dearborn Street, Chicago, 1906-15'. *A.L.S.*, X, 1982, 344-57.

Lindsay, Norman. 'Miles Franklin'. *Bohemians of the Bulletin* (Sydney: A.& R., 1965), 143-5.

Martin, David. '1954: Meeting Miles for the Last Time'. *Overland*, No. 62, 1975, 36-37.

---. 'Miles Franklin'. *An Overland Muster*, edited by Stephen Murray-Smith (Brisbane: Jacaranda Press, 1965), 13-15.

Martin, Sylvia. 'Relative Correspondence: Franklin's *My Brilliant Career*, and the Influence of Nineteenth-century Australian Women's Writing'. In *The Time to Write: Australian Women Writers 1890-1930*, edited by Kay Ferres (Ringwood, Vic.: Penguin, 1993), 54-70.

---. 'Miles Franklin in London: The Story of a Friendship'. *Meanjin*, 51.1, 1992, 35-44.

Mathew, Ray. *Miles Franklin.* (Melbourne: Lansdowne Press, 1963). Australian Writers and their Work series.

Matthews, Brian. 'Disguises and Persecutions: Miles Franklin, Louisa Lawson, Barbara Baynton'. In his *Romantics and Mavericks: The Australian Short Story.* (Townsville, Qld.: James Cook University of North Queensland, 1987), 4-15. The

Colin Roderick Lectures; 1986. Monograph/Foundation for Australian Literary Studies, No. 14.
---. 'An Uncongenial Life: Miles Franklin's *My Brilliant Career*'. In *Making Connections: Introducing Nine Texts for Senior English Students*, edited by Graham Tulloch and Annie Greet (Adelaide: CRNLE/Flinders University of SA and Trinity Gardens/SAETA), 59-65.
McInherny, Frances. 'Miles Franklin, *My Brilliant Career* and the Female Tradition'. *A.L.S.*, IX, 1980, 275-85. Reprinted in *Who is She?*, edited by Shirley Walker (St Lucia: U.Q.P., 1983), 71-83.
Muir, Nigel. 'Miles Franklin Confesses'. *S.M.H.*, 16 July, 1966, 15.
Perosa, Sergio. 'Notes on Miles Franklin's *My Career Goes Bung*'. In *Saggi e ricerche sulle culture extraeuropee*, edited by G. Bellini, C. Gorlier and S. Zoppi (Rome: Bulzoni, 1985), 19-28. Africa, America, Asia, Australia, 1.
Olubas, Brigitta. '"Infinite Rehearsal" in the Work of Miles Franklin'. *New Literatures Review*, No. 18, 1990, 37-47.
Pybus, Cassandra. 'The Real Miles Franklin?' *Meanjin*, XLII, 1983, 459-68.
Roderick, Colin. *Miles Franklin: Her Brilliant Career*. (Adelaide: Rigby, 1982). Reviewed by B. Davis, *Overland*, No. 91, 1983 23-27; D. Gallagher, *LiNQ*, X, No. 3, 1982/83, 68-72; J. Hanrahan, *ABR*, No. 49, 1983, 21-22; N. Keesing, *Age Saturday Extra*, 4 September, 1982, 15; V. Kent, *A.L.S.*, XI, 1983, 132-36; C. Treloar, *Advertiser*, 16 October, 1982, 30.
Roe, Jill. 'The Appeal of Biography'. In *Writing Lives: Feminist Biography and Autobiography*, edited by Susan Magarey, Caroline Guerin, and Paula Hamilton (Adelaide: Australian Feminist Studies, Research Centre for Women's Studies U of Adelaide, 1992 / *Australian Feminist Studies*, 16, 1992, special issue), 3-10. On Franklin.
---. 'For Australians Only - Jill Roe Writes About the Life and Work of Miles Franklin'. *London Review of Books*, X, No. 4, 1988, 10.
---. 'Forcing the Issue: Miles Franklin and Australian Identity'. *Hecate*, 17.1, 1991 (special issue *Women/Australia/Theory*), 67-73.
---. 'Miles Franklin's Library'. In *Books, Readers, Reading*, edited by David Walker with Julia Horne and Martyn Lyons, *Australian Cultural History*, 11, 1992, 51-66.
---. 'The Significant Silence: Miles Franklin's Middle Years'. *Meanjin*, XXXIX, 1980, 48-59.
---. '"Tremenjus Good For What Ails Us": The Correspondence of Miles Franklin and C. Hartley Grattan'. In *Perspectives on Australia: Essays on Australiana in the Collections of the Harry Ransom Humanities Research Center*, edited by Dave Oliphant (Austin: Harry Ransom Humanities Research Center, University of Texas, 1989), 70-101.
Roe, Phil. '*Sybyllascape*: Language and Landscape - Intervening in the Historical Space of Literary Narrative'. *SPAN*, 32, 1991, 24-31.
Roff, Sue. 'Rites of Passage: Six Australian Authors in Search of the Same Character'. *Australian Society*, III, No. 9, 1984, 33-34.
Rose, Paulette. 'Miles Franklin: Chronicler of the Australian Bush and Early Feminist'. In *Faith of a (Woman) Writer*, edited by Alice Kessler-Harris and William McBrien (Westport, Ct: Greenwood Press, 1988), 119-27.
Rutherford, Anna. 'Miles Franklin: The Outside Track'. In *Multiple Worlds, Multiple Words: Essays in Honour of Irene Simon*, edited by Hena Maes-Jelinek, Pierre Michel and Paulette Michel-Michot (Liege: Dept. of English, University of Liege, 1988), 239-56.
Sheridan, Sue. 'Louisa Lawson, Miles Franklin and Feminist Writing', 1888-1901'. *Australian Feminist Studies*, Nos. 7 and 8, 1988, 29-47.
Sircar, Sanjay. 'Artfully Artless: Miles Franklin and *My Brilliant Career*'. *Folio* (Folio Society, London), Winter, 1983, 20-27.

---. 'Miles Franklin's *Bring The Monkey*'. *Clues: A Journal of Mystery and Detection*, 15.2, 1994, 15-37.

---. '"Tea with Alice of *Alice in Wonderland*" by Miles Franklin: With an Introduction and Cultural Critique'. *Children's Literature* (Yale UP), 22, 1994, 127-38.

Strauss, Jennifer. 'Portrait of the Artist as a Young Woman: Cultural Contexts and the Quest for Identity in Alice Munro's *Lives of Girls and Women* and in Miles Franklin's *My Brilliant Career* and *My Career Goes Bung*'. *Australian-Canadian Studies*, 8.2, 1991, 41-55.

Sutherland, Bruce. 'Stella Miles Franklin's American Years'. *Meanjin*, XXIV, 1965, 439-54.

Thomas, Glen. 'Reading Women's Writing: The Critical Reception of Miles Franklin'. *LiNQ*, 20.2, 1993, 78-82.

Tolchard, Clifford. 'Miles Franklin - and All That Swagger'. *Walkabout*, XXXIII, No. 1, 1967, 16-19.

Walker, Shirley. 'The Boer War: Paterson, Abbott, Brennan, Miles Franklin and Morant'. *A.L.S.*, XII, No. 2, 1985, 207-222.

Wills, David. 'Antipodean Semiotics: "French Theory" in Australia and the Practice of Antipodean Cinema'. *Commonwealth* (Paris), VI, No. 2, 1984, 95-103. Film of *My Brilliant Career*, directed by Gillian Armstrong.

Wongar, B. '"Hands Warmer than the Sun": B. Wongar on Miles Franklin'. *ABR*, 176, 1995, 14.

FULLERTON, MARY ELIZA

Critical Material

Burke, Colleen Zeita. 'Expanding the Horizons: Researching Neglected Australian Women Poets and Writers'. In *The Book of Poets on the Heath*, edited by Kerry Leves and Ellyn Lewis (Katoomba, N.S.W.: Windowledge Publications, 1993), 126-31.

Hooton, Joy. 'Mary Fullerton: Pioneering and Feminism'. In *The Time to Write: Australian Women Writers 1890-1930*, edited by Kay Ferres (Ringwood, Vic.: Penguin, 1993), 38-53.

Martin, Sylvia. 'Miles Franklin in London: The Story of a Friendship'. *Meanjin*, 51.1, 1992, 35-44.

---. 'Rethinking Passionate Friendships: The Writing of Mary Fullerton'. *Women's History Review*, 2.3, 1993, 395-406.

FURPHY, JOSEPH

Collection

Joseph Furphy. Edited with an introduction by John Barnes. (St Lucia: U.Q.P., 1981). Portable Australian Authors.

Reviewed by V. Brady, *Westerly*, XXVII, No. 1, 1982, 85-88; R. Eaden, *CRNLE Reviews Journal*, No. 1, 1982, 28-31; J. Hanrahan, *ABR*, No. 42, 1982, 32-33; A.M. Stewart, *Quadrant*, XXVII, No. 9, 1983, 84-85; K. Stewart, *A.L.S.*, X, 1982, 541-43.

Fiction

The Annotated Such Is Life: Being Certain Extracts from the Diary of Tom Collins. Introduction and notes by Frances Devlin-Glass, Robin Eaden, Lois Hoffmann and G.W. Turner. (Melbourne: O.U.P., 1991).

Reviewed by J. Barnes, *Bibliographical Society of Australia and New Zealand Bulletin*, 16.3, 1992, 117-24; J. Croft, *A.L.S.*, 15.3, 1992, 235-38; C. Wallace-Crabbe, *ABR*, 132, 1991, 14-15.

The Buln-Buln and the Brolga and Other Stories. Introduction by Kevin Gilding.

(Adelaide: Rigby, 1971). Seal Australian Fiction. *The Buln-Buln and the Brolga* first published Sydney: A.& R., 1948.
Rigby's Romance. Introduction by G.W. Turner. (Adelaide: Rigby, 1971). Seal Australian Fiction. First published as a serial 1905-06 and in full as a book, Melbourne: De Garis, 1921.
Such Is Life. With an introduction by John Barnes. (Penrith, N.S.W.: Discovery Press, 1968). First published Sydney: Bulletin, 1903.

   Non-Fiction
Bushman and Bookworm: Letters of Joseph Furphy. Edited by John Barnes and Lois Hoffman. (Melbourne: O.U.P., 1995).

   Critical Material
Hoffman, Lois. 'Joseph Furphy: An Annotated Checklist of Items in Periodicals'. *A.L.S.*, IX, 1984, 409-16.
Lebedewa, Nina. 'Furphy Criticism Since 1955: A Checklist'. *A.L.S.*, III, 1967, 149-150.
Antonini, Maria. 'Il Romanzo Australiano *Such Is Life* di Joseph Furphy'. *Convivium*, XXXV (1967), 746-55.
Arthur, Kateryna Olijnyk. 'Fencing Furphy: Form of the Chronotope in *Such is Life*'. *Span*, No. 25, 1987, 47-58.
Barnes, John (ed.). *The Writer in Australia*. See particularly Joseph Furphy and A.G. Stephens, 'On Publishing a Novel: A Correspondence', 117-27, and Furphy's 'A Review of *Such is Life*', 128-30.
Barnes, John. '"Every Man Can Write at Least One Book": Joseph Furphy' *Australian Cultural History*, No. 8, 1989, 7-23.
---. 'Furphy and the View from Groper Land'. *Notes & Furphies*, No. 18, 1987, 17-18.
---. *Joseph Furphy*. (Melbourne: Lansdowne Press, 1963). Australian Writers and their Work series.
---. *Joseph Furphy*. (Melbourne: O.U.P., 1967). Great Australians Series.
---. 'On Misreading *Such is Life*'. *Westerly*, 38.3, 1993, 39-49.
---. 'Joseph Furphy and Miles Franklin'. *Overland*, No. 119, 1990, 78-86.
---. *The Order of Things: A Life of Joseph Furphy* (Melbourne: O.U.P., 1990). Reviewed by N. Birns, *Antipodes*, 6.2, 1992, 163-66; V. Brady, *Westerly*, 36.3, 1991, 116-18; B. Matthews, *Overland*, 123, 1991, 85-87; P. Mead, *ABR*, 131, 1991, 28-29; C. Munro, *Weekend Australian*, 23-24 March, 1991, Review 4; P. Pierce, *S.M.H.*, 16 February, 1991, 43; Vivian Smith, *Quadrant*, 35.7-8, 1991, 107-09; K. Stewart, *A.L.S.*, 15.3, 1992, 228-32; C. Wallace-Crabbe, *Age*, 26 January, 1991, Saturday Extra 7.
---.' *Such is Life* and the Observant Reader'. In *Bards, Bohemians, and Bookmen*, edited by Leon Cantrell (St Lucia: U.Q.P., 1976), 153-69.
Buckley, Vincent. 'Imagination's Home'. *Quadrant*, XXXIII, No. 3, 1979, 24-29, rptd. in *Between Two Worlds*, edited by Axel Clark, John Fletcher and Robin Marsden (Sydney: Wentworth Press, 1979), 73-89.
Croft, Julian. 'Between Hay and Booligal: Tom Collins' Land and Joseph Furphy's Landscape'. In *Mapped But Not Known: The Australian Landscape of the Imagination*, edited by P.R. Eaden and F.H. Mares (Netley, S.A.: Wakefield Press, 1986), 154-170.
---. *The Federal and National Impulse in Australian Literature, 1890-1958* The Colin Roderick lectures, Monograph 18 (Townsville, Qld.: Foundation for Australian Literary Studies, 1988). Contains paper on Furphy.
---. 'A Letter to Tom Collins'. *Overland*, 132, 1993, 35-36.
---. *The Life and Opinions of Tom Collins: A Study of the Works of Joseph Furphy*. (St. Lucia: U.Q.P., 1991). Reviewed by J. Barnes, *Quadrant*, 36.1-2, 1992, 99-103;

N. Birns, *Antipodes*, 5.2, 1991, 154; K. Stewart, *A.L.S.*, 15.3, 1992, 228-32; C. Wallace-Crabbe, *ABR*, 132, 1991, 14-15.

---. '"Who is She?" The Image of Woman in the Novels of Joseph Furphy'. In *Who is She?*, edited by Shirley Walker (St Lucia: U.Q.P., 1983), 1-11.

Darby, Robert. 'Furphies: A Comment on a Note on Furphy'. *Notes and Furphies*, No. 17, 1986, 29-30.

---. 'Penguin and the Man-o'-War Hawk: Joseph Furphy's Critical Reputation, 1903-1947'. *A.L.S.*, XIII, No. 2, 1987, 210-223.

Douglas, Dennis. 'Joseph Furphy and the Picaresque: A Generic Re-appraisal of *Such is Life*'. *Overland*, No. 73, 1978, 15-24.

---. 'Tom Collins's Conscience'. *Australian Quarterly*, No. 4, 1964, 75-82.

Dugan, Michael. 'C.J. De Garis as Publisher'. *Biblionews and Australian Notes & Queries*, 2nd ser., IV, No. 2, 1970, 18-18. Publisher of *Rigby's Romance* in 1921.

Dutton, Geoffrey. 'Gentlemen vs. Lairs'. *Quadrant*, IX, No. 1, 1965, 14-20.

Ewers, John K. 'No Ivied Walls'. *Westerly*, No. 4, 1969, 60-68.

Glass, Frances Devlin. 'Furphy and the Land: The Feminine as a Metaphor for Landscape'. *Westerly*, 36.4, 1991, 39-44.

---. 'Joseph Furphy's Novels: Naked Capers in the Riverina'. In *The Australian Experience: Critical Essays on Australian Novels*, edited by W.S. Ramson (Canberra: Australian National University Press, 1974), 73-96.

Grant, Don. 'The House that Furphy Built: Tom Collins House'. *Notes & Furphies*, 30, 1993, 2-5.

Green, Dorothy. 'The Tradition of Social Responsibility in the Australian Novel: Richardson and Furphy'. *Literary Criterion*, XV, Nos. 3-4, 1980, 23-34.

Guo Zhaokang. 'On *Such is Life*'. *Oceanic Literature*, No. 5, 1983, 372-80. In Chinese.

Hadgraft, Cecil. 'The Whirligig and Furphy'. *A.L.S.*, VII, 1976, 229-40.

Hamer, Clive. 'The Christian Philosophy of Joseph Furphy'. *Meanjin*, XXIII, No. 2, 1964, 142-53.

Hartley, Robert. 'Tom Collins, Clot Or Ham?: A Literary Contract Re-examined'. *Southern Review*, IX, No. 2, 1987, 154-172.

Indyk, Ivor. 'Reading Men Like Signboards: The Egalitarian Semiotic of *Such is Life*'. *A.L.S.*, XII, No. 3, 1986, 303-15.

Johnson, Robert L. 'The Road Out in Australian and American Fiction: A Study of Four Spokesmen'. *Southern Review*, I, No. 3, 1965, 20-31.

Keogh, Susan. 'Land, Landscape and *Such is Life*'. *Southerly*, 49, No. 1, 1989, 54-63.

Kiernan, Brian. 'The Comic Vision of *Such is Life*'. *Meanjin*, XXIII, No. 2, 1964, 132-41.

---. 'Society and Nature in *Such is Life*'. *A.L.S.*, I, No. 1, 1963, 75-88.

Knight, Nina. 'Furphy and Romance: *Such is Life* Reconsidered'. *Southerly*, XXIX, 1969, 243-55.

Lang, Jean. 'Some Real Furphies'. *Notes & Furphies*, No. 12, 1984, 10-12.

Lawson, Alan. 'As Plain as the Nose on Your Face: Two Notes on Furphy'. *Notes and Furphies*, No. 17, 1986, 30-31.

Lee, S.E. 'The Story of Mary O'Halloran'. *Drylight*, 1966, 66-75.

Lindsay, Norman. 'Tom Collins'. *Bohemians of the Bulletin* (Sydney: A.& R., 1965), 146-7.

Maidment, W.M. 'Australian Literary Criticism'. *Southerly*, XXIV, 1964, 20-41.

McDougall, R. *Australia Felix: Joseph Furphy and Patrick White*. (Canberra: A.N.U. Press, 1966). C.L.F. lectures.

McKenzie, K.A. 'Joseph Furphy, Jacobean'. *A.L.S.*, II, 1966, 266-77.

Martin, Susan. 'Why Do All these Women Have Moustaches? Gender, Boundary and Frontier in *Such is Life* and "Monsieur Caloche"'. *Southern Review*, 25.1, 1992, 68-

77.
Mead, Philip. 'Reversible Empires: Melville/Shakespeare/Furphy'. In *Shakespeare's Books: Contemporary Cultural Politics and the Persistence of Empire*, edited by Philip Mead and Marion Campbell (Parkville, Vic.: Department of English, U of Melbourne, 1993), 26-49.
Mudie, Ian. 'Fifty Years of *Rigby's Romance*'. *Issue*, I, No. 3, 1971, 27-28.
Oliver, H.J. 'Joseph Furphy'. In *The Literature of Australia*. Revised edition, edited by Geoffrey Dutton (Ringwood, Vic.: Penguin, 1976), 337-50.
---. 'Lawson and Furphy'. In *The Literature of Australia*, edited by Geoffrey Dutton (Adelaide: Penguin Books, 1964), 296-305.
Osland, Dianne. 'Life, and the Opinions of Tom Collins'. *Southerly*, XLV, No. 2, 1985, 227-242.
Pons, Xavier. 'Joseph Furphy, Democratic Artist'. In *Individual and Community in Commonwealth Literature*, edited by Massa Daniel (Msida, Malta: Old University Press, 1979), 115-22.
Richters, Z.P. 'The Moral History of Tom Collins'. *Southerly*, XXXIX, 1979, 246-64.
Rodriguez, Judith. 'The Original Nosey Alf'. *A.L.S.*, VII, 1975, 176-84.
Scheckter, John. 'The Lost Child in Australian Fiction'. *Modern Fiction Studies*, XXVII, No. 1, 1981, 61-72.
Sharkey, Michael. 'The Crow and the King-Bird: Coincidence, or Thought for Jack the Shellback?'. *Notes & Furphies*, No. 13, 1984, 23.
---. 'The Echuca Coffee Palace and the Farmer's Arm'. *Notes & Furphies*, No. 1, 1978, 12.
---. 'Place Names in *Such is Life*'. *Notes & Furphies*, No. 1, 1978, 9.
Smith, Graeme Kinross. 'Joseph Furphy'. *Westerly*, No. 4, 1975, 41-49.
---. 'Joseph Furphy, Bushman & Bookworm'. *This Australia*, I. No. 2, 1982, 21-23.
Turner, G.W. 'The Bandicoot i' the Adage: The Local and the Exotic in Furphy's Literary Landscape'. In *Mapped But Not Known: The Australian Landscape of the Imagination*, edited by P.R. Eaden and F.H. Mares (Netley, S.A.: Wakefield Press, 1986), 171-85.
---. *The English Language in Australia and New Zealand*. (London: Longmans, 1966), passim.
---. 'Joseph Furphy and Narrative Art'. In *Aspects of Australian Fiction: Essays Presented to John Colmer*, edited by Alan Brissenden (Nedlands, WA: University of Western Australia Press, 1990), 41-52.
Walker, David. 'The Palmer Abridgement of *Such is Life*'. *A.L.S.*, VIII, 1978, 491-98.
Wallace-Crabbe, Chris. 'Furphy's "Masculine Strength"'. *The Literary Criterion* (Mysore), VI, No. 3, 1964, 83-92. Reprinted as 'Masculine Strength', in his *Melbourne or the Bush: Essays on Australian Literature and Society*. (Sydney: A.& R., 1974), 14-23.
Whelen, J.A. 'Some Remarks (and possible furphies) on a Literary Anniversary'. *Notes & Furphies* 30, 1993, 5-7. Followed by an 'Index of Furphiana published in previous *Notes & Furphies*'.
White, R.S. *Furphy's Shakespeare*. (Nedlands, WA:, University of Western Australia, 1989). With Appendices by Rebecca Hiscock and Patricia Kotai-Ewers.
Wieland, James. 'Australian Literature and the Question of Historical Method: Reading Lawson and Furphy'. *Journal of Commonwealth Literatures*, XX, No. 1, 1985, 16-35.
Wilding, Michael. *The Radical Tradition: Lawson, Furphy, Stead*. (Townsville, Qld: Foundation for Australian Literary Studies / James Cook U of North Queensland, 1993).
Wilkes, G.A. *Joseph Furphy's 'Such is Life'*. (Melbourne: Shillington House, 1985).

JOSEPH FURPHY 119

Essays in Australian Literature.
---. 'The Australian Image in Literature: *Such is Life* Reconsidered'. *The Teaching of English*, No. 6, 1965, 5-16.
Williams, Justina. *Tom Collins & His House*. (Perth: Tom Collins Press for the Fellowship of Australian Writers, W.A. Section, 1973).
Wilson, Robert R. 'Bushmen in Porcelain Palaces: Knowing and Mistaking in *Such is Life*'. *Southerly*, XXXIX, 1979, 123-42.
Zeller, Robert. 'Delayed Furphy: More of Nejd Arab'. *Notes & Furphies*, 26, 1991, 19.
---. '"I Hope Here Be Truths"': R.G. Howarth as Editor of Joseph Furphy'. In *Perpectives on Australia: Essays on Australiana in the Collections of the Harry Ransom Humanities Research Center*, edited by Dave Oliphant (Austin: Harry Ransom Humanities Research Center, 1989), 103-19.
---. 'Yarning About Yarning: The Buln-Buln and the Brolga and the Rhetoric of *Such is Life*'. *Antipodes*, II, No. 1, 1988, 44-48.

GARNER, HELEN

Fiction

The Children's Bach. (Fitzroy, Vic.: McPhee Gribble; Ringwood, Vic.: Penguin, 1985). First published McPhee Gribble, 1984.
Reviewed by K. Ahearne, *Going Down Swinging*, No. 7, 1986, 44-49; D. Anderson, *National Times*, 30 November-6 December, 1984, 35; R. Beeby, *Age*, 13 December, 1984, 14; K. England, *Advertiser Saturday Review*, 8 December, 1984, 9; C. Gerrish, *Womanspeak*, IX, No. 2, 1985, 25; K. Goldsworthy, *ABR*, No. 68, 1985, 22-24; M. Halligan, *Canberra Times*, 12 January, 1985, 13; V. Horn, *ABR*, No. 71, 1985, 39-40; K. Houghton, *Sunday Mail* (Brisbane), 16 June, 1985, 26; E. Jolley, *Scripsi*, III, Nos. 2-3, 1985, 17-20; N. Jose, *Age Monthly Review*, V, No. 6, 1985, 17-18; P. Koch, *Courier-Mail*, 19 January, 1985, 31; A. Mitchell, *Weekend Australian Magazine*, 8-9 December, 1984, 16; D. Parker, *Quadrant*, XXIX, No. 3, 1985, 70-72; E. Perkins, *CRNLE Reviews Journal*, No. 2, 1985, 9-10; P. Pierce, *Age Saturday Extra*, 1 December, 1984, 18; C. Semmler, *Bulletin*, 20 August, 1985, 82-84; R. Stone, *S.M.H.*, 1 December, 1984, 40; G. Windsor, *Bulletin*, 8 January, 1985, 74.

Cosmo Cosmolino. (Ringwood, Vic.: McPhee Gribble/Penguin, 1992).
Reviewed by G. Bastin, *CRNLE Reviews Journal*, 1, 1992, 49-55; C. Bliss, *World Literature Today*, 67.3, 1993, 667-68; V. Brady, *Westerly*, 37.3, 1992, 87-89; D. Brooks, *Voices*, 2.2, 1992, 89-92; L. Cataldi, *Northern Perspective*, 15.2, 1992, 112-14; P. Craven, *Weekend Australian*, 7-8 March, 1992, Review 7; H. Daniel, *Age*, 29 February, 1992, Saturday Extra 7; S. Dowse, *Modern Times*, March, 1992, 28; A. van Herk, *SPAN*, 37, 1993, 249-52; J. Mead, *Island*, 53, 1992, 66-69; J. Nieuwenhuizen, *ABR*, 139, 1992, 17-18; E. Perkins, *LiNQ*, 19.2, 1992, 169-75; C.K. Stead, *London Review of Books*, 15.2, 1993, 19; A. Stretton, *Bulletin*, 10 March, 1992, 108; N. Walker, *T.L.S.*, 8 January, 1993, 17; J. Waterman *Antipodes*, 6.2, 1992, 147.

Honour & Other People's Children: Two Stories. (Melbourne: McPhee Gribble, 1980).
Reviewed by N. Adams, *Westerly*, XXVI, No. 2, 1981, 75-77; H. Daniel, *Age*, 15 November, 1980, 31; G. Dutton, *Bulletin*, 13 January, 1981, 56; B. Jefferis, *S.M.H.*, 22 November, 1980, 21; P. Pierce, *Meanjin*, XL, 1981, 111-13; C. See, *New York Times Book Review*, 4 April, 1982, 12 & 28; A. Summers, *National Times*, 23-29 November, 1980, 44; H. Thompson, *CRNLE Reviews Journal*, No. 1, 1983, 66-69; G. Windsor, *Quadrant*, XXV, No. 6, 1981, 71-74.

Monkey Grip. (Melbourne: McPhee Gribble, 1977).
Reviewed by E. Carew, *S.M.H.*, 5 November, 1977, 17; R. Conway, *Quadrant*, XXII, No. 5, 1978, 77; S. Edgar, *Canberra Times*, 4 March, 1978, 12; J. Larkin,

Age, 22 October, 1977, 24; N. Shrimpton, *New Statesman*, XCIX, 1980, 174-75; G. Strawson, *T.L.S.*, 18 January, 1980, 54.

Postcards From Surfers. (Fitzroy, Vic.: McPhee Gribble; Ringwood, Vic.: Penguin, 1985). Reviewed by D.R. Burns, *National Times*, 29 November-5 December, 1985, 45; G. Burns, *Age Saturday Extra*, 9 November, 1985, 14; D. Durrant, *London Magazine*, 29, Nos 3-4, 1989, 130; P. Goldsworthy, *S.M.H.*, 21 November, 1985, 48; R. Gostand and S. Cassidy, *Social Alternatives*, V, No. 4, 1986, 56-57; S. Hosking, *Overland*, No. 103, 1986, 67-69; L. Jacobs, *CRNLE Reviews Journal*, No. 2, 1985, 39-42; N. Jose, *Age Monthly Review*, V, No. 10, 1986, 22; C. Jurrist, *Antipodes*, I, No. 2, 1987, 124; A. Mitchell, *Weekend Australian Magazine*, 2-3 November, 1985, 15; S. Moore, *ABR*, No. 77, 1985, 32-34; K. Saunders, *Courier-Mail Magazine: The Great Weekend*, 1 February, 1986, 7; S. Trigg, *Scripsi*, IV, No. 2, 1986, 197-201.

Non-Fiction

The First Stone: Some Questions about Sex and Power. (Sydney: Picador Pan Macmillan, 1994).
Reviewed by P. Craven, *Weekend Australian*, 25-26 March, 1995, Review 7; G. Duncan, *Quadrant*, 39.5, 1995, 75-77; M. Fraser, *Age*, 25 March, 1995, Saturday Extra 7 and *Voices* 5.4, 1995-96, 110-13; F. Giles, *Meanjin*, 54.2, 1995, 384-90; K. McDonald, *Arena Magazine*, 17, 1995, 44-48; C. Pybus, *ABR*, 170, 1995, 6-8 (see also interview with Garner and Pybus by R. Koval, 9-12); M. Rayner, *Eureka Street*, 5.3, 1995, 31-35; R. Sorensen, *S.M.H.*, 25 March, 1995, Spectrum 9A; A. Wertheim, *Antipodes*, 9.2, 1995, 177-78. See also 'Three Perspectives on H. Garner's *The First Stone*' by J. Hanrahan, M. Lake and G. Little, *ABR*, 174, 1995, 25-28.

'Helen Garner on *The Children's Bach* and "Two Friends"'. In *Writers in Action: The Writer's Choice Evenings*, edited by Gerry Turcotte ed. (Sydney: Currency Press, 1990), 161-78.

Critical Material

'Interview - Helen Garner'. *Going Down Swinging*, No. 7, 1986, 50-57.
Ashcroft, W.D. 'The Language of Music: Helen Garner's *The Children's Bach*'. *A.L.S.*, 14, No. 4, 1990, 489-98.
Baker, Candida. 'Helen Garner'. In her *Yacker: Australian Writers Talk About Their Work* (Sydney: Picador, 1986), 128-56.
Bertrand, Ina. '"Woman's Voice": The Autobiographical Form in Three Australian Filmed Novels'. *Literature/Film Quarterly*, 21.2, 1993, 130-37. Discusses works by Franklin, Garner, and Gunn.
Bice, Kathryn. 'Helen Garner Has to Murder Her Darlings'. *Australian Financial Review Magazine: Weekend Review*, No. 19, 1986, 10-11.
Brophy, Kevin. 'Helen Garner's *Monkey Grip*: The Construction of an Author and Her Work'. *A.L.S.*, 15.4, 1992, 270-81.
Brydon, Diana. 'Contracts with the World: Redefining Home, Identity and Community in [Four Women Novelists:] Aidoo, Brodber, Garner and Rule'. In *The Commonwealth Novel Since 1960*, edited by Bruce King (Houndmills, Basingstoke, Hampshire and London: Macmillan, 1991), 198-215.
Burns, D.R. 'The Active Passive Inversion: Sex Roles in Garner, Stead and Harrower'. *Meanjin*, XLV, No. 3, 1986, 346-53.
Chisholm, Anne. 'A Love of Language'. *National Times*, 4-10 January, 1981, 31. Interview.
Clower, John. 'The Anarchistic Craft of *The Children's Bach*'. *Australian & New Zealand Studies in Canada*, 6, 1991. 55-75.
Craven, Peter. 'Of War and Needlework: The Fiction of Helen Garner'. *Meanjin*, XLIV, No. 2, 1985, 209-218.
Curthoys, Ann. 'Helen Garner's *The First Stone*'. *Australian Feminist Studies*, 21,

1995, 203-11.

Ellison, Jennifer. 'Helen Garner'. In her *Rooms of Their Own* (Ringwood, Vic.: Penguin, 1986), 132-151.

Grandy, Karen. 'Serving the Home Guard: Housekeepers and Homemakers in *The Children's Bach* and *Dancing in the Dark*'. *Australian & New Zealand Studies in Canada*, 6, 1991, 76-89.

Grenville, Kate, and Sue Woolfe. *Making Stories: How Ten Australian Novels Were Written*. (St Leonards, NSW: Allen & Unwin, 1993). Includes contribution on *The Children's Bach*.

Hope, Deborah. 'Helen Garner: Reflections on Life as Writer and Artist'. *Bulletin*, 5 November, 1985, 82-84.

Kelly, Philippa. 'The Language of Subversion: Discourses of Desire in *Painted Woman, The Children's Bach* and *Messages from Chaos*'. *Southerly*, 54.1, 1994, 143-56.

---. 'Transgressive Spaces: Helen Garner's *Cosmo Cosmolino*'. *Westerly*, 40.1, 1995, 19-25.

Levy, Bronwen. 'Third Time Lucky, or After the Wash-up'. *Imago*, 7.3, 1995, 108-17. Discusses the public debate concerning *The First Stone* and H. Darville Demidenko's *The Hand that Signed the Paper*.

Liddelow, Eden. 'Helen Garner: A Retrospective, with Angels'. *Scripsi*, 7.3, 1992, 106-18.

McDonald, Roger. *Gone Bush* (Sydney: Bantam, 1990), 93-108. Talk with Garner.

Mansfield, Nicholas. '"A Pleasant, Meaningless Discord": Helen Garner's *The Children's Bach*'. *Westerly* 36.2, 1991, 17-22.

Rogers, Shelagh. '"You Don't Really Know What It is Until You Go Away and Come Back": Interviews with Four Australian Writers'. *Australian and New Zealand Studies in Canada*, No. 1, 1989, 33-43.

Shepherd, Greg. 'An Interview with Helen Garner'. *English in Australia*, No. 66, 1984, 44-48.

Taylor, Andrew. 'Desire and Repetition in the Novels of Helen Garner'. In *Aspects of Australian Fiction: Essays Presented to John Colmer*, edited by Alan Brissenden (Nedlands, WA: University of Western Australia Press, 1990), 113-26.

Wachtel, Eleanor. '"I'm Writing to Save Myself": An Interview with Helen Garner'. *Australian & New Zealand Studies in Canada*, 19, 1993, 57-65.

Willbanks, Ray. 'Helen Garner'. In his *Speaking Volumes: Australian Writers and Their Work* (Ringwood, Vic.: Penguin, 1991).

GAUNT, MARY

Fiction

Kirkham's Find. Introduction by Kylie Tennant; afterword by Dale Spender. (Ringwood, Vic.: Penguin, 1988). First published London: Methuen, 1897.

Reviewed by S. Roff, *Antipodes*, 3.1, 1989, 34.

Critical Material

Bradstock, Margaret. 'Gaunt and Cambridge: The Warrnambool Connection'. *Bibliographical Society of Australia and New Zealand Bulletin*, 16.4, 1992, 155-57.

---. 'Mary Gaunt in China'. *Southerly*, 53.3, 1993, 151-60.

Jones, Dorothy. 'Water, Gold and Honey: A Discussion of *Kirkham's Find*'. In *Debutante Nation: Feminism Contests the 1890s*, edited by Susan Magarey, Sue Rowley, and Susan Sheridan (St Leonards, NSW: Allen & Unwin, 1993), 175-84.

Martin, Sue. '"Sad Sometimes, Lonely Often . . . Dull Never": Mary Gaunt, Traveller and Novelist'. In *A Bright and Fiery Troop: Australian Women Writers of the Nineteenth Century*, edited by Debra Adelaide (Ringwood: Penguin, 1988), 183-97.

McPherson, Bernice. 'A Colonial Feminine Ideal: Femininity and Representation'.

Journal of Australian Studies, 42, 1994, 5-17. Includes discussion of Cambridge and Gaunt.
Whitlock, Gillian. '"A Most Improper Desire": Mary Gaunt's Journey to Jamaica'. *Kunapipi*, 15.3, 1993, 86-95.

GELLERT, LEON

Critical Material
Wieland, James. 'Leon Gellert's *Songs of a Campaign*: Reading an Un-read Poem'. *Southerly*, 52.2, 1992, 82-98.

GEOGHEGAN, EDWARD

Drama
The Currency Lass; or, My Native Girl: A Musical Play in Two Acts. Edited by Roger Covell (Sydney: Currency Press; London: Eyre Methuen, 1976). The National Theatre.
Reviewed by D. Gyger, *24 Hours*, II, No. 3, 1977, 51; E. Riddell, *Australian*, 26 June, 1976, 40; H. Van Der Poorten, *Theatre-Australia* (New Lambton Heights, N.S.W.), I, No. 1, 1976, 52; A.W., *Theatrescope* (Sydney), No. 2, 1976, 26.

Critical Material
Oppenheim, Helen. 'The Author of *The Hibernian Father*: An Early Colonial Playwright'. *A.L.S.*, II, 1966, 278-88.
---. '*The Hibernian Father*: Mysteries Solved and Unsolved'. *A.L.S.*, III, 1967, 66-67.
Weiner, Albert B. '*The Hibernian Father*: The Mystery Solved'. *Meanjin*, XXV, 1966, 456-64.

GIBBS, MAY

Critical Material
Guide to the Papers of May Gibbs in the Mitchell Library, State Library of New South Wales. (Sydney: State Library of NSW, 1990). Reviewed by G. Powell, *Archives and Manuscripts*, 19.2, 1991, 239-41.

Lang, Jean. *Pathway to Magic: The Story of May Gibbs in Western Australia*. (Perth, WA: Challenge Bank, 1991).
Walsh, Maureen. *May Gibbs: Mother of the Gumnuts*. (Sydney: A.& R., 1994). Reviewed by M. Jones, *S.M.H.*, 13 August, 1994, Spectrum 9A, P. Loiterton, *Redoubt*, 20, 1995, 127-28.

GILBERT, KEVIN

Fiction
Me and Mary Kangaroo. (Ringwood, Vic.: Viking, 1994).
Reviewed by A. Baillie, *ABR*, 168, 1995, 58; L. Davison, *Age*, 18 March, 1995, Saturday Extra 9; A. Horsfield, *Australian Multicultural Book Review*, 3.2, 1995, 44.

Poetry
Black from the Edge. (South Melbourne: Hyland House, 1994).
Reviewed by D. Headon, *Weekend Australian*, 28-29 May, 1994, Review 7; G. Rowlands, *Overland*, 137, 1994, 70-71; T. Rowse, *Age*, 21 May, 1994, Saturday Extra 8.

The Blackside: People are Legends and Other Poems. (South Yarra, Vic.: Hyland House, 1990).
Reviewed by P. Stewart, *Webber's*, 3, 1991, 84-90.

Child's Dreaming. (South Yarra, Vic.: Hyland House, 1992).
Reviewed by Jack Davis, *Age*, 27 February, 1993, Saturday Extra 7.

End of Dreamtime. (Sydney: Island P., 1971).
Reviewed by R. Dunlop, *Poetry Australia*, 43, 1972, 53-64; M. McPhee, *S.M.H.*, 12 November, 1971, 22; J. Tulip, *Bulletin*, 8 January 1972, 35.
People are Legends. (St Lucia: U.Q.P., 1978).
Reviewed by M. Boyes, *ABR*, 7, 1978, 22; L. Murray, *S.M.H.*, 7 October, 1978, 16; E. Perkins, *LiNQ*, 7.1, 1979, 94-98; N. Perkins, *Weekend Australian*, 30-31 December, 1978, Weekend 6; [anon.] *Virginia Quarterly Review*, 55, 1979, 148; E. Watson, *Social Alternatives*, 1.4, 1979, 88.

Drama

The Cherry Pickers. (Canberra: Burrambinga Books, 1988).
Reviewed by K. Brisbane, *ABR*, 102, 1988, 38,40; A. Shoemaker, *Australasian Drama Studies*, 17, 1990, 221-24; J. Wright, *Overland*, 112, 1988, 73-74.

Non-Fiction

Because a White Man'll Never Do It. (Sydney: A.& R., 1974).
Reviewed by J. Lapsley, *Australian*, 9 February, 1974, 46; K. Walker, *Nation Review*, 29 March - 4 April, 1974, 760; O. White, *Age*, 29 January 1974: 6.
Living Black: Blacks Talk to Kevin Gilbert. (Ringwood, Vic.: Penguin, 1978).
Reviewed by J. Beckett, *S.M.H.*, 14 October 1978: 17; I. Eriksen, *Luna*, 3.2, 1979, 36-38; H. Morphy, *Age*, 1 April, 1978, 24; N. Perkins, *Australian*, 8 April, 1978; E. Webby, *Overland*, 73, 1978, 61-62.

Critical Material

Beston, John B. 'The Aboriginal Poets and English: Kath Walker, Jack Davis and Kevin Gilbert'. *Meanjin*, 36.4, 1972, 446-62.
Gilbert, Helen. 'De-scribing Orality'. In *De-scribing Empire: Post-colonialism and Textuality*, edited by Chris Tiffin and Alan Lawson (London and New York: Routledge, 1994), 98-111. Includes discussion of theatre of Gilbert.
Langford Ginibi, Ruby. 'A Poet Who Never Gave Up'. *Australian Short Stories No 43*, edited by Bruce Pascoe (Apollo Bay, Vic.: Pascoe Publishing, 1993), 7-9. Obituary.
Page, Geoff. 'Kevin Gilbert'. In his *A Reader's Guide To Contemporary Australian Poetry* (St. Lucia: U.Q.P., 1995), 74-76.
McMillan, Pauline. 'Kevin Gilbert and *Living Black*'. *Journal of Australian Studies*, 45, 1995, 1-14.
Mudrooroo, *Age*, 17 April, 1993, Saturday Extra 7. Obituary. see also A. Shoemaker, *Notes & Furphies*, 31, 1993, 1-2.
Nelson, Emmanuel S. 'Black America and the Australian Aboriginal Literary Consciousness'. *Westerly*, 30.4, 1985, 43-54.

GILES, ZENY

Critical Material

Nickas, Helen. 'Interview with Zeny Giles'. In *Australian Writing Now*, edited by Manfred Jurgensen and Robert Adamson (Ringwood, Vic.: Outrider/Penguin, 1988), 308.
---. *Migrant Daughters: The Female Voice in Greek-Australian Prose Fiction*. (Melbourne: Owl Publishing, 1992).

GILMORE, MARY

Poetry

Mary Gilmore. Edited with an introduction by R.D. FitzGerald. (Sydney: A.& R., 1963). Australian Poets.
The Passionate Heart and Other Poems. (Sydney: A.& R., 1979). First published as *Selected Verse*, A.& R., 1969.

Reviewed by D. Modjeska, *Meanjin*, XLI, 1982, 228-35; E. Perkins, *CRNLE Reviews Journal*, No. 2, 1979, 30-34.

Selected Verse. Enlarged edition. (Sydney: A.& R., 1969). First edition 1948. Foreword by R.D. FitzGerald, who with T. I. Moore selected additional poems from her *Fourteen Men* (1954).
Reviewed by B. Bennett, *Westerly*, No. 4, 1970, 54-56; T.I. Moore, *Canberra Times*, 1 November, 1969, 19; H. Tabrett, *Makar*, VI, No. 3, 1970, 39-41.

> *Non-Fiction*

Letters. Selected and edited by W.H. Wilde & T. Inglis Moore. (Carlton: M.U.P., 1980).
Reviewed by D. Carter, *Helix*, No. 7-8, 1981, 183-85; G. Dutton, *Bulletin*, 22 July, 1980, 92-93; K. England, *Advertiser*, 26 July, 1980, 23; R.G. Geering, *Journal of the Royal Australian Historical Society*, LXVIII, No. 1, 1982, 74-76; D. Green, *Hemisphere*, XXV, No. 4, 1981, 126-29; N. Keesing, *ABR*, No. 23, 1980, 8-9; B. Kingston, *Labour History*, No. 40, 1981, 127-28; F.H. Mares, *A.L.S.*, X, 1981, 139-43; D. Martin, *Age*, 26 July, 1980, 27; D. Modjeska, *Meanjin*, XLI, 1982, 228-35; A.A. Phillips, *Overland*, No. 83, 1981, 65-67; B. Plews, *CRNLE Reviews Journal*, No. 2, 1980, 27-30; P. Thompson, *S.M.H.*, 5 July, 1980, 20; G. Windsor, *Quadrant*, XXIV, No. 11, 1980, 66-67.

Old Days: Old Ways. (North Ryde, N.S.W.: A.& R., 1986). First published Sydney: A.& R., 1934.
Reviewed by J.A. Mead, *ABR*, No. 85, 1986, 26-27.

'Some Mary Gilmore Letters'. *A.L.S.*, V, 1972, 417-30. Letters to I.M. Foster, edited by I.M. Foster and L.T. Hergenhan.

> *Critical Material*

Mary Gilmore: A Tribute. (Sydney: Australasian Book Society, 1965) With an introduction by T. Inglis Moore; a Foreword by Dymphna Cusack; Biographical Notes by Barrie Ovenden; and Bibliography by Walter Stone. Reviewed by A.R. Chisholm, *Age*, 14 August, 1965, 24; B. Elliott, *ABR*, IV, 1965, 226; C. Hadgraft, *Meanjin*, XXIV, 1965, 535-7; D. Martin, *Australian*, 14 August, 1965, 10; M. McCallum, *Nation*, 21 August, 1965, 21-2; W. Stone, *The Bridge*, II, No. 1, 1965, 57-8; V. Vallis, *A.L.S.*, II, No. 2, 1965, 150-1.

Balkin, Mary. 'Mary and William Gilmore: A Family Note'. *A.L.S.*, V, 1972, 430-31.

Bayley, William A. *Dame Mary Gilmore and Silverton Public School*. (Silverton: The author, 1967). [Duplicated].

Brooksbank, Anne. *All My Love*. Port Melbourne: Heinemann, 1991). Fictionalised account of the alleged love affair between Lawson and Mary Gilmore. Reviewed by J. Messer, *S.M.H.*, 9 February, 1991, 48; E. Riddell, *ABR*, 128, 1991, 11; J. Stephens, *Australian Society*, 10.3, 1991, 42-43.

Cato, Nancy. 'Woman and Poet'. *Overland*, No. 26, 1963, 28.

Foster, I.M. 'Mary Gilmore: A Memoir'. *A.L.S.*, V, 1972, 414-16.

Green, Eleanor. 'Mary Gilmore, An Impression'. An address given to the English Association, Sydney, on 3 April, 1963. *Makar*, No. 19, 1964, 24-7.

Heseltine, H.P. 'C. Hartley Grattan in Australia: Some Correspondence, 1937-38'. *Meanjin*, XXIX, 1970, 356-64. Includes letters from Gilmore.

Holloway, Barbara. 'White Steps on the Way to the International Year of Indigenous People: The Difficulties and Lines of Flight of Mary Gilmore'. *SPAN*, 37, 1993, 93-107.

Lawson, Sylvia. *Mary Gilmore*. (Melbourne: O.U.P., 1966). Great Australians Series. Reviewed by G.Souter,*S.M.H.*, 22 April, 1967, 20.

Mares, F.H. 'Dame Mary Gilmore'. *Southerly*, XXV, No. 4, 1965, 234-45.

Pearce, Sharyn. 'Fishing for Women: Mary Gilmore's Journalism in the *Worker*'. In

The Time to Write: Australian Women Writers 1890-1930 edited by Kay Ferres (Ringwood, Vic.: Penguin, 1993), 88-107.

Robertson, Constance. 'Mary Gilmore'. *Southerly*, XXV, No. 4, 1965, 247-50.

Roderick, Colin. 'The Teaching Life of Mary Gilmore'. *Education Gazette*, LVII, 1963, 131-3 and *Teachers' Journal*, XLVI, 1963, 16-23.

S., W. W. [Walter W. Stone]. 'The Conservation of Literary Relics'. *Biblionews and Australian Notes & Queries*, Series 3, II, No. 1, 1977, 14-15. Inscriptions on Henry Lawson's collars.

Sheridan, Sue. 'Conflicting Discourses on Race and Nationalism in Mary Gilmore's Poetry'. *Social Alternatives*, 8, No. 3, 1989, 23-25.

---. 'Mary Gilmore's and Katharine Prichard's representations of Aborigines'. In her *Along the Faultlines: Sex, Race and Nation in Australian Women's Writing 1880s-1930s* (St Leonards, NSW: Allen & Unwin, 1995), 135-52.

Smith, Graeme Kinross. '"Woman-Wise, and Woman-Waked"'. *Hemisphere*, XX, No. 9, 1976, 33-38.

Souter, Gavin. *A Peculiar People: The Australians in Paraguay.* (Sydney: A.& R., 1968).

Stewart, Douglas. 'The Paradoxes of Mary Gilmore'. *S.M.H.*, 14 August, 1965, 15.

Strauss, Jennifer. 'Stubborn Singers of Their Full Song: Mary Gilmore and Lesbia Harford'. In *The Time to Write: Australian Women Writers 1890-1930* edited by Kay Ferres (Ringwood, Vic.: Penguin, 1993), 108-38.

Tennant, Kylie. 'Vale - Mary Gilmore'. *Westerly*, September, 1963, 42-5.

Tolchard, Clifford. 'Mary Gilmore: Crusader and Poet'. *Walkabout*, XXXIV, No. 3, 1968, 12-15; see also letter to the editor by Elizabeth Pack, *Walkabout*, XXXIV, No. 6, 1968, 5, and by William Bayley in the same issue, 6.

Toms, Bruce. 'Mary Gilmore's Life of Service'. *Realist*, No. 19, 1965, 6-7.

Walker, Shirley. *Vanishing Edens: Responses to Australia in the Works of Mary Gilmore, Judith Wright and Dorothy Hewett.* Monograph 23. (Townsville, Qld.: Foundation for Australian Literary Studies / James Cook U of North Queensland, 1992). Reviewed by S. Bennett, *Imago*, 5.3, 1993, 95-97; N. Birns, *Antipodes*, 7.2, 1993, 167-68.

Webster, Owen. 'Frank Dalby Davison'. *Overland*, No. 44, 1970, 35-37.

Wilde, W.H. *Courage a Grace: A Biography of Dame Mary Gilmore.* (Carlton, Vic.: M.U.P., 1988). Reviewed by E. Campion, *Bulletin*, 13 December, 1988, 129-130; P. Grimshaw, *Australian Journal of Politics and History*, 36, No. 3, 1990, 462-3; N.J. Kyle, *Journal of the Royal Australian Historical Society*, 75, No. 4, 1990, 333-4; S. Magarey, *Australian Historical Studies*, 23, No. 93, 1989, 488-90; P. Morgan, *Age Saturday Extra*, 7 January, 1989, 11; C. Munro, *A.L.S.*, 14, No. 1, 1989, 138-42; S. J. Paolini, *Antipodes*, 3.2, 1989, 155; M. Sharkey, *Overland*, No. 114, 1989, 92-94; N. Wheatley, *S.M.H.*, 26 November, 1988, 89.

---. *Three Radicals.* (Melbourne: O.U.P., 1969). Australian Writers and Their Work. Discusses Gilmore, Maurice and O'Dowd. Reviewed by A. Mitchell, *A.L.S.*, V, 1971, 99-100.

--- .'"The Crows kept flying'up": Old Bush Song or Mary Gilmore Ballad?' *A.L.S.*, X, 1981, 105-11.

--- 'Dame Mary Gilmore's "Descent into Hell": A Restless Spirit Caged on a Lonely Farm'. *National Times*, May 6-11, 1974, 42-44.

--- 'Mary Gilmore and 1942'. *Bulletin*, 22 July, 1980, 77-81.

--- 'Mary Gilmore: The Hidden Years'. *Meanjin*, XXXII, 1973, 425-32.

Wood, W.A. 'The Best of Mary Gilmore'. *Realist Writer*. No. 11, 1963, 8-12.

---. 'Mary Gilmore's heaven; a letter to a friend'. *Realist*, No. 19, 1965, 14-16.

Wright, Judith. 'Tribute to Mary Gilmore'. In *An Overland Muster*, edited by S. Murray-Smith (Brisbane: Jacaranda Press, 1965), 19-20. Originally published *Overland*, No. 4, 1955, 8.

GOLDHAR, PINCHAS
Critical Material
Brezniak, H. *Pinchas Goldhar: The First Yiddish Writer In Australia: An Assessment.*
(Sydney: The Wentworth Press, 1968). Also contains two short stories.
MacLean, Pam. 'The Australian-Yiddish Writer, Pinchas Goldhar (1901-1947)'.
Southerly, 55.2, 1995, 29-34.

GOLDSWORTHY, PETER
Fiction
Bleak Rooms. (Cowandilla, SA: Wakefield P, 1988).
Reviewed by H. Daniel, *Age*, 19 March, 1988, Saturday Extra 11; H. Falkner,
Weekend Australian, 2-3 April, 1988, Weekend 14; S. McKernan, *ABR*, 100, 1988,
14-15; Y. Rousseau, *Age Monthly Review*, 8.5, 1988, 22-23; A. Stretton, *S.M.H.*, 4
June, 1988, 80.

Honk if You Are Jesus. (Pymble, NSW: A.& R., 1992).
Reviewed by C. Blanche, *Quadrant*, 37.5, 1993, 80-82; K. Goldsworthy, *Voices*, 3.2,
1993, 110-14; J. Keens, *ABR*, 146, 1992, 21; L. Murray, *T.L.S.*, 3 December, 1993,
11; P. Pierce, *Bulletin*, 19 January, 1993, 88; A. Riemer, *S.M.H.*, 12 December,
1992, 1993, 48; G. Windsor, *Weekend Australian*, 28-29 November, 1992, 1993,
Review 4.

Little Deaths. (Pymble, NSW: A.& R., 1993).
Reviewed by M. Condon, *Overland*, 136, 1994, 85-86; H. Falkiner, *ABR*, 156, 1993,
17-18 (see also interview by C. Keneally, 18-19); P. Loiterton, *Redoubt*, 18, 1994,
134-35; P. O'Connor, *Age*, 5 February, 1994, Saturday Extra 8; E. Riddell, *Bulletin*,
19 October, 1993, 97; A. Riemer, *S.M.H.*, 6 November, 1993, Spectrum 11A; L.
Trainor, *Weekend Australian*, 11-12 December, 1993, Review 7.

Maestro. (Sydney: A.& R, 1989).
Reviewed by K. Goldsworthy, *Voices*, 3.2, 1993, 110-14; J. Hanrahan, *Weekend
Australian*, 2-3 December, 1989, Weekend 12; J. Livett, *Island*, 55, 1993, 66-69; S.
McKernan, *Bulletin*, 12 December, 1989, 116-17; D.J. O'Hearn, *Age*, 25 November,
1989, Saturday Extra 10; A.P. Riemer, *S.M.H.*, 11 November, 1989, 86; W.
Tonetto, *Mattoid*, 37.2, 1990, 124-31; G. Windsor, *ABR*, 116, 1989, 15-16.

With Brian Matthews. *Magpie.* (Kent Town, SA: Wakefield P., 1992).
Reviewed by C. Blanche, *Quadrant*, 36.11, 1992, 86-88; P. Craven, *Age*, 21 March,
1992, Saturday Extra 9; D. Davison, *Weekend Australian*, 11-12, April, 1992,
Review 4; K. Goldsworthy, *Voices*, 3.2, 1993, 110-14; C. Greenfield and P.
Williams, *Hecate*, 19.1, 1993, 155-63; P. Pierce, *S.M.H.*,7 March, 1992, 44; T.
Smith, *Scarp*, 20, 1992, 67; J. Stephens, *Modern Times*, May, 1992, 30.

This Goes with This. (Crows Nest, NSW: ABC, 1988).
Reviewed by D. Brooks, *Age Monthly Review*, July, 1989, 6-7; V. Buckley, *Age*, 25
June, 1988, Saturday Extra 14; J. Grant, *Weekend Australian*, 7-8 January, 1989,
Weekend 6; S. McKernan, *Bulletin*, 3 May, 1988, 127; B. Merry, *LiNQ*, 16.3, 1988,
114-21; E. Riddell, *Overland*, 112, 1988, 78-80; S. Trigg, *Island Magazine*, 36,
1988. 22-29.

Wish. (Sydney: A.& R.), 1995).
Reviewed by R. Lucas, *Bulletin*, 14 Nov., 1995, 97; A. Riemer, *S.M.H.*, 28 Oct.,
1995, Spectrum 11A; M. Sharkey, *Weekend Australian*, 4-5 Nov., 1995, Review 9.

Zooing. (North Ryde, NSW: A.& R., 1986).
Reviewed by H. Daniel, *Age*, 8 March, 1986, Saturday Extra 14; H. Falkner,
Australian, 5 March, 1986, 10; F. Kellaway, *Overland*, 104, 1986, 64-65; E. Webby,
S.M.H., 22 March, 1986, 46; G. Windsor, *ABR*, 78, 1986, 24-25.

Poetry
Archipelagoes. (Sydney: A.& R., 1982).
Reviewed by V. Brady, *Island Magazine*, 13, 1982, 52-54; M. Brakmanis, *Words and Visions*, 12, 1983, 24-28; A. Brewster, *Ash Magazine*, 10, 1982, 30; G. Dutton, *Bulletin*, 13 July, 1982, 122-124; M. Lord, *ABR*, 48, 1983, 31-32; J. Tranter, *S.M.H.*, 21 August, 1982, 37.
Readings from Ecclesiastes: Poems. (Sydney: A.& R, 1982).
Reviewed by A. Brewster, *Ash Magazine*, 11, 1982, 33-34; G. Catalano, *Age*, 3 July, 1982, Saturday Extra 14; G. Dutton, *Bulletin*, 13 July, 1982, 122-124; M. Duwell, *Weekend Australian*, 19-20, June, 1982, Weekend 9; M. Lord, *ABR*, 48, 1983, 31-32; L.A. Murray, *S.M.H.*, 6 March, 1982, 44; G. Page, *Quadrant*, 26.8, 1982, 75-77; R. Pybus, *Stand*, 5.3, 1984, 56-62; M. Richards, *Island Magazine*, 14, 1983, 51-52.
This Goes with That: Selected Poems 1970-1990. (North Ryde, NSW: A.& R., 1991).
Reviewed by M. Duwell, *Weekend Australian*, 20-21 April, 1991, Review 4; K. Goldsworthy, *Voices*, 3.2, 1993, 110-14; M. Hulse, *PN Review*, 19.5, 1993, 64; J. Owen, *Quadrant* 35.6, 1991, 79-81.

Non-Fiction
'Ask Not For Whom the Bleeper Bleeps...'. In *Toads: Australian Writers: Other Work, Other Lives*, edited by Andrew Sant (North Sydney: Allen & Unwin/Susan Haynes, 1992), 36-43.
'The Detroit of the South'. *Overland*, 104, 1986, 38-40.
'Honk if You Love Science'. *Island Magazine*,54, 1993, 40-43. Paper presented at the Salamanca Writers Weekend, 1992.
'On Blood, Sweat, Ink, and the Death of the Novel'. *Island Magazine*, 43-44, 1990, 80-82.
'What's Left After They Take Away My Theory'. *Island Magazine*, 45, 1990, 8-9.

Critical Material
Catalano, Gary. 'Words & Music'. *Island*, 53, 1992, 54-57.
Guess, J. 'Peter Goldsworthy: The Provincial Advantage'. *Ash Magazine*, 12, 1983, 9-10.
Matthews, Brian. 'The List of No Answers: In the Matter of P. Goldsworthy'. In *Southwords: Essays on South Australian Writing*, edited by Philip Butterss (Kent Town, SA: Wakefield, 1995), 178-88.
Page, Geoff. 'Peter Goldsworthy'. In his *A Reader's Guide To Contemporary Australian Poetry* (St. Lucia: U.Q.P., 1995), 79-80.
Riemer, Andrew. *The Ironic Eye: The Poetry and Prose of Peter Goldsworthy*. (Pymble, NSW: A.& R., 1994). Reviewed by J. Croft, *Weekend Australian*, 4-5 June, 1994, Review 7; D. Gilbey, *ABR*, 163, 1994, 23-25; R. Gostand, *Social Alternatives*, 13.2, 1994, 55-56; V. Ikin, *S.M.H.*, 26 February, 1994, Spectrum 9A; B. Kiernan, *A.L.S.*, 17.2, 1995, 198-202; P. Loiterton, *Redoubt*, 18, 1994, 135-36.

GORDON, ADAM LINDSAY
Collection
Adam Lindsay Gordon. Edited by Brian Elliott. (Melbourne: Sun Books, 1973). Three Colonial Poets, Book 3.
Reviewed by J. Blight, *Nation Review*, 16-22 November, 1973, 167.

Poetry
The Feud; and the traditional ballad The Dowie Dens O'Yarrow. (Adelaide: Rigby, 1965). With notes by Hugh Anderson.

Non-Fiction
Last Letters, 1868-1870: Adam Lindsay Gordon to John Riddoch. Edited with an introduction by Hugh Anderson. (Melbourne: Hawthorn Press, 1970).
Reviewed by L. Kramer, *A.L.S.*, V, 1971, 102-04; T.I. Moore, *Meanjin*, XXX,

1971, 354; K. Slessor, *Daily Telegraph*, Sydney, 21 November, 1970, 55.

Critical Material

McLaren, Ian F. *Adam Lindsay Gordon: A Comprehensive Bibliography*. (Parkville, Vic.: University of Melbourne Library, 1986). Reviewed by D.H. Borchardt, *Reference Australia*, 3, 1989, 51-7; M. Ehrhardt, *A.L.S.*, XIII, No. 2, 1987, 249-50; B. Hubber, *Biblionews and Australian Notes and Queries*, 14, No. 1, 1989, 16-21.

Ackland, Michael. 'A Martial Code: Meditation and Action in the Verse of Adam Lindsay Gordon'. *Westerly*, 38.2, 1993, 53-65.

Alderson, John J. *Clanalder Sennachie*, No. 32, 1966, 10. Reconstructing Gordon's house in Brighton.

Bernstein, D.L. *First Tuesday in November: The Story of the Melbourne Cup*. (Melbourne: Heinemann, 1969), 288.

Cameron, Roderick. *Australia: History and Horizons*. (London: Weidenfeld and Nicolson, Sydney: Hicks Smith, 1971), 231-35.

Cavell, Norma. 'A Poet Gone Where the Last Year's Leaves Go'. *S.M.H.*, 22 July, 1967, 18.

Cleland, John B. 'Margaret Kiddle's *Men of Yesterday* and Adam Lindsay Gordon'. *Journal of the Royal Australian Historical Society*, Part 2, 1964, 156-8. Contains reference to one of his poems.

Elliott, Brian. 'Adam Lindsay Gordon: A Small Discovery'. *A.L.S.*, VI, 1973, 203-04.

---. 'Antipodes: An Essay in Attitudes'. *Australian Letters*, VII, No. 3, 1966, 51-70.

---. 'The Colonial Poets'. In *The Literature of Australia*, edited by Geoffrey Dutton (Adelaide: Penguin Books, 1964), 236-242.

Gray, Martin. 'Adam Lindsay Gordon as Hero'. In *Myths, Heroes and Anti-heroes: Essays on the Literature and Culture of the Asia-Pacific Region*, edited by Bruce Bennett and Dennis Haskell (Nedlands, WA: Centre for Studies in Australian Literature, U of Western Australia, 1992), 98-106.

Harris, Max. 'Adam Lindsay Gordon's Last Leap'. *Weekend Australian Magazine*, 3-4 May, 1980, 9.

Hinton, Edith. *Recollections of the South-East*. (Adelaide: Griffin Press, 1971), 39-54.

Holloway, Barbara. 'What Made the Sick Stockrider Sick? The Function of Horses and Fever in A.L. Gordon's "The Sick Stockrider"'. *Westerly*, 38.1, 1993, 35-42.

Hutton, Geoffrey. *Adam Lindsay Gordon: The Man and the Myth*. (London: Faber, 1978). Reviewed by L. Blake, *Age*, 16 September, 1979, 25; C. Flower, *Bulletin*, 21 November, 1978, 68; B. Matthews, *Advertiser*, 4 November, 1978, 22; W.D. Maxwell-Mahon, *UNISA English Studies*, (Pretoria), XVII, No. 2, 1979, 61-62; C. Roderick, *Townsville Daily Bulletin*, 2 December, 1978, 4; V. Smith, *Quadrant*, XXIII, Nos. 1-2, 1979, 116-17; R. Stow, *T.L.S.*, 25 August, 1978, 944; M. Thorpe, *English Studies*, LXI, No. 1, 1978, 66.

Jamison, Greeba. 'Adam Lindsay Gordon'. *Walkabout*, XXXVI, No. 6, 1970, 48-51.

Jordan, Richard Douglas. 'Adam Lindsay Gordon: The Australian Poet' *Westerly*, XXX, No. 2, 1985, 45-56.

Kelleher, Bryan J. 'Adam Lindsay Gordon (1833-1870) - A Note'. *Notes and Furphies*, No. 16, 1986, 17.

Kramer, Leonie. 'The Literary Reputation of Adam Lindsay Gordon'. *A.L.S.*, I, No. 1, 1963, 42-56.

MacRae, C.F. *Adam Lindsay Gordon*. (New York: Twayne, 1968). Twayne's World Authors Series, 41. Reviewed by L. Kramer, *A.L.S.*, V, 1971, 102-04; A.L. McLeod, *Books Abroad*, XLIV, 1970, 126-27.

Magarey, Kevin. 'Place, Landscape, Saussure, Region, and Two Australian Colonial Poets: Some Footnotes'. In *Mapped But Not Known: The Australian Landscape of the Imagination*, edited by P.R. Eaden and F.H. Mares (Netley, S.A.: Wakefield Press,

1986), 105-127.
Sellick, Robert. 'Burke and Wills and the Colonial Hero: Three Poems'. *A.L.S.*, V, 1971, 180-89.
Smith, Martin. 'Martin Smith Tells the Extraordinary Story of Adam Lindsay Gordon'. *Campaign*, Sydney, No. 27, 1977, 17-19.
Stivens, Dal. 'Myth of the Songless Bird'. *Canberra Times*, 16 April, 1966, 9.
Tenison-Woods, Julian E. *Personal Reminiscences of Adam Lindsay Gordon.* (Canberra: [E.O. Eriksen], 1995). First published *Melbourne Review*, 1884.
Wilde, W.H. *Adam Lindsay Gordon.* (Melbourne: O.U.P., 1972). Australian Writers and Their Work. Reviewed by M. Dunlevy, *Canberra Times*, 16 June, 1973, 10; A. Mitchell, *A.L.S.*, VI, 1974, 332-36; J. Waten, *Age*, 21 April, 1973, 13.
Wilding, Michael. 'A.L. Gordon in England: The Legend of the Steeplechase'. *Southerly*, XXV, No. 2, 1965, 99-107.
Woods, Julian Tenison. 'Personal Reminiscences of Adam Lindsay Gordon'. *Australian Literary Supplement*, 6-7 June, 1987, 12. First published *Melbourne Review*, 9, 1884, 131-41.
Wright, Judith. 'Adam Lindsay Gordon and Barcroft Boake', *Preoccupations in Australian Poetry*. (Melbourne: O.U.P., 1965), 57-67.

GOULD, ALAN

Fiction
Close Ups. (Port Melbourne: Heinemann, 1994).
Reviewed by M. Condon, *Weekend Australian*, 25-26 June, 1994, Review 6; K. Cummings, *ABR*, 162, 1994, 16-17 (see also interview by R. Sorensen 17-19); J. Hanrahan, *Age*, 9 July, 1994, Saturday Extra 8; R. Lucas, *Bulletin*, 12 July, 1994, 88-89; R. McDonald, *Quadrant*, 37.10, 1994, 78-79; A. Riemer, *S.M.H.*, 4 June: Spectrum 10A.
The Enduring Disguises: Three Novellas. (North Ryde, NSW.: A.& R., 1988).
Reviewed by D. Johnson, *S.M.H.*, 16 July, 1988, 78; M. Jurgensen, *Weekend Australian*, 16-17 July, 1988, Weekend 16.
The Man Who Stayed Below. (Sydney: A.& R., 1984).
Reviewed by K. Ahearne, *Age Saturday Extra*, 27 October, 1984, 12; G. Dutton, *Bulletin*, 4 December, 1984, 77-78; M. Halligan, *Canberra Times*, 15 December, 1984, 18; N. Keesing, *Weekend Australian Magazine*, 29-30 September, 1984, 15; R. Lucas, *S.M.H.*, 15 December, 1984, 33; S. McKernan, *Australian Book Review*, No. 68, 1985, 24-25.
To the Burning City. (Port Melbourne: Heinemann, 1991).
Reviewed by I. Buchanan, *Southerly*, 52.4, 1992, 182-86; F. Capp, *Age*, 26 October, 1991, Saturday Extra 8; J. Carroll, *ABR*, 135, 1991, 40; D. Davison, *Weekend Australian*, 26-27 October, 1991, Review 6; A.P. Riemer, *S.M.H.*, 8 August, 1992, 41.

Poetry
Astral Sea. (Cremorne Junction: A.& R., 1981).
Reviewed by D. Brooks, *Canberra Times*, 15 August, 1981, 16; J. Clanchy, *Muse*, No. 9, 1981, 13; G. Page, *National Times*, 7-13 June, 1981, 62; T. Shapcott, *Age*, 21 November, 1981, 23.
Formerlight: Selected Poems. (Sydney: A.& R., 1992).
Reviewed by L. Bourke, *Voices*, 2.3, 1992, 104-07; T. Collins, *Imago*, 4.2, 1992, 105-06; B. Hill, *Age*, 9 May, 1992, Saturday Extra 10; J. Owen, *Quadrant*, 36.9, 1992, 83-85.
Icelandic Solitaries. (St Lucia: U.Q.P., 1978).
Reviewed by G. Page, *Canberra Times*, 29 June, 1978, 13; E. Perkins, *LiNQ*, 6, No. 2, 1978, 85-87; C. Pollnitz, *Southerly*, 39, 1978, 342-357; V. Young, *Parnassus*, 7,

No. 1, 1978, 76-95.

Momentum. (Melbourne: Heinemann, 1992).
Reviewed by M. Dugan, *Overland*, 131, 96; J. Foulcher, *Island*, 55, 1993, 69-72;
P. Nelson, *Quadrant*, 37.7-8, 1993, 117-19; A. Wilson, *ABR*, 146, 1992, 50-51.

The Pausing of the Hours. (Sydney: A.& R., 1984).
Reviewed by G. Catalano, *Age Saturday Extra*, 26 May, 1984, 16; B. Tully, *Muse Communique*, No 34, 1984, 25-27.

The Twofold Place. (North Ryde, NSW: A.& R., 1986).
Reviewed by J. Rodriguez, *S.M.H.*, 17 January, 1987, 46; F. Zwicky, *Weekend Australian Magazine*, 14-15 June, 1986, 16.

Years Found in Likeness. (North Ryde, NSW: A.& R., 1988).
Reviewed by M. Duwell, *ABR*, No. 113, 31; D. Reiter, *Redoubt*, No. 5, 1989, 61-65.

Critical Material
Page, Geoff. 'Alan Gould'. In his *A Reader's Guide To Contemporary Australian Poetry* (St. Lucia: U.Q.P., 1995), 83-85.

GOULD, NAT.

Critical Material
Welcome, John. 'Nat Gould - Novelist of the Turf'. *London Magazine*, VII, No. 5, 1967, 54-59.

GOW, MICHAEL

Drama
All Stops Out. (Sydney: Currency Press, 1991).
Reviewed by P. Makeham, *Australasian Drama Studies*, 25, 1994, 193-95.

Away. Introduction by May-Brit Akerholt and Richard Wherrett (Sydney: Currency Press/Playbox Theatre Co., 1988).
Reviewed by J. MacCallum, *Australasian Drama Studies*, Nos. 15-16, 1988/89, 199-202.

1841. (Sydney: Currency Press/State Theatre Company of SA, 1988).
Reviewed by J. MacCallum, *Australasian Drama Studies*, Nos. 15-16, 1988/89, 199-202.

Europe. On Top of the World. Introduction by Peter Kingston (Sydney: Currency Press, 1987).
Reviewed by M-B. Akerholt, *Australasian Drama Studies*, Nos. 12-13, 1988, 195-200.

Furious. (Sydney: Currency Press/ Playbox Theatre Centre of Monash U, 1994).
Reviewed by N. Fletcher, *Australasian Drama Studies*, 27, 1995, 156-61.

The Kid. (Sydney: Currency Press, 1983).
Reviewed by N. Fletcher, *Australasian Drama Studies*, 2, No. 2, 1984, 115-18; M. McLeod, *Kunapipi*, 6, No. 1, 1984, 79-83; *National Times*, 16-22 March, 1984, 31.

Critical Material
Akerholt, May-Brit. 'Interview: Michael Gow Talks to May-Brit Akerholt'. *Australasian Drama Studies*, Nos. 12-13, 1988, 73-84.
D'cruz, Glenn. 'A "Dark" Ariel? Shakespeare and Australian Theatre Criticism'. In *Shakespeare's Books: Contemporary Cultural Politics and the Persistence of Empire*, edited by Philip Mead and Marion Campbell (Parkville, Vic.: Department of English, U of Melbourne, 1993), 165-74. Discusses critical responses to *Away*.
De Roeper, Julia. 'Michael Gow', *New Theatre Australia*, No. 4, 1988, 29-31.
Eccles, Jeremy. 'Creation and Clash: *1841*: Australia's Bicentenary and the Critics'.

Blast, No. 8, 1988/89, 22-25.

Gay, Penny. 'Michael Gow's *Away*: The Shakespeare Connection'. In *Reconnoitres: Essays in Australian Literature in Honour of G.A. Wilkes*, edited by Margaret Harris and Elizabeth Webby (South Melbourne: O.U.P. in association with Sydney U.P., 1992), 204-13.

Gilbert, Helen. 'Monumental Moments: Michael Gow's *1841*, Stephen Sewell's *Hate*, Louis Nowra's *Capricornia* and Australia's Bicentenary'. *Australasian Drama Studies*, 24, 1994, 29-45.

Mitchell, Tony. 'Great White Hope or Great White Hype? Re Critical Construction (and Demolition) of Michael Gow'. *Spectator Burns*, No. 3, 1989, 17-27.

Pearson, John M. 'An Interview with Michael Gow'. *Southerly*, 52.2, 1992, 116-31.

Schaffeld, Norbert. '"Shakespeare at the Beach": Europa-Referenzen als Vehikel australischer Identitätssuche in den Dramen Michael Gows'. In *Australien zwischen Europa und Asien*, edited by Gerhard Stilz and Rudolf Bader (Bern: Peter Lang, 1993), 135-50.

Simon, Luke. *Michael Gow's Plays: A Thematic Approach*. (Sydney: Currency Press, 1991).

Thomas, Martin. '"Page or Stage?"' Michael Gow's *Away*'. *New Theatre Australia*, No. 9, 1989, 38-40.

Webby, Elizabeth. *Modern Australian Plays*. Horizon Studies in Literature. (Sydney: Sydney UP in association with O.U.P., 1990). Includes discussion of *Away*.

GRANO, PAUL

Critical Material

'Death of Poet'. *Courier-Mail*, 14 January, 1975, 8.

Hadgraft, Cecil. 'Paul Grano, Witness'. *Meanjin*, XXXII, 1973, 459-65.

GRANT, JOHN

Critical Material

Richards, Michael. 'A Convict Voice'. *National Library of Australia News*, 1.8, 1991, 7.

Syson, Ian. 'John Grant: Australia's First *Really* Radical Poet'. *A.L.S.*, 16.3, 1994, 297-311.

GRATTAN, C. HARTLEY

Non-Fiction

'C. Hartley Grattan's View of Australian Literature in 1928'. *Antipodes*, II, No. 1, 1988, 20-24. This essay by C.H. Grattan was first published in *The Bookman* (New York), LXVII, No. 6, 1928, 625-631. It was later reprinted as *Australian Literature* (Seattle, Wash.: University of Washington Bookstore, 1929). University of Washington Chapbooks, No. 29.

Critical Material

Barrett, John. 'History and Hartley Grattan'. *Overland*, 122, 1991, 28-29. Response to L. Hergenhan, 'Recovering American Connections'. *Overland*, 121, 1990, 70-76.

Hergenhan, Laurie. 'C. Hartley Grattan and Australian-American Connections'. *Southerly*, XLVII, No. 2, 1987, 223-231.

---. 'C. Hartley Grattan: Foreign Observer Extraordinary'. *Newsletter of the American Association of Australian Literary Studies*, II, No. 2, 1986, 6-7.

---. 'The C Hartley Grattan Manuscript Collection: A Critical Introduction'. In *Perspectives on Australia: Essays on Australiana in Collections of the Harry Ransom Humanities Research Center*, edited by Dave Oliphant (Austin: Harry Ransom Humanities Research Centre, University of Texas, 1989), 51-75.

---. 'History and Hartley Grattan'. *Overland*, 124, 1991, 40. Response to J. Barrett,

Overland, 122, 1991, 28-29.
---. *No Casual Traveller: Hartley Grattan and Australia-US Connections*. (St Lucia: U.Q.P., 1995). Reviewed by E. Campion, *Bulletin*, 1 Aug., 1995, 91; R. Fitzgerald, *Queensland Review*, 2.2, 1995, 81-83; J. Hanrahan, *ABR*, 173, 1995, 26-27 (see also response by R. Fitzgerald, *ABR*, 175, 1995, 5-6); H. McQueen, *Independent*, Dec. 1995/Jan. 1996, 84-86; B. Matthews, *S.M.H.*, 2 Sept., 1995, Spectrum 10A; P. Spearritt, *Age*, 23 Dec., 1995, Saturday Extra 6.
---. 'Recovering American Connections'. *Overland*, No. 121, 1990, 70-76.
Jamkhandi, Sudakhar R. 'Australian Literary Publications in the C. Hartley Grattan Collection'. In *Perspectives on Australia: Essays on Australiana in Collections of the Harry Ransom Humanities Research Center*, edited by Dave Oliphant (Austin: Harry Ransom Humanities Research Centre, University of Texas, 1989), 39-49.
Poyas, Frank B. 'C. Hartley Grattan: The Man and the Collection'. In *Perspectives on Australia: Essays on Australiana in Collections of the Harry Ransom Humanities Research Center*, edited by Dave Oliphant (Austin: Harry Ransom Humanities Research Centre, University of Texas, 1989), 11-37.

GRAY, ROBERT

Poetry
Certain Things. (Port Melbourne: Heinemann, 1993).
Reviewed by H. Cam, *S.M.H.*, 28 August, 1993, 49; M. Duwell, *Weekend Australian*, 14-15 August, 1993, Review 6; J. Foulcher, *Quadrant*, 38.6, 1994, 82-85; K. Hart, *Age*, 5 February, 1994, Saturday Extra 8; R. Handicott, *LiNQ*, 22.1, 1995, 126-29.
Creek Water Journal. (St Lucia: U.Q.P., 1974). Paperback Poets, Second Series, No. 3.
Reviewed by S.E. Lee, *Southerly*, XXXVI, 1976, 331-56; G. Page, *Canberra Times*, 26 September, 1975, 14 and *New Poetry*, XXIII, No. 1, 1974, 75-77 and *Hemisphere*, XIX, No. 7, 1975, 40; P. Porter, *T.L.S.*, 9 April, 1976, 432; J. Rodriguez, *Luna*, No. 3, 1976, 19-20.
Grass Script. (Sydney: A.& R., 1979).
Reviewed by R. Adamson, *New Poetry*, XXVII, No. 4, 1980, 67-70; G. Catalano, *Meanjin*, XXXIX, 1980, 89-90; R. Handicott, *LiNQ*, X, No. 2, 1982, 113-24; M. Harrison, *S.M.H.*, 17 May, 1980, 22; D. Haskell, *Southerly*, XL, 1980, 226-40; P. Kocan, *24 Hours*, IV, No. 12, 1980, 70; G. Page, *ABR*, No. 21, 1980, 23-24.
New and Selected Poems. (Port Melbourne: Heinemann, 1995).
Reviewed by H. Cam, *S.M.H.*, 9 Dec., 1995, Spectrum 14; K. Hart, *ABR*, 176, 1995, 53-54; D. McCooey, *Age*, 30 Dec., 1995, Saturday Extra 6.
Piano. (North Ryde, N.S.W.: A.& R., 1988).
Reviewed by L. Bourke, *Poetry Australia*, No. 118, 1989, 29-40; H. Cam, *S.M.H.*, 1 October, 1988, 74; J. Grant, *Weekend Australian*, 1-2 October, 1988, Weekend 10; P. Mead, *Age Saturday Extra*, 8 October, 1988, 14; A. Urquhart, *Westerly*, 34, No. 2, 1989, 106-108.
Selected Poems 1963-1983. (North Ryde, N.S.W.: A.& R., 1985).
Reviewed by J. Rodriguez, *S.M.H.*, 22 March, 1986, 47; K. Russell, *Quadrant*, XXXI, Nos. 1-2, 1987, 109-115; esp. 112.
Selected Poems 1985. Revised and expanded edition of above (North Ryde, N.S.W.: A.& R.1990).
Reviewed by J. Grant, *Quadrant*, 34, Nos. 7-8, 1990, 59-63; W. Wynne, *ABR*, No. 122, 1990, 39-41.
The Skylight. (London; Sydney: A.& R., 1984).
Reviewed by G. Bitcon, *Southerly*, XLV, No. 3, 1985, 352-359; G. Catalano, *Age Monthly Review*, IV, No. 7, 1984, 11-12; P. Lugg, *Canberra Times*, 22 December,

1984, 15; V. O'Sullivan, *Helix*, Nos. 21-22, 1985, 122-128; G. Page, *Quadrant*, XXIV, No. 4, 1985, 71-75; M. Richards, *ABR*, No. 69, 1985, 35.

Non-Fiction

'Poetry and Living: An Evaluation of the American Poetic Tradition'. In *The American Model: Influence and Independence in Australian Poetry*, edited by Joan Kirkby (Sydney: Hale & Iremonger, 1982), 117-136.

Critical Material

Gould, Alan. 'Robert Gray'. *Quadrant*, 38.3, 1994, 64-66.

Haskell, Dennis. 'Humanism and Sensual Awareness in the Poetry of Robert Gray'. *Southerly*, XLVI, No. 3, 1986, 261-70.

Hawke, John. 'Robert Gray and the Vitalist Tradition'. *Southerly*, 55.4, 1995, 96-105.

Page, Geoff. 'Robert Gray'. In his *A Reader's Guide To Contemporary Australian Poetry* (St. Lucia: U.Q.P., 1995), 89-92.

Sant, Andrew. 'An Interview with Robert Gray'. *Island Magazine*, No. 7, 1981, 15-20.

Spurr, Barry. *The Poetry of Robert Gray*. (Glebe, NSW: Pascal P, 1995).

Stephens, John. 'Evoking Empathy: Structures of Language and Feeling in Robert Gray's Poetry'. *A.L.S.*, 14, No. 4, 1990, 450-63.

Urquhart, Alan. 'Objectivity and Other Stances in the Poetry of Robert Gray'. *Westerly*, XXXIII, No. 3, 1988, 45-58.

Williams, Barbara. 'An Interview with Robert Gray'. *Southerly*, 50, No. 1, 1990, 27-44.

GRAY, TOM

Critical Material

Moran, Rod. 'Tracing the Life of Tom Gray, Stockman, Poet and Soldier'. *Voices*, 1.4, 1991-92, 55-68.

GREEN, DOROTHY

See Auchterlonie, Dorothy.

GRENVILLE, KATE

Fiction

Bearded Ladies: Stories. (St Lucia: U.Q.P., 1985). First published: St Lucia: U.Q.P., 1984.

Reviewed by K. Ahearne, *Age Saturday Extra*, 11 August, 1984, 15; M. Eldridge, *ABR*, No. 76, 1985, 25-28; T. Forshaw, *Quadrant*, XXIX, No. 3, 1985, 77-79; L. Frost, *Overland*, No. 97, 1984, 66-68; C. Gerrish, *Womanspeak*, IX, No. 1, 1984, 24; M. Hulse, *PN Review*, XIII, No. 5, 1987, 80-81; J. Motion, *T.L.S.*, 18 October, 1985, 1173; C. Peake, *S.M.H.*, 29 September, 1984, 47.

Dark Places. (Sydney: Macmillan, 1994).

Reviewed by L. Altomari, *Antipodes*, 9.1, 1995, 49-50; D. Anderson, *S.M.H.*, 2 July, 1994, Spectrum 9A; P. Craven, *Meanjin*, 53.3, 1994, 566-570; M. Fraser, *Voices*, 4.4, 1994-95, 91-98; K. Goldsworthy, *ABR*, 162, 1994, 7-9 (see also interview by R. Sorensen 8-10); I. Indyk, *Weekend Australian*, 9-10 July, 1994, Review 7; L. Knight, *T.L.S.*, 2 September, 1994, 10; R. Lucas, *Bulletin*, 19 July, 1994, 89; J. Maiden, *Overland*, 141, 1995, 82-84; R. Sorensen, *Age*, 23 July, 1994, Saturday Extra 7.

Dreamhouse. (New York: Viking, 1987). First published St Lucia: U.Q.P., 1986.

Reviewed by K. Ahearn, *Overland*, No. 106, 1987, 76-78; J. Cotter, *ABR*, No. 85, 1986, 5-7; B. Edwards, *Mattoid*, No. 27, 1987, 82-84; B. Farmer, *ABR*, No. 96, 1987, 6-8; esp. 7; B. Jefferis, *Weekend Australian Magazine*, 6-7 September, 1986,

14; M. Luke, *Fremantle Arts Review*, II, No. 2, 1987, 12; S. McKernan, *Bulletin*, 30 September, 1986, 92, 95; M. Peacock, *New York Times and Book Review*, 22 November, 1987, 24; P. Pierce, *Age Saturday Extra*, 13 September, 1986, 10; K. Saunders, *Courier-Mail: The Great Weekend*, 27 September, 1986, 6; V. Sen, *Canberra Times*, 13 September, 1986, B2; C. Thompson, *Scripsi*, IV, No. 3, 1987, 61-68.

Joan Makes History: A Novel. (St Lucia: U.Q.P.; Latham, New York: British American, 1988).
Reviewed by D. Anderson, *S.M.H.*, 30 April, 1988, 70; D. Bird, *Westerly*, XXXIII, No. 3, 1988, 87-88; C. Bliss, *World Literature Today*, 63.3, 1989, 533; M. Clark, *ABR*, No. 100, 1988, 9-10; M. Flanagan, *Overland*, No. 112, 1988, 77-78; M. Hardie, *Southerly*, 49, No. 1, 1989, 113-17; B. Matthews, *Age Saturday Extra*, 30 April, 1988, 15; B. Merry, *LiNQ*, 16, No. 2, 1988, 108-17; S. McKernan, *Bulletin*, 3 May, 1988, 127; S. Morrison, *Weekend Australian*. *Weekend Magazine*, 14-15 May, 1988, 19; D. Reiter, *Redoubt*, No. 3, 1988, 71-76; K. Veitch, *Fremantle Arts Review*, III, No. 9, 1988, 15; J. Wells, *Lilith*, No. 6, 1989, 155-58; N. Willard, *New York Times Book Review*, 18 December, 1988, 7.

Lilian's Story. (Sydney: George Allen & Unwin, 1985; New York: Viking Penguin, 1986).
Reviewed by D. Anderson, *National Times*, 28 June-4 July, 1985, 32; A. Brewster, *CRNLE Reviews Journal*, No. 2, 1985, 27-31; K. Bucknell, *T.L.S.*, 10 October, 1986, 1130; L. Clancy, *Age Saturday Extra*, 17 August, 1985, 13; M. Eldridge, *ABR*, No. 76, 1985, 25-28; J. Emery, *Antipodes*, 3.1, 1989, 50-51; K. England, *Advertiser Saturday Review*, 17 August, 1985, 7; K. Goldsworthy, *Age Monthly Review*, V, No.5, 1985, 17-19; M. Halligan, *Canberra Times*, 19 October, 1985, B2; B. Jefferis, *Overland*, No. 103, 1986, 65-66; E. Jolley, *S.M.H.*, 29 June, 1985, 42; A. McGregor, *Courier-Mail*, 24 August, 1985, 30; S. McKernan, *Bulletin*, 23 July, 1985, 78, 80; A. Mitchell, *Weekend Australian Magazine*, 22-23 June, 1985, 15; J. Purdy, *New York Times Book Review*, 7 September, 1986, 27.

Lilian's Story. (North Sydney: Allen & Unwin, 1991). Revised edition of 1985 publication, containing changes and additions made for US publication.

Non-Fiction
With Sue Woolfe. *Making Stories: How Ten Australian Novels Were Written*. (St Leonards, NSW: Allen & Unwin, 1993). Includes discussion of *Lilian's Story*.
'Self-Portrait'. *ABR*, No. 87, 1987, 17-18.
'Why I Write As I Do'. *Australian Literature Quarterly*, 6-7 June, 1987, 6.

Critical Material
Baker, Candida. 'Kate Grenville'. In her *Yacker 3* (Sydney: Picador, 1989), 100-129
Bartlett, Alison. 'Other Stories: The Representation of History in Recent Fiction by Australian Women Writers'. *Southerly*, 53.1, 1993, 165-80.
Craven, Peter. 'The Gothic Grenville, or Kate Makes Rhetoric'. *Scripsi*, 6, No. 3, 1990, 239-58.
Ellison, Jennifer. 'Kate Grenville'. In her *Rooms of Their Own* (Ringwood, Vic.: Penguin, 1986), 152-171.
Goulston, Wendy. 'Herstory's Re/vision of History: Women's Narrative Subverts Imperial Discourse in Kate Grenville's *Joan Makes History*'. *Australian & New Zealand Studies in Canada*, 7, 1992, 20-27.
Haynes, Roslynn D. 'Fatalism and Feminism in the Fiction of Kate Grenville'. *WLWE*, 31.1, 1991, 60-79.
Herk, Aritha. van. 'Post-Modernism: Homesick for Homesickness'. In *The Commonwealth Novel Since 1960*, edited by Bruce King (Houndmills, Basingstoke, Hampshire and London: Macmillan, 1991), 216-30. Includes discussion of *Joan Makes History*.

Jones, Dorothy. 'Living in the Country: A Woman's Reading'. *Australian-Canadian Studies*, 10.2, 1992, 87-98. Includes discussion of Grenville.

Livett, Jennifer. 'History That Might Have Happened'. *Island Magazine*, No. 36, 1988, 83-85.

Mercer, Gina. 'Newer Voices 2: Kate Grenville'. *Southerly*, XLV, No. 3, 1985, 295-300.

Midalia, Susan. 'Re-writing Woman: Genre Politics and Female Identity in Kate Grenville's *Dreamhouse*'. *A.L.S.*, 16.1, 1993, 30-37.

Nugent, Ann. 'Does Joan Make History? If So, in Which Generation?' *Blast*, Nos. 6-7, 1988, 22-24.

Perkins, Elizabeth. 'Characters in Search of History: Five Contemporary Australian Novels'. In *Australian Writing 1988*, edited by M. Jurgensen and R. Adamson, Bicentennial issue of *Outrider*. Published in association with Penguin as *Australian Writing Now* (Ringwood, Vic.: Penguin, 1988), 58-71.

Prentice, Chris. 'The Interplay of Place and Placelessness in the Subject of Post-colonial Fiction'. *SPAN*, 31, 1991, 63-80. Discusses Grenville's *Lilian's Story* and Sally Morgan's *My Place*.

Rogers, Shelagh. '"You Don't Really Know What It Is Until You Go Away and Come Back": Interviews with Four Australian Writers'. *Australian and New Zealand Studies in Canada*, No. 1, 1989, 33-43.

Turcotte, Gerry. 'The Story-teller's Revenge: Kate Grenville Interviewed by Gerry Turcotte'. *Kunapipi*, 16.1, 1994, 147-58.

---. 'Telling Those Untold Stories: An Interview with Kate Grenville'. *Southerly*, 47, No. 3, 1987, 284-99.

---. '"The Ultimate Oppression": Discourse Politics in Kate Grenville's Fiction'. *WLWE*, 29, No. 1, 1989, 64-85.

Willbanks, Ray. 'Kate Grenville'. In his *Speaking Volumes: Australian Writers and Their Work* (Ringwood, Vic.: Penguin, 1991).

GRIMSTONE, MARY LEMAN

Critical Material

Roe, Michael. 'Mary Leman Grimstone (1800-1850?): For Women's Rights and Tasmanian Patriotism'. *Tasmanian Historical Research Association. Papers and Proceedings*, 36, No. 1, 1989, 8-32.

GUNN, JEANNIE

Critical Material

Bertrand, Ina. '"Woman's Voice": The Autobiographical Form in Three Australian Filmed Novels'. *Literature/Film Quarterly*, 21.2, 1993, 130-37. Discusses works by Franklin, Garner, and Gunn.

Larbalestier, Jan. 'Amity and Kindness in the Never-Never: Ideology and Aboriginal-European Relations in the Northern Territory'. *Social Analysis*, No. 27 (Special Issue; Writing Australian Culture), 1990, 70-82. Discusses Gunn's *The Little Black Princess* and *We of the Never-Never*.

McQueen, Humphrey. 'Racism and Australian Literature'. In *Racism: The Australian Experience. A Study of Race Prejudice in Australia. Volume I. Prejudice and Xenophobia*, edited by F.S. Stevens (Sydney: Australia and New Zealand Book Company, 1971), 115-22.

Myers, David. 'From Empire Feudalism and Racism to Commonwealth Citizenship: The View of Four Female Intruders in the Colonial Tropics'. In *Australian Literature Today*, edited by R.K. Dhawan and David Kerr (New York: Indian Society for Commonwealth Studies/ Advent P, 1993), 80-97. Includes discussion of Gunn.

HACKSTON, JAMES

Fiction

Father Clears Out. With a Foreword by Douglas Stewart (Sydney: A.& R., 1966).
Reviewed by Nancy Keesing, *Bulletin*, 24 September, 1966, 61.

Critical Material

Hetherington, John. 'A Sentimental Bloke Named Hal Gye'. *Age*, 24 September, 1966, 22.
Stewart, Douglas. 'The Re-appearance of Hal Gye'. *S.M.H.*, 27 August, 1966, 20.

HALL, RODNEY

Fiction

Captivity Captive. (Fitzroy, Vic.: McPhee Gribble; London: Faber; New York: Farrar, Straus, Giroux; Toronto: Collins Publishers, 1988).
Reviewed by V. Brady, *ABR*, No. 104, 1988, 27-29; A. Broinowski, *S.M.H.*, 3 September, 1988, 81; H. Daniel, *Weekend Australian*, 3-4 September, 1988, Weekend 12; B. Edwards, *Mattoid*, No. 32, 1988, 116-19; A. Gamerman, *New Statesman*, 1 April, 1988, 24; R. Gostand, *Social Alternatives*, 8, No. 1, 1989, 63-5; A. Gurr, *Australian Studies*, No. 4, 1990, 127-29; P. Lewis, *Stand Magazine*, 30, No. 3, 1989, 66-73; M. Lord, *Overland*, No. 113, 1988, 85-87; B. Matthews, *Age Saturday Extra*, 10 September, 1988, 15; J. Mellors, *London Magazine*, XXVIII, Nos. 1-2, 1988, 133-136; P. Pierce, *Bulletin*, 13 September, 1988, 122-123; R. Schieder, *Books in Canada*, XVII, No. 7, 1988, 30-31.

A Dream More Luminous than Love: The Yandilli Trilogy. (Sydney: Picador, 1994). Trilogy consists of *Captivity Captive*, *The Second Bridegroom* and *The Grisly Wife*.
Reviewed by J. Kinnane, *Overland*, 138, 1995, 70-71; B. Matthews, *Age*, 16 July, 1994, Saturday Extra 8, M. McGirr, *Eureka Street*, 4.8, 1994, 41-42.

The Grisly Wife. (Chippendale, NSW: Pan Macmillan, 1993).
Reviewed by L. Alomarl, *Antipodes*, 8.1, 1994, 74-75; H. Daniel, *Age*, 2 October, 1993, Saturday Extra 8; N. Krauth and R. Holden, *ABR*, 156, 1993, 5-8; R. Lucas, *S.M.H.*, 16 October, 1993, Spectrum 11A; P. Pierce, *Bulletin*, 16 November, 1993, 105; I. Salusinszky, *Weekend Australian*, 30-31 October, 1993, Review 6; P. Sharrad, *World Literature Today*, 68.2, 1994, 424; V. Smith, *T.L.S.*, 24 September, 1993, 21.

Just Relations. (Ringwood, Vic.: Penguin, 1982).
Reviewed by J. Bryson, *S.M.H.*, 15 May, 1982, 42; V. Coleman, *Quadrant*, XXVII, No. 8, 1983, 79-80; J. Davidson, *National Times*, 2-8 May, 1982, 20; A. Diffey, *Weekend Australian Magazine*, 7-8 August, 1982, 10; M. Halligan, *Canberra Times*, 26 June, 1982, 14; R. Haupt, *Age Monthly Review*, II, No. 2, 1982, 4-5; B. Jefferis, *Hemisphere*, XXVIII, No. 2, 1983, back cover; M. Lord, *Overland*, No. 90, 1982,

53-56; J. McLaren, *ABR*, No. 43, 1982, 28; J. Neville, *T.L.S.*, 24 June, 1983, 682; P. Pierce, *Age Saturday Extra*, 8 May, 1982, 15; J. Pritchard, *Westerly*, XXVII, No. 3, 1982, 72-74; E. Riddell, *Bulletin*, 1 June, 1982, 68; F. Taliaferro, *Harper's*, March, 1983, 74-75; J. Tulip, *Southerly*, XLIII, 1983, 117-18; M. Williams, *Courier-Mail*, 1 October, 1983, 29.

Kisses of the Enemy. (Ringwood, Vic.: Penguin, 1987; New York: Farrar, Straus & Giroux, 1989).
Reviewed by K. Ahearne, *Australian Society*, VIII, No. 1, 1988, 42-43; P. K. Bell, *New York Times Book Review*, 27 November, 1988, 9; J. Brett, *ABR*, No. 99, 1988, 31-32; K. Brophy, *Westerly*, XXXIII, No. 3, 1988, 85-87; H. Daniel, *Weekend Australian. Weekend Magazine*, 21-22 November, 1987, 15; J. Hanrahan, *Age Saturday Extra*, 16 December, 1987, 10; T. James, *Quadrant*, XXXII, No. 3, 1988, 58; C. Jurrist, *Antipodes*, II, No. 1, 1988, 61; P. Lewis, *Stand Magazine*, 30, No. 3, 1989, 66-73; S. McKernan, *Bulletin*, 12 April, 1988, 84-86; P. Pierce, *S.M.H.*, 14 November, 1987, 90.

A Place Among People. (St Lucia: U.Q.P., 1975).
Reviewed by D. Gilbey, *Southerly*, XXXVII, 1977, 464-67; M. Macleod, *S.M.H.*, 16 August, 1975, 15.

The Second Bridegroom. (Ringwood, Vic.: McPhee Gribble; London: Faber, 1991).
Reviewed by J. Coe, *London Review of Books*, 13.17, 1991, 12; H. Daniel, *Age*, 5 October, 1991, Saturday Extra 10; L. Davison, *Editions*, 13, 1992, 12; B. Edwards, 41, 1991, 143-48; J. Grossman, *New York Times Book Review*, 1 September, 1991, 11; P. Kane, *World Literature Today*, 66.4, 1992, 774; S. Knight, *S.M.H.*, 19 October, 1991, 49; M. Lord, *Overland*, 127, 1992, 86-88; J. Motion, *ABR*, 136, 1991, 16; E. Perkins, *LiNQ*, 19.1, 1992, 143-49; P. Rolfe, *Bulletin*, 26 November, 1991, 116-17; I. Salusinszky, *Weekend Australian*, 2-3 November, 1991, Review 5; A. Sykes, *T.L.S.*, 6 September, 1991, 21; D. Tacey, *Island*, 53, 1992, 58-62.

The Ship on the Coin. (St Lucia: U.Q.P., 1972). Paperback Prose, 2.
Reviewed by B. Bennett, *Westerly*, No. 4, 1972, 67-68; A.R. Chisholm, *Age*, 23 September, 1972, 14; B. Jefferis, *S.M.H.*, 14 October, 1972, 23; N. Keesing, *Bulletin*, 16 September, 1972, 50-52; B. Kiernan, *Australian*, 9 September, 1972, 33; E.S. Lindsay, *LiNQ*, II, No. 3, 1973, 40-41; W.A. Murray, *ABR*, XI, 1973, 73; D.J. O'Hearn, *Overland*, No. 56, 1973, 60-61; D. Rowbotham, *Courier Mail*, 14 October, 1972, 15.

Poetry

Autobiography of a Gorgon. (Melbourne: Cheshire, 1968).
Reviewed by D. Anderson, *Southerly*, XXIX, 1969, 74-75; B. Beaver, *S.M.H.*, 22 February, 1969, 21; G. Curtois, *Poetry Magazine*, No. 2, 1969, 33-35; D. Douglas, *Age*, 25 January, 1969, 10; M. Duwell, *Makar*, V, No. 1, 1969, 25-27; G. Lehmann, *Bulletin*, 8 February, 1969, 70-71; D. Malouf, *Australian*, 21 December, 1968, 14; M. Richards, *Meanjin*, XXVIII, 1969, 276; R. Ward, *ABR*, VIII, 1969, 70-71; F. Zwicky, *Westerly*, No. 1, 1970, 48-50.

Black Bagatelles (St Lucia: U.Q.P., 1978).
Reviewed by V. Brady, *ABR*, No. 5, 1978, 22-23; G. Dutton, *Bulletin*, 21 November, 1978, 67; [S.E. Lee], *Southerly*, XXXIX, 1979, 455-56; E. Lindsay, *24 Hours*, III, No. 10, 1978, 70.

Eyewitness. (Sydney: South Head Press, 1967).
Reviewed by B. Beaver, *S.M.H.*, 24 June, 1967, 18; L.J. Clancy, *Overland*, No. 39, 1968, 50-51; D. Douglas, *Age*, 12 August, 1967, 24; R. Dunlop, *Southerly*, XXVII, 1967, 293-94; S. Hume, *Telegraph* (Brisbane), 21 June, 1967, 56; M. Irvin, *Twentieth Century*, XXII, 1967, 83-86; A. King, *Meanjin*, XXVII, 1968, 174-76; S.E. Lee, *Poetry Australia*, No. 18, 1967, 45; R. Ward, *ABR*, VI, 1967, 145; J. Wright, *Australian*, 8 July, 1967, 12.

Heaven, in a Way. (St Lucia: U.Q.P., 1970). Paperback Poets, 3.
Reviewed by B.A. Breen, *Twentieth Century*, XXV, 1971, 280-82; M. Duwell, *Makar*, VI, No. 1, 1970, 21-24; C. Harrison-Ford, *Poetry Magazine*, XVIII, No. 6, 1970, 47-48 and *Union Recorder*, L, No. 11, 1970, 5-6; S. Lawson, *Australian*, 23 May, 1970, 19; P. Roberts, *S.M.H.*, 15 August, 1970, 24; J. Saunders, *Stand*, XIII, No. 3, 1972, 79; T.W. Shapcott, *ABR*, IX, 1970, 255-56; R.A. Simpson, *Age*, 15 August, 1970, 17; J. Tulip, *Southerly*, XXXI, 1971, 77-79.

The Law of Karma: A Progression of Poems. (Canberra: Australian National University Press, 1968).
Reviewed by B. Beaver, *S.M.H.*, 19 April, 1969, 24; C. Harrison-Ford, *Poetry Magazine*, No. 4, 1969, 5-11; F. Kellaway, *Overland*, No. 46, 1970/71, 39; G. Lehmann, *Bulletin*, 8 February, 1969, 70-71; G. Page, *Canberra Times*, 1 March, 1969, 11; G. Rowlands, *Makar*, V, No. 1, 1969, 28-30; T. Shapcott, *Australian*, 22 February, 1969, 18; R. Ward, *ABR*, VIII, 1968, 44; F. Zwicky, *Westerly*, No. 1, 1970, 48-50.

The Most Beautiful World. (St Lucia: U.Q.P., 1981).
Reviewed by D. Carter, *Age*, 26 September, 1981, 27; B. Giles, *ABR*, No. 47, 1982, 28-29; S. McKernan, *Canberra Times*, 11 September, 1982, 13; J. Tranter, *Meanjin*, XLI, 1982, 399-400.

Rodney Hall Reads Romulus and Remus. With music by Richard Mills. (St Lucia: U.Q.P., 1970). Poets on Record, 1. Record and booklet. Booklet includes notes by Rodney Hall and selected bibliography.
Reviewed by M. Duwell, *Makar*, VII, No. 1, 1971, 43-45; S.E. Lee, *Southerly*, XXXI, 1971, 238-39; A.C. Lyons, *Twentieth Century*, XXVI, 1971, 181-83; G. Page, *Canberra Times*, 27 March, 1971, 15; J.D. Pringle, *S.M.H.*, 3 April, 1971, 24; R.A. Simpson, *Age*, 27 February, 1971, 17; K. Slessor, *Daily Telegraph*, (Sydney), 2 January, 1971, 10; J. Tulip, *Bulletin*, 6 March, 1971, 46.

Selected Poems. (St Lucia: U.Q.P., 1975).
Reviewed by H.H. Anniah Gowda, *Literary Half-Yearly*, XVIII, No. 1, 1977, 239-41; G. Dutton, *Nation Review*, 9-15 January, 1976, 335; A. Gould, *Canberra Poetry*, 1976, 71; J. Griffin, *Advertiser*, 3 July, 1976, 22; G. Harwood, *Overland*, No. 63, 1976, 67-68; [S.E. Lee], *Southerly*, XXXIX, 1979, 454-55; J. McLaren, *Segment*, No. 5, 1976, 58; P. Porter, *T.L.S.*, 9 April, 1976, 432; J. Rodriguez, *Luna*, I, No. 2, 1976, 46-50; T. Shapcott, *Australian*, 21 February, 1976, 29; J. Tulip, *Age*, 13 March, 1976, 23; V. Young, *Hudson Review*, XXXI, 1978-79, 681-82.

A Soapbox Omnibus. (St Lucia: U.Q.P., 1973). Paperback Poets, 16.
Reviewed by R. Adamson, *Australian*, 14 September, 1974, 39.

Non-Fiction

Focus on Andrew Sibley. (St Lucia: U.Q.P., 1968). Artists in Queensland.
Reviewed by P. Cleary, *Twentieth Century*, XXIII, 1969, 380; E. Lynn, *Art and Australia*, VI, 1969, 279, and in *Bulletin*, 18 January, 1969, 57-58; P. McCaughey, *Age*, 11 January, 1969, 13.

'Confessions of a Poetry Editor'. *Australian*, 11 April, 1970, 17. See also letter to the editor by L. Drake, *Australian*, 22 April, 1970, 12.

Critical Material

Beeby, Rosslyn. 'The Cultural Cringe is Waning: Author'. *Age*, 20 May, 1983, 10.
Broinowski, Alison. 'An Experienced Weaver of Spells'. *National Times*, 6-12 June, 1982, 19. Interview.
Covell, Roger. 'Theme on Rebirth of Single Soul'. *S.M.H.*, 18 November, 1972, 16.
Dalton, Warwick. 'To Ask: To Dig: Perhaps to Find Meaning'. *Australian*, 27 July, 1968, 11.
Davidson, Jim. 'Rodney Hall'. *Meanjin*, XL, 1981, 312-27. Interview. Reprinted in

his *Sideways from the Page* (Melbourne: Fontana, 1983), 303-323.

Dean, Peter. 'Novelist Strikes Gold'. *Courier-Mail*, 20 May, 1983, 2.

Duwell, Martin, and McLeod, N.J. 'The End of a Beginning: An Interview with Rodney Hall'. *Makar*, X, No. 1, 1974, 1-13.

Hall, Sandra. 'The Other Poets'. *Bulletin*, 28 September, 1968, 43-45.

Harvey, Oliver. 'Writing so Hard to Make a Crust'. *Courier-Mail*, 26 May, 1982, 5.

Hawley, Janet. 'Poets in the Pen'. *Australian*, 28 December, 1973, 10.

Krause, Tom. 'Rodney's Bound for the Literary Hall of Fame'. *Australian*, 18 May, 1983, 9.

Malouf, David. 'Some Volumes of Selected Poems of the 1970s, II'. *A.L.S.*, X, 1982, 304-05.

Page, Geoff. 'Rodney Hall'. In his *A Reader's Guide To Contemporary Australian Poetry* (St. Lucia: U.Q.P., 1995), 96-99.

Pons, Xavier. '"Savage Paradise": History, Violence and Family in Recent Australian Fiction by Hall, Keneally and Malouf'. In *European Perspectives: Contemporary Essays on Australian Literature*, edited by Giovanna Capone (*A.L.S.* 15.2 (special issue)/ St. Lucia: U.Q.P., 1991), 72-82

Plunkett, Felicity. '"All Those Layered and Clotted Images": An Interview with Rodney Hall'. *Australian & New Zealand Studies in Canada*, 11, 1994, 56-67.

Rees, Jacqueline. 'The Pursuit of Excellence'. *Bulletin*, 15 January, 1977, 37-38.

Riddell, Elizabeth. 'Broadsheet Muse'. *Australian*, 5 March, 1977, 30.

Sayers, Stuart. 'Why Rodney Hall Keeps his Relations on File'. *Age Saturday Extra*, 15 May, 1982, 14.

Shapcott, Thomas. 'The Early Volumes of Rodney Hall'. *Makar*, V, No. 1, 1969, 21-24.

Sutton, Ray. 'The Poet who Celebrates the Land'. *S.M.H.*, 24 October, 1981, 50.

HANRAHAN, BARBARA

Fiction

The Albatross Muff. (London: Chatto & Windus, 1977).
Reviewed by G. Dutton, *Bulletin*, 24 September, 1977, 85.

Annie Magdalene. (London: Chatto & Windus/Hogarth Press, 1985).
Reviewed by J. Colmer, *Weekend Australian Magazine*, 1-2 June, 1985, 16; P.F. Edelson, *Antipodes*, I, No. 1, 1987, 53; K. Goldsworthy, *Age Saturday Extra*, 30 November, 1985, 14; M. Gollan, *S.M.H.*, 22 June, 1985, 45; M. John, *ABR*, No. 72, 1985, 16-17; C. Leonard, *National Times*, 17-23 May, 1985, 31; J. Motion, *T.L.S.*, 18 October, 1985, 1173; D. Parker, *Quadrant*, XXX, Nos. 7 & 8, 1986, 126-30.

A Chelsea Girl. (London: Grafton, 1988).
Reviewed by P. F. Edelson, *Antipodes*, 5.2, 1991, 151; N. Keesing, *S.M.H.*, 6 August, 1988, 76; J. Maiden, *Weekend Australian*, 20-21 August, 1988, Weekend 15; R. Sorensen, *Age Saturday Extra*, 20 August, 1988, 16.

Dove. (St Lucia: U.Q.P., 1982). Paperback prose.
Reviewed by R. Barnes, *National Times*, 15-21 August, 1982, 22; A. Brewster, *Ash Magazine*, No. 10, 1982, 31-32; G. Dutton, *Bulletin*, 6 July, 1982, 53-54; T. Forshaw, *Age Saturday Extra*, 3 April, 1982, 13; M. Glastonbury, *New Statesman*, 3 December, 1982, 29; G. Harwood, *S.M.H.*, 27 March, 1982, 46; M. Luke, *Westerly*, XXVII, No. 3, 1982, 65-67; S. Walker, *ABR*, No. 45, 1982, 11; F. Weldon, *Weekend Australian Magazine*, 12-13 June, 1982, 7.

Dream People. (London, Sydney: Grafton Books; London, Sydney: Paladin, 1987).
Reviewed by C. Bird, *Age Saturday Extra*, 22 August, 1987, 12; S. Dowrick, *Times on Sunday*, 9 August, 1987, 32; S. McKernan, *Bulletin*, 19 January, 1988, 70; B. Turner, *S.M.H.*, 14 November, 1987, 92.

Flawless Jade. (St Lucia: U.Q.P., 1989).

Reviewed by C. Bird, *Age Saturday Extra*, 21 October, 1989, 9; D. Dunstan, *ABR*, No. 116, 1989, 5; S. Geok-Lin Lim, *Antipodes*, 4.1, 1990, 65: T. Glyde, *T.L.S.*, 14-20 September, 1990, 980; M. Halligan, *ABR*, No. 116, 1989, 3-5; J. Hanrahan, *Overland*, No. 118, 1990, 81-82; G. Hopkins, *Studio*, No. 39, 1990, 31; M.R. Liverani, *Weekend Australian Magazine*, 25-26 November, 1989, Weekend 7; G. McFall, *New York Times Book Review*, 23 December, 1990, 12; M. Nedeljkovic, *Commonwealth* (France), 13, No. 1, 1990, 87-94; N. Stasko, *Phoenix Review*, No. 6, 1990, 116-19.

The Frangipani Gardens. (St Lucia: U.Q.P., 1980).
Reviewed by L. Frost, *CRNLE Reviews Journal*, No. 1, 1981, 61-63; B. Jefferis, *National Times*, 12-18 October, 1980, 64; N. Jillett, *Age*, 31 January, 1981, 29; F. McInherny, *ABR*, No. 28, 1981, 8; J. Miles, *Advertiser*, 18 October, 1980, 25; P. Ward, *Weekend Australian Magazine*, 15-16 November, 1980, 18.

Good Night, Mr Moon. (St. Lucia: U.Q.P., 1992).
Reviewed by C. Blanche, *Quadrant*, 36.11, 1992, 86-88; L. Clancy, *Age*, 18 April, 1992, Saturday Extra 8; D. Davison, *Weekend Australian*, 25-26 July, 1992, Review 7; A. van Herk, *SPAN*, 37, 1994, 249-52; C. Keneally, *ABR*, 140, 1992, 6-7; A.P. Riemer, *S.M.H.*, 21 March, 1992, 47.

Iris in Her Garden: Eight Stories. With relief etchings by the author. (Canberra: Officina Brindabella, 1991). Reprinted St Lucia: U.Q.P., 1992.
Reviewed by C. Blanche, *Quadrant*, 37.3, 1993, 84-86; F. Capp, *Age*, 20 June, 1992, Saturday Extra 9.

Kewpie Doll. (London: Chatto & Windus, 1984).
Reviewed by J. Bedford, *National Times*, 9-15 March, 1984, 34; B. Clunies Ross, *Kunapipi*, VI, No. 3, 1984, 103-105; M. Doulton, *Weekend Australian Magazine*, 10-11 March, 1984, 15; T. Forshaw, *Quadrant*, XXVIII, No. 9, 1984, 81; M. Glastonbury, *New Statesman*, 20 January, 1984, 24; K. Goldsworthy, *Age Saturday Extra*, 7 April, 1984 19; R. Lucas, *S.M.H.*, 31 March, 1984, 41; J. Neville, *T.L.S.*, 20 January, 1984, 70; G. Sutherland, *Tribune*, 16 May, 1984, 11.

Michael and Me and the Sun. (St Lucia: U.Q.P., 1992).
Reviewed by J. Cooke, *S.M.H.*, 26 December, 1992, 31; B. Josephi, *Westerly*, 38.2, 1993, 86-87; L. Trainor, *Weekend Australian*, 30-31 January, 1993, Review 7; H. Elliott, *ABR*, 146, 1992, 6-7.

The Peach Groves. (St Lucia: U.Q.P., 1979).
Reviewed by N. Jillett, *Age*, 24 November, 1979, 27; J. Neville, *S.M.H.*, 24 November, 1979, 20; S. Ramsey, *T.L.S.*, 30 May, 1980, 606; P. Ward, *Weekend Australian Magazine*, 8-9 December, 1979, 13.

The Scent of Eucalyptus. (Sydney: Collins, 1980). Fontana Books. First published Chatto & Windus, 1973.
Reviewed by N. Keesing, *ABR*, No. 22, 1980, 16.

Sea-green. (Sydney: Collins, 1980). Fontana Books. First published Chatto & Windus, 1974. Reviewed by E. Hackett, *Advertiser*, 5 October, 1974, 24; N. Keesing, *ABR*, No. 22, 1980, 16; J. Tittensor, *Nation Review*, 11-17 October, 1974, 1653.

Where the Queens all Strayed. (St Lucia: U.Q.P., 1978). Paperback Prose.
Reviewed by E. Carew, *S.M.H.*, 2 December, 1978, 17; R. Claremont, *Quadrant*, XXIII, No. 5, 1979, 69-70; R. Nicholls, *Age*, 27 January, 1979, 26; G. Page, *Canberra Times*, 10 February, 1979, 21.

    Critical Material
ABR, No. 116, (November) 1989, 3-13. Special Section on Hanrahan, with an interview by R. Sorensen and articles by A. Taylor, 'Hanrahan's Double Life', and B. Walker, 'Mimicry and Authority'.

'Focus on Barbara Hanrahan'. With contributions by Pearl Bowman and Phyllis Fahrie Edelson. *Antipodes* 6.2, 1992. 103-12.

Adam, Ian. 'Margin? Center? The Polychromagic Realism of *The Frangipani Gardens*'. *Antipodes*, 5.1, 1991, 47-50.

Baker, Candida. 'Barbara Hanrahan'. In her *Yacker 2: Australian Writers Talk About Their Work* (Sydney: Picador, 1987), 72-92.

Brydon, Diana. 'Barbara Hanrahan's Fantastic Fiction'. *Westerly*, XXVII, No. 3, 1982, 41-49.

Capone, Giovanna. 'Barbara Hanrahan e *The Albatross Muff*: il racconto e il ritorno'. In *Percorsi immaginati: Viaggio, metafora e modello in scrittori anglofoni d'Africa, Asia, America, Australia*, edited Giovanna Capone (Bologna: Cooperativa Libraria Universitaria Editrice Bologna, 1993), 163-78.

Carrol, Alison. *Barbara Hanrahan: Printmaker*. (Cowandilla, S.A.: Wakefield Press, 1986). Reviewed by S. Hosking, *ABR*, No. 89, 1987, 16-18.

Colmer, John. 'Autobiography and Three Women Writers: Barbara Hanrahan, Oriel Gray and Kylie Tennant'. In his *Australian Autobiography: A Personal Quest* (Melbourne: O.U.P., 1989), 128-146.

Dolan, David. 'Parallel Lives: Barbara Harvey Zerbini and Barbara Hanrahan'. *Voices*, 4.1, 1993, 22-30.

England, Katharine. 'Too many Echoes'. *Advertiser*, 3 March, 1984, 35. *Kewpie Doll* and *The Scent of Eucalyptus*.

Goldsworthy, Kerryn. '"Your Only Entry into the World": Barbara Hanrahan's Adelaide'. In *Southwords: Essays on South Australian Writing*, edited by Philip Butterss (Kent Town, SA: Wakefield, 1995), 144-59.

Johnston, Richard. 'Unexplored Country'. *London Magazine*, N.S. XX, Nos. 8-9, 1980, 63-70.

Kirkby, Joan. 'Daisy Miller Down Under: The Old World/New World Paradigm in Barbara Hanrahan'. *Kunapipi*, VIII, No. 3, 1986, 10-27.

Laughton, Verity. 'Barbara Hanrahan'. *Ash Magazine*, No. 6, 1981, 6-7.

Lindsay, Elaine. 'Finding a Voice: From the Diaries of Barbara Hanrahan'. *Southerly*, 55.3, 1995, 114-30.

---. 'A Mystic in Her Garden: Spirituality and the Fiction of Barbara Hanrahan'. In *Claiming Our Rites: Studies in Religion by Australian Women Scholars*, edited by Joy Morny and Penelope Magee (Adelaide: AASR, 1994), 19-35.

---. 'Women Rising: Spirituality in the Writings of Barbara Hanrahan'. *Kunapipi*, 16.1, 1993, 13-21.

Malone, John. 'A Morning with Barbara Hanrahan'. *English in Australia*, No. 82, December, 1987, 50.

Mott, Julie. 'Interview with Barbara Hanrahan'. *A.L.S.*, XI, 1983, 38-46.

Palmer, Jenny. 'An Interview with Barbara Hanrahan'. *Bulletin*, 21-28 December, 1982, 203-06.

Roff, Sue. 'Rites of Passage: Six Australian Authors in Search of the Same Character'. *Australian Society*, III, No. 9, 1984, 33-34.

Salzman, Paul. 'Barbara Hanrahan's *Annie Magdalene*: The Inside Story'. *Southerly*, 52.4, 1992, 105-18.

Sayers, Stuart. 'Out of the Print Box to Become a Novelist'. *Age*, 3 November, 1979, 29.

Stevens, John. 'An Author Who Finds Little Joy in Her Task of Writing'. *Age Saturday Extra*, 15 June, 1985, 15.

---. 'Ordinary People Seen Through a Writer's Extra-ordinary Eye'. *S.M.H.*, 22 June, 1985, 41.

---. 'Writer by Chance in Love with Sinister Adelaide'. *Advertiser Saturday Review*, 22 June, 1985, 4.

Stewart, Annette. 'Barbara Hanrahan 1939-1991'. *Island*, 50, 1992, 8-10. Obituary.

See also A. Carroll, *Art & Australia*, 29.4, 1992, 442-43; R. Sorensen, *ABR*, 140, 1992, 7; A. Stewart, *Notes & Furphies*, 28, 1992, 27.
---. 'Barbara Hanrahan's Grotesquerie'. *Quadrant*, XXXII, Nos. 1&2, 1988, 59-65.
Sykes, Alrene. 'Barbara Hanrahan's Novels'. *A.L.S.*, XI, 1983, 47-57.
---. '*The Scent of Eucalyptus*: Gothic Autobiography'. *A.L.S.*, 14, No. 3, 1990, 306-15.
Thomas, Sue. 'Writing the Self: Barbara Hanrahan's *The Scent of Eucalyptus*'. *Kunapipi*, 11, No. 3, 1990, 53-66.
Walker, Brenda. 'Tea Rose and The Confetti-dot Goddess: Images of the Woman Artist in Barbara Hanrahan's Novels'. In *Who is She?*, edited by Shirley Walker (St Lucia: U.Q.P., 1983), 204-19.
Ward, Peter. 'Seeking a Writer's Secret Treasure in Magical Thebarton'. *Weekend Australian Magazine*, 7-8 January, 1984, 5.

HARCOURT, J.M.

Fiction
Upsurge: A Novel. With an introduction by Richard A. Nile. (Nedlands, W.A.: University of Western Australia Press, 1986). First published London: John Long, 1934. Facsimile edition.
Reviewed by P. Cowan, *Fremantle Arts Review*, II, No. 10, 1987, 14.

HARDY, FRANK

Collection
A Frank Hardy Swag; edited by Clement Semmler. (Sydney: Harper & Row, 1982).
Reviewed by B. Hunter, *Courier-Mail*, 29 May, 1982, 24; J. McLaren, *Overland*, No. 92, 1983, 61-62; B. Oakley, *ABR*, No. 43, 1982, 26-27; G. Turner, *Age Saturday Extra*, 17 July, 1982, 13.

Fiction
Billy Borker Yarns Again. (Melbourne: Nelson Australia, 1967).
Reviewed by J. Miles, *Adelaide Advertiser*, 9 September, 1967, 22; B. Porter, *Australian*, 2 September, 1967, 11; R. Robinson, *S.M.H.*, 14 October, 1967, 25.
But the Dead are Many. (London: Bodley Head, 1975).
Reviewed by E. Aarons, *Tribune*, 1 October, 1975, 7; P. Ackroyd, *Spectator*, 9 August, 1975, 188; G. Adler, *Direct Action*, 12 February, 1976, 13, see also letter from Hardy, 4 March, 1976, 2; K.D. Gott, *Quadrant*, XX, No. 3, 1976, 58-59; B. Kiernan, *Age*, 11 October, 1975, 17; E. Korn, *T.L.S.*, 1 August, 1975, 865; T.J. McKenna, *Australian*, 18 October, 1975, 39; A. Roberts, *Advertiser*, 4 October, 1975, 24; C. Semmler, *S.M.H.*, 11 October, 1975, 16; R. Wade, *Contemporary Review*, CCXXVII, 1975, 213.
The Great Australian Lover and Other Stories. (Melbourne: Nelson, 1972).
Reviewed by J. Miles, *Advertiser*, 23 December, 1972, 16; L. Murray, *S.M.H.*, 10 February, 1973, 18; R. Park, *Sunday Telegraph*, 14 January, 1973, 23.
Great Australian Legends. (Surry Hills, N.S.W.: Hutchinson, 1988).
Reviewed by C. Semmler, *Weekend Australian*, 14-15 January, 1988, Weekend 6.
It's Moments like These. (Melbourne: Gold Star Publications, 1972). Revised version of *Legends from Benson's Valley* London: Werner Laurie, 1963.
Reviewed by M. Wood, *National Times*, 2-7 October, 1972, 23.
The Loser Now Will Be Later to Win. (Carlton, Vic.: Pascoe, 1985).
Reviewed by J. Colmer, *Weekend Australian Magazine*, 26-27 April, 1986, 12; M. Gregory, *Tribune*, No. 2418, 1986, 11; S. Knight, *S.M.H.*, 15 February, 1986, 46; V. Lindesay, *ABR*, No. 78, 1986, 14-15; C. Semmler, *Courier-Mail Magazine: The Great Weekend*, 15 February, 1986, 6.

The Obsession of Oscar Oswald. (Carton: Pascoe Publishing, 1983).
Reviewed by H. Brown, *Canberra Times*, 24 March, 1984, 22; H. Daniel, *Age Saturday Extra*, 17 December, 1983, 14; G. Hutchinson, *National Times*, 16-22 December, 1983, 31; N. Keesing, *Weekend Australian Magazine*, 14-15 January, 1984, 12; L. McGuarr, *ABR*, No. 58, 1984, 26-27.

The Outcasts of Foolgarah. (Melbourne: Allara Publishing, 1971).
Reviewed by P. and R. Cahill, *Australian Left Review*, No. 33, 1971, 78-79; A.R. Chisholm, *Age*, 23 October, 1971, 14; S. Edgar, *Canberra Times*, 16 October, 1971, 14; C. Harrison-Ford, *Nation*, 2 October, 1971, 22-23; W. Hedley, *Tribune*, 13 October, 1971, 7; A. Henries, *Bulletin*, 30 October, 1971, 51-53; K. Kemp, *National Times*, 11-16 October, 1971, 22; B. Kiernan, *Australian*, 11 September, 1971, 19; A. Roberts, *Advertiser*, 28 August, 1971, 20; A. Robertson, *Tribune*, 13 October, 1971, 7.

Power without Glory. Introduction by Jack Lindsay. (London: Sphere Books, 1968). First published Melbourne: Realist, 1950.
Reviewed by R. Williams, *Australian Left Review*, No. 5, 1968, 77-79.

Warrant of Distress, by Oscar Oswald. (Carlton: Pascoe Publishing, 1983).
Reviewed by H. Brown, *Canberra Times*, 24 March, 1984, 22; H. Daniel, *Age Saturday Extra*, 17 December, 1983, 14.

Who Shot George Kirkland? A Novel About the Nature of Truth. (Melbourne: Edward Arnold (Australia), 1981).
Reviewed by D.R. Burns, *ABR*, No. 28, 1981, 10-11; M. Cotter, *Overland*, No. 88, 1982, 63-64; H. Daniel, *Age*, 22 November, 1980, 29; D. Freney, *Tribune*, 17 December, 1980, 10; M. Halligan, *Canberra Times*, 27 June, 1981, 15; P. Pierce, *Meanjin*, XL, 1981, 110-11; A. Roberts, *Advertiser*, 14 March, 1981, 25; C. Semmler, *S.M.H.*, 6 December, 1980, 21.

The Yarns of Billy Borker. Illustrated by Vane; introduced by Clement Semmler. (Sydney: A.& R., 1977). A.& R. Modern Comedies. First published Sydney: Reed, 1965.
Reviewed by T. Forshaw, *Quadrant*, XXI, No. 7, 1977, 72-73.

Non-Fiction

A series of articles by Hardy with some autobiographical content appeared in *Bulletin*, 4 January, 1969 through to 1 February, 1969. A reply '*Literaturnaya Gazeta* Answers the Australian Author', *Soviet News Bulletin* (Canberra), No. 2/174, 1969, 1-3, was reprinted in *Bulletin*, 8 February, 1969, 16-17.

The Hard Way: The Story behind Power without Glory. (Hawthorn, Vic.: Gold Star Publications, 1971). First published Sydney: Australasian Book Society; London: T. Werner Laurie, 1961.
Reviewed by C. Harrison-Ford, *Australian*, 27 February, 1972, 25.

The Unlucky Australians. (Melbourne: Nelson Australia, 1968).
Reviewed by G. Farwell, *S.M.H.*, 22 June, 1968, 17; J. Paterson, *Australian*, 31 August, 1968, 13; A.R., *Australian Left Review*, No. 4, 1968, 78-79; L. Radic, *Age*, 29 June, 1968, 15; P. Rappolt, *Advertiser*, 8 June, 1968, 14; C.D. Rowley, *Bulletin*, 13 July, 1968, 64, 66; Scrutarius, *Walkabout*, XXXIV, No. 9, 1968, 45, 48; R. Ward, *ABR*, VII, 1968, 180.

'Environment and Ideology in Australian Literature: A Personal View'. In *Literary Australia*, edited by Clement Semmler and Derek Whitelock (Melbourne: Cheshire, 1966), 69-80. Includes comment about his writing.
'Frank Hardy on Commitment'. *Quadrant*, XI, No. 1, 1967, 15-21. Transcript of television interview with Tony Morphett. Includes discussion of *Power Without Glory* and his other works.
'Lawson v. Kramer: No Contest'. *S.M.H.*, 24 April, 1985, 10. Letter to the editor

attacking Leonie Kramer's attitude to Henry Lawson.
'Self-portraits'. *ABR*, No. 52, 1983, 13-14. Autobiographical.
'Series Made Against the Stream'. *Australian*, 16 May, 1977, 6. Letter to the editor on 'Power without glory' TV series.
'The Prophet without Glory'. *S.M.H.*, 21 July, 1984, 38. Autobiographical.

    Critical Material
'Contrast of Two Authors'. *Socialist*, 22 October, 1975, 6.
'Frank Hardy's Struggle to Publish *The Outcasts*'. *Review* (Melbourne), 27 August, 1971, 1304-05.
'Hardy: A "Cultural" John Wren'. *National U*, 4 April, 1977, 16.
'Long-haired Promotion'. *Nation*, 1 November, 1969, 13-14. Mentions the sale of film rights of Hardy's books.
'The Outcasts Await the Final Verdict'. *Australian*, 17 September, 1971, 9.
'Snedden Won't Talk about Grant to Hardy'. *Australian*, 5 March, 1969, 1. Report of a question by Mr. Uren on a C.L.F. grant to Hardy (see *Parliamentary Debates*, H. of R. LXII, 1969, 322).
Beasley, Jack. *Journal of an Era: Notes from the Red Letter Days*. (Earlwood, N.S.W.: Wedgetail Press, 1988), 29-39.
---. '"The hero of my own life"'. In his *Red Letter Days*. (Sydney: Australasian Book Society, 1979), 53-95.
Beattie, Max. 'Frank Hardy's "Treason" Amuses the Upper Crust'. *Age*, 11 December, 1971, 2.
Brady, Veronica. 'Television, Power Without Glory'. *Westerly*, No. 3, 1976, 111-12.
Brennan, Niall. *John Wren, Gambler: His Life and Times*. (Melbourne: Hill of Content, 1971). See especially Pt. 2, Ch. 4, 'Libels and Reputations'. Reviewed by F. Hardy, *Review* (Melbourne), 20-26 November, 1971, 186-87.
---. 'The John Wren Myth'. *National Times*, 20-25 September, 1976, 22-23, 26-28.
Capp, Fiona. *Writers Defiled: Security Surveillance of Australian Authors and Intellectuals 1920-1960*. (Ringwood, Vic.: McPhee Gribble, 1993). Includes discussion of Hardy.
Childs, K. 'Tall Tales'. In his *A Month of Lunches: Twenty-Eight Lives Celebrate Melbourne*. (Melbourne: O.U.P., 1984), 73-76. Interview.
Costigan, Michael. 'Hardy Justifies Power'. *Weekend Australian Magazine*, 10-11 January, 1981, 9.
Denoon, Donald. 'Guilt and the Gurinji'. *Meanjin*, XXIX, 1970, 253-65.
Derriman, Philip. 'John Wren: His Family Breaks its Silence'. *S.M.H.*, 17 December, 1983, 25-26.
Docker, John. 'A Study in Context: And the Dead are Many'. *Arena*, No. 41, 1976, 48-61.
Fatchen, Max. 'Frank Hardy Hits at Censorship'. *Advertiser*, 9 September, 1971, 3.
Frow, John. 'Who Shot Frank Hardy? Intertextuality and Textual Politics'. *Southern Review*, XV, 1982, 22-39.
Gheorghiu, Manuela. 'Frank Hardy: Un Martor Patetic al Vietii'. *Secolul*, XX, 1976, Nos. 7-8, 62-65.
Gleghorn, Geoffrey. 'The Trade-Union Big Noise with a Voice Louder than a Jack Hammer'. *National Times*, 30 July-4 August, 1973, 40.
Hadgraft, Cecil. 'Indulgence: David Martin's *The Hero of Too*, Frank Dalby Davison *The White Thorntree*, Dal Stivens's *A Horse of Air*, David Malouf's *Johnno*, and Frank Hardy's *But the Dead are Many*'. In *Studies in the Recent Australian Novel*, edited by K.G. Hamilton (St Lucia: U.Q.P., 1978), 194-224.
Hall, James. 'Foreword'. *Australian*, 23 August, 1969, 18. On a N.S.W. literary grant to Frank Hardy.
Harris, Max. 'Browsing'. *Australian*, 6 September, 1975, 11.
Henderson, Gerard. 'Would you Believe?'. *Quadrant*, XX, No. 12, 1976, 31-33.

Hurst, John. 'The Four Obsessions of Frank Hardy'. *National Times*, 16-21 November, 1980, 50.

Larkin, John. 'Gone Carringbush'. *Age*, 12 November, 1980, 11.

Lindsay, Jack. 'Frank Hardy's *Power Without Glory*'. In his *Decay and Renewal*. (Sydney: Wild & Woolley, 1976), 349-63.

Lockwood, Rupert. 'One Night in the Life of Frank Hardy'. *Nation Review*, 17-23 October, 1975, 24.

McNay, Michael. '"Suicide is an Attempt to Annex Death into Life... by Choosing Death I can Shape People's Memories of Me"'. *Australian*, 9 August, 1975, 27. Interview.

Minogue, Dennis. 'An Outcast Returns'. *Age*, 25 October, 1975, 15.

Molloy, Bruce. 'An Interview with Frank Hardy (1973)'. *A.L.S.*, VII, 1976, 356-74.

Monks, John. '*Power Without Glory* Game on Again - 25 Years Later'. *Australian*, 5 June, 1976, 3.

Morgan, Patrick. 'The Hard and the Soft Way'. *Quadrant*, XX, No. 12, 1976, 25-30.

Neville, Jill. 'Australian Essence, Distilled in France'. *S.M.H.*, 4 November, 1978, 13.

Simons, Margaret. 'A Hardyspeak in Carringbush'. *Age Saturday Extra*, 14 January, 1984, 9.

Simper, Errol. 'Frank Hardy: Still a Revolutionary'. *Canberra Times*, 3 July, 1976, 11. Interview.

Stevens, John. 'Basking in Reflective Glory'. *Age*, 8 June, 1976, 2.

Thomson, Robert. 'Hardy Skips the First Race to Praise his Latest Book'. *S.M.H.*, 29 December, 1983, 7.

Walker, Tony. 'Frank Hardy's Passion: A City where they Don't Say "Have a Nice Day"'. *S.M.H.*, 12 October, 1983, 9.

Waten, Judah. [Letter to the editor about his association with Hardy and the Realists]. *Quadrant*, XIII, No. 3, 1969, 80.

Webster, Owen. 'That Hardy Book: Publisher Denies He Chickened'. *Review* (Melbourne), 3 September, 1971, 1348.

Wells, Fred. 'The Hardy Episode'. *Quadrant*, XIII, (wrongly numbered as XIV), No. 2, 1969, 58-61.

Williams, Peter. 'Gambling with Socialism: A Hardy Obsession'. *Southern Review*, XX, No. 1, 1987, 69-87.

---. 'Interventions and Obsessions: The Work of Frank Hardy'. *Southern Review*, XIV, 1981, 168-91. See also Beasley, Jack, and Williams, Peter. '"Intervention and Obsessions": An Exchange between Beasley and Williams'. *Southern Review*, XV, 1982, 234-39.

---. 'Plagiarism and Rewriting: The Case of Frank Hardy'. *New Literature Review*, No. 10, 1982, 45-53.

HARFORD, LESBIA

Fiction

The Invaluable Mystery. Foreword by Helen Garner, introduction by Richard Nile and Robert Darby. (Fitzroy, Vic.: McPhee Gribble/Penguin, 1987).
Reviewed by A. Gurr, *Australian Studies*, No. 4, 1990, 127-29; S. McKernan, *Times on Sunday*, 23 August, 1987, 30; H. Thomson, *ABR*, No. 95, 1987, 15-16.

Poetry

The Poems of Lesbia Harford. Introduced by D. Modjeska. (North Ryde, N.S.W.: Sirius Books, 1985).
Reviewed by E. Jolley, *Fremantle Arts Review*, I, No. 12, 1986, 15; J. Strauss, *Age Monthly Review*, VI, No. 5, 1986, 5-6.

Critical Material

Coates, Donna. 'Lesbia Harford's Homefront Warrior and Women's World War I

Writing'. *A.L.S.*, 17.1, 1995, 19-28.
Strauss, Jennifer. 'Stubborn Singers of Their Full Song: Mary Gilmore and Lesbia Harford'. In *The Time to Write: Australian Women Writers 1890-1930* edited by Kay Ferres (Ringwood, Vic.: Penguin, 1993), 108-38.

HARPUR, CHARLES

Collection
Charles Harpur. Edited by Adrian Mitchell. (Melbourne: Sun Books, 1973). Three Colonial Poets, Book 1.
Reviewed by J. Blight, *Nation Review*, 16-22 November, 1973, 167.
Charles Harpur, Selected Prose and Poetry. Edited by Michael Ackland. (Ringwood, Vic.: Penguin, 1986).
Reviewed by C. Castan, *Social Alternatives*, 7, No. 1, 1988, 67.

Drama
Stalwart the Bushranger; with *The Tragedy of Donohoe*. Edited by Elizabeth Perkins. Foreword by Dorothy Green. (Sydney: Currency Press; St Lucia: Australasian Drama Studies, 1987).
Reviewed by P. Mead, *Age Monthly Review*, VIII, No. 9, 1988, 16-17; K. Stewart, *A.L.S.*, 14, No. 1, 1989, 122-26.

Poetry
Charles Harpur. Edited by Donovan Clarke. (Sydney: A.& R., 1963).
Reviewed by A. King, *A.L.S.*, I, No. 4, 1964, 274-9.
Poetical Works. Edited with introduction and bibliography by Elizabeth Perkins. (Sydney: A.& R., 1984).
Reviewed by M. Ackland, *Meridian*, IV, No. 1, 1985, 65-69; D. Carter, *Age Saturday Extra*, 1 September, 1984, 16; G. Dutton, *Bulletin*, 29 May, 1984, 92 & 97; D. Headon, *Overland*, No. 97, 1984, 68-69; A. Mitchell, *A.L.S.*, XI, 1984, 541-46; C. Semmler, *Weekend Australian Magazine*, 26-27 May, 1984, 18; G.A. Wilkes, *Southerly*, XLV, No. 2, 1985, 244; J. Wright, *ABR*, No. 62, 1984, 14-15.

Critical Material
Ackland, Michael. 'Charles Harpur and his Editors'. *Bibliographical Society of Australia and New Zealand Bulletin*, IX, No. 1, 1985, 1-13.
---. 'Charles Harpur for a New Generation'. *Quadrant*, XXVIII, No. 6, 1984, 65-71.
---. 'Charles Harpur's Republicanism'. *Westerly*, XXIX, No. 3, 1984, 75-88.
---. 'Charles Harpur's "The Bush Fire" and "A Storm in the Mountains": Sublimity, Cognition and Faith', *Southerly*, XLIII, 1983, 459-74.
---. 'Cognitive Man and Divinity in the Short Descriptive Verse of Charles Harpur'. *Southern Review*, XVI, 1983, 389-401.
---. 'God's Sublime Order in Harpur's "The Creek of the Four Graves"'. *A.L.S.*, IX, 1984, 355-70.
---. 'Inspiration Versus Moonshine in Charles Harpur's "The Importance of a Rhyme"'. *Southerly*, 49, No. 4, 1989, 636-42.
---. 'Nature Through Currency Lad Eyes: Wentworth, Harpur, Kendall and the Australian Landscape'. In *Mapped But Not Known: The Australian Landscape of the Imagination*, edited by P.R. Eaden and F.H. Mares (Netley, S.A.: Wakefield Press, 1986), 73-85.
---. 'Plot and Counter-Plot in Charles Harpur's "The Bushrangers"'. *Australasian Drama Studies*, No. 8, 1986, 49-61.
---. 'Poetic Ideal versus "The Hard Real" in Charles Harpur's "The Tower of the Dream"'. *Southerly*, XLVII, No. 2, 1987, 380-394.
---. '"Though Urged by Doubt..." Charles Harpur and the Nineteenth Century Crisis of Faith'. *AUMLA*, No. 64, 1985, 154-174.
Cantrell, Leon. 'Marvell and Charles Harpur'. *A.L.S.*, VI, 1973, 88-90.

De Groen, Frances. 'Harpur's Biographer, J.N. Rawling: Background Information and Papers'. *Notes & Furphies*, No. 3, 1979, 1-3.

Devlin, F.M. 'The Problems of Charles Harpur: A Semi-Historical Note'. *Makar*, V, No. 2, 1969, 24-25.

Dixon, Robert. 'Charles Harpur and John Gould'. *Southerly*, XL, 1980, 315-29.

Elliott, Brian. 'Antipodes: An Essay in Attitudes'. *Australian Letters*, VII, No. 3, 1966, 51-70.

---. 'The Colonial Poets'. In *The Literature of Australia*, edited by Geoffrey Dutton (Adelaide: Penguin Books, 1964), 228-31.

Heseltine, H.P. 'Criticism and the Individual Talent'. *Meanjin*, XXXI, 1972, 10-24. Includes discussion of 'The Tower of the Dream'.

Indyk, Ivor. 'Pastoral and Priority: The Aboriginal in Australian Pastoral'. *New Literary History*, 24.4, 1994, 837-55. Includes discussion of writing by Harpur.

Jordens, Ann-Mari. *The Stenhouse Circle: Literary Life in Mid-Nineteenth Century Sydney*. (Carlton: M.U.P., 1979).

Kane, Paul. 'Charles Harpur and the Myth of Origins'. *A.L.S.*, XIII, No. 2, 1987, 146-160.

Kramer, Leonie. 'Imitation and Originality in Australian Colonial Poetry: The Case of Charles Harpur'. *Yearbook of English Studies*, XIII, 1983, 116-32.

Macainsh, Noel. 'Charles Harpur's "Midsummer Noon" - A Structuralist Approach'. *A.L.S.*, VIII, 1978, 435-45.

---. 'A Fair Menace: Images of Womanhood in Early Australian Poetry'. *Westerly*, XXXIII, No. 3, 1988, 25-32.

Magarey, Kevin. 'Place, Landscape, Saussure, Region, and Two Australian Colonial Poets: Some Footnotes'. In *Mapped But Not Known: The Australian Landscape of the Imagination*, edited by P.R. Eaden and F.H. Mares (Netley, S.A.: Wakefield Press, 1986), 105-127.

Marsh, Elizabeth. 'Two Notes on Charles Harpur's "A Midsummer Noon in the Forest"' [sic]. *Southerly*, XXXIX, 1979, 104-14.

Mead, Philip. 'Charles Harpur's Disfiguring Origins: Allegory in Colonial Poetry'. *A.L.S.*, 14, No. 3, 1990, 279-96. Republished in *Imagining Romanticism: Essays on English and Australian Romanticisms*, edited by Deirdre Coleman and Peter Otto (West Cornwall, CT: Locust Hill P., 1992), 217-40.

Mishra, Vijay C. 'Charles Harpur's Reputation 1853-1858: The Years of Controversy' *A.L.S.*, VIII, 1978, 446-56.

---. 'Early Literary Responses to Charles Harpur'. *Westerly*, No. 4, 1977, 88-93.

---. 'The Literary Reputation of Charles Harpur'. *Southerly*, XXXVI, 1976, 432-40.

Mitchell, Adrian. 'Writing Up a Storm: Natural Strife and Charles Harpur'. *Southerly*, 53.2, 1993, 90-113.

Normington-Rawling, J. *Charles Harpur: An Australian*. (Sydney: A.& R., 1962). Reviewed by M. Aurousseau, *Meanjin*, XXII, No. 1, 1963, 69-79; A.D. Hope, *A.L.S.*, I, No. 1, 1963, 66-9.

---. 'Charles Harpur'. *Bulletin*, 18 April, 1964, 42. Letter containing factual correction of Donovan Clarke's preface to *Charles Harpur*, see above.

---. 'A Currency Lad Poet: the Significance of Charles Harpur'. *Quadrant*, VII, 1963, 11-25.

Perkins, Elizabeth. 'An Early Australian Short Story by Harpur'. *A.L.S.*, VII, 1976, 327-32.

---. 'Emerson and Charles Harpur'. *A.L.S.*, VI, 1973, 82-88.

---. 'Harpur's Notes [to "The Kangaroo Hunt"] and Kendall's "Bell Birds"'. *A.L.S.*, V, 1972, 277-84.

---. 'Rhetoric and the Man: Charles Harpur and the Call to Armed Rebellion'. *Age Monthly Review*, VI, No. 5, 1986, 14-17.

---. 'The Religious Faith of Charles Harpur'. *Quadrant*, XXIII, No. 6, 1979, 29-35, reprinted in *Between Two Worlds*, edited by Axel Clark, John Fletcher and Robin Marsden (Sydney: Wentworth Books, 1979), 3-22.

Prance, Jon. 'The Graves of Harpur's Hill'. *Canberra Times*, 14 May, 1977, 13.

Wright, Judith. *Charles Harpur*. (Melbourne: Lansdowne Press, 1963). Australian Writers and their Work series. Reviewed by A. Lawson, *A.L.S.*, VIII, 1978, 382-87.

---. 'Charles Harpur'. In her *Preoccupations in Australian Poetry* (Melbourne: O.U.P., 1965), 1-18.

HARRIS, ALEXANDER

Fiction

Settlers and Convicts: or, Recollections of Sixteen Years' Labour in the Australian Backwoods, by an Emigrant Mechanic. Forword by C.M.H. Clark. (Carlton: M.U.P., 1953). Reprinted with revised foreword 1964, 1969. First published London: C. Cox, 1847. Reviewed by C.M.H. Clark, *Hemisphere*, XIV, No. 6, 1970, 30-31.

The Emigrant Family, or, The Story of an Australian Settler, ed. by W.S. Ramson. (Canberra: Australian National University Press, 1967). First published 1849. Reviewed by C.M.H. Clark, *Historical Studies*, XIII, 1968, 265-66; D. Green, *Canberra Times*, 6 April, 1968, 11; T. Keneally, *ABR*, VII, 1968, 84; L. Kramer, *S.M.H.*, 2 March, 1968, 20; C. Turnbull, *Age*, 27 January, 1968, 21; G.A.W., *Southerly*, XXVIII, 1968, 231.

Critical Material

Anderson, Hugh. *Farewell to Old England: A Broadside History of Early Australia*. (Adelaide: Rigby, 1964), 165-86.

[Crittenden, Victor.] 'A 19th-century Literary Controversy'. *Margin*, 37, 1995, 34-35. Discusses *Settlers and Convicts* including an article by Patricia Miles, 'In Search of Alexander Harris', *Push: A Journal of Early Australian Social History*, 30, 1992, 46-69.

Green, Dorothy. "The Road Not Taken?" *Southerly*, 49, No. 3, 1989, 288-99.

Ramson, W.S. '*The Emigrant Family*: The Delineation of Actual Life'. In his collection, *The Australian Experience: Critical Essays on Australian Novels*. (Canberra: Australian National University Press, 1974), 1-18.

---. 'Early Australian English: The Vocabulary of an Emigrant Mechanic'. *Southerly*, XXV, No. 2, 1965, 116-30.

Sinnett, Frederick. *The Fiction Fields of Australia*. (Brisbane: U.Q.P., 1966), 42-3 and passim. Reprinted in *The Writer in Australia*, edited by John Barnes, 8-32. This essay first published in *Illustrated Journal of Australia*, 1, 1856, 97-105, 199-208.

HARRIS, MAX

See also Malley, Ern.

Collection

The Best of Max Harris. (North Sydney: Allen & Unwin, 1986). Reviewed by H. Daniel, *Age Saturday Extra*, 12 April, 1986, 13.

Poetry

Poetic Gems. (Adelaide: Mary Martin Books, 1979).
Reviewed by J. McLaren, *ABR*, No. 18, 1980, 38-39.

A Window at Night. Edited by Robert Clark. (Adelaide: ABR Publications, 1967). Reviewed by A. King, *Meanjin*, XXVII, 1968, 178; F.H. Mares, *Southerly*, XXVIII, 1968, 74-79.

Non-Fiction

The Angry Eye. Introduced by Rupert Murdoch. (Potts Point, N.S.W.: Pergamon Press (Australia), 1973).
Reviewed by E. Hatchett, *Advertiser*, 15 December, 1973, 20; E. Riddell, *Australian*,

26 January, 1974, 48; T. Stephens, *Sunday Telegraph*, 23 December, 1973, 18; J. Waten, *Age*, 1 December, 1973, 12.

Ockers: Essays on the Bad Old New Australia. (Adelaide: Maximus Books, 1974). Reviewed by D. Horne, *Meanjin*, XXXIV, 1975, 462-67; J. Miles, *Advertiser*, 13 September, 1975, 21.

'Conflicts in Australian Intellectual Life 1940-1964'. In *Literary Australia*, edited by Clement Semmler and Derek Whitelock (Melbourne: Cheshire, 1966), 69-80.

 Critical Material
Clancy, L.J. 'Max Harris and the Academics'. *Dissent*, No. 20, 1967, 43-45.
Dutton, Geoffrey. 'The Public and the Private Max'. *Overland*, 139, 1995, 56-58. Obituary.
Goldsworthy, Kerryn. 'Max Harris: A Salute (1921-1995)'. *Notes & Furphies*, 34, 1995, 10-11. Obituary.
Macainsh, Noel. 'Busted Penguins - Max Harris and Ern Malley'. *Quadrant*, XXIV, No. 7, 1980, 19-24.
McGregor, Craig. 'Conversations with Max Harris'. *National Times*, 29 August-3 September, 1977, 19-24.
Ward, Peter. 'The Intellectual Swaggie: The Long and Angry Road of Max Harris'. *Weekend Australian*, 17-18 February, 1979, 9.
---. 'Poet's Fugitive World'. *Australian*, 17 January, 1980, 8.

HARRIS, ROBERT

 Poetry
The Abandoned. (Sydney: Senor Press, 1979).
Reviewed by G. Catalano, *Meanjin*, 39, 1980, 81-93; K. Goodwin, *Weekend Australian*, 29-30 September, 1979, Weekend 10.

The Cloud Passes Over. (North Ryde, NSW: A.& R, 1986).
Reviewed by M. Glover, *Age Monthly Review*, February, 1987, 22; A. Gould, *Quadrant*, 30.10, 1986, 69-74; K. Hart, *Overland*, 104, 1986, 71-72; M. Heyward, *ABR*, 79, 1986, 36; P. Mead, *Island Magazine*, 29, 1986, 32-40; F. Zwicky, *Weekend Australian*, 15-16 March, 1986, Weekend 15.

Jane, Interlinear & Other Poems. (Sydney: Paper Bark, 1992).
Reviewed by D. Barbour, *Australian-Canadian Studies*, 11.1 and 2, 1993, 172-80; H. Cam, *S.M.H.*, 12 September, 1992, 42; G. Catalano, *Age*, 23 May, 1992, Saturday Extra 7; D. Fahey, *Voices*, 3.1, 1993, 118-22; J. Forbes, *Scripsi*, 8.2, 1992, 211-17; M. Langford, *Southerly*, 53.1, 1993, 215-21; R. Pretty, *ABR*, 143, 1992, 51-52; R. D. Randall, *Antipodes*, 6.2, 1992, 152-54; N. Rowe, *Literature and Aesthetics*, 2, 1992, 103-06.

Localities. (Greensborough, Vic.: Seahorse Publications, 1973).
Reviewed by *Contempa*, 6, 1973, 50; *Ear in the Wheatfield*, 2, 1973, 67-69; J. Grant, *Contempa*, series 2.3, 1977, 50-53.

Translations from the Albatross. (Collingwood, Vic.: Outback P., 1976).
Reviewed by A. Gould, *Nation Review*, 22-28 December, 1977, 17; J. Grant, *Contempa*, ser.2.3, 1977, 53-55; T. Thorne, *Australian*, 13 November, 1976, 44; J. Tranter, *Australian*, 26 February, 1977, 29.

 Non-Fiction
'To John Kinsella, Poet, of Jane R'. *Scripsi*, 9.2, 1994, 29. Letter discussing his *Jane, Interlinear*.

 Critical Material
Adamson, Robert. 'The Shadow of Doubt and "Derivations" in Australian Poetry'. *Meanjin*, 49.3, 1990. 537-48.

---. *Age*, 10 April: Saturday Extra 7 and *Weekend Australian*, 10-11 April, 1993, Review 6. Obituary. See also T. Thorne and D. Lawton, *Overland*, 131, 1993, 15-16 (feature on Harris 5-16 includes previously unpublished pieces).
Jenkins, John. 'The Poetry of Robert Harris'. *Overland*, 127, 1992, 16-19.
Page, Geoff. 'Robert Harris'. In his *A Reader's Guide To Contemporary Australian Poetry* (St. Lucia: U.Q.P., 1995), 102-105.

HARROWER, ELIZABETH

Fiction
The Catherine Wheel. (Sydney: A.& R., 1979). Sirius Books. First published London: Cassell, 1960.
Reviewed by N. Adams, *Westerly*, XXV, No. 3, 1980, 108-13; J. Bedford, *National Times*, 14 April, 1979, 33; V. Ikin, *CRNLE Reviews Journal*, No. 1, 1980, 10-14.
The Long Prospect. (Sydney: A.& R., 1979). Sirius Books. First published London: Cassell, 1958.
Reviewed by N. Adams, *Westerly*, XXV, 3, 1980, 108-13, (also discusses *Down in the City* (London: Cassell, 1957) and *The Watch Tower* (London: Macmillan, 1966; Sydney: A.& R., 1979)); J. Bedford, *National Times*, 14 April, 1979, 33.
The Watch Tower. (London: Macmillan, 1966).
Reviewed by A.R. Chisholm, *Age*, 10 December, 1966, 24; L.J. Clancy, *Australian*, 18 March, 1967, 10; J. Colmer, *ABR*, V, 1966, 218-9; W. Grono, *Westerly*, No. 4, 1966, 45-46; N. Keesing, *Southerly*, XXVII, 1967, 139-141; H.G. Kippax, *S.M.H.*, 19 November, 1966, 15; J. Laird, *Canberra Times*, 7 January, 1967, 10; G. Lehmann, *Bulletin*, 12 November, 1966, 54-6; *T.L.S.*, 10 November, 1966, 1028.

Critical Material
Burns, D.R. 'The Active Passive Inversion: Sex Roles in Garner, Stead and Harrower'. *Meanjin*, XLV, No. 3, 1986, 346-53.
Burns, Robert. 'The Underdog-Outsider: The Achievement of Mathers' *Trap*'. *Meanjin*, XXIX, 1970, 95-105. Discusses *Trap* in relation to *The Watch Tower* and other recent novels.
Clancy, Laurie. 'Fathers and Lovers: Three Australian Novels'. *A.L.S.*, X, 1982, 459-67. Deals with *The Watch Tower*.
Claremont, Robyn. 'The Novels of Elizabeth Harrower'. *Quadrant*, XXIII, No. 11, 1979, 16-21.
Coleman, Deidre. '*The Watch Tower*: Bluebird's Castle'. In *(Un)Common Ground: Essays in Literatures in English*, edited by Andrew Taylor and Russell McDougall (Adelaide: CRNLE/Flinders University of South Australia, 1990), 97 107.
Davidson, J. 'Elizabeth Harrower'. *Meanjin*, XXXIX, 1980, 163-74. Interview. Reprinted in his *Sideways from the Page* (Melbourne: Fontana, 1983), 247-262.
Ferrier, Carole. 'Is an "Images of Woman" Methodology Adequate for Reading Elizabeth Harrower's *The Watch Tower*?' In *Who is She?* edited by Shirley Walker (St Lucia: U.Q.P., 1983), 191-203.
Geering, R.G. *Recent Fiction*. (Melbourne: O.U.P., 1974). Australian Writers and Their Work. Reviewed by C. Hadgraft, *A.L.S.*, VI, 1974, 441-2.
---. 'Elizabeth Harrower's Novels: A Survey'. *Southerly*, XXX, 1970, 131-47.
Giuffre, Giulia. 'Interview with Elizabeth Harrower'. In her *A Writing Life: Interviews with Australian Women Writers* (Sydney: Allen and Unwin, 1990), 41-55.
Gunew, Sneja. 'What Does Woman Mean? Reading, Writing and Reproduction'. *Hecate*, IX, 1983, 111-22.
McInherny, Frances. 'Deep into the Destructive Core: Elizabeth Harrower's *The Watch Tower*'. *Hecate*, IX, 1983, 123-34. Reprinted in *Gender, Politics and Fiction: Twentieth Century Women's Novels*, edited by Carole Ferrier (St Lucia: U.Q.P.,

1985), 150-62.
Mansfield, Nicholas. '"The Only Russian in Sydney": Modernism and Realism in *The Watch Tower*'. *A.L.S.*, 15.3, 1992, 131-40.
Yeo, Rosie. '*Down in the City*: Elizabeth Harrower's "Lost" Novel'. *Southerly*, 50, No. 4, 1990, 491-98.

HARRY, J.S.

Poetry
A Dandelion for Van Gogh. (Sydney: Island Press, 1985).
Reviewed by J. Irving, *ABR*, No. 73, 1985, 28-29; G. Page, *ABR*, No. 75, 1985, 31-33; J. Rodriguez, *S.M.H.*, 31 May, 1986, 46; K. Russell, *Quadrant*, XXXI, Nos. 1&2, 1987, 109-115.
The Deer Under the Skin. (St Lucia: U.Q.P., 1970). Paperback Poets, No. 6.
Reviewed by G. Curtis, *Makar*, VII, No. 1, 1971, 39-41; R. Dunlop, *Poetry Australia*, No. 40, 1971, 52-56; K.L. Goodwin, *Meanjin*, XXXI, 1972, 499-500; D. Hewett, *Westerly*, No. 4, 1971, 55-59; I. Indyk, *The Bridge*, VI, No. 1, 1971, 80-82; M. Johnston, *S.M.H.*, 12 June, 1971, 21; T. Shapcott, *ABR*, No. 10, 1971, 148-150; R.A. Simpson, *Age*, 24 April, 1971, 15; J. Tulip, *Bulletin*, 1 May, 1971, 48.
Hold for a Little While and Turn Gently. (Sydney: Island Press, 1979).
Reviewed by K. Goodwin, *Weekend Australian. Weekend Magazine*, 22-23 March, 1980, 15; G. Page, *National Times*, 4-10 May, 1980, 45-46; J. Rodriguez, *ABR*, No. 22, 1980, 27-28; R.A. Simpson, *Age*, 12 January, 1980, 24.
The Life on Water and the Life Beneath. (Sydney: A.& R, 1995).
Reviewed by P. Brown, *ABR*, 169, 1995, 45; H. Cam, *S.M.H.*, 11 Feb., 1995, Spectrum 10A; M. Duwell, *Weekend Australian*, 24-25 June, 1995, Review 7; H. Horton, *Imago*, 7.2, 1995, 96-98; D. Leadbetter, *Overland*, 141, 1995, 86-88.
Selected Poems. (Ringwood, Vic.: Penguin, 1995).
Reviewed by J. Jones, *Ulitarra* 8, 1995, 121-23; C. Wallace-Crabbe, *ABR*, 174, 1995, 51-52.

Critical Material
Duwell, Martin. 'Both Sides of the Curtain: The Poetry of J.S. Harry', *Overland*, No. 106, 1987, 40-45.
Lucas, Rose. '"In the spaces of the sky . . . our eyes hunt stars": Creating Possibilities in the Poetry of J.S. Harry'. In *Poetry and Gender: Statements and Essays in Australian Women's Poetry and Poetics*, edited by David Brooks and Brenda Walker (St Lucia: U.Q.P., 1989), 231-41.
Maiden, Jennifer. 'When Worlds Collide: a Brief Response to One Aspect of the Work of J.S. Harry'. *Southerly*, 52.3, 1992, 97-100.
Page, Geoff. 'J.S. Harry'. In his *A Reader's Guide To Contemporary Australian Poetry* (St. Lucia: U.Q.P., 1995), 105-108.
Tulip, J. 'Contemporary Australian Poetry II: Transition and Advance'. *Southerly*, XXXII, 1972, 176-195, esp. 186-188.

HART, KEVIN

Poetry
The Departure. (St Lucia: U.Q.P., 1978).
Reviewed by R.D. Jones, *Makar*, 14, No. 2, 1980, 54-61; R. Gray, *S.M.H.*, 3 March, 1979, 18; G. Page, *Canberra Times*, 29 July, 1978, 13; E. Perkins, *LiNQ*, 6, No. 2, 1978, 85-7; C. Pollnitz, *Southerly*, 39, 1987, 342-57, esp. 352-3; T. Shapcott, *ABR*, No. 1, 1987, 19-20; C. Treloar, *24 Hours*, 3, No. 6, 1978, 65; C. Wallace-Crabbe, *Age*, 2 September, 1987, 21.
The Lines of the Hand. (Sydney: A.& R., 1982).

Reviewed by G. Catalano, *Meanjin*, 40, 1981, 349-60; J. Croft, *Island Magazine*, No. 11, 1982, 43-5; M. Duwell, *Image*, 5, No. 2, 1982, 15-16; B. Giles, *ABR*, No. 52, 1983, 26-27; D. Haskell, *Southerly*, 41, 1982, 348-60, esp. 357-8; J. Maiden, *S.M.H.*, 12 June, 1982, 37; G. Page, *National Times*, 7-13 June, 1981, 62; T. Shapcott, *Age*, 21 November, 1981, 23; C. Wallace-Crabbe, *T.L.S.*, 19 November, 1982, 1282.

New and Selected Poems. (Pymble, NSW: A.& R., 1995).
Reviewed by A. Croggon, *Voices*, 5.3, 1995, 106-09; R. Darling, *Antipodes*, 9.2, 1995, 160-61; M. Duwell, *Weekend Australian*, 19-20 Aug., 1995, Review 10; D. Leadbetter, *Overland*, 141, 1995, 86-88; D. McCooey, *Age*, 5 Aug., 1995, Saturday Extra 8; P. Salom, *ABR*, 168, 1995, 51-52.

Peniel. (Hawthorn, Vic.: Golvan Arts, 1990).
Reviewed by M. Duwell, *Weekend Australian*, 29-30 June, 1991, Review 4; J. Foulcher, *Island*, 48, 1991, 64-67; L. McCredden, *Editions*, 12, 1991, 24; D. Micholson, *Mattoid*, 42.1, 1992, 154-55; P. Nelson, *Quadrant*, 36.1-2, 1992, 111-12; G. Rowlands, *CRNLE Reviews Journal*, 2.2, 1990, 87-89; T. Shapcott, *Age*, 4 May, 1991, Saturday Extra 7; P. Steele, *Overland*, 122, 1991, 71-73; A. Taylor, *Voices*, 1.2, 1991, 106-07.

Your Shadow. (Sydney: A.& R., 1984).
Reviewed by B. Beaver, *Weekend Australian*, 25-26 August, 1984, 15; G. Bitcon, *Southerly*, 45, No. 3, 1985, 352-59, esp. 353-55; G. Catalano, *Age Monthly Review*, 4, No. 7, 1984, 11-12; G. Dutton, *Bulletin*, 2 October, 1984, 80-81; F. Kellaway, *Overland*, No. 99, 1985, 70-2; V. O'Sullivan, *Helix*, Nos. 21-22, 1985, 122-28; G. Page, *Island Magazine*, No. 21, 1984, 51-52 and *Quadrant*, 29, No. 4, 1985, 71-5; M. Richards, *ABR*, No. 69, 1985, 35; J. Rodriguez, *S.M.H.*, 21 November, 1985, 46; C. Vleeskens, *CRNLE Reviews Journal*, No. 2, 1984, 44-45.

    Critical Material
'Interview with Kevin Hart'. *Mattoid*, No. 6, 1979, 3-14.
Catalano, Gary. 'The Weight of Things'. *Overland*, No. 104, 1986, 23-26.
McCooey, David. '"Secret Truths": The Poetry of Kevin Hart'. *Southerly*, 55.4, 1995, 109-21.
Page, Geoff. 'Kevin Hart'. In his *A Reader's Guide To Contemporary Australian Poetry* (St. Lucia: U.Q.P., 1995), 108-110.

HART-SMITH, WILLIAM

    Poetry
Hand in Hand: A Garnering: With Uncollected Poems and Essays on his Life and Work. Edited by Barbara Petrie. (Springwood, NSW: Butterfly Books, 1991).
Reviewed by H. Horton, *Imago*, 4.1, 1992, 113-14; L. Jacobs, *CRNLE Reviews Journal*, 1, 1992, 98-101; A. Lansdown, *Quadrant*, 37.9, 1993, 86-88.

With Mary Morris. *Let Me Learn the Steps* (Fremantle: Fremantle Arts Centre Press, 1977).
Reviewed by C. Harrison-Ford, *S.M.H.*, 10 December, 1977, 17; S. Kobulniczky, *Artlook*, III, No. 6, 1977, 32; M. Macleod, *Quadrant*, XXII, No. 3, 1978, 76-77; T. Thorne, *Weekend Australian Magazine*, 14-15 January, 1978, 7.

MiniPoems. [Perth].
Reviewed by H. Colebatch, *Westerly*, No. 3, 1974, 74-75.

Selected Poems 1936-1984. Edited by Brian Dibble. (North Ryde, N.S.W.: A.& R., 1985).
Reviewed by B. Beaver, *Weekend Australian Magazine*, 11-12 May, 1985, 15; G. Catalano, *Age Monthly Review*, V, No. 2, 1985, 17-18; B. Elliott, *CRNLE Reviews Journal*, No. 2, 1985, 75-76; R. Gray, *Island Magazine*, No. 24, 1985, 58-59; M.

Haig, *Quadrant*, XXIX, No. 8, 1985, 86-89; G. Page, *ABR*, No. 70, 1985, 28-29; C. Wallace-Crabbe, *Age Saturday Extra*, 27 April, 1985, 14.

The Talking Clothes. (Sydney: A.& R., 1966).
Reviewed by B. Beaver, *S.M.H.*, 24 September, 1966, 17; E.A.M. Colman, *Poetry Magazine*, No. 6, 1966, 27-8; D. Douglas, *Age*, 3 December, 1966, 23; R. Dunlop, *Poetry Australia*, No. 14, 1967, 46; R. Hall, *Bulletin*, 29 October, 1966, 42; A. Hamilton, *Books and Bookmen*, XI, No. 11, 1966, 34; S.E. Lee, *Southerly*, XXVII, 1967, 69-71; B. Nesbitt, *Australian*, 17 December, 1966, 12; T. W. Shapcott, *ABR*, V, 1966, 237.

   Critical Material
Brady, Veronica and Bennett, Bruce. 'An Interview: William Hart-Smith'. *Westerly*, No. 1, 1976, 25-32.
Brady, Veronica. 'Islands of Light: The Recent Poetry of W. Hart-Smith'. *Westerly*, No. 1, 1976, 33-42.
Dibble, Brian. '"He Will Be Lonely in Heaven": Australasian Poet William Hart-Smith, 23 November 1911 - 15 April 1990'. *Southern Review*, 23.3, 1990, 191-99.
Lansdown, Andrew. 'An Interview with W. Hart-Smith on the Jindyworobaks'. *A.L.S.*, IX, 1979, 200-06.
---. 'A Legacy of Joy: In Memory of William Hart-Smith'. *Quadrant*, 34, No. 12, 1990, 51-53. Revised version printed in *Studio*, 45, 1991-92, 26-29.
---. 'Twenty-four Poems by W. Hart-Smith'. *Artlook*, V, No. 7, 1979, 35-36. Introduction.
Page, Geoff. 'William Hart-Smith'. In his *A Reader's Guide To Contemporary Australian Poetry* (St. Lucia: U.Q.P., 1995), 110-112.

HARWOOD, GWEN

   Poetry
Bone Scan. (North Ryde, N.S.W.: A.& R., 1988).
Reviewed by T. Bishop, *Antipodes*, 3.2, 1989, 148; H. Cam, *S.M.H.*, 20 May, 1989, 84; V. O'Sullivan, *Island Magazine*, No. 40, 1989, 29-33; D. Reiter, *Redoubt*, No. 5, 1989, 61-65.

Collected Poems. (Oxford; Melbourne: O.U.P., 1991).
Reviewed by F. Adcock, *T.L.S.*, 24 January, 1992, 23.

The Lion's Bride. (Sydney: A.& R., 1981).
Reviewed by B. Beaver, *Meanjin*, XLI, 1982, 403-05; M. Heyward, *Age Saturday Extra*, 2 October, 1982, 13; E. Marsh, *ABR*, No. 41, 1982, 29-30 and *Luna*, No. 15, 1982, 31-32; R. Morse, *PN Review*, XII, No. 3, 1985, 64-65; M. Scott, *Island Magazine*, No. 12, 1982, 9-12; N. Talbot, *Quadrant*, XXVII, No. 4, 1983, 90-92; C. Wallace-Crabbe, *T.L.S.*, 19 November, 1982, 1282.

Poems. (Sydney: A.& R., 1963).
Reviewed by J.M. Couper, *Poetry Magazine*, No. 2, 1964, 35-6; P. Jeffery, *Westerly*, 1964, No. 4, 55-9; E. Jones, *Prospect*, VII, No. 2, 1964, 27-8; S.E. Lee, *Southerly*, XXIV, No. 2, 1964, 133-4; D. Moody, *Meanjin*, XXII, 1963, 418-21; *T.L.S.*, 10 September, 1964, 842.

Poems: Volume Two. (Sydney: A.& R., 1968).
Reviewed by B. Beaver, *S.M.H.*, 24 August, 1968, 23; L.J. Clancy, *Overland*, No. 39, 1968, 51; D. Douglas, *Age*, 4 January, 1969, 11; M. Dunlevy, *Canberra Times*, 29 June, 1968, 14; R. Dunlop, *Poetry Australia*, No. 28, 1969, 36-37; G. Dutton, *ABR*, VII, 1968, 162; K. England, *Advertiser*, 20 July, 1968, 20; R. Hall, *Australian*, 14 September, 1968, 12; E. Jones, *Nation*, 23 November, 1968, 22-23; S.E. Lee, *Southerly*, XXVIII, 1968, 306-08; G. Lehmann,*Bulletin*, 17 August, 1968, 82; C. Wallace-Crabbe, *Meanjin*, XXVIII, 1969, 264-67.

The Present Tense. Edited by Alison Hoddinott. (Potts Point, NSW: Imprint, 1995).
Reviewed by H. Cam, *S.M.H.*, 9 Dec., 1995, Spectrum 14; P. Steele, *Age*, 14 Oct.,
1995, Saturday Extra 8; S. Trigg, *ABR*, 177, 1995, 53-54.

Selected Poems. (Sydney: A.& R., 1975). A.& R. Poetry Classics.
Reviewed by J. Beston, *S.M.H.*, 18 October, 1975, 20; D. Dodwell, *Westerly*, No.
2, 1977, 73-79; R. Hall, *New Poetry*, XXIV, No. 2, 1976, 23-30; J. Tulip,
Australian, 6 December, 1975, 40.

Selected Poems. (North Ryde, NSW: A.& R, 1990). Revised edition, originally
published 1975.
Reviewed by D. Menon, *Literary Criterion*, 26.4, 1991, 83-85.

Non-Fiction
*Blessed City: The Letters of Gwen Harwood to Thomas Riddell January to September
1943*. (North Ryde, N.S.W.: A.& R., 1990).
Reviewed by K. Goldsworthy, *ABR*, No. 126, 1990, 10; P. Goldsworthy, *Voices* 1.1,
1991, 101-02; F. Kellaway, *Overland*, 124, 1991, 93-94; R. Leach, *Westerly*, 36.1,
1991, 93-94; A. Peek, *Antipodes*, 5.2, 1991, 157; T. Shapcott, *Island Magazine*, No.
45, 1990, 58-60;J. Sullivan, *Age*, 1 December, 1990, Saturday Extra 11.

'Lamplit Presences'. *Southerly*, XL, 1980, 247-54. Autobiographical.
'Words and Music'. *Southerly*, XLVI, No. 4, 1986, 367-76.

Critical Material
McLean, Kathy. *Gwen Harwood: An Annotated Bibliography*. Computer file.
(Canberra: ALIA P, 1993).
Shaw, Patricia, and Peter Campbell. 'Seeking Pearls in a Magpie's Nest: The Larry
Sitsky Papers'. *Voices*, 5.1, 1995, 47-60. Contains information about Harwood MSS.
'Refrain: Poetry Review'. With feature on Gwen Harwood; contributions by G.
Kratzman, S. Trigg, J. Strauss and G. Harwood. *ABR*, 143, 1992, 38-44.
Baker, Candida. 'Gwen Harwood'. In her *Yacker 3* (Sydney: Picador, 1989), 130-
157.
Beston, John. 'Artists and Academics in the Poetry of Gwen Harwood'. *Quadrant*,
XVIII, No. 3, 1974, 21-27.
---. 'An Interview with Gwen Harwood'. *Quadrant*, XIX, No. 7, 1975, 84-88.
Bishop, T. G. 'An Afternoon with Gwen Harwood'. *Antipodes*, 4.2, 1990, 92-94.
---. 'Gwen Harwood: Life Sentences'. In *International Literature in English: Essays
on the Major Writers*, edited by Robert L. Ross (New York: Garland, 1991), 621-35.
Brissenden, R.F. *A Fire-Talented Tongue: Some Notes on the Poetry of Gwen
Harwood* (Sydney: Wentworth Press, 1978). Seventh Herbert Blaiklock Memorial
Lecture. Also published in *Southerly*, XXXVIII, 1978, 3-6.
Carter, David. 'The Death of Satan and the Persistence of Romanticism'. *Literary
Criterion* (Mysore), XV, Nos. 3-4, 1980, 62-65.
Davies, Mark. 'Interview with Poet Gwen Harwood'. *Northern Perspective*, 18.1,
1995, 55-62.
Douglas, Dennis. 'Gwen Harwood: The Poet as Doppelganger'. *Quadrant*, XIII,
(wrongly numbered as XIV), No. 2, 1969, 15-19.
---. 'A Prodigious Dilemma: Gwen Harwood's Professor Eisenbart and the Vices of
the Intellect'. *A.L.S.*, VI, 1973, 77-82.
Edgar, Stephen. 'An Interview with Gwen Harwood'. *Island Magazine*, No. 25-26,
1986, 74-76.
Frizell, Helen. '10,000 Accolades for Poet'. *S.M.H.*, 17 November, 1978, 7. See also
p.3.
Harrex, Syd. 'Island Lyrics: Vivian Smith, Gwen Harwood and James McAuley'.
Island Magazine, No. 25-26, 1986, 67-73.
Hoddinot, Alison. 'Gwen Harwood and the Philosophers'. *Southerly*, XLI, 1981,
272-87.

---. *Gwen Harwood: The Real and the Imagined World*. (North Ryde, NSW: Collins/A.& R, 1991). Reviewed by P. Mead, *A.L.S.*, 16.2, 1993, 140-51; T. Shapcott, *Age*, 20 July, 1991, Saturday Extra 7; M. Sharkey, *Overland*, 124, 1991, 91-93; S. Trigg, *Island*, 52, 1992, 62-66.

Hope, A.D. 'Gwen Harwood and the Professors'. *A.L.S.*, V, 1972, 227-32.

Lawson, Elizabeth. *The Poetry of Gwen Harwood*. (South Melbourne: Sydney U.P./O.U.P., 1991). Reviewed by G. Kratzmann, *Meridian*, 12.2, 1993, 186-90; P. Mead, *A.L.S.*, 16.2, 1993, 140-51; M. Sharkey, *Overland*, 124, 1991, 91-93; S. Trigg, *Island*, 52, 1992, 62-66.

---. '"They trust me with the axe": The Poetry of Gwen Harwood". In *Poetry and Gender: Statements and Essays in Australian Women's Poetry and Poetics*, edited by David Brooks and Brenda Walker (St Lucia: U.Q.P., 1989), 145-64.

---. 'Toward the Heart's True Speech: Voice-conflict in the Poetry of Gwen Harwood'. *Southerly*, XLIII, 1983, 45-72.

Lear, Anne. 'Interview with Gwen Harwood'. *Span*, No. 26, 1988, 1-11.

Makeham, Patricia. *The Poetry of Gwen Harwood: An Introduction*. (Sydney: English Teachers' Association of N.S.W., 1983). Reviewed by R. Leonarder, *English in Australia*, No. 69, 1984, 40.

Malouf, David. 'Some Volumes of Selected Poems of the 1970s'. *A.L.S.*, X, 1981, 13-21.

Page, Geoff. 'Gwen Harwood'. In his *A Reader's Guide To Contemporary Australian Poetry* (St. Lucia: U.Q.P., 1995), 113-115.

Rama, R.P. '[Interview with] Gwen Harwood'. *Dialogues with Australian Poets*. (Calcutta: P. Lal/Writers Workshop, 1993), 9-22.

Riddell, Elizabeth. 'Making Good Books after a Late Start (Encounters with Poets)'. *Australian*, 24 January, 1970, 17.

Sant, Andrew, ed. *Toads: Australian Writers: Other Work, Other Lives*, edited by Andrew Sant (Sydney: Allen & Unwin, 1992). Collection of autobiographical essays on writing and money. Includes Harwood.

Sellick, Robert (ed.). *Gwen Harwood*. (Bedford Park, S.A.: CRNLE, Flinders University). CRNLE Essays and Monographs Series, No. 3, 1987. Reviewed by T. Bishop, *Antipodes*, II, No. 1, 1988, 64-65; M. Macleod, *A.L.S.*, XIII, No. 3, 1988, 393-395.

Simpson, R.A. 'Happy Reward for Poet of Mischief and Fine Verse'. *Age*, 17 November, 1978, 11.

Strauss, Jennifer. *Boundary Conditions: The Poetry of Gwen Harwood*. (St Lucia: U.Q.P., 1992). Reviewed by G. Kratzmann, *Meridian*, 12.2, 1993, 186-90; P. Mead, *A.L.S.*, 16.2, 1993, 140-51; N. Potter, *Antipodes*, 6.2, 1992, 162-63; S. Trigg, *Island*, 52, 1992, 62-66.

---. 'Elegies for Mothers: Reflections on Gwen Harwood's "Mother Who Gave Me Life" and Les Murray's "Three Poems in Memory of My Mother"'. *Westerly*, 34, No. 4, 1989, 58-63.

---. 'The Poetry of Dobson, Harwood & Wright: "Within the Bounds of Feminine Sensibility?"'. *Meanjin*, XXXVIII, 1979, 334-49. Reprinted in *Still the Frame Holds: Essays on Women Poets and Writers*, edited by Sheila Roberts and Yvonne Pacheco Tevis (San Bernadino, CA: Borgo P, 1993), 79-99.

---. 'She/I/You/It: Constructing Mothers and Motherhood in the Writing of Gwen Harwood'. *Southerly*, 52.1, 1992, 1-19.

Talbot, Norman. '... Truth beyond the Language Game: The Poetry of Gwen Harwood'. *A.L.S.*, VII, 1976, 241-58.

---. 'Two Figures of the Artist: John Shaw Neilson and Gwen Harwood'. In *South Pacific Images*, edited by Chris Tiffin (St Lucia: SPACLALS, 1978), 145-57.

---. 'Women and Men (both dong and ding): Gwen Harwood's Poetry'. *Luna*, No. 10, 1980, 16-24.

Taylor, Andrew. 'Gwen Harwood: The Golden Child Aloft on Discourse'. In his *Reading Australian Poetry* (St Lucia: U.Q.P., 1987), 112-125.
Trigg, Stephanie. *Gwen Harwood*. (Melbourne: O.U.P., 1994). Reviewed by T. Bishop, *Antipodes*, 9.1, 1995, 66; J. Croft, *Weekend Australian* 4-5 June, 1993, Review 7; R. Sorensen, *Age*, 23 April, 1993, Saturday Extra 8; A. Taylor, *Voices*, 5.4, 1995-96, 114-18.
Williams, Barbara. 'An Interview with Gwen Harwood'. *Westerly*, XXXIII, No. 4, 1988, 53-58.

HASLUCK, NICHOLAS

Collection
With C.J. Koch. *Chinese Journey*. (Fremantle: Fremantle Arts Centre Press, 1985). Reviewed by M. Jones, *S.M.H.*, 7 December, 1985, 46.

Fiction
The Bellarmine Jug. (Ringwood, Vic.: Penguin, 1984).
Reviewed by L. Clancy, *Age Saturday Extra*, 8 September, 1984, 19; J. Crace, *T.L.S.*, 8 March, 1985, 266; G. Dutton, *Bulletin*, 28 August, 1984, 67-68; D. Foster, *S.M.H.*, 8 December, 1984, 35; D. Grant, *Fremantle Arts Centre Broadsheet*, 4, No. 1, 1985, 2-3; J. Grant, *Age Monthly Review*, 4, No. 5, 1984, 18; J. Hanrahan, *ABR*, No. 69, 1985, 14-15; V. Horn, *ABR*, No. 71, 1985, 39-40; N. Keesing, *Weekend Australian*, 28-29 July, 1984, Weekend 15; G. Lord, *National Times*, 17-23 August, 1984, 30; J. McLaren, *CRNLE Reviews Journal*, No. 2, 1985, 47-51; H. McQueen, *S.M.H.*, 11 August, 1984, 44; G. Windsor, *Overland*, No. 98, 1985, 68-69.

The Blosseville File. (Ringwood, Vic.: Penguin, 1992).
Reviewed by C. Blanche, *Quadrant*, 36.11, 1992, 86-88; P. Hutchings, *S.M.H.*, 28 March, 1992, 47; R. O'Grady, Age, 28 March, 1992, Saturday Extra 8; P. Pierce, *Bulletin*, 10 March, 1992, 108; J. Stephens, *Modern Times*, March, 1992, 29; L. Trainor, *Weekend Australian*, 28-29 March, 1992, Review 7.

The Blue Guitar. (South Melbourne, Macmillan, 1980). Reprinted Ringwood, Vic.: Penguin, 1989.
Reviewed by V. Brady, *ABR*, No. 26, 1980, 12; H. Daniel, *Age*, 9 August, 1980, 27; M. Macleod, *S.M.H.*, 21 June, 1980, 27; B. Martin, *New Statesman*, 4 April, 1980, 523; C. Pybus, *ABR*, No. 109, 1989, 28-29; S. Ruddell, *Weekend Australian*, 13-14 December, 1980, Weekend 12; F. Tuohy, *T.L.S.*, 18 April, 1980, 430.

The Country Without Music. (Ringwood, Vic.: Viking, 1990).
Reviewed by V. Brady, *Australian Society*, 9, No. 9, 1990, 38-39; H. Daniel, *Age*, 11 August, 1990, Saturday Extra 9; J. Forbes, *S.M.H.*, 11 August, 1990, 73; M. Halligan, *Weekend Australian*, 22-23 September, 1990, Review 6; J. Kernick, *Editions*, 11, 1991, 10; E. Perkins, *LiNQ*, 19.1, 1992, 143-49; P. Pierce, *Bulletin*, 27 November, 1990, 135; T. Shapcott, *ABR*, No. 124, 1990, 9-10.

A Grain of Truth. (Ringwood, Vic.: Penguin, 1994).
Reviewed by H. Horton, *Imago*, 7.2, 1995, 100-01; A. Peek, *ABR*, 164, 1994, 17 (see also interview by R. Sorensen 18-19); M. Reid, *FAR*, 9.5, 1994, 12; M. Sexton, *S.M.H.*, 27 August, 1994, Spectrum 12A; M. Sharky, *Weekend Australian*, 24-25 September, 1994, Review 7.

The Hand That Feeds You. (Fremantle: Fremantle Arts Centre Press, 1982).
Reviewed by D.R. Burns, *ABR*, No. 57, 1983/84, 13-14; H. Daniel, *Age Saturday Extra*, 22 January, 1983, 10; G. Dutton, *Bulletin*, 18 January, 1983, 56-57; A. Hildyard, *Island Magazine*, Nos. 18-19, 1984, 40-44; G. Lord, *S.M.H.*, 18 December, 1982, 30; G. Sheridan, *Quadrant*, 27, No. 8, 1983, 85-87; G. Windsor, *Overland*, No.92, 1983, 65-67; D.I. Yeats, *Fremantle Arts Centre Broadsheet*, 2, No. 2, 1983, 7.

The Hat on the Letter O. (Fremantle: Fremantle Arts Centre Press, 1978).
Reviewed by K. O. Arthur, *Westerly*, 35, No. 2, 1990, 86-88; L. Clancy, *Helix*, No. 4, 1979, 84-85; D. Colmer, *Weekend Australian*, 24-25 February, 1979, Weekend 11; K. Cummings, *S.M.H.*, 23 December, 38; B. Dibble, *ABR*, No. 8, 1979, 25; C. Hanna, *Southerly*, 39, 1979, 224-27; C. Kelly, *National Times*, 30 September, 1978, 37; D.J. O'Hearn, *Overland*, No. 74, 1979, 52-54; S. J. Paolini, *Antipodes*, 4.2, 1990, 139; E. Webby, *Meanjin*, 40, 1981, 200-208.

Quarantine. (South Melbourne: Macmillan, 1978; New York: Holt Rhinehart and Winston, 1979; Ringwood, Vic.: Penguin, 1986).
Reviewed by S. Cassidy and R. Gostand, *Social Alternatives*, 6, No. 3, 1987, 62; D. Colmer, *Weekend Australian*, 27 May, 1978, Weekend 8; B. Dibble, *ABR*, No. 2, 1978, 10-11; C. Hanna, *Southerly*, 39, 1979, 224-27; N. Jillet, *Age*, 1 July, 1978, 23; S. Kobulniczky, *Westerly*, XXIII, No. 3, 1978, 86-88; M. Macleod, *Kunapipi*, 1, No. 2, 1979, 137-41, esp 139 and *S.M.H.*, 15 July, 1978, 17; J. Maddocks, *Quadrant*, 22, No. 12, 1978, 70; D. Matthews, *CRNLE Reviews Journal*, No. 2, 1986, 104-106; P. Pierce, *Meanjin*, 37, 1978, 393-401; E. Platt, *Artlook*, 4, No. 5, 1978, 36; C. Roderick, *Townsville Daily Bulletin*, 17 February, 1979, 4; *Virginia Quarterly Review*, Vol. 55, 1979, 100.

Truant State. (Ringwood, Vic.: Penguin Books, 1987).
Reviewed by T. Forshaw, *Weekend Australian. Weekend Magazine*, 17-18 October, 1987, 15; T. James, *Quadrant*, XXXII, Nos. 1 & 2, 1988, 118-119; L.V. Kepert, *S.M.H.*, 21 November, 1987, 88; M.R. Liverani, *Overland*, No. 110, 1988, 70-72; S. McKernan, *Bulletin*, 19 January, 1988, 70; H. McQueen, *Times on Sunday*, 18 October, 1987, 33; R. O'Grady, *Age Saturday Extra*, 17 October, 1987, 14; M.E. Pitts, *Antipodes*, II, No. 1, 1988, 64; G. Windsor, *Fremantle Arts Review*, II, No. 11, 1987, 14.

Poetry

Anchor and Other Poems. (Fremantle: Fremantle Arts Centre Press, 1976).
Reviewed by F. Kellaway, *Overland*, No. 67, 1977, 77; F. Kelly, *National Times*, 24-29 January, 1977, 16; J. Maddocks, *Quadrant*, 22, No. 12, 1978, 70; P. Neilsen, *Age*, 12 March, 1977, 18; K. Weller, *Artlook*, 2, No. 11, 1976, 7-8; F. Zwicky, *Westerly*, XXIII, No. 2, 1978, 88-91.

With William Grono. *On the Edge*. (Claremont: Freshwater Bay Press, 1980).
Reviewed by L.R. Burrows, *Westerly*, 26, No. 1, 1989, 56-62; G. Catalano, *Meanjin*, 40, 1981, 114-23, esp. 120-21; G. Dutton, *Bulletin*, 27 January, 1981, 62-63; M. Duwell, *Weekend Australian*, 1-2 November, 1980, Weekend 16; V. Ikin, *Quadrant*, 25, No. 5, 1981, 75-76; B. Pascoe, *ABR*, No. 35, 1981, 22-23; G. Rowlands, *Overland*, No. 84, 1981, 71; T.A. Williams, *Artlook*, 6, No. 11, 1980, 50.

Non-Fiction

'The Making of *The Country Without Music*: The Antipodean Panoptique'. *Quadrant*, 36.4, 1992, 46-51.

Offcuts from a Legal Literary Life. (Nedlands, WA: U of Western Australia P., 1993).
Reviewed by L. Clancy, *Age*, 22 May, 1993, Saturday Extra 8; K. Dolin, *Westerly*, 38.3, 1993, 92-94; G. Dutton, *ABR*, 153, 1993, 16-17; C. Semmler, *Quadrant*, 37.9, 1993, 84-85; M. Sharkey, *Weekend Australian*, 17-18 April, 1993, Review 6; G. Watt, *Antipodes*, 7.2, 1993, 159-60.

'The Past's Deceitful Dream'. *Island Magazine*, No. 39, 1989, 76-83. Discusses relationship between history and fiction.

'A Sense of Time and Place'. *Quadrant*, 31, No. 12, 1987, 66-68. Discusses *A Blue Guitar*.

'Untitled Prose Piece VII'. *Fremantle Arts Review*, 2, No.5, 1987, 12. Discusses the relationship of a title to a literary work.

'A Writer's Story: "The legal Dr Jekyll or the literary Mr Hyde"?'. *Quadrant*, 33, No. 9, 1989, 50-52.
'Writing Places'. *Journal of Australian Literature*, 1, No. 1, 1990, 70-78. Autobiographical.

Critical Material

'Just as It Was on the Goldfields: Veronica Brady Discusses with Nicholas Hasluck the Political Background to *Truant State*'. *Australian Society*, VII, No. 4, 1988, 49-52.
Baker, Candida. 'Nicholas Hasluck'. In her *Yacker: Australian Writers Talk About Their Work* (Sydney: Picador, 1986), 158-182.
Brady, Veronica. 'An Approach to Vigilance: The Politics of Nicholas Hasluck's *The Country without Music*'. *Westerly*, 36.1, 1991, 47-58.
Daniel, Helen. *Liars: Australian New Novelists*. (Ringwood, Vic.: Penguin, 1988), 231-261.
---. 'The Moral "Faszad": The Novels of Nicholas Hasluck'. *Westerly*, XXV, No. 4, 1980, 63-67.
Dolin, Kieran. 'Legal Fictions and Nicholas Hasluck's *The Bellarmine Jug*'. *Westerly*, 37.4, 1992, 47-54.
Feng, Ji. 'Nicholas Hasluck's *Quarantine*'. *Oceanic Literature*, No. 5, 1983, 350-54. In Chinese.
Johnstone, Richard. 'Unexplored Country'. *London Magazine*, 20, Nos. 8-9, 1980, 63-70. Discusses *The Blue Guitar*.

HAY, WILLIAM

Critical Material

Edwards, Peter. 'The Daunting Doubts of William Hay'. In *Bards, Bohemians, and Bookmen*, edited by Leon Cantrell (St Lucia: U.Q.P., 1976), 218-35.
Gosse, Fayette. *William Gosse Hay*. (Melbourne: Lansdowne Press, 1965). Reviewed by D. Douglas, *A.L.S.*, II, 1966, 227.
Hergenhan, L.T. 'The Strange World of Sir William Heans (and The Mystery of William Hay)'. *Southerly*, XXVII, 1967, 118-137. Reprinted in his *Unnatural Lives*. (St Lucia: U.Q.P., 1983), 75-90.
Herring, Thelma. '*The Escape of Sir William Heans*: Hay's Debt to Hawthorne and Meredith'. *Southerly*, XXVI, 1966, 75-92.
Horner, J.C. 'The Themes of Four Convict Novels'. *Tasmanian Historical Research Association, Papers and Proceedings*, XV, 1967, 1-32.
McDonald, Avis G. 'Displaced Images in *The Escape of the Notorious Sir William Heans*'. *Southerly*, 50, No. 1, 1990, 58 69.
Muecke, I.D. '"The Return of Robert Wasterton": A Commentary on an Unfinished Novel'. *South Australiana*, VII, 1968, 84-105.
---. 'William Hay and History: A Comment on Aims, Sources and Method'. *A.L.S.*, II, No. 2, 1965, 117-37.

HAZZARD, SHIRLEY

Fiction

The Bay of Noon. (Boston: Little, Brown & Co., Atlantic Monthly Press; London: Macmillan, 1970).
Reviewed by M. Cavell, *Partisan Review*, XXXVIII, 1971, 118-19; S. Despoja, *Advertiser*, 22 August, 1970, 18; M. Dick, *S.M.H.*, 5 September, 1970, 20; T. Forshaw, *Australian*, 6 February, 1971, 22; A. Fremantle, *Commonwealth* XCII, 1970, 323-24; R. Macauley, *New York Times Book Review*, 5 April, 1970, 4-5; E. Morgan, *Listener*, LXXXIII, 1970, 768; J. Raban, *New Statesman*, LXXIX, 1970, 667; O. Ruhen, *Age*, 5 September, 1970, 15; J. Whitwell, *Canberra Times*, 19 September, 1970, 13.

The Evening of the Holiday. (London: Macmillan, 1966).
Reviewed by J. Colmer, *ABR*, V, 1966, 218-9; D. Craig, *New Statesman*, 3 June, 1966, 817; S. Edgar, *Canberra Times*, 22 October, 1966, 12; D. Galloway, *Southern Review* (Baton Rouge, La.), N.S. IV, 859; L.V. Kepert, *S.M.H.*, 15 October, 1966, 17; L. Kramer, *Bulletin*, 10 September, 1966, 44-5; *Time*, 14 January, 1966, 67.

People in Glass Houses. (New York: Knopf; London: Macmillan, 1967).
Reviewed by J. Colmer, *ABR*, VII, 1968, 63; S. Despoja, *Advertiser*, 13 January, 1968, 18; T.B. Millar, *Canberra Times*, 9 March, 1968, 10; F. Raphael, *New York Times Book Review*, 15 October, 1967, 5; L. Wellein, *Studies in Short Fiction*, V, 1968, 392-94.

The Transit of Venus. (New York: Viking Press; London: Macmillan, 1980).
Reviewed by J. Beston, *S.M.H.*, 5 July, 1980, 21 and *WLWE*, XIX, 1980, 198-200; D. Bird, *Westerly*, XXVI, No. 1, 1981, 54-56; E. Chesnick, *Nation* (New York), CCXXX, 1980, 633-34; R. Creswell, *ABR*, No. 23, 1980, 7; V. Cunningham, *T.L.S.*, 4 April, 1980, 382; B. D'Alpuget, *Financial Review*, 4 July, 1980, 37; R.G. Geering, *Overland*, No. 83, 1981, 69-71; G. Godwin, *New York Times Book Review*, 16 May, 1980, 7, 16-17; N. Jillett, *Age*, 16 July, 1980, 26; N. Keesing, *24 Hours*, V, No. 10, 1980, 72; D. Kubal, *Hudson Review*, XXXIII, 1980, 442-43; P. Pierce, *Meanjin*, XL, 1981, 109-10; E. Riddell, *Bulletin*, 26 August, 1980, 70, 72; D. Rowbotham, *Courier-Mail*, 29 November, 1980, 24; F. Taliaferro, *Harper's*, February, 1980, 84-85; M. Vernon, *Weekend Australian Magazine*, 31 May-1 June, 1980, 37.

Non-Fiction

Defeat of an Ideal: A Study of the Self-Destruction of the United Nations. (New York: Little, Brown; London: Macmillan, 1973).
Reviewed by A. Astrachan, *Book World*, 4 March, 1973, 6-7; W.M. Ball, *Age*, 23 June, 1973, 18; M. Dunlevy, *Canberra Times*, 28 September, 1973, 13; J. Hallows, *Australian*, 23 June, 1973, 37; K. Kyle, *Listener*, 26 April, 1973, 556; K. Tennant, *S.M.H.*, 30 June, 1973, 26; *T.L.S.*, 20 April, 1973, 433-34 (see also S. Hazzard, *T.L.S.*, 4 May, 1973, 501).

Postscripts: 1988 Boyer Lectures. (Crows Nest, N.S.W.: A.B.C. Books, 1989).
'Problems Facing Contemporary Novelists'. *A.L.S.*, IX, 1979, 179-81.
'We Need Silence to Find Out What We Think'. *New York Times Book Review*, 14 November, 1982, 11 & 28-29.

Critical Material

Beston, John B. 'A Bibliography of Shirley Hazzard'. *WLWE*, XX, 1981, 236-54.
Scheick, William J. 'A Bibliography of Writings by Shirley Hazzard'. *Texas Studies in Literature and Language*, XXV, 1983, 249-53.

Anderson, Don. 'Indian-Wrestling a Jellyfish'. *National Times*, 7-13 December, 1984, 29. Boyer Lectures.
Anthony, Susan. 'An Unexpected Recognition of Serious Writing'. *Bulletin*, 17 June, 1980, 78, 81.
Baym, Nina. 'Artifice and Romance in Shirley Hazzard's Fiction'. *Texas Studies in Literature and Language*, XXV, 1983, 222-48.
Bird, Delys. 'Text Production and Reception - Shirley Hazzard's *The Transit of Venus*'. *Westerly*, XXX, No. 1, 1985, 38-51.
Broyard, Anatole. 'Generous Love'. *New York Times Book Review*, 13 June, 1982, 39.
Capone, Giovanna. 'Shirley Hazzard: Transit and *The Bay of Noon*'. *A.L.S.*, XIII, No. 2, 1987, 172-183.
Colmer, John. 'Patterns and Preoccupations of Love: The Novels of Shirley Hazzard'. *Meanjin*, XXIX, 1970, 461-67.

---. 'Shirley Hazzard's *The Transit of Venus*'. *Journal of Commonwealth Literature*, XIX, No. 1, 1984, 10-21.

Cotton, Judy. 'The Transit of Hazzard'. *Vogue Australia*, October, 1980, 112-13.

Dalley, Helen. 'Australian Author Shirley Hazzard Makes her Mark Overseas'. *Australian Women's Weekly*, 17 November, 1982, 21 & 23.

Danvers, Dennis. 'A Conversation with Shirley Hazzard'. *Antipodes*, I, No. 1, 1987, 40-43.

Doyle, H.M. 'A Letter From Shirley Hazzard'. *A.L.S.*, XII, No. 3, 1986, 400-02. Letters from Hazzard to Doyle regarding influence of poets on her writing.

Dutton, Geoffrey. 'Shirley Hazzard: Chance and the Transit of Pleasure'. *Bulletin*, 28 August, 1984, 50-51.

Evans, Trish. 'Shirley's "Transit" is a Rare Event'. *Weekend Australian Magazine*, 29-30 November, 1980, 13.

Freedman, Helen Rosengren. 'A Writer who Took on the U.N.'. *Age*, 8 January, 1981, 9.

Garrett, Jan. 'The Transits of Hazzard'. *Look & Listen*, I, No. 4, 1984, 36-39.

Geering, R.G. *Recent Fiction*. (Melbourne: O.U.P., 1974). Australian Writers and Their Work. Reviewed by C. Hadgraft, *A.L.S.*, VI, 1974, 441-2.

Harris, Max. 'A Face to Remember'. *Australian*, 14 May, 1966, 10.

Hergenhan, Laurie. 'The "I" of the Beholder: Representations of Tuscany in Some Recent Australian Literature'. *Westerly*, 36.4, 1991, 107-14. Discusses works by Hazzard and others.

Hill, Barry. 'Boyer Opens up'. *Look & Listen*, I, No. 3, 1984, 73-74.

Jennings, Kate. 'Going against the Grain: Interview with Shirley Hazzard'. *Island*, 50, 1992, 20-27.

Jones, Margaret. 'Author Says Australia Has Come of Age'. *Canberra Times*, 18 August, 1984, 17. See also her 'Shirley Hazzard versus the Bureaucrats', *Age Saturday Extra*, 18 August, 1984, 12.

Kavanagh, Paul. 'Shirley Hazzard, Astronomer of Souls'. *Southerly*, XLV, No. 2, 1985, 209-219. Reprinted in their *Conversations: Interviews with Australian Writers* (North Ryde, NSW: Collins/A.& R, 1991), 95-110.

Lehmann, Geoffrey. 'The Novels of Shirley Hazzard: An Affirmation of Venus'. *Quadrant*, XXV, No. 3, 1981, 33-36. See also Susan Moore. 'A Response to "The Novels of Shirley Hazzard"', No. 7, 1981, 62-63.

Levy, Bronwen. 'Constructing the Woman Writer: The Reviewing Reception of Hazzard's *The Transit of Venus*'. In *Gender, Politics and Fiction: Twentieth Century Women's Novels*, edited by Carole Ferrier (St Lucia: U.Q.P., 1985), 179-99.

McCarthy, Phillip. 'The Reluctant Transit of Shirley Hazzard'. *Good Weekend* (*S.M.H.* supplement), 27 October, 1984, 22-25.

MacDermott, Doireann. 'Stones for Glass Houses: Some Reflexions on the United Nations Organization'. *Revista Canaria de Estudios Ingleses* (Tenerife, Spain), Nos. 13-14, 1987, 249-258.

McDougall, Russell. 'Beyond Humanism? The Black Drop of Shirley Hazzard's *Transit of Venus*'. *Journal of Commonwealth Literature*, 30.2, 1995, 119-33.

Mattei Anna Grazia. 'The Novel as "Work in Progress": Shirley Hazzard's *The Transit of Venus*'. In *European Perspectives: Contemporary Essays on Australian Literature*, edited by Giovanna Capone (*A.L.S.* 15.2 (special issue)/ St. Lucia: U.Q.P., 1991), 117-27.

Miller, Pat. 'Australian-born Writer Pulls No Punches on Issues of Conscience'. *Woman's Day*, 21 March, 1977, 34-5.

Moon, E.B. '"Indispensable Humanity": Saviours and Destroyers and Major and Minor Characters, in Shirley Hazzard's *The Transit of Venus*'. *Southerly*, XLV, No. 1, 1985, 94-108.

---. 'Fate, Individual Action and the Shape of Life in Shirley Hazzard's *The Transit of Venus'. Southerly*, XLIII, 1983, 332-44.

Moore, Susan. 'Meaning and Value'. *Quadrant*, XXVIII, No. 5, 1984, 75-79.

Neri, Algerina. 'Ripening in the Sun: Shirley Hazzard's Heroines in Italy'. *Westerly*, XXVIII, No. 4, 1983, 37-42.

Nichterlein, Sue. 'Shirley Hazzard: First since McCullough'. *National Times*, 8-14 June, 1980, 12.

Olubas, Brigitta. 'Rewriting the Past: Exploration and Discovery in *The Transit of Venus'. A.L.S.*, 15.3, 1992, 155-64.

Palmer, Jenny. 'Shirley Hazzard, an Interview in New York with Australia's Top Novelist of 1981'. *Bulletin*, 13 October, 1981, 84-88.

Priessnitz, Horst. 'Shirley Hazzard: Glimpses of Paradise'. In *International Literature in English: Essays on the Major Writers*, edited by Robert L. Ross (New York: Garland, 1991), 335-50.

Rainwater, Catherine and Scheick, William J. '"Some Godlike Grammar"; An Introduction to the Writings of Hazzard, Ozick and Redmon'. *Texas Studies in Literature and Language*, XXV, 1983, 181-211.

---. 'An Interview with Shirley Hazzard (Summer 1982)'. *Texas Studies in Literature and Language*, XXV, 1983, 213-21.

Riemer, A.P. 'This World, the Next, and Australia - the Emergence of a Literary Commonplace'. *Southerly*, XLIV, 1984, 251-270.

Roff, Sue. 'Rites of Passage: Six Australian Authors in Search of the Same Character'. *Australian Society*, III, No. 9, 1984, 33-34.

Sellick, Robert. 'Shirley Hazzard: Dislocation and Continuity'. *A.L.S.*, IX, 1979, 182-88.

---. '"Some Godlike Grammar": The Narrator in *The Transit of Venus'*. In *Aspects of Australian Fiction: Essays Presented to John Colmer*, edited by Alan Brissenden (Nedlands, W.A.: University of Western Australia Press, 1990), 87-96.

Simes, Gary. 'Irony's Best when it's Sincere'. *S.M.H.*, 3 December, 1983, 45. Discusses Penguin editions of *The Evening of the Holiday; People in Glass Houses; The Bay of Noon*, first published London: Macmillan, 1965, 1967 and 1970 respectively.

Tayloe, Nancy Dew. 'An Introduction to Shirley Hazzard's *The Transit of Venus'*. *WLWE*, XXIV, No. 2, 1984, 287-295.

Tully, Bill. 'The *Blast* Interview: Shirley Hazzard'. *Blast*, 25, 1994, 4-5.

Twidale, K.M. 'Discontinuous Narrative and Aspects of Love in Shirley Hazzard's Short Stories'. *Journal of Commonwealth Literature*, 26.1, 1991, 101-16.

Wieland, James. '"Antipodean Eyes": Ways of Seeing in Shirley Hazzard's *The Transit of Venus'. Kunapipi*, V, No. 2, 1983, 36-49.

---. 'Going through with Things: Men and Women in *The Transit of Venus'*. *Commonwealth Novel in English*, III, No. 1, 1984, 1-20.

Wynhausen, Elizabeth. 'Critics' Glittering Prize for a Venus Seven Years in Transit'. *S.M.H.*, 10 January, 1981, 15.

HEMENSLEY, KRIS

Fiction

Here We Are. (Sydney: Wild & Woolley, 1975).
Reviewed by R. Adamson, *Australian*, 8 May, 1976, 30 and *New Poetry*, XXIV, No. 1, 1976, 79; L.S. Fallis, *Books Abroad*, L, 1976, 480; R. Garfitt, *T.L.S.*, 9 April, 1976, 445; C. Harrison-Ford, *S.M.H.*, 12 April, 1975, 13 and *Stand*, XVI, No. 3, 1975, 42-43; F. Kelly, *National Times*, 9-14 June, 1975, 17; J. Tittensor, *Nation Review*, 21-27 March, 1975, 612.

The Rooms. (Melbourne: Outback Press, 1974).
Reviewed by C. Harrison-Ford, *S.M.H.*, 7 June, 1975, 15; F. Kelly, *National Times*, 9-14 June, 1975, 17.

Poetry

Domestications, A Selection of Poems 1968-72. (Melbourne: Sun Books, 1974).
Reviewed by W. Billeter, *Etymspheres*, Series 1, No. 1, 1975 (?), 39-41; K.L. Macrae, *New Poetry*, XXIII, No. 2, 1975, 83-84; G. Page, *Canberra Times*, 8 November, 1974, 10; C. Sansom, *Nation Review*, 20-26 September, 1974, 1574.

Love's Voyages. (St Lucia: Makar, 1974). Gargoyle Poets, No. 7.
Reviewed by F. Kelly, *National Times*, 31 March-5 April, 1975, 29; D. Petersen, *LiNQ*, IV, No. 1-2, 1975, 32-33; G. Rowlands, *Issue*, V, No. 1, 1975, 49-50.

The Poem of the Clear Eye. (Melbourne: The Paper Castle, 1975).
Reviewed by R. Adamson, *New Poetry*, XXIII, No. 3, 1975, 85-86 and *Australian*, 8 May, 1976, 30 and *New Poetry*, XXIV, No. 1, 1976, 78-79; T. Harrington, *Contempa*, I, No. 2, 1976, 57-62; J. Jenkins, *Magic Sam*, No. 2, 1976; R.D. Jones, *Makar*, XII, No. 1, 1976, 54-56; J. Maiden, *New Poetry*, XXIV, No. 1, 1976, 74-75.

Sulking in the Seventies. (Melbourne: Rigmarole of the Hours, 1975).
Reviewed by M. Dugan, *Age*, 1 May, 1976, 20; J. Jenkins, *Magic Sam*, No. 2, 1976.

Non-Fiction

'"... The Wild Assertion of Vitality"'. *A.L.S.*, VIII, 1977, 226-39.

Critical Material

Duwell, Martin. 'Where We Are Now: An Interview with Kris Hemensley'. *Makar*, 13, No. 1, 1977, 3-18. Reprinted in his *A Possible Contemporary Poetry* (Brisbane: Makar Press, 1982), 50-66.
Harrison-Ford, Carl. 'Poetics before Politics. A Note on Kris Hemensley's "New Australian Poetry"'. *Meanjin*, XXIX, 1970, 226.
Sayers, Stuart. 'Down among the Dead Ships'. *Age*, 21 October, 1972, 15.
Tulip, James. 'Towards an Australian Modernism: New Writings of Kris Hemensley'. *Southerly*, XXXVII, 1977, 142-51.

HENNESSEY, JOHN DAVID

Fiction

The Dis-Honourable. With an introduction by Nancy Bonnin. (St Lucia: U.Q.P., 1975). First published in Sydney: Intercolonial Press Agency, 1895.

HENNING, RACHEL

Non-Fiction

The Letters of Rachel Henning. Edited by David Adams, with a foreword and illustrations by Norman Lindsay. (New York: Penguin Books, 1985; Ringwood, Vic.: Penguin, 1986). First published Sydney: Bulletin, 1952.
Reviewed by J. Emery, *Antipodes*, I, No. 2, 1987, 123-124; *New Yorker*, 24 March, 1986, 127-128.

Critical Material

Allingham, Anne. 'Challenging the Editing of the Rachel Henning Letters'. *A.L.S.*, 16.3, 1994, 262-79.
Jones, Dorothy. 'Ladies in the Bush: Catherine Traill, Mary Backer and Rachel Henning'. *Span*, No. 21, 1985, 96-120.

HENSHAW, MARK

Fiction

Out of the Line of Fire. (Ringwood, Vic.: Penguin. 1988).
Reviewed by K. Ahearne, *Australian Society*, 7, No. 10, 1988, 49; H. Daniel, *Weekend Australian*, 4 June, 1988, Weekend 15; M. Flanagan, *Overland*, No. 112, 1988, 77-78; Y. Gooneratne, *Southerly*, 49, No. 4, 1989, 652-53; M. Luke, *Fremantle Arts Review*, 3, No. 9, 1988, 14; P. Magee, *Redoubt*, No. 4, 1988, 70-72;

G. Manning, *Scripsi*, 5, No. 3, 1989, 213-21; B. Matthews, *Scripsi*, 5, No. 3, 1989, 207-12; W. Ommundsen, *Mattoid*, No. 32, 1988, 77-81; E. Riddell, *ABR*, No. 101, 1988, 26-27; R. Usher, *Age Saturday Extra*, 2 July, 1988, 13.

Critical Material
Arthur, Katerina Olijnyk. 'Interview with Mark Henshaw'. *Span*, No. 28, 1989, 1-10.
Gelder, Ken. 'Postmodernism's "Lost Objects": Desire in the Recent Fiction of Murnane, Brooks, Henshaw and Jones'. *Island Magazine*, No.41, 1989, 49-53.
Gillett, Sue. 'Tactics in Evasion: Mark Henshaw's *Out of the Line of Fire*'. *Southern Review*, 27.2, 1994, 178-86.
Hart, Kevin, 'Where Truth Actually Lies'. *Island Magazine*, No. 36, 1988, 80-82.
Hillman, Roger. 'Mark Henshaw's *Out of the Line of Fire*: Australian Text and European Context'. In *German-Australian Cultural Relations Since 1945*, edited by Manfred Jurgensen, German-Australian Studies 9, (Bern: Peter Lang, 1995), 208-140.
Carroll, John. 'Deconstructing the Mandala: Mark Henshaw's *Out of the Line of Fire*'. *Meanjin*, 48, No. 2, 1989, 407-18.
Ommundsen, Wenche. 'Engendering the Bicentennial Reader: Sally Morgan, Mark Henshaw and the Critics'. In *Postcolonial Fictions*, edited by Michèle Drouart (special issue in two volumes including SPACLALS Conference Proceedings, *SPAN*, 36, 1993), 251-63.
---. 'The Reader in Contemporary Metafiction: Freedom or Constraint'. *AUMLA*, No. 74, 1990, 169-84.

HERBERT, XAVIER

Collection
Xavier Herbert: Episodes from Capricornia, Poor Fellow My Country and other Fiction, Nonfiction and Letters. Edited with an introduction by Frances de Groen and Peter Pierce. (St Lucia: U. Q. P., 1992).
Reviewed by N. Birns, *Antipodes*, 6.2, 1992, 163-66; J. McLaren, *A.L.S.*, 16.1, 1993, 119-21.

Fiction
Capricornia. Introduction by Laurie Hergenhan. (Sydney: A.& R., 1972). Reprinted 1977; First published Sydney: Publicist, 1938.
Capricornia. (London: A.& R., 1977). First published Sydney: Publicist, 1938.
Reviewed by C.P. Snow, *Financial Times*, 10 March, 1978, 15.
Capricornia. Introduction by Mudrooroo Nyoongah. (North Ryde, NSW: Collins/A.& R, 1990). First published Sydney: Publicist, 1938.
Reviewed by L. Clancy, *Weekend Australian,* 26-27 January, 1991, Review 6; J. McLaren, *A.L.S.*, 16.1, 1993, 119-21.

Dream Road Illus. Ray Crooke (Sydney: Collins, 1977). Extract from *Poor Fellow My Country*.
Reviewed by G.R. Lansell, *ABR.*, No. 1, 1978, 33; P. Rappolt, *Canberra Times*, 21 January, 1978, 14.
Larger than Life. (Sydney: A.& R., 1963).
Reviewed by R. Wilson, *Southerly*, XXIV, No. 2, 1964, 141-3.

Poor Fellow My Country. (Sydney, London: Collins, 1975).
Reviewed by C.M.H. Clark, *Canberra Times*, 12 September, 1975, 10; B. Elliott, *Advertiser*, 13 September, 1975, 20; G. Farwell, *S.M.H.*, 13 September, 1975, 15; C. Harrison-Ford, *S.M.H.*, 13 September, 1975, 15; J. Hepworth, *Nation Review*, 17-23 October, 1975, 23; H. Heseltine, *Australian*, 13 September, 1975, 41; L.V. Kepert, *Sun-Herald*, 14 September, 1975, 114; B. Kiernan, *Age*, 13 September, 1975, 19; E. Kynaston, *Overland*, No. 62, 1975, 76-78; A. Lundkvist, *Dagens Nyheter* (Stockholm), 7 February, 1977; H. McQueen, *Arena*, No. 41, 1976, 79-91; D.

Rowbotham, *Courier-Mail*, 13 September, 1975, 17; R. Stow, *T.L.S.*, 9 April, 1976, 417, reprinted *National Times*, 2-7 August, 1976, 28-29.

South of Capricornia: Short Stories 1925-1958. Edited with an introduction by Russell McDougall. (Melbourne: O.U.P., 1990).
Reviewed by L. Clancy, *Weekend Australian*, 26-27 January, 1991, Review 6; J. Healy, *CRNLE Reviews Journal*, 2, 1993, 130-32; M. Lord, *ABR*, 129, 1991, 36; J. McLaren, *A.L.S.*, 16.1, 1993, 119-21; E. Watts, *Antipodes*, 5.1, 1991, 69-70.

Non-Fiction
Disturbing Element. (Melbourne: Cheshire, 1963).
Reviewed by J. Lindsay, *Meanjin*, XXIII, No. 4, 1964, 443; S. Murray-Smith, *ABR*, III, 1963, 33.
'The Agony - And the Joy'. *Overland*, Nos. 50-51, 972, 65-68.
'The Writing of *Capricornia*'. *A.L.S.*, IV, 1970, 207-14. Speech delivered at the Adelaide Arts Festival, 1962.

Critical Material
Ehrhardt, Marianne and Stuart, Lurline. 'Xavier Herbert: A Checklist'. *A.L.S*, VIII, 1978, 499-511.
'Author Xavier Herbert Dies at 83 in N.T.', *Canberra Times*, 12 November, 1984, 1. For other obituaries see *Courier-Mail*, 12 November, 1984, 1.
'Non-Crawling Herbert Says No to Warana'. *Courier-Mail*, 20 August, 1975, 10; similar report *S.M.H.*, 20 August, 1975, 15.
'A Roller-Coaster Ride with Xavier'. *Bulletin*, 27 November, 1984, 112-13. 'Batman's Melbourne' column.
'The Signing of the Peace Treaty: Xavier Herbert Describes the Ending of his War of Independence'. *Australian*, 29 March, 1975, 14.
'Xavier Herbert Backs Whitlam'. *Courier-Mail*, 24 November, 1975, 2; similar report *Australian*, 26 November, 1975, 2.
'Xavier Herbert...the Literary Rebel in the Bush'. *S.M.H.*, 12 November, 1984, 5
Baker, Mark. 'Strange Fella, This Other Country'. *Age*, 20 September, 1975, 2.
'Batman'. 'A Man's Reason for Being'. *Bulletin*, 9 August, 1975, 44-45.
Birt, Gordon R. 'The Xavier He Knew'. *National Times*, 25-31 January, 1985, 45.
Borschmann, Gregg. 'Last Tango in Paradise. Author is Charged up for Latest Book'. *Sunday Sun*, 20 November, 1983, 52-53.
---. 'Xavier Herbert's Final Round-up'. *Age Saturday Extra*, 17 December, 1983, 12.
Burns, D.R. 'Vague Vision and Savage Substance: *Poor Fellow My Country* as the Sum of Opposing Parts'. *Overland*, No. 113, 1988, 45-51.
Casey, Constance. 'Down Under, Out Back and Over There'. [*Washington Post*] *Book World*, 4 October, 1981, 15.
Clancy, Laurie. *Xavier Herbert*. (Boston: Twayne, 1981). Twayne's World Author's Series: TWAS 552: Australia. Reviewed by D. Grant, *ABR*, No. 40, 1982, 33-34; J.J. Healy, *A.L.S.*, X, 1982, 535-41; L.T. Hergenhan, *Modern Language Review*, LXXX, No. 2, 1985, 448-449; J. Waten, *Age Saturday Extra*, 25 June, 1983, 8.
---. 'The Design of *Capricornia*'. *Meanjin*, XXXIV, 1975, 150-56.
---. '*Poor Fellow My Country*: Herbert's Masterpiece?' *Southerly*, XXXVII, 1977, 164-75.
Cornford, Philip. 'Far Out in the North Queensland Bush Xavier Herbert Talks about His 70 Years of Life and the Last Book He Will Write'. *Sunday Australian*, 2 May, 1971, 45.
Daniel, Helen. 'Outsiders and Society: *Poor Fellow my Country*'. *Westerly*, XXIII, No. 4, 1978, 37-47.
De Groen, Frances. 'Three Background Studies of *Poor Fellow My Country*'. *Notes & Furphies*, No. 18, 1987, 29-33.
---. *Xavier Herbert's Birth: The Documentary Record*. (Canberra: English

Department, University College, Australian Defence Force Academy, 1988). Occasional Paper, No. 11.

---. 'Xavier Herbert, Journalist?'. *A.L.S.*, 16.1, 1993, 116-18.

Drewe, Robert. 'A Peep into the Cocoon'. *Bulletin*, 7 August, 1976, 46-47. Interview with Prof. Michio Ochi, working on a Japanese translation of *Poor Fellow My Country*.

Dunstan, Keith. 'Life with the Octopus'. *Courier-Mail*, 19 July, 1975, 13.

---. 'Xavier (Alfred Francis) Herbert'. In his *Ratbags*. (Sydney: Golden Press, 1979), 149-62. See also *S.M.H.*, 14 April, 1979, 11-12.

Fatchen, Max. 'A Literary Leviathan on the Slipway'. *Advertiser*, 15 July, 1975, 4.

Gissing, Phil. 'Herbert Returns to his Beloved [Northern] Territory...Pen in Hand'. *S.M.H.*, 18 September, 1984, 2.

---. 'The Life of a Literary Recluse'. *Tribune*, 12 December, 1984, 15.

Goldie, Terry. *Fear and Temptation: The Image of the Indigene in Canadian, Australian and New Zealand Literatures*. (Kingston, Ontario: McGill University Press, 1989).

Grant, Don. 'Xavier Herbert's Botch'. *Overland*, No. 65, 1976, 43-47.

Green, Kevin. 'Xavier Herbert, H.G. Wells and J.S. Huxley'. *A.L.S.*, XII, No. 1, 1985, 47-64.

Hassall, Anthony J. (ed.). *The Making of Xavier Herbert's Poor Fellow My Country*. (Townsville, Qld.: Foundation for Australian Literary Studies, 1988). Monograph 14.

Healy, J.J. 'Grant Watson and the Aborigine: A Tragic Voice in an Age of Optimism'. *A.L.S.*, VII, 1975, 24-38.

Hergenhan, Laurie. 'An Australian Tragedy: Xavier Herbert's *Poor Fellow My Country*'. In *Studies in the Recent Australian Novel*, edited by K.G. Hamilton (St Lucia: U.Q.P., 1978), 29-60. An expanded version of an article of the same title, *Quadrant*, XXI, No. 2, 1977, 62-70.

---. 'Rebuttal, a Defence of Xavier Herbert's *Poor Fellow My Country*'. *Overland*, No. 67, 1977, 41-42. On the article by Don Grant in *Overland*, No. 65, 1977, 43-47.

---. 'Xavier Herbert, Writer in Residence'. *Alumni News* (University of Queensland), VIII, No. 2, 1976, 10-11.

Heseltine, Harry. *Xavier Herbert*. (Melbourne: O.U.P., 1973). Australian Writers and Their Work. Reviewed by K.L. Goodwin, *Notes & Queries* n.s. XXIII, No. 1, 1976, 42-43; C. Hadgraft, *A.L.S.*, V, 1974, 438-40; M. Thorpe, *English Studies*, LV, 1974, 550.

---. 'Xavier Herbert's Magnum Opus'. *Meanjin*, XXXIV, 1975, 133-36.

James, Trevor. 'Xavier Herbert (1901-1984)'. *London Magazine*, XXV, Nos. 5-6, 1985, 111-118.

Indyk, Ivor. 'Pastoral and Priority: The Aboriginal in Australian Pastoral'. *New Literary History*, 24.4, 1993, 837-55. Includes discussion of writing by Herbert.

Johnston, Elizabeth. 'Mr. Herbert Misses his Own Funeral'. *Australian*, 23 March, 1976, 11.

Kelly, David. 'Landscape in *Poor Fellow My Country*'. *Overland*, No. 67, 1977, 43-46.

Kiernan, Brian. 'Xavier Herbert: *Capricornia*'. *A.L.S.*, IV, 1970, 360-70.

Killam, G.D. 'Great Steel-Rails in the Fictions of Xavier Herbert and Rudy Wieke'. In *Australian/Canadian Literatures in English: Comparative Perspectives*, edited by Russell McDougall and Gillian Whitlock (North Ryde, N.S.W.: Methuen Australia, 1987), 170-186.

Lawson, Elizabeth. '"Oh Don't You Remember Black Alice?" or How Many Mothers had Norman Shillingsworth'. *Westerly*, XXXII, No. 3, 1987, 29-40.

---. 'Lucy's Gold, *The Pommy Cow*, in Herbertland: Sarah Campion's "Mo Burdekin" Novels'. *LiNQ*, XV, No. 2, 1987, 71-79.

McDougall, Russell. '*Capricornia*: Recovering the Imaginative Vision of a Polemical

Novel'. *A.L.S.*, X, 1981, 67-78.

McEwen, Mike. 'Reformer or Reactionary?'. *Advertiser*, 16 October, 1985, 12.

McGrath, Ann. 'Trespassing on Male Territory: Women on Men'. In *Writing Lives: Feminist Biography and Autobiography*, edited by Susan Magarey, Caroline Guerin, and Paula Hamilton (Adelaide: Australian Feminist Studies, Research Centre for Women's Studies U of Adelaide, 1992 / *Australian Feminist Studies*, 16, 1992, special issue), 87-92. On Herbert.

McKenzie, C.J. 'Xavier Looks at Death as Final Drama. No Bitterness in his Plan to "Vanish Away"'. *Sunday Telegraph* (Sydney), 28 August, 1983, 9.

McLaren, John. *Xavier Herbert's Capricornia and Poor Fellow My Country*. (Melbourne: Shillington House, 1981). Essays in Australian Literature. Reviewed by J. Croft, *A.L.S.*, X, 1982, 400-01; V. Ikin, *Westerly*, XXVII, No. 3, 1982, 70-72; R. McDougall, *ABR*, No. 29, 1981, 34.

---. 'The Image of Reality in our Writing'. *Overland*, Nos. 27-28, 1963, 43-7. Contains specific references to Herbert's work.

McQueen, Humphrey. 'Poor Fellow my Country'. In his *Gallipoli to Petrov*. (Sydney: Allen & Unwin, 1984), 153-66. First published in *Arena*, No. 41, 1976, 79-91.

McQueen, Humphrey. 'Racism and Australian Literature'. In *Racism: The Australian Experience. A Study of Race Prejudice in Australia. Volume I. Prejudice and Xenophobia*, edited by F.S. Stevens (Sydney: Australia and New Zealand Book Company, 1971), 115-22.

Monahan, Sean. '*Poor Fellow My Country*: A Question of Genre'. *Westerly*, XXXII, No. 3, 1987, 45-56.

---. 'Xavier Herbert's *Capricornia*: In Praise of the Swagman Spirit?' *Westerly*, XXX, No. 4, 1985, 15-24.

Morgan, Patrick. 'In Memoriam: Xavier Herbert'. *Quadrant*, XXVIII, No. 12, 1984, 7.

Mudge, Neil. '*Capricornia*: Seasonal, Diurnal and Colour Patterns'. *A.L.S.*, IX, 1979, 156-66.

Munro, Craig. 'Some Facts about a Long Fiction: The Publication of *Capricornia*'. *Southerly*, XLI, 1981, 82-104.

---. 'Xavier Herbert: A Disturbing Element'. *This Australia*, II, No. 2, 1983, 11-16.

Murray-Smith, Stephen. 'Obituary: Mr Xavier Herbert, Chronicler of Australian Outback'. *Times*, 13 November, 1984, 18.

---. 'Swag'. *Overland*, No. 97, 1984, 25 & 26.

Nicklin, Lenore. 'Xavier Herbert Puts the Boot In'. *S.M.H.*, 6 September, 1975, 12.

Pascoe, Michael. 'Old 'Orrible: Xavier Herbert'. *Semper Floreat*, XLVI, No. 4, 7 April, 1976, 38-40.

---. 'The Quiet Woman Behind the Man of a Million Words'. *Courier-Mail*, 16 September, 1975, 5.

Pons, Xavier. 'Caste and Castration: The Personal Element in *Capricornia*'. *Caliban*, XIV, 1977, 133-47.

Price, Cecil. 'Xavier Herbert'. *Anglo-Welsh Review*, XXVI, No. 57, 1976, 148-53.

Reid, Ian. 'A Splendid Bubble: Publishing and Fiction-Writing in the Thirties'. *Meanjin*, XXXIII, 1974, 266-71.

Reid, Robert. 'Playboy Interview: Xavier Herbert'. *Australian Playboy*, June, 1982, 33-39 & 129-36.

Richards, Dave. 'Me and My Shadow'. *National Times*, 25-31 January, 1985, 20-22. Interview.

---. 'Xavier Returns to the Mulga'. *Courier-Mail*, 19 September, 1984, 5.

Robertson, Robert T. 'Form into Shape: *His Natural Life* and *Capricornia* in a Commonwealth Context'. In *Commonwealth Literature and the Modern World*, edited by Hena Maes-Jelinek (Brussels: Didier, 1975), 137-46.

Rolfe, Patricia. '"Old 'Orrible" Loves Australia'. *Bulletin*, 5 January, 1974, 32-34.
Ross, Robert L. 'Xavier Herbert's *Poor Fellow My Country*: In Search of an American Audience'. *Journal of Popular Culture*, 23, No. 2, 1989, 55-62.
Rowbotham, David. '"Old 'Orrible" Delivers an Octopus'. *Courier-Mail*, 24 August, 1974, 3. Other news reports about Herbert, *Bulletin*, 13 July, 1974, 27; *S.M.H.*, 27 July, 1974, 9; *Bulletin*, 30 November, 1974, 12-13.
---. 'Final Journey for our Literary Giant'. *Courier-Mail*, 12 November, 1984, 2.
Sawer, Geoffrey. 'National Criticism Writ Large on an Immense Canvas'. *Canberra Times*, 26 May, 1976, 2.
Sayers, Stuart. 'When Xavier Herbert Comes to Town'. *Age*, 13 September, 1975, 19.
Waite, Eric. 'Assault and Pepper at a Literary Lunch'. *National Times*, 6-12 April, 1980, 19-20. Letters in reply from D. Bowman; J.L. Fitzgerald; D. Forbes; D.L. Hackett; P. Hackett; D. Hawken; W. Hedley; X. Herbert, *National Times*, 11-17 May, 1980, 27; and D.Ogilvie, *National Times*, 25-31 May, 1980, 21.
Wevers, Lydia. 'Terra Australis: Landscape as Medium in *Capricornia* and *Poor Fellow My Country*'. *A.L.S.*, 17.1, 1995, 38-48.
White, Robert. *Australia Lost: Paintings from Poor Fellow My Country, by Xavier Herbert*. (Sydney: Collins, 1978).
Willey, Keith. 'Alone among the Immigrant Rabble, Xavier Herbert Winds Up His Most Ambitious Work'. *National Times*, 30 April-5 May, 1973, 24.
Williams, Graham. 'The Loves and Hates of Xavier Herbert'. *S.M.H.*, 15 July, 1978, 2.
Yeomans, John. 'The Long-Distance Novelist'. *Herald* (Melbourne), 25 August, 1975, 4.

HEWETT, DOROTHY

Fiction

Bobbin Up. (London: Virago, 1985). First published Melbourne: Australasian Book Society, 1959.
Reviewed by V. Brady, *Australian Society*, V, No. 2, 1986, 40-42; L. Clancy, *Age Saturday Extra*, 8 February, 1986, 14; N. Jose, *Age Monthly Review*, V, No. 10, 1986, 23; M. Macleod, *S.M.H.*, 13 July, 1985, 46; K.C. O'Brien, *Listener*, 16 May, 1985, 28-29; J. Roe, *Sydney Gazette*, No. 8, 1986, 65-67; C. Semmler, *Courier-Mail*, 6 July, 1985, 30.

The Toucher. (Ringwood, Vic.: McPhee Gribble, 1993).
Reviewed by N. Albinski, *Antipodes*, 7.2, 1993, 161; L. Barrett, *Meanjin*, 52.3, 1993, 598-601; P.M. Beckerling, *SPAN*, 37, 1993, 244-45; C. Blanche, *Quadrant*, 37.11, 1993, 78-80; B. Brook, *Australian Women's Book Review*, 5.4, 1993, 6-7; H. Daniel, *Age*, 12 June, 1993, Saturday Extra 9; D. English, *Weekend Australian*, 19-20 June, 1993, Review 6; E. Lindsay, *ABR*, 151, 1993, 6-7 (see also interview by R. Sorensen, 8-10); R. Lucas, *Bulletin*, 22 June, 1993, 97; P. Pierce, *S.M.H.*, 26 June, 1993, 47; J. Rodriguez, *Overland*, 132, 1993, 79-82; N. Stasko, *Southerly*, 53.4, 1993, 174-82.

Drama

Bon-Bons and Roses for Dolly. The Tatty Hollow Story: Two Plays. Introduced by Arthur Ballet. (Sydney: Currency Press, London: Eyre Methuen, 1976).
Reviewed by M. Leask, *Theatrescope*, No. 1, 1976, 16; *Theatre-Australia*, I, No. 3, 1976, 56; G. Page, *Canberra Times*, 12 February, 1977, 15.

The Chapel Perilous (or The Perilous Adventures of Sally Banner). Introduced by Aarne Neeme; preface by Sylvia Lawson. (Sydney: Currency Press, 1972). Currency Playtexts, Series I, No. 4.
Reviewed by R. Blair, *Nation Review*, 25-30 November, 1972, 201; J. Gibson,

Canberra Times, 30 September, 1972, 12; A. Kruse, *Southerly*, XXXIII, 1973, 245-46; A.A. Phillips, *Meanjin*, XXXII, 1973, 193-94; L. Radic, *Age*, 30 September, 1972, 14; R. Wissler, *Makar*, IX, No 1, 1973, 45-48.

Collected Plays. Vol. 1. Introduced by Kristin Williamson. (Sydney: Currency Press, 1992).
Reviewed by A. Cromwell, *Antipodes*, 7.1, 1993, 70-72; E. Perkins, *Australasian Drama Studies*, 22, 1993, 146-50; C. Pickett, *Meridian*, 11.2, 1992, 89-93; M. Williams, *ABR*, 144, 1992, 27-28.

The Golden Oldies, and Susannah's Dreaming. (Sydney: Currency Press, 1981).
Reviewed by M. Lord, *ABR*, No. 37, 1981, 15-16.

The Man from Mukinupin. (Fremantle: Fremantle Arts Centre Press, Sydney: Currency Press, 1979).
Reviewed by A. Godfrey-Smith, *ABR*, No. 18, 1980, 21-22; J. McCallum, *Theatre-Australia*, IV, No. 4, 1979, 55; L. Radic, *Age*, 21 April, 1980, 10; E. Webby, *CRNLE Reviews Journal*, No. 1, 1980, 116-18.

This Old Man Comes Rolling Home. Introduced by Jack Beasley, with a note by Merv Lilley (Sydney: Currency Press; London: Eyre Methuen, 1976).
Reviewed by M. Jones, *S.M.H.*, 20 November, 1976, 13; *Theatre-Australia*, I, No. 3, 1976, 56.

'Bon-bons and Roses for Dolly'. *Westerly*, No. 4, 1972, 22-36. Extract from Play.

    Poetry

Alice in Wormland. (Sydney: Paper Bark Press, 1987).
Reviewed by G. Harwood, *Westerly*, XXXII, No. 4, 1987, 101-102; J. Heath, *Weekend Australian. Weekend Magazine*, 8-9 August, 1987, 13; E. Jones, *Age Saturday Extra*, 14 November, 1987, 17; L. McCredden, *ABR*, No. 95, 1987, 26-27; J. Rodriguez, *S.M.H.*, 10 October, 1987, 46; J. Strauss, *Overland*, No. 110, 1988, 80; *New Theatre Australia*, No. 1, 1987, 42-43; F. Zwicky, *ABR*, No. 95, 1987, 25-26.

Greenhouse. (Sydney: Big-Smoke Books, 1979).
Reviewed by C. Pollnitz, *Southerly*, XLI, 1981, 237-40; A. Taylor, *ABR*, No. 21, 1980, 11-12; J. Tranter, *Age*, 5 January, 1980, 19.

Peninsula. (South Fremantle: Fremantle Arts Centre P., 1994).
Reviewed by H. Cam, *S.M.H.*, 26 February, 1994, Spectrum 10A; M. Johnson, *Antipodes*, 9.2, 1995, 166-68; C. Mansell, *Overland*, 137, 1994, 68-70; M. Polain, *FAR*, 9.3, 1994, 9; N. Rowe, *Voices*, 4.4, 1994-95, 109-16; T. Ryan, *Westerly*, 39.2, 1994, 87-88; S. Schwartz, *ABR*, 159, 1994, 36-37; J. Strauss, *Age*, 7 May, 1994, Saturday Extra 8.

Rapunzel in Suburbia. (Sydney: Prism Poets, 1975).
Reviewed by H. Colebatch, *Westerly*, No. 3, 1975, 80-84; K. Metcalfe, *New Poetry*, XXIII, No. 2, 1975, 78-80; T. Thorne, *Australian*, 12 July, 1975, 27.

Selected Poems. Edited with an introduction by Edna Longley. (Fremantle, WA: Fremantle Arts Centre P., 1991). Reprinted as *Alice in Wormland: Selected Poems*. (Newcastle upon Tyne: Bloodaxe, 1990).
Reviewed by K. Brophy, *ABR*, 131, 1991, 16-18; M. Duwell, *Weekend Australian*, 29-30 June, 1991, Review 4; C. Harrison-Ford, *Voices*, 1.3, 1991, 92-96; M. Hulse, *PN Review*, 17.6, 1991, 72-73; S.K. Kelen, *Southerly*, 52.1, 1992, 173-77; L. Norfolk, *T.L.S.*, 5 July, 1991, 21-22.

A Tremendous World in Her Head: Selected Poems. (Sydney: Dangaroo Press, 1989).
Reviewed by L. Bourke, *Westerly*, 35, N0. 4, 105-07; F. Rummery and J. Millbank, *Antithesis*, 4, No. 1, 1990, 169-73.

Windmill Country. (Melbourne: Overland, 1968).

Reviewed by D. Anderson, *Southerly*, XXIX, 1969, 75-76; D. Douglas, *Age*, 15 February, 1969, 13; R. Dunlop, *Poetry Australia*, No. 24, 1968, 38; F. Haynes, *Critic* (Perth), IX, 1968, 53-54; F. Kellaway, *Overland*, No. 40, 1968, 36-37; G. Lehmann, *Bulletin*, 12 October, 1968, 80; M. Richards, *Meanjin*, XXVIII, 1969, 273-74; R. Ward, *ABR*, VIII, 1968, 44; B. Williams, *Westerly*, No. 4, 1968, 67-71.

Non-Fiction

Wild Card: An Autobiography 1923-1958. (South Yarra, Vic.: McPhee Gribble, 1990).

Reviewed by N. B. Albinski, *Antipodes*, 5.2, 1991, 121-23; J. Brett, *Australian Society*, 9, No. 9, 1990, 37-38; E. Campion, *Bulletin*, 2 October, 1990, 112; J.M. Hearn, *Overland*, 122, 1991, 64-65; C. Ferrier, *Australian Historical Studies*, 99, 1992, 354-55; C. Lawrence, *Westerly*, 35, No. 2, 1990, 102-3; L. McCredden, *Australian Women's Book Review*, 2, No. 4, 1990, 18-19; M. Missen, *Age*, 11 August, 1990, Saturday Extra 10; J. Palmer, *Southerly*, 51.1, 1991, 176-82; T. Robertson, *Weekend Australian*, 25-26 August, 1990, Review 7; C. Wallace-Crabbe, *ABR*, No. 125, 1990, 43; J. Williams, *Westerly*, 35, No. 4, 1990, 103-05.

'Autobiographically Speaking'. In, *The View from Tinsel Town*, edited by Tom Thompson (Ringwood, Vic.: Southerly/Penguin, 1985, 37-41.

'Can't Stop the Music'. *Theatre Australia*, V, No. 2, 1980, 15-17.

'Creating Heroines in Australian Plays'. *Hecate*, V, No. 2, 1979, 73-79.

'Dorothy Hewett: Two Early Essays'. Previously unpublished; with note by Ian Syson. *Hecate*, 21.2, 1995, 129-36.

'The Garden and the City'. *Westerly*, XXVII, No. 4, 1982, 99-104. Autobiographical.

'Isis in Search'. *New Poetry*, XXVIII, No. 1, 1980, 49-56.

'A Peculiar Form of Masochism'. *Critic*, Perth, XI, 1970, 14-15. On her career as a playwright.

'The Story of My Life'. *Zeitschrift fur Anglistik und Amerikanistik*, XV, 1967, 343-46.

'Thoughts into Words'. *Fremantle Arts Review*, 5, No. 11, 1990/91, Supplement [1-4].

'Women in the Arts'. *'Artforce*, No. 46, 1984, 12. Report of an address.

'Writer's View'. *Theatre-Australia*, IV, No. 2, 1979, 15-16.

'Writing a Novel: Notes on *The Toucher*'. *Meridian*, 13.1, 1994, 3-77.

Critical Material

'No Bon-bons for Dorothy?'. *S.M.H.*, 29 June, 1973, 12.

Akerholt, May-Brit. 'Female Figures in the Plays of Dorothy Hewett and Patrick White'. *Westerly*, XXIX, No. 1, 1984, 69-77.

Baker, Candida. 'Dorothy Hewett'. In her *Yacker: Australian Writers Talk About Their Work* (Sydney: Picador, 1986), 184-209.

Barbour, Judith. 'Privileged, Authentic, Transcendent, Arcane: Limits of Naturalism in some Contemporary Australian Plays'. *Southerly*, XXXVII, 1977, 77-92.

Baschiera, Carla Dente. 'Dramatic Conventions and Techniques in *The Chapel Perilous* by Dorothy Hewett'. *Linguistica E Letteratura*, VIII, Nos. 1-2, 1983, 303-28.

Bennett, Bruce, ed. *Dorothy Hewett: Selected Critical Essays*. (South Fremantle, WA: Fremantle Arts Centre P, 1995). Reviewed by F. Capp, *Age*, 18 Feb., 1995, Saturday Extra 8; A. Gardiner, *Hecate*, 21.2, 1995, 137-41; V. Ikin, *S.M.H.*, 25 Feb., 1995, Spectrum 11A; M. Johnson, *Antipodes*, 9.2, 1995, 166-68; M. Polain, *FAR*, 9.8, 1995, 15; J. Rodriguez, *ABR*, 169, 1995, 50-51.

Bertinetti, Paolo. 'The Plays of Dorothy Hewett'. In *Saggi e ricerche sulle culture extraeuropee*, edited by G. Bellini, C. Gorlier and S. Zoppi (Rome: Bulzoni, 1986), 17-24. Africa, America, Asia, Australia, 2.

Campbell, Lance. 'From the Heart'. *Advertiser*, 9 August, 1980, 30. Interview.

Capp, Fiona. *Writers Defiled: Security Surveillance of Australian Authors and*

Intellectuals 1920-1960. (Ringwood, Vic.: McPhee Gribble, 1993). Includes discussion of Hewett.

Carlisle, Wendy. 'Dorothy Hewett Living Down Her Past'. *Tribune*, 7 August, 1985, 15. Interview.

Davidson, Jim. 'Dorothy Hewett'. *Meanjin*, XXXVIII, 1979, 350-67. Interview. Reprinted in his *Sideways from the Page* (Melbourne: Fontana, 1983), 184-208.

Davies, Lloyd. *In Defence of My Family*. (Cottesloe, W.A.: Peppy Gully Press, 1987). An account of several libel actions taken by the author and his family against Dorothy Hewett.

Dean, Michael. 'Trial by Ordeal'. *Australian*, 8 April, 1976, 12.

Denholm, Michael. 'Dorothy Hewett'. *Tasmanian Review*, I, No. 1, 1979, 6-8. Interview.

Digby, Jenny. 'Representations of Female Identity in the Poetry of Dorothy Hewett'. *Southerly*, 53.2, 1993, 167-89.

Drewe, Robert. 'Goodbye Dolly'. *Australian*, 13 October, 1972, 9.

Dunstone, Bill. 'Performance and Difference in Dorothy Hewett's *The Man from Mukinupin*'. *New Literatures Review*, 19, 1990, 72-81.

Fitzpatrick, Peter. 'Dorothy Hewett'. In his *After 'The Doll'* (Melbourne: Edward Arnold, 1979), 145-56.

Ferrier, Carole. 'Dorothy Hewett: Australian Dramatist'. *Lip* (Carlton, Vic.), 30 October, 1976, 2-5.

Galbraith, Larry. 'Dorothy Hewett Casting Theatrical Spells'. *Campaign*, No. 86, 1983, 38-39.

Garlick, Barbara. 'Beyond Social Realism: The Woman's Voice'. *Social Alternatives*, VII, No. 1, 1988, 68-70. Discusses D. Hewett's *Bobbin Up* and C. Rohan's *Down by the Dockside* and *The Delinquents*.

Gilman, Marvin. 'Lines of Intersection: The two Dorothys and Marxism'. *New Literatures Review*, 28/29, 1995-96, 23-28. On D. Hewett and Canadian writer Dorothy Livesay.

Goodall, Julie. 'Dorothy Hewett'. *The Press*, (University of Queensland, Students' Union), XLIX, No. 8/4, 1979, 7. Interview for 4ZZZ.

Gostand, Reba. 'Quest or Question? Perilous Journey to the Chapel'. In *Bards, Bohemians, and Bookmen*, edited by Leon Cantrell (St Lucia: U.Q.P., 1976), 289-304.

Green, Kristin. 'Dorothy Hewett: A Censored Look at a Revolutionary Romantic'. *Theatre-Australia*, III, No. 9, 1979, 16-17, 38.

Griffiths, Gareth. 'Experiments with Form in Recent Australian Drama'. *Kunapipi*, II, No. 1, 1980, 77-81.

Hawley, Janet. 'Too Bad If People Are Shocked, Says Author'. *Australian*, 22 June, 1973, 3.

Hoad, Brian. 'Something for the Censors to Chew Over'. *Bulletin*, 24 February, 1981, 77. *The Man from Mukinupin*.

Hooton, Joy. 'Writing the Self'. *Island*, 48, 1991, 18-22.

Hopkins, Lekkie. 'Language, Culture and Landscape in *The Man from Mukinupin*'. *Australasian Drama Studies*, No. 10, 1987, 91-106.

Kavanagh, Paul. 'An Interview with Dorothy Hewett'. *Southerly*, 1984, 123-42. Reprinted in *Conversations: Interviews with Australian Writers*, edited by Paul Kavanagh and Peter Kuch (North Ryde, NSW: Collins/A.& R, 1991), 111-135.

Kemp, Kevon. 'An Excited Playwright Looks into the Crater of the Big Time'. *National Times*, 30 September-5 October, 1974, 22; (see also letter to the editor by M.. Maslen, *National Times*, 14-19 October, 1974, 4).

---. 'For Women, A Work that Will Make Things Suddenly and Blindingly Clear. Dorothy Hewett Writes the Roles She Would Love to Play'. *National Times*, 4-9 September, 1972, 20.

---. 'A Real Voice for Women'. *National Times Magazine*, 29 April-3 May, 1974, 28.

Kiernan, Brian. 'Seeing her Own Mischance: the Poetry and Plays of Dorothy Hewett'. *Overland*, No. 64, 1976, 16-23.

Larkin, John. 'Living with a Libel'. *Age*, 16 October, 1976, 13; other reports on the libel case: *Bulletin*, 28 February, 1976, 41; *Overland*, No. 64, 1976, 55; *Age*, 3 July, 1976, 2.

Luke, Margot. 'Insight and Outrage: Dorothy Hewett's New Play'. *Westerly*, No. 4, 1972, 37-40.

Modjeska, Drusilla. 'Dorothy Hewett: Talking with Drusilla Modjeska'. In *Writing Lives: Conversations Between Women Writers*, edited by Mary Chamberlain (London: Virago, 1988), 85-97.

Moffitt, Ian. 'The Legend Finds *her* Australia'. *Bulletin*, 10 April, 1976, 44.

Moran, Rod. 'Rapunzel in Windmill Country'. *Fremantle Arts Review*, II, No. 12, 1987, 3-5.

Neller, Shelley. 'The Life and Times of Dorothy Hewett'. *Weekend Australian Magazine*, 31 January-1 February, 1981, 8.

Page, Geoff. 'Dorothy Hewett'. In his *A Reader's Guide To Contemporary Australian Poetry* (St. Lucia: U.Q.P., 1995), 119-124.

Page, Robert. 'Dorothy Hewett: A Major Australian Writer'. *Artlook*, V, No. 4, 1979, 33-35.

Porter, Pip. 'Dorothy Hewett: An Interview'. *Hecate*, III, No. 1, 1977, 7-15.

Robins, Brian. 'Defamation Settlement Leaves in Doubt Author's Rights'. *Australian Financial Review*, 13 December, 1978, 14.

Smith, Martin. '"... being a Communist almost destroyed my creativity...". Martin Smith talks with famed Australian playwright Dorothy Hewett'. *Campaign*, No. 26, 1977, 11, 12, 14.

Sykes, Alrene. 'Dorothy Hewett: Playwright of Splendid Moments'. *WLWE*, XVII, No. 1, 1978, 106-13.

Taylor, Andrew. 'Dorothy Hewett as Poet: The Only Escape from the Labyrinth Is within the Labyrinth'. *Southerly*, XLIV, 1984, 423-40. Revised version appears in his *Reading Australian Poetry* (St Lucia: U.Q.P., 1987), 126-138.

Thomas, Sue. 'Writing Autobiography: An Interview with Dorothy Hewett'. *Meridian*, VII, No. 2, 1988, 153-159.

Tompkins, Joanne. '"I Was a Rebel in Word and Deed": Dorothy Hewett's *The Chapel Perilous* and Contemporary Australian Feminist Writing'. *Australian & New Zealand Studies in Canada*, 19, 1993, 41-56.

Walker, Shirley. *Vanishing Edens: Responses to Australia in the Works of Mary Gilmore, Judith Wright and Dorothy Hewett*. Monograph 23. (Townsville, Qld.: Foundation for Australian Literary Studies / James Cook U of North Queensland, 1992). Reviewed by S. Bennett, *Imago*, 5.3, 1993, 95-97; N. Birns, *Antipodes*, 7.2, 1993, 167-68.

Weller, Guy. 'The Man from Muckinupin [sic]. New Dorothy Hewett Play at the Playhouse. *Artlook* Interviews the Director Stephen Barry'. *Artlook*, V, No. 8, 1979, 3-5.

White, Patrick. 'The Perils of Art in Sydney Town'. *S.M.H.*, 2 November, 1974, 16.

Whitehead, Jean. 'Ordeal by Freedom: A Carve-Up of Sally or Society?' *Westerly*, No. 1, 1971, 41-44. A Discussion of *The Chapel Perilous*, a play which is itself printed in part in *Westerly*, No. 1, 1971, 33-40.

Williams, Bruce. 'Dorothy Hewett: Confession and Beyond'. *Overland*, No. 64, 1976, 24-29.

Williams, Margaret. *Dorothy Hewett: The Feminine as Subversion*. (Sydney: Currency Press, 1992). Reviewed by A. Cromwell, *Antipodes*, 7.1, 1993, 70-72; S. Lever, *A.L.S.*, 16.2, 1993, 229-33; E. Perkins, *Australasian Drama Studies*, 22, 1993, 146-50; C. Pickett, *Meridian*, 11.2, 1992, 89-93; T. Radic, *Australian Women's Book*

Review, 4.3, 1992, 3-4.
Williamson, Kristin. 'Unrepentant Spirit'. *National Times*, 8-14 February, 1981, 40-41.

HIBBERD, JACK

Fiction
The Life of Riley. (Port Melbourne: Heinemann/Mandarin Australia, 1991).
Reviewed by P. Bryan, *ABR*, 130, 1991, 21; N. Jose, *Weekend Australian*, 11-12 May, 1991, Review 6; D.L. O'Hearn, *Age*, 6 April, 1991, Saturday Extra 6.
Perdita. (Ringwood, Vic.: McPhee Gribble, 1992).
Reviewed by N. Phelan, *S.M.H.*, 10 October, 1992, 40; I. Salusinszky, *Weekend Australian*, 10-11 October, 1992, Review 7; M. Sharkey, *ABR*, 145, 1992, 55-57.
Memoirs of an Old Bastard. Fitzroy, Vic.: McPhee Gribble, 1989).
Reviewed by A. Bull, *Fremantle Arts Review*, 4, No. 5, 1989, 14-15; M. Copland, *Age Saturday Extra*, 4 March, 1989, 12; H. Daniel, *S.M.H.*, 11 February, 1989, 81; G. Griffiths, *Westerly*, 34, No. 1, 1989, 92-94; J. Hooker, *Weekend Australian*, 11-12 March, 1989, Weekend 12; J. Macgregor, *ABR*, No. 108, 1989, 37-38; P. Morgan, *Quadrant*, 33, No. 6, 1989, 66-67; P. Pierce, *Bulletin*, 14 March, 1989, 114.

Drama
Dimboola: A Wedding Reception Play. (Harmondsworth, Middlesex, Ringwood, Vic.: Penguin, 1974). Bound with John Powers, *The Last of the Knucklemen*.
Reviewed by D. Rowbotham, *Courier-Mail*, 22 March, 1975, 17.

Peggy Sue, or, The Power of Romance. Preface by David Kendall (Montmorency, Vic.: Yackandandah Playscripts, 1982).

A Stretch of the Imagination. Introduced by the author; preface by Margaret Williams. (Sydney: Currency Press, 1973). Currency Playtexts, Series 2.
Reviewed by J. Grillo, *Gambit*, No. 25, 1974, 107; H. Hewitt, *Canberra Times*, 23 June, 1973, 10; K. Jamieson, *Makar*, X, No. 1, 1974, 46-50; M. Jones, *S.M.H.*, 14 April, 1973, 28; A. Kruse, *Southerly*, XXXIII, 1973, 243; A.A. Phillips, *Meanjin*, XXXII, 1973, 194-95.

Three Popular Plays. (Melbourne: Outback Press, 1976). Contents: 'One of Nature's Gentlemen'; 'A Toast to Melba'; 'The Les Darcy Show'.
Reviewed by J. McCaughey, *Meanjin*, XXXV, 1976, 412-15; H. van der Poorten, *Theatre-Australia*, I, No. 7, 1977, 56.

'White with Wire Wheels' and 'Who?'. Included in *Plays*, edited by Graeme Blundell (Ringwood, Vic., Harmondsworth, Middlesex: Penguin, 1970).
Reviewed by T. Sturm, *Bulletin*, 9 January, 1971, 37-38.

Critical Material
'"Dimboola" Celebrates First 12 Months'. *Canberra Times*, 14 August, 1975, 19.
'Dimboola, Play to Film'. *Theatre Australia*, III, No. 4, 1978, 13-15.
'Dimboola Returns to Canberra'. *Canberra Times*, 11 February, 1975, 11.
'Ideology Drama "no no" - Plays Stands on own [sic]'. *Australian Jewish News*, 8 October, 1976, 15.
'Jack Hibberd'. *Lot's Wife*, 16 September, 1974, 22-23. Interview.
'Talking to Jack: Geraldine Pascall Interviews Dramatist Jack Hibberd'. *Australian*, 20 June, 1973, 12.
Baker, Candida. 'Jack Hibberd'. In her *Yacker 2: Australian Writers Talk About Their Work* (Sydney: Picador, 1987), 94-115.
Baschiera, Carla Dente. 'Allusion/Illusion: A Stretch of the Imagination Di Jack Hibberd'. *Quaderni di Anglistica*, No. 4, 1986, 133-148.
Beston, John B. 'An Interview with Jack Hibberd'. *WLWE*, XV, 1976, 367-72.

Brisbane, Katharine. 'Rewarding Wander off the Beaten Track'. *Australian*, 27 April, 1968, 10.

Butler, Chris. 'Dr. Jack brings New Life to Dame Nellie'. *Advertiser*, 19 January, 1976, 4.

Chisholm, Anne. 'Jack Hibberd Returns with "a theatrical slice of mind"'. *National Times*, 2-8 November, 1980, 38.

Davidson, Jim. 'Jack Hibberd'. *Meanjin*, 37, 1978, 443-455. Interview. Reprinted in his *Sideways from the Page* (Melbourne: Fontana, 1983), 128-45.

Drewe, Robert. 'A Toast to Jack Hibberd'. *Bulletin*, 27 March, 1976, 54.

Duigan, Virginia. 'Jack Hibberd's Myth and Epic now Toasts Dame Nellie'. *National Times*, 5-10 January, 1976, 32.

Fitzpatrick, Peter. 'Jack Hibberd'. In his *After 'The Doll'*. (Melbourne: Edward Arnold, 1979), 129-44.

Gantner, Carillo. 'An Australian Play in China'. *Overland*, No. 110, 1988, 27-35. On the Shanghai production of *A Stretch of the Imagination*.

Hainsworth, John (ed.). *Hibberd*. (North Ryde, N.S.W.: Methuen, 1987). Reviewed by M. Copland, *Age Saturday Review*, 1 October, 1988, 16.

Heinrichs, Paul. 'Dimboola Steps into the Movies'. *Age*, 24 December, 1977, 16.

Hosking, Martin. 'The Coffee Afterwards'. *Island*, 60-61, 1994, 38, 40-43. Reflects on the achievements of the Australian Performing Group with which Hibberd was closely identified in the 1960s and '70s.

Hutchinson, Garrie. 'Two Faces of Melba'. *Theatrescope*, No. 2, 1976, 18-19.

Lochner, Juliane. 'A Conversation with Jack Hibberd'. *Antipodes*, 9.2, 1995, 131-34.

McGillick, Paul. *Jack Hibberd*. (Amsterdam: Rodopi, 1988). Australian Playwrights Monograph Series edited by Ortrun Zuber-Skerritt, 3. Reviewed by P.P. Heckenberg, *ABR*, No. 103, 1988, 8-10; L. Sutton, *CRNLE Reviews Journal*, No. 2, 1989, 54-56.

---. 'Jack Hibberd's Anti-Naturalism'. *Quadrant*, XXIII, No. 3, 1979, 42-47.

Molloy, Susan. 'Hibberd Takes up the Cudgels for Melbourne'. *National Times*, 25 November-1 December, 1983, 35. Interview.

O'Flahertie, Sue. 'Leila and the Car Lovers'. *Daily Telegraph* (Sydney), 15 November, 1972, 36.

Peake, Cathy. 'A Man of Many Parts'. *Theatre Australia*, V, No. 4, 1980, 13.

Perkins, Elizabeth. 'Jack Hibberd - Interview'. *LiNQ*, XI, No. 1, 1983, 5-21.

Pierce, Peter. 'Revaluing Australian Legends: Some Plays by Jack Hibberd'. *A.L.S.*, VIII, 1978, 342-50.

Radic, Leonard. 'Jack Hibberd Rips Open our "Cultural Cocoon"'. *Age*, 10 April, 1976, 18.

Roberts, Alan. 'It's Just what the Doctor Ordered'. *Advertiser*, 30 July, 1977, 26.

Robinson, Ian. 'Melba Lives - Warts, Chewing Gum and All'. *National Times*, 29 March-3 April, 1976, 25.

Shine, Chris. 'Interview with Jack Hibberd'. *Australasian Drama Studies*, No. 10, 1987, 79-90.

Sirmai, Geoff. 'An Interview with Jack Hibberd'. *Southerly*, XLV, No. 3, 1985, 260-265.

Sykes, Alrene. 'Jack Hibberd and the New Wave Drama'. In *Bards, Bohemians, and Bookmen*, edited by Leon Cantrell (St Lucia: U.Q.P., 1976), 305-19.

Sykes, Jill. 'Ordered Chaos in the Life of Jack Hibberd'. *S.M.H.*, 2 July, 1977, 16.

Thomas, Laurie. 'Playwright Who Likes It Here'. *Australian*, 15 June, 1968, 9.

Timlin, John. 'How Pirated *Dimboola* got Everyone a Buck except Jack Hibberd'. *Australian Financial Review*, 22 December, 1978, 10.

Tittensor. John. 'Jack Hibberd and Australian Popular Theatre'. *Commonwealth* (France), 12, No. 1, 1989, 81-86.

Usher, Robin. 'Another Play in the Life of Jack Hibberd'. *Age*, 15 November, 1980, 27.

HIGGINS, BERTRAM

Non-Fiction
'Some Autobiographical Notes: 'Twenties, Oxford and London; Early 'Thirties, Melbourne'. *Quadrant*, XIII, No. 6, 1969, 51-54.

Critical Material
Chisholm, A.R. 'Notes on Bertram Higgins's "Under the Sign of the Fisher"'. *Meanjin*, XXX, 1971, 90-93. Introduction followed by poems.
---. 'The Poetry of Bertram Higgins'. *Quadrant*, XI, No. 4, 1967, 90-92.
---. 'The Poetry of Bertram Higgins'. *Quadrant*, XII, No. 2, 1968, 81-83. Reprint of *Quadrant*, XI, 1967, No. 4, 90-92.

HIGHAM, CHARLES

Poetry
Noonday Country. (Sydney: A.& R., 1966).
Reviewed by J.M. Allen, *Poetry Magazine*, No. 6, 1966, 29-30; B. Beaver, *S.M.H.*, 27 August, 1966, 20; J.J. Bray, *ABR*, V, 1966, 222-3 and see also C. Higham, *ABR*, VI, 1966, 16 and reply by J.J. Bray, VI, 1966, 40; M. Dodsworth, *London Magazine*, VII, No. 1, 1967, 113; D. Douglas, *Age*, 3 December, 1966, 23; R. Dunlop, *Poetry Australia*, No. 14, 1967, 46-47; H.G. Kippax, *S.M.H.*, 27 August, 1966, 20; S.E. Lee, *Southerly*, XXVII, 1967, 63-64; J.McAuley, *Bulletin*, 30 July, 1966, 44; T. I. Moore, *Canberra Times*, 19 November, 1966, 10; B. Nesbitt, *Australian*, 17 December, 1966, 12; J.M. Pearse, *Adelaide Advertiser*, 20 August, 1966, 14.

The Voyage to Brindisi and Other Poems, 1966-1969. (Sydney: A.& R., 1970).
Reviewed by R. Connor, *Poetry Magazine*, XVIII, No. 3, 1970, 40-43; G. Curtis, *Makar*, VI, No. 2, 1970, 35-38; R. Dunlop, *Poetry Australia*, No. 38, 1971, 62; C. Harrison-Ford, *Union Recorder*, L, No. 14, 1970, 12-13; G. Lehmann, *Bulletin*, 10 October, 1970, 57; P. Roberts, *S.M.H.*, 26 September, 1970, 24.

Critical Material
Hall, Sandra. 'The Other Poets'. *Bulletin*, 28 September, 1968, 43-45.

HILL, ERNESTINE

Non-Fiction
Kabbarli: A Personal Memoir of Daisy Bates. (Sydney: A.& R., 1973).
Reviewed by K. England, *Advertiser*, 16 June, 1973, 28; G. Farwell, *S.M.H.*, 30 June, 1973, 26; T. Forshaw, *Australian*, 23 June, 1973, 38; B. McKinlay, *Nation Review*, 29 June-5 July, 1973, 1154.

Critical Material
Dunlevy, Maurice. 'The Writer and Her Country'. *Canberra Times*, 23 August, 1972, 9. Other reports or comments on Ernestine Hill's death, *Age*, 23 August, 1972, 4; *Canberra Times*, 23 August, 1972, 1; *S.M.H.*, 23 August, 1972, 1 & 9.
Moffitt, Ian. 'Tell Only of the Travel...'. *Australian*, 26 August, 1972, 32.
Morris, Meaghan. 'I Don't Really Like Biography'. In *Writing Lives: Feminist Biography and Autobiography*, edited by Susan Magarey, Caroline Guerin, and Paula Hamilton (Adelaide: Australian Feminist Studies, Research Centre for Women's Studies U of Adelaide, 1992 / *Australian Feminist Studies*, 16, 1992, special issue), 13-23. On Hill.
Morrison, John. 'The Diamond 88'. *Realist*, No. 28, 1968, 53-56. Reprinted in his *The Happy Warrior* (Fairfield, Vic.: Pascoe Publishing, 1987), 122-126.
Pohlmeyer, G. 'Ernestine Hill'. *North*, No. 3, 1966, 19-20.

HOPE, A.D.

Drama

Ladies From the Sea: A Play in Three Acts. (Carlton, Vic.: M.U.P., 1987).
Reviewed by M. Armstrong, *Quadrant*, XXXII, No. 10, 1988, 59-60; A.P. Riemer, *S.M.H.*, 14 May, 1988, 73.

The Tragical History of Doctor Faustus. By Christopher Marlowe; purged and amended by A.D. Hope. (Canberra: Australian National University Press, 1982).
Reviewed by R. Elliott, *Canberra Times*, 7 August, 1982, 16; E. Jones, *ABR*, No. 60, 1984, 34-35.

Poetry

A.D. Hope. With an introduction by the author. (Sydney: A.& R, 1963).
Reviewed by R.F. Brissenden, *A.L.S.*, I, No. 4, 1964, 283-6.

A.D. Hope Reads from His Own Work. (St Lucia: U.Q.P., 1972). Poets on Record, 8. Record and booklet. Booklet includes notes by the author and selected bibliography.
Reviewed by M. Duwell, *Makar*, VIII, No. 2, 1972, 47-48; *New Poetry*, XX, No. 4, 1972, 49.

The Age of Reason. (Carlton, Vic.: M.U.P., 1985).
Reviewed by B. Beaver, *Weekend Australian*, 8-9 June, 1985, 14; M. Dunlevy, *Canberra Times*, 18 May, 1985, 14; J. Leonard, *Meanjin*, XLIV, No. 3, 1985, 413-419; P. Neilsen, *Overland*, No. 100, 1985, 93-94; P. Porter, *ABR*, No. 75, 1985, 30-31; J. Rodriguez, *S.M.H.*, 3 August, 1985, 46.

Antechinus: Poems 1975-1980. (Sydney: A.& R., 1981).
Reviewed by D. Brooks, *Westerly*, XXVII, No. 4, 1982, 127-28; M. Dunlevy, *Canberra Times*, 20 February, 1982, 12; G. Dutton, *Bulletin*, 4 May, 1982, 68 & 71-72; M. Heyward, *Age Saturday Extra*, 1 October, 1982, 13; E. Jones, *ABR*, No. 53, 1983, 26-27; R. Pybus, *Meanjin*, XLII, 1983, 253-56.

A Book of Answers. (Sydney: A.& R., 1978).
Reviewed by K. Goodwin, *Weekend Australian Magazine*, 1-2 July, 1978, 9; H.P. Heseltine, *Meanjin*, XXXVIII, 1979, 117-19; P. Martin, *ABR*, No. 3, 1978, 5-6; D. Stewart, *S.M.H.*, 20 May, 1978, 19.

Collected Poems 1930-1965. (Sydney: A.& R.; New York: Viking Press, 1966). With a Preface.
Reviewed by M. Baldwin, *Books and Bookmen*, XII, No. 3, 1966, 51-2; R.F. Brissenden, *Comment*, June, 1966, 19-20; L. Cantrell, *Poetry Australia*, No. 13, 1966, 32-7; L.J. Clancy, *Nation*, 30 April, 1966, 22-3; E.A.M. Colman, *Poetry Magazine*, No. 3, 1966, 26-30 and *Poetry Magazine*, No. 1, 1967, 3; G. Cross, *S.M.H.*, 26 February, 1966, 19; D. Douglas, *Age*, 18 June, 1966, 23; M. Dunlevy, *Canberra Times*, 19 March, 1966, 11 and *Canberra Times*, 31 December, 1966, 10; R. Fuller, *Meanjin*, XXV, 1966, 224-6; H. Gregory, *New York Times Book Review*, 5 February, 1967, 2; D. Hine, *Poetry*, CXIII, 1968, 47-52; D. Kalstone, *Partisan Review*, XXXIV, 1967, 619-22; P. Martin, *Twentieth Century*, XXI, 1966, 178-82; S.F. Morse, *Contemporary Literature*, IX, 1968, 114-15; V. Smith, *Bulletin*, 12 March, 1966, 44-5; A. Taylor, *Overland*, No. 35, 1966, 55-6; *T.L.S.*, 18 August, 1966, 744; G.A. Wilkes, *Southerly*, XXVI, 1966, 214.

Collected Poems, 1930-1970. First paperback edition (Sydney: A.& R., 1972). This edition introduced by Leonie Kramer.
Reviewed by C. Harrison-Ford, *Sunday Australian*, 16 April, 1972, 24.

The Drifting Continent. Illustrated by Arthur Boyd. (Canberra: Brindabella Press, 1979).
Reviewed by D. Stewart, *S.M.H.*, 18 August, 1979, 17.

Dunciad Minor: An Heroick Poem. (Carlton: M.U.P., 1970).
Reviewed by L. Cantrell, *Makar*, VII, No. 1, 1971, 33-35; M. Dunlevy, *Canberra Times*, 14 November, 1970, 14 and *Hemisphere*, XV, No. 3, 1971, 38-39; D. Green, *Meanjin*, XXIX, 1970, 424-29; S.E. Lee, XXXI, 1971, 239-40; R. Lindsay, *Chauntecleer*, No. 4, 1971, 73-80; C. McIntosh, *Philological Quarterly*, LI, 1972, 745-46; A.A. Phillips, *Bulletin*, 5 December, 1970, 54-55; E. Riddell, *Australian*, 7 November, 1970, 18; P. Roberts, *S.M.H.*, 5 December, 1970, 24; T.W. Shapcott, *ABR*, X, 1970/71, 44; R.A. Simpson, *Age*, 5 December, 1970, 17.

A Late Picking: Poems 1965-1974. (Sydney: A.& R., 1975).
Reviewed by R. Gray, *S.M.H.*, 24 January, 1976, 17; J. Griffin, *Advertiser*, 13 March, 1976, 24; E. Jones, *Age*, 14 February, 1976, 18; D. Kirby, *T.L.S.*, 7 April, 1978, 394; D. Malouf, *Nation Review*, 31 October-6 November, 1975, 74-75; L. Murray, *National Times*, 12-17 April, 1976, 23-24; M. O'Connor, *Canberra Poetry*, 1976, 64-66, 69-71; G. Page, *Canberra Times*, 9 January, 1976, 6; P. Porter, *Observer* (London), 7 May, 1978, 33; F. Zwicky, *Westerly*, No. 2, 1977, 86-89.

New Poems, 1965-1969. (Sydney: A.& R., 1969).
Reviewed by K.O. Arvidson, *Australian University*, X, 1973, 187-89; R. Dunlop, *Poetry Australia*, No. 32, 1970, 56-57; J.H., *Harper's Magazine*, CCXLI, 1970, 109; D. Hoffman, *New York Times Book Review*, 2 February, 1971, 7, 28; J.W. Hughes, *Saturday Review*, 8 August, 1970, 34; E. Jones, *Nation*, 25 July, 1970, 23-24; F. Kellaway, *Overland*, No. 46, 1970/71, 38; G. Lehmann, *Bulletin*, 10 January, 1970, 38-39; A. Riddell, *S.M.H.*, 22 November, 1969, 16; R.A. Simpson, *Age*, 28 February, 1970, 13; V. Smith, *Poetry Magazine*, XVIII, No. 4, 1970, 39-40; P. Ward, *ABR*, IX, 1970, 127-28; [C. James], *T.L.S.*, 23 July, 1970, 832; E. Webb, *Journal of Commonwealth Literature*, VI, No. 2, 1971, 148-51. See also K. Slessor, *Daily Telegraph* (Sydney), 27 June, 1970, 14.

Orpheus. (North Ryde, NSW: A.& R., 1991).
Reviewed by D. Brooks, *ABR*, 137, 1991, 13-14, *Redoubt*, 13, 1992, 75-80; M. Duwell, *Weekend Australian*, 23-24 November, 1991, Review 7; D. Fahey, *Southerly*, 52.1, 1992, 140-48; M. Flanagan, *Age*, 24 August, 1991, Saturday Extra 6; K. Hart, *Voices*, 1.4, 1991, 109-12; J. Owen, *Quadrant*, 35.12, 1991, 86-88.

Selected Poems. (Sydney: A.& R., 1973). Preface by the author. This selection differs from that in the Australian Poets series (1963).

Selected Poems. Chosen and introduced by Ruth Morse. (Manchester: Carcanet, 1986).
Reviewed by N. Corcoran, *T.L.S.*, 22 August, 1986, 919; M. Hulse, *PN Review*, XIII, No. 4, 1987, 62-64; B. Morrison, *London Review of Books*, VIII, No. 20, 1987, 11; A. Pollard, *British Book News*, July, 1986, 429.

Selected Poems. Edited with an Introduction by David Brooks. (Pymble, NSW: A.& R., 1992).
Reviewed by L. Kramer, *Literature and Aesthetics*, 3, 1993, 117-20; C. Wallace-Crabbe, *Age*, 13 March, 1993, Saturday Extra 8.

Tre Volti Dell'Amore. Translated [into Italian] by Giovanni Distefano. (Venice: Edizioni Helvetia, 1983). Reviewed by D. Malouf, *S.M.H.*, 12 November, 1983, 40.

Non-Fiction

The Cave and the Spring. (Adelaide: Rigby, 1965). Includes discussion of critical views of Hope's 'Imperial Adam'.
Reviewed by D. Hoffman, *New York Times Book Review*, 2 February, 1971, 7, 28; C. Wallace-Crabbe, *Books Abroad*, XV, 1966, 469-70 and *Meanjin*, XXV, 1966, 15-19.

Chance Encounters. With a Memoir by Peter Ryan. (Carlton: Melbourne UP, 1992).
Reviewed by E. Campion, *Bulletin*, 30 June, 1992, 93; L. Clancy, *Age*, 11 July,

1992, Saturday Extra 7; R. Darling, *Antipodes*, 7.1, 1993, 59-60; K. Hart, *ABR*, 142, 1992, 21-22; C. Wallace-Crabbe, *Weekend Australian*, 18-19 July, 1992, Review 7. Introduction by P. Ryan reprinted in *Quadrant*, 36.7-8, 1992, 30-40.

The Literary Influence of Academies, the Annual Lecture Delivered to Australian Academy of the Humanities at its First Annual General Meeting at Canberra on 19 May 1970. (Sydney: Sydney University Press for the Australian Academy of the Humanities, 1970). Also published in *Australian Academy of the Humanities, Proceedings, 1970*.
Reviewed by L. Cantrell, *Makar*, VII, No. 4, 1971, 46-47.

A Midsummer Eve's Dream: Variations on a Theme by William Dunbar. (Canberra: Australian National University Press, 1970).
Reviewed by T.P. Dobson, *Age*, 25 July, 1970, 17; M. Dunlevy, *Canberra Times*, 18 July, 1970, 14; D. Fox, *Notes & Queries*, N.S. XIX, 1972, 31-32; R. Hall, *Australian*, 1 August, 1970, 19; D. Hoffman, *New York Times Book Review*, 2 February, 1971, 7, 28; I.W.A. Jamieson, *Historical Studies*, XIV, 1971, 638-40; A.M. Kinghorn, *Yearbook of English Studies*, II, 1972, 246-47; S. Knight, *Poetry Magazine*, XVIII, No. 6, 1970, 3-9; B. Martin, *Bulletin*, 29 August, 1970, 50; J.D. Pringle, *Quadrant*, XIV, No. 4, 1970, 73-75; C.J. Watson, *Meanjin*, XXIX, 1970, 430-33. J. Wordsworth, *Review of English Studies*, XXII, 1971, 475-76.

Native Companions: Essays and Comments on Australian Literature, 1936-1966. (Sydney: A.& R., 1974). Perspectives in Australian Literature.
Reviewed by M. Dunlevy, *Canberra Times*, 15 November, 1974, 8; J. Waten, *Age*, 26 October, 1974, 18.

The New Cratylus: Notes on the Craft of Poetry. (Melbourne: O.U.P., 1979).
Reviewed by G. Dutton, *Bulletin*, 11 September, 1979, 80-82; K. Goodwin, *Weekend Australian Magazine*, 8-9 September, 1979, 10; H.P. Heseltine, *Overland*, No. 79, 1980, 76-77; E. Jones, *Age*, 14 July, 1979, 20; F. Kellaway, *ABR*, No. 15, 1979, 8-9; B. King, *WLWE*, XIX, 1980, 43-45; D. Malouf, *Meanjin*, XXXIX, 1980, 150-62; P. Pierce, *National Times*, 28 July, 1979, 40; C. Semmler, *S.M.H.*, 6 October, 1979, 19; C.K. Stead, *AUMLA*, No. 53, 1980, 95-98.

The Pack of Autolycus. (Canberra: A.N.U. Press, 1978).
Reviewed by K. Goodwin, *Weekend Australian Magazine*, 26-27 May, 1979, 11; M. Halligan, *Canberra Times*, 7 April, 1979, 16; H.P. Heseltine, *Overland*, No. 79, 1980, 76-77; J. Waten, *Age*, 12 May, 1979, 24.

'Anna Akhmatova's *Secrets of the Craft*'. In *Essays to Honour Nina Christesen: Founder of Russian Studies in Australia*, edited by Judith Armstrong and Rae Slonck (Kew, Vic.: Australia International Press & Publications, 1979), 64-79.

'The Frontiers of Literature'. *Quarterly Journal of the Library of Congress*, XXVII, 1970, 99-103.

'My Debt to Tennyson'. *Educational Magazine*, XXXVI, No. 4, 1979, 13.

'Payments for Poets'. *Australian Author*, I, No. 4, 1969, 7-9.

'Perception and Poetry; or, The New Cratylus'. *Meanjin*, XXVI, 1967, 385-395.

'These Are the Books that Really Matter'. *S.M.H.*, 14 August, 1982, 30.

Critical Material

Hooton, Joy. *A.D. Hope*. (Melbourne: O.U.P., 1979). Australian Bibliographies. Reviewed by L. Cantrell, *A.L.S.*, IX, 1980, 427.

O'Brien, Patricia. *A.D. Hope: A Bibliography*. (Adelaide: Libraries Board of South Australia, 1968). Bibliographies of Australian Writers. Reviewed by L. Cantrell, *A.L.S.*, V, 1971, 87-91.

State Library of South Australia. 'Bibliographies of Australian Writers Supplements. In *Index of Australian Book Reviews*, IV, 1968, 262-267; V, 1969, 247-50, 265-66; VI, 1970, 307-13; VII, 1971, 288-90; VIII, 1972, 239-248; IX, 1973; X, 1974, 155-61; XI, 1975, 205-11.

'A.D. Hope Papers for Library'. *Canberra Times*, 21 July, 1978, 3. Similar reports *S.M.H.*, 21 July, 1978, 3, and *S.M.H.*, 22 July, 1978, 19.

'Announcement of Prize Awards for 1969'. *Poetry*, Chicago, CXV, 1969/70, 133.

'A Rich, Complex Personality'. *S.M.H.*, 5 March, 1966, 14.

'The Stockman's Whip'. *T.L.S.*, 15 January, 1970, 60.

Abraham, Lyndy. 'A.D. Hope and the Poetry of Allusion'. *A.L.S.*, IX, 1979, 167-78.

Argyle, Barry. 'The Poetry of A.D. Hope'. *Journal of Commonwealth Literature*, No. 3, 1967, 87-96.

Baker, Candida. 'A.D. Hope'. In her *Yacker 3* (Sydney: Picador, 1989), 158-180.

Besses, Pierre. 'La Sphere, l'Espace et l'Homonculus: l'Anthithese comme Structure de l'Imaginaire dans "The Cheek" de A.D. Hope (1944-1945)'. *Commonwealth* (Toulouse), IV, 1979-1980, 97-194. In French.

---. 'La Terre et le Soleil: La Femme dans la Poesie Australienne de A.D. Hope (143-1969)'. *Caliban* (Toulouse), XVII, 1980, 169-78. In French.

Bowers, Neil. 'Form as Substance in the Poetry of A.D. Hope'. *Shenendoah*, 44.1, 1994, 68-80.

Brissenden, R.F. 'A.D. Hope's *New Poems*'. *Southerly*, XXX, 1970, 83-96.

---. 'A.D. Hope's "The Double Looking Glass": A Reading'. *A.L.S.*, VI, 1974, 339-51.

---. 'Art and the Academy - The Achievement of A.D. Hope'. In *The Literature of Australia*, edited by Geoffrey Dutton, revised edition (Ringwood, Vic.: Penguin, 1976), 406-26.

---. '"Intellectualised Pornography": "Imperial Adam" and Kenneth Slessor'. *Southerly*, 49, No. 3, 1989, 383-90.

---. 'Talking With Alec Hope and the Art of Conversation'. *Quadrant*, XXXI, No. 9, 1987, 28-30.

Brissenden, R.F. and Brooks, David. Preface to Special Festschrift Issue For A.D. Hope. *Phoenix Review*, Winter,1987, Special Issue, 5.

Brooks, David. 'A.D. Hope: The Oxford Letters'. *Voices*, 5.1, 1995, 90-102.

Brooks, David, ed. *Security of Allusion: Essays in Honour of A.D. Hope*. (Canberra: Phoenix Review/Bistro Editions with Australian National U, Faculty of Arts, 1992). Special issue of *Phoenix Review*. Includes essays by Ann McCulloch, Susan McKernan, Vincent Buckley, Ruth Morse and David Brooks.

Buckley, Vincent. *Poetry and the Sacred*. (London: Chatto & Windus, 1968), 8-9, 11-12.

Chisholm, Anne. 'Something Comes into your Head. . . ' *National Times*, 17-23 May, 1981, 36-37.

Cross, Gustav. 'Australian Poetry in the 'Sixties'. *Poetry Australia*, No. 5, 1965, 33-8.

---. 'The Poetry of A.D. Hope'. In *The Literature of Australia*, edited by Geoffrey Dutton (Adelaide: Penguin Books, 1964), 377-88.

Cross, K.G.W. and Marsh, D.R.C. *Poetry Reading and Understanding*. (Melbourne: F.W. Cheshire, 1966), 217-21. Discusses 'The Death of the Bird'.

Darling, Robert. 'A.D. Hope: The Mythology of the Actual'. In *International Literature in English: Essays on the Major Writers*, edited by Robert L. Ross (New York: Garland, 1991), 647-58.

Deane, Patrick. 'A.D. Hope, T.S. Eliot, and the "Counter-Revolution" in Modern Poetry'. *Australian & New Zealand Studies in Canada*, 5, 1991, 97-114.

Denison, Vera. 'The Vice Age: Parody No. 12'. *Australian*, 17 April, 1971, 18.

Docker, John. 'Sex and Nature in Modern Poetry'. *Arena*, No. 22, 1970, 5-24.

---. 'The Image of Woman in A.D. Hope's Poetry'. In his *Australian Cultural Elites: Intellectual Traditions in Sydney and Melbourne*. (Sydney: A.& R., 1974), 42-58.

Dunlevy, Maurice. 'Time to Write Poetry'. *Canberra Times*, 29 November, 1969, 14.

Elkin, P.K. 'The Lower Slopes'. *Poetry Magazine*, No. 1, 1964, 2-4.

180   A.D. HOPE

Graham, Suzanne. 'Myth and the Poetry of A.D. Hope'. *A.L.S.*, VII, 1975, 130-40.
Green, Dorothy. 'The Chameleon Poet'. *Adult Education* (Melbourne), XII, No. 2, 1967, 6-12.
Harcourt, Bill. 'The Push'. *National Times*, 3-8 February, 1975, 28-31. See also letter to the editor by Donald Horne, *National Times*, 10-15 February, 1975, 2.
Hart, Kevin. *A.D. Hope*. (Melbourne: O.U.P., 1992). Reviewed by D. Coad, *World Literature Today*, 67.3, 1993, 669; P. Coleman, *Weekend Australian*, 9-10 January, 1993, Review 6; P. Craven, *Age*, 12 September, 1992, Saturday Extra 10; R. Darling, *Antipodes*, 8.1, 1994, 85-86; R.P. Deane, *Australian & New Zealand Studies in Canada*, 11, 1994, 113-16; I. Donaldson, *Voices*, 3.1, 1993, 123-25; G. Dutton, *Overland*, 129, 1992, 94-96; B. Gadd, *World Literature Today*, 68.1, 1994, 209; J. Hanrahan, *ABR*, 147, 1992, 25-26; L. Kramer, *Literature and Aesthetics*, 3, 1993, 117-20; S. Lever, *Southerly*, 53.1, 1993, 210-15; R.M., *T.L.S.*, 1 January, 1993, 25; P. Mead, *A.L.S.*, 16.2, 1993, 140-51; P. Pierce, *Quadrant*, 37.11, 1993, 75-77; T. Shapcott, *Voices*, 2.4, 1992, 122-24. An edited extract from the book, '"Among All Those Kangaroos"' published *Overland*, 128, 1992, 59-62.
---. '"Ghosts That Haunt the Heart's Possession": A Tribute to A.D. Hope'. *Southerly*, 52.3, 1992, 45-56.
---. '"To Have Heard the Sirens Sing": Reading A.D. Hope'. *Scripsi*, 7.3, 1992, 43-65.
Hartman, Geoffrey H. 'The Maze of Modernism: Reflections on Louis Macneice, Robert Graves, A.D. Hope, Robert Lowell, and Others'. In his *Beyond Formalism: Literary Essays, 1958 - 1970*. (New Haven, Conn.: Yale University Press, 1970), 258-80.
Heseltine, H.P. 'Paradise Within: A.D. Hope's New Poems'. *Meanjin*, XXIX, 1970, 405-20.
Horne, Donald. *The Education of Young Donald*. (Sydney: A.& R., 1967), 229-234, 327.
James, Clive. 'Australian Poets'. *T.L.S.*, 18 December, 1987, 1403.
Jones, Dorothy. 'A.D. Hope. "Clover Honey"'. In *Australian Poems in Perspective*, edited by P.K. Elkin (St Lucia: U.Q.P., 1978), 101-15.
Kavanagh, Paul and Peter Kuch, eds. *Conversations: Interviews with Australian Writers*. (North Ryde, NSW: Collins/A.& R, 1991). Includes interview with Hope.
Kelly, Frances. 'Hope for Fairies'. *Canberra Times*, 28 July, 1970, 14. Interview.
King, Bruce. 'A.D. Hope and Australian Poetry'. *Sewanee Review*, LXXXVII, 1979, 119-41.
---. 'A.D. Hope: Isolation and Reintegration'. *Literary Half-Yearly*, XX, No. 1, 1979, 28-36.
Kramer, Leonie. 'Judith Wright, Hope, McAuley'. *Literary Criterion* (Mysore), XV, Nos. 3-4, 1980, 83-92.
Krause, Tom. 'Where there's Hope there's Life'. *Weekend Australian Magazine*, 9-10 October, 1982, 11.
Kuch, Peter and Kavanagh, Paul. 'Daytime Thoughts About the Night Shift'. *Southerly*, XLVI, No. 2, 1986, 221-31.
Macainsh, Noel. 'A.D. Hope's Malthusian Muse'. *Quadrant*, XXIX, No. 3, 1985, 58-63.
---. 'Fine Wine and Triumphant Music - A.D. Hope's Poetic'. *Westerly*, XXXI, No. 3, 1986, 25-35.
---. 'The Suburban Aristocrat: A.D. Hope and Classicism'. *Meridian*, IV, No. 1, 1985, 19-30.
Martin, Philip, 'A.D. Hope, Nonconformist'. *Journal of Popular Culture*, 23, No. 2, 1989, 47-53.
Mathur, Malati. 'A. D. Hope's "Ulysses" and Kate Llewllyn's "Penelope": Two Modern Voices from the Past'. *The Commonwealth Review*, 2.1-2, 1990-91, 86-95.

---. 'The Music Motif in A.D. Hope's Poetry'. *Literary Criterion*, 30.1&2, 1995, 81-96.

McAuley, James. 'Memoirs and Memories'. *Quadrant*, XX, No. 4, 1976, 8-10.

McGregor, Craig (ed.). *In the Making*. (Melbourne: Nelson Australia, 1969), 229-35.

McKernan, Susan. 'Uncommitted Modern Man: A.D. Hope'. In her *A Question of Commitment: Australian Literature in the Twenty Years after the War*. (Sydney: Allen and Unwin, 1989), 96-119.

Maver, Igor. 'An Antipodean Byron? A.D. Hope's Affiliations with Lord Byron's Poetry'. *Commonwealth*, 15.2, 1992, 97-105.

---. 'The Discreet Charm of *Dunciad Minor*: The Cases of A.D. Hope and Alexander Pope'. In *Commonwealth Literary Cultures: New Voices, New Approaches*, edited by Giovanna Capone, Claudio Gorlier, and Bernard Hickey (Lecce: Edizioni del Grifo, 1993), 201-14.

Mezger, Ross. 'Alienation and Prophecy: The Grotesque in the Poetry of A.D. Hope'. *Southerly*, XXXVI, 1976, 268-83.

Millar, Daniel. 'The Poetry of A.D. Hope'. *Review of English Literature*, XV, No. 4, 1964, 29-38.

Moore, Susan. 'A.D. Hope's "Three Faces of Love"'. *A.L.S.*, X, 1982, 389-91.

Morse, Ruth. 'Editing A.D. Hope'. *A.L.S.*, XII, No. 4, 1986, 499-509.

---. 'The Poetry of A.D. Hope'. *PN Review*, No. 41, 1984, 34-37.

---. 'Security of Allusion: Andre Chenier and the Poetry of A.D. Hope'. *Quadrant*, XXXII, Nos. 1&2, 1988, 101-109.

Nagarajan, S. 'Aspects of the Poetic Thought of A.D. Hope'. *Journal of Commonwealth Literature*, VI, No. 1, 1971, 31-41.

---. 'Some Aspects of the Poetic Thought of A.D. Hope'. In *Studies in Australian and Indian Literature*, edited by C.D. Narasimhaiah and S. Nagarajan (New Delhi: Indian Council for Foreign Relations, 1971), 112-24. Discussion, 125-27.

Narasimhaiah, C.D. 'A.D. Hope: A Poetry of Shocked Sensibility'. *ACLALS Bulletin*, Series 4, No. 4, 1976, 6-15.

---. 'Introduction'. *Literary Criterion* (Mysore), XV, Nos. 3-4, 1980, xiii-xix.

Padgham, S.G. 'Days of A.D. Hope - The Phoenix Review'. *Muse*, No. 66, 1987, 10-11.

Page, Geoff. 'A.D. Hope'. In his *A Reader's Guide To Contemporary Australian Poetry* (St. Lucia: U.Q.P., 1995), 130-132.

Paolucci, Anne and Henry. 'Poet-Critics on the Frontiers of Literature: A.D. Hope, T.S. Eliot, and William Carlos Williams'. *Review of National Literatures*, XI, 1982, 146-91.

Perrine, L. 'A.D. Hope's "Agony Column"'. *Notes on Contemporary Literature*, II, 1972, 2-3.

Pratt, Noel. 'The Gentle Satirist'. *Australian*, 21 March, 1970, 21.

Rexroth, Kenneth. 'What is There to Alienate From?' *Bulletin*, 29 April, 1967, 34. Rexroth's opinion on Hope and Wright: interview with Charles Higham.

Rama, R.P. '[Interview with] Alec Derwent Hope'. *Dialogues with Australian Poets*. (Calcutta: P. Lal/Writers Workshop, 1993). 23-30.

Roper, Sheila L. 'An Exhumation: A.D. Hope's Short Pathology of Imagism'. *Helix*, Nos. 13-14, 1983, 191-94.

Sharma, Anurag. 'A.D. Hope: A Distinct Voice Crying in the Wilderness'. *Journal of Australian Literature*, 1, No. 1, 1990, 66-69.

Smith, Vivian. 'A.D. Hope: Poet of Many Contradictions'. *S.M.H.*, Mid-year study guide, 12 June, 1973, 1.

---. 'Australian Poetry in the '60's: Some Mid-Century Notes'. *Balcony*, No. 4, 1966, 46-51.

---. 'Experiment and Renewal: A Missing Link in Modern Australian Poetry'. *Southerly*, XLVII, No. 1, 1987, 3-18; esp. 7-18.

Somapala, Wijetunga. 'Australia in Poetry'. *Hemisphere*, XII, No. 2, 1968, 8-10.
Souter, Gavin. 'Hope Springs Eternal'. *S.M.H.*, 28 February, 1981, 6.
Taylor, Andrew. 'A. D. Hope: The Double Tongue of Harmony'. *Southern Review*, XVII, 1984, 81-95. Reprinted in his *Reading Australian Poetry* (St Lucia: U.Q.P., 1987), 70-84.
---. 'Poets, Urban and Rural'. *Advertiser*, 22 August, 1978, 22.
Thompson, John. 'Poetry in Australia: A.D. Hope'. *Southerly*, XXVI, 1966, 237-46. Transcript of an interview by John Thompson first telecast in 1965.
Tonetto, Walter. 'A.D. Hope: Between the Demonic and Genius'. *Journal of Australian Literature*, 1, No. 1, 1990, 48-65.
---. *A.D. Hope: Questions of Poetic Strength*. (New Delhi: Indian Society for Commonwealth Studies, 1993). Reviewed by E. Martinez, *Commonwealth Review*, 4.1, 1992-93, 168-71.
Wallace-Crabbe, Chris. 'Three Faces of Hope'. *Meanjin*, XXVI, 1967, 396-407.
---. 'True and False Alike Work by Suggestion: The Poetry of A.D. Hope'. *A.L.S.*, 14, No. 4, 1990, 415-24.
Walsh, William. 'A.D. Hope'. In his *A Manifold Voice: Studies in Commonwealth Literature*. (London: Chatto & Windus, 1970), 125-53.
Webb, E. 'Dualities and Their Resolution in the Poetry of A.D. Hope'. *Southerly*, XXXII, 1972, 210-25.
Wieland, James. 'A.D. Hope's Latter-Day Ulysses: "The End of a Journey" and the Literary Background'. *A.L.S.*, X, 1982, 468-77.
---. *The Ensphering Mind: History, Myth and Fictions in the Poetry of Allen Curnow, Nissim Ezekiel, A.D. Hope, A.M. Klein, Christopher Okigbo, and Derek Walcott*. (Washington D.C.: Three Continents, 1988). Reviewed by B. King, *Ariel*, 20.2, 1989, 84-86.
---. 'Some Recent Australian Writing: Questions of "Meaning"'. *Span*, Nos. 16-17, 1983, 88-113.
Wilkes, G.A. 'The Poetry of A.D. Hope'. *Australian Quarterly*, XXXVI, 1964, 41-51.
Wright, Judith. 'A.D. Hope'. In her *Preoccupations in Australian Poetry*. (Melbourne: O.U.P., 1965), 181-92; and passim.
Zwicky, Fay. 'Another Side of Paradise: A.D. Hope and Judith Wright'. *Southerly*, XLVIII, No. 1, 1988, 3-21.

HOPEGOOD, PETER

Poetry
Snake's-eye View of a Serial Story. (Sydney: Edwards and Shaw, 1964).
Reviewed by D. Hewett, *Overland*, No. 32, 1965, 46-7.

Critical Material
Clarke, Donovan. 'The Poetry of Peter Hopegood'. *Poetry Magazine*, No. 2, 1964, 26-31.

HORNE, DONALD

Fiction
But What If There Are No Pelicans?. (Sydney: A.& R., 1971).
Reviewed by A.R. Chisholm, *Age*, 24 April, 1971, 16; M. Clark, *Bulletin*, 8 May, 1971, 52-53; C. Eagle, *Overland*, No. 49, 1971, 48; S. Edgar, *Canberra Times*, 29 May, 1971, 14; N. Keesing, *Quadrant*, XV, No. 4, 1971, 73-74; B. Kiernan, *Australian*, 1 May, 1971, 20; M. Lemming, *ABR*, X, 1971, 153; B. Oakley, *Sunday Australian*, 9 May, 1971, 31; M. Thomas, *Sunday Review*, 25 April, 1971, 827; M. Vintner, *S.M.H.*, 22 May, 1971, 23.
His Excellency's Pleasure: A Satire. (Melbourne: Nelson, 1977).

Reviewed by D. Pryor, *24 Hours*, II, No. 6, 1977, 53.

The Permit. (Melbourne: Sun Books, 1965).
Reviewed by H.G. Kippax, *S.M.H.*, 6 November, 1965, 19; L. Kramer, *Bulletin*, 13 November, 1965, 53; K. Thomas, *Nation*, 13 November, 1965, 23.

   Non-Fiction
Confessions of a New Boy. (Ringwood, Vic.: Viking, 1985). Second volume of autobiography of which the first is *The Education of Young Donald*.
Reviewed by D. Anderson, *National Times*, 29 November-5 December, 1985, 44; V. Buckley, *Quadrant*, XXX, No. 3, 1986, 76-79; E. Campion, *Bulletin*, 5 November, 1985, 97; J. Hanrahan, *Age Saturday Extra*, 9 November 1985, 13; K. Saunders, *Courier-Mail Magazine: The Great Weekend*, 18 January, 1986, 7.

The Education of Young Donald. (Sydney: A.& R., 1967).
Reviewed by V. Buckley, *Bulletin*, 2 December, 1967, 78-79; C.M.H. Clark, *Overland*, No. 38, 1968, 39-40; A. Hughes, *Dissent*, No. 22, 1968, 49-50; H.G. Kippax, *S.M.H.*, 7 October, 1967, 17; M. Lemming, *ABR*, VII, 1967, 6; B. McPherson, *Canberra Times*, 20 January, 1968, 10; A. Roberts, *Adelaide Advertiser*, 28 October, 1967, 18; J. Waten, *Age*, 4 November, 1967, 23.

Ideas for a Nation. (Sydney: Pan, 1989).
Reviewed by D. Altman, *Weekend Australian*, 2-3 December, 1989, Weekend 12; B. Buckley, *Quadrant*, 34, No. 3, 1990. 74-5; J. Kitson, *ABR*, No. 117, 1989/90, 18-19; S. MacIntyre, *Editions*, 5, No. 1, 1989/90, 25-26.

Portrait of an Optimist. (Ringwood, Vic.: Penguin, 1988).
Reviewed by S. Alomes, *Journal of Australian Studies*, No. 29, 1990, 85-86; M. Cathcard, *ABR*, No. 107, 1988, 14-16.

'Writing *The Education of Young Donald*'. *Quadrant*, XV, No. 2, 1971, 42-46.

   Critical Material
Anderson, Don. 'Portraits of the Artist as a Young Man: *The Education of Young Donald; Unreliable Memoirs*; *The Watcher on the Cast Iron Balcony*'. *Meanjin*, XLII, 1983, 339-48.
Colmer, John. 'Australian Autobiography: A Hole in the Literary Landscape'. *Southerly*, XLV, No. 2, 1985, 165-186.
---. 'Autobiography or Sociography? Donald Horne'. In his *Australian Autobiography: A Personal Quest*. (Melbourne: O.U.P., 1989).
Harris, Susan. 'Five by Five: An Educational Sampling'. [Adelaide] *A.L.S. Working Papers*, I, No. 1, 1975, 54-64.
Rowse, Tim. 'Culture as Myth, Criticism as Irony: The Middle Class Patriotism of Donald Horne'. *Island Magazine*, No. 37, 1988, 12-22.
Thomas, Mark. 'Donald Horne'. In his *Australia in Mind: Thirteen Influential Australian Thinkers*. (Sydney: Hale and Iremonger, 1989), 115-130.

HORNE, RICHARD HENGIST

   Fiction
Memoirs of a London Doll, Written by Herself, Edited by Mrs Fairstar. With an introduction and notes by Margery Fisher. (London: Deutsch; New York: Macmillan, 1967). First published pseudonymously London: Bohn, 1846.
Reviewed by E. Bray, *Canberra Times*, 20 April, 1968, 10; N.L. Magid, *New York Times Book Review*, 24 November, 1968, 44; I. Southall, *Age*, 27 January, 1968, 21.
   Critical Material
Blainey, Ann. *The Farthing Poet: A Biography of Richard Hengist Horne, 1802-84, a Lesser Literary Lion*. (London: Longmans, 1968). Reviewed by M. Dunlevy, *Canberra Times*, 15 June, 1968, 15; B. Elliott, *A.L.S.*, IV, 1969, 85-87; K. England, *Advertiser*, 15 June, 1968, 18; K.J. Fielding, *Meanjin*, XXVIII, 1969, 130-31; N.

Keesing, *Bulletin*, 22 June, 1968, 75-77;S. Murray-Smith, *Historical Studies*, XV, 1971, 190-92.
Elliott, Brian. 'An R.H. Horne Poem on Burke and Wills'. *A.L.S.*, I, No.2, 1963, 122-6.
Paroissien, David. 'Mrs Browning's Influence on and Contributions to *A New Spirit of the Age* (1844)'. *English Language Notes*, VIII, 1971, 274-81.
Sellick, Robert. 'Burke and Wills and the Colonial Hero: Three Poems'. *A.L.S.*, V, 1971, 180-89.
Turnbull, Clive. 'Mulberry Leaves: The Story of Charles Whitehead'. *Australian Lives* (Melbourne: Cheshire, 1965), 1-22.
Walker, Mary Howitt. *Come Wind, Come Weather: A Biography of Alfred Howitt*. (Carlton: M.U.P., 1971).
Walker, R.B. '"Orion" Horne and the Bushranger Daniel Morgan'. *A.L.S.*, XI, 263-65.

HOSPITAL, JANETTE TURNER

Fiction

Borderline. (Sydney: Hodder & Stoughton, 1985; St Lucia: U.Q.P., 1987).
Reviewed by S. Achilles, *Editions*, No. 3, 1989, 9-11; C. Cremen, *Australian Financial Review Magazine*, 3 October, 1986, 14; D. Grant, *ABR* No. 79, 1986, 10-11; J. Hanrahan, *Times on Sunday*, 27 December, 1987, 30; S. Hosking, *CRNLE Reviews Journal*, No. 2, 1985, 37-38; B. Little, *Weekend Australian*, 10-11 August, 1985, Weekend, 15; M. Luke, *Fremantle Arts Review*, 3, No. 4, 1988, 15; P.T. O'Connor, *New York Times Book Review*, 10 May, 1987, 34; C. Thompson, *Scripsi*, 5, No. 2, 1989, 167-75.

Charades. (St Lucia: U.Q.P., 1988; New York: Bantam, 1989).
Reviewed by S. Achilles, *Editions*, 3, 1989, 9-11; E. Barry, *Antipodes*, 3.2, 1989, 147; B. Birskys, *Imago*, 1, No. 1, 1989, 47; L. Clancy, *Age Saturday Extra*, 24 September, 1988, 12; F. Davis, *Fremantle Arts Review*, 3, No. 12, 1988, 14; M. Eldridge, *Weekend Australian*, 1-2 October, 1988, Weekend 9; L. Frost, *ABR*, No. 105, 1988, 32-33; M. Lord, *Overland*, No. 113, 1988, 85-87; M. McClusky, *S.M.H.*, 10 September, 1988, 76; S. McKernan, *Bulletin*, 24 January, 1989, 92-93; N. Stasko, *Phoenix Review*, No. 6, 1990, 116-19; C. Thompson, *Scripsi*, 5, No. 2, 1989, 167-75; G. Turcotte, *Southerly*, 49, No. 1, 1989, 121-23.

Charades. (Virago, 1990). First published St Lucia: U.Q.P., 1988.
Reviewed by U. Holden, *London Magazine*, 30.5/6, Aug.-Sept. 1990, 142-44.

Collected Stories 1970-1995. (St Lucia: U.Q.P., 1995).
Reviewed by G. Cork, *S.M.H.*, 28 Oct., 1995, Spectrum 11A; J. Croft, *Weekend Australian*, 18-19 Nov., 1995, Review 8; L. Frost, *ABR*, 175, 1995, 29-30.

Dislocations. (Toronto: McClelland & Stewart, 1986; St Lucia: U.Q.P., 1987; New York: W.W. Norton, 1990).
Reviewed by S. Achilles, *Editions*, 3, 1989, 9-11; G. Burns, *Age Saturday Extra*, 28 November, 1987, 15; H. Falkner, *Weekend Australian*, 26-27 December, 1987, Weekend 12; R. Groves, *ABR*, No. 97, 1987/88, 10-11; S. Hall, *Bulletin*, 15 December, 1987, 95; J. Hanrahan, *Times on Sunday*, 27 December, 1987, 30; D. Johnson, *S.M.H.*, 14 November, 1987, 90; M.A. Mueller, *Queen's Quarterly*, 94, No. 3, 1987, 692-94; N. Potter, *Antipodes*, 4.2, 1990, 133-35.

Isobars. (St Lucia: U.Q.P., 1990; Baton Rouge: Louisiana State U.P.; Toronto: McClelland and Stewart, 1991).
Reviewed by R. Burgin, *New York Times Book Review*, 29 September, 1991, 18; C. Clutterback, *Southerly*, 51.1, 1991, 159-65; H. Daniel, *S.M.H.*, 18 August, 1990, 75; D. Danvers, *Antipodes*, 5.2, 1991, 148; A. Fremd, *Imago*, 3.1, 1991, 80-81; M. Halligan, *ABR*, No. 123, 1990, 3-4; A. Hussein, *T.L.S.*, 3 July, 1992, 25; P. Kelly,

LiNQ, 19.2, 1992, 176-78; T. Shapcott, *Age*, 1 September, 1990, Saturday Extra 10.
The Ivory Swing. (Toronto: McClelland & Stewart, 1982; London: Hodder & Stoughton, 1983).
Reviewed by F. Manvell, *British Book News*, December, 1983, 776; S. Scobie, *Queen's Quarterly*, 92, No. 1, 1985, 179-82.
The Ivory Swing. (St. Lucia: U.Q.P., 1991). First published Toronto: McClelland & Stewart, 1982.
Reviewed by C. Baker, *SPAN*, 34&35, 1992-93, 392-95; S. Milnes, *CRNLE Reviews Journal*, 1, 1992, 106-08; J. Stephens, *Australian Society*, 10.7, 1991, 43-44; K. Veitch, *S.M.H.*, 27 July, 1991, 39.
The Last Magician. (St Lucia: U.Q.P.; Virago; New York: Holt, 1992). Excerpts published in *Island*, 50, 1992, 48-49.
Reviewed by C. Baker, *SPAN*, 34&35, 1992-93, 392-95; C. Blanche, *Quadrant*, 36.11, 1992, 86-88; V. Brady, *ABR*, 141, 1992, 14-15; L. Clancy, *Age*, 2 May, 1992, Saturday Extra 7; J. Coe, *London Review of Books*, 14.18, 1992, 22; W. Goulston, *Antipodes*, 6.2, 1992, 150-51; E. Hower, *New York Times Book Review*, 13 September, 1992, 15; A. Hussein, *T.L.S.*, 3 July, 1992, 25; E. Liddelow, *Modern Times*, July, 1992, 32; P. Pierce, *Bulletin*, 2 June, 1992, 98; A.P. Riemer, *S.M.H.*, 16 May, 1992, 49; G. Turcotte, *Weekend Australian*, 16-17 May, 1992, Review 7; R. Willbanks, *World Literature Today*, 68.1, 1994, 209-10.
The Tiger in the Tiger Pit. (Toronto: McClelland & Stewart, 1983; Hornsby, N.S.W.: Hodder & Stoughton, 1984).
Reviewed by K. Cummings, *S.M.H.*, 26 May, 1990, 78; N. Jillett, *Age Saturday Extra*, 24 November, 1984, 17; E. Lindsay, *S.M.H.*, 23 March, 1985, 40; R. Macklin, *Weekend Australian*, 29-30 December, 1984, Weekend 12; C. Rooke, *Malahat Review*, 67, 1984, 139; S. Scobie, *Queen's Quarterly*, 92, No. 1, 1985, 179-82.
The Tiger in the Tiger Pit. 1983. (London: Virago, 1991). First published Toronto: McClelland & Stewart, 1983.
Reviewed by A. Bartlett, *CRNLE Reviews Journal*, 1, 1991, 82-86.
Juniper, Alex [pseud.]. *A Very Proper Death*. (Ringwood, Vic.: Penguin, 1990).
Reviewed by R.F. Brissenden, *Voices*, 1.2, 1991, 100-02; R. Wallace-Crabbe, *Weekend Australian*, 16-17 February, 1992, Review 6.

Non-Fiction

'An Expatiation on Expatriation'. *Overland*, No. 114, 1989, 35-39.
'I Feel in Transit. I Don't Belong Anywhere'. *Australian Author*, 17, No. 3, 1985, 3-9. Interview.
'The Interview'. *Weekend Australian. Literary Magazine*, 29-30 March, 1986, 4.
'Janette Turner Hospital on *Dislocations, Borderline*, and *Charades*'. In *Writers in Action: The Writer's Choice Evenings*, edited by Gerry Turcotte (Sydney: Currency Press, 1990), 63-85.
'Letter to a New York Editor'. *Meanjin*, 42, No. 3, 1988, 560-61.

Critical Material

Store, Ron. 'Janette Turner Hospital: A Preliminary Bibliography 1973-1988'. *LiNQ*, 17, No.2, 1990, 148-59.
LiNQ, 17, No. 1, 1990. A special issue on Hospital, containing interviews, articles by Elizabeth Perkins, Sue Lovell, Joan Davis, and reviews.
Baker, Candida. 'Janette Turner Hospital'. In her *Yacker 2: Australian Writers Talk About Their Work* (Sydney: Picador, 1987), 248-278.
Brydon, Diana. 'The Stone's Memory: An interview with Janette Turner Hospital'. *Commonwealth Novel in English*, 4.1, 1991, 14-23.
Clutterbuck, Charlotte. 'A Shared Depository of Wisdom: Connection and

Redemption in *Tiger in the Tiger Pit* and *Possession'*. *Southerly*, 53.2, 1993, 121-29.
Gillett, Sue. '*Charades*: Searching for Father Time: Memory and the Uncertainty Principle'. *New Literatures Review*, 21, 1991, 68-81.
Hamelin, Christine. '"Novelist as Urgent Quester": An Interview with Janette Turner Hospital'. *Australian & New Zealand Studies in Canada*, 9, 1993, 106-11.
Langer, Beryl. 'Interview with Janette Turner Hospital'. *Australian-Canadian Studies*, 9.1&2, 1991, 143-50.
Lovell, Sue. 'The Inheritance of Difference: An Interview with Janette Turner Hospital'. *Imago*, 1, No. 1, 1989, 8-9.
Pearlman, Mickey, ed. *Listen to Their Voices: Twenty Interviews with Women Who Write* (New York; London: W.W. Norton, 1993), 47-58.
Temby, Kate. 'Gender, Power and Postmodernism in *The Last Magician'*. *Westerly*, 40.3, 1995, 47-55.
Zwar, Desmond. 'Boringly Lengthy Interview'. *Australian Author*, 17, No. 4, 1985, 16. Letter to the Editor.

HOWARTH, R.G.

Critical Material
'Prof R.G. Howarth Dies'. *S.M.H.*, 23 January, 1974, 11.
'R.G. Howarth: Two Reminiscences'. *Southerly*, XXXIV, 1974. By W.G. Cassidy and Thelma Herring, pp. 385-97; by Margaret Trist, pp. 397-402.
Howarth, Geoff. 'Guy'. *Southerly*, 49, No. 4, 1989, 649-51. Biographical piece by the author's son.
Keesing, Nancy. 'Professor R.G. Howarth'. *Australian Author*, VI, No. 2, 1974, 41.
McLeod, A.L. 'R.G.H. as Poet and Teacher: A Reminiscence'. *Poetry Australia*, No. 53, 1974, 70-75.
---. 'R.G. Howarth as Poet: Lyricist, Aphorist, Satirist'. *Southerly*, 49, No. 3, 1989, 363-73.
O., H.J. [ie H.J. Oliver]. 'Professor R.G. Howarth'. *Southerly*, XXXIV, 1974, 107-110.

HUME, FERGUS

Fiction
Madame Midas. Introduction by Stephen Knight. (London: Hogarth Press, 1985). First published London: Hansom Cab Pub. Co., 1888.
The Mystery of a Hansom Cab. Introduction by Stephen Knight. (London: Hogarth Press, 1985). First published London: Kemp & Boyce, 1886.
Reviewed by T. Heald, *Books and Bookmen*, No. 363, January 1986, 30-31.

Critical Material
'A Literary Mystery'. *Age*, 30 October, 1965, 21.
[Note on rarity of early elditions.] *Biblionews*, Second series, II, No. 1, 1967, 28. Reprinted from *T.L.S.*, 8 December, 1966.
Dixon, Robert. 'Closing the Can of Worms: Enactments of Justice in *Bleak House*, *The Mystery of a Hansom Cab* and *The Tax Inspector'*. *Westerly*, 37.4, 1992, 37-45.
Fredman, Lionel. 'Follow that Cab'. *Quadrant*, XXI, No. 4, 1977, 63-65.
Irvin, Eric. 'Random Notes and Questions'. *Margin*, No. 22, 1989, 1-3. Contains a note on plays by Hume.
Knight, Stephen. 'The Case of the Missing Genre: In Search of Australian Crime Fiction'. *Southerly*, XLVIII, No. 3, 1988, 235-249.
Ryan, J.S. 'Melbourne's Century Old Mystery - Who Was Fergus Hume?' *Margin*, No. 14, 1985, 17-20.
Sussex, Lucy. 'Madam Midas and Henry Lawson'. *Notes & Furphies*, No. 21, 1988, 18.

HUMPHRIES, BARRY

Fiction

Barry McKenzie Holds His Own: An Original Photoplay. Written in collaboration with Bruce Beresford. (Melbourne: Sun Books, 1974).
Reviewed by J.D. Pringle, *S.M.H.*, 21 December, 1974, 13.

The Barry Humphries Book of Innocent Austral Verse. (Melbourne: Sun Books, 1968).
Reviewed by R. Ward, *ABR*, 7, No. 12, 1968, 218-219.

Bazza Pulls It Off: More Adventures of Barry McKenzie. With drawings by Nicholas Garland (Melbourne: Sun Books, 1971).
Reviewed by J. McAuley, *Sunday Australian*, 12 December, 1971, 29.

The Complete Barry McKenzie. By Barry Humphries and Nicholas Garland. (London: Methuen, 1988; Sydney: Allen & Unwin, 1989).
Reviewed by J. Davidson, *Weekend Australian*, 11-12 February, 1989, Weekend 8; C. Welch, *Spectator*, 12 November, 1988, 35,38.

Dame Edna's Bedside Companion. Crofted by Dame Edna Everage. With forewords by Beverly Nichols, Margaret Drabble and Beryl Bainsbridge. (Sydney: Corgi, 1982).
Reviewed by A. Diffey, *Weekend Australian Magazine*, 6-7 November, 1982, 9.

Dame Edna's Coffee Table Book. (London: Harrop, 1976).
Reviewed by D. Jones, *Listener*, 30 December, 1976, 85.

The Humour of Barry Humphries. Selected by John Allen, illustrated by Barry Humphries (Sydney: Currency Press, 1984).
Reviewed by H. Colebatch, *Quadrant*, 29, No. 6, 1985, 83-84.

The Life and Death of Sandy Stone. Introduced and edited by Colin O'Brien (Sydney: Macmillan, 1990).
Reviewed by K. Daniel, *Australian Bookseller and Publisher*, 70, No. 1009, 1990, 27-8; R. Fitzgerald, *Age Saturday Extra*, 17 November, 1990, 7.

My Gorgeous Life: An Adventure. By Dame Edna Everage, with vignettes by John Richardson (Melbourne: Macmillan, 1989).
Reviewed by M. Carlton, *S.M.H.*, 14 October, 1989, 81; G. Flynn, *Weekend Australian*, 7-8 October, 1989, 9; R. Fitzgerald, *Quadrant*, 34, Nos. 1-2, 1990, 111-112; J. Nieuwenhuizen, *Australian Bookseller and Publisher*, 69, No. 996, 1989, 36; D. Pryor, *Age Saturday Extra*, 21 October, 1989, 11.

A Nice Night's Entertainment: Sketches and Monologues, 1956-1981. Introduced by R.F. Brissenden (Woolahra, N.S.W.: Currency Press; London: Granada, 1981).
Reviewed by P. Blazey, *S.M.H.*, 25 July, 1981, 44; J. Jebb, *Spectator*, 16 January, 1982, 21-22; M. McLeod, *Span*, No. 14, 1982, 20-4; D. Pryor, *Overland*, No. 86, 1981, 63-4; L. Radic, *Age*, 8 August, 1981, 25.

Women in the Background. (Melbourne: Heinemann, 1995).
Reviewed by A. Riemer, *S.M.H.* 18 Nov.: Spectrum 12A; M. Sharkey, *Weekend Australian*, 2-3 Dec., 1995, Review 7; M. Shmith, *Age*, 18 Nov., 1995, Saturday Extra 9.

The Wonderful World of Barry McKenzie. With drawings by Nicholas Garland (Melbourne: Sun Books, 1971).
Reviewed by M. Boddy, *Bulletin*, 6 February, 1971, 50; B. Ellis, *Nation*, 20 February, 1971, 22; R. Murray, *National Times*, 1 March, 1971, 28; S. Sayers, *Age*, 16 January, 1971, 14; M. Thomas, *Sunday Review*, 24 January, 1971, 462-3.

Poetry

Neglected Poems and Other Creatures. (North Ryde, NSW: A.& R., 1991).
Reviewed by D. Haskell, *Voices*, 2.1, 1992, 109-11; E. Jurman, *S.M.H.*, 4 November, 1991, 26; J. Owen, *Quadrant*, 36.12, 1992, 86-88; P. Pierce, *S.M.H.*, 28 December, 1991, 31; M. Ricketson, *Age*, 7 December, 1991, Saturday Extra 8

and *Weekend Australian*, 11-12 January, 1992, Review 4.

Non-Fiction

More Please: An Autobiography. (Ringwood, Vic.: Viking, 1992).
Reviewed by J. Bayley, *London Review of Books*, 14.20, 1992, 23-24; G. Bloom, *Southerly*, 53.1, 1993, 222-25; I. Britain, *Voices*, 3.3, 1993, 112-16; E. Campion, *Bulletin*, 20 October, 1992, 84; P. Coleman, *Weekend Australian*, 3-4 October, 1992, Review 7; J. Davidson, *Editions*, 14, 1992, 6; R. Drewe, *Age*, 3 October, 1992, Saturday Extra 10; S. Hughes, *S.M.H.*, 26 September, 1992, 47; C. Semmler, *Quadrant*, 37.1-2, 1993, 119-20; N. Walker, *T.L.S.*, 27 November, 1992, 11.

Critical Material

Adams, Philip. 'Coming to Terms with Our Larrikins'. In *The Larrikin Streak: Australian Writers Look at the Legend*, edited by Clem Gorman (Sth Melbourne, Vic.: Sun Books, 1990), 121-4.

Armstrong, David Malet. 'Barry Humphries: At *Quadrant*, at 50'. *Quadrant*, 28, No. 5, 1984, 12.

Blackman, Barbara. 'Days of Wine and Roses'. *Quadrant*, 35.1/2, 1991, 100-03.

Coleman, Peter. 'How Dare You Make Us Laugh?'. *Quadrant*, 13, No. 8, 62-8.

---. 'The Mark of Bazza'. *Quadrant*, 33, No. 4, 1989, 60-61.

---. *The Real Barry Humphries*. (London: Robson Books, 1990). Reviewed by G. Flynn, *Weekend Australian*, 2-3 February, 1991, Review 6.

Davidson, Jim. 'The Babe Among the Gladdies Is Perambulating Nicely Thank You'. *Meanjin Quarterly*, 33, 1974, 443-5.

---. 'A Fugitive Art'. *Meanjin*, 45, No. 2, 1986, 149-168.

Hooton, Joy. 'Australian Autobiography and the Question of National Identity: Patrick White, Barry Humphries, and Manning Clark'. *A-B: Auto-Biography Studies*, 9.1, 1994, 43-63.

James, Clive. 'Approximately in the Vicinity of Barry Humphries'. In his *Snakecharmers in Texas: Essays 1980-1987* (London: Jonathan Cape, 1988), 30-44.

Kitson, Jill. 'A Conversation with Barry Humphries on Patrick White'. *Quadrant*, 37.4, 1993, 53-57.

Kramer, Leonie. 'A Tribute'. *Quadrant*, 28, No. 5, 1984, 13.

Lahr, John. *Dame Edna Everage and the Rise of Western Civilisation: Backstage with Barry Humphries*. (London: Bloomsbury, 1991). Reviewed by E. Campion, *Bulletin*, 24 December, 1991, 182; R. Davenport-Hines, *T.L.S.*, 27 December, 1991, 28; J. Davidson, *Australian Society*, 11.1&2, 1992, 24-25, 27; S. Hughes, *Age*, 7 December, 1991, Saturday Extra 8; P. Pierce, *S.M.H.*, 28 December, 1991, 31; M. Ricketson, *Weekend Australian*, 11-12 January, 1992, Review 4; C.K. Stead, *London Review of Books*, 14.2, 1992, 18.

Munster, George. 'Black Thoughts, Bright Laughter'. In *Contemporary Australian Drama: Perspectives Since 1955*, edited by Peter Holloway (Sydney: Currency Press, 1981), 161-66.

Oakley, Barry. 'Barry Humphries' Bestiary'. In *Contemporary Australian Drama: Perspectives Since 1955*, edited by Peter Holloway (Sydney: Currency Press, 1981), 167-169.

Pateshall, Harry. 'The Sins of Barry Humphries, Or the Trouble with Craig McGregor'. *Quadrant*, 27, Nos. 1-2, 1983, 30-34.

HUNGERFORD, T.A.G.

Fiction

Hungerford Short Fiction. Compiled and introduced by Peter Cowan (Fremantle, W.A.: Fremantle Arts Centre Press, 1989).
Reviewed by V. Brady, *Age Saturday Extra*, 9 September, 1989, 11; R.F. Brissenden, *Weekend Australian*, 14-15 October, 1989, Weekend 7; S. Matchett, *ABR*, No. 113, 1989, 44-45.

Non-Fiction
A Knockabout With a Slouch Hat: An Autobiographical Collection 1942-1951.
(Fremantle, W.A.: Fremantle Arts Centre Press, 1985).
Reviewed by L. Clancy, *ABR*, No. 73, 1985, 18-19; D. Grant, *CRNLE Reviews Journal*, No. 2, 1985, 16-18; N. Keesing, *S.M.H.*, 27 July, 1985, 44; S. McKernan, *Canberra Times*, 30 November, 1985, B2; W. Noonan, *Weekend Australian Magazine*, 17-18 August, 1985, 15.

Red Rover All Over: An Autobiographical Collection, 1952-1986. (Fremantle, W.A.: Fremantle Arts Centre Press, 1986).
Reviewed by G. Dutton, *Weekend Australian. Weekend Magazine*, 14 March, 1987, 14-15; S. Sayers, *Age Saturday Extra*, 25 April, 1987, 14.

Stories From Suburban Road: An Autobiographical Collection, 1920-1939.
(Fremantle, W.A.: Fremantle Arts Centre Press, 1983).
Reviewed by D. Buchbinder, *ABR*, No. 64, 1984, 27-28; E. Campion, *Bulletin*, 28 February, 1984, 67, 69; D. Carter, *Age Saturday Extra*, 21 April, 1984, 15; T. Forshaw, *Quadrant*, XXVIII, No. 9, 1984, 81-84; A. Gunter, *Idiom*, XV, No. 2, 1980, 37-38; N. Keesing, *Weekend Australian Magazine*, 11-12 February, 1984, 13; A. Sant, *ABR*, No. 60, 1984, 20-21; M. Wright, *Fremantle Arts Centre Broadsheet*, III, No. 1, 1984, 7.

'I Write Basically Because...'. *A.L.S.*, XII, No. 2, 1985,263-264. Response to a questionnaire on the theme Australian literature and war.
'The Ridge and the River'. *Voices*, 5.4 1995-96, 5-10. Discusses *The Ridge and the River* and his memories of the war in the islands.

Critical Material
Hosking, Rick. 'The Usable Past: Australian War Fiction of the 1950s'. *A.L.S.*, XII, No. 2, 1985, 234-247.
O'Neill, Marnie. 'Interview with T.A.G. Hungerford and notes on his work'. In Hammond, Derryn; O'Neill, Marnie and Reid, Jo-Anne. *Autobiography, the Writer's Story* by Derryn Hammond, Marnie and Reid O'Neill (Fremantle: Fremantle Arts Centre Press, 1988), 33-47.
Sayers, Stuart. 'Miles Franklin's Advice Paid Off'. *Age Saturday Extra*, 13 July, 1985, 16.
Wright, Mary. 'Knocking About'. *Fremantle Arts Centre Broadsheet*, IV, No. 2, 1985, 3-4.

HUXLEY, HENRIETTA
Critical Material
Hadgraft, Cecil. 'Henrietta Huxley'. *Southerly*, XXXII, 1972, 227-32.

IDRIESS, ION

Critical Material

Bonnin, Margriet. 'Ion Idriess: "Rich Australia"'. In *Nellie Melba, Ginger Meggs and Friends: Essays in Australian Cultural History*, edited by Susan Dermody, John Docker and Drusilla Modjeska (Malmsbury, Vic.: Kibble Books, 1982), 234-49.

Casey, Gavin. 'A Handshake for Ion Idriess'. *Meanjin*, XXIII, No. 4, 1964, 348-52.

Eley, Beverley. *Ion Idriess*. (Potts Point, NSW: ETT Imprint, 1995). Reviewed by P. Coleman, *Weekend Australian*, 22-23 July, 1995, Review 7; R. Hall, *ABR*, 173, 1995, 12-13; P. Ryan, *S.M.H.* 5 Aug., 1995, Spectrum 10A.

Ruhen, Olaf. 'Frontiersman with a Pen'. *ABR*, No. 14, 1979, 30-31. Obituary.

INGAMELLS, REX

Non-Fiction

'Conditional Culture'. In *The Writer in Australia*, edited by John Barnes (Melbourne: O.U.P., 1969), 245-65. This essay first published 1938.

Critical Material

Spate, Oskar. 'Quiros and the Poets'. *Overland*, No. 112, 1988, 69-72. Discusses poems by Rex Ingamells, Douglas Stewart and James McAuley.

IRELAND, DAVID

Fiction

Archimedes and the Seagle. (Ringwood, Vic.: Penguin, 1986). First published Ringwood, Vic.: Viking, 1984.

Reviewed by W.R. Cole, *New York Times Book Review*, 3 May, 1987, 44; H. Daniel, *Age Saturday Extra*, 18 August, 1984, 15; G. Dutton, *Bulletin*, 7 August, 1984, 58; K. England, *Advertiser Saturday Review*, 15 September, 1984, 36; T. Forshaw, *Quadrant*, XXIX, Nos. 1-2, 1985, 138-140; T. Glad, *Social Alternatives*, VI, No. 2, 1987, 75; K. Goldsworthy, *Overland*, No. 97, 1984, 76-77; M. Harrison, *Look & Listen*, I, No. 3, 1984, 88; J.D. Pringle, *S.M.H.*, 25 August, 1984, 44; V. Sen, *Canberra Times*, 20 October, 1984, 18; M. Turnbull, *ABR*, No. 65, 1984, 8.

Bloodfather. (Ringwood, Vic.: Viking, 1987).

Reviewed by D. Anderson, *S.M.H.*, 5 December, 1987, 74; G. Dutton, *Weekend Australian. Weekend Magazine*, 12-13 December, 1987, 15; K. Goldsworthy, *Age Saturday Extra*, 23 January, 1988, 12; P. Lewis, *Australian Studies*, No. 3, 1988, 112-15; M.R. Liverani, *Overland*, No. 110, 1988, 70-72; S. McKernan, *Bulletin*, 22 March, 1988, 95-96; L. Nowra, *Times on Sunday*, 13 December, 1987, 32; D.J. O'Hearn, *ABR*, No. 98, 1988, 19; J.S. Ryan, *Span*, No. 29, 1989, 100-104; A. Stewart, *Quadrant*, XXXII, No. 6, 1988, 61-62; A. Wallace, *Social Alternatives*, 8, No. 2, 1989, 70-72.

Burn. (Sydney: A.& R., 1974).

Reviewed by R.F. Brissenden, *Australian*, 31 May, 1975, 27; S. Edgar, *Canberra Times*, 5 September, 1975, 12; K. England, *Advertiser*, 10 May, 1975, 24; V. Ikin,

Southerly, XXXVI, 1976, 112-15; E. Kynaston, *Overland*, No. 63, 1976, 57-58; D.J. O'Hearn, *Age*, 14 June, 1975, 21; K. Tennant, *S.M.H.*, 12 April, 1975, 13; J. Tittensor, *Nation Review*, 2-8 May, 1975, 765.

The Chantic Bird. (Sydney: A.& R., 1968). Reprinted Sydney: A.& R., 1979.
Reviewed by A. Brissenden, *Advertiser*, 24 February, 1968, 20; N. Freehill, *Realist*, No. 30, 1968, 77-78; N. Keesing, *Bulletin*, 6 April, 1968, 73; B. Kiernan, *Australian*, 27 April, 1968, 12; J. McLaren, *ABR*, No. 16, 1979, 16; M. Vinter, *S.M.H.*, 11 May, 1968, 20; M. Wilding, *Southerly*, XXX, 1970, 74.

City of Women. (Ringwood, Vic.: Allen Lane, 1981).
Reviewed by D. Bird, *Westerly*, XXVI, No. 4, 1981, 76-78; H. Daniel, *Overland*, No. 85, 1981, 72-73; K. Gelder, *CRNLE Reviews Journal*, No. 1, 1982, 1-2; K. Goldsworthy, *National Times*, 9-15 August, 1981, 36; M. Halligan, *Canberra Times*, 10 October, 1981, 12; L. Kelly, *Weekend Australian Magazine*, 19-20 September, 1981, 14; J. Legasse, *ABR*, No. 37, 1981, 31-32; M. Morris, *Financial Review*, 7 August, 1981, 31; D.J. O'Hearn, *Age*, 8 August, 1981, 25; J. Palmer, *National Times*, 9-15 August, 1981, 36; E. Riddell, *Bulletin*, 11 August, 1981, 64; M. Roberts, *Island Magazine*, No. 8, 1981, 42-43; A. Stewart, *Quadrant*, XXV, No. 11, 1981, 66-68.

The Flesheaters. (Sydney: A.& R., 1972).
Reviewed by L.J. Clancy, *Age*, 5 August, 1972, 15; J. Hepworth, *Nation Review*, 5-11 August, 1972, 1218; T. Keneally, *S.M.H.*, 15 July, 1972, 21; V. Kepert, *Sun-Herald*, 2 July, 1972, 59; W.L. Marshall, *Sunday Telegraph*, 30 July, 1972, 22; A. Mitchell, *Advertiser*, 22 July, 1972, 18; *National Times*, 2-7 October, 1972, 23; L. Sandercock, *Canberra Times*, 9 December, 1972, 10.

The Glass Canoe. (South Melbourne: Macmillan, 1976).
Reviewed by D.R. Burns, *Nation Review*, 2-8 July, 1977, 937; M. Dunlevy, *Canberra Times*, 29 May, 1976, 9; K. England, *Advertiser*, 24 July, 1976, 20; C.J. Hanna, *Southerly*, XXXVII, 1977, 111-13; C. Harrison-Ford, *Meanjin*, XXXVI, 1977, 246-52; J. Modder, *Courier-Mail*, 7 August, 1976, 17; D.J. O'Hearn, *Age*, 31 July, 1976, 22; M. Poole, *New Statesman*, 28 May, 1982, 25; O. Ruhen, *Overland*, No. 64, 1976, 66-67; D. Stewart, *S.M.H.*, 22 May, 1976, 15.

The Unknown Industrial Prisoner. (Sydney: A.& R., 1971).
Reviewed by H. Brown, *Canberra Times*, 26 February, 1972, 12; D. Crick, *S.M.H.*, 15 January, 1972, 22; J. Hepworth, *Review*, 18-24 December, 1971, 304; B. Kiernan, *Australian*, 20 November, 1971, 19; J. McLaren, *Overland*, Nos. 50-51, 1972, 96; A. Mitchell, *Advertiser*, 13 November, 1971, 18; *National Times*, 8-13 November, 1971, 23; B. Oakley, *Sunday Australian*, 21 November, 1971, 33; C. Tolchard, *Bulletin*, 27 November, 1971, 52-53.

A Woman of the Future. (Harmondsworth: Allen Lane, 1979).
Reviewed by D. Altman, *Nation Review*, November, 1980, 52; D. Bird, *Westerly*, XXV, No. 1, 1980, 102-05; M. Clark, *S.M.H.*, 10 November, 1979, 18; R. Creswell, *ABR*, No. 16, 1979, 4-5; M. Dunlevy, *Canberra Times*, 22 December, 1979, 12; R. Farquhar, *Australian Playboy*, February, 1980, 174; C. Hanna, *Southerly*, XL, 1980, 120-24; V. Ikin, *Quadrant*, XXIV, No. 5, 1980, 68-69; B. Muirden, *Advertiser*, 10 November, 1979, 24; W. Noonan, *Weekend Australian Magazine*, 14-15 June, 1980, 26; D.J. O'Hearn, *Age*, 17 November, 1979, 28; P. Pierce, *Meanjin*, XXXIX, 1980, 267-69; A. Pollard, *CRNLE Reviews Journal*, No. 1, 1980, 38-40; E. Riddell, *Bulletin*, 20 November, 1979, 96-98; J. Rodriguez, *Kunapipi*, II, No. 2, 1980, 159-61 and *24 Hours*, V, No. 1, 1980, 60-61; P. Trundle, *Courier-Mail*, 8 December, 1979, 20.

Non-Fiction
[Statement in reply to a questionnaire on his fiction]. *A.L.S.*, VIII, 1977, 192-93.

Critical Material

'The Ellicott Papers, the Vetoing of the *Unknown Prisoner*'. *Cinema Papers*, No. 16, 1978, 18-19, 81.

'The Unknowable David Ireland'. *ABR*, 136, 1991, 4-14. Special feature on the work of David Ireland, with contributions by R. Sorensen, A. Peek, K. Gelder, F. Capp, M. Sorensen and N. Turnbull.

Antonini, Maria. 'Gli "Alienati" di David Ireland'. *Spicilegio Moderno* (Bologna), No. 8, 1977, 197-202.

Burns, D.R. 'Filthy Fable as Visionary Monster Novel: The Definitive Role of David Ireland's *A Woman of the Future*'. *Overland*, No. 121, 1990, 15-20.

Cantrell, Leon. 'The New Novel: David Ireland's *The Unknown Industrial Prisoner*, Michael Wilding's *The Short Story Embassy*, and Frank Moorhouse's *The Electrical Experience*'. In *Studies in the Recent Australian Novel*, edited by K.G. Hamilton (St Lucia: U.Q.P., 1978), 225-57.

Chance, Ian. 'Interview: David Ireland'. *Words and Visions*, No. 12, 1983, 6-7.

Chisholm, Anne. 'Ireland Pattern'. *National Times*, 31 January-6 February, 1982, 34.

Dale, Brian. 'David Ireland is a Sponge Absorbing People, Words and Events for New Masterpieces'. *National Times*, 1-6 January, 1973, 14.

Daniel, H.E. 'Ways of Resistance in David Ireland's *The Unknown Industrial Prisoner*'. *Westerly*, No. 2, 1977, 59-66.

Daniel, Helen. *Double Agent*. (Ringwood, Vic.: Penguin, 1982). Reviewed by R. Blaber, *CRNLE Reviews Journal*, No. 1, 1983, 8-9; L. Clancy, *Age Saturday Extra*, 13 November, 1982, 12; K. Gelder, *A.L.S.*, XI, 1983, 139-41; F. McInherny, *ABR*, No. 54, 1983, 28-29; S. McKernan, *Canberra Times*, 22 January, 1983, 15; X. Pons, *Meridian*, II, 1983, 188-89.

---. *Liars: Australian New Novelists*. (Ringwood, Vic.: Penguin, 1988), 111-137.

---. 'Disconnecting Reality'. *Age Monthly Review*, II, No. 2, 1982, 11-12. About *The Chantic Bird*; *The Unknown Industrial Prisoner*; *The Flesheaters*; *The Glass Canoe*; *A Woman of the Future*; *City of Women*.

---. 'Mosaic of Change'. *Overland*, No. 80, 1980, 45-47.

---. 'Observer and Accomplice: the Narrator in Ireland's *The Flesheaters*'. *Westerly*, No. 3, 1977, 39-46.

---. 'Purpose and the Racial Outsider: *Burn* and *The Chant of Jimmie Blacksmith*'. *Southerly*, XXXVIII, 1978, 25-43.

---. 'Recoil from Disorder: David Ireland's *The Chantic Bird*'. *A.L.S.*, VIII, 1978, 471-84.

Elkin, P.K. 'David Ireland: A Male Metropolis'. In *Who is She?*, edited by Shirley Walker (St Lucia: U.Q.P., 1983), 163-77.

Fabre, Michel. 'Words and Writing in the Novels of David Ireland'. *Commonwealth Essays and Studies* (Paris), VI, No. 1, 1983, 107-24.

---. 'Writing as Meta-Fiction in David Ireland's *The Flesheaters*'. In *Australian Papers: Yugoslavia, Europe and Australia*, edited by Mirko Jurak (Ljubljana: Edward Cardelj University, 1983), 159-66.

Field, Michele. 'David Ireland Sees Inside Women's Heads'. *S.M.H.*, 25 July, 1981, 47.

Gelder, Ken. *Atomic Fiction: The Novels of David Ireland*. (St Lucia: U.Q.P., 1993). Reviewed by N. Birns, *Antipodes*, 7.2, 1993, 167-68; C. Bliss, *World Literature Today*, 68.2, 1994, 423-24; C. Colebrook, *SPAN*, 37, 1993 242-43; E. Lindsay, *ABR*, 155, 1993, 20-21; P. Pierce, *A.L.S.*, 16.3, 1994, 352-55.

---. 'David Ireland's Novels: Australia, Community and the "Illegality" of Fiction'. *Journal of Narrative Technique*, 21.1, 1991, 32-42.

---. 'David Ireland's *Prisoner* and *The Flesheaters*'. *A.L.S.*, IX, 1980, 535-38.

---. '"Trans-what?" Sexuality and the Phallus in *A Dutiful Daughter* and *The Flesheaters*'. *Southerly*, 49, No. 1, 1989, 3-15.

Grenville, Kate, and Sue Woolfe. *Making Stories: How Ten Australian Novels Were Written*. (St Leonards, NSW: Allen & Unwin, 1993). Includes contribution on *A Woman of the Future*.

Gunew, Sneja. 'What Does Woman Mean? Reading, Writing and Reproduction'. *Hecate*, IX, 1983, 111-22.

Hall, Sandra. 'Male Writer Enters the Female Mind'. *Bulletin*, 10 June, 1980, 68.

Hastwell, Rosalie. 'The Chantic Bird Motif'. *Adelaide A.L.S. Working Papers*, III, 1979, 29-33.

Hawley, Janet. 'Ireland's Lonely Journey'. *Age*, 10 November, 1979, 23.

Hay, Sheridan. 'An Interview with David Ireland'. *Science Fiction* (Perth, W.A.), III, No. 3, 1981, 110-16.

Herk, Aritha van. 'CrowB(e)ars and Kangaroos of the Future: the Post-Colonial Ga(s)p'. *WLWE*, 30.2, 1990, 42-54. Discusses *A Woman of the Future* and D.H. Lawrence's *Kangaroo*.

Hicks, Ian. 'Battle Rages Over *Woman of the Future*'. *S.M.H.*, 7 June, 1980, 2. For reports of the Miles Franklin Award see e.g. *Age*, 3 June, 1980, 11; *Courier-Mail*, 4 June, 1980, 5. Other reports of the controversy e.g. *Courier-Mail*, 6 June, 1980, 2. See also 'N.B.C. Book Awards, 1980', *ABR*, No. 25, 1980, 24.

Jones, Margaret. 'Novel with Political Theme Wins [Miles Franklin Award]'. *S.M.H.*, 29 March, 1972, 8.

Littlemore, Stuart. '"The Writer has Got me. I've no Other Life. The Program is Writing me now"'. *National Times*, 3-8 May, 1976, 22.

Macleod, Mark. 'David Ireland'. *Kunapipi*, III, No. 1, 1981, 64-75. Interview.

Mitchell, Adrian. 'Paradigms of Purpose: David Ireland's Fiction'. *Meanjin*, XXXIV, 1975, 189-97.

Moorhouse, Frank. 'Asylums and Prisons'. *Bulletin*, 22 July, 1972, 50.

Partridge, Colin. 'Butterflies Flew Free: David Ireland's Australia'. *True North/Down Under* (Lantzville, British Columbia), No. 2, 1984, 75-86.

Pons, Xavier. 'The Dead Heart of Australia'. *Overland*, No. 80, 1980, 38-44.

---. 'Paranoia as a Way of Life'. *Quadrant*, XXVI, Nos. 1-2, 1982, 96-103. Discusses *The Chantic Bird* and *The Unknown Industrial Prisoner*.

Salzman, Paul. 'Working the Self: Issues of Form and Gender in Australian Fiction'. *Meanjin*, XLVI, No. 4, 1987, 513-524.

Sayers, Stuart. 'Only the Work Counts with David Ireland'. *Age*, 27 October, 1973, 15. Reprinted in *Advertiser*, 17 November, 1973 23.

---. 'A Title Sought and Found its Book'. *Age*, 12 June, 1976, 18.

Stewart, Annette M. 'Recent Australian Fiction'. *WLWE*, XXII, 1983, 212-23. Discusses *City of Women*.

Stewart, Douglas. 'David Ireland: An Under-Rated, Unpredictable Author in Progress'. *National Times*, 3-8 May, 1976, 21.

JAMES, BRIAN

Fiction

The Big Burn: Short Stories. (Sydney: A.& R., 1965). Selected and with an Introduction by Norman Lindsay.
Reviewed by M. Dunlevy, *Canberra Times*, 2 April, 1966, 11; K. Tennant, *S.M.H.*, 19 March, 1966, 15.

Critical Material

Tierney, Alan J.H. *Brian James: A Checklist, 1942-1971*. (Castle Hill, N.S.W.: the author, 1973).

Concannon, John. 'Mostly about Brian James'. *North*, No. 2, 1966, 9-10.
Martin, Gary. 'An Insight into Brian James'. *Westlife*, I, No. 3, 1972, 13-14.
Semmler, Clement. *The Art of Brian James and Other Essays on Australian Literature*. (St Lucia: U.Q.P., 1972).
Turner, Ian. 'Bunyip's Not Always a Joke'. In *An Overland Muster*, edited by Stephen Murray-Smith (Brisbane: Jacaranda Press, 1965), 47-50. Originally published *Overland*, No. 10, 1957, 33-34.

JAMES, JOHN STANLEY

Non-Fiction

The Vagabond Papers. Edited and with an introduction by Michael Cannon. (Carlton: M.U.P., 1969). Abridged from the first editions of 1877-78 published Melbourne: G. Robertson.
Reviewed by G. Hawkins, *Australian*, 25 October, 1969, 23; L.T. Hergenhan, *A.L.S.*, IV, 1970, 307-09; N. Keesing, *Bulletin*, 15 November, 1969, 61-62; S. Lawson, *Nation*, 20 September, 1969, 22-23; S. Murray-Smith, *ABR*, IX, 1969, 24-25; B.R. Penny, *Canberra Times*, 25 October, 1969, 17; C. Turnbull, *Age*, 20 September, 1969, 14.

Critical Material

Anderson, Hugh. 'Vagabond Journalist'. *Walkabout*, XXXIV, No. 2, 1968, 16-19.
Irvin, Eric. '"The Vagabond" as Playwright'. *Southerly*, XLI, 1981, 106-20.
Prout, Denton, and Feely, Fred. *50 Years Hard*. (Adelaide: Rigby, 1967), esp. 196-203. James worked in Pentridge to gather material for articles on penology.

JOHNSON, COLIN

See under Mudrooroo. (In 1988 as a Bicentennial Project Colin Johnson changed his name to Mudrooroo Nyoongah and later to Mudrooroo Narogin.)

JOHNSTON, GEORGE

Fiction

A Cartload of Clay. Preface by John Douglas Pringle. (Sydney: Collins, 1971).
Reviewed by C. Harrison-Ford, *Nation*, 22 January, 1972, 21-22; B. Jefferis, *S.M.H.*, 9 October, 1971, 18; N. Keesing, *Bulletin*, 23 October, 1971, 62-63; B. Kiernan, *Australian*, 16 October, 1971, 18; J. Lleonart, *Canberra Times*, 16 October, 1971, 15;

S.M.H., 9 October, 1971, 18; N. Keesing, *Bulletin*, 23 October, 1971, 62-63; B. Kiernan, *Australian*, 16 October, 1971, 18; J. Lleonart, *Canberra Times*, 16 October, 1971, 15; J. McLaren, *Overland*, Nos. 50-51, 1972, 97; A. Mitchell, *Advertiser*, 16 October, 1971, 20; J. Moses, *Sunday Australian*, 2 January, 1972, 15.

Clean Straw for Nothing. (London, Sydney: Collins, 1969).
Reviewed by L. Cantrell, *Meanjin*, XXX, 1971, 139; E. Castle, *Overland*, No. 43, 1969, 53-54; S. Hall, *Bulletin*, 23 August, 1969, 56; I. Hicks, *Canberra Times*, 23 August, 1969, 13; B. Kiernan, *Australian*, 16 August, 1969, 20; H.G. Kippax, *S.M.H.*, 23 August, 1969, 18; C. Semmler, *ABR*, VIII, 1969, 246; O. Webster, *Age*, 23 August, 1969, 10 and *Southerly*, XXIX, 1969, 315-17.

The Far Road. (Sydney: Fontana Collins, 1987). First published London: Collins, 1962.
Reviewed by R. Lucas, *S.M.H.*, 13 June, 1987, 48.

With Charmian Clift. *High Valley*. Afterword by Nadia Wheatley. (North Ryde, N.S.W., 1990).
Reviewed by P. Nelson, *Canberra Times*, 10 June, 1990, 18; V. Sen, *Weekend Australian*, 23-24 June, 1990, Review 10.

The Meredith Trilogy. Introduction by Garry Kinnane (Sydney: Collins, 1988). Comprises *My Brother Jack* (1964), *Clean Straw for Nothing* (1969) and *A Cartload of Clay* (1971).

My Brother Jack. (Sydney: Collins, 1964). Reprinted with introduction by Brian Matthews, North Ryde, N.S.W.: A.& R., 1990.
Reviewed by H.P. Heseltine, *Meanjin*, XXIII, No. 2, 1964, 220-2; F.H. Mares, *Southerly*, XXIV, No. 4, 1964, 244-7; A. Marshall, *ABR*, III, 1964, 95; J. McLaren, *Overland*, No. 30, 1964, 55; K. Thomas, *Nation*, 4 April, 1964, 20.

With Charmian Clift. *Strong Man from Piraeus and Other Stories*. Chosen and introduced by Garry Kinnane. (Melbourne: Thomas Nelson, 1984).
Reviewed by C. Castan, *Social Alternatives*, V, No. 4, 1986, 58; P. Corris, *National Times*, 6-12 April, 1984, 33; H. Daniel, *Age Saturday Extra*, 19 May, 1984, 17; B. Farmer, *ABR*, No. 62, 1984, 15-16; K. Gelder, *CRNLE Reviews Journal*, No. 2, 1985, 43-46; M. Halligan, *Canberra Times*, 23 June, 1984, 16; B. Little, *Weekend Australia*, 28-29 April, 1984, 13; R. Lucas, *S.M.H.*, 28 April, 1984, 40; P. Rolfe, *Bulletin*, 8 May, 1984, 82-83.

   Non-Fiction
War Diary 1942. (Sydney: Collins, 1984).
Reviewed by I. Champion, *Canberra Times*, 6 June, 1985, 22; M. Kennedy, *ABR*, No. 71, 1985, 10 12; P. Ryan, *Age Saturday Extra*, 6 July, 1985, 13.

'ANZAC... A Myth For All Mankind'. *Educational Gazette*, LX, 1966, 71-5. Contains autobiographical comment.
'As Myths Fade - We Need an Identity'. *Walkabout*, XXXVI, No. 2, 1970, 5-8. Some autobiographical content.
Introduction, *The World of Charmian Clift*. (Sydney: Ure Smith, 1970).
'Why Buy Books?'. *ABR*, VIII, 1969, 241.

   Critical Material
'Author Leaves Family $39,999'. *Australian*, 4 November, 1970, 5. Similar report in *Canberra Times*, 4 November, 1970, 11.
'Coming Late Into the Light - Our Brother George and the Johnston Story as Recent Australian History'. *Westerly*, XXXII, No. 1, 1987, 21-42.
'Writer Wins Second Franklin Award'. *S.M.H.*, 15 April, 1970, 5.
Ashbolt, Allan. 'George Johnston: Man of Artistic Toughness'. *S.M.H.*, 23 July, 1970, 8. See also report on p. 1.
Clift, Charmian. *Peel Me a Lotus*. (Sydney, London: Collins Australia, 1969). First

published London: Hutchinson, 1959. Contains material on Johnston's family life in Greece.
---. 'My Husband George'. *Pol*, No. 9, 1969, 83-85.
Colmer, John. 'Australian Autobiography: A Hole in the Literary Landscape'. *Southerly*, XLV, No. 2, 1985, 165-186.
---. 'Autobiography and Fiction: George Johnston's Meredith Trilogy'. In his *Australian Autobiography: A Personal Quest* (Melbourne: O.U.P., 1989), 32-49.
Cunningham, James. 'George Johnston'. *S.M.H.*, 28 August, 1965, 14.
Dunlevy, Maurice. 'George Johnston'. *Canberra Times*, 23 July, 1970, 20.
Eagle, Chester. 'George's Brother Jack'. *Helix*, Nos. 11-12, 1982, 154-69.
---. 'Myth, Mockery and Expatriation - Love/Hate of Australia in George Johnston's *My Brother Jack*'. *Commonwealth* (Paris), VI, No. 2, 1984, 35-41.
Fraser, Virginia. 'George Johnston Wins Second Franklin Award'. *Australian*, 15 April, 1970, 1.
Goodwin, A.E. 'Voyage and Kaleidoscope in George Johnston's Trilogy'. *A.L.S.*, VI, 1973, 143-51.
Greer, Patrick. 'George Johnston in Hydra'. *London Magazine*, N.S. XX, Nos. 8-9, 1980, 109-15.
H[all], S[andra]. 'Time to Face a Modern Australia'. *Bulletin*, 23 August, 1969, 56-57. Report of an interview with Johnston.
Hall, James. 'And Now It's Two for the Load'. *Australian*, 23 November, 1968, 12.
Hall, Sandra. 'Why Write Novels?' *Bulletin*, 26 October, 1968, 52-54.
Hergenhan, Laurie. 'War in Post-1960s Fiction: Johnston, Stow, McDonald, Malouf and Les Murray'. *A.L.S.*, XII, No. 2, 1985, 248-260.
Hutton, Geoffrey. 'He Died Alive'. *Age*, 23 July, 1970, 6.
Johnson, Greer and Tiffin, Chris. 'The Evolution of George Johnston's David Meredith'. *A.L.S.*, XI, 1983, 162-70.
Johnston, Martin. 'Concerning *A Cartload of Clay*'. *S.M.H.*, 25 September, 1971, 19. This also appeared in *Advertiser*, 16 October, 1971, 21, and *Age*, 2 October, 1971, 11 (there entitled 'The Final Cartload of Clay').
Jones, Margaret. 'Australia in Search of a Soul'. *S.M.H.*, 16 August, 1969, 16.
Keavney, Kay. 'From George, with Sadness'. *Australian Women's Weekly*, 3 September, 1969, 13.
Kinnane, Garry. *George Johnston: A Biography*. (Melbourne: Nelson, 1986). Reviewed by C. Eagle, *Age Saturday Extra*, 11 October, 1986, 20; A. Mitchell, *Weekend Australian Magazine*, 4-5 October, 1986, 14; P. Morgan, *ABR*, No. 88, 1987, 10-11; J.D. Pringle, *S.M.H.*, 18 October, 1986, 48; E. Riddell, *Bulletin*, 7 October, 1986, 86-88; D. Rowbotham, *Courier-Mail: The Great Weekend*, 8 November, 1986, 6.
---. 'The Artist and Two Authors'. *Age Saturday Extra*, 10 April, 1982, 9. Interview with Sidney Nolan about George Johnston and Patrick White.
---. 'The Reconstruction of Self: Background and Design in George Johnston's Meredith Trilogy'. *A.L.S.*, XI, 1984, 435-46.
---. 'Reply to Graeme Kinross Smith'. *Westerly*, XXXIII, No. 1, 1988, 83. The original article appeared in *Westerly*, XXXII, No. 3, 1987, 75-77.
Knuckey, Marie. 'In Search of Charmian's Island'. *S.M.H.*, 1 June, 1972, Look! section, 10.
Lawson, Alan. '"Where a Man Belongs": Hal Porter's *The Paper Chase* and George Johnston's *Clean Straw for Nothing*'. In *Studies in the Recent Australian Novel*, edited by K.G. Hamilton (St Lucia: U.Q.P., 1978), 168-93.
Mares, F.H. 'Biography and Fiction: George Johnston's Meredith Trilogy and Garry Kinnane's Biography'. *A.L.S.*, XIII, No. 3, 1988, 357-364.
Mellick, J.S.D. 'The New and the Old - Responses to Translocation'. *Commonwealth* (Paris), VI, No. 2, 1984, 29-34.

O'Hara, John. 'The Early and the Late George Johnston'. *Review*, 11-17 March, 1972, 589.

Riddell, Elizabeth. 'George, for Whom Working is Therapy'. *Australian*, 16 August, 1969, 18.

---. 'George Johnston'. *Australian Author*, II, No. 4, 1970, 43.

---. 'Writing near the Brink: A Personal Recollection of the Author-Journalist George Johnston'. *Australian*, 23 July, 1970, 11. See also report on p. 1.

Rowley, Hazel. 'The Beautiful and the Damned: George Johnston and Auto/Biographical Fictions'. *Island Magazine*, Nos. 34-35, 1988, 148-156.

Sayers, Stuart. 'Moomba Book Prize to Johnston'. *Age*, 28 February, 1970, 2.

Scheckter, John. '"Before It Is too Late": George Johnston and the Doppler Effect'. *Australian & New Zealand Studies in Canada* 5, 1991, 115-30.

Simpson, Colin. *Greece: The Unclouded Eye*. (Sydney: A.& R., 1968), 102-07.

Smith, Barry. 'George Johnston's Anzac: the Role of Sidney Nolan and Peter Finch'. *Quadrant*, XXI, No. 6, 1977, 66-69.

Smith, Graeme Kinross. 'Brother George Looks Over Biographer's Shoulders'. *Westerly*, XXXII, No. 3, 1987, 75-77.

Thurley, Geoffrey. '*My Brother Jack*: An Australian Masterpiece?' *Ariel* (Calgary), V, No. 3, 1974, 61-80.

Tolchard, Clifford. 'My Husband George: My Wife Charmian: The Johnston-Clift Partnership'. *Walkabout*, XXXV, No. 1, 1969, 26-29.

JOHNSTON, MARTIN

Collection

Martin Johnston: Selected Poems and Prose. Edited with an introduction by John Tranter. (St Lucia: U.Q.P., 1993).

Reviewed by D. Anderson, *S.M.H.*, 17 July, 1993, 47; K. Bolton, *Overland*, 133, 1993, 42-44; A. Bullen, *Eureka Street*, 4.5, 1994, 48-50; H. Cam, *S.M.H.*, 10 July, 1993, 45; B. Gadd, *World Literature Today*, 68.3, 1994, 631; I. Indyk, *Weekend Australian*, 31 July-1 August, 1993, Review 6; K. Jennings, *Bulletin*, 19 October, 1993, 90; J. Leonard, *Social Alternatives*, 12.4, 1994, 56-57; S. O'Brien, *T.L.S.*, 20 August, 1993, 6; C. Wallace-Crabbe, *ABR*, 155, 1993, 50-51.

Fiction

Cicada Gambit. (Sydney: Hale & Iremonger; 1983).

Reviewed by J. Hawkes, *Aspect*, 31, 1984, 71-72; N. Jillett, *Age*, 18 February, 1984, 14; E. Jones, *Age Monthly Review*, 4.2, 1984, 14-15; N. Keesing, *Australian*, 2-3 March, 1984, 13; N. Krauth, *ABR*, 60, 1984, 14; E. Perkins, *Quadrant*, 28.11, 1984, 85-86; C. Wallace-Crabbe, *Scripsi*, 3.1, 1985, 175-77; N. Wheatley, *S.M.H.*, 7 January, 1984, 34.

Poetry

Ithaka: Modern Greek Poetry in Translation. Translated by Martin Johnston. (Sydney: Island Press, 1973).

The Sea-Cucumber. (St Lucia: U.Q.P., 1978).

Reviewed by R.D. Jones, *Makar*, 14.2, 1980, 59-61; E. Perkins, *LiNQ*, 6.2, 1978, 85-87; C. Pollnitz, *Southerly*, 3, 1978, 342-57; T. Shapcott, *ABR*, 1, 1978, 19-20; J. Tranter, *National Times*, 26 August, 1978, 42; C. Wallace-Crabbe, *Age*, 2 September, 1978, 21.

Shadowmass: Poems. (Sydney: Arts Society University of Sydney, 1971).

Reviewed by T. Shapcott, *ABR*, 11, 1972, 250.

The Typewriter Considered as a Bee-Trap. (Sydney: Hale & Iremonger; 1984).

Reviewed by G. Catalano, *Age*, 29 June, 1985, 16; S. Edgar, *Island Magazine*, 25-26, 1986, 118-20; M. Heyward, *Scripsi*, 3.2-3, 1985, 223-28; E. Jones, *ABR*, 77, 1985-86, 41-42; J. Rodriguez, *S.M.H.*, 22 March, 1986, 47.

Non-Fiction

'Growing Up in Greece'. In *Changing Places: Australian Writers in Europe 1960s-1990s*, edited by Laurie Hergenhan and Irmtraud Petersson (St Lucia: UQP, 1994), 16-19.

Critical Material

'Curse of Tragedy Claims Poet Son'. *S.M.H.*, 22 June, 1990, 4. For further obituaries see *Australian*, 22 June, 1990, 4; *Age*, 22 June, 1990, 14.

Duwell, Martin. 'Exiled by Circumstance and Inclination: Martin Johnston 1947-1990'. *Editions*, 8-9, 1990, 9-10. Reprinted in *Martin Johnston: Selected Poems and Prose*, edited by John Tranter (St Lucia: U.Q.P., 1993), 273-276.

Page, Geoff. 'Martin Johnston'. In his *A Reader's Guide To Contemporary Australian Poetry* (St. Lucia: U.Q.P., 1995), 136-140.

Roberts, Mark. 'Towards a New Diversity: Martin Johnston and the New Australian Poetry'. *Island*, 58, 1994, 60-63.

Ryan, Gig. 'Martin Johnston (1947-1990)'. *Scripsi*, 7.3, 1992, 229-44.

Tranter, John. 'A Beautiful but Useless Game'. *Makar*, 14.2, 1980, 4-11. Interview.

JOLLEY, ELIZABETH

Fiction

Cabin Fever. (Ringwood, Vic.: Viking, 1990).

Reviewed by F. Busch, *New York Times Book Review*, 7 July, 1991, 9; P. Craig, *T.L.S.*, 25 January, 1991, 20; P. Craven, *Age*, 8 September, 1990, Saturday Extra, 8; G. Dutton, *ABR*, No. 124, 1990, 12; C. Floyd, *SPAN*, 33, 1992, 177-81; L. Graeber, *New York Times Book Review*, 26 July, 1992, 24; D. Modjeska, *Scripsi*, 6, No. 3, 1990, 129-34; A. Nettelbeck, *Westerly*, 36.3, 1991, 114-15; P. Pierce, *Bulletin*, 23 October, 1990, 118-19; P. Quick, *Mattoid*, 40, 1991, 126-28; A.P. Riemer, *S.M.H.*, 8 September, 1990, 77; R. Willbanks, *Antipodes*, 6.2, 1992, 148-49.

The Georges' Wife. (Ringwood, Vic.: Viking, 1993).

Reviewed by H. Bowers, *Imago*, 6.2, 1994, 99-101; P. Craven, *Weekend Australian* 2-3 October, 1993, Review 6; H. Daniel, *ABR*, 155, 1993, 8-9; J. Hanrahan, *Age*, 2 October, 1993, Saturday Extra 7; E. Liddelow, *Editions*, 18, 1993, 19-20 (also discusses *Cabin Fever* and *My Father's Moon*); R. Lucas, *Bulletin*, 26 October, 1993, 89; P. Pierce, *S.M.H.*, 2 October, 1993, Spectrum 13A; N. Potter, *Antipodes*, 8.1, 1994, 72-73.

Foxybaby. (St Lucia: U.Q.P., 1985).

Reviewed by M. Brown, *CRNLE Reviews Journal*, No. 2, 1985, 1-3; E. Butel, *National Times*, 6-12 September, 1985, 30; L. Chamberlain, *T.L.S.*, 13 June, 1986, 645; V. Chapple, *Courier-Mail: The Great Weekend*, 23 November, 1985, 7; J. Colmer, *Weekend Australian Magazine*, 7-8 September, 1985, 17; H. Daniel, *Age Saturday Review*, 7 September, 1985, 13; B. Dibble, *ABR*, No. 77, 1985, 29-31; K. England, *Advertiser*, 7 September, 1985, 7; C. Gerrish, *Womanspeak*, X, No. 1, 1986, 26; B. Jefferis, *Overland*, No. 103, 1986, 65-66; S. McKernan, *Bulletin*, 26 November, 1985, 99-100; E. Perkins, *Quadrant*, XXX, No. 3, 1986, 80-83; S. Trigg, *Scripsi*, IV, No. 1, 1986, 265-74; B. Walker, *Westerly*, XXXI, No. 1, 1986, 91-94; E. Webby, *S.M.H.*, 14 September, 1985, 47.

Milk and Honey. (Fremantle, W.A.: Fremantle Arts Centre Press, 1984; New York: Persea Books, 1986).

Reviewed by P. Ackroyd, *New York Times Book Review*, 15 June, 1986, 12; I. Baranay, *S.M.H.*, 13 October, 1984, 41; M. Brown, *CRNLE Reviews Journal*, No. 2, 1985, 1-3; L. Clancy, *Age Saturday Extra*, 3 November, 1984, 19; K. England, *Advertiser Saturday Extra*, 13 October, 1984, 38; T. Forshaw, *Quadrant*, XXIX, No. 3, 1985, 77-79; L. Frost, *Overland*, No. 97, 1984, 66-68; M. Halligan, *Canberra*

Times, 23 December, 1984, 8; D. Hanaor, *Antipodes*, I, No. 1, 1987, 53; M. Harrison, *Age Monthly Review*, V, No. 1, 1985, 16-19; D. Jones, *Westerly*, XXXI, No. 2, 1986, 35-49; N. Jose, *Age Monthly Review*, V, No. 6, 1985, 17-18; B. Little, *Weekend Australian Magazine*, 22-23 September, 1984, 14; J. Motion, *T.L.S.*, 18 October, 1985, 1173.

Miss Peabody's Inheritance. (St. Lucia: U.Q.P., 1983; New York: Viking Press, 1984).
Reviewed by H. Allan, *LiNQ*, XII, No. 1-3, 1985, 75-77; T. Forshaw, *Quadrant*, XXVIII, No. 4, 1984, 81-82; G.G. Fraser, *New York Times Book Review*, 17 November, 1985, 50; M. Glastonbury, *New Statesman*, 10 May, 1985, 25-26; D. Jones, *Westerly*, XXIX, No. 4, 1984, 77-88; D.A.N. Jones, *London Review of Books*, VII, No. 9, 1986, 22-23; J. Motion, *T.L.S.*, 18 October, 1985, 1173; W. Noonan, *Weekend Australian Magazine*, 22-23 October, 1983, 14; P. Pierce, *Age Saturday Extra*, 19 November, 1983, 18; K. Purnell. *Luna*, No. 18, 1984, 40-43; S. Wyndham, *S.M.H.*, 29 October, 1983, 42.

Mr. Scobie's Riddle. (Ringwood, Vic.: Penguin, 1983). Reviewed by T. Forshaw, *Quadrant*, XXVIII, No. 4, 1984, 81-82; M. Glastonbury, *New Statesman*, 10 May, 1985, 25-26; D. Jones, *London Review of Books*, VII, No. 9, 1986, 22-23; G. Lord, *National Times*, 13-19 March, 1983, 32; J. Motion, *T.L.S.*, 18 October, 1985, 1173; T. Shapcott, *Courier-Mail*, 12 March, 1983, 26; C.K. Stead, *S.M.H.*, 29 January, 1983, 33.

My Father's Moon. (Ringwood, Vic.: Viking, 1989).
Reviewed by B. Abel, *Contemporary Review*, 255, No. 1485, 1989, 213-16; P. Craven, *Weekend Australian Magazine*, 22-23 April, 1989, Weekend 10; H. Daniel, *Age Saturday Extra*, 15 April, 1989, 11; B. Edwards, *Mattoid*, No. 34, 1989, 183-86; H. Garner, *Scripsi*, 6, No. 1, 199081-86; D. Glazer, *Margin*, No. 22, 1989, 33-34; V. Gornick, *New York Times Book Review*, 30 April, 1989, 9; M. Hardie, *Southerly*, 49, No. 4, 1989, 654-60; D. Jones, *Span*, No. 29, 1989, 113-15; S. McKernan, *Bulletin*, 11 April, 1989, 121; D. Reiter, *Redoubt*, No. 6, 1989, 65-70; A.P. Riemer, *ABR*, No. 110, 1989, 27-28; N. Stasko, *Phoenix Review*, No. 6, 116-19; E. Webby, *S.M.H.*, 15 April, 1989, 89; P. Wolfe, *Antipodes*, 4.2, 1990, 136.

The Newspaper of Claremont Street. (Fremantle, W.A.: Fremantle Arts Centre Press, 1981).
Reviewed by B. Dibble, *ABR*, No. 40, 1982, 29-39; L. Frost, *Westerly*, XXVII, No. 3, 1982, 67-68; V. Ikin, *CRNLE Reviews Journal*, No. 2, 1982, 5-10; T. Platek, *Antipodes*, II, No. 1, 1988, 56; R.P. Sinkler, *New York Times Book Review*, 20 December, 1987, 16.

The Orchard Thieves. (Ringwood, Vic.: Viking Penguin, 1995).
Reviewed by M. Fraser, *S.M.H.*, 30 Sept., 1995, Spectrum 12A; J. Kitson, *ABR*, 175, 1995, 23; M. Wilding, *Weekend Australian*, 14-15 Oct., 1995, Review 9.

Palomino. (Collingwood, Vic.: Outback Press, 1980; New York: Stanley Moss/Persea, 1987).
Reviewed by L. Clancy, *Age Saturday Extra*, 3 November, 1984, 19; K. England, *Advertiser Saturday Review*, 13 October, 1984, 38; L. Frost, *Overland*, No. 97, 1984, 66-68; C. Gerrish, *Womanspeak*, IX, No. 1, 1984, 24; J. Hendin, *New York Times Book Review*, 19 July, 1987, 11; N. Keesing, *ABR*, No. 28, 1983, 34-35; P. Lewis, *London Magazine*, XXV, Nos. 1-2, 1985, 148-152; J. Motion, *T.L.S.*, 18 October, 1985, 1173; T. Shapcott, *Westerly*, XXV, No. 4, 1980, 73-75.

Stories: Five Acre Virgin: The Travelling Entertainer. (Fremantle, W.A.: Fremantle Arts Centre Press, 1984). First published 1976 and 1979 respectively.
Reviewed by G. Burns, *Age Saturday Extra*, 14 July, 1984, 13; G. Dutton, *Bulletin*, 29 May, 1984, 97; M. Halligan, *Canberra Times*, 29 September, 1984, 16.

The Sugar Mother. (Fremantle, W.A.: Fremantle Arts Centre Press; New York: Harper & Row, 1988).
Reviewed by B. Abel, *Contemporary Review*, 254, No. 1479, 1989, 213-16; P. Craven, *Age Saturday Extra*, 23 April, 1988, 12; M. Hardie, *Southerly*, 49, No. 1, 1989, 113-17; M. Harris, *ABR*, No. 98, 1988, 32-33; S. McKernan, *Bulletin*, 29 March, 1988, 112; J.L. Myles, *Antithesis*, 2, No. 1, 1989, 93-95; C. Peake, *S.M.H.*, 16 April, 1988, 72; D. Reiter, *Redoubt*, No. 6, 1989, 65-70; N. E. Schaumberger, *Antipodes*, 3.1, 1989, 30; B. Walker, *Westerly*, XXXIII, No. 3, 1988, 90-91; *New Yorker*, 5 September, 1988, 101.

The Travelling Entertainer and Other Stories. (Fremantle: Fremantle Arts Centre Press, 1979).
Reviewed by D.R. Burns, *ABR*, No. 19, 1980, 20-32; B. Williams, *Westerly*, XXV, No. 2, 1980, 104-07.

The Well. (Ringwood, Vic.: Viking, 1986; Ringwood, Vic.: Penguin, 1987).
Reviewed by J. Cadzow, *Weekend Australian. Weekend Magazine*, 6-7 June, 1987, 12; R. Coover, *New York Times Book Review*, 16 November, 1986, 1, 44-45; P. Craig, *T.L.S.*, 15 August, 1986, 894; H. Daniel, *Age Saturday Extra*, 27 September, 1986, 12; B. Dibble, *Overland*, No. 106, 1987, 80-82; G. Dutton, *Weekend Australian Magazine*, 20-21 September, 1986, 15; B. Edwards, *Mattoid*, No.27, 1987, 85-87; D. Glazer, *Margin*, No. 18, 1987, 20-21; M. Halligan, *Canberra Times*, 29 November, 1986, B2; S. McKernan, *Bulletin*, 18 November, 1986, 101; D. Modjeska, *S.M.H.*, 13 September, 1986, 44; S.J. Paolini, *Antipodes*, I, No. 2, 1987, 117; J. Rodriguez, *Fremantle Arts Review*, I, No. 12, 1986, 14-15; S. Trigg, *ABR*, No. 86, 1986, 5-6.

Woman in a Lampshade. (Ringwood, Vic.: Penguin, 1983; New York: King Penguin/Penguin Books, 1986).
Reviewed by R. Coover, *New York Times Book Review*, 6 November, 1986, 1, 44-45; T. Forshaw, *Quadrant*, XXVIII, No. 4, 1984, 81-82; A. Hildyard, *Island Magazine*, Nos. 18-19, 1984, 40-44; N. Keesing, *Weekend Australian Magazine*, 12-13 March, 1983, 16; G. Lord, *National Times*, 13-19 March, 1983, 32.

Drama

Off the Air: Nine Plays for Radio. Edited with an introduction and commentary by Delys Bird. (Ringwood, Vic.: Penguin, 1995).
Reviewed by P. Craven, *ABR*, 169, 1995, 14-15; M. Drouart, *FAR*, 9.8, 1995, 18-19; V. Ikin, *S.M.H.*, 25 Feb., 1995, Spectrum 11A; N. Jillett, *Age*, 8 Apr., 1995, Saturday Extra 9; C. Keneally, *AWBR*, 7.2, 1995, 6-7.

Non-Fiction

Central Mischief: Elizabeth Jolley on Writing, Her Past and Herself. Edited with an introduction by Caroline Lurie. Ringwood, Vic.: Viking, 1992).
Reviewed by S. Chenery, *Weekend Australian*, 13-14 June, 1992, Review 7; H. Daniel, *Age*, 2 May, 1992, Saturday Extra 8; R. Lucas, *Voices*, 2.3, 1992, 107-10; T. Meszaros, *CRNLE Reviews Journal*, 2, 1993, 121-24; B. Milech, *Antipodes*, 6.2, 1992, 169-70; P. Pierce, *S.M.H.*, 9 May, 1992, 4-6; A. Riemer, *ABR* 141, 1992, 43-44; P. Rolfe, *Bulletin*, 2 June, 1992, 98-99.

Diary of a Weekend Farmer. (Nedlands, WA: Fremantle Arts Centre P., 1993).
Reviewed by J. Burke, *Age*, 24 July, 1993, Saturday Extra 8; B. Milech, *Antipodes*, 8.1, 1994, 79; J. Tranter, *S.M.H.*, 12 June, 1993, 45.

'A Child Went Forth'. *ABR*, No. 56, 1983, 5-8. Self-Portraits 5.
'Cloisters of Memory'. *Meanjin*, 48, No. 3, 1989, 531-39. Autobiographical.
'The Inward Eye'. *This Australia*, VI, No. 4, 1987, 36-39.
'On Being An Australian Author - "Living on One Leg Like a Bird"'. *Island Magazine*, No. 30, 1987, 25-31.

'727 Chester Road'. *Southern Review*, 21, No. 3, 1988, 261-64. Autobiographical Note relating to *My Father's Moon* and 'Little Lewis Has Had a Lovely Sleep'.
'Who Talks of Victory?' *Meanjin*, XLVI, No. 1, 1987, 4-15. Autobiographical.

Critical Material

Guide to the Papers of Elizabeth Jolley in the Mitchell/State Library of New South Wales. (Sydney: Library Council of New South Wales, 1988).

Baker, Candida. 'Elizabeth Jolley'. In her *Yacker: Australian Writers Talk About Their Work* (Sydney: Picador, 1986), 210-233.

Bennett, Bruce. 'Versions of Ageing: Olga Masters and Elizabeth Jolley'. In *Olga Masters: An Autumn Crocus*, Proceedings of the Olga Masters Memorial Conference 8-10 July, 1988, edited by W. McGaw and P. Sharrad (Wollongong: New Literatures Research Centre, University of Wollongong, 1990), 84-96.

Bird, Delys, and Brenda Walker, eds. *Elizabeth Jolley: New Critical Essays*. (North Ryde, NSW: A.& R., 1991). Reviewed by L. Clancy, *Age*, 22 June, 1991, Saturday Extra 7; M. Lord, *ABR*, 131, 1991, 20; S. McKernan, *Westerly*, 37.1, 1992, 92-93; P. Pierce, *A.L.S.*, 16.3: 352-55.

Cadzow, Jane. 'A Compulsive Writer who Sifts Shadows from Another World'. *Weekend Australian Magazine*, 22-23 Sepember, 1984, 16.

Caporaletti, Silvana. 'The Echoes of the Echoing Well: Reading into the Darkness of Elizabeth Jolley's *The Well*'. In *Commonwealth Literary Cultures: New Voices, New Approaches*, edited by Giovanna Capone, Claudio Gorlier, and Bernard Hickey (Lecce: Edizioni del Grifo, 1993), 171-90.

Buffi, Roberta. 'Perth and Naples: Two "Corrupted" Mediterranean Cities'. *Westerly*, 39.4, 1994, 14-19. Includes discussion of the representation of Perth in works by Jolley.

Carr, Julie. 'The Dancing Body: Somatic Expression in Elizabeth Jolley's Fiction'. *Westerly*, 39.2, 1994, 75-80.

Clancy, Laurie. 'Love, Longing and Loneliness: The Fiction of Elizabeth Jolley'. *ABR*, No. 56, 11983, 8-12.

Coover, Robert. 'Dotty and Disorderly Conduct'. *New York Times Book Review*, 16 November, 1986, 44-45. Review article dealing especially with *The Well* and *Woman in a Lampshade*.

Daniel, Helen. *Liars: Australian New Novelists*. (Ringwood, Vic.: Penguin, 1988), 267-300.

---. 'Elizabeth Jolley: Variations on a Theme'. *Westerly*, XXXI, No. 2, 1986, 50-63.

D'Cruz, Doreen. 'Contesting the "One Law — the One Sublimating Transcendent Guarantor": Elizabeth Jolley's *The Well* and *Sugar Mother*'. *SPAN*, 40, 1995, 54-71.

Ellison, Jennifer. 'Elizabeth Jolley'. In her *Rooms of Their Own* (Ringwood, Vic.: Penguin, 1986), 172-191.

Garner, Helen. 'Elizabeth Jolley: An Appreciation'. *Meanjin*, XLII, 1983, 153-57.

Gillett, Sue. '*The Well*: Beyond Representation, the Active Space of Desire and Creativity'. *Westerly*, 37.1, 1992, 33-41.

Goddard, Kerry. 'Women off the Market: Possession and Desire in Elizabeth Jolley's *The Well*'. *SPAN*, 37, 1993, 201-11.

Goldsworthy, Kerryn. 'Voices in Time: *A Kindness Cup* and *Miss Peabody's Inheritance*'. *A.L.S.*, XII, No. 4, 1986, 471-81.

Grenville, Kate, and Sue Woolfe. *Making Stories: How Ten Australian Novels Were Written*. (St Leonards, NSW: Allen & Unwin, 1993). Includes contribution on *Mr Scobie's Riddle*.

Headon, David. 'Elizabeth Jolley'. *Meanjin*, XLIV, No. 1, 1985, 39-46. Interview.

Howells, Coral Ann. 'In Search of Lost Mothers: Margaret Laurence's *The Diviners* and Elizabeth Jolley's *Miss Peabody's Inheritance*'. *Ariel*, XIX, No. 1, 1988, 57-70.

Jones, Dorothy. 'Olivia and Chloe: Fictions of Female Friendship'. *A.L.S.*, 14, No. 1, 1989, 3-14. Includes discussion of Jolley's fiction.

Joussen, Ulla. 'An Interview with Elizabeth Jolley'. *Kunapipi*, 15.2, 1993, 37-43.

Kavanagh, Paul. 'This Self the Honey of All Beings - A Conversation with Elizabeth Jolley'. *Southerly*, 49, No. 3, 1989, 438-51. Reprinted in *Conversations: Interviews with Australian Writers*, edited by Paul Kavanagh and Peter Kuch (North Ryde, NSW: Collins/A.& R, 1991), 153-176.

Kirkby, Joan. 'The Call of the Mother in the Fiction of Elizabeth Jolley'. *Span*, No. 26, 1988, 46-63.

---. 'The Nights Belong to Elizabeth Jolley'. *Meanjin*, XLIII, 1984, 484-92.

---. 'The Spinster and the Missing Mother in the Fiction of Elizabeth Jolley'. In *Old Maids to Radical Spinsters: Unmarried Women in the Twentieth Century Novel*, edited by Laura L. Doan (Champaign: U of Illinois P., 1991), 235-58.

Livett, Jennifer. 'Against the Grain: Dream Narrative in Elizabeth Jolley's *Foxybaby*'. In *Postcolonial Fictions*, edited by Michèle Drouart (special issue in two volumes including SPACLALS Conference Proceedings, *SPAN*, 36, 1993), 211-19.

---. 'Two Answers to Every Question: Elizabeth Jolley's Fictions, Ethics and Criticism'. *A.L.S.*, 17.1, 1995, 10-18.

Manning, Gerald F. 'Sunsets and Sunrises: Nursing Home As Microcosm in "Memento Mori" and *Mr. Scobie's Riddle*'. *Ariel*, XVIII, No. 2, 1987, 27-34.

Mayman, Jan. 'A Literary Flowering in Suburbia'. *National Times*, 13-19 March, 1983, 29.

McCowan, Sandra, ed. *Elizabeth Jolley's World*. (South Fremantle, WA: Fremantle Arts Centre P., 1994). For secondary school students.

McDonald, Roger. *Gone Bush*. (Sydney: Bantam, 1990), 1-11.

Milech, Barbara, and Brian Dibble. 'Aristophanic Love-Dyads: Community, Communion, and Cherishing in Elizabeth Jolley's Fiction'. *Antipodes*, 7.1, 1993, 3-10.

Modjeska, Drusilla. 'Extra to Real Life: Drusilla Modjeska Reflects on Elizabeth Jolley's Trilogy'. *ABR*, 169, 1995, 15-16.

Paolini, Shirley. 'Narrative Strategies in Elizabeth Jolley's *The Well* and African Folktales'. *Antipodes*, 7.1, 1993, 11-13.

Riemer, A.P. 'Between Two Worlds - An Approach to Elizabeth Jolley's Fiction'. *Southerly*, XLIII, 1983, 239-52.

---. 'Displaced Persons - Some Preoccupations in Elizabeth Jollcy's Fiction'. *Westerly*, XXXI, No. 2, 1986, 64-79.

---. 'New Worlds and Old'. In *International Literature in English*, edited by Robert Ross (New York: Garland, 1991), 371-82.

---. 'This World, the Next, and Australia - the Emergence of a Literary Commonplace'. *Southerly*, XLIV, 1984, 251-70.

Salzman, Paul. 'Elizabeth Jolley: Fiction and Desire'. *Meridian*, V, No. 1, 1986, 53-62.

---. *Helplessly Tangled in Female Arms and Legs: Elizabeth Jolley's Fictions*. (St Lucia: U.Q.P., 1993). Reviewed by P. Bagworth, *Westerly*, 38.4, 1993, 121-23; N. Birns, *Antipodes*, 7.2, 1993 167-68; C. Colebrook, *SPAN*, 37, 1993, 242-43; E. Lindsay, *ABR*, 155, 1993, 20-21; T. Meszaros, *CRNLE Reviews Journal* 2, 1993, 121-24; P. Pierce, *A.L.S.*, 16.3, 1994, 352-55; M.E. Ryan, *Overland*, 135, 1994, 74-75.

Sant, Andrew, ed. *Toads: Australian Writers: Other Work, Other Lives*, edited by Andrew Sant (Sydney: Allen & Unwin, 1992). Collection of autobiographical essays on writing and money. Includes Jolley.

Soulier, Anne-Marie. 'Elizabeth Jolley et le Pays des Autres'. *Commonwealth*, 17.1, 1994, 45-50. French with English abstract.

Thomson, Helen. 'Elizabeth Jolley's Trilogy: *My Father's Moon, Cabin Fever, The Georges' Wife*: The Fiction of Pain'. In her *Bio-fictions: Brian Matthews, Drusilla Modjeska and Elizabeth Jolley*. Monograph 25. (Townsville: James Cook U of North

Queensland, Foundation for Australian Literary Studies, 1994). 36-54.
Trigg, Stephanie. 'An Interview with Elizabeth Jolley'. *Scripsi*, IV, No. 1, 1986, 245-64.
White, Terri-Ann. 'A Fine Line Between Truth and Fiction'. *Fremantle Arts Review*, III, No. 2, 1988, 12.
Willbanks, Ray. 'Elizabeth Jolley'. In his *Speaking Volumes: Australian Writers and Their Work* (Ringwood, Vic.: Penguin, 1991).
---. 'A Conversation with Elizabeth Jolley'. *Antipodes*, 3.1, 1989, 27-29.
Wimmer, Adi. 'Dualism and the Austrian Connection in Elizabeth Jolley's Fiction'. *Southerly*, 52.2, 1992, 44-55. Reprinted in *The Making of Pluralist Australia 1950-1990*, selected papers from the inaugural EASA Conference 1991, (Bern: Peter Lang, 1992).

JONES, EVAN

Poetry
Left at the Post. (St Lucia: U.Q.P., 1984).
Reviewed by J. Barnie, *Kunapipi*, VI, No. 3, 1984, 107-122; M. Hulse, *PN Review*, XIII, No. 1, 1986, 72; E. Lawson, *ABR*, No. 60, 1984, 35-36; P. Porter, *Scripsi*, III, No. 1, 1985, 67-71.
Recognitions. (Canberra: A.N.U. Press, 1978).
Reviewed by K. Goodwin, *Weekend Australian Magazine*, 17-18 March, 1979, 11; J. Legasse, *Westerly*, No. 4, 1978, 83-84; G.K. Smith, *Age*, 24 February, 1979, 25; T. Thorne, *New Poetry*, XXVII, No. 2, 1979, 80-82; J.M. Wright, *Quadrant*, XXV, No. 4, 1981, 51-52.
Understandings. (Melbourne: M.U.P., 1967).
Reviewed by B. Beaver, *S.M.H.*, 6 January, 1968, 16; L.J. Clancy, *Overland*, No. 39, 1968, 51; M. Colman, *Poetry Magazine*, No. 3, 1968, 27-30; R. Dunlop, *Poetry Australia*, No. 20, 1968, 41-42; M. Jurgensen, *Makar*, IV, No. 4, 1968, 44-47; S.E. Lee, *Southerly*, XXVIII, 1968, 151-52; G. Page, *Canberra Times*, 18 May, 1968, 12; T. Shapcott, *Bulletin*, 9 December, 1967, 84; P. Steele, *Twentieth Century*, XXII, 1968, 376-79 and *Meanjin*, XXVIII, 1969, 122; R. Ward, *ABR*, VII, 1968, 93.

Critical Material
Page, Geoff. 'Evan Jones'. In his *A Reader's Guide To Contemporary Australian Poetry* (St. Lucia: U.Q.P., 1995), 140-143.

JONES, RAE DESMOND

Fiction
The Lemon Tree. (North Ryde, N.S.W.: A.& R., 1990).
Reviewed by S. Lake, *ABR*, No. 120, 1990, 11.
Walking the Line. (North Sydney: Red Press, 1979).
Reviewed by H. Daniel, *Age*, 19 April, 1980, 26; R. Hall, *S.M.H.*, 2 August, 1980, 22; C. Munro, *ABR*, No. 21, 1980, 22-23.
Wisdom. (Sydney: Black Wattle, 1995).
Reviewed by E. Lindsay, *Weekend Australian*, 10-11 June, 1995, Review 7.

Poetry
The Mad Vibe. (Cammeray: Saturday Centre, 1975). Saturday Centre Poets' Series, No. 9.
Reviewed by R. Hall, *Australian*, 16 August, 1975, 30.
Orpheus with a Tuba. (St Lucia: Makar, 1973). Gargoyle Poets, No. 6.
Reviewed by J.E. Tranter, *New Poetry*, XXII, No. 1, 1974, 54-55.
The Palace of Art. (St Lucia: Makar Press, 1981).
Reviewed by G. Rowlands, *Overland*, No. 90, 1982, 61-64; G. Ryan, *Scripsi*, II,

Nos. 2-3, 1983, 225-227.

Shakti. (St Lucia: Makar Press, 1977).
Reviewed by G. Catelano [sic], *Luna*, III, No. 2, 1979, 32-34, see also G. Rowlands, 'Reply to Gary Catalano', *Luna*, IV, No. 1, 1979, 38-40; C. Harrison, *S.M.H.*, 8 April, 1978, 17; T. Shapcott, *Australian Weekend Review*, 18-19 February, 1978, 9; A. Taylor, *National Times*, 27 May, 1978, 31.

Critical Material

Duwell, Martin. 'The Mad Vibe, an Interview'. *Makar*, X, No. 2, 1974, 1-8. Reprinted in his *A Possible Contemporary Poetry* (St Lucia: Makar Press, 1982), 107-115, with supplementary interview 115-120.
Irwin, Trevor Q. 'The Drama of the Separate Self in Rae Desmond Jones' *The Mad Vibe*'. *A.L.S.*, IX, 1979, 207-13.
Page, Geoff. 'Rae Desmond Jones'. In his *A Reader's Guide To Contemporary Australian Poetry* (St. Lucia: U.Q.P., 1995), 143-146.

JONES, ROD

Fiction

Billy Sunday. (Sydney: Pan Macmillan Picador, 1995).
Reviewed by Don Anderson, *ABR*, 171, 1995, 5-6 (see also interview by R. Koval, 7-8); H. Daniel, *Age*, 3 June: Saturday Extra 7; M. McGirr, *Eureka Street*, 5.5, 1995, 44; J. Maiden, *Overland*, 141, 1995, 82-84; P. Nelson, *Weekend Australian*, 17-18 June, 1995, Review 10.

Julia Paradise. (Fitzroy, Vic.: McPhee Gribble/Penguin, 1986).
Reviewed by C. Bird, *Age Monthly Review*, February, 1987, 6; A.M. Conway, *T.L.S.*, 26 February-3 March, 1988, 215; T. Forshaw, *Weekend Australian*, 3-4 January, 1987, Weekend 10; W. Herbert, *New York Times Book Review*, 11 October, 1987, 12; D. Hewett, *Overland*, No. 108, 1987, 83-6; B. Hickey, *Span*, No. 26, 1988, 112-16; E. Liddelow, *Fine Line*, No. 1, 1987, 11-16; D. Modjeska, *S.M.H.*, 20 December, 1986, 28; K.D. Murray, *Antithesis*, 1, No. 1, 1987, 105-14; D. Parker, *Phoenix Review*, No. 2, 1987-8, 110-12; B. Pascoe, *Times on Sunday*, 4 January, 1987, 29; C. Pybus, *Island Magazine*, No. 32, 1987, 63; P. Salzman, *ABR*, No. 87, 1986-7, 4-5; A. Sant, *Age*, 29 November, 1986, Saturday Extra 16.

Prince of the Lilies. (Ringwood, Vic.: McPhee Gribble, 1991).
Reviewed by D. Anderson, *S.M.H.*, 4 May, 1991, 44; D. Brooks, *SPAN*, 34&35, 1992-93, 384-91; J. Bulman-May, *Southerly*, 52.1, 1992, 170-72; D. Davison, *Weekend Australian*, 18-19 May, 1991, Review 5; B. Merry, *LiNQ*, 20.1, 1993, 106-09; A.P. Riemer, *ABR*, 130, 1991, 4-5; A. Sant, *Voices*, 1.3, 1991, 109-10; R. Sorensen, *Age*, 4 May, 1991, Saturday Extra 6; J. Stephens, *Australian Society*, 10.7, 1991, 43-44.

Critical Material

Gelder, Ken. 'Postmodernism's "Lost Objects": Desire in the Recent Fiction of Murnane, Brooks, Henshaw and Jones'. *Island Magazine*, No. 41, 1989, 49-53.
Murray, Kevin. '"Come Into My Parlour": Rod Jones and the Reviewers'. *Antithesis*, 1, No. 1, 1987, 105-114.

JONES, T. HARRI

Poetry

The Collected Poems of T. Harri Jones. Ed. by Julian Croft and Don Dale-Jones (Llandysul: Gomer Press, 1977).
Reviewed by A.J. Hassall, *Southerly*, XXXVIII, 1978, 113-18; B. Humfrey, *Anglo-Welsh Review*, No. 60, 1978, 136-38; W.G.H., *UNE Convocation Bulletin and Alumni News*, No. 43, 1978, 25-26.

The Colour of Cockcrowing. (London: Hart Davis, 1966). Reviewed by J.J. Bray, *ABR*, V, 1966, 222-3, see also C. Higham, *ABR*, VI, 1966, 16 and reply by J.J. Bray, *ABR*, VI, 1966, 40; D. Douglas, *Age*, 3 December, 1966, 23.

    Critical Material
Croft, Julian. *T.H. Jones*. (Cardiff: University of Wales Press for the Welsh Arts Council, 1976). Writers of Wales. Reviewed by A.J. Hassall, *Southerly*, XXXVIII, 1978, 113-18; L.T. Hergenhan, *A.L.S.*, VIII, 1977, 110; G. Jones, *Anglo-Welsh Review*, XXVI, No. 58, 1977, 161-65; W.G.H., *UNE Convocation Bulletin and Alumni News*, No. 43, 1978, 25-26.
---. 'A Word Not Lightly Said'. *Poetry Magazine*, No. 2, 1965, 3-7.
Partridge, Colin John. 'The Weeping of My Love: The Verse of Thomas Henry Jones'. *Southern Review*, II, No. 1, 1966, 59-63.
Talbot, Norman. 'In Memoriam: T.H. Jones'. *The Australian Highway*, XLV, No. 3, 1965, 24-7.
---. 'To Write Simply: The Poetry of T.H. Jones'. *Quadrant*, IX, No. 5, 1965, 35-42.

JOSE, NICHOLAS

    Fiction
Avenue of Eternal Peace. (Ringwood, Vic.: Penguin, 1989).
Reviewed by A. Broinowski, *S.M.H.*, 7 October, 1989, 81; D. Davison, *Weekend Australian*, 18-19 November, 1989, 8; P. Ellingsen, *Age*, 9 December 1989, Saturday Extra, 9; R. Gostand, *Social Alternatives*, 9.3, 1990, 66-67; J. McLaren, *Overland*, 116, 1989, 23; P. Salzman, *ABR*, 115, 1989, 7-8.

Feathers or Lead: Short Fiction. (Ringwood, Vic.: Penguin, 1986).
Reviewed by D. English, *Age Saturday Extra*, 9 August, 1986, 12; T. Forshaw, *Weekend Australian Magazine*, 17-18 June, 1986, 17; R. Gostand, *Social Alternatives*, 6.3, 1987, 63-65; J.A. Mead, *ABR*, 84, 1986, 14-16.

Paper Nautilus. (Ringwood, Vic.: Penguin, 1987).
Reviewed by H. Daniel, *Age Saturday Extra*, 15 August, 1987, 15; B. Garlick, *Social Alternatives*, 7.4, 1989, 63-64; J. Hanrahan, *Overland*, 111, 1988, 97-101; H. McQueen, *S.M.H.*, 3 October, 1987, 46; D.M. Roskies, *Antipodes*, 2.2, 1988, 130-31; C. Thompson, *ABR*, 96, 1987, 26-27; C. van Langenberg, *The Book Magazine*, 1.3, 1987-88, 24.

The Possesion of Amber. (St Lucia: UQP; 1980).
Reviewed by D.R. Burns, *ABR*, 27, 1980, 11-12; G. Dutton, *Bulletin*, 26 August, 1980, 72; T. Forshaw, *S.M.H.*, 15 November, 1980, 21; N. Jillett, *Age*, 4 April, 1981, 28; R. Jones, *Ash Magazine*, 5, 1981, 33; C. Stead, *Age*, 13 December, 1980, 19; M. Vernon, *Weekend Australian Magazine*, 15-16 November, 1980, 18; E. Webby, *Meanjin*, 40, 1981, 200-08; G. Windsor, *Quadrant*, 25.6, 1981, 71-74.

The Rose Crossing. (London: Hamish Hamilton, 1994).
Reviewed by N. Clee, *T.L.S.*, 6 January, 1995, 20; J.C. Hawley, *Antipodes*, 9.2, 1995, 155-56; H. Horton, *Imago*, 7.2, 1995, 99-100; S. Hughes, *Sunday Age*, 7 May, 1995, 10; P. Looker, *Voices*, 5.2, 1995, 121-24; P. Nelson, *Weekend Australian*, 24-25 December, 1994, Review 4; S. Patton, *Island*, 60-61, 1994, 48-51; N. Phelan, *ABR*, 165, 1994, 17-18; J. Wilson, *Westerly*, 40.3, 1995, 89-92.

Rowena's Field. (Adelaide: Rigby, 1984).
Reviewed by D. Anderson, *National Times*, 18-24 January, 1985, 33; L. Clancy, *Age Saturday Extra*, 23 March, 1985, 15; H. Daniel, *ABR*, 72, 1985, 26; S. Dowse, *Island Magazine*, 23, 1985, 59-60; H. McQueen, *S.M.H.*, 2 February, 1985, 41; D. Parker, *Quadrant*, 29.3, 1985, 70-72.

Non-Fiction
Chinese Whispers: Cultural Essays. (Kent Town, SA: Wakefield, 1995).
Reviewed by C. Weng-Ho, *ABR*, 172, 1995, 6-7.
'Asian Impersonations'. *Island*, 60-61, 1994, 47-49.
'At Cross Purposes: Behind the Forbidden Door'. *Quadrant*, 31.6, 1987, 54-56.
'Hamlet, Marwell and the Times'. *Critical Review*, 28, 1986, 47-62
'Sensitive New Asian Country'. *Island*, 53, 1992, 43-47.
Critical Material
Jacobs, Lyn. 'Nicholas Jose: "Travellers among Mountains and Streams"'. In
Southwords: Essays on South Australian Writing, edited by Philip Butterss (Kent
Town, SA: Wakefield P, 1995), 160-77.

JURGENSEN, MANFRED

Fiction
A Difficult Love; Break-Out: A Legend of the Seventies. (Brisbane: Phoenix, 1987).
Reviewed by D. Amalushi, *LiNQ*, 15, No. 3, 1987, 88-90; A. Bock, *LiNQ*, 15, No.
1, 1987, 106-109; R. Gostand, *Social Alternatives*, 7, No. 1, 1988, 64-66; M. Lange,
Outrider, 4, No. 1, 1987, 188-92; E. Perkins, *Outrider*, 1988, 58-71.
Intruders. (Brisbane: Phoenix Publications, 1992).
Reviewed by W. Brumley, *ABR*, 144, 1992, 30; H. Horton, *Imago*, 5.1, 1993, 93-94;
N. Phelan, *S.M.H.*, 21 November, 1992, 50; N. Potter, *Antipodes*, 7.1, 1993, 76.

Poetry
A Kind of Dying. (Melbourne: Hawthorn, 1977). Hawthorn Poets, 19.
Reviewed by F. Kellaway, *Overland*, No. 72, 1978, 53-7.
My Operas Can't Swim. (Milton, Qld.: Jacaranda, 1989).
Reviewed by H. Horton, *Imago*, 2, No. 1, 1990, 80-82; E. Perkins, *ABR*, No. 122,
1990, 17; W. Tonetto, *Southerly*, 50, No. 2, 1990, 255-61.
The Partiality of Harbours. (Brooklyn, N.S.W.: Paper Bark, 1989).
Reviewed by D. Barbour, *Australian-Canadian Studies*, 11.1-2, 1993, 172-80; K.
Brophy, *Going Down Swinging*, Nos. 10-11, 1990, 253-4; H. Cam, *S.M.H.*, 23
September, 1989, 81; R. Darling, *Antipodes*, 4.1, 1990, 68; E. Perkins, *ABR*, No.
122, 17; W. Tonetto, *Southerly*, 50, No. 2, 1990, 255-61 and *LiNQ*, 18.1, 1991, 127-
28.
Selected Poems: 1972-86. Edited and Introduced by D. Tsaloumas (Newstead, Qld.:
Albion Press, 1987).
Reviewed by K. Russell, *Quadrant*, 32, No. 7, 1988, 40-42.
Shadows of Utopia. (Rockhampton: U of Central Queensland P. in association with
Australian Scholarly Publishing, Melbourne, 1994).
Reviewed by M.O'Flynn, *ABR*, 164, 1994, 56-57; G. Rowlands, *Overland*, 137,
1994, 70-71.
Signs and Voices. Paperback poets 17 (St Lucia: U.Q.P., 1973).
Reviewed by M. Lange, *Makar*, 10, No. 1, 1974, 40-43; F. Zwicky, *Westerly*, No.
1, 1975, 68-73.
The Skin Trade. (Indooroopilly, Qld.: Phoenix, 1983).
Reviewed by J. Maiden, *S.M.H.*, 13 August, 1983, 38; M. Morgan, *ABR*, No. 52,
1983, 23-4; E. Perkins, *Image*, 6, No. 3, 1983, 17-18 and *Outrider*, 1, No. 1, 1984,
169-71.
South African Transit. (Johannesburg: Raven Press, 1979).
Reviewed by T. James, *CRNLE Reviews Journal*, 1, 1981, 76-81.
Stationen. (Bern: Lukianos Verlag Hans Erpf, 1968).
Reviewed by M. McInnes, *Makar*, 4, 1968, 53-56.

Waiting for Cancer. (Brisbane: Queensland Community Press, 1985).
Reviewed by B. Beaver, *Weekend Australian*, 21-22 December, 1985.
A Winter's Journey:(1976-1977): Diary Poems. (Sydney: Edwards & Shaw, 1979).
Reviewed by G. Dutton, *Bulletin*, 26 June, 1979, 66-7; K. Goodwin, *Weekend Australian*, 16-17 June, 1979, Weekend 10; J. Rodriguez, *ABR*, 16, 1979, 24.

Critical Material
Perkins, Elizabeth. '"Three Suns I Saw": Geography, Art and Desire in Manfred Jurgensen's *A Winter's Journey*'. In *The German Presence in Queensland over the Last 150 Years*, edited by Manfred Jurgensen and Alan Corkhill (St Lucia Qld.: German Department, University of Queensland, 1988), 326-39.
---. 'Translating the Next Sentence: Language as Theme in Some Poetry of Manfred Jurgensen'. *LiNQ*, 13, No. 2, 1985, 1-14.
Tonetto, Walter. 'Biting the Ploughed Reticence: Raw Energy and Sublime Longing in the Poetry of Manfred Jurgensen'. *Outrider*, [10.1&2], 1993, 297-310.

JURY, CHARLES RISCHBIETH

Non-Fiction
Well Measur'd Song: Quantitative and Quasiquantitative Vere in English. (Melbourne: Cheshire, 1968). Edited by Barbara Wall and D.C. Muecke.
Reviewed by *ABR*, 7, 1968, 117; S.E. Lee, *Southerly*, 2, 1968, 145-60.

Critical Material
'Poetic Justice'. *Nation*, 11 March, 1967, 10-11.
Dale, Leigh. 'Classical and Colonial: Reading the Homoerotic in Charles Jury's *Icarius*'. *Meridian*, 14.1, 1995, 45-58.
Ryan, J. S. 'Forgotten Poetic Sensibilities: The Plays of Charles Jury and Ray Mathew'. In *Australian Drama 1920-1955: Papers Presented to a Conference at the University of New England, Armidale, September 1-4, 1984.* (Armidale, NSW: University of New England, Department of Continuing Educayion, 1986), 71-88.
Wall, Barbara. 'Charles Rischbieth Jury: Poet of Adelaide'. *South Australiana*, 4, 1966, 79-114.
---. 'C.R. Jury and the Authorship of "Fiction: A University Satire": A Correction'. *South Australiana*, 22, 1983, 142.

KALAMARAS, VASSO

Collection
The Same Light. (Fremantle, W.A.: Fremantle Arts Centre Press, 1989).
Reviewed by E. Hatzimanolis, *Antithesis*, 4, No. 1, 1990, 181-6; L. Houbein, *ABR*, No. 115, 1989, 14; A. Pitsis, *Editions*, Nos. 8-9, 1990, 11; B. Roberts, *Australian Women's Book Review*, 1, No. 2, 1989, 4-5.

Drama
The Bread Trap. (Box Hill, Vic.: Elikia Books, 1986).
Reviewed by C. Castan, *Australasian Drama Studies*, No. 10, 1987, 119-122.

Poetry
Twentytwo Poems. (Daglish: Kalamaras, 1977).
Reviewed by M. Jurgensen, *Outrider*, 1, No. 1, 1984, 182-84.

Critical Material
Castan, Con. *Conflicts of Love.* (Brisbane: Phoenix Publications, 1986). Reviewed by A. Corkhill, *A.L.S.*, 14, No. 2, 1989, 271-73; M. Koundoura, *Outrider*, III, No. 2, 1986, 204-06 and *ABR*, No. 87, 1987, 24-25.
---. 'Greek-Australian Plays'. *Australasian Drama Studies*, Nos. 12-13, 1988, [17]-33.
---. 'Vasso Kalamaras: A Tale of Two Countries'. *Meanjin*, 44, No. 1, 1985, 87-92.
Nickas, Helen. *Migrant Daughters: The Female Voice in Greek-Australian Prose Fiction.* (Melbourne: Owl Publishing, 1992), 49-89; 203-224.

KEESING, NANCY

Poetry
Hails and Farewells, and Other Poems. (Sydney: Edwards & Shaw, 1977).
Reviewed by D. Green, *Nation Review*, 26 January-1 February, 1978, 16; J. Griffin, *Advertiser*, 10 September, 1977, 25; C. Harrison-Ford, *S.M.H.*, 10 December, 1977, 17; E. Lindsay, *Weekend Australian Magazine*, 13-14 August, 1977, 12.

The Woman I Am: Poems. Selected and introduced by Meg Stewart. (Sydney: State Library of NSW P, 1994).
Reviewed by M. McLeod, *S.M.H.* 21 Jan., 1995, Spectrum 12A.

Non-Fiction
Riding the Elephant. (Sydney: Allen & Unwin, 1988).
Reviewed by B. Farmer, *Mattoid*, No. 31, 1988, 134-36; M. Gollan, *S.M.H.*, 9 July, 1988, 74; S.E. Lee, *Southerly*, XLVIII, No. 3, 1988, 336-339; R. Ward, *Overland*, No. 111, 1988, 101-102.

Non-Fiction
'Black? White? Grey? How "Readers" Read'. *Australian Author*, V, No. 3, 1973, 32-3.

Critical Material

Bowen, Jill. 'A Weather-Eye on Literature'. *Australian*, 10 January, 1984, 8.
Costigan, Michael. 'Nancy Keesing: In Memoriam'. *Southerly*, 53.1, 1993, 1-4.
Frizell, Helen. 'Poet and Housewife'. *S.M.H.*, 2 July, 1974, 7.
Sayers, Stuart. 'Fire is the Final Critic'. *Age*, 23 September, 1978, 24.

KEFALA, ANTIGONE

Fiction

Alexia: A Tale of Two Cultures. (Sydney: Ferguson, 1985).
Reviewed by L. Forsyth, *ABR*, No. 73, 1985, 15-17.
The First Journey: Two Short Novels. (Sydney: Wild and Woolley, 1975).
Reviewed by R. Garfitt, *T.L.S.*, 9 April, 1976, 445; R.D. Jones, *Makar*, 12, No. 1, 1976, 61-2; D. Kim, *S.M.H.*, 26 June, 1976, 17.
The Island. (Sydney: Hale and Iremonger, 1984).
Reviewed by F. Davis, *Fremantle Arts Centre Broadsheet*, 4, No. 4, 1985, 4; T. Forshaw, *Quadrant*, 29, No. 3, 1985, 77-79; M. Harrison, *Age Monthly Review*, 5, No. 1, 1985, 16-19; M. Jurgensen, *Outrider*, 1, No. 2, 1984, 231-32; E. Lawson, *Phoenix Review*, No. 1, 1986/87, 119-21; S. McKernan, *ABR*, No. 68, 1985, 24-25; W. Noonan, *Weekend Australian*, 27-28 October, 1984, Weekend 15; C. Peake, *S.M.H.*, 22 December, 1984, 36.

Poetry

Absence: New and Selected Poems. (Sydney: Hale & Iremonger, 1992).
Reviewed by C. Bateson, *Australian Women's Book Review*, 5.1, 1993, 5-6; M. Duwell, *Weekend Australian*, 31 October-1 November, 1992, Review 7; S. Gardner, *Imago*, 4, 3, 1992, 92-93; K. Hart, *Age*, 28 November, 1992, Saturday Extra 9; P. Kane, *World Literature Today*, 68.1, 1994, 210; D. Randall, *Antipodes* 7.2, 1993, 147-48.
The Alien. Gargoyle poets 5 (St Lucia: Makar, 1973).
Reviewed by M. Haley, *Twentieth Century*, No. 28, 1973, 181-2; E.S. Lindsay, *LiNQ*, 2, No. 3, 1973, 38-39; G. Rowlands, *Expression Australia*, 12, No. 6, 1973, 18-19; T. Shapcott, *ABR*, No. 11, 1973, 134-36; J. Tranter, *New Poetry*, 22. No. 1, 1974, 43-61, esp. 52-4.
European Notebook. (Sydney: Hale and Iremonger, 1988).
Reviewed by J. Grant, *Weekend Australian*, 7-8 January, 1989, Weekend 6; D. McCooey, *Westerly*, 34, No. 1, 1989, 91-92; N. Papastergiados, *Age Monthly Review*, 9, No. 4, 1989, 3-5; C. Wallace-Crabbe, *Age Saturday Extra*, 28 January, 1989, 13.
Thirsty Weather. (Melbourne: Outback Press, 1978).
Reviewed by R. Allingham, *Poetry Australia*, No. 70, 1979, 59-62; G. Dutton, *Bulletin*, 25 July, 1978, 62; A. Gibbs, *Weekend Australian*, 9-10 September, 1978, Weekend 9; K. Hemensley, *Australasian Small Press Review*, Nos. 7-8, 1979, 56-61, esp. 58-59; J. Rodriguez, *S.M.H.*, 30 December, 1978, 17; B. Vaughan, *ABR*, No 8, 1979, 24.

Critical Material

'Interview'. *Aspect*, 5, Nos. 1-2, 1980, 68-74.
Brett, Judith. 'The Process of Becoming: Antigone Kefala's *The First Journey* and *The Island*'. *Meanjin*, 44, No. 1, 1985, 125-33.
Castan, Con. 'Antigone Kefala'. *Outrider*, 1, No. 2, 1984, 18-21.
Fremd, Angelika. 'Interview with Antigone Kefala'. *Outrider*, 1, No. 2, 1984, 9-18.
Gunew, Sneja. 'Ania Walwicz and Antigone Kefala: Varieties of Migrant Dreaming'. *Arena*, No. 76, 1986, 65-80.
---. 'Antigone Kefala: Re-viewing Reviewers who Domesticate the Alien'. *Outrider*,

1, No. 2, 1984, 21-24.
---. 'In Journeys Begin Dreams: Antigone Kefala and Ania Walwicz'. In her *Framing Marginality: Multicultural Literary Studies* (Carlton, Vic.: MUP, 1994), 71-92.
---. 'Migrant Women Writers: Who's on Whose Margins'. *Meanjin*, 42, No. 1, 1983, 16-26.
Gunew, Sneja, and Kateryna O. Longley, eds. *Striking Chords: Multicultural Literary Interpretations*. North Sydney: Allen & Unwin, 1992.
Hatzimanolis, Efi. 'The Politics of Nostalgia: Community and Difference in Migrant Writing'. *Hecate*, 16, Nos. 1-2, 1990, 120-27.
Nickas, Helen. *Migrant Daughters: The Female Voice in Greek-Australian Prose Fiction*. (Melbourne: Owl Publishing, 1992), 151-161; 225-243.
Page, Geoff. 'Antigone Kefala'. In his *A Reader's Guide To Contemporary Australian Poetry* (St. Lucia: U.Q.P., 1995), 146-149.
Rama, R.P. '[Interview with] Antigone Kefala'. *Dialogues with Australian Poets*. (Calcutta: P. Lal/Writers Workshop, 1993), 31-44.
Tsokos, Michelle. 'Memory and Absence: The Poetry of Antigone Kefala'. *Westerly* 39.4, 1994, 51-60.

KENDALL, HENRY

Collection
Henry Kendall. Selected by Leonie Kramer. Introduction by A.D. Hope (Melbourne: Sun Books, 1973). Three Colonial Poets, Book 2.
Reviewed by J. Blight, *Nation Review*, 16-22 November, 1973, 167.
Henry Kendall: Poetry, Prose & Selected Correspondence. Edited by Michael Ackland. (St Lucia: U.Q.P., 1993).
Reviewed by V. Smith, *A.L.S.*, 16.2, 1993, 242-44.

Poetry
Bellbirds and Other Verses. Edited by T. Inglis Moore. (North Ryde, N.S.W.: A.& R., 1988). First published as *Selected Poems of Henry Kendall* (Sydney: A.& R., 1957).
Henry Kendall. Edited with an introduction by T. Inglis Moore. (Sydney: A.& R., 1963). Australian Poets Series.
Reviewed by D. Ambrose, *Poetry Magazine*, No. 6, 1966, 30-2; A. King, *A.L.S.*, I, No. 4, 1964, 276-7.
The Poetical Works of Henry Kendall. Edited by T.T. Reed with a Preface, Introduction, Notes, Bibliography and Appendix ('Poems by Basil Edward Kendall' and 'Poems by Melinda Kendall'). (Adelaide: Libraries Board of South Australia, 1966).
Reviewed by D. Douglas, *Age*, 10 September, 1966, 23; G.J., *Australian*, 9 April, 1966, 9; J. McAuley, *A.L.S.*, III, 1968, 314; T.I. Moore, *Canberra Times*, 28 May, 1966, 10 and *Meanjin*, XXVI, 1967, 101-103; A.W. Thomson, *Journal of Commonwealth Literature*, No. 5, 1968, 131-32; G.A. Wilkes, *Southerly*, XXVI, 1966, 213-4.

Critical Material
McLaren, Ian F. *Henry Kendall: A Comprehensive Bibliography*. (Parkville, Vic.: University of Melbourne Library, 1987). Reviewed by M. Ackland, *Bibliographical Society of Australia and New Zealand Bulletin*, 13, No. 2, 1989 (issued 1990), 73-77; J. Fletcher, *Biblionews and Australian Notes and Queries*, 14, No. 1, 1989, 13-15.
Ackland, Michael. '"Behind the Veil": Metamorphosis and Alienation in the Poetry of Henry Kendall'. *Southerly*, 51, 4, 1991, 105-22.
---. *Henry Kendall: The Man and the Myths*. (Carlton, Vic.: Melbourne UP/Miegunyah P, 1995). Reviewed by R. Hall, *ABR*, 172, 1995, 28-29; L. Kramer, *S.M.H.*, 17 June, 1995, Spectrum 11A; K. Stewart, *Weekend Australian*, 15-16 July,

1995, Review 9.

---. 'Nature Through Currency Lad Eyes: Wentworth, Harpur, Kendall and the Australian Landscape'. In *Mapped But Not Known: The Australian Landscape of the Imagination*, edited by P.R. Eaden and F.H. Mares (Netley, S.A.: Wakefield Press, 1986), 73-85.

---. 'No Easy Age for Faith or Verse: *Songs from the Mountains* and Henry Kendall's Burden of Election'. In Russell McDougall ed. *Henry Kendall: The Muse of Australia* (Armidale: Centre for Australian Language and Literature Studies, Uni of New England, 1992), 385-404.

---. 'Publishing Practice and Poetic Reputation: The Case of Henry Kendall'. *Bibliographical Society of Australia and New Zealand Bulletin*, 15, 1, 1991, 21-31.

---. 'Towards "The Shadow": Henry Kendall and the Mid-Century Crisis of Faith'. *Westerly*, 35, No. 3, 1990, 71-78. Reprinted in Russell McDougall ed. *Henry Kendall: The Muse of Australia* (Armidale: Centre for Australian Language and Literature Studies, Uni of New England, 1992), 275-288.

Bennett, F. '1870 Poem'. *S.M.H.*, 12 May, 1970, 2. Letter to the editor.

Burke, Iris. *Foreshadowings*. (Sydney: Australian Documentary Facsimile Society, 1963). Includes 'Four Extracts from a Chronology (in preparation) of the Rev T.H. Kendall and his Descendants', 'A Draft List of the Prose Writings of Heny Kendall'. Appendix III and Appendix IV. The 'Draft List' does not give dates of articles.

Clarke, Donovan. 'Henry Kendall: A Study in Imagery'. In Russell McDougall ed. *Henry Kendall: The Muse of Australia* (Armidale: Centre for Australian Language and Literature Studies, Uni of New England, 1992), 1-24.

---. 'Kendall's Views on Contemporary Writers: A Survey of His Correspondence'. *A.L.S.*, I, No. 3, 1964, 170-9.

---. 'New Light on Henry Kendall'. *A.L.S.*, II, 1966, 211-3.

Dingley, Robert. 'Double Vision: Aspects of Aboriginality in Kendall's Writing'. In Russell McDougall ed. *Henry Kendall: The Muse of Australia* (Armidale: Centre for Australian Language and Literature Studies, Uni of New England, 1992), 405-417.

---. 'The Track to Ogygia: A Note on Henry Kendall'. *Southerly*, XLVI, No. 3, 1986, 352-58.

Elliott, Brian. 'Antipodes: An Essay in Attitudes'. *Australian Letters*, VII, No. 3, 1966, 51-70.

---. 'The Colonial Poets'. In *The Literature of Australia*, edited by Geoffrey Dutton (Adelaide: Penguin Books, 1964), 231-6.

Gaffney, Carmel. 'Aspects of Kendall's Pastoral Muse'. In Russell McDougall ed. *Henry Kendall: The Muse of Australia* (Armidale: Centre for Australian Language and Literature Studies, Uni of New England, 1992), 150-164.

Goldie, Terry. 'The Aboriginal Connection: A Study of Charles Mair's *Tecumseh* and Henry Kendall's "The Glen of Arrawatta"'. *WLWE*, XXI, 1982, 287-97.

Heseltine, H.P. 'The Metamorphoses of Henry Kendall'. *Southerly*, XLI, 1981, 367-89. The eleventh Blaiklock Memorial Lecture.

Hope, A.D. 'Henry Kendall: A Dialogue with the Past'. *Southerly*, XXXII, 1972, 163-73. The 1st Herbert Blaiklock Memorial Lecture, University of Sydney, 14 July, 1971. Also published separately with the same title (Surry Hills, N.S.W.: Wentworth Press, 1972). Reprinted in Russell McDougall ed. *Henry Kendall: The Muse of Australia* (Armidale: Centre for Australian Language and Literature Studies, Uni of New England, 1992), 25-36.

Jordens, Ann-Mari. *The Stenhouse Circle: Literary Life in Mid-Nineteenth Century Sydney*. (Carlton: M.U.P., 1979). Includes commentary on Kendall.

Mitchell, A.C.W. 'The Radiant Dream: Notes on Henry Kendall'. *A.L.S.*, IV, 1969, 99-114. Reprinted in Russell McDougall ed. *Henry Kendall: The Muse of Australia* (Armidale: Centre for Australian Language and Literature Studies, Uni of New England, 1992), 37-53.

McDougall, Russell. *Henry Kendall: The Muse of Australia*. (Armidale: Centre for Australian Language and Literature Studies, Uni of New England, 1992). Reviewed by P. Kane, *Antipodes*, 7.1, 1993, 67-70; P. Mead, *Weekend Australian*, 17-18 October, 1992, Review 6; V. Smith, *A.L.S.*, 16.2, 1993, 242-44.

Otto, Peter. 'Kendall's Sublime Melancholy'. In Russell McDougall ed. *Henry Kendall: The Muse of Australia* (Armidale: Centre for Australian Language and Literature Studies, Uni of New England, 1992), 418-433.

Perkins, Elizabeth. 'Harpur's Notes [to "The Kangaroo Hunt"] and Kendall's "Bell Birds"'. *A.L.S.*, V, 1972, 277-84. Reprinted in Russell McDougall ed. *Henry Kendall: The Muse of Australia* (Armidale: Centre for Australian Language and Literature Studies, Uni of New England, 1992), 139-149.

Pringle, John Douglas. 'A Death on the Clarence'. In his *On Second Thoughts: Australian Essays*. (Sydney: A.& R, 1971, 134-49. Principally on Kendall's associate, James Lionel Michael.

Redden, W.J. 'Henry Kendall'. *S.M.H.*, 7 December, 1972, 7. Letter to the editor on the Henry Kendall Memorial Association.

Reed, T.T. 'Kendall's Satirical Humour'. *Southerly*, XLII, 1982, 363-84. The twelfth Blaiklock Memorial Lecture.

Ryan, J.S. 'Henry Kendall's Vital Association with the Grafton Area, Particularly in 1862-63'. In Russell McDougall ed. *Henry Kendall: The Muse of Australia* (Armidale: Centre for Australian Language and Literature Studies, Uni of New England, 1992), 54-86.

Sellick, Robert. 'Burke and Wills and the Colonial Hero: Three Poems'. *A.L.S.*, V, 1971, 180-89.

Stewart, Ken. '"A Careworn Writer for the Press": Henry Kendall in Melbourne'. In Russell McDougall ed. *Henry Kendall: The Muse of Australia* (Armidale: Centre for Australian Language and Literature Studies, Uni of New England, 1992), 165-205.

---. 'Henry Kendall and "The Legacy of Guilt"'. *Southerly*, 51, 4, 1991, 48-62. Reprinted in Russell McDougall ed. *Henry Kendall: The Muse of Australia* (Armidale: Centre for Australian Language and Literature Studies, Uni of New England, 1992), 289-303.

Stuart, Julian. *Part of the Glory: Reminiscences of the Shearers' Strike, Queensland, 1891*. Foreword by Lyndall Hadow. (Sydney: Australasian Book Society, 1967), 61-62, 67. Includes remarks on Kendall.

Swancott, Charles. *Gosford and the Henry Kendall Country (Koolewong to Lisarow)*. (Woy Woy: The Author, 1966).

Tolchard, Clifford. 'Thomas Kendall: Australia's Unhappy Pilgrim'. *Walkabout*, XXXIII, No. 5, 1967, 30.

Wilde, W.H. *Henry Kendall*. (Boston: Twayne, 1976). Twayne's World Author series: 387. Reviewed by V. Smith, *A.L.S.*, VIII, 1978, 527-28.

Wilding, Michael. '"My Name is Rickeybockey": The Poetry of Robert Adamson and the Spirit of Henry Kendall'. *Southerly*, XLVI, No. 1, 1986, 25-43.

Wilkes, G.A. 'Going Over the Terrain in a Different Way: An Alternative View of Australian Literary History'. *Southerly*, XXXV, 1975, 141-56.

Wilkins, Una J. 'Is it all "Bell Birds"?' *Drylight* (Sydney), 1966, 16-24.

Williams, T.L. 'Henry Kendall: A National Australian Poet'. *Journal of the Royal Queensland Historical Society*, VIII, 1967, 388-96.

Wright, Judith. 'Henry Kendall'. In her *Preoccupations in Australian Poetry*. (Melbourne: O.U.P., 1965), 19-44.

KENEALLY, THOMAS

Fiction

[pseud.] William Coyle. *Act of Grace*. (London: Chatto & Windus, 1992). Reviewed by D. Davison, *Weekend Australian*, 21-22 March, 1992, Review 7.

Blood Red, Sister Rose. (London, Sydney: Collins; New York: Viking, 1974).
Reviewed by P. Ackroyd, *Spectator*, CCXXXIII, 1975, 310; R.F. Brissenden, *Australian*, 9 November, 1974, 29; E. Campion, *Bulletin*, 23 November, 1974, 49-50; C. Egerton, *Nation Review*, 29 November-5 December, 1974, 203; J. Flanagan, *S.M.H.*, 9 November, 1974, 15; N. Hepburn, *Listener*, XCIII, 1975, 190; B. Jefferis, *Hemisphere*, XIX, No. 6, 1975, 40-41; B. Kiernan, *Age*, 9 November, 1974, 16; A.G. Mojtabai, *New York Times Book Review*, 9 February, 1975, 7; F. Moorhouse, *National Times*, 3-8 February, 1975, 23; P. Prince, *New Statesman*, LXXXVIII, 1974, 513; E. Riddell, *Australian*, 2 November, 1974, 35; S. Sayers, *Age*, 5 November, 1974, 8.

Bring Larks and Heroes. (Melbourne: Cassell Australia, 1967; New York: Viking Press, 1968; London: Quartet, 1973).
Reviewed by P. Adams, *Atlantic*, CCXXII, No. 2, 1968, 96; R. Baker, *Books and Bookmen*, XIII, No. 4, 1968, 30-31; N. Braham, *Twentieth Century*, XXIII, 1968, 86-88; R. Burns, *Nation*, 18 November, 1967, 22-23; K. Cantrell, *Australian Left Review*, No. 1, 1968, 73-75; S. Despoja, *Advertiser*, 16 December, 1967, 14; C. Gorchels, *Library Journal*, XCIII, 1968, 2259; P. Gough, *Bulletin*, 7 October, 1967, 80; D. Halliwell, *Spectator*, 1 March, 1968, 267-68; R. Hughes, *Times*, 24 February, 1968, 21; N. Jillett, *Age*, 14 October, 1967, 23; L. Kramer, *S.M.H.*, 11 November, 1967, 19; F.H. Mares, *Adelaide Advertiser*, 11 November, 1967, 18; J. McLaren, *Overland*, No. 38, 1968, 41-42; T.J.B. Spencer and M. Wilding, *Year Book of World Affairs*, XXIII, 1969, 333; *T.L.S.*, 26 October, 1973, 1299 (see also letter to the editor by R. Howard, *T.L.S.*, 2 November, 1973, 1346); D. Whitelock, *Australian*, 14 October, 1967, 14; R. Wighton, *ABR*, VI, 1967, 194.

The Chant of Jimmie Blacksmith. (New York: Viking; Sydney: A.& R., 1972; Harmondsworth, Middlesex; Ringwood, Vic.: Penguin, 1973).
Reviewed by P. Bell, *LiNQ*, II, No. 2, 1973, 48-52; J.B. Beston, *WLWE*, XI, No. 2, 1972, 65-66 and *Journal of Commonwealth Literature*, IX, 1974, 71-73; D.R. Burns, *Nation*, 29 April, 1972, 21-22; M. Costigan, *Review*, 8-14 April, 1972, 701; V. Cunningham, *Listener*, LXXXVIII, 1972, 345; I. Hamilton, *New Statesman*, XCVII, 2 March, 1979, 298; C. Harrison-Ford, *Bulletin*, 8 April, 1972, 44; H. Hewitt, *Canberra Times*, 6 May, 1972, 13; D. Hinch, *National Times*, 30 October-4 November, 1972, 37; B. Jefferis, *Hemisphere*, XVI, No. 10, 1972, 37; M. Jones, *S.M.H.*, 15 April, 1972, 23; B. Kiernan, *Meanjin*, XXXI, 1972, 489-93 and *Australian*, 8 April, 1972, 16; J. McLaren, *Overland*, No. 52, 1972, 52-53; A. Mitchell, *Advertiser*, 8 April, 1972, 16; W.A. Murray, *ABR*, XI, 1972, 8-9; D.J. O'Hearn, *Age*, 8 April, 1972, 12; C. Porterfield, *Time* (Aust. ed.), 28 August, 1972, 58, 60; W. Pradhan, *Union Recorder*, LII, 1972, 171-72; A. Thwaite, *New York Times Book Review*, 27 August, 1972, 3, 24; *T.L.S.*, 15 September, 1972, 1041; S. Toulson, *New Statesman*, LXXXIV, 11972, 295; J. Yardley, *Book World*, VI, No. 33, 1972, 13 August, 8.

[pseud.] William Coyle. *Chief of Staff.* (London: Chatto & Windus, 1991).
Reviewed by J. Hanrahan, *Age*, 11 January, 1992, Saturday Extra 6; P. Rolfe, *Bulletin*, 28 January, 1992, 194.

Confederates. (Sydney: Collins, 1979; New York: Harper & Row, 1980).
Reviewed by K. England, *Advertiser*, 15 March, 1980, 28; B. Jefferis, *S.M.H.*, 23 February, 1980, 18; N. Jillett, *Age*, 1 March, 1980, 27; B. King, *Sewanee Review*, LXXXIX, 1981, 461-69; F. King, *Spectator*, 17 November, 1979, 26-27; J. Mellors, *Listener*, 1 November, 1979, 611; A. Motion, *T.L.S.*, 23 November, 1979, 11; P. Pierce, *Meanjin*, XXXIX, 1980, 263-65; G. Radcliffe, *ABR*, No. 18, 1980, 9; D. Rowbotham, *Courier-Mail*, 23 February, 1980, 22; M. Thomas, *Canberra Times*, 15 March, 1980, 13; G.A. Wilkes, *Weekend Australian Magazine*, 5-6 April, 1980, 12.

The Cut-Rate Kingdom. (Sydney: Bulletin and Wildcat Press, 1980). Reprinted

Ringwood, Vic.: Penguin, 1984.
Reviewed by D. Cusack, *Bowyang*, No. 5, 1981, 46; D. English, *ABR*, No. 24, 1980, 40; R. Hall, *S.M.H.*, 30 August, 1980, 21; H. Hewitt, *Canberra Times*, 18 October, 1980, 22; N. Jillett, *Age*, 30 August, 1980, 25; J. Mellors, *Listener*, 5 July, 1984, 27; D. Rowbotham, *Courier-Mail*, 30 August, 1980, 22, and *Courier Mail*, 31 March, 1984, 28; G. Trigoldby, *New Statesman*, 15 June, 1984, 26; G. Windsor, *Overland*, No. 96, 1984, 66-68; M. Wood, *T.L.S.*, 24 August, 1984, 935.

A Dutiful Daughter. (Sydney: A.& R.; New York: Viking Press, 1971).
Reviewed by J.B. Beston, *Westerly*, No. 4, 1971, 61-63 and *Makar*, VII, No. 2, 1971, 38-41 and *Journal of Commonwealth Literature*, VII, 1972, No. 2, 154-55; A. Carter, *New York Times Book Review*, 12 September, 1971, 53; M. Costigan, *Sunday Review*, 16 May, 1971, 915; M. Dook, *Union Recorder*, LIV, 1974, 132; R. Evans, *LiNQ*, II, No. 2, 1973, 52-56; C. Harrison-Ford, *Bulletin*, 15 May, 1971, 48-49; H. Hewitt, *Canberra Times*, 29 May, 1971, 15; B. Jefferis, *Hemisphere*, XV, No. 11, 1971, 35-36; M. Jones, *S.M.H.*, 8 May, 1971, 22; B. Kiernan, *Australian*, 15 May, 1971, 19; M. Lemming, *ABR*, X, 1971, 152; M.M., *Time*, 7 June, 1971, 62-64; J. McLaren, *Overland*, Nos. 50-51, 1972, 97; B. Oakley, *Sunday Australian*, 16 May, 1971, 32; D.J. O'Hearn, *Age*, 8 May, 1971, 19; A. Roberts, *Advertiser*, 1 May, 1971, 26; D. Rowbotham, *Courier-Mail*, 5 June, 1971, 13.

A Family Madness. (London, Sydney: Hodder & Stoughton, 1985; New York: Simon & Schuster, 1986).
Reviewed by K. England, *Advertiser*, 5 October, 1985, 7; L. Forsyth, *ABR*, No. 77, 1985, 27-28; M. Glastonbury, *New Statesman*, 4 October, 1985, 28-29; E. Jolley, *S.M.H.*, 28 September, 1985, 46; B. Kiernan, *National Times*, 25-31 October, 1985, 62; S. McKernan, *Bulletin*, 8 October, 1985, 84; J. Mellors, *Listener Guide*, 24 October, 1985, 29; A. Mitchell, *Weekend Australian Magazine*, 28-29 September, 1985, 17; P.T. O'Conner, *New York Times Book Review*, 15 March, 1987, 28; N. Philip, *British Book News*, January, 1986, 48; D. Rowbotham, *Courier-Mail*, 12 October, 1985, 30; J. Sutherland, *London Review of Books*, 7 November, 1985, 24; R. Towers, *New York Times Book Review*, 16 March, 1986, 9; R. Wade, *Contemporary Review*, CCXLVIII, No. 1440, 1986, 45-49; M. Wood, *T.L.S.*, 18 October, 1985, 1169.

The Fear. (London: Cassell, 1965).
Reviewed by P. Gough, *Bulletin*, 17 July, 1965, 50; J. McLaren, *Overland*, No. 33, 1966, 44; C. Semmler, *S.M.H.*, 24 July, 1965, 14; D. Whitelock, *ABR*, IV, 1965, 182; M. Wilding, *Southerly*, XXVI, 1966, 60-1.

Flying Hero Class. (Sydney; London: Hodder & Stoughton; New York: Warner Books, 1991).
Reviewed by J. Chimonyo, *Age*, 9 March, 1991, Saturday Extra 8; T. P. Coakley, *Antipodes*, 5.2, 1991, 149; E. Hower, *New York Times Book Review*, 7 April, 1991, 9; J. Kitson, *ABR*, 129, 1991, 5-6; P. Nelson, *Quadrant*, 35.9, 1991, 83-84; I. Salusinszky, *Weekend Australian*, 23-24 March, 1991, Review 5; R. Sorensen, *S.M.H.*, 9 March, 1991, 47.

Gossip from the Forest. (London: Collins, 1975; New York: Harcourt, Brace, Jovanovich, 1976).
Reviewed by R.F. Brissenden, *Australian*, 29 November, 1975, 45; D.R. Burns, *Nation Review*, 5-11 December, 1975, 210; B. Courtis, *Age*, 25 April, 1980, 2; A. Duchene, *T.L.S.*, 19 September, 1975, 1041; K. England, *Advertiser*, 29 November, 1975, 24; P. Fussell, *New York Times Book Review*, 11 April, 1976, 7-8; B. Kiernan, *Age*, 22 November, 1975, 17; M. Lurie, *National Times*, 1-6 March, 1976, 20; M. Macleod, *S.M.H.*, 29 November, 1975, 15; R.E. McDowell, *World Literature Today*, LI, No. 1, 1977, 157; S. O'Grady, *Weekend Australian Magazine*, 26-27 April, 1980, 11; M. Thorpe, *English Studies*, LVIII, No. 1, 1977, 47.

Jacko. (Port Melbourne: Heinemann, 1993).
Reviewed by J. Flintoff, *T.L.S.*, 18 March, 1994, 13; P. Kane, *Age*, 23 October, 1993, Saturday Extra 8; B. King, *World Literature Today*, 68.4, 1994, 879-80; A. Peek, *ABR*, 156, 1993, 15-16; P. Pierce, *S.M.H.*, 2 October, 1993, Spectrum 12A; M. Sharkey, *Weekend Australian*, 30-31 October, 1993, Review 7; T. Ware, *Antipodes*, 9.2, 1995, 146-47.

Moses the Lawgiver. (New York: Harper & Row; London: Collins, 1975).
Reviewed by J. Bentley, *Australian*, 19 June, 1976, 40; K. England, *Advertiser*, 17 July, 1976, 20; C. Semmler, *S.M.H.*, 16 October, 1976, 19.

Ned Kelly and the City of the Bees. (London: Cape, 1978; Ringwood, Vic.: Penguin, 1980; Boston: D.R. Godine, 1981).
Reviewed by D. English, *ABR*, No. 27, 1980, 20; E. Finnin, *Advertiser*, 27 January, 1979, 21.

Passenger. (London: Collins; New York: Harcourt Brace Jovanovich, 1979).
Reviewed by V. Brady, *Westerly*, XXV, No. 2, 1980, 61-75; L. Clancy, *Overland*, No. 80, 1980, 51-52; K. England, *Advertiser*, 14 April, 1979, 17; D. English, *ABR*, No. 11, 1979, 1 and 3; E. Fuller, *Sewanee Review*, LXXXVIII, 1980, ii, iv, vi; C. Hanna, *Southerly*, XL, 1980, 120-24; M. Hope, *Spectator*, 20 January, 1979, 23; N. Jillett, *Age*, 5 May, 1979, 27; M. Macleod, *S.M.H.*, 16 June, 1979, 19; B. Morrison, *New Statesman*, XCVII, 19 January, 1979, 88; J. Neville, *National Times*, 14 July, 1979, 36; C.C. Park, *Hudson Review*, XXXII, 1980, 573-75; D. Rowbotham, *Courier-Mail*, 21 April, 1979, 19; R. Sellick, *CRNLE Reviews Journal*, No. 2, 1979, 39-44.

The Place at Whitton. (London: Cassell, 1964).
Reviewed by N. Buckley, *Bulletin*, 28 November, 1964, 54; A. Glover, *S.M.H.*, 30 January, 1965, 13; P. Gough, *Nation*, 19 September, 1964, 22-3; M. Harris, *ABR*, III, 1964, 168.

The Playmaker. (London, Sydney: Hodder & Stoughton, 1987; New York: Simon and Schuster, 1988).
Reviewed by J. Atlas, *New York Times Book Review*, 20 September, 1988, 7, (A letter to the editor by A.H. Peacock about this review appears in the *New York Times Book Review*, 20 March, 1988, 41); M. Clark, *S.M.H.*, 10 October, 1987, 47; P. Craven, *ABR*, No. 97, 1987/88, 12-13; H. Daniel, *Age Saturday Extra*, 10 October, 1987, 13; B. Edwards, *Mattoid*, No. 33, 1989, 192-95; D. English, *Times on Sunday*, 11 October, 1987, 33; B. Leithauser, *New Yorker*, 8 February, 1988, 99-100; N. Lezard, *Spectator*, 12 September, 1987, 34; S. McKernan, *Bulletin*, 20 October, 1987, 105; A. Mitchell, *Weekend Australian*. *Weekend Magazine*, 10-11 October, 1987, 15; N. Potter, *Antipodes*, II, No. 1, 1988, 8; R. Stone, *New York Times Book Review*, 1 October, 1989, 1; J. Sutherland, *London Review of Books*, IX, No. 17, 1987, 18-19; P. Vansittart, *London Magazine*, 27, No. 8, 1987, 105-7.

A River Town. (Port Melbourne, Vic.: Heinemann, 1995).
Reviewed by L. Clancy, *ABR*, 170, 1995, 50; L. Frost, *Age*, 15 Apr., 1995, Saturday Extra 9; S. Henighan, *T.L.S.*, 24 March, 1995, 20; J.T. Hospital, *London Review of Books*, 17.10, 1995, 22-23; D. Matthews, *Weekend Australian*, 15-16 Apr., 1995, Review 9; E. Riddell, *S.M.H.*, 8 Apr., 1995, Spectrum 9A; T. Ware, *Antipodes*, 9.2, 1995, 146-47.

Schindler's Ark. (London: Hodder & Stoughton; New York: Simon & Schuster [as *Schindler's List*], 1982).
Reviewed by E. Campion, *Bulletin*, 23 November, 1982, 82 & 84; D.J. Enright, *T.L.S.*, 29 October, 1982, 1189; M. Glastonbury, *New Statesman*, 5 November, 1982, 25; J. Hanrahan, *ABR*, No. 48, 1983, 24-25; H. Hewitt, *Canberra Times*, 18 December, 1982, 16; M. Hulse, *London Magazine*, n.s. XXII, No. 11, 1983, 103-05; P. Kemp, *Listener*, 14 October, 1982, 31; F. King, *New Statesman*, 30 October,

1982, 28-29; M. Lurie, *National Times*, 5-11 December, 1982, 23; D.J. O'Hearn, *Age Saturday Extra*, 11 December, 1982, 12; D. Rowbotham, *Courier-Mail*, 6 November, 1982, 25; R. Taubman, *London Review of Books*, V, No. 1, 1983, 23; R. Wade, *Contemporary Review*, No. 1404, 1983, 45-46; A.N. Wilson, *Encounter*, No. 352, 11983, 70-71.

Season in Purgatory. (London: Collins, 1976; New York: Harcourt Brace Jovanovich, 1977).
Reviewed by K. England, *Advertiser*, 27 November, 1976, 25; N. Hepburn, *Listener*, XCVI, 1976, 317; J. Miller, *T.L.S.*, 3 September, 1976, 1069; I. Murray, *Financial Times*, 16 September, 1976, 15; L. Murray, *Bulletin*, 8 January, 1977, 54-55; D.J. O'Hearn, *Age*, 18 December, 1976, 20; D. Rowbotham, *Courier-Mail*, 13 November, 1976, 19; A. Rutherford, *Commonwealth Newsletter*, No. 11, 1977, 29 and *Literary Half-Yearly*, XVIII, No. 1, 1977, 211-17; C. Semmler, *S.M.H.*, 6 November, 1976, 15; T. Shapcott, *National Times*, 18-23 October, 1976, 61; R.A. Sokolov, *New York Times Book Review*, 27 February, 1977, 30; N. Totton, *Spectator*, 4 September, 1976, 17; J.Treglown, *New Statesman*, XCII, 3 September, 1976, 313.

The Survivor. (Sydney: A.& R., 1969; New York: Viking, 1970).
Reviewed by R. Burns, *Nation*, 29 November, 1969, 21-22; L. Cantrell, *Meanjin*, XXX, 1971, 129-31; S. Edgar, *Canberra Times*, 15 November, 1969, 15; R.W.V. Elliott, *Australian University*, VIII, 1970, 83-85; M. Jones, *S.M.H.*, 1 November, 1969, 17; N. Keesing, *Bulletin*, 8 November, 1969, 58-59; B. Kiernan, *Australian*, 1 November, 1969, 22; M. Levin, *New York Times Book Review*, 27 September, 1970, 48; J. McLaren, *Overland*, No. 43, 1969, 50-51; J. Waten, *Age*, 1 November, 1969, 17 (see also letter to the editor by Keneally,*Age*, 8 November, 1969, 14); D. Whitelock, *ABR*, IX, 1969/70, 55; M. Wilding, *Southerly*, XXX, 1970, 71-72.

Three Cheers for the Paraclete. (Sydney: A.& R., 1968; New York: Viking Press, 1969).
Reviewed by P. Adams, *Atlantic*, CCXXIII, No. 4, 1969, 146; N. Braham, *Twentieth Century*, XXIII, 1968, 182-83; L.J. Clancy, *Meanjin*, XXVIII, 1969, 414-16; P. Cuneo, *Saturday Review*, LII, 1969, 94; C.H. Ford, *Australian Left Review*, No. 2, 1969, 74-76; R. Hall, *Nation*, 21 December, 1968, 21-22; H.P. Heseltine, *ABR*, VIII, 1968, 4-5; N. Keesing, *Bulletin*, 26 October, 1968, 83, 85; B. Kiernan, *Australian*, 12 October, 1968, 12; H.G. Kippax, *S.M.H.*, 19 October, 1968, 23; M. Levin, *New York Times Book Review*, 13 April, 1969, 46; F.H. Mares, *Advertiser*, 12 October, 1968, 12; J. McLaren, *Overland*, No. 40, 1968, 39-40; J.N. Molony, *Canberra Times*, 19 October, 1968, 14; D. O'Grady, *Commonweal*, XCI, 24 October, 1969, 108-09; D.J. O'Hearn, *Age*, 12 October, 1968, 12.

Towards Asmara: An African Novel. (London; Sydney: Hodder & Stoughton; New York: Warner Books [as *To Asmara*], 1989).
Reviewed by B. Abel, *Contemporary Review*, 255, 1485, 1989, 213-16; V. Brady, *ABR*, No. 117, 1989/90, 33-34; J. Carmody, *Quadrant*, 34, No. 11, 1990, 79-80; T. P. Coakley, *Antipodes*, 4.1, 1990, 64; M. Costigan, *S.M.H.*, 7 October, 1989, 81; D. English, *Weekend Australian*, 14-15 October, 1989, Weekend 6; J. Harding, *London Review of Books*, 12, No. 5, 1990, 14-15; G. Ingoldby, *New Statesman and Society*, 2, 69, 1989, 38-39; J. Larkin, *Age Saturday Extra*, 7 October, 1989, 9; P. Pierce, *Bulletin*, 17 October, 1989, 127-28; R.B. Sykes, *Editions*, 1, No. 5, 1989/90, 22; M. Thorpe, *World Literature Today*, 64.2, 1990, 360.

A Victim of the Aurora. (Sydney: Collins, 1977; New York: Harcourt Brace Jovanovich, 1978).
Reviewed by C. Hanna, *Southerly*, XL, 1980, 120-24; N. Hepburn, *The Listener*, XCVIII, 1977, 382-83; J. Keates, *New Statesman*, XCVI, 1977, 343; J. Mills, *Queen's Quarterly*, LXXXV, 1978-79, 643-46.

Woman of the Inner Sea. (Rydalmere, NSW: Hodder & Stoughton, 1992).

Reviewed by C. Blanche, *Quadrant*, 37.5, 1993, 80-82; R. Brain, *T.L.S.*, 26 June, 1992, 20; D.R. Burns, *Overland*, 129, 1992, 84-86; M. Luke, *ABR*, 141, 1992, 10-11; D.J. O'Hearn, *Age*, 20 June, 1992, Saturday Extra 9; P. Pierce, *Bulletin*, 16 June, 1992, 106; A.P. Riemer, *S.M.H.*, 13 June, 1992, 42; M. Sharkey, *Weekend Australian*, 13-14 June, 1992, Review 7; C.K. Stead, *London Review of Books*, 14, 18, 1992, 20; R. Willbanks, *World Literature Today*, 68.2, 1994, 425-26.

Non-Fiction

Homebush Boy: A Memoir. (Port Melbourne: Heinemann Minerva, 1995).
Reviewed by T. Bowden, *Weekend Australian* 4-5 Nov., 1995, Review 9; E. Campion, *Bulletin*, 14 Nov., 1995, 96; J. Hanrahan, *Age*, 30 Dec., 1995, Saturday Extra 6; T. Shapcott, *ABR*, 177, 1995, 13-14.

Memoirs from a Young Republic. (London: Heinemann, 1993).
Reviewed by D. Davie, *T.L.S.*, 5 November, 1993, 25.

Now and in Time to Be: Ireland and the Irish. (London: Ryan Publ.; Sydney: Pan Macmillan, 1991; New York: Norton, 1992).
Reviewed by D.J. O'Hearn, *Age*, 21 December, 1991, Saturday Extra 6; P. Pierce, *Bulletin*, 28 January, 1992, 193; K. Weber, *New York Times Book Review*, 19 April, 1992, 12.

Our Republic. (Melbourne: Heinemann, 1993).
Reviewed by E. Campion, *Bulletin*, 11 May, 1993, 97; E. Cox, *ABR*, 152, 1993, 20; J. Davidson, *Age*, 8 May, 1993, Saturday Extra 9; R. Murray, *Quadrant*, 38.4, 1994, 76-78; J.D. Pringle, *S.M.H.*, 15 May, 1993, 47; I. Salusinszky, *Weekend Australian*, 29-30 May, 1993, Review 5.

Outback. (Sydney: Hodder & Stoughton, 1983). Travel book.
Reviewed by D. Altman, *Weekend Australian Magazine*, 19-20 November, 1983, 15; W.R. Mead, *London Review of Books*, VI, No. 4, 1984, 22; C. Morehead, *Spectator*, 26 November, 1983, 28-29; E.C. Rolls, *S.M.H.*, 3 December, 1983, 46; A. Ross, *T.L.S.*, 16 December, 1983, 1393; M. Thomas, *Canberra Times*, 11 December, 1983, 12.

The Place Where Souls are Born. (Rydalmere, NSW: Hodder & Stoughton; New York: Simon & Schuster, 1992).
Reviewed by D.R. Burns, *Overland*, 129, 1992, 84-86; R. Houston, *New York Times Book Review*, 26 April 1992, 22; D.J. O'Hearn, *Age*, 20 June, 1992, Saturday Extra 9; J. Williams, *T.L.S.*, 25 December, 1992, 25.

'The Australian Novel'. *Age*, 3 February, 1968, 22.
'A Family Madness'. In *The View from Tinsel Town*, edited by Tom Thompson (Ringwood, Vic.: Southerly/Penguin, 1985), 53-58.
'Doing Research for Historical Novels'. *The Australian Author*, 7, No. 1, 1975, 27-29.
'Keneally on Critics: Have a Chocolate-coated Funnel-webb'. *National Times*, 15-20 May, 1972, 5.
'The Novelist's Poison'. *Australian Author*, I, No. 4, 1969, 3-6.
'Origin of a Novel'. *Hemisphere*, XIII, No. 10, 1969, 9-13. Discusses the writing of *The Survivor*.
'"Trap" that Can Snare a Priest'. *S.M.H.*, 14 February, 1968, 6.
'The World's Worse End?' *Antipodes*, II, No. 1, 1988, 5-8. Originally published in *Caliban*, XIV, 1977, 81-89. Discusses perceptions of Australia in Australian literature.
'Writers' View'. *Theatre Australia*, IV, No. 8, 1980, 17-18.

Critical Material

Ehrhardt, Marianne. 'Thomas Keneally: A Checklist'. *A.L.S.*, IX, 1979, 98-117.
'Author Share $5,000 Prize in Literary Contest'. *Australian*, 27 October, 1970, 1.

'The Breelong Blacks'. See also poem by Arthur Noonan. *Armidale & District Historical Society. Journal & Proceedings*, No. 18, 51-57.

'Bullie's House'. *Identity*, IV, No. 1, 1980, 15-17. An Aboriginal point of view.

'Keneally Wins Booker Prize with War Story'. *Canberra Times*, 21 October, 1982, 1.

'Keneally by Nimrod'. *Canberra Times*, 22 February, 1980, 10.

'The Path Paved with Rejection Slips'. *Australian*, 29 July, 1969, 5.

'Thomas Keneally Wins Herald $2,500 Award for Novel'. *S.M.H.*, 21 October, 1972, 1. Related report, *S.M.H.*, 26 October, 1972, 2.

Antonini, Maria. '*Blood Red, Sister Rose* e la Trilogia Europea di Thomas Keneally'. In *Australiana*, edited by Paolo Bertinetti and Claudio Gorlier (Rome: Bulzoni, 1982), 197-207; abstract 268-69.

Baker, Candida. 'Thomas Keneally'. In her *Yacker 2: Australian Writers Talk About Their Work* (Sydney: Picador, 1987), 116-142.

Bayliss, John F. 'Slave and Convict Narratives: A Discussion of American and Australian Writing'. *Journal of Commonwealth Literature*, No. 8, 1969, 142-49.

Beston, John B. 'An Awful Rose: Thomas Keneally as a Dramatist'. *Southerly*, XXXIII, 1973, 36-42.

---. 'The Hero's "Fear of Freedom" in Keneally'. *A.L.S.*, V, 1972, 374-87.

---. 'An Interview with Thomas Keneally'. *WLWE*, XII, No. 1, 1973, 48-56.

---. 'Novelist's Vital Professionalism'. *Hemisphere*, XVII, No. 10, 1973, 23-26.

Brady, Veronica. 'The Most Frightening Rebellion: The Recent Novels of Thomas Keneally'. *Meanjin*, XXXVIII, 1979, 74-86.

---. 'The Utopian Impulse in Australian Literature with Special Reference to P. White and T. Keneally'. *Caliban*, XIV, 1977, 109-21.

Breitinger, Eckhard. 'Thomas Keneally's "Historical" Novels'. *Commonwealth Newsletter*, No. 10, 1976, 16-20.

Bruer, Mark. 'The Force that Was with Oskar Schindler'. *Advertiser*, 24 December, 1982, 20.

Buckridge, Patrick. 'Gossip and History in the Novels of Brian Penton and Thomas Keneally'. *A.L.S.*, 14, No. 4, 1990, 436-49.

Burns, Robert. 'Out of Context: A Study of Thomas Keneally's Novels'. *A.L.S.*, IV, 1969, 31-48.

---. 'The Underdog-Outsider: The Achievement of Mathers' *Trap*'. *Meanjin*, XXIX, 1970, 95-105. Discusses *Trap* in relation to *The Fear* and other recent novels.

Cadzow, Jane. 'Keneally's Zest for Life'. *Weekend Australian Magazine*, 24-25 March, 1984, 2.

Cameron, Richard. 'The Art of Being a Writer'. *Bulletin*, 6 July, 1968, 34. Comment on seminar organized by the Society of Authors in Melbourne.

Cantrell, Kerin. 'Perspective on Thomas Keneally'. *Southerly*, XXVIII, 1968, 54-67.

Casey, Constance. 'Down Under, Out Back and Over There'. [*Washington Post*] *Book World*, 4 October, 1981, 14.

Clancy, Jack. '*The Chant of Jimmie Blacksmith*: The Film of the Book'. *A.L.S.*, IX, 1979, 95-97.

Clancy, L.J. 'Conscience and Corruption: Thomas Keneally's Three Novels'. *Meanjin*, XXVII, 1968, 33-41.

Coakley, Thomas P. 'Thomas Keneally: Cycle and Redemption'. In *International Literature in English: Essays on the Major Writers*, edited by Robert L. Ross (New York: Garland, 1991), 425-35.

Cole-Adams, Peter. 'Novelist in Search of the Irreplaceable'. *Age*, 17 November, 1973, 15. Interview.

Coleman, Richard. 'Tom Keneally, Older and Wiser, Discovers the Theatre's Magic'. *S.M.H.*, 23 April, 1983, 40.

Cotter, Michael. 'The Image of the Aboriginal in Three Modern Australian Novels'.

Meanjin, XXXVI, 1977, 582-91.

Darroch, Robert. 'Tom Keneally's Winning Words'. *Bulletin*, 9 November, 1982, 116-17 & 119. Booker Prize. See also K. England, *Advertiser*, 19 November, 1982, 4; and P. Morgan, *Advertiser*, 23 October, 1982, 22.

Dawson, Sally. 'Consuming Theatre: Linguistic Colonialism in Thomas Keneally's *The Playmaker*'. *Australian Studies*, No. 4, 1990, 27-34.

Denis, Yves. '*Three Cheers for the Paraclete*: Roman du Radicalisme Religieux'. *Etudes Anglaises*, XXV, 1972, 229-31.

Dunlevy, Maurice. 'Copyright, Plagiarism and a Long Literary Tradition'. *Canberra Times*, 27 September, 1980, 14. *A Season in Purgatory*.

Eccles, Jeremy. 'Keneally War Story on Stage'. *S.M.H.*, 30 April, 1983, 14.

English, David. 'History and the Refuge of Art: Thomas Keneally's Sense of the Past'. In *The Writer's Sense of the Past: Essays on Southeast Asian and Australasian Literature*, edited by Kirpal Singh (Singapore University Press, 1987), 160-169. Also published in *Meridian*, VI, No. 1, 1987, 23-29.

Fabre, Michel. 'Thomas Keneally: An Interview'. *Caliban*, XIV, 1977, 101-08.

---. 'Voices and Gossip: Destiny and History in the Latter Novels of Thomas Keneally'. *Caliban*, XIV, 1977, 91-99.

Ferres, Kay. 'Keneally and Gare: Boundary Riders and Fringe Dwellers'. *LiNQ*, XIV, No. 2, 1986, 48-56.

Field, Michele. 'Tom Keneally: A Well-written Life'. *S.M.H.*, 21 October, 1983, 7.

Frizell, Helen. 'Author Asks Thomas Keneally to Take his Book off Market'. *S.M.H.*, 8 December, 1978, 2. See also 'Keneally Sued over Book's Copyright', *S.M.H.*, 9 June, 1979, 19. *A Season in Purgatory*.

---. 'Saint Joan Exorcised'. *S.M.H.*, 16 November, 1974, 11.

Frow, John. 'The Chant of Thomas Keneally'. *A.L.S.*, X, 1982, 291-99.

Gaffney, Carmel. 'Keneally's Faction: Schindler's Ark'. *Quadrant*, XXIX, No. 7, 1985, 75-77.

Geering, R.G. *Recent Fiction*. (Melbourne: O.U.P., 1974). Australian Writers and Their Work. Reviewed by C. Hadgraft, *A.L.S.*, VI, 1974, 441-2.

Gelder, Ken. '"Trans-what?" Sexuality and the Phallus in *A Dutiful Daughter* and *The Flesheaters*'. *Southerly*, 49, No. 1, 1989, 3-15.

Grenville, Kate, and Sue Woolfe. *Making Stories: How Ten Australian Novels Were Written*. (St Leonards, NSW: Allen & Unwin, 1993). Includes contribution on *The Chant of Jimmie Blacksmith*.

Gurr, Andrew. 'Is He a Camera? Keneally's *A Family Madness*'. *Australian Studies*, No. 4, 1990, 113-21.

Hall, Sandra. 'Writing for Dear Life'. *Bulletin*, 30 March, 1968, 31-32.

Hawley, Janet. 'Keneally Finds Rich Lode in Our Past'. *Age*, 2 February, 1980, 19.

Heiland, Donna. 'History and Sublimity in Keneally's *The Playmaker*'. *Australian & New Zealand Studies in Canada*, 11, 1994, 12-22.

Hergenhan, Laurie. 'Interview with Thomas Keneally'. *A.L.S.*, XII, No. 4, 1986, 453-57.

---. 'The Past as "The Present Rendered Fabulous"': The Confronting of European Origins in *Bring Larks and Heroes* and *A Fringe of Leaves*'. In *Australian Papers: Yugoslavia, Europe and Australia*, edited by Mirko Jurak (Ljubljana: Edvard Cardelj University, 1983), 269-74. Reprinted in revised form in his *Unnatural Lives*. (St Lucia: U.Q.P., 1983), 139-50.

Hollington, Michael. 'The Ned Kelly of Cracow: Keneally's *Schindler's Ark*'. *Meanjin*, XLII, 1983, 42-46.

Hospital, Janette T. 'Keneally's Reluctant Prophets'. *Commonweal*, XIII, 1976, 295-300.

Hulse, Michael. 'Virtue and the Philosophic Innocent'. *Quadrant*, XXVII, No. 5, 1983, 69-71.

Hutton, Geoffrey. 'Keneally on Stage'. *Age*, 2 March, 1968, 7. Fairly detailed discussion of the relation of *Halloran's Little Boat* to *Bring Larks and Heroes*.

Indyk, Ivor. 'Pastoral and Priority: The Aboriginal in Australian Pastoral'. *New Literary History*, 24.4, 1993: 837-55. Includes discussion of writing by Kendall.

Jenkyn, D. 'Purgatory is Booked Out'. *Nation Review*, 17-23 March, 1977, 508. Accusations of plagiarism. See also Tom Keneally, 'In Reply to D. Jenkyn', *Nation Review*, 24-30 March, 1977, 53; J.W. Benson, 'Honest Tom', *Nation Review*, 31 March-6 April, 1977, 554. *A Season in Purgatory*.

Jillett, Neil. 'Thomas Keneally'. *Age*, 11 November, 1967, 24.

Johnson, Manly. 'Thomas Keneally's Nightmare of History'. *Antipodes*, 3.2, 1989, 101-04.

Jones, Margaret. 'The Hero as Victim'. *S.M.H.*, 16 September, 1972, 17.

Kiernan, Brian. 'Thomas Keneally and the Australian Novel: A Study of *Bring Larks and Heroes*'. *Southerly*, XXVIII, 1968, 189-99.

Knightley, Phillip. 'Tom Keneally Changes Pace and Style: The Result is "Totally Seductive"'. *National Times*, 15-20 November, 1976, 20.

Krausmann, Rudi. 'Thomas Keneally'. *Aspect*, IV, Nos. 1-2, 1979, 48-58. Interview.

Laigle, Geneviève. 'The White World and its Relationship with the Aborigines in Keneally's *Chant of Jimmy Blacksmith*'. *Commonwealth*, 14,1, 1991, 102-10.

Lapsley, John. 'Novel Touch'. *Australian*, 15 November, 1974, 14.

Larkin, John. 'A Great Australian Writer Goes Looking for a Great Australian Outlaw'. *Age*, 28 August, 1980, 11. Ned Kelly.

Macleod, Mark. 'Thomas Keneally's *Passenger* and the Middle Voice'. *Literary Criterion* (Mysore), XV, Nos. 3-4, 1980, 183-94.

Mann, Paul. 'Playboy Interview: Thomas Keneally'. *Australian Playboy*, April, 1985, 33-39.

Mansfield, Paul. 'The Chat of Tom Keneally'. *Age Saturday Extra*, 21 January, 1984, 11.

Marechal, Patricia. 'Thomas Keneally: *Passenger*'. *Commonwealth* (Toulouse), IV, 1979-1980, 69-76. In French.

McGregor, Craig (ed.). *In the Making*. (Melbourne: Nelson Australia, 1969), 252-55.

McInherny, Frances. '*Bring Larks and Heroes*: The Moral and the Dream'. *Southerly*, XXXVII, 1977, 68-75.

---. 'Thomas Keneally's "Innocent Men"'. *A.L.S.*, X, 1981, 57-66.

---. 'Woman and Myth in Thomas Keneally's Fiction'. *Meanjin*, XL, 1981, 248-58.

Mitchell, Adrian. 'Thomas Keneally and the Scheme of Things'. *A.L.S.*, IX, 1979, 3-13.

Molloy, F.C. 'An Irish Conflict in *Bring Larks and Heroes*'. *A.L.S.*, VII, 1976, 389-98.

Molloy, Susan. 'Thomas Keneally Wrestles with the Cultural KGB'. *S.M.H.*, 13 March, 1982, 46.

Monk, Patricia. 'Eden Upside-Down: Thomas Keneally's *Bring Larks and Heroes* as Anti-Pastoral'. *WLWE*, XXI, 1982, 297-303.

Moore, Gloria J. 'On Tom Keneally's Catholic Novels'. *Quadrant*, 38.4, 1994, 66-68.

Morgan, Patricia. 'Thomas Keneally is There with the Literary Ghosts'. *Sunday Mail* (Brisbane), 9 December, 1973, 25. Interview.

Musgrove, Brian, and Chris Lee. '"The Best Tricks Are in the Book": An Interview with Tom Keneally'. *Coppertales*, 1, 1995, 147-57.

O'Hearn, Tim. '*Schindler's Ark* and *Schindler's List*: One for the Price of Two'. *Commonwealth Novel in English*, 5.2, 1993, 9-15.

Oyabu, Tsutomu. 'An Interview with Thomas Keneally'. *Research Reports of Kurume Technical College*, No. 31, 1979, 59-69.

Petersson, Irmtraud. '"White Ravens" in a World of Violence: German Connections in Thomas Keneally's Fiction'. *A.L.S.*, 14, No. 2, 1989, 160-73.

Pierce, Peter. 'The Australian Literature of the Viet Nam War'. *Meanjin*, XXXIX, 1980, 290-303.

---. *Australian Melodramas: Thomas Keneally's Fiction*. (St Lucia: U.Q.P., 1995). Reviewed by A. Mitchell, *ABR*, 173, 1995, 25-26; A. Riemer, *S.M.H.*, 26 Aug., 1995, Spectrum 11A. See also Salusinszky below.

---. '"The Critics Made Me": The Receptions of Thomas Keneally and Australian Literary Culture'. *A.L.S.*, 17.1, 1995, 99-103.

---. 'The Sites of War in the Fiction of Thomas Keneally'. *A.L.S.*, XII, No. 4, 1986, 442-52.

Pons, Xavier. '"Savage Paradise": History, Violence and Family in Recent Australian Fiction by Hall, Keneally and Malouf'. In *European Perspectives: Contemporary Essays on Australian Literature*, edited by Giovanna Capone (*A.L.S.* 15.2 (special issue)/ St. Lucia: U.Q.P., 1991), 72-82.

Quartermaine, Peter. *Thomas Keneally*. (London; New York; Melbourne; Auckland: Edward Arnold, 1991). Reviewed by R. Brown, *Australian Studies*, 8, 1994, 146-50; P. Pierce, *A.L.S.*, 15.4, 1992, 360-62.

Ramson, W.S. '*The Chant of Jimmie Blacksmith*: Taking Cognisance of Keneally'. In his *The Australian Experience: Critical Essays on Australian Novels*. (Canberra: Australian National University Press, 1974), 325-44.

Reynolds, Henry. 'Jimmy Governor and Jimmie Blacksmith'. *A.L.S.*, IX, 1979, 14-25.

Riddell, Elizabeth. 'Keneally, Just Talking'. *Australian*, 20 November, 1971, 15. Interview.

---. 'A "Literary Juggler" Comes Home'. *Australian*, 23 October, 1971, 14.

Rolfe, Patricia. 'The Flavor of Life'. *Bulletin*, 4 September, 1965, 30. An interview.

Rowse, Tim. 'Thomas Keneally: A Review of His Last Three Novels'. *Union Recorder*, XLIX, No. 27, 1969, 129-32.

Rutherford, Anna. 'Re-appraisal of a Myth: *The Chant of Jimmie Blacksmith*'. *Commonwealth* (Rodez), I, 1974-75, 104-12.

Ryan, Colleen. 'Trade Unions, Wombats not Commercial Winners'. *Financial Review*, 29 August, 1980, 34-35.

Ryan, J.S. 'Furphy 1: The Red Cord: A Neglected Folk Motif in the Early Fiction of Thomas Keneally'. *Notes & Furphies*, 26, 1991, 2-3.

---. 'Some Convict Sources in Keneally and FitzGerald'. *A.L.S.*, IX, 1980, 385-87.

---. 'Thomas Keneally in Armidale'. *Journal and Proceedings of the Armidale and District Historical Society*, No. 15, 1971/72, 80-89.

Sait, J.E. 'Thomas Keneally's *Blood Red, Sister Rose* and Robertson Davies' *Fifth Business*: Two Modern Hagiographies'. *Journal of Commonwealth Literature*, XVI, No. 1, 1981, 96-108.

Salusinszky, Imre. 'Thomas Keneally: My Part in His Downfall'. *Quadrant*, 39.10, 1995, 23-26.

Souter, Gavin. 'Refugee from Good Old Irish Theology'. *S.M.H.*, 4 November, 1967, 18.

Sterel, Elisabeth. 'Keneally's Win Causes a Mild Controversy'. *Age*, 21 October, 1982, 14.

Sturm, Terry. 'Thomas Keneally and Australian Racism: *The Chant of Jimmie Blacksmith*'. *Southerly*, XXXIII, 1973, 261-74.

Trewin, Ion. 'The Booker: Handling a High-Flying Winner'. *The Bookseller*, 5 March, 1983, 816-818.

Trundle, Peter. 'Keneally: The Pain and the Happiness'. *Courier-Mail*, 18 December, 1982, 22. Interview.

Walker, Shirley. 'Thomas Keneally and "The Special Agonies of Being a Woman"'. In *Who is She?*, edited by Shirley Walker (St Lucia: U.Q.P., 1983), 150-62.

Ware, Tracy. 'Of Irony and Institutions: Thomas Keneally's *Three Cheers for the Paraclete'*. *Australian and New Zealand Studies in Canada*, No. 2, 1989, 74-85.
Webster, Owen. 'The Literary Life of Australia'. *Overland*, No. 45, 1970, 27-32.
Willbanks, Ray. 'Thomas Keneally'. In his *Speaking Volumes: Australian Writers and Their Work* (Ringwood, Vic.: Penguin, 1991).
Wilding, Michael. 'Two Cheers for Keneally'. *Southerly*, XXIX, 1969, 131-38.
Wills, Garry. 'Catholic Faith and Fiction'. *New York Times Book Review*, 16 January, 1972, 1-2, 14, 16, 20.
Zeller, Robert. 'Tales of the Neutral Ground: James Fenimore Cooper, Thomas Keneally and the Historical Novel'. *WLWE*, 33.2&34.1, 1993-94, 24-30.

KENNA, PETER

Drama

Furtive Love. (Sydney: Currency Press, 1981).
Reviewed by M. Lord, *ABR*, No. 37, 1981, 15-16.

A Hard God. Introduced by Philip Hickie; preface by Cyril Pearl (Sydney: Currency Press; London: Eyre Methuen, 1973). Currency Methuen Plays Series III, No. 1.
Reviewed by R. Cavan, *Plays and Players*, XXII, No. 6, 1975, 39; J. Coleby, *Drama*, No. 116, 1975, 92.

The Slaughter of St. Teresa's Day. Introduced by Philip Hickie; preface by Cyril Pearl. (Sydney: Currency Press, 1972). Currency Playtexts, Series 1.
Reviewed by R. Cavan, *Plays and Players*, XXII, No. 6, 1975, 39; A. Kruse, *Southerly*, XXXIII, 1973, 241-42; R. Wissler, *Makar*, IX, No. 1, 1973, 45-48.

Three Plays: Talk to the Moon; Listen Closely; Trespassers will be Prosecuted. (Sydney: Currency Press, 1977).
Reviewed by G. Davies, *Words'worth*, XI, No. 1, 1978, 51; A. Godfrey-Smith, *ABR*, No. 2, 1978, 19-20; H. Hewitt, *Canberra Times*, 18 February, 1978, 13.

Critical Material

Biven, Angela. 'Few Pauses by Supertongued Playwright'. *Advertiser*, 17 February, 1981, 6.
Bladwell, Frank. 'Peter Kenna's *A Hard God'*. *Southerly*, XXXIX, 1979, 155-71.
Brisbane, Katharine. 'A New Lease of Life'. *National Times*, 14-19 June, 1976, 24.
---. 'Obituary'. *New Theatre Australia*, No. 3, 1988, 4-5.
Brady, Veronica. *Playing Catholic: Essays on Four Catholic Plays*. (Sydney: Currency Press, 1991). Discusses *A Hard God*.
Emeljanow, Victor. 'Unrepentant Australian'. *National Times*, 23 December, 1978, 41.
Goodyear, Paula. 'Playwright With a Pet Theory'. *S.M.H.*, 9 May, 1972, 8.
Griffiths, Gareth. 'Experiments with Form in Recent Australian Drama'. *Kunapipi*, II, No. 1, 1980, 75-76.
McCallum, John. 'Peter Kenna and the Search for Intimacy'. *Meanjin*, XXXVII, 1978, 317-23.
Nicklin, Lenore. 'Sister's Gift Rescues a Writer. A Tyrant of Time, Energy: The Kidney Machine'. *S.M.H.*, 11 January, 1975, 8.
Oakley, Barry. 'Three Times Across a Tightrope'. *National Times*, 20-25 March, 1978, 39.
Parr, Bruce. 'Peter Kenna's *The Cassidy Album*: A Call for Re-viewing'. *Australasian Drama Studies*, 24, 1994, 77-98.
Reid, Don. 'Study Guide'. *Theatre-Australia*, II, No. 3, 1977, 68-69. On *A Hard God*.
Webby, Elizabeth. *Modern Australian Plays*. Horizon Studies in Literature. (Sydney: Sydney UP in assoc. with O.U.P., 1990). Includes discussion of A Hard God

KINGSLEY, HENRY

Collection

Henry Kingsley. Edited with an introduction by J.S.D. Mellick. (St Lucia: U.Q.P., 1982). Portable Australian Authors.
Reviewed by T. Goldie, *WLWE*, XXIV, No. 2, 1984, 299-301; K. Stewart, *A.L.S.*, X, 1982, 541-43.

Fiction

The Hillyars and the Burtons: A Story of Two Families, with an introduction by Leonie Kramer. Facsimile edition (Sydney: Sydney University Press, 1973). Australian Literary Reprints. First published London: Macmillan, 1865.
Reviewed by J. Beston, *S.M.H.*, 29 September, 1973, 27; J. Hay, *Canberra Times*, 30 June, 1973, 11; O. Ruhen, *Australian*, 5 May, 1973, 16; M. Wilding, *Southerly*, XXXV, 1975, 97-99.

The Recollections of Geoffry Hamlyn. 1859. Introduction by Susan K. Martin. (Sydney: A.& R., 1993). First published London: Macmilla, 1859

Critical Material

Anderson, Hugh. 'The Composition of *Geoffry Hamlyn*: A Comment'. *A.L.S.*, IV, 1969, 79-80. Discusses Brian Elliott's article, *A.L.S.*, III, 1968, 271-89.
Barnes, John. *Henry Kingsley and Colonial Fiction*. (Melbourne: O.U.P., 1971). Australian Writers and Their Work. Reviewed by C. Harrison-Ford, *Sunday Australian*, 21 November, 1971, 32; B. Kiernan, *Australian*, 6 November, 1971, 18; L. Kramer, *A.L.S.*, V, 1972, 433-37.
---. '"A Young Man Called Kingsley"'. *Meanjin*, XXX, 1971, 72-84.
Baxter, Rosilyn. 'Henry Kingsley and the Australian Landscape'. *A.L.S.*, IV, 1970, 395-98.
Croft, Julian. 'Is *Geoffry Hamlyn* a Creole Novel?' *A.L.S.*, VI, 1974, 269-76.
Dixon, R. 'Kingsley's *Geoffry Hamlyn* and the Art of Landscape'. *Southerly*, XXXVII, 1977, 274-99.
Eggert, Paul. 'A Cautionary Tale: Stop-Press Corrections in *The Recollections of Geoffry Hamlyn* (1859)'. *BSANZ Bulletin*, 19.4, 1995, 267-70.
Elliott, Brian. 'The Composition of *Geoffry Hamlyn*: The Legend and the Facts'. *A.L.S.*, III, 1968, 271-89.
Friederich, Werner P. *Australia in Western Imaginative Prose Writings 1600-1960: An Anthology and a History of Literature*. (Chapel Hill: University of North Carolina Press: 1967), 72-91.
Hamer, Clive. 'Henry Kingsley's Australian Novels'. *Southerly*, XXVI, 1966, 40-57.
Hergenhan, L.T. '*Geoffry Hamlyn* Through Contemporary Eyes'. *A.L.S.*, II, 1966, 289-95.
Horner, J.C. '*Geoffry Hamlyn* and its Australian Setting'. *A.L.S.*, I, No. 1, 1963, 3-15.
Lee, Christopher. 'Representing Failure: Gender and Madness in Henry Kingsley's *The Hillyars and the Burtons*'. *AUMLA*, 82, 1994, 35-48.
McLaren, John. '*Geoffry Hamlyn* & the Australian Myth'. *Segment*, II, 1973, 6-12.
Mellick, J. Stanton. 'The Elusive Henry Kingsley'. In *Autobiographical and Biographical Writing in the Commonwealth*, edited by Doireann MacDermott (Sadabell, Barcelona: Editorial AUSA, 1984), 153-156.
---. 'Henry Kingsley and the "Dear Old Station": The "Baroona" of *Geoffry Hamlyn*?' *A.L.S.*, 16.2, 1993, 216-17.
---. 'Henry Kingsley - Mounted Policeman?' *A.L.S.*, VII, 1976, 416-20.
---. 'Henry Kingsley in Australia'. *A.L.S.*, VI, 1973, 91-94.
---. *The Passing Guest: A Life of Henry Kingsley*. (St Lucia: U.Q.P., 1983). Reviewed by J. Barnes, *ABR*, No. 64, 1984, 24-25; P. Botsman, *Courier-Mail*, 24 September, 1983, 30; B. Elliott, *A.L.S.*, IX, 1984, 419-22; G. Hutchinson, *S.M.H.*,

20 August, 1983, 36; L. Kramer, *Overland*, No. 96. 1984, 60-61; K. Stewart, *CRNLE Reviews Journal*, No. 2, 1984, 66-68; G.A. Wilkes, *Southerly*, XL, No. 2, 1985, 244; R. Winch, *Canberra Times*, 12 November, 1983, 19.

Morgan, Patrick. 'The Australian Origins of *Geoffry Hamlyn*'. *Margin*, 37, 1995, 3-5.

Ryan, J.S. 'The Prose Style of Henry Kingsley'. *Armidale & District Historical Society. Journal & Proceedings*, No. 19, 1976, 62-63.

Scheckter, John. 'The Lost Child in Australian Fiction'. *Modern Fiction Studies*, XXVII, No. 1, 1981, 61-72.

Scheuerle, W.H. 'Henry Kingsley, a Study'. *Dissertation Abstracts* (Syracuse, N.Y.), XXV, 1964, 1200-01.

---. *The Neglected Brother: A Study of Henry Kingsley*. (Tallahassee: Florida State University Press, 1971). Reviewed by L. Kramer, *A.L.S.*, V, 1972, 433-37; G.B. Tennyson, *Nineteenth Century Fiction*, XXVII, 1972, 120.

---. 'Romantic Attitudes in *Geoffry Hamlyn*'. *A.L.S.*, II, No. 2, 1965, 79-91.

Wellings, N.G. 'Henry Kingsley: *Ravenshoe*'. *A.L.S.*, IV, 1969, 115-29.

Wilkes, G.A. 'Kingsley's *Geoffry Hamlyn*: A Study in Literary Survival'. *Southerly*, XXXII, 1972, 243-54. Reprinted in revised form in *The Australian Experience: Critical Essays on Australian Novels*, edited by W.S. Ramson (Canberra: Australian National University Press, 1974), 61-72.

KNOWLES, LEE

Poetry

Cool Summer: Poems. (Fremantle, WA: Fremantle Arts Centre Press, 1977).
Reviewed by F. Kellaway, *Overland*, 72, 1978, 53-57; J. Rodriguez, *ABR*, 2, 1978, 33-34; F. Zwicky, *Westerly*, 23.2, 1978, 88-91.

Dial Marina: Poems. (Fremantle, WA: Fremantle Arts Centre Press, 1986).
Reviewed by G. Page, *Island Magazine*, 30, 1987, 64-67.

Sirocco Days. (South Fremantle, WA: Fremantle Arts Centre Press, 1993).
Reviewed by A. Bartlett, *ABR*, 149, 1993, 38; M. Duwell, *Weekend Australian*, 6-7 March, 1993, Review 12.

Critical Material

Colebatch, Hal. 'A Hard Freedom - The Poetry of Lee Knowles'. *Westerly*, 39.2, 1994, 61-69.

Page, Geoff. 'Lee Knowles'. In his *A Reader's Guide To Contemporary Australian Poetry* (St. Lucia: U.Q.P., 1995), 154-157.

KOCAN, PETER

Fiction

The Cure. (Sydney: A.& R., 1983).
Reviewed by H. Daniel, *Age Saturday Extra*, 16 April, 1983, 11; G. Dutton, *Bulletin*, 19 April, 1983, 66-67; A. Hildyard, *Island Magazine*, Nos. 18-19, 1984, 40-44; D.A.N. Jones, *London Review of Books*, V, No. 15, 1983, 23; P. Kay, *Canberra Times*, 13 August, 1983, 16; M. Lord, *ABR*, No. 53, 1983, 24; S. McInerney, *S.M.H.*, 21 May, 1983, 38; P. Pierce, *Meanjin*, XLII, 1983, 407-08.

Flies of a Summer. (North Ryde, N.S.W.: A.& R., 1988).
Reviewed by M. Gressor, *S.M.H.*, 28 May, 1988, 78; T. Lintermans, *Age Saturday Extra*, 28 May, 1988, 15; J. Macgregor, *Weekend Australian*, 2-3 July, 1988, Weekend 16; P. Pierce, *Bulletin*, 28 June, 1988, 138; A. Urquhart, *Westerly*, 34, No. 2, 1989, 112-14.

The Treatment. (Sydney: A.& R., 1980).
Reviewed by W. Bacon, *National Times*, 26 October-1 November, 1980, 60; G. Disher, *Island Magazine*, No. 7, 1981, 41-43; G. Dutton, *Bulletin*, 2 December, 1980, 89; G. Hawkins, *Weekend Australian Magazine*, 1-2 November, 1980, 17; M.

Lord, *ABR*, No. 53, 1983, 24; J. Neville, *S.M.H.*, 8 November, 1980, 20; O. Ruhen. *Age*, 7 February, 1981, 27.

The Treatment; and The Cure. (Sydney: A.& R., 1984). *The Treatment* first published Sydney: A.& R.,1980; *The Cure* first published Sydney: A.& R., 1983.
Reviewed by N. Keesing, *ABR*, No. 60, 1984 23-24; G. Zdenkowski, *S.M.H.*, 28 April, 1984, 41.

Poetry

Armistice. (Sydney: A.& R., 1980).
Reviewed by J. Rodriguez, *ABR*, No. 29, 1981, 29-30.

Freedom to Breathe. (North Ryde, N.S.W.: A.& R., 1985).
Reviewed by A. Lansdown, *Quadrant*, XXXI, No. 3, 1987, 78-79.

The Other Side of the Fence. (St Lucia: U.Q.P., 1975).
Reviewed by A. Gould, *Nation Review*, 2-8 April, 1976, 621; J. Grant, *Contempa*, Series 2, No. 2, 1976, 49-50; P. Kavanagh, *Southerly*, XXXVI, 1976, 478; A. Korvisianos, *Union Recorder*, LVI, No. 8, 1976, 32-33; J. McLaren, *Segment*, V, 1976, 56; G. Page, *Canberra Times*, 24 July, 1976, 13; T. Shapcott, *Age*, 17 July, 1976, 23.

Standing with Friends. (Melbourne: Heinemann, 1992).
Reviewed by J. Foulcher, *Island*, 55, 1993, 69-72; K. Hart, *Age*, 17 October, 1992, Saturday Extra 9; A. Lansdown, *Quadrant*, 37.9, 1993, 86-88.

Critical Material

'Prison Poet Talks of Life on the Inside'. *S.M.H.*, 13 August, 1976, 3.
'Rehabilitation and now Poetic Justice'. *Age*, 12 August, 1976, 3; for other comments on the Commonwealth Poetry Prize see *S.M.H.*, 10 August, 1976, 3; *The Bookseller* (London), 21 August, 1976, 1419.
Drewe, Robert. '"With the Whole Sky in his Eyes"'. *Bulletin*, 28 February, 1976, 66-68.
Hawley, Janet. 'The Poetic Persuasion of a Gunman'. *Age*, 16 March, 1983, 11.
Heseltine, Harry. '"How Do You Feel Within Yourself?"': The Case of Peter Kocan'. In *Psychopathology in Australian Life*, edited by Harry Heseltine (Canberra, A.C.T.: English Department, University College, Australian Defence Force Academy, 1988).
Krause, Thomas. 'Poetic Justice Saves an "Insider"'. *Weekend Australian Magazine*, 19-20 March, 1983, 12.
Page, Geoff. 'Peter Kocan'. In his *A Reader's Guide To Contemporary Australian Poetry* (St. Lucia: U.Q.P., 1995), 158-161.

KOCH, C.J.

Fiction

Across the Sea Wall. (London: Heinemann, 1965).
Reviewed by E. Corsellis, *S.M.H.*, 15 May, 1965, 16; M. Lord, *ABR*, No. 47, 1982, 27-28; R. Marsden, *Quadrant*, XXVI, No. 12, 1982, 81-82; J. McLaren, *Overland*, No. 32, 1965, 44; E. Riddell, *National Times*, 9-16 May, 1982, 21; A. Roberts, *ABR*, IV, 1965, 151 (and see letter by N. Cato, ibid., IV, 1965, 192); N. Scott, *Weekend Australian Magazine*, 11-12 September, 1982, 10; P. Shrubb, *Bulletin*, 29 May, 1965, 55; S. Smith, *S.M.H.*, 29 May, 1982, 41; G. Turner, *Age Saturday Extra*, 17 July, 1982, 13.

The Boys in the Island. 2nd Ed. (Sydney: A.& R., 1974). First published London: Hamish Hamilton, 1958.
Reviewed by A.R. Chisholm, *Age*, 15 February, 1975, 15; J. McLaren, *ABR*, No. 16, 1979, 36.

The Doubleman. (London: Chatto & Windus, 1985).
Reviewed by D. Anderson, *National Times*, 26 April-2 May, 1985, 32; J. Bayley,

London Review of Books, 4 July, 1986, 13; V. Brady, *Westerly*, XXX, No. 3, 1985, 89-94; L. Clancy, *Age Saturday Extra*, 18 May, 1985, 14; B. Clunies Ross, *Kunapipi*, VI, No. 3, 1984, 101-103; M. Collins, *Weekend Australian Magazine*, 29-30 June, 1985, 16; K. England, *Advertiser*, 4 May, 1985, 7; C. Fein, *New York Times Book Review*, 23 February, 1986, 22; P. Fuller, *Canberra Times*, 18 May, 1985, 13; M. Hulse, *PN Review*, XIII, No. 5, 1987, 80-81; M. John, *ABR*, No. 71, 1985, 5-6; R. Jones, *Listener*, 2 May, 1985, 27-28; P. Lewis, *London Magazine*, XXV, Nos. 1-2, 1985, 148-152; R. Lewis, *New Statesman*, 19 April, 1985,32, 34; A. Mitchell, *Weekend Australian Magazine*, 27-28 April, 1985, 13; L. Murray, *S.M.H.*, 27 April, 1985, 36; D. Rowbotham, *Courier-Mail*, 4 May, 1985, 30; A. Sant, *Age Monthly Review*, V, No. 2, 1985, 5-7; P. Sharrad, *Overland*, No. 100, 1985, 96-98; P. Smelt, *T.L.S.*, 7 June, 1985, 644; J. Stevens, *Age Saturday Extra*, 27 April, 1985, 11; G. Windsor, *Bulletin*, 7 May, 1985, 92.

The Doubleman. 1985. Rev. ed. with new introduction and new scene in final chapter. (Pymble, NSW: Collins A.& R./Imprint, 1992). First published London: Chatto & Windus, 1985

Highways to a War. (Port Melbourne, Vic.: Heinemann, 1995).
Reviewed by N. Birns, *Antipodes*, 9.2, 1995, 143 (see also: 'Antipodes interviews Christopher J. Koch' 144-45); R. Gerster, *ABR*, 173, 1995, 6-7 (see also interview by H. Daniel 7-9); M. Gressor, *S.M.H.*, 1 July: Spectrum 10A; J. Hanrahan, *Age*, 8 July, 1995, Saturday Extra 8; N. Hasluck, *Quadrant*, 39.11, 1995, 77-78; D. Matthews, *Weekend Australian*, 15-16 July, 1995, Review 7; P. Pierce, *Bulletin*, 18 July, 1995, 91; A. Riemer, *Independent*, July, 1995, 102.

The Year of Living Dangerously. (Melbourne: Nelson (Australia), 1978).
Reviewed by B. Beaver, *ABR*, No. 8, 1979, 22-23; T. Bowden, *National Times*, 23 December, 1978, 40; V. Brady, *Westerly*, XXV, No. 2, 1980, 61-75; L. Clancy, *Overland*, No. 80, 1980, 52; P.K. Cowie, *CRNLE Reviews Journal*, No. 1, 1980, 24-26; G. Fairbairn, *Bulletin*, 26 December-2 January, 1979, 39; J. Hodgkinson, *Canberra Times*, 2 December, 1978, 15; G. Lehmann, *Quadrant*, XXIII, No. 3, 1979, 68-70; J. Miles, *Advertiser*, 24 March, 1979, 25; L. Murray, S.M.H., 21 October, 1978, 17; L. Oakes, *Age*, 2 December, 1978, 26; G. O'Grady, *Nation Review*, 15-21 December, 1978, 20; P. Pierce, *Meanjin*, XXXVIII, 1979, 226-28; C. Semmler, *24 Hours*, III, No. 12, 1979, 68-69; L. Strahan, *Helix*, Nos. 9 & 10 Supplement 'Fresh Flounder', 1981, 28-35; P. Ward, *Weekend Australian Magazine*, 13-14 January, 1979, 6.

Non-Fiction
Crossing the Gap: A Novelist's Essays. (London: Hogarth Press/Chatto and Windus, 1987).
Reviewed by T. Aitken, *T.L.S.*, 31 July, 1987, 823; E. Campion, *Bulletin*, 6 June, 1987, 95-96; P. Craven, *Weekend Australian. Weekend Magazine*, 6-7 June, 1987, 11; S. Donnelly, *New Literatures Review*, No. 16, 1988, 64-68; D.R. Ewen, *CRNLE Reviews Journal*, 1, 1991, 87-89; M. Flanagan, *Age Saturday Extra*, 23 May, 1987, 12; K. Hart, *ABR*, No. 93, 1987, 15-16; P.R. Hay, *Island*, 57, 1993, 74-76; B. Hill, *Times on Sunday*, 26 April, 1987, 30; M. Hulse, *PN Review*, No. 60, 1987, 65-66; R. Marsden, *Quadrant*, XXXI, No. 8, 1987, 76-78; P. Pierce, *S.M.H.*, 11 April, 1987, 46; J.D. Pringle, *Overland*, No. 109, 1987, 74-75.

'Crossing the Gap'. *Quadrant*, XXV, Nos. 1-2, 1981, 4-9. Autobiographical.
'Koch on Koch: *The Year of Living Dangerously*'. In *Making Connections: Introducing Nine Texts for Senior English Students*, edited by G. Tulloch and A. Greet (Adelaide: CRNLE/Flinders University of South Australia and Trinity Gardens: SAETA, 1990), 23-40.
Letter in *Quadrant*, XI, No. 5, 1967, 65-68. Discusses reviewing of his own novels.
'The New Heresy Hunters'. *Overland*, No. 102, 1986, 43-46.

'Serving No Masters'. *Quadrant*, XXX, No. 12, 1986, 83-85. Speech at Quadrant 30th anniversary dinner.
'Who Wants the Novel? Fiction in the Era of Film and Television'. *Quadrant*, XXVI, No. 12, 1982, 8-11.

Critical Material

Baker, Candida. 'Christopher Koch'. In her *Yacker 3* (Sydney: Picador, 1989), 182-211.
Balajee, B.N. 'The Fusion of Myth and Topicality in Christopher Koch's *The Year of Living Dangerously*'. *The Literary Criterion* (Mysore), XXIII, 1988, 34-37.
---. 'An Interview with Chris Koch'. *Commonwealth* (Paris), X, No. 2, 1988, 70-74.
Campbell, Felicia. 'Silver Screen, Shadow Play: The Tradition of the Wayang Kulit in *The Year of Living Dangerously*'. *Journal of Popular Culture*, 28.1, 1994, 163-69.
Clancy, Laurie. 'The Envenomed Dreams of C.J. Koch'. *Island Magazine*, No. 23, 1985, 52-58.
Claremont, Robyn. 'The Novels of C.J. Koch'. *Quadrant*, XXIV, No. 7, 1980, 25-29.
Cowie, Phillip K. 'The Architectonics of Doubleness in C.J. Koch's Novels, With Particular Emphasis on *The Year of Living Dangerously* (1978) and *The Doubleman* (1985)'. In *Saggi e ricerche sulle culture extraeuropee*, edited by G. Bellini, C. Gorlier and S. Zoppi (Rome: Bulzoni, 1986), 83-97. Africa, America, Asia, Australia, 2.
Dever, Maryanne. 'A View of Asia from Down Under: The Politics of Representation in *The Year of Living Dangerously*'. *WLWE*, 29, No. 2, 1989, 35-50.
Dobson, Rosemary. 'Major Literary Prizes to Novelist and Biographer'. *ABR*, No. 15, 1979, 6-7. See also *Artforce*, No. 25, 1979, 1; D. Rowbotham, *Courier-Mail*, 13 October, 1979, 19; S. Sayers, *Age*, 13 October, 1979, 27; *Weekend Australian Magazine*, 3-14 October, 1979, 11.
Feng Ji. 'Christopher Koch and his Novel *The Boys in the Island*'. *Oceanic Literature*, No. 3, 1982, 342-45. In Chinese.
Frizell, Helen. 'The Re-emergence of a Major Novelist'. *S.M.H.*, 2 December, 1978, 12.
Headon, David. *Northern Perspective*, IX, No. 2, 1987, 90-93. Interview.
Hulse, Michael. 'Christopher Koch in conversation with Michael Hulse in London'. *Quadrant*, XXIX, No. 6, 1985, 17-25.
Inamdar, F.A., 'C.J. Koch's Feminine Perspective'. In *Australian Literature Today*, edited by R.K. Dhawan and David Kerr (New York: Indian Society for Commonwealth Studies/ Advent P, 1993), 98-104.
Inamdar, F.A., and Yasmin Shaikh. 'Image Patterns in *The Boys in the Island*: Themes of Illusion and Reality and the Colonial Perspective', *Journal of Australian Literature* (India), 1, 2, 1991, 15-24.
Ingalls, Rachel. 'Getting out of Djakarta'. *London Review of Books*, V, No. 15, 1983, 22-23. Film of *The Year of Living Dangerously*, directed by Peter Weir.
Kerr, David and Edmonds, Phillip. 'Christopher Koch Speaking'. *Weekend Australian Magazine*, 6-7 April, 1985, 4. Interview.
Kumaraswarmy Raju, M. 'Male Loneliness in Koch's *Double Man*'. *The Commonwealth Review*, 2.1-2, 1990-91, 21-29.
Maack, Annegret. '"Can We Ever Understand Alien Cultures?": Christopher Koch and Blanche D'Alpuget'. In Gerhard Stilz and Rudolf Bader (eds.) *Australien zwischen Europa und Asien* (Bern: Peter Lang, 1993), 123-33.
Maes-Jelinek, Hena. 'History and the Mythology of Confrontation in *The Year of Living Dangerously*'. *Kunapipi*, VIII, No. 1, 1986, 27-35.
---. 'A Web of Horizons: "Otherland" in Christopher Koch's *The Doubleman*'. In *Multiple Worlds, Multiple Words: Essays in Honour of Irene Simon*, edited by H. Maes-Jelinek, P. Michel and P. Michel-Michot (Liege: Department of English,

University of Liege, [1988]), 161-73.
Mansfield, Nicholas. 'Realism and Strangeness: C.J. Koch's *The Doubleman*'. *Ariel*, 23.2, 1992, 47-61.
McGregor, Adrian. 'Christopher Koch: Creating a New Australian Mythology'. *Courier-Mail*, 14 May, 1985, 4.
McGregor, Grant. 'The Australian City of Christopher Koch'. *Quadrant*, XX, No. 6, 1976, 66-71.
McInerney, Sally. 'Chris Koch Author'. *S.M.H. Magazine Good Weekend*, 16 February, 1985, 46.
McKernan, Susan. 'C.J. Koch's Two-Faced Vision'. *Meanjin*, XLIV, No. 4, 1985, 432-439.
Miller, Karl. 'Diary'. *London Review of Books*, 2 May, 1985, 21. Article on Christopher Koch's *The Doubleman*.
Mitchell, Adrian. 'Christopher Koch on *The Doubleman*'. *Southerly*, XLV, No. 2, 1985, 129-151. Interview.
Nettelbeck, Amanda. 'Expanding Boundaries: Changing Perceptions of "Asia" in Two Australian Novels'. *Kunapipi*, 16.2, 1994, 13-23. Discusses *The Year of Living Dangerously* and G. Lee's *Troppo Man*.
---. '"The Two Halves": Questions of Post-Colonial Theory and Practice in Christopher Koch's *The Year of Living Dangerously*'. *SPAN*, 32, 1991, 3-8.
Neville, Jill. 'The Insider's View'. *National Times*, 20 October, 1980, 33.
Pierce, Peter. 'Defection and Dislocation: The Fiction of Christopher Koch'. *Westerly*, 35, No. 2, 1990, 47-55.
Pons, Xavier. 'Oedipus in the Tropics: A Psychoanalytical Interpretation of C.J. Koch's *The Year of Living Dangerously*'. In *Colonisations*, edited by X. Pons and M. Rocard (Toulouse: Universite de Toulouse-Le Mirail, 1985), 109-17.
Ram, Alur Janaki. 'Chris Koch, India and *Across the Sea Wall*: Some Observations'. *The Literary Criterion* (Mysore), XXIII, 1988, 24-33.
Rolfe, Patricia. 'The Novelist's Chances'. *Bulletin*, 19 June, 1965, 33. An interview.
Roskies, D.M. 'A View of Asia from Down Under. The Politics of Representation in *The Year of Living Dangerously*'. *WLWE*, 29.2, 1989, 35-50. Reprinted in *Commonwealth Novel in English*, 5.2, 1993, 66-82.
Sayers, Stuart. 'Novel in a Slice of History'. *Age*, 2 December, 1978, 25.
Shapcott, Thomas. 'Breaking the Drought'. *London Magazine*, N.S. XX, Nos. 8-9, 1980, 70-75.
Sharrad, Paul. 'Living Dangerously - Christopher Koch and Cultural Tradition'. *Quadrant*, XXIX, No. 9, 1985, 64-68.
---. 'Pastoral, Romance and Post-colonial Consciousness: Spenser and Koch'. *Commonwealth*, 14.1, 1991, 111-22.
---. '*Pour mieux Sauter*: Christopher Koch's Novels in Relation to White, Stow and the Quest for a Post-Colonial Fiction'. *WLWE*, XXIII, 1984, 208-23.
Thieme, John. 'Christopher J. Koch: Interview'. *Kunapipi*, 8, No. 1, 1986, 19-27.
---. 'Re-Mapping the Australian Psyche: The Asian Novels of C.J. Koch'. *Southerly*, XLVII, No. 4, 1987, 451-461.
Tiffin, Helen. 'Asia, Europe and Australian Identity: The Novels of Christopher Koch'. *A.L.S.*, X, 1982, 326-35.
---. 'Christopher Koch: An Interview with Helen Tiffin'. *Commonwealth Novel in English*, 5.1, 1992, 1-10.
---. 'Indian Motifs in the Novels of Christopher Koch'. *Rajasthan University Studies in English*, XV, 1982-1983, 57-63.

LAMBERT, ERIC

Fiction

The Long White Night. (London: Muller, 1965).
Reviewed by L.V. Kepert, *S.M.H.*, 15 January, 1966, 15; G. Robin, *Australian*, 5 March, 1966, 12.

Critical Material

Hosking, Rick. 'The Usable Past: Australian War Fiction of the 1950s'. *A.L.S.*, XII, No. 2, 1985, 234-247.
Mullett, Jack. 'Eric Lambert'. *Overland*, No. 34, 1966, 19-20.
O'Leary, Zoe. *The Desolate Market: A Biography of Eric Lambert*. Research assistant, Marjorie Pizer. (Sydney: Edwards and Shaw, 1974). Reviewed by D. Freney, *Tribune*, 3 September, 1974, 10; E. Kynaston, *Nation Review*, 5-11 July, 1974, 1251; D. Martin, *Overland*, No. 59, 1974, 66-69; H. McQueen, *Canberra Times*, 9 August, 1974, 9; J. Waten, *Age*, 10 August, 1974, 16.

LANE, WILLIAM

Fiction

The Workingman's Paradise, an Australian Labour Novel. By 'John Miller'; with an introduction by Michael Wilding. (Sydney: Sydney University Press, 1980). First published Sydney: Edwards Dunlop & Co., 1892.
Reviewed by L. Clancy, *ABR*, No. 29, 1981, 39-40; H. Daniel, *Age*, 30 May, 1981, 25; A.A. Phillips, *S.M.H.*, 28 February, 1981, 50.

Critical Material

Gobbett, Don, and Malcolm Saunders. *With Lane in Paraguay: Harry Taylor of 'The Murray Pioneer' 1873-1932.* (Rockhampton, Qld: Central Queensland UP in association with *The Murray Pioneer*, 1995).
Solness, Peter. 'Ginger Meggs in Paraguay'. *S.M.H.: Good Weekend*, 25 January, 1986, 6-11.
Souter, Gavin. *A Peculiar People: The Australians in Paraguay.* (Sydney: A.& R., 1968).
Wilding, Michael. 'William Lane and the Worker Book Fund. "Progressive Books at Cost"'. *Southerly*, XLI, 1981, 329-34.
---. 'William Lane's *The Workingman's Paradise*: Pioneering Socialist Realism'. In *Words and Worlds: Studies in the Social Role of Verbal Culture*, edited by Stephen Knight and S.N. Mukherjee (Sydney: Sydney Association for Studies in Society and Culture, 1983), 31-54. Sydney in Society and Culture No. 1.

LANG, JOHN HENRY

Fiction

Botany Bay or True Tales of Early Australia. Australian Books on Demand 8. (Canberra: Mulini Press, 1994) First published London: W. Tegg, 1859.
Lucy Cooper (An Australian Tale). (Canberra: Mulini Press, 1992). First published

1846. Includes introduction by Victor Crittenden giving 'evidence' for attributing this book to John Lang.
Reviewed by L. Clancy, *Weekend Australian*, 20-21 March, 1993, Review 6.

Critical Material

Bond, Ruskin. 'Looking for John Lang's Grave'. *Blackwood's Magazine*, CCCXI, 1972, 237-42.

Hadgraft, Cecil, and Webby, Elizabeth. 'More Substance to Fisher's Ghost?' *A.L.S.*, III, 1968, 190-200.

Hosking, Rick. 'Magnetic Amalgams? John Lang's *Wanderings in India* (1859), Rudyard Kipling and Henry Lawson'. *Literary Criterion*, 30.1&2, 1995, 59-80.

Irvin, Eric. 'Was John Lang Really a Four-Word Dramatist?' *Australasian Drama Studies*, No. 11, 1987, 23-26.

Keesing, Nancy. *John Lang & "The Forger's Wife": A True Tale of Early Australia*. (Sydney: John Ferguson, 1979). Biography and reprint of novel. Reviewed by M. Dunlevy, *Canberra Times*, 14 July, 1979, 18; H. King, *Journal of the Royal Australian Historical Society*, LXVIII, 1981, 178-80; P. Linnett, *Australian Jewish News*, 30 November, 1979, 21; D. Stewart, *S.M.H.*, 29 September, 1979, 18; P. Thompson, *24 Hours*, IV, No. 10, 1979, 79.

---. 'Not a Pure Merino'. *Hemisphere*, XXIV, No. 2, 1980, 84-88; see also Ruskin Bond. 'Coda to Nancy Keesing's Article "Not a Pure Merino"'. *Hemisphere*, XXIV, No. 2, 1980, 89.

Narasimhaiah, C.D. 'Introduction'. *Literary Criterion* (Mysore), XV, Nos. 3-4, 1980, xx-xxi.

Roderick, Colin. 'John Lang (1816-1864): First Australian-born Novelist'. *Royal Australian Historical Society Journal and Proceedings*, LI, 1963, 100-35. Biographical study.

Routh, S.J. 'The Australian Career of John Lang, Novelist'. *A.L.S.*, I, No. 3, 1964, 206-7. Evidence of Lang's authorship of the *Legends of Australia*.

LANGFORD GINIBI, RUBY

Non-Fiction

Don't Take Your Love to Town. (Ringwood, Vic.: Penguin, 1988).
Reviewed by J. Wright, *Social Alternatives*, 8.3, 1989, 67.

My Bundjalung People. (St Lucia: U.Q.P., 1994).
Reviewed by L. Connors, *LiNQ*, 22.2, 1995, 127-31; A. Curthoys, *Age*, 18 Feb., 1995, Saturday Extra 8; J. Huggins, *Imago*, 7.1, 1995, 89-90; A. Jackson-Nakano, *Australian Aboriginal Studies*, 2, 1994, 79-80; P. Mamajun Torres, *Weekend Australian*, 29-30 October, 1994, Review 5; B. Marshall-Stoneking, *Overland*, 138, 1995, 74-76; M. Smith, *ABR*, 166, 1994, 15-16; V.M. Speechley-Golden, *AWBR*, 7.1, 1995, 9-10.

Real Deadly. (Pymble, NSW: Collins/A & R, 1991).
Reviewed by R. Dingli, *Northern Perspective*, 16.2, 1993, 138-39; S. Hosking, *CRNLE Reviews Journal*, 1, 1992, 14-17; A. Inglis, *Modern Times*, April, 1992, 31-32; M.R. Liverani, *Weekend Australian*, 28-29 March, 1992, Review 6 (reply by the author *Weekend Australian*, 2-3 May, 1992, Review 6; M. Nyoongah, *SPAN*, 34 & 35, 1992-93, 376-83; B. Roberts, *ABR*, 139, 1992, 8-9; J. Robertson, *Hecate*, 18.1, 1992, 117-30; A. Shoemaker, *Imago*, 4.3, 1992, 91-92; S. Thomas, *Meridian*, 12.2, 1993, 173-75.

'The Fencing Circus'. In *Australia for Women: Travel and Culture*, edited by Susan Hawthorne and Renate Klein (North Melbourne, Vic.: Spinifex Press, 1994), 252-259.

'Grandfather Sam Anderson'. In *Australian Writing Now*, edited by Manfred Jurgensen and Robert Adamson (Ringwood, Vic.: Penguin, 1988), 40-43.

'Mission Life Memories'. *Ulitarra*, 2, 1992, 45-48.
'Nobby's Story'. *Meanjin*, 53.1, 1994, 51-60.
'A Poet Who Never Gave Up'. *Australian Short Stories No 43*, edited by Bruce Pascoe (Apollo Bay, Vic.: Pascoe Publishing, 1993), 7-9. Obituary for Kevin Gilbert.
'Tracing My Roots'. *Independent Monthly*, December-January, 1990, 8.
'Tribute to Oodgeroo of the Noonuccal Tribe'. *Australian Women's Book Review*, 6.1, 1994, 2-3.

   Critical Material
Gelder, Ken. 'Aboriginal Narrative and Property'. *Meanjin*, 50.2-3, 1991, 353-65. Discusses Ruby Langford Ginibi and Sally Morgan.
---. 'The Politics of the Sacred'. *World Literature Today*, 67.3, 1993, 499-504. Discusses Ruby Langford Ginibi and Sam Watson.
Holloway, Barbara. 'Finding a Position: Non-Aboriginal Reviewing of Aboriginal Women's Writing'. *Australian Women's Book Review*, 5.1, 1993, 20. Includes discussion of *Real Deadly*.
Little, Janine. 'Talking with Ruby Langford Ginibi'. *Hecate*, 20.1, 1994, 100-21.
McGrath, Caitlin, and Phillipa Sawyer. '"It is Our Turn": An Interview with Ruby Langford Ginibi'. *Meridian*, 13.1, 1994, 79-87.
Rowse, Tim. 'The Aboriginal Subject in Autobiography: Ruby Langford's *Don't Take Your Love to Town*'. *A.L.S.*, 16.1, 1993, 14-28.
Turcotte, Gerry, ed. *Writers in Action: The Writer's Choice Evenings*. (Sydney: Currency Press, 1990), 113-37.

LANGLEY, EVE

   Fiction
The Pea Pickers. (Sydney: A.& R., 1966). First published Sydney: A.& R., 1942. Reviewed by B. Elliott, *ABR*, V, 1966, 134-5; R. Lesley, *Canberra Times*, 14 May, 1966, 13; M. Macleod, *S.M.H.*, 28 February, 1976, 15.
The Pea-Pickers. (North Ryde, NSW: A.& R., 1991). Introduction by Lucy Frost. First published Sydney: A.& R., 1942.

   Critical Material
Arkin, Marian. 'Literary Transvestism in Eve Langley's *The Pea-Pickers*'. *Modern Fiction Studies*, XXVII, No. 1, 1981, 109-16.
Frizell, Helen. 'Eve Langley Rediscovered'. *S.M.H.*, 26 July, 1975, 12.
Frost, Lucy. 'Body in the Vault: The Unpublished Novels of Eve Langley'. *A.L.S.*, 16.1, 1993, 50-56.
McLeod, Aorewa. 'The New Zealand Novels of Eve Langley'. *Southerly*, 55.2, 1995, 160-78.
Porter, Hal. *The Extra*. (Melbourne: Thomas Nelson (Australia), 1975), 141-51.
Segerberg, Anita. '"Strangled by a Bad Tradition"? The Work of Eve Langley'. *Journal of New Zealand Literature*, 10, 1992, 55-73.
Thwaite, Joy. 'Eve Langley: Personal and Artistic Schism'. In *Gender, Politics and Fiction: Twentieth Century Women's Novels*, edited by Carole Ferrier (St Lucia: U.Q.P., 1985), 118-35.
---. *The Importance of Being Eve Langley*. (North Ryde, N.S.W.: A.& R., 1990). Reviewed by L. Clancy, *Age*, 10 February, 1990, Saturday Extra 12; M. Harris, *Weekend Australian*, 27-28 January, 1990, Weekend 7; C. Munro, *A.L.S.*, 15.1, 1991, 89-93.
Vallis, Val. 'Three Lyric Poets: Riddell, Mathew, Langley'. In his *Heart's Reasons These . . .: Commentaries on Five Australian Poets*. The Colin Roderick Lectures, Monograph 16 (Townsville, Qld.: Foundation for Australian Literary Studies, 1988), 51-70.

LAWLER, RAY

Drama
The Doll Trilogy. (Sydney: Currency Press, 1978).
Reviewed by G. Dutton, *Weekend Australian Magazine*, 10-11 February, 1979, 8; A. Godfrey-Smith, *ABR*, No. 2, 1978, 18-21; H. Hewitt, *Canberra Times*, 5 May, 1979, 17; J. McCallum, *Theatre Australia*, 3, No. 8, 1979, 49; L. Radic, *Age*, 17 March, 1979, 23.

Critical Material
'The Doll-maker: Almost a Stranger in his own Land'. *S.M.H.*, 3 September, 1983, 39.
'Nothing's Plenty for a Brilliant Author'. *Artforce*, No. 11, 1977, 4-5. Interview.
Baker, Candida. 'Ray Lawler'. In her *Yacker 2: Australian Writers Talk About Their Work* (Sydney: Picador, 1987), 144-171.
Baker, J.G. *Companion to Ray Lawler, 'The Summer of the Seventeenth Doll' and Alan Seymour, 'The One Day of the Year'*. (Sydney: A.& R., 1965).
Brennan, Niall. 'Dawn of the 17th doll'. *Age*, 18 December, 1965, 21.
Brisbane, Katharine. 'The Late Flowering of Ray Lawler'. *Bulletin*, 19 March, 1977, 47-48.
Carrick, John. 'Encore for the Modest Master'. *Advertiser*, 21 May, 1977, 28.
Dare, Tim. 'Tuned in to Today's Accent'. *Australian*, 18 September, 1971, 16. Interview. See also report in *Australian*, 10 September, 1971, 4.
Davison, P.H. 'Three Australian Plays: National Myths under Criticism'. *Southerly*, XXIII, No. 2, 1963, 110-27. Contains comment on *Summer of the Seventeenth Doll*.
Fitzpatrick, Peter. 'Ray Lawler'. In his *After 'The Doll'*. (Melbourne: Edward Arnold, 1979), 19-33.
Fletcher, Nadia. 'Humour in *The Doll* Trilogy'. *Australasian Drama Studies*, No. 7, 1985, 53-68.
Goldsworthy, Kerryn. 'Is It a Boy or a Girl? Gendering the Seventeenth Doll'. *Southerly*, 55.1, 1995, 89-105.
Grealy, Michael. 'It's the First Summer for Another Doll'. *Advertiser*, 8 January, 1976, 22. Interview.
Healey, Ken. 'Top Author Says he is Really an Actor'. *Canberra Times*, 12 July, 1981, 8.
Hibberd, Jack. 'After Many a Summer: The *Doll* Trilogy'. *Meanjin*, XXXVI, 1977, 106-09.
Hooton, Joy. 'Lawler's Demythologizing of the *Doll*: *Kid Stakes* and *Other Times*'. *A.L.S.*, XII, No. 3, 1986, 335-46.
Hurst, John. 'There's Life in the Old Doll Yet'. *Australian*, 5 December, 1975, 12.
Leask, Margaret. 'An Interview with Ray Lawler'. *Elizabethan Trust News*, No. 18, 1976, 3-4.
Marks, Stan. 'Another Summer, Another Doll'. *Theatre-Australia*, I, No. 5, 1976-1977, 42-43.
McCallum, John. 'The *Doll* and the Legend'. *Australasian Drama Studies*, III, No. 2, 1985, 33-44.
Milliken, Robert. 'Ray Lawler's *Doll* Trilogy Revived in Triumph'. *National Times*, 21-26 February, 1977, 50.
Nicklin, Lenore. '13 Summers after *The Doll* Ray Lawler Tackles Governor Bligh and the Rum Corps'. *S.M.H.*, 17 September, 1971, 7. Also published in *Advertiser*, 2 October, 1971, 25.
O'Grady, Suellen. 'Exploring Life after *The Doll*'. *Weekend Australian Magazine*, 14-15 July, 1984, 17.
Ponton, F. '*Summer of the Seventeenth Doll*'. *Teaching of English*, No. 14, 1969, 43-47.
Porteous, Alexander. 'Some Recent Australian Plays, and Problems of Their

Criticism'. *A.L.S.*, III, 1967, 83-97.
Radic, Leonard. '... And Now - It's the Summer of the First Doll'. *Age*, 15 November, 1975, 16.
Robinson, Ian. 'The Summers Before Lawler's 17th Doll'. *National Times*, 29 December, 1975-3 January, 1976, 32.
Salusinszky, Imre. 'What's Bugging Olive: A New Reading of *The Doll*'. *Southerly*, 50, No. 2, 1990, 170-81.
Scheller, Bernhard. 'Ray Lawler und einige Entwicklungstendenzen im Australischen Drama'. *Zeitschrift fur Anglistik und Amerikanistik*, XXVI, 1978, 115-30.
Smark, Peter. 'Lawler, Hatching Plots in Ireland'. *Australian*, 31 July, 1971, 20.
Sykes, Alrene. 'Ray Lawler Talks to Alrene Sykes'. *Australasian Drama Studies*, III, No. 2, 1985, 21-31.
Sykes, Jill. 'Snared in the Past of *The Doll*'. *S.M.H.*, 28 February, 1976, 11.
Webby, Elizabeth. *Modern Australian Plays*. Horizon Studies in Literature. (Sydney: Sydney UP in assoc. with O.U.P., 1990). Includes discussion of *The Summer of the Seventeenth Doll*.

LAWRENCE, D.H.

Fiction

With M.L. Skinner. *The Boy in the Bush*. Preface by Harry T. Moore. (South Melbourne: Macmillan, 1980). First published London: Secker, 1924.
Reviewed by D. Allen, *National Times*, 28 December-3 January, 1981, 37; M. Dunlevy, *Canberra Times*, 6 January, 1973, 8; P. Eggert *ABR*, No. 31, 1981, 23; T. Forshaw, *S.M.H.*, 3 February, 1973, 25; P. Jones, *Ash Magazine*, No. 7, 1981, 29-30; S. Ruddell, *Canberra Times*, 31 January, 1981, 17; J. Waten, *Age*, 20 January, 1973, 19.
With M.L. Skinner. *The Boy in the Bush*. Edited by Paul Eggert. (Cambridge; New York; Melbourne: Cambridge UP, 1990).
Reviewed by D. Carter, *Weekend Australian*, 27-28 April, 1991, Review 6; E. Delavenay, *Études Anglaises*, 25.2, 1992, 228-29; B. Steele, *Overland*, 123, 1991, 88-90.
Kangaroo. Edited by Bruce Steele. (Cambridge: Cambridge UP., 1994).
Reviewed by F. Devlin Glass, *Australian Studies*, 44, 1995, 103-04; F. Kermode, *London Review of Books*, 21, 1994, 24-25.
Kangaroo: The Corrected Edition. Foreword by Raymond Southall (Sydney: Collins, 1990).
Reviewed by L. Clancy, *Weekend Australian*, 31 March-1 April, 1990, Weekend 5; R. Ross, *Antipodes*, 5.2, 1991, 163; S. Trigg, *ABR*, No. 118, 1990, 29-30.

Critical Material

Alexander, John. 'D.H. Lawrence's *Kangaroo*: Fantasy, Fact or Fiction?' *Meanjin*, XXIV, 1965, 179-97. Comment by Curtis Atkinson in *Meanjin*, XXIV, 1965, 358-9.
Bartlett, Norman. 'Mollie Skinner and *The Boy in the Bush*'. *Quadrant*, XXVIII, Nos. 7-8, 1984, 73-75.
Bjorksten, Ingmar. 'I tvivelaktigt sallskap' [In Dubious Company]. *Svenska Dagbladet* (Stockholm), 19 August, 1977.
Darroch, Robert. *D.H. Lawrence in Australia*. (South Melbourne: Macmillan, 1981).
Reviewed by E. Campion, *Bulletin*, 18 August, 1981, 87-90; T.M. Fitzgerald, *S.M.H.*, 1 August, 1981, 44; D. Leitch, *National Times*, 2-8 August, 1981, 26-27; R. Mainsbridge, ABR, No. 35, 1981, 15-16; P. Pierce, *Age*, 15 August, 27; L.L. Robson, *Journal of Australian Studies*, No. 10, 1982, 83-84.
---. 'D.H. Lawrence's Australia'. *Overland*, No. 113, 1988, 34-38.
---. 'D.H. Lawrence's *Bulletin* Connection'. *Bulletin*, 18 August, 1981, 94-101.
---. '*Kangaroo*: The Darroch Thesis'. *Meridian*, 11.1, 1992, 23-30.

---. 'The Man Who Was Kangaroo'. *Quadrant*, XXXI, No. 9, 1987, 56-60.
---. 'More on Lawrence in Australia'. *D.H. Lawrence Review*, 20.1, 1988, 39-59.
---. 'The Mystery of *Kangaroo* and the Secret Army'. *Australian*, 15 May, 1976, 26, 28.
---. 'So Many of the Best People Join Secret Armies'. *Australian*, 15 January, 1977, 21. 26.
Davis, Joseph. *D.H. Lawrence at Thirroul*. (Sydney: Collins, 1989). Reviewed by L. Clancy, *Weekend Australian*, 31 March-1 April, 1990, Weekend 5; P. Eggert, *Age*, 13 January, 1990, Saturday Extra 8; M. Hellyer, *Editions*, Nos. 8-9, 1990, 35-36; R. Ross, *Antipodes*, 5.2, 1991, 163; S. Trigg, *ABR*, No. 118, 1990, 29-30.
---. 'D.H. Lawrence at Thirroul: A Reply to Andrew Moore'. *Overland*, No. 121, 1990, 44-5.
Eggert, Paul. 'Lawrence, The Secret Army, and the West Australian Connexion: Molly Skinner'. *Westerly*, XXVII, No. 4, 1982, 123-26. Discusses Robert Darroch. *D.H. Lawrence in Australia*.
---. 'The Literary work of a Readership: *The Boy in the Bush* in Australia, 1924-1926'. *Bibliographical Society of Australia and New Zealand Bulletin*, 12, No. 4, 1988 (issued 1990), 149-66.
Ellis, David. 'Lawrence in Australia: The Darroch Controversy'. *D.H. Lawrence Review*, 21.2, 1989, 167-74.
Friederich, Werner P. *Australia in Western Imaginative Prose Writings 1600-1960: An Anthology and a History of Literature*. (Chapel Hill: University of North Carolina Press, 1967), 226-35.
Hall, Richard and Ruffels, John K. 'Shipboard Talk: Did D.H. Lawrence Meet Fr O'Reilly'. *Overland*, No. 117, 1990, 11-14.
Heuzenroeder, John. 'D. H. Lawrence's Australia'. *A.L.S.*, IV, 1970, 319-33.
Hope, A.D. 'D.H. Lawrence's *Kangaroo*: How It Looks to an Australian'. In *The Australian Experience: Critical Essays on Australian Novels*, edited by W.S. Ramson (Canberra: Australian National University Press, 1974), 157-73.
Lee, Robert. 'D.H. Lawrence and the Australian Ethos'. *Southerly*, XXXIII, 1973, 144-51.
Maddox, Brenda. *The Married Man: A Life of D.H. Lawrence*. (London: Sinclair-Stevenson, 1994). Includes discussion of Lawrence's Australian sojourn and the political background to *Kangaroo*. Reviewed by F. Kermode, *London Review of Books*, 16.21, 1994, 24-25.
Mather, Rodney. 'Patrick White and Lawrence: A Contrast'. *Critical Review*, No. 13, 1970, 34-50.
McQueen, Humphrey. 'Kangaroo Revisited'. *24 Hours*, July, 1994, 66-69.
Moore, Andrew. 'Anticipating the Cambridge *Kangaroo*: A Reply to Bruce Steele'. *Meridian*, 11.1, 1992, 31-37. Response to Bruce Steele in *Meridian*, 10.1, 1991, 19-34.
---. 'On Ferroequinology and D.H. Lawrence: A Reply to Joseph Davis'. *Overland* 123, 1991, 45-46. See also *Overland* 120, 1990, 41-44, and 121, 1990, 44-45.
---. 'The Historian as Detective: Pursuing the Darroch Thesis and D.H. Lawrence's Secret Army'. *Overland*, No. 113, 1988, 39-44.
---. 'Thirroul and the Literary Establishment Strike Back'. *Overland*, No. 120, 1990, 41-44.
Niven, Alastair. *D.H. Lawrence*. (Cambridge: Cambridge University Press, 1978). British Authors, introductory critical studies.
Peek, Andrew. 'The Sydney *Bulletin* and D.H. Lawrence's *Kangaroo*'. *Notes & Queries*, N.S. XXVI, 1979, 337-38.
--- 'Tim Burstall's *Kangaroo*'. *Westerly*, XXV, No. 4, 1980, 39-42. Interview with film director.
Riemer, A.P. 'This World, the Next, and Australia - the Emergence of a Literary

Commonplace'. *Southerly*, XLIV, 1984, 251-70.
Roff, Sue. 'Mating and Courtship: Misogyny in West Australia'. *Newsletter of the A.A.A.L.S.*, I, No. 2, 1985, 6.
---. 'The Lure of Mateship. Australia Had a Marked Effect on the Fantasies of D.H. Lawrence' *Australian Society*, III, No. 5, 1984, 33-34.
Skinner, M.L. *The Fifth Sparrow: An Autobiography*. With a foreword by Mary Durack [Edited by Mary Durack and Marjorie Rees]. (Sydney: Sydney University Press, 1972). Reviewed by M. Dunlevy, *Canberra Times*, 6 January, 1973, 8; N. Keesing, *Southerly*, XXXIII, 1973, 86-88; W.A. Murray, *ABR*, XI, 1972, 36-37; A.A. Phillips, *Nation Review*, 16-22 December, 1972, 295; O. Ruhen, *Australian*, 9 December, 1972, 37; *T.L.S.*, 1 June, 1973, 625; J. Waten, *Age*, 20 January, 1973, 19; M. Williams, *S.M.H.*, 3 March, 1973, 25.
St. John, Edward. 'D.H. Lawrence and Australia's Secret Army'. *Quadrant*, XXVI, No. 6, 1982, 53-57.
Steele, Bruce. '*Kangaroo*: Fiction and Fact'. *Meridian*, 10.1, 1991, 19-34.
Tacey, David. 'On Not Crossing the Gap: Lawrence and Our Genius Loci'. *Quadrant*, 34, No. 11, 1990, 69-73.
Tolchard, Clifford. 'D.H. Lawrence in Australia'. *Walkabout*, XXXIII, No. 11, 1967, 28-31.
Van Herk, Aritha. 'CrowB(e)ars and Kangaroos of the Future: the Post-Colonial Ga(s)p'. *WLWE*, 30.2, 1990, 42-54. Discusses *Kangaroo*.
Waten, Judah. 'Books and the Bottle-O's Son'. *S.M.H.*, 12 April, 1969, 19.
Wilding, Michael. 'Between Scylla and Charybdis: *Kangaroo* and the Form of the Political Novel'. *A.L.S.*, IV, 1970, 334-48.
--- 'D.H. Lawrence in Australia: Some Recently Published Letters'. *A.L.S.*, IX, 1980, 373-77.
---. '"A New Show": The Politics of *Kangaroo*'. *Southerly*, XXX, 1970, 20-40. Reprinted as '*Kangaroo*: "A New Show"'. In his *Political Fictions*. (London: Routledge & Kegan Paul, 1980), 150-91.

LAWSON, HENRY

Collection

Collected Prose. Edited by Colin Roderick. Memorial edition (Sydney: A.& R., 1972), Vol.1: Short stories and sketches, 1888-1922. Vol.2: Autobiographical and other writings, 1887-1922.
Reviewed by P. Coleman, *Bulletin*, 5 August, 1972, 37; M. Dunlevy, *Canberra Times*, 1 July, 1972, 14; A.N. Jeffares, *Journal of Commonwealth Literature*, X, No. 1, 1975, 77-79; T. Keneally, *S.M.H.*, 19 August, 1972, 22; B. Kiernan, *Australian*, 8 July, 1972, [28]; A.A. Phillips, *Age*, 5 August, 1972, 15; G.A.W., *Southerly*, XXXIII, 1973, 346-47. Vol. 1 reviewed by L. Cantrell, *A.L.S.*, VI, 1973, 99-104. Vol. 2 reviewed by S. Murray-Smith, *A.L.S.*, VI, 1973, 105-06.

The Complete Works of Henry Lawson. Edited by Leonard Cronin; with introductions by Brian Kiernan. Vol. 1 *A Camp-Fire Yarn*; Vol. 2 *A Fantasy of Man* (Sydney: Lansdowne, 1984).
Reviewed by A. Barker, *S.M.H.*, 13 October, 1984, 40; J. Barnes, *ABR*, No. 68, 1985, 26-29; H. Hewitt, *Canberra Times*, 21 October, 1984, 10; J. McLaren, *ABR*, No. 66, 1984, 37; A. Mitchell, *Weekend Australian Magazine*, 10-21 October, 1984, 17; A. Mole, *Advertiser Saturday Review*, 27 October, 1984, 38; C. Semmler, *Bulletin*, 2 October, 1984, 70-72.

The Essential Henry Lawson: The Best Works of Australia's Greatest Writer. Selection and biography by Brian Kiernan. (Melbourne: Currey O'Neil, 1983).
Reviewed by J. Barnes, *ABR*, No. 49, 1983, 34-35.

Henry Lawson. Selected and edited with an introduction and bibliography by Brian

Kiernan. (St Lucia: U.Q.P., 1976). Portable Australian Authors.
Reviewed by L.S. Fallis, *World Literature Today*, LI, No. 3, 1977, 498; J. Maddocks, *Quadrant*, XXI, No. 7, 1977, 75-76.

The Picador Henry Lawson. Edited and introduced by Geoffrey Dutton. (Chippendale, NSW: Pan/Macmillan Picador, 1991).

The World of Henry Lawson. Edited by Walter Stone (Dee Why West: Paul Hamlyn, 1974). Includes biographical introduction and notes.

   Fiction

The Bush Undertaker and Other Stories. Selected by Colin Roderick. (Sydney: A.& R., 1970). Revised edition with preface by Colin Roderick. (Pymble, NSW: A.& R., 1994). Includes 'A Fragment of Autobiography', 223-47, and commentary (predominantly textual) by the editor, 248-72.
Reviewed by B. Kiernan, *Australian*, 20 February, 1971, 24.

The Drover's Wife and Other Stories. Selection, introduction and glossary by Alan Brissenden (Hornsby, N.S.W.: Hodder and Stoughton (Australia); London: Coronet Books, 1974).

Grandfather's Courtship: A Christmas Story. Introduction by Colin Roderick. (Sydney: A.& R., 1982).
Reviewed by G. Hutton, Age Saturday Extra, 24 December, 1982, 7.

Henry Lawson the Master Story-Teller: Prose Writings. Edited by Colin Roderick. (Sydney: A.& R., 1984).
Reviewed by C. Semmler, *Weekend Australian Magazine*, 16-17 June, 1984, 15; V. Sen, *Canberra Times*, 21 July, 1984, 18.

Henry Lawson's Best Stories. (Sydney: A.& R., 1966). Selected and with a Preface by Cecil Mann.
Reviewed by R.F. Brissenden, *Australian*, 31 December, 1966, 9; A.R. Chisholm, *Age*, 22 October, 1966, 21; C. Hadgraft, *Bulletin*, 29 October, 1966, 39; I. Hamilton, *New Statesman*, 16 December, 1966, 911; George Johnston, *S.M.H.*, 12 November, 1966, 19; Grahame Johnston, *Canberra Times*, 3 December, 1966, 11.

Humorous Stories. Compiled by Cecil Mann. (Sydney: A.& R., 1967).
Reviewed by F.H. Mares, *Adelaide Advertiser*, 17 June, 1967, 20.

The Penguin Henry Lawson Short Stories. Edited with an introduction by John Barnes. (Ringwood, Vic.: Penguin, 1986).

Selected Stories. Introduction by Brian Matthews. (Adelaide: Rigby, 1971). Seal Australian Fiction.

The Stories of Henry Lawson. Edited and with an introduction and critical commentary by Cecil Mann. (Sydney: A.& R., 1965).
Reviewed by M. Dunlevy, *Canberra Times*, 17 April, 1965, 9; D. Green, *Nation*, 4 September, 1965, 21-2; M. Harris, *ABR*, IV, 1965, 137; L. Kramer, *Bulletin*, 12 June, 1965, 54-5; A.A. Phillips, *Age*, 5 June, 1965, 24; *T.L.S.*, 16 September, 1965, 794.

Two Sundowners and Other Stories. (Tokyo: Kenkyusha, 1964). Edited with notes by Mikio Hiramatsu.

While the Billy Boils. Introduction by Chris Wallace-Crabbe (Sydney: A.& R., 1991). First published Sydney: A.& R., 1896.

   Poetry

Collected Verse. Edited by Colin Roderick. *Vol. I: 1885-1900*. (Sydney: A.& R., 1967).
Reviewed by L.N.C., *Australian Left Review*, No. 6, 1967, 80; D. Douglas, *Overland*, No. 38, 1968, 47-48, *Southerly*, XXVII, 1967, 298-99 and *Age*, 21 October, 1967, 24; B. Elliott, *A.L.S.*, III, 1967, 154-157; F.H. Mares, *Adelaide*

Advertiser, 17 June, 1967, 20; S. Murray-Smith, *Overland*, No. 42, 1969, 44-45; E. Perkins, *Makar*, IV, No. 4, 1968, 48-52; R. Ward, *S.M.H.*, 23 December, 1967, 17.

Collected Verse. Edited by Colin Roderick. *Vol. II: 1901-1909*. (Sydney: A.& R., 1968).
Reviewed by L. Cantrell, *Australian Left Review*, No. 2, 1969, 79-80; T.I. Moore, *Canberra Times*, 7 September, 1968, 15.

Collected Verse. Edited by Colin Roderick. *Vol. III: 1910-1922*. (Sydney: A.& R., 1968, 1969).
Reviewed by L. Cantrell, *Australian Left Review*, No. 23, 1970, 9-80.

Poems. Selected by Walter Stone, illustrated by Pro Hart. (Sydney: Ure Smith, 1973). Introduction by Walter Stone.

Poems. With preface and chronology by Colin Roderick. (Sydney: John Ferguson, 1979).
Reviewed by B. Elliott, *Advertiser*, 11 August, 1979, 28; M. Pettigrove, *Canberra Times*, 14 July, 1979, 19; W. Stone, *S.M.H.*, 4 August, 1979, 18; K. Tennant, *Hemisphere*, XXIV, No. 3, 1980, 142-43.

Selected Poems of Henry Lawson. (Sydney: A.& R., 1980).
Reviewed by M. Eldridge, *Canberra Times*, 21 June, 1980, 15.

    Non-Fiction
Letters, 1890-1922. Edited with introduction and notes by Colin Roderick. (Sydney: A.& R., 1970).
Reviewed by D. Ball, *S.M.H.*, 25 July, 1970, 24; A.R. Chisholm, *Age*, 1 August, 1970, 16; M. Dunlevy, *Canberra Times*, 25 July, 1970, 12; A.N. Jeffares, *Journal of Commonwealth Literature*, X, No. 1, 1975, 77-79; N. Keesing, *Bulletin*, 15 August, 1970, 43-44; W. Stone, *Australian*, 29 August, 1970, 21; G.A.W., *Southerly*, XXXIII, 1973, 346-47.

Recollections: A Selection of Autobiographical Works. Edited by Leonard Cronin. (Frenchs Forest, N.S.W.: Reed, 1987).

    Critical Material
Arnold, John and Thorn, Frances. 'Checklist of Henry Lawson Manuscripts in the Lothian Collection'. *La Trobe Library Journal*, VII, 1981, 101-04.
Chaplin, Harry F. *Henry Lawson: his Books, Manuscripts, Autograph Letters and Association Copies, Together with Publications by Louisa Lawson*. (Sydney: Wentworth Press, 1974). Studies in Australian Bibliography, No. 21. Reviewed by L. Cantrell, *Southerly*, XXXV, 1975, 103-04.
Stone, Walter. *Henry Lawson: A Chronological Checklist of his Contributions to the Bulletin, 1887-1924*. Second edition. (Sydney: Wentworth, 1964). *Studies in Australian Bibliography*, 1.

La Trobe Library Journal: Henry Lawson Issue. (Melbourne: The Friends of the La Trobe Library, 1981). Reviewed by A.A. Phillips, *Age Saturday Extra*, 27 February, 1982, 15.
'100 Years of Henry Lawson'. *Tribune*, 14 June, 1967, 5-8. Includes very brief articles by R.F. Brissenden, A.D. Hope, and many others.
'The Lawson Industry'. *Bulletin*, 8 July, 1967, 13.
'Pleas from the Heart from Prisoner 117'. *Age*, 3 January, 1986, 5. About the release of previously unpublished correspondence, short stories and poems.
'Reality and Fictional World: Henry Lawson'. *Australian Literature Bulletin* (Venice), II, No. 1, 1979, 20.
'A Rose for Hannah [Thorburn]'. *Australian*, 7 February, 1972, 3.
Adams, Phillip. 'Henry's Centenary'. *Bulletin*, 22 July, 1967, 43. Referring to the Play *Lawson* by Oriel Gray.
---. 'Lawson: Too Little with Us'. *Australian*, 28 September, 1968, 11. On a

238 HENRY LAWSON

television production of 'The Drover's Wife'.
Arens, Werner. 'The Ironical Fate of "The Drover's Wife": Four Versions from Henry Lawson (1892) to Barbara Jefferis (1980)'. In *The Story Must Be Told: Short Narrative Prose in the New English Literatures*, edited by Peter O. Stummer (Wurzburg: Konighausen und Neumann, 1986), 119-133.
Arnold, John and Thorn, Frances. 'Henry and Bertha Lawson: Some Unpublished Letters and Stories'. *La Trobe Library Journal*, VII, 1981, 73-75.
Arnold, Rollo. 'Henry Lawson: The New Zealand Visits'. *A.L.S.*, III, 1968, 163-89.
---. 'Henry Lawson: "The Sliprails and the Spur" at Pahiatua?' *A.L.S.*, IV, 1970, 286-92.
Barnes, John (ed.). *The Writer in Australia* (Melbourne: O.U.P., 1969), passim, but see particularly Lawson's '"Pursuing Literature" in Australia', 71-79 (first published 1899), and A.G. Stephens, 'Henry Lawson: Collected Criticism 1896-1922', 80-105.
Barnes, John. *Henry Lawson's Short Stories*. (Melbourne: Shillington House, 1985). Essays in Australian Literature.
---. 'Henry Lawson in England: The "High Tide": A Revaluation'. *Quadrant*, XXVII, No. 8, 1983, 60-69.
---. 'Henry Lawson in London'. *Quadrant*, XXIII, No.7, 1979, 24-35.
---. 'Lawson and the Short Story in Australia'. *Westerly*, No. 2, 1968, 83-87.
---. 'Textual Criticism'. *Quadrant*, XXVII, No. 9, 1983, 4. Letter of correction to his 'Henry Lawson in England'.
---. '"What has he done for our National Spirit?" - A Note on Lawson Criticism'. *A.L.S.*, VIII, 1978, 485-91.
Barton, Hilton. 'Bret Harte and Henry Lawson: Democratic Realists'. *Realist*, No. 26, 1967, 7-10.
Baxter, Rosilyn. 'Henry Lawson and Gertrude Moore'. *A.L.S.*, V, 1971, 91-93.
Beasley, Jack. *Journal of An Era: Notes From the Red Letter Days*. (Earlwood, N.S.W.: Wedgetail Press, 1988), 21-28.
Beatty, Bill. *Around Australia*. (Melbourne: Cassell, 1966), 197-201.
Brooksbank, Anne. *All My Love*. (Port Melbourne: Heinemann, 1991). Fictionalised account of the alleged love affair between Lawson and Mary Gilmore. Reviewed by J. Messer, *S.M.H.*, 9 February, 1991, 48; E. Riddell, *ABR*, 128, 1991, 11; J. Stephens, *Australian Society*, 10.3, 1991, 42-43.
Burns, Greg. 'Lawson on Westralia'. *Westerly*, XXVII, No. 4, 1982, 117-21.
Carswell, Doreen. 'Kipling and Lawson, Contemporaries'. *Expression*, VIII, No. 2, 1969, 50-52.
Clark, Manning. *In Search of Henry Lawson*. (Melbourne: Macmillan, 1978). Republished as *Henry Lawson: The Man and the Legend*. (Carlton, Vic.: Melbourne UP, 1995). Reviewed by E. Campion, *Bulletin*, 9 May, 1978, 68; J. Docker, *National Times*, 2 June, 1978, 20; M. Dunlevy, *Canberra Times*, 10 June, 1978, 16; F.D. Glass, *Journal of Australian Studies*, No. 3, 1978, 99-100; D. Green, *Nation Review*, 15-21 June, 1978, 14; B. Matthews, *Advertiser*, 19 June, 1978, 29; J. McLaren, *ABR*, No. 1, 1978, 26-27; B. Pearson, *A.L.S.*, IX, 1980, 410-13; A.A. Phillips, *Meanjin*, XXXVII, 1978, 257-61; C. Roderick, *Townsville, Daily Bulletin*, 19 May, 1978, 4 reprinted in *S.M.H.*, 12 May, 1978 (see correspondence and comments from H. Frizell, *S.M.H.*, 12 May, 1978, 1; *S.M.H.*, 13 May, 1978, 3; E.C.B. MacLaurin and P. White, *S.M.H.*, 17 May, 1978, 6; J. Gunning and C. Roderick, *S.M.H.*, 18 May, 1978, 6; A.H. Gibbs, H.W. Piper and R. Tzannes, *S.M.H.*, 19 May, 1978, 6; B. Courcier and E.C.B. MacLaurin, *S.M.H.*, 23 May, 1978, 6; P. White, *S.M.H.*, 24 May, 1978, 6; Mrs M. Johnston and C. Roderick, *S.M.H.*, 25 May, 1978, 6; G.J.V. Hart, P. Kenna and M.I. Smythe, *S.M.W.*, 26 May, 1978, 6; H. Frizell, *S.M.H.*, 1 June, 1978, 7; M. Abraham, *Advertiser*, 10 June, 1978, 26;, 7-8); C. Semmler, *Canberra Times*, 10 June, 1978, 16; J. Waten, *Age*, 29 April, 1978, 22.

---. 'Henry Lawson'. In *The Literature of Australia*, Revised edition, edited by Geoffrey Dutton (Ringwood, Vic.: Penguin, 1976), 322-36.

Cleverly, J.F. 'The Schooldays of Henry Lawson'. *Education*, XLIV, July, 1963, 3-4.

Cocchi, Raffaele. 'Henry Lawson: Figlio del Popolo; Poeta della Solitudine e della Disperazione'. In *Australiana*, edited by Paolo Bertinetti and Claudio Gorlier (Rome: Bulzoni, 1982), 187-96; abstract 266-68.

Cranny-Francis, A. 'Henry Lawson and the *Labour Leader*'. *A.L.S.*, XI, 1983, 266.

---. 'Pacifying the Socialist: the "Reform" of Henry Lawson's "The Hymn of the Socialists"'. *A.L.S.*, X, 1982, 511-15.

Dobrez, Livio. 'The Craftsmanship of Lawson Revisited'. *A.L.S.*, VII, 1976, 375-88.

Docker, John. 'Manning Clark's Henry Lawson'. *Labour History*, No. 37, 1979, 1-14.

Douglas, Dennis. 'The Text of Lawson's Prose'. *A.L.S.*, II, 1966, 254-65.

Downing, Sheila M. 'Blazing the Trail: Henry Lawson's Short Fiction'. In *Percorsi immaginati: Viaggio, metafora e modello in scrittori anglofoni d'Africa, Asia, America, Australia*, edited Giovanna Capone (Bologna: Cooperativa Libraria Universitaria Editrice Bologna, 1993), 121-35.

Dunlevy, Maurice. 'The Price of a Decent Brass Band'. *Canberra Times*, 17 June, 1967, 11.

Dyson, L. 'Centenary for Henry Lawson'. *Australian*, 2 June, 1967, 6. Letter to editor concerning commemoration of the Lawson centenary, answered by Walter Stone, 8 June, 1967, 8; and P. Clancy, 16 June, 1967, 6.

E[lliott], B[rian] R. 'Ben Trovato!' *Adelaide A.L.S. Working Papers*, II, No. 2, 1977, 79-80.

Fox, Len. 'Henry Lawson and Ragnar Redbeard'. *Overland*, No. 38, 1968, 31-34. Deals with Lawson in relation to Arthur Desmond.

---. 'Lawson: The Centenary Symposium Continues: Humanism and Mateship'. *Tribune*, 21 June, 1967, 14.

Gerson, Stanley. 'A Great Australian Dickensian'. *Dickensian*, LXVIII, 1972, 74-89. Deals with Lawson as imitator of Dickens.

Hall, Richard. 'Bureaucratic Bastardry and Henry Lawson's Legacy'. *Australian Financial Review*, 13 May, 1983, 25 & 30.

Hanna, Clifford. 'A Gift Recovered: A Henry Lawson Inscription'. *A.L.S.*, X, 1982, 516.

Hardy, Bobbie. *Their Work was Australian: The Story of the Hudson Family*. (Sydney: Hudson Family, 1970), 39-40. On Lawson's employment at Hudson Brothers' railway carriage works.

Hardy, Frank. 'The Genius of Henry Lawson: Time, Place and Circumstances', Part I. *Realist Writer*, No. 13, 1963, 10-14.

---. 'The Genius of Henry Lawson, Time, Place and Circumstances', Part II. *Realist*, No. 14, 1964, 8-13.

Harris, Max. 'Our Most Successful Failure?'. *Australian*, 17 June, 1967, 6.

Harvey, Oliver. 'Henry Lawson: Loser who Left a Priceless Legacy'. '*Courier-Mail*, 22 September, 1984, 26.

---. 'The Works of Henry Lawson'. *Age Saturday Extra*, 22 September, 1984, 7.

Hawley, Janet. 'New Insight on Lawson in London'. *Age Saturday Extra*, 27 November, 1982, 3 & 5. See also *Courier-Mail*, 27 November, 1982, 27; *Advertiser*, 4 December, 1982, 31.

---. 'The Works of Henry Lawson'. *Age Saturday Extra*, 22 September, 1984, 7.

Heinrichs, Paul. 'Lawson's Mother was Quite a Character Too'. *Age*, 12 October, 1977, 2.

Hersey, April. Letter to the Editor. *Bulletin*, 19 November, 1966, 5.

Heseltine, H.P. 'The Australian Nineties: An Experiment in Critical Method'. *The*

Teaching of English, No. 6, 1965, 17-32.
---. 'Between Living and Dying: The Ground of Lawson's Art'. *Overland*, No. 88, 1982, 19-26.
Hewett, Dorothy. 'The Journey of Henry Lawson'. *Australian Left Review*, No. 3, 1967, 29-32; and No. 4, 1967, 56-62.
Hickey, Bernard. 'Some Henry Lawson Letters to Edward Garnett'. *A.L.S.*, XII, No. 1, 1985, 128-131.
Hosking, Rick. 'Magnetic Amalgams? John Lang's *Wanderings in India* (1859), Rudyard Kipling and Henry Lawson'. *Literary Criterion*, 30.1&2, 1995, 59-80.
Jarvis, D.R. 'Narrative Technique in Lawson'. *A.L.S.*, IX, 1980, 367-73.
---. 'Lawson, the *Bulletin* and the Short Story'. *A.L.S.*, XI, 1983, 58-66.
Johansson, Bertil. 'Henry Lawson and his letters'. Review article. *Henry Lawson. Letters 1890-1922.* Edited by Colin Roderick. (Sydney: A.& R., 1970). *Moderna sprak*, Stockholm, No. 4, 1976.
Johnson, Robert L. 'The Road Out in Australian and American Fiction: A Study of Four Spokesmen'. *Southern Review*, I, No. 3, 1965, 20-31.
Johnston, Grahame. 'His Yarns Endure'. *Canberra Times*, 17 June, 1967, 11.
Jones, Alex I. 'Sound Sybolism in Henry Lawson's Poetry'. In *Reconnoitres: Essays in Australian Literature in Honour of G.A. Wilkes*, edited by Margaret Harris and Elizabeth Webby (South Melbourne: O.U.P. in association with Sydney U.P., 1992), 54-60.
Jones, Joseph. *The Union Honors Its Dead: Henry Lawson Commemorative Gathering Number thirty-nine.* (Hong Kong: the Author, 1966). Re-printed from *United College Journal* (Hong Kong), IV, June, 1965.
Kempster, Chris. *The Songs of Henry Lawson.* (Ringwood, Vic.: Viking O'Neil, 1989). Reviewed by E. Toohey, *ABR*, No. 118, 1990, 46.
Kevans, Denis. 'Lawson: The Centenary Symposium Continues: Part of Our Heritage'. *Tribune*, 21 June, 1967, 14.
Kiernan, Brian. *Henry Lawson: Sketches and Stories.* (Sydney: English Association, 1987). A lecture for the English Association, 19 June, 1987.
---. 'A correction'. *A.L.S.*, XI, 1983, 119. To his article in X, 1982, 503-07.
---. 'Some Previously Unpublished Lawson Material in Australian Libraries'. *A.L.S.*, X, 1982, 503-07.
---. 'Ways of Seeing: Henry Lawson's "Going Blind"'. *A.L.S.*, IX, 1980, 298-308.
Lawson, Alan. 'The Framing of "The Loaded Dog": The Story, Source and Tradition'. *Quadrant*, XXIX, No. 5, 1985, 63-65.
Lawson, Bertha, and Brereton, J.L. (eds.). *Henry Lawson by His Mates.* (Sydney: A.& R., 1973). First published Sydney: A.& R., 1931. Reviewed by M. Dunlevy, *Canberra Times*, 23 June, 1973, 10; R. Park, *Sunday Telegraph*, 17 June, 1973, 22.
Lawson, Sylvia. 'Please Don't Put the Boot Into Henry Lawson's Mum'. *National Times*, 15-21 November, 1985, 35. Article refers to *Henry Lawson, Out of Eden* by Xavier Pons.
Lee, Christopher. 'The Emasculation of Henry Lawson'. *Meridian*, 13.1, 1994, 3-14.
---. 'Man, Work and Country: The Production of Henry Lawson'. *A.L.S.*, 15.3, 1992, 110-22.
---. 'The National Myth and the Stereotype: "The Bush Undertaker" Goes to the Bhabha'. *Australian-Canadian Studies*, 10.2, 1992, 136-41.
---. 'What Colour Are the Dead? Madness, Race and the National Gaze in Henry Lawson's "The Bush Undertaker"'. *Kunapipi*, 13.3, 1992, 14-25.
Long, Gavin. 'Young Paterson and Young Lawson'. *Meanjin*, XXIII, No. 4, 1964, 403-13.
Mackaness, George. 'Henry Lawson's First Book'. In *Bibliomania: An Australian Book Collector's Essays.* (Sydney: A.& R., 1965), 53-7.
Maddocks, John. 'Dickens and Lawson'. *Quadrant*, XXII, No. 2, 1978, 42-46.

---. 'Narrative Technique in Lawson's Joe Wilson Stories'. *Southerly*, XXXVII, 1977, 97-107.

Matthews, Brian. *The Receding Wave: Henry Lawson's Prose*. (Carlton: M.U.P., 1972). Reviewed by L. Cantrell, *A.L.S.*, VI, 1973, 99-104; M. Dunlevy, *Canberra Times*, 31 March, 1973, 13; G. McGregor, *Ariel*, IV, 1973, 106-07; J. McLaren, *Overland*, No. 61, 1975, 56-58; H. McQueen, *Arena*, No. 31, 1973, 44-51; A. Mitchell, *Advertiser*, 14 October, 1972, 20; A.A. Phillips, *Meanjin*, XXXI, 1972, 486-88; C. Semmler, *S.M.H.*, 21 April, 1973, 19; J. Waten, *Age*, 25 November, 1972, 17.

---. '"The Drover's Wife" Writ Large: One Measure of Lawson's Achievement'. *Meanjin*, XXVII, 1968, 54-66.

---. 'Eve Exonerated: Henry Lawson's Unfinished Love Stories'. In *Who is She?*, edited by Shirley Walker (St Lucia: U.Q.P., 1983), 37-55.

---. 'Henry Lawson: The Real and the Fictional Worlds after Darwin'. In *Individual and Community in Commonwealth Literature*, edited by Daniel Massa (Msida, Malta: Old University Press, 1979), 99-107.

---. 'Henry Lawson and the Work Ethic'. *Literary Criterion* (Mysore), XV, Nos. 3-4, 1980, 108-16.

---. 'Henry Lawson's Fictional World'. In *Bards, Bohemians, and Bookmen*, edited by Leon Cantrell (St Lucia: U.Q.P., 1976), 170-202.

---. 'Louisa and Henry and Gertie and the Drover's Wife'. *A.L.S.*, IX, 1980, 286-97.

---. '"The Nurse and Tutor of Eccentric Minds": Some Developments in Lawson's Treatment of Madness'. *A.L.S.*, IV, 1970, 251-57.

McQueen, Humphrey. *A New Britannia*. (Ringwood, Vic.; Harmondsworth, Middlesex: Penguin, 1970). See particularly pp. 101-16.

Melville, Rosemary. 'The Newcastle That Henry Lawson Knew'. *Kunapipi*, 12.3, 1990, 22-26.

Mitchell, Adrian. 'Henry Lawson: Truth in Ragged Trousers'. *Issue*, III, No. 9, 1973, 26-28.

---. *The Short Stories of Henry Lawson*. Horizon Studies in Literature. (South Melbourne: Sydney UP/O.U.P., 1995).

Murdoch, Walter. 'Afterthoughts'. *Australian*, 15 July, 1967, 6.

---. 'Lawson the Luckless'. *Australian*, 24 June, 1967, 8.

Murray-Smith, Stephen. *Henry Lawson*. First edition published Melbourne: Lansdowne, 1962, reprinted Melbourne: O.U.P., 1963. New edition Melbourne: O.U.P., 1975. Reviewed by J. Waten, *Age*, 29 May, 1976, 22.

Nesbitt, Bruce. 'Literary Nationalism and the 1890s'. *A.L.S.*, V, 1971, 3-17.

---. 'Some Notes on Lawson's Contributions to the *Bulletin*, 1887-1900'. *Biblionews*, Second series, II, No. 1, 1967, 17-20.

O'Grady, Desmond. 'Henry Lawson'. *Opinion*, IX, 1965, 34-44. Reprinted from *Southerly*, No. 2, 1957.

O'Mallee, Myall. 'Lawson: The Centenary Symposium Continues: Lawson and O'Dowd'. *Tribune*, 21 June, 1967, 14.

O'Neill, Phillip. 'Aborigines and Women in Lawson's "The Bush Undertaker"'. *Australian & New Zealand Studies in Canada*, 8, 1992, 59-70.

Oliver, H.J. 'Lawson and Furphy'. In *The Literature of Australia*, edited by Geoffrey Dutton (Adelaide: Penguin Books, 1964), 288-96.

Pagliaro, Teresa. 'Jose's Editing of *While the Billy Boils*'. *Bibliographical Society of Australia and New Zealand Bulletin*, 14.3, 1990, 81-93.

Pearl, Cyril. 'Don't Hide Lawson...'. *S.M.H.*, 11 January, 1969, 18. Brief references to the Henry Lawson scrap books in the Mitchell Library.

Pearson, W.H. *Henry Lawson among Maoris*. (Canberra: Australian National University Press, 1968). Reviewed by R.D. Arnold, *Historical Studies*, XIV, 1969, 137-39; K. England, *Advertiser*, 4 January, 1969, 22; N. Keesing, *Bulletin*, 30

November, 1968, 83-84; B. Kiernan, *Australian*, 28 December, 1968, 10; I. Reid, *ABR*, VIII, 1969, 158; C. Roderick, *Journal of the Royal Australian Historical Society*, LVII, 1971, 263-66; T.L. Sturm, *Southerly*, XXX, 1970, 231-34; J.M. Woodward, *Westerly*, No. 2, 1969, 60-61.

---. 'Henry Lawson among Maoris'. *Meanjin*, XXVII, 1968, 67-73.

---. 'Henry Lawson's New Zealand Visits: A Comment'. *A.L.S.*, IV, 1969, 68-73. Discusses Rollo Arnold, 'Henry Lawson: The New Zealand Visits', *A.L.S.*, III, 1968, 163-89. Reply by Arnold, *A.L.S.*, IV, 1969, 73-79.

---. 'Lawson Manuscripts in New Zealand, and a Note on Lawson's Autobiographies'. *Biblionews*, Second series, II, Nos. 3-4, 1967, 6.

Perry, R.R. 'Lawson - Bard of the Tribe'. *S.M.H.*, 17 June, 1967, 14.

Petrikovskaya, Alla. 'Henry Lawson and the Soviet Reader'. *Soviet Literature* (Moscow), No. 7, 1967, 171-73.

Phillips, A.A. *Henry Lawson.* (New York: Twayne, 1970). Twayne's World Authors series, 133. Reviewed by L. Cantrell, *A.L.S.*, VI, 1973, 99-104; B. Kiernan, *Meanjin*, XXXI, 1972, 346-50 and *Australian*, 3 June, 1972, 19; B. Matthews, *Overland*, No. 53, 1972, 59-61; A. Mitchell, *Advertiser*, 29 July, 1972, 18; J. Waten, *Age*, 10 June, 1972, 13.

---. 'The Craftsmanship of Lawson'. *Oceanic Literature*, No. 5, 1983, 298-317. In Chinese, translated from *The Australian Tradition*, chapter 1.

---. 'Henry Lawson Revisited'. *Meanjin*, XXIV, 1965, 5-17.

---. 'Henry Lawson's Rise and Fall'. In his *Responses: Selected Writings*. (Kew, Vic.: Australian International Press & Publications, 1979), 115-18. Review of Denton Prout *Henry Lawson, the Grey Dreamer* first published in *Meanjin*, XXII, 1963, 426-29.

Plews, Barry. 'Lawson, Lost and Found'. *Bowyang*, (Flinders University), No. 3, 1980, 106-10.

Pons, Xavier. *Out of Eden: Henry Lawson's Life and Works: A Psychoanalytic View.* (Sydney: A.& R., 1984). Reviewed by J. Barnes, *ABR*, No. 68, 1985, 26-29; P. Carter, *Overland*, No. 100, 1985, 69-73; M. Clark, *S.M.H.*, 18 August, 1984, 43 See also *S.M.H.*, 4 December, 1984, 8 for a letter to the editor by Xavier Pons in response to Manning Clark's review *S.M.H.*, 18 August, 1984, 43; B. Matthews, *A.L.S.*, XII, No. 1, 1985, 148-151; C. Roderick, *Courier-Mail*, 6 October, 1984, 30; C. Semmler, *Weekend Australian Magazine*, 20-21 October, 1984, 17; J. Waten, *Age Saturday Extra*, 22 September, 1984, 16.

---. 'Henry Lawson and Tom Mutch: "The Parsin for Edgerkashun"'. *Journal of Commonwealth Literature*, VII, No. 2, 1972, 148-53.

---. 'Henry Lawson's Literary Vocation'. *Meanjin*, XXXIX, 1980, 237-49.

---. 'La Polemique Lawson-Paterson'. *Etudes Anglaises*, XXV, 1972, 220-28.

Prout, Denton. *Henry Lawson: The Grey Dreamer.* (Adelaide: Rigby, 1963). Reviewed by H.P. Heseltine, *A.L.S.*, I, No. 3, 1964, 212-5; H. Hughes, *Overland*, No. 29, 1964, 59; S. Lawson, *Nation*, 24 August, 1963, 21-2; A.A. Phillips, *Meanjin*, XXII, No. 4, 1963, 426-9; W. Stone, *Southerly*, XXIV, 1964, 139-41; *T.L.S.*, 16 January, 1964, 49; H.G. Trabing, *AUMLA*, No. 21, 1964, 124-5.

Prout, Denton and Frizell, Helen. 'Seeking out the Facts about Henry Lawson'. *S.M.H.*, 1 June, 1978, 7.

Quartermaine, Peter. 'The "Literary Photographs" of Henry Lawson'. *A.L.S.*, VIII, 1978, 419-34.

Roderick, Colin (ed.). *Henry Lawson Criticism 1894-1971.* Edited with introduction and bibliography by Colin Roderick. (Sydney: A.& R., 1972). Reviewed by L. Cantrell, *A.L.S.*, VI, 1973, 99-104; M. Harris, *ABR*, XI, 1972, 23; *New Poetry*, XX, No. 5-6, 1972, 79-80; A.A. Phillips, *Age*, 23 December, 1972, 12.

Roderick, Colin. *Henry Lawson, Commentaries on His Prose Writings.* (London; Sydney: A.& R., 1985). Cover title: *Henry Lawson, the Master Story Teller: Commentaries on His Prose Writings*. Reviewed by P. Carter, *Overland*, No. 100,

1985, 69-73; J. Colmer, *Weekend Australian Magazine*, 23-24 March, 1985, 11; B. Kiernan, *S.M.H.*, 9 March, 1985, 42; J. Pausacker, *Age Saturday Extra*, 13 April, 1985, 13; C. Semmler, *Courier-Mail*, 6 April, 1985, 27.
---. *Henry Lawson: A Life*. (North Ryde, NSW: Collins/A.& R., 1991) Reviewed by J. Barnes, *Quadrant*, 35.7-8, 1992, 99-102; R. Bouyssou, *Commonwealth*, 15.1, 1992, 102; and *Etudes Anglaises*, 26.1, 1993, 108; E. Campion, *Bulletin*, 21 May, 1991, 122; B. Kiernan, *Weekend Australian*, 18-19 May, 1991, Review 5; T. Pagliaro, *Bibliographical Society of Australia and New Zealand Bulletin*, 15.1, 1991, 43-44; T. Pagliaro, *Overland*, 124, 1991, 78-79; M. Sharkey, *ABR*, 132, 1991, 8-11; K. Stewart, *A.L.S.*, 15.3, 1992, 228-32; D.J. Tacey, *Age*, 1 June, 1991, Saturday Extra 7.
---. *Henry Lawson: Poet and Short Story Writer*. (Sydney: A.& R., 1966). Contains a Bibliography, 68-70. Reviewed by R.F. Brissenden, *Australian*, 31 December, 1966, 9; A.R. Chisholm, *Age*, 22 October, 1966, 21; C. Hadgraft, *Bulletin*, 29 October, 1966, 39; George Johnston, *S.M.H.*, 12 November, 1966, 19.
Grahame Johnston, *Canberra Times*, 3 December, 1966, 11.
---. *The Real Henry Lawson*. (Adelaide: Rigby, 1982). Reviewed by J. Barnes, *ABR*, No. 49, 1983, 34-35; E. Kynaston, *Weekend Australian Magazine*, 25-26 December, 1982, 10; D. Robinson, *A.L.S.*, XI, 1983, 277-79; J. Waten, *Age Saturday Extra*, 8 January, 1983, 8.
---. 'Henry Lawson and Albert Lee-Archer on the *Damascus*, 1900'. *Overland*, 127, 1992, 70-74.
---. 'Henry Lawson: Man and Myth'. *Southerly*, XLII, 1982, 457-69.
---. 'Henry Lawson: The Middle Years, 1893-1896'. *Journal of the Royal Australian Historical Society*, LIII, 1967, 101-121.
---. 'Henry Lawson: The Middle Years. Part 2: 1896-1900'. *Journal of the Royal Australian Historical Society*, LV, 1969, 328-54.
---. 'Henry Lawson and Hannah Thorburn'. *Meanjin*, XXVII, 1968, 74-89.
---. 'Henry Lawson to W.W. Head (W.A. Woods)'. *Meanjin*, XXV, 1966, 81-5. See also John Reynolds. 'Walter Alan ("Father") Woods'. *Meanjin*, XXV, 1966, 86-8.
---. 'Henry Lawson's Joe Wilson - Skeleton Novel or Short Story Sequence?' *Overland*, No. 66, 1977, 35-47.
---. 'Lawson the Poet'. In *Bards, Bohemians, and Bookmen*, edited by Leon Cantrell (St Lucia: U.Q.P., 1976), 203-17.
---. 'Was Lawson Born In A Tent?' *North*, No. 5, 1966, 14-21. Reprinted in *Quadrant*, XXVI, No. 11, 1982, 70-72.
S[tone], W[alter] W. 'The Conservation of Literary Relics'. *Biblionews and Australian Notes & Queries*, Series 3, II, No. 1, 1977, 14-15.
Saillens, Emile. 'Henry Lawson: A Contemporary French View', tr. by Colin Roderick. *Southerly*, XXX, 1970, 190-208. Original published in *Mercure de France* in 1910.
Sargeson, Frank. 'Henry Lawson: Some Notes after Re-reading'. *Landfall*, XX, 1966, 156-62. Reprinted in *Translation*, edited by Nancy Keesing (Sydney: A.& R., 1970), 105-11.
Sayers, Stuart. 'Moscow Expert on Lawson'. *Age*, 30 September, 1972, 14.
Schaffer, Kay. 'Henry Lawson, the Drover's Wife and the Critics'. In *Debutante Nation: Feminism Contests the 1890s*, edited by Susan Magarey, Sue Rowley, and Susan Sheridan (St Leonards, NSW: Allen & Unwin, 1993), 199-210.
---. 'Henry Lawson: The People's Poet'. In her *Women and the Bush: Forces of Desire in the Australian Cultural Tradition* (Melbourne: Cambridge University Press, 1988), 112-47.
Semmler, Clement. 'Paterson and Lawson'. *The Banjo of the Bush*. (Melbourne: Lansdowne Press, 1966), 78-87 and passim.
Sharkey, Michael. 'Zora, Dave and Henry: Some Recollections of Henry Lawson by

Zora Cross'. *Overland*, No. 117, 1990, 67-72.

Simpson, Lindsay. 'Released...Lawson's Prison Letters to his Landlady'. *S.M.H.*, 3 January, 1986, 1.

Stewart, Ken. '"The Loaded Dog": A Celebration'. *A.L.S.*, XI, 11983, 152-61.

Stokes, John. 'Henry Lawson in Perth'. *Western Australian Teachers' Journal*, LIV, 1964, 127-8. Biography only.

Sunderland, Lynn. *The Fantastic Invasion: Kipling, Conrad and Lawson*. (Carlton, Vic.: M.U.P., 1989).

Sussex, Lucy. 'Madam Midas and Henry Lawson'. *Notes & Furphies*, No. 21, 1988, 18.

Tennant, Kylie. 'A Question of Authenticity'. *S.M.H.*, 25 January, 1975, 15.

Thomas, Dean. *Short Stories of Henry Lawson: Lawson Anecdotes, From His Birth to His Death*. (Sydney: Hodder & Stoughton, 1988).

Tierney, William J. 'The Lost Verse of "Eurunderee"'. *Endeavour* (Sunshine Coast Literary Society, Buderim, Q.), IV, No. 3, Autumn 1975, 31-32.

Wallace-Crabbe, Chris. 'Lawson's *Joe Wilson*: A Skeleton Novel'. *A.L.S.*, I, No. 3, 1964, 147-54.

Waters, Edgar. 'Sydney or the Bush? The Stories of Henry Lawson'. *Overland*, No. 34, 1966, 41-2.

Whitlock, Gillian. 'The Bush, the Barrack-Yard and the Clearing: "Colonial Realism" in the Sketches and Stories of Susanna Moodie, C.L.R. James and Henry Lawson'. *Journal of Commonwealth Literature*, XX, No. 1, 1985, 36-48.

Wieland, James. 'Australian Literature and the Question of Historical Method: Reading Lawson and Furphy'. *Journal of Commonwealth Literature*, XX, No. 1, 1985, 16-35.

Wilding, Michael. 'Henry Lawson'. In *La Nouvelle de Langue Anglaise. The Short Story*. (Paris: Service des Publications de la Sorbonne Nouvelle, 1988), 157-67.

---. 'Henry Lawson - Ethnic Writer'. *Outrider*, 9.1, 1992, 104-09.

---. 'Henry Lawson's Radical Vision'. In *Rise of Socialist Fiction 1880-1914*, edited by G. Klaus (Sussex: Harvester Press; New York: St Martin's Press, 1987), 203-30.

---. *The Radical Tradition: Lawson, Furphy, Stead*. ([Townsville, Qld]: Foundation for Australian Literary Studies/James Cook U of North Queensland, 1993).

Wilkes, G.A. 'Henry Lawson Reconsidered'. *Southerly*, XXV, No. 4, 1965, 264-75.

Wright, Judith. *Henry Lawson*. (Melbourne: O.U.P., 1966). Great Australians Series. Reviewed by F.H. Mares, *Adelaide Advertiser*, 17 June, 1967, 20; I. Pratt, *S.M.H.*, 24 June, 1967, 17.

---. 'The Reformist Poets'. In her *Preoccupations in Australian Poetry*, 1965, 68-79.

Zaunbrecher, Marian. 'Henry Lawson's Religion'. *Journal of Religious History*, XI, 1980, 308-19.

Zinkhan, E.J. 'Louisa Lawson's "The Australian Bush-Woman" -A Source for "The Drover's Wife" and "Water them Geraniums"?' *A.L.S.*, X, 1982, 495-99.

LAWSON, LOUISA

Poetry

The Lonely Crossing and Other Poems. (Dubbo, N.S.W.: Review Publications, 1986). Facsimile reprint. First published Sydney: Dawn, 1905.

Non-Fiction

The First Voice of Australian Feminism: Excerpts from Louisa Lawson's 'The Dawn' 1885-1895. Edited by Olive Lawson (Sydney: New Endeavour Press/Simon and Schuster, 1990).

Reviewed by M. Dewar, *Northern Perspective*, 13, No.2, 1990, 117-118; B. Hutton, *Age*, 21 April, 1990, Saturday Extra, 10; B. Matthews, *ABR*, No. 119, 1990, 19-21; R. Munro, *CRNLE Reviews Journal*, No. 2, 1990, 67-8; C. Williams, *S.M.H.*, 24 March, 1990, 77.

Critical Material

Docker, John. 'A Note on Brian Matthews' *Louisa*', *Meanjin*, 48, No. 2, 1989, 397-406. Reply by B. Matthews, 'A Letter about Curious Elisions', *Meanjin*, 48, No. 3, 1989, 572-73.

Grimshaw, Patricia. 'Female Lives and the Tradition of Nation-Making'. *Voices*, 5.3, 1995, 30-44. Includes discussion of Louisa Meredith and Louisa Lawson.

Matthews, Brian. *Louisa*. (Melbourne: McPhee Gribble, 1987). Biography. Reviewed by D. Adelaide, *Southerly*, 48, No. 2, 1988, 229-31; J. Allen, *Australian Historical Studies*, XXIX, No. 91, 1988, 219-220; P. Clarke, *Canberra Historical Journal*, New Series, No. 21, 1988, 46-47; M. Johnson, *Antipodes*, II, No. 1, 1988, 72; B. Kingston, *A.L.S.*, XIII, No. 3, 1988, 383-386; R. Nile, *Westerly*, XXXIII, No. 3, 1988, 91-93; X. Pons, *Meridian*, VII, No. 1, 1988, 83-84; P. Quartermaine, *Australian Studies*, No. 3, 1989, 121-23; K. Stewart, *A.L.S.*, XIII, No. 3, 1988, 386-389; N. Wheatley, *Scripsi*, V, No. 1, 1988, 155-164.

---. 'Australian Colonial Women and their Autobiographies'. *Kunapipi*, 7, Nos. 2&3, 1985, 36-46.

---. 'Disguises and Persecution: Miles Franklin, Louisa Lawson, Barbara Baynton'. In his *Romantics and Mavericks: The Australian Short Story*. (Townsville, Qld.: James Cook University of North Queensland, 1987), 4-15. The Colin Roderick Lectures; 1986. Monograph/Foundation for Australian Literary Studies No. 14.

---. 'It Was a Story That Needed Rounding Off...'. *Australian Society*, VI, No. 10, 1987, 37-39. Discusses writing Louisa Lawson's biography.

---. 'Louisa Lawson: Tentative Notes Towards a Work Possibly in Progress'. *Meanjin*, XLVI, No. 1, 1987, 94-102.

Sheridan, Sue. 'Louisa Lawson, Miles Franklin and Feminist Writing, 1888-1901'. *Australian Feminist Studies*, Nos. 7&8, 1988, 29-47.

Thomson, Helen. 'Brian Matthews' *Louisa*: Competing Voices'. *Bio-fictions: Brian Matthews, Drusilla Modjeska and Elizabeth Jolley*. Monograph 25. (Townsville: James Cook U of North Queensland, Foundation for Australian Literary Studies, 1994). 1-18.

Zinkhan, Elaine. 'In Shadow Too Long: The Life of Louisa Lawson'. *Age Monthly Review*, February, 1988, 3-5. Review article on Brian Matthews, *Louisa* (Melbourne: McPhee Gribble, 1987).

---. 'Louisa Albury Lawson: Feminist and Patriot'. In *A Bright and Fiery Troop: Australian Women Writers of the Nineteenth Century*, edited by Debra Adelaide (Ringwood: Penguin, 1988), 217-32.

LEAKEY, CAROLINE

Fiction

The Broad Arrow: The Story of Maida Gwynnham, a 'Lifer' in Van Diemen's Land. (North Ryde, N.S.W.: A.& R., 1988). First published London: Bentley, 1859.

The Broad Arrow. Introduction by Jenna Mead. (Sydney: A.& R., 1992). First published London: Bentley, 1859.

Critical Material

Hergenhan, L.T. '*The Broad Arrow*: An Early Novel of the Convict System'. *Southerly*, XXXVI, 1976, 141-59. Reprinted as 'A Woman "Lifer": Caroline Leakey's *The Broad Arrow*', in his *Unnatural Lives*. (St Lucia: U.Q.P., 1983), 31-46.

Horner, J.C. 'The Themes of Four Convict Novels'. *Tasmanian Historical Research Association, Papers and Proceedings*, XV, 1967, 1-32.

Mead, Jena. 'Biodiscourse: Oliné Keese and Caroline Leakey'. *Australian Feminist Studies*, 20, 1994, 53-76.

---. '(Re)producing a Text: Caroline Leakey's *The Broad Arrow*'. *Meridian*, 10.1, 1991, 81-88.

Poole, Joan E. '*The Broad Arrow* - A Re-appraisal'. *Southerly*, XXVI, 1966, 117-24.

Raggio, Janice. *'The Broad Arrow* and *Clara Morison*. Studies of Early Colonial Life'. *Adelaide A.L.S. Working Papers*, III, 1979, 36-51.
Rutherford, Anna. 'The Wages of Sin: Caroline Leakey's *The Broad Arrow*'. In *The Commonwealth Writer Overseas*, edited by Alastair Niven (Brussels: Didier, 1976), 245-54.
Scheckter, John. *'The Broad Arrow*: Conventions, Convictions and Convicts'. *Antipodes*, I, No. 2, 1987, 89-91.
Walker, Shirley. '"Wild and Wilful" Women: Caroline Leakey and *The Broad Arrow*'. In *A Bright and Fiery Troop: Australian Women Writers of the Nineteenth Century*, edited by Debra Adelaide (Ringwood: Penguin, 1988), 85-99.

LEHMANN, GEOFFREY

Fiction
A Spring Day in Autumn. (Melbourne, London: Nelson, 1974). Reviewed by L. Murray, *S.M.H.*, 26 October, 1974, 16.

Poetry
Children's Games. (North Ryde, N.S.W.: A.& R., 1990).
Reviewed by H. Cam, *S.M.H.*, 22 September, 1990, 76; M. Duwell, *Weekend Australian*, 5-6 January, 1991, 7; P. Salom, *ABR*, No. 126, 1990, 15-16; T. Shapcott, *Age*, 22 September, 1990, Saturday Extra, 7.

Conversation with a Rider. (Sydney: A.& R., 1972).
Reviewed by L. Cantrell, *Makar*, IX, No. 3, 1974, 41-43; K. England, *Advertiser*, 26 May, 1973, 20; J. Forbes, *New Poetry*, XXII, Nos. 2 & 3, 1974, 75-77; P. Law, *Poetry Australia*, No. 47, 1973, 75-77; P. Roberts, *S.M.H.*, 14 July, 1973, 24; R.A. Simpson, *Age*, 12 May, 1973, 15; J. Tulip, *Southerly*, XXXIII, 1973, 236-37.

Extracts from Ross' Poems. (Sydney: A.& R., 1976). Poets of the Month.
Reviewed by V. Ikin, *Quadrant*, XXI, No. 9, 1977, 78-79.

With Les A. Murray. *The Ilex Tree*. (Brisbane: Jacaranda Press, 1965).
Reviewed by D. Douglas, *Age*, 10 September, 1966, 23; R. Dunlop, *Poetry Australia*, No. 10, 1966, 32-4; W. Hart-Smith, *Poetry Magazine*, No. 1, 1966, 28-30; F. Haynes, *Westerly*, No. 3, 1966, 90-4; S.E. Lee, *Southerly*, XXVI, 1966, 129-30; B. Nesbitt, *Australian*, 11 June, 1966, 8; V. Smith, *Bulletin*, 12 February, 1966, 48.

Nero's Poems: Translations of the Public and Private Poems of the Emperor Nero. (Sydney: A.& R., 1981).
Reviewed by D. Brooks, *Canberra Times*, 28 August, 1982, 15; G. Dutton, *Bulletin*, 24 November, 1981, 80-82; M. Duwell, *Weekend Australian Magazine*, 7-8 November, 1981, 8; C.J. Koch, *National Times*, 18-24 October, 1981, 38; P. Mead, *Island Magazine*, No. 14, 1983, 48-51; J.D. Pringle, *S.M.H.*, 12 September, 1981, 43; C. Wallace-Crabbe, *Age*, 28 November, 1981, 23.

Ross' Poems. (Sydney: A.& R., 1978).
Reviewed by A. Gould, *National Review*, 14-20 July, 1978, 18-19; R. Gray, *Poetry Australia*, No. 70, 1979, 68; R. Hall, *Weekend Australian Magazine*, 4-5 March, 1978, 8; E. Lindsay, *Quadrant*, XXIII, No. 3, 1979, 70; N. Macainsh, *ABR*, No. 4, 1978, 9-10; G. Page, *Canberra Times*, 3 March, 1979, 15; J. Rodriguez, *S.M.H.*, 8 July, 1978, 19; C. Wallace-Crabbe, *Age*, 2 September, 1978, 21.

Selected Poems. (Sydney: A.& R., 1976).
Reviewed by A. Gould, *Nation Review*, 17-23 February, 1977, 429 and *Poetry Australia*, No. 64, 1977, 68-73; [S.E. Lee], *Southerly*, XXXIX, 1979, 459-61; T. Thorne, *Australian*, 19 March, 1977, 30.

Spring Forest. (Pymble, NSW: A.& R., 1992) Reviewed by C. Pollnitz, *Weekend Australian*, 16-17 January, 1993, Review 5; K. Hart, *Age*, 28 November, 1992, Saturday Extra 9.

A Voyage of Lions. (Sydney: A.& R., 1968).
Reviewed by B. Beaver, *S.M.H.*, 22 February, 1969, 21; D. Douglas, *Age*, 25 January, 1969, 10; R. Hall, *Australian*, 26 April, 1969, 17; G.K. Holzknecht, *Makar*, V, No. 3, 1969, 31-33; E. Jones, *Nation*, 13 December, 1969, 22-23; N. Keesing, *Bulletin*, 22 February, 1969, 71-72; S.E. Lee, *Southerly*, XXIX, 1969, 223-25; M. Richards, *Meanjin*, XXVIII, 1969, 277-79; R. Ward, *ABR*, VIII, 1969, 92.

Critical Material
Davies, Mark. 'Geoffrey Lehmann: A Short Appreciation'. *Northern Perspective*, 13, No. 2, 1990, 105-6.
Malouf, David. 'Some Volumes of Selected Poems of the 1970s, II'. *A.L.S.*, X, 1982, 305-06.
Morgan, Michelle. 'A Governor, a Farmer, an Emperor: Rome and Australia in Geoffrey Lehmann'. *A.L.S.*, XI, 1983, 14-24.
Page, Geoff. 'Geoffrey Lehmann'. In his *A Reader's Guide To Contemporary Australian Poetry* (St. Lucia: U.Q.P., 1995), 171-174.
Sharkey, Michael. 'Geoffrey Lehmann's *Nero's Poems*'. *Quadrant*, XXVIII, No. 6, 1984, 72-75.

LETTERS, FRANCIS J.H.

Critical Material
Ryan, J.S. 'Francis J.H. Letters (1897-1964): Poet and Scholar'. *Notes & Furphies*, No. 21, 1988, 7-11.

LINDSAY, JACK

Fiction
The Blood Vote. (St. Lucia: U.Q.P., 1985).
Reviewed by S. Altinel, *T.L.S.*, 9 May, 1986, 498; J. Colmer, *Weekend Australian Magazine*, 25-26 May, 1985, 16; M. Duwell, *Overland*, No. 101, 1985, 92-94; I. Hicks, *S.M.H.*, 15 June, 1985, 43; M. Hulse, *PN Review*, XIII, No. 5, 1987, 80-81; C. Leonard, *National Times*, 3-9 May, 1985, 33; S. McKernan, *Canberra Times*, 22 June, 1985, B2; J. McLaren, *ABR*, No. 72, 1985, 31-32; P. Shannon, *Tribune*, No. 2399, 1985, 11; G. Windsor, *Bulletin*, 11 June, 1985, 94-97. See also Rowbotham, Jill. 'The Forgotten Novel Jack Lindsay Wrote About Brisbane', *Courier Mail: The Great Weekend*, 20 April, 1985, 28.
Thunder Underground. (London: Frederick Muller, 1966).
Reviewed by R.F. Brissenden, *Australian*, 16 April, 1966, 10; E. Corsellis, *S.M.H.*, 2 October, 1965, 17.

Non-Fiction
Life Rarely Tells: An Autobiography in Three Volumes. Introduction by Michael Wilding. Three volumes in one (Ringwood, Vic.: Penguin, 1982).
Reviewed by L. Clancy, *Island Magazine*, No. 17, 1983, 31-35; M. Dunlevy, *Canberra Times*, 8 May, 1982, 14; D. den Hartog, *ABR*, No. 43, 1982, 25-26; D. Holbrook, *Age Monthly Review*, II, No. 3, 1982, 5-6. See also 'Jack Lindsay Replies', *Age Monthly Review*, II, No. 4, 1982, 2, and D. Holbrook, 'Lindsay: Without Inhibitions', *Age Monthly Review*,II, No. 5, 1982, 2, & 14; H. Reade, *Weekend Australian Magazine*, 3-4 July, 1982, 9.
'Expatriate Publishing'. *Meanjin*, XXXIII, 1974, 176-79.

Critical Material
Arnold, John. 'Jack Lindsay: Towards a Bibliography'. *Overland*, No. 83, 1981, 50-55.
Chaplin, Harry F. *Jack Lindsay: A Catalogue of his First Editions and Other Writings.* (Cremorne, N.S.W.: Book Collectors' Society of Australia, 1983).
Reviewed by J. McLaren, *Biblionews and Australian Notes & Queries*, IX, No. 2,

1984, 62-63.

'Jack Lindsay Honoured'. *Meanjin*, XXXII, 1973, 317.

Arnold, John. 'The Franfrolico Press: Workers, Friends and Supporters'. *Biblionews and Australian Notes and Queries*, 13, No. 3, 1988, 68-76 and 13, No. 4, 1988, 100-106.

---. 'Jack Lindsay: A Personal Memoir'. *Overland*, No. 121, 1990, 77-79.

Barker, Anthony. 'Jack Lindsay: Prodigious, Brilliant - and Largely Unknown'. *S.M.H.*, 26 January, 1985, 36.

Corbett, James. 'Jack Lindsay: A Man for the Moment'. *Overland*, No. 52, 1972, 38-40.

Field, Michele. 'Jack Lindsay: Writer-in- Exile'. *S.M.H.*, 6 August, 1985, 25.

FitzGerald, Robert D. 'Textures and Developments'. *Southerly*, XLI, 1981, 409-20.

Fotheringham, Richard. 'Expatriate Publishing: Jack Lindsay and the Fanfrolico Press'. *Meanjin*, XXXI, 1972, 55-61.

Gillen, Paul, ed. *Jack Lindsay: Faithful to the Earth*. (Pymble, NSW: A.& R., 1993). Reviewed by J. Arnold, *Editions*, 17, 1993, 21.

Gillen, Paul. 'Jack Lindsay's Romantic Communism'. *Westerly*, 36.2, 1991, 65-77.

---. 'The Last Man of Letters?'. *Westerly*, 39.3, 1994, 83-87.

Hall, Robert Lowe. 'Expatriate Publishing'. *Meanjin*, XXXIII, 1974, 170-76.

Hecker, Manfred. 'Besonderheiten des sozialistischen Realismus in Jack Lindsays Romanen zur englischen Geschichte'. *Zeitschrift fur Anglistik und Amerikanistik*, XXI, 1973, 137-60.

Hetherington, John. 'Down at Bangslappers with Jack Lindsay'. *Age*, 14 September, 1968, 11.

Jacque, Valentina. 'Jack Lindsay and Soviet Readers'. *Soviet Literature*, No. 2, 1966, 170-73.

Johnson, Nancy. 'Unusual Facets of Lindsayana'. *Biblionews and Australian Notes & Queries*, XI, No. 1, 1986, 3-14.

Mackie, Robert. (ed.) *Jack Lindsay: The Thirties and Forties*. (London: University of London. Institute of Commonwealth Studies, Australian Studies Centre, 1984). Reviewed by G. Windsor, *Bulletin*, 12 February, 1985, 56, 58.

---. 'Jack Lindsay: Prodigious Man of Letters'. *BASA Magazine*, II, No. 1, 1985, 25-26.

Maiden, Tony. 'Jack Lindsay'. *National Times*, 19-24 January, 1976, 18.

Miles, Bernard. 'Cleopatra and her Latest Lover: Jack Lindsay and the Theatre'. *Notes & Furphies*, No. 10, 1983, 1-4.

Phillips, A.A. 'The Sea Coast of Bohemia'. In his *Responses: Selected Writings*. (Kew, Vic.: Australian International Press & Publications, 1979), 67-69. Review of *The Roaring Twenties* first published as 'King's Cross Bohemia' in *Overland*, No. 18, 1960, 53-54.

Robieson, Sinclair. 'Jack Lindsay at 80'. *Weekend Australian Magazine*, 11-12 October, 1980, 8.

Rowbotham, David. 'University Honour for a Veteran "Radical"'. *Courier Mail*, 2 December, 1972, 5.

Seehase, Georg. 'Kapitalistische Entfremdung und humanistische Integration: Bemerkungen zum englischen proletarischen Gegenwartsroman'. *Zeitschrift fur Anglistik und Amerikanistik*, XV, 1967, 383-400.

Sitwell, Edith. 'Letters to Jack Lindsay'. *Meanjin*, XXV, 1966, 76-80.

Smith, Bernard (ed.). *Culture and History: Essays Presented to Jack Lindsay*. (Sydney: Hale & Iremonger, 1984). Reviewed by P. Botsman, *Courier-Mail*, 1 December, 1984, 31; L. Clancy, *Age Saturday Extra*, 9 March, 1985, 12; J. Colmer, *Weekend Australian Magazine*, 27-28 October, 1984, 1; J.C. Doyle, *ABR*, No. 78, 1986, 12-13; B. Elliott, *CRNLE Reviews Journal*, No. 2, 1985, 85-90; D. Greason, *National Times*, 28 December-3 January, 1985, 32; J. McLaren, *Meridian*, IV, No.

2, 1985, 189-192; N. Morpeth, *Overland*, No. 101, 1985, 99-102; G. Windsor, *Bulletin*, 12 February, 1985, 56, 58.
---. 'Jack Lindsay'. *A.L.S.*, XI, 1983, 216-26.
---. 'Jack Lindsay's Marxism'. *Arena*, No. 71, 1985, 138-151.
---. 'A Man with his own Vision'. *Age Monthly Review*, II, No. 4, 1982, 2 & 14.
Stevens, John. 'After 82 years and 150 Books, Jack Lindsay Begins to Be Noticed'. *Age*, 21 November, 1984, 11.
---. 'Belated Recognition for Jack Lindsay'. *S.M.H.*, 15 November, 1984, 11.
Stewart, Douglas. 'Aristophanes in Australia'. *S.M.H.*, 23 April, 1966, 18.
Stone, Walter. 'Beating the Salvage Bag'. *Biblionews*, I, No. 4, 1966, 3-6.
Waten, Judah. 'Some Australians and Iris Murdoch'. *Age*, 19 February, 1966, 22.
Wilding, Michael. 'Jack Lindsay'. *Overland*, No. 83, 1981, 40-43.
Wright, Judith. 'Vision'. In her *Preoccupations in Australian Poetry*. (Melbourne: O.U.P., 1965), 131-139.
Young, Edith. *Inside Out*. (London: Routledge & Kegan Paul, 1971), 125-36.

LINDSAY, JOAN

Fiction

Picnic at Hanging Rock. (Melbourne: Cheshire, 1967).
Reviewed by *ABR*, VII, 1968, 88; *T.L.S.*, 11 April, 1968, 365; M. Vintner, *S.M.H.*, 3 January, 1968, 18.

The Secret of Hanging Rock: Joan Lindsay's Final Chapter. With an introduction by John Taylor and a commentary by Yvonne Rousseau. (North Ryde, N.S.W.: A.& R., 1987). Contains the final chapter of Joan Lindsay's *Picnic at Hanging Rock*. Correspondence about this edition can be found in letters to the Editor *Australian Bookseller and Publisher*, No. 970, 14 and No. 971, 1987, 18. Reviewed by K. Gelder, *ABR*, No. 89, 1987, 28-30.

Non-Fiction

Time without Clocks. (Melbourne: Cheshire, 1962). Autobiography.
Reviewed by M. Casey, *ABR*, II, 1963, 50; H. Hewitt, *Canberra Times*, 12 March, 1977, 12.

Critical Material

'Death of Lady Lindsay Ends Career of "Remarkable Woman"'. *Australian*, 27 December, 1984, 5.
'Writer, Artist, Lady Joan Lindsay Dies'. *S.M.H.*, 24 December, 1984, 2. For other obituaries see *Age*, 24 December, 1984, 5; *Canberra Times*, 24 December, 1984, 3; *Weekend Australian Magazine*, 5-6 January, 1985, 2.
Barrett, Donald. 'Picnicking with E.M. Forster, Joan Lindsay et al'. *LiNQ*, XV, No. 1, 1987, 79-86.
---. 'The Mythology of Pan and Picnic at Hanging Rock'. *Southerly*, XLII, 1982, 299-308.
---. 'Some Correspondence with Joan Lindsay'. *A.L.S.*, 14, No. 1, 1989, 104-107.
Crittenden, Anne. '*Picnic at Hanging Rock*: A Myth and its Symbols'. *Meanjin*, XXXV, 1976, 1967-74.
Bushell, Maureen. *A Storm in a Tea-cup: The Solution to the Mystery of Hanging Rock*. (Brisbane: Mermaid, 1993).
Downes, Stephen. 'Rock Keeps its Secret'. *Age*, 22 March, 1977, 16; Interview.
Hartigan, K. V. 'Artemis in South Australia: Classical Allusions in *Picnic at Hanging Rock*'. *Classical and Modern Literature*, 11.1, 1990, 93-98.
Hunter, Ian. 'Corsetway to Heaven: Looking Back at Hanging Rock'. *Arena*, No. 41, 1984, 9-1.
Kirkby, Joan. 'Old Orders, New Lands: The Earth Spirit in *Picnic at Hanging Rock*'. *A.L.S.*, VIII, 1978, 255-68.

McGregor, Adrian. 'An End to the Mystery at Hanging Rock'. *S.M.H.*, 22 January, 1986, 11.
O'Neill, Terence. 'Literary Cousins: *Picnic at Hanging Rock*'. *A.L.S.*, X, 1982, 375-78.

LINDSAY, NORMAN

Fiction

Age of Consent. Introduction by Barry Oakley. North Ryde, NSW: A.& R., 1991). First published 1938.
Reviewed by C. Semmler, *Weekend Australian*, 24-25 August, 1991, Review 4.

A Curate in Bohemia. Introduction by Barry Oakley. (North Ryde, NSW: A.& R., 1991). First published 1913.
Reviewed by C. Semmler, *Weekend Australian*, 24-25 August, 1991, Review 4.

The Flyaway Highway. (Melbourne: Lansdowne Press, 1973). First published Sydney: A.& R., 1936.
Reviewed by K. England, *Advertiser*, 6 October, 1973, 20; F.M. Witsenhuysen, *Canberra Times*, 21 December, 1973, 8.

Micomicana. (Carlton: M.U.P., 1979).
Reviewed by J.B. Gadsdon, *S.M.H.*, 24 February, 1979, 17.

Rooms & Houses. (Sydney: Ure Smith, 1968).
Reviewed by E. Hackett, *ABR*, VIII, 1968, 37; B. Kiernan, *Australian*, 23 November, 1968, 15; G. Lehmann, *Bulletin*, 25 January, 1969, 65-66; N. Parker, *Canberra Times*, 1 March, 1969, 10; K. Rushbrooke, *Realist*, No. 33, 1969, 77-78; C. Turnbull, *Age*, 16 November, 1968, 15.

The Magic Pudding. (Ringwood, Vic.: Penguin, 1972). First published Sydney: A.& R., 1918. Reviewed by P. Ryan, *Nation*, 22 July, 1972, 20.

The Magic Pudding. 2nd. ed. (Sydney: A.& R., 1963). First published Sydney: A.& R., 1918.
Reviewed by C. MacInnes, *Bulletin*, 30 May, 1964, 51-2.

Poetry

Puddin' Poems. (London: A.& R., 1978).
Reviewed by R. Stow, *T.L.S.*, 29 September, 1978, 1084.

Non-Fiction

Bohemians at the Bulletin. (Sydney: A.& R., 1977). First published as *Bohemians of the Bulletin*, 1965.
Reviewed by G. Sprod, *S.M.H.*, 12 November, 1977, 20.

Bohemians of the Bulletin. (Sydney: A.& R., 1965).
Reviewed by J. Allison, *Southerly*, XXVI, 1966, 69-70; M.H. Ellis, *Bulletin*, 28 August, 1965, 28-9; J. Hetherington, *Age*, 28 August, 1965, 21; R. McCuaig, *Canberra Times*, 21 August, 1965, 12; S. Murray-Smith, *ABR*, IV, 1965, 199; J.D. Pringle, *S.M.H.*, 21 August, 1965, 16; C. Semmler, *Meanjin*, XXIV, 1965, 539-41; Scrutarius, *Walkabout*, XXXII, No. 1, 1966, 46-8.

The Letters of Norman Lindsay. Edited by R.G. Howarth and A.W. Barker. (Sydney: A.& R., 1979).
Reviewed by B. Elliott, *Advertiser*, 14 July, 1979, 25 and *A.L.S.*, IX, 1979, 253-57; J.B. Gadsdon, *S.M.H.*, 26 May, 1979, 17; C. Wallace-Crabbe, *Age*, 14 July, 1979, 21.

My Mask: For What Little I Know of the Man Behind It: An Autobiography. (Sydney: A.& R., 1970).
Reviewed by K. Cantrell, *Southerly*, XXX, 1970, 238-40; J. Hetherington, *Age*, 22 August, 1970, 14; N. Keesing, *Bulletin*, 29 August, 1970, 50; W.S. Ramson,

Canberra Times, 15 August, 1970, 13; C. Semmler, *S.M.H.*, 22 August, 1970, 19; L. Thomas, *Australian*, 15 August, 1970, 17. See also letter to the editor by Daryl Lindsay, *Overland*, No. 45, 1970, 35.

Norman Lindsay on Art, Life and Literature. Edited by Keith Wingrove. (St Lucia: U.Q.P., 1990).
Reviewed by P. Buckridge, *Imago*, 2, No. 2, 1990, 81-2; P. Butterss, *Australian Historical Studies*, 24.97, 1991, 472-74; G. Burns, *Age*, 19 May, 1990, Saturday Extra 10; C. Keneally, *ABR*, No. 121, 1990, 43; P. Kirkpatrick, *Southerly*, 50, No. 4, 1990, 532-34; C. Semmler, *Weekend Australian*, 30 June-1 July, 1990, Review 7.

Pencil Drawings. (Sydney: A.& R., 1969). Foreword by A.D. Hope, reprinted as 'The Pencil Drawings', *Quadrant*, XIII, No. 6, 1969, 16-17.
Reviewed by C. Turnbull, *Age*, 6 December, 1969, 17.

The Scribblings of an Idle Mind. (Melbourne: Lansdowne Press, 1966).
Reviewed by I. Turner, *ABR*, VI, 1966, 23.

Selected Pen Drawings. (Sydney: A.& R., 1968). Introduction by Douglas Stewart; preface by Norman Lindsay.

Siren and Satyr: The Personal Philosophy of Norman Lindsay. Introduced by A.D. Hope. (South Melbourne: Sun Books, 1976). Sun-Academy Series.
Reviewed by U. Prunster, *Art and Australia*, XIV, Nos. 3-4, 1977, 246-47.

'Have We Reached Maturity?'. *Age*, 16 July, 1966, 25.
'Looking Back in Anger'. *Age*, 9 July, 1966, 21.
'Unpublished Letters: Norman Lindsay to Lionel Lindsay'. *Southerly*, XXX, 1970, 289-300.

Critical Material

Chaplin, Harry F. (ed.). *Norman Lindsay: His Books, Manuscripts, and Autograph Letters in the Library of, and Annotated by, Harry F. Chaplin*. Foreword by Norman Lindsay. (Sydney: Wentworth Press, 1969). Studies in Australian and Pacific Bibliographies. Includes extensive extracts from letters to and from Norman Lindsay. Reviewed by K. Cantrell, *A.L.S.*, IV, 1970, 296-98. See also correction note, *A.L.S.*, IV, 1970, 425.

The opening of a Norman Lindsay memorial appeal was accompanied by brief reports, reproductions of his sketches, etc., almost daily in the *Australian* from 28 February, 1970, and some elsewhere, e.g., *Bulletin*, 30 May, 1970, 21, and 29 August, 1970, 51.

Kemsley, James. 'A Gentle Mania 2: Norman Lindsay'. *Biblionews and Australian Notes & Queries*, 19.2, 1994, 53-54. Brief note on collecting 'Lindsayana'.

'Lindsay Left $65,697 Estate'. *Australian*, 10 April, 1970, 4. See also related report, *S.M.H.*, 10 April, 1970, 8.

'Norman Lindsay Dies at Age of 90'. *S.M.H.*, 22 November, 1969, 1.

Allison, Jack. '"Futurity": Norman Lindsay's Creative Stimulus'. *Meanjin*, XXIX, 1970, 346-55. Includes comments by Jack Lindsay, 354-55.

Bloomfield, Lin (ed.). *The World of Norman Lindsay*. (Melbourne: Macmillan, 1979). Reprinted Melbourne: Sun Books, 1983. Reviewed by N. Keesing, *S.M.H.*, 3 November, 1979, 18 and *ABR*, No. 55, 1983, 14-15.

Blunden, Godfrey. 'The Ninety Years of Norman Lindsay'. In Norman Lindsay, *Watercolours*. (Sydney: Ure Smith, 1969), 9-28. Revised edition of *Norman Lindsay Water Colour Book* (Sydney: Springwood Press, 1939).

Burns, D.R. 'Of Sex and Other Eruptions: The Novels of Norman Lindsay'. *Meanjin*, XXXII, 1973, 67-72.

Cawley, A.C. 'Love's Fool Paradise'. *Meanjin*, XXIII, No. 2, 1964, 179-85. Discusses the setting of Lindsay's *Halfway to Anywhere*.

Chaplin, Harry F. 'The "Jubilee" *Magic Pudding*'. *Biblionews and Australian Notes*

& *Queries*, Second series, III, No. 2, 1969, 27-28. Includes notes from correspondence and conversations on the origin of *The Magic Pudding*.

Colebatch, Hal. 'Norman Lindsay and "The Magic Pudding" - A Marxist Reading'. *Westerly*, No. 1, 1976, 83-86. Joke.

Commins, Kathleen. *'The Magic Pudding'*. *S.M.H.*, 9 July, 1968, 10. Principally a statement by Norman Lindsay about the writing of *The Magic Pudding*.

Day, Kerin M. 'Norman Lindsay's Novels: An Aspect of Their Ethics'. In *The Australian Experience: Critical Essays on Australian Novels*, edited by W.S. Ramson (Canberra: Australian National University Press, 1974), 141-56.

Docker, John. 'Norman Lindsay's *Creative Effort*: Manifesto for an Urban Intelligentsia'. *A.L.S.*, VI, 1973, 24-35.

---. 'Norman Lindsay, Kenneth Slessor, and the Artist-Aristocracy'. In his *Australian Cultural Elites: Intellectual Traditions in Sydney and Melbourne*. (Sydney: A.& R., 1974), 22-41. Revised from *A.L.S.*, 1973.

Griffith, Michael. 'Francis Webb and Norman Lindsay'. *Southerly*, 49, No. 1, 1989, 32-43.

Hall, Sandra. 'Canonisation of a Larrikin'. *Bulletin*, 9 September, 1972, 44-45.

---. 'Norman Lindsay: Preparing His Lifetime for the National Trust'. *Bulletin*, 30 August, 1969, 45-47.

Hetherington, John. *Norman Lindsay*. (Melbourne: O.U.P., 1969) 3rd. edition [revised]. Australian Writers and Their Work. First published Melbourne: Landsdowne Press, 1968. Reviewed by K. Cantrell, *A.L.S.*, IV, 1970, 295-96. See also correction note, *A.L.S.*, IV, 1970, 425; B. Elliott, *ABR*, VIII, 1969, 247-48; K.L. Goodwin, *Notes & Queries*, N.S., XIX, 1972, 359-60.

---. *Norman Lindsay: The Embattled Olympian*. (Melbourne: O.U.P., 1973). Reviewed by G. Farwell, *S.M.H.*, 15 December, 1973, 15; C. Flower, *Bulletin*, 5 January, 1974, 35; C. Hadgraft, *A.L.S.*, VI, 1974, 328-32; C. Harrison-Ford, *Modern Language Review*, LXXI, 1976, 391-93; J. Lindsay, *Meanjin*, XXXIII, 1974, 27-41; H. McQueen, *Canberra Times*, 4 January, 1974, 9; A. Mitchell, *Advertiser*, 24 November, 1973, 26; C. Pearl, *Nation Review*, 14-20 December, 1973, 294; J. Roe, *Historical Studies*, XVI, 1975, 465-66; B. Smith, *Australian Journal of Politics and History*, XXI, No. 2, 1975, 122-23; C. Tolchard, *Sunday Telegraph*, 11 November, 1973, 54; C. Turnbull, *Age*, 27 October, 1973, 12.

Holroyd, John. 'Norman Lindsay in Novels'. *Biblionews and Australian Notes & Queries*, Series 3, III No. 1, 1978, 6-8.

---. 'Norman Lindsay's Widow dies in Sydney'. *S.M.H.*, 24 May, 1978, 8. Similar report in *Canberra Times*, 24 May, 1978, 3.

Jackson, Nigel. 'In Defence of Norman Lindsay'. *Quadrant*, XIII, (wrongly numbered as XIV), No. 2, 1969, 20-28. See also letter by Jackson, *Quadrant*, XIII, No. 6, 1969, 80.

Johnson, Nancy. 'Unusual Facets of Lindsayana'. *Biblionews and Australian Notes & Queries*, XI, No. 1, 1986, 3-14.

Jones, Margaret. 'A Shrill Cicada Dirge for "Our Only Genius"'. *S.M.H.*, 25 November, 1969, 7. Includes some brief extracts from Douglas Stewart's funeral oration.

Keesing, Nancy. 'Norman Lindsay'. *Quadrant*, XIII, No. 6, 1969, 13-15.

Kelly, Frances. 'Norman Lindsay'. *Canberra Times*, 29 November, 1969, 13.

Lindsay, Jack. 'The Life and Art of Norman Lindsay'. *Meanjin*, XXXIII, 1974, 27-41.

---. 'Norman Lindsay as Novelist'. In *Bards, Bohemians, and Bookmen*, edited by Leon Cantrell (St Lucia: U.Q.P., 1976), 251-65.

---. 'Norman Lindsay: Problems of His Life and Work'. *Meanjin*, XXIX, 1970, 39-48.

Lindsay, Jane. *Portrait of Pa: Norman Lindsay*. (Pymble, NSW: A.& R., 1994).

Reviewed by G. Dutton, *ABR*, 158, 1994, 61. First published Sydney: A.& R., 1973.
Lindsay, Lionel. *Comedy of Life: An Autobiography*. (Sydney: A.& R., 1967).
Lindsay, Rose. *Model Wife: My Life with Norman Lindsay*. (Sydney: Ure Smith, 1967).
Mackaness, George. 'Collecting Norman Lindsay'. In his *Bibliomania: An Australian Book Collector's Essays*. (Sydney: A.& R., 1965), 94-115.
Maidment, W.M. 'Australian Literary Criticism'. *Southerly*, XXIV, 1964, 20-41. Refers extensively to *Creative Effort*.
Manifold, John. 'Obituary: Norman Lindsay'. *Australian Left Review*, No. 23, 1970, 35-36.
Marshall, Alan. 'It's the "Alice" of Australia'. *Age*, 8 February, 1975, 12. *The Magic Pudding*.
McQueen, Humphrey. 'Norman Lindsay's *Vision*'. In his *Gallipoli to Petrov*. (Sydney: Hale & Iremonger, 1984), 35-43. First published as 'The Lindsays and Vision - a Marxist Reading'. *Westerly*, XX, 1975, 50-56.
---. 'The Thinker from The Bush: Norman Lindsay'. In his *Gallipoli to Petrov*. (Sydney: Hale & Iremonger, 1984), 82-85. First published as 'Life Without Hope', *Nation Review*, 28 April-4 May, 1977, 673.
Muir, Marcie. 'Norman Lindsay and the Magic Pudding'. *Voices*, 3.4, 1993, 45-56.
Rickard, John. 'The Magic of the Pudding'. *Meanjin*, XLVII, No. 4, 1988, 717-722. Discusses *The Magic Pudding* in the context of Lindsay's work.
Robinson, Desmond. 'Lifelong Battle with Australia's Mrs Grundy: Norman Lindsay: Artist, Writer and Bohemian'. *S.M.H.*, 22 November, 1969, 2.
Saxby, H.M. *A History of Australian Children's Literature, 1841-1941*. (Sydney: Wentworth Books, 1969), 75, 106-13, 120, 189.
Slessor, Kenneth. *Bread and Wine: Selected Prose*. (Sydney: A.& R., 1970), 111-127.
---. 'Lindsay at Ninety'. *Age*, 22 February, 1969, 14.
Stewart, Douglas. *Norman Lindsay: A Personal Memoir*. (Melbourne: Thomas Nelson (Australia), 1975). Reviewed by R.F. Brissenden, *Australian*, 13 March, 1976, 30; B. Elliott, *Advertiser*, 29 November, 1975, 24; D. Malouf, *Nation Review*, 28 November-4 December, 1975, 181 and *Sun-Herald*, 19 October, 1975, 84; R. Rivett, *Age*, 15 November, 1975, 15; C. Semmler, *S.M.H.*, 20 December, 1975, 15; B. Smith, *T.L.S.*, 9 April, 1976, 423; E. Webby, *A.L.S.*, VII, 1976, 438.
---. 'A Genius with Sex as his Religion'. *Bulletin*, 27 February, 1979, 50-56.
---. 'Lindsay's Legend'. *Australian*, 28 February, 1970, 18.
---. 'Rebel's Palace'. *Walkabout*, XXXIX, No. 9, 1973, 10-15. About Springwood.
---. 'A Send-off for Norman Lindsay'. *Southerly*, XXX, 1970, 53-54.
Sturm, T.L. 'Kenneth Slessor's Poetry and Norman Lindsay'. *Southerly*, XXXI, 1971, 281-306.
Wright, Judith. 'The Affirmation of Hugh McCrae'. In her *Preoccupations in Australian Poetry* (Melbourne: O.U.P., 1965, 98-110, 131-9. Discusses Lindsay's influence on McCrae.

LLEWELLYN, KATE

Fiction
Dear You. (Hawthorn, Vic.: Hudson, 1988).
Reviewed by M. Halligan, *Weekend Australian*, 10-11 September, 1988, Weekend Magazine 10; D. Porter, *Editions*, 6, 1990, 29; D. Simmonds, *S.M.H.*, 3 September, 1988, 81.

Poetry
Crosshatched. (Pymble, NSW: A.& R., 1994).
Reviewed by P. Brown, *Overland*, 139, 1995, 86-88; H. Cam, *S.M.H.*, 23 July, 1994, Spectrum 11A; M. Duwell, *Weekend Australian*, 4-5 Feb., 1995, Review 7;

M. Freer, *Imago*, 7.1, 1995, 94-95; J. Jones, *Southerly*, 55.2, 1995, 191-200; D. McCoohey, *Westerly*, 39.3, 1994, 95-97; W. Wynne, *ABR*, 166, 1994, 53-54.
Figs: Poems. (Hawthorn, Vic.: Hudson, 1990).
Reviewed by H. Cam, *S.M.H.*, 2 March, 1990, 47.

Honey: Poems. (Hawthorn, Vic.: Hudson, 1988).
Reviewed by H. Cam, *S.M.H.* 1 October, 1988, 74; E. Riddell, *Overland*, 112, 1988, 78-80.

Luxury. (Broadway, NSW: Redress P, 1985).
Reviewed by P. Mead, *Island Magazine*, 29, 1986, 32-40; J. Rodriguez, *S.M.H.* 31 May, 1986, 46; G. Rowlands, *Overland*, 106, 1987, 73-74; S.J. Williams, *ABR*, 80, 1986, 30-31.

The Mountain. (Hawthorn, Vic.: Hudson, 1989).
Reviewed by D. Davison, *Weekend Australian*, 16 December, 1989, Review 9; A. Gunter, *Overland*, 117, 1990, 88-90; J. Hanrahan, *ABR*, 118, 1990, 17-18; D. Johnson, *S.M.H.*, 18 November, 1989, 91; M. Missen, *Age*, 2 December, 1989, Saturday Extra 7; D. Porter, *Editions*, 6, 1990, 29; N. Stasko, *Phoenix Review*, 6 1990, 116-19.

Selected Poems. (Hawthorn, Vic.: Hudson, 1992).
Reviewed by T. Shapcott, *Age*, 9 May, 1992, Saturday Extra 10.

Trader Kate and the Elephants. (Unley, SA: Friendly Street Poets, 1982).
Reviewed by G. Dutton, *Bulletin*, 4 May, 1982, 68, 71-72; K. Goldsworthy, *Age*, 21 August, 1982, Saturday Extra 15; J. Grant, *CRNLE Reviews Journal*, 2, 1983, 35-38; D. Haskell, *Island Magazine*, 13, 1982, 54-55; A. Kefala, *Aspect*, 25, 1982, 73-78; V. Laughton, *Ash Magazine*, 9, 1982, 33; J. McLaren, *ABR*, 39, 1982, 21-24; J. Maiden, *S.M.H.*, 12 June, 1982, 37; P. Neilsen, *Image*, 5.2, 1982, 14; R. Nissen, *Luna*, 16, 1983, 36-38; C. Vleeskens, *Fling*, 2.1, 1982, 41-44; C. Vleeskens, *Compass*, 4.4, 1983, 58-60.

The Waterlily: A Blue Mountains Journal. (Hawthorn, Vic.: Hudson, 1987).
Reviewed by N. Dutton, *Overland*, 109, 1987, 82-83; P. Hodgins, *Age*, 30 May, 1987, 16; D. Johnson, *S.M.H.*, 6 June, 1987, 48; M.R. Liverani, *Weekend Australian*, 13-14 June, 1987, 15; D. Porter, *Editions*, 6, 1990, 29; B. Roberts, *Times on Sunday*, 28 June, 1987, 35.

Non-Fiction

Angels and Dark Madonnas: Travels in India and Italy. (Hawthorn, Vic.: Hudson, 1991).
Reviewed by A. Kennor, *Age*, 21 December, 1991, Saturday Extra 7; P. Nelson, *Weekend Australian*, 28-29 September, 1991, Review 5.

The Floral Mother and Other Essays. (Sydney: A.& R., 1995).
Reviewed by K. England, *ABR*, 172, 1995, 16-17.

Lilies, Feathers & Frangipani. (Pymble, NSW: A & R., 1993).
Reviewed by R. Cassin, *Voices*, 4.1, 1994, 118-22; D. Leadbetter, *ABR*, 154, 1993, 32.

Critical Material

Ash, Jennifer. 'Paradise and Australian Women Poets'. *Southerly*, 48.3, 1988, 259-73.
Gunter, Anne. 'Mapping the Unpredictable: The Art of Kate Llewellyn'. *Overland*, 127, 1992, 63-68.
Martin, Philip. 'Anne Elder and Kate Llewellyn'. In *Poetry and Gender: Statements and Essays in Australian Women's Poetry and Poetics*, edited by David Brooks and Brenda Walker (St Lucia: U.Q.P., 1989), 221-29. See also 'Statement', 52-53.
Mathur, Malati. 'A. D. Hope's "Ulysses" and Kate Llewllyn's "Penelope": Two Modern Voices from the Past'. *The Commonwealth Review*, 2.1-2, 1990-91, 86-95.

Page, Geoff. 'Kate Llewellyn'. In his *A Reader's Guide To Contemporary Australian Poetry* (St. Lucia: U.Q.P., 1995), 177-180.
Tomnay, Susan. 'Alone Again Naturally'. *Portfolio*, April, 1988, 98-100.

LOCKE, SUMNER (Helena Sumner Locke Elliott)
Critical Material
Albinski, Nan Bowman. 'Helena Sumner Locke - Careful! She Might Hear You'. *Antipodes*, 8.1, 1994, 47-53.

LOYAU, GEORGE
Critical Material
Anderson, Hugh. *George Loyau: The Man Who Wrote Bush Ballads*. Together with *The Queenslanders' New Colonial Camp Fire Song Book* and *The Sydney Songster*. Studies in Australian Folklore 6. (Ascot Vale, Vic.: Red Rooster P., 1991). Reviewed by R. Ovcrcll, *Bibliographical Society of Australia and New Zealand Bulletin*, 15.1, 1991, 42; R. Ward, *Bulletin*, 10 September, 1991,126-27.

LOUKAKIS, ANGELO
Fiction
For the Patriarch. (St Lucia: U.Q.P., 1981).
Reviewed by R. Barnes, *National Times*, 8-14 March, 1981, 48; H. Eliot, *Island Magazine*, Nos. 9-10, 1982, 77-78; V. Laughton, *Ash Magazine*, No. 11, 1982, 30; J. Murray, *CRNLE Reviews Journal*, No. 1, 1982, 11-13; E. Webby, *Meanjin*, 42, No. 1, 1983, 34-41; V. Wright, *Weekend Australian*, 26-27 January, 1985, Weekend 12.

Messenger. (Ringwood, Vic.: Penguin, 1992).
Reviewed by D. Adelaide, *S.M.H.*, 12 December, 1992, 50; H. Daniel, *Age*, 16 January, 1993, Saturday Extra 8; R. McDonald, *Bulletin*, 16 February, 1993, 92; S. Masson, *ABR*, 148, 1993, 37-38; G. Windsor, *Weekend Australian*, 19-20 December, 1992, Review 6.

Vernacular Dreams. (St Lucia: U.Q.P., 1986).
Reviewed by H. Falkner, *Weekend Australian*, 22-23 March, 1986, Weekend 13; L. Forsyth, *Age Saturday Extra*, 6 September, 1986, 13; R. Gostand, *Social Alternatives*, 6, No. 2, 1987, 75-77; P. Hanley, *Muse*, No. 66, 1987, 33-34; M. Jurgensen, *Outrider*, 3, No. 1, 1986, 174-75; P. Salzman, *ABR*, No. 80, 1986, 15-16.

Critical Material
Raizis, M. Byron. 'The Image of the Greek in Australian Literature'. In *Yugoslavia, Europe and Australia*, edited by Mirko Jurak (Ljubljana: Edvard Cardelj University, 1983), 115-32. Discusses *For the Patriarch*.

LURIE, MORRIS
Fiction
Dirty Friends. (Ringwood, Vic.: Penguin, 1981).
Reviewed by R. Barnes, *National Times*, 13-19 September, 1981, 42; H. Eliot, *Island Magazine*, Nos. 9-10, 1982, 77; T. Krause, *Weekend Australian Magazine*, 22-23 August, 1981, 11; F. McInerney [sic, ie McInherny], *ABR*, No. 37, 1981, 30-31; S. McKernan, *Overland*, No. 88, 1982, 57; D.J. O'Hearn, *Age*, 5 September, 1981, 28; T. Shapcott, *Courier-Mail*, 20 March, 1982, 27.

The English in Heat. (Sydney: A.& R., 1972).
Reviewed by A. Macdonald, *S.M.H.*, 21 April, 1972, 20.

Flying Home. (Melbourne: Outback Press, 1978).
Reviewed by D.R. Burns, *Nation Review*, 22-28 June, 1978, 15; G. Dutton, *Bulletin*,

2 May, 1978, 62; H. Hewitt, *Canberra Times*, 15 July, 1978, 12; C. Kelly, *National Times*, 20 May, 1978, 32; J. McLaren, *ABR*, No. 2, 1978, 26-27; M. Macleod, *S.M.H.*, 22 April, 1978, 16; R.M. McConchie, *Overland*, No. 75, 1979, 62-64; D.J. O'Hearn, *Age*, 29 April, 1978, 24; E. Perkins, *Quadrant*, XXII, No. 9, 1978, 76-77; P. Pierce, *Meanjin*, XXXVII, 1978, 393-401; E. Riddell, *24 Hours*, IV, No. 1, 1979, 54; T. Roberts, *Advertiser*, 20 May, 1978, 25.

Inside the Wardrobe. (Melbourne: Outback Press, 1975). Reviewed by S. Dawson, *Australian*, 17 July, 1976, 41; P. Edmonds, *Luna*, II, No. 2, 1977, 49-50; K. England, *Advertiser*, 5 June, 1976, 20; B. Kiernan, *National Times*, 2-7 August, 1976, 36-37; J. King, *Weekend Australian Magazine*, 30-31 July, 1977, 13; M. Macleod, *S.M.H.*, 8 May, 1976, 15; D.J. O'Hearn, *Age*, 19 June, 1976, 19; O. Ruhen, *Overland*, No. 64, 1976, 66.

Madness. (North Ryde, NSW: A.& R, 1991).
Reviewed by H. Daniel, *Age*, 6 July, 1991, Saturday Extra 8; J. Hanrahan, *ABR*, 132, 1991, 40-41; S. Hughes, *S.M.H.*, 3 August, 1991, 43; P. Pierce, *Bulletin*, 6 August, 1991, 96; I. Salusinszky, *Weekend Australian*, 10-11 August, 1991, Review 4.

My Life as a Movie: and Other Gross Conceits. (Ringwood, Vic.: McPhee Gribble/Penguin, 1988).
Reviewed by D. Stone, *Australian Jewish News*, 55, No.19, 9.

The Night We Ate the Sparrow: A Memoir and Fourteen Stories. (Fitzroy, Vic.: McPhee Gribble; Ringwood, Vic.: Penguin, 1985).
Reviewed by G. Burns, *ABR*, No. 79, 1986, 9-10; H. Daniel, *Age Saturday Extra*, 21 December, 1985, 8; H. Falkner, *Weekend Australian Magazine*, 25-26 January, 1986, 12; S. Hosking, *Overland*, No. 103, 1986, 67-69; T. Thompson, *S.M.H.*, 28 December, 1985, 30.

Outrageous Behaviour. (Ringwood, Vic.: Penguin, 1984).
Reviewed by J. Colmer, *Weekend Australian Magazine*, 22-23 December, 1984, 11; H. Daniel, *Age Saturday Extra*, 26 January, 1985, 12; P. Goldsworthy, *S.M.H.*, 9 February, 1985, 44.

Public Secrets. (South Melbourne: Sun Books, 1980).
Reviewed by H. Daniel, *Age*, 27 June, 1981, 25; M. Nayman, *ABR*, No. 32, 1981, 19.

Rappaport's Revenge. (London, Sydney: A.& R., 1973).
Reviewed by J. Hepworth, *Nation Review*, 27 July-2 August, 1973, 1283; A. Macdonald, *S.M.H.*, 22 September, 1973, 21; D.J. O'Hearn, *Age*, 22 September, 1973, 13.

Running Nicely. (Melbourne: Nelson (Australia), 1979). Reviewed by B. Grant, *ABR*, No. 14, 1979, 12-13; R. Hall, *S.M.H.*, 7 July, 1979, 18; P. Kocan, *Weekend Australian Magazine*, 7-8 July, 1979, 10; R. Macklin, *Bulletin*, 10 July, 1979, 78; D.J. O'Hearn, *Age*, 16 June, 1979, 23; E. Perkins, *Quadrant*, XXIII, No. 12, 1979, 68.

Seven Books for Grossman. (Ringwood, Vic.: Penguin, 1983).
Reviewed by F. McInherny, *ABR*, No. 60, 21-22; A. Stretton, *S.M.H.*, 7 April, 1984, 42.

Snow Jobs. (Carlton, Vic.: Pascoe, 1985).
Reviewed by A. Buzo, *ABR*, No. 77, 1985, 27; S. Knight, *S.M.H.*, 15 February, 1986, 46.

The String. (Ringwood, Vic.: McPhee Gribble Penguin, 1995).
Reviewed by G. Cork, *S.M.H.*, 26 Aug., 1995, Spectrum 10A; S. Kiernan, *Weekend Australian*, 9-10 Sept., 1995, Review 7; M. Manne, *ABR*, 174, 1995, 42-43 (see also interview by R. Koval, 43-44).

Two Brothers Running; Seventeen Stories and a Movie. (Ringwood, Vic.: Penguin, 1990).
Reviewed by J. Chimonyo, *Age*, 12 May, 1990, Saturday Extra, 7; L. Trainor, *Weekend Australian*, 5-6 May, 1990, Weekend 6; R. Lucas, *S.M.H.*, 11 August, 1990, 72.

Non-Fiction
Hackwork. (Melbourne: Outback Press, 1977).
Reviewed by J. Flanagan, *S.M.H.*, 11 February, 1978, 19; J. McLaren, *ABR*, No. 2, 19788, 26; D. O'Grady, *Quadrant*, XXII, No. 5, 1978, 78; D.J. O'Hearn, *Age*, 28 January, 1978, 25; I. Richards, *Advertiser*, 20 May, 1978, 25; J. Tranter, *National Times*, 20-25 February, 1978, 32.
Whole Life: An Autobiography. (Melbourne: McPhee Gribble, 1987).
Reviewed by E. Campion, *Bulletin*, 12 May, 1987, 87; A. Clare, *S.M.H.*, 23 May, 1987, 48 and *Age Saturday Extra*, 23 May, 1987, 11; R. Elisha, *ABR*, No. 93, 1987, 11-12; S. Liberman, *Overland*, No. 108, 1987, 95-96; A. Mitchell, *Weekend Australian. Weekend Magazine*, 2-3 May, 1987, 14; P. O'Connor, *Fine Line*, 2 September, 1987, 56-57.
'Crazy Reading, Reading Crazy: A Few Words from a Non-Bookish Kid'. *Educational Magazine*, XXXV, No. 2, 1978, 20-21.
'Self Portrait'. *ABR*, No. 77, 1985, 26.

Critical Material
'Out of the Wasteland'. *Walkabout*, March, 1974, 57-58. Abridged from the *Age*.
Colmer, John. 'Autobiography and the Jewish Migrant Experience: Morris Lurie'. In his *Australian Autobiography: A Personal Quest* (Melbourne: O.U.P., 1990), 147-152.
Duigan, Virginia. 'Morris Lurie Came Right When He Got Up, Ate Well, Wrote a Book, Married Girl Next Door'. *National Times*, 27 August-1 September, 1973, 24.
Haddock, Y. 'The Prose Fiction of Jewish Writers of Australia. 1945-1969. Part II'. *Journal of Proceeding of the Australian Jewish Historical Society*, VIII, No. 1, 1975, 56-60.
O'Hearn, D.J. 'Morris Lurie: The Humor of Survival'. *Overland*, No. 89, 1982, 24-28.
Riemer, A.P. 'This World, the Next, and Australia - the Emergence of a Literary Commonplace'. *Southerly*, XLIV, 1984, 251-70.
Sayers, Stuart. '*Flying Home* Comes to Roost'. *Age*, 1 May, 1976, 20. Interview.
---. 'Launching a Stubborn Book'. *Age*, 25 February, 1978, 24.
---. 'The "Miracles" in the Life of Morris Lurie'. *Age*, 13 October, 1973, 14. Interview. Reprinted in *Advertiser*, 3 November, 1973, 23.

McAULEY, JAMES

See also Malley, Ern

Collection
James McAuley: Poetry, Essays and Personal Commentary. Edited by Leonie Kramer. (St Lucia: U.Q.P., 1988).
Reviewed by M. Hulse, *PN Review*, No. 69, 1989, 52-53; L. McCredden, *ABR*, No. 101, 1988, 29-30; P. Mead, *A.L.S.*, 14, No. 4, 1990, 518-22; E. Perkins, *LiNQ*, 16, No. 1, 1988, 13-20; J. Strauss, *Phoenix Review*, No. 3, 1988, 109-114; R. Zeller, *Antipodes*, 4.1, 1990, 69.

Poetry
Captain Quiros. (Sydney: A.& R., 1964).
Reviewed by V. Buckley, *Prospect*, VII, No. 3, 1964, 30; L.R. Burrows, *Westerly*, No. 2, 47-9; R.G. Geering, *Bulletin*, 1 August, 1964, 49; D. Hewett, *Overland*, No. 32, 1965, 46-7; A.D. Hope, *Twentieth Century*, XIX, 1964, 107-16; P. Mares, *ABR*, III, 1964, 208; P. Steele, *Meanjin*, XXIII, No. 4, 1964, 439; N. Talbot, *Quadrant*, VIII, No. 4, 1964, 69-75.

Collected Poems, 1936-1970. (Sydney: A.& R., 1971).
Reviewed by M. Dunlevy, *Canberra Times*, 22 May, 1971, 15; R. Dunlop, *Poetry Australia*, No. 40, 1971, 52-54; K.L. Goodwin, *Makar*, VII, No. 4, 1971, 37-39; C. Harrison-Ford, *Sunday Australian*, 16 May, 1971, 31; E. Irvin, *S.M.H.*, 15 May, 1971, 23; P. Joseph, *New Poetry*, XIX, No. 3, 1971, 39-42; L. Kramer, *Bulletin*, 29 May, 1971, 46-47; D. Malouf, *Australian*, 30 October, 1971, 17; C. Semmler, *Hemisphere*, XV, No. 12, 1971, 40-41; R.A. Simpson, *Age*, 26 June, 1971, 13; K. Slessor, *Daily Telegraph* (Sydney), 17 April, 1971, 12.

Collected Poems. (Pymble, NSW: A.& R., 1994).
Reviewed by P. Pierce, *Quadrant* 39.4: 88-90.

James McAuley Reads from His Own Work. (St Lucia: U.Q.P., 1970). Poets on Record, 3. Record and booklet. Booklet includes notes by James McAuley and selected bibliography.
Reviewed by M. Duwell, *Makar*, VII, No. 1, 1971, 43-45; S.E. Lee, *Southerly*, XXXI, 1971, 238-39; A.C. Lyons, *Twentieth Century*, XXVI, 1971, 181-83; G. Page, *Canberra Times*, 27 March, 1971, 15; J.D. Pringle, *S.M.H.*, 3 April, 1971, 24; R.A. Simpson, *Age*, 27 February, 1971, 17; K. Slessor, *Daily Telegraph* (Sydney), 2 January, 1971, 10; J. Tulip, *Bulletin*, 6 March, 1971, 46.

James McAuley. With an introduction by the author. (Sydney: A.& R., 1963). Australian Poets series.
Reviewed by R.F. Brissenden, *A.L.S.*, I, No. 4, 1964, 283-6.

Music Late at Night: Poems 1970-73. (Sydney: A.& R., 1976). Poets of the Month.
Reviewed by V. Ikin, *Quadrant*, XXI, No. 9, 1977, 78-79; C. Pollnitz, *Southerly*, XXXVI, 1976, 466-7.

Music in the Mirabell Garden. Translated by James McAuley from the poetry of Georg Trakl. (Hobart: New Albion Press, 1982).
Reviewed by G. Dutton, *Bulletin*, 8 March, 1983, 58; S. Smith, *S.M.H.*, 26 February, 1983, 38; C. Wallace-Crabbe, *Age Saturday Extra*, 22 October, 1983, 14.

Surprises of the Sun. (Sydney: A.& R., 1969).
Reviewed by B. Beaver, *S.M.H.*, 14 June, 1969, 18; R. Dunlop, *Poetry Australia*, No. 32, 1970, 55-56; K. England, *Advertiser*, 3 January, 1970, 14; C. Harrison-Ford, *Poetry Magazine*, 17, No. 4, 1969, 5-11; E. Jones, *Nation*, 4 April, 1970, 21; M. Jurgensen, *Makar*, V, No. 3, 1969, 25-30; G. Lehmann, *Bulletin*, 21 June, 1969, 77-78; G. Page, *Canberra Times*, 13 September, 1969, 17; T.W. Shapcott, *ABR*, 1969, 182-83; R.A. Simpson, *Age*, 25 October, 1969, 16; N. Stock, *Togatus: University of Tasmania Student Magazine*, XL, No. 9, 1969, 24-25; *T.L.S.*, 15 January, 1970, 60; J. Tulip, *Southerly*, XXIX, 1969, 309-12.

A World of its Own. Paintings by P. Giles. (Canberra: A.N.U. Press, 1978).
Reviewed by D. Stewart, *S.M.H.*, 18 February, 1978, 18; C. Treloar, *Australian*, 3 April, 1978, 6.

Non-Fiction

The Grammar of the Real: Selected Prose, 1959-1974. Preface by Grahame Johnston. (Melbourne: O.U.P., 1975).
Reviewed by S. Amanuddin, *World Literature Today* (Norman Oklahoma), LI, No. 1, 1977, 158; R.F. Brissenden, *A.L.S.*, VII, 1976, 444; J. Colmer, *Quadrant*, XX, No. 7, 1976, 78-80; S. Jobson, *Australian*, 20 March, 1976, 30; G. Lehmann, *S.M.H.*, 8 May, 1976, 17; P. Quartermaine, *Notes & Queries*, n.s. XXVI, 1979, 85-6; J. Waten, *Age*, 29 May, 1976, 22.

The Personal Element in Australian Poetry. (Sydney: A.& R., 1970). Monograph of the Foundation for Australian Literary Studies, No. 3.
Reviewed by M. Duwell, *Makar*, VI, No. 3, 1970, 42-4; C. Harrison-Ford, *Union Recorder*, L, No. 19, 1970, 8-9; A. Mitchell, *A.L.S.*, V, 1971, 101; P. Roberts, *S.M.H.*, 15 August, 1970, 24; C. Semmler, *ABR*, IX, 1970, 211-12; J. Tulip, *Bulletin*, 28 November, 1970, 62-3.

A Primer of English Versification. (Sydney: Sydney University Press, 1966). Published in an American edition as *Versification: A Short Introduction.* (East Lansing: Michigan State University Press, 1966).
Reviewed by J.J. Bray, *ABR*, V, 1966, 222-3; J.M. Couper, *Bulletin*, 15 October, 1966, 58; J. McMichael, *Southern Review* (Baton Rouge, La.), N.S. III, 1967, 441-43.

'The First 15 Years'. *Quadrant*, XV, No. 5, 1971, 13-16. On *Quadrant*.
'The McAuley Affair'. *Quadrant*, XI, No. 5, 1967, 17-20. On his exclusion from a Soviet anthology 'for civic and political considerations'.

Critical Material

'An Interview with James McAuley'. *Togatus: University of Tasmania Student Magazine*, XL, No. 9, 1969, 7-8.
'Biographical Note'. *Poetry*, XCC, 1972, 336.
'Poet Wins $10,000 Award: Britannicas Also to Musician, Scientists'. *Australian*, 29 November, 1972, 3. For similar reports see *Canberra Times*, 29 November, 1972 3; *S.M.H.*, 29 November, 1972, 2.

Quadrant, XXI, No. 3, 1977. Memorial number. The articles are listed below under their authors' names.

Angus, Max. 'Two Tasmanian Painters Remember: II'. *Quadrant*, XXI, No. 3, 1977, 30.

Balzidis, Despina. 'James McAuley's Radical Ingredients'. *Meanjin*, XXXIX, 1980, 374-82.

Bartholomeusz, Dennis. 'James McAuley. *Terra Australis*'. In *Australian Poems in Perspective*, edited by P.K. Elkin (St Lucia: U.Q.P., 1978), 161-69.

Bradley, David. 'James McAuley - The Landscape of the Heart'. In *The Literature of Australia*, edited by Geoffrey Dutton (Adelaide: Penguin Books, 1964), 389-406.

Brissenden, R.F. 'The Wounded Hero: James McAuley's *Collected Poems, 1936-1970*'. *Southerly*, XXXII, 1972, 267-78.

Bushell, Gerald. 'Captain Quiros: James McAuley and Celsus Kelly, O.F.M.' *Quadrant*, XXI, No. 3, 1977, 24-29.

Coleman, Peter. *The Heart of James McAuley: Life and Work of the Australian Poet.* (Sydney: Wildcat Press, 1980). Reviewed by A. Brissenden, *Advertiser*, 29 February, 1981, 27; E. Campion, *Bulletin*, 16 December, 1980, 77; M. Duwell, *The Australian*, 3 January, 1981; S. McKernan, *Island Magazine*, Nos. 9-10, 1982, 79-80; J.D. Pringle, *S.M.H.*, 27 December, 1980, 25; T. Shapcott, *Courier-Mail*, 7 November, 1981, 24; G. Windsor, *ABR*, No. 28, 1981, 18.

Connolly, Richard. 'Music Late at Night'. *Quadrant*, XXI, No. 3, 1977, 75-77.

Cross, Gustav. 'Australian Poetry in the 'Sixties'. *Poetry Australia*, 13, No. 5, 1965, 33-8.

Dobrez, Livio. 'The Three McAuleys'. *Southern Review*, IX, 1976, 171-84.

Dobson, Rosemary. 'James McAuley, Poet'. *Quadrant*, XXV, No. 5, 1981, 30-31. See also Conway, Ronald. 'James McAuley, Catholic', 26-29; and Hunt, Peter. 'More on McAuley'[letter], No. 11, 1981, 76-77.

Docker, John. 'James McAuley: The Poetry and the Attitude'. *Arena* (Melbourne), No. 26, 1971, 73-86.

Dunlevy, Maurice. 'The Mind and Art of James McAuley'. *Canberra Times*, 10 January, 1981, 14.

---. 'Vis-a-vis McAuley'. *Canberra Times*, 5 August, 1967, 7-8.

Elliott, Brian. 'James McAuley, 1917-76'. *Southern Review*, IX, 1976, 170.

Gaffney, Carmel. 'Music out of Decay: McAuley's Later Poetry and Georg Trakl'. *Southerly*, XXXVI, 1976, 407-19.

Giles, Patricia. 'Two Tasmanian Painters Remember: I'. *Quadrant*, XXI, No. 3, 1977, 30.

Green, Dorothy. 'Letters from a Young Poet'. *Quadrant*, XXI, No. 3, 1977, 18-21.

Harcourt, Bill. 'The Push'. *National Times*, 3-8 February, 1975, 23-31. See also letter by Donald Horne, *National Times*, 10-15 February, 1975, 2.

Harrex, Syd. 'Island Lyrics: Vivian Smith, Gwen Harwood and James McAuley'. *Island Magazine*, Nos. 25-26, 1986, 67-73.

Harwood, Gwen. 'Gentleness'. *Quadrant*, XXI, No. 3, 1977, 15-16.

---. 'A Memory of James McAuley'. *Age*, 21 January, 1978, 25.

Hastings, Peter. 'A Kind of Tolerance'. *Quadrant*, XXI, No. 3, 1977, 49-50.

Horne, Donald. *The Education of Young Donald.* (Sydney: A.& R., 1967), 224 and passim.

---. 'In a Private Requiem'. *Quadrant*, XXI, No. 3, 1977, 31-32.

Jackman, Harry. 'Jim and the Kiaps - "A Performing Flea in A.A. Conlon's Remarkable Circus"'. *Quadrant*, XXI, No. 3, 1977, 71, 73-74.

Johnston, Grahame. 'A Sort of Lifeline'. *Quadrant*, XXI, No. 3, 1977, 14.

Keesing, Nancy. 'James McAuley'. *Australian Author*, IX, No. 1, 1977, 35. Obituary.

King, Bruce. 'A.D. Hope and Australian Poetry'. *Sewanee Review*, LXXXVII, 1979,

119-41.

Kirkpatrick, Peter. 'Patience and Despair: James McAuley's Pessimism'. *Southerly*, XLIV, 1984, 191-205.

Kramer, Leonie. 'James McAuley'. *Quadrant*, XX, No. 11, 1976, 5.

---. 'James McAuley's *Captain Quiros*: The Rational Paradise'. *Southerly*, XXV, No. 3, 1965, 147-61.

---. 'James Phillip McAuley (1917-1976)'. *Australian Academy of the Humanities. Proceedings*, 1977, 35-37.

---. 'Judith Wright, Hope, McAuley'. *Literary Criterion* (Mysore), XV, Nos. 3-4, 1980, 83-92.

---. 'The Later James McAuley'. *Quadrant*, XXX, No. 11, 1986, 68-69.

---. 'What Did James McAuley Do With His Life?' *Quadrant*, XXIX, No. 10, 1985, 36-40.

Krygier, Richard. 'Twenty Years'. *Quadrant*, XXI, No. 3, 1977, 58-59.

Lawrence, Peter. 'The Colleague'. *Quadrant*, XXI, No. 3, 1977, 68-70.

Macainsh, Noel. 'The Late Poems of James McAuley'. *Southerly*, XLV, No. 3, 1985, 330-342. Reprinted in his *Pathos of Distance* (Bern: Peter Lang, 1992), 214-28.

---. 'Music in Mirabell'. *Quadrant*, XXVIII, No. 9, 1984, 18-23. Reprinted in his *Pathos of Distance* (Bern: Peter Lang, 1992), 199-213.

McCredden, Lyn. 'Any Hope of Self-Construction? McAuley's Poems about Autobiography'. *Southern Review*, 22, No. 1, 1989, 61-74.

---. 'Between Position and Desire: The Love Poetry of James McAuley'. *Southerly*, 51.1, 1991, 35-54.

---. *James McAuley*. (Melbourne: O.U.P., 1992). Reviewed by D. Coad, *World Literature Today*, 68.1, 1994, 210-11; P. Coleman, *Weekend Australian*, 9-10 January, 1993, Review 6; P. Craven, *Age*, 12 September, 1992, Saturday Extra 10; R. Darling, *Antipodes*, 8.1, 1994, 85-86; I. Donaldson, *Voices*, 3.1, 1993, 123-25; J. Hanrahan, *ABR*, 147, 1992, 25-26; J.S. Leonard, *Overland*, 130, 1993, 87-89; S. Lever, *Southerly*, 53.1, 1993, 210-15; P. Mead, *A.L.S.*, 16.2, 1993, 140-51; P. Pierce, *Quadrant*, 37.11, 1993, 75-77.

---. 'James McAuley's *Captain Quiros*'. *A.L.S.*, XIII, No. 1, 1987, 54-56.

---. 'Mastering Romanticism: The Struggle for Vocation in the Texts of James McAuley'. In *Imagining Romanticism: Essays on English and Australian Romanticisms*, edited by Deirdre Coleman and Peter Otto (West Cornwall, CT: Locust Hill P., 1992), 265-73.

McGillick, P.E. 'The Thirty Years' War in Australian Literature'. *Aspect*, II, No. 4, 1977, 35-38.

McKernan, Susan. 'James McAuley's Quest'. In her *A Question of Commitment: Australian Literature in the Twenty Years after the War* (Sydney: Allen and Unwin, 1989), 70-95.

McLaughlin, D.C. 'McAuley in Malley's "Dürer: Innsbruck, 1495"'. *Westerly*, 38.1, 1993, 59-62.

Maver, Igor. 'The Mirabell Garden Revisited: Poets of the Ghostly-pale Moon and Leaden Sky - James McAuley and Georg Trakl'. *Outrider*, 1990, 106-21.

Moore, Deirdre. 'Jimmy'. *Overland*, No. 117, 1990, 48-9. Brief reminiscence of McAuley's student days at Sydney University.

Murray, Les. 'In Passion so Eloquent: A Personal Appreciation'. *S.M.H.*, 16 October, 1976, 10.

Nagarajan, S. 'The Personal Element in the Poetry of James McAuley'. *ACLALS Bulletin*, Series 4, No. 4, 1976, 26-31.

Pascoe, Elaine. 'James McAuley'. *English in Australia*, No. 39, 1977, 3-4.

Reid, Owen W. 'James McAuley - The Academic Poet'. *Tasmanian Education*, XVI, 1964, 79-83.

Ridland, John. '"Kindness and Courage": Eight Letters from James McAuley'.

Quadrant, 38.7-8, 1994, 67-75.

Robinson, Dennis. 'The Traditionalism of James McAuley'. *A.L.S.*, XI, 1983, 205-15.

Rowe, Noel. 'The Catholic element in James McAuley's Poetry'. *Quadrant*, XXVIII, No. 5, 1984, 45-48.

Ryan, J.S. '"Under Aldebaran": Edmund Spenser and the Early James McAuley'. *Notes and Furphies*, No. 18, 1987, 15-16.

Santamaria, B.A. 'So Clean a Spirit'. *Quadrant*, XXI, No. 3, 1977, 51-54.

Scheps, Leo. 'Unkellying Quiros. A Gloss of Part II of James McAuley's "Captain Quiros"'. *Journal of Australian Studies*, 42, 1994, 8-31.

Smith, Vivian. *James McAuley*. (Melbourne: Lansdowne Press, 1965). Australian Writers and Their Work. Reviewed by A. Brissenden, *ABR*, V, 1966, 63; D. Douglas, *A.L.S.*, II, 1966, 226-8; W. Hart-Smith, *Bulletin*, 5 February, 1966, 34 and see also letter by Vivian Smith, *Bulletin*, 19 February, 1966, 35-6; R. McCuaig, *Canberra Times*, 29 January, 1966, 11.

---. 'Australian Poetry in the '60's: Some Mid-Century Notes'. *Balcony*, No. 4, 1966, 46-51.

---. 'The Editor'. *Quadrant*, XXI, No. 3, 1977, 13-14.

---. 'Experiment and Renewal: A Missing Link in Modern Australian Poetry'. *Southerly*, XLVII, No. 1, 1987, 3-18; esp. 10-18.

---. 'James McAuley'. *A.L.S.*, VIII, 1977, 3-6.

---. 'James McAuley's Recent Poetry'. (Canberra: Australian National University, 1964). Commonwealth Literary Fund Lecture, 1962.

Spate, Oskar. 'Quiros and the Poets'. *Overland*, No. 112, 1988, 69-72. Discusses poems by Rex Ingamells, Douglas Stewart and James McAuley.

Stewart, Douglas. 'The Requiem'. *Quadrant*, XXI, No. 3, 1977, 79-80.

Strauss, Jennifer. 'From Heroism to *Pietas*: The Anti-Modernist's Progress in the Poetry of James McAuley'. *Meanjin*, 48, No. 3, 1989, 597-610.

Thompson, John. 'Poetry in Australia: James McAuley'. *Southerly*, XXVII, 1967, 96-106. Transcript of an interview by John Thompson telecast in 1965.

Tikoo, S. K. 'McAuley, Eliot and English Poetic Tradition'. *The Commonwealth Review*, 2.1-2, 1990-91, 64-75.

Traill, John D. 'A Note on James McAuley'. *Quadrant*, XXI, No. 4, 1977, 61.

Wallace-Crabbe, Chris. '"Beware of the Past": James McAuley's Early Poetry'. *Meanjin*, XXX, 1971, 323-30.

Wright, Judith. 'J.P. McAuley'. In her *Preoccupations in Australian Poetry* (Melbourne: O.U.P., 1965), 170-80.

McCRAE, HUGH

Poetry

Hugh McCrae: Selected Poems. (Sydney: A.& R., 1966). Australian Poets Series. Edited and with an Introduction by Douglas Stewart.
Reviewed by J.M. Allen, *Poetry Magazine*, No. 5, 1966, 31; R. McCuaig, *Canberra Times*, 18 June, 1966, 11.

Non-Fiction

Letters. Selected by Robert D. FitzGerald. (Sydney: A.& R., 1970). Includes Norman Cowper, 'McCrae the Man', originally published in *Southerly*, XIX, 1958, 67-75, and brief biographical and other notes.
Reviewed by D. Ball, *S.M.H.*, 25 July, 1970, 24; K. Cantrell, *Southerly*, XXX, 1970, 234-38; A.R. Chisholm, *Age*, 1 August, 1970, 16; N. Keesing, *Bulletin*, 15 August, 1970, 43-44; T.I. Moore, *Meanjin*, XXX, 1971, 353-56; N. Palethorpe, *Walkabout*, XXXVII, No. 8, 1971, 56; K. Slessor, *Daily Telegraph*, Sydney, 18 July, 1970, 16; W. Stone, *Australian*, 29 August, 1970, 21; T. Sturm, *A.L.S.*, V, 1971, 217-18.

'My Life and My Books (A Little Bit of Each)'. *Southerly*, XXXIII, 1973, 222-29.
  Critical Material
Chaplin, Harry F. (ed.). *A McCrae Miscellany: Georgiana Huntly McCrae, George Gordon McCrae, and Hugh Raymond McCrae: Their Books, Manuscripts, Letters and Drawings in the Library of Harry F. Chaplin*. (Sydney: Wentworth Press, 1967). Studies in Australian Bibliography, No. 16.
Hetherington, John. 'Hugh McCrae: The Laughing Poet'. *Etruscan*, XXII, No. 1, 1973, 13-16.
Lindsay, Norman. *My Mask*. (Sydney: A.& R., 1970), 184-91.
Macainsh, Noel. 'Hugh McRae [sic] and the Centaurs'. *Quadrant*, XXIII, No. 10, 1979, 19-26.
Mackaness, George. 'Collecting Hugh McCrae'. In his *Bibliomania: An Australian Book Collector's Essays* (Sydney: A.& R., 1965), 38-43.
Slessor, Kenneth. 'Hugh McCrae'. In his *Bread and Wine: Selected Prose*. (Sydney: A.& R., 1970).
Webb, John. 'The "Dark" Element in Hugh McCrae'. *A.L.S.*, VI, 1973, 197-202.
Wright, Judith. 'The Affirmation of Hugh McCrae'. In her *Preoccupations in Australian Poetry* (Melbourne: O.U.P., 1965), 98-110, 131-9.

McCUAIG, RONALD

  Fiction
Gangles. (Sydney: A.& R., 1973).
Reviewed by D. Stewart, *S.M.H.*, 8 December, 1973, 13.

  Poetry
Selected Poems. (Pymble, NSW: A.& R., 1992).
Reviewed by L. Bourke, *Southerly*, 52.4, 1992, 158-64; G. Catalano, *Age*, 23 May, 1992, Saturday Extra 7; J. Croft, *Voices*, 2.3, 1992, 100-03; A. Gould, *Quadrant*, 37.10, 1992, 81-83; M. Sharkey, *ABR*, 143, 1992, 48-49.

  Critical Material
Stewart, Douglas. 'Ronald McCuaig's Poetry'. In his *Writers of the Bulletin*. (Sydney: Australian Broadcasting Commission, 1977), 45-57.

McCULLOUGH, COLLEEN

  Fiction
A Creed for the Third Millennium. First Australian ed. (Sydney: Harper & Row, 1985).
Reviewed by G. Curran, *S.M.H.*, 6 July, 1985, 46; J. Fraser, *Weekend Australian Magazine*, 6-7 July, 1985, 15; J. Hanrahan, *Age Saturday Extra*, 3 August, 1985, 13; L. Jodrell, *Courier-Mail*, 6 July, 1985, 30; D. Matthews, *ABR*, No. 79, 1986, 16; D. Mitchell, *National Times*, 26 July-1 August, 1985, 31; W. Strieber, *New York Times Book Review*, 26 May, 1985, 14.

The First Man in Rome. (London; Sydney; Johannesburg: Century; New York: Morrow, 1990).
Reviewed by M. Halligan, *Weekend Australian*, 15-16 December 1990, Review 5; J. McGregor, *Age*, 9 February, 1991, Saturday Extra 8; C. E. Rinzler, *New York Times Book Review*, 4 November, 1990, 19.

Fortune's Favourites. (London: Century; New York: Morrow, 1993).
Reviewed by M. Buck. *New York Times Book Review*, 24 October, 1993, 22; K. Hunt, *Weekend Australian*, 30-31 October, 1993, Review 5; D. Pryor, *Age*, 20 November, 1993, Saturday Extra 8; N.J. Richey, *World Literature Today*, 68.3, 1994, 632.

The Grass Crown. (Milsons Point, NSW: Random House, 1991).

Reviewed by G. Flynn, *Weekend Australian*, 30 November-1 December, 1991, Review 7; J. Hanrahan, *Age*, 2 November, 1991, Saturday Extra 7.

An Indecent Obsession. (New York: Harper & Row, 1981).
Reviewed by H. Daniel, *Age*, 31 October, 1981, 25; G. Dutton, *Bulletin*, 8 December, 1981, 98; D. Green, *Weekend Australian Magazine*, 31 October-1 November, 1981, 10; G. Lord, *S.M.H.*, 7 November, 1981, 44; C. Rumens, *T.L.S.*, 11 December, 1981, 1448.

The Ladies of Missalonghi. (Melbourne, London: Hutchinson; New York: Harper and Row, 1987).
Reviewed by C. Bird, *Age Saturday Extra*, 18 April, 1987, 10; D. Colmer, *Weekend Australian. Weekend Magazine*, 16-17 May, 1987, 14; N. Phelan, *S.M.H.*, 2 May, 1987, 47; J. Yolen, *New York Times Book Review*, 26 April, 1987, 15.

The Thorn Birds. (New York: Harper and Row, London: Macdonald and Jane's, 1977).
Reviewed by A. Brookner, *T.L.S.*, 7 October, 1977, 1135; D.R. Burns, *Nation Review*, 9-15 June, 1977, 16; D. Green, *Quadrant*, XXI, No. 7, 1977, 70-72, see also letter by M. MacLeod, *Quadrant*, XXI, No. 10, 1977, 71-72; A. Heller, *Atlantic Monthly*, CCXXXIX, No. 6, 1977, 91; I. Hicks, *S.M.H.*, 11 April, 1977, 7; D.J. O'Hearn, *Age*, 21 May, 1977, 18; J.D. Pringle, *S.M.H.*, 21 May, 1977, 15; A. Roberts, *Advertiser*, 21 May, 1977, 29; D. Rowbotham, *Courier-Mail*, 21 May, 1977, 19.

Critical Material

Brady, Veronica. 'Colleen McCullough and the Savage God'. *Quadrant*, XXIV, No. 8, 1980, 48-52.
Demarest, Michael. 'Colleen McCullough's Outback Superhit'. *Time* (Australia), 30 May, 1977, 10-14.
Dutton, Geoffrey. 'A Bird in the Bush is Worth Millions'. *Bulletin*, 28 May, 1977, 60, 63.
Morris, Gwen. 'An Australian Ingredient in American Soap: *The Thorn Birds* by Colleen McCullough'. *Journal of Popular Culture*, 24.4, 1991, 59-69.
Osbourne, Richard. 'Interpreting Popular Literature'. *Arena*, No. 60, 88-98. Discusses *The Thorn Birds*.
Simpson, Colin. 'Suddenly an Australian's Novel Makes Her a Millionaire'. *Australian Author*, IX, No. 2, 1977, 11-16.
Sykes, Jill. 'Living with a Best Seller Can Have Its Problems'. *S.M.H.*, 29 June, 1977, 7.
Wearne, Heather. Contemporary Culture, Romance Fiction and *The Thorn Birds*'. *Meanjin*, 51.1, 1992, 169-79.
Whitlock, Gillian, David Saunders and Peter Anderson. 'Double Trouble, Part One: One or Two Women; Part Two: The Work and Its Double: Literary Resemblances and the Law; Part Three: Don Quixote on Wall Street'. *Meanjin*, 48, No. 2, 1989, 269-90. Discusses connections between *The Ladies of Missalonghi* and Lucy Maud Montgomery's *The Blue Castle*.

McDONALD, ROGER

Fiction

1915. (St Lucia: U.Q.P., 1979).
Reviewed by V. Brady, *Westerly*, XXV, No. 2, 1980, 61-75; L. Clancy, *Overland*, No. 80, 1980, 53-54; M. Dunlevy, *Canberra Times*, 7 April, 1979, 16; S. Edgar, *National Times*, 7 April, 1979, 37; R. Hall, *S.M.H.*, 21 April, 1979, 17; B. Kiernan, *Age*, 7 April, 1979, 23; R. McBride, *Bulletin*, 5 June, 1979, 77-78; J. McLaren, *ABR*, No. 13, 1979, 11; B. Muirden, *Advertiser*, 14 April, 1979, 17; E. Riddell, *24 Hours*, IV, No. 6, 1979, 66; C. Roderick, *Townsville Daily Bulletin*, 21 April, 1979,

4; D. Rowbotham, *Courier-Mail*, 7 April, 1979, 23; G. Sprod, *Quadrant*, XXIII, No. 8, 1979, 77-78; C. Vleeskens, *Time-Off* (University of Queensland Students' Union), XLIX, No. 4, 1979, 44-45; C. Wallace-Crabbe, *T.L.S.*, 11 January, 1980, 30.

Rough Wallaby. (Sydney: Bantam, 1989).
Reviewed by D. Johnson, *S.M.H.*, 4 November, 1989, 84; B. Pascoe, *ABR*, No. 117, 1989/90, 35-36; P. Pierce, *Bulletin*, 9 January, 1990, 80-81; A. Wearne, *Weekend Australian*, 4-5 November, 1989, Weekend 9.

The Shearer's Motel. (Chippendale: Pan Macmillan/Picador, 1992).
Reviewed by D. Anderson, *S.M.H.*, 19 September, 1992, 43; G. Dutton, *ABR*, 145, 1992, 19-20; J. Hooker, *Weekend Australian*, 26-27 December, 1992, Review 5; R. Zeller, *Antipodes*, 8.2, 1994, 80.

Slipstream. (St Lucia: U.Q.P., 1982).
Reviewed by G. Dutton, *Bulletin*, 25 May, 1982, 71; M. Halligan, *Canberrra Times*, 14 August, 1982, 19; N. Keesing, *ABR*, No. 41, 1982, 6-7; M. Lord, *Overland*, No. 90, 1982, 53-56; D.J. O'Hearn, *ABR*, No. 41, 1982, 7-8; D. Rowbotham, *Courier-Mail*, 29 May, 1982, 24; C. Semmler, *Weekend Australian Magazine*, 29-30 May, 1982, 12; A. Stewart, *Quadrant*, XXVII, No. 6, 1983, 86-87; J. Tulip, *Southerly*, XLIII, 1983, 116-17; C. Wallace-Crabbe, *Age Saturday Extra*, 8 May, 1982, 15.

Water Man. (Sydney: Picador, 1993).
Reviewed by K. England, *Voices*, 4.2, 1994, 111-17; T. Gilling, *Bulletin*, 14 September, 1993, 105; A. Gould, *Quadrant*, 38.3, 1994, 81-82; I. Hamilton, *T.L.S.*, 20 August, 1993, 5; J. Hanrahan, *ABR*, 155, 1993, 10-12; K. Hart, *Age*, 26 February, 1994, Saturday Extra 9; A. Riemer, *S.M.H.*, 4 September, 1993, Spectrum 11A; M. Sharkey, *Weekend Australian*, 9-10 October, 1993, Review 6.

Poetry

Airship. (St Lucia: U.Q.P., 1975). Paperback Poets, second series, 4. Reviewed by K.L. Goodwin, *Makar*, XI, No. 2, 1975, 50-51; R. Gray, *Poetry Australia*, No. 58, 1976, 79-80; P. Neilsen, *Age*, 12 June, 1976, 19; P. Rappolt, *Canberra Times*, 9 April, 1976, 14; R. Tamplin, *T.L.S.*, 9 April, 1976, 443.

Citizens of Mist. (St Lucia: U.Q.P., 1968).
Reviewed by P. Annand, *Makar*, 5, No. 1, 1969, 47-8 (see W. Gould, *Makar*, 5, No. 3, 1969, 33-6); D. Douglas, *Age*, 25 January, 1969, 10; R. Hall, *Australian*, 26 April, 1969, 17; G. Lehmann, *Bulletin*, 15 March, 1969, 80-1; *T.L.S.*, 8 May, 1969, 480.

Non-Fiction
'When I Began *1915* . . .'. *A.L.S.*, XII, No. 2, 1985, 264-265. Response to a questionnaire on the theme Australian literature and war.

Critical Material
Andrews, Barry. 'The Empire Strikes Back: *1915* and the Australian Sense of the Past'. In *Australian Papers: Yugoslavia, Europe and Australia*, edited by Mirko Jurak (Ljubljana: Edvard Cardelj University, 1983), 173-82.
Baker, Candida. 'Roger McDonald'. In her *Yacker 2: Australian Writers Talk About Their Work* (Sydney: Picador, 1987), 172-186.
Broinowski, Alison. 'Roger McDonald's ... Biggles for Grown-Ups'. *National Times*, 16-22 May, 1982, 30.
Brown, Wallace. 'At Last, the Great Australian Novel?' *Courier-Mail*, 17 March, 1979, 17.
Catalano, Gary. 'The Poetry of Roger McDonald'. *Quadrant*, 36.10, 1992, 70-73.
Hergenhan, Laurie. 'War in Post-1960s Fiction: Johnston, Stow, McDonald, Malouf and Les Murray'. *A.L.S.*, XII, No. 2, 1985, 248-260.
Howells, Coral Ann. '"'Tis Sixty Years since": Timothy Findley's *The Wars* and

Roger McDonald's *1915*'. *WLWE*, XXIII, 1984, 129-36.
McInerney, Sally. 'From the Central West to Gallipoli'. *S.M.H.*, 14 April, 1979, 16.
Neville, Jill. 'The Insider's View'. *National Times*, 20 October, 1979, 33.
Page, Geoff. 'Roger McDonald'. In his *A Reader's Guide To Contemporary Australian Poetry* (St. Lucia: U.Q.P., 1995), 191-195.
Rodriguez, Judith. 'McDonald's Marathon - Unexaggerated Achievements in Australian Poetry'. *Luna*, No. 3, 1976, 15-24.

McINNES, COLIN

Fiction

June in Her Spring. (London: Penguin Books, 1965).
Reviewed by R. Ward, *ABR*, IV, 1965, 55.

Critical Material

Gould, Tony. *Inside Outsider: The Life and Times of Colin McInnes*. (London: Chatto & Windus/Hogarth Press, 1983). Reviewed by C. Hawtree, *Spectator*, 10 September, 1983, 20; G. Murnane, *S.M.H.*, 26 November, 1983, 44; P. Pierce, *Age Saturday Extra*, 14 January, 1984, 11; E. Riddell, *Bulletin*, 6 December, 1983, 99 & 101.
---. 'How Colin McInnes Found Liberation in Australia's Bush'. *Weekend Australian Magazine*, 19-20 November, 1983, 5.

McINNES, GRAHAM

Non-Fiction

The Road to Gundagai. (London: Hamish Hamilton, 1965). Reviewed by L.V. Kepert, *S.M.H.*, 26 June, 1965, 15; J. Lindsay, *ABR*, IV, 1965, 162; I. Mair, *Age*, 19 June, 1965, 24; S. Murray-Smith, *ABR*, IV, 1965, 143; C. Osborne, *The London Magazine*, October, 1965, 98-101; H. Porter, *Bulletin*, 3 July, 1965, 50-1; *T.L.S.*, 6 May, 1965, 347.

Critical Material

Hall, Basil. 'The Track Winding Back: Memories of Boyhood'. *Age*, 29 May, 1965, 22.
Harris, Susan. 'Five by Five: An Educational Sampling'. [*Adelaide*] *A.L.S. Working Papers*, I, No. 1, 1975, 54-64.

McKAY, HUGH

Critical Material

Kirkpatrick, Peter. '"His Name Is Not in *Who's Who in Australia*": The Life and Some of the Opinions of "A Modest Genius", Hugh McKay'. *Southerly*, 50, No. 2, 1990, 222-39.

McKEE WRIGHT, DAVID

Critical Material

Sharkey, Michael. 'Apollo in George Street: A Reappraisal of David McKee Wright'. *Southerly*, XLVI, No. 4, 1986, 444-55.
---. 'David McKee Wright: By Any Name a Virtuoso'. *Notes & Furphies*, No. 12, 1984, 9.
---. 'David McKee Wright's Roman Novel'. *Southerly*, 51.1, 1991, 71-87.
---. 'A Lost Satire on the 1890s *Bulletin* Writers and Bohemians'. *A.L.S.*, XII, No. 4, 1986, 509-27.

MACK, LOUISE

Fiction

The World is Round. Introduced by Nancy Phelan (Pymble, NSW: A.& R., 1993). First published London: T. Fisher Unwin,1896.

Reviewed by E. Morrison, *ABR*, 155, 1993, 22-23.

Critical Material

Phelan, Nancy. *The Romantic Lives of Louise Mack*. (St. Lucia: U.Q.P., 1991). Final chapter 'Envoy' published in *Overland*, 122, 1991, 50-54. Reviewed by M. Gollan, *Voices*, 1.4, 1991, 99-102; V. Lawson, *S.M.H.*, 11 May, 1991, 49; S.K. Martin, *Australian Women's Book Review*, 3.2, 1991, 3-4; T. Pagliaro, *Overland*, 124, 1991, 76-77; E. Riddell, *Bulletin*, 9 April, 1991, 104-05; M. Sharkey, *ABR*, 130, 1991, 16-17; S. Yarwood, *Weekend Australian*, 4-5 May, 1991, Review 4.

MACKELLAR, DOROTHEA

Poetry

My Country and Other Poems. (Melbourne: Currey O'Neil, 1982).
Reviewed by R. Elliott, *Canberra*, 21 August, 1982, 13.

Poems. (Adelaide: Rigby, 1971). Includes a memoir by Adrienne Matzenik.
Reviewed by E. Kynaston, *Review* (Melbourne), 5 November, 1971, 103; A. Mitchell, *Advertiser*, 4 September, 1971, 30; T. Shapcott, *ABR*, X, 1971, 186.

A Sunburnt Country. Paintings by Bill Beavan. (Adelaide: Rigby, 1978). Includes biography and notes on the poem 'My Country'.

Non-Fiction

I Love a Surburnt Country: The Diaries of Dorothea MacKellar. Edited by Jyoti Brunsdon. (North Ryde, N.S.W., A.& R., 1990).
Reviewed by V. Smith, *Quadrant*, 34, No. 9, 1990, 78-79.

Critical Material

'Almost a Signature: Dorothea Mackellar's 63 Year Old Poem'. *Canberra Times*, 16 January, 1968, 11. Comments by T. Inglis Moore, D. Green, and J. Lynravn.
'Miss Dorothea Mackellar, Poet, Dies at 82'. *S.M.H.*, 16 January, 1968, 4.
Bladen, Peter. '"My Country"'. *Expression*, VII, No. 1, 1968, 13-15.
Hankel, Valmai. 'Notes on the Publication of Dorothea Mackellar's Poem, "My Country"'. *South Australiana*, VIII, 1969, 11-16.
Howley, Adrienne. *My Heart, My Country: The Story of Dorothea Mackellar*. (St Lucia: U.Q.P., 1989). Reviewed by H. Elliott, *Weekend Australian*, 28-29 October, 1989, Weekend 8; M. Lord, *ABR*, No. 116, 1989, 20-22.

MACKENZIE, KENNETH

Also published as Seaforth Mackenzie.

Fiction

Dead Men Rising. (Sydney: Pacific Books, 1969). First published London: Cape, 1951.
Reviewed by P. Cowan, *Westerly*, No. 3, 1969, 48; S. Despoja, *Advertiser*, 14 June, 1969, 14; B. Kiernan, *Australian*, 8 November, 1969, 20.

The Refuge: A Confession. (Melbourne: Sun Books, 1969). First published London: Cape, 1954.
Reviewed by B. Kiernan, *Australian*, 8 November, 1969, 20.

The Young Desire It. With an introduction by Douglas Stewart. (Sydney: A.& R., 1963). First published London: Cape, 1937.

Poetry

The Poems of Kenneth Mackenzie. Edited with an introduction by Evan Jones and Geoffrey Little. (Sydney: A.& R., 1972).
Reviewed by D. Hewett, *Westerly*, No. 4, 1972, 59-62; *New Poetry*, XXI, No. 1, 1973, 42; S.E. Lee, *Southerly*, XXXIII, 1973, 336-38; R. Simpson, *Age*, 4 November, 1972, 15.

Critical Material
Davis, Diana. 'A Checklist of Kenneth Mackenzie's Works, including Manuscript Material'. *A.L.S.*, IV, 1970, 398-404.
'Seaforth Mackenzie Issue'. *Westerly*, No. 1, 1968, 63. Corrections to texts of poems published in *Westerly*, 1966, No. 3.
Clarke, Donovan. 'Seaforth Mackenzie: Novelist of Alienation'. *Southerly*, XXV, No. 2, 1965, 75-90.
Cowan, Peter. 'Seaforth Mackenzie's Novels'. *Meanjin*, XXIV, 1965, 298-307.
Davis, Diana. 'The Genesis of a Writer: The Early Years of Kenneth Mackenzie'. *A.L.S.*, III, 1968, 254-70.
---. 'Seaforth Mackenzie'. *Westerly*, No. 3, 1966, 4-12.
Dossetor, R.F. 'Reminiscences of Kenneth Seaforth Mackenzie and E.L. Grant Watson'. *A.L.S.*, XIII, No. 1, 1987, 99-104.
Geering, R.G. 'Seaforth Mackenzie's Fiction'. *Southerly*, XXVI, 1966, 25-39.
Jones, Evan. *Kenneth Mackenzie*. (Melbourne: O.U.P., 1969). Australian Writers and Their Work. Reviewed by P. Cowan, *Westerly*, No. 3, 1969, 48; B. Elliott, *ABR*, VIII, 1969, 247-48; R.G. Geering, *A.L.S.*, IV, 1970, 305-07; K.L. Goodwin, *Notes & Queries*, N.S., XIX, 1972, 359-60.
---. 'A Dead Man Rising: The Poetry of Kenneth Mackenzie'. *Australian Quarterly*, XXXVI, 1964, 70-9.
---. 'Kenneth Mackenzie's Hospital Poems'. *Westerly*, No. 3, 1966, 13-38. Critical essay 13-14; poems printed, 15-38.
---. 'Prose and Short Stories'. *Westerly*, No. 3, 1966, 39-84. Critical comment, 39; prose and stories, 40-84.
Neggo, O. 'Seaforth Mackenzie: An Introduction to an Australian Writer'. *W.A. Teachers' Journal*, LVI, 1966, 424-5.

McKINNEY, J.P.

Drama
The Well. In *Khaki, Bush, and Bigotry*, edited by Eunice Hanger (St Lucia: U.Q.P., 1968).

Critical Material
Walker, Shirley. 'A Checklist of the Writings of J.P. McKinney'. *A.L.S.*, IX, 247.

McMASTER, RHYLL

Poetry
The Brineshrimp. (St. Lucia: U.Q.P., 1972).
Reviewed by M. Dugan, *Age*, 1 April, 1972, 13; M. Haley, *Twentieth Century*, 27, 1973, 283; C. Harrison-Ford, *Nation*, 13 May 1972, 21-22; I. Indyk, *The Bridge*, 7.2, 1972, 58; F. Kellaway, *Overland*, 53, 1973, 62; S. Lee, *Southerly*, 32, 1972, 310-11; D. Malouf, *Australian*, 17 June, 1972, 18; G. Rowlands, *Makar*, 8.1, 1972, 43-45; T. Shapcott, *ABR*, 11, 1972, 249-50; *T.L.S.*, 12 October, 1973, 1216; J. Tulip, *Bulletin*, 1 July, 1972, 47-48.

Flying the Coop: New and Selected Poems 1972-1994. (Port Melbourne, Vic.: Heinemann, 1994).
Reviewed by H. Cam, *S.M.H.*, 11 Feb., 1995, Spectrum 10A.; A. Gould, *Quadrant*, 39.5, 1995, 78-81; D. Leadbetter, *Overland*, 141, 1995, 86-88; M. Lynch, *AWBR*, 7.2, 1995, 5-6; G. Page, *Voices*, 5.2, 1995, 113-17; P. Salom, *ABR*, 168, 1995, 51-52.

On My Empty Feet. (Port Melbourne, Vic.: Heinemann, 1993).
Reviewed by A. Bullen, *Voices*, 4.3, 1994, 107-10; H. Cam, *S.M.H.*, 18 September, 1993, Spectrum 13A; J. Foulcher, *ABR*, 155, 1993, 45-46 (see also autobiographical note by Rhyll McMaster, 44); K. Hart, *Age*, 5 February, 1994, Saturday Extra, 8;

R. Munro, *Australian Women's Book Review*, 6.1, 1994, 13-14; P. Nelson, *Quadrant*, 38.5, 1994, 85-86; M. Roberts, *Overland*, 135, 1994, 84-85; C. Wallace-Crabbe, *Meanjin*, 53.2, 1994, 380-81.

Washing the Money: Poems with Photographs. (North Ryde, NSW: A.& R., 1986). Reviewed by P. Mead, *Island Magazine*, 29, 1986, 32-40; G. Page, *ABR*, 78, 1986, 27; J. Rodriguez, *S.M.H.*, 25 April, 1987, 44; J. Strauss, *Age*, 18 October, 1986, Saturday Extra, 12; F. Zwicky, *Weekend Australian Magazine*, 14-15 June, 1986, 16.

Critical Material

Alexander, Peter. '"Vital Organ with Strings Attached": The Poetry of Rhyll McMaster'. *Southerly*, 55.4, 1995, 14-20.

Catalano, Gary. 'The Poetry of Rhyll McMaster'. *Island*, 59, 1994, 66-68.

Gould, Alan. 'Being Observant, Keeping Faith'. *Quadrant*, 39.4, 1995, 40-44.

Page, Geoff. 'Rhyll McMaster'. In his *A Reader's Guide To Contemporary Australian Poetry* (St. Lucia: U.Q.P., 1995), 195-198.

MACNAMARA, FRANK

Critical Material

Butterss, Philip. 'The Less Rebellious Frank the Poet'. *Overland*, No. 112, 1988, 58-62.

---. 'James Lester Burke, Martin Cash and Frank the Poet'. *A.L.S.*, 15.3, 1992, 22-25.

Meredith, John and Whalan, Rex. *Frank the Poet: The Life and Works of Francis MacNamara*. (Melbourne: Red Rooster, 1979). Reviewed by W. Fahey, *Labour History*, No. 40, 1981, 137-39; K. Goodwin, *Weekend Australian Magazine*, 15-16 September, 1979, 13; J. Griffin, *Advertiser*, 11 August, 1979, 27; C. Hector, *National Times*, 15 September, 1979, 41; N. Keesing, *S.M.H.*, 9 February, 1980, 20; D. Kevans, *Tribune*, 14 November, 1979, 10; L.L. Robson, *Victorian Historical Journal*, LI, No. 1, 1980, 52-54 and *A.L.S.*, IX, 1980, 559-61.

Meredith, John. 'Frank the Poet: A Postscript'. *Overland*, No. 112, 1988, 63.

Reece, Bob. 'Frank the Poet'. In *Exiles from Erin: Convict Lives in Ireland and Australia*, edited Bob Reece (Houndmills, Basingstike, and London: Macmillan, 1991), 151-83.

McNEIL, JIM.

Drama

Collected Plays. (Sydney: Currency Press, 1987).
Reviewed by P. King, *Times on Sunday*, 24 May, 1987, 32.

How Does Your Garden Grow. Introduced by Katharine Brisbane; preface by Les Newcombe. (Sydney: Currency Press, London: Eyre Methuen, 1974). Currency Methuen plays series, 3. Reviewed by L. Radic, *Age*, 29 March, 1975, 14; A.W., *Elizabethan Trust News*, No. 14, 1975, 12.

Critical Material

'Top Prize for Prison Playwright McNeil'. *Age*, 18 July, 1975, 4; similar report *Canberra Times*, 18 July, 1975, 6.

Ellis, Bob. 'How I Killed Jim McNeil, the Dustbin of the Yard'. *S.M.H.*, 19 October, 1985, 51.

Kenna, Peter. 'A Convict of Society who Beat Man's Worst Enemy'. *S.M.H.*, 2 June, 1984, 45. Obituary.

Price, Antony. 'Jim McNeil and the Quest for a Dramatic Language'. *Journal of Commonwealth Literature*, XVIII, No. 1, 1983, 14-26.

MALLEY, ERN

(Malley was a hoax figure invented by Harold Stewart and James McAuley)

Poetry

Collected Poems. Commentary by Albert Tucker. (Pymble, NSW: A.& R., 1993).
Reviewed by D. Anderson, *S.M.H.*, 12 June, 1993, 45; P. Coleman, *Weekend Australian*, 29-30 May, 1993, Review 6; V. Ikin, *S.M.H.*, 28 August, 1993, 49; B. Lloyd, *Meridian*, 12.2, 1993, 152-58; P. Pierce, *Age*, 28 August, 1993, Saturday Extra 7; T. Shapcott, *ABR*, 154, 1993, 41-42.

Ern Malley's Poems. With an introduction by Max Harris. (Adelaide: Mary Martin, 1970). First published as 'The Darkening Ecliptic', *Angry Penguins*, Autumn, 1944, 1-33.
Reviewed by R. Hall, *Australian*, 30 May, 1970, 20; T.W. Shapcott, *ABR*, IX, 1970, 185.

The Poems of Ern Malley: Comprising the Complete Poems. Commentaries by Max Harris and Joanna Murray-Smith. (Sydney: Allen & Unwin, 1988).
Reviewed by D. Hewett, *Overland*, No. 112, 1988, 84-85; P. Rolfe, *Bulletin*, 22 November, 1988, 134.

Critical Material

Anderson, Peter. 'The Greatest Australian Poet that (N)ever Lived'. *Southern Review*, 24.2, 1991, 121-31.

Brooks, David. 'Ern Malley and *Les Déliquescences d'Adoré Floupette*'. *A.L.S.*, 15.1, 1991, 78-81.

Cooper, Derek. *The Gullibility Gap*. (London: Routledge and Kegan Paul, 1974).

Elliott, Brian. 'After Many a Summer'. *Helix*, No. 7-8, 1981, 139-55.

Francis, Ivor. '"Malley" - Last Laugh'. *Advertiser*, 6 September, 1975, 20.

Harris, Max. 'Malley among the Angry Penguins'. *Weekend Australian Magazine*, 3-4 November, 1984, 20.

Harrison-Ford, Carl. 'The Well-Wrought Ern'. *Southerly*, 54.3, 1994, 84-100.

Heyward, Michael. *The Ern Malley Affair*. Introduced by Robert Hughes. (St Lucia: U.Q.P.; London: Faber & Faber, 1993). Edited extract published in *Overland* 130, 1993, 16-19. Reviewed by M. Ford, *London Review of Books*, 9 September, 1993, 17-18; I. Hamilton, *T.L.S.*, 20 August, 1993, 5; G. Hassall, *Meanjin*, 25.4, 1993, 794-97; H. Horton, *Imago*, 5.3, 1993, 99-101; E. Jones, *Overland*, 135, 1994, 70-71; G. Jones, *Voices*, 4.1, 1994, 104-07; T. Keeley, *Scarp*, 26, 1995, 62-64; A. Kershaw, *ABR*, 154, 1993, 40-41; P. Kirkpatrick, *Journal of Australian Studies*, 42, 1994, 104-05; B. Lloyd, *Meridian*, 12.2, 1993, 152-58.

---. 'Extracts from *The Ern Malley Hoax*'. *Scripsi*, 6, No. 3, 1990, 7-34.

Lehman, David. 'The Ern Malley Hoax: Australia's "National Poet"'. *Shenandoah*, 34.4, 1983, 47-73.

Lewis, David. 'Ern Malley's Namesake'. *Quadrant*, 39.3, 1995, 14-15.

Macainsh, Noel. 'Busted Penguins - Max Harris and Ern Malley'. *Quadrant*, XXIV, No. 7, 1980, 19-24.

McLaughlin, D.C. 'McAuley in Malley's "Dürer: Innsbruck, 1495"'. *Westerly*, 38.1, 1993, 59-62.

Mead, Philip. 'Cultural Pathology: What Ern Malley Means'. *A.L.S.*, 17.1, 1995, 83-87.

Priessnitz, Horst. 'Ossian in Australien: Ein Nachtrag zum "Ern Malley Hoax"'. *Poetica* (Amsterdam), X, 1978, 66-87.

Roskolenko, Harry. 'Ern'. *Quadrant*, XXI, No. 3, 1977, 50.

Wilson, Barbara Ker. 'Black Swan of Trespass'. *Overland*, No. 68, 1977, 41-46.

Joke: Ern Malley's hidden years in Melbourne.

Wright, Judith. 'Poets of the 'Forties And 'Fifties'. In her *Preoccupations in Australian Poetry* (Melbourne: O.U.P., 1965), 193-210.

MALOUF, DAVID

Collection

David Malouf: *'Johnno', Short Stories, Poems, Essays and Interview*. Edited by James Tulip. (St. Lucia: U.Q.P., 1990).
Reviewed by L. Clancy, *Age*, 16 February, 1991, Saturday Extra 9; I. Indyk, *A.L.S.*, 15.3, 1992, 232-35.

Fiction

Antipodes. (London: Chatto & Windus: Hogarth Press, 1985).
Reviewed by D. Anderson, *National Times*, 22-28 March, 1985, 31; P. Buckridge, *Kunapipi*, VIII, No. 3, 1986, 138-140; C. Castan, *Social Alternatives*, V, No. 4, 1986, 58; P. Duguid, *T.L.S.*, 8 February, 1985, 140; M. Halligan, *Canberra Times*, 13 April, 1985, 18; J. Hanrahan, *ABR*, No. 70, 1985, 17-18; B. Jefferis, *Weekend Australian Magazine*, 16-17 March, 1985, 12; N. Jose, *Age Monthly Review*, V, No. 6, 1985, 17-18; J. Mellors, *Listener*, 9 January, 1986, 29; D. O'Hearn, *Age Saturday Extra*, 4 May, 1985, 14; D. Parker, *Age Monthly Review*, V, No. 3, 1985, 6; J. Pringle, *S.M.H.*, 30 March, 1985, 44; S. Smith, *Quadrant*, XXIX, No. 7, 1985, 83-85; B. Walker, *Westerly*, XXX, No. 3, 1985, 87-89; G. Windsor, *Bulletin*, 19 March, 1985, 66.

Child's Play with Eustace and The Prowler. (London: Chatto & Windus, 1982).
Reviewed by L. Clancy, *ABR*, No. 44, 1982, 24-25; M. Eldridge, *Canberra Times*, 11 September, 1982, 12; K. England, *Advertiser*, 9 October, 1982, 23; H. Garner, *National Times*, 4-10 July, 1982, 21; D. Green, *Hemisphere*, XXVII, 1983, 385; P. Rolfe, *Bulletin*, 19 October, 1982, 98-99; D. Rowbotham, *Courier-Mail*, 3 July, 1982, 22; N. Scott, *Weekend Australian Magazine*, 24-25 July, 1982, 10; P. Sharrad, *CRNLE Reviews Journal*, No. 1, 1983, 54-58; C.K. Stead, *S.M.H.*, 31 July, 1982, 37; J. Tittensor, *Overland*, No. 89, 1982, 62-63; J. Tulip, *Southerly*, XLIII, 1983, 114-15.

Fly Away Peter. (London: Chatto & Windus, 1982).
Reviewed by A. Brownjohn, *T.L.S.*, 15 October, 1982, 1141; L. Clancy, *ABR*, No. 44, 1982, 25; J. Davidson, *S.M.H.*, 25 September, 1982, 34; H. Garner, *National Times*, 12-18 September, 1982, 23; M. Halligan, *Canberra Times*, 23 October, 1982, 17; R. Haupt, *Age Saturday Extra*, 20 November, 1982, 12; R. Marsden, *Quadrant*, XXVII, No. 6, 1983, 83-84; P. Rolfe, *Bulletin*, 19 October, 1982, 98-99; D. Rowbotham, *Courier-Mail*, 18 September, 1982, 26; P. Sharrad, *CRNLE Reviews Journal*, No. 1, 1983, 54-58; J. Tulip, *Southerly*, XLIII, 1983, 113-14; R. Wade, *Contemporary Review*, No. 1404, 1983, 47-48.

The Great World. (London: Chatto & Windus, 1990; New York: Pantheon, 1991).
Reviewed by R. Brain, *T.L.S.*, 6-12 April, 1990, 375; H. Daniel, *Age*, 24 February, 1990, Saturday Extra 8; J. Hooker, *Weekend Australian*, 24-25 February, 1990, Weekend 6; J. Maddocks, *Editions*, Nos. 8-9, 1990, 8-9; P. Nelson, *Quadrant*, 35.11, 1991, 84-86; V. Passaro, *New York Times Book Review*, 31 March, 1991, 20; P. Pierce, *Bulletin*, 28 February, 1990, 90; A.P. Riemer, *S.M.H.*, 17 February, 1990, 79; R. Willbanks, *World Literature Today*, 65.3, 1991, 543; G. Windsor, *ABR*, No. 119, 1990, 7-8.

Harland's Half Acre. (Harmondsworth, Middlesex; Ringwood, Vic.: Penguin, 1985). First published London: Chatto & Windus, Hogarth Press, 1984.
Reviewed by S. Bann, *London Review of Books*, VI, No. 12, 1984, 18-19; J. Bedford, *National Times*, 22-28 June, 1984, 32; L. Clancy, *ABR*, No. 65, 1984, 6-7; J. Crace, *T.L.S.*, 15 June, 1984, 658; J. Davidson, *Overland*, No. 97, 1984, 74; F. Davis, *Fremantle Arts Centre Broadsheet: Books*, IV, No. 5, 1985, 2-3; K. England, *Advertiser Saturday Review*, 23 June, 1984, 35; M. Harrison, *Look & Listen*, I, No. 1, 1984, 95; B. Jefferis, *Weekend Australian Magazine*, 2-3 June, 1984, 13; J. McLaren, *CRNLE Reviews Journal*, No. 2, 1985, 47-51; J. Mellors, *Listener*, 5 July,

1984, 27; D.J. O'Hearn, *Age Saturday Extra*, 2 June, 1984, 18; C. Oakley, *Quadrant*, XXIX, Nos. 1-2, 1985, 140-141; D. Rowbotham, *Courier-Mail*, 16 June, 1984, 26; T. Shapcott, *S.M.H.*, 2 June, 1984, 41; P. Sharrad, *Compass*, V, No. 4, 1985, 4; J. Tulip, *Age Monthly Review*, V, No. 3, 1985, 5; G. Windsor, *Bulletin*, 22 May, 1984, 86.

An Imaginary Life. (London: Chatto & Windus, 1978).
Reviewed by V. Brady, *Westerly*, XXV, No. 2, 1980, 61-75; L. Clancy, *Overland*, No. 80, 1980, 54; G. Dutton, *Bulletin*, 17 October, 1978, 75-76; H. Frizell, *S.M.H.*, 20 May, 1978, 17; K. Hart, *Canberra Times*, 28 October, 1978, 15; R. Just, *T.L.S.*, 22 September, 1978, 1056; B. Kiernan, *Age*, 28 October, 1978, 26; P. Martin, *Overland*, No. 74, 1979, 59-60; R. Mason, *Campaign Australia*, No. 124, 1986, 46-47; R. McAllister, *S.M.H.*, 30 September, 1978, 17; P. McGillick, *National Times*, 21-27 March, 1986, 37; J. McLaren, *ABR*, No. 5, 1978, 15; P. Pierce, *Meanjin*, XXXVIII, 1979, 231-33; K. Pollitt, *New York Times Book Review*, 23 April, 1978, 10-11, reprinted in *Weekend Australian Magazine*, 15-16 July, 1978, 8; N.J. Richey, *World Literature Today*, LX, No. 1, 1986, 175; E. Riddell, *24 Hours*, III, No. 10, 1978, 66; D. Rowbotham, *Courier-Mail*, 18 November, 1978, 19; A.L. Urban, *Australian*, 21 February, 1986, 13.

Johnno: A Novel. (St Lucia: U.Q.P., 1975).
Reviewed by R. Ericksen, *Meanjin*, XXXV, 1976, 332-33; D. Gilbey, *Southerly*, XXXVI, 1976, 444-47; G. Hutchinson, *Makar*, XI, No. 3, 1975, 42-51; G. Page, *Canberra Times*, 13 June, 1975, 8; F. Pike, *T.L.S.*, 9 April, 1976, 445; E. Riddell, *Australian*, 19 April, 1975, 37; D. Rowbotham, *Courier-Mail*, 5 April, 1975, 15; D. Stewart, *S.M.H.*, 5 April, 1975, 11; A. Summers, *Advertiser*, 5 July, 1975, 18; J. Tittensor, *Nation Review*, 2-8 May, 1975, 765; J. Tulip, *Quadrant*, XIX, No. 3, 1974, 95-96; J. Waten, *Age*, 26 April, 1975, 16.

Remembering Babylon. (Milsons Point, NSW: Chatto & Windus/Random House Australia; New York: Pantheon, 1993).
Reviewed by S. Berne, *New York Times Book Review*, 17 October, 993, 7; C. Blanche, *Quadrant*, 38.1-2, 1994, 115-17; M. Bramwell, *Editions*, 16, 1993, 21-22; J. Carr, *Island*, 56, 1993, 71-72; J. A. Cincotti, *New York Times Book Review*, 17 October, 993, 7; D. Coad, *World Literature Today*, 68.4: 880; H. Daniel, *Age*, 24 April, 1993, Saturday Extra 7; D. English, *Overland*, 132, 1993, 21-22; S. Falkiner, *Voices*, 3.2, 1993, 117-20; R. Gray, *T.L.S.*, 7 May, 1993, 20; C. Keneally, *ABR*, 150, 1993, 8-9; J. Kinnane, *Overland*, 138, 1995, 70-71; P. Knox-Shaw, *Antipodes*, 9.1, 1995, 42-43; D. Myers, *Commonwealth Review*, 5.2, 1993-94, 172-74; A. Nettelbeck, *CRNLE Reviews Journal*, 2, 1993, 30-32; P. Otto, *Meanjin*, 52.3, 1993, 545-58; P. Pierce, *Bulletin*, 27 April, 1993, 98; A. Riemer, *S.M.H.*, 17 April, 1993, 47; I. Salusinszky, *Weekend Australian*, 24-25 April, 1993, Review 7; C.K. Stead, *London Review of Books*, 15.11, 1993, 28-29; P. Straus, *ABR*, 150, 1993, 6-7; A. Taylor, *Westerly*, 38.4, 1993, 123-25.

Drama
Blood Relations. (Sydney: Currency Press, 1988).
Reviewed by H. Gilbert, *Australasian Drama Studies*, 19, 1991, 124-28; M. Lord, *Australian Society*, VII, No. 10, 1988, 49-51; L. Nowra, *New Theatre Australia*, No. 1, 1987, 22-24.

Poetry
Bicycle. (St Lucia: U.Q.P., 1970).
Reviewed by P. Annand, *Makar*, 6, 1970, 14; C. Harrison-Ford, *Union Recorder*, 50, No. 11, 1970, 5-6; J.S. Harry, *Poetry Magazine*, 18, No. 6, 1970, 49-52; J. Tulip, *Southerly*, 30, 1970, 157-60; D. Hewett, *Westerly*, No. 4, 1971, 59; F. Kellaway, *Overland*, No. 53, 1972, 61-3; J. Saunders, *Stand*, 13, No. 3, 1972, 79.
First Things Last. (St Lucia: U.Q.P., 1980).

Reviewed by D. Carter, *Scripsi*, I, No. 2, 1981, 48-51; G. Catalano, *Meanjin*, XL, 1981, 117-19; M. Duwell, *Weekend Australian Magazine*, 18-19 July, 1981, 10; M. Harrison, *S.M.H.*, 3 January, 1981, 37; P. Martin, *Helix*, Nos. 9-10 Supplement 'Fresh Flounder', 17-20; P. Mead, *Island Magazine*, No. 7, 1981, 39-41; L. Murray, *Compass*, III, Nos. 2-3, 1981, 89-92; M. O'Connor, *Kunapipi*, IV, No. 1, 1982, 178-82; G. Page, *Canberra Times*, 3 January, 1981, 12; E. Perkins, *LiNQ*, IX, No. 1, 1981, 173-78; J. Tulip, *Southerly*, XLI, 1981, 392-401; P. van Schaick, *UNISA English Studies* (Pretoria), XX, No. 1, 1982, 44-45; C. Wallace-Crabbe, *ABR*, No. 27, 1980, 15.

Neighbours in a Thicket. (St Lucia: U.Q.P., 1974).
Reviewed by B. Beaver, *S.M.H.*, 23 November, 1974, 15; K. England, *Advertiser*, 4 October, 1975, 24; R. Garfitt, *Stand*, XVII, No. 1, 1975, 66-67; A. Gould, *Canberra Poetry*, II, No. 1, 1975, 64-65; R. Gray, *Poetry Australia*, No. 58, 1976, 77-79; S. Kantarizis, *New Poetry*, XXIII, No. 3, 1975, 67-69; S.E. Lee, *Southerly*, XXXV, 1975, 298-302; G. Page, *Canberra Times*, 18 April, 1975, 8 and *Hemisphere*, XIX, No. 7, 1975, 40; P. Porter, *T.L.S.*, 9 April, 1976, 431; J. Tranter, *Australian*, 14 December, 1974, 21; J. Tulip, *Age*, 28 June, 1975, 20; R. Wissler, *Makar*, X, No. 3, 1975, 46-47.

Selected Poems. (Sydney: A.& R., 1981).
Reviewed by D. Carter, *Scripsi*, I, No. 2, 1981, 48-51; M. Duwell, *Weekend Australian Magazine*, 18-19 July, 1981, 10; P. Martin, *Helix* Nos. 9-10 Supplement 'Fresh Flounder', 1981, 17-20; J. Ohmart, *Canberra Times*, 23 May, 1981, 14; G. Page, *National Times*, 7-13 June, 1981, 62; J. Rodriguez, *Age*, 11 April, 1981, 26; C. Wallace-Crabbe, *Meanjin*, XL, 1981, 500-06.

Selected Poems. (North Ryde, NSW: A.& R., 1991).
Reviewed by D. Gilbey, *ABR*, 136, 1991, 40-41; M. Hulse, *PN Review*, 19.5, 1993, 64-65; J. Owen, *Quadrant*, 36.12, 1992, 86-88.

Selected Poems 1959-89. (St Lucia: U.Q.P., 1992).
Reviewed by L. Cataldi, *CRNLE Reviews Journal*, 2, 1993, 78-85; W. Fiennes, *T.L.S.*, 6 January, 1995, 22; C. Pollnitz, *Weekend Australian*, 23-24 January, 1993, Review 7; F. Rouse, *Outrider*, [10.1&2], 1993, 124-25.

Wild Lemons. (Sydney: A.& R., 1980).
Reviewed by D. Carter, *Scripsi*, I, No. 2, 1981, 48-51; P. Martin, *Helix*, Nos. 9-10 Supplement 'Fresh Flounder', 1981, 17-20; J. Rodriguez, *ABR*, No. 29, 1981, 29-30.

Non-Fiction

12 Edmondstone Street. (London: Chatto & Windus, 1985).
Reviewed by L. Clancy, *ABR*, No. 78, 1986, 38; J. Davidson, *Age Saturday Extra*, 7 December, 1985, 13; R. Dobson, *S.M.H.*, 30 November, 1985, 46; J. Hooton, *Overland*, No. 103, 1986, 60-62; S. Kiernan, *National Times*, 3-9 January, 1986, 28; G. Phelps, *London Review of Books*, VIII, No. 8, 1986, 19; E. Riddell, *Bulletin*, 26 November, 1985, 99; D. Rowbotham, *Courier-Mail: The Great Weekend*, 16 November, 1985, 6; V. Sen, *Canberra Times*, 23 November, 1985, B2; I. Thomson, *The Listener*, 13 February, 1986, 28; J. Tulip, *Age Monthly Review*, V, No. 10, 1986, 11.

A.L.S., XII, No. 2, 1985, 265-268. Response to a questionnaire on the theme Australian literature and war.
'David Malouf on *12 Edmondstone St*'. In *Writers in Action: The Writer's Choice Evenings*, edited by Gerry Turcotte (Sydney: Currency Press, 1990), 43-62.
'First Experiences and First Places'. *Alumni News* (Univ. of Qld.), XVI, No. 2, 1984, 4-7.
'A First Place: The Mapping of a World'. *Southerly*, XLV, No. 1, 1985, 3-10.
'The Making of Literature'. *Overland*, No. 106, 1987, 5-6. Speech (edited form) given at the Premier's Literary Awards, Melbourne, 1986.

'Oh, for Those Backwater Days'. *Courier-Mail*, 27 September, 1974, 8.
'Opera: The Most Contemporary Art'. *ABR*, 136, 1991, 25-29.
'A Personal Multi-cultural Biography'. *Australian Studies*, 5. Special issue: Europe and Australia, 73-80.
'Three Talks: David Malouf, Les Murray and David Rowbotham'. *A.L.S.*, XI, 1984, 316-20. See also 'Selections from Question Time', 322-23. Session at Warana Writers Weekend.

Critical Material

Giffuni, Cathe. 'The Prose of David Malouf: A Bibliography'. *Australian & New Zealand Studies in Canada*, 7, 1992, 53-62.

'Academic Wins Best Book Award'. *Australian*, 7 June, 1975, 5; similar report in *Courier-Mail*, 7 June, 1975, 18.

Ashcroft, Bill. 'The Return of the Native: *An Imaginary Life* and *Remembering Babylon*'. *Commonwealth*, 16.2, 1993, 51-60.

Attar, Samar. 'A Lost Dimension: The Immigrant's Experience in the Work of David Malouf'. *A.L.S.*, XIII, No. 3, 1988, 308-321.

---. 'Samar Attar interviews David Malouf'. *Outrider*, 6, No. 1, 1989, 89-110.

---. '"Yearning of Grandsons for a Language the Dead Still Speak": Exile and Loss of Language in David Malouf's Work'. In *Provisional Maps: Critical Essays on David Malouf*, edited by Amanda Nettelbeck (Nedlands, WA: U of Western Australia, 1994), 51-69.

Baker, Candida. 'David Malouf'. In her *Yacker: Australian Writers Talk About Their Work* (Sydney: Picador, 1986), 234-63.

Bartsch, Kurt. '"Und den Mythos zerstört man nicht ohne Opfer": Zu den Ovid-Romanen *An Imaginary Life* von David Malouf und *Die letzte Welt* von Christoph Ransmayr'. In *Lesen und Schreiben: Literatur - Kritik - Germanistik*, edited by Volker Wolf (Tübingen and Basel: Francke, 1995), 15-22.

Bedford, Jean. 'David Malouf's Search for Emotional Reality'. *National Times*, 9-15 September, 1985, 26.

Bishop, Peter. 'David Malouf and the Language of Exile'. *A.L.S.*, X, 1982, 410-28. *An Imaginary Life*.

Bramwell, Murray. 'Maps of Migration: David Malouf's *Fly Away Peter*'. In *Making Connections: Introducing Nine Texts for Senior Students*, edited by Graham Tulloch and Annie Greet (Adelaide: CRNLE/Flinders Uni of South Australia and Trinity Gardens SAETA, 1990), 66-72.

Buckridge, Patrick. 'Astonished by Everything: The Functions of Sublime Discourse in David Malouf's Fiction'. In *Provisional Maps: Critical Essays on David Malouf*, edited by Amanda Nettelbeck (Nedlands, WA: U of Western Australia, 1994), 163-181.

---. 'Colonial Strategies in the Writing of David Malouf'. *Kunapipi*, VIII, No. 3, 1986, 48-58.

Chambers, Ross. *Room for Maneuver: Reading (the) Oppositional (in) Narrative*. (Chicago and London: U of Chicago P, 1991). Includes discussion of *An Imaginary Life*.

Colakis, Marianthe. 'David Malouf's and Derek Mahon's Visions of Ovid in Exile'. *Classical and Modern Literature: A Quarterly*, 13.3, 1993, 229-39.

Copeland, Julie. 'Interview with David Malouf'. *A.L.S.*, X, 1982, 429-36.

Craven, Peter. 'Crooked Versions of Art: The Novels of David Malouf'. *Scripsi*, III, No. 1, 1985, 99-126.

Dale, Leigh and Helen Gilbert. 'Edges of the Self: Topographies of the Body in the Writing of David Malouf'. In *Provisional Maps: Critical Essays on David Malouf*, edited by Amanda Nettelbeck (Nedlands, WA: U of Western Australia, 1994), 85-100.

Daniel, Helen. 'Narrator and Outsider in *Trap* and *Johnno*'. *Southerly*, XXXVII,

1977, 184-95.

Davidson, Jim. 'David Malouf'. *Meanjin*, XXXIX, 1980, 323-34. Interview. Reprinted in his *Sideways From the Page* (Melbourne: Fontana, 1983), 263-279.

Delrez Marc. 'Antipodean Dialogue: R. Stow and D. Malouf'. In *Crisis and Creativity in the New Literatures in English*, edited by Geoffrey Davis and Hena Maes-Jelinek. Cross/Cultures 1 (Amsterdam; Atlanta, Ga.: Rodopi, 1990), 291-307.

Dever, Maryanne. 'Place, Possession, Power: The Politics of Space in David Malouf's *Harland's Half Acre*'. In *Provisional Maps: Critical Essays on David Malouf*, edited by Amanda Nettelbeck (Nedlands, WA: U of Western Australia, 1994), 117-131.

---. 'Secret Companions: The Continuity of David Malouf's Fiction'. *WLWE*, XXVI, No. 1, 1986, 62-75.

Dommergues, Andre. 'Traditions and Dream in David Malouf's *An Imaginary Life*'. *Commonwealth* (Paris), X, No. 1, 1987, 61-67.

Ewans, Michael. '*Voss*: White, Malouf, Meale'. *Meanjin*, 48, No. 3, 1989, 513-25.

Fabre, Genevieve. 'Exil et Imaginaire dans *An Imaginary Life* de David Malouf'. *Commonwealth* (Toulouse) IV, 1979-1980, 51-58. In French.

Fabre, Michel. 'Roots and Imaginations: An Interview with David Malouf'. *Commonwealth* (Toulouse) IV, 1979-1980, 59-67.

Ferrier, Elizabeth. 'Mapping the Local in the Unreal City'. *Island Magazine*, No. 41, 1989, 65-69. Includes discussion of work by Malouf.

Gilbert, Helen. 'The Boomerang Effect: Canonical Counter-discourse and David Malouf's *Blood Relations* as an Oppositional Reworking of *The Tempest*'. *WLWE*, 31.2, 1991, 50-64.

Griffiths, Gareth. 'Being there, being There: Postmodernism and Post-Colonialism: Kosinsky and Malouf'. *Ariel*, 20, No. 4, 1989, 132-48. Republished in *Past the Last Post: Theorizing Post-Colonialism and Postmodernism* edited by Ian Adam and Helen Tiffin (Hemel Hampstead: Harvester Wheatsheaf, 1991), 153-66.

---. 'Culture and Identity: Politics and Writing in Some Recent Post-Colonial Texts'. In *From Commonwealth to Post-Colonial* edited by Anna Rutherford (Sydney; Aarhus: Dangaroo P, 1992), 436-43.

---. '*An Imaginary Life*: The Post-Colonial Text as Transformative Representation'. *Commonwealth*, 16.2, 1993, 61-69.

Hadgraft, Cecil. 'Indulgence: David Martin's *The Hero of Too*, Frank Dalby Davison's *The White Thorntree*, Dal Stivens's *A Horse of Air*, David Malouf's *Johnno*, and Frank Hardy's *But the Dead are Many*'. In *Studies in the Recent Australian Novel*, edited by K.G. Hamilton (St Lucia: U.Q.P., 1978), 194-224.

Hallows, John. 'David Malouf is Beating the Odds'. *Weekend Australian Magazine*, 12-13 October, 1985, 12.

Hansson, Karen. 'David Malouf and the Image of Australia'. In *Commonwealth Literary Cultures: New Voices, New Approaches*, edited by Giovanna Capone, Claudio Gorlier, and Bernard Hickey (Lecce: Edizioni del Grifo, 1993), 191-200.

---. *Sheer Edge: Aspects of Identity in David Malouf's Writing*. Lund Studies in English 83. (Lund: Lund UP, 1991). Reviewed by I. Indyk, *A.L.S.*, 15.3, 1992, 232-35.

Haskell, Dennis. '"Smoke Drifting up at Dawn": Individual Identity in the Poetry of David Malouf'. In *Provisional Maps: Critical Essays on David Malouf*, edited by Amanda Nettelbeck (Nedlands, WA: U of Western Australia, 1994), 13-27.

Hay, John. 'Trying to Capture that Fine Careless Rapture'. *Courier-Mail*, 22 December, 1979, 29. Visit to Brisbane.

Hergenhan, Laurie. 'Discoveries and Transformations: Aspects of David Malouf's Work'. *A.L.S.*, XI, 1984, 328-41.

---. 'The "I" of the Beholder: Representations of Tuscany in Some Recent Australian Literature'. *Westerly*, 36.4, 1991, 107-14. Discusses work by Malouf and others.

---. 'War in Post-1960s Fiction: Johnston, Stow, McDonald, Malouf and Les Murray'. *A.L.S.*, XII, No. 2, 1985, 248-260.

Heseltine, Harry. *'An Imaginary Life* - The Dimensions of Self'. *A.L.S.*, 14, No. 1, 1989, 26-40.

Huggan, Graham. '(Un)co-ordinated Movements: The Geography of Autobiography in David Malouf's *12 Edmondstone St* and Clark Blaise's *Resident Alien'. Australian and New Zealand Studies in Canada*, No. 3, 1990, 56-65.

Indyk, Ivor. 'The Australian Exploration of Masculinity'. *Commonwealth: Essays and Studies/Melanges*, III, 1977-1978, 89-96.

---. *David Malouf.* (Melbourne: O.U.P., 1993). Reviewed by D. English, *Weekend Australian*, 15-16 May, 1993, Review 6; S. Lever, *A.L.S.*, 16.2, 1993, 229-33; P. O'Neill, *Antipodes*, 9.1, 1995, 65-66; P. Pierce, *Quadrant*, 37.11, 1993, 75-77; J. Scheckter, *World Literature Today*, 68.2, 1994, 424-25; R. Sorensen, *Age*, 20 March, 1993, Saturday Extra 8

Jolly, Roslyn. 'Transformation of Caliban and Ariel: Imagination and Language in David Malouf, Margaret Atwood and Seamus Heaney'. *WLWE*, XXVI, No. 2, 1986, 295-330.

Jones, Margaret. 'Yes, Writers Are Born - but under the House'. *S.M.H.*, 11 August, 1984, 38. Interview.

Josephi, Beate. 'Interview with David Malouf'. In *Provisional Maps: Critical Essays on David Malouf*, edited by Amanda Nettelbeck (Nedlands, WA: U of Western Australia, 1994), 29-34.

Kavanagh, Paul. 'Elegies of Presence: Malouf, Heidegger and Language'. In *Provisional Maps: Critical Essays on David Malouf*, edited by Amanda Nettelbeck (Nedlands, WA: U of Western Australia, 1994), 150-162.

---. 'With Breath Just Condensing On It: An Interview with David Malouf'. *Southerly*, XLVI, No. 3, 1986, 247-59. Republished in *Conversations: Interviews with Australian Writers*, edited by Paul Kavanagh and Peter Kuch (North Ryde, NSW: Collins/A.& R, 1991).

Kerr, David. 'Uniting the Hemispheres: David Malouf's Fiction'. In *Australian Literature Today*, edited by R.K. Dhawan and David Kerr (New York: Indian Society for Commonwealth Studies/ Advent P, 1993), 61-73.

Kirby, Stephen. 'Homosocial Desire and Homosexual Panic in the Fiction of David Malouf and Frank Moorhouse'. *Meanjin*, XLVI, No. 3, 1987, 385-393.

Knox-Shaw, Peter. 'An Art of Intersection: David Malouf's Kunstellerom, *Harland's Half Acre'. Antipodes*, 5.1, 1991, 31-39.

---. 'Malouf's Epic and the Unravelling of National Stereotype'. *Journal of Commonwealth Literature*, 26.1, 1991, 79-100.

Laigle, Geneviève. 'Approaching Prayer, Knowledge, One Another: David Malouf's *Remembering Babylon'. Commonwealth*, 18.1, 1995, 78-91.

---. '"Entering the Dimensions of my Self": Malouf's *An Imaginary Life'. Commonwealth*, 16.2, 1993, 70-78.

Leer, Martin. 'At the Edge: Geography and the Imagination in the Work of David Malouf'. *A.L.S.*, XII, No. 1, 1985, 3-21.

McDonald, Avis G. 'Beyond Language: David Malouf's *An Imaginary Life'. Ariel*, XIX, No. 1, 1988, 45-54.

McInerney, Sally. 'Only David Malouf Could Find Brisbane Like Vienna'. *S.M.H.*, 24 April, 1982, 44. Interview.

Mansfield, Nick. 'Body Talk: The Prose of David Malouf'. *Southerly*, 49, No. 2, 1989, 230-38.

Murphy, Damien. 'Culture Reaches Brisbane at Last'. *Age*, 23 April, 1985, 14.

Neilsen, Philip. 'Breaking the Myth: David Malouf's *Fly Away Peter'. Outrider*, 6, No. 1, 1989, 75-88.

---. 'The Conflict between Australia and Europe in David Malouf's *Johnno* and *An*

Imaginary Life'. Earth Wings: The Outrider 91 Almanach, 175-79.

---. *Imagined Lives: A Study of David Malouf*. (St. Lucia: U.Q.P., 1990). Reviewed by L. Clancy, *Age*, 16 February, 1991, Saturday Extra 9; M. Delrez, *ABR*, No. 127, 1990, 17, 43; I. Indyk, *A.L.S.*, 15.3, 1992, 232-35; V. Muller, *Imago* 3.1, 1991, 91-92.

Nettelbeck, Amanda. 'Imagining the Imaginary in *An Imaginary Life*'. *Southern Review*, 26.1, 1993, 28-38.

---. '"The Mapping of the World": Discourses of Power in David Malouf's *Fly Away Peter*'. *Kunapipi*, 11, No. 3, 1989, 84-97.

---. 'Myths of a Nation: History as Narrative Invention in David Malouf's *The Great World*'. In *Myths, Heroes and Anti-heroes: Essays on the Literature and Culture of the Asia-Pacific Region*, edited by Bruce Bennett and Dennis Haskell (Nedlands, WA: Centre for Studies in Australian Literature, U of Western Australia, 1992), 132-41.

---. 'Narrative Invention as "Spatial History" in *The Great World*'. *Australian & New Zealand Studies in Canada*, 7, 1992, 41-52.

---. 'The Pattern of History: Discursive Conflicts in David Malouf's *Child's Play*'. *Span*, No. 29, 1989, 31-44.

Nettelbeck, Amanda, ed. *Provisional Maps: Critical Essays on David Malouf*. (Nedlands, WA: Centre for Studies in Australian Literature, U of Western Australia, 1994). Reviewed by S. Scott, *Westerly*, 39.4, 1994, 144-46. Reviewed by B. Kiernan, *A.L.S.*, 17.2, 1995, 198-202.

---. 'Rewriting an Explorer Mythology: The Narration of Space in David Malouf's Work'. In *Provisional Maps: Critical Essays on David Malouf*, edited by Amanda Nettelbeck (Nedlands, WA: U of Western Australia, 1994), 101-115.

Nicklin, Lenore. 'Malouf Returns, only to Leave'. *S.M.H.*, 25 January, 1979, 7.

O'Brien, Susie. 'The Theme of Transformation in *An Imaginary Life* and *The Bone People*'. *SPAN*, 30, 1990, 79-91.

---. *Reading David Malouf*. Horizon Studies in Literature. (South Melbourne: Sydney UP/O.U.P., 1995).

O'Grady, Desmond. 'Journeys Inside the Skull'. *National Times*, 2-8 November, 1980, 53.

O'Hearn, D.J. 'The Life and Reality of Malouf's World'. *Age*, 19 March, 1985, 22.

Page, Geoff. 'David Malouf'. In his *A Reader's Guide To Contemporary Australian Poetry* (St. Lucia: U.Q.P., 1995), 183-186.

Papastergiadis, Nikos. 'David Malouf and Languages for Landscape: An Interview'. *Ariel*, 25.3, 1994, 83-94.

---. 'Languages for Landscapes: David Malouf in Conversation with Nikos Papastergiadis'. *Crossings*, 20, 1994, 18-21.

Pati, Madhusudan. '*Banaghattaki Atmakatha* and *An Imaginary Life*: A Comparison in Sensibility'. *Literary Criterion*, 29.2, 1994, 1-17.

Patrick, Annie. 'David Malouf the Librettist'. In *Provisional Maps: Critical Essays on David Malouf*, edited by Amanda Nettelbeck (Nedlands, WA: U of Western Australia, 1994), 133-47.

Perera, Suvendrini. 'Unspeakable Bodies: Representing the Aboriginal in Australian Critical Discourse'. *Meridian*, 13.1, 1994, 15-26. Discusses *Remembering Babylon*.

Perkins, Elizabeth, and Jurgensen, Manfred. 'A Place of Our Own: David Malouf Talks with *Outrider*'. *Outrider*, II, No. 2, 1985, 59-71.

Pierce, Peter. 'David Malouf's Fiction'. *Meanjin*, XLI, 1982, 526-34.

---. 'Problematic History, Problems of Form: David Malouf's *Remembering Babylon*'. In *Provisional Maps: Critical Essays on David Malouf*, edited by Amanda Nettelbeck (Nedlands, WA: U of Western Australia, 1994), 183-96.

Pons, Xavier. 'Broken Lines, Broken Lives: Discontinuities in David Malouf's *The Great World*'. *Commonwealth*, 16.2, 1993, 79-87.

---. '"Savage Paradise": History, Violence and Family in Recent Australian Fiction by Hall, Keneally and Malouf'. In *European Perspectives: Contemporary Essays on Australian Literature*, edited by Giovanna Capone (*A.L.S.* 15.2 (special issue)/ St. Lucia: U.Q.P., 1991),72-82.

Porter, Peter. 'Brisbane Comes Back'. *Quadrant*, XIX, No. 6, 1975, 53-58.

Riem, Antonella. 'The "Double" Character and the Growing up Process in David Malouf's *Johnno* and Randolph Stow's *The Merry-Go-Round in the Sea*'. In her *The Labyrinths of Self: A Collection of Essays on Australian and Caribbean Literature*. (Leichhardt, N.S.W.: FILEF. Italo-Australian Publications, 1987), 181-195.

---. 'The Quest Motif in David Malouf's *An Imaginary Life* and Patrick White's *The Aunt's Story*'. In her *The Labyrinths of Self: A Collection of Essays on Australian and Caribbean Literature*. (Leichhardt, N.S.W.: FILEF. Italo-Australian Publications, 1987), 99-109.

Rogers, Shelagh. '"You Don't Really Know What It is Until You Go Away and Come Back": Interviews with Four Australian Writers'. *Australian and New Zealand Studies in Canada*, No. 1, 1989, 33-43.

Rorato, Laura. *Arte e vita nei romanzi di David Malouf: un viaggio attraverso il continente uomo*. (Florence: Firenze Atheneum, 1991).

Rowbotham, Jill. 'Australia May Not Be All That Wonderful'. *Courier-Mail*, 31 January, 1985, 4. Concerns David Malouf's reaction to attitudes to Australia in Britain and the U.S.

---. 'Brisbane - The View from a Small Italian Village'. *Courier-Mail*, 30 April, 1983, 24. Interview.

---. 'David Malouf: Home Writings from Abroad'. *Bulletin*, 29 May, 1984, 79 & 82.

Sayers, Stuart. 'Don't Ignore the Middle Ground, Says Malouf'. *Age Saturday Extra*, 1 October, 1983, 18.

Shapcott, Tom. 'David Malouf: An Interview'. *Quadrant*, XXII, No. 10, 1978, 27-31.

---. 'The Evidence of Anecdote'. In *Provisional Maps: Critical Essays on David Malouf*, edited by Amanda Nettelbeck (Nedlands, WA: U of Western Australia, 1994), 1-11.

Smith, Linda. 'David Malouf: Public Face of a Private Author'. *Weekend Australian Magazine*, 6-7 April, 1985, 4.

Spinks, Lee. 'Allegory, Space, Colonialism: *Remembering Babylon* and the Production of Colonial History'. *A.L.S.*, 17.2, 1995, 166-74.

Stewart, Annette. 'Art and the Australian Artist: In White, Malouf, Murnane and Bail'. *Quadrant*, XXXI, No. 8, 1987, 52-59.

Taylor, Andrew. '*The Great World*, History, and Two or One Other Things'. In *Provisional Maps: Critical Essays on David Malouf*, edited by Amanda Nettelbeck (Nedlands, WA: U of Western Australia, 1994), 35-50.

---. 'Postmodern Romantic: The Imaginary in David Malouf's *An Imaginary Life*'. In *Imagining Romanticism: Essays on English and Australian Romanticisms*, edited by Deirdre Coleman and Peter Otto (West Cornwall, CT: Locust Hill P., 1992), 275-90.

Thomas, Mark. 'David Malouf'. In his *Australia in Mind: Thirteen Influential Australian Thinkers* (Sydney: Hale and Iremonger, 1989), 99-113.

Thwaites, Tony. 'The Site of the Beholder: David Malouf's *Child's Play*'. *Southern Review*, XX, No. 1, 1987, 16-35.

Tipping, Richard Kelly. 'An Interview with David Malouf'. *Southerly*, 49, No. 3, 1989, 492-502.

Tulip, James. 'David Malouf, Francis Webb and Australian Religious Consciousness'. In *Reconnoitres: Essays in Australian Literature in Honour of G.A. Wilkes*, edited by Margaret Harris and Elizabeth Webby (South Melbourne: O.U.P. in association with Sydney U.P., 1992), 226-37.

Turner, John P. Jnr. '"I am there": Language and Metamorphosis in David Malouf's *An Imaginary Life*'. *SPAN*, 30, 1990, 92-101.

Ward, Peter. 'Bird of Passage Flies High'. *Australian*, 1 June, 1982, 12. Interview.
---. 'Literary View'. *Weekend Australian Magazine*, 15-16 July, 1978, 8.
Wertheim, Albert. 'Inscape and Creation in David Malouf's *Harland's Half Acre*'. *Commonwealth*, 14.2, 1992, 106-13.
Wearne, Heather. 'The "Fortunate" and the "Imagined": Landscape, Myth and Created Self in A.B. Facey and David Malouf'. In *The Making of Pluralist Australia 1950-1990*, selected papers from the inaugural EASA Conference 1991, (Bern: Peter Lang, 1992).
Whitlock, Gillian. 'The Child in the (Queensland) House: David Malouf and Regional Writing'. In *Provisional Maps: Critical Essays on David Malouf*, edited by Amanda Nettelbeck (Nedlands, WA: U of Western Australia, 1994), 71-84.
Wieland, James. 'Some Recent Australian Writing: Questions of "Meaning"'. *Span*, Nos. 16-17, 1983, 88-113.
Willbanks, Ray. 'A Conversation with David Malouf'. *Antipodes*, 4.1, 1990, 13-18.
---. 'David Malouf'. In his *Speaking Volumes: Australian Writers and Their Work* (Ringwood, Vic.: Penguin, 1991).
Williams, Barbara, and Shelagh Rogers. 'Two Interviews with David Malouf'. *Australian & New Zealand Studies in Canada 5*, 1991, 81-96.
Williams, Barbara. 'Malouf, Martin, Murray: The Artists on Their Craft'. *Nimrod*, 36.2, 1993, 135-37. Interview.
Winner, Anthony. 'David Malouf's *Child's Play*: Narrative Traditions in a Postmodern Game'. *Southerly*, 54.4, 1994-95, 116-30.
Woods, Stephen. 'David Malouf's *Child Play* and "the Death of the Author"'. *A.L.S.*, XIII, No. 3, 1988, 322-333.
Wright, John M. 'David Malouf, Lyrical Epicurean'. *Quadrant*, XXV, No. 12, 1981, 58-59.

MANIFOLD, JOHN

Poetry
Collected Verse. (St Lucia: U.Q.P., 1978).
Reviewed by J. Croft, *Quadrant*, XXIII, Nos. 1-2, 1979, 118-19; G. Dutton, *Bulletin*, 16 May, 1978, 70; C. Frost, *LiNQ*, VII, Nos. 2 & 3, 1979, 104-09; A. Gould, *Nation Review*, 8-14 June, 14-15; J. Grant, *Poetry Australia*, No. 68, 57-58; R.D. Jones, *National Times*, 14 October, 1978, 40; [S.E. Lee], *Southerly*, XXXIX, 1979, 452-54; E. Lindsay, *24 Hours*, III, No. 8, 1978, 68, 72; D. Malouf, *Overland*, No. 73, 1978, 47-54; W.H. Pritchard, *Hudson Review*, XXXII, 1979, 260; T. Shapcott, *ABR*, No. 6, 1978, 18-20; C. Treloar, *Weekend Australian Magazine*, 18-19 March, 1978, 8; C. Vleeskens, *Semper*, XLVIII, No. 9, 1978, 30.

On My Selection. With a preface by A.D. Hope. (Adelaide: Bibliophile Books, 1983).
Reviewed by B. Beaver, *Weekend Australian Magazine*, 29-30 October, 1983, 15; S. McKernan, *Canberra Times*, 1 September, 1985, 15; D. Rowbotham, *Courier-Mail*, 5 November, 1983, 30; G. Rowlands, *Overland*, No. 96, 1984, 27 28; M. Sharkey, *S.M.H.*, 31 December, 1983, 32.

Op. 8: Poems, 1961-69. (St Lucia: U.Q.P., 1971).
Reviewed by G. Curtis, *Makar*, VII, No. 2, 1971, 41-43; R. Dunlop, *Poetry Australia*, XL, 1971, 55-56; D. Green, *Canberra Times*, 29 May, 1971, 15; R. Hall, *Australian*, 3 July, 1971, 20; C. Harrison-Ford, *New Poetry*, XIX, No. 2, 1971, 32-33; S.E. Lee, *Southerly*, XXXI, 1971, 229-30; T.W. Shapcott, *ABR*, X, 1971, 90-91; J. Tulip, *Bulletin*, 14 August, 1971, 48.

Six Sonnets on Human Ecology. (Brisbane: Communist Arts Group, 1974).
Reviewed by M. Ehrhardt, *Tribune*, 15 October, 1974, 10.

Non-Fiction

Who Wrote the Ballads?. Notes on Australian Folksong. (Sydney: Australasian Book Society, 1964).
Reviewed by G.A. Wilkes, *Southerly*, XXIV, No. 3, 1964, 249-50.

Critical Material

Hall, Rodney. *J.S. Manifold*. (St Lucia: U.Q.P., 1978). Reviewed by J. Croft, *Quadrant*, XXIII, Nos. 1-2, 1979, 118-19; M. Dunlevy, *Canberra Times*, 17 June, 1978, 12; G. Dutton, *Bulletin*, 16 May, 1978, 70; M. Ehrhardt, *Tribune*, 29 March, 1978, 8; C. Frost, *LiNQ*, VII, Nos. 2-3, 1979, 104-09; A. Gould, *Nation Review*, 8-14 June, 1978, 14-15; C. Hanna, *A.L.S.*, IX, 1979, 129-31; E. Lindsay, *24 Hours*, III, No. 8, 1978, 72; D. Malouf, *Overland*, No. 73, 1978, 47-54; T. Shapcott, *ABR*, No. 6, 1978, 18-20; P. Thompson, *S.M.H.*, 1 July, 1978, 19; C. Treloar, *Weekend Australian Magazine*, 18-19 March, 1978, 8; R. Ward, *Meanjin*, XXXVIII, 1979, 246-52.

Morse, Ruth. 'John Manifold: Poet at Cambridge'. *A.L.S.*, XIII, No. 3, 1988, 369-380.

Murray-Smith, Stephen. 'Vale John Manifold'. *ABR*, No. 71, 1985, 15-16. For other obituaries see *Age*, 22 April, 1985, 6; *The Border Issue*, 1985, 69; *Courier-Mail*, 20 April, 1985, 2; *Foque Newsletter*, No. 11, 1985, 3-5; *Notes & Furphies*, No. 15.

MANN, LEONARD

Fiction

Flesh in Armour. (Sydney: Unwin Paperbacks, 1985). First published Melbourne: Phaedrus, 1932.
Reviewed by L. Clancy, *ABR*, No. 80, 1986, 24-25.

Venus Half-Caste. (London: Hodder and Stoughton, 1963).
Reviewed by H.P. Heseltine, *Meanjin*, XXII, No. 4, 1963, 422-6; C. Semmler, *ABR*, II, 1963, 195.

Non-Fiction

'A Double Life (Australian Writers in Profile, 6)'. *Southerly*, XXIX, 1969, 163-74.

Critical Material

Darby, Robert. 'Patrick White and "the dun-coloured offspring..."'. *Notes & Furphies*, No. 18, 1987, 16-17.

Phillips, A.A. 'The Australian Puritans'. In his *Responses: Selected Writings*. (Kew, Vic.: Australian International Press and Publications, 1979), 53-54. Review of *Andrea Caslin*. First published in *Adult Education*, II, 1959.

Smith, Graeme Kinross. 'Leonard Mann - a Profile'. *A.L.S.*, VII, 324-27.

Vintner, Maurice. 'Rediscovery, 1: Leonard Mann's *A Murder in Sydney*'. *Overland*, No. 44, 1970, 39-40.

MANNING, FREDERIC

Fiction

Her Privates We. (London: Heinemann, 1964). First published London: Peter Davies, 1930.
Reviewed by S. Murray-Smith, *ABR*, III, 1964, 229; G. Scott, *Bulletin*, 24 October, 1964, 51-2.

The Middle Parts of Fortune: Somme & Ancre, 1916. (London: Peter Davies; New York: St Martin's Press, 1977; London: Granada, 1978). First published in a limited edition London: Piazza Press, 1929.
Reviewed by A. Bell, *Age*, 28 October, 1978, 25; G. Dutton, *Bulletin*, 10 January, 1978, 53; P. Fussell, *New York Times Book Review*, 23 October, 1977, 26; J. Grieve, *Canberra Times*, 17 September, 1977, 12; G. Marcus, *Rolling Stone* (Aust. ed.), 6

April, 1978; R. Nicholls, *S.M.H.*, 29 October, 1977, 17; W.H. Pritchard, *Hudson Review*, XXXI, 1978, 524-25; J. Symons, *T.L.S.*, 19 August, 1977, 997 (see also letters by R. Cody, *T.L.S.*, 9 September, 1977, 1081, and J. Symons, *T.L.S.*, 30 September, 1977, 1108); M. Taylor, *Commonwealth*, 19 January, 1979, 26-27.
The Middle Parts of Fortune: Somme and Ancre, 1916. Introduced by Paul Fussell. (New York; London; Ringwood, Vic.: Penguin Books, 1990). First published in a limited edition London: Piazza Press, 1929.

Critical Material

Clunies Ross, Bruce. 'Frederic Manning and the Tragedy of War'. *Overland*, No. 75, 1979, 45-49.

Cody, Richard. *Newsletter of the Friends of the Amherst College Library*, Fall 1977. Issue devoted to Manning.

Coleman, Verna. *The Last Exquisite: A Portrait of Frederic Manning* (Carlton, Vic.: M.U.P., 1990). Reviewed by A. Caesar, *Meridian*, 10.1, 1991, 76-78; E. Campion, *Bulletin*, 15 May, 1990, 116; H. Carpenter, *T.L.S.*, 21-27 December, 1990, 1368; L. Clancy, *Age*, 11 August, 1990, Saturday Extra 9; R. Harrison, *Weekend Australian*, 15-16 September, 1990, Review 6; C. Munro, *A.L.S.*, 15.1, 1991, 89-93; C. Semmler, *Quadrant*, 34, No. 6, 1990, 70-73; V. Smith, *ABR*, No. 122, 1990, 22.

---. 'The Last Exqusite: Forgotten Fred Manning, Expatriate'. *Quadrant*, 34, Nos. 1-2, 1990, 29-32. Reprint of Introduction to her *The Last Exquisite: A Portrait of Frederic Manning* (Carlton, Vic.: M.U.P., 1990).

Haq, Kaiser. 'Forgotten Fred: A Portrait of Frederic Manning'. *London Magazine*, N.S. XXIII, Nos. 9-10, 1983-1984, 54-78.

Hergenhan, L.T. 'Ezra Pound, Frederic Manning and James Griffyth Fairfax'. *A.L.S.*, XI, 1984, 395-99. See also his 'A Checklist of Recent Manning Criticism'. 399-400.

---. 'Novelist at War: Frederic Manning's *Her Privates We*'. *Quadrant*, XIV, No. 4, 1970, 19-29.

---. 'A Private Life: Frederic Manning'. *Quadrant*, 33, No. 8, 1989, 33-35.

---. 'Some Unpublished Letters from T.E. Lawrence to Frederic Manning'. *Southerly*, XXIII, No. 4, 1963, 242-52.

---. 'Two Expatriates: Some Correspondence from Frederic Manning to James Griffyth Fairfax', *Southerly*, XXXIX, 1979, 59-95.

Klein, H.M. 'In the Midst of Beastliness: Concepts and Ideals in Manning's *Her Privates We*'. *Journal of Commonwealth Literature*, XII, No. 2, 1978, 136-52.

---. 'The Structure of Frederic Manning's War Novel *Her Privates We*'. *A.L.S.*, VI, 1974, 404-17.

Marwil, Jonathan. 'Combative Companions: Ezra Pound and Frederic Manning'. *Helix*, Nos. 13-14, 1983, 9-15.

---. 'Frederic Manning: A Retrospective in the Form of an Introduction'. *Saint Louis Literary Supplement*, I, No. 4, 1977, 12-14.

---. *Frederic Manning: An Unfinished Life.* (Durham, N.C.: Duke University Press; North Ryde, N S W.: A.& R., 1988). Reviewed by L. Clancy, *Age Saturday Extra*, 27 August, 1988, 15; C. Eagle, *ABR*, No. 108, 1989, 12-14; A. Kershaw, *Weekend Australian*, 11-12 June, 1988, Weekend 15.

---. 'Frederic Manning's Passionate Perfection'. *S.M.H.*, 25 November, 1978, 12.

Parfitt, George. 'Frederic Manning and the Great War'. *Journal of Commonwealth Literature*, XVI, 1981, No. 1, 87-95.

Pringle, J.M. Douglas. '*Her Privates We*: An Aesthete Goes to War'. In *The Australian Experience: Critical essays on Australian Novels*, edited by W.S. Ramson (Canberra: Australian National University Press, 1974), 121-40. Reprinted from Pringle's *On Second Thoughts* Sydney: A.& R., 1971.

Raleigh, John Henry. '"The Finest and Noblest Book of Men in War": Frederic Manning's *Her Privates We*'. In *Critical Reconstructions: The Relationship of Fiction *and Life*, edited by Robert M. Polhemus and Roger B. Henkle (Stanford: Stanford UP, 1994), 231-50.

Rutherford, Andrew. 'The Common Man as Hero - Literature of the Western Front'. In his *The Literature of War: Five Studies in Heroic Virtue*. (London: Macmillan, 1978), 64-112, esp. 99-112.

Smith, C.N. 'The Very Plain Song of It: Frederic Manning, *Her Privates, We*'. In *The First World War in Fiction*, edited by Holger Klein (London: Macmillan, 1976), 174-82.

MARSHALL, ALAN

Collection

Alan Marshall's Australia. (Melbourne: Hyland House, 1981).
Reviewed by V. Lindesay, *ABR*, No. 35, 1981, 14; A.A. Phillips, *Age*, 26 September, 1981, 27.

Alan Marshall's Battlers. Compiled by Gwen Hardisty. (Melbourne: Hyland House, 1983). Reviewed by K. Ahearne, *National Times*, 20-26 January, 1984, 34; B. Jefferis, *Weekend Australian Magazine*, 7-8 January, 1984, 11; K. Tennant, *Hemisphere*, XXVIII, 1984, 364; J. Waten, *Age Saturday Extra*, 5 November, 1983, 15.

Fiction

The Complete Stories. (Melbourne: Nelson, 1977).
Reviewed by D. Green, *National Times*, 7-12 November, 1977, 53; J. Hepworth, *Nation Review*, 12-18 January, 1978, 16; J. McLaren, *ABR*, No. 1, 1978, 26-27; A. Mitchell, *Quadrant*, XXII, No. 6, 1978, 76-77; B. Morrow, *Advertiser*, 5 November, 1977, 25.

How Beautiful Are Thy Feet. (Melbourne: Gold Star, 1972). First published Melbourne: Chesterhill Press, 1949.
Reviewed by S. Despoja, *Advertiser*, 18 November, 1972, 22; A.A. Phillips, *Nation Review*, 30 September-6 October, 1972, 1477; M. Wood, *National Times*, 2-7 October, 1972, 23.

Short Stories. (South Melbourne, London: Nelson, 1973). Includes Jack Lindsay, 'Alan Marshall's Writing', reprinted from *Meanjin*, 1969.
Reviewed by R. Campbell, *Bulletin*, 16 March, 1974, 47; P. Harding, *Nation Review*, 12-18 October, 1973, 1655; N. Keesing, *S.M.H.*, 6 October, 1973, 22; R. Park, *National Times*, 15-20 October, 1973, 24 (see also D. Goodall, *National Times*, 5-10 November, 1973, 41).

Non-Fiction

Alan Marshall Talking. Ed. Edward Harding (Melbourne: Longman Cheshire, 1978).
Reviewed by M. Clarke, *24 Hours*, IV, No. 1, 1979, 52-53; M. Eldridge, *Canberra Times*, 24 February, 1979, 17; G. Hutton, *Age*, 30 September, 1978, 25; E. Lindsay, *ABR*, No. 6, 1978, 5-6; G. Sprod, *S.M.H.*, 28 October, 1978, 19; B. Wannan, *National Times*, 14 October, 1978, 42; M. Williams, *Courier-Mail*, 16 September, 1978, 19.

Hammers Over the Anvil. (Melbourne: Thomas Nelson (Australia), 1975).
Reviewed by W. Blaxland, *S.M.H.*, 20 December, 1975, 17; K. Tennant, *Hemisphere*, XX, No. 8, 1976, 28-29; J. Waten, *Age*, 18 October, 1975, 18.

I Can Jump Puddles; This Is the Grass; In Mine Own Heart. These titles were republished in Melbourne by Cheshire, 1971; 1972; 1972 respectively. They were originally published by Cheshire in 1955; 1962 and 1963 respectively.
Reviewed by N. Keesing, *Bulletin*, 25 March, 1972, 47-49; E. Kynaston, *Review*, 4-10 March, 1972, 557; J. Murray, *Australian*, 29 April, 1972, 19.

These Are my People. (Melbourne: Currey O'Neil, 1984). First published Melbourne:

Cheshire, 1944. Reviewed by D. Grant, *CRNLE Reviews Journal*, No. 2, 1985, 16-18; B. Hunter, *Courier-Mail*, 28 April, 1984, 26; A.A. Phillips, *Nation Review*, 30 September-6 October, 1972, 1477; L. Ward, *Canberra Times*, 16 June, 1984, 18; J. Waten, *Age Saturday Extra*, 5 May, 1984, 16.

'Some Aspects of the Writer's Craft: A Talk'. *Opinion*, X, No. 2, 1966, 20-30.

    Critical Material

'Author to Receive Award'. *Canberra Times*, 8 July, 1972, 17. Other news reports *Age*, 6 May, 1972, 14; *Age*, 23 September, 1972, 14; *Canberra Times*, 23 September, 1972, 1; *S.M.H.*, 8 November, 2; *Age*, 18 December, 1972, 2.

'Frank Cheshire Tells his Story'. *Age*, 5 April, 1975, 23. Marshall's publisher.

Adams, Phillip. 'A Bank for the Precious, Unused Years'. *Age*, 13 July, 1974, 9. Similar article, 'The Story-Teller Supreme', in *S.M.H.*, 20 July, 1974, 9.

---. 'Alan Marshall: Last Work from Sick Bed'. *S.M.H.*, 23 January, 1984, 4. Obituary.

---. 'The Puddles that still Shine in the Afterglow'. *Weekend Australian Magazine*, 4-5 February, 1984, 2.

Aiton, Douglas. 'Still Jumping Puddles'. *Age*, 20 October, 1973, 9.

Bain, Phillip. 'A Portrait of Alan Marshall'. *Tribune*, 26 September, 1979, 12.

Baster, Peter. 'Alan Marshall's Last Interview'. *Overland*, No. 96, 1984, 25-26.

Beasley, Jack. 'Gurrawilla the Song Maker: Alan Marshall: Writer Versus Cult Figure'. In his *Red Letter Days*. (Sydney: Australasian Book Society, 1979), 1-52.

Collins, Martin. 'Gurawilla [sic] proves that a good story is still best'. *Australian*, 18 July, 1967, 16.

Colmer, John. 'Alan Marshall's Autobiographical Trilogy'. In his *Australian Autobiography: A Personal Quest* (Melbourne: O.U.P., 1989), 16-31.

Dunlevy, Maurice. 'Alan Marshall - Still "Jumping" at 79'. *Canberra Times*, 7 June, 1981, 7.

---. 'The Literary Puddles That Grew to a Flood'. *Canberra Times*, 16 November, 1973, 14.

Innes, Prue. 'Russia Honours Alan Marshall'. *Age*, 22 July, 1977, 2.

Irving, Freda, and Collins, Martin. 'Alan's Best Gift Was Showing how to Jump Puddles'. *Weekend Australian Magazine*, 28-29 January, 1984, 20.

Lindsay, Elaine. 'A Neglected Novel: Alan Marshall's Factory'. *Overland*, No. 73, 1978, 42-44. *How Beautiful are thy Feet.*

Lindsay, Jack. 'A Triumph over Adversity: Comments on Alan Marshall's Writing'. *Meanjin*, XXVIII, 1969, 437-45. Reprinted in his *Decay and Renewal*. (Sydney: Wild & Woolley, 1976), 335-48.

Loughrey, Lance. 'Under Alan Marshall's Spell'. *Age Saturday Extra*, 28 January, 1984, 11.

Marks, Harry. *I Can Jump Oceans: The World of Alan Marshall*. (Melbourne: Thomas Nelson (Australia), 1976). Reviewed by M. Armitage, *Advertiser*, 13 November, 1976, 21; L. Clancy, *Overland*, No. 69, 1978, 68-71; J. Croft, *A.L.S.*, IX, 1979, 125-27; M. Macleod, *S.M.H.*, 18 December, 1976, 13; A.A. Phillips, *Age*, 27 November, 1976, 19; P. Thompson, *Australian*, 23 March, 1977, 10.

---. 'Journey over Plains and Peaks'. *Australian*, 29 April, 1972, 19. Interview.

---. 'Talking to Alan Marshall: Notes for a Biography'. *Overland*, No. 57, 1973/74, 12-13.

McLaren, John. 'Discontinuous Autobiography: Some Work of Alan Marshall and Bruce Beaver'. In *Autobiographical and Biographical Writing in the Commonwealth*, edited by Doireann MacDermott (Sadabell, Barcelona: Editorial AUSA, 1984, 147-151.

---. 'Looking Back from the Hilltops'. *ABR*, No. 58, 1984, 18-19.

Morrison, John. *The Happy Warrior*. (Fairfield, Vic.: Pascoe Publishing, 1987). Contains four essays on Alan Marshall. 'Alan Marshall', 11-14, reprinted from

Walkabout, XVI, No. 12, 8-9; 'The Writer and the Swagman', 15-30, reprinted from *Overland*, No. 42, 1969, 15-21, also reprinted in John Morrison, *Australian by Choice* (Adelaide: Rigby, 1973), 71-86; 'The Big Drink', 31-39, reprinted from *Age*, 5 September, 1964, 21, also reprinted in *Transition*, edited by Nancy Keesing (Sydney: A.& R., 1970), 186-92; 'The Happy Warrior', 40-50, reprinted from *Overland*, No. 96, 1984, 21-24.
Mudie, Ian. 'Alan Marshall, Storyteller'. *Issue*, II, No. 5, 1972, 24-25.
O'Grady, Suellen. 'Broth of a Boy Becomes a Braw Old Man'. *Weekend Australian Magazine*, 13-14 June, 1981, 13.
Phillips, A.A. 'A Fighter with a Gift for Friendship'. *Age*, 23 January, 1984, 9.
Sayers, Stuart. 'Two Letters from Katrina'. *Age*, 22 December, 1973, 12.
---. 'Unusual Man and his World'. *Age*, 20 November, 1976, 18.
Waten, Judah. 'Alan Marshall - an Obituary'. *Australian Author*, XVI, No. 1, 1984, 15.
---. 'Sydney *and* the Bush'. *S.M.H.*, 10 January, 1970, 16.
White, John. *Alan Marshall and the Victorian Writers' League*; with a brief preface by Dick Diamond. (Kuranda, Qld.: Rams Skull Press, 1987).

MARTIN, CATHERINE

Fiction
An Australian Girl. Introduction by Elizabeth Webby. (London, Sydney: Pandora, 1988). First published London: Bentley, 1890.
Reviewed by B. Levy, *Australian Society*, VII, No. 10, 1988, 48-49; M. McClusky, *ABR*, No. 104, 1988, 30-32.
The Incredible Journey. Introduction by Margaret Allen (Sydney: Pandora, 1987). First published London: Jonathon Cape, 1923.
Reviewed by S. McKernan, *Times on Sunday*, 23 August, 1987, 33; P. Pierce, *Age Saturday Extra*, 5 September, 1987, 13; H. Thomson, *ABR*, No. 91, 1987, 6-7.
The Silent Sea. Edited by Rosemary Foxton. (Sydney: U of New South Wales P., 1995). Colonial Texts 4. Originally published London: Bentley, 1892.

Critical Material
Ackland, Michael. '"Wrecked! Through All Eternity!": Faith and Gender Issues in Catherine Martin's *The Explorers and Other Poems*'. *Southerly*, 54.2, 1994, 149-68.
Allen, Margaret. 'Catherine Martin : An Australian Girl?'. In *A Bright and Fiery Troop: Australian Women Writers of the Nineteenth Century*, edited by Debra Adelaide (Ringwood: Penguin, 1988), 151-64.
---. 'Catherine Martin, Writer: Her Life and Ideas'. *A.L.S.*, XIII, No. 2, 1987, 184-197. Includes bibliography.
---. 'Reading Catherine Martin's *An Australian Girl*'. In *Southwords: Essays on South Australian Writing*, edited by Philip Butterss (Kent Town, SA: Wakefield, 1995), 46-61.
Bradstock, Margaret. 'Landscape and Environment in the Novels of Catherine Martin'. *Margin*, 36, 1995, 13-15.
Foxton, Rosemary. '"Another Fresh Australian Tale": The American Publication of Catherine Martin's *The Silent Sea*'. *A.L.S.*, 15.4, 1992, 350-54.
Lee, Christopher. 'The Australian Girl Catches the First Feminist Wave'. *Hecate*, 19.1, 1993, 124-33.
---. 'Strategies of Power and Catherine Martin's *An Australian Girl*'. *Southerly*, 51.2, 1991, 189-206.
---. 'Women, Romance and the Nation: The Reception of Catherine Martin's *An Australian Girl*'. *Australian Feminist Studies*, 17, 1993, 67-80.

MARTIN, DAVID
Fiction
Foreigners. (Adelaide: Rigby, 1981).
Reviewed by D. Carter, *Age*, 24 October, 1981, 24; M. Eldridge, *Canberra Times*, 6 February, 1982, 18; N. Keesing, *ABR*, No. 38, 1982, 27-28; C. Semmler, *ABR*, No. 43, 1982, 31; G. Windsor, *S.M.H.*, 24 October, 1981, 49.

Frank and Francesca. (Melbourne: Nelson (Australia), 1972). Reviewed by D. Dugan, *Age*, 30 September, 1972 14; A.B. Ingram, *S.M.H.*, 25 November, 1972, 23; W. McVitty, *Nation Review*, 4-10 November, 1972, 98; R. Park, *Sunday Telegraph*, 5 November, 1972, 25; S. Sayers, *Age*, 16 September, 1973, 14; *T.L.S.*, 15 June, 1973, 680; R. Wighton, *ABR*, XI, 1972, 46-47.

The Hero of Too. (Melbourne: Cassell, 1965). Also published as *The Hero of the Town.* (New York: Morrow, 1965).
Reviewed by R.F. Brissenden, *Australian*, 11 September, 1965, 10; G.K.W. Johnston, *Canberra Times*, 18 September, 1965, 13; N. Keesing, *ABR*, IV, 1965, 207 and *The Bridge*, II, No. 2, 1966, 55-6; L.V. Kepert, *S.M.H.*, 28 August, 1965, 16; J. McLaren, *Overland*, No. 33, 1966, 43-4; Scrutarius, *Walkabout*, XXXII, No. 4, 1966, 48; R.T., *Twentieth Century*, XX, 1966, 374-5; M. Wilding, *Southerly*, XXVI, 1966, 58-9.

Hughie. (Melbourne: Nelson, 1971).
Reviewed by E. Collins, *Sunday Australian*, 22 August, 1971, 22; G. Hutchings, *Canberra Times*, 16 October, 1971, 15; N. Keesing, *Bulletin*, 31 July, 1971, 49.

The King Between. (Melbourne: Cassell, 1966). Also published as *The Littlest Neutral* (New York: Crown, 1966).
Reviewed by M. Dunlevy, *Canberra Times*, 21 May, 1966, 11; N. Jillett, *Age*, 28 May, 1966, 25; J.M[anifold]., *Overland*, No. 35, 1966, 57; D. Mortier, *Australian Left Review*, No. 2, 1966, 59-60; I. Rowlands, *ABR*, V, 1966, 159; Scrutarius, *Walkabout*, XXXII, No. 10, 1966, 49-51; K. Thomas, *Nation*, 9 July, 1966, 23; R.M. Wilding, *Bulletin*, 30 July, 1966, 45-6.

Where a Man Belongs. (Melbourne: Cassell Australia, 1969). Reviewed by T. Forshaw, *Nation*, 23 August, 1969, 22-23 (see also letters to the editor by P. Adams, *Nation*, 6 September, 1969, 15, and D. Whitington, *Nation*, 20 September, 1969, 14); H. Hewitt, *Canberra Times*, 26 April, 1969, 12; B. Kiernan, *Australian*, 3 May, 1969, 19; J. McLaren, *Overland*, No. 42, 1969, 39-40; M. Vintner, *S.M.H.*, 12 April, 1969, 21; D. Whitlock, *ABR*, VIII, 1969, 86-87; M. Wilding, *Southerly*, XXX, 1970, 70-71; M. Wolkowsky, *Bulletin*, 5 April, 1969, 64.

Poetry
The Gift: Poems 1959-1965. (Brisbane: Jacaranda Press, 1966).
Reviewed by T.I. Moore, *Canberra Times*, 19 November, 1966, 10; T. Shapcott, *ABR*, V, 1966, 180; V. Smith, *Bulletin*, 30 July, 1966, 47; A. Taylor, *Overland*, No. 35, 1966, 55-6.

The Idealist. (Brisbane: Jacaranda Press, 1968).
Reviewed by D. Anderson, *Southerly*, XXIX, 1969, 76; B. McPherson, *Canberra Times*, 12 April, 1969, 12; R. Ward, *ABR*, VIII, 44.

Non-Fiction
Fox on My Door: A Journey through My Life. (Blackburn, Vic.: Collins Dove, 1987).

Reviewed by M. Dunkle, *Times on Sunday*, 26 July, 1987, 32; M. Walker, *Fremantle Arts Review*, II, No. 11, 1987, 15; P. Weiniger, *Australian Jewish News*, 16 October, 1987, 10; N. Wheatley, *ABR*, No. 96, 1987, 20-21.

My Strange Friend: An Autobiography. (Sydney: Macmillan, 1991).
Reviewed by L. Clancy, *Age*, 9 November, 1991, Saturday Extra 6; W. Crocker,

Overland, 123, 1991, 87-88; S. Liberman, *ABR*, 136, 1991, 30-31; J. McLaren, *Weekend Australian*, 29-30 June, 1991, Review 5; A.P. Riemer, *S.M.H.*, 15 June, 1991, 41; P. Rolfe, *Bulletin*, 30 July, 1991, 106-07.

On the Road to Sydney. (Melbourne: Nelson, 1971).
Reviewed by A. Macdonald, *S.M.H.*, 26 December, 1970, 11; J.D. Pringle, *Bridge*, VI, No. 1, 1971, 75-76; O. Thomson, *Australian*, 5 December, 1970, 27; C. Turnbull, *Age*, 5 December, 1970, 16; L. Ward, *Canberra Times*, 1 May, 1971, 14.

'Between the Lines'. *Bulletin*, 5 April, 1983, 72. Third in a series.

'David Martin on David Martin (Australian Writers in Profile, 9)'. *Southerly*, XXXI, 1971, 163-69.

'Portrait of the Novel as Play'. *Australian*, 9 April, 1966, 10. Discusses the play, *The Young Wife*, and its relation to the novel.

'Spanish Generation and Cousinhood of Man'. *Bridge*, V, No. 1, 1970, 49-54.

'We of the Thirties'. *Bridge*, VI, No. 2, 1971, 9-14.

'What Do We Write for Today's Young People?' *Age*, 8 July, 1972, 17.

    Critical Material

Buckley, Brian. 'The Improbable Australian'. *Bulletin*, 18 September, 1965, 32.

Factor, June. 'David Martin's Writing for Children'. *Overland*, No. 79, 1980, 47-54.

Green, Cliff. 'David Martin: Our Most Improbable Friend'. *Overland*, 141, 1995, 25-27.

Haddock, Y. 'The Prose Fiction of Jewish Writers of Australia. 1945-1969. Part II'. *Journal of Proceedings of the Australian Jewish Historical Society*, VIII, 1975, 50-56.

Hadgraft, Cecil. 'Indulgence: David Martin's *The Hero of Too*, Frank Dalby Davison's *The White Thorntree*, Dal Stivens's *A Horse of Air*, David Malouf's *Johnno*, and Frank Hardy's *But the Dead are Many*'. In *Studies in the Recent Australian Novel*, edited by K.G. Hamilton (St Lucia: U.Q.P., 1978), 194-224.

Keesing, Nancy. 'Where Does a Man Belong? David Martin and his Work'. *Overland*, No. 63, 1976, 10-13, 15.

McLaren, John. 'David Martin at Eighty'. *ABR*, 177, 1995, 58.

McVitty, Walter. 'Alienation and Belonging:Ivan Southall'. In his *Innocence and Experience: Essays on Contemporary Australian Children's Writers* (Melbourne: Thomas Nelson Australia, 1981), 163-195. Includes notes by Martin and bibliography.

Middleton, Delys E.J. 'Villain or Hero? The Bushranger in *Ralph Rashleigh*, *Robbery under Arms*, and *The Hero of Too*'. *Armidale and District Historical Society Journal and Proceedings*, No. 13, 1970, 27-36.

Neville, Jill. 'On a Children's Walkabout'. *S.M.H.*, 18 November, 1978, 13. Interview.

Raizis, M. Byron. 'The Image of the Greek in Australian Literature'. In *Australian Papers: Yugoslavia, Europe and Australia*, edited by Mirko Jurak (Ljubljana: Edvard Cardelj University, 1983), 115-32.

Sayers, Stuart. 'David Martin Comes Home'. *Age*, 1 March, 1969, 13.

MARTIN, PHILIP

    Poetry

A Bone Flute. (Canberra: A.N.U. Press, 1974).
Reviewed by M. Jurgensen, *Makar*, 10, No. 3, 1975, 43-6; S.E. Lee, *Southerly*, 35, 1975, 304-305; F. Zwicky, *Westerly*, No. 1, 1975, 68-73.

A Flag for the Wind. (Melbourne: Longman Cheshire, 1982).
Reviewed by G. Burn, *Meanjin*, 43, No. 3, 1984, 460-62; A. Caesar, *CRNLE Reviews Journal*, No. 2, 1985, 64-7; K. Goldsworthy, *Age*, 23 July, 1983, 12; F. Kellaway, *Overland*, No. 91, 1983, 56-7; G. Page, *Quadrant*, 29, No. 4, 1985, 71-5.

New and Selected Poems. (Melbourne: Longman Cheshire, 1988).
Reviewed by T. Bishop, *Antipodes*, 4, No. 2, 1990, 140-1; L. Bourke, *Poetry*

Australia, No. 118, 1988, 29-40; H. Cam, *S.M.H.*, 9 July, 1988, 74; J. Grant, *Age Saturday Extra*, 14 May, 1988, 16; K. Hart, *Overland*, No. 113, 1988, 95-6; P. Hodgins, *Antipodes*, 2, No. 2, 1988, 119-120; P. Salom, *ABR*, No. 102, 1988, 36-38.

Voice Unaccompanied. (Canberra: A.N.U. Press, 1970).
Reviewed by M. Irvin, *Twentieth Century*, 25, 1970, 182-4; G. Rowlands, *Makar*, 7, No. 1, 1971, 42.

     Critical Material
Page, Geoff. 'Philip Martin'. In his *A Reader's Guide To Contemporary Australian Poetry* (St. Lucia: U.Q.P., 1995), 188-189.
Rowe, Noel. 'Emotions of a Destiny: The Poetry of Philip Martin'. *Southerly*, 46, No. 1, 1986, 93-113.
Williams, Barbara. 'A Conversation with Philip Martin'. *Antipodes*, 9.1, 1995, 37-38.
---. Interview. 'Malouf, Martin, Murray: The Artists on Their Craft'. *Nimrod*, 36.2, 1993, 135-37.

MASTERS, OLGA

     Fiction
Amy's Children. (St Lucia: U.Q.P., 1987). Republished New York: Norton, 1987.
Reviewed by J. Carrol, *Age Saturday Extra*, 25 April, 1987, 13; B. Jefferis, *Australian Weekend Magazine*, 18-19 April, 1987, 11; N. Keesing, *S.M.H.*, 18 April, 1987, 31; B. Matthews, *Times on Sunday*, 26 April, 1987, 30; S. McKernan, *Bulletin*, 12 May, 1987, 87-88; D.J. O'Hearn, *ABR*, No. 90, 1987, 6-7; B. Walker, *Fremantle Arts Review*, II, No. 7, 1987, 14-15; R. Willbanks, *World Literature Today*, 63.3, 1989, 534; V. Wright, *Weekend Australian. Weekend Magazine*, 31 October-1 November, 1987, 22.

The Home Girls. (St Lucia: U.Q.P., 1982).
Reviewed by E. Jolley, *Fremantle Arts Centre Broadsheet: Books*, IV, No. 1, 1985, 3-4; S. McKernan, *Canberra Times*, 21 January, 1984, 18; L. Potter, *Ash Magazine*, No. 12, 1983, 30-31.

A Long Time Dying. (St Lucia: U.Q.P., 1985).
Reviewed by E. Butel, *National Times*, 6-12 September, 1985, 30; H. Daniel, *Age Saturday Extra*, 14 September, 1985, 15; G. Dutton, *Weekend Australian Magazine*, 7-8 September, 1985, 16; M. Eldridge, *Canberra Times*, 12 October, 1985, B3; K. England, *Advertiser*, 14 September, 1985, 7; K. Goldsworthy, *Island Magazine*, Nos. 25-26, 1986, 116-17; P. Goldsworthy, *S.M.H.*, 5 October, 1985, 46; B. Jefferis, *Overland*, No. 103, 1986, 65-66; E. Perkins, *Quadrant*, XXX, No. 3, 1986, 80-83; J. Perlez, *New York Times Book Review*, 15 March, 1987, 16; L. Shrubb, *Quadrant*, XXXI, No. 3, 1987, 72-74.

Loving Daughters. (St Lucia: U.Q.P., 1985). First published: 1984. Reprinted in paperback: 1985. Also published New York, W. W. Norton, 1993.
Reviewed by J. Bedford, *National Times*, 7-13 September, 1984, 32; H. Daniel, *Age Saturday Extra*, 14 September, 1985, 15; S. Day, *Island Magazine*, No. 22, 1985, 55-56; G. Dutton, *Bulletin*, 25 September, 1984, 98, 100; K. England, *Advertiser Saturday Review*, 27 October, 1984, 39; T. Forshaw, *Quadrant*, XXIX, Nos. 1-2, 1985, 138-140; K. Goldsworthy, *Overland*, No. 97, 1984, 75-77; P. Koch, *Courier-Mail*, 22 September, 1984, 29; J. Lewis, *Fremantle Arts Centre Broadsheet: Books*, III, No. 6, 1984, 2; S. McInerney, S.M.H., 20 October, 1984, 41; A. Mitchell, *Weekend Australian Magazine*, 29-30 September, 1984, 14; H. F. Mosher, *New York Times Book Review*, 16 May, 1993, 10; J. Motion, *T.L.S.*, 18 October, 1985, 1173; G. Rogers, *Womanspeak*, IX, No. 1, 1984, 25; V. Sen, *Canberra Times*, 23 June, 1985, 8; N. Wallace, *LiNQ*, XII, Nos. 1-3, 1985, 78-81.

The Rose Fancier. (St Lucia: U.Q.P.; New York: Norton, 1988).
Reviewed by D. Anderson, *ABR*, No. 102, 1988, 28-30; A. Bellis, *Redoubt*, No. 6,

1989, 70-74; M. Gollan, *S.M.H.*, 2 July, 1988, 75; A. Gurr, *Australian Studies*, No. 4, 1990, 127-29; J. Hanrahan, *Age Saturday Extra*, 9 July, 1988, 11; M. Harris, *Antipodes*, 3.1, 1989, 47; B. Matthews, *Australian Society*, VII, No. 9, 1988, 44-46; W. Noonan, *Weekend Australian*, 23-24 July, 1988, Weekend 16; J. O'Meara, *Lot's Wife*, 28, No. 14, 1988, 56-57; A. Wallace, *Social Alternatives*, 8, No. 2, 1989, 73-4.

Drama
A Working Man's Castle. (Sydney: Currency Press in association with Theatre South, Wollongong, 1988).
Reviewed by D. Jones, *Australasian Drama Studies*, No. 14, 152-54.

Non-Fiction
Olga Masters: Reporting Home: Her Writings as a Journalist. Ed. Deirdre Coleman (St Lucia: U.Q.P., 1990).
Reviewed by C. Baker, *SPAN*, 33, 1992, 175-76; K. Cummings, *S.M.H.*, 11 August, 1990, 73; K. Veitch, *ABR*, No. 124, 1990, 42-43.
'*A Long Time Dying*'. In *A View from Tinsel Town*, edited by Tom Thompson (Ringwood, Vic.: Southerly/Penguin, 1985), 42-46.
'War Gave Women a First Taste of Liberation'. *S.M.H.*, 13 August, 1985, 11.

Critical Material
'Late Starter Who Wrote It Her Way'. *S.M.H.*, 7 October, 1986, 17. Obituary.
Bennett, Bruce. 'Ageing and the Question of "Home" - Olga Masters and Elizabeth Jolley'. In Olga Masters: An Autumn Crocus, edited by William McGaw and Paul Sharrad (Wollongong: New Literatures Research Centre, University of Wollongong, 1990). Reprinted in his *An Australian Compass: Essays on Place and Direction in Australian Literature*. (Fremantle, WA: Fremantle Arts Centre P, 1991), 132-145.
Cotes, Alison, and Randall, D'Arcy. 'A Tribute to Olga Masters'. *ABR*, No. 86, 1986, 4-5. Obituary.
Edelson, Phyllis. 'Olga Masters' Plain Fiction Tells Home Truths'. *Antipodes*, I, No. 2, 1987, 68-70. Review article which discusses *Amy's Children, The Home Girls, Long Time Dying* and *Loving Daughters*.
Ellison, Jennifer. 'Olga Masters'. In her *Rooms of Their Own* (Ringwood, Vic.: Penguin, 1986), 212-229.
Jones, Dorothy. 'Digging Deep: Olga Masters, Storyteller'. *Kunapipi*, VIII, No. 3, 1986, 28-35.
---. 'Drama's Vitallest Expression: The Fiction of Olga Masters'. *A.L.S.*, XIII, No. 1, 1987, 3-14.
---. 'The Fiction of Olga Masters'. *Scarp*, No. 12, 1988, 14-16.
---. 'Writable Realism: The Fiction of Olga Masters'. *SPAN*, 30, 1990, 69-78.
Lewis, Julie. *Olga Masters: A Lot of Living*. (St. Lucia: U.Q.P., 1991). Reviewed by L. Clancy, *Age*, 29 February, 1992, Saturday Extra 7; H. Dakin, *Southerly*, 52.2, 1992, 155-59; D. Fontaine, *Antipodes*, 6.1, 1992, 93; J. Hooton, *Westerly*, 37.2, 1992, 83-84; M. Jones, *S.M.H.*, 30 November, 1991, 49; C. Keneally, *Weekend Australian*, 19-20 October, 1991, Review 5; M. Lord, *Overland*, 126, 1992, 94-95; A. Sant, *ABR*, 137, 1991, 12; F. Thompson, *Northern Perspective*, 15.2, 1992, 114-15. See also Marion Dixon, 'A Conversation with Julie Lewis'. *Westerly*, 37.2, 1992, 57-67. Extract, 'The Worst of Times', published in *Island*, 46, 1991, 24-27.
---. 'Scrambled Lives'. *Hecate*, 17.1, 1991, special issue *Women/Australia/Theory*, 74-78.
Lord, Mary. 'Celebrating Olga Masters'. *ABR*, No. 103, 1988, 32-34. Discusses the memorial conference on Olga Masters held at the University of Wollongong, 10-12 July, 1988. Also reviews *A Working Man's Castle* (see above) which was performed at the conference. A letter to the editor from Sandra Gorman about this review appeared in *ABR*, No. 105, 1988, 4-5.

McGaw, William and Sharrad, Paul eds. *Olga Masters: An Autumn Crocus* (Wollongong: New Literatures Research Centre, University of Wollongong, 1990). Proceedings of Olga Masters Memorial Conference, 8-10 July, 1988.

Randall, D'Arcy. 'Keeping Mum: A Memoir of Olga Masters'. *Island*, 50, 1992, 54-58. Reprinted in *Antipodes*, 6.1, 1992, 66-72.

Riem, Antonella. 'Isolation in Olga Masters' *The Home Girls* and Beverley Farmer's *Milk*'. In her *The Labyrinths of Self: A Collection of Essays on Australian and Caribbean Literature*. (Leichhardt, N.S.W.: FILEF. Italo-Australian Publications, 1987), 141-151.

Suárez Lafuente, Maria, and Isabel Carrera Suárez. 'The Voices of Silence in Olga Masters' Narrative'. *Commonwealth* (France), 13.2, 1991, 109-14.

Wright, Mary. 'To Marry the Pen with Imagination'. *Fremantle Arts Review*, II, No. 6, 1987, 6-7.

MATHERS, PETER

Fiction

A Change for the Better. (Adelaide: Words and Visions Publications, 1984).
Reviewed by D. Anderson, *National Times*, 13-19 April, 1984, 33; R. Blaber, *CRNLE Reviews Journal*, No. 2, 1985, 32-33; J. Gitzen, *ABR*, No. 61, 1984, 20-21; N. Phelan, *S.M.H.*, 21 April, 1984, 28; G. Turner, *Age Saturday Extra*, 21 April, 1984, 14; G. Windsor, *Overland*, No. 96, 1984, 66-68.

Trap. (Melbourne: Cassell, 1966).
Reviewed by J. Barbour, *Southerly*, XXVI, 1966, 279-80; L.J. Clancy, *Meanjin*, XXV, 1966, 485-8; M. Dunlevy, *Canberra Times*, 18 June, 1966, 10; M. MacCallum, *Nation*, 23 July, 1966, 23; D. Martin, *Age*, 21 May, 1966, 21; J. McLaren, *Overland*, No. 34, 1966, 50; G. Scott, *Bulletin*, 25 June, 1966, 43; M. Vintner, *S.M.H.*, 4 June, 1966, 14; D. Whitelock, *ABR*, V, 1966, 153 and see also comment by S. Murray-Smith, *ABR*, VI, 1966, 3.

The Wort Papers. (North Melbourne: Cassell Australia, 1972).
Reviewed by D. Anderson, *Bulletin*, 16 December, 1972, 56; C. Harrison-Ford, *Australian*, 17 February, 1973, 31; B. Jefferis, *S.M.H.*, 16 December, 1972, 20 and *Hemisphere*, XVII, No. 8, 1973, 37-38; N. Keesing, *Southerly*, XXXIII, 1973, 345-46; D.J. O'Hearn, *Age*, 9 December, 1972, 16; M. Perrin, *Canberra Times*, 10 March, 1973, 11; A. Roberts, *Advertiser*, 18 November, 1972, 22. O. Webster, *Overland*, No. 55, 1973, 56-58; M. Wilding, *National Times*, 15-20 January, 1973, 18.

Non-Fiction

'Extractions (Australian Writers in Profile, 10)'. *Southerly*, XXXI, 1971, 210-15.

'Pittsburgh Identity: 0000000621'. *Overland*, No. 39, 1968, 12-16. Autobiographical.

Critical Material

Buckley, Vincent. 'Peter Mathers' *Trap*', *Ariel* (Calgary), V, No. 3, 1974, 115 27.

Burns, Robert. 'The Underdog-Outsider. The Achievement of Mathers' *Trap*'. *Meanjin*, XXIX, 1970, 95-105.

Cameron Richard. 'The Art of Being a Writer'. *Bulletin*, 6 July, 1968, 34. Comment on seminar organized by the Society of Authors in Melbourne.

Clancy, L.J. 'Peter Mathers' Words'. *Meanjin*, XXXIII, 1974, 272-77.

---. 'An Interview with Peter Mathers'. *A.L.S.*, VIII, 1977, 197-201.

Collinson, Laurence. 'Seeing Mathers Subjectively'. *Overland*, No. 35, 1966, 11-12.

Daniel, Helen. *Liars: Australian New Novelists*. (Ringwood, Vic.: Penguin, 1988), 43-70.

---. 'Narrator and Outsider in *Trap* and *Johnno*'. *Southerly*, XXXVII, 1977, 184-95.

Dare, Tim. 'Mathers' Utopia'. *Australian*, 15 May, 1971, 17.

Dovey, Teresa. 'A Late Entry in the Uppersass Reporting Prize: Another "Writing" of Peter Mathers' *Trap* and *The Wort Papers*'. *Southern Review*, XVII, 1984, 188-202.

McGregor, Craig (ed.). *In the Making*. (Melbourne: Nelson Australia, 1969), 38-43.

O'Hearn, D.J. 'Re-Reading Peter Mathers'. *Overland*, No. 85, 1981, 47-58.

Watson, Betty L. 'The Australian Image: Social Realism, Send-Up and Satire'. *English in Australia*, No. 18, 1971, 11-21.

MAURICE, FURNLEY (FRANK WILMOT)

Critical Material

Headon, David. 'Frank Wilmot, the First Australian Modernist'. *Meanjin*, XLI, 1982, 469-78.

Heuzenroeder, John. 'Poet and Populace: Frank Wilmot's Poetry'. *Meanjin*, XXXIII, 1974, 47-55.

Palmer, Vance. 'Frank Wilmot'. In *The Writer in Australia*, edited by John Barnes (Melbourne: O.U.P., 1969), 171-90. This essay first published Melbourne: Frank Wilmot Memorial Committee, 1942.

Stone, Leon. '"Furnley Maurice" vs. "The Red Pagan"'. *Biblionews and Australian Notes & Queries*, IV, Nos. 3-4, 1970, 10-12.

Walker, David. *Dreams and Disillusion: A Search for Australian Cultural Identity*. (Canberra: A.N.U. Press, 1976).

Wilde, W.H. *Three Radicals*. (Melbourne: O.U.P., 1969). Australian Writers and Their Work. Discusses Maurice, Gilmore and O'Dowd. Reviewed by A. Mitchell, *A.L.S.*, V, 1971, 99-100.

MEREDITH, LOUISA ANNE

Critical Material

Ellis, Vivienne Rae. *Louisa Anne Meredith: Tigress in Exile* (Sandy Bay, Tasmania: Blubber Head Press, 1979). Biography.

Grimshaw, Patricia. 'Female Lives and the Tradition of Nation-Making'. *Voices*, 5.3, 1995, 30-44. Includes discussion of Louisa Meredith and Louisa Lawson.

Johnston, Judith. '"Woman's Testimony": Imperialist Discourse in the Professional Colonial Travel Writing of Meredith and Traill'. *Australian & New Zealand Studies in Canada*, 11, 1994, 34-55.

MILLER, ALEX

Fiction

The Ancestor Game. (Ringwood, Vic.: Penguin, 1992).

Reviewed by H. Daniel, *Age*, 15 August, 1992, Saturday Extra, 9; S. Masson, *ABR*, 143, 1992, 4-5; P. Pierce, *Bulletin*, 15 September, 1992, 100-01; A. Riemer, *S.M.H.*, 15 August, 1992, 43; T. Shapcott, *Overland*, 128, 1992, 79-81; G. Windsor, *Weekend Australian*, 15-16 August, 1992, Review 4.

The Sitters. (Ringwood, Vic.: Viking, 1995).

Reviewed by V. Brady, *ABR*, 170, 1995, 43-44 (see also interview with Miller by H. Daniel, 44-46); J. Chimonyo, *24 Hours* (June), 1995, 32, 34; A. Coombs, *Weekend Australian*, 27-28 May, 1995, Review 8; H. Horton, *Imago*, 7.3, 1995, 139; M. McGirr, *Eureka Street*, 5.5, 1995, 44; J. Maiden, *Overland*, 141, 1995, 82-84; A. Riemer, *S.M.H.*, 6 May, 1995, Spectrum 13A; J. Rodriguez, *Age*, 29 April, 1995, Saturday Extra 8.

The Tivington Nott. (London: Robert Hale; Cheltenham, Vic.: Princeton Books, 1989).

Reviewed by J. Dabbs, *ABR*, 113, 1989, 47; M. Halligan, *Weekend Australian*, 22-23 July, 1989, Weekend 8; J. Larkin, *Age*, 17 June, 1989, Saturday Extra, 10; G. Manning, *Age Monthly Review*, 9.7, 1989, 5-6.

Watching the Climbers on the Mountain. (Sydney: Pan Books, 1988).
Reviewed by G. Flynn, *Weekend Australian*, 19-20 November, 1988, 9; N. Keesing, *S.M.H.*, 17 September, 1988, 78; H. Willis, *Age*, 15 October, 1988, Saturday Extra 15.

Non-Fiction
'Chasing My Tale'. *Kunapipi*, 15.3, 1993, 1-6. Discusses *The Ancestor Game*.
'This is How Its Going to be Then'. *ABR*, 127, 1990-91, 30. Discusses *The Tivington Nott*.
'The Limits of Democracy'. *Eureka Street*, 4.4, 1994, 29-32. Autobiographical.

Critical Material
Caterson, Simon. 'Playing the Ancestor Game: Alex Miller Interviewed by Simon Caterson'. *Journal of Commonwealth Literature*, 29.2, 1994, 5-11.
Jacobs, Lyn. 'Ancestral Furies: The Fiction of Beth Yahp, Ding Xiaoqui and Alex Miller'. *New Literatures Review*, 28/29, 1995-96, 153-64.
Jørgensen, Mette. 'Readings of Dialogue in Alex Miller's *The Ancestor Game*'. *Kunapipi*, 15.3, 1993, 12-20.
Sorensen, Rosemary. 'Reputations Made and Unmade: Rosemary Sorensen Talks to Evan Green, Alex Miller and Peter Carey'. *ABR*, 134, 1991, 10-11.

MILLER, E. MORRIS

Non-Fiction
'Some Public Library Memoirs, 1900-1913'. Introduced and edited by Derek Drinkwater. *La Trobe Library Journal*, IX, 1985, 49-83. Memoirs of his work in what is now the State Library of Victoria.

Critical Material
E.M.M.: A Handlist of the Published Works and Manuscripts of Edmund Morris Miller. (Hobart: Morris Miller Library, University of Tasmania, 1970).
'E. Morris Miller as University Librarian'. *Australian Academic and Research Libraries*, XV, No. 4, 1984, 216-225.
Borchardt, D.H. 'E. Morris Miller'. *Australian Library Journal*, XXIV, 1975, 500-01. Letter to the editor.
Hadgraft, Cecil. 'Frederick T. Macartney's Autobiography'. *Meanjin*, XXVIII, 1969, 552-57.
McVilly, David. 'Personalities From the Past: Edmund Morris Miller, 1881-1964: A Proposal for a Biography'. *Australian Library Journal*, XXIV, 1975, 315-17.
Rich, Joe. 'A Renegade Victorian Librarian on the Warpath'. *Age Saturday Extra*, 27 July, 1985, 15.
Roe, Michael. 'Edmund Morris Miller: 1881-1964'. In his *Nine Australian Progressives: Vitalism in Bourgeois Social Thought 1890-1960*. (St Lucia: U.Q.P., 1984), 280-314.

MODJESKA, DRUSILLA

Fiction
The Orchard. (Port Melbourne: Macmillan, 1994).
Reviewed by D. Carter, *Weekend Australian*, 22-23 October, 1994, Review 5; L. Davison, *ABR*, 164, 1994, 11-12 (see also interview by R. Sorensen 12-14); D. Falconer, *Age*, 10 September, 1994, Saturday Extra 9; M. Fraser, *Voices*, 4.4, 1994-95, 91-98; D. Hecq, *AWBR*, 6.4, 1994, 2-3; M. Jones, *S.M.H.*, 17 September, 1994, Spectrum 11A; S.K. Martin, *Meanjin*, 53.4, 1994, 767-69; H. Neilson, *Westerly*, 40.1, 1995, 84-85; M. Ryan, *Overland*, 138, 1995, 80-81.

Poppy. (Ringwood, Vic.: McPhee Gribble, 1990).
Reviewed by B. Brook, *Australian Women's Book Review*, 3.1, 1991, 7-8; E. Campion, *Bulletin*, 2 October, 1990, 112; M. de Gabrielle, *Span*, 32, 1991, 126-27;

R. Gerster, *Age*, 13 October, 1990, Saturday Extra 10; K. Jennings, *S.M.H.*, 13 October, 1990, 78;M. Lord, *Overland*, 122, 1991, 65-66; B. Milech, *Antipodes*, 7.2 (1993): 155-56; S. Powell, *Australian Society*, 9.10, 1990, 34; T. Prenzler, *Social Alternatives*, 10.1, 1991, 67-68; P. Quick, *Mattoid*, 40, 1991, 129-31; L. Trainor, *Weekend Australian*, 3-4 November, 1990, Review 7; S. Trigg, *Scripsi*, 6.3, 1990, 137-42; B. Tully, *Blast*, 13-14, 1990, 32; G. Whitlock, *Southerly*, 51.2, 1991, 316-19; W. Wynne, *ABR* 124, 1990, 18.

Non-Fiction
Exiles at Home: Australian Women Writers 1925-1945. (Sydney: A.& R., 1981). Reviewed by M. Barnard, *S.M.H.*, 12 December, 1981, 40; J. Breen, *New Statesman*, 12 March, 1982, 19-20; H. Clarke, *Social Alternatives*, 3.2, 1983, 71; C. Ferrier, *Hecate*, 8.1, 1982, 77-81; G. Jones, *Westerly*, 27.2, 1982, 100-04; M. McLeod, *Span*, 14, 1982, 20-24; C. Munro, *ALS*, 10, 1982, 533-35; R. Pringle, *Labour History*, 44, 1983, 135-36; E. Riddell, *Bulletin*, 26 January, 1982, 90; B. Roberts, *Historical Studies*, 20, 1983, 483-84; S. Sheridan, *Meanjin*, 41, 1982, 89-96; K. Stewart, *Meridian*, 1.2, 1982, 68-70;J. Turner, *ABR*, 40, 1982, 4-5; S. Walker, *Island Magazine*, 13, 1982, 55-57.

Critical Material
Duncan, Catherine. 'Exile Abroad'. *Meanjin*, 42, 1983, 276-79.

Hopkins, Lekkie. 'Reading *Poppy*'. *Island*, 64, 1995, 52-55.

Koval, Ramona. 'Drusilla Modjeska'. Interview. In her *One to One* (Sydney: ABC Enterprises, 1992), 18-24.

Levy, Bronwen. 'Looking in Mirrors: Reflecting on *Poppy*'. *Australian Feminist Studies*, 16, 1992, 159-69.

Smith, S. 'Re-Citing, Re-Siting, and Re-Sighting Likeness: Reading the Family Archive in Drusilla Modjeska's *Poppy*, Donna Williams' *Nobody Nowhere* and Sally Morgan's *My Place*'. *Modern Fiction Studies*, 40.3, 1994, 509-42.

Thomson, Helen. 'Drusilla Modjeska's *Poppy*: The Feminist Quest'. In her *Biofictions: Brian Matthews, Drusilla Modjeska and Elizabeth Jolley*. Monograph 25. (Townsville: James Cook U of North Queensland, Foundation for Australian Literary Studies, 1994), 19-35.

Whitlock, Gillian. 'Graftworks: Australian Women's Writing 1970-1990'. In *Gender, Politics and Fiction: Twentieth Century Australian Women's Novels* 2nd Edition, edited by Carole Ferrier (St Lucia: U.Q.P., 1992), 236-58.

MOLL, ERNEST G.

Poetry
The Road to Cactus-Land: A Group of Poems. (Sydney: Edwards and Shaw, 1971). Reviewed by K. England, *Advertiser*, 16 October, 1971, 20; E. Irvin, *S.M.H.*, 19 June, 1971, 21; T.W. Shapcott, *ABR*, X, 1971, 150; K. Slessor, *Daily Telegraph* (Sydney), 24 April, 1971, 10.

Critical Material
Gardiner, Thomas J. 'The Poetry of E.G. Moll'. *Southerly*, XXV, No. 3, 1965, 173-81.

MOORE, T. INGLIS

Critical Material
'Literature-Study Pioneer dies in Canberra'. *Canberra Times*, 24 July, 1978, 3. Other obituary notices and comments from Helen Frizell, *S.M.H.*, 5 August, 1978, 19; L. Rees, *Australian Author*, X, No. 4, 1978, 31-32; *S.M.H.*, 25 July, 1978, 10; Douglas Stewart, *S.M.H.*, 10 August, 1978, 6.

Christesen, Clem. 'T. Inglis Moore'. *A.L.S.*, IX, 1979, 117-19. Eulogy.

Hope, A.D. 'In Memoriam: T. Inglis Moore'. *Notes & Furphies*, No. 2, 1979, 1.

---. 'Tom Inglis Moore: A Pioneer in Australian Literary Studies'. *Meanjin*, XXVI, 1967, 177-179.

MOOREHEAD, ALAN

Non-Fiction

Cooper's Creek. (London: Hamilton, 1963).
Reviewed by G. Dutton, *ABR*, III, 1964, 96; M.H. Ellis, *Bulletin*, 8 February, 1964, 42-3.

Critical Material

Heyward, Michael. 'Alan Moorehead'. *Voices*, 5.1, 1995, 79-89. Also published in *Quadrant*, 39.6, 1995, 23-28.
Pocock, Tom. *Alan Moorehead*. (London: Bodley Head, 1990). Reviewed by T. Bonyhady, *ABR*, No. 123, 1990, 31-32; P. Knightley, *S.M.H.*, 17 March, 1990, 80.
Semmler, Clement. 'War Correspondents in Australian Literature: an Outline'. *A.L.S.*, XII, No. 2, 1985, 194-206.

MOOREHEAD, FINOLA

Fiction

A Modern Classic: Handwritten. (Fitzroy, Vic.: Sybylla Co-operative, 1986).
Reviewed by K. Hemensley, *Age Monthly Review*, 6.3, 1986, 3-4.

Quilt: A Collection of Prose. (Melbourne: Sybylla Co-operative, 1985).
Reviewed by T. Chartay, *Tribune*, 6 November, 1988, 11; S. Hawthorne, *Age*, 20 December, 1986, Saturday Extra 10; K. Hemensley, *Age Monthly Review*, 6.3, 1986, 3-4; S. McKernan, *ABR*, 81, 1986, 6-7; B. Saxby, *Muse Communique*, 5, December 1985 - January 1986, 27-28; *Womanspeak*, 9.5, 1985/86, 24.

Remember the Tarantella. (Sydney: Primavera P, 1987).
Reviewed by K. Constable, *Antithesis*, 3.2, 1990, 208-10; H. Daniel, *S.M.H.*, 2 January, 1988, 39; J. Hanrahan, *Times on Sunday*, 24 January, 1988, 33; S. Hawthorne, *Age*, 16 January, 1988, Saturday Extra 11; M. Moss, *ABR*, 98, 1988, 33-34; S. Soldatow, *Weekend Australian*, 26-27 December, 1987, Weekend 11; *Womanspeak*, 11.4, 1988, 23.

Still Murder. (Ringwood, Vic.: Penguin, 1991).
Reviewed by K. Ahearne, *Age*, 23 March, 1991, Saturday Extra 8; R. Brissenden, *Voices*, 1.2, 1991, 100-03; H. Daniel, *ABR*, 129, 1991, 7-8; M. Hawkins, *Editions*, 11, 1991 30-31; S. Knight, *S.M.H.*, 23 February, 1991, 48; W. Larcombe, *Australian Women's Book Review*, 3.3, 1991, 23-24; N. Richardson, *Meanstreets*, 2, 1991, 58-59; J. Stephens, *Australian Society*, May, 1991, 43; G. Whitlock, *Southerly*, 52.1, 149-51.

Critical Material

Grenville, Kate, and Sue Woolfe. *Making Stories: How Ten Australian Novels Were Written*. (St Leonards, NSW: Allen & Unwin, 1993). Includes contribution on *Remember the Tarantella*.
Hampton, Susan. 'Finola Moorhead: *Remember the Tarantella*'. *Southerly*, 48.1, 1988, 55-68.
Thompson, Denise. 'Finola's Dilemma, or: If Literature and Politics Don't Mix, What Am I Doing Here?' *Southerly*, 55.2, 1995, 113-25.

MOORHOUSE, FRANK

Fiction

The Americans, Baby: A Discontinuous Narrative of Stories and Fragments. (Sydney: A.& R., 1972).
Reviewed by I. Bedford, *Nation*, 22 July, 1972, 23; P. Dunn, *Nation Review*, 14-20

October, 1972, 1549; M. Halligan, *Canberra Times*, 14 October, 1972, 11 (see also letters to the editor of *Canberra Times* from 19 October to 9 November, 1972); B. Jefferis, *S.M.H.*, 22 July, 1972, 23; B. Kiernan, *Australian*, 29 July, 1972, 28 and *National Times*, 2-7 August, 1976, 36-37; J. Miles, *Advertiser*, 22 July, 1972, 18; *National Times*, 24-29 July, 1972, 20-21; R. Nicholls, *Age*, 22 July, 1972, 12; D. Rowbotham, *Courier-Mail*, 3 March, 1973, 13; I. Turner, *Bulletin*, 19 August, 1972, 46-47.

Coca-Cola Kid. Traduit de l'anglais par Jean-Paul Delamotte. (Paris: Presses de la Renaissance). Reviewed by B. Genies, *Le Monde*, 29 November, 1985, 20.
Conference-Ville. (Sydney: A.& R., 1976). A.& R. Original Fiction Paperback.
Reviewed by I. Dunn, *Nation Review*, 31 March-6 April, 1977, 576; P. Elkin, *Quadrant*, XXI, No. 6, 1977, 78-79, see also reply by Moorhouse, *Quadrant*, XXI, No. 8, 1977, 42; S. Hall, *Australian*, 26 February, 1977, 28; J. McLaren, *Overland*, No. 68, 1977, 65; L. Murray, *S.M.H.*, 22 January, 1977, 15.
The Electrical Experience: A Discontinuous Narrative. (Sydney: A.& R., 1974).
Reviewed by D. Green, *Hemisphere*, XIX, No. 5, 1975, 38-39; G. Hutchinson, *Makar*, X, No. 3, 1974, 47-49; M. Johnston, *S.M.H.*, 30 November, 1974, 15; T. Keneally, *National Times*, 3-8 February, 1975, 22; B. Kiernan, *Age*, 7 December, 1974, 19 and *Meanjin*, XXXIV, 1975, 38; J. Teerds, *Courier-Mail*, 17 January, 1976, 19.
The Everlasting Secret Family. (Sydney: A.& R., 1979). Reviewed by J. Bedford, *National Times*, 30 March-5 April, 1980, 29; L. Clancy, *ABR*, No. 21, 1980, 27; G. Dutton, *Bulletin*, 23 April, 1980, 86-87; S. Edgar, *Quadrant*, XXIV, No. 11, 1980, 64-66; M. Eldridge, *Canberra Times*, 19 July, 1981, 15; K. England, *Advertiser*, 24 May, 1980, 22; J. Freebury, *Australian Society*, VII, No. 4, 1988, 50-51; J. Legasse, *Westerly*, XXV, No. 4, 1980, 76-78; P. Lewis, *T.L.S.*, 31 October, 1980, 1240; M. Macleod, *S.M.H.*, 17 May, 1980, 20; J. Mellors, *London Magazine*, N.S. XX, Nos. 8-9, 1980, 115-17; R. Neill, *Bulletin*, 23 February, 1988, 66-68; D.J. O'Hearn, *Age*, 3 May, 1980, 27; I. Reid, *CRNLE Reviews Journal*, No. 2, 1980, 37-39; E. Webby, *Meanjin*, XL, 1981, 206-08.
Forty-Seventeen. (Ringwood, Vic.: Viking, 1988; New York: Harcourt, Brace, Jovanovich, 1989).
Reviewed by D. Bird, *ABR*, No. 98, 1988, 34-36; A. Carter, *New York Times Book Review*, 13 August, 1989, 3; B. Edwards, *Mattoid*, No. 33, 1989, 183-86; R. Gostand, *Social Alternatives*, 8, No. 2, 1989, 73-74; J. Hanrahan, *Age Saturday Extra*, 26 March, 1988, 12; A. Loukakis, *Weekend Magazine*, 16-17 April, 1988, 15; G. Raines, *Australian Studies* (British Australian Studies Association), No. 1, 1988, 106-111; A.P. Riemer, *S.M.H.*, 19 March, 1988, 74; N. Stasko, *Phoenix Review*, No. 3, 1988, 118-120; R. Willbanks, *World Literature Today*, 64.2, 1990, 360.
Futility and Other Animals. (Sydney: Gareth Powell Associates, 1969).
Reviewed by R. Burns, *Nation*, 12 July, 1969, 21-22; P. Cowan, *Westerly*, No. 3, 1969, 48-49; T. Forshaw, *S.M.H.*, 4 August, 1973, 20; C. Harrison-Ford, *Australian Left Review*, No. 5, 1969, 77-78; B. Kiernan, *Australian*, 5 July, 1969, 18; M. Wilding, *Southerly*, XXIX, 1969, 231-36 and *Meanjin*, XXX, 1971, 265.
Grand Days. (Chippendale, NSW: Pan Macmillan, 1993).
Reviewed by A. Broinowski, *S.M.H.*, 4 September, 1993, Spectrum 9A; J. Davidson, *Age*, 2 October, 1993, Saturday Extra 8; G. Dutton and C. Bird, *ABR*, 156, 1993, 9-11; N. Jose, *Meanjin*, 35.1, 1994, 179-82; B. Tully, *Blast*, 24, 1994, 20-21; P. Pierce, *Bulletin*, 7 September, 1993, 105; J. Scheckter, *World Literature Today*, 69.1, 1995, 219; N. Walker, *T.L.S.*, 24 September, 1993, 21, G. Windsor, *Voices*, 3.4, 1993, 102-05; P. Wolfe, *Antipodes*, 8.1, 1994, 73.
Lateshows. (Sydney: Pan/Picador, 1990).
Reviewed by J. Forbes, *Weekend Australian*, 24-25 November, 1990, Review 5; P.

Pierce, *Age*, 20 October, 1990, Saturday Extra 9; T. Shapcott, *ABR*, No. 125, 1990, 38-39; A. Wearne, *S.M.H.*, 10 November, 1990, 80.

Loose Living. (Sydney: Picador, 1995).
Reviewed by B. Dickins, *Meanjin*, 54.4, 1995, 742-43; G. Papaellinas, *ABR*, 175, 1995, 14-15; P. Pierce, *S.M.H.*, 23 Sept., 1995, Spectrum 11A; M. Sharkey, *Weekend Australian*, 7-8 Oct., 1995, Review 9; M. Shmith, *Age*, 21 Oct., 1995, Saturday Extra 8.

Room Service: Comic Writings of Frank Moorhouse. (Ringwood, Vic.: Viking Press, 1985).
Reviewed by K. Ahearne, *ABR*, No. 85, 1986, 8-9; F. Giles, *Overland*, No. 102, 1986, 79-80; B. Jefferis, *Weekend Australian Magazine*, 28-29 December, 1985, 12; P. Pierce, *Age Saturday Extra*, 21 December, 1985, 8; T. Thompson, *S.M.H.*, 28 December, 1985, 30; V. Wright, *Weekend Australian. Weekend Magazine*, 2-3 May, 1987, 14.

Selected Stories. (Sydney: A.& R., 1983). Republished as *The Coca-Cola Kid: Selected Stories*. (North Ryde, N.S.W.: A.& R., 1985).
Reviewed by R. Gaind, *Canberra Times*, 17 April, 1986, 13; D. Taylor, *London Magazine*, N.S. XXIII, No. 4, 1983, 95.

Tales of Mystery and Romance. (Sydney: A.& R., 1977). Reviewed by J. Cadzow, *Courier Mail*, 27 August, 1977, 19; R. Creswell, *24 Hours*, II, No. 8, 1977, 58-59; J. Davidson, *Age*, 30 July, 1977, 21; I. Dunn, *Nation Review*, 4-10 August, 1977, 16; D. Green, *National Times*, 12-17 September, 1977, 19-20; S. Hall, *Weekend Australian Magazine*, 13-14 August, 1977, 13; T. Heald, *Australian*, 25 June, 1977, 28; R. Nicholls, *S.M.H.*, 18 June, 1977, 17; A. Summers, *Advertiser*, 30 July, 1977, 25.

Non-Fiction

'Censors of Centre and Secondarity in Australian Culture'. In *The View from Tinsel Town*, edited by Tom Thompson (Ringwood, Vic.: Southerly/Penguin, 1985), 102-105.
'Childhood Reading without a Library'. *Educational Magazine*, XXXV, No. 5, 1978, 47-48.
'What Happened to the Short Story?' *A.L.S.*, VIII, 1977, 179-82.
'What HAS Happened to the Short Story?' *Australian Author*, IX, No. 4, 1977, 19-22.

Critical Material

'Author's Book Gets an R Rating in Victoria'. *Age*, 12 August, 1975, 1; further articles and letters on censorship of *The Americans, Baby* appeared in *Age*, 14 August, 1975, 7; *Age*, 15 August, 1975, 8 and 9; *Australian*, 18 August, 1975, 7; *Age*, 21 August, 1975, 2; *Age*, 22 August, 1975, 4 and 8; *Age*, 23 August, 1975, 3; *Bulletin*, 23 August, 1975, 23; *Age*, 27 August, 1975; *Age*, 29 August, 1975, 2; *Australian Library News*, September, 1975, 11; *Bulletin*, 6 September, 1975, 5. On revocation of R rating *Bulletin*, 13 December, 1975, 16.
Anderson, Don. 'Frank Moorhouse's Discontinuities'. *Southerly*, XXXVI, 1976, 26-38.
Arens, Werner. 'The Ironical Fate of "The Drover's Wife". Four Versions from Henry Lawson (1892) to Barbara Jefferis (1980)'. In *The Story Must Be Told: Short Narrative Prose in the New English Literatures*, edited by Peter O. Stummer (Wurzburg: Konighausen und Neumann, 1986), 119-133.
Baker, Candida. 'Frank Moorhouse'. In her *Yacker 3* (Sydney: Picador, 1989), 212-235.
Belmont, Winifred. 'Frank Moorhouse: An Interview'. *Notes & Furphies*, No. 7, 1981, 1-4.

Bennett, Bruce. 'Frank Moorhouse and the New Journalism'. *Overland*, No. 70, 1978, 6-10.

Birns, Nicholas. 'Beyond Disillusionment: Frank Moorhouse's *Grand Days* and Post-Colonial Idealism'. *Westerly*, 40.1, 1995, 67-71.

Bredow, Susan. 'How Coca-Cola Kid Came to Be'. *Australian*, 30 August, 1985, 10.

Butler, Chris. 'The Long and the Short of it All'. *Advertiser*, 1 March, 1978, 28. Interview.

Cantrell, Leon. 'The New Novel: David Ireland's *The Unknown Industrial Prisoner*, Michael Wilding's *The Short Story Embassy*, and Frank Moorhouse's *The Electrical Experience*'. In *Studies in the Recent Australian Novel*, edited by K.G. Hamilton (St Lucia: U.Q.P., 1978), 225-57.

Casey, Constance. 'Down Under, Out Back and Over There'. *[Washington Post] Book World*, 4 October, 1981, 14.

Clunies Ross, Bruce. 'Laszlo's Testament or Structuring the Past and Sketching the Present in Contemporary Short Fiction, Mainly Australian'. *Kunapipi*, I, No. 2, 1979, 110-123.

Davidson, Jim. 'Frank Moorhouse'. *Meanjin*, XXXVI, 1977, 156-71. Interview. Reprinted in his *Sideways from the Page* (Melbourne: Fontana, 1983), 11-33.

Drewe, Robert. 'W.A. Bans Royal Wedding Gift'. *Bulletin*, 4 August, 1981, 70, 72. See also Sullivan, Jane. 'Writer Claims a Classic of Pornography'. *Age*, 28 August, 1981, 3.

Gillard, G.M. 'The New Writing: Whodunnit?'. *Meanjin*, XL, 1981, 167-74.

Harrison-Ford, Carl. 'The Short Stories of Wilding and Moorhouse'. *Southerly*, XXXIII, 1973, 167-78.

Graham, Don. 'Koka Kola Kulture: Reflections Upon Things American Down Under'. *Southwest Review*, 78.2, 1993, 231-44. Australian-USA literary connections including discussion of Michael Wilding and Frank Moorhouse.

Horne, Donald. 'Frank Moorhouse: The Guru of Conferences'. *National Times*, 31 January-5 February, 1977, 18.

Jost, John. 'A Rosy Future for the Miracle Worker'. *Age*, 22 December, 1973, 14.

Kanaganayakam, C. 'Form and Meaning in the Short Stories of Frank Moorhouse'. *WLWE*, XXV, No. 1, 1985, 67-76.

Kiernan, Brian. 'Frank Moorhouse: A Retrospective'. *Modern Fiction Studies*, XXVII, No. 1, 1981, 73-94.

---. 'Notes on Frank Moorhouse'. *Overland*, No. 56, 1973, 9-11.

Kirby, Stephen. 'Homosocial Desire and Homosexual Panic in the Fiction of David Malouf and Frank Moorhouse'. *Meanjin*, XLVI, No. 3, 1987, 385-393.

Legasse, Jim. 'Telling a Self: More on Moorhouse's Family'. *Westerly*, XXVII, No. 1, 1982, 73-83. *The Everlasting Secret Family*.

McDonald, Roger ed. *Gone Bush*. (Sydney: Bantam, 1990), 161-85.

MacNeill, Ian. 'Flight and Retrieval'. *Campaign*, No. 54, 1980, 35-36.

McQueen, Humphrey. 'The Thinker from The Push: Frank Moorhouse', in his *Gallipoli to Petrov*. (Sydney: Hale & Iremonger, 1984), 101-06. First published as 'A Light Vintage', *Island Magazine*, No. 6, 1976, 2-4.

Oost, Victor. 'Culture and Literature - Heterosexual Relations in Four Australian Short Stories'. *Antipodes*, 8.1, 1994, 25-30. Includes discussion of 'Going into the Heartland with the Wrong Person at Christmas'.

Osborne, David. 'Frank Moorhouse: Alive and Living from Writing in Sydney, Lord Help Him'. *National Times*, 1-6 July, 1974, 22.

Parigi, Frank. 'Frank Moorhouse and Michael Wilding - and Internationalism'. *Antipodes*, 8.1, 1994, 15-20.

Perlez, Jane. '"Letters to Twiggy" - Favourable Reply'. *Australian*, 27 November, 1971, 12.

Pope, William. 'Frank Moorhouse's *Tales of Mystery and Romance*: A Study in

Narrative Method'. *Southerly*, XLII, 1982, 412-23.

Quartermaine, Peter. 'Cultural Correspondence: Frank Moorhouse's *Forty-Seventeen'*. *Australian Studies*, 6, 1992, 60-67.

Quinnell, Ken. 'Frank Moorhouse'. *Cinema Papers* (Richmond, Vic.), 1974, 138-40.

Raines, Gay. 'The Short Story Cycles of Frank Moorhouse'. *A.L.S.*, 14, No. 4, 1990, 425-35.

Reid, Ian. 'Writing from the Third Position: Frank Moorhouse's Recent Fiction'. *Meanjin*, XXXVII, 1978, 165-70.

Rogers, Shelagh. '"You Don't Really Know What It is Until You Go Away and Come Back": Interviews with Four Australian Writers'. *Australian and New Zealand Studies in Canada*, No. 1, 1989, 33-43.

Rowse, Tim. 'The Pluralism of Frank Moorhouse'. In *Nellie Melba, Ginger Meggs and Friends: Essays in Australian Cultural History*, edited by Susan Dermody, John Docker and Drusilla Modjeska (Malmsbury, Vic.: Kibble Books, 1982), 250-67.

Smith, Graeme Kinross. 'Liberating Acts - Frank Moorhouse, his Life, his Narratives'. *Southerly*, XLVI, No. 4, 1986, 391-423.

Smith, Martin. 'There's No Such Thing as a Gay Novel'. *Campaign*, No. 21, 1977, 19-20. Interview.

Thomas, Mark. 'Frank Moorhouse'. In his *Australia in the Mind: Thirteen Influential Australian Thinkers*. (Sydney: Hale & Iremonger, 1989), 165-78.

Trikha, Pradip. 'The Short Stories of Frank Moorhouse'. *Journal of Australian Literature* (India), 1.2, 1991, 25-28.

van Hattem, Margaret. 'Where Ideas Spill Over like Beer on a Hot Day'. *Australian*, 10 July, 1972, 7. Interview.

Vauthier, Simone. 'Ventriloquist's Act: Frank Moorhouse's "Pledges, Vows and Pass this Note"'. *RANAM (Recherches Anglaises et Nord-Americaines)*, 21, 1988.

Willbanks, Ray. 'Frank Moorhouse'. In his *Speaking Volumes: Australian Writers and Their Work* (Ringwood, Vic.: Penguin, 1991).

MORANT, HARRY HARBORD ('BREAKER')

Poetry

The Poetry of 'Breaker' Morant: from *The Bulletin* 1891-1903. Foreword by David McNicoll. (Gladesville: Golden Press, 1980). Reviewed by K. Goodwin, *Weekend Australian Magazine*, 12-13 July, 1980, 16.

Critical Material

Bedford, Jean. 'The Secret Life of Daisy Bates and The Breaker'. *National Times*, 11-17 November, 1983, 28.

Cumming, Fia. 'Breaking New Ground on Morant'. *Bulletin*, 26 July, 1983, 54.

Denton, Kit. *The Breaker*. (Sydney: A.& R., 1973). A novel. Reviewed by D. McNicoll, *Bulletin*, 13 April, 1974, 44-46; C. Semmler, *S.M.H.*, 6 April, 1974, 15.

Denton, Kit. *Closed File*. (Adelaide: Rigby, 1983). Reviewed by D. Grant, *ABR*, No. 67, 1984, 29-30.

Foster, R.T. 'Banjo Didn't Like the Breaker'. *S.M.H.*, 18 July, 1981, 46. Biographical.

Fuller, Peter. 'Author's New Book not Meant to Destroy "Breaker" Legend'. *Canberra Times*, 23 October, 1983, 9.

Macken, Deirdre. 'Breaker Morant Unmasked but who will Believe the Facts?' *Age*, 9 August, 1983, 11.

McNicoll, David. '"The Breaker" Died Bravely'. *Bulletin*, 9 June, 1973, 40-43. See also Kit Denton, 'The Morant Hush-up Job', *Bulletin*, 30 June, 1973, 48-49, and letter to the editor by R.M. Hawkins, *Bulletin*, 21 July, 1973, 5.

Walker, Shirley. 'The Boer War: Paterson, Abbott, Brennan, Miles Franklin and Morant'. *A.L.S.*, XII, No. 2, 1985, 207-222.

MORGAN, SALLY

Non-Fiction

My Place. (Fremantle, W.A.: Fremantle Arts Centre Press, 1987; New York: Seaver Books/Henry Holt, 1989).
Reviewed by R. Dizard, *Australian Studies*, No. 4, 1990, 134-39; R. Gostand, *Social Alternatives*, VII, No. 1, 1988, 64-66; D. Hill, *Australian Aboriginal Studies*, No. 2, 1988, 135-36; J. T. Hospital, *New York Times Book Review*, 19 February, 1989, 13-14; B. Jefferis, *Weekend Australian. Weekend Magazine*, 4-5 July, 1987, 14; A. Lacey, *Muse*, No. 66, 1988, 34; J. Mulvaney, *Overland*, No. 111, 1988, 92-95; H. Reynolds, *T.L.S.*, 1-7 January, 1988, 2; H. Smith, *Australian Studies*, 6, 1992, 140-42; S. Thomas, *Meanjin*, XLVII, No. 4, 1988, 755-761.

Wanamurraganya: The Story of Jack McPhee. (Fremantle, W.A.: Fremantle Arts Centre Press, 1989).
Reviewed by B. Hutton, *Age Saturday Extra*, 4 November, 1989, 10; T. Kelly, *Weekend Australian*, 11-12 November, 1989, Weekend 8; A. Riemer, *ABR*, No. 115, 1989, 38-40.

Critical Material

Attwood, Bain. 'Portrait of an Aboriginal as an Artist: Sally Morgan and the Construction of Aboriginality'. *Australian Historical Studies*, 99, 1992, 302-18. See responses to this article in *Australian Historical Studies*, 100, 1993: Tony Birch. 'Half Caste' [poem] 458; Huggins, Jackie. 'Always Was Always Will Be' 459-64; Rowse, Tim. 'Sally Morgan's Kaftan' 465-68; Tarrago, Isabel. 'Response to Sally Morgan and the Construction of Aboriginality' 469. See also Reed, Elizabeth. 'Sally Morgan: A Black Tall Poppy?' *Australian Historical Studies* 101, 1993, 637-39 [a response to Attwood's and Huggins' articles].
Bird, Delys, and Dennis Haskell, eds. *Whose Place? A Study of Sally Morgan's My Place*. (Pymble, NSW: A.& R., 1992). Reviewed by B. Perrett, *ABR*, 147, 1992, 27; S. Thomas, *Meridian*, 12.2, 1993, 170-73.
Bliss, Carolyn. 'The Mythology of Family: Three Texts of Popular Australian Culture'. *New Literatures Review*, No. 18, 1989, 60-72. Includes discussion of *My Place*.
Colmer, John. 'The Quest for Roots: Vincent Buckley and Sally Morgan'. In his *Australian Autobiography: A Personal Quest*. (Melbourne: O.U.P., 1989), 98-116.
Cooper, Annabel. 'Talking about *My Place*/ My Place: Feminism, Criticism and the Other's Autobiography'. *Southern Review*, 28.2, 1995, 140-53.
Elder, Arlene A. 'Silence as Expression: Sally Morgan's *My Place*'. *Kunapipi*, 14.1, 1992, 16-24.
Ferrier, Elizabeth. 'Mapping the Local in the Unreal City'. *Island Magazine*, No. 41, 1989, 65-69.
Gelder, Ken. 'Aboriginal Narrative and Property'. *Meanjin*, 50.2-3, 1991, 353-65. Discusses Ruby Langford Ginibi and Morgan.
Griffiths, Gareth. 'The Myth of Authenticity'. In *De-scribing Empire: Post-colonialism and Textuality*, edited by Chris Tiffin and Alan Lawson (London and New York: Routledge, 1994), 70-85. Discusses *My Place*.
Hogan, Eleanor. '"A Little Bit of the Other Side of the Story": Genealogies in Sally Morgan's *My Place*'. *Meridian*, 11.1, 1992, 14-22.
Jaireth, Subhash. 'The "I" in Sally Morgan's *My Place*: Writing of a Monologised Self'. *Westerly*, 40.3, 1995, 69-78.
Newman, Joan. 'Reader-Response to Transcribed Oral Narrative: *A Fortunate Life* and *My Place*'. *Southerly*, XLVIII, No. 4, 1988, 376-388.
Ommundsen, Wenche. 'Engendering the Bicentennial Reader: Sally Morgan, Mark Henshaw and the Critics'. In *Postcolonial Fictions*, edited by Michèle Drouart (special issue in two volumes including SPACLALS Conference Proceedings, *SPAN*, 36,

1993), 251-63.

Prentice, Chris. 'The Interplay of Place and Placelessness in the Subject of Post-colonial Fiction'. *SPAN*, 31, 1991, 63-80. Discusses *My Place*.

Reid, Jo-Anne. Interview with Sally Morgan and notes on her work. In *Autobiography, The Writer's Story*, edited by Derryn Hammond, Marnie O'Neill and Jo-Anne Reid (Fremantle: Fremantle Arts Centre Press, 1988), 9-13.

Robertson, Jo. 'Talking to; Talking about; or Talking for? Enunciative Politics for Non-Aboriginal Literary Critics'. *Imago*, 7.3, 1995, 84-92.

Sheridan, Susan. 'Different Lives: Two Aboriginal Women's Stories'. *Antipodes*, 3.1, 1989, 20-23. Discusses Sally Morgan and Ruby Langford-Ginibi.

Smith, S. 'Re-Citing, Re-Siting, and Re-Sighting Likeness: Reading the Family Archive in Drusilla Modjeska's *Poppy*, Donna Williams' *Nobody Nowhere* and Sally Morgan's *My Place*. *Modern Fiction Studies*, 40.3, 1994, 509-42.

Trees, Kathryn. '*My Place* as a Counter-Memory'. *SPAN*, 32, 1991, 60-74.

Wright, Mary. 'A Fundamental Question of Identity'. *Fremantle Arts Review*, II, No. 7, 1987, 3-5. Revised version in *Kunapipi*, 10, Nos. 1-2, 1988, 92-109.

MORRISON, JOHN

Fiction

The Best Stories of John Morrison. Introduced by Stephen Murray-Smith (Ringwood, Vic.: Penguin, 1988).

Reviewed by G. Raines, *Australian Studies*, No. 3, 1989, 124-28; R. Schmedding, *Redoubt*, No. 5, 1989, 69-71; D. Sourile, *Social Alternatives*, 8, No. 2, 1989, 72-73; N. Stasko, *Phoenix Review*, No. 4, 1989, 115-119.

North Wind. (Ringwood, Vic.: Penguin, 1982).

Reviewed by H. Daniel, *Age Saturday Extra*, 17 April, 1982, 13; G. Dutton, *Bulletin*, 18 May, 1982, 77-78 & 80; J. McLaren, *ABR*, No. 43, 1982, 27; G. Windsor, *S.M.H.*, 1 May, 1982, 45.

Selected Stories. Introduction by Ian Reid. (Adelaide: Rigby, 1972). Seal Australian Fiction.

Reviewed by J. Hetherington, *Age*, 12 August, 1972, 17; N. Keesing, *Sunday Telegraph*, 1 October, 1972, 23; H. Rosenbloom, *Nation Review*, 28 October-3 November, 1972, 64.

Stories of the Waterfront. (Ringwood, Vic.: Penguin, 1984).

Reviewed by B. Hickey, *ABR*, No. 63, 1984, 31-32; G. Lord, *National Times*, 9-15 March, 1984, 35; R. Lucas, *S.M.H.*, 31 March, 1984, 41; W. Noonan, *Weekend Australian Magazine*, 21-22 April, 1984, 14; B. Roberts, *Meanjin*, XLIII, 1984, 408-13.

This Freedom. (Ringwood, Vic.: Penguin, 1985).

Reviewed by H. Anderson, *Tribune*, No. 2407, 18 December, 1985, 10; D.R. Burns, *National Times*, 25-31 October, 1985, 63; L. Clancy, *ABR*, No. 77, 1985, 36-38; H. Daniel, *Age Saturday Extra*, 7 December, 1985, 14; T. Forshaw, *Weekend Australian Magazine*, 12-13 October, 1985, 20; R. Gostand and S. Cassidy, *Social Alternatives*, V, No. 4, 1986, 56-57; R. Stevenson, *T.L.S.*, 19 June, 1987, 668; E. Webby, *S.M.H.*, 16 November, 1985, 47.

Non-Fiction

Australian by Choice. (Adelaide: Rigby, 1973).

Reviewed by D. Stewart, *S.M.H.*, 29 June, 1974, 18; C. Turnbull, *Age*, 26 January, 1974, 13.

The Happy Warrior. (Fairfield, Vic.: Pascoe Publishing, 1987). Literary and critical essays.

'The Books that Drove me on'. *Educational Magazine*, XXXV, No. 2, 1978, 22-24.

'How True is That Story?'. *Overland*, No. 55, 1973, 50-55.
'Our Own Standard Library'. *Age*, 20 June, 1970, 15.
'Pommy in Wonderland'. *Meanjin*, XXX, 1971, 227-33.

Critical Material

Aiton, Douglas. 'Little-Known Talent Spins a Good, Old-Fashioned Yarn'. *Age*, 23 February, 1974, 15.
Dunlevy, Maurice. 'Life: An Author's Starting Point'. *Canberra Times*, 1 February, 1974, 14.
Indyk, Ivor. 'The Economics of Realism: John Morrison'. *Meanjin*, XLVI, No. 4, 1987, 502-512.
Loh, Morag. 'John Morrison: Writers at Work'. *Meanjin*, XLVI, No. 4, 1987, 496-501.
Phillips, A.A. 'The Short Stories of John Morrison'. *Overland*, No. 58, 1974, 31-35.

MORTLOCK, J.F.

Non-Fiction

Experiences of a Convict. (Sydney: Sydney University Press, 1965). Edited by G.A. Wilkes and A.G. Mitchell.
Reviewed by F.C. Ball, *Books and Bookmen*, XII, No. 2, 1966, 46; J.K. Fletcher, *Australian Quarterly*, XXXVIII, No. 3, 1966, 122-3; D.R. Hainsworth, *ABR*, V, 1965, 34; N. Keesing, *Southerly*, XXVI, 1966, 66-9; N. McLachlan, *Historical Studies Australia and New Zealand*, XII, 1966, 446-9; L.L. Robson, *Age*, 4 December, 1965, 24; W. Stone, *Biblionews*, I, No. 2, 1966, 30-1.

Critical Material

Wilkes, G.A. 'The Literary Career of J.F. Mortlock'. Commonwealth Literary Fund Lectures, 1963.

MUDIE, IAN

Poetry

Look, the Kingfisher! (Melbourne: Hawthorn Press, 1970).
Reviewed by K. England, *Advertiser*, 12 September, 1970, 18; G. Page, *Canberra Times*, 9 January, 1971, 12; P. Roberts, *S.M.H.*, 26 September, 1970, 24; K. Slessor, *Daily Telegraph*, Sydney, 15 August, 1970, 13.

Selected Poems 1934-1974. (Melbourne: Thomas Nelson (Australia), 1976).
Reviewed by J. Griffin, *Advertiser*, 27 November, 1976, 25; [S.E. Lee], *Southerly*, XXXIX, 1979, 449-51; R.A. Simpson, *Age*, 5 February, 1977, 23.

Critical Material

Tonkin, J.J., and Van Wageningen, J. *Ian Mudie: A Bibliography*. (Adelaide: Libraries Board of South Australia, 1970). Bibliographies of Australian Writers.
'Bibliographies of Australian Writers - Supplement'. *Index to Australian Book Reviews*, VI, No. 4, 1970, 313-20; VII, No. 4, 1971, 290-91; VIII, No. 4, 1972, 248-9; IX, No. 4, 1973, 148-51; X, No. 4, 1974, 162-65, 190-91; XI, No. 4, 1975, 211-214.
'Death of Poet Ian Mudie'. *S.M.H.*, 30 October, 1976, 15.
Griffin, John. 'Mateship and Ian Mudie'. *Advertiser*, 27 November, 1976, 25. Obituary.
Muirden, Bruce. *The Puzzled Patriots: The Story of the Australia First Movement*. (Melbourne: M.U.P., 1968).
'Spotlight on Ian Mudie'. *Expression Australasia*, XVIII, 1974, No. 1, 17.

MUDROOROO

(see also Colin Johnson; previously known as Mudrooroo Nyoongah/Narogin)

Fiction

Doctor Wooreddy's Prescription for Enduring the Ending of the World. (Melbourne: Hyland House, 1983).
Reviewed by N. Bushnell, *Courier-Mail*, 28 January, 1984, 30; H. Daniel, *Age Saturday Extra*, 26 November, 1983, 16; J. Duffy, *ABR*, No. 58, 1984, 23-24; B. Marshall-Stoneking, *Weekend Australian Magazine*, 18-19 February, 1984, 14; F. Moore, *Tribune*, 14 September, 1983, 12; S. Muecke, *Meridian*, IV, No. 1, 1985, 41-48; G. Windsor, *Overland*, No. 96, 1984, 66-68.

Doin Wildcat: A Novel Koori Script. (Melbourne: Hyland House, 1988).
Reviewed by H. Dakin, *Southerly*, 49, No. 2, 1989, 260-262; H. Daniel, *Age Saturday Extra*, 15 October, 1988, 14.

The Kwinkan. (Pymble, NSW: Collins A.& R., 1993).
Reviewed by J. Turner Hospital, *T.L.S.*, 20 August: 4; B. Marshall-Stoneking, *Overland*, 134, 1994, 72-74; N. Rigby, *World Literature Today*, 68.3, 1994, 632-33; S. Ruta, *New York Times Book Review*, 9 January, 1994, 21; J. Wilson, *ABR*, 150, 1993, 11-12; G. Windsor, *Weekend Australian*, 12-13 June, 1993, Review 7.

Long Live Sandawarra. (Melbourne: Quartet, 1979).
Reviewed by B. d'Alpuget, *24 Hours*, 4, No. 12, 1980, 68-69; S. Edgar, *National Times*, 8 December, 1979, 42; K. England, *Advertiser*, 7 June, 1980, 24; R. Hall, *S.M.H.*, 29 December, 1979, 18; G. Pascall, *Weekend Australian Magazine*, 24-25 November, 1979, 14; T. Shapcott, *Westerly*, 25, No. 2, 1980, 121-22; J. Waten, *Age*, 29 September, 1979, 26.

Master of the Ghost Dreaming. (North Ryde, NSW: A.& R., 1991).
Reviewed by M. Flanagan, *Age*, 4 May, 1991, Saturday Extra 7; P. Jones, *S.M.H.*, 9 March, 1991, 46; S. Masson, *ABR*, 128, 1991, 8; A. Shoemaker, *Editions*, 13, 1992, 15.

Wild Cat Falling. (Sydney: A.& R., 1965).
Reviewed by E. Corsellis, *S.M.H.*, 3 April, 1965, 18; A. King, *Westerly*, 1, 1965, 70; C. Koch, *Bulletin*, 1 May, 1965, 54; L. Strahan, *Meanjin*, 24, No. 3, 1965, 385-86; D. Whitelock, *ABR*, 4, No. 7, 1965, 126.

Wild Cat Screaming. (Pymble, NSW: A.& R., 1992).
Reviewed by H. Daniel, *ABR*, 145, 1992, 17-18; J. Davis, *Age*, 31 October, 1992, Saturday Extra 8; B. Perret, *Meridian*, 12.1, 1993, 93-95; S. Ruta, *New York Times Book Review*, 9 January, 1994, 21; R. Sykes, *S.M.H.*, 3 October, 1992, 48; L. Trainor, *Weekend Australian*, 17-18 October, 1992, Review 7.

Poetry

Dalwurra, the Black Bittern: A Poem Cycle. Edited by Veronica Brady; associate editor Susan Miller. (Nedlands, W.A.: Centre for Studies in Australian Literature, University of Western Australia, 1988).
Reviewed by K. Arthur, *Westerly*, 34, No. 1, 1989, 90-91; H. Cam, *S.M.H*, 3 September, 1988, 82; A. Riach, *CRNLE Reviews Journal*, No. 2, 1989, 61-4; J.S. Ryan, *Span*, No. 28, 1989, 109-112.

The Garden of Gethsemane: Poems from the Lost Decade. (South Yarra, Vic.: Hyland House, 1991).
Reviewed by M. Duwell, *Weekend Australian*, 16-17 May, 1992, Review 7; P. Mead, *Modern Times*, April, 1992, 32-33; G. Page, *Island*, 51, 1992, 62-64.

The Song Circle of Jacky and Selected Poems. (Melbourne: Hyland House, 1986).
Reviewed by V. Brady, *Westerly*, XXXII, No. 2, 1987, 97-100; A. Diamond, *Meanjin*, XLVI, No. 2, 1987, 230-234; M. Macleod, *Times on Sunday*, 29 March,

1987, 32; J. Patterson, *English in Australia*, No. 80, 1987, 41-42; B. Perrett, *Meridian*, VI, No. 1, 1987, 91-93; K. Russell, *Quadrant*, XXXI, No. 9, 1987, 61-66 esp. 63; K. Singh, *CRNLE Reviews Journal*, No. 1, 1989, 48-50; J. Wright, *Australian Aboriginal Studies*, No. 1, 1987, 119-120.

   Non-Fiction

Aboriginal Mythology: An A-Z Spanning the History of the Australian Aboriginal Peoples from the Earliest Legends to the Present Day. (London: Aquarian/Harper Collins, 1994). Reviewed by H. Horton, *Imago*, 7.3, 1995, 140-41; A. Shoemaker, *ABR*, 168, 1995, 23-24.

Us Mob: History, Culture, Struggle: An Introduction to Indigenous Australia. (Pymble, NSW: A.& R., 1995).
Reviewed by P. Morrissey, *ABR*, 176, 1995, 19-20; J. Sabbioni, *FAR*, 10.4, 1995–96, 19–20.

Writing From the Fringe: A Study of Modern Aboriginal Literature in Australia. (South Yarra, Vic.: Hyland House, 1989).
Reviewed by G. Duncan, *Australian Society*, 9, No. 6, 1990, 38; S. During, *ABR*, No. 118, 1990, 21-23; M. Flanagan, *Age*, 5 May, 1990, Saturday Extra 8; B. Hodge and V. Mishra, *Westerly*, 35, No. 3, 1990, 91-93; E. Nelson, *Southerly*, 50, No. 4, 1990, 521-23; A. Shoemaker, *Weekend Australian*, 28-29 July, 1990, Review 9.

'Aboriginal Responses to the "Folk Tale"'. *Southerly*, XLVIII, No. 4, 1988, 363-370.
'A Literature of Aboriginality'. *Ulitarra*, 1, 1992, 28-33.

   Critical Material

MacGregor, Justin. 'An Annotated Bibliography of Mudrooroo Narogin (Colin Johnson)'. *WLWE*, 31.2, 1991, 84-99.

Albinski, Nan Bowman. 'Restoring Broken Houses: The Indigenous Novelists'. In *The Commonwealth Novel Since 1960*, edited by Bruce King (Houndmills, Basingstoke, Hampshire and London: Macmillan, 1991), 231-46. Includes discussion of *Wild Cat* novels.

Arthur, Kateryna. 'Fiction and the Rewriting of History: A Reading of Colin Johnson'. *Westerly*, XXX, No. 1, 1985, 55-60.

---. 'Neither Here Nor There: Towards a Nomadic Reading'. *New Literatures Review*, No. 17, 1989, 31-42. Includes discussion of work by Narogin.

Ballyn, Susan. 'Colin Johnson: A Survey'. In *Commonwealth Literary Cultures: New Voices, New Approaches*, edited by Giovanna Capone, Claudio Gorlier, and Bernard Hickey (Lecce: Edizioni del Grifo, 1993), 419-28.

Bau, Susanne. 'A Conversation with Mudrooroo'. *Antipodes*, 8.2, 1994, 120-22.

Beier, Ulli. 'The Aboriginal Novelist Who Found Buddha'. *Quadrant*, XXIX, No. 9, 1985, 69-75. Interview.

Bennett, B. and Lockwood, L. 'Colin Johnson: An Interview'. *Westerly*, No.3, 1975, 33-37.

Brown, Jodie. 'Mudrooroo's *Doctor Wooreddy's Prescription for Enduring the End of the World* and Robert Drewe's *The Savage Crows*'. *Westerly*, 38.3, 1993, 71-78.

Cotter, Michael. '"Perth or the bush?": Sense of Place in the Novels of Colin Johnson'. In *A Sense of Place in the New Literatures in English*, edited by Peggy Nightingale (St Lucia: U.Q.P., 1986), 97-111.

Daniel, Helen. 'Mudrooroo's Shadow Boxing'. *Island*, 55, 1993, 44-47.

Devins, Ron 'Mudrooroo's Use of Utopian and Dystopian Genre Conventions in *Master of the Ghost Dreaming*'. *SPAN*, 40, 1995, 18-33.

Fee, Margery. 'The Signifying Writer and the Ghost Reader: Mudrooroo's *Master of the Ghost Dreaming* and *Writing from the Fringe*'. *Australian & New Zealand Studies in Canada*, 8, 1992, 18-32.

Fielder, John. 'Postcoloniality and Mudrooroo Narogin's Ideology of Aboriginality'. *SPAN*, 32, 1991, 43-54.

---. 'Wildcat Reading: *Wildcat Falling*, Assimilation and Ambivalence'. *New Literatures Review*, 27, 1994, 19-28.

Fischer, Gerhard. 'Australian-German Intercultural Dramaturgy: On Mudrooroo's Play'. In *German-Australian Cultural Relations Since 1945*, edited by Manfred Jurgensen, German-Australian Studies 9, (Bern: Peter Lang, 1995), 225-44.

Fischer, Gerhard, ed. *The Mudrooroo/Müller Project: A Theatrical Casebook*. (Kensington: New South Wales UP, 1993). Includes a play by Heiner Müller, 'The Commission - Memory of a Revolution', and a new play by Mudrooroo, 'The Aboriginal Protesters Confront the Declaration of the Australian Republic on 26 January 2001 with the Production of *The Commission* by Heiner Müller'. Reviewed by A. Cromwell, *Antipodes*, 7.2, 1993, 163-64; H. Daniel, *Age* 1 May, 1993, Saturday Extra 9; R. Fotheringham, *ABR*, 154, 1993, 45, 49; H. Gilbert, *CRNLE Reviews Journal*, 2, 1993, 135-38; B. Marshall-Stoneking, *Overland*, 134, 1994, 72-74; A Shoemaker, *Australasian Drama Studies*, 24, 1994, 203-06.

Healy, J.J. 'Colin Johnson/Mudrooroo Narogin: An Imaginative Movement across Cultural Boundaries'. In *International Literature in English: Essays on the Major Writers*, edited by Robert L. Ross (New York: Garland, 1991), 21-38.

Hosking, Sue. 'Two Corroborees: Constructions of Myth by Katharine Susannah Prichard and Mudrooroo'. In *Myths, Heroes and Anti-heroes: Essays on the Literature and Culture of the Asia-Pacific Region*, edited by Bruce Bennett and Dennis Haskell (Nedlands, WA: Centre for Studies in Australian Literature, U of Western Australia, 1992), 11-19.

Little, Janine. 'A Conversation with Mudrooroo'. *Hecate*, 19.1, 1993, 143-54.

McDonald, Roger. *Gone Bush* (Sydney: Bantam, 1990), 109-23. Talk with Mudrooroo Narogin.

McGregor, Justin. 'A Dialogue Between Margins: Colin Johnson and Mudrooroo, *Wild Cat Falling* and *Doin Wildcat*'. In *Postcolonial Fictions*, edited by Michèle Drouart (special issue in two volumes including SPACLALS Conference Proceedings, *SPAN*, 36, 1993), 647-60.

---. 'A Margin's History: Mudrooroo Narogin's *Doctor Wooreddy's Prescription for Enduring the Ending of the World*'. *Antipodes*, 6.2, 1992, 113-18.

---. 'Towards a Hybrid Discourse: The Poetry of Mudrooroo'. *Kunapipi*, 14.1, 1992, 24-36.

Muecke, S. 'Discourse, History, Fiction: Language and Aboriginal History'. *Australian Journal of Cultural Studies*, 1, No. 1, 1983, 71-79.

Nelson, Emmanuel S. 'Black America and the Australian Aboriginal Literary Consciousness'. *Westerly*, 30, No. 4, 1985, 43-54.

---. 'Connecting with the Dreamtime: The Novels of Colin Johnson'. *Southerly*, XLVI, No. 3, 1986, 337-43.

---. 'The Missionary in Aboriginal Fiction'. *Southerly*, XLVIII, No. 4, 1988, 451-457. Discusses *Dr. Wooreddy's Prescription for Enduring the Ending of the World*.

O'Connor, Mark. 'Aboriginal Literature Becomes a Force'. *Kunapipi*, 10, Nos 1&2, 1988, 246-53.

Page, Geoff. 'Mudrooroo'. In his *A Reader's Guide To Contemporary Australian Poetry* (St. Lucia: U.Q.P., 1995), 202-205.

Pércopo, Maureen Lynch. 'Mostri Bianchi: La Colonizzazione della Terra Australis Incognita'. In *Metamorfosi, Mostri, Labirinti*, edited by G. Cerina, M. Domenichelli, P. Tucci, M. Virdis (Rome: Bulzoni, 1991), 379-97. Discusses *Dr Wooreddy* and Robert Drewe's *The Savage Crows*.

Pons, Xavier. 'Writing Koori: Mudrooroo Narogin and Aboriginal Fiction'. In *The Making of Pluralist Australia 1950-1990*, selected papers from the inaugural EASA Conference 1991, (Bern: Peter Lang, 1992).

Rama, R.P. '[Interview with] Mudrooroo Nyoongah'. *Dialogues with Australian Poets*

(Calcutta: P. Lal/Writers Workshop, 1993), 55-70.
Rudolphy, Ron and Williamson, John. 'Mudrooroo Narogin (Colin Johnson): An Interview'. *Westerly*, 34, No. 2, 1989, 83-89.
Shaw, Bruce. 'Response to Colin Johnson's "Captured Discourse, Captured Lives"'. *Aboriginal History*, 13, Nos. 1-2, 1989, 149-51. Johnson's article appeared in *Aboriginal History*, 11, Nos. 1-2, 1987, 27-32.
Shoemaker, Adam. 'Fact and Historical Fiction: Ion L. Idriess and Colin Johnson'. *Westerly*, 27, No. 4, 1982, 73-9.
---. 'It's the Quest which Matters. Interview with Mudrooroo'. *Island*, 55, 1993, 38-44.
---. *Mudrooroo: A Critical Study*. (Sydney: A.& R., 1993). Reviewed by M. Hayes, *Australian Canadian Studies*, 12.2, 1994, 85-88; G. Rossner, *New Literatures Review*, 26, 1993, 77-80.
---. 'The Short Stories of Colin Johnson, Jack Davis and Archie Weller'. In *Connections: Essays on Black Literatures*, edited by Emmanuel Nelson (Canberra: Aboriginal Studies Press, 1989), 53-59.
Tapping, Craig. 'Literary Reflections of Orality: Colin Johnson's *Dr. Wooreddy's Prescription for Enduring the Ending of the World*'. *WLWE*, 30.2, 1990, 55-61.
---. 'Oral Cultures and the Empire of Literature'. *Kunapipi*, 11, No. 1, 1989, 86-96.
Tiffin, Chris. 'Colin Johnson: Aboriginal Novelist'. *Rajasthan University Studies in English*, No. 15, 1982/83, 64-68.
Tompkins, Joanne. '"It All Depends On What Story You Hear": Historiographic Metafiction and Colin Johnson's *Dr. Wooreddy's Prescription For Enduring the Ending of the World* and Witi Ihimaera's *The Matriarch*'. *Modern Fiction Studies*, 36, No. 4, 1990, 483-98.
van Toorn, Penny. 'Mudrooroo and the Power of the Post: Alternative Inscriptions of Aboriginalist Discourse in a Post-Aboriginalist Age'. *Southern Review*, 28.2, 1995, 121-39.
Watego, Cliff. 'Cultural Adaptation in the South Pacific Novel'. *WLWE*, No. 23, 1984, 488-496.
Webb, Hugh. 'Doin the Post-Colonial Story? Neidjie, Narogin and the Aboriginal Narrative Intervention...' *SPAN*, 32, 1991, 32-40.
---. 'Mudrooroo: Passionate Writer from the Fringe'. *FAR*, 9.7, 1995, 7-8.
---. 'Poetry as Guerilla Warfare: Colin Johnson's Semiotic Bicentennial Gift'. *New Literatures Review*, No. 17, 1989, 43-49.
---. 'The Work of Mudrooroo Narogin: 31 Years of Literary Production, 1960-1991'. *SPAN*, 33, 1992, 52-71.

MURDOCH, WALTER

Non-Fiction
Walter Murdoch and Alfred Deakin on Books and Men: Letters and Comment, 1900 - 1918. Edited by J.A. La Nauze and Elizabeth Nurser. (Carlton: M.U.P., 1974). Reviewed by M. Roe, *Meanjin*, XXXIII, 1974, 198-200.

Critical Material
'Memorial Tribute to Sir Walter Murdoch'. *S.M.H.*, 10 August, 1970, 8. Report of speech by Sir Paul Hasluck. Similar report in *Australian*, 10 August, 1970, 3.
'The Preacher from Pitsligo'. *Canberra Times*, 1 August, 1970, 10.
'Prof. Murdoch Left $164,000'. *Age*, 17 October, 1970, 8.
'Sir Walter Murdoch Philosopher'. *S.M.H.*, 1 August, 1970, 13.
'Walter Murdoch: A Request for Documents'. *Meanjin*, XXXII, 1973, 206.
Craig, Clifford. 'Memories of Walter Murdoch'. *Overland*, No. 45, 1970, 34-35.
Dale, Leigh. 'Walter Murdoch: "A Humble Protest"?' *A.L.S.*, 16.2, 1993, 179-89.
Dunlevy, Maurice. 'Australia's Great Essayist Wrote Unrivalled Prose'. *Canberra Times*, 6 August, 1977, 12.

Durack, Mary. 'Walter Murdoch: The Man in the Mirror'. *Meanjin*, XXVIII, 1969, 217-20.
Hasluck, Paul. 'Sir Walter Murdoch'. *University News* (University of Western Australia), I, No. 6, 1970, 1-6. Memorial address.
La Nauze, John. *Walter Murdoch, a Biographical Memoir*. (Carlton: M.U.P., 1977). Reviewed by M. Armitage, *Advertiser*, 1 October, 1977, 29; G.C. Bolton, *Journal of Australian Studies*, No. 2, 1977, 129-31; K. Fitzpatrick, *Historical Studies*, XVIII, No. 70, 1978, 161-64; P. Hasluck, *Studies in Western Australian History*, No. 2, 1978, 75-77; B.E. Mansfield, *Royal Australian Historical Society. Journal*, LXIV, No. 1, 1978, 63-65; R. Rivett, *24 Hours*, II, No. 10, 1977, 55 and *Age*, 3 September, 1977, 22; C. Semmler, *S.M.H.*, 13 August, 1977, 17; V. Smith, *Quadrant*, XXI, No. 9, 1977, 74; C.T. Stannage, *Australian Journal of Politics and History*, XXIV, 1978, 276-77; P. Thompson, *Weekend Australian Magazine*, 6-7 August, 1977, 12.
---. 'Sir Walter Murdoch, the Essayist'. In Lyall Hunt (ed.). *Westralian Portraits* (Nedlands: University of W.A. Press, 1979), 222-26.
Oliver, Harold J. 'He Reached His Public with Good Personal Talk: Sir Walter Murdoch - A Master of the Essay'. *Australian*, 1 August, 1970, 4.
Phillips, A.A. 'Walter Murdoch'. In his *Responses: Selected Writings*. (Kew, Vic.: Australian International Press & Publications, 1979), 167-69. Obituary, first published as 'Walter Murdoch: The Art of Good-Humoured Devastation'. *Meanjin*, XXVIII, 1969, 221-23.
Triebel, Louis. 'Walter Murdoch: Essayist'. *Meanjin*, XXVIII, 1969, 209-16.

MURNANE, GERALD

Fiction
Emerald Blue. (Ringwood, Vic.: McPhee Gribble, 1995).
Reviewed by P. Craven, *Weekend Australian*, 3-4 June, 1995, Review 7; D. Matthews, *ABR*, 171, 1995, 9-10; D. Tacey, *Age*, 8 July, 1995, Saturday Extra 8.
Inland. (Richmond, Vic.: Heinemann, 1988).
Reviewed by K. Brophy, *Westerly*, XXXIII, No. 3, 1988, 85-87; A. Enstice, *Lot's Wife*, XXVIII, No. 1, 1988, 20; S. Gillett, *Antithesis*, 2, No. 1, 1988, 85-88; K. Goldsworthy, *Age Saturday Extra*, 2 April, 1988, 11; S. Hall, *ABR*, No. 98, 1988, 16-17; B. Matthews, *Scripsi*, V, No. 1, 1988, 143-149; D.O. Matthews, *Overland*, No. 112, 1988, 87-88; S. McCauley, *Fremantle Arts Review*, III, No. 7, 1988, 14; S. McKernan, *Bulletin*, 19 April, 1988, 118; P. Morgan, *Antipodes*, 3.2, 1989, 146; P. Pierce, *S.M.H.*, 16 April, 1988, 73; J. Tittensor, *Meanjin*, XLVII, No. 4, 1988, 751-754.
Landscape With Landscape. (Ringwood, Vic.: Penguin, 1987). First published Carlton, Vic.: Norstrilia, 1985.
Reviewed by D. Anderson, *National Times*, 24-30 March, 1985, 31; H. Daniel, *Age Saturday Extra*, 22 June, 1985, 17; B. Haneman, *ABR*, No. 72, 1985, 27-8; P. Hueston, *Scripsi*, III, Nos. 2-3, 1985, 64-73; N. Lucy, *Westerly*, XXXII, No. 2, 1987, 103-105; B. Oakley, *S.M.H.*, 8 June, 1985, 46; D.J. O'Hearn, *Weekend Australian*, 15-16 June, 1985, 14; A. Preston, *Age Monthly Review*, July, 1985, 17-18; G. Windsor, *Bulletin*, 25 June, 1985, 93.
A Lifetime on Clouds. (Ringwood, Vic.: Heinemann, 1976). Reprinted St. Kilda, Vic.: Penguin, 1986.
Reviewed by D.R. Burns, *Nation Review*, 24-30 March, 1977, 549; M. Costigan, *Weekend Australian Magazine*, 21-22 June, 1986, 15; C. Harrison-Ford, *Meanjin*, XXXVI, 1977, 246-52; L. Murray, *S.M.H.*, 19 February, 1977, 17; J. Tittensor, *Age*, 4 December, 1976, 22.
Velvet Waters. (Ringwood, Vic.: McPhee Gribble, 1990).

Reviewed by I. Adam, *Westerly*, 37.1, 1992, 88-89; D. Brooks, *SPAN*, 34&35, 1992-93, 384-91; P. Craven, *Age*, 24 November, 1990, Saturday Extra 8; J. Forbes, *Weekend Australian*, 24-25 November, 1990, Review 5; N. Hasluck, *Voices*, 1.1, 1991, 90-94; D.J. O'Hearn, *ABR*, No. 127, 1990, 12-13; A.P. Riemer, *S.M.H.*, 1 December, 1990, 48.

Non-Fiction

'Pure Ice'. *Meridian*, VII, No. 2, 1988, 160-162. Text of a speech given at the launching of *Inland* in Adelaide, 9 March, 1988.

'Title to be Announced: A Lecture on *The Plains*'. *Age Monthly Review*, VIII, No. 9, 1988, 10-14. This is an edited version of a text read by Gerald Murnane at La Trobe University, 1 July, 1988.

'The Typescript Stops Here: Or: Who Does the Consultant Consult?' *Meanjin*, 48, No. 1, 1989, 190-94. On Murnane's work as fiction consultant for *Meanjin*.

'Why I Write What I Write'. *Meanjin*, XLV, No. 4, 1986, 514-17.

Critical Material

Salusinszky, Imre. *Gerald Murnane: An Annotated Bibliography of Primary and Secondary Sources*. (Melbourne: Footprint P of the Victoria U of Technology, 1993).

Adam, Ian. 'The Referentiality of the Deconstructed: Gerald Murnane's *The Plains*'. *Westerly*, 36.1, 1991, 25-29.

Anderson, Don. 'A "Terrible Denudation": Gerald Murnane's *Emerald Blue*'. *Southerly*, 55.3, 1995, 73-83.

Baker, Candida. 'Gerald Murnane'. In her *Yacker 2: Australian Writers Talk About Their Work* (Sydney: Picador, 1987), 188-217.

Bird, Carmel. 'Gerald Murnane's Tasmania: Island in a Dream Atlas'. *Fine Line*, No. 2, 1987, 38-44.

Birns, Nicholas. 'Gerald Murnane and the Power of Landscape'. *New Literatures Review*, No. 18, 1989, 73-82.

---. 'Indefinite Desires: Love and the Search for Truth in the Fiction of Gerald Murnane'. *Southerly*, 55.3, 1995, 48-62.

Daniel, Helen. *Liars: Australian New Novelists*. (Ringwood, Vic.: Penguin, 1988), 43-70, 307-341.

Gelder, Kenneth. 'History, Politics and the (Post) modern: Receiving Australian Fiction'. *Meanjin*, XLVII, No. 3, 1988, 551-559. Discusses the work of Gerald Murnane, Alan Wearne and Peter Carey.

---. 'Postmodernism's "Lost Objects": Desire in the Recent Fiction of Murnane, Brooks, Henshaw and Jones'. *Island Magazine*, No. 41, 1989, 49-53.

Gillett, Sue. 'Gerald Murnane's *The Plains*: A Convenient Source of Metaphors'. *Ariel*, 26.2, 1995, 25-39.

---. 'Inland with Gerald Murnane: An Interview'. *Meridian*, VII, No. 2, 1988, 163-174.

---. 'Loving and Hating the *Inland* Reader: Postmodern Ploys or Romantic Reaction?' *SPAN*, 30, 1990, 59-68.

Hanrahan, John ed. *Gerald Murnane*. (Footscray, Vic.: Footscray Foundation for Australian Studies, 1987). Footprint New Writers 2. Includes an autobiographical essay, criticism, an interview and a bibliography.

Hecq, Dominique. 'The Inescapable Plain of Trespass: On Translating *The Plains*'. *Southerly*, 55.3, 1995, 63-72.

Kolsky, Stephen. 'Exploring *Inland*'. *Earth Wings: The Outrider 91 Almanach*. (Brisbane: Phoenix Publications, 1991), 97-109.

Koval, Ramona. 'An Interview with Gerald Murnane'. *ABR*, 172, 1995, 56-57.

Salusinszky, Imre. *Gerald Murnane*. (Melbourne: O.U.P., 1993). Reviewed by D. English, *Weekend Australian*, 15-16 May, 1993, Review 6; S. Lever, *A.L.S.*, 16.2, 1993, 229-33; P. Pierce, *Quadrant*, 37.11, 1993, 75-77; J. Scheckter, *World*

Literature Today, 68.2, 1994, 424-25; R. Sorensen, *Age*, 20 March, 1993, Saturday Extra 8.
---. 'Murnane, Husserl, Derrida: The Scene of Writing'. *A.L.S.*, 14, No. 2, 1989, 188-98.
---. 'On Gerald Murnane'. *Meanjin*, XLV, No. 4, 1986, 518-29.
---. 'A *Tamarisk Row* Form Guide'. *Scripsi*, 8.2, 1992, 157-70.
---. 'That Hilarious Supplement: Gerald Murnane's *A Lifetime on Clouds*'. *A.L.S.*, 15.4, 1992, 294-303.
Stewart, Annette. 'Art and the Australian Artist: In White, Malouf, Murnane and Bail'. *Quadrant*, XXXI, No. 8, 1987, 52-59.
Tittensor, John. 'Inner Australia: The Novels of Gerald Murnane'. In *Colonisations*, edited by X. Pons and M. Rocard (Toulouse: Universite de Toulouse-Le Mirail, 1985), 97-107.

MURRAY, ANNA MARIA

Wilson, Gwendoline. *Murray of Yarralumla*. (Melbourne: O.U.P., 1968). On her authorship of *The Guardian*, by 'An Australian' (1838), see particularly 88-94.
Reviewed by D. Rogers, *ABR*, VII, 160.
---. 'Anna Maria Murray: Authoress of *The Guardian*'. *A.L.S.*, III, 1967, 148-149.

MURRAY, LES A.

Poetry
The Boys Who Stole the Funeral. (Sydney: A.& R., 1980; London: Carcanet, 1989; New York: Farrar, Straus & Giroux, 1991).
Reviewed by J. Barnie, *Kunapipi*, IV, No. 1, 1982, 172-78; G. Catalano, *Meanjin*, XXXIX, 1980, 351-55; P Corcoran, *London Review of Books*, 12, No. 2, 1990, 15-16; M. Dunlevy, *Canberra Times*, 1 November, 1980, 14; J. Forbes, *New Poetry*, XXVIII, No. 1, 1980, 60-63; B. Giles, *ABR*, No. 24, 1980, 4-5; M. Imlah, *T.L.S.*, 18-24 May, 1990, 521-22; M. Johnson, *World Literature Today*, 65.1, 1991, 185-86; C.J. Koch, *Quadrant*, XXIV, No. 9, 1980, 40-42; G. Page, *National Times*, 4-10 May, 1980, 45; J.D. Pringle, *S.M.H.*, 15 March, 1980, 14; J. Shapcott, *New Statesman and Society*, 2, No. 27, 1989, 38; C. Wallace-Crabbe, *Age*, 19 July, 1980, 23.
Collected Poems. (North Ryde, NSW: A.& R., 1991).
Reviewed by P. Mead, *Australian Society*, 10.8, 1991, 40-42; C. Pollnitz, *Age*, 13 July, 1991, Saturday Extra 8.
Collected Poems. (Manchester: Carcanet, 1992).
Reviewed by G. Foden, *T.L.S.*, 29 May, 1992, 24, J. Symons, *London Review of Books*, 14.5, 1992, 27.
Collected Poems. (Port Melbourne, Vic.: Heinemann, 1994).
Reviewed by D. Leadbetter, *Overland*, 141, 1995, 74-75; G. Page, *Voices*, 5.2, 1995, 113-17; C. Wallace-Crabbe, *ABR*, 168, 1995, 48-49
The Daylight Moon. (North Ryde, N.S.W.: A.& R., 1987; Manchester: Carcanet Press, 1988).
Reviewed by V. Buckley, *Age Saturday Extra*, 2 January, 1988, 8; A. Gould, *Muse*, No. 69, 1988, 19-21; M. Imlah, *T.L.S.*, 18-24 May, 1990, 521-22; E. Jones, *Times on Sunday*, 27 December, 1987, 30; P. Kane, *Antipodes*, II, No. 1, 1988, 67; G. Lehmann, *Weekend Australian*. *Weekend Magazine*, 27-28 February, 1988, 14; A.D.F. Macrae, *Australian Studies* (British Australian Studies Association), No. 1, 1988, 100-105; P. Porter, *Scripsi*, V, No. 1, 1988, 191-196; K. Russell, *Overland*, No. 110, 1988, 82-83; C.K. Stead, *London Review of Books*, X, No. 4, 1988, 11-12; J. Tulip, *Poetry Australia*, No. 120, 1989, 12-25; A. Urquhart, *Westerly*, XXXIII, No. 4, 1988, 89-91.

Dog Fox Field. (North Ryde, N.S.W.: A.& R., 1990).
Reviewed by H. Cam, *S.M.H.*, 27 April, 1991, 41; J. Croft, *ABR*, No. 126, 1990, 6-7; K. Hart, *Overland*, 122, 1991, 69-71; M. Hulse, *PN Review*, 17.6, 1991, 72-73; L. Norfolk, *T.L.S.*, 5 July, 1991, 21-22; C. Pollnitz, *Age*, 13 July, 1991, Saturday Extra 8; N. Rowe, *Southerly*, 51.2, 1991, 319-30; I. Salusinszky, *Weekend Australian*, 9-10 February, 1991, Review 7; C.K. Stead, *London Review of Books*, 13.10, 1991, 10-11.

Equanimities. (Copenhagen: Razorback Press, 1982).
Reviewed by I. Stephen, *Kunapipi*, IV, No. 2, 1982, 154-55.

Ethnic Radio. (Sydney: A.& R., 1978).
Reviewed by A. Gould, *Nation Review*, 14-20 July, 1978, 18-19; R. Gray, *Poetry Australia*, No. 70, 1979, 68-69; J. Griffin, *Advertiser*, 25 February, 1978, 25; R. Hall, *Weekend Australian Magazine*, 4-5 March, 1978, 8; [S.E. Lee], *Southerly*, XXXIX, 1979, 443-45; E. Lindsay, *Quadrant*, XXIII, No. 3, 1979, 70; N. Macainsh, *ABR*, No. 4, 1978, 10; M. O'Connor, *Kunapipi*, (Aarhus) I, No. 1, 1979, 40-52; G. Page, *Canberra Times*, 14 October, 1978, 17; J. Rodriguez, *S.M.H.*, 8 July, 1978, 19; T. Shapcott, *Age*, 1 July, 1978, 23; J. Tranter, *24 Hours*, III, No. 6, 1978, 70-71.

The Idyll Wheel: Cycle of a Year at Bunyah, New South Wales, April 1986-April 1987. Engravings by Rosalind Atkins. (Canberra: Officina Brindabella, 1989).
Reviewed by H. Cam, *S.M.H.*, 29 July, 1989, 78; M. Duwell, *Weekend Australian*, 19-20 August, 1989, Weekend 9.

Lunch & Counter Lunch. (Sydney: A.& R., 1974).
Reviewed by K. England, *Advertiser*, 7 December, 1974, 28; R. Garfitt, *Stand*, XVII, No. 1, 1975, 67-68; M. Johnston, *S.M.H.*, 9 November, 1974, 15; D. Malouf, *Poetry Australia*, No. 57, 1975, 70-72; P. Rappolt, *Canberra Times*, 15 November, 1974, 8; R.A. Simpson, *Age*, 8 March, 1975, 16; J. Tranter, *Australian*, 2 November, 1974, 37.

The People's Otherworld. (Sydney: A.& R., 1983).
Reviewed by D. Anderson, *National Times*, 23-29 December, 1983, 28; J. Barnie, *Kunapipi*, VI, No. 3, 1984, 107-122; V. Brady, *Helix*, Nos. 21-22, 1985, 112-120; J. Croft, *ABR*, No. 62, 1984, 19-20; G. Dutton, *Bulletin*, 6 December, 1983, 99; M. Duwell, *Weekend Australian Magazine*, 5-6 November, 1983, 19; A. Gould, *Age Saturday Extra*, 3 December, 1983, 15; D. Haskell, *Westerly*, XXIX, No. 4, 1984, 73-76; G. Lehmann, *S.M.H.*, 12 November, 1983, 41; P. Lugg, *Canberra Times*, 4 February, 1984, 14; B. Morrison, *T.L.S.*, 9 August, 1985, 873, reprinted in *Age Monthly Review*, V, No. 5, 1985, 4-5; R. Morse, *PN Review*, No. 44, 1985, 68; B. O'Donohue, *Arts National*, II, No. 4, 1985, 59, 106; G. Page, *Quadrant*, XXVIII, Nos. 1-2, 1984, 134-26; R. Pybus, *Stand*, XXVI, No. 3, 1985, 62-69; M. Richards, *Island Magazine*, Nos. 18-19, 1984, 52-57; S. Trigg, *Scripsi*, II, No. 4, 1984, 109-48; F. Zwicky, *Overland*, No. 98, 1985, 42-46.

Poems Against Economics. (Sydney: A.& R., 1972).
Reviewed by G. Curtis, *Makar*, VIII, No. 2, 1972, 43-45; C. Harrison-Ford, *New Poetry*, XX, No. 3, 1972, 40-41; E. Kynaston, *Nation Review*, 5-11 August, 1972, 1215; R. McDonald, *Poetry Australia*, No. 47, 1973, 71-73; G. Page, *Canberra Times*, 14 October, 1972, 10; P. Roberts, *S.M.H.*, 26 August, 1972, 20; T. Shapcott, *ABR*, XI, 1972, 42-43; J. Tulip, *Bulletin*, 5 August, 1972, 38-39 and *Southerly*, XXXIII, 1973, 234-35.

Selected Poems. (Manchester: Carcanet, 1986). Poetry Signatures Series.
Reviewed by N. Corcoran, *T.L.S.*, 22 August, 1986, 919; M. Hulse, *PN Review*, XIII, No. 4, 1987, 62-64; A. Pollard, *British Book News*, July, 1986, 429; C.K. Stead, *London Review of Books*, X, No. 4, 1988, 11-12.

Selected Poems: The Vernacular Republic. (Sydney: A.& R., 1976).
Reviewed by G. Catalano, *Meanjin*, XXXVI, 1977, 67-72; A. Gould, *Nation Review*, 26 November-2 December, 1976, 141; R. Gray, *S.M.H.*, 11 September, 1976, 15; R. McDonald, *National Times*, 18-23 October, 1976, 64-65; P. Nelson, *Poetry Australia*, No. 64, 1977, 74-78; J. Tranter, *Australian*, 29 January, 1977, 30.

Translations from the Natural World. (Sydney: Isabella P, 1992; New York: Farrar, Straus & Giroux, 1994).
Reviewed by D. Coad, *World Literature Today*, 69.1, 1995, 219-20; J. Foulcher, *Island*, 55, 1993, 69-72; P. Goldsworthy, *Voices*, 2.3, 1992, 98-100; K. Hart, *Age*, 17 October, 1992, Saturday Extra 9; L. Mackinnon, *T.L.S.*, 20 August, 1993, 6.

The Vernacular Republic: Poems 1961-1981. (Sydney: A.& R.; New York: Persea Books, 1982).
Reviewed by F. Adcock, *T.L.S.*, 30 July, 1982, 830; C. Benfey, *Parnassus: Poetry in Review*, XI, No. 2, 1983/84, 236-252; J. Grant, *Age Monthly Review*, II, No. 4, 1982, 9-10; J. Lucas, *New Statesman*, 7 May, 1982, 20-21; J.D. McClatchy, *Poetry* (Chicago), CXLIII, 1983, 172-74; S. Trigg, *Scripsi*, II, No. 4, 1984, 139-48.

The Weatherboard Cathedral. (Sydney: A.& R., 1969).
Reviewed by R. Dunlop, *Poetry Australia*, No. 32, 1970, 51-52; R. Hall, *Australian*, 24 January, 1970, 19; E. Jones, *Nation*, 13 December, 1969, 22-23; F. Kellaway, *Overland*, No. 45, 1970/71, 39; G. Lehmann, *Bulletin*, 7 February, 1970, 43-44; R. McDonald, *Makar*, V, No. 4, 1969, 28-31; A. Riddell, *S.M.H.*, 22 November, 1969, 16; G. Rowlands, *Makar*, V, No. 4, 1969, 32-34; R.A. Simpson, *Age*, 6 December, 1969, 17; J. Tulip, *Southerly*, XXX, 1970, 148-51; P. Ward, *ABR*, IX, 1969/70, 61.

'The Liberated Plague'. This poem was published in the *London Review of Books*, 29 October, 1987, provoking a series of letters and replies including those of Alan Wearne, *London Review of Books*, IX, No. 22, 1987, 4; Les Murray, *London Review of Books*, X, No. 1, 1988, 4; John Fletcher, *London Review of books*, X, No. 3, 1988, 4; Les Murray, *London Review of Books*, X, No. 4, 1988, 4; John Fletcher, *London Review of Books*, X, No. 7, 1988, 4-5.

'Walking to the Cattle Place: A Meditation'. *Poetry Australia*, No. 42, 1972, 4-23.
Reviewed by D. Malouf, *Australian*, 29 April, 1972, 20.

Non-Fiction

Blocks and Tackles: Articles and Essays 1982 to 1990. (North Ryde, N.S.W.: A.& R., 1990).
Reviewed by J. Croft, *ABR*, No. 126, 1990, 6-7; K. Jennings, *S.M.H.*, 17 November, 1990, 81; C. Pollnitz, *Age*, 13 July, 1991, Saturday Extra 8; N. Rowe, *Southerly*, 51.2, 1991, 319-30; I. Salusinszky, *Weekend Australian*, 9-10 February, 1991, Review 7; A. Sharma, *Antipodes*, 7.1, 1993, 65, J. Strauss, *Overland*, 123, 1991, 47-50.

The Paperbark Tree: Selected Prose. (Manchester: Carcanet, 1992).
Reviewed by D. Davie, *London Review of Books*, 14.21, 1992, 26-27; R. Francis, *PN Review*, 19.3, 1993, 52-54; M. Fraser, *S.M.H.*, 23 January, 1993, 38; M. Wormald, *T.L.S.*, 21 May, 1993, 27.

The Peasant Mandarin. (St Lucia: U.Q.P., 1978).
Reviewed by G. Dutton, *Bulletin*, 21 November, 1978, 68; M. Duwell, *A.L.S.*, IX, 1979, 259-62; *Helix*, No. 2, 1978, 54; C. Kelly, *National Times*, 30 September, 1978, 37; L. Lowe, *Campaign*, No. 37, 1978, 50; M. Macleod, *Meanjin*, XXXIX, 1980, 103-11; P. Monaghan, *Canberra Times*, 3 February, 1979, 17; D.A. Myers, *International Fiction Review*, VII, No. 1, 1980, 69-70; W. Noonan, *24 Hours*, III, No. 10, 1978, 67; M. Richards, *Helix*, No. 4, 1979, 73-80; J. Tulip, *S.M.H.*, 30 September, 1978, 17.

Persistence in Folly. (Sydney: A.& R., 1984). Sirius Books.

Reviewed by J. Grant, *S.M.H.*, 1 September, 1984, 41; J. McLaren, *ABR*, No. 69, 1985, 14; A. Mitchell, *Weekend Australian Magazine* 4-5 August, 1984, 15; B. Morrison, *T.L.S.*, 9 August, 1985, 873, reprinted in *Age Monthly Review*, V, No. 5, 1985, 4-5; R. Morse, *PN Review*, XII, No. 5, 1986, 49; C. Roderick, *Courier-Mail*, 15 December, 1984, 31; J. Rodriguez, *Meridian*, IV, No. 1, 1985, 72-75.

'The Human-Hair Thread'. *Meanjin*, XXXVI, 1977, 550-71.

'Interview with Les A. Murray: "I'm the Regius Professor of Idle Yarning"'. *Union Recorder* (Sydney), LXV, No. 6, 1985, 14-15.

'Les Murray on *The Daylight Moon*'. In *Writers in Action: The Writer's Choice Evenings*, edited by Gerry Turcotte (Sydney: Currency Press, 1990), 87-112.

'My Earliest Childhood...'. *A.L.S*, XII, No. 2, 268. Response to a questionnaire on the theme Australian literature and war.

'On Being Subject Matter'. *Bulletin*, 5 April, 1983, 60-64, 67-68 & 70-71.

'Poemes and the Mystery of Embodiment'. *Meanjin*, XLVII, No. 3, 1988, 519-533. This essay is complementary to one titled 'Poems and Poesies', first published in the *Age Monthly Review* [VI, No. 8, 1986-87, 3-6] and then in an expanded version in the British journal, *P.N. Review* [XIV, No. 3, 1988, 25-31]'.

'The Suspect Captivity of the Fisher King: "Scholars help us with our immortality - and we help them to theirs"'. *Quadrant*, 34, No. 9, 1990, 16-19. Reprinted in his *Blocks and Tackles*.

'Three Talks: David Malouf, Les Murray and David Rowbotham'. *A.L.S.*, XI, 1984, 320-21. See also 'Selections from Question Time', 322-23. Session at Warana Writers' Weekend.

Critical Material

'Literary Prize after Lean Times'. *Canberra Times*, 28 October, 1970, 3.

'NBC Book Awards 1980'. *ABR*, No. 25, 1980, 24.

Ailwood, Dianne. 'The Poetry of Les Murray'. *Southerly*, XXXI, 1971, 188-99.

Almon, Bert. 'Fullness of Being in Les Murray's "Presence: Translations from the Natural World"'. *Antipodes*, 8.2, 1994, 123-26, 128, 130.

Baker, Candida. 'Les A. Murray'. In her *Yacker 2: Australian Writers Talk About Their Work* (Sydney: Picador, 1987), 218-246.

Barnie, John. 'The Poetry of Les Murray'. *A.L.S.*, XII, No. 1, 1985, 22-34.

Bennett, Bruce. 'Versions of the Past in the Poetry of Les Murray and Peter Porter' in Singh, Kirpal (ed.). *The Writer's Sense of the Past: Essay on Southeast Asian and Australasian Literature* (Singapore: Singapore University Press, 1987), 178-188. Revised as 'Patriot and Expatriate: Les A. Murray and Peter Porter'. In his *An Australian Compass: Essays on Place and Direction in Australian Literature*. Fremantle, WA: Fremantle Arts Centre P, 1991), 38-51.

Bourke, L.H. '"The Ballad Trap": Les A. Murray and Pegasus'. *Meridian*, VI, No. 1, 1987, 31-40.

---. '"Digging Under the Horse": Surface As Disguise in the Poetry of Les A. Murray'. *Southerly*, XLVII, No. 1, 1987, 26-41.

---. 'Family and the Father in the Poetry of Les A. Murray'. *A.L.S.*, XIII, No. 3, 1988, 282-295.

---. 'Les A. Murray: Interview'. *Journal of Commonwealth Literature*, 21, No. 1, 1986, 167-87.

---. 'The Rapture of Place: From Immanence to Transcendence in the Poetry of Les A. Murray'. *Westerly*, XXXIII, No. 1, 1988, 41-51.

Bourke, Lawrence. *A Vivid Steady State: Les Murray and Australian Poetry*. (Kensington, NSW: New South Wales UP, and Strawberry Hills, NSW: New Endeavour P, 1992). Reviewed by D. Haskell, *Westerly* 37.4, 1992, 104-05; P. Mead, *A.L.S.*, 16.2, 1993, 140-51; P. Nelson, *ABR*, 140, 1992, 54-55; C. Pollnitz, *Weekend Australian*, 2-3 May, 1992, Review 6; N. Rowe, *Southerly*, 52.2, 1992, 165-74; T. Shapcott, *Age*, 2 May, 1992, Saturday Extra 8.

Capp, Fiona. 'Les Murray. An Interview'. *ABR*, No. 69, 1985, 12-14.
Carter, David. 'The Death of Satan and the Persistence of Romanticism'. *Literary Criterion* (Mysore), XV, Nos. 3-4, 1980, 77-82.
Clunies Ross, Bruce. 'Les Murray's Vernacular Republic'. In *Diversity Itself: Essays in Australian Arts and Culture*, edited by Peter Quartermaine (Exeter: Exeter University, 1986), 21-37.
---. 'A Poetic Novel for The Vernacular Republic: Les Murray's *The Boys Who Stole the Funeral*'. In *Aspects of Australian Fiction: Essays Presented to John Colmer*, edited by Alan Brissenden (Nedlands, W.A.: University of Western Australia Press, 1990), 173-90.
Crawford, Robert. 'Les Murray: Shaping an Australian Voice'. In his *Identifying Poets: Self and Territory in Twentieth Century Poetry* (Edinburgh: Edinburgh University Press, 1993), 73-101.
Daly, Martin. 'Les Murray: A Lot More than Just Any Old Poet'. *Courier-Mail, The Great Weekend*, 9 November, 1985, 8.
Davidson, Jim. 'Les A. Murray'. *Meanjin*, XLI, 1982, 112-29. Interview. Reprinted in his *Sideways from the Page*, (Melbourne: Fontana, 1983), 346-71.
Filkins, Peter. 'The Dark & Light of the Daylight Moon: The Poetry of Les Murray'. *New England Review*, 15.3, 1993, 197-207.
Frizell, Helen. 'Les Murray Takes Off'. *S.M.H.*, 23 February, 1980, 17.
Gaffney, Carmel. 'Les Murray Again'. *Quadrant*, XXXII, Nos. 1&2, 1988, 66-71.
---. 'Les Murray's Otherworld'. *Quadrant*, XXVIII, Nos. 7-8, 1984, 55-58.
Goodwin, K.L. 'Les Murray. *Toward the Imminent Days*'. In *Australian Poems in Perspective*, edited by P.K. Elkin (St Lucia: U.Q.P., 1978), 185-202.
Gould, Alan. 'A Verse Novel'. *Helix*, Nos. 21-22, 1985, 120-122. On *The Boys Who Stole the Funeral*.
---. '"With the Distinct Timbre of an Australian Voice": The Poetry of Les Murray'. *Antipodes*, 6.2, 1992, 121-29.
Gray, Robert. 'An Interview with Les Murray'. *Quadrant*, XX, No. 12, 1976, 69-72.
Hart, Kevin. '"Interest" in Les Murray'. *A.L.S.*, 14, No. 2, 1989, 147-59.
Headon, David. 'An Interview with Les Murray'. *LiNQ*, XIII, No. 3, 1986, 7-16.
Hergenhan, Laurie. 'War in Post-1960s Fiction: Johnston, Stow, McDonald, Malouf and Les Murray'. *A.L.S.*, XII, No. 2, 1985, 248-260.
Heseltine, H.P. 'Criticism and the Individual Talent'. *Meanjin*, XXXI, 1972, 10-24. Includes discussion of 'An Absolutely Ordinary Rainbow'.
Kane, Paul. 'Les Murray: Relegation and Convergence'. In *International Literature in English: Essays on the Major Writers*, edited by Robert L. Ross (New York: Garland, 1991), 437-46.
---. 'Sydney and the Bush: The Poetry of Les A. Murray'. In *From Outback to City: Changing Preoccupations in Australian Literature of the Twentieth Century*, edited by Alexandra Cromwell (New York: American Association of Australian Literary Studies, 1988), 15-22.
Kavanagh, Paul, and Kuch, Peter. 'An Interview with Les Murray'. *Southerly*, XLIV, 1984, 367-78. Reprinted in *Conversations: Interviews with Australian Writers*, edited by Paul Kavanagh and Peter Kuch (North Ryde, NSW: Collins/A.& R, 1991).
Leer, Martin. '"Contour-line by Contour": Landscape Change as an Index of History in the Poetry of Les Murray'. *A.L.S.*, 16.3, 1994, 249-61.
Lucas, John. 'An English Reading of Les Murray'. *Meridian*, 12.1, 1993, 76-83.
Malouf, David. 'Some Volumes of Selected Poems of the 1970s, II'. *A.L.S.*, X, 1982, 306-09.
Marsden, Peter H. 'Paradise Mislaid: The Hostile Reception of Les A. Murray's Poem "The Liberated Plague"'. In *Crisis and Creativity in the New Literatures in English*, edited by Geoffrey V. Davis and Hena Maes-Jelinek (Amsterdam; Atlanta, Ga.: Rodopi, 1990), 265-89.

McDonald, Roger. *Gone Bush* (Sydney: Bantam, 1990), 29-47.

McGrath, Sandra. 'An Otherworld of Dreaming in Poetry'. *Weekend Australian Magazine*, 5-6 November, 1983, 17.

Moffit, Ian. 'The Poet of the Republic'. *Bulletin*, 15 January, 1977, 36-37.

O'Connor, Ursula. 'Life, Said the Poet, Was Hardly a Bed of Roses'. *S.M.H.*, 30 June, 1969, 6.

Page, Geoff. 'Les Murray'. In his *A Reader's Guide To Contemporary Australian Poetry* (St. Lucia: U.Q.P., 1995), 205-209.

Peacock, Noel. '"Embracing the Vernacular": An Interview with Les A. Murray'. *Australian & New Zealand Studies in Canada*, 7, 1992, 28-40.

Perrett, Bill. 'Les A. Murray and the "Aboriginal Way"'. *Meridian*, VII, No. 1, 1988, 73-79.

Pollnitz, Christopher. 'The Bardic Pose: A Survey of Les A. Murray's Poetry'. Part I, *Southerly*, XL, 1980, 367-87, Part II, XLI, 1981, 52-74; Part III, XLI, 1981, 188-210.

Porter, Peter. 'Country Poetry and Town Poetry: A Debate with Les Murray'. *A.L.S.*, IX, 1979, 39-48.

---. 'Les Murray: An Appreciation'. *Journal of Commonwealth Literature*, XVII, No. 1, 1982, 45-52.

---. 'Les Murray Interviewed by Peter Porter'. *Australian Studies*, No. 4, 1990, 77-87.

Pratt, Noel. 'Showbiz of the Solitary Man'. *Australian*, 7 November, 1970, 19.

Richards, Max. 'Les Murray's Vocation: Gone with Cattle'. *Helix*, No. 4, 1979, 73-80.

Rowlands, Graham. 'Behind the Weatherboard Mask'. *Nation Review*, 6-12 October, 1978, 18.

Shapcott, Thomas. 'John Tranter and Les Murray'. *A.L.S.*, X, 1982, 381-88. *The Boys who Stole the Funeral*.

Sharkey, Michael. 'Les Murray's Single-Minded Many-Sidedness'. *Overland*, No. 82, 1980, 19-25.

Sharma, Anurag. 'Biography and Art: Murray on his Mother'. *Rajasthan University Studies in English*, 21-22, 1989-90, 29-36.

---. 'The Image of India in Les Murray's Poetry'. *The Literary Criterion* (Mysore), 25, No. 2, 1990, 47-57.

---. 'Les Murray's Indianness: The Celebratory Mode of His Poetry: An Analysis of Some of His Indian Poems'. *Literary Criterion* 27.1&2, 1992, 106-15.

Singh, Kirpal. 'Landscape as Revelation: The Case of Les Murray'. *Span*, No. 28, 1989, 90-96.

Smith, Graeme Kinross. '"... The Frequent Image of Farms" - a Profile of Les Murray'. *Westerly*, XXV, No. 3, 1980, 39-52.

Strauss, Jennifer. 'Elegies for Mothers: Reflections on Gwen Harwood's "Mother Who Gave Me Life" and Les Murray's "Three Poems in Memory of My Mother"'. *Westerly*, 34, No. 4, 1989, 58-63.

Sykes, Nick. 'Les A. Murray'. *Studio*, No. 33, 1988/89, 13-20. Interview.

Taylor, Andrew. 'Past Imperfect? The Sense of the Past in Les A. Murray'. *Southern Review*, XIX, No. 1, 1986, 89-103. Reprinted in *The Writer's Sense of the Past: Essays on Southeast Asian and Australasian Literature*, edited by Kirpal Singh (Singapore: Singapore University Press, 1987), 189-197 and in Taylor, Andrew. *Reading Australian Poetry* (St Lucia: U.Q.P., 1987), 139-155.

Throsby, Margaret. 'The Search for "Ah!"' *Look & Listen*, I, No. 1, 1984, 68-71. Interview.

Treloar, Carol. 'Literary View'. *Weekend Australian Magazine*, 22-23 July, 1978, 8, reprinted as 'Writers in Residence: Les Murray at New England'. *Notes & Furphies*, No. 1, 1978, 19-20.

Tulip, James. 'Les Murray in the 1980's: A New Religious Equanimity'. *Southerly*, XLIV, 1984, 281-96.
Williams, Barbara. 'An Interview with Les A. Murray'. *Westerly*, 37.2, 1992, 45-56.
---. 'Malouf, Martin, Murray: The Artists on Their Craft'. *Nimrod*, 36.2, 1993, 135-37. Interview.
Wilmer, Clive. 'Les Murray in Conversation'. *PN Review*, 18.4, 1992, 15-18.

NEILD, JAMES EDWARD ('Jacques')

Critical Material
Blake, L.J. 'The Facts about "Jacques"'. *Australian*, 4 July, 1967, 6.
Brisbane, Katharine. 'The More We Change The More We Don't'. *Australian*, 24 June, 1967, 11.
Love, Harold. '"Are you Christopher Sly?": Actors, Journalists and Murderers on the Nineteenth-century Melbourne Stage'. In *Masks of Time: Drama and Its Contexts*, edited by A.M. Gibbs (Papers from the Australian Academy of the Humanities Symposium 1993. Occasional Paper 16), (Canberra: Australian Academy of the Humanities, 1994), 165-76.
---. *James Edward Neild: Victorian Virtuoso.* (Carlton: M.U.P., 1989). Reviewed by M. Ackland, *Bibliographical Society of Australia and New Zealand Bulletin*, 13, No. 2, 1989, 73-77; J. Carmody, *ABR*, No. 114, 1989, 40-2; V. Kelly, *A.L.S.*, 14, 1990, 408-12.

NEILSON, JOHN SHAW

Collection
John Shaw Neilson: Poetry, Autobiography and Correspondence. Edited by Cliff Hanna. (St. Lucia: U.Q.P., 1991).
Reviewed by A. Collett, *Australian Studies*, 6, 1992, 113-15; H. Jaffa, *Antipodes*, 6.2, 1992, 159-61; A. Rawlins, *ABR*, 136, 1991, 39-40.

Poetry
Green Days and Cherries. Edited by Hugh Anderson and Les Blake. (Ascot Vale, Vic.: Red Rooster Press, 1981).
Reviewed by J. Griffin, *Advertiser*, 6 June, 1981, 25; L. Jacobs, *ABR*, No. 43, 1982, 33-34; R. Tranter, *24 Hours*, VI, No. 6, 1981, 76.

The Poems of Shaw Neilson. (Sydney: A.& R., 1973). Edited and with an introduction by A.R. Chisholm. Revised and enlarged edition. First published Sydney: A.& R., 1965.
Reviewed by J.F. Burrows, *Southerly*, XXXIV, 1974, 98-101; J. Devaney, *Meanjin*, XXIV, 1965, 256-9; D. Douglas, *Age*, 17 April, 1965, 17; S. Lawson, *Nation*, 12 June, 1965, 21-2; V. Smith, *Bulletin*, 10 April, 1965, 53.

Selected Poems. Edited and introduced by Robert Gray. (Pymble, NSW: A.& R., 1992).
Reviewed by P. Nelson, *Quadrant*, 37.7-8, 1993, 117-19.

Shaw Neilson. Edited with an introduction by Judith Wright. (Sydney: A.& R., 1963). Australian Poets series.
Reviewed by A. King, *A.L.S.*, I, No. 4, 1964, 274-6.

Some Poems of Shaw Neilson. Selected and with wood engravings by Barbara Hanrahan. (Canberra: Brindabella Press, 1984).
Reviewed by B. Beaver, *Weekend Australian Magazine*, 21-22 December, 1985, 13.

The Sun Is Up: Selected Poems. Introduced by Richard Keam. (Dromana, Vic.: Loch Haven Books, 1991). Reprinted from Neilson's *Collected Poems* (1934).

Witnesses of Spring: Unpublished Poems. Selected by Judith Wright and Val Vallis from material assembled by Ruth Harrison, edited by Judith Wright. (Sydney: A.& R., 1970).
Reviewed by D. Douglas, *A.L.S.*, V, 1971, 218-23; R. Hall, *Australian*, 28 November, 1970, 23; P. Roberts, *S.M.H.*, 31 July, 1971, 20; K. Slessor, *Daily Telegraph* (Sydney), 15 August, 1970, 13; *Canberra Times*, 28 November, 1970, 13 (see also letters to the editor in *Canberra Times* by D. Green, 2 December, 1970, 2; R.S. Jones, 5 December, 1970, 2; T.I. Moore, 3 December, 1970, 28).

Non-Fiction

The Autobiography. Introduced by Nancy Keesing. (Canberra: National Library of Australia, 1978).
Reviewed by J. Bedford, *National Times*, 10 February, 1979, 30; L. Blake, *Age*, 10 February, 1979, 25; D. Douglas, *ABR*, No. 12, 1979, 12; K. England, *Advertiser*, 19 May, 1979, 21; B. Jefferis, *S.M.H.*, 27 January, 1979, 17.

Critical Material

Anderson, Hugh. *Shaw Neilson: An Annotated Bibliography and Checklist, 1893-1964*. Revised edition. (Sydney: Wentworth Press, 1964). Studies in Australian Bibliography, 3. First published Cremorne: W.W. Stone, 1956.

Chaplin, Harry F. (ed.). *A Neilson Collection*: An Annotated Catalogue of First Editions, Inscribed Copies, Letters, Manuscripts and Association Items; collected and collated by Harry F. Chaplin. (Sydney: Wentworth Books, 1964). Studies in Australian Bibliography, 13. Reviewed by W.M. Maidment, *Southerly*, XXIV, No. 4, 1964, 250-53.

'Nhill Honours Its Poet'. *Western Historian*, No. 33, 1974, 4-8.

Anderson, Hugh and Blake, L.J. *John Shaw Neilson*. (Adelaide: Rigby, 1972). Reviewed by D. Douglas, *Age*, 13 May, 1972, 13; D. Green, *Canberra Times*, 5 August, 1972, 11; C. Harrison-Ford, *S.M.H.*, 27 May, 1972, 27; B. Kiernan, *Australian*, 2 September, 1972, 33; A. Mitchell, *Advertiser*, 4 March, 1972, 24; L. Paul, *Victorian Historical Magazine*, XLIII, 1972, 873-75; A.A. Phillips, *Review*, 13-19 May, 1972, 839; A. Stewart, *A.L.S.*, VI, 1973, 108-12; V. Vallis, *Meanjin*, XXXII, 1973, 225-26.

Ballyn, Susan. 'John Shaw Neilson's Concept of Love'. *Commonwealth*, 14.1, 1991, 97-101.

---. 'Nature and the Concept of Death in John Shaw Neilson's Verse'. *Revista Canaria de Estudios Ingleses* (Tenerife, Spain), No. 12, 1986, 113-121.

Blake, L.J. 'Restoring Poet's Pioneer Home'. *Age*, 26 January, 1972, 9. Letter to the editor; see also related reports, *Australian*, 14 February, 1972, 9; *S.M.H.*, 19 February, 1972, 22; *Age*, 19 February, 1972, 14; *Age*, 8 April, 1972, 12.

---. 'Talking to Ted'. *Overland*, No. 35, 1966, 50-1. Ted Harrington on Neilson.

Burrows, J.F. 'Shaw Neilson's Originality'. *Southerly*, XXXII, 1972, 118-44.

Chaplin, H.F. 'Shaw Neilson & A.G. Stephens, a Note on the Copyrights'. *Biblionews and Australian Notes & Queries*, series 3, I, No. 2, 1976, 20-26.

Davidson, Jim. *Lyrebird Rising: Louise Hanson-Dyer of Oiseau-Lyre 1884-1962*. (Carlton, Vic.: MUP, 1994). Of biographical interest.

Devaney, James. 'One of the Rare People: James Devaney Recalls Shaw Neilson'. *Makar*, VIII, No. 2, 1972, 27-30.

Douglas, Dennis. 'The Imagination of John Shaw Neilson'. *A.L.S.*, V, 1971, 18-23.

Dunlevy, Maurice. 'Unpublished Story of a Bush Poet'. *Canberra Times*, 10 February, 1972, 12.

Gaffney, Carmel. '"The Green Singer": Neilson's Pastoral Poetry'. *Southerly*, 54.2, 1994, 82-96.

Hadgraft, Cecil. 'A Tribute to James Devaney'. *Meanjin*, XXIV, 1965, 215-21.

Hanna, Cliff. 'The Dual Nature of Shaw Neilson's Vision'. *A.L.S.*, V, 1972, 254-76.

---. *The Folly of Spring: A Study of John Shaw Neilson's Poetry* (St Lucia: U.Q.P., 1990). Reviewed by M. Duwell, *A.L.S.*, 14, No. 4, 1990, 522-25; C. Gaffney, *Southerly*, 51.1, 1991, 170-76; A. Ward, *Redoubt*, No. 9, 1990, 70-71.

---. 'The Incongruousness of his Poetry and his Calling: The Effect of Biography on the Poetry of John Shaw Neilson'. In *Autobiographical and Biographical Writing in the Commonwealth*, edited by D. MacDermott (Sadabell, Barcelona: Editorial AUSA, 1984) 101-107.

---. '"The Orange Tree" and the Limitations of Poetry'. *A.L.S.*, VIII, 1978, 280-95.

---. 'The Public Image of John Shaw Neilson'. *A.L.S.*, XII, No. 3, 1986, 397-400.

---. 'Shaw Neilson's "1912" Notebook: A Diary of Lost Love'. *Meridian*, 9, No. 2, 1990, 111-21.

Harris, Max. 'John Shaw Neilson'. *Australian Letters*, VI, Nos. 3-4, 1964, 16-21.

Harrison, Ruth and Burrows, J.F. 'More of Neilson's Fugitives'. *Southerly*, XXXV, 1975, 276-93.

Harrison, Ruth, Burrows, J.F., and Hanna, Clifford. 'A Gathering of Fugitives: An Account of Some Neilson Manuscripts'. *Southerly*, XXXIII, 1973, 313-22.

Harrison, Ruth. 'Towards a Reassessment of the MSS of Shaw Neilson'. *A.L.S.*, III, 1968, 305-12.

Haskell, Dennis. 'Landscape at the Edge of Promise: Neilson and Australian Romanticism'. *Meridian*, 9, No. 2, 1990, 133-42. Shortened version reprinted in *Imagining Romanticism: Essays on English and Australian Romanticisms*, edited by Deirdre Coleman and Peter Otto (West Cornwall, CT: Locust Hill P., 1992), 203-215.

Keesing, Nancy. 'Neilson's Own Story'. Overland, No. 74, 1979, 54-56. On editing the *Autobiography*.

Kuch, Peter. 'Shaw Neilson and Padraic Colum'. *Meridian*, 9, No. 2, 1990, 122-32.

Lane, Mary L. 'The Miracle of John Shaw Neilson'. *Expression*, VIII, No. 3, 1969, 33-38.

Macainsh, Noel. 'John Shaw Neilson and the Cult of the Child'. *Quadrant*, XXII, No. 9, 1978, 18-23.

---. 'John Shaw Neilson and the Floral Metaphor'. *LiNQ*, XIII, No. 2, 1986, 56-74.

Maidment, W.M. 'Australian Literary Criticism'. *Southerly*, XXIV, 1964, 25-26.

McAuley, James. 'Shaw Neilson's Poetry'. *A.L.S.*, II, 1966, 235-53.

Oliver, H.J. *Shaw Neilson*. (Melbourne: O.U.P., 1968). Australian Writers and Their Work. Reviewed by *ABR*, VIII, 1969, 114; M. Dunlevy, *Canberra Times*, 17 May, 1969, 13; F.H. Mares, *A.L.S.*, IV, 1969, 189-90.

Phillips, John H. *Poet of the Colours: The Life of John Shaw Neilson*. (Sydney: Allen & Unwin/Haynes, 1988). Reviewed by J. Green, *Age Saturday Extra*, 29 October, 1988, 16; C. Hanna, *A.L.S.*, 14, No. 2, 1989, 273-76; G. Lehmann, *Weekend Australian*, 11-12 February, 1989, Weekend 8.

Reid, Owen W. 'John Shaw Neilson'. *Tasmanian Education*, XVI, 1964, 13-17.

Richards, Max. 'Shaw Neilson: Simple Singer or Complex Artist?. *Meridian*, 9, No. 2, 1990, 143-50.

Riem Natale, Antonella. 'Hail Holy Light! John Shaw Neilson's "The Orange Tree": An Unorthodox Reading'. *Literary Criterion*, 30.1&2, 1995, 128-32.

Riem, Antonella. 'The "Larger" and "Sadder" Mysteries of Life in the Poetry of Christopher Brennan and John Shaw Neilson'. In her *The Labyrinths of Self: A Collection of Essays on Australian and Caribbean Literature*. (Leichhardt, N.S.W.: FILEF. Italo-Australian Publications, 1987), 111-123.

Robinson, Dennis. 'Native Craft: Some Considerations of John Shaw Neilson'. *Southerly*, XLI, 1981, 336-54.

S[tone], W[alter] W. *Biblionews and Australian Notes & Queries*, Series 3, II, No.

1, 1977, 13. Stephens' alterations to a Neilson poem.
Srinath, C.N. 'A Vision of the Many Coloured Presence: A Note on Shaw Neilson's Poetry'. *ACLALS Bulletin*, Series 4, No. 4, 1976, 32-38.
Stewart, Annette. 'A New Light on "The Orange Tree"?' *A.L.S.*, V, 1971, 24-30.
---. 'Shaw Neilson. *The Orange Tree*'. In *Australian Poems in Perspective*, edited by P.K. Elkin (St Lucia: U.Q.P., 1978), 37-50.
Stone, Walter. 'Neilson's Problems and a Query'. *Biblionews and Australian Notes & Queries*, Series 3, I, No. 4, 1977, 62-63.
Talbot, Norman. 'Two Figures of the Artist: John Shaw Neilson and Gwen Harwood'. In *South Pacific Images*, edited by Chris Tiffin (St Lucia: SPACLALS, 1978), 145-57.
Tennant, Kylie. 'Poet with the Plough'. *Hemisphere*, XXIV, No. 2, 1980, 110-13.
Vallis, Val. 'John Shaw Neilson: An Appreciation'. In his *Heart Reasons, These . . .: Commentaries on Five Australian Poets* (Townsville, Qld.: Foundation for Australian Literary Studies, 1989), 1-26. The Colin Roderick Lectures, Monograph 16.
Wright, Judith. 'John Shaw Neilson'. In her *Preoccupations in Australian Poetry* (Melbourne: O.U.P., 1965), 111-30.
---. 'Meaning, Value, and Poetry'. *Meanjin*, XXVII, 1968, 244-49.

NEWLAND, SIMPSON
Critical Material
White, Graham. 'Beyond Windswept Branches: Simpson Newland's Images of Central Australia'. *Westerly*, 36.4, 1991, 63-69.

NIBBI, GINO
Critical Material
O'Grady, Desmond. 'Between Australia and Italy: The Achievement of Gino Nibbi'. In *Australia and Italy: Contributions to Intellectual Life*, edited by Giovanna Capone (Ravenna: Longo Editore/Universita di Bologna, 1989), 92-102.

NORMAN, N.W.
Critical Material
Roe, Michael. 'N.W. Norman (1901-81): Novelist of Australia's Outback and Outsiders'. *Journal of Australian Studies* 36, 1993, 36-50.

NOWRA, LOUIS
Fiction
The Misery of Beauty, the Loves of Frogmun. (Sydney: A.& R., 1976).
Reviewed by S. Hall, *Australian*, 26 February, 1977, 28; C. Harrison-Ford, *S.M.H.*, 7 May, 1977, 17; A. Mitchell, *Quadrant*, XXII, No. 2, 1978, 76-77.
Palu. (Sydney: Picador, 1987; New York, St Martin's Press, 1989).
Reviewed by J. Colmer, *Weekend Australian. Weekend Magazine*, 8-9 August, 1987, 16; J. Davidson, *Times on Sunday*, 16 August, 1987, 33; M. Johnson, *Antipodes*, 4.1, 1990, 65; D. Myers, *LiNQ*, 17, No. 1, 1990, 165-7; D.J. O'Hearn, *Age Saturday Extra*, 5 September, 1987, 13; T. Shapcott, *ABR*, No. 97, 1987/88, 16-17; M. Taylor, *Antithesis*, 1, No. 2, 1987, 108-110; G. Turcotte, *CRNLE Reviews Journal*, No. 1, 1989, 43-47; B. Turner, *S.M.H.*, 22 August, 1987, 48.

Drama
Capricornia. (Sydney: Currency Press, 1988). Stage adaptation of Xavier Herbert's novel.
Reviewed by A. Cromwell, *Antipodes*, 4.1, 1990, 68; J. Eccles, *S.M.H.*, 23 April, 1988, 74; G. Turcotte, *Australasian Drama Studies*, Nos. 15-16, 1989/1990, 189-91.

Cosi. (Sydney: Currency Press, 1991).
Reviewed by H. Thomson, *Australasian Drama Studies*, 23, 1993, 175-78.
The Golden Age. (Sydney: Currency Press; Melbourne: Playbox Theatre Company, 1985).
Reviewed by P. Fitzpatrick, *Australasian Drama Studies*, No. 7, 1985, 139-144.
Inner Voices. (Sydney: Currency Press, 1977).
Reviewed by F. de Groen, *CRNLE Reviews Journal*, No. 1, 1980, 102-09.
Inside the Island; The Precious Woman. With music score by Sarah de Jong. (Woollahra, N.S.W.: Currency Press, 1981).
Reviewed by M. Lord, *ABR*, No. 45, 1982, 25-26; E. Perkins, *LiNQ*, XI, No. 1, 1983, 89-100; L. Radic, *Age Saturday Extra*, 7 August, 1982, 15.
Radiance. (Sydney: Currency Press, 1993).
Reviewed by A. Cromwell, *Antipodes*, 9.2, 1995, 166; P. Makeham, *Australasian Drama Studies*, 25, 1994, 193-95.
Summer of the Aliens. (Sydney: Currency Press, 1992).
Reviewed by A. Cromwell, *Antipodes*, 7.1, 1993, 70-72; H. Thomson, *Australasian Drama Studies*, 23, 1993, 175-78.
Sunrise. (Sydney: Currency Press/State Theatre Company of South Australia, 1983).
Reviewed by V. Kelly, *Australasian Drama Studies*, II, No. 2, 1984, 124-6.
The Temple. (Sydney: Currency Press, 1993).
Reviewed by P. Fitzpatrick, *Australasian Drama Studies* 25, 1994, 199-201.
Visions. (Sydney: Currency Press, 1979).
Reviewed by F. de Groen, *CRNLE Reviews Journal*, No. 1, 1980, 102-09; A. Godfrey-Smith, *ABR*, No. 18, 1980, 21-22; S. Hoass, *Canberra Times*, 26 January, 1980, 18; J. McCallum, *Theatre-Australia*, IV, No. 4, 1979, 55; L. Radic, *Age*, 21 April, 1980, 10.

Non-Fiction

'How I Became Stagestruck'. *S.M.H. Magazine: Good Weekend*, 12 January, 1985, 34-35.
'*Inner Voices* and the First Coil'. *A.L.S.*, IX, 1979, 189-99.
'Madness and Ergot'. *National Times*, 4-10 October, 1985, 51. Letter to the Editor concernig *Inside the Island*.
'The Short, Nasty, Brutal Life of the Playwright'. *Island*, 63, 1995, 3-8.
'The Shrinking Vision', *Island Magazine*, No. 39, 1989, 11-13. Discusses developments and changes in Australian theatre in the 1980s.
'Translating for the Australian Stage (A Personal Viewpoint)'. *A.L.S.*, X, 1982, 336-43.

Critical Material

Baker, Candida. 'Louis Nowra'. In her *Yacker 3* (Sydney: Picador, 1989), 236-258. Interview.
Campbell, Lance. 'Not Mushroom for Failure'. *Advertiser*, 24 May, 1982, 24. Interview.
Davidson, Jim. 'Louis Nowra'. *Meanjin*, XXXIX, 1980, 479-95. Interview. Reprinted in his *Sideways From the Page* (Melbourne: Fontana, 1983), 280-302.
Duigan, Virginia. 'Louis Nowra: The Annals of the Cheated'. *National Times*, 6-11 December, 1976, 42.
Gilbert, Helen. 'De-scribing Orality'. Includes discussion of Aboriginal drama, Jack Davis, Kevin Gilbert, Louis Nowra. In *De-scribing Empire: Post-colonialism and Textuality*, edited by Chris Tiffin and Alan Lawson (London and New York: Routledge, 1994), 98-111.
---. 'Ghosts in a Landscape: Louis Nowra's *Inside the Island* and Janis Balodis' *Too Young for Ghosts'. Southern Review*, 27.4, 1994, 432-47.
---. 'Monumental Moments: Michael Gow's *1841*, Stephen Sewell's *Hate*, Louis

Nowra's *Capricornia* and Australia's Bicentenary'. *Australasian Drama Studies*, 24, 1994, 29-45.

---. 'Postcolonial Grotesques: Re-membering the Body in Louis Nowra's *Visions* and *The Golden Age*'. In *Postcolonial Fictions*, edited by Michèle Drouart (special issue in two volumes including SPACLALS Conference Proceedings, *SPAN*, 36, 1993), 618-33.

Griffiths, Gareth. 'Australian Subjects and Australian Style: The Plays of Louis Nowra'. *Commonwealth* (Paris), VI, No. 2, 1984, 42-48.

Harris, Samela. 'Reluctant Elitist Writes with Dedicated Fervor'. *Australian*, 20 May, 1982, 8.

Kelly, Veronica. 'Lest We Forget: Louis Nowra's "Inside the Island"'. *Island Magazine*, No. 23, 1985, 19-23.

Kelly, Veronica (ed.). *Louis Nowra*. (Amsterdam: Rodopi, 1987), Australian Playwrights No. 1. Reviewed by R. Corballis, *Modern Drama*, 34.1, 1991, 163-67; A. Cromwell, *Antipodes*, 4.1, 1990, 68; H. Thomson, *Meridian*, 8, No. 1, 1989, 91-93; G. Turcotte, *Span*, No. 25, 1987, 109-112.

---. 'Louis Nowra'. In *Post-Colonial English Drama: Commonwealth Drama since 1960*, edited by Bruce King (London: Macmillan; New York: St Martin's, 1992), 50-66.

---. 'A Mirror for Australia: Louis Nowra's Emblematic Theatre'. *Southerly*, XLI, 1981, 431-58.

---. '"More Character-Driven": An Interview with Louis Nowra'. *Coppertales*, 2, 1995, 79-92.

---. '"Nowt More Outcastin": Utopian Myth in Louis Nowra's *The Golden Age*'. In *A Sense of Exile*, edited by Bruce Bennett (Nedlands, W.A.: The Centre for Studies in Australian Literature, 1988), 101-110.

Kiernan, Brian. 'Some Contemporary Developments in Australian Drama: Louis Nowra and Stephen Sewell'. In *Australian Papers: Yugoslavia, Europe and Australia*, edited by Mirko Jurak (Ljubljana: Edvard Cardelj University, 1983), 1983-89.

Le Moignan, Michael. 'The Strange World of Louis Nowra'. *National Times*, 23-29 November, 1980, 40.

McCallum, John. 'The World Outside: Cosmopolitanism in the Plays of Nowra and Sewell'. *Meanjin*, XLIII, 1984, 286-96.

Makeham, Paul. 'The Black Hole of Our History: Paul Makeham Talks to Playwright Louis Nowra about Australian Theatre, Nationalism and the Process of Writing'. *Canadian Theatre Review*, 74, 1993, 27-31.

Milliken, Robert. 'Nowra Carves into the Upper Crust'. *National Times*, 18-24 November, 1983, 34.

Morley, Michael. 'Louis Nowra on Translating and Adapting *Lulu*'. *Theatre Australia*, V, No. 10, 1981, 23. Interview.

Nicklin, Leonore. 'Writing about the Cut-Off People'. *S.M.H.*, 17 August, 1978, 7.

Radic, Leonard. 'Louis Nowra Learns to Adapt'. *Age Saturday Extra*, 25 August, 1984, 14.

Ridgman, Jeremy 'Interview: Louis Nowra, Stephen Sewell and Neil Armfield talk to Jeremy Ridgman'. *Australasian Drama Studies*, I, No. 2, 1985, 105-23.

Sykes, Jill. 'Sources Close to Home'. *S.M.H.*, 9 August, 1980, 19.

Turcotte, Gerry. '"The Circle is Burst": Eschatological Discourse in Louis Nowra's *Sunrise* and *The Golden Age*'. *Australasian Drama Studies*, No. 11, 1987, 65-77. Also published in *Span*, No. 24, 1987, 63-80.

---. 'Perfecting the Monologue of Silence: An Interview with Louis Nowra'. *Kunapipi*, IX, No. 3, 1987, 51-67.

---. '"Speaking the Formula of Abjection": Hybrids and Gothic Discourses in Louis Nowra's Novels'. *Westerly*, 36.3, 1991, 61-72.

OAKLEY, BARRY

Fiction

The Craziplane. (Sydney: Hodder & Stoughton, 1989).
Reviewed by M. Copland, *Age Saturday Extra*, 23 September, 1989, 9; P. Pierce, *S.M.H.*, 9 September, 1989, 79; T. Scott, *Weekend Australian*, 30 September-1 October, 1989, Weekend 8; L. Trainor, *ABR*, No. 115, 1989, 13-14.

Let's Hear It for Prendergast. (Melbourne: Heinemann Australia, 1970).
Reviewed by D. Ball, *Bulletin*, 19 December, 1970, 47; L. Cantrell, *Meanjin*, XXX, 1971, 135-37; A.R. Chisholm, *Age*, 19 December, 1970, 17; C. Harrison-Ford, *Overland*, No. 48, 1971, 59-60; B. Kiernan, *Australian*, 26 December, 1970, 10; J.D. Pringle, *S.M.H.*, 19 December, 1970, 20; W.S. Ramson, *Canberra Times*, 30 January, 1971, 12.

A Salute to the Great McCarthy. (Melbourne: Heinemann Australia, 1970, Ringwood, Vic.: Penguin, 1971).
Reviewed by R. Burns, *Nation*, 25 July, 1970, 20-22 (see also letters to the editor by B. Oakley, 8 August, 1970, 14, and by R. Burns, 22 August, 1970, 16); L. Cantrell, *Meanjin*, XXX, 1971, 135; T. Forshaw, *S.M.H.*, 15 August, 1970, 22; D. Haworth, *New Statesman*, 5 February, 1971, 188; N. Keesing, *Bulletin*, 12 September, 1970, 50-52; B. Kiernan, *Australian*, 25 July, 1970, 20; J. Larkin, *Age*, 27 June, 1970, 13; M. Lemming, *ABR*, IX, 1970, 282; J. Lleonart, *Canberra Times*, 8 August, 1970, 13; I. Turner, *Overland*, No. 45, 1970, 44-45.

Walking Through Tigerland. (St Lucia: U.Q.P., 1977).
Reviewed by W. Blaxland, *S.M.H.*, 19 November, 1977, 17; D.R. Burns, *Nation Review*, 1-7 December, 1977, 16; P. Corris, *24 Hours*, III, No. 1, 1978, 55; G. Davenport, *Hudson Review*, XXXII, 1979, 139-40; D. Green, *National Times*, 7-12 November, 1977, 53; S. Hall, *Weekend Australian Magazine*, 3-4 December, 1977, 10; V. Ikin, *Quadrant*, XXII, No. 8, 1978, 76; S. Kobulniczky, *Westerly*, No. 1, 1978, 96-100; B. Morrow, *Advertiser*, 31 December, 1977, 17; D. Rowbotham, *Courier-Mail*, 17 December, 1977, 17; M. Smith, *Campaign*, No. 28, 1978, 54.

A Wild Ass of a Man. (Melbourne: Cheshire, 1967, Ringwood, Vic.: Penguin, 1970).
Reviewed by A.R. Chisholm, *Age*, 11 November, 1971, 1967, 23; S. Edgar, *ABR*, VII, 1967/68, 46; T. Forshaw, *Quadrant*, XXI, No. 7, 1977, 72-73; C. Harrison-Ford, *Sunday Australian*, 28 February, 1971, 33; W.S. Ramson, *Canberra Times*, 30 January, 1971, 12; M. Vintner, *S.M.H.*, 11 November, 1967, 19.

Drama

Bedfellows. (Sydney: Currency Press, London: Eyre Methuen, 1975).

Reviewed by L. Radic, *Age*, 1 November, 1975, 20.

Beware of Imitations. (Montmorency, Vic.: Yackandandah Playscripts, 1985).
Reviewed by H. Thomson, *ABR*, No. 85, 1986, 23-24.

The Feet of Daniel Mannix. Music by Lorraine Milne (Sydney: A.& R., 1975). A.&
R. playtexts. Introduction by Leonard Radic.
Reviewed by L. Radic, *Age*, 1 November, 1975, 20.

The Great God Mogadon and Other Plays. (St Lucia: U.Q.P., 1980).
Reviewed by M. Lord, *ABR*, No. 22, 1980, 10; J. McCallum, *Theatre Australia*, V,
No. 4, 1980, 44; L. Radic, *Age*, 21 April, 1980, 10; P. Thompson, *S.M.H.*, 15
March, 1980, 15.

A Lesson in English. (Sydney: Currency Press; London: Eyre Methuen, 1976).
Currency Double Bill. Bound with Ron Blair, *The Christian Brothers*.
Reviewed by H. Van Der Poorten, *Theatre-Australia*, I, No. 2, 1976, 56.

Marsupials and Politics: Two Comedies. (St Lucia: U.Q.P., 1981). Contemporary
Australian Plays, 10.
Reviewed by M. Lord, *ABR*, No. 37, 1981, 15-16; D. Rowbotham, *Courier-Mail*, 15
August, 1981, 24.

The Ship's Whistle. (Melbourne: Monash New Plays, 1979).
Reviewed by J. McCallum, *Theatre-Australia*, IV, No. 4, 1979, 55; E. Webby,
CRNLE Reviews Journal, No. 1, 1980, 116-18.

'Witzenhausen, Where Are You?' In *6 One-Act Plays*, edited by Eunice Hanger (St
Lucia: U.Q.P., 1971).

Non-Fiction

Scribbling in the Dark. (St Lucia: U.Q.P., 1985). Revised edition (St Lucia: U.Q.P.,
1993).
Reviewed by D. Anderson, *National Times*, 25 April-1 May, 1986, 43; H. Daniel,
Age Saturday Extra, 12 April, 1986, 13; B. Dickins, *ABR*, No. 82, 1986, 24-25; F.
Kellaway, *Overland*, No. 104, 1986, 64-65; S. Knight, *S.M.H.*, 19 April, 1986, 46;
J. Moses, *Weekend Australian Magazine*, 21-22 June, 1986, 16; D. Rowbotham,
Courier-Mail Magazine: The Great Weekend, 29 March, 1986, 6; V. Sen, *Canberra
Times*, 31 May, 1986, B3; G. Windsor, *Bulletin*, 10 June, 1986, 107.

'An Author's Private Library. Barry Oakley Reveals his Reading History'. *Australian
Library News*, XII, No. 7, 1981, 4.
'Great Rivalries: Sydney, Melbourne and Pina Wima'. In *The View from Tinsel Town*,
edited by Tom Thompson (Ringwood, Vic.: Southerly/Penguin, 1985), 91-94.
'The Montague Avenue Gang'. *National Times*, 23-29 November, 1980, 35-36.
Autobiographical.
'On Being a Writer in Australia'. *Dissent*, No. 29, 1972, 1-5.
'Self Portrait'. *ABR*, No. 78, 1986, 34-35.
'The Writer in Australia'. *Westerly*, No. 3, 1975, 65-70. Autobiographical.
'Writers' View'. *Theatre-Australia*, IV, No. 4, 1979, 24-25.

Critical Material

'Authors Share $5,000 Prize in Literary Contest'. *Australian*, 27 October, 1970, 1.
'Barry Oakley'. *Lot's Wife*, 26 August, 1974, 10-11. Interview.
Campbell, Lance. 'Kendall's Legacy ...'. *Advertiser*, 6 October, 1980, 24.
Coleman, Richard. 'From Acting at School to Comic Reality of Stage'. *S.M.H.*, 2
August, 1980, 23.
Collins, Martin. 'Author Sees Us as a Pretty Bloody Lot'. *Australian*, 26 June, 1970,
20.
Daniel, Helen. 'The Picaro in Disguise: The Novels of Barry Oakley'. *Westerly*,
XXV, No. 2, 1980, 51-57.
Dare, Tim. 'Heroic Victims'. *Australian*, 19 September, 1970, 16.

Duigan, Victoria. 'Prepare for New Life Satires from Barry Oakley, Father of Six'. *National Times*, 8-13 January, 1973, 17.

Hack, Iola. 'Melbourne Attacked in Prize-Winning Novel'. *Age*, 28 October, 1970, 13.

Hawley, Janet. 'A Playwright Back in his Moderate Pond'. *Age*, 29 September, 1979, 23.

---. 'Three-Way Split'. *Australian*, 16 April, 1974, 12. Oakley's current writing projects.

Larkin, John. '500 Words a Night in the Wilds of Richmond'. *Age*, 27 June, 1970, 2.

Nicklin, Lenore. 'Cruel Fate of an Aussie Rules Champ'. *S.M.H.*, 6 August, 1970, 7.

O'Connor, Ursula. 'Third Try Lucky for Cook Novel Winner'. *S.M.H.*, 27 October, 1970, 8.

Sayers, Stuart. 'Old Walhalla on Parade'. *Age*, 12 December, 1970, 16.

---. 'Play Writing is the Phase in the Ascendant'. *Age*, 11 November, 1978, 25.

Thomas, Keith. 'Cathartic Delight'. *Weekend Australian Magazine*, 26-27 July, 1980, 13.

Watson, Betty L. 'Barry Oakley and the Satiric Mode'. *A.L.S.*, VII, 1975, 50-63.

White, Sally. 'Barry Oakley Lives Up to His Own "Terrifying" Expectations'. *Age*, 20 October, 1973, 15. Reprinted in *Advertiser*, 10 November, 1973, 21.

O'BRIEN, JOHN

Non-Fiction

The Men of '38 and Other Pioneer Priests. Edited by T.J. Linane and F.A. Mecham. (Kilmore, Vic.: Lowden, 1975). Biographical introductions by F.A. Mecham and Cardinal James Freeman.

Discussed by S. Sayers, *Age*, 7 June, 1975, 17.

Critical Material

Gill, Alan. 'Father Pat - the Poet who outsold Lawson'. *S.M.H.*, 6 March, 1976, 13.

Mecham, Frank. *"John O'Brien" and the Boree Log*. (Sydney: A.& R., 1981). Reviewed by J. Barry, *ABR*, No. 45, 1982, 13-14; E. Campion, *Bulletin*, 2 March, 1982, 67; C. Hadgraft, *A.L.S.*, X, 1982, 547-48; J.S. Murray, *Weekend Australian Magazine*, 20-21, 1982, 10; C. Semmler, *Courier-Mail*, 10 April, 1982, 20; V. Sen, *Canberra Times*, 15 May, 1982, 15.

O'DOWD, BERNARD

Poetry

Bernard O'Dowd. Edited with an introduction by A.A. Phillips. (Sydney: A.& R., 1963). Australian Poets series.

Critical Material

Anderson, Hugh. *Bernard O'Dowd (1866-1953): An Annotated Bibliography*. (Sydney: Wentworth Books, 1963). Studies in Bibliography, No. 12. General Editor: Walter W. Stone.

Anderson, Hugh. *Bernard O'Dowd*. (New York: Twayne, 1968).

---. *The Poet Militant: Bernard O'Dowd*. (Melbourne: Hill of Content, 1969). Revised and enlarged edition of *Bernard O'Dowd* (New York: Twayne, 1968). Reviewed by R. Baxter, *Journal of the Royal Australian Historical Society*, LVII, 1971, 257-59; B. Elliott, *ABR*, IX, 1969/70, 61-63; C. Harrison-Ford, *Union Recorder*, University of Sydney, 22 July, 1970, 4-5; S. Lawson, *Nation*, 29 November, 1969, 23; T. Sturm, *A.L.S.*, IV, 1970, 417-21.

Docker, John. 'Politics and Poetics: Bernard O'Dowd's *Dawnward*? and Nineteenth-Century Chartist Poetry'. *Southerly*, 53.2, 1993, 13-33.

Macartney, Frederick T. 'The Poet Militant'. *Age*, 9 April, 1966, 15.
McQueen, Humphrey. *A New Britannia: An Argument Concerning the Social Origins of Australian Radicalism and Nationalism.* (Ringwood, Vic., Harmondsworth, Middlesex: Penguin, 1970), 101-103.
O'Dowd, Rudel ('Pat'). 'O'Dowd Paterfamilias'. *Overland*, No. 39, 1968, 17-23.
O'Mallee, Myall. 'Lawson: The Centenary Symposium Continues: Lawson and O'Dowd'. *Tribune*, 21 June, 1967, 14.
Pearce, Harry H. 'Bernard O'Dowd'. *Bernard O'Dowd Centenary Souvenir* (Melbourne: Australian Poetry Lovers' Society, 1966). See also *Clanalder Sennachie*, No. 30, 1966, 2.
Wilde, W.H. *Three Radicals.* (Melbourne: O.U.P., 1969). Australian Writers and Their Work. Discusses O'Dowd, Maurice and Gilmour. Reviewed by A. Mitchell, *A.L.S.*, V, 1971, 99-100.
Wright, Judith. 'Meaning, Value, and Poetry'. *Meanjin*, XXVII, 1968, 244-49.
---. 'The Reformist Poets'. In her *Preoccupations in Australian Poetry* (Melbourne: O.U.P., 1965), 68-79.

OGILVIE, W.H.

Critical Material

Barton, Hilton. 'Will Ogilvie: An Imperialistic Minstrel'. *Realist Writer*, No. 12, 1963, 23-4.
Keesing, Nancy. '"Anon" and Detection'. *Southerly*, XXX, 1970, 221-25.
Ogilvie, George T.A. *Will H. Ogilvie: Balladist of Border and Bush.* (Seascale, Cumbria: G.T. Ogilvie, 1994).
Semmler, Clement. 'Two Australian Balladists: W.H. Ogilvie and E.J. Brady'. *Antipodes*, II, No. 1, 1988, 33-38.
Tapp, Dorothy. 'Will Ogilvie'. *Broken Hill Historical Society, Journal and Proceedings*, IV, 1968, 25-29.

OODGEROO NOONUCCAL
(previously Kath Walker)

Collection

Kath Walker in China. Foreword by Manning Clark. Translated by Gu Zixin. (Milton, Qld.: Jacaranda Press and International Culture Publishing Corporation, 1988). Bilingual edition.
Reviewed by G. Jennings, *Arena*, 95, 1991, 170-73; S. Patton, *ABR*, No. 122, 1990, 13; E. Smith, *Queensland Writer*, 2.1, 1990, 17.

Poetry

The Dawn is at Hand. (Brisbane: Jacaranda, 1966).
Reviewed by L. Cantrell, *Poetry Magazine*, 1, 1967, 31-32; B. Gill, *Australian*, 5 November, 1966, 9; S.E. Lee, *Southerly*, 27, 1967, 60-71; R. McCuaig, *Literary Letter*, 42, 1966, 4; R. Robinson, *S.M.H.*, 12 November, 1966, 20; T. Shapcott, *ABR*, 6, 1966-67, 33; A. Taylor, *Overland*, 36, 1967, 44.

My People. (Milton, Qld.: Jacaranda, 1970). 2nd edition, 1981; 3rd edition, 1990.
Reviewed by R. Hall, *Australian*, 24 April, 1971, 20; S.E. Lee, *Southerly*, 31, 1971, 233-34; R. Robinson, *Makar*, VII, No. 1, 1971, 7-9; N. Wilkinson, *New Guinea*, 6.3, 1971, 62; *Union Recorder*, 51.3, 1971, 7.

Stradbroke Dreamtime. (Pymble, NSW: A.& R, 1993). Revised edition. Originally published Sydney: A.& R., 1972.
Reviewed by M. Dunkle, *ABR*, No. 31, 1981, 34-6; S. Lees, *The Review* (Melbourne), 24-30 June, 1972, 1025; W. McVitty, *Age*, 16-17 October, 1982, Saturday Extra, 12; D. Moore, *Bulletin*, 3 June, 1972, 52; R. Robinson, *S.M.H.*, 3 June, 1972, 21; S. Shivaprakash, *Literary Criterion*, 30.1&2, 1995, 133-36; *T.L.S.*,

14 July, 1972, 813.
We Are Going. (Brisbane: Jacaranda Press, 1964).
Reviewed by A. Brissenden, *Southerly,* 24, 1964, 248-49; D.Douglas, *Age Literary Review,* 8 August, 1964, 22; J. Hellyer, *Hemisphere,* No. 12, 1964, 17-18; D. Jones, *Poetry Magazine,* 3, 1964, 31; R. McCuaig, *Bulletin,* 22 August, 1964, 52; *T.L.S.,* 10 September, 1964, 842; I. Turner, *Australian,* 26 September, 1964.

Non-Fiction
'I Used My Art For Sanity's Sake' and 'Hijack'. In *Long Water: Aboriginal Art and Literature,* edited by Ulli Beier and Rudi Krausmann. A special edition of *Aspect,* 34, 1986, 52-57; 83-86.

Critical Material
Little, Janine. 'Oodgeroo: A Selective Checklist'. *A.L.S.,* 16.4, 1994, 178-187.
'An Interview with Kath Walker'. *Aspect,* 5, 1963, 7-11.
Anderson, Michael. 'A Call for Justice'. *Identity,* I, No. 8, 1973, 17.
Baker, Candida. 'Kath Walker'. In her *Yacker 2: Australian Writers Talk About Their Work* (Sydney: Picador, 1987), 280-301.
Beston, John. 'The Aboriginal Poets in English: Kath Walker, Jack Davis, and Kevin Gilbert'. *Meanjin,* XXXVI, 1977, 446-62.
Brewster, Anne. 'Oodgeroo: Orator, Poet, Storyteller'. In *Oodgeroo: A Tribute,* edited by Adam Shoemaker (St Lucia: *Australian Literary Studies* and U.Q.P., 1994), 92-104.
Cochrane, Kathie. *Oodgeroo.* With a contribution by Judith Wright. Illustrated by Ron Hurley. (St Lucia: U.Q.P., 1994). Reviewed by L. Connors, *LiNQ,* 22.2: 127-31; J. Griffin, *Eureka Street,* 5.5, 1995, 40-41; H. Horton, *Imago,* 7.1, 1995, 99-101; J. Little, *AWBR,* 7.1, 1995, 18-19; P. Mamajun Torres, *Weekend Australian,* 29-30 October, 1993, Review 5; J. McDonell, *Southerly,* 55.4, 1995, 197-203; B. Marshall-Stoneking, *Overland,* 138, 1995, 74-76; P. Morrissey, *ABR,* 166, 1993, 13-14; M. Strelau, *Antipodes,* 9.2, 1995, 174.
Collins, John. 'Oodgeroo Noonuccal: A Celebration'. *Imago,* 7.1, 1995, 65-66.
---. 'Oodgeroo of the Tribe Noonuccal'. *Race & Class,* 35.4, 1994, 77-87.
Davidson, Jim. 'Kath Walker'. *Meanjin,* XXXVI, 1977, 428-41. Interview. Reprinted in his *Sideways from the Page* (Melbourne: Fontana, 1983), 52-70.
Dexter, Nancy. 'Kath's in Town with a Few Bitter Truths'. *Age,* 30 July, 1975, 19.
Doobov, Ruth. 'The New Dreamtime: Kath Walker in Australian Literature'. *A.L.S.,* VI, 1973, 46-55.
Fox, Len. 'Kath Walker: Aboriginal Poet'. *Realist Writer,* 16, 1964, 24-25.
Grassby, A.J. *Oodgeroo Noonuccal: Poet, Painter and Elder of Her People.* (South Melbourne: Macmillan, 1991).
Hodge, Bob. 'Poetry and Politics in Oodgeroo: Transcending the Difference'. In *Oodgeroo: A Tribute,* edited by Adam Shoemaker (St Lucia: *Australian Literary Studies* and U.Q.P., 1994), 63-76.
Indyk, Ivor. 'Pastoral and Priority: The Aboriginal in Australian Pastoral'. *New Literary History,* 24.4, 1993 837-55. Includes discussion of writers including Oodgeroo.
Lauer, Margaret Read. 'Kath Walker at Moongalba: Making the New Dreamtime'. *WLWE,* XVII, No. 1, 1978, 83-95.
Mason, Bobbie Ann. 'Kath Walker, Aboriginal Poet'. *Denver Quarterly,* XV, No. 4, 1981, 63-75.
McCredie, Jane. 'Black Poet Thankful for Life Between two Worlds'. *Age,* 3 October, 1981, 16.
Mudrooroo. 'Obituary'. *Island,* 57, 1993, 3. See other obituaries: K. Cochrane, *Australian Aboriginal Studies,* 19.2, 1993, 129-30, Ruby Langford Ginibi, *Australian Women's Book Review,* 6.1, 1994, 2-3, A. Shoemaker, *ABR,* 156, 1993, 4 and *Notes*

& *Furphies*, 31, 1993, 1-2.
---. 'The Poetemics of Oodgeroo of the Tribe Noonuccal'. In *Oodgeroo: A Tribute*, edited by Adam Shoemaker (St Lucia: *Australian Literary Studies* and U.Q.P., 1994), 57-62.
Page, Geoff. 'The Poetry of Oodgeroo'. *Island*, 57, 1993, 4-5.
---. 'Oodgeroo'. In his *A Reader's Guide To Contemporary Australian Poetry* (St. Lucia: U.Q.P., 1995), 217-221.
Rama, R.P. '[Interview with] Oodgeroo Noonuccal'. In *Dialogues with Australian Poets*, (Calcutta: P. Lal/Writers Workshop, 1993), 45-53.
Rask Knudsen, Eva. 'From Kath Walker to Oodgeroo Noonuccal? Ambiguity and Assurance in *My People*'. In *Oodgeroo: A Tribute*, edited by Adam Shoemaker (St Lucia: *Australian Literary Studies* and U.Q.P., 1994), 105-118.
Rider, Sue. 'Oodgeroo's Work and Its Theatrical Potential'. In *Oodgeroo: A Tribute*, edited by Adam Shoemaker (St Lucia: *Australian Literary Studies* and U.Q.P., 1994), 153-63.
Scott, L.E. 'The Lady in Black Seeking Truth in the Night'. *Pacific Quarterly Moana*, IV, No. 4, 1979, 426.
Shoemaker, Adam, ed. *Oodgeroo: A Tribute*. (St Lucia: *Australian Literary Studies* and U.Q.P., 1994). Special issue *A.L.S.*, 16.4. Includes biographical material, reminiscences, appreciation of Oodgeroo's social, educational and political achievements as well as critical articles listed separately under their authors. Reviewed by L. Connors, *LiNQ*, 22.2, 1995, 127-31; R. Hall, *Age*, 18 Feb., 1995, Saturday Extra 7; H. Horton, *Imago*, 7.2, 1995, 101; J. McDonell, *Southerly*, 55.4, 1995, 197-203; G. Papaellinas, *ABR*, 168, 1995, 25; M. Strelau, *Antipodes*, 9.2, 1995, 174.
---. 'Performance for the People'. In *Oodgeroo: A Tribute*, edited by Adam Shoemaker (St Lucia: *Australian Literary Studies* and U.Q.P., 1994), 164-77.
Smith, Angela. 'Long Memoried Women: Oodgeroo Noonuccal and Jamaican Poet, Louise Bennett'. In *Oodgeroo: A Tribute*, edited by Adam Shoemaker (St Lucia: *Australian Literary Studies* and U.Q.P., 1994), 77-91.
Turcotte, Gerry. 'Recording the Cries of the People: An Interview with Oodgeroo (Kath Walker)'. *Kunapipi*, 10, Nos. 1&2, 1988, 16-30.
Wallis, John. 'Kath Walker: Poetry or Propaganda'. *Checkpoint*, No. 10, 1972, 22-24.
Weiniger, Peter. 'Kath Walker and the New Dreamtime'. *Age*, 18 August, 1981, 11.
Wright, Judith. 'The Koori Voice: A New Literature'. *Australian Author*, V, No. 4, 1973, 38-44.

O'REILLY, DOWELL

Critical Material
Heseltine, H.P. '"Cyrus Brown of Sydney Town": Christopher Brennan and Dowell O'Reilly'. In *Bards, Bohemians, and Bookmen*, edited by Leon Cantrell (St Lucia: U.Q.P., 1976), 136-52.

O'REILLY, JOHN BOYLE

Fiction
Moondyne. Introduction by Brian Elliott (Adelaide: Rigby, 1975).

Non-Fiction
Selected Poems, Speeches, Dedications and Letters of John Boyle O'Reilly: 1844-1890. Edited by Liam Barry (Australind, WA: National Gaelic Publications, 1994).

Critical Material
Brady, Veronica. 'History, Literature and J.B. O'Reilly'. *Westerly*, No. 4, 1977, 47-59.
---. 'The Return of the Repressed: J.B. O'Reilly and the Politics of Desire'. *Westerly*,

XXXIII, No. 2, 1988, 105-113.
Elliot, Ian. *Moondyne Joe: The Man and the Myth*. (Nedlands: University of W.A. Press, 1978). The original of O'Reilly's 'Moondyne'.
Mackaness, George. 'John Boyle O'Reilly'. *Bibliomania: An Australian Book Collector's Essays* (Sydney: A.& R., 1965), 172-8.
Rosen, Bruce. 'The "Catalpa" Rescue'. *Royal Australian Historical Society Journal*, LXV, 73-88.
Rutherford, L.M. '*The Wild Goose*: A Manuscript Convict Newspaper'. *Bibliographical Society of Australia and New Zealand Bulletin*, 16.1, 1992, 1-17. Includes reproduction of an issue of *The Wild Goose*.
Brady, Veronica. 'The Innocent Gaze: John Boyle O'Reilly's "The King of the Vasse"'. *Kunapipi*, 16.2 1994, 1-6.

PI O (π.ο.).

Poetry
24 Hours. (Melbourne: Collective Effort Press, 1995).
Reviewed by I. Indyk, *Southerly*, 55.4, 1995, 66-72.

Fitzroy Poems. (Melbourne: Collective Effort, 1989).
Reviewed by H. Cam, *S.M.H.*, 20 May, 1989, 84; J.H. Duke, *Age Monthly Review*, June, 1989, 8-10; M. Lysenko, *Going Down Swinging*, 9, 1989, 121-22; A. Selenitsch, *Overland*, 116, 1989, 86-88; A. Wearne, *ABR*, 113, 1989, 34-36.

Off the Record. Edited by Pi O. (Ringwood, Vic.: Penguin, 1985).
Reviewed by K. Brophy, *Age Monthly Review*, December/January, 1986-87, 12-13; P. Pierce, *Age*, 12 April, 1986, Saturday Extra 14; M. Sharkey, *Meanjin*, 44.4, 1985, 446-51.

Panash. (Carlton, Vic.: Collective Effort Press, 1978).
Reviewed by L. Buttrose, *Nation Review*, 15 February, 1979, 332; R.D. Jones, *Makar*, 14.3, 1980, 61-63.

Pi O Revisited. (Sydney: Wild & Woolley, 1976).
Reviewed by T. Thorne, *Australian*, 16 April, 1977, 31.

Poems by Pi O. (Melbourne, Fitzrot Publications, 1974).
Reviewed by R.D. Jones, *Makar*, 10.1, 1974, 43-46.

Street Singe. (Melbourne: Pi Omega, 1976).
Reviewed by L. Abraham, *Autralian Small Press Review*, 4, 1976, 20-22; M. Dugan, *Age*, 24 July, 1976, 23; A. Wearne, *Contempa*, 2.2, 1976, 52.

Critical Material
Kanarakis, George. 'The Literary Contribution of the Greek Macedonians in Australia'. In *Macedonian Hellenism*, edited by A.M. Tamis (Dalesford, Vic.: River Seine Press, 1990), 314-323.
Koval, Ramona. 'π.ο.'. In her *One to One* (Sydney: ABC Enterprises, 1992), 49-60. Interview.
Marshall-Stoneking, Billy. 'π.ο.: An Appreciation'. *Southerly*, 55.4, 1995, 40-53.
Page, Geoff. 'π.ο.'. In his *A Reader's Guide To Contemporary Australian Poetry* (St. Lucia: U.Q.P., 1995), 209-213.
Tsokalidou, Roula. 'π.ο.: The Poet Who Cracked the Code'. *Southerly*, 55.4, 1995, 54-65.

PAGE, GEOFF

Fiction

Benton's Conviction. (North Ryde, N.S.W.: A.& R., 1985).
Reviewed by G. Catalano, *Age Monthly Review*, V, No. 4, 1985, 4-5; L. Clancy, *Age Saturday Extra*, 16 November, 1985, 12; P. Goldsworthy, *S.M.H.*, 3 August, 1985, 47; D. Mathews, *ABR*, No. 77, 1985, 38-39; S. McKernan, *Bulletin*, 20 August, 1985, 97; W. Noonan, *Weekend Australian Magazine*, 17-18 August, 1985, 15; E. Perkins, *Quadrant*, XXX, No. 3, 1986, 80-83; S. Sayers, *Age*, 28 September, 1985, 12; P. Sharrad, *Overland*, No. 100, 1985, 96-98.

Invisible Histories. (Sydney: Picador, 1990).
Reviewed by J. Barcelon, *ABR*, No. 118, 1990, 14-15; M. Duwell, *Weekend Australian*, 10-11 March, 1990, Weekend 8; H. Horton, *Imago*, 3.1, 1991, 89-91; M. Jones, *S.M.H.*, 10 February, 1990, 75; R. O'Grady, *Age*, 24 February, 1990, Saturday Extra 9; P. Rolfe, *Bulletin*, 13 March, 1990, 100.

Winter Vision. (St Lucia: U.Q.P., 1989).
Reviewed by D. English, *Weekend Australian*, 30 September-1 October, 1989, Weekend 8; J. Hanrahan, *ABR*, No. 114, 1989, 35-36; J.T. Hospital, *Age Saturday Extra*, 9 September, 1989, 10; M. Jones, *S.M.H.*, 10 February, 1990, 75; R. Moran, *Overland*, No. 117, 1990, 86-87.

Poetry

Cassandra Paddocks. (Sydney: A.& R., 1980).
Reviewed by G. Catalano, *Meanjin*, XXXIX, 1980, 359-61; R. Gray, *S.M.H.*, 15 March, 1980, 16; R. Handicott, *LiNQ*, X, No. 2, 1982, 113-24; L. Trainor, *Canberra Times*, 17 May, 1980, 15.

Clairvoyant in Autumn. (Sydney: A.& R., 1983).
Reviewed by B. Beaver, *Quadrant*, XXVII, No. 7, 1983, 118-19.

Collected Lives. (North Ryde, N.S.W.: A.& R., 1986).
Reviewed by D. Brooks, *Weekend Australian. Weekend Magazine*, 20-21 February, 1988, 13; K. Hart, *ABR*, No. 92, 1987, 18-19; D. Haskell, *Island Magazine*, No. 33, 1987, 66-67; V. O'Sullivan, *Meanjin*, XLVI, No. 3, 1987, 347-354; esp. 351; P. Porter, *Age Saturday Extra*, 4 July, 1987, 13.

Footwork. (North Ryde, N.S.W.: A.& R., 1988).
Reviewed by V. Buckley, *Age Saturday Extra*, 19 November, 1988, 16; H. Cam, *S.M.H.*, 29 October, 1988, 87; J. Grant, *Weekend Australian*, 7-8 January, 1989, Weekend 6; S. Lee, *Southerly*, 49, No. 2, 1989, 249-59.

Gravel Corners. (Pymble, NSW: A.& R., 1992).
Reviewed by J. Davies, *Southerly*, 52.4, 1992, 169-76; K. Hart, *Age*, 28 November,

1992, Saturday Extra 9; P. Nelson, *Quadrant*, 37.3, 1993, 87-88; C. Pollnitz, *Weekend Australian*, 19-20 September, 1992, Review 6.

Human Interest. (Melbourne: Heinemann, 1994).
Reviewed by K. Brophy, *Overland*, 139, 1995, 74-76; M. Duwell, *Weekend Australian*, 26-27 November, 1994, Review 4; H. Horton, *Imago*, 6.3, 1994, 96-98; N. Rowe, *Voices*, 4.4, 1994-95, 109-16.

Selected Poems. (North Ryde, NSW: A.& R., 1991).
Reviewed by D. Callahan *Australian Studies*, 6, 1992, 142-45; M. Duwell, *Weekend Australian*, 23-24 November, 1991, Review 7; J. Owen, *Quadrant*, 35.6, 1991, 79-81.

Smalltown Memorials. (St Lucia: U.Q.P., 1975). Paperback Poets, Second Series, No. 5.
Reviewed by R. Gray, *Poetry Australia*, No. 58, 1976, 80; J. Griffin, *Advertiser*, 20 December, 1975, 20; K. Hart, *Canberra Poetry*, 1975, 50-51; S.E. Lee, *Southerly*, XXXVI, 1976, 331-56; P. Porter, *Australian*, 2 August, 1975, 28; P. Rappolt, *Canberra Times*, 9 April, 1976, 14; J. Rodriguez, *Luna*, No. 3, 1976, 20-21; R. Tamplin, *T.L.S.*, 9 April, 1976, 443; D. Thwaites, *New Poetry*, XXIV, No. 2, 1976, 96-98.

Smiling in English, Smoking in French: A Journal. (Deakin, A.C.T.: Brindabella, 1988).
Reviewed by S. Padgham, *Muse* (Canberra), No. 69, 1988, 22.

   Non-Fiction
'A Month on the U.S. Poetry Circuit'. *Island Magazine*, Nos. 25-26, 1986, 22-23.
'Poetry and the Public Past'. *Ulitarra*, 8, 1995, 75-81.
A Reader's Guide to Contemporary Australian Poetry. (St Lucia: U.Q.P., 1995).
Reviewed by C. Pollnitz, *Weekend Australian*, 6-7 May, 1995, Review 9; T. Shapcott, *ABR*, 168, 1995, 50; C. Wallace-Crabbe, *Voices*, 5.3, 1995, 102-05.

   Critical Material
Catalano, Gary. 'Bends in the River'. *Quadrant*, 39.3, 1995, 61-65.
Collett, Anne. 'Geoff Page Interviewed by Anne Collett'. *Germinal*, No. 2, 1986, 11-19.
Gould, Alan. 'Geoff Page'. *Quadrant*, 36.5, 1992, 62-63.
Hart, Kevin. 'Location and Detail'. *Makar*, XII, No. 1, 1976, 37-43. Interview.
Wieland, James. 'Some Recent Australian Writing: Questions of "Meaning"'. *Span*, Nos. 16-17, 1983, 88-113.

PALMER, NETTIE

   Collection
Nettie Palmer: Her Private Journal 'Fourteen Years', Poems, Reviews and Literary Essays. Edited with an introduction by Vivian Smith. (St Lucia: U.Q.P., 1988).
Reviewed by C. Burns, *ABR*, No. 115, 1989, 5-6; K. Gallagher, *Australian Studies*, No. 3, 1989, 128-32; D.F. Porter, *Weekend Australian*, 17-18 September, 1988, Weekend 10; C. Wallace-Crabbe, *A.L.S.*, 14, No. 2, 1989, 262-64; J. Wells, *Lilith*, No. 6, 1989, 153-54; N. Wheatley, *Fremantle Arts Review*, 4, No. 2, 1989, 14.

   Non-Fiction
Letters of Vance and Nettie Palmer 1915-1963. Selected and edited by Vivian Smith. (Canberra: National Library of Australia, 1977).
Reviewed by G. Dutton, *Bulletin*, 25 April, 1978, 58; D.Green, *National Times*, 10-15 April, 1978, 32-33; E. Lindsay, *Weekend Australian Magazine*, 29 April, 1978, 8; M. Lord, *ABR*, No. 14, 1979, 18; C. Maguire, *Australian Library Journal*, XXVII, No. 6, 1978, 93-94; A. Mitchell, *A.L.S.*, VIII, 1978, 517-20; B. Muirden, *Advertiser*, 18 March, 1978, 25; A.A. Phillips, *Age*, 14 January, 1978, 25; C.

Semmler, *24 Hours*, III, No. 5, 1978, 56-57; V.S. Sharma, *Canberra Times*, 23 September, 1978, 17; P. Thompson, *S.M.H.*, 11, February, 1978, 17.

Critical Material

Smith, Vivian. 'Nettie Palmer: A Checklist of Literary Journalism 1918-1936'. *A.L.S.*, VI, 1973, 190-96. See also entries listed for Vance Palmer.

Ashbolt, Allan. 'A Love Affair with the World of Ideas'. *S.M.H.*, 24 August, 1985, 43. Includes Nettie Palmer.

Baracchi, Guido. 'Nettie Palmer'. *Overland*, No. 32, 1965, 37-8.

Hergenhan, L.T. 'Convict Legends, Australian Legends: Price Warung and the Palmers'. *A.L.S.*, IX, 1980, 337-45.

Heseltine, Harry. 'C. Hartley Grattan in Australia: Some Correspondence, 1937-38'. *Meanjin*, XXIX, 1970, 356-64.

Hickey, Bernard. '"Strengthening the Powers that Fence the Heart": The Work of Vance and Nettie Palmer'. In *Individual and Community in Commonwealth Literature*, edited by Daniel Massa (Msida, Malta: Old University Press, 1979), 108-14.

Jordan, Deborah. 'Nettie Palmer as Critic'. In *Gender, Politics and Fiction: Twentieth Century Women's Novels*, edited by Carole Ferrier (St Lucia: U.Q.P., 1985), 59-84.

---. 'Towards a Biography of Nettie Palmer'. *Hecate*, VI, No. 2, 1980, 65-72.

Levey, Esther. 'Yours As Ever... NP'. *Meanjin*, XXIV, 1965, 329-33.

McLeod, Jessie. 'Nettie Palmer - Some Personal Memories'. *Overland*, No. 31, 1965, 20-1.

Semmler, Clement. 'The Palmers: The Authentic Voices of Our Literature'. *Bulletin*, 20 August, 1985, 82-85. Includes Nettie Palmer.

Sendy, John. 'Vance & Nettie Palmer: A Literary Debt Repaid'. *This Australia*, IV, No. 3, 1985, 14-19.

Smith, Vivian. *Vance and Nettie Palmer*. (New York: Twayne, 1975). Twayne's World Authors series, 332. Reviewed by S. Amanuddin, *Books Abroad*, I, No. 4, 1978, 959; M. Dunlevy, *Canberra Times*, 6 June, 1975, 8; C. Hadgraft, *A.L.S.*, VII, 1975, 219-21; H.P. Heseltine, *Overland*, No. 66, 1977, 70-71; M. Macleod, *S.M.H.*, 19 July, 1975, 19; J. Waten, *Age*, 28 June, 1975, 18.

---. 'Australia of the Spirit: Some Aspects of the Work of Vance and Nettie Palmer 1938-48'. In *Bards, Bohemians, and Bookmen*, edited by Leon Cantrell (St Lucia: U.Q.P., 1976), 236-50.

Tipping, Marjorie. 'Remembrance of Palmers Past'. *Overland*, No. 100, 1985, 10-18. Includes Nettie Palmer.

Walker, David. *Dream and Disillusion: A Search for Australian Cultural Identity*. (Canberra: A.N.U. Press, 1976).

---. 'The Prophets Downcast: The Palmers and their Nationalism'. *Meanjin*, XXXV, 1976, 149-57.

PALMER, VANCE

Fiction

Golconda. (St Lucia: U.Q.P., 1972). First published Sydney: A.& R., 1948. Reviewed by N. Keesing, *Bulletin*, 21 October, 1972, 55; K. Tennant, *S.M.H.*, 28 October, 1972, 20.

Non-Fiction

Intimate Portraits and Other Pieces: Essays and Articles. Selected with an introduction by H.P. Heseltine. (Melbourne: Cheshire, 1969). Reviewed by S. Edgar, *Canberra Times*, 28 March, 1970, 10; B. Elliott, *ABR*, IX, 1970, 92; D. Hewett, *Westerly*, No. 1, 1971, 67-70; N. Keesing, *Bridge*, V, No. 2, 1970, 52; C. Semmler, *S.M.H.*, 27 December, 1969, 12; J. Waten, *Age*, 3 January, 1970, 12.

The Legend of the Nineties. (South Yarra, Vic.: Currey O'Neil, 1983). First published

Melbourne: M.U.P., 1954.
Reviewed by J. Harley, *Royal Historical Society of Victoria Journal*, LVI, No. 2, 1985, 52-54; C. Wesley, *Tasmanian Historical Research Association Papers and Proceedings*, XXX, 1983, 129-30.

Letters of Vance and Nettie Palmer 1915-1963. Selected and edited by Vivian Smith. (Canberra: National Library of Australia, 1977).
Reviewed by G. Dutton, *Bulletin*, 25 April, 1978, 58; D.Green, *National Times*, 10-15 April, 1978, 32-33; E. Lindsay, *Weekend Australian Magazine*, 29 April, 1978, 8; M. Lord, *ABR*, No. 14, 1979, 18; C. Maguire, *Australian Library Journal*, XXVII, No. 6, 1978, 93-94; A. Mitchell, *A.L.S.*, VIII, 1978, 517-20; B. Muirden, *Advertiser*, 18 March, 1978, 25; A.A. Phillips, *Age*, 14 January, 1978, 25; C. Semmler, *24 Hours*, III, No. 5, 1978, 56-57; V.S. Sharma, *Canberra Times*, 23 September, 1978, 17; P. Thompson, *S.M.H.*, 11, February, 1978, 17.

'An Australian National Art'. In *The Writer in Australia*, edited by John Barnes (Melbourne: O.U.P., 1969), 168-70.
'Frank Wilmot'. In *The Writer in Australia*, edited by John Barnes (Melbourne: O.U.P., 1969), 171-90.
'A.G. Stephens'. In *An Overland Muster*, edited by S. Murray-Smith (Brisbane: Jacaranda Press, 1965), 123-7. First published *Overland*, No. 17, 1960, 30-1.

Critical Material

National Library of Australia, Manuscript Section. *Palmer Papers: A Guide to the Papers of Vance and Nettie Palmer held in the National Library of Australia.* (Canberra: National Library of Australia, 1973).

'Vance Palmer'. In *An Overland Muster*, edited by S. Murray-Smith (Brisbane: Jacaranda Press, 1965), 110. First published in *Overland*, No. 15, 1959, 3.
Ashbolt, Allan. 'A Love Affair with the World of Ideas'. *S.M.H.*, 24 August, 1985, 43.
Barnes, John (ed.). *The Writer in Australia* (Melbourne: O.U.P., 1969). See particularly Palmer's 'An Australian National Art'. 168-70 (first published 1905), his 'Frank Wilmot', 171-90 (first published 1942), and Louis Esson, 'Letters from London, 1920-1921', 191-99.
Burns, D.R. 'Vance Palmer and the Unguarded Awareness'. *A.L.S.*, VI, 1974, 259-68.
Capp, Fiona. *Writers Defiled: Security Surveillance of Australian Authors and Intellectuals 1920-1960.* (Ringwood, Vic.: McPhee Gribble). Includes discussion of Palmer.
Dunlevy, Maurice. 'Writers Leave Australia to Get Out of the Cold'. *Canberra Times*, 17 December, 1977, 10.
Hergenhan, L.T. 'Convict Legends, Australian Legends: Price Warung and the Palmers'. *A.L.S.*, IX, 1980, 337-45.
Heseltine, Harry. *Vance Palmer.* (St Lucia: U.Q.P., 1970). Reviewed by M. Dunlevy, *Canberra Times*, 26 September, 1970, 12; D. Green, *A.L.S.*, V, 1971, 205-14; C. Hadgraft, *Makar*, VI, No. 4, 1970, 46-48; M. Harris, *ABR*, X, 1971, 151-52; D. Hewett, *Westerly*, No. 1, 1971, 67-70; N. Keesing, *Bulletin*, 14 November, 1970, 61-62; A.A. Phillips, *Meanjin*, XXIX, 1970, 523-25; C. Semmler, *S.M.H.*, 17 October, 1970, 21; G. Serle, *Historical Studies*, XV, 1972, 310-11. K. Tennant, *Twentieth Century*, XXV, 1970, 186-89; J. Waten, *Age*, 3 October, 1970, 14.
---. 'C. Hartley Grattan in Australia: Some Correspondence, 1937-38'. *Meanjin*, XXIX, 1970, 356-64.
Hickey, Bernard. '"Strengthening the Powers that Fence the Heart": The Work of Vance and Nettie Palmer'. In *Individual and Community in Commonwealth Literature*, edited by Daniel Massa (Msida, Malta: Old University Press, 1979), 108-14.

Ho Xiaoxi, Hu Yifeng, and Pan Yong. 'Synopses of Vance Palmer's Trilogy - *Golconda, Seedtime* and *The Big Fellow*'. Oceanic Literature, No. 3, 1982, 328-41. In Chinese.

Indyk, Ivor. 'Vance Palmer and the Social Function of Literature'. *Southerly*, 50, No. 3, 1990, 346-58.

Kent, David. 'Vance Palmer on the "Barambah": Some Additional War Poems'. *Notes & Furphies*, No. 11, 1983, 3-5.

---. 'Vance Palmer on the "Euripides": Further War Poems'. *Notes and Furphies*, No. 17, 1986, 21-22.

Lindsay, Jack. 'The Novels of Vance Palmer'. In his *Decay and Renewal*. (Sydney: Wild & Woolley, 1976), 267-303.

Matthews, Brian. 'Vance Palmer's Long Journey'. In his *Romantics and Mavericks: The Australian Short Story*. (Townsville, Qld.: James Cook University of North Queensland, 1987),23-33. The Colin Roderick Lectures, 1986. Foundation for Australian Literary Studies, Monograph No. 14.

McGregor, G. 'Vance Palmer's "The Swayne Family"'. *Westerly*, XXIV, No. 4, 1979, 51-60.

Palmer, Helen. 'Boyhood in Perspective'. *ABR*, X, 1972, 219. Review of Roy Bulcock, *No Wider Land*, comparing it to *The Passage*.

Phillips, A.A. 'Portrait of Vance Palmer'. In his *Responses: Selected Writings*. (Kew, Vic.: Australian International Press & Publications, 1979), 170-7. First published in *Meanjin*, XXIX, 1970, 523-25, review of Harry Heseltine, *Vance Palmer*.

---. 'Vance Palmer'. In his *Responses: Selected Writings*. (Kew, Vic.: Australian International Press & Publications, 1979), 55-56. First published in the *Age*, 18 July, 1959, 20.

Semmler, Clement. 'The Palmers: The Authentic Voices of Our Literature'. *Bulletin*, 20 August, 1985, 82-85.

Sendy, John. 'Vance & Nettie Palmer: A Literary Debt Repaid'. *This Australia*, IV, No. 3, 1985, 14-19.

Smith, Graeme Kinross. 'Vance Palmer'. *Westerly*, No. 1, 1978, 39-47.

Smith, Vivian. *Vance Palmer*. (Melbourne: O.U.P., 1971). Australian Writers and Their Work. Reviewed by C. Harrison-Ford, *Sunday Australian*, 21 November, 1971, 32; B. Kiernan, *Australian*, 6 November, 1971, 18; L. Kramer, *A.L.S.*, V, 1972, 433-37; W. Walsh, *Notes and Queries*, n.s. XXII, 1975, 219-20; J. Waten, *Age*, 23 September, 1972, 15 and *S.M.H.*, 1 July, 1972, 20.

---. *Vance and Nettie Palmer*. (New York: Twayne, 1976). Twayne's World Authors series, 332. Reviewed by S. Amanuddin, *Books Abroad*, I, No. 4, 1978, 959; M. Dunlevy, *Canberra Times*, 6 June, 1975, 8; C. Hadgraft, *A.L.S.*, VII, 1975, 219-21; H.P. Heseltine, *Overland*, No. 66, 1977, 70-71; M. Macleod, *S.M.H.*, 19 July, 1975, 19; J. Waten, *Age*, 28 June, 1975, 18.

---. 'Australia of the Spirit: Some Aspects of the Work of Vance and Nettie Palmer 1938-48'. In *Bards, Bohemians, and Bookmen*, edited by Leon Cantrell (St Lucia: U.Q.P., 1976), 236-50.

---. 'Vance and Nettie Palmer: The Literary Journalism'. *A.L.S.*, VI, 1973, 115-27.

Smythe, Percy. *A Critical Survey of 'The Passage'*. (Sydney: College Press, 1965).

Thomas Sue. 'Vance Palmer in London 1906-1907'. *Bibliographical Society of Australia and New Zealand Bulletin*, X, No. 1, 1986, 25-30.

Tipping, Marjorie. 'Remembrance of Palmers Past'. *Overland*, No. 100, 1985, 10-18.

Torre, Stephen. 'Psyche as Text: The Short Stories of Vance Palmer'. *LiNQ*, XV, No. 1, 1987, 64-78.

Walker, David. 'The Palmer Abridgement of *Such is Life*'. *A.L.S.*, VIII, 1978, 491-98.

---. 'The Prophets Downcast: The Palmers and their Nationalism'. *Meanjin*, XXXV,

1976, 149-57.
Waten, Judah. 'Vance Palmer and His Literary Contribution'. *Realist Writer*, No. 11, 1963, 22-4.
Young, Edith. *Inside Out*. (London: Routledge and Kegan Paul, 1971), 108-12.

PARK, RUTH

Fiction
Missus. (Melbourne: Nelson, 1985). The first book in *The Harp in the South* Trilogy.
Reviewed by K. Ahearne, ABR, No. 74, 1985, 18-20; E. Butel, *National Times*, 23-29 August, 1985, 30; J. Cohen, *New York Times Book Review*, 8 February, 1987, 24; H. Daniel, *Age Saturday Extra*, 5 October, 1985, 13; G. Dutton, *Weekend Australian Magazine*, 7-8 September, 1985, 16; J.A. Mead, *ABR*, No. 86, 1986, 32-33; N. Phelan, *S.M.H.*, 31 August, 1985, 47; R. Stevenson, *T.L.S.*, 19 June, 1987, 668.
My Sister Sif. (Ringwood, Vic.: Viking Kestrel, 1986). Reviewed by W. McVitty, *Weekend Australian. Weekend Magazine*, 20-21 December, 1987, 13; J. Motion, *T.L.S.*, 4 September, 1987, 964.

Non-Fiction
A Fence around the Cuckoo. (Ringwood, Vic.: Penguin/Viking, 1992).
Reviewed by F. Adolph, *Westerly*, 38.3, 1993, 91-92; G. Appleton, *Voices*, 2.4, 1992, 115-18; C. Baker, *Age*, 12 September, 1992, Saturday Extra 10; H. Elliott, *Overland*, 130, 1993, 89-90; A. Inglis, *Editions*, 14, 1992, 9-10; M. Luke, *ABR*, 144, 1992, 20-22; A. Riemer, *S.M.H.*, 5 September, 1992, 41; S. Yarwood, *Weekend Australian*, 19-20 September, 1992, Review 6.
Fishing in the Styx. (Ringwood, Vic.: Viking, 1993).
Reviewed by L. Beasley, *Redoubt*, 19, 1994, 115-16; C. Creagh, *Weekend Australian*, 30-31 October, 1993, Review 6; J. Hanrahan, *Age*, 30 October, 1993, Saturday Extra 7; H. Lindsay, *Southerly*, 54.2, 1994, 174-78; C. Pybus, *S.M.H.*, 30 October, 1993, Spectrum 9A; H. Rowley, *ABR*, 156, 1993, 20 (see also Interview by K. Veitch, 20-21).
'A Short Voyage: Into the Hole in My Head'. *National Times*, 27 October-1 November, 1975, 22.

Critical Material
'Ruth Park's Time Machine'. *24 Hours*, X, No. 9, 1985, 89-91.
Gaertner, George. 'Ruth Park - It's Back to Writing in Earnest Again'. *Age*, 2 August, 1975, 23.
Hawley, Janet. 'Real Life is Sometimes ... Too Fictional'. *S.M.H.*, 31 August, 1985, 43.
---. 'Three Murders Helped to Blood Novelist Ruth Park'. *Age Saturday Extra*, 31 August, 1985, 10.
Jodrell, Linda. 'Ruth Plays with Time', *Courier-Mail*, 23 August, 1985, 12.
Molloy, F.C. '"Hearts of Gold and a Happy Ending": The Appeal of *The Harp in the South*'. *A.L.S.*, 14, No. 3, 1990, 316-24.

PARTRIDGE, ERIC

Non-Fiction
Frank Honywood, Private: A Personal Record of the 1914-1918 War. Introduced and annotated by Geoffrey Serle. (Carlton, Vic.: M.U.P., 1987).
Reviewed by J. Wieland, *A.L.S.*, 14, No. 1, 1989, 130-35.
Critical Material
'Eric Partridge: Slanguage Expert'. *The Macquarie Dictionary Society*, 11, No. 4, 1984, 2-3.

Barnes, Julian. 'Eric Partridge 1894-1979'. *New Statesman*, XCVII, 8 June, 1979, 831-32.
Elliott, Ralph. 'For "hell" read "heaven": to Eric Partridge on his Seventieth Birthday'. *Meanjin*, XXIII, No. 1, 1964, 83-8.
---. 'Serving a Life Sentence: Eric Partridge 1894-1979'. *Meanjin*, XXXVIII, 1979, 516-20.
Fotheringham, Richard. 'Expatriate Publishing: Eric Partridge and the Scholartis Press'. *Meanjin*, XXXI, 1972, 338-42.
Green, Benny. 'Eric Partridge'. *Spectator*, 9 June, 1979, 25.
Hall, Robert Lowe. 'Expatriate Publishing'. *Meanjin*, XXXIII, 1974, 170-76.
Pearse, A.E. 'E.H. Partridge, Lexicographer Extraordinary'. *Alumni News* [University of Queensland Alumni Association], VII, No. 2, 1975, 7-9.

PATERSON, A.B.

Collection
A.B. 'Banjo' Paterson: Bush Ballads, Poems, Stories and Journalism. Edited by Clement Semmler. (St. Lucia: U.Q.P., 1992).
Reviewed by J. Croft, *ABR*, 152, 1993, 52-53; K. Stewart, *Weekend Australian*, 28-29 March, 1992, Review 5.
Banjo Paterson: His Poetry and Prose. Selected and introduced by Richard Hall. (St Leonards, NSW: Allen & Unwin, 1993).
Reviewed by G. Dutton, *S.M.H.*, 21 August, 1993, 47; R. Lucas, *Bulletin*, 31 August, 1993, 88-89.
Complete Works Vol.1 *Singer of the Bush*; Vol.2 *Song of the Pen.* (Melbourne: Lansdowne, 1983).
Reviewed by L. Carlyon, *Age Saturday Extra*, 31 December, 1983, 9; C. Semmler, *Weekend Australian Magazine*, 10-11 December, 1983, 13.
The World of 'Banjo' Paterson: His Stories, Travels, War Reports and Advice to Racegoers. Selected and introduced by Clement Semmler. (Sydney: A.& R., 1967).
Reviewed by A.R. Chisholm, *Age*, 16 September, 1967, 23; M. Dunlevy, *Canberra Times*, 26 August, 1967, 13; B.R. Elliott, *ABR*, VI, 1967, 179; N. Keesing, *Bulletin*, 26 August, 1967, 61; F.H. Mares, *Adelaide Advertiser*, 5 August, 1967, 12; R. Ward, *S.M.H.*, 23 December, 1967, 17.

Fiction
Short Stories. (Sydney: Lansdowne, 1980).
Reviewed by T. Shapcott, *Courier-Mail*, 4 October, 1980, 25.

Poetry
The Banjo's Best-Loved Poems. Chosen by Rosamund Campbell and Philippa Harvie. (Sydney: Lansdowne, 1985).
Reviewed by B. Hunter, *Courier-Mail Magazine: The Great Weekend*, 25 January, 1986, 7.
The Collected Verse of Banjo Paterson: An Anthology of Poems by Australia's Best Known Bush Balladist. Selected and introduced by Clement Semmler. (South Yarra, Vic.: Viking O'Neil, 1992).
The Man From Snowy River and Other Verses. Introduced by Jonathan King. Commemorative Centennial edition. (Pymble, NSW: A.& R., 1995).
The Penguin Banjo Paterson Collected Verse. Selected and introduced by Clement Semmler. (Ringwood, Vic.: Penguin, 1993). First published as *Collected Verse of Banjo Paterson.* (Ringwood, Vic.: Viking O'Neil, 1992).
Reviewed by J. Croft, *ABR*, 152, 1993, 52-53; G. Dutton, *S.M.H.*, 21 August, 1993, 47.
Song of the Wheat. An Illuminated Manuscript by Gordon Nicol. (Canberra: National

Library of Australia, 1988). Facsimile reproduction of text and illuminations of ms. executed ca. 1925.

Critical Material

'Letter Proves Authorship: "Waltzing Matilda" by A.B. Paterson'. *Canberra Times*, 8 July, 1970, 22.

'Whose Matilda?'. *Nation*, 27 November, 1965, 9-10. Copyright.

Andreeva, M.G. 'K Voprosu o Stanovlenii Natsional'noi Avstraliiskoi Poezii (Tvorchestvo A. Patersona)'. [The Origins of an Australian National Poetry: The Work of A.B. Paterson]. *Vestnik Moskovskogo Universiteta. Seriia Philologiia*, No. 2, 1977, 22-31.

Blake, Les. 'Jack Riley: His Life and Legend'. *Royal Historical Society of Victoria Journals*, LV, No. 3, 1984, 22-28. Possibly the original Man from Snowy River.

Blazey, Peter. 'The Bush discovers "Banjo" - an Authentic Australian Hero'. *Weekend Australian Magazine*, 3-4 March, 1984, 11.

Driscoll, Judith. 'A Thaw on Snowy River'. *A.L.S.*, V, 1971, 190-95.

E.,R. 'More About Waltzing Matilda'. *Northern Folk*, No. 16, 1967, 10.

Edwards, Ron. 'Josephine Peney and "Waltzing Matilda"'. *Northern Folk*, No. 4, 1966, 8-11.

Fairbairn, Anne. '"Waltzing Matilda" - from Australia across the Arab World to India'. *Rajasthan University Studies in English*, XV, 1982-1983, 100-05.

Forster, N.H.W. 'Mirage and Matilda'. *Walkabout*, XXXIV, No. 1, 1968, 5. See also letters to the editor by Oscar Mendelsohn, *Walkabout*, XXXIV, No. 3, 1968, 5; Richard Magoffin, *Walkabout*, XXXIV, No. 8, 1968, 8; Oscar Mendelsohn, *Walkabout*, XXXIV, No. 11, 1968, 5.

Foster, R.T. 'Banjo Didn't Like the Breaker'. *S.M.H.*, 18 July, 1981, 46. Biographical.

Grenard, Philip. 'The Banjo Industry Gets "The Works"'. *Bulletin*, 18 October, 1983, 28-29.

---. '"New" Poem Written by the Banjo'. *Bulletin*, 2 August, 1983, 30-32.

Haley, Martin. '"Banjo" Paterson was born one hundred years ago'. *Catholic Leader* (Brisbane), 4 June, 1964, 8.

Harvey, Oliver. 'Opening New Doors on Banjo Paterson'. *Courier-Mail*, 8 October, 1983, 31.

Hawley, Janet. '"Banjo" Paterson's Treasure Chests Opened'. *Canberra Times*, 8 October, 1983, 17.

---. 'Old Tin Trunks Yield New "Banjo" Treasures'. *Age Saturday Extra*, 8 October, 1983, 3.

Heseltine, H.P. 'The Australian Nineties: An Experiment in Critical Method'. *The Teaching of English*, No. 6, 1965, 17-32.

---. '"Banjo" Paterson: A Poet Nearly Anonymous'. *Meanjin*, XXIII, No. 4, 1964, 386-402.

Lahey, John. 'Waltzing Matilda - the True Story'. *Age*, 23 November, 1983, 11.

Long, Gavin. 'Young Paterson and Young Lawson'. *Meanjin*, XXIII, No. 4, 1964, 403-13.

Macartney, Frederick T. 'Jostling Matilda'. *Meanjin*, XXIV, 1965, 359-63. With reply by A.A. Phillips.

---. 'The Matilda Muddle'. *Meanjin*, XXVI, 1967, 211-216.

---. 'A Postscript on "Waltzing Matilda"'. *Meanjin*, XXIX, 1970, 143. Supplements his 'The Matilda Muddle', *Meanjin*, XXVI, 1967, 211-115.

Magoffin, Richard. *Fair Dinkum Matilda*. (Charters Towers, Q.: Mimosa Press, 1973). Reviewed by F.T. Macartney, *Southerly*, XXXIV, 1974, 80-82.

---. 'The Origins of Matilda'. *Australian*, 15 June, 1973, 8. Letter to the editor. See also letters to the editor about the date and origins of 'Waltzing Matilda', *Age*, 28 August, 1973, 8; *Age*, 6 September, 1973, 8; *Age*, 15 September, 1973, 10.

Manifold, J.S. 'Ballads and Folk-legends'. In *Australia, New Zealand and the South Pacific: A Handbook*, edited by Charles Osborne (London: Blond, 1970), 298-302.
---. '"The Banjo"'. In *An Overland Muster*, edited by S. Murray-Smith (Brisbane: Jacaranda Press, 1965), 1-12. Originally published in *Overland*, No. 1, 1954, 14-16, No. 2, 1954-5, 22-24.
---. 'The Changing Face of Realism'. *Realist*, No. 34, 1969, 34-41.
---. 'The Long March With Matilda'. *Australian Left Review*, No. 40, 1973, 18-21. See reply by Harry H. Pearce, *Australian Left Review*, No. 41, 1973, 53-54. See also related report, Gavin Souter, 'Once a Jolly Swagman Named Hoffmeister...', *S.M.H.*, 8 June, 1973, 7, reprinted in *Advertiser*, 16 June, 1973, 25.
McInerney, Sally. 'Banjo Wrote Matilda No Buts About it, Granddaughters Say'. *S.M.H.*, 17 July, 1982, 39.
Mendelsohn, Oscar. *A Waltz With Matilda*. (Melbourne: Lansdowne Press, 1966). Authorship of the words and music of 'Waltzing Matilda'. Reviewed by T. Forshaw, *Nation*, 29 October, 1966, 22-3; G. Hutton, *Age*, 8 October, 1966, 24; W. Noonan, *S.M.H.*, 15 October, 1966, 16; K. Randall, *Australian*, 10 September, 1966, 8 and see also letters to the editor by William A. Schueler, H.V. Howe, Charles V. Nathan, ibid., 20 September, 1966, 8 and reply by Oscar Mendelsohn, ibid., 13 October, 1966, 8; Scrutarius, *Walkabout*, XXXIII, No. 1, 1967, 44-46.
---. '"Waltzing Matilda" Again'. *Meanjin*, XXIX, 1970, 377-79. Reply to Macartney, *Meanjin*, XXIX, 1970, 143.
Nedeljkovic, Maryvonne. '"Banjo" Paterson, *the* Poet of the Bush'. *Commonwealth* (Toulouse), IV, 1979-1980, 87-95.
Ollif, Lorna. *Andrew Barton Paterson*. (New York: Twayne, 1972). Twayne's World Authors series, 120. Reviewed by A. Mitchell, *Advertiser*, 29 July, 1972, 18; J. Waten, *Age*, 8 July, 1972, 15.
Palmer, Helen. *A.B. 'Banjo' Paterson*. (Melbourne: Longmans, 1965). Great People in Australian History Series.
Pearce, Harry Hastings. *On the Origins of 'Waltzing Matilda': Expression, Lyric, Melody*. (Melbourne: Hawthorn Press, 1971). Reviewed by M. Dunlevy, *Canberra Times*, 28 August, 1971, 14; D. Gyger, *Australian*, 28 August, 1971, 18; N. Keesing, *Bulletin*, 4 September, 1971, 42-43 (see also letter to the editor by J.R.Y. Bartlam, *Bulletin*, 9 October, 1971, 8-10); G.W. Leeper, *Meanjin*, XXX, 1971, 478-83; N. Phelan, *S.M.H.*, 16 October, 1971, 21; C. Turnbull, *Age*, 28 August, 1971, 15.
Pons, Xavier. 'La Polemique Lawson-Paterson'. *Etudes Anglaises*, XXV, 1972, 220-28.
---. 'Waltzing Matilda'. *Australian Tradition*, No. 26, 1971, 8-11, 15.
Roderick, Colin. *Banjo Paterson: Poet by Accident*. (St Leonards, NSW: Allen & Unwin, 1993). Reviewed by M. Ackland, *Journal of Australian Studies*, 39, 1993, 89 and *A.L.S.*, 17.2, 1995, 204-07; A. Bell, *ABR*, 152, 1993, 51-52; G. Dutton, *S.M.H.*, 1 May, 1993, 45; R. Lucas, *Bulletin*, 27 April, 1993, 98; C. Semmler, *Weekend Australian*, 22-23 May, 1993, Review 7 and *Overland*, 134, 1994, 78-79.
Roulston, Barbara. Letter to the Editor. *Nation*, 8 January, 1966, 18.
Semmler, Clement. *A.B. (Banjo) Paterson*. (Melbourne: Lansdowne Press, 1965). Australian Writers and Their Work. Reviewed by D. Douglas, *A.L.S.*, II, 1966, 226; W. Hart-Smith, *Bulletin*, 5 February, 1966, 34.
---. *A.B. Paterson*. (Melbourne: O.U.P., 1967). Great Australians. Reviewed by A.H. Chisholm, *Journal of the Royal Australian Historical Society*, LIV, 1968, 420-22.
---. *The Banjo of the Bush: The Work, Life and Times of A.B. Paterson*. (Melbourne: Lansdowne Press, 1966). With an Introduction by Maie Casey. Includes a Bibliography. Reviewed by D. Green, *Canberra Times*, 12 November, 1966, 10; J. Hall, *Australian*, 12 November, 1966, 12; H.P. Heseltine, *A.L.S.*, III, 1967, 73-75; G. Hutton, *Age*, 19 November, 1966, 23; S. Lawson, *Nation*, 28 January, 1967, 21-22; A. Porteous, *Overland*, No. 36, 1967, 41-42; C.A. Roderick, *ABR*, VI, 1967,

48-49; G. Scott, *Bulletin*, 10 December, 1966, 57; K. Tennant, *S.M.H.*, 12 November, 1966, 19.

---. *The Banjo of the Bush: The Life and Times of A.B. Paterson*. Second edition (St Lucia: U.Q.P., 1974). First published Melbourne: Lansdowne, 1966. Includes additional Preface (pp. xi-xv) and illustrations.

---. *The Banjo of the Bush: The Life and Times of A.B. "Banjo" Paterson*. (St Lucia: U.Q.P., 1984). First published Melbourne: Lansdowne, 1966. Reviewed by N. Krauth, *ABR*, No. 61, 1984, 18-20; L. Ward, *Canberra Times*, 24 June, 1984, 8.

---. 'A.B. (Banjo) Paterson. *The Man from Snowy River*'. In *Australian Poems in Perspective*, edited by P.K. Elkin (St Lucia: U.Q.P., 1978), 1-10.

---. 'Banjo Paterson and the 1890's'. *Southerly*, XXIV, No. 3, 1964, 176-187.

---. 'The Greatest of our Folk-Poets'. *Bulletin*, 22-29 December, 1981, 116-18.

---. 'Kipling and A.B. Paterson: Men of Empire and Action'. *Australian Quarterly*, XXXIX, No. 2, 1967, 71-78.

---. 'Some Notes on the Literature of the Shearers' Strikes of 1891 and 1894'. *Australian Quarterly*, XLI, No. 4, 1969, 75-87.

---. 'War Correspondents in Australian Literature: an Outline'. *A.L.S.*, XII, No. 2, 1985, 194-206.

Smilde, Roelof, and Byrne, Reg. 'The Racetrack Writings of Banjo Paterson'. *Nation Review*, 13-19 July, 1973, 1207.

Sussex, Lucy. 'A Source for Banjo Paterson's "A Bush Christening"'. *Notes and Furphies*, No. 25, 1990, 11-15

Walker, Shirley. 'The Boer War: Paterson, Abbott, Brennan, Miles Franklin and Morant'. *A.L.S.*, XII, No. 2, 1985, 207-222.

Wallace-Crabbe, Chris. 'Popular Paterson'. *Overland*, No. 70, 1978, 34-38.

Walsh, Richard. '"Banjo" Paterson, A Poet By No Means Anonymous'. *Weekend Australian Magazine*, 21-22 December, 1985, 5.

---. 'Correspondence'. Letter relating to Shirley Walker's segment in 'The Boer War: Paterson, Abbott, Brennan, Miles Franklin and Morant', *A.L.S.*, XII, No. 2, 1985, 207-22. Response by Walker, *A.L.S.*, XII, No. 3, 1986, 424-25.

Wright, Judith. 'The Reformist Poets'. In her *Preoccupations in Australian Poetry* (Melbourne: O.U.P., 1965), 68-79.

PENTON, BRIAN

Fiction

Landtakers. (Sydney: A.& R., 1963). First published Sydney: Endeavour Press, 1934. Reviewed by G. Dutton, *Nation*, 8 February, 1964, 21-2.

Landtakers: The Story of an Epoch. Introduction by Donald Grant. (Sydney: A.& R., 1972). Paperback edition. First published Sydney: Endeavour Press, 1934.

The Landtakers. Revised edition. Edited by Patrick Buckridge. (North Ryde, NSW: Collins/ A.& R., 1991). First published Sydney: Endeavour Press, 1934.

Critical Material

Chaplin, Harry F. (ed.). *Norman Lindsay: His Books, Manuscripts, and Autograph Letters in the Library of, and Annotated by, Harry F. Chaplin*. Foreword by Norman Lindsay. (Sydney: Wentworth Press, 1969), 28-30, 35-36. Studies in Australian and Pacific Bibliographies.

Smith, Ross and Taylor, Cheryl. 'Brian Con Penton (1904-1951): A Bibliography'. *LiNQ*, XV, No. 1, 1987, 122-128.

Buckridge, Patrick. 'Biography as Social Knowledge: An Anthropological Perspective'. *Southern Review*, 22, No. 1, 1989, 4-16.

---. 'Gossip and History in the Novels of Brian Penton and Thomas Keneally'. *A.L.S.*, 14, No. 4, 190, 436-49.

---. 'The Penton Scandal: Rhetoric and Lifestyle in the Career of an Australian

Intellectual'. *Southerly*, XLVIII, No. 1, 1988, 31-45.
---. 'Reflections on Awards and Reviews'. *Imago*, 7.1, 1995, 67-69.
---. *The Scandalous Penton: A Biography of Brian Penton*. (St Lucia: U.Q.P., 1994).
Reviewed by E. Campion, *Bulletin*, 29 March, 1994, 105; R. Cassin, *Voices*, 4.4,
1994-95, 122-25; A. Deamer, *S.M.H.*, 2 April, 1994, Spectrum 8A; K. Goodwin,
Queensland Review, 2.1, 1995, 88; I. Indyk, *A.L.S.*, 17.1, 1995, 95-99; C. Lee,
Coppertales, 2, 1995, 121-22; J. McLaren, *Overland*, 137, 1994, 67-68; T.
O'Connor, *ABR*, 160, 1994, 28-29; N. O'Reilly, *Weekend Australian*, 2-3 April,
1994, Review 7; A. Wearne, *Age*, 2 April, 1994, Saturday Extra 8.
Hergenhan, L.T. 'Brian Penton's 1930s Novels: The "Roots of the New Psyche"'. In
Culture & History: Essays Presented to Jack Lindsay, edited by Bernard Smith
(Sydney: Hale & Iremonger, 1984), 72-88. Reprinted in his *Unnatural Lives*. (St
Lucia: U.Q.P., 1983), 91-107.

PERRY, GRACE

Poetry
Berrima Winter. (Sydney: South Head Press, 1974).
Reviewed by B. Beaver, *S.M.H.*, 11 January, 1975, 17.

Black Swans at Berrima. (Sydney: South Head Press, 1972).
Reviewed by B. Andrews, *Sun-Herald*, 8 October, 1972, 65; J.E. Chamberlin,
Hudson Review, XXVI, 1973, 389-91; F. Holzknecht, *Makar*, VIII, No. 3, 1972,
40-42; A.L. McLeod, *Books Abroad*, No. 47, 1973, 608; G. Page, *Canberra Times*,
5 May, 1973, 13; P. Roberts, *S.M.H.*, 4 November, 1972, 23; J. Tulip, *Southerly*,
XXXIII, 1973, 233-34.

Frozen Section. (Sydney: Edwards & Shaw, 1967).
Reviewed by B. Beaver, *S.M.H.*, 2 June, 1967, 19; D. Douglas, *Age*, 12 August,
1967, 24; R. Hall, *Australian*, 23 September, 1967, 11; T. Shapcott, *ABR*, VI, 1967,
124; J. Tulip, *Poetry Australia*, No. 19, 1967, 39-40 and *Southerly*, XXVIII, 1968,
69-71.

Journal of a Surgeon's Wife. (Sydney: South Head Press, 1976). Reviewed by B.
Beaver, *S.M.H.*, 29 May, 1976, 15; J. Griffin, *Advertiser*, 29 January, 1977, 21; E.
Lindsay, *Australian*, 31 July, 1976, 40.

Red Scarf. (Sydney: Edwards and Shaw, 1963).
Reviewed by P.K. Elkin, *Poetry Magazine*, No. 1, 1964, 4-5; A.D. Hope, *Poetry
Magazine*, No. 2, 1964, 32-3; S.E. Lee, *Southerly*, XXIV, No. 2, 1964, 135.

Snow in Summer. (Sydney: South Head Press, 1980).
Reviewed by L. Jacobs, *ABR*, No. 42, 1982, 33-34; G. Schien, *National Times*, 10-16
May, 1981, 60; M. Scott, *Island Magazine*, No. 8, 1981, 39; T. Shapcott, *S.M.H.*,
17 January, 1981, 42.

Two Houses. (Sydney: South Head Press, 1969).
Reviewed by J. Tulip, *Southerly*, XXIX, 1969, 313-14; P. Ward, *ABR*, IX, 1969 and
1970, 61.

'Be Kind to Animals'. *Poetry Australia*, No. 93, 1984, (whole issue).
Reviewed by J. Rodriguez, *S.M.H.*, 31 March, 1984, 40.

Critical Material
Jaffa, Herbert C. 'In Memory: Dr. Grace Perry, 1927-1987'. *Antipodes*, I, No. 2,
1987, 107.
New, William H. 'Grace Perry's House of Poetry'. *Poetry Australia*, No. 45, 1972,
45-55.
Tulip, James. 'Evolution of a Poet'. *Poetry Australia*, Nos. 74-75, 1980, 50-53.

PHILLIPS, A.A.

Non-Fiction
Responses: Selected Writings. (Kew, Vic.: Australian International Press & Publications: 1979).
Reviewed by B. Elliott, *A.L.S.*, IX, 1980, 539-41; J. McLaren, *Age*, 21 June, 1980, 25; D.J. O'Hearn, *ABR*, No. 22, 1980, 5; P. Pierce, *National Times*, 27 April-3 May, 1980, 39.
   Critical Material
Bennett, Bruce. 'Provincial and Metropolitan'. *Overland*, No. 86, 1981, 39-45.
Charlwood, Don. 'Obituary'. *Overland*, No. 102, 1986, 62-63.
Davidson, Jim. 'A.A. Phillips'. *Meanjin*, XXXVI, 1977, 286-97. Interview. Reprinted in his *Sideways From the Page*. (Melbourne: Fontana, 1983), 34-51.
S.,G. 'A.A. Phillips, 1900-1985'. *Meanjin*, XLIV, No. 4, 1985, 431. For other obituaries see *ABR*, No. 77, 1985, 86-87; *Age*, 7 November, 1985, 11; *Age Monthly Review*, V, No. 8, 1985, 35.

PORTEOUS, RICHARD SYDNEY

   Critical Material
Smith, Ross and Taylor, Cheryl. 'Richard Sydney ("Skip") Porteous (1897-1963): A Bibliography'. *LiNQ*, XV, No. 3, 1987, 102-111.

PORTER, DOROTHY

   Fiction
Rookwood. (St Lucia: U.Q.P., 1991).
Reviewed by M. McCarthy, *Australian Women's Book Review*, 3.4, 1991, 25-26.
The Witch Number. (St Lucia: U.Q.P., 1993).
Reviewed by S. Matthews, *ABR*, 149, 1993, 57-58; J. Pausacker, *Age*, 20 March 1993: Saturday Extra 8; N. Robinson, *Weekend Australian*, 3-4 April 1993: Review 4.
   Poetry
Akhenaten. (St Lucia: U.Q.P., 1992).
Reviewed by L. Bourke, *Southerly*, 52.4, 1992, 158-64; G. Dutton, *Voices*, 2.2, 1992, 86-88; J. Maiden, *ABR*, 140, 1992, 42-43; T. W. Shapcott, *Age*, 9 May 1992, Saturday Extra 10; A. Wearne, *S.M.H.*, 16 May 1992, 48.
Bison. (Sydney: Prism Books, 1979).
Reviewed by W. Dyson, *Compass*, 3.2-3, 1981, 95-96; K. Goodwin, *Weeked Australian Magazine*, 19-22 April, 1980, 16; P. Kerr, *ABR*, 47, 1982-3, 40.
Driving Too Fast. (St Lucia: U.Q.P., 1989).
Reviewed by J. Beveridge, *Phoenix Review* , 7-8, 1992, 154-56; H. Cam, *S.M.H.*, 20 January, 1990, 71; J. Millbank, *Antithesis*, 4.1, 1990, 169-73; G. Kinross Smith, *Age*, 6 January 1990: Saturday Extra 7; S. Patton, *ABR* 117, 1989, 43-44; A. Wallace, *Social Alternatives*, 9.2, 1990, 58-59.
Little Hoodlum. (Sydney: Prism Books, 1975).
Reviewed by R. Adamson, *Australian*, 13 December, 1975, 45; J. Grant, *Poetry Australia*, 65, 1977, 64-65; T. Thorne, *Australian*, 13 November, 1976, 44.
The Monkey's Mask. (South Melbourne: Hyland House, 1994).
Reviewed by H. Cam, *S.M.H.*, 3 September, 1994, Spectrum 11A; L. Cataldi, *Overland*, 140, 1995, 82-83; M. Day, *S.M.H.*, 3 September 1994, Spectrum 11A; J. Digby, *ABR*, 165, 1994, 43-44; H. Kristin, *Age*, 22 October 1994, Saturday Extra 9; C. Miner, *Antipodes*, 9.2, 1995, 150-51.
The Night Parrot. (Wentworth Falls, NSW: Black Lightning Press, 1984).
Reviewed by B. Beaver, *Weekend Australian Magazine*, 11-12 May, 1985, 15; G.

Dutton, *Bulletin*, 25 June, 1985, 93-94; B. Giles, *ABR*, 65, 1984, 40; F. G. Kellaway, *Overland*, 99, 1985, 70-72; E. Lawson, *Phoenix Review*, 1, 1987, 119-21; J. Rodriguez, *S.M.H.*, 10 November, 1984, 41.

Critical Material

Digby, Jenny. 'Festive, Fun and Dangerous'. Interview. *Island*, 57, 1993, 34-39.

Fallon, Kathleen Mary. 'Ham-Fists in those "Male Size Golf Gloves"'. *Southerly*, 55.3, 1995, 191-97. Response to F. Moorhead's reading of *The Monkey's Mask* below.

McCredden, Lyn. 'Literary Reputation: Dorothy Porter'. *Notes & Furphies*, 34, 1995, 6-9.

---. 'The Mask Slips: Dorothy Porter and the Politics of Literary Reputation'. *Arena Magazine*, 17, 1995, 48-50.

Moorhead, Finola. '"She Doesn't Prove Who Did It, Anyway"'. *Southerly*, 55.1, 1995, 177-92. Discusses *The Monkey's Mask*. For response see Fallon above.

Page, Geoff. 'Dorothy Porter'. In his *A Reader's Guide To Contemporary Australian Poetry* (St. Lucia: U.Q.P., 1995), 225-228.

PORTER, HAL

Collection

Hal Porter. Edited by Mary Lord. (St Lucia: U.Q.P., 1980). Portable Australian Authors. Reviewed by D.R. Burns, *ABR*, No. 23, 1980, 1, 3-5; K. Stewart, *LiNQ*, VIII, No. 2, 1980, 78-81.

Hal Porter: A Handful of Pennies, Short Stories, Film Outline, Poems, Autobiography and Commentary. Edited by Mary Lord. (St Lucia: U.Q.P., 1989). Originally published as *Hal Porter*, 1980.
Reviewed by L. Kramer, *ABR*, No. 109, 1989, 16-17, see also letter in reply by L. Hergenhan, *ABR*, No. 113, 1989, 48.

Fiction

The Cats of Venice. (Sydney: A.& R., 1965).
Reviewed by T. Astley, *S.M.H.*, 9 April, 1966, 13; S. Lawson, *Canberra Times*, 12 March, 1966, 10; R. Mathew, *London Magazine*, V, No. 11, 1966, 93; W. Noonan, *Australian*, 26 March, 1966, 8; T.W. Shapcott, *ABR*, V, 1966, 119; M. Wilding, *Southerly*, XXVI, 1966, 208-12.

The Clairvoyant Goat and Other Stories. (Melbourne: Nelson, 1981).
Reviewed by R. Barnes, *National Times*, 31 January-6 February, 1982, 37; R.G. Geering, *Southerly*, XLII, 1982, 109-14; E. Riddell, *Bulletin*, 23 February, 1982, 62 & 66; G. Windsor, *Age Weekend Review*, 12 December, 1981, 27.

Fredo Fuss Love Life. (Sydney: A.& R., 1974).
Reviewed by M. Armitage, *Advertiser*, 21 December, 1974, 16; D. Benn, *Westerly*, No. 1, 1975, 80-81; A.R. Chisholm, *Age*, 30 November, 1974, 17; A. Diffey, *S.M.H.*, 16 November, 1974, 16; C. Harrison-Ford, *Australian*, 2 November, 1974, 37; B. Kiernan, *Meanjin*, XXXIV, 1975, 36-37.

Mr Butterfry and Other Tales of New Japan. (Sydney: A.& R., 1970).
Reviewed by A.R. Chisholm, *Age*, 26 December, 1970, 11; C. Harrison-Ford, *Overland*, No. 48, 1971, 59-60; H. Hewitt, *Canberra Times*, 30 January, 1971, 13; B. Kiernan, *Australian*, 21 November, 1970, 22; F. Moorhouse, *Bulletin*, 12 December, 1970, 54-55; M. Wilding, *Meanjin*, XXX, 1971, 265-67.

The Right Thing. (Adelaide: Rigby, 1971).
T. Forshaw, *Age*, 30 October, 1971, 16; C. Harrison-Ford, *Bulletin*, 27 November, 1971, 51-52; B. Jefferis, *S.M.H.*, 13 November, 1971, 23; B. Kiernan, *Australian*, 20 November, 1971, 19; A. Mitchell, *Advertiser*, 2 October, 1971, 24; J. Moses, *Sunday Australian*, 12 January, 1972, 15; *National Times*, 29 November-4 December,

1971, 38; B. Palfrey, *Canberra Times*, 11 December, 1971, 13; M. Thomas, *Review* (Melbourne), 6-12 November, 1971, 134.

Selected Stories. Chosen with an introduction by Leonie Kramer. (Sydney: A.& R., 1971).
Reviewed by R. Collings, *Sunday Review*, 25 April, 1971, 827; T. Forshaw, *Age*, 15 May, 1971, 15; A. Henries, *Bulletin*, 15 May, 1971, 49; M. Lemming, *ABR*, X, 1971, 153; B. Palfrey, *Canberra Times*, 12 June, 1971, 15; M. Thorpe, *English Studies*, LIII, 1972, 284; R.B.J. Wilson, *Meanjin*, XXXI, 1972, 223-25; M. Wolkowsky, *Sunday Australian*, 23 May, 1971, 32.

Selected Stories. Introduced by Fay Zwicky. (North Ryde, NSW: A.& R., 1991).

The Tilted Cross. (London: Faber, 1961). Reprinted with introduction by Adrian Mitchell (Adelaide: Rigby, 1971); reprinted with introduction by Laurie Hergenhan. (St Lucia: U.Q.P., 1989).
Reviewed by B. Burns, *Prospect*, VII, No. 1, 1964, 27; R. Gostand, *Social Alternatives*, 8, No. 2, 1989, 73-74; L. Kramer, *ABR*, No. 109, 1989, 16-17; W. Tonetto, *Mattoid*, No. 36, 1990, 155-67.

Drama
Eden House. (Sydney: A.& R., 1969).
Reviewed by R. Geering, *Southerly*, XXX, 1970, 314-15; H. Hewitt, *Canberra Times*, 14 March, 1970, 13; D. Whitelock, *ABR*, X, 1970, 14.

The Professor. (London: Faber and Faber, 1966).
Reviewed by P. Adams, *Bulletin*, 27 August, 1966, 47; K. Cantrell, *Southerly*, XXVII, 1967, 185-87; A. Downing, *Australian*, 30 July, 1966, 8; F. Evers, *ABR*, V, 1966, 202; H. Hewitt, *Canberra Times*, 3 September, 1966, 11.

Poetry
Elijah's Ravens. (Sydney: A.& R., 1968).
Reviewed by B. Beaver, *S.M.H.*, 6 April, 1968, 18; R. Dunlop, *Poetry Australia*, XXVIII, 1969, 37-39; M. Irvin, *Bulletin*, 30 March, 1968, 67; S.E. Lee, *Southerly*, XXVIII, 154-55; G. Page, *Canberra Times*, 18 May, 1968, 12; M. Richards, *Meanjin*, XXVIII, 1969, 271-72; T.W. Shapcott, *ABR*, VII, 131.

In an Australian Country Graveyard - and Other Poems. (Melbourne: Thomas Nelson (Australia), 1974).
Reviewed by B. Andrews, *Sun Herald*, 22 December, 1974, 62; D. Bean, *Westerly*, No. 1, 1975, 80-81; B. Beaver, *S.M.H.*, 1 February, 1975, 15; S.E. Lee, *Southerly*, XXXV, 1975, 302-04; W. Walsh, *T.L.S.*, 9 April, 1976, 443.

Non-Fiction
The Actors: An Image of New Japan. (Sydney: A.& R., 1968).
Reviewed by A. Broinowski, *Australian*, 19 October, 1968, 12; K. England, *Advertiser*, 12 October, 1968, 12; R.G. Geering, *Southerly*, XXIX, 1969, 156-58; E. Hackett, *ABR*, VIII, 1968, 9; H. Morita, *Nation*, 23 November, 1968, 20-21; H. Mukai, *Dissent*, No. 24, 1969, 42-43; A.A. Phillips, *Overland*, No. 41, 1969, 43; R. Raymond, *Bulletin*, 16 November, 1968, 88-89; J. Waten, *Age*, 19 October, 1968, 13.

Bairnsdale: Portrait of an Australian Country Town. (Sydney: Ferguson, 1977).
Reviewed by *Canberra Times*, 7 January, 1978, 10; C. Eagle, *Age Saturday Extra*, 1 February, 1986, 14; R.G. Geering, *Southerly*, XXXVIII, 1978, 357-60; *Journal of Australian Studies*, No. 2, 1977, 150-1; A.A. Phillips, *Age*, 2 July, 1977, 23; H. Tanner, *24 Hours*, II, No. 8, 1977, 56-57; P. Thompson, *Weekend Australian Magazine*, 8-9 February, 1986, 13.

The Extra. (Melbourne: Thomas Nelson (Australia), 1975; reprinted St Lucia: U.Q.P., 1987).
Reviewed by D.R. Burns, *Nation Review*, 3-9 October, 1975, 1310; R. Campbell,

Bulletin, 27 September, 1975, 46; F. Devine, *National Times*, 6-11 October, 1975, 20; T. Forshaw, *Quadrant*, XIX, No. 9, 1975, 87-88; T. Glad, *Social Alternatives*, VI, No. 4, 1987, 68-69; esp. 69; L. Kramer, *Overland*, No. 63, 1976, 62-64; M. Macleod, *S.M.H.*, 18 October, 1975, 17; J. Waten, *Age*, 20 September, 1975, 15; E. Webby, *A.L.S.*, VII, 1976, 436-37.

The Paper Chase. (Sydney: A.& R., 1966).
Reviewed by A. Ashbolt, *ABR*, VI, 1966, 21; R.G. Geering, *Southerly*, XXVII, 1967, 180-85; M. Harris, *Australian*, 26 November, 1966, 12; H.G. Kippax, *S.M.H.*, 12 November, 1966, 18; L. Kramer, *Bulletin*, 19 November, 1966, 58; M. McCallum, *Nation*, 28 January, 1967, 23; A.A. Phillips, *Age*, 19 November, 1966, 23; M. Wilding, *London Magazine*, VII, No. 5, 1967, 99-100.

Stars of Australian Stage and Screen. (Adelaide: Rigby, 1965).
Reviewed by A. Bagot, *ABR*, IV, 1965, 231; H.G. Kippax, *S.M.H.*, 28 August, 1965, 16.

The Watcher on the Cast-Iron Balcony. (London: Faber, 1963).
Reviewed by K. Ewers, *Westerly*, No. 4, 1963, 90-6; J. Lindsay, *Meanjin*, XXIII, No. 4, 1964, 443-4; *T.L.S.*, 1 November, 1963, 883; P. Ward, *ABR*, II, 1963, 192.

'Answers to the Funny, Kind Man (Australian Writers in Profile, 4)'. *Southerly*, XXIX, 1969, 3-14. Reprinted in *Hal Porter*, edited by Mary Lord (St Lucia: U.Q.P., 1980), 379-391.
'Childhood Reading'. *Educational Magazine*, XXXVI, No. 5, 1979, 21-23.
'Chores of a Writer in Residence'. *Bulletin*, 2 October, 1979, 59-62. Correspondence from D. Gallagher, 30 October, 1979, 19; M.-E. Ryan, 6 November, 1979, 14; and P. Webb, 27 November, 1979, 17-18.
'Gavin's Diary: An Unused Last Chapter of *The Right Thing*'. *Southerly*, XXXIII, 1973, 355-63. Includes brief introduction by Hal Porter.
'Hal Porter's Australia'. *Australian Letters*, VI, Nos. 3-4, 1964, 22-50. Of autobiographical and stylistic interest.

        Critical Material
Finch, Janette H. *Bibliography of Hal Porter*. (Adelaide: Libraries Board of South Australia, 1965). Bibliographies of Australian Writers series. Reviewed by M. Wilding, *A.L.S.*, III, 1967, 142-148.
State Library of South Australia. 'Bibliographies of Australian Writers - Supplement'. *Index to Australian Book Reviews*. II, No. 4, 1966, 227-8; III, No. 4, 1967, 215-217; IV No. 4, 1968, 251-58; V, No. 4, 1969, 251-53; VI, No. 4, 1970, 320-23; VII, No. 4, 1971, 291-96; VIII, No. 4, 1972, 250-52; IX, No. 4, 1973, 151-54; X, No. 4, 1975, 166-70, 191.
Lord, Mary. 'A Contribution to the Bibliography of Hal Porter'. *A.L.S.*, IV, 1970, 405-09.

'Hal Porter Dies at 73'. *Age*, 1 October, 1984, 3. For other obituaries see *Age*, 1 October, 1984, 11; *Canberra Times*, 3 October, 1984, 26; *S.M.H.*, 1 October, 1984, 3. See also Forshaw, Thelma, 'Some Remarks on the Late Great Hal Porter', *A.L.S.*, XII, No. 1, 1985, 89-91.
'Tension on the Reel'. *Overland*, No. 71, 1978, 2-41. Special section on Hal Porter's story 'The Jetty' and its relation to 'The Child' segment of the film *Libido*. Contributions by Porter, Tim Burstall, David Baker, John Murray, Fred Schepisi.
Anderson, Don. 'Portraits of the Artist as a Young Man: *The Education of Young Donald; Unreliable Memoirs*; *The Watcher on the Cast Iron Balcony*'. *Meanjin*, XLII, 1983, 339-48.
Barnes, John. 'New Tracks to Travel: The Stories of White, Porter and Cowan'. *Meanjin*, XXV, 1966, 154-70.
Bennett Bruce. 'Australian Perspectives on the Near North: Hal Porter and Randolph Stow'. In *South Pacific Images*, edited by Chris Tiffin (St Lucia: SPACLALS, 1978),

124-44.
Burns, Robert. 'A Sort of Triumph over Time: Hal Porter's Prose Narratives'. *Meanjin*, XXVIII, 1969, 19-28.
Capone, Giovanna. 'Aesthete at Antipodes: Hal Porter and the Tilted Cross'. In *Saggi e ricerche sulle culture extraeuropee*, edited by G. Bellini, C. Gorlier, S. Zoppi (Rome: Bulzoni, 1987), 7-28. Africa, America, Asia, Australia, 3.
---. 'Hal Porter, *The Tower* and the Quintessence of Porterism'. In *European Perspectives: Contemporary Essays on Australian Literature*, edited by Giovanna Capone (*A.L.S.* 15.2 (special issue)/ St. Lucia: U.Q.P., 1991), 162-72.
---. *Incandescent Verities: The Fiction of Hal Porter*. (Roma (Italy): Bulzoni, 1990). Reviewed by B. Bennett, *Westerly*, 35, No. 3, 1990, 94-96; L. Clancy, *Age*, 1 June, 1991, Saturday Extra 8; C.J. Koch, *A.L.S.*, 15.1, 1991, 87-89; M. Lord, *ABR*, No. 126, 1990, 38.
Colmer, John. 'Australian Autobiography: A Hole in the Literary Landscape'. *Southerly*, XLV, No. 2, 1985, 165-186.
---. 'Autobiography as Art: Hal Porter'. In his *Australian Autobiography: A Personal Quest*. (Melbourne: O.U.P., 1990), 50-70.
---. 'Hal Porter: The Watcher on the Cast-Iron Balcony'. In *Autobiographical and Biographical Writing in the Commonwealth*, edited by D. MacDermott (Sabadell, Barcelona: Editorial AUSA, 1984), 57-62.
Duncan, R.A. 'Hal Porter's Writing and the Impact of the Absurd'. *Meanjin*, XXIX, 1970, 468-73.
Geering, R.G. 'Hal Porter, The Watcher'. *Southerly*, XXIV, No. 2, 1964, 92-103.
---. 'Hal Porter: The Controls of Melodrama'. *Southerly*, XXXIII, 1973, 18-33.
---. 'Hal Porter's Autobiography'. *Southerly*, XXXVI, 1976, 123-33.Gostand, Reba. 'Repetition and Menace in Hal Porter's *The Tower*'. *A.L.S.*, VI, 1973, 36-45.
Hall, Sandra. 'Japan Puts Porter under a Microscope'. *Bulletin*, 2 September, 1980, 76.
Harris, Max. 'A Comeback From a Cast-Iron Balcony'. *Australian*, 2 January, 1965, 9.
---. 'The Disciplined Solitude of Lusty Prince Hal'. *Australian*, 12 April, 1969, 18.
---. 'Divided Spirit that Was Hal Porter'. *Weekend Australian Magazine*, 13-14 October, 1984, 14.
Harris, Susan. 'Five by Five: An Educational Sampling'. [*Adelaide*] *A.L.S. Working Papers*, I, No. 1, 1975, 54-64.
Hawley-Crowcroft, Jean. 'Hal Porter's Asian Stories'. *Quadrant*, XXVIII, Nos. 7-8, 1984, 41-45.
Hergenhan, L.T. '*The Tilted Cross*: The "Duties of Innocence"'. *Southerly*, XXXIV, 1974, 157-67. Reprinted in his *Unnatural Lives*. (St Lucia: U.Q.P., 1983), 130-38.
Jobling, Lee. 'Trick Chinese Boxes: Hal Porter's Art of Autobiography'. *Southerly*, XL, 1980, 159-73.
Koch, C.J. 'In Memoriam: Hal Porter'. *Quadrant*, XXVIII, No. 11, 1984, 7-8.
---. 'Loss of the Self-Watcher, a Man apart'. *Australian*, 1 October, 1984, 10.
Lawson, Alan. "Where a Man Belongs": Hal Porter's *The Paper Chase* and George Johnston's *Clean Straw for Nothing*'. In *Studies in the Recent Australian Novel*, edited by K.G. Hamilton (St Lucia: U.Q.P., 1978), 168-93.
Lord, Mary. *Hal Porter*. (Melbourne: O.U.P., 1974). Australian Writers and Their Work. Reviewed by C. Hadgraft, *A.L.S.*, VI, 1974, 440-41.
---. *Hal Porter: A Man of Many Parts*. (Milsons Point, NSW: Random House, 1993). Reviewed by J. Davidson, *Age* 20 November, 1993, Saturday Extra 9; G. Dutton, *S.M.H.*, 6 November, 1993, Spectrum 11A; H. Elliott, *ABR*, 157, 1993/1994, 11-12; K. Gasmier, *FAR*, 9.1, 1994, 13-15; I. Indyk, *A.L.S.*, 17.1, 1995, 95-99; L. Kramer, *Weekend Australian*, 4-5 December, 1993, Review 5; P. Pierce, *Bulletin*, 7 December, 1993, 89; P. Porter, *Meanjin*, 53.2, 1994, 376-80.

---. 'Hal Porter's Comic Mode'. *A.L.S.*, IV, 1970, 371-82.
---. 'Interview with Hal Porter'. *A.L.S.*, VIII, 1978, 269-79. See also Hal Porter's letter, *A.L.S.*, IX, 1979, 140.
Manning, Barbara. '*Eden House* as Battleground'. *Bulletin*, 5 April, 1969, 38-39.
Matthews, Brian. 'Ruminating Among the Ruins'. In his *Romantics and Mavericks: The Australian Short Story*. (Townsville, Qld.: James Cook University of North Queensland, 1987), 34-48. The Colin Roderick Lectures, 1986. Monograph/Foundation for Australian Literary Studies No. 14.
McGregor, Craig (ed.). *In the Making*. (Melbourne: Nelson Australian, 1969), 154-59.
Miles, John. 'Hal and a God Called Hughie'. *Advertiser*, 10 March, 1970, 2. Interview with Hal Porter as winner of *Advertiser* Literary Competition for the novel. Also reported in *Age*, 14 March, 1970, 14.
Munday, Rosemary. 'Hal Porter Passes on Some Truths about Famous People He's Watched as an Extra'. *National Times*, 30 September-5 October, 1974, 20.
Murray, Kevin. 'A Tribute to Hal Porter'. *ABR*, No. 66, 1984, 16.
Murray-Smith, Stephen. 'Swag'. *Overland*, No. 97, 1984, 25 & 26.
Newman, Joan. 'The Self Observed: Hal Porter's Australian Autobiography, *The Watcher on the Cast Iron Balcony*'. *A-B: Auto-Biography Studies*, 8.1, 1993, 91-101.
Onslow, Annette. 'Hal Porter Revisited'. *Aspect*, V, No. 4, 1981, 83-86.
Radic, Leonard. 'The Play That Took a Fortnight to Write'. *Age*, 22 March, 1969, 9. Discusses *Eden House* and Porter's interest in the theatre generally.
Rolfe, Patricia. 'Hal Porter: The Middle Age of Innocence'. *Bulletin*, 14 December, 1963, 35-7. A biographical note.
Rutherford, Anna. 'The Cross Tilted to Fall: Hal Porter's *The Tilted Cross*'. In *Commonwealth Literature and the Modern World*, edited by Hena Maes-Jelinek (Brussels: Didier, 1975), 27-35.
Smith, Graeme Kinross. 'Hal Porter: A Profile'. *A.L.S.*, VII, 1975, 208-12.

PORTER, PETER

Poetry
After Martial. (London: O.U.P., 1972).
Reviewed by G. Ewart, *Encounter*, XL, No. 3, 1973, 64-65; C. Harrison-Ford, *New Poetry*, XXI, No. 1, 1973, 36-37; S.E. Lee, *Southerly*, XXXIII, 1973, 338-39; *T.L.S.*, 3 November, 1972, 1304; A. Taylor, *ABR*, XI, 1973, 70-71.

The Automatic Oracle. (Oxford; Melbourne: O.U.P., 1987).
Reviewed by B. Bennett, *ABR*, No. 100, 1988, 36-37; T. Dooley, *T.L.S.*, 15-21 January, 1988, 56; E. Jones, *Age Saturday Extra*, 16 April, 1988, 13; B. Morrison, *London Review of Books*, X, No. 5, 1988, 13-14; M. O'Connor, *Weekend Australian. Weekend Magazine*, 28-29 May, 1988, 14; C. Pollnitz, *Scripsi*, V, No. 1, 1988, 197-209; M.H. Simpson, *Unisa English Studies*, 24.1, 1991, 47-49; A. Wallace, *Southerly*, XLVIII, No. 3, 1988, 350-355.

The Chair of Babel. (Melbourne: O.U.P., 1992).
Reviewed by N. Corcoran, *T.L.S.*, 8 May, 1992, 22; M. Duwell, *Scripsi*, 8.2, 1992, 191-98; E. Jones, *Age*, 19 September, 1992, Saturday Extra 10; C. Pollnitz, *Weekend Australian*, 5-6 September, 1992, Review 6.

Collected Poems. (London: O.U.P., 1983).
Reviewed by J. Ash, *PN Review*, No. 33, 1983, 74-75; A. Brownjohn, *Encounter*, No. 358, 1983, 80-84; V. Buckley, *ABR*, No. 63, 1984, 21-22; A. Cleary, *Thames Poetry*, II, No. 13, 1983, 41-44; D. Davis, *Listener*, 18 August, 1983, 20-21; D. Dunn, *London Magazine*, N.S. XXIII, No. 3, 1983, 74-78; G. Dutton, *Bulletin*, 20 September, 1983, 88 & 91; P. Goldsworthy, *Ash Magazine*, Nos. 14-15, 1983-1984, 32-33; D. Green, *Hemisphere*, XXVIII, 1984, 297-98; E. Jones, *Scripsi*, II, No. 4,

1984, 69-75; P. Levi, *Spectator*, 23 April, 1983, 24; J. Lucas, *New Statesman*, 1 April, 1983, 21; A. Murray, *S.M.H.*, 18 June, 1983, 37; C. Raine, *London Review of Books*, V, No. 18, 1983, 5-7; G. Szirtes, *Poetry Review*, LXXIII, No. 1, 1983, 34-36; C. Wallace-Crabbe, *Age Saturday Extra*, 28 May, 1983, 8.

The Cost of Seriousness. (London: O.U.P., 1978).
Reviewed by F. Adcock, *Encounter*, No. 299, 1978, 88-89; B. Beaver, *Age*, 16 December, 1978, 27; J. Fenton, *New Review*, V, No. 1, 1978, 117-18; E. Fisher, *Spectator*, 8 July, 1978, 25; J. Fuller, *New Statesman*, 2 June, 1978, 742; K. Goodwin, *Weekend Australian Magazine*, 2-3 December, 1978, 8; D. Graham, *Stand*, XX, 1978/79, 68-69; J. Grant, *Poetry Australia*, No. 69, 1979, 68-71; *Helix*, No. 2, 1978, 55-56; P. Law, *Quadrant*, XXII, No. 8, 1978, 76-77; [S.E. Lee], *Southerly*, XXXIX, 1979, 442-43; H. Lomas, *London Magazine*, N.S. XX, Nos. 8-9, 1980, 126-30; A. Stevenson, *Listener*, C, 1978, 62; N. Wheale, *Poetry Review*, LXVIII, No. 2, 1978, 54-55.

English Subtitles. (London: O.U.P., 1981).
Reviewed by J. Grant, *Age*, 19 December, 1981, 21; M. Hulse, *PN Review*, No. 21, 1981, 63; E. Jones, *Scripsi*, I, No. 2, 1981, 8-11; J. Lasdun, *Spectator*, 18 April, 1981, 21-22; L. Lerner, *Encounter*, LVII, No. 3, 1981, 62-63; H. Lomas, *London Magazine*, N.S. XXI, No. 3, 1981, 73-75; E. Longley, *New Statesman*, 24 April, 1981, 19; J. Lucas, *T.L.S.*, 17 April, 1981, 429; P. Mead, *Island Magazine*, No. 14, 1983, 48-51; M. O'Neill, *Poetry Review*, LXXII, No. 1, 1982, 62; G. Page, *Hemisphere*, XXVII, No. 1, 1982, 27; C. Rawson, *London Review of Books*, III, 1981, No. 13, 1982, 14; *Thames Poetry*, II, No. 10, 1982, 29-31; J. Tranter, *S.M.H.*, 17 October, 1981, 50; F. Zwicky, *Westerly*, XXVII, No. 2, 1982, 106-09.

Fast Forward. (Oxford: O.U.P., 1984).
Reviewed by J. Bate, *London Review of Books*, VI, Nos. 22-23, 1984, 19-20; G. Ewart, *British Book News*, January, 1985, 52-53; M. Hulse, *Quadrant*, XXIX, No. 3, 1985, 86-87; E. Jones, *ABR*, No. 77, 1985, 41-42; L. Mackinnon, *T.L.S.*, 11 January, 1985, 54; C.B. McCully, *PN Review*, No. 45, 1985, 77-80; I. McMillan, *Argo*, VI, No. 2, 1985, 45-46; J. Saunders, *Stand Magazine*, XXVIII, No. 2, 1987, 73; W. Tonetto, *Phoenix Review*, No. 1, 1986/87, 113-115; C. Wallace-Crabbe, *Age Saturday Extra*, 27 April, 1985, 14.

With Arthur Boyd. *Jonah*. (London: Secker and Warburg; St Kilda: Heinemann Australia, 1973).
Reviewed by R. Adamson, *Australian*, 5 January, 1974, 36; A. Brownjohn, *New Statesman*, 4 January, 1974, 23; R. Garfitt, *London Magazine*, XIII, No. 6, 1974, 102-03; P. Roberts, *S.M.H.*, 9 February, 1974, 15; C. Sansom, *Nation Review*, 4-10 January, 1974, 381.

The Lady and the Unicorn. (London: Secker & Warburg, 1975).
Reviewed by N. Borlase, *S.M.H.*, 17 September, 1977, 16.

The Last of England. (London: O.U.P., 1970).
Reviewed by A. Brownjohn, *New Statesman*, LXXX, 1970, 384; A. Cluysenaar, *Stand* (Newcastle-upon-Tyne), XII, No. 1, 1971, 72-76; D. Dunn, *Encounter*, XXXVI, No. 3, 1971, 68-70; J. Fuller, *Listener*, 24 December, 1970, 888; C. Harrison-Ford, *Nation*, 26 June, 1971, 21-22; C. James, *Review* (London), No. 24, 1970, 53-61; P. Joseph, *New Poetry*, XIX, No. 4, 1971, 35-37; R. Milliss, *Review* (Melbourne), 22-28 January, 1972, 392; *New Poetry*, XX, No. 1-2, 1972, 62; N. Rennie, *London Magazine*, N.S. X, No. 12, 1971, 92-95; P. Roberts, *S.M.H.*, 3 July, 1971, 19; M. Schmidt, *Poetry*, CXX, 1972, 177-79; R.A. Simpson, *Age*, 11 September, 1971, 18; J. Smith, *Poetry Review*, LXI, 1970/71, 364; *T.L.S.*, 30 October, 1970, 1245.

Living in a Calm Country. (London: O.U.P., 1975).
Reviewed by P. Beer, *T.L.S.*, 7 May, 1976, 540; R. Davies, *New Statesman*, XC,

24 October, 1975, 515-16; D. Dunn, *Encounter*, XLVI, No. 2, 1976, 75-76; D. Graham, *Stand*, XVII, No. 3, 1976, 77-78; C. Hope, *London Magazine*, N.S. XVI, No. 2, 1976, 89-91; P. Law, *Nation Review*, 26 March-1 April, 1976, 596; L. Murray, *S.M.H.*, 14 February, 1976, 15; T. Shapcott, *Australian*, 24 April, 1976, 27; C. Wallace-Crabbe, *Age*, 22 May, 1976, 22; P. Washington, *Spectator*, 8 November, 1975. 602.

Machines. (Hitchin, Herts.: Mandeville Press, 1986).
Reviewed by I. McMillan, *Poetry Review*, LXXVII, No. 1, 1987, 49.

With Arthur Boyd. *Mars* (London: Andre Deutsch, 1988).
Reviewed by B. Bennett, *CRNLE Reviews Journal*, No. 2, 1989, 1-4; L. Bourke, *Westerly*, 34, No. 2, 1989, 103-106; J. Mendelssohn, *S.M.H.*, 12 November, 1988, 90.

Millennial Fables. (Melbourne: O.U.P., 1995).
Reviewed by N. Powell, *T.L.S.*, 10 March, 1995, 26; P. Steele, *Age*, 8 Apr., 1995, Saturday Extra 9; J. Tranter, *ABR*, 169, 1995, 40-41.

With Arthur Boyd. *Narcissus*. (London: Secker and Warburg, 1984).
Reviewed by W. Tonetto, *Phoenix Review*, No. 1, 1986/87, 113-115.

Peter Porter Reads from His Own Work. (St Lucia: U.Q.P., 1974). Poets on Record, 12. Record and booklet. Booklet includes notes by Peter Porter and selected biliography.
Reviewed by J. Beston, *S.M.H.*, 6 July, 1974, 15; R.M. Beston, *Makar*, X, No. 2, 1974, 47-48.

Poems Ancient and Modern. (London: Scorpion Press, 1965).
Reviewed by E. Jones, *Australian*, 5 June, 1965, 11.

A Porter Folio: New Poems. (Lowestoft: Scorpion Press, 1969).
Reviewed by M. Dodsworth, *Listener*, LXXXII, 1969, 285-86; C. Harrison-Ford, *Poetry Magazine*, XVIII, No. 3, 1970, 35-40; B. Jones, *London Magazine*, N.S. IX, No. 7, 1969, 95-99; A. Thwaite, *New Statesman*, LXXVIII, 1969, 53-54.

A Porter Selected. (Melbourne, O.U.P., 1989).
Reviewed by L. Bourke, *Westerly*, 35, No. 2, 1990, 76-78; H. Cam, *S.M.H.*, 3 February, 1990, 78; P. Carter, *Overland*, No. 117, 1990, 20-24; C. Harrison-Ford, *Island Magazine*, Nos. 43-44, 1990, 66-70; S. O'Brien, *T.L.S.*, 15-21 December, 1989, 1392; A. Wallace, *Southerly*, 50, No. 1, 1990, 103-08; W. Wynne, *ABR*, No. 122, 1990, 39-41.

Possible Worlds. (Melbourne: O.U.P., 1989).
Reviewed by L. Bourke, *Westerly*, 35, No. 2, 1990, 76-78; H. Cam, *S.M.H.*, 3 February, 1990, 78; P. Carter, *Overland*, No. 117, 1990, 20-24; P. Corcoran, *London Review of Books*, 12, No.2, 1990, 15-16; C. Harrison-Ford, *Island Magazine*, Nos. 43-44, 1990, 66-70; M. Hulse, *Quadrant*, 33, No. 12, 1989, 48-49; E. Jones, *Age*, 23 June, 1990, Saturday Extra 9; S. O'Brien, *T.L.S.*, 15-21 December, 1989, 1392; J. Shapcott, *New Statesman & Society*, 27 October, 1989, 38; A. Wallace, *Southerly*, 50, No. 1, 1990, 103-08.

Preaching to the Converted. (London: O.U.P., 1972).
Reviewed by D. Dunn, *Encounter*, XL, No. 3, 1973, 66-69; T. Eagleton, *Stand*, XIV, No. 2, 1973, 77-78; G. Ewart, *New Statesman*, LXXXIV, 1972, 873; J. Galassi, *Poetry*, CXXIII, 1973, 113-14; C. Harrison-Ford, *New Poetry*, XXI, No. 1, 1973, 34-37; S.E. Lee, *Southerly*, XXXIII, 1973, 339-41; A. Maclean, *Listener*, LXXXIX, 1973, 389; P. Roberts, *S.M.H.*, 21 April, 1973, 18; *T.L.S.*, 3 November, 1972, 1304; A. Taylor, *ABR*, XI, 1973, 70-71; M. Thorpe, *English Studies*, LV, 1974, 550.

Non-Fiction

'Australian Expatriate Writers in Britain'. In *A Passage to Somewhere Else*, edited by Doireann MacDermott and Susan Ballyn, Proceedings of the Commonwealth Conference, University of Barcelona, 30 September- 2 October, 1987 (Barcelona: Promociones y Publicaciones Universitarias, 1988), 135-41.

'Australian Poetry Today'. *Aquarius*, Nos. 15-16, 1983-1984, 11-13.

'Brisbane Comes Back'. *Quadrant*, XIX, No. 6, 53-58. Autobiographical.

'Country Poetry and Town Poetry: A Debate with Les Murray'. *A.L.S.*, IX, 1979, 39-48.

'An Expatriate's Reaction to His Condition'. *Westerly*, 32.2, 1987, 43-7.

'A Land Fit for Conservatives'. *T.L.S.*, 30 July, 1971, 891-93. Principally autobiographical.

'Les Murray: An Appreciation'. *Journal of Commonwealth Literature*, XVII, No. 1, 1982, 45-52.

'Les Murray Interviewed by Peter Porter'. *Australian Studies*, No. 4, 1990, 77-87.

'Opinion'. *Review* (London), No. 22, 1970, 34-39.

'Saving from the Wreck'. *Scripsi*, III, Nos. 2-3, 1985, 195-216. Article on literary translation.

'Sunburned Neurosis?' *Hemisphere*, XX, No. 4, 1976, 14-21.

'Viewpoint'. T.L.S., 7 July, 1972, 774. Partly about his own reading.

'What I Have Written...'. *Hemisphere*, XXVIII, 1983, 150-56. Interview.

'Working with Arthur Boyd'. *Westerly*, XXXII, No. 1, 1987, 69-78.

Critical Material

Kaiser, John R. *Peter Porter: A Bibliography, 1954-1986*. (London: Mansell, 1990).

'The Poet in the Sixties: Vices and Virtues- A Recorded Conversation with Peter Porter'. In *British Poetry Since 1960: A Critical Survey*, by Michael Schmidt and Grevel Lindop (South Hinksey, Oxford: Carcanet Press, 1972), 202-12.

Baker, Candida. 'Peter Porter'. In her *Yacker 3* (Sydney: Picador, 1989), 260-283.

Beaver, Bruce. 'The Cosmopolitan Eye: Peter Porter and Arthur Boyd'. *Phoenix Review*, 7 & 8, 1992, 99-109.

Bennett, Bruce. 'The Bright Locked World'. *Overland*, 124, 1991, 47-52. Part of a chapter of his *Spirit in Exile*, see below.

---. 'Passports to Paradise: Peter Porter and Clive James'. In *A Sense of Exile*, edited by Bruce Bennett (Nedlands, W.A.: The Centre for Studies in Australian Literature, 1988), 67-79.

---. 'Peter Porter's Expatriate Vision'. In *Poetry of the Pacific Region*, edited by Robert Sellick (Adelaide: Centre for the Research in the New Literatures in English, 1984), 19-30.

---. 'Peter Porter in Profile'. *Westerly*, XXVII, No. 1, 1982, 45-47.

---. *Spirit in Exile: Peter Porter and His Poetry*. (Melbourne: O.U.P., 1991). Reviewed by L. Bourke, *Westerly*, 37.4, 1992, 107-09; H. Dakin, *Southerly*, 52.2, 1992, 155-59; M. Duwell, *A.L.S.*, 15.4, 1992, 362-64; M. Gray, *Yearbook of English Studies*, 24, 1994, 344-45; K. Hart, *Overland*, 127, 1992, 90-92; H.C. Jaffa, *Antipodes*, 7.2, 1993, 174-78; E. Jones, *Age*, 12 October, 1991, Saturday Extra 7; S. O'Brien, *T.L.S.*, 24 January, 1992, 23; G. Page, *ABR*, 135, 1991, 32-33; C. Pollnitz, *Weekend Australian*, 21-22 September, 1991, Review 5; J. Rodriguez, *Voices*, 2.1, 1992, 94-96; T. Shapcott, *S.M.H.*, 21 September, 1991, 42.

---. 'Versions of the Past in the Poetry of Les Murray and Peter Porter'. In *The Writer's Sense of the Past: Essays on Southeast Asian and Australasian Literature*, edited by Kirpal Singh (Singapore: Singapore University Press, 1987), 178-188.

Brownjohn, Alan. 'Alan Brownjohn Talks to Peter Porter'. *The Literary Review*, 59, 1983, 18-22.

---. 'The Martial Art'. *Poetry Review*, LXXIII, No. 1, 1983, 32-33.

Coleman, Richard. 'A Man of Many Places'. *S.M.H.*, 12 April, 1980, 15.

Dooley, Tim. 'Acting against Oblivion'. *Poetry Review*, LXXIII, No. 1, 1983, 27-29.

Douglas, Dennis. 'Conversation with Peter Porter'. *Overland*, No. 44, 1970, 33-34.

Dunlevy, Maurice. 'A Journey into a Double Past'. *Canberra Times*, 19 August, 1972, 10.

Ewart, Gavin. 'From Notions to Emotions'. *T.L.S.*, 19 May, 1978, 550.

Gordon, Nancy, and Lindsay, Elaine. 'Interview with Peter Porter'. *Issue*, (Adelaide), IV, No. 14, 1974, 48-51.

Gray, Robert. 'Peter Porter and Australia'. *Poetry Review*, LXXIII, No. 1, 1983, 16-20.

Harrison, Martin. 'Peter Porter Interviewed by Martin Harrison'. *A.L.S.*, XI, 1984, 458-67.

Hergenhan, Laurie. 'The "I" of the Beholder: Representations of Tuscany in Some Recent Australian Literature'. *Westerly*, 36.4, 1991, 107-14. Discusses works by Porter and others.

Horder, John. 'Peter Porter: Expatriate Poet'. *Canberra Times*, 28 May, 1966, 9.

Hulse, Michael. 'Love and Death: Nine Points of Peter Porter'. *Quadrant*, XXVII, No. 9, 1983, 31-38.

James, Clive. 'The Boy from Brisbane'. *Poetry Review*, LXXIII, No. 1, 1983, 25-27. Reprinted in his *Snakecharmers in Texas: Essays 1980-87* (London: Jonathan Cape, 1988), 44-48.

Kavanagh, Paul. 'Little Harmonic Labyrinths: An Interview with Peter Porter'. *Southerly*, XLV, No. 1, 1985, 12-22. Reprinted in *Conversations: Interviews with Australian Writers* edited by Paul Kavanagh and Peter Kuch (North Ryde, NSW: Collins/A.& R., 1991).

Kemp, Peter. 'Intimations of Mortality'. *T.L.S.*, 31 May, 1985, 609.

Kinsella, John. 'John Kinsella Interviews Peter Porter Regarding Collaboration between Peter Porter and Arthur Boyd'. *Westerly*, 40.3, 1995, 19-38.

Krausmann, Rudi. 'Poet ... Politics ... Apocalypse'. *Aspect*, Spring 1975, 5-9, 11-12.

Long, Angela. 'A Season in Terra Primitivis'. *National Times*, 17-23 June, 1983, 29.

Martin, Philip. 'Interview with Peter Porter'. *Quadrant*, XVIII, No. 1, 1974, 9-19.

Murche, John. 'An Expatriate Poet Makes Objects of Desire his Reward'. *Weekend Australian Magazine*, 25-26 February, 1984, 15.

Murray, Les. 'The Boeotian Strain'. *Kunapipi*, II, No. 1, 1980, 45-64.

---. 'Peter Porter. *On First Looking into Chapman's Hesiod*'. In *Australian Poems in Perspective*, edited by P.K. Elkin (St Lucia: U.Q.P., 1978), 171-84. Reprinted as 'On Sitting Back and Thinking About Porter's Boeotia', in his *Peasant Mandarin: Prose Pieces by Les Murray* (St. Lucia: U.Q.P., 1978), 172-84.

Nicklin, Lenore. 'Peter Porter - An Atheist who Prays'. *S.M.H.*, 19 July, 1975, 11.

Neill, Edward. 'Peter Porter's Poetry: An Appreciation'. *Basa Magazine*, 2.2, 1985, 9-14.

O'Neill, Michael. 'The Lying Art: An Aspect of the Poetry of Peter Porter'. *Durham University Journal*, 48, 1987, 367-72.

Orr, Peter (ed.). *The Poet Speaks*. (London: Routledge and Kegan Paul, 1966), 179-84. An interview.

Owen, Margaret. 'Peter Porter and The Group'. *Poetry Review*, LXXIII, No. 1, 1983, 12-13. *Poetry Review*, LXXIII, No. 1, 1983, the Peter Porter number also contains poems by Edwin Brock, George Szirtes, Dannie Abse, D.J. Enright, Gavin Ewart and Vernon Scannell in honour of Peter Porter.

Patterson, Lee. 'Expatriate Poet Makes It Pay'. *S.M.H.*, 3 January, 1970, 11.

Page, Geoff. 'Peter Porter'. In his *A Reader's Guide To Contemporary Australian Poetry* (St. Lucia: U.Q.P., 1995), 228-233.

Richards, Max. 'The Citizenship of Peter Porter'. *A.L.S.*, VIII, 1978, 351-59.

---. 'The Province of Peter Porter'. *Meridian*, 12.1, 1993, 84-90.

Rolph, John. 'A Note on the Scorpion Press'. *Poetry Review*, LXXIII, No. 1, 1983,

13.
Rowbotham, David. 'Peter Porter Pops in with Poems'. *Courier-Mail*, 30 March, 1974, 5.
Selzer, David. 'Porter Major'. *Phoenix*, 10, 1973, 83-85.
Steele, Peter. *Peter Porter*. (Melbourne: O.U.P., 1992). Reviewed by P. Coleman, *Weekend Australian*, 9-10 January, 1993, Review 6; P. Craven, *Age*, 12 September, 1992, Saturday Extra 10; I. Donaldson, *Voices*, 3.1, 1993, 123-25; M. Duwell, *Scripsi*, 8.2, 1992, 191-98; J. Hanrahan, *ABR*, 147, 1992, 25-26; H.C.Jaffa, *Antipodes*, 7.2, 1993, 175; J.S. Leonard, *Overland*, 130, 1993, 87-89; P. Mead, *A.L.S.*, 16.2, 1993, 140-51; P. Pierce, *Quadrant*, 37.11, 1993, 75-77.
---. 'The Radiation of Peter Porter'. *Westerly*, XXIX, No. 3, 1984, 65-77.
Stratford, Jenny. 'The Market in Authors' Manuscripts'. *T.L.S.*, 24 July, 1969, 817-18. See also letter to the editor by Peter Porter, *T.L.S.*, 31 July, 1969, 859.
Throssell, Ric. 'Perhaps to Open a Door'. *Australian*, 18 November, 1972, 33.
Thwaite, Anthony. 'Porter: Man and Poet'. *Poetry Review*, LXXIII, No. 1, 1983, 22-23.
Uhlmann, Anthony. 'Peter Porter and the Automatic Oracle'. *Active: Reactive* (Sydney: Persona Press, 1987), 2-4. Interview with Peter Porter.
Waten, Judah. 'Some Australians and Iris Murdoch'. *Age*, 19 February, 1966, 22.
Williams, Barbara. '"I Am a Characteristic Australian": An Interview with Peter Porter'. *Australian and New Zealand Studies in Canada*, No. 2, 1989, 65-73.
---. 'Peter Porter: An Interview'. *Westerly*, 35, No. 2, 1990, 57-73.
Williams, David. '"A Map of Loss": The Recent Poetry of Peter Porter'. *Critical Quarterly*, XXV, No. 4, 1983, 55-62.

PRAED, ROSA CAMPBELL

Fiction
The Bond of Wedlock. Introduced by Lynne Spender. (London, Sydney: Pandora, 1987). First published London: White, 1887.
Reviewed by L. Downes, *LiNQ*, 17, No. 2, 1990, 135-40; R. Lucas, *S.M.H.*, 4 July, 1987, 46; S. McKernan, *Times on Sunday*, 23 August, 1987, 33; P. Pierce, *Age Saturday Extra*, 5 September, 1987, 13; H. Thomson, *ABR*, No. 91, 1987, 6-7.
The Bond of Wedlock. Introduced by Elizabeth Webby. Australian Books on Demand 7. (Canberra: Mulini Press, 1993). First published London: White, 1887.
Lady Bridget in the Never-Never Land: A Story of Australian Life. Introduced by Pam Gilbert. (London, Sydney: Pandora, 1987). First published London: Heinemann, 1891.
Reviewed by S. McKernan, *Times on Sunday*, 23 August, 1987, 33; P. Pierce, *Age Saturday Extra*, 5 September, 1987, 13; H. Thomson, *ABR*, No. 91, 1987, 6-7.
Outlaw and Lawmaker. Introduction by Dale Spender. (London, Sydney: Pandora, 1988). First published London: Chatto & Windus, 1893.
Reviewed by B. Levy, *Australian Society*, VII, No. 10, 1988, 48-49.

Critical Material
Tiffin, Chris. *Rosa Praed (Mrs Campbell Praed) 1851-1934: A Bibliography*. Victorian Fiction Research Guides 15 (St Lucia: Department of English, University of Qld., 1989). Reviewed by D. Hecq, *Meridian*, 9, No. 1, 1990, 94-96; G. Whitlock, *A.L.S.*, 14, No. 3, 1990, 400-03.
Tiffin, Chris, and Lynette Baer, comps. *The Praed Papers: A Listing and Index*. (Brisbane: Library Board of Queensland, 1994). Reviewed in *Margin*, 35, 1995, 33.
Dixon, Robert. *Writing the Colonial Adventure: Race, Gender and Nation in Anglo-Australian Popular Fiction, 1875-1914*. (Melbourne: Cambridge UP, 1995). Discusses Praed.
Elliott, Brian. 'Tea on the Piazza with Mrs Campbell Praed'. In *Commonwealth*

Literature: Unity and Diversity in a Common Culture, edited by John Press (London: Heinemann, 1965), 64-81.

Ferres, Kay. 'Rewriting Desire: Rosa Praed, Theosophy, and the Sex Problem'. In *The Time to Write: Australian Women Writers 1890-1930* edited by Kay Ferres (Ringwood, Vic.: Penguin, 1993), 238-55.

---. 'Women Making a Spectacle of Themselves: Rosa Praed's *Ariane*, Melodrama, and Marriage Reform'. *Australasian Drama Studies*, 23, 1993, 56-64.

Higgins, Susan. '"That Singular Anomaly, the Lady Novelist" in 1888'. *Australia 1888 Bulletin*, No. 7, 1981, 68-73.

Macainsh, Noel. 'The Hidden Civilization of North Queensland - Mrs Campbell Praed's *Fugitive Anne*'. *LiNQ*, X, No. 1, 1981, 1-18.

Pierce, Peter. '"Weary With Travelling Through Realms of Air ...": Romance Fiction of "Boldrewood", Haggard, Wells and Praed'. *Westerly*, XXXII, No. 2, 1987, 79-90.

Sharkey, Michael. 'Rosa Praed's Colonial Heroines'. *A.L.S.*, X, 1981, 48-56. Reprinted in *Who is She?*, edited by Shirley Walker (St Lucia: U.Q.P., 1983), 26-36.

Spender, Dale. 'Rosa Praed: Original Australian Writer'. In *A Bright and Fiery Troop: Australian Women Writers of the Nineteenth Century*, edited by Debra Adelaide (Ringwood: Penguin, 1988), 199-215.

Tiffin, Chris. 'Final Intention, Revision and Genetic Text: Editing Rosa Praed's *My Australian Girlhood*'. In *Editing in Australia*, edited by Paul Eggert, Occasional Paper 17 (Canberra: English Department, University College ADFA, 1990), 125-36.

PRIBAC, BERT

Critical Material

Maver, Igor. 'The Mediterranean in Mind: Bert Pribac, a Slovene Poet in Australia'. *Westerly*, 39.4, 1994, 123-29.

---. 'The Poetry of Slovene Immigrants in Australia: Bert Pribac'. *Earth Wings: The Outrider 91 Almanach* (Brisbane: Phoenix Publications, 1991), 210-24.

PRICHARD, KATHARINE SUSANNAH

Fiction

The Black Opal. Introduction by Dymphna Cusack. (Sydney: A.& R., 1973). A.& R. Classics. Paperback edition. First published London: Heinemann, 1921.

Coonardoo. Introduction by Douglas Stewart (Sydney: A.& R., 1964). Reprinted with introduction by Drusilla Modjeska, 1990. First published London: Cape, 1929.

Golden Miles. Introduction by Drusilla Modjeska (London: Virago, 1984). First published Sydney: Australasian Publishing Company, 1948.

Reviewed by L. Clancy, *ABR*, No. 75, 1985, 20-22; D. Bird, *CRNLE Reviews Journal*, No. 2, 1985, 52-54; B. Josephi, *CRNLE Reviews Journal*, No. 2, 1984, 59-63.

Happiness: Selected Short Stories. (Sydney: A.& R., 1967).

Reviewed by *Biblionews*, 2nd Series, II, No. 2, 1967, 38; M. Dunlevy, *Canberra Times*, 3 June, 1967, 13; H.P. Heseltine, *Westerly*, No. 2, 1968, 79-83; M. Hitchcock, *ABR*, VI, 1967, 122; K. Tennant, *S.M.H.*, 3 June, 1967, 19; D. Whitelock, *Southerly*, XXVII, 1967, 297-98.

Haxby's Circus: The Lightest, Brightest Little Show on Earth. Introduction by Justina Williams. (Sydney: A.& R., 1973). A.& R. Classics. Paperback edition. First published London: Cape, 1930.

Intimate Strangers. Introduced by Ric Throssell. (North Ryde, N.S.W.: A.& R., 1990). First published London: Cape, 1937.

Reviewed by L. Clancy, *Weekend Australian*, 20-21 October, 1990, Review 5.

The Roaring Nineties. Introduction by Drusilla Modjeska (London: Virago, 1983). First published London: Cape, 1946.

Reviewed by L. Clancy, *ABR*, No. 75, 1985, 20-22; S. Dowrick, *S.M.H.*, 20 August, 1983, 38; B. Josephi, *CRNLE Reviews Journal*, No. 2, 1984, 59-63; J. Waten, *Age Saturday Extra*, 20 August, 1983, 12.

On Strenuous Wings. (Berlin, East Germany: Seven Seas Books, 1966). A Selection edited and with an introduction by Joan Williams.
Reviewed by A. Palmer, *Overland*, No. 33, 1966, 50.

Subtle Flame. (Sydney: Australasian Book Society, 1967).
Reviewed by A.R. Chisholm, *Age*, 12 August, 1967, 23; M. Dunlevy, *Canberra Times*, 19 August, 1967, 11; C. Grimm, *ABR*, VI, 1967, 175; N. Keesing, *Bulletin*, 19 August, 1967, 64-65; M. Vintner, *S.M.H.*, 7 October, 1967, 17; D. Whitelock, *Southerly*, XXVII, 1967, 296-97.

Tribute: Selected Stories of Katharine Susannah Prichard. Edited by Ric Throssell. (St Lucia: U.Q.P., 1988).
Reviewed by J. Clark and B. Brooks, *S.M.H.*, 4 March, 1989, 88; B. Merry, *LiNQ*, 18.1, 1991, 132-36; A. Wallace, *Social Alternatives*, 8, No. 2, 1989, 70-72.

The Wild Oats of Han. (Revised edition. Melbourne: Lansdowne, 1968). First published Sydney: A.& R., 1928.
Reviewed by R. Wighton, *ABR*, VII, 1968, 225.

Winged Seeds. Introduction by Drusilla Modjeska (London: Virago, 1984). First published Sydney: Australasian Publishing Company, 1950.
Reviewed by L. Clancy, *ABR*, No. 75, 1985, 20-22; B. Josephi, *CRNLE Reviews Journal*, No. 2, 1984, 59-63.

Working Bullocks. With an introduction by John A. Hay. (Sydney: A.& R., 1972). A.& R. Classics. Paperback edition. Reprinted 1980 in A.& R.'s Sirius Quality Paperbacks. First published London: Cape, 1926.

Working Bullocks. Introduced by Ivor Indyk. (North Ryde, NSW: A.& R., 1991). First published London: Cape, 1926.
Reviewed by R. Sorensen, *ABR*, 130, 1991, 41-42.

Drama

Brumby Innes and Bid Me to Love. Edited by Katharine Brisbane, with a preface by Ric Throssell and notes on the Aboriginals in *Brumby Innes* by Carl von Brandenstein (Sydney: Currency Press; London: Eyre Methuen, 1974). The National Theatre.
Reviewed by D. Green, *Hemisphere*, XIX, No. 12, 1975, 40-41; A. W[ales], *Elizabethan Theatre Trust News*, No. 15, 1975, 24.

Non-Fiction

As Good as a Yarn with You: Letters between Miles Franklin, Katharine Susannah Prichard, Jean Devanny, Marjorie Barnard, Flora Eldershaw and Eleanor Dark. Edited by Carole Ferrier. (Cambridge: Cambridge UP, 1992). For reviews see Barnard, Marjorie.

Child of the Hurricane. (Sydney: A.& R., 1963).
Reviewed by A. Ashworth, *Southerly*, 24, No. 3, 1964, 206-7; J. Lindsay, *Meanjin*, XXIII, No. 4, 1964, 442; K. Tennant, *Realist Writer*, No. 13, 1963, 17-18.

Straight Left: Articles and Addresses in Politics, Literature and Women's Affairs over almost 60 Years from 1910 to 1968. Collected and introduced by Ric Throssell. (Sydney: Wild & Woolley, 1982).
Reviewed by J. McLaren, *Overland*, No. 92, 1983, 62-63; S. Walker, *A.L.S.*, XI, 1983, 280-81; M. Whitlam, *S.M.H.*, 20 November, 1982, 37.

'Deakin and Evatt'. *Realist*, No. 30, 1968, 14-22. Includes some autobiographical information.

'Some Perceptions and Aspirations (Australian Writers in Profile, 3)'. *Southerly*, XXVIII, 1968, 235-44.

Critical Material
'Australian Writer Dies: Books Read in 19 Languages'. *Canberra Times*, 4 October, 1969, 1.
'Contrast of Two Authors'. *Socialist*, 22 October, 1975, 6.
'K.S. Prichard, Literary Giant, Dies at 85'. *Tribune*, 8 October, 1969, 14.
'Katharine Susannah Prichard: "Excess of Love"? Some Comments'. *Overland*, No. 44, 1970, 25-28. Comments by a number of writers on Dorothy Hewett, 'Excess of Love: The Irreconcilable in Katharine Susannah Prichard', *Overland*, No. 43, 1969/70, 27-31.
'Papers of Katharine Susannah Prichard Presented to the National Library'. *Australian Library Journal*, XIX, 1970, 97. See also *Canberra Times*, 25 March, 1970, 22.
Arthur, Kateryna. 'Katharine Susannah Prichard and the Negative Text'. In *Katharine Susannah Prichard: Centenary Essays* edited by John Hay and Brenda Walker (Nedlands WA: Centre for Studies in Australian Literature, U of Western Australia, 1984), 35-48.
Bartlett, Norman. 'Perth in the Turbulent Thirties'. *Westerly*, No. 4, 1977, 61-69.
Beasley, Jack. *A Gallop of Fire: Katharine Susannah Prichard: On Guard for Humanity: A Study of Creative Personality*. (Earlwood, NSW: Wedgetail P, 1992). Reviewed by P. Pierce, *A.L.S.*, 16.3, 1994, 352-55.
---. *The Rage for Life: The Work of Katharine Susannah Prichard*. (Sydney: Current Book Distributors, 1964).
---. 'My Unilateral Debate: Katharine Susannah Prichard, Rebel Heroes and Matters Pertaining'. *A.L.S.*, XI, 1983, 246-55.
Biggins, D. 'Katharine Susannah Prichard and Dionysos: *Bid me to Love and Brumby Innes*'. *Southerly*, XLIII, 1983, 320-31.
Breen, Jennifer. 'Katharine Susannah Prichard's Fiction: Women, Sexuality and Work'. In *Katharine Susannah Prichard: Centenary Essays* edited by John Hay and Brenda Walker (Nedlands WA: Centre for Studies in Australian Literature, U of Western Australia, 1984), 29-34.
---. 'Women at Work'. *New Statesman*, 8 July, 1983, 24-25.
Brady, Veronica. 'Katharine Susannah Prichard and the Tyranny of History, *Intimate Strangers*'. *Westerly*, XXVI, 1981, No. 4, 65-71.
Buckridge, Pat. 'Katharine Susannah Prichard and the Literary Dynamics of Political Commitment'. In *Gender, Politics and Fiction: Twentieth Century Women's Novels*, edited by C. Ferrier (St Lucia: U.Q.P., 1985), 85-100.
Burchill, Sandra. 'The Early Years of Katharine Susannah Prichard: The Growth of her Political Conscience'. *Westerly*, XXXIII, No. 2, 1988, 89-100.
---. 'Katharine Susannah Prichard: "She Did What She Could"'. In *The Time to Write: Australian Women Writers 1890-1930* edited by Kay Ferres (Ringwood, Vic.: Penguin, 1993), 139-61.
Cameron, Annette. 'Katharine Susannah Prichard Remembered'. *Tribune*, No. 2361, 1985, 15.
Capp, Fiona. 'Secret Lives: ASIO and Australian Writers'. *Age Monthly Review*, 10, No. 1, 1990, 6-8.
---. *Writers Defiled: Security Surveillance of Australian Authors and Intellectuals 1920-1960*. (Ringwood, Vic.: McPhee Gribble, 1993). Includes discussion of Prichard.
Colebatch, Hal. 'New Light on Katharine Susannah Prichard'. *Antipodes*, 4.2, 1990, 125-29.
Cusack, Dymphna. 'Katharine Susannah Prichard'. *Realist*, No. 14, 1964, 14-16.
D.D. and M.M.M. 'A Note on *Brumby Innes*'. *Kosmos*, II, 1972, 139-40.
Dale, Leigh. '*Coonardoo* and Truth'. In *Tilting at Matilda: Literature, Aborigines, Women and the Church in Contemporary Australia*, edited by Dennis Haskell (South Fremantle, WA: Fremantle Arts Centre P., 1994), 129-40.

Doecke, Brenton. 'Australian Historical Fiction and the Popular Front: Katharine Susannah Prichard's Goldfields Trilogy'. *Westerly*, 39.3, 1994, 25-36.

Drake-Brockman, Henrietta. *Katharine Susannah Prichard*. (Melbourne: O.U.P., 1967). Reviewed by M. Dunlevy, *Canberra Times*, 19 August, 1967, 11; H.P. Heseltine, *Westerly*, No. 2, 1968, 79-83.

Ellis, Cath. 'A Tragic Convergence: A Reading of Katharine Susannah Prichard's *Coonardoo*'. *Westerly*, 40.2, 1995, 63-71.

Ewers, John K. 'The Katharine I Didn't Know'. *Westerly*, No. 2, 1977, 83-85.

Ferrier, Carole. 'Jean Devanny, Katharine Susannah Prichard, and the "Really Proletarian Novel"'. In *Gender, Politics and Fiction: Twentieth Century Women's Novels*, edited by C. Ferrier (St Lucia: U.Q.P., 1985), 101-17.

---. 'Women of Letters and the Uses of Memory'. In *Wallflowers and Witches: Women and Culture in Australia 1910-1945*, edited by Maryanne Dever (St Lucia: U.Q.P., 1994), 73-90. Discusses Prichard.

---. 'The "Working Class Novel" in Australia: Katharine Susannah Prichard and Jean Devanny'. In *Katharine Susannah Prichard: Centenary Essays* edited by John Hay and Brenda Walker (Nedlands WA: Centre for Studies in Australian Literature, U of Western Australia, 1984), 13-28.

Gunew, Sneja. 'Katharine Prichard's Political Writings and the Politics of Her Writing'. In *Katharine Susannah Prichard: Centenary Essays* edited by John Hay and Brenda Walker (Nedlands WA: Centre for Studies in Australian Literature, U of Western Australia, 1984), 49-60.

Hadow, Lyndall. 'Flawed Portraits of Aboriginal Women'. *Tribune*, 4 March, 1975, 7.

Hardy, Frank. 'Page from a Diary'. *Australian Left Review*, No. 6, 1969, 34-35. Describes a visit to Katharine Susannah Prichard in 1964. Reprinted in *Australian Author*, II, No. 3, 1970, 40-42.

Hay, J.A. 'Betrayed Romantics and Compromised Stoics: K.S. Prichard's Women'. In *Who is She?*, by Shirley Walker (St Lucia: U.Q.P., 1983), 98-117.

---. 'Katharine Susannah Prichard: The Perspectives of Bibliography and Criticism'. In *Katharine Susannah Prichard: Centenary Essays* edited by John Hay and Brenda Walker (Nedlands WA: Centre for Studies in Australian Literature, U of Western Australia, 1984), 61-70.

---. 'Katharine Susannah Prichard, the Writer'. In *Westralian Portraits*, edited by Lyall Hunt (Nedlands: University of W.A. Press, 1979), 199-206.

Headlam, K.B. (Thea). 'My Aunt - Katharine Susannah Prichard'. *LiNQ*, XI, No. 2, 1983-1984, 45-53. Biography.

Heseltine, H.P. 'C. Hartley Grattan in Australia: Some Correspondence, 1937-38'. *Meanjin*, XXIX, 1970, 356-64.

---. '"Wind-Waif upon the Shore": *Coonardoo*'. In his *Acquainted with the Night*. (Townsville: Townsville Foundation for Australian Literary Studies, 1979), 19-38.

Hewett, Dorothy. 'Excess of Love: The Irreconcilable in Katharine Susannah Prichard'. *Overland*, No. 43, 1969/70, 27-31.

---. 'Girl in a White Muslin Dress'. *Westerly*, December, 1963, 63-5. Review of *Child of the Hurricane*.

---. 'Happy Birthday, Brave Red Witch'. *National Times*, 25 November-1 December, 1983, 29.

Hosking, Sue. 'Two Corroborees: Constructions of Myth by Katharine Susannah Prichard and Mudrooroo'. In *Myths, Heroes and Anti-heroes: Essays on the Literature and Culture of the Asia-Pacific Region*, edited by Bruce Bennett and Dennis Haskell (Nedlands, WA: Centre for Studies in Australian Literature, U of Western Australia, 1992), 11-19.

Ikin, Van. 'The Political Novels of Katherine Susannah Prichard'. *Southerly*, XLIII, 1983, 80-102 'I: The Metaphysical Perspective: *The Black Opal* and *Working*

Bullocks'; 203-26 'II: The Nature of Man: *Coonardoo* and *Intimate Strangers*'; 296-312 'III: The Surrender to Ideology - The Goldfields Trilogy and *Subtle Flame*'.

Iseman, Kay. 'Katharine Susannah Prichard: Of an End a New Beginning'. *Arena*, No. 54, 1979, 70-96. Reprinted in *Nellie Melba, Ginger Meggs and Friends: Essays in Australian Cultural History*, edited by Susan Dermody, John Docker and Drusilla Modjeska (Malmsbury, Vic.: Kibble Books, 1982), 124-61.

Jankovic, Vida. 'Echoes of Emerson in the Works of Katharine Susannah Prichard'. In *Australian Papers: Yugoslavia, Europe and Australia*, edited by Mirko Jurak (Ljubljana: Edvard Cardelj University, 1983), 167-71.

Lever, Susan. 'Aboriginal Subjectivities and Western Conventions: A Reading of *Coonardoo*'. *Australian & New Zealand Studies in Canada*, 19, 1993, 23-29.

Lindsay, Jack. 'The Novels of Katharine Susannah Prichard'. In his *Decay and Renewal*. (Sydney: Wild & Woolley, 1976), 304-34. Originally published in *Meanjin*, XX, 1961, 366-387.

Makeham, Paul. 'Framing the Landscape: Prichard's *Pioneers* and Esson's *The Drovers*'. *Australasian Drama Studies*, 23, 1993, 121-34.

Malos, Ellen. 'Jack Lindsay's Essay on Katharine Susannah Prichard's Novels'. *Meanjin*, XXII, No. 4, 1963, 413-16. Jack Lindsay in reply, 416-17.

---. 'Some Major Themes in the Novels of Katharine Susannah Prichard'. *A.L.S.*, I, No. 1, 1963, 32-41.

Martin, David. 'Katharine Susannah Prichard the Writer'. *Tribune*, 15 October, 1969, 6.

Morse, Ruth. 'Impossible Dreams! Miscegenation and Building Nations'. *Southerly*, XLVIII, No. 1, 1988, 80-96.

Nile, Richard. *The Making of a Really Modern Witch: Katharine Susannah Prichard 1919-1969*. Working Papers in Australian Studies 56 (London: Sir Robert Menzies Centre for Australian Studies, Institute of Commonwealth Studies, U of London, 1990).

O'Brien, Patrick. 'Zhdanov in Australia'. *Quadrant*, XVIII, No. 5, 1974, 37-55.

O'Grady, Suellen. 'In Praise of Katharine Sussanah [sic] Prichard'. *Weekend Australian Magazine*, 11-12 July, 1981, 13.

Roff, Sue. 'Mating and Courtship: Misogyny in West Australia'. *Newsletter of the A.A.A.L.S.*, I, No. 2, 1985, 6.

Roland, Betty. 'Requiem for K.S.P.'. *Overland*, No. 44, 1970, 29-31.

Schaffer, Kay. 'Critical Dilemmas: Looking for Katharine Susannah Prichard'. *Hecate*, X, No. 2, 1984, 45-52.

Sellick, Robert. 'Prichard, *Brumby Innes* and the Frontier'. In *(Un)Common Ground: Essays in Literatures in English*, edited by Andrew Taylor and Russell McDougall. Essays and Monograph Series 4 (Adelaide: CRNLE/Flinders University of S.A., 1990), 75-83.

Sheridan, Sue. '*Coonardoo*: A 1988 Reading of a 1928 Novel'. *Blast*, Nos. 6-7, 1988, 5-6.

---. 'Mary Gilmore's and Katharine Prichard's Representations of Aborigines'. In her *Along the Faultlines: Sex, Race and Nation in Australian Women's Writing 1880s-1930s*. (St Leonards, NSW: Allen & Unwin, 1995), 135-52.

---. 'Response to Ric Throssell'. *Blast*, No. 8, 1988/89, 45.

Sutherland, Gail. 'Katharine Susannah Prichard - the Pen as a political Weapon'. *Tribune*, 30 November, 1984, 8-9.

Thomas, Sue. 'Interracial Encounters in Katharine Susannah Prichard's *Coonardoo*'. *WLWE*, XXVII, No. 2, 1987, 234-244.

Throssell, Ric '*Coonardoo*: A Counter Blast from Ric Throssell'. *Blast*, No. 8, 1988/89, 44.

---. 'Delos of a Sun God's Race or Mammon's Desmesne: Katharine Susannah Prichard's Australia'. *Kunapipi*, VI, No. 2, 1984, 98-104.

---. Katharine's Still Subtle Flame'. *Age*, 2 December, 1983, 17.

---. 'Katharine Susannah Prichard: A Reluctant Daughter of Mark Twain'. *Antipodes*, 3.2, 1989, 89-93.

---. 'Katharine Susannah Prichard: A Standard of Value'. In *Katharine Susannah Prichard: Centenary Essays* edited by John Hay and Brenda Walker (Nedlands WA: Centre for Studies in Australian Literature, U of Western Australia, 1984), 7-12.

---. *Wild Weeds and Wind Flowers: The Life and Letters of Katharine Susannah Prichard*. (Sydney: A.& R., 1975). Reviewed by A. Beattie, *Union Recorder*, LVIII, No. 7, 1978, 16-17; B. Bennett, *Meanjin*, XXXV, 1976, 324-29; V. Brady, *Studies in Western Australian History*, No. 1, 1977, 69-71; R.F. Brissenden, *Australian*, 24 January, 1976, 29; J.A. Hay, *Westerly* No. 2, 1977, 80-82; A.A. Phillips, *Overland*, No. 65, 1976, 72-74; F.B. Vickers, *Tribune*, 5 November, 1975, 10; E. Webby, *A.L.S.*, VII, 1976, 435-36; M. Williams, *S.M.H.*, 18 October, 1975, 20.

---. 'Writing about Katharine Susannah Prichard'. *Segment* (Darling Downs Institute of Advanced Education), III, 1974, 5-8.

Waten, Judah. 'Books and the Bottle-O's Son'. *S.M.H.*, 12 April, 1969, 19. Waten's early reading.

Wells, Julie. '"Red Witches": Perceptions of Communist Women Writers'. In *Wallflowers and Witches: Women and Culture in Australia 1910-1945*, edited by Maryanne Dever (St Lucia: U.Q.P., 1994), 147-62. Discusses Prichard.

Williams, Joan. 'Katharine Susannah Prichard the Communist'. *Tribune*, 15 October, 1969, 7.

Williams, Justina. *The First Furrow*. (Willagee, W.A.: Lone Hand Press, 1976), 65-70.

Williams, Margaret. 'Natural Sexuality: Katherine Prichard's *Brumby Innes*'. *Meanjin*, XXXII, 1973, 91-93.

RICHARDSON, HENRY HANDEL

Fiction

The Adventures of Cuffy Mahony. (Sydney: A.& R., 1979). Sirius Books. Collects previously published short fiction.
Reviewed by J. Bedford, *National Times*, 14 April, 1979, 33; K. Button, *Meridian* (La Trobe University), I, No. 2, 1982, 49-53; E. Perkins, *CRNLE Reviews Journal*, No. 2, 1979, 30-34.

The End of a Childhood: The Short Stories of Henry Handel Richardson. Edited and introduced by Carol Franklin. (Sydney: A.& R., 1992).
Reviewed by M. Dyson, *CRNLE Reviews Journal*, 2, 1993, 58-61.

The Fortunes of Richard Mahony. With an introduction by Leonie Kramer. (Harmondsworth, Middlesex, Ringwood, Vic.: Penguin, 1971; reprt. 1982). 3 volumes: *Australia Felix* first published London: Heinemann, 1917; *The Way Home*, first published 1925; *Ultima Thule*, first published 1929.
Reviewed by K. McLeod, *T.L.S.*, 4 June, 1982, 608; K.R. Srinivasa Iyengar, *Literary Half-yearly*, XXII, No. 2, 1981, 143-47, reprinted from *Federated India*, 4 February, 1931; K. Stewart, *Overland*, No. 53, 1972, 54-56.

The Fortunes of Richard Mahony. With an introduction by G.A. Wilkes. (Penrith, N.S.W.: Discovery Press, 1968). First published in one volume London: Heinemann, 1930.

The Fortunes of Richard Mahony. Afterword by Dorothy Green. (Harmondsworth: Penguin, 1982). 3 volumes in one.

The Getting of Wisdom. With an introduction by Leonie Kramer. (Penrith, N.S.W.: Discovery Press, 1968). Reprinted with an introduction by Germaine Greer. (London: Virago, 1981). First published London: Heinemann, 1910.
Reviewed by F. Adcock, *T.L.S.*, 15 May, 1981, 537, see also letter from T. Beal, 637; J. Cooke, *New Statesman*, 17 April, 1981, 20; C. Moorehead, *Spectator*, 20 June, 1981, 24.

Maurice Guest. (Melbourne: Sun Books, 1965). With a Preface by A.N. Jeffares. Reprinted with an introduction by Karen McLeod (London: Virago, 1981). First published London: Heinemann, 1908.
Reviewed by F. Adcock, *T.L.S.*, 15 May, 1981, 537; J. Barbour, *Nation*, 5 February, 1966, 21-2; A.R. Chisholm, *Age*, 12 February, 1966, 24; J. Cooke, *New Statesman*, 17 April, 1981, 21; M. Eldridge, *Canberra Times*, 27 June, 1981, 15.

Non-Fiction

Myself When Young. (Melbourne: Heinemann, 1964). With the following: a foreword by Edna Purdie; Roncoroni, O.M. '1895-1903'; Robertson, J.G. 'The Art of Henry Handel Richardson'; 'A List of the Writings of Henry Handel Richardson'.
Reviewed by C. Bolton, *ABR*, III, 1964, 184.

Southerly, XXIII, No. 1, 1963. This issue is devoted to a collection of the author's writings, some previously unpublished, which are relevant to the novels.

Critical Material

Borchardt, D.H. *Catalogue of a Collection of Books Relating to Richard Wagner and His Circle Used by Henry Handel Richardson as Sources for The Young Cosima (1939) and Housed in the University of Tasmania Library*, with a note on the annotations by Maureen Mann (Melbourne, 1973). Monash University English Department Bibliographical Checklists, No. 2.

Howells, Gay. *Henry Handel Richardson, 1870-1946: A Bibliography to Honour the Centenary of Her Birth*. (Canberra: National Library of Australia, 1970).

Wittrock, Verna D. 'Henry Handel Richardson: An Annotated Bibliography of Writings About Her'. In *English Literature in Transition: 1880-1920*. (Indiana: Purdue University, 1964), 146-186.

Henry Handel Richardson 1870-1946: Papers Presented at a Centenary Seminar. (Canberra: National Library of Australia, 1972). Reviewed by J. Beston, *S.M.H.*, 9 September, 1972, 22; P. Cowan, *Westerly*, No. 4, 1972, 70-71; B. Elliott, *Australian University*, X, 1972, 308-10.

'H.H.R. is Gone, But Olga Keeps Her Memory Green'. *S.M.H.*, Look! Section, 13 September, 1973, 3.

'Olga Roncoroni'. *Notes & Furphies*, No. 9, 1982, 9. Obituary.

Arkin, Marian. 'Henry Handel Richardson: A More Fortunate Reading Strategy'. In *International Literature in English: Essays on the Major Writers*, edited by Robert L. Ross (New York: Garland, 1991), 315-29.

---. 'A Reading Strategy for Henry Handel Richardson's Fiction'. *WLWE*, 30.2, 1990, 120-30.

Bader, Rudolf. 'Henry Handel Richardson (Die Literatur Australiens IV)'. *Der Kleine Bund* (Supplement to *Der Bund*, Berne), 2 October, 1982, 2-3.

---. 'Lawrence of Arabia and H.H. Richardson'. *A.L.S.*, XI, 1983, 99-101.

Barfoot, C.C. 'Current Literature 1985 II. Criticism, Literary Theory and Literary History, Biography'. *English Studies*, LXVII, No. 6, 1987, 539.

Barnes, John. 'Henry Handel Richardson'. *Biblionews and Australian Notes & Queries*, 2nd ser., III, No. 3, 1970, 23-25. Includes text of review of *Australia Felix* by Arthur H. Adams.

Bennett, Jack W. 'The Frontier Legacy: Willa Cather and Henry Handel Richardson'. *Antipodes*, I, No. 1, 1987, 35-39.

---. 'Sense of the Past in Willa Cather and Henry Handel Richardson'. In *The Writer's Sense of the Past: Essays on Southeast Asian and Australasian Literature*, edited by Kirpal Singh (Singapore: Singapore University Press, 1987), 77-82.

Beresford, Bruce. 'Getting *The Getting of Wisdom*'. *Quadrant*, XXI, No. 10, 1977, 25-27.

Bird, Delys. 'Towards an Aesthetics of Australian Women's Fiction: *My Brilliant Career* and *The Getting of Wisdom*'. *A.L.S.*, XI, 1983, 171-81.

Bock, Hanne K. 'Henry Handel Richardson: Letters to Brandes'. *Southerly*, XLIII, 1983, 438-49.

---. 'Her Own Room: The Gendering of Henry Handel Richardson'. In *The Time to Write: Australian Women Writers 1890-1930* edited by Kay Ferres (Ringwood, Vic.: Penguin, 1993), 185-99.

---. 'The Reviewer and Miss Robertson'. *A.L.S.*, XI, 1984, 404-08.

Brady, Veronica. '"A Thick Crumbly Slice of Life". *The Fortunes of Richard Mahony* as a Cultural Monument'. *Westerly*, No. 3, 1977, 47-56.

Buckley, Vincent. *Henry Handel Richardson*. (Melbourne: Lansdowne Press, 1962). Australian Writers and Their Work. Reviewed by V.D. Wittrock, *English Literature in Transition*: 1880-1920, VII, No. 3, 1965, 190-1.

---. *Henry Handel Richardson* 2nd ed. (Melbourne: O.U.P., 1970). Australian Writers and Their Work.

Butcher, Margaret K. 'From *Maurice Guest* to *Martha Quest*: The Female *Bildungsroman* in Commonwealth Literature'. *WLWE*, XXI, 1982, 254-62.

Capon, Margaret. 'Olga Maria Roncoroni - A Last Link with Henry Handel Richardson'. *LiNQ*, X, No. 3, 1982/83, 5-23.

Clark, Axel. *Henry Handel Richardson: Fiction in the Making*. (Brookvale, N.S.W.: Simon & Schuster/New Endeavour Press, 1990). Reviewed by A. Blainey, *Scripsi*, 7.1, 1991, 95-99; E. Campion, *Bulletin*, 20 March, 1990, 134-35; C. Franklin, *Southerly*, 51.2, 1991, 331-38; J. Hanrahan, *Weekend Australian*, 7-8 April, 1990, Weekend 7; L. Kramer, *ABR*, No. 121, 1990, 18-19; K. McLeod, *Meridian*, 10.1, 1991, 79-80; C. Munro, *A.L.S.*, 15.1, 1991, 89-93; B. Niall, *Overland*, No. 120, 1990, 86-87; H. Rowley, *Age*, 28 April, 1990, Saturday Extra 10; L. Sussex, *CRNLE Reviews Journal*, No. 2, 1989, 18-20; C. Williams, *S.M.H.*, 24 March, 1990, 77.

---. '"A Great Liar": Henry Handel Richardson's First Three Years at P.L.C. Melbourne'. *Scripsi*, 5, No. 4, 1989, 199-215.

Clark, Dymphna. 'The Aurora Borealis: Henry Handel Richardson as a Translator'. *Quadrant*, XVII, No. 1, 1973, 21-30.

Clutton-Brock, M.A. 'The Melancholy Optimist: An Account of Walter Lindesay Richardson and His Family'. *Meanjin*, XXIX, 1970, 192-208.

---. 'Mrs. Lins: Sister of Henry Handel Richardson'. *Southerly*, XXVII, 1967, 46-59.

Corones, Eva Jarring. *The Portrayal of Women in the Fiction of Henry Handel Richardson*. (Lund: Gleerup, 1983). Reviewed by D. Green, *CRNLE Reviews Journal*, No. 2, 1984, 36-37; A. McDonald, *WLWE*, XXV, No. 1, 1986, 76-77; E. Webby, *A.L.S.*, XII, No. 4, 1986, 534-38.

Douglas, Dennis. *Maurice Guest: Henry Handel Richardson*. (Melbourne: Edward Arnold (Australia), 1978). Studies in Australian Literature. Reviewed by F.D. Glass, *Span*, No. 7, 1978, 62-64; J. McLaren, *ABR*, No. 9, 1979, 22-23; A. Mitchell, *A.L.S.*, IX, 1979, 250-51; J. Waten, *Age*, 14 October, 1978, 26.

Dutton, Geoffrey. 'Gentlemen vs. Lairs'. *Quadrant*, IX, No. 1, 1965, 14-20.

Dyson, Mandy. '"those marvellous perhapses": Form and the Feminine in *The Getting of Wisdom*'. *LiNQ*, 20.2, 1993, 83-88.

Elliott, William D. *Henry Handel Richardson (Ethel Florence Lindesay Richardson)*. (Boston, Mass.: Twayne, 1975). Twayne's World Author Series, TWAS 366. Reprinted Sydney: A.& R., 1977. Reviewed by J. Colmer, *A.L.S.*, VII, 1976, 439-40; D. Green, *Nation Review*, 7-13 April, 1977, 600; J. Waten, *Age*, 16 July, 1977, 23.

---. 'The Fortunes of Richard Mahony: A Critical Appraisal'. *Dissertation Abstracts*, XXVIII (1967): 2243 A (Mich.).

---. 'French Influences in *The Fortunes of Richard Mahony*'. *Discourse*, IX, 1968, 108-15.

--- 'H.H. Richardson: The Education of an Australian Realist'. *Studies in the Novel*, IV, 1972, 141-53.

---. 'Richardson's Realism and *The Getting of Wisdom*'. *Discourse*, XII, 1969, 112-16.

---. 'Scandinavian Influences in the Novels of H.H. Richardson'. *Discourse*, XII, 1969, 249-54.

Foster, I.M. '"Richard Mahony's Tragedy"'. *A.L.S.*, IV, 1970, 279-80. Includes text of a letter by H.H.R. on the theme of *The Fortunes of Richard Mahony*.

Foster, R.T. 'HHR's Epic Cries out for a Film'. *S.M.H.*, 26 September, 1981, 48.

Franklin, Carol. '"A Depressed Amor": Richardson's "The Bathe: a Grotesque"'. *A.L.S.*, 15.3, 1992, 165-78.

---. 'The Female *Kuenstlerroman*: Richardson *versus* Bjornson'. *Southerly*, XLIII, 1983, 422-36.

---. 'H.H. Richardson's "Two Hanged Women": Our Own True Selves and

Compulsory Homosexuality'. *Kunapipi*, 14.1, 1992, 41-52.
---. 'Mansfield and Richardson: A Short Story Dialectic'. *A.L.S.*, XI, 1983, 227-33.
---. 'The Not-so-objective-correlative. "Germany" in the Work of Four Antipodean Women Writers'. *Kunapipi*, 12, No. 1, 1990, 56-69.
---. 'The Resisting Writer: H.H. Richardson's Parody of Gogol'. *AUMLA*, No. 68, 1987, 233-250.
Green, Dorothy. *Henry Handel Richardson and Her Fiction*. (Sydney: Allen and Unwin, 1986). First published Canberra: Australian National University Press, 1973 with title *Ulysses Bound*. Reviewed by H. Bock, *Overland*, No. 107, 1987, 74-76; A. Diamond, *ABR*, No. 88, 1987, 17-19; A. Mitchell, *Weekend Australian. Weekend Magazine*, 10-11 January, 1987, 11.
---. *Ulysses Bound: Henry Handel Richardson and Her Fiction*. (Canberra: Australian National University Press, 1973). Reviewed by M. Eldridge, *Canberra Times*, 19 October, 1973, 11; F.D. Glass, *Hemisphere*, XVIII, No. 1, 1974, 40-41; B. Hickey, *Journal of Commonwealth Literature*, No. 3, 1976, 81-84; L.V. Kepert, *Sun-Herald*, 16 September, 1973, 76; L. Kramer, *ABR*, No. XI, 1973, 125; *T.L.S.*, 23 November, 1973, 1454 (see also M. Bishop, *T.L.S.*, 21 December, 1973, 1567); E. Perkins, *AUMLA*, XLVI, 1976, 307-09; A.A. Phillips, *Meanjin*, XXXIII, 1974, 80-85; J. Roe, *Historical Studies*, XVI, 1974, 308-10 and *Refractory Girl*, No. 6, 1974, 5-8; K. Stewart, *A.L.S.*, VI, 1974, 320-24; K. Tennant, *S.M.H.*, 6 October, 1973, 24; E. Webby, *Southerly*, XXXIV, 1974, 95-58.
---. 'The Flesh and the Spirit'. *Prometheus*, Australian National University [2 pp., unnumbered].
---. 'The Fortunes of Olga Roncoroni'. *Age*, 23 June, 1982, 17. Obituary.
---. 'Henry Handel Richardson minus Ned Kelly'. *Meanjin*, XXXI, 1972, 162-66. Discusses Alexander Brooke Smith, the original of Purdy Smith.
---. '"*I* Will Say Music, Too...": A Note on Henry Handel Richardson's Songs'. *Meanjin*, XXXII, 1973, 466-67.
---. 'The Pilgrim Soul: The Philosophical Structure of *The Fortunes of Richard Mahony*'. *Meanjin*, XXVIII, 1969, 328-37.
---. 'A Poet in Prose Who Saw "With Energy"'. *Hemisphere*, XIII, No. 11, 1969, 22-27.
---. 'Pot and Kettle'. *Overland*, No. 74, 1979, 39-41, 43-44. Reply to Elizabeth Summons, No. 72. See also Summons, Elizabeth. 'A Reply'. *Overland*, No. 74, 1979, 45-46.
---. 'Power-Games in the Novels of Henry Handel Richardson'. In *Who is She?*, edited by Shirlet Walker (St Lucia: U.Q.P., 1983), 84-97.
---. 'The Tradition of Social Responsibility in the Australian Novel: Richardson and Furphy'. *Literary Criterion* (Mysore), XV, Nos. 3-4, 1980, 23-34.
---. 'Walter Lindesay Richardson: The Man, the Portrait, and the Artist'. *Meanjin*, XXIX, 1970, 5-20.
---. *The Young Cosima*'. *A.L.S.*, IV, 1970, 215-26.
Greer, Germaine. 'The Getting of Wisdom'. *Scripsi* (Melbourne), I, Nos. 3-4, 1982, 4-12.
Heseltine, H.P. 'Criticism and the Individual Talent'. *Meanjin*, XXXI, 1972, 10-24.
---. '"Fear No More": *The Fortunes of Richard Mahony*'. In his *Acquainted with the Night*. (Townsville: Townsville Foundation for Australian Literary Studies, 1979), 1-18.
Jamison, Greeba. 'House of Fleeting Fame'. *Walkabout*, XXXVI, No. 1, 1970, 50-52.
Jeffares, A. Norman. '*The Fortunes of Richard Mahony* Reconsidered'. *Sewanee Review*, LXXXVII, 1979, 158-64.
---. 'Richard Mahony, Exile'. *Journal of Commonwealth Literature*, No. 6, 1969, 106-19.

Kiernan, Brian. 'The Fortunes of Richard Mahony'. *Southerly*, XXIX, 1969, 199-209.
---. 'Literature Grew Up with a Child'. *Age*, 3 January, 1970, 13.
---. 'Romantic Conventions and *Maurice Guest*'. *Southerly*, XXVIII, 1968, 286-94.
Kramer, Leonie. *Henry Handel Richardson*. (Melbourne: O.U.P., 1966). Great Australians Series. Reviewed by N. Keesing, *Bulletin*, 1 July, 1967, 66; J. Kimber, *ABR*, VI, 1967, 192.
---. *Myself When Laura: Fact and Fiction in Henry Handel Richardson's School Career*. (Melbourne: Heinemann for the Australian Association for the Teaching of English, 1966). *English In Australia* Monograph No. 1.
---. 'Henry Handel Richardson'. In *The Literature of Australia*, edited Geoffrey Dutton (Adelaide: Penguin Books, 1964), 318-31.
Kranendonk, A.G. van. 'A Neglected Masterpiece'. *Southerly*, XXXVII, 1977, 229-40. Translated from the Dutch with an introduction by Noel Macainsh.
Liljegren, S.B. *Ballarat and the Great Gold Rush According to the Richard Mahony Trilogy; A Study in the Literary Use of Sources*. (Uppsala: A. B. Lundequistska Bokhandeln; Copenhagen: Ejnar Munksgaard, 1964). Australian Essays and Studies, No. 4.
Loder, Elizabeth. 'The Fortunes of Richard Mahony: Dream and Nightmare'. *Southerly*, XXV, No. 4, 1965, 251-63.
---. '*Maurice Guest*: An Innocent Abroad'. *Balcony*, No. 4, 1966, 34-7.
---. '*Maurice Guest*: Some Nineteenth-Century Progenitors'. *Southerly*, XXVI, 1966, 94-105.
Macainsh, Noel. 'Not a True Love Story: Henry Handel Richardson's *Maurice Guest*'. *Westerly*, XXX, No.1, 1985, 77-86. Reprinted in his *The Pathos of Distance* (Bern: Peter Lang, 1992), 142-156.
---. 'Point-of-View and Consequent Naturalism in the Novels of Henry Handel Richardson'. *Westerly*, XXIX, No. 2, 1984, 61-70. Reprinted in his *The Pathos of Distance* (Bern: Peter Lang, 1992), 127-141.
---. 'Richard Mahony as Papa Hamlet: Consequent Nationalism in *The Fortunes*'. *AUMLA*, No. 62, 1984, 133-150. Reprinted in his *The Pathos of Distance* (Bern: Peter Lang, 1992), 109-126.
---. 'The Shock of Recognition - Henry Handel Richardson and J.P. Jacobsen's *Niels Lyhne*'. *Southerly*, XXXVI, 1976, 99-111.
Mackenzie, Manfred. 'The Way Home'. *Span*, No. 28, 1989, 63-84. A comparative study of Henry James' *Roderick Hudson* and Richardson's *Maurice Guest*.
Maidment, W.M. 'Australian Literary Criticism'. *Southerly*, XXIV, 1964, 20-41.
Mann, Maureen C. 'The Genesis of *The Young Cosima*: Henry Handel Richardson's most Neglected Novel'. *WLWE*, XVII, No. 1, 1978, 96-105.
---. 'Some Misinterpretations of Henry Handel Richardson's Marginalia in Eckart's Biography of Cosima Wagner'. *Bibliographical Society of Australia and New Zealand Bulletin*, V, 1981, 69-73.
McFarlane, Brian. '*The Getting of Wisdom*: Not "Merry" At All'. *A.L.S.*, VIII, 1977, 51-63.
---. 'Power in Dark Places: *The Fortunes of Richard Mahony*'. *Southerly*, XXXVII, 1977, 211-28.
McLeod, Karen. *Henry Handel Richardson: A Critical Study*. (Melbourne: Cambridge University Press, 1985). Reviewed by M. Butcher, *British Book News*, January, 1986, 54; L. Clancy, *Island Magazine*, No. 30, 1987, 70-72; A. Clark, *National Times*, 31 January-6 February, 1986, 29; J. Colmer, *Weekend Australian Magazine*, 18-19 January, 1986, 13; L.J. Kramer, *Yearbook of English Studies*, XVIII, 1988, 352; M. Tomlinson, *Age Saturday Extra*, 22 March, 1986, 14; E. Webby, *A.L.S.*, XII, No. 4, 1986, 534-38.
Mead, Philip. 'Death and Home-work: The Origins of Narrative in *The Fortunes of Richard Mahony*'. *A.L.S.*, 17.2, 1995, 115-23.

Morgan, Patricia. 'The Last Friend Remembers "HHR"'. *Advertiser*, 2 February, 1974, 21.

---. 'Olga: My Life with H.H.R.'. *Herald* (Melbourne), 6 September, 1973, 31.

Narasimhaiah, C.D. 'Introduction'. *Literary Criterion*, XV, Nos. 3-4, 1980, xxi-xxii.

New, William H. 'Convention and Freedom: A Study of *Maurice Guest*'. *English Studies* (Anglo-Amer. Supp.), 1969, lxii-lxviii.

Odeen, Elizabeth. '*Maurice Guest*': *A Study*. (Austin: University of Texas Press, 1964).

Palmer, Anthony J. 'A Link with Late Nineteenth-Century Decadence in *Maurice Guest*'. *A.L.S.*, V., 1972, 366-73.

Phillips, A.A. 'A Harmony of Minds'. In his *Responses: Selected Writings*. (Kew, Vic.: Australian International Press & Publications, 1979), 194-200. Review of Dorothy Green. *Ulysses Bound*. First published in *Meanjin*, XXXIII, 1974, 80-85.

Pratt, Catherine. 'Fictions of Development: Henry Handel Richardson's *The Getting of Wisdom*'. *Antipodes*, 9.1, 1995, 3-9.

---. "What Had She to Do with Angels?" Gender and Narrative in *The Fortunes of Richard Mahony*'. *A.L.S.*, 16.2, 1993, 152-60.

Riemer, A.P. '"Influenced by D'Annunzio": *Maurice Guest* and the Romantic Agony'. In *Reconnoitres: Essays in Australian Literature in Honour of G.A. Wilkes*, edited by Margaret Harris and Elizabeth Webby (South Melbourne: O.U.P. in association with Sydney U.P., 1992), 61-78.

---. 'The Young Cosima - A Reconsideration'. *Southerly*, XL, 1980, 190-203.

Roff, Sue. 'Rites of Passage: Six Australian Authors in Search of the Same Character. *Australian Society*, III, No. 9, 1984, 33-34.

Spies, Marion. 'Swedenborg and Mahony: A Note'. *Meridian*, 9, No. 1, 1990, 83-89.

Stewart, Ken. 'Dr. Richardson and Dr. Mahony'. *Southerly*, XXXIII, 1973, 74-79.

---. '*The Fortunes of Richard Mahony*: Symphony and Naturalism'. In *The Australian Experience: Critical Essays on Australian Novels*, edited by W.S. Ramson (Canberra: Australian National University Press, 1974), 97-120.

---. 'History and Fiction in *The Fortunes of Richard Mahony*'. *Teaching History*, IV, No. 3, 1970, 24-39.

---. '*Lake View*, Chiltern Victoria'. *Notes & Furphies*, No. 3, 1979, 11-12.

---. '*Maurice Guest* and the Siren Voices'. *A.L.S.*, V, 1972, 352-65.

---. 'The Prototype of Richard Mahony'. *A.L.S.*, IV, 1970, 227-40.

---. 'Their Road to Life: A Note on Richard Mahony and Walter Richardson'. *Meanjin*, XXIX, 1970, 505-08.

Stoller, Alan and Emmerson, R.H. 'The Fortunes of Walter Lindesay Richardson'. *Meanjin*, XXIX, 1970, 21-33.

Strahan, Lynn. '"Lakeview", Victoria'. in *Historic Houses of Australia*. (North Melbourne: Cassell Australia for Australian Council of National Trusts, 1974), 186-95.

Summers, Anne. 'The Self Denied: Australian Women Writers - Their Image of Women'. *Refractory Girl*, No. 2, 1973, 4-11.

Summons, Elizabeth. 'Ethel and Florence and Arthur and Mattie'. *Overland*, No. 72, 1978, 24-30.

Tennison, Patrick. 'Great Australians'. *Walkabout*, XXXIV, No. 12, 1968, 68.

Thomson, A.K. 'Henry Handel Richardson's *The Fortunes of Richard Mahony*'. *Meanjin*, XXVI, 1967, 423-434.

Triebel, Louis. *Henry Handel Richardson, Australian Novelist and Lover of Wisdom: the Inter-Relation of her Life and Work, Together with an Assessment of the Influence of her Husband, Professor J.G. Robertson, Fellow of the British Academy, and Some Appraisals of Important Relevant Criticisms on H.H.R. from 1908 to 1975: An Essay.* (Hobart: Cat & Fiddle Press, 1976).

Wattie, Nelson. 'Henry Handel Richardson and the German *Bildungsroman*'.

Commonwealth (Paris), VI, No. 2, 1984, 22-28.
Wilkes, G.A. 'Henry Handel Richardson: Some Associations'. *Southerly*, XLVII, No. 2, 1987, 207-213.
Wood, Ray Sinclair. 'Henry Handel Richardson's *The Fortunes of Richard Mahony*: A Note on the Nature of its Tragedy'. *Adelaide A.L.S. Working Papers*, III, 1979, 3-16.
Zwicky, Fay. 'Maurice the Obscure: Provincial Expatriate in Search of a Voice'. *Meridian*, IV, No. 2, 1985, 99-111.

ROBERTS, PHILIP

Poetry
Crux. Drawings by Margo Lewers. (Sydney: Island Press, 1973).
Reviewed by R. Adamson, *Australian*, 25 August, 1973, 45; J. Croft, *S.M.H.*, 30 June, 1973, 26; M. Lange, *Makar*, X, No. 2, 1974, 45-47; T. Stubbin, *Australasian Small Press Review*, No. 1, 1975, 20-21.
Selected Poems. (Sydney: Island Press, 1978).
Reviewed by D. Haskell, *Compass*, III, Nos. 2-3, 1981, 29-34; J. Rodriguez, *S.M.H.*, 24 February, 1979, 17; C. Treloar, *Weekend Australian Magazine*, 29 April, 1978, 9.
Will's Dream. (St Lucia: U.Q.P., 1975).
Reviewed by R. Adamson, *Australian*, 31 January, 1976, 25; A. Gould, *Nation Review*, 2-8 April, 1976, 621; K. Hart, *Canberra Poetry*, 1976, 74; K. Heinzelman, *Poetry*, CXXXI, No. 4, 1978, 232-34; G. Page, *Canberra Times*, 24 July, 1976, 13; P. Porter, *T.L.S.*, 9 April, 1976, 431-32; T. Shapcott, *Age*, 17 July, 1976, 23; A. Taylor, *Poetry Australia*, No. 58, 1976, 73-77.

ROBINSON, ROLAND

Poetry
Altjeringa and Other Aboriginal Poems. (Sydney: A.H. & A.W. Reed, 1970).
Reviewed by B.A. Breen, *Twentieth Century*, XXVI, 1971, 175-77; R. Dunlop, *Poetry Australia*, No. 40, 1971, 56; K. England, *Advertiser*, 26 December, 1970, 12; S.E. Lee, *Southerly*, XXXI, 1971, 237-38; P. Roberts, *S.M.H.*, 31 July, 1971, 20; T.W. Shapcott, *ABR*, X, 1970/71, 44; K. Slessor, *Daily Telegraph*, Sydney, 19 December, 1970, 45.
Grendel. (Brisbane: Jacaranda Press, 1967).
Reviewed by B. Beaver, *S.M.H.*, 4 November, 1967, 21; A. Brissenden, *Adelaide Advertiser*, 14 October, 1967, 14; N. Keesing, *Poetry Magazine*, No. 6, 1967, 31-33; A.C.L., *Twentieth Century*, XXII, 1968, 270-72; S.E. Lee, *Southerly*, XXVIII, 1968, 156-57; E. Marsh, *Westerly*, No. 3, 1968, 54-55; V. Smith, *Bulletin*, 25 November, 1967, 83.
The Hooded Lamp. (Sydney: Edwards & Shaw, 1976).
Reviewed by J. Griffin, *Advertiser*, 18 December, 1976, 25; D. Stewart, *S.M.H.*, 28 August, 1976, 19; C. Treloar, *24 Hours*, I, No. 12, 1977, 47-48.
Selected Poems (1944-1982). Edited by A.J. Bennett and Michael Sharkey. (Armidale, N.S.W.: Kardoorair Press, 1983).
Reviewed by J. Barnie, *Kunapipi*, VI, No. 3, 1984, 107-122; E. Lawson, *ABR*, No. 56, 1983, 31; V. Newsom, *Compass*, V, No. 3, 1985, 8; T. Scanlon, *Northern Perspective*, VI, Nos. 1-2, 1984, 27-28.
Selected Poems. (Sydney: A.& R., 1971).
Reviewed by K. England, *Advertiser*, 12 February, 1972, 18; C. Harrison-Ford, *Sunday Australian*, 16 January, 1972, 20; F. Holzknecht, *Makar*, VIII, No. 1, 1972, 37-40; P. Joseph, *Review* (Melbourne), 27 November-3 December, 1971, 221; D.

Malouf, *Australian*, 12 February, 1972, 15; G. Page, *Canberra Times*, 24 December, 1971, 9; A. Pollard, *Journal of Commonwealth Literature*, X, No. 3, 1976, 77; P. Roberts, *S.M.H.*, 25 March, 1972, 19 (see also letter to the editor by D. Stewart, *S.M.H.*, 29 March, 1972, 6); T. Shapcott, *ABR*, X, 1971, 186.

Non-Fiction

The Drift of Things: An Autobiography, 1914 - 52. (South Melbourne: Macmillan, 1973).
Reviewed by A.T. Brissenden, *Advertiser*, 16 February, 1974, 20; M. Dunlevy, *Canberra Times*, 26 July, 1974, 8; G. Farwell, *Bulletin*, 26 January, 1974, 45; C. Harrison-Ford, *Australian*, 19 January, 1974, 46; L.V. Kepert, *Sun-Herald*, 23 December, 1973, 45; I. Mudie, *Age*, 5 January, 1974, 12; C. Sansom, *Nation Review*, 26 April-2 May, 1974, 890; K. Tennant, *S.M.H.*, 12 January, 1974, 17.

A Letter to Joan: An Autobiography 1962-73. (Melbourne: Macmillan, 1978).
Reviewed by P. Kocan, *Quadrant*, XXIII, No. 5, 1979, 71-72; M. MacDonald, *24 Hours*, IV, No. 1, 1979, 50; B. Muirden, *Advertiser*, 23 September, 1978, 25; C. Pollnitz, *ABR*, No. 7, 1978-79, 28-29; J. Waten, *Age*, 28 October, 1978, 26.

The Shift of Sands: An Autobiography 1952-62. (South Melbourne: Macmillan, 1976).

Reviewed by A. Brissenden, *Advertiser*, 8 May, 1976, 20; R.F. Brissenden, *Australian*, 17 July, 1976, 41; M. Halligan, *Canberra Times*, 15 January, 1977, 12; M. Macleod, *S.M.H.*, 3 April, 1976, 19; R. McDonald, *Nation Review*, 14-20 May, 1976, 765.

The Nearest the White Man Gets. (Sydney: Hale & Iremonger, 1989).
Reviewed by N. Cato, *Imago* 3.2, 1991, 98-100.

Critical Material

Darby, Robert. 'The Grass Tree Spears'. *Independent Australian*, IV, 1981, No. 3, 16-19.
Harrison-Ford, Carl. 'Poems Where I Make My Fires: The Poetry of Roland Robinson'. *New Poetry*, XIX, No. 5, 1971, 3-8.
Headon, David and Scanlon, Tony. 'Interview with D[arwin] C[ommunity] C[ollege]'s Writer-in-Residence, Roland Robinson'. *Northern Perspective*, VI, Nos. 1-2, 1984, 24-27.
Manifold, John. 'Black Legends Influence White Poet's Work'. *Tribune*, 22 September, 1976, 8.
Sayers, Stuart. 'Poet, Historian Win Awards'. *Age*, 18 October, 1974, 14. Related reports in *Advertiser*, 18 October, 1974, 7; *S.M.H.*, 18 October, 1974, 2; *Age*, 19 October, 1974, 20; *Age*, 23 November, 1974, 19.

RODRIGUEZ, JUDITH

Poetry

The House by Water: New and Selected Poems. (St Lucia: U.Q.P., 1988).
Reviewed by H. Cam, *S.M.H.*, 1 October, 1988, 74; L. Knowles, *Fremantle Arts Review*, III, No. 12, 1988, 15; T. Lintermans, *Age Saturday Extra*, 12 November, 1988, 24.

Mudcrab at Gambaro's. (St Lucia: U.Q.P., 1980).
Reviewed by A. Brewster, *Ash Magazine*, No. 8, 1982, 29-30; J. Grant, *Age*, 27 December, 1980, 18; M. Harrison, *S.M.H.*, 3 January, 1981, 37; V. Ikin, *Quadrant*, XXV, No. 5, 1981, 75-76; R. Nissen, *Luna*, No. 13, 1981, 30-32; E. Perkins, *LiNQ*, IX, No. 1, 1981, 173:78; M. Scott, *Island Magazine*, No. 8, 1981, 39; C. Wallace-Crabbe, *ABR*, No. 27, 1980, 14-15.

Nu-plastik Fanfare Red. (St Lucia: U.Q.P., 1973). Paperback poets 14.
Reviewed by P. Annand, *Makar*, IX, No. 1, 1973, 43-45.

Water Life. With linocuts by the author. (St Lucia: U.Q.P., 1976).
Reviewed by A. Gould, *Nation Review*, 17-23 March, 1977, 524-25; J. Strauss, *Luna*, II, No. 2, 38-40; J. Tranter, *Weekend Australian Magazine*, 6-7 August, 1977, 13.
Witch Heart. (Melbourne: Sisters Publishing, 1982).
Reviewed by K. Goldsworthy, *Age Saturday Extra*, 23 July, 1983, 12; S. Hawthorne, *Social Alternatives*, III, No. 3, 1983, 80; R. Johnson, *CRNLE Reviews Journal*, No. 1, 1984, 45-48; J. Maiden, *Meanjin*, XLII, 1983, 256-58; S. McKernan, *Canberra Times*, 7 May, 1983, 12; R. Nissen, *Luna*, No. 17, 1983, 22-24; A. Stewart, *Island Magazine*, No. 16, 1983, 45-47; J. Strauss, *ABR*, No. 49, 1983, 29.

Non-Fiction
'Archimedes' Platform, Images of Poetry, Woman Writing'. *Meanjin*, XLVII, No. 2, 1988, 313-321.

Critical Material
Bird, Delys. 'The White Witch and the Red Witch: The Poetry of Judith Rodriguez'. In *Poetry and Gender: Statements and Essays in Australian Women's Poetry and Poetics*, edited by David Brooks and Brenda Walker (St Lucia: U.Q.P., 1989), 195-203.
Forster, Deborah. 'From the Heart of the Poet'. *Age Saturday Extra*, 19 November, 1982, 16.
Kerr, David and Edmonds, Phillip. 'Judith Rodriguez and Her Poetry'. *Bulletin*, 25 December, 1984-1 January, 1985, 180-183.
O'Donohue, Barry. 'Interview: Judith Rodriguez'. *Image*, III, No. 2, 1979, 10-14.
Page, Geoff. 'Judith Rodriguez'. In his *A Reader's Guide To Contemporary Australian Poetry* (St. Lucia: U.Q.P., 1995), 245-248.
Rama, R.P. '[Interview with] Judith Rodriguez'. *Dialogues with Australian Poets*. (Calcutta: P. Lal/Writers Workshop, 1993), 71-86.
Sayers, Stuart. 'Poetry was her Craft from the Age of Eight'. *Age*, 8 December, 1973, 15.
Strauss, Jennifer. '"A Lifetime Devoted to Literature": A Tribute to Judith Rodriguez'. *Southerly*, 52.3, 1992, 168-75.

ROHAN, CRIENA

Fiction
The Delinquents. (Ringwood: Vic.: Penguin, 1986).
Reviewed by H. Daniel, *Age Saturday Extra*, 1 March, 1986, 13; J. Factor, *Meanjin*, XLV, No. 3, 1986, 423-28; K.H., *Womanspeak*, X, No. 2, 1986, 25; C. Thompson, *ABR*, No. 88, 1987, 19-20.
Down by the Dockside. (Ringwood, Vic.: Penguin, 1984).
Reviewed by L. Barwick, *CRNLE Reviews Journal*, No. 2, 1985, 80-82; V. Brady, *Australian Society*, V, No. 2, 1986, 40-42; L. Clancy, *ABR*, No. 69, 1985, 15-16; J. Factor, *Meanjin*, XLV, No. 3, 1986, 423-28; C. Gerrish, *Womanspeak*, IX, No. 4, 1985, 26-27; M. Lord, *Overland*, No. 99, 1985, 78-79; J. McLaren, *Overland*, No. 30, 1964, 54; P. Pierce, *Age Saturday Extra*, 26 January, 1985, 12; C. Shute, *Tribune*, 20 March, 1985, 10; A. Stretton, *S.M.H.*, 2 March, 1985, 40; G. Windsor, *Bulletin*, 5 March, 1985, 64-65.

Critical Material
Factor, June. 'Criena Rohan'. *Overland*, No. 30, 1964, 46. An article inspired by her death: tells of her life and achievement.
Garlick, Barbara. 'Beyond Social Realism: The Woman's Voice'. *Social Alternatives*, VII, No. 1, 1988, 68-70. Discusses D. Hewett's *Bobbin Up* and C. Rohan's *Down by the Dockside* and *The Delinquents*.

ROLAND, BETTY

Fiction

Beyond Capricorn. (London: Collins, 1976).
Reviewed by A.R. Chisholm, *Age* 28 August, 1976, 23; R. Macklin, *S.M.H.*, 17 July, 1976, 15.

Drama

The Touch of Silk. (Sydney: Currency Press, 1975 and 1988). First published Carlton: MUP, 1942.
Reviewed by O. Delroy, *Words' Worth*, 11.2, 1978 33; F. Kelly, *National Times*, 18-23 August, 1975, 25; J. Morgan, *Australian Quarterly*, 14.4, 1942, 110; L. Radic, *Age*, 29 March, 1975, 14; *Elizabethan Trust News*, 14, March 1975, 12.

Non-Fiction

Caviar for Breakfast. (Melbourne: Quartet Books, 1979; Sydney: Collins Imprint, 1989).
Reviewed by E. Campion, *Bulletin*, 18 December, 1979, 68-69; F. Capp, *Age*, 7 October, 1989, Saturday Extra 10; D. Cusack, *ABR*, 18, 1980, 7-8; G. Jamison, *Age*, 3 November, 1979, 1992, 30; P. Nelson, *Weekend Australian*, 24 September, 1989, Review 9; N. Phelan, *S.M.H.*, 17 November, 1979, 13; A. Ravenscroft, *Australian Women's Book Review*, 1.1, 1989, 28-30.

The Devious Being. (North Ryde, NSW: A.& R., 1990).
Reviewed by D. McCooey, *Southerly*, 51.1, 1991, 165-70; T.-A. White, *ABR*, 127, 1990, 7-8.

The Eye of the Beholder. (Sydney: Hale & Iremonger, 1984).
Reviewed by G. Dutton, *Bulletin*, 30 October, 1984, 94-95; G. Hutton, *Age*, 1 December, 1984, Saturday Extra 16; S. McInerney, *S.M.H.*, 17 November, 1984, 17; D.J. O'Hearn, *Weekend Australian*, 15-16 December, 1984, Weekend 14; D. Martin, *Overland*, 97, 1984, 22-24; R. Pascoe, *ABR*, 68, 1985, 40; J. Stone, *Biblionews and Australian Notes and Queries*, 10.3, 1985, 80-81; J. Teichman, *Quadrant*, 29.6, 1985, 26-29.

An Improbable Life. (North Ryde, NSW: A.& R, 1989).
Reviewed by F. Capp, *Age*, 10 June 1989, Saturday Extra 9; M. Keon, *Weekend Australian*, 20-21 May 1989, Review 10; M. McClusky, *Independent Monthly*, August 1989, 37; P. Shrubb, *Quadrant*, 34.7-8, 1990, 64-68; A. Ravenscroft, *Australian Women's Book Review*, 1.1, 1989, 28-30.

Critical Material

Barbour, Judith. 'Privileged, Authentic, Transcendent, Arcane: Limits of Naturalism in some Contemporary Plays'. *Southerly*, 37.1, 1977, 77-92.
Giuffré, Giulia. *A Writing Life: Interviews with Australian Women Writers.* (Sydney: Allen & Unwin, 1990), 1-13.
Gorman, Clem. 'Betty Roland - A Defiant Life'. In *The Larrikin Streak: Australian Writers Look at the Legend* edited by Clem Gorman (South Melbourne: Sun Books, 1990), 245-50.
Modjeska, Drusilla. 'Interview: Betty Roland Talks to Drusilla Modjeska'. *Australasian Drama Studies*, 8, 1986, 63-69.
Moore, Nicole. 'The Burdens Twain or Not Forgetting Yourself: The Writing of Betty Roland's Life'. *Hecate*, 18.1, 1992, 6-26.

ROMERIL, JOHN

Drama

The Floating World. With notes on the Yellow Peril and comment from Allan Ashbolt, Katharine Brisbane and the *Official History of Australia in the Second World War* (Sydney: Currency Press, London: Eyre Methuen, 1975).

Reviewed by L. Radic, *Age*, 1 November, 1975, 20.

I Don't Know Who to Feel Sorry For. Introduced by Graeme Blundell; preface by Margery M. Morgan. (Sydney: Currency Press, London: Eyre Methuen, 1973). Currency Playtexts, Series 2.
Reviewed by H. Hewitt, *Canberra Times*, 14 June, 1974, 11; K. Jamieson, *Makar*, X, No. 1, 1974, 46-50.

　　Non-Fiction
'Street Theatre'. *Arena*, No. 20, 1969, 14-21. See also Henrie R. Ellis, 'Street Theatre', *Arena*, No. 21, 1970, 52-53.

　　Critical Material
Butler, Chris. 'He Makes the Stage a "Soap Box"'. *Advertiser*, 29 November, 1974, 7.
Dare, Tim. 'The Performing Pram'. *Australian*, 17 July, 1971, 20.
Davidson, Jim. 'John Romeril'. *Meanjin*, XXXVII, 1978, 300-12. Interview. Reprinted in his *Sideways from the Page* (Melbourne: Fontana, 1983), 109-127.
Elias, Sophie. 'Political Drama in Australia. Why and Wherefore?' An interview with John Romeril, playwright. *Commonwealth* (Toulouse) IV, 1979-1980, 145-54.
Garner, Helen. 'The Respectable John Romeril'. *National Times*, 18-24 April, 1982, 19.
Griffiths, Gareth. 'Experiments with Form in Recent Australian Drama'. *Kunapipi*, II, No. 1, 1980, 84-87.
Griffiths, Gareth ed. *John Romeril*. (Amsterdam and Atlanta: Rodopi, 1993). Reviewed by P. Makeham, *Australasian Drama Studies*, 27, 1995, 188-91.
---. '"Unhappy the Land That Has a Need of Heroes": John Romeril's Asian Plays'. In *Myths, Heroes and Anti-heroes: Essays on the Literature and Culture of the Asia-Pacific Region*, edited by Bruce Bennett and Dennis Haskell (Nedlands, WA: Centre for Studies in Australian Literature, U of Western Australia, 1992), 142-54.
Knappett, Bruce. 'A People's Playwright'. *Bulletin*, 10 July, 1971, 43-46.
Marks, Harry. 'Painter and Playwright with Joint Targets'. *Age*, 23 October, 1971, 16.
Mercer, Leah. '"A Fairly Hybrid Talent": An Interview with John Romeril'. *Australasian Drama Studies*, No. 17, 1990, 51-57.
Ray, John J. 'Play Accused of Stirring up Hatred against the Japanese'. *S.M.H.*, 2 October, 1975, 7; see also answer from Katharine Brisbane, *S.M.H.*, 4 October, 1975, 8.
Robinson, Ian. 'With *The Floating World* a Hit, John Romeril Plans a Play about Holdens'. *National Times*, 26-31 August, 1974, 27.
Tompkins, Joanne. 'Re-Orienting Australasian Drama: Staging Theatrical Irony'. *Ariel*, 25.4, 1994, 117-33. Includes discussion of *The Floating World*.
Watson, Maggie. 'Romeril's Theatre of Ideas'. *National Times*, 5-11 July, 1981, 35.
Webby, Elizabeth. *Modern Australian Plays*. Horizon Studies in Literature. (Sydney: Sydney UP in assoc. with O.U.P., 1990). Includes discussion of *The Floating World*.
Williamson, Kristin. 'Romeril'. *National Times*, 18-24 October, 1985, 28.

ROWBOTHAM, DAVID

　　Poetry
All the Room. (Brisbane: Jacaranda Press, 1964).
Reviewed by A. Glad, *Poetry Australia*, No. 4, 1965, 29-31; R. Hodge, *Westerly*, No. 4, 1964, 59-60; F. Kellaway, *ABR*, III, 1964, 253; S.E. Lee, *Southerly*, XXV, 1965, 134-5.

Bungalow and Hurricane. (Sydney: A.& R., 1967).
Reviewed by R. Adamson, *Poetry Magazine*, No. 5, 1968, 31-32; P. Annand, *Makar*, IV, No. 3, 1968, 21-22, 24; B. Beaver, *S.M.H.*, 4 May, 1968, 19; R. Dunlop, *Poetry*

Australia, No. 20, 1968, 39-40; M. Irvin, *Bulletin*, 9 December, 1967, 81-82; A. King, *Meanjin*, XXVII, 1968, 181-82; S.E. Lee, *Southerly*, XXVIII, 1968, 153-54; B. Matthews, *Overland*, No. 38, 1968, 47; B. Medlin, *ABR*, VII, 1967, 41.

The Makers of the Ark. (Sydney: A.& R., 1970).
Reviewed by R. Hall, *Australian*, 20 March, 1971, 22; C. Harrison-Ford, *Union Recorder*, L, No. 27, 1970, 14-15; G. Page, *Canberra Times*, 9 January, 1971, 12; P. Roberts, *S.M.H.*, 17 July, 1971, 24; G. Rowlands, *Makar*, VII, No. 1, 1971, 32-33; K. Slessor, *Daily Telegraph*, Sydney, 19 December, 1970, 45; J. Tulip, *Bulletin*, 20 March, 1971, 60.

Maydays. (St Lucia: U.Q.P., 1980).
Reviewed by G. Catalano, *Age*, 27 September, 1980, 26; E. Perkins, *LiNQ*, IX, No. 1, 1981, 173-78; T. Shapcott, *ABR*, No. 23, 1980, 5-6.

The Pen of Feathers. (Sydney: A.& R., 1971).
Reviewed by P. Annand, *Makar*, VII, No. 4, 1971, 40-41; R. Dunlop, *Poetry Australia*, No. 43, 1972, 60-62; C. Harrison-Ford, *Sunday Australian*, 16 January, 1972, 20; P. Joseph, *Review* (Melbourne), 27 November-3 December, 1971, 221; D. Malouf, *Australian*, 27 November, 1971, 18; P. Roberts, *S.M.H.*, 25 March, 1972, 19 (see also letter to the editor by D. Stewart, *S.M.H.*, 29 March, 1972, 6); T. Shapcott, *ABR*, X, 1971, 186; J. Tulip, *Bulletin*, 8 January, 1972, 35.

Selected Poems. (St Lucia: U.Q.P., 1975).
Reviewed by J. McLaren, *Segment* (Toowoomba), V, 1976, 58; P. Neilsen, *Age*, 31 January, 1976, 15; T. Shapcott, *Australian*, 1 January, 1977, 18; R. Tamplin, *T.L.S.*, 9 April, 1976, 443.

Non-Fiction

'Statement of Discovery'. *Poetry Magazine*, No. 3, 1966, 5-7.
'Three Talks: David Malouf, Les Murray and David Rowbotham'. *A.L.S.*, XI, 1984, 324-27. Session at Warana Writers' Weekend.

Critical Material

Malouf, David. 'Some Volumes of Selected Poems of the 1970s, II'. *A.L.S.*, X, 1982, 300-03.
Strugnell, John. *David Rowbotham*. (St Lucia: U.Q.P., 1969). Artists in Queensland.
Reviewed by M. Dugan, *Twentieth Century*, XXV, 1970, 83-84; R. Mills, *Makar*, VI, No. 2, 1970, 42-43; R.A. Simpson, *Age*, 13 June, 1970, 15.

ROWCROFT, CHARLES

Critical Material

Barnes, John. *Henry Kingsley and Colonial Fiction*. (Melbourne: O.U.P., 1971), 33-35. Australian Writers and Their Work.
Hadgraft, Cecil. 'Charles Rowcroft, For Example'. *A.L.S.*, II, 1966, 171-8.
Healy, J.J. 'The Treatment of the Aborigine in Early Australian Fiction, 1840-70'. *A.L.S.*, V, 1972, 233-53.
Shipley, John B. 'Charles Rowcroft: An Unpublished Memoir'. *A.L.S.*, III, 1967, 116-125.
Sinnett, Frederick. *The Fiction Fields of Australia*. (Brisbane: U.Q.P., 1966), 43-6 and passim. Reprinted in *The Writer in Australia*, edited by John Barnes (Melbourne: O.U.P., 1969), 8-32. This essay first published in *Illustrated Journal of Australia*, 1, 1856, 97-105, 199-208.
Zinkhan, E.J. 'Charles Rowcroft: Information, Corrections, Additions'. *A.L.S.*, XI, 1983, 238-45.
---. 'Charles Rowcroft's *Chronicles of 'The Fleet Prison'*. *The Dickensian*, No. 407, 1985, 130-139.

ROWLAND, J.R.

Poetry

The Clock Inside. (Sydney: A.& R., 1979).
Reviewed by C. Pollnitz, *Southerly*, XLI, 1981, 225; R.A. Simpson, *Age*, 12 January, 1980, 24; M. Thwaites, *Canberra Times*, 31 May, 1980, 14.

The Feast of Ancestors. (Sydney: A.& R., 1965).
Reviewed by E.A.M. Colman, *Poetry Magazine*, No. 5, 1965, 30-4; D. Douglas, *Age*, 13 November, 1965, 23; R. Dunlop, *Poetry Australia*, No. 7, 1965, 39-43; B. Elliott, *ABR*, IV, 1965, 232; F. Haynes, *Westerly*, No. 3, 1966, 90-4; E. Jones, *Nation*, 22 January, 1966, 22-3; S.E. Lee, *Southerly*, XXVI, 1966, 128-9; V. Smith, *Bulletin*, 25 September, 1965, 53-4; N. Talbot, *Meanjin*, XXV, 1966, 119-21; A. Taylor, *Overland*, No. 35, 1966, 55-6.

Sixty. (North Ryde, N.S.W.: A.& R., 1989).
Reviewed by I. Indyk, *S.M.H.*, 25 November, 1989, 88.

   Critical Material
Fabre, Michel. 'Landscape and the Clock: The Poetry of John Russel Rowland'. *WLWE*, XX, No. 1, 1981, 75-85.
Jockel, Gordon. 'Diplomat and Poet'. *Australian*, 20 November, 1965, 9.

RUDD, STEELE

   Fiction
The Complete Steele Rudd. (St Lucia: U.Q.P., 1987). Boxed set of four volumes, with an introduction by Cecil Hadgraft (1987): *On Our Selection* contains also *Our New Selection*, *Sandy's Selection*, *Back at Our Selection*, and a bibliography; *The Rudd Family* contains also *Stocking Our Selection*, *From Selection to City*, *The Book of Dan*, *Grandpa's Selection and Other Stories*, and *The Poor Parson*; *A City Selection* contains also *Dad in Politics and Other Stories*, *Me an' th' Son*, *The Dashwoods*, *We Kaytons*, *The Miserable Clerk*, *On an Australian Farm*, and *Memoirs of Corporal Keely*; *The Old Homestead* contains also *In Australia*, *For Life and Other Stories*, *On Emu Creek*, *The Romance of Runnibede*, *Green Grey Homestead*. See below for original publication details of individual volumes.
Reviewed by D. Anderson, *Times on Sunday*, 11 October, 1987, 33.

The Dashwoods: A Sequel to On an Australian Farm [and] *Grandpa's Selection and Other Stories.* (St Lucia: U.Q.P., 1970). These titles are also published separately in paperback. Brief introductions by Eric Davis. First published Sydney: NSW Bookstall Co., 1911 and 1919 respectively.
Reviewed by A.R. Chisholm, *Age*, 13 March, 1971, 14; C. Harrison-Ford, *Nation*, 10 July, 1971, 21.

From Selection to City [and] *On an Australian Farm.* (St Lucia: U.Q.P., 1969) These titles are also published separately in paperback. Brief introductions by Eric Davis. *From Selection to City* first published in book form Sydney: NSW Bookstall Co., 1909; *On an Australian Farm* first published Sydney: NSW Bookstall Co., 1910.

In Australia or The Old Selection. Adapted by Richard Fotheringham. (St Lucia: U.Q.P., 1987).
Reviewed by K. Stewart, *A.L.S.*, 14, No. 1, 1989, 122-26.

In Australia [and] *For Life and Other Stories.* (St Lucia: U.Q.P., 1968). These titles are also published separately in paperback. Brief introductions by Eric Davis. *In Australia* first published Sydney: Pratten, 1908; *For Life* first published Sydney: NSW Bookstall Co., 1909.
Reviewed by A.R. Chisholm, *Age*, 19 July, 1969, 10; N. Keesing, *Bulletin*, 7 June, 1969, 70-71.

Me an' th' Son [and] *The Miserable Clerk.* (St Lucia: U.Q.P., 1973). These titles are

also separately published in paperback. Brief introductions by Eric Davis. First published in Sydney: Pratten, 1924 and Sydney: NSW Bookstall Co., 1926 respectively.
Reviewed by O. Ruhen, *Australian*, 29 August, 1973, 14; C. Semmler, *S.M.H.*, 24 November, 1973, 15.

The Old Homestead [and] *Memoirs of Corporal Keeley*. (St Lucia: U.Q.P., 1971). These titles are also published separately in paperback. Brief introductions by Eric Davis. First published in book form Sydney: NSW Bookstall Co., 1917 and 1918 respectively.
Reviewed by M. Haley, *Twentieth Century*, XXVII, 1973, 284-85; C. Harrison-Ford, *Nation*, 10 July, 1971, 21; J. O'Hara, *Review* (Melbourne), 20 August, 1971, 1278.

On Emu Creek [and] *We Kaytons*. (St Lucia: U.Q.P., 1972). These titles are also separately published in paperback. Brief introductions by Eric Davis. First published Sydney: NSW Bookstall Co., 1923 and London: Hodder & Stoughton, 1921 respectively.
Reviewed by *ABR*, XI, 1972, 54; B. Jeffrey, *Canberra Times*, 10 February, 1973, 11; K. Smithyman, *Journal of Commonwealth Literature*, XII, No. 1, 1977, 72-73.

On Our Selection. Introduced by Philip Butterss. (Sydney: A.& R., 1992). First published Sydney: Bulletin, 1899.

The Poor Parson [and] *Dad in Politics and Other Stories*. (St Lucia: U.Q.P., 1968). These titles are also published separately in paperback. Brief introductions by Eric Davis. First published Sydney: NSW Bookstall Co., 1907 and 1908 respectively.
Reviewed by N. Keesing, *Bulletin*, 22 February, 1969, 72; K. Rushbrooke, *Realist*, No. 33, 1969, 74-77.

The Romance of Runnibede [and] *Green Grey Homestead*. (St Lucia: U.Q.P., 1975). These titles are also separately published in paperback. Brief introductions by Eric Davis. First published Sydney: NSW Bookstall Co., 1927 and Sydney: Macquarie Head Press, 1934 respectively.
Reviewed by A.R. Chisholm, *Age*, 21 June, 1975, 19; D. Kim, *S.M.H.*, 5 July, 1975, 16; J. King, *Courier-Mail*, 30 August, 1975, 15.

A Steele Rudd Selection: The Best Dad and Dave Stories with Other Rudd Classics. Chosen by Frank Moorhouse. (St Lucia: U.Q.P., 1986).
Reviewed by K. Stewart, *ABR*, No. 91, 1987, 8-9.

Stocking Our Selection [and] *The Book of Dan*. (St Lucia: U.Q.P., 1970). These titles are also published separately in paperback. Brief introductions by Eric Davis. First published Sydney: NSW Bookstall Co., 1909 (see Miller and Macartney) and 1911 respectively.
Reviewed by K. Slessor, *Daily Telegraph*, Sydney, 8 August, 1970, 59.

Critical Material

'Memorial Gestures'. *Canberra Times*, 13 June, 1975, 8. Proposed memorial on the Darling Downs.
Birch, R.J. 'Toowoomba Remembers Steele Rudd'. *Bulletin*, 17 May, 1969, 67-68.
Carlyon, Les. 'Preserving Dad and Dave for Another Generation'. *Courier-Mail*, 23 October, 1984, 4.
Chisholm, Alex H. 'Some Queensland Personalities at Close Range'. *Royal Historical Society of Queensland. Journal Year-book of Proceedings*, IX, No. 4, 1973, 63-64.
Davis, Eric D. '"Steele Rudd", and His Gift of Laughter: An Australian Literary Heritage'. *Royal Historical Society of Queensland Journal*, IX, 1969/70, 127-43.
Davis, Eric Drayton. *The Life and Times of Steele Rudd Creator of On Our Selection,' Dad and Dave*. (Melbourne: Lansdowne, 1976). Reviewed by L. Cantrell, *A.L.S.*, VIII, 1978, 378-82; I.S. Davidson, *Courier-Mail*, 1 May, 1976, 17; B. Elliott, *Advertiser*, 17 April, 1976, 16; S. Sayers, *Age*, 10 January, 1976, 14; B. Wannan,

Age, 27 March, 1976, 18; J. Waten, *S.M.H.*, 20 April, 1976, 7.

Dermody, Susan. 'Two Remakes: Ideologies of Film Production, 1919-1921'. In *Nellie Melba, Ginger Meggs and Friends: Essays in Australian Cultural History*, edited by Susan Dermody, John Docker and Drusilla Modjeska (Malmsbury, Vic.: Kibble Books, 1982), 33-59.

Dowsley, Geoff. 'Steele Rudd (Arthur Hoey Davis)'. *Tasmanian Journal of Education*, II, 1968, 205-09.

Edwards, Peter. 'Cranky Jacks: Men Without Women in Steele Rudd's *On Our Selection* and Lennie Lower's *Here's Luck*'. In *Reconnoitres: Essays in Australian Literature in Honour of G.A. Wilkes*, edited by Margaret Harris and Elizabeth Webby (South Melbourne: O.U.P. in association with Sydney U.P., 1992), 79-90.

Ellingsen, Peter. 'The Tarnish on our Steele Rudd'. *Bulletin*, 3 July, 1984, 110.

Fletcher, A.R. 'The Greatness of Steele Rudd'. *Expression*, VIII, No. 1, 1969, 22-25.

Fotheringham, Richard. 'Arthur Hoey Davis and Several "Steele Rudds": Imagining the Pseudonymous Author'. *A.L.S.*, 14, No. 3, 1990, 297-305.

---. *In Search of Steele Rudd: Author of the Classic Dad & Dave Stories*. (St Lucia: U.Q.P., 1995). Reviewed by N. Jillett, *Age*, 18 Nov., 1995, Saturday Extra 9; H. McQueen, *Independent*, Dec. 1995/Jan. 1996, 84-86; P. Pierce, *ABR*, 177, 1995, 12-13; C. Semmler, *Weekend Australian*, 14-15 Oct., 1995, Review 9.

---. 'The Plays of Steele Rudd'. *Australasian Drama Studies*, 26, 1995, 81-100.

Fowler, J. Beresford. *The Green-Eyed Monster: Autobiography*. (Ilfracombe, Devon: A.H. Stockwell, 1968), 59-62, 79-81, 130-31. References to stage productions of *On Our Selection*.

French, Maurice. 'Steele Rudd's Dad: An Exiled Convict?' *A.L.S.*, XIII, No. 1, 1987, 95-99.

Green, Dorothy. 'No Laughing Matter'. *Bulletin Literary Supplement*, 30 September, 1980, 29-35.

Ikin, Van. 'Steele Rudd as Failed Artist'. *Southerly*, XXXVI, 1976, 363-76.

Irvin, Eric. 'The Great Australian Play'. *Quadrant*, XX, No. 1, 1976, 19-24. Dramatisation of *On Our Selection* by Albert Edmunds and Beaumont Smith.

Jeffrey, Brian. 'The Man with a "Rich Gift of Honest Laughter"'. *Canberra Times*, 11 October, 1980, 21.

Lindsay, Norman. 'Steele Rudd'. In his *Bohemians of the Bulletin*. (Sydney: A.& R., 1965), 63-7.

Palmer, Vance. *Intimate Portraits*, ed. H.P. Heseltine. (Melbourne: Cheshire, 1969), 88-92.

Putnis, Peter. *Steele Rudd's Australia*. (Toowoomba: Darling Downs Institute Press, 1988). Reviewed by K. Stewart, *A.L.S.*, 14, No. 1, 1989, 122-26.

Semmler, Clement. 'The Bush Chronicles of Steele Rudd and Clement Semmler'. *Bulletin*, 23 October, 1984, 100-01 & 104.

S

SACCHI, FILIPPO

Critical Material
Bettoni, Camilla. 'La Casa in Oceania - Sacchi's Ingham Novel'. *LiNQ*, X, No. 2, 1982, 103-12.

SALOM, PHILIP

Fiction
Playback. (Fremantle, WA: Fremantle Arts Centre P, 1991).
Reviewed by D. Davison, *Weekend Australian*, 13-14 July, 1991, Review 4; R. Dessaix, *ABR*, 131, 1991, 15-16; W. Goulston, *Antipodes*, 6.1, 1992, 90-91; P. Hutchings, *S.M.H.*, 29 June, 1991, 47; A. Kennon, *Age*, 31 August, 1991, Saturday Extra 8.

Poetry
Barbecue of the Primitives. (St Lucia: U.Q.P., 1989).
Reviewed by M. Heald, *Westerly*, 34, No. 3, 1989, 92-94; S. Patton, *ABR*, No. 113, 1989, 30-31.

Feeding the Ghost. (Ringwood, Vic.: Penguin, 1993).
Reviewed by M. Duwell, *Weekend Australian*, 20-21 March, 1993, Review 7; D. Gilbey, *ABR*, 149, 1993, 37-38; K. Hart, *Age*, 20 March, 1993, Saturday Extra 8; S. Miller, *Westerly*, 38.2, 1993, 87-89; P. Nelson, *Quadrant*, 38.1-2, 1994, 117-18; S. O'Brien, *T.L.S.*, 20 August, 1993, 6; J. Owen, *Meanjin*, 52.3, 1993, 573-81.

The Projectionist. (Fremantle: Fremantle Arts Centre Press, 1983).
Reviewed by H. Allen, *LiNQ*, XI, No. 2, 1983-1984, 118-120; J. Barnie, *Kunapipi*, VI, No. 3, 1984, 107-122; B. Beaver, *Weekend Australian. Weekend Magazine*, 29-30 October, 1983, 15; L.R. Leavis and J.M. Blom, *English Studies*, LXV, 1984, 446-451; K. Llewellyn, *S.M.H.*, 3 March, 1984, 42; M. Macleod, *Meanjin*, XLIII, No. 4, 1984, 457-460 and *Kunapipi*, VI, No. 1, 1984, 79-83; S. McCauley, *Westerly*, XXIX, No. 2, 1984, 109-111; M. Richards, *Island Magazine*, Nos. 18-19, 1984, 52-57; G. Rowlands, *Overland*, Nos. 94-95, 1984, 82-84; A. Taylor, *ABR*, No. 61, 1984, 35-36; C. Wallace-Crabbe, *T.L.S.*, 20 July, 1984, 819.

The Silent Piano. (Fremantle: Fremantle Arts Centre Press, 1980).
Reviewed by R. Bennett, *ABR*, No. 29, 1981, 27; L.R. Burrows, *Westerly*, XXVI, No. 1, 1981, 56-62; M. Diesendorf, *Vista*, XVI, No. 3, 1983, 2; G. Dutton, *Bulletin*, 27 January, 1981, 62-63; M. Duwell, *Weekend Australian. Weekend Magazine*, 3-4 January, 1981, 10; K.L. Goodwin, *WLWE*, XXI, No. 1, 1982, 79-82; J. Guess, *Ash Magazine*, No. 6, 1981, 31; M. Harris, *Bulletin*, 22-29 December, 1981, 70; A. Lansdown, *Artlook*, VI, No. 11, 1980, 49; A. Niven, *English Studies*, LXIII, 1982, 339-340; B. O'Donohue, *Image* (Brisbane), IV, Nos. 1-2, 1981, 64-65 and *LiNQ*, X,

No. 1, 1981, 126-132; G. Rowlands, *Overland*, No. 84, 1981, 69-71.

Sky Poems. (Fremantle, W.A.: Fremantle Arts Centre Press, 1987).
Reviewed by B. Giles, *ABR*, No. 94, 1987, 32-34; P. Goldsworthy, *Island Magazine*, No. 33, 1988, 70-71; P. Neilsen, *Age Saturday Extra*, 20 August, 1987, 13; K. Russell, *Quadrant*, 33, No. 4, 1989, 62-64; A. Taylor, *Fremantle Arts Review*, II, No. 9, 1987, 14-15.

Critical Material
Holst Petersen, Kirsten, and Rutherford, Anna. 'Sojourn in the Sky: Conventions of Exile in Philip Salom's *Sky Poems*'. *Westerly*, XXXIII, No. 2, 1988, 67-74.
Page, Geoff. 'Philip Salom'. In his *A Reader's Guide To Contemporary Australian Poetry* (St. Lucia: U.Q.P., 1995), 257-261.
Patton, Simon. 'The Poet's Progress: Interview with Philip Salom by Simon Patton'. *ABR*, 134, 1991, 20-21.
1Williams, Barbara. 'Interview with Philip Salom'. *Westerly*, XXXIII, No. 4, 1988, 59-65.

SAVERY, HENRY
Fiction
The Bitter Bread of Banishment, Formerly Quintus Servinton: A Tale Founded upon Incidents of Real Occurence. (Kensington: N.S.W. University Press, 1984). First published anonymously Hobart: Henry Melville, 1830-1831.
Reviewed by R. Block, *S.M.H.*, 15 September, 1984, 47; L. Clancy, *ABR*, No. 65, 1984, 32-33; C. Semmler, *Weekend Australian Magazine*, 11-12 August, 1984, 17.

Quintus Servinton: A Tale founded Upon Incidents of Real Occurrences. Edited with a biographical Introduction by Cecil Hadgraft (Brisbane: Jacaranda Press, 1962). First published anonymously Hobart: Henry Melville, 1830-1.
Reviewed by B. Elliott, *A.L.S.*, I, No. 1, 1963, 70-2; M.H. Ellis, *Bulletin*, 5 January, 1963, 38; L.T. Hergenhan, *Quadrant*, VII, No. 2, 1963, 77-9.

Non-Fiction
The Hermit in Van Diemen's Land. (Brisbane: U.Q.P., 1965). Edited and with an introduction by Cecil Hadgraft and Margriet Roe. First published in book form Hobart Town: Andrew Bent, 1829-30.
Reviewed by K. Tennant, *ABR*, IV, 1965, 58.

Critical Material
Hadgraft, Cecil. 'In Quest of a Quaker: A Note on Henry Savery's *Nom de Plume*'. *A.L.S.*, I, No. 1, 1963, 57.
McDonald, Avis G. 'The Bitter Banishment of Quintus Scrvinton'. *WLWE*, XXVIII, No. 1, 1988, 66-74.
Woodberry, Joan *Andrew Bent and the Freedom of the Press in Van Diemen's Land*. (Hobart: Fullers Bookshop, 1972). Bent was Savery's first publisher.

SCHLUNKE, E.O.
Fiction
Stories of the Riverina. (Sydney: A.& R., 1965). Selected and with an Introduction by Clement Semmler.
Reviewed by M. Dunlevy, *Canberra Times*, 2 April, 1966, 11; K. Tennant, *S.M.H.*, 19 March, 1966, 15; M. Wolkowsky, *Bulletin*, 16 July, 1966, 47.

Critical Material
Semmler, Clement. 'E.O. Schlunke: An Appreciation'. *Meanjin*, 20, 1961, 407-18. Reprinted in *For the Uncanny Man: Essays, Mainly Literary*. (Melbourne: Cheshire, 1963), 147-59.

SCOTT, JOHN A.

Fiction

Blair. (Fitzroy, Vic.: McPhee Gribble/Penguin; New York: New Directions, 1988).
Reviewed by C. Bliss, *Antipodes*, 64.3, 1990, 524; H. Daniel, *Age Saturday Extra*, 2 April, 1988, 12; M. Gressor, *S.M.H.*, 9 April, 1988, 74; M. Roberts, *LiNQ*, 16, No. 3, 1988, 123-4; M. Sharkey, *ABR*, No. 98, 1988, 18-19.

What I Have Written. (Ringwood, Vic.: McPhee Gribble, 1993; New York: W. W. Norton, 1994).
Reviewed by D. Davison, *Weekend Australian*, 7-8 August, 1993, Review 5; S. Hughes, *S.M.H.*, 24 July, 1993, 45; N. Krauth, *ABR*, 152, 1993, 12-13 (see also interview 13-14); N.D. Smart, *Antipodes*, 9.1, 1995, 48-49; A. Wearne, *Overland*, 132, 1993, 82-83.

Poetry

The Barbarous Sideshow. (St Lucia: Makar Press, 1975).
Reviewed by R. Adamson, *New Poetry*, 24, No. 1, 1976, 78-81; J. Tranter, *Australian*, 10 April, 1976, 43.

From the Flooded City. (St Lucia: Makar Press, 1982).
Reviewed by B. Giles, *ABR*, No. 45, 1982, 20; A. Korvisianos, *Muse*, No. 18, 1982, 22; J. Maiden, *S.M.H.*, 12 June, 1982, 37; B. O'Donohue, *Image*, 5, No. 1, 22-23; G. Rowlands, *Overland*, No. 90. 1982, 63-64; J. Tranter, *Scripsi*, 1, Nos 3-4, 1982, 94-96; C. Vleeskens, *Fling*, 2, No. 2, 1982, 41-44.

The Quarrel with Ourselves; and Confession. (Clifton Hill, Vic.: Rigmarole Books, 1984).
Reviewed by A.-H. Ball, *Words and Visions*, No. 18, 1985, 38-39; B. Beaver, *Weekend Australian Magazine*, 28-29 July, 1984, 14; G. Catalano, *Age Saturday Extra*, 27 October, 1984, 13; M. Hulse, *PN Review*, XII, No. 5, 1986, 56; G. Rowlands, *Overland*, No. 97, 1984, 71-72.

St. Clair: Three Narratives. (St Lucia: U.Q.P., 1986).
Reviewed by M. Hulse, *PN Review*, XIV, No. 1, 1987, 61-62; P. Mead, *Island Magazine*, No. 29, 1986, 43-40; G. Page, *ABR*, No. 78, 1986, 27-28; C. Pollnitz, *Scripsi*, IV, No. 2, 1986, 255-263; A. Taylor, *Canberra Times*, 10 May, 1986, B3; F. Zwicky, *Weekend Australian Magazine*, 12-13 April, 1986, 15.

St. Clair. Introduction by Christopher Pollnitz. (Sydney: Pan/Picador, 1990). Revised edition, originally published St Lucia: U.Q.P., 1986.
Reviewed by L. Bourke, *Southerly*, 51.4, 1991, 142-51; M. Duwell, *Weekend Australian*, 16-17 February, 1991, Review 5.

Selected Poems. (St Lucia: U.Q.P., 1995).
Reviewed by M. Duwell, *Weekend Australian*, 25-26 Nov., 1995, Review 9; P. Rose, *ABR*, 169, 1995, 42-43.

Singles: Shorter Works 1981-1986. (St Lucia: U.Q.P., 1989).
Reviewed by R. Adamson, *Scripsi*, 6, No. 1, 1990, 213-19; M. Duwell, *Weekend Australian*, 8-9 July, 1989, Weekend 11; J. Forbes, *Editions*, No. 3, 1989, 11-12; L. Jacobs, *ABR*, No. 113, 1989, 25-26; R. Usher, *Age Saturday Extra*, 27 May, 1989, 10.

Translation. (Sydney: Pan/Picador, 1990).
Reviewed by M. Duwell, *Weekend Australian*, 16-17 February, 1991, Review 5; K. Hart, *Voices*, 1.1, 1991, 97-101; P. Kane, *World Literature Today*, 65.4, 1991, 765; S. Patton, *ABR*, No. 127, 1990, 19-20; T. Shapcott, *Age*, 15 December, 1990, Saturday Extra 7.

Non-Fiction

'A Stitching of Water: Notes towards a Poetic'. *Meanjin*, 52.2, 1993, 400-12.

Critical Material

Craven, Peter and Heyward, Michael. 'An Interview with John A. Scott'. *Scripsi*, II, Nos. 2-3, 1983, 231-246.
Duwell, Martin. 'Enlarging Our Experiments with Narrative: John A. Scott's Trilogy with Annotations'. *A.L.S.*, 15.3, 1992, 179-91.
McDowell, Colin. 'John A. Scott The Covering Cherub'. *Scripsi*, II, Nos. 2-3, 1983, 247-256.
Page, Geoff. 'John A. Scott'. In his *A Reader's Guide To Contemporary Australian Poetry* (St. Lucia: U.Q.P., 1995), 261-263.
Salusinszky, Imre. 'The Poetry of John A. Scott'. *Scripsi*, III, No. 1, 1985, 185-192.
Thwaites, Tony. 'Two Tales: John A. Scott, Seymour Chatman and Some Occlusions of Narrative'. *Journal of Narrative Technique*, 21.1, 1991, 98-120.

SEWELL, STEPHEN

Drama

The Blind Giant is Dancing. (Sydney: Currency Press/State Theatre Company of South Australia, 1983).
Reviewed by R. Archer, *Australian Left Review*, No. 90, 1984, 41-43; P. Fitzpatrick, *Australasian Drama Studies*, III, No. 2, 1985, 145-148; R. Green, *Canberra Times*, 27 June, 1984, 24.

The Garden of Granddaughters. (Sydney: Currency Press, 1993).
Reviewed by H. Thomson, *Australasian Drama Studies*, 25, 1994, 204-09.

Hate. (Sydney: Currency Press/Playbox Theatre Co., Melbourne and Belvoir Street Theatre, Sydney, 1988).
Reviewed by P. Fitzpatrick, *Australasian Drama Studies*, Nos. 15-16, 1989/90, 202-05; J. McCallum and J. Waites, *New Theatre Australia*, No. 8, 1989, 24-26.

Traitors. (Sydney: Alternative Publishing Co-operative/Nimrod Theatre, 1983).
Reviewed by L. Radic, *Age*, 16 July, 1983, 10.

Welcome the Bright World. (Sydney: Alternative Publishing Co-operative/Nimrod Theatre, 1983).
Reviewed by M. Lord, *ABR*, No. 54, 1983, 29; J. McCallum, *S.M.H.*, 14 May, 1983, 35; L. Radic, *Age*, 16 July, 1983, 10.

Critical Material

'A Playwright Walks the Corridors of Power'. *S.M.H.*, 9 June, 1984, 48.
Bolton, Matthew. 'Seeker after Truth', *Age*, 8 September, 1983, 14.
Caulfield, Carl. '"What the Bomb Does to Our Minds": Sewell's *Welcome the Bright World* and Brenton's *The Genius*'. *Australasian Drama Studies*, No. 14, 1989, 19-32.
Fitzpatrick, Peter. *Stephen Sewell: The Playwright as Revolutionary*. (Sydney: Currency Press, 1991). Reviewed by R. Corballis, *Australasian Drama Studies*, 22, 1993, 156-58; D. Emmerson, *ABR*, 142, 1994, 54.
---. 'Sewell's *Dreams* at the Adelaide Festival'. *Australasian Drama Studies*, No. 9, 1986, 35-51.
Gilbert, Helen. 'Monumental Moments: Michael Gow's *1841*, Stephen Sewell's *Hate*, Louis Nowra's *Capricornia* and Australia's Bicentenary'. *Australasian Drama Studies*, 24, 1994, 29-45.
Healey, Ken. 'Exciting Young Dramatist Brings "Dancing Giant" to Canberra'. *Canberra Times*, 10 June, 1984, 8.
Hunter, Mary Ann. 'Casebook: Sewell's *Miranda*'. *Australasiasn Drama Studies*, No. 14, 1989, 47-63. Discusses production of premiere in Brisbane, 1989.
---. 'Interview: Stephen Sewell Talks to Mary Ann Hunter'. *Australasian Drama Studies*, No. 14, 1989, 33-45.
Kay, Shelley. 'Stephen Sewell - On Human Relations and the Left'. *Tribune*, 25 July, 1984, 15. Interview.

Kiernan, Brian. 'Some Contemporary Developments in Australian Drama: Louis Nowra and Stephen Sewell'. In *Australian Papers: Yugoslavia, Europe and Australia*, edited by Mirko Jurak (Ljubljana: Edvard Cardelj University, 1983), 183-89.

McCallum, John. 'The World Outside: Cosmopolitanism in the Plays of Nowra and Sewell'. *Meanjin*, XLIII, 1984, 286-96.

Morley, Michael. 'Trotsky Cassidy & Dancing Giants'. *National Times*, 7-13 October, 1983, 31.

Ridgman, Jeremy. 'Interview: Louis Nowra, Stephen Sewell and Neil Armfield Talk to Jeremy Ridgeman'. *Australasian Drama Studies*, 1, No. 2, 1983, 105-23.

---. 'Stephen Sewell - Political Playwright'. *Theatre Australia*, IV, No. 9, 1980, 12.

SEYMOUR, ALAN

Fiction

The Coming Self-Destruction of the United States of America. (London: Souvenir Press, 1969).
Reviewed by O. Ruhen, *Age*, 29 November, 1969, 14.

The One Day of the Year. (London: Souvenir Press, 1967). Novel based on the play of the same name.
Reviewed by *ABR*, 7, 1968, 69; H. Hewitt, *Canberra Times*, 27 January, 1968, 10; N. Jillett, *Age*, 23 December, 1967, 22; N. Keesing, *Bulletin*, 23 December, 1967, 51; T. Keneally, *Australian*, 27 January, 1968, 12; M. Vintner, *S.M.H.*, 3 February, 1968, 18.

Non-Fiction

'Comment from Alan Seymour in Turkey'. *Masque*, I, No. 3, 1968, 40.

'One Image of Australia'. *Meanjin*, XXVI, 1967, 223-229. On productions of *The One Day of The Year* in France and Australia.

'Who Has Disregarded Whom?' *Masque*, I, No. 6, 1968, 26-27.

With Mordecai Gorelik. 'Words and Music'. *Masque*, No. 11, 1969, 18-30. Discussions of modern theatre. See also letters to the editor by Alan Seymour, *Masque*, No. 12, 1969, 40-41, and Clem Gorman, 41.

Critical Material

'And Tell Sad Tales'. *Masque*, No. 12, 1969, 39-40.

Baker, J.G. *Companion to Ray Lawler, 'The Summer of the Seventeenth Doll', and Alan Seymour, 'The One Day of the Year'.* (Sydney: A.& R., 1965).

Courtis, Brian. 'Seymour's still in there Fighting'. *Age*, 8 September, 1979, 20.

Davison, P.H. 'Three Australian Plays: National Myths under Criticism'. *Southerly*, XXIII, No. 2, 1963, 110-27. Commentary on *The One Day of The Year*.

Drewe, Robert. 'Remember Seymour'. *Australian*, 14 February, 1973, 11.

Duncan, Catherine. 'French Production of Alan Seymour's *One Day of the Year*'. *Meanjin*, XXV, 1966, 229-37.

Frizell, Helen. 'Playwright Back To a Theatre Boom'. *S.M.H.*, 3 March, 1973, 23.

Hutton, Geoffrey. 'Home is An Author - Briefly'. *Age*, 8 March, 1973, 9.

Kelly, Frances. 'Exile with a Cause, and a Script'. *Australian*, 17 January, 1978, 8.

Murphy, Damien. 'Seymour's Sacrilegious Anzac Study Undergoes a Rewrite'. *S.M.H.*, 2 June, 1984, 44. See also his 'Seymour Classic Revised', *Age Saturday Extra*, 9 June, 1984, 15.

Porteous, Alexander. 'Some Recent Australian Plays, and Problems of Their Criticism'. *A.L.S.*, III, 1967, 83-97.

Pratt, Noel. 'Writer Meets Actor and a Play is Born: Noel Pratt on the Playwrights' Conference'. *Australian*, 15 March, 1973, 11.

Scott, Graham. 'Indigenous Drama and *The One Day of the Year*'. *Idiom*, No. 9, 1969, 15-21.

Sykes, Alrene and Richards, Keith. 'Another Look at the Old War-Horse: Alan

Seymour's *The One Day of the Year'*. *Australasian Drama Studies*, II, No. 2, 1984, 65-89.

Sykes, Alrene. 'Alan Seymour'. *A.L.S.*, VI, 1974, 277-87.

SHAPCOTT, THOMAS W.

Fiction

The Birthday Gift, A Novel. (St Lucia: U.Q.P., 1982).

Reviewed by M. Brakmanis, *Ash Magazine*, No. 12, 1983, 28-29; G. Dutton, *Bulletin*, 18 January, 1983, 56-57; M. Halligan, *Canberra Times*, 5 December, 1982, 11; J. Modder, *Courier-Mail*, 1 January, 1983, 24; P. Pierce, *Age Saturday Extra*, 4 October, 1982, 13; C.K. Stead, *S.M.H.*, 18 September, 1982, 32; J. Tulip, *Southerly*, XLIII, 1983, 115-16; C. Vleeskens, *Fling*, II, Nos 3-4, 1983, 74-76.

Hotel Bellevue. (London: Chatto and Windus, 1986).

Reviewed by J. Davidson, *Overland*, No. 106, 1987, 69-70; K. Goodwin, *Courier-Mail: The Great Weekend*, 20 September, 1986, 6; M. Halligan, *Canberra Times*, 6 December, 1986, B3; P. Lewis, *Stand Magazine*, XXVII, No. 4, 1986, 71 and *London Magazine*, 26, Nos. 9-10, 1986/87, 152-56; S. McKernan, *Bulletin*, 2 December, 1986, 88; A. Mitchell, *Weekend Australian Magazine*, 27-28 September, 1986, 15; G. Murnane, *ABR*, No. 87, 1987, 7-8; P. Pierce, *S.M.H.*, 20 September, 1986, 47; A. Sattin, *T.L.S.*, 7 November, 1986, 1255; G. Turner, *Age Saturday Extra*, 20 September, 1986, 15.

Limestone and Lemon Wine. (London: Chatto & Windus, 1988).

Reviewed by H. Daniel, *Age Saturday Extra*, 23 April, 1988, 12; M. Stimpson, *T.L.S.*, 26 February-3 March, 1988, 215; A. Stretton, *S.M.H.*, 14 May, 1988, 74.

Mona's Gift. (Ringwood, Vic.: Penguin, 1993).

Reviewed by V. Armanno, *Imago*, 5.3, 1993, 87-88; K. Brophy, *Overland*, 134, 1994, 79-81; K. England, *ABR*, 154, 1993, 17-18 (see also interview by N. Myatt, 18-19); H.C. Jaffa, *Antipodes*, 8.1, 1994, 77; R. Lucas, *Bulletin*, 28 September, 1993, 89; M. Missen, *Age*, 18 September, 1993, Saturday Extra 10; G. Ratcliffe, *Australian Canadian Studies*, 12.2, 1994, 92-96; G. Turcotte, *Weekend Australian*, 9-10 October, 1993, Review 8; G. Windsor, *S.M.H.*, 11 September, 1993, Spectrum 12A.

The Search for Galina. (London: Chatto and Windus, 1989).

Reviewed by J. Hanrahan, *Age*, 3 November, 1990, Saturday Extra 8; M. Luke, *ABR*, No. 112, 1989, 12-13; A.P. Riemer, *S.M.H.*, 17 June, 1989, 83; I. Salusinszky, *Weekend Australian*, 15-16 July, 1989, Weekend 10.

What You Own: Stories. (North Ryde, NSW: A.& R., 1991).

Reviewed by A. Di Carlo, *ABR*, 134, 1991, 18; D. Davison, *Weekend Australian*, 28-29 September, 1991, Review 4; I. Dunn, *S.M.H.*, 12 October, 1991, 45; A. Peek, *Age*, 9 November, 1991, Saturday Extra 7.

White Stag of Exile. (Ringwood, Vic.: Allen Lane, 1984).

Reviewed by N. Amadio, *Arts National*, II, No. 3, 1985, 57-59, 109; B. Beaver, *Quadrant*, XXVIII, No. 5, 1984, 86-87; E. Benson, *CRNLE Reviews Journal*, No. 2, 1984, 9-10; *British Book News*, December, 1984, 750; J. Davidson, *Meanjin*, XLIII, 1984, 231-35; S. Dowrick, *National Times*, 2-8 March, 1984, 35; G. Dutton, *Bulletin*, 3 April, 1984, 17-78; K. Goldsworthy, *Age Saturday Extra*, 3 March, 1984, 17; M. Halligan, *Canberra Times*, 16 June, 1984, 18; J. Hanrahan, *ABR*, No. 59, 1984, 23-24; E. Jolley, *Fremantle Arts Centre Broadsheet: Books*, III, No. 6, 1984, 3-4; N. Jose, *Age Monthly Review*, IV, No. 2, 1984, 3-4; D. Myers, *S.M.H.*, 10 March, 1984, 41; E. Perkins, *Island Magazine*, No. 20, 1984, 53-54; D. Rowbotham, *Courier-Mail*, 3 March, 1984, 30; J. Taylor, *Weekend Australian Magazine*, 10-11 March, 1984, 16; G. Windsor, *Overland*, No. 98, 1984, 66-68.

Poetry

Begin with Walking. (St Lucia: U.Q.P., 1972). Paperback Poets, 11.
Reviewed by R. Adamson, *Australian*, 31 March, 1973, 33; D. Douglas, *Overland*, No. 56, 1973, 50-52; G. Page, *Canberra Times*, 17 February, 1973, 11; P. Roberts, *S.M.H.*, 7 April, 1973, 23; C. Sansom, *Nation Review*, 5-11 January, 1973, 376; R.A. Simpson, *Age*, 7 April, 1973, 13; *T.L.S.*, 12 October, 1973, 1216; J. Tulip, *Southerly*, XXXIII, 1973, 239 and *Bulletin*, 13 January, 1973, 42.

The City of Home. (St Lucia: U.Q.P., 1995).
Reviewed by B. Beaver, *ABR*, 174, 1995, 50-51; H. Cam, *S.M.H.*, 30 Sept., 1995, Spectrum 14A; K. Hart, *Age*, 18 Nov., 1995, Saturday Extra 8.

Fingers at Air: Experimental Poems 1969. (Ipswich: printed privately, 1969).
Reviewed by R. Dunlop, *Poetry Australia*, No. 38, 1971, 62-63; R. Hall, *Australian*, 9 May, 1970, 20; C. Harrison-Ford, *Poetry Magazine*, XVIII, No. 1, 1970, 31-34; S.E. Lee, *Southerly*, XXX, 1970, 309-10; I. McKay, *Makar*, VI, No. 2, 1970, 31-34.

Interim Report: Some Poems 1970-1971. (Ipswich: The Author, 1971).
Reviewed by C. Bowen, *New Poetry*, XIX, No. 6, 1971, 37.

Inwards to the Sun. (St Lucia: U.Q.P., 1969).
Reviewed by G. Curtois, *Poetry Magazine*, XVIII, No. 1, 1970, 37; K. Goodwin, *Makar*, VI, No. 1, 1970, 28-30; R. Hall, *Australian*, 9 May, 1970, 20; F. Kellaway, *Overland*, No. 46, 1970/71, 39; G. Lehmann, *Bulletin*, 10 October, 1970, 57; G. Page, *Canberra Times*, 28 March, 1970, 11; P. Roberts, *S.M.H.*, 17 January, 1970, 18; R.A. Simpson, *Age*, 24 January, 1970, 11; J. Tulip, *Southerly*, XXXI, 1971, 72-73.

The Mankind Thing. (Brisbane: Jacaranda Press, 1964).
Reviewed by R. Dunlop, *Poetry Australia*, No. 1, 1965, 23-5; B. Elliott, *ABR*, IV, 1965, 178; E. Jones, *Australian*, 13 March, 1965, 11; S.E. Lee, *Southerly*, XXV, No. 2, 1965, 135-6; G. Lehmann, *Bulletin*, 16 January, 1965, 40-1.

Selected Poems. (St Lucia: U.Q.P., 1978).
Reviewed by R. Allingham, *Poetry Australia*, No. 70, 1979, 59-60; B. Beaver, *Age*, 16 December, 1978, 27; V. Brady, *ABR*, No. 7, 1978-79, 27; G. Dutton, *Bulletin*, 21 November, 1978, 67; K. Goodwin, *Weekend Australian Magazine*, 25-26 November, 1978, 8; [S.E. Lee], *Southerly*, XXXIX, 1979, 456-58; S. Morrell, *24 Hours*, IV, No. 2, 1979, 63; J. Rodriguez, *S.M.H.*, 24 February, 1979, 17.

Selected Poems: 1956-1988. (St. Lucia: U.Q.P., 1989).
Reviewed by L. Bourke, *Westerly*, 35, No. 1, 1990, 79-81; M. Duwell, *Weekend Australian*, 30 September-1 October, 1989, Weekend 10; B. Merry, *LiNQ*, 18.1, 1991, 142-48; J. Strauss, *Age Saturday Extra*, 28 October, 1989, 9; W. Wynne, *ABR*, No. 122, 1990, 39-41.

The Seven Deadly Sins. Poem for the opera by Thomas W. Shapcott: music of the opera by Colin Brumby (Ipswich: T.W. Shapcott in conjunction with the Queensland Opera Company, 1970). Booklet with record.
Reviewed by C. Harrison-Ford, *Poetry Magazine*, XVIII, No. 5, 1970, 43-44.

Seventh Avenue Poems. (Sydney: A.& R., 1976). Poets of the Month.
Reviewed by V. Ikin, *Quadrant*, XXI, No. 9, 1977, 78-79.

Shabbytown Calendar. (St Lucia: U.Q.P., 1975).
Reviewed by A. Gould, *Nation Review*, 13-19 February, 1976, 453; R. Gray, *S.M.H.*, 6 March, 1976, 18; J. Griffin, *Advertiser*, 16 October, 1976, 24; K. Hart, *Canberra Poetry*, 1976, 72-73; K. Heinzelman, *Poetry*, CXXXI, No. 4, 1978, 234-35; P. Law, *Poetry Australia*, No. 62, 1977, 69-70; J. McLaren, *Segment*, V, 1976, 55; P. Neilsen, *Age*, 31 January, 1976, 15; C. Pollnitz, *Southerly*, XXXVI, 1976, 469-70; P. Porter, *T.L.S.*, 9 April, 1976, 431; G. Rowlands, *Overland*, No. 111, 1988, 103.

Stump & Grape & Bopple-Nut: Prose Inventions. (Brisbane: Bullion Publications, 1981).
Reviewed by J. Legasse, *Westerly*, XXVII, No. 1, 1982, 94-95.
A Taste of Salt Water. (Sydney: A.& R., 1967).
Reviewed by B. Beaver, *S.M.H.*, 18 November, 1967, 21; A. Brissenden, *Adelaide Advertiser*, 14 October, 1967, 14; R. Dunlop, *Poetry Australia*, No. 20, 1968, 40; K. Goodwin, *Makar*, IV, No. 3, 1968, 23-24; R. Hall, *Australian*, 14 October, 1967, 15; H.P. Heseltine, *Poetry Magazine*, No. 2, 1968, 30-33; M. Irvin, *Twentieth Century*, XXII, 1968, 379-81; A. King, *Meanjin*, XXVII, 1968, 180-81; E. Marsh, *Westerly*, No. 3, 1968, 52-53; T. I. Moore, *Canberra Times*, 11 November, 1967, 13; A. Taylor, *Overland*, No. 38, 1968, 45; J. Tulip, *Southerly*, XXVIII, 71-73; R. Ward, *ABR*, VI, 1967, 197.

Travel Dice. (St Lucia: U.Q.P., 1987).
Reviewed by B. Beaver, *Scripsi*, IV, No. 4, 1987, 117-120; esp. 119-120; J. Davis, *LiNQ*, XV, No. 3, 1987, 92-93; K. Hart, *ABR*, No. 92, 1987, 18-19; C. James, *T.L.S.*, 27 November-3 December, 1987, 1327; K. Llewellyn, *S.M.H.*, 25 July, 1987, 47; G. Page, *Phoenix Review*, No. 2, 1987/88, 112-114; P. Porter, *Age Saturday Extra*, 4 July, 1987, 13; G. Rowlands, *Overland*, No. 108, 1987, 92-94; esp. 93; K. Russell, *Quadrant*, XXXII, No. 7, 1988, 40-42; P. Salom, *Fremantle Arts Review*, II, No. 9, 1987, 14-15.

Turning Full Circle. (Sydney: New Poetry, 1979).
Reviewed by S. Morell, *24 Hours*, V, No. 1, 1980, 57.

Welcome! (St Lucia: U.Q.P., 1983).
Reviewed by B. Beaver, *WLWE*, XXIV, No. 2, 1984, 302-303 and *Scripsi*, IV, No. 4, 1987, 117-120; esp. 117-119; G. Catalano, *Age Saturday Extra*, 4 February, 1984, 17; B. Giles, *ABR*, No. 56, 1983, 29-30; F. Jussawalla, *CRNLE Reviews Journal*, No. 2, 1984, 87-90; S. McKernan, *Canberra Times*, 19 November, 1983, 23; M. Sariban, *Image*, VI, No. 3, 1983, 20-22.

Non-Fiction

Biting the Bullet: A Literary Memoir. (Brookvale, N.S.W.: Simon & Schuster/New Endeavour Press, 1990).
Reviewed by K. Cummings, *S.M.H.*, 6 October, 1990, 79; J. Hanrahan, *Age*, 3 November, 1990, Saturday Extra 8; M. O'Connor, *Quadrant*, 36.5, 1992, 75-77. (See also letter about this article by R. Wighton, *Quadrant*, 36.6, 1992, 7-8, rejoinder from M. O'Connor, *Quadrant*, 36.9, 1992, 70-71, and letter from T. Shapcott, *Quadrant*, 36.10, 1992, 6-7); M. Sharkey, *Weekend Australian*, 13-14 October, 1990, Review 7; J. Strauss, *Overland*, 123, 1991, 47-50.

Focus on Charles Blackman. (Brisbane: U.Q.P., 1967).
Reviewed by M. Drysdale, *Art and Australia*, V, 1967, 501; H. Knorr, *Twentieth Century*, XXII, 1968, 382-3; E. Lynn, *Bulletin*, 20 January, 1968, 47; J. Reed, *ABR*, VII, 1968, 69; R. Wallace-Crabbe, *Canberra Times*, 17 February, 1968, 10.

The Literature Board: A Brief History. (St Lucia: U.Q.P., 1988).
Reviewed by P. Bowler, *Canberra Times*, 9 April, 1988, B5; P. Pierce, *Age*, 16 April, 1988, Saturday Extra 13; E. Williams, *ABR*, No. 99, 1988, 3-4.

'Between the Lines'. *Bulletin*, 5 April, 1983, 71. Second in a series.
'Beware of Broken Glass: Models in a Room of Mirrors'. In *The American Model: Influence and Independence in Australian Poetry*, edited by Joan Kirkby (Sydney: Hale & Iremonger, 1982), 28-41.
'Letter from Tom Shapcott'. *Meanjin*, XLIV, No. 1, 1985, 146-148. A response by Thomas Shapcott, as Director of the Literature Board, to a review referring to themes in Australian literature, by Bev Roberts in *Meanjin*, XLIII, No. 3, 1984. 'Some Sources of *White Stag of Exile*'. *A.L.S.*, XII, No. 3, 1986, 402-05.

Critical Material

'Reading by Ipswich Poet'. *Canberra Times*, 7 June, 1968, 14.

Allart, John. 'Thomas Shapcott'. *Artlook*, V, No. 11, 1979, 3-4. Interview.

Baker, Candida. 'Thomas Shapcott'. In her *Yacker: Australian Writers Talk About Their Work* (Sydney: Picador, 1986), 264-288.

Cadzow, Jane. 'How a Few Coins Make our Literary Gems Glitter'. *Weekend Australian Magazine*, 10-11 March, 1984, 17.

Clancy, L.J. 'The Poetry of Thomas W. Shapcott'. *Meanjin*, XXVI, 1967, 182-187.

Davidson, Jim. 'Thomas Shapcott'. *Meanjin*, XXXVIII, 1979, 56-68. Interview. Reprinted in his *Sideways From the Page* (Melbourne: Fontana, 1983), 146-63.

Duwell, Martin and Neilsen, Philip. 'An Act of Exorcism: An Interview with Thomas W. Shapcott'. *Makar*, XI, No. 3, 1975, 4-16.

Frizell, Helen. 'Varied Rewards of Verse'. *S.M.H.*, 23 February, 1979, 7. Interview.

Harrison-Ford, Carl. 'The Dance of Form: The Poetry of Thomas W. Shapcott'. *Meanjin*, XXXI, 1972, 300-07.

Malouf, David. 'Some Volumes of Selected Poems of the 1970s, II'. *A.L.S.*, X, 1982, 303-04.

Maver, Igor. 'Thomas Shapcott's Verse From a European Perspective'. *A.L.S.*, 14, No. 4, 1990, 507-509.

Page, Geoff. 'Thomas Shapcott'. In his *A Reader's Guide To Contemporary Australian Poetry* (St. Lucia: U.Q.P., 1995), 265-267.

Porter, Peter. 'Markers to the Millenium. Thomas Shapcott's Poetry: A Retrospective'. *A.L.S.*, 14, No. 4, 1990, 505-507.

Sant, Andrew. 'Thomas Shapcott'. *Tasmanian Review*, No. 2, 1979, 6-8. Interview.

Williams, Barbara. 'Tom Shapcott: An Interview'. *Westerly*, 34, No. 1, 1989, 43-52.

SHEARER, JILL

Drama

Catherine: A Play in Two Acts. (Melbourne: Edward Arnold, 1977).

Reviewed by A. Godfrey-Smith, *ABR*, 4, 1978, 21-23; J. Ward, *English in Australia*, 45, 1978, 48.

Echoes and Other Plays. (Brisbane: Playlab, 1980).

Reviewed by M. Lord, *ABR*, 30, 1981, 28-29; J. McCallum, *Theatre Australia*, 5.7, 1981, 52.

The Foreman. (Sydney: Currency Press, 1977). Bound with *The New Life*, by Mary Gage.

Reviewed by R. Arnold, *English in Australia*, 45, 1978, 47-48; A. Godfrey-Smith, *ABR*, 2, 1978, 18-21; D. Oberg, *Words'worth*, 11.2, 1978, 35; D. Pfeiffer, *Opinion*, 8.3, 1979, 31.

Shimada. (Sydney: Currency Press, 1989).

Rviewed by V. Kelly, *Australasian Drama Studies*, 17, 1990, 224-27.

Non-Fiction

'Diary of a Play'. *Scope*, 31.4, 1986, 17.

'Shaping the Script'. *Queensland Writer*, 1.4, 1989, 21-22. Discuses *Shimada*.

Critical Material

Dale, Leigh, and Helen Gilbert. 'Disguising Desire: Gender and Imperialism in Jill Shearer's *Shimada*'. In *Myths, Heroes and Anti-heroes: Essays on the Literature and Culture of the Asia-Pacific Region*, edited by Bruce Bennett and Dennis Haskell (Nedlands, WA: Centre for Studies in Australian Literature, U of Western Australia, 1992), 47-57.

Gilbert, Helen. 'The Catherine Wheel: Travel, Exile and the (Post) Colonial Woman'. *Southerly*, 53.2, 1993, 58-77. Discusses *Catherine*.

---. 'Telling It in Multiple Layers: An Interview with Jill Shearer'. *Australasian*

Drama Studies, 21, 1992, 138-53.
O'Neill, Errol. 'Liberties with the Truth'. *Australian Author*, 24.4, 1992-93, 18-21. Edited transcript of a speech for Warana Writers' Week, September 1992. Discusses *Shimada*.

SIMPSON, R.A.

Poetry

After the Assassination and Other Poems. (Brisbane: Jacaranda Press; San Francisco: Tri-Ocean Books, 1968).
Reviewed by B. Beaver, *S.M.H.*, 27 July, 1968, 23; L.J. Clancy, *Westerly*, No. 1, 1969, 63-64; D. Douglas, *Age*, 4 January, 1969, 11; F. Haynes, *Critic* Perth, IX, 1969, 85; E. Jones, *Nation*, 13 December, 1969, 22-23; S. Knight, *Canberra Times*, 3 August, 1968, 14; S.E. Lee, *Southerly*, XXVIII, 1968, 303-304; M. Randall, *Poetry*, Chicago, CXV, 1969, 49-50; M. Richards, *Meanjin*, XXVIII, 1969, 274; P. Steele, *Meanjin*, XXVIII, 1969, 122; R. Ward, *ABR*, VII, 1968, 165.

Dancing Table: Poems and Drawings 1986-1991. (Ringwood, Vic.: Penguin, 1992).
Reviewed by D. Gilbey, *ABR*, 140, 1992, 45-46; B. Hill, *Age*, 9 May, 1992, Saturday Extra 10; P. Nelson, *Quadrant*, 38.1-2, 1994, 117-18.

Diver. (St Lucia: U.Q.P., 1972). Paperback Poets, 7.
Reviewed by R. Adamson, *New Poetry*, XX, Nos. 5-6, 1972, 73-74; G. Curtis, *Makar*, VIII, No. 1, 1972, 40-43; S.E. Lee, *Southerly*, XXXII, 1972, 302-317; *T.L.S.*, 12 October, 1973, 1216; G. Page, *Canberra Times*, 26 August, 1972, 13; P. Roberts, *S.M.H.*, 20 May, 1972, 12; J. Tulip, *Bulletin*, 1 July, 1972, 47-49.

The Forbidden City. (Sydney: Edwards & Shaw, 1979).
Reviewed by G. Catalano, *Meanjin*, XXXIX, 1980, 359-61; R. Harland, *New Poetry*, XXVIII, No. 2, 1980, 57-58; B. Pascoe, *ABR*, No. 24, 1980, 18; T. Shapcott, *Age*, 26 January, 1980, 26; M. Thwaites, *Canberra Times*, 31 May, 1980, 14.

Poems from Murrumbeena. (St Lucia: U.Q.P., 1976). Paperback Poets. Second Series, 12.
Reviewed by S. Amanuddin, *World Literature Today*, LII, 1978, 176; J. Forbes, *24 Hours*, II, No. 10, 1977, 64; F. Kellaway, *Overland*, No. 67, 1977, 76-77; E. Lindsay, *Weekend Australian Magazine*, 16-17 July, 1977, 12; M. Macleod, *Quadrant*, XXII, No. 3, 1978, 75-76; C. Pollnitz, *Southerly*, XXXVII, 1977, 452-53; L.V. Robinson, *LiNQ*, V, No. 3, 1977, 75-76; T. Thorne, *Weekend Australian Magazine*, 14-15 January, 1978, 7; J. Tulip, *Age*, 19 February, 1977, 17.

Selected Poems. (St Lucia: U.Q.P., 1981).
Reviewed by P. Neilsen, *Age*, 26 December, 1981, 14; G. Page, *Quadrant*, XXVI, No. 8, 1982, 75-76; G. Rowlands, *Overland*, No. 88, 1982, 66-67; P. Steele, *ABR*, No. 46, 1982, 22-23.

This Real Pompeii. (Brisbane: Jacaranda Press, 1964).
Reviewed by E.A.M. Colman, *Poetry Magazine*, No. 1, 1965, 27-8; R. Dunlop, *Poetry Australia*, No. 1, 1965, 23-5; D. Hewett, *Overland*, No. 32, 1965, 46-7; R. Hodge, *Westerly*, No. 4, 1964, 59-60; E. Jones, *Australian*, 13 March, 1965, 11; F. Kellaway, *ABR*, III, 1964, 253; S.E. Lee, *Southerly*, XXV, No. 2, 1965, 132-3; G. Lehmann, *Bulletin*, 24 October, 1964, 56.

Words For a Journey: Poems 1970-1985. (Carlton, Vic.: M.U.P., 1986).
Reviewed by H. Heseltine, *Overland*, No. 105, 1986, 46-53; E. Jones, *Phoenix Review*, No. 3, 1988, 116-118; P. Neilsen, *Age Saturday Extra*, 12 July, 1986, 12; V. O'Sullivan, *Meanjin*, XLVI, No. 3, 1987, 347-354; esp. 352-353; K. Russell, *Quadrant*, XXXI, Nos. 1-2, 1987, 109-115; esp. 110.

Critical Material

'Interview'. *Image* (Brisbane), III, No. 4, 1979, 3-5.

Catalano, Gary. 'Spiralling Ghosts: The Poetry of R.A. Simpson'. *Quadrant*, 37.9, 1993, 65-68.
Page, Geoff. 'R.A. Simpson'. In his *A Reader's Guide To Contemporary Australian Poetry* (St. Lucia: U.Q.P., 1995), 267-269.
Riddell, Elizabeth. 'Alone with His Visions'. *Australian*, 7 February, 1970, 19.
Sayers, Stuart. 'The Poems Began in Rome'. *Age*, 28 January, 1978, 25.

SINNETT, FREDERICK

Critical Material
The Fiction Fields of Australia. Edited by C.H. Hadgraft. (Brisbane: U.Q.P., 1966). First published anonymously in *Illustrated Journal of Australia*, 1, 1856, 97-105, 199-208. Reprinted in *The Writer in Australia*, edited by John Barnes (Melbourne: O.U.P., 1969), 8-32.
Reviewed by J. Alderson, *Clanalder Sennachie*, No. 41, 1967, 5; B. Elliott, *ABR*, VI, 1967, 68; G.A.W., *Southerly*, XXVII, 1967, 142-143.

SKINNER, M.L.

Fiction
With D.H. Lawrence. *The Boy in the Bush*. Preface by Harry T. Moore. (South Melbourne: Macmillan, 1980). First published London: Secker, 1924.
Reviewed by D. Allen, *National Times*, 28 December-3 January, 1981, 37; M. Dunlevy, *Canberra Times*, 6 January, 1973, 8; P. Eggert *ABR*, No. 31, 1981, 23; T. Forshaw, *S.M.H.*, 3 February, 1973, 25; P. Jones, *Ash Magazine*, No. 7, 1981, 29-30; S. Ruddell, *Canberra Times*, 31 January, 1981, 17; J. Waten, *Age*, 20 January, 1973, 19.
With D.H. Lawrence. *The Boy in the Bush*. Edited by Paul Eggert. (Cambridge; New York; Melbourne: Cambridge UP, 1990).
Reviewed by D. Carter, *Weekend Australian*, 27-28 April, 1991, Review 6; B. Steele, *Overland*, 123, 1991, 88-90.

Non-Fiction
The Fifth Sparrow: An Autobiography. With a foreword by Mary Durack [Edited by Mary Durack and Marjorie Rees]. (Sydney: Sydney University Press, 1972). Reviewed by M. Dunlevy, *Canberra Times*, 6 January, 1973, 8; N. Keesing, *Southerly*, XXXIII, 1973, 86-88; W.A. Murray, *ABR*, XI, 1972, 36-37; A.A. Phillips, *Nation Review*, 16-22 December, 1972, 295; O. Ruhen, *Australian*, 9 December, 1972, 37; *T.L.S.*, 1 June, 1973, 625; J. Waten, *Age*, 20 January, 1973, 19; M. Williams, *S.M.H.*, 3 March, 1973, 25.

Critical Material
Bartlett, Norman. 'Mollie Skinner and *The Boy in the Bush*'. *Quadrant*, XXVIII, Nos. 7-8, 1984, 73-75.
Eggert, Paul. 'Lawrence, The Secret Army, and the West Australian Connexion: Molly Skinner'. *Westerly*, XXVII, No. 4, 1982, 123-26. Discusses Robert Darroch. *D.H. Lawrence in Australia*.
---. 'The Literary work of a Readership: *The Boy in the Bush* in Australia, 1924-1926'. *Bibliographical Society of Australia and New Zealand Bulletin*, 12, No. 4, 1988 (issued 1990), 149-66.
Martin, Sylvia. 'Mollie Skinner: Quaker Spinster and "The Witch of Wellaway"'. In *The Time to Write: Australian Women Writers 1890-1930* edited by Kay Ferres (Ringwood, Vic.: Penguin, 1993), 200-17.
Newman, Joan. 'Constructing the Self: Mollie Skinner'. *Hecate* (special issue *Women/Australia/Theory)* 17.1, 1991, 79-87.

SLESSOR, KENNETH

Collection

Kenneth Slessor: Poetry, Essays, War Despatches, War Diaries, Journalism, Autobiographical Material and Letters. Edited by Dennis Haskell. (St. Lucia: U.Q.P., 1991).
Reviewed by L. Jacobs, *CRNLE Reviews Journal*, 1, 1992, 90-93; H. Jaffa *Antipodes*, 6.2, 1992, 159-61.

Poetry

Backless Betty from Bondi. (Sydney: A.& R., 1983).
Reviewed by B. Kennedy, *Weekend Australian Magazine*, 27-28 August, 1983, 14; M. Lord, *ABR*, No. 68, 1984, 18.

Collected Poems. Edited by Dennis Haskell and Geoffrey Dutton. (Pymble, NSW: A.& R., 1994). Reviewed by H.C. Jaffa, *Antipodes*, 9.1, 1995, 53-54; T. Shapcott, *ABR*, 173, 1995, 49-50.

Darlinghurst Nights. Drawings by Virgil Reilly. (Sydney: A.& R., 1981). First published Sydney: F.C. Johnson, 1932.
Reviewed by B. Kennedy, *Weekend Australian Magazine*, 4-5 July, 1981, 11; M. Lord, *ABR*, No. 37, 1981, 33-34.

Poems. With an introduction by Clement Semmler and notes by the author. (Sydney: A.& R., 1972). Reprinted as *Selected Poems* (Sydney: A.& R., 1975). First published as *One Hundred Poems: 1919-1939* (Sydney: A.& R., 1944).

Non-Fiction

Bread and Wine: Selected Prose. (Sydney: A.& R., 1970). Reviewed by K. England, *Advertiser*, 1 August, 1970, 76; A.M. Gibbs, *A.L.S.*, IV, 1970, 410-12; N. Keesing, *Bulletin*, 6 June, 1970, 52; S. Lawson, *Australian*, 2 May, 1970, 20; J.D. Pringle, *S.M.H.*, 11 July, 1970, 21; J. Waten, *Age*, 2 May, 1970, 14.

The War Despatches of Kenneth Slessor. Edited by Clement Semmler. (St Lucia: U.Q.P., 1987).
Reviewed by A. Ashbolt, *S.M.H.*, 28 November, 1987, 87; K. Goodwin, *Australian Journal of Politics and History*, XXXIV, No. 2, 1988, 283-285; D. McNicoll, *Quadrant*, XXXII, Nos. 1-2, 1988, 117-118; M. Williams, *Age Saturday Extra*, 21 November, 1987, 18.

The War Diaries of Kenneth Slessor: Official Australian Correspondent, 1940-1944. Edited by Clement Semmler. (St Lucia: U.Q.P., 1985).
Reviewed by D.M. Davin, *PN Review*, XIII, No. 4, 1987, 73; M.Dunlevy, *Canberra Times*, 28 September, 1985, B2; G. Dutton, *Weekend Australian Magazine*, 19-20 October, 1985, 20; A. Gould, *Quadrant*, XXX, No. 5, 1986, 76-78; K. Hart, *ABR*, No. 82, 1986, 10-11; D. McCarthy, *S.M.H.*, 26 October, 1985, 46; D. McNicoll, *Bulletin*, 8 October, 1985, 82; B. Ord, *Sunday Mail* (Brisbane), 1 December, 1985, 34; G. Page, *Age Monthly Review*, VI, No. 1, 1986, 8-9; M. Williams, *Age Saturday Extra*, 5 October, 1985, 13.

'Australian Poetry and Hugh Mccrae'. In *Critical Essays on Kenneth Slessor*, edited by A.K. Thomson (Brisbane: Jacaranda, 1968), 172-83. Originally published in *Southerly*, XVII, 1956, 128-37.
'Australian Poetry and Norman Lindsay'. In *Critical Essays on Kenneth Slessor*, edited by A.K. Thomson (Brisbane: Jacaranda, 1968), 157-71. Originally published in *Southerly*, XVI, 1955, 62-72.
'Modern English Poetry'. *Southerly*, XXXI, 1971, 272-80. First published 1931. Reprinted in *Critical Essays on Kenneth Slessor*, edited by A.K. Thomson (Brisbane: Jacaranda, 1968), 139-146.
'The Poet Tells of the Birth of a Poem'. *Opinion*, XII, No. 3, 1968, 44-47. Discusses 'Five Visions of Captain Cook'.

'The Quality of Magic'. *Southerly*, XXXI, 1971, 249-55.
'Reply to Elliott'. In *Critical Essays on Kenneth Slessor*, edited by A.K. Thomson (Brisbane: Jacaranda, 1968), 65-66. Originally published in *Meanjin*, IV, 1945, 221-223. Reply to Elliott's review of *One Hundred Poems*.
'Spectacles For the Fifties'. In *Critical Essays on Kenneth Slessor*, edited by A.K. Thomson (Brisbane: Jacaranda, 1968), 86-90. Originally published on *Southerly*, XIII, 1952, 215-19.
'Writing Poetry: The Why and the How'. In *Critical Essays on Kenneth Slessor*, edited by A.K. Thomson (Brisbane: Jacaranda, 1968), 152-6. Originally published in *Southerly*, IX, 1948, 166-71.

Critical Material

Fryer Memorial Library of Australian Literature. 'Bibliography'. In *Critical Essays on Kenneth Slessor*, edited by A.K. Thomson (Brisbane: Jacaranda, 1968), 204-09.
'$99,000 Left by Poet to Son'. *S.M.H.*, 17 September, 1971, 10. Similar report in *Australian*, 17 September, 1971, 3.
'Kenneth Slessor, Poet and Gentleman . . . An Earth Visitor Moves on'. *Woman's Day*, 26 July, 1971, 7.
'Manuscripts: Kenneth Slessor'. *National Library of Australia Acquisitions Newsletter*, No. 11, 1972, 1.
'A Reputation That Endures'. *S.M.H.*, 1 July, 1971, 7. See also letter to the editor by Barbara Revill, *S.M.H.*, 12 July, 1971, 6.
'Tribute to Kenneth Slessor'. *Canberra Times*, 2 July, 1971, 13. Report of statement by Hon. P. Howson.
Aldington, Richard. 'Kenneth Slessor'. In *Critical Essays on Kenneth Slessor*, edited by A.K. Thomson (Brisbane: Jacaranda, 1968), 124-27. Originally published in *Australian Letters*, I, No. 3, 1958, 11-3.
Buckley, Vincent. 'The Poetry of Kenneth Slessor'. In *Critical Essays on Kenneth Slessor*, edited by A.K. Thomson (Brisbane: Jacaranda, 1968), 70-76. Originally published in *Meanjin*, XI, 1952, 23-30.
Burns, Graham. *Kenneth Slessor*. (Melbourne: O.U.P., 1975). Australian Writers and Their Work. Reviewed by J. Colmer, *A.L.S.*, VII, 1976, 440; C. James, *T.L.S.*, 9 April, 1976, 422; J. Waten, *Age*, 29 May, 1976, 22.
Burrows, Leonard. 'Kenneth Slessor. *Captain Dobbin*'. In *Australian Poems in Perspective*, edited by P.K. Elkin (St Lucia: U.Q.P., 1978), 51-74.
Caesar, Adrian. *Kenneth Slessor*. (Melbourne: O.U.P., 1995). Reviewed by A. Taylor, *Voices*, 5.4, 1995-96, 114-18; T. Shapcott, *ABR*, 173, 1995, 49-50.
Campbell, Ross. 'Ken Slessor, Noted Poet and Journalist, Dies'. *Daily Telegraph* (Sydney), 1 July, 1971, 10.
Cantrell, Leon. 'Slessor'. *Makar*, VII, No. 3, 1971, 1-3. Obituary.
Chien Chiao-ju. 'Some Notes on Slessor's "Music" Sequence'. *Southerly*, XLII, 1982, 398-405.
Croft, Julian. 'Notes on Slessor's "Five Visions"'. *A.L.S.*, IV, 1969, 172-74. Discusses his previous article in *A.L.S.* in relation to Slessor's in *Opinion*, XII, No. 3, 1968, 44-47.
---. 'The One Rip of Darkness: Time in Slessor's "Captain Dobbin" and "Out of Time"'. *Southerly*, XXXI, 1971, 307-15.
---. 'Slessor's "Five Visions of Captain Cook"'. *A.L.S.*, IV, 1969, 3-17.
---. 'The World Outside Time: Slessor's "Five Bells"'. *A.L.S.*, V, 1971, 121-32.
Dobrez, L.A.C. 'Portrait of the Man of Sentiment: Kenneth Slessor'. *Southerly*, XXXVII, 1977, 16-32.
Docker, John. 'Norman Lindsay, Kenneth Slessor and the Artist-Aristocracy'. In his *Australian Cultural Elites: Intellectual Traditions in Sydney and Melbourne*. (Sydney: A.& R., 1974), 22-41. Revised from *A.L.S.*, 1973.
Dunlevy, Maurice. 'Image of the Punctilious and Perfectionist Poet'. *Canberra Times*,

30 July, 1977, 12.
---. 'Kenneth Slessor Dies in Sydney'. *Canberra Times*, 1 July, 1971, 3.
Dutton, Geoffrey. '"Intellectualized Pornography": "Imperial Adam" and Kenneth Slessor'. *Southerly*, 49, No. 3, 1989, 383-90.
---. *Kenneth Slessor: A Biography*. (Ringwood, Vic.: Viking, 1991). Reviewed by R.F. Brissenden, *Weekend Australian*, 16-17 February, 1991, Review 7; J. Croft, *A.L.S.*, 15.3, 1992, 235-38; L. Jacobs, *CRNLE Reviews Journal*, 1, 1992, 94-97; H. C. Jaffa, *Antipodes*, 5.2, 1991, 91-95; N. Keesing, *Southerly*, 51.2, 1991, 311-16; H. McQueen, *ABR*, 128, 1991, 34-35; P. Mead, *Australian Society*, 10.3, 1991, 38-39; J.D. Pringle, *S.M.H.*, 2 February, 1991, 41; C. Semmler, *Overland*, 123, 1991, 65-69; Vivian Smith, *Quadrant*, 35.7-8, 1991, 107-09; C. Wallace-Crabbe, *Voices*, 1.1, 1991, 95-97.
---. 'Slessor & Biography: Decoding the Past'. *Voices*, 1.4, 1991, 81-92.
Elkin, P.K. 'Kenneth Slessor. *Five Bells*'. In *Australian Poems in Perspective*, edited by P.K. Elkin (St Lucia: U.Q.P., 1978), 75-87.
Elliott, Brian. 'Review of *One Hundred Poems 1919-1939*'. In *Critical Essays on Kenneth Slessor*, edited by A.K. Thomson (Brisbane: Jacaranda, 1968), 62-4. Originally published in *Meanjin*, IV, 1945, 135-7.
FitzGerald, Robert D. 'Kenneth Slessor'. *A.L.S.*, V, 1971, 115-20.
Frost, Alan. 'Captain James Cook and the "Passage into the Dark"'. *A.L.S.*, IV, 1970, 293-94.
Gordon, J.J. et al. *Notes on Kenneth Slessor's Poetry*, by J.J. Gordon, D.E. Sheridan & R.K. Sadler. (Sydney: Methuen, 1976).
Harris, Max. *Kenneth Slessor*. (Melbourne: Lansdowne Press, 1963). Australian Writers and their Work series.
Hart, Kevin. '"Differant Curioes"'. *Southerly*, 49, No. 2, 1989, 182-196.
Haskell, Dennis. 'Conceptions of Time and Death in the Work of Kenneth Slessor'. *Voices*, 1.1, 1991, 5-22.
---. 'A Cure of Souls, and Satin Boots: Kenneth Slessor as Satirist'. In his *Australian Poetic Satire*. Monograph 26. ([Townsville]: Foundation for Australian Literary Studies, James Cook U of North Queensland, 1995), 22-43.
---. 'Hyperborea vs Uninteresting Facts: Kenneth Slessor's Journalism in the Early 1920s'. *Southerly*, 52.4, 1992, 15-29.
---. '"My Rather Tedious Hero": A Portrait of Kenneth Slessor'. *Westerly*, 36.3, 1991, 27-36.
---. '"The Nothing ... neither long nor short": Attitudes to Death in the Work of Kenneth Slessor'. In *Reconnoitres: Essays in Australian Literature in Honour of G.A. Wilkes*, edited by Margaret Harris and Elizabeth Webby (South Melbourne: O.U.P. in association with Sydney U.P., 1992), 115-27.
---. 'Sheer Voice and Fidget Wheels: A Study of "Five Bells"'. *A.L.S.*, XIII, No. 3, 253-265.
Hope, A.D. 'Slessor 20 Years After'. *Bulletin*, 1 January, 1963, 37-8.
Hope, A.D. 'Slessor Twenty Years After'. In *Critical Essays on Kenneth Slessor*, edited by A.K. Thomson (Brisbane: Jacaranda, 1968), 128-30. Originally published in *The Bulletin*, 1 June, 1963, 37-38. Review of *Poems* (Sydney: A.& R., 1963).
Howarth, R.G. 'Sound in Slessor's Poetry'. In *Critical Essays on Kenneth Slessor*, edited by A.K. Thomson (Brisbane: Jacaranda, 1968), 95-103. Originally published in *Southerly*, XVI, 1955, 189-96.
Jaffa, Herbert C. *Kenneth Slessor*. (New York: Twayne, 1971). Twayne's World Authors series, 145. Reviewed by B.A. Breen, *Opinion*, XV, No. 4, 1971, 38-39; D. Green, *Nation Review*, 7-13 April, 1977, 600; C. Harrison-Ford, *Sunday Australian*, 16 January, 1972, 20; R. McCuaig, *A.L.S.*, V, 1971, 200-205; T. I. Moore, *Meanjin*, XXX, 1971, 471-73; C. Semmler, *S.M.H.*, 26 June, 1971, 22; R.A. Simpson, *Age*, 16 October, 1971, 16; D. Stewart, *Southerly*, XXXI, 1971, 316-17; J. Waten, *Age*,

16 July, 1977, 23.

---. 'Aspects of Modern Poetry: Kenneth Slessor, 1901-1971'. *Poet Lore*, LXVIII, 1973, 191-99.

Keesing, Nancy. 'Kenneth Slessor'. *Australian Author*, III, No. 4, 1971, 5-6.

Kirkpatrick, Peter. 'Joe Lynch, Bohemian Hero of "Five Bells"'. *A.L.S.*, XIII, No. 3, 1988, 365-369.

---. 'An Uncollected Poem by Kenneth Slessor'. *A.L.S.*, 15.3, 1992, 213-16.

Kramer, Leonie. 'The Landscapes of Slessor's Poetry'. *Southerly*, XXXVII, 1977, 3-14.

Lindsay, Jack. 'Aids to Vision'. In *Critical Essays on Kenneth Slessor*, edited by A.K. Thomson (Brisbane: Jacaranda, 1968), 91-2. Originally published in *Southerly*, XIV, 1953, 204-5.

---. 'Vision of the Twenties'. In *Critical Essays on Kenneth Slessor*, edited by A.K. Thomson (Brisbane: Jacaranda, 1968), 77-85. Originally published in *Southerly*, XIII, 1952, 62-71.

Lindsay, Norman. 'Reflections on *Vision*'. In *Critical Essays on Kenneth Slessor*, edited by A.K. Thomson (Brisbane: Jacaranda, 1968), 93-4. Originally published in *Southerly*, XIV, 1953, 267-9.

Macainsh, Noel. 'Aestheticism and Reality in the Poetry of Kenneth Slessor'. *Westerly*, XXVII, No. 1, 1982, 31-41.

---. 'Kenneth Slessor and the "Image of Actual Experience"'. *Southerly*, XL, 1980, 439-49.

Macartney, F.T. 'The Poetry of Kenneth Slessor'. In *Critical Essays on Kenneth Slessor*, edited by A.K. Thomson (Brisbane: Jacaranda, 1968), 104-12. Originally published in *Meanjin*, XVI, 1957, 265-72. Review of *Poems* (Sydney: A.& R., 1957).

Macdonald, Alexander. 'Requiem for a Poet'. In his *The Ukulele Player under the Red Lamp*. (Sydney: A.& R., 1972), 250-65. Reviewed by J.D. Pringle, *S.M.H.*, 11 November, 1972, 20. See also letters to the editor by C. Pearl and A. Macdonald, *S.M.H.*, 17 November, 1972, 7.

McCrae, Hugh. 'Kenneth Slessor's Poetry'. In *Critical Essays on Kenneth Slessor*, edited by A.K. Thomson (Brisbane: Jacaranda, 1968), 59-61. Originally published in *Australian Quarterly*, XII, No. 3, 1940, 95-97.

McAuley, James. 'An Imprint of Slessor'. *Quadrant*, XVII, No. 1, 1973, 5-10.

---. 'On Some of Slessor's Discarded Poems'. *Southerly*, XXXIII, 1973, 118-28.

McCallum, Gerald. 'Slessor's Cook: The Imprudent Hero'. *AL.S.*, V, 1971, 176-78.

McCuaig, Ronald. 'An Afternoon and Evening with Kenneth Slessor'. *Australian Literary Quarterly*, 3-4 October, 1987, 12.

---. 'Kenneth Slessor's Poetry'. In *Critical Essays on Kenneth Slessor*, edited by A.K. Thomson (Brisbane: Jacaranda, 1968), 52-58. Originally published in his *Tales Out of Bed* (Sydney: Allied Authors and Artists, 1944), 87-94.

McGregor, Craig. 'Conversation with Kenneth Slessor'. *S.M.H.*, 30 October, 1965, 18.

Maidment, W.M. 'Australian Literary Criticism'. *Southerly*, XXIV, 1964, 20-41.

Malouf, David. 'Where in the World was Kenneth Slessor? A Personal View of the Slessor Tribute at the Adelaide Writers' Week, 1974'. *Southerly*, XXXIV, 1974, 202-06.

Mitchell, A.C.W. 'Kenneth Slessor and the Grotesque'. *A.L.S.*, I, No. 4, 1964, 242-50. Reprinted in *Critical Essays on Kenneth Slessor*, edited by A.K. Thomson (Brisbane: Jacaranda, 1968), 131-38.

---. 'On the Personal Element in Kenneth Slessor's Poetry'. *Antipodes*, 5.2, 1991, 84-90.

Moore, T. Inglis. 'Kenneth Slessor'. In *Critical Essays on Kenneth Slessor*, edited by A.K. Thomson (Brisbane: Jacaranda, 1968), 113-23. Originally published in *Southerly*, VIII, 1947, 194-205.

Olsen, John. *Salute to Five Bells: John Olsen's Opera House Journal*. Photographs by Robert Walker (Sydney: A.& R., 1973). Includes foreword by Laurie Thomas and an essay and a poem by Douglas Stewart.

Palmos, Frank. 'Kenneth Slessor - A View from Knee-High, 1955-1959'. *Westerly*, 36.3, 1991, 37-39.

Poole, Gaye. 'Casebook: *Darlinghurst Nights*'. *Australasian Drama Studies*, Nos. 12 & 13, 1988, 102-123.

Porter, Hal. *The Extra*. (Melbourne: Thomas Nelson (Australia), 1975), 85-108. Reminiscences. An extract was published as 'Wine, Wives and Ham on the Bone'. *Bulletin*, 13 September, 1975, 48-51. See also letter from Robin C. Slessor, *Bulletin*, 18 October, 1975, 5.

---. 'Melbourne in the Thirties'. *The London Magazine*, V, No. 6, 1965, 31-47.

Pringle, John Douglas. 'Poets' Corner'. *Quadrant*, XV, No. 4, 1971, 65-66. See also letter to the editor by Nancy Keesing, 'Kenneth Slessor', *Quadrant*, XV, No. 6, 1971, 5-60.

Riddell, Elizabeth. 'Pioneer Poet Who Just Couldn't Help Writing'. *Australian*, 1 July, 1971, 11.

Riem, Antonella. 'Kenneth Slessor's Stylistic Elegance'. In her *The Labyrinths of Self: A Collection of Essays on Australian and Caribbean Literature*. (Leichhardt, N.S.W.: FILEF. Italo-Australian Publications, 1987), 111-123, 161-167.

Rowe, Noel. *Modern Australian Poets*. (Sydney: Sydney UP in assoc. with O.U.P., 1994). Includes discussion of the poetry of Slessor.

Semmler, Clement. *Kenneth Slessor*. (Melbourne: Longmans in association with the British Council, 1966). Writers and Their Work Series, No. 194. Reviewed by M. Armitage, *Adelaide Advertiser*, 17 June, 1967, 20; B. Beaver, *S.M.H.*, 6 May, 1967, 16; B. Elliott, *ABR*, VI, 1967, 103; W. Grono, *Westerly*, No. 4, 1966, 47-53; R. Hall, *Australian*, 4 March, 1967, 8; H. Heseltine, *A.L.S.*, III, 1967, 72-73; S. Lawson, *Nation*, 28 January, 1967, 21; T.W. Shapcott, *Bulletin*, 17 December, 1966, 48-9.

---. 'Poetry in Australia, Kenneth Slessor'. *Southerly*, XXVI, 1966, 190-8. Transcript of an interview by John Thompson telecast, 7 November, 1962.

---. 'Slessor and Eliot: Some Personal Musings'. *Southerly*, XXXI, 1971, 267-71.

---. 'War Correspondents in Australian Literature: an Outline'. *A.L.S.*, XII, No. 2, 1985, 194-206.

---. 'What Kenneth Slessor was Writing During his 30 Silent Years'. *National Times*, 27 September-2 October, 1976, 26-27.

Shephard, L.I. 'Poetry with New Vision'. In *Critical Essays on Kenneth Slessor*, edited by A.K. Thomson (Brisbane: Jacaranda, 1968), 67-69. Originally published in *Australasian Book News*, II, 1948, 341-2, 359.

Slessor, Robert C. 'Some Personal Notes'. *Southerly*, XXXI, 1971, 243-47.

Smith, Graeme Kinross. 'Kenneth Slessor'. *Westerly*, No. 2, 1978, 51-59.

Smith, Vivian. 'The Ambivalence of Kenneth Slessor'. *Southerly*, XXXI, 1971, 256-66.

---. 'Australian Modernism: The Case of Kenneth Slessor'. In *Reconnoitres: Essays in Australian Literature in Honour of G.A. Wilkes*, edited by Margaret Harris and Elizabeth Webby (South Melbourne: O.U.P. in association with Sydney U.P., 1992), 128-41.

Spurr, Barry. *The Poetry of Kenneth Slessor*. (Glebe, NSW: Pascal P, 1994).

Stewart, Douglas. *A Man of Sydney: An Appreciation of Kenneth Slessor*. (Melbourne: Thomas Nelson (Australia), 1977). Reviewed by R. Campbell, *Bulletin*, 23 July, 1977, 55; J. Croft, *A.L.S.*, IX, 1979, 127-28; G. Dutton, *24 Hours*, II, No. 9, 1977, 53-54; D. Green, *Nation Review*, 8-14 September, 1977, 16; A.A. Phillips, *Overland*, No. 69, 1978, 74-75; I. Reid, *Advertiser*, 20 August, 1977, 26; C. Semmler, *S.M.H.*, 30 July, 1977, 17; V. Smith, *Quadrant*, XXI, No. 9, 1977, 74.

---. 'Kenneth Slessor's Poetry'. *Meanjin*, XXVIII, 1969, 149-68.
---. 'Kenneth Slessor's Prose'. *Southerly*, XXXV, 1975, 112-31.
---. 'A Portrait of Kenneth Slessor'. *Southerly*, XXXIV, 1974, 323-41.
---. 'Slessor and "Vision"'. *Quadrant*, XIX, No. 4, 1975, 68-76.
---. 'Slessor: More to Come?'. *Sunday Australian*, 11 July, 1971, 22.
Sturm, T.L. 'Kenneth Slessor's Poetry and Norman Lindsay'. *Southerly*, XXXI, 1971, 281-306.
Taylor, Andrew. 'Kenneth Slessor's Approach to Modernism'. In his *Reading Australian Poetry*. (St Lucia: U.Q.P., 1987), 53-69.
Thomson, A.K. (ed.). *Critical Essays on Kenneth Slessor*. (Brisbane: Jacaranda, 1968). Articles are listed under authors' names. Reviewed by J. Croft, *A.L.S.*, IV, 1969, 193-96.
---. 'Kenneth Slessor: An Essay in Interpretation'. In *Critical Essays on Kenneth Slessor*, edited by A.K. Thomson (Brisbane: Jacaranda, 1968), 1-51.
Thomson, A.K. and Sherry, Bev. 'Appendix: An Analysis of "Music"'. In *Critical Essays on Kenneth Slessor*, edited by A.K. Thomson (Brisbane: Jacaranda, 1968), 184-203.
Wallace-Crabbe, Chris. 'Kenneth Slessor and the Powers of Language'. In *The Literature of Australia*, edited by Geoffrey Dutton (Adelaide: Penguin Books, 1964), 342-52.
Watson, K.D. 'Slessor and Cleveland: A Footnote to "Adventure Bay"'. *A.L.S.*, V, 1971, 179.
Wright, Judith. 'Kenneth Slessor - Romantic and Modern'. In her *Preoccupations in Australian Poetry*, (Melbourne: O.U.P., 1965), 140-53; and passim.

SMITH, HAZEL

Poetry
Abstractly Represented: Poems and Performance Texts 1982-1990. (Springwood, NSW: Butterfly Books, 1991).
Reviewed by H. Cam, *S.M.H.*, 16 November, 1991, 48; K. Brophy, *ABR*, 138, 1992, 40-42; J. Owen, *Quadrant*, 36, 1992, 83-85.

Critical Material
Wallace, Joy. '"In the game I make of sense": The Poetry of Hazel Smith'. *Southerly*, 55.4, 1995, 136-46.

SMITH, JAMES

Critical Material
A Very Busy Smith: An Annotated Checklist of the Works of James Smith: Nineteenth-century Melbourne Journalist and Critic. Compiled and introduced by Lurline Stuart. (Clayton, Vic.: Centre for Bibliographical and Textual Studies / National Centre for Australian Studies, Monash U, 1992).
Stuart, Lurline. *James Smith: The Making of a Colonial Culture*. (North Sydney: Allen & Unwin, 1989). Reviewed by J. Davidson, *Australian Historical Studies*, 24.96, 1991, 248-50; V. Kelly, *A.L.S.*, 14.3, 1990, 408-12; G. Melleuish, *ABR*, 114, 1989, 44-45; J. Rickard, *Australian Society*, 8.8, 1989, 43; G. Shaw, *Australian Journal of Politics and History*, 36.3, 1990, 461-62; K. Stewart, *Weekend Australian*, 7-8 October, 1990, Weekend 10.

SMITH, VIVIAN

Poetry
Familiar Places. (Sydney: A.& R., 1978). Poets of the Month, Series 4.
Reviewed by R. Claremont, *Quadrant*, XXIII, No. 7, 1979, 71; E. Lindsay, *24 Hours*, III, No. 12, 1979, 65; E. Perkins, *LiNQ*, Nos. 2-3, 1979, 112-13.

An Island South. (Sydney: A.& R., 1967).
Reviewed by D. Anderson, *Australian Highway*, XLVII, No. 3, 1967, 15-16; B. Beaver, *S.M.H.*, 18 November, 1967, 21; A. Brissenden, *Adelaide Advertiser*, 14 October, 1967, 14; R. Dunlop, *Poetry Australia*, No. 20, 1968, 42; W. Hart-Smith, *Poetry Magazine*, No. 3, 1968, 33-35; M. Irvin, *Twentieth Century*, XXII, 1967, 186-88; G. Johnston, *Bulletin*, 4 November, 1967, 83-84; A. King, *Meanjin*, XXVII, 1968, 183; T.I. Moore, *Canberra Times*, 11 November, 1967, 13; A. Taylor, *Overland*, No. 38, 1968, 45; J. Tulip, *Southerly*, XXVIII, 1968, 73-74; R. Ward, *ABR*, VI, 1967, 197.

New Selected Poems. (Sydney: A.& R., 1995).
Reviewed by M. Costigan, *ABR*, 170, 1995, 53; H.C. Jaffa, *Antipodes*, 9.2, 1995, 163-65; D. Leadbetter, *Overland*, 141, 1995, 86-88.

Selected Poems. (North Ryde, N.S.W.: A.& R., 1985).
Reviewed by B. Beaver, *Weekend Australian Magazine*, 21-22 December, 1985, 13; G. Bitcon, *Southerly*, XLV, No. 3, 1985, 352-359; G. Catalano, *Meanjin*, XLV, No. 1, 1986, 103-06; M. Haig, *Age Monthly Review*, V, No. 7, 1985, 11-13; M. Hulse, *PN Review*, No. 69, 1989, 52-53; M. Jurgensen, *Outrider*, III, No. 1, 1986, 170-172; J. Strauss, *Overland*, No. 103, 1986, 62-63.

Tide Country. (Sydney: A.& R., 1982).
Reviewed by G. Dutton, *Bulletin*, 14 June, 1983, 76 & 78; B. Giles, *ABR*, No. 47, 1982, 28-29; K. Goldsworthy, *Age Saturday Extra*, 23 July, 1983, 12; C. Koch, *National Times*, 26 September-2 October, 1982, 21; E. Perkins, *Quadrant*, XXVII, No. 3, 1983, 79-81; M. Scott, *Island Magazine*, No. 15, 1983, 49-53.

Non-Fiction

'Tasmanian Artists'. *Island Magazine*, No. 36, 1988, 77-79. Includes autobiograhical comment.
'Translating: Some Personal Notes'. *Outrider*, III, No. 1, 1986, 37-40.

Critical Material

Catalano, Gary. 'Vivian Smith'. *Quadrant*, 39.12, 1995, 57-60.
Gaffney, Carmel. 'The Poetry of Vivian Smith: "A Sense of Sure Precision"'. *Quadrant*, 33, No. 7, 1989, 61-65.
Harrex, Syd. 'Island Lyrics: Vivian Smith, Gwen Harwood and James McAuley'. *Island Magazine*, Nos. 25-26, 1986, 67-73.
Irvin, Margaret. '"That Subtle Country of My Heart": The Poetry of *The Other Meaning*'. *Poetry Magazine*, No. 1, 1969, 33-36.
McCooey, David. 'An Interview with Vivian Smith'. *A.L.S.*, 17.2, 1995, 182-86.
——. 'Still Life: Art and Nature in Vivian Smith's Poetry'. *A.L.S.*, 17.2, 1995, 157-65.
Page, Geoff. 'Vivian Smith'. In his *A Reader's Guide To Contemporary Australian Poetry* (St. Lucia: U.Q.P., 1995), 278-281.
Rama, R.P. '[Interview with] Vivian Smith'. In *Dialogues with Australian Poets* (Calcutta: P. Lal/Writers Workshop, 1993), 87-97.
Rowe, Noel. 'Patience and Surprise: The Poetry of Vivian Smith'. *Southerly*, XLVI, No. 2, 1986, 178-94.

SOUTHALL, IVAN

Fiction

Ash Road. (Sydney: A.& R., 1965).
Reviewed by K. Commins, *S.M.H.*, 13 November, 1965, 21; C. Green, *Overland*, 36, 1967, 46; D. Hall, *ABR*, 5, 1965-66, 45.

Blackbird. (Port Melbourne, Vic.: Mammoth Australia, 1992).
Reviewed by A. Nieuwenhuizen, *Age*, 4 April, 1992, Saturday Extra 8.

Bread and Honey. (Sydney: A.& R., 1970).

Reviewed by A. Bower Ingram, *S.M.H.*, 10 July, 1971, 24; R. Brekvist, *New York Times Book Review*, 2 May, 1971, 14; N. Donkin, *Australian*, 10 July, 1971, 24; D. Dugan, *Age*, 12 January, 1971, 12; H. Schoenheimer, *The Review*, 16 July, 1971, 1137.

Chinaman's Reef is Ours. (Sydney: A.& R., 1970).
Reviewed by A. Bower Ingram, *S.M.H.*, 5 September, 1970, 20; D. Dugan, *Age*, 8 August, 1970, 16; M. Saxby, *Australian*, 12 December, 1970, 28.

Christmas in the Tree. (Sydney, Hodder & Stoughton, 1985).
Reviewed by S. McInerney, *S.M.H.*, 15 February, 1986, 47.

A City Out of Sight. (Sydney: A.& R., 1985; Ringwood, Vic.: Puffin, 1986).
Reviewed by S. Hayes, *T.L.S.*, 29 March, 1985, 347; S. McInerney, *S.M.H.*, 30 August, 1986, 43; M. Saxby, *ABR*, 69, 1985, 22.

The Curse of Cain. (Sydney: A.& R., 1968).
Reviewed by K. Commins, *S.M.H.*, 8 June, 1968, 20; J. Kimber, *ABR*, 3, 1968, 169.

Finn's Folly. (Sydney: A.& R., 1969).
Reviewed by *T.L.S.*, 3 April, 1969, 349; K. Commins, *S.M.H.*, 9 August, 1969, 18; A. Bower Ingram, *S.M.H.*, 11 July, 1970, 23; M. Saxby, *Australian*, 11 July, 1970, 23.

Fly West. (Sydney: A.& R., 1975).
Reviewed by P. Dowling *24 Hours*, 1.5, 1976, 55-56; D. Dugan, *Age*, 7 June, 1975, 18; T.W.Millett, *Australian*, 30 August, 1975, 30; P.T. Plowman, *Bulletin*, 19 April, 1975, 47.

The Fox Hole. (London, Sydney: Methuen, 1967, reprinted 1980; London: Pan, 1972).
Reviewed by M. Dunkle, *ABR*, 26, 1980, 16; D. Hall, *ABR*, 7, 1968, 72-73; A. Bower Ingram, *S.M.H.*, 27 November, 1972, 23.

The Golden Goose. (Sydney: Methuen, 1981).
Reviewed by M. Dunkle, *ABR*, 39, 1982, 27-29; M. Maher, *Idiom*, 17.2, 1982, 25; A. Thwaite, *T.L.S.*, 20 November, 1981, 1356.

Head in the Clouds. (London, Sydney: A.& R., 1973).
Reviewed by R. Crossley-Holland, *Spectator*, 14 April, 1973, 230; A. Bower Ingram, *S.M.H.*, 7 April, 1973, 23; D. Orgel, *New York Times Book Review*, 29 April, 1973, 10.

Indonesian Journey. (Melbourne: Lansdowne, 1966).
Reviewed by A. Ashbolt, *ABR*, 4.5, 1965, 80; K. Commins, *S.M.H.*, 4 December, 1965, 19; D. Hall, *ABR*, 5, 1966, 70.

Josh. (Sydney: A.& R., 1971).
Reviewed by N. Babbitt, *New York Times Book Review*, 15 October, 1972, 8; D. Dugan, *Age*, 20 November, 1971, 11; R. Park, *Sunday Australian*, 30 January, 1972, 23; A. Thwaite, *New Statesman*, 12 November, 1971, 660-62: *T.L.S.*, 22 October, 1971, 1319.

King of the Sticks. (Sydney: Collins, 1979).
Reviewed by L. Anderson, *Words'worth*, 13.1, 1980, 52-53; M. Dunkle, *ABR*, 24, 1980, 31; D. Oberg, *Words'worth*, 15.1, 1982, 48; E. Stodart, *Weekend Australian Magazine*, 12-13 July, 1980, 14.

Let The Balloon Go. (London: Methuen/Hicks Smith, 1969).
Reviewed by K. Commins, *S.M.H.*, 12 July, 1969, 21; D. Hall, *ABR*, 8.2-3, 1968-69, 48-49.

The Long Night Watch. (London, Sydney: Methuen, 1983).
Reviewed by D. Hibberd, *T.L.S.*, 24 February, 1984, 202; W. McVitty, *Age*, 24 March, 1984, Saturday Extra 14; P. Skene-Catling, *Spectator*, 10 December, 1983,

30-31.

Matt and Jo. (London, Sydney: A.& R., 1973).
Reviewed by A. Carter, *T.L.S.*, 6 December, 1974, 1373; D. Dugan, *Age*, 12 January, 1974, 14; A. Bower Ingram, *S.M.H.*, 9 March, 1974, 13; C. Odell, *National Times*, 10-15 December, 1973, 31.
Over the Top. (London: Methuen, 1972; New York: Macmillan [as *Benson Boy*], 1972).
Reviewed by D. Dugan, *Age*, 29 July, 1972, 12 and 9 December, 1972, 18; A. Bower Ingram, *S.M.H.*, 14 October, 1972, 23; D. Orgel, *New York Times Book Review*, 29 April, 1973, 10; *T.L.S.*, 14 July, 1972, 803; R. Wighton, *ABR*, 11, 1972, 46-47.
Rachel. (North Ryde, NSW: A.& R., 1986).
Reviewed by S. McInerney, *S.M.H.*, 30 August, 1986, 43; *ABR*, 89, 1987, 26-27.
To the Wild Sky. (Sydney, A.& R., 1967, reprinted 1977; Hyde Park, SA: Peacock, 1981).
Reviewed by D. Dugan, *Age Literary Supplement*, 20 May, 1967, 23 and *Age*, 13 August, 1977, 26; D. Hall, *ABR*, 6, 1967, 104; H. Frizell, *S.M.H.*, 10 December, 1977, 19; H. Hume, *Australian Weekend Magazine*, 30-31 July, 1977, 13; W. McVitty, *Nation Review*, 18-24 August, 1977, 17; D. Oberg, *Words'worth*, 15.1, 1982, 48; N. Tucker, *T.L.S.*, 15 July, 1977, 861; P. Young, *National Times*, 15 July, 1978, 25.

   Non-Fiction
'An Inner Life Style'. In *The Written World: Youth and Literature*, edited by Agnes Nieuwenhuizen (Port Melbourne, Vic.: D.W. Thorpe, 1994), 55-68.
'Function and Purposes: A Statement by a Writer for Children'. *ABR*, 8, 1969. 165-66.
A Journey of Discovery: On Writing for Children. (Ringwood, Vic.: Penguin, 1975).
Reviewed by H. Frizell, *S.M.H.*, 1 May, 1976, 16; R. Wighton, *24 Hours*, 1.1, 1976, 41-42; B. Ker Wilson, *Age*, 6 December, 1975, 21.
'Key to Being Human'. *Australian Library News*, 6.8, 1976, 3. Text of a talk on books and reading.
Seventeen Seconds. (Sydney: Hodder & Stoughton, 1974). Special edition for young people of *Softly Tread the Brave* (Sydney: A.& R., 1960).
Reviewed by D. Dugan, *Age*, 17 November, 1973, 13; A. Bower Ingram, *S.M.H.*, 6 October, 1973, 23; W. McVitty, *Nation Review*, 25-31 January, 1974, 474.

   Critical Material
Hetherington, John. 'Ivan Southall: The Riddle and the Answer'. In his *Forty-Two Faces* (Melbourne: F.W. Cheshire, 1962), 207-13.
Hosking, Rick. 'The Usable Past: Australian War Fiction of the 1950s'. *ALS*, 12.2, 1985, 234-47.
Ingram, Anne Bower. 'Ivan Southall: The Novelist'. *Australian Postwar Novelists*, edited by Nancy Keesing (Brisbane: Jacaranda P, 1975), 124-28.
McCorry, P. 'Growing Up Male: Ivan Southall's View'. *Refractory Girl*, 4, 1973, 37-40.
McVitty, Walter. 'Ivan Southall: Wounding and Regeneration'. In his *Innocence and Experience: Essays on Contemporary Australian Children's Writers* (Melbourne: Thomas Nelson Australia, 1981), 233-72. Includes notes by Southall and bibliography.
Nieuwenhuizen, Agnes. 'Interview with Ivan Southall'. *Meanjin*, 51.3, 1992, 653-59.
Pausacker, Jenny. 'Not under Glass: The Novels of Ivan Southall'. *Meanjin*, 51.3, 1992, 660-69.

SPENCE, CATHERINE HELEN

Collection
Catherine Helen Spence. Edited with an introduction by Helen Thomson. (St Lucia: U.Q.P., 1987). Portable Australian Authors.
Reviewed by L. Frost, *ABR*, No. 92, 1987, 20-22; N. Keesing, *S.M.H.*, 30 May, 1987, 48; S. Magarey, *Times on Sunday*, 31 May, 1987, 32; J. Roe, *A.L.S.*, XIII, No. 2, 1987, 242-245; D.J. Tacey, *Meridian*, 9, No. 1, 1990, 60-62.

Fiction
Clara Morison. Introduction by Susan Eade (Adelaide: Rigby, 1971). Seal Australian Fiction. First published London: John W. Parker, 1854.
Reviewed by B.H. Bennett, *A.L.S.*, VI, 1973, 220-24; J. Wightman, *Meanjin*, XXXIII, 1974, 89-92.

Clara Morison: A Tale of Australia During the Gold Fever. Introduction and Notes by Susan Magarey (Adelaide: Wakefield Press, 1986). First published London: John W. Parker, 1854.
Reviewed by D.J. Tacey, *Meridian*, 9, No. 1, 1990, 60-62.

Gathered In. Introduction by B.L. Waters and G.A. Wilkes (Sydney: Sydney University Press, 1977). Australian Literary Reprints. First book publication.
Reviewed by N. Keesing, *Hemisphere*, XXII, No. 7, 1978, 28-29; M. Macdonald, *24 Hours*, II, No. 11, 1977, 67; R. Nicholls, *S.M.H.*, 17 September, 1977, 17; A. Summers, *Advertiser*, 3 December, 1977, 28.

Handfasted. Edited with a preface and afterword by Helen Thomson. (Ringwood, Vic.: Penguin, 1984).
Reviewed by L. Clancy, *ABR*, No. 64, 1984, 11-12; H. Daniel, *Age Saturday Extra*, 9 June, 1984, 16; G. Dutton, *Bulletin*, 5 June, 1984, 88 & 91; M. Gollan, *S.M.H.*, 23 June, 1984, 42; B. Josephi, *CRNLE Reviews Journal*, No. 2, 1984, 59-63; S. Magarey, *Meridian*, IV, No. 2, 1985, 178-180; R. O'Grady, *Advertiser Saturday Review*, 15 September, 1984, 37.

Mr. Hogarth's Will. With an introduction by Helen Thomson. (Ringwood, Vic.; New York: Penguin, 1988;). First published London: Richard Bentley, 1865.
Reviewed by S. Paolini, *Antipodes*, 3.1, 1989, 34.

Non-Fiction
An Autobiography. (Adelaide: Libraries Board of South Australia, 1975). Australiana Facsimile Editions 199. First published in book form Adelaide: Thomas, 1910.
Reviewed by M. Dunlevy, *Canberra Times*, 19 September, 1975, 11; C. Wagner, *Nation Review*, 7-13 November, 1975, 102; E. Webby, *A.L.S.*, VII, 1976, 434-35.

A Week in the Future. With an introduction & notes by Lesley Durrell Ljungdahl. (Sydney: Hale & Iremonger, 1987). Reproduces the original text serialised in *The Centennial Magazine: An Australian Monthly* from December 1888 to July 1889.
Reviewed by M. Gollan, *S.M.H.*, 20 February, 1988, 73.

Critical Material
Gunton, E.J. *Bibliography of Catherine Helen Spence.* (Adelaide: Libraries Board of South Australia, 1967).

Albinski, Nan Bowman. '*Handfasted*: An Australian Feminist's American Utopia'. *Journal of Popular Culture*, 23, No. 2, 1989, 15-31.

Barnes, John. *Henry Kingsley and Colonial Fiction.* (Melbourne: O.U.P., 1971), 38-41. Australian Writers and Their Work.

Bennett, Bruce. 'Catherine Spence, George Eliot and the Contexts of Literary Possibility'. *Journal of Commonwealth Literature*, XXVI, No. 1, 1986, 202-210.

Bridge, Carl. 'Catherine Helen Spence and the South Australian Institute: A Note'. *South Australiana*, XXII, No. 1, 1983, 74-76.

Collins, Lyn. '*Clara Morison*: A Tribute to Frederick Sinnett'. *Adelaide A.L.S.*

Working Papers, I, No. 2, 1975, 4-11.
Cooper, Janet. *Catherine Spence*. (Melbourne: O.U.P., 1972). Great Australians. Reviewed by B.H. Bennett, *A.L.S.*, VI, 1973, 220-24.
Cooper, M. 'A Woman of Vision'. *Parade*, No. 308, 1976, 36-37.
Daniels, Kay. 'Catherine Spence'. History Teachers' Association of N.S.W. *Women and History Conference*, 1976, 54-65.
---. 'Political Pathfinders and a Strange Sexual Radical'. *National Times*, 9-16 January, 1983, 24-25.
Magarey, Susan. 'Catherine Helen Spence: Novelist'. In *Southwords: Essays on South Australian Writing*, edited by Philip Butterss (Kent Town, SA: Wakefield, 1995), 27-45.
---. 'Feminist Visions Across the Pacific: Catherine Helen Spence's *Handfasted*'. *Antipodes*, 3.1, 1989, 31-33.
---. *Unbridling the Tongues of Women: A Biography of Catherine Helen Spence*. (Sydney: Hale & Iremonger, 1985). Reviewed by K. Bail, *Weekend Magazine*, 8-9 February, 1986, 13; L. Clancy, *Meridian*, V, No. 2, 1986, 185-86; S. Dowrick, *S.M.H.*, 1 March, 1986, 45; B. Kingston, *A.L.S.*, XII, No. 4, 1986, 550-52; L. Meldrum, *Canberra Times*, 5 April, 1986, B2; H. Thomson, *Island Magazine*, No. 27, 1986, 66-67; A.T. Yarwood, *Age Saturday Extra*, 18 January, 1986, 11.
Partington, Geoffrey. 'Catherine Helen Spence and the Wonderful 19th Century: "The Advancement of Women"'. *Quadrant*, 34, Nos. 1-2, 1990, 63-67.
Raggio, Janice. '*The Broad Arrow* and *Clara Morison*. Studies of Early Colonial Life'. *Adelaide A.L.S. Working Papers*, III, 1979, 36-51.
Ramsland, John. 'Catherine Helen Spence: Writer, Public Speaker and Social and Political Reformer, 1825-1910'. *South Australiana*, XXII, No. 1, 1983, 36-73.
Sinnett, Frederick. *The Fiction Fields of Australia*. (Brisbane: U.Q.P., 1966), 34-42 and passim. Reprinted in *The Writer in Australia*, edited by John Barnes (Melbourne: O.U.P., 1969), 8-32.
Smith, Martin. 'Catherine Helen Spence and Rose Scott'. *Campaign*, No. 26, 1978, 15-17.
---. 'Martin Smith Acquaints You with Two Great Women from Our Past'. *Campaign*, No. 26, 1977, 15-16.
Thomson, Helen. 'Catherine Helen Spence: Pragmatic Utopian'. In *Who is She?*, edited by Shirley Walker (St Lucia: U.Q.P., 1983), 12-25.
---. 'Love and Labour: Marriage and Work in the Novels of Catherine Helen Spence'. In *A Bright and Fiery Troop: Australian Women Writers of the Nineteenth Century*, edited by Debra Adelaide (Ringwood: Penguin, 1988), 101-115.
Walker, R.B. 'Catherine Helen Spence and South Australian Politics'. *Australian Journal of Politics and History*, XV, 1969, 35-46.
---. 'Catherine Helen Spence, Unitarian Utopian'. *A.L.S.*, V, 1971, 31-41.

SPIELVOGEL, NATHAN FREDERICK

Critical Material

Blake, Les. 'Nathan Spielvogel'. *Australian Jewish Historical Society Journal of Proceedings*, IX, 1984, 403-16. Biographical.
Fredman, L.E. 'How My Life Was Spent: The Autobiography of Nathan F. Spielvogel'. *Australian Jewish Historical Society Journal and Proceedings*, VI, Part I, 1964, 1-26.
Indyk, Ivor. 'The Ancient Legend of the Wandering Gumsucker'. *Bridge*, VII, No. 1, 1972, 49-51.

STEAD, CHRISTINA

Collection

A Christina Stead Reader. Edited by Jean B. Read. (Sydney: A.& R., 1982). First

published New York: Random House, 1978.
Reviewed by D. Anderson, *ABR*, No. 42, 1982, 7-9; D. Modjeska, *ABR*, No. 42, 1982, 10; T. Shapcott, *Courier-Mail*, 17 April, 1982, 24.

Christina Stead: Selected Fiction and Nonfiction. Edited by R.G. Geering and A. Segerberg. (St Lucia: U.Q.P., 1994).
Reviewed by M. Fraser, *Voices*, 4.4, 1994-95, 91-98; C. Lee, *Coppertales*, 1, 1995, 159-66.

Fiction

The Beauties and Furies. With a new introduction by Hilary Bailey. (London: Virago, 1982). First published London: Peter Davies, 1936.
Reviewed by A. Carter, *London Review of Books*, IV, No. 17, 1982, 11-13; H. Thompson, *CRNLE Reviews Journal*, No. 1, 1983, 66-69.

Cotter's England. (London: Secker & Warburg, 1967). First published as *Dark Places of the Heart.* (New York: Holt, Rinehart & Winston, 1966).
Reviewed by J. Barbour, *Nation*, 4 November, 1967, 22; J. Baxter, *Bulletin*, 27 January, 1968, 51; N. Braybrooke, *Canberra Times*, 20 May, 1967, 10; A. Gyger, *Australian*, 29 July, 1967, 11; B. Jefferis, *S.M.H.*, 23 September, 1967, 18; N. Jillett, *Age*, 19 August, 1967, 22; G.R. Lansell, *ABR*, VI, 1967, 185; *T.L.S.*, 3 August, 1967, 701; M. Wilding, *London Magazine*, VII, No. 8, 1967, 98-100.

Dark Places of the Heart. (New York: Holt, Rinehart and Winston, 1966).
Reviewed by *Time*, 23 September, 1966, 76.

For Love Alone. Introduction by Terry Sturm. (Sydney: A.& R., 1973). Paperback edition. First published New York: Harcourt Brace, 1944. Then London: Virago, 1978; then Sydney: A.& R., 1979 (Sirius Books); then, with an introduction by Peter Craven, (North Ryde, N.S.W.: A.& R., 1990).
Reviewed by A. Duchene, *T.L.S.*, 8 September, 1978, 985; S. Edgar, *Canberra Times*, 8 October, 1966, 10; R.G. Howarth, *Bulletin*, 12 November, 1966, 56; B. Jefferis, *S.M.H.*, 8 October, 1966, 20; N. Jillett, *Age*, 8 October, 1966, 25; E. Perkins, *Quadrant*, XXIII, No. 9, 1979, 70 and *CRNLE Reviews Journal*, No. 2, 1979, 30-34; C. Seaton, *Australian*, 12 November, 1966, 15; C. Tomalin, *New Statesman*, 21 July, 1978, 95, reprinted in *Nation Review*, 27 October-2 November, 1978, 21.

House of All Nations. (Sydney, London: A.& R., 1974). A.& R. Classics. First published London: Davies, 1938.
Reviewed by C. Egerton, *Nation Review*, 18-24 October, 1974, 20; E. Feinstein, *New Statesman*, 14 June, 1974, 856; T. Forshaw, *Australian*, 7 September, 1974, 39; K. Tennant, *S.M.H.*, 24 August, 1974, 16.

I'm Dying Laughing: The Humourist. Edited by R.G. Geering. (London: Virago, 1986). Republished Ringwood, Vic.: Penguin, 1989.
Reviewed by L. Adler, *Times on Sunday*, 19 April, 1987, 30; D. Anderson, *ABR*, No. 92, 1987, 6-8; A. Blake, *Meanjin*, XLVII, No. 1, 1988, 135-143; D. Hewett, *Overland*, No. 108, 1987, 83-86; esp. 83-84 and *Fremantle Arts Review*, II, No. 7, 1987, 14; J. Motion, *T.L.S.*, 24 April, 1987, 435; E. Riddell, *Bulletin*, 7 April, 1987, 74-75; A. Riemer, *S.M.H.*, 28 March, 1987, 47; S. Roff, *Antipodes*, I, No. 2, 1987, 122-123; *New Yorker*, 28 December, 1987, 123; H. Rowley, *Age Saturday Extra*, 4 April, 1987, 12.

Letty Fox: Her Luck. (Sydney: A.& R., 1974). A.& R. Classics. Introduction by Meaghan Morris. First published New York: Harcourt Brace, 1946. Reprinted London: Virago, 1978. Reprinted with introduction by Susan Sheridan (North Ryde, N.S.W., 1991).
Reviewed by A. Duchene, *T.L.S.*, 8 September, 1978, 985; D. Malouf, *Age Monthly Review*, II, No. 5, 1982, 11-12; C. Tomalin, *New Statesman*, 21 July, 1978, 95,

reprinted in *Nation Review*, 27 October-2 November, 1978, 21.

The Little Hotel. (London, Sydney: A.& R., 1973).
Reviewed by P. Ackroyd, *Spectator*, 1 June, 1974, 678; B.L. Baer, *Nation* (New York) CCXX, 1975, 501-03; C. Egerton, *Nation Review*, 18-24 October, 1974, 20; E. Feinstein, *New Statesman*, 14 June, 1974, 856; T. Forshaw, *Australian*, 7 September, 1974, 39; B. Kiernan, *Age*, 14 September, 1974, 15; S. Koch, *Saturday Review*, 31 May, 1975, 28; K. Tennant, *S.M.H.*, 24 August, 1974, 16; *T.L.S.*, 24 May, 1974, 545; M. Thorpe, *English Studies*, LVI, 1975, 538.

The Little Hotel. (New York: Henry Holt, 1992). First published London, Sydney: A.& R., 1973.
Reviewed by L. Graeber, *New York Times Book Review*, 4 October, 1992, 32.

A Little Tea, a Little Chat. With a new introduction by Hilary Bailey (London: Virago, 1981). First published New York: Harcourt Brace, 1948.
Reviewed by A. Duchene, *T.L.S.*, 25 September, 1981, 1110; D. Malouf, *Age Monthly Review*, II, No. 5, 1982, 11-12.

The Man Who Loved Children. (New York: Holt, Rinehart and Winston, 1976). First published New York: Simon & Schuster, 1940.
Reviewed by J. Beston, *The Island Times* (Honolulu), I, No. 3, 1976, 38; E. Connell, *Harper's Magazine*, July, 1976, 75-76; K. Dick, *Sunday Times* (London), 26 June, 1966, 48; S. Edgar, *Canberra Times*, 8 October, 1966, 10; N. Jillett, *Age*, 25 June, 1966, 25; D. Martin, *Bulletin*, 16 July, 1966, 44-5; R.Z. Sheppard, *Time* (Australian edition), 7 June, 1976, 61-62.

Miss Herbert (The Suburban Wife). (New York: Random House, 1976). Reprinted London: Virago, 1979.
Reviewed by B. Atkinson, *Nation Review*, 1980, 79; J. Beston, *The Island Times*, I, No. 3, 1976, 38; D. Brydon, *WLWE*, XVII, No. 1, 1978, 114-15; E. Connell, *Harper's Magazine*, July, 1976, 76; K. England, *Advertiser*, 31 May, 1980, 20; E. Fisher, *Spectator*, 17 November, 1979, 27; N. Keesing, *S.M.H.*, 16 February, 1980, 18; J. Langford, *Weekend Australian Magazine*, 1-2 March, 1980, 16; J. Naughton, *Listener*, 18 October, 1979, 535; T. Shapcott, *Australian*, 30 April, 1977, 28; R.Z. Sheppard, *Time* (Australian edition), 7 June, 1976, 61-62; K. Thomas, *Weekend Australian Magazine*, 1-2 March, 1980, 16; J. Yglesias, *National Times*, 5-10 July, 1976, 19.

Ocean of Story: The Uncollected Stories of Christina Stead. Edited with an afterword R.G. Geering. (Ringwood, Vic.: Viking, 1985). Reprinted Ringwood, Vic.: Penguin, 1986.
Reviewed by B. Birskys, *Scope*, XXXII, No. 1, 1987, 4-5; A. Blake, *Meridian*, V, No. 2, 1986, 117-22; A. Clark, *Age Monthly Review*, V, No. 11, 1986, 10-11; V. Coleman, *Quadrant*, XXX, No. 9, 1986, 68-69; H. Garner, *Scripsi*, IV, No. 1, 1986, 191-94; M. Harris, *National Times*, 24-30 January, 1986, 34; N. Jillett, *Age Saturday Extra*, 14 December, 1985, 13; F. Kellaway, *Overland*, No. 103, 1986, 76-77; B. King, *World Literature Today*, LXI, No. 1, 1987, 154-155; D.J. O'Hearn, *Weekend Australian Magazine*, 14-15 December, 1985, 17; C.K. Stead, *London Review of Books*, 4 September, 1986, 13; E. White, *New York Times Book Review*, 25 May, 1986, 7 and *Australian Financial Review Magazine: Weekend Review*, 6 June, 1986, 38.

The Palace with Several Sides: A Sort of Love Story. Edited by R.G. Geering; wood engravings by Mike Hudson. (Canberra: Brindabella, 1986). Republished North Ryde, N.S.W.: A.& R., 1990.

The People with the Dogs. With a new introduction by Judith Kegan Gardiner. (London: Virago, 1981). First published Boston: Little Brown, 1952.
Reviewed by A. Duchene, *T.L.S.*, 25 September, 1981, 1110; B. Greenwell, *New*

Statesman, 21 August, 1981, 21; D. Malouf, *Age Monthly Review*, II, No. 5, 1982, 11-12.

The Puzzleheaded Girl. (New York: Holt, Rinehart & Winston, 1967; London: Secker & Warburg, 1968). Reprinted with a new introduction by Angela Carter, London: Virago, 1984.
Reviewed by J. Baxter, *Bulletin*, 21 September, 1968, 67-68; D. Edmonds, *Studies in Short Fiction*, VI, 1968, 110-12; F.H. Gardner, *Nation* (New York), 1 January, 1968, 21-22; T. Keneally, *Australian*, 31 August, 1968, 12; L. Kramer, *S.M.H.*, 27 July, 1968, 24; P. MacManus, *Saturday Review*, 14 October, 1967, 34, 99-100; A. Morris, *New York Times Book Review*, 10 December, 1967, 54; R. Sale, *Hudson Review*, XX, 1967/68, 667; C.T. Samuels, *New Republic*, 9 September, 1967, 30-31; R. Sokolov, *Newsweek*, 11 September, 1967, 55-56; R. Throssell, *Weekend Australian Magazine*, 9-10 February, 1985, 11; R. Ward, *ABR*, VII, 1968, 143; M. Wilding, *London Magazine*, N.S., VIII, 1968, 112-13 and *Meanjin*, XXX, 1971, 263.

The Salzburg Tales. (Melbourne: Sun Books, 1966). First published London: Davies, 1934.
Reviewed by J. Battersby, *S.M.H.*, 11 June, 1966, 18; M. Dunlevy, *Canberra Times*, 25 June, 1966, 10; T. Forshaw, *Australian*, 7 September, 1974, 39; N. Jillett, *Age*, 25 June, 1966, 25; B. Oakley, *Secondary Teacher*, No. 117, 1966, 33; C. Semmler, *ABR*, V, 1966, 155; C.K. Stead, *London Review of Books*, 4 September, 1986, 13; K. Tennant, *S.M.H.*, 24 August, 1974, 16.

The Salzburg Tales. Introduction by Susan Sheridan. (North Ryde, NSW: A.& R., 1991). First published London: Davies, 1934.
Reviewed by M. Lord, *Voices*, 1.1, 1991, 103-06.

Seven Poor Men of Sydney. With an Introduction by Ron Geering (Sydney: A.& R., 1965). First published London: Davies, 1934.
Reviewed by J. Battersby, *S.M.H.*, 11 June, 1966, 18; R. Burns, *Nation*, 11 June, 1966, 21; L.J. Clancy, *Australian*, 19 March, 1966, 9; I. Cross, *Bulletin*, 23 April, 1966, 56; K. Dick, *Sunday Times* (London), 26 June, 1966, 48; M. Dunlevy, *Canberra Times*, 26 February, 1966, 10; C. Semmler, *ABR*, V, 1966, 137.

Seven Poor Men of Sydney. Introduced by Margaret Harris. (North Ryde, NSW: Collins/A.& R, 1990). First published London: Davies, 1934.
Reviewed by L. Clancy, *Weekend Australian*, 26-27 January, 1991, Review 6.

Non-Fiction

'[The International Symposium on the Short Story. Part 1:] England'. *Kenyon Review*, XXX, 1968, 444-50.

'It Is All a Scramble for Boodle: Christina Stead Sums up America'. *ABR*, 141, 1992, 22-24. Edited version of unpublished notes written by C.S. during her first visit to America.

Talking into the Typewriter: Selected Letters (1973-1983). Edited with preface and annotations by R.G. Geering. (Pymble, NSW: A.& R. 1992); *A Web of Friendship: Selected Letters (1928-1973)*. Edited with preface and annotations by R.G. Geering. (Pymble, NSW: A.& R., 1992).
Reviewed by A. Blake, *Meridian*, 11.2, 1992, 84-86; M. Halligan, *Voices*, 2.4, 1992, 112-15; M. Harris, *ABR*, 141, 1992, 20-21; E. Harrower, *Overland*, 128, 1992, 77-79; W. Jamrozik, *S.M.H.*, 17 June, 1992, 38; M. Lord, *Weekend Australian*, 20-21 June, 1992, Review 7; M. Missen, *Age*, 6 June, 1992, Saturday Extra 9; V. Muller, *Imago*, 5.2, 1993, 94-95; E. Riddell, *Bulletin*, 30 June, 1992, 92-93.

'A Writer's Friends: Piece on "A Writer's Life"'. *Southerly*, XXVIII, 1968, 163-68.

Critical Material

Beston, Rose Marie. 'A Christina Stead Bibliography'. *WLWE*, XV, No. 1, 1976, 96-103.

Ehrhardt, Marianne. 'Christina Stead: A Checklist'. *A.L.S.*, IX, 1980, 508-35.

Thomson, Helen. 'Bibliography'. *ABR*, No. 42, 1982, 14-15.

'Author Here to Take Up ANU Fellowship'. *Canberra Times*, 4 August, 1969, 7.

'Christina Stead: A Celebration'. *Stand*, XXIII, No. 4, 1982, also contains a biographical note, a list of her books and two of the Salzburg Tales.

'Christina Stead: Australian Novelist of Marked Originality'. *Times*, 7 April, 1983, 12.

'White Prize for Christina Stead'. *S.M.H.*, 14 November, 1974, 13. Similar reports in other newspapers of this date.

Anderson, Don. 'Christina Stead's Unforgettable Dinner-Parties'. *Southerly*, XXXIX, 1979, 28-45.

Bader, Rudolf. 'Christina Stead and the Bildungsroman'. *WLWE*, XXIII, 1984, 31-39.

Baker, Rebecca. 'Christina Stead: The Nietzsche Connection'. *Meridian*, 2, 1983, 116-20.

Barbour, Judith. 'Christina Stead: The Sublime Lives of Obscure Men'. *Southerly*, XXXVIII, 1978, 406-16.

Barnes, John. 'Australian Books in Print: Filling Some Gaps'. *Westerly*, No. 2, 1967, 60-63.

---. 'Christina Stead (1902-1983)'. *ABR*, No. 51, 1983, 10.

---. 'Christina Stead: The Drama of the Person'. In *Essays on Contemporary Post-Colonial Fiction*, edited by Hedwig Bock and Albert Wertheim (Munchen: Huber, 1986), 333-53.

Bedford, Jean. 'One of our Foremost ...'. *National Times*, 8-14 April, 1983, 34.

Beston, John B. 'A Brief Biography of Christina Stead'. *WLWE*, XV, No. 1, 1976, 79-86.

---. 'An Interview with Christina Stead'. *WLWE*, XV, No. 1, 1976, 87-95.

Bindella, Maria Teresa. 'Searchlights and the Search for History in Christina Stead's *Seven Poor Men of Sydney*'. In *European Perspectives: Contemporary Essays on Australian Literature*, edited by Giovanna Capone (*A.L.S.* 15.2 (special issue)/ St. Lucia: U.Q.P., 1991), 95-106.

Blain, Virginia. '*A Little Tea, A Little Chat*: Decadent Pleasures and the Pleasure of Decadence'. *Southerly* 53.4, 1993: 20-35.

---. 'Stead for Real'. *ABR*, 141, 1992, 25-26.

Blake, Ann. 'Christina Stead's English Short Stories'. *Southerly*, 53.4, 1993, 146-60.

---. 'Christina Stead's *Miss Herbert (The Suburban Wife)* and the English Middle Class'. *Journal of Commonwealth Literature*, 26.1, 1991, 49-64.

Boone, Joseph A. 'Of Fathers, Daughters, and Theorists of Narrative Desire: At the Crossroads of Myth and Psychoanalysis in *The Man Who Loved Children*'. *Contemporary Literature*, 31.4, 1990, 512-14.

Boyers, Robert. 'The Family Novel'. *Salmagundi* (Flushing, N.Y.), No. 26 Spring 1974, 21-25.

Brady, Veronica. '*The Man who Loved Children* and the Body of the World'. *Meanjin*, XXXVII, 1978, 229-39.

Brown, Denise. 'Christina Stead's "Drama of the Person"'. *A.L.S.*, XIII, No. 2, 1987, 139-145.

Brydon, Diana. *Christina Stead*. (New York: Barnes & Noble Books; London: Macmillan Education, 1987). Reviewed by J. Gribble, *A.L.S.*, 14, No. 3, 1990, 398-400; M. Johnson, *Antipodes*, I, No. 2, 1987, 121; H. Rowley, *Westerly*, 34, No. 1, 1989, 86-89.

---. '"Other Tongues than Ours": Christina Stead's *I'm Dying Laughing*'. *Australian and New Zealand Studies in Canada*, No. 2, 1989, 17-26.

---. 'Resisting "the Tyranny of What Is Written": Christina Stead's Fiction'. *Ariel*, XVII, No. 4, 1986, 3-15.

Burns, D.R. 'The Active Passive Inversion: Sex Roles in Garner, Stead and

Harrower'. *Meanjin*, XLV, No. 3, 1986, 346-53.

Burns, Graham. 'The Moral Design of *The Man Who Loved Children*'. *Critical Review*, (Melbourne), No. 14, 1971, 38-61.

Calisher, Hortense. 'Stead'. *Yale Review*, LXXVII, No. 2, 1987, 169-177.

Carter, Angela. 'In Love with the Tempest'. *Sunday Times* (London), 10 April, 1983, 44.

---. 'Unhappy Families - Angela Carter on the Scope of Christina Stead's Achievement'. *London Review of Books*, IV, No. 17, 1982, 11-13.

Chisholm, Anne. 'Christina Stead at 80 and Still Writing'. *Bulletin*, 27 July, 1982, 26-27.

---. 'Stead'. *National Times*, 29 March-4 April, 1981, 32,34.

Clancy, Laurie. 'Arabesques and Banknotes'. *ABR*, No. 42, 1982, 10-14.

---. *Christina Stead's The Man Who Loved Children and For Love Alone*. (Melbourne: Shillington House, 1981). Reviewed by J. Croft, *A.L.S.*, X, 1982, 400-01; S. Higgins, *ABR*, No. 29, 1981, 37; J. Waten, *Age*, 7 February, 1981, 28.

---. 'The Economy of Love: Christina Stead's Women'. In *Who is She?*, edited by Shirley Walker (St Lucia: U.Q.P., 1983), 136-49.

---. 'Fathers and Lovers: Three Australian Novels'. *A.L.S.*, X, 1982, 459-67. *The Man who Loved Children*.

---. '"The Natural Outlawry of Womankind": Christina Stead's The Man Who Loved Children'. *Viewpoints: H.S.C. English Literature*, edited by B. McFarlane (Melbourne: 1982, 159-164.

Dizard, Robin. 'Love Stories'. In *From Commonwealth to Post-Colonial*, edited by Anna Rutherford (Sydney; Aarhus: Dangaroo P, 1992), 399-403. Discusses *The Beauties and Furies*.

Drewe, Robert. 'Christina Stead's Silent Return'. *Bulletin*, 4 October, 1975, 43-45.

---. 'An Interview with Christina Stead'. *Scripsi*, IV, No. 1, 1986, 183-90. Previously published in *Yacker, Australian Writers Talk About Their Work*, edited by Candida Baker (Sydney: Picador, 1986), 14-26.

---. 'A Last Interview'. *Mode Australia*, June-July, 1983, 94-96.

Duffy, Julia. 'The Grain of the Voice in Christina Stead's *The Man Who Loved Children*'. *Antipodes*, 4.1, 1990, 48-51.

Edelson, Phyllis Fahrie. 'Christina Stead: Gender and Power'. In *International Literature in English: Essays on the Major Writers*, edited by Robert L. Ross (New York: Garland, 1991), 241-49.

Fagan, Robert. 'Christina Stead'. *Partisan Review*, XLVI, 1979, 262-70.

Ferrier, Carole. 'The Death of the Family in Some Novels by Women of the Forties & Fifties'. *Hecate*, II, No. 2, 1976, 48-61.

Gardiner, Judith Kegan. '"Caught but not caught": Psychology and Politics in Christina Stead's "The Puzzleheaded Girl"'. *WLWE*, 21.1, 1992 26-41.

---. *Rhys, Stead, Lessing and the Politics of Empathy*. (Bloomington: Indiana University Press, 1989).

Geering, R.G. *Christina Stead*. Australian Writers and Their Work. (Melbourne: O.U.P., 1969). Reviewed by M. Wilding, *A.L.S.*, IV, 1970, 412-16.

---. *Christina Stead*. (New York: Twayne, 1969). Twayne's World Authors Series, No. 95. Revised edition, Sydney: A.& R., 1979. Reviewed by D. Ball, *S.M.H.*, 4 July, 1970, 19; R. Burns, *Nation*, 22 August, 1970, 21-22 (see also letter to the editor by G. Murnane, *Nation*, 5 September, 1970, 16); B. Elliott, *ABR*, VIII, 1969, 247-48; K.L. Goodwin, *Notes & Queries*, N.S. XIX, 1972 359-60; D. Green, *Meanjin*, XXX, 1971, 251-53 and *Hemisphere*, XVI, No. 3, 1972, 39; N. Keesing, *Bulletin*, 20 June, 1970, 45-46; B. Kiernan, *Australian*, 25 April, 1970, 20; M. Wilding, *A.L.S.*, IV, 1970, 412-16.

---. 'Christina Stead in the 1960's'. *Southerly*, XXVIII, 1968, 26-36.

---. 'From the Personal Papers of Christina Stead: Extracts and Commentaries'.

Southerly, 50, No. 4, 1990, 399-425.

---. 'From the Personal Papers of Christina Stead: Extracts & Commentaries (cont.)'. *Southerly*, 51.1, 1991, 5-17.

---. '*I'm Dying Laughing*: Behind the Scenes'. *Southerly*, XLVII, No. 3, 1987, 309-317.

---. 'Talking into the Typewriter: The Letters of Christina Stead'. *Southerly*, 50, No. 1, 1990, 3-19.

---. 'What is Normal? Two Recent Novels by Christina Stead'. *Southerly*, XXXVIII, 1978, 462-73. *The Little Hotel* and *Miss Herbert*.

Giuffre, Giulia. 'Christina Stead Interviewed'. *Stand*, XXIII, No. 4, 1982, 22-29. Reprinted in her *A Writing Life: Interviews with Australian Women Writers*. (Sydney: Allen and Unwin, 1990), 73-87.

Green, Dorothy. 'Chaos, or a Dancing Star? Christina Stead's *Seven Poor Men of Sydney*'. *Meanjin*, XXVII, 1968, 150-61.

---. 'Christina Stead (d. 31 March 1983)'. *Notes & Furphies*, No. 11, 1983, 1-2.

---. 'Christina Stead Wrote Because She Loved to'. *S.M.H.*, 8 April, 1983, 6. Also as 'A Vision with the Touch of Genius'. *Age*, 8 April, 1983, 11; and 'She Wrote Because She Loved to'. *Courier-Mail*, 16 April, 1983, 28.

Gribble, Jennifer. 'The Beauties and Furies'. *Southerly*, XLVII, No. 3, 1987, 324-337.

---. 'Books of Laughter and Forgetting'. *Meridian*, VI, No. 2, 1987, 158-164.

---. *Christina Stead*. (Melbourne: O.U.P., 1994). Reviewed by J. Croft, *Weekend Australian*, 4-5 June, 1994, 7; G. Dow, *Overland*, 137, 1994, 77-78; D. Gilbey, *ABR*, 163, 1994, 23-25; B. Kiernan, *A.L.S.*, 17.2, 1995, 198-202; R. Sorensen, *Age*, 23 April, 1994, Saturday Extra 8; K.M. Stern, *Antipodes*, 9.1, 1995, 60.

---. 'Christina Stead's *For Love Alone*'. *Critical Review*, 31, 1991, 17-27.

---. '*The Man Who Loved Children*: Storm in a Tea-Cup'. In *The Australian Experience: Critical Essays on Australian Novels*, edited by W.S. Ramson (Canberra: Australian National University Press, 1974), 174-208.

Grimm, Cherry. 'Return to Australia of Christina Stead'. *S.M.H.*, 19 July, 1969, 18.

Hamilton, K.G. 'Two Difficult Young Men: Martin Boyd's *A Difficult Young Man* and Christina Stead's *The People with the Dogs*'. In *Studies in the Recent Australian Novel*, edited by K.G. Hamilton (St Lucia: U.Q.P., 1978), 141-67.

Hardwick, Elizabeth. 'The Neglected Novels of Christina Stead'. In her *A View of My Own: Essays in Literature and Society*. (London: Heinemann, 1964), 41-8.

Harris, Margaret. 'Christina Stead's Human Comedy: The American Sequence'. *WLWE*, 21.1, 1992, 42-51.

---. 'Christina Stead in 1993'. *Southerly*, 53.4, 1993, 161-65.

---. 'Christina Stead in *Southerly*'. *Southerly*, 49, No. 3, 1989, 514-28.

---. '"To Hell with Conservatories": Christina Stead and the Fiction of William J. Blake'. *Meridian*, 8, No. 2, 1989, 161-73.

---. 'Names in Stead's *Seven Poor Men of Sydney*'. In *Reconnoitres: Essays in Australian Literature in Honour of G.A. Wilkes*, edited by Margaret Harris and Elizabeth Webby (South Melbourne: O.U.P. in association with Sydney U.P., 1992), 142-53.

Henke, Suzette. 'An American Looks at Christina Stead's America'. *Notes & Furphies*, 28, 1992, 2-4.

Hergenhan, Laurie. 'An Australian "Odyssey": Christina Stead's *For Love Alone*'. *Rajasthan University Studies in English*, XV, 1982-1983, 42-56.

Heseltine, Harry. '"Those Easier Dead": *Seven Poor Men of Sydney*'. In his *Acquainted with the Night*. (Townsville: Townsville Foundation for Australian Literary Studies, 1979), 39-58.

Higgins, Susan. 'Christina Stead's *For Love Alone*: A Female Odyssey?' *Southerly*, XXXVIII, 1978, 428-45.

Hill, Barry. 'Christina Stead at 80 Says Love is her Religion'. *S.M.H.*, 17 July, 1982, 33.

---. 'Christina Stead in Command'. *Age*, 28 February, 1980, 2. Review of the broadcast interview with Wetherell.

---. 'The Woman who Loved Silence'. *Age Saturday Extra*, 17 July, 1982, 2.

Holmes, Bruce. 'Character and Ideology in Christina Stead's *House of All Nations*'. *Southerly*, XLV, No. 3, 1985, 266-278.

Hooton, Joy. 'Christina Stead, an Original Novelist'. *Hemisphere*, XXVI, 1982, 341-45.

---. 'Mermaid and Minotaur in *The Man Who Loved Children*'. *Meridian*, 8, No. 2, 1989, 127-39.

Hurtley, Jacqueline. 'Christina Stead: Spain Remembered. Towards a Definition of the Impact of the Country on Her Work'. In *A Passage to Somewhere Else*, edited by Doireann MacDermott and Susan Ballyn. Proceedings of the Commonwealth Conference held in the University of Barcelona, 30 September-2 October, 1987 (Barcelona: Promociones y Publicaciones Universitarias, 1988), 85-90.

Jamison, Greeba. 'Christina Stead - "Can't Help Being Original"'. *Walkabout*, XXXVI, No. 2, 1970, 36-37.

Jones, Dorothy. '"A Kingdom and a Place of Exile": Women Writers and the World of Nature'. *WLWE*, XXIV, No. 2, 1984, 257-273.

Jose, Nicholas. 'The Dream of Europe: *For Love Alone, The Aunt's Story* and *The Cardboard Crown*'. *Meridian*, VI, No. 2, 1987, 113-125; esp. 113-119.

Keavney, Kay. 'Ranked with the Immortals - Christina Stead'. *Australian Women's Weekly*, 17 November, 1976, 71-72.

Krause, Tom. 'Novelist's Late Laurels'. *Australian*, 7 December, 1982, 7.

Law, Pamela. 'Letty Fox, Her Luck'. *Southerly*, XXXVIII, 1978, 448-53.

Lawson, Elizabeth. 'Louie's Mother: The Feminist Inscape of *The Man Who Loved Children*'. *Meridian*, 8, No. 2, 1989, 114-26.

Legge, Kate. 'Christina Stead, an Australian who Wrote for the World'. *Age*, 7 April, 1983, 3.

Lever, Susan. '"The Night of Which No One Speaks": Christina Stead's Art as Struggle'. *SPAN*, 37, 1993, 108-19.

Lidoff, Joan. *Christina Stead*. (New York: Ungar, 1982). Reviewed by M. Harris, *Southerly*, XLIV, 1984, 233-35.

---. 'Christina Stead: An Interview'. *Aphra*, (Springtown, PA), VI, No. 3 & 4, 1976, 39-64.

---. 'Domestic Gothic: The Image of Anger, Christina Stead's *Man Who Loved Children*'. *Studies in the Novel*, XI, 1979, 201-15.

---. 'The Female Ego: Christina Stead's Heroines'. *New Boston Review*, II, No. 3, 1977, 19-20.

---. 'Home is where the Heart is: The Fiction of Christina Stead'. *Southerly*, XXXVIII, 1978, 363-75.

Lilley, Kate. 'The New Curiosity Shop: Marketing Genre and Femininity in Stead's *Miss Herbert (The Suburban Wife)*'. *Southerly*, 53.4, 1993, 5-12.

Lord, Mary. 'Christina Stead Supplement'. *ABR*, No. 42, 1982, 7. Introduction.

Lundkvist, Artur. 'En Egensinnig Forfattarinna'. *Dagens Nyheter*, 3 April, 1977, 4. English title: 'A Self-Willed Author'

Macainsh, Noel. 'The Art of Compromise - Christina Stead's *For Love Alone*'. *Westerly*, XXXII, No. 4, 1987, 79-88.

Malouf, David. 'Stead is Best at Egotistical Monsters'. *S.M.H.*, 17 July, 1982, 36.

McDonald, Marion. 'Christina Stead: The Exile Returns, Unhappily'. *National Times*, 22-27 November, 1976, 21-22.

McDonnell, Jennifer. 'Christina Stead's *The Man Who Loved Children*'. *Southerly*, XLIV, 1984, 394-413.

McDowell, Edwin. 'Christina Stead, Novelist, Was 80'. *New York Times*, 13 April, 1983, D23.

McGregor, Grant. '*Seven Poor Men of Sydney*: The Historical Dimension'. *Southerly*, XXXVIII, 1978, 380-404.

Mansfield, Nick. '"This Is not Understanding": Christina Stead's *For Love Alone*'. *Southerly*, 52.1, 1992, 77-89.

Mercer, Gina. 'Christina Stead - A Radical Author: Patterns of Thesis and Antithesis'. *Span*, XXI, 1985, 137-51.

Miller, Anthony. '*Seven Poor Men of Sydney*'. *Westerly*, No. 2, 1968, 61-66.

Molloy, Susan. 'Christina Stead Debunks some Myths: She is neither Bitter, nor a Recluse. . .'. *S.M.H.*, 20 January, 1983, 8. Interview.

Muncaster, Tina. 'The Pleasures of Text and Table: Appetite and Consumption in *I'm Dying Laughing*'. *Southerly*, 53.4, 1993, 106-15.

Nestor, Pauline. 'An Impulse to Self-Expression: *The Man Who Loved Children*'. *Critical Review*, No. 18, 1976, 61-78.

O'Grady, Desmond. 'Christina Stead. Sabba Familiare'. *Australian Literature Bulletin* (Venice), II, No. 1, 1979, 36-37.

Perkins, Elizabeth. 'Learning to Recognize Wicked People: Christina Stead's *A Little Tea, A Little Chat*'. *WLWE*, 21.1, 1992, 13-25.

Pybus, Rodney. '*Cotter's England*: In Appreciation'. *Stand*, XXIII, No. 4, 1982, 40-47.

---. 'The Light and the Dark: The Novels of Christina Stead'. *Stand*, X, No. 1, 1969, 30-37.

Raskin, Jonah. 'Christina Stead in Washington Square'. *London Magazine*, N.S., IX, No. 11, 1970, 70-77. Interview.

Reid, Ian. 'Form and Expectation in Christina Stead's Novellas'. *Literary Criterion* (Mysore), XV, Nos. 3-4, 1980, 48-58.

Riddell, Elizabeth. 'Collector's Stead'. *Australian*, 5 September, 1973, 12.

Riem, Antonella. 'Deepening Consciousness Through Love in Christina Stead's *For Love Alone*'. In her *The Labyrinths of Self: A Collection of Essays on Australian and Caribbean Literature*. (Leichhardt, N.S.W.: FILEF. Italo-Australian Publications, 1987), 197-207.

Riemer, Andrew. 'Critics Can Be Creative, Too' (The Invention of Christina Stead). *Independent Monthly*, 5.11, 1994, 76-80.

---. 'This World, the Next, and Australia - the Emergence of a Literary Commonplace'. *Southerly*, XLIV, 1984, 251-70.

Roff, Sue. 'Rites of Passage: Six Australian Authors in Search of the Same Character'. *Australian Society*, III, No. 9, 1984, 33-34.

Ross, Robert L. 'Christina Stead's Encounter with "The True Reader": The Origin and Outgrowth of Randall Jarrell's Introduction to *The Man Who Loved Children*'. In *Perspectives on Australia: Essays on Australiana in the Collections of the Harry Ransom Humanities Research Center*, edited by Dave Oliphant (Austin: Harry Ransom Humanities Research Center, University of Texas, 1989), 161-79.

Rowley, Hazel. 'Christina Stead: The Battleground of Life'. *Scripsi*, 8.3, 1993, 17-52.

---. *Christina Stead: A Biography*. (Port Melbourne: Heinemann, 1993). Reviewed by D. Bird, *Journal of Australian Studies*, 40, 1994, 89-90; A. Blake, *Editions*, 16, 1993, 3-4; V. Brady, *Australian Historical Studies*, 103, 1994, 340-41; D.R. Burns, *Overland*, 132, 1993, 77-79; D. Coad, *World Literature Today*, 68.3, 1994, 633; P. Craven, *Age*, 29 May, 1993, Saturday Extra 7; J. Davidson, *Meanjin*, 25.4, 1993, 783-86; H. Elliott, *Weekend Australian*, 5-6 June, 1993, Review 5; C. Ferrier, *A.L.S.*, 16.3, 1994, 348-51; A. Inglis, *Voices*, 3.4, 1993, 114-20; D. Modjeska, *S.M.H.*, 5 June, 1993, 45; A. Peek, *Island*, 57, 1993, 68-70; E. Riddell, *Bulletin*, 27 July, 1993, 89; L. Sage, *T.L.S.*, 20 August, 1993, 3-4; A. Segerberg, *Antipodes*, 9.1,

1995, 58-60; C. Semmler, *Quadrant*, 37.12, 1993, 82-84; C.K. Stead, *London Review of Books*, 17.11, 1995, 36; K.M. Stern, *Antipodes*, 9.1, 1995, 57-58; K. Stewart, *Southerly*, 53.4, 1993, 166-73; M. Wilding and K. Llewellyn, *ABR*, 152, 1993, 8-11 (see also interview with Hazel Rowley by R. Sorensen, *ABR*, 152, 1993, 5-7).

---. 'Christina Stead: Politics and Literature in the Radical Years, 1935-1942'. *Meridian*, 8, No. 2, 1989, 149-159.

---. 'Christina Stead: Un-Australian?' *Southerly*, 53.4, 1993, 47-57.

---. 'Christina Stead: The Voyage to Cythera'. *Span*, No. 26, 1988, 33-45.

---. 'A "Wanderer": Christina Stead'. *Westerly*, XXXIII, No. 1, 1988, 15-21.

S[tewart], K.A. '"Lydham Hall", Bexley, Sydney: Home of Christina Stead 1907-1917'. *Notes & Furphies*, No. 1, 1978, 10-11.

Sage, Lorna. 'Inheriting the Future: *For Love Alone*'. *Stand*, XXIII, No. 4, 1982, 34-39.

Schofield, R.J. 'The Man Who Loved Christina Stead'. *Bulletin*, 22 May, 1965, 29-31.

Scopes, Evelyn. *Christina Stead. The Man Who Loved Children*. (Ringwood, Vic.: Penguin, 1984).

Segerberg, Anita. 'A Christina Stead Letter'. *A.L.S.*, XIII, No. 2, 1987, 198-201.

---. 'Christina Stead in New York'. *Antipodes*, 3.1, 1989, 15-19.

---. 'A Fiction of Sisters: Christina Stead's *Letty Fox* and *For Love Alone*'. *A.L.S.*, 14, No. 1, 1989, 15-25.

---. 'Getting Started: The Emergence of Christina Stead's Early Fiction'. *A.L.S.*, XIII, No. 2, 1987, 121-138.

Semmler, Clement. 'The Novels of Christina Stead'. In *The Literature of Australia*, edited by Geoffrey Dutton. Revised edition (Ringwood, Vic.: Penguin, 1976), 485-99.

Sheinberg, J. 'Sam Pollit: A Psychological Case Study'. *Notes & Furphies*, No. 1, 1978, 11.

Sheridan, Susan. *Christina Stead*. (Hemel Hempstead, Herts.: Harvester Wheatsheaf; Indiana: Indiana U.P., 1988). Reviewed by M. Arkin, *Antipodes*, 4.1, 1990, 75; P. F. Edelson, *Modern Fiction Studies*, 35.4, 1989, 872; J. Gribble, *A.L.S.*, 14, No. 3, 1990, 398-400; L. Niall, *ABR*, No. 109, 1989, 17-18; H. Rowley, *Westerly*, 34, No. 1, 1989, 86-89.

---. '*The Man Who Loved Children* and the Patriarchal Family Drama'. In *Gender, Politics and Fiction: Twentieth Century Women's Novels*, edited by C. Ferrier (St Lucia: U.Q.P., 1985), 136-49.

---. 'Re-reading Christina Stead'. *Southerly*, 53.4, 1993, 42-46.

---. 'The Woman Who Loved Men: Christina Stead as Satirist in *A Little Tea, a Little Chat* and *The People with the Dogs*'. *WLWE*, 21.1, 1992, 2-12.

Smith, Graeme Kinross. 'Christina Stead - A Profile'. *Westerly*, No. 1, 1976, 67-75.

Southerly. XLIV, No. 1, 1984. Special Christina Stead issue. Reviewed by L. Clancy, *Age Saturday Extra*, 14 July, 1984, 14; A. Mitchell, *Weekend Australian Magazine*, 9-10 June, 1984, 14.

Spencer, T.J.B., and Wilding, M. 'A Report on Contemporary Literature'. *Year Book of World Affairs*, XXIII, 1969, 331-39.

Stern, Kate Macomber. *Christina Stead's Heroine: The Changing Sense of Decorum*. American University Studies, series 4, English Language and Literature 87 (New York: Peter Lang, 1989). Reviewed by J. Gribble, *A.L.S.*, 14, No. 3, 1990, 398-400; N. Lee-Jones, *Antipodes*, 4.1, 1990, 74.

Stewart, Ken. 'Heaven and Hell in *The Man Who Loved Children*'. *Meridian*, II, 1984, 121-27.

---. 'Male Chauvinism: The Origin of a Phrase'. *Age Monthly Review*, VI, No. 8, 1986, 15-16.

Stivens, Dal. 'Obituaries'. *Australian Author*, XV, No. 3, 1983, 21.

Sturm, Terry. 'Christina Stead's New Realism: *The Man Who Loved Children* and *Cotters' England*'. In *Cunning Exiles: Studies of Modern Prose Writers*, edited by Don Anderson and Stephen Knight (Sydney: A.& R., 1974), 9-35.

Summers, Anne. 'The Self Denied: Australian Women Writers - Their Image of Women'. *Refractory Girl*, No. 2, 1973, 4-11.

Sykes, Jill. 'Portrait of a Private Writer'. *S.M.H.*, 17 June, 1976, 7.

Thomas, Tony. 'Christina Stead: *The Salzburg Tales, Seven Poor Men of Sydney*'. *Westerly*, No. 4, 1970, 46-53.

Tracy, Lorna. 'The Virtue of the Story: *The Salzburg Tales*'. *Stand*, XXIII, No. 4, 1982, 48-53.

Truscott, Hilary. 'The Question of National Identity in *Seven Poor Men of Sydney*'. *Australian Studies*, No. 3, 1989, 72-80.

Walker, Shirley. 'Language, Art and Ideas in *The Man who Loved Children*'. *Meridian*, II, No. 1, 1983, 11-19.

Waten, Judah. 'Some Australians and Iris Murdoch'. *Age*, 19 February, 1966, 22.

West, Rebecca. 'Christina Stead - A Tribute'. *Stand*, XXIII, No. 4, 1982, 31-33.

Wetherell, Rodney. 'Christina Stead Talks to Rodney Wetherell'. *Overland*, No. 93, 1983, 17-29. Previously published as 'Christina Stead Looks Back' in *24 Hours*, V, No. 2, 1980, 62-63 (abridged), and *A.L.S.*, X, 1980, 431-48.

Whitehead, Ann. 'Christina Stead: An Interview'. *A.L.S.*, VI, 1974, 230-48. Transcript of an A.B.C. interview.

Wilding, Michael. 'Christina Stead'. *A.L.S.*, XI, 1983, 150-51.

---. 'Christina Stead's Australian Novels'. *Southerly*, XXVII, 1967, 20-23.

---. 'Christina Stead's *The Puzzleheaded Girl*: The Political Context'. In *Words and Wordsmiths: A Volume for H.L. Rogers*, edited by Geraldine Barnes et al. (Sydney: Dept. of English, University of Sydney, 1989), 147-73.

---. 'I Like Him to Write'. [Part-biographical] *Meanjin*, 53.2, 1994, 197-207.

---. *The Radical Tradition: Lawson, Furphy, Stead*. (Townsville, Qld: Foundation for Australian Literary Studies/James Cook U of North Queensland, 1993).

Williams, Chris. *Christina Stead: A Life of Letters*. (Melbourne: McPhee Gribble; London: Virago, 1989). Reviewed by F. Capp, *Australian Women's Book Review*, 1, No. 1, 1990, 2-3; L. Clancy, *Meridian*, 8, No. 2, 1989, 175-78; K. Goldsworthy, *Weekend Australian*, 19-20 August, 1989, Weekend 9; J. Gribble, *A.L.S.*, 14, No. 3, 1990, 398-400; M. Harris, *S.M.H.*, 12 August, 1989, 79; N. Lee-Jones, *Antipodes*, 4.1, 1990, 74; K. Llewellyn, *ABR*, No. 113, 1989, 11-12; S. McKernan, *Bulletin*, 18 July, 1989, 112, J. Mead, *Editions*, No. 2, 1989, 15; L. Sage, *T.L.S.*, 26 January- 1 February, 1990, 85; J. Stone, *Biblionews and Australian Notes and Queries*, 14, No. 4, 1989, 105-109; C. Wallace-Crabbe, *Age Saturday Extra*, 12 August, 1989, 11.

---. 'Christina Stead's Australia - "Easily the Largest Island"'. *Southerly*, 53.1, 1993, 80-95.

---. 'David Stead: The Man Who Loved Nature'. *Meridian*, 8, No. 2, 1989, 101-13.

Woodward, Wendy. 'Calling a Spade a Muck Dig: Discourse and Gender in Some Novels by Christina Stead'. In *Crisis and Creativity in the New Literatures in English*, edited by Geoffrey V. Davis and Hena Maes-Jelinek. Cross/Cultures 1 (Amsterdam; Atlanta Ga.: Rodopi, 1990), 249-64.

---. 'Concealed Invitations: The Use of Metaphor in Some of Christina Stead's Narratives'. *Southerly*, 53.4, 1993, 80-95.

Yelin, Louise. 'Christina Stead in 1991'. *WLWE*, 21.1, 1992, 52-54.

---. 'Sexual Politics and Female Heroism in the Novels of Christina Stead'. In *Faith of a (Woman) Writer*, edited by Alice Kessler-Harris and William McBrien (Westport, Ct.: Greenwood Press, 1988), 191-98.

STEPHENS, A.G.

Non-Fiction

A.G. Stephens: Selected Writings. Edited by Leon Cantrell. (Sydney: A.& R., 1977). Perspectives in Australian Literature. Reprinted Sydney: A.& R., 1979. Reviewed by D. Green, *Meanjin*, XXXVIII, 1979, 495-500; D. Jarvis, *A.L.S.*, IX, 1980, 417-18; G. Sprod, *S.M.H.*, 12 August, 1978, 17; P. Thompson, *24 Hours*, III, No. 10, 1978, 72; D. Walker, *National Times*, 4 November, 1978, 49.

The Writer in Australia, edited by John Barnes (Melbourne: O.U.P., 1969), passim, but see particularly Section 2, 'Discovering Australia', 65-157, reprinting Stephens on Lawson, Furphy, and Brennan.

Critical Material

Mackaness, George. 'Alfred George Stephens: A Check List'. In his *Bibliomania*: *An Australian Book Collector's Essays*. (Sydney: A.& R., 1965), 179-81.

Anderson, Hugh, and Blake, L.J. *John Shaw Neilson*. (Adelaide: Rigby, 1972). Deals with Stephens as editor.

Barnes, John. 'A.G. Stephens and the Critic's Tasks'. *Meanjin*, XXVII, 1968, 459-71.

Cantrell, Leon. 'A.G. Stephens, *The Bulletin*, and the 1890s'. In *Bards, Bohemians, and Bookmen*, edited by Leon Cantrell (St Lucia: U.Q.P., 1976), 98-113.

Chaplin, H.F. 'Shaw Neilson & A.G. Stephens, a Note on the Copyrights'. *Biblionews and Australian Notes & Queries*, series 3, I, No. 2, 1976, 20-26.

Kiernan, Brian. 'A.G. Stephens's *Bookfellow* in New Zealand'. *A.L.S.*, 16.2, 1993, 211-15.

Lawson, Valerie. *Connie Sweetheart*. (Melbourne: Heinemann, 1990). Contains material on Connie Sweetheart Robertson's father, A.G. Stephens, and his times. Reviewed by P. Butterss, *Australian Historical Studies*, 24.97, 1991, 472-74; S.E. Lee, *Southerly*, 51.1, 1991, 153-58.

Lee, S.E. '*The Bulletin* - J.F. Archibald and A.G. Stephens'. In *The Literature of Australia*, edited by Geoffrey Dutton (Adelaide: Penguin Books, 1964), 273-87.

--- 'A.G. Stephens: The Critical Credo'. *A.L.S.*, I, No. 4, 1964, 219-41.

---. 'A.G. Stephens as Literary Editor'. *Southerly*, XXIV, 1964, 101-73.

Maidment, W.M. 'A.G. Stephens and the "Gympie Miner"'. *Southerly*, XXIV, No. 3, 1964, 190-205.

Palmer, Vance. *Intimate Portraits*, ed. H.P. Heseltine. (Melbourne: Cheshire, 1969), 108-12.

Semmler, Clement. 'A.G. Stephens as Editor of Barcroft Boake's Poems'. *A.L.S.*, III, 1968, 228-30.

Stephens, Alison. 'A.G. Stephens as Editor of Barcroft Boake's Poems: A Comment'. *A.L.S.*, IV, 1969, 80-83. Discusses Clement Semmler's article.

Stone, Leon. '"Furnley Maurice" vs. "The Red Pagan"'. *Biblionews and Australian Notes & Queries*, IV, No. 3-4, 1970, 10-12.

Stone, Walter. 'A.G. Stephens and F.A. Malcolm'. *Biblionews and Australian Notes & Queries*, Second Series, VI, Nos. 1-2, 1972, 7-8.

---. 'Beating the Salvage Bag'. *Biblionews*, I, No. 4, 1966, 3-6.

Webb, John. 'Poets versus Critics'. *A.L.S.*, V, 1972, 312-16.

Whitlock, Gillian. 'A.G. Stephens: An Internationalist Critic'. *A.L.S.*, VIII, 1977, 82-91.

STEPHENS, JAMES BRUNTON

Critical Material

Hadgraft, Cecil. *James Brunton Stephens*. (St Lucia: U.Q.P., 1969). Reviewed by M. Dunlevy, *Canberra Times*, 3 January, 1970, 14; B. Elliott, *ABR*, IX, 1970, 92; S. Lawson, *Nation*, 18 April, 1970, 23; A. Mitchell, *A.L.S.*, IV, 1970, 303-05; E.

Perkins, *Makar*, VI, No. 1, 1970, 32-38.
Semmler, Clement. 'Brunton Stephens as Literary Critic'. *A.L.S.*, II, No. 2, 1965, 92-102.

STEPHENSEN, P.R.

Non-Fiction

The Foundations of Culture in Australia. With a new introduction by Craig Munro. (Sydney: Allen and Unwin, 1986). First published Gordon, N.S.W.: Miles, 1936. Reviewed by V. Brady, *Australian Society*, VI, No. 1, 1987, 40-42; D. Dolan, *Canberra Times*, 20 December, 1986, B3; D. English, *ABR*, No. 92, 1987, 33-34; A. Mitchell, *Weekend Australian. Weekend Magazine*, 10-11 January, 1987, 11.

'The Foundations of Culture in Australia: An Essay towards National Self-respect'. In *The Writer in Australia*, edited by John Barnes (Melbourne: O.U.P., 1969), 204-44. First published 1935.

Critical Material

Arnold, John. 'Jack Lindsay, P.R. Stephensen and the Publication of D.H. Lawrence's Paintings'. *A.L.S.*, IX, 1979, 242-43.
Doecke, Brenton. 'P.R. Stephensen, "Fascism"'. *Westerly*, 38.2, 1993, 17-28.
Fotheringham, Richard. 'Expatriate Publishing: Jack Lindsay and the Fanfrolico Press'. *Meanjin*, XXXI, 55-61.
---. 'Expatriate Publishing: P.R. Stephensen and the Mandrake Press'. *Meanjin*, XXXI, 1972, 183-88.
Hall, Robert Lowe. 'Expatriate Publishing'. *Meanjin*, XXXIII, 1974, 170-76.
Kershaw, Alister. 'P.R. Stephensen'. *Southerly*, XLIII, 1983, 185-99. Reminiscences.
Lindsay, Jack. 'Expatriate Publishing'. *Meanjin*, XXXIII, 1974, 176-79.
---. 'Mouthpiece of the Unruly. *Overland*, No. 96, 1984, 47-50.
---. 'Zarathustran Walkabout'. *T.L.S.*, 9 April, 1976, 423.
Muirden, Bruce. *The Puzzled Patriots: The Story of the Australia First Movement* Amended edition. (Carlton: M.U.P.; London, New York: Cambridge University Press, 1968).
Munro, Craig. *Wild Man of Letters: The Story of P.R. Stephensen*. (Carlton: M.U.P., 1984). Reprinted St Lucia: U.Q.P., 1992. Reviewed by D. Anderson, *National Times*, 20-26 July, 1984, 30; A. Barker, *S.M.H.*, 21 July, 1984, 48; P. Botsman, *Courier-Mail*, 25 August, 1984, 28; P. Bowman, *Antipodes*, 7.1, 1993, 82; A. Clark, *Quadrant*, XXVIII, No. 9, 1984 75-77; R. Fitzgerald, *Imago*, 5.1, 1993, 84-86; J. Fletcher, *Biblionews and Australian Notes & Queries*, IX, 1984, 123-28; D. Green, *Meanjin*, XLIV, No. 2, 1985, 193-208; M. Harrison, *Look & Listen*, I, No. 3, 1984, 88; P. Hasluck, *Age Saturday Extra*, 28 July, 1984, 15; P. Lloyd, *Advertiser*, 11 August, 1984, 41; R. McDonald, *Age Monthly Review*, IV, No. 4, 1984, 3-4; H. McQueen, *Australian Society*, IV, No. 1, 1985, 36-37; A. Mitchell, *Weekend Australian Magazine*, 7-8 July, 1984, 15; B. Muirden, *ABR*, No. 64, 5-6; E. Perkins, *LiNQ*, XIII, No. 3, 1985, 57-61; V. Smith, *A.L.S.*, XII, No. 3, 1986, 417-21; J. Walter, *Meanjin*, XLV, No. 4, 1986, 479-87; G. Windsor, *Bulletin*, 10 July, 1984, 72-73.
--- 'The D.H. Lawrence - P.R. Stephensen Letters'. *A.L.S.*, XI, 1984, 291-315.
---. 'P.R. Stephensen and the Early Workers' Theatre Movement in London'. *Australasian Drama Studies*, 1, No. 2, 1983, 125-37.
---. 'Some Facts about a Long Fiction: The Publication of *Capricornia*'. *Southerly*, XLI, 1981, 82-104. Stephensen was the book's publisher.
---. 'Two Boys from Queensland: P.R. Stephensen and Jack Lindsay'. In *Culture & History*, edited by Bernard Smith (Sydney: Hale & Iremonger, 1984), 40-71.
Ormsby, Myles G. 'Inky Stephensen'. *Quadrant*, XXVIII, No. 11, 1984, 3. Letter to the editor.
Reid, Ian. 'A Splendid Bubble: Publishing and Fiction-Writing in the 'Thirties'.

Meanjin, XXXIII, 1974, 266-71.
Roe, Michael. 'P.R. Stephensen & Aleister Crowley'. *Meanjin*, XXXIII, 1974, 180.
Stone, Walter. 'Collecting Books and Manuscripts for Australia's Libraries'.
University of Queensland Alumni News, III, No. 3, 1971, 29-38.
Trundle, Peter. 'Stephensen: The Radical Who Loved Words'. *Courier-Mail*, 30 June,
1984, 24.

STEWART, DOUGLAS

Drama
The Fire on the Snow. (Sydney: A.& R., 1977). Playtexts. First published Sydney:
A.& R., 1944.
Reviewed by K. Brisbane, *24 Hours*, II, No. 4, 1977, 56.

Poetry
Australian Poets: Douglas Stewart. (Sydney: A.& R., 1963). Reprinted as *Selected
Poems*, Australian Poets (Sydney: A.& R., 1966).
Reviewed by *T.L.S.*, 16 September, 1965, 799.

Collected Poems, 1936-1967. (Sydney: A.& R., 1967).
Reviewed by A. Brissenden, *Adelaide Advertiser*, 14 October, 1967, 14; E.A.M.
Colman, *Poetry Magazine*, No. 1, 1968, 27-31; B. Dawe, *Overland*, No. 40, 1968,
41; M. Dunlevy, *Canberra Times*, 4 November, 1967, 11; D. Green, *Nation*, 3
February, 1968, 20-21; F. Haynes, *Westerly*, No. 1, 1968, 53-55; A. King, *Meanjin*,
XXVII, 1968, 172-73; S.E. Lee, *Southerly*, XXVIII, 1968, 157-59; G. Lehmann,
S.M.H., 11 November, 1967, 20; C. Semmler, *ABR*, VII, 1967, 41; V. Smith,
Bulletin, 21 October, 1967, 89-90.

Douglas Stewart Reads from His Own Work. (St Lucia: U.Q.P., 1971). Poets on
Record, 6. Record and booklet. Booklet includes notes by the author and selected
bibliography.
Reviewed by P. Annand, *Makar*, VII, No. 4, 1971, 42-43; *New Poetry*, XX, No. 4,
1972, 49; A.C. Lyons, *Twentieth Century*, XXVI, 1971, 183; D. Malouf, *Australian*,
18 December, 1971, 16; P. Roberts, *S.M.H.*, 29 April, 1972, 16; R.A. Simpson,
Age, 8 January, 1972, 11.

Selected Poems. (Sydney: A.& R., 1973). Foreword by the author. This selection
differs from that in the Australian Poets series (1966).
Reviewed by R. Campbell, *Bulletin*, 2 June, 1973, 54-55.

Selected Poems. (Pymble, NSW: A.& R., 1992). First published Sydney: A.& R.,
1973.
Reviewed by P. Nelson, *Quadrant* 37.7-8, 1993, 117-19.

Non-Fiction
Douglas Stewart's Garden of Friends. Illustrated by Margaret Coen; afterword by
Meg Stewart. (Ringwood, Vic.: Penguin, 1988). Corrected edition. First published
Ringwood, Vic.: Viking, 1987.
Reviewed by M. Gollan, *S.M.H.*, 7 November, 1987, 81; P. Hasluck, *Fremantle Arts
Review*, III, No. 1, 1988, 15; B. Reid, *Overland*, No. 109, 1987, 79-80; C. Semmler,
Weekend Australian. Weekend Magazine, 16-17 January, 1988, 1.

The Seven Rivers. (Sydney: A.& R., 1966).
Reviewed by M. Clark, *Bulletin*, 26 November, 1966, 57; T. Forshaw, *Nation*, 15
October, 1966, 23-4; D. Macdonald, *Canberra Times*, 19 November, 1966, 11; J.
Pringle, *S.M.H*, 12 November, 1966, 8; O. Ruhen, *ABR*, VI, 1966, 27.

Springtime in Taranaki: Autobiography of Youth. (Sydney: Hale & Iremonger, 1983).
Reviewed by M. Dunlevy, *Canberra Times*, 19 November, 1983, 22; R.D.
FitzGerald, *Overland*, Nos. 94-95, 1984, 84-85; T. Forshaw, *Quadrant*, XXVIII,
Nos. 1-2, 1984, 139-49; C. Hadgraft, *A.L.S.*, XII, No. 1, 1985, 142-143; N.

Keesing, *Weekend Australian Magazine*, 5-6 November, 1983, 18; L. Kramer, *S.M.H.*, 5 November, 1983, 43; N. Phelan, *Age Saturday Extra*, 10 December, 1983, 15; C. Semmler, *ABR*, No. 58, 1984, 16-17.

'On Being a Verse Playwright'. *Meanjin*, XXIII, No. 3, 1964, 272-7.

   Critical Material

'Douglas Stewart Dies'. *S.M.H.*, 16 February, 1985, 1. For other obituaries see *ABR*, No. 69, 1985, 5-6; *Age Saturday Extra*, 23 February, 1985, 14; *Bulletin*, 5 March, 1985, 39, 41; *S.M.H.*, 16 February, 1985, 11; *Overland*, No. 98, 1985, 30-31; *Quadrant*, XXIX, No. 4, 1985, 11-12; *Weekend Australian*, 16-17 February, 1985, 4.

'Rewritten "Matilda" Withdrawn'. *Canberra Times*, 12 July, 1973, 1. Similar report in *S.M.H.*, 12 July, 1973, 1. Deals with Stewart's contribution to the Australian National Anthem quest.

Ashworth, Arthur. 'From a Discussion of the Poetry of Douglas Stewart'. *Poetry Magazine*, No. 5, 1966, 3-6. Includes comments by Douglas Stewart.

Ballyn, Susan. 'A Family affair: Douglas Stewart's *Garden of Friends*'. *Revista Canaria de Estudios Ingleses* (Teneriffe, Spain), No. 16, 1988, 205-11.

---. 'Man and Nature in Douglas Stewart's *The Birdsville Track*'. *Commonwealth* (Paris), VI, No. 2, 1986, 25-29.

Bourke, Lawrence. 'Making the Crossing: Douglas Stewart the Expatriate Patriot'. *Southerly*, 53.2, 1993, 40-53.

Burrows, J.F. 'An Approach to the Plays of Douglas Stewart'. *Southerly*, XXIII, No. 2, 1963, 94-108.

Drewe, Robert. 'Foreword'. *Australian*, 2 June, 1973, 37. Retirement from Angus & Robertson.

FitzGerald, R.D. 'Motif in the Work of Douglas Stewart'. In his *The Elements of Poetry*. (Brisbane: U.Q.P., 1963).

Gooneratne, Yasmine. 'Douglas Stewart. *The Silkworms*'. In *Australian Poems in Perspective*, edited by P.K. Elkin (St Lucia: U.Q.P., 1978), 117-40.

Kavanagh, Paul. 'Preternatural Mimicry: The Lyric Poetry of Douglas Stewart'. *Southerly*, XLIII, 1983, 265-81.

Keesing, Nancy. *Douglas Stewart*. (Melbourne: Lansdowne Press, 1965). Revised edition (Melbourne: O.U.P., 1969). Reviewed by A. Brissenden, *ABR*, V, 1966, 63; W. Hart-Smith, *Bulletin*, 5 February, 1966, 34; R. McCuaig, *Canberra Times*, 29 January, 1966, 11.

Kramer, Leonie. 'Two Perspectives in the Poetry of Douglas Stewart'. *Southerly*, XXXIII, 1973, 286-99.

Lawson, Max. *Companion to Douglas Stewart: Ned Kelly*. (Sydney: A.& R., 1965). Foreword by Douglas Stewart.

---. *Companion to Douglas Stewart: The Fire On The Snow*. (Sydney: A.& R., 1965). Introduction by Douglas Stewart.

Lindsay, Norman. *The Scribblings of an Idle Mind*. (Melbourne: Lansdowne Press, 1966), 92 6 and passim.

McAuley, James. 'Douglas Stewart'. In *The Literature of Australia*, edited by Geoffrey Dutton (Adelaide: Penguin Books, 1964), 362-76.

McGregor, Craig (ed.). *In the Making*. (Melbourne: Nelson Australia, 1969), 108-13.

McKernan, Susan. 'Douglas Stewart and the *Bulletin*'. In her *A Question of Commitment: Australian Literature in the Twenty Years after the War*. (Sydney: Allen and unwin, 1989), 120-40.

O'Brien, Geraldine. 'A Gardening Poet who Sings the Universe into Shape'. *S.M.H.*, 1 October, 1983, 47.

Phillips, A.A. 'Hallowing a Ghost'. In his *Responses: Selected Writings*. (Kew, Vic.: Australian International Press & Publications, 1979), 70-71. Review of *Fisher's Ghost* first published in the *Bulletin*, 26 October, 1960, 74.

---. 'The Poetry of Douglas Stewart'. In his *Responses: Selected Writings*. (Kew, Vic.: Australian International Press & Publications, 1979), 158-66. First published in *Meanjin*, XXVIII, 1969, 97-104.

Pringle, John Douglas. 'Pringle and Stewart'. *24 Hours*, I, No. 12, 1977, 45-46. Radio interview.

Robinson, Dennis. 'Douglas Stewart's Nature Lyrics'. *Southerly*, XLVII, No. 1, 1987, 52-69.

---. 'Douglas Stewart's *Rutherford*'. *Southerly*, XLVII, No. 2, 1987, 150-163.

Rowbotham, David. 'Profile of a Poet: Nature Inspires Douglas Stewart'. *Courier-Mail*, 25 May, 1971, 16.

Sayers, Stuart. 'Writers and Readers'. *Age*, 21 December, 1968, 10. On literary awards made to Douglas Stewart during 1968.

Semmler, Clement. *Douglas Stewart*. (New York: Twayne Publishers, 1974). Twayne's World Authors series, 327. Reviewed by B. Elliott, *Advertiser*, 20 September, 1975, 28; C. Hadgraft, *A.L.S.*, VII, 1975, 217-19 (see also C. Semmler's letter, *A.L.S.*, VII, 1976, 342-44 and Hadgraft's reply *A.L.S.*, VII, 1976, 445); C. Harrison-Ford, *Age*, 19 July, 1975, 18; N. Keesing, *S.M.H.*, 17 May, 1975, 17; D. Martin, *Overland*, No. 64, 1976, 58-60; J. Waten, *Age*, 16 July, 1977, 23; D. Whitelock, *Australian*, 26 July, 1975, 29.

Smith, Ross. 'Douglas Stewart: "Terra Australis"'. *LiNQ*, II, No. 2, 1973, 29-34.

Smith, Vivian. 'Experiment and Renewal: A Missing Link in Modern Australian Poetry'. *Southerly*, XLVII, No. 1, 1987, 3-18; esp. 10-18.

---. 'Lyric Poet'. *Meanjin*, XXVI, 1967, 41-50.

---. 'McAuley and Stewart'. Letter to the Editor. *Bulletin*, 19 February, 1966, 35-6. Deals with authorship of books in the Australian Writers and Their Work Series.

Spate, Oskar. 'Quiros and the Poets'. *Overland*, No. 112, 1988, 69-72. Discusses poems by Rex Ingamells, Douglas Stewart and James McAuley.

Thompson, John. 'Poetry in Australia: Douglas Stewart'. *Southerly*, XXVII, 1967, 188-98. Transcript of an interview with John Thompson telecast in 1965.

STEWART, HAROLD

See also Malley, Ern.

Poetry

By the Old Walls of Kyoto. (New York: Weatherhill, 1981). Reviewed by *T.L.S.*, 30 October, 1981, 1272; H. Bolitho, *Age*, 5 September, 1981, 27; C. Pearson, *Advertiser*, 29 May, 1982, 25; V. Sen, *Canberra Times*, 31 October, 1981, 14; M. South, *Hemisphere*, XXVI, 1982, 264-65; P. Warner, *Weekend Australian Magazine*, 26-27 September, 1981, 11.

A Chime of Windbells: A Year of Japanese Haiku in English Verse. Translations with an essay (Melbourne, Sydney: Paul Flesch; Rutland, Vt., Tokyo: Charles E. Tuttle, 1969).
Reviewed by B. Beaver, *S.M.H.*, 21 June, 1969, 2; D. Green, *Canberra Times*, 19 July, 1969, 15; G. Lehmann, *Bulletin*, 16 August, 1969, 53-54; R.A. Simpson, *Age*, 25 October, 1969, 17.

Critical Material

Ackland, Michael. 'Harold Stewart: A Tribute'. *Quadrant*, 39.11, 1995, 30-33. Obituary.

Dunlop, Ronald. 'Pilgrim's Origress in Japan: Discovering Harold Stewart'. *Southerly*, XLIII, 1983, 167-81.

---. 'Some Aspects of the Poetry of Harold Stewart'. *Southerly*, XXIII, No. 4, 1963, 222-34.

Green, Dorothy. 'Ern Malley's Other Half: Harold Stewart's "By the Old Walls of Kyoto"'. *Quadrant*, XXI, No. 8, 1977, 33-39.

---. 'Poet's Progress'. *Hemisphere*, XVII, No. 12, 1973, 12-21.
Horne, Donald. *The Education of Young Donald*. (Sydney: A.& R., 1967), 229 and passim thereafter.

STIVENS, DAL

Fiction

A Horse of Air. (Sydney: A.& R., 1970). Reprinted Ringwood, Vic.: Penguin, 1986.
Reviewed by D. Ball, *Bulletin*, 12 December, 1970, 59; R. Campbell, *Daily Telegraph* (Sydney), 27 March, 1971, 52; T. Glad, *Social Alternatives*, VI, No. 2, 1987, 75; M. Lemming, *ABR*, X, 1971, 152-53; D. Matthews, *Overland*, No. 106, 1987, 80-82; E. Morgan, *Listener*, 29 April, 1971, 559; M. Vintner, *S.M.H.*, 16 January, 1971, 20.

Jimmy Brockett. (Ringwood, Vic.: Penguin, 1983). First published London: Britannicus Liber, 1951.
Reviewed by D. Carter, *Age Saturday Extra*, 31 December, 1983, 8; L. Clancy, *Overland*, No. 96, 1984, 73-74; P. Eggert, *ABR*, No. 60, 1984, 33; V. Ikin, *Westerly*, XXIX, No. 1, 1984, 91-93; C.K. Stead, *S.M.H.*, 29 October, 1983, 41.

Selected Stories, 1936-1968. Introduction by H.P. Heseltine. (Sydney: A.& R., 1969).
Reviewed by M.Dunlevy, *Canberra Times*, 16 August, 1969, 12; S. Hall, *Bulletin*, 16 August, 1969, 51; E. Rice, *Age*, 20 September, 1969, 14; C. Semmler, *ABR*, VIII, 1969, 268-69; M. Vintner, *S.M.H.*, 9 August, 1969, 17; M. Wilding, *Meanjin*, XXX, 1971, 261-63.

Three Persons Make a Tiger. (Melbourne: Cheshire, 1968).
Reviewed by N. Keesing, *ABR*, VII, 1968, 115; B. Kiernan, *Australian*, 6 April, 1968, 14 (see also letters to the editor by J. Clarke, *Australian*, 16 April, 1968, 6; A.D. Hope, 22 April, 1968, 8; B. Kiernan, 8 May, 1968, 8; and 'J. Swift' [D. Stivens] 8 May, 1968, 8); F. King, *Bulletin*, 20 April, 1968, 68; J. McLaren, *Overland*, No. 40, 1968, 40-41; S. Sayers, *Age*, 26 October, 1968, 12.

The Unicorn and Other Tales. (Sydney: Wild & Woolley, 1976).
Reviewed by D.R. Burns, *Nation Review*, 30 December, 1976-5 January, 1977, 261; A.R. Chisholm, *Age*, 30 October, 1976, 18; R. Creswell, *24 Hours*, II, No. 3, 1977, 48-49.

Non-Fiction
'A *Bulletin* Short Story'. *Southerly*, XL, 1980, 211-21.

Critical Material
'Manuscripts: Dal Stivens'. *National Library of Australia, Acquisitions Newsletter*, No. 9, 1971, 1-2.
Hadgraft, Cecil. 'Indulgence: David Martin's *The Hero of Too*, Frank Dalby Davison's *The White Thorntree*, Dal Stivens's *A Horse of Air*, David Malouf's *Johnno*, and Frank Hardy's *But the Dead are Many*'. In *Studies in the Recent Australian Novel*, edited by K.G. Hamilton (St Lucia: U.Q.P., 1978), 194-224.
Hawley, Janet. 'Dal Stivens is Bored with His Prize Book'. *Australian*, 25 March, 1971, 3.
Hickman, Lorraine. '"I Get Obsessed"'. *Australian Women's Weekly*, 21 July, 1971, 65.
O'Connor, Ursula. 'A Winner, but He Still Has Obsessions'. *S.M.H.*, 25 March, 1971, 3.

STONE, LOUIS

Fiction
Jonah. With an introduction by Ronald McCuaig. (Sydney: A.& R., 1965). First

published London: Methuen, 1911.
Reviewed by J. Barbour, *Nation*, 18 September, 1965, 22 (and see letter by R. McCuaig, *Nation*, 16 October, 1965, 17); M. Dunlevy, *Canberra Times*, 21 August, 1965, 12; D. Green, *Australian*, 18 September, 1965, 11; N. Keesing, *Bulletin*, 28 August, 1965, 55; J. McLaren, *ABR*, IV, 1965, 223; *T.L.S.*, 6 January, 1966, 6.

   Critical Material
Chaplin, Harry F. (ed.). *Norman Lindsay: His Books, Manuscripts, and Autograph Letters in the Library of, and Annotated by Harry F. Chaplin*. Foreword by Norman Lindsay. (Sydney: Wentworth Press, 1969), 87-89. Studies in Australian and Pacific Bibliographies.
Cranston, C.A. 'Sentimental Jonah's Heart of Stone'. *A.L.S.*, 14, No. 2, 1989, 216-28.
Green, Dorothy. 'Louis Stone's *Jonah*: A Cinematic Novel'. *A.L.S.*, II, No. 1, 1965, 15-31.
Oliver, H.J. *Louis Stone*. (Melbourne: O.U.P., 1968). Australian Writers and Their Work. Reviewed by M. Dunlevy, *Canberra Times*, 17 May, 1969, 13; F.H. Mares, *A.L.S.*, IV, 1969, 189-90.

STOW, RANDOLPH

   Collection
Randolph Stow: 'Visitants', Episodes From Other Novels, Poems, Interviews and Essays. Edited by Anthony J. Hassall (St Lucia: U.Q.P., 1990).
Reviewed by I. Indyk, *A.L.S.*, 15.3, 1992, 232-35; G. Jones, *SPAN*, 33, 1992, 173-74; C. Semmler, *Weekend Australian*, 10-11 November, 1990, Review 7.

   Fiction
The Girl Green as Elderflower. (London: Secker & Warburg, 1980).
Reviewed by B. Clunies Ross, *Kunapipi*, II, No. 1, 1980, 184-85; V. Cunningham, *T.L.S.*, 16 May, 1980, 548; M. Dunlevy, *Canberra Times*, 26 July, 1981, 16; G. Dutton, *Bulletin*, 26 August, 1980, 72, 74; J. Hanrahan, *ABR*, No. 27, 1980, 8-9; A.J. Hassall, *Overland*, No. 90, 1982, 59-60; B. Jefferis, *S.M.H.*, 2 August, 1980, 20 and *Hemisphere*, XXVII, 1983, 257; N. Jillett, *Age*, 30 August, 1980, 25; B. King, *Sewanee Review*, LXXXIX, 1981, 461-69; J. Mellors, *Listener*, 22 May, 1980, 661; N. Shrimpton, *New Statesman*, XCIX, 1980, 936-37; H. Watson-Williams, *Westerly*, XXV, No. 4, 1980, 68-72.

The Merry-go-round in the Sea. (London: Macdonald; New York: Morrow, 1965). Reprinted London: Secker & Warburg, 1984.
Reviewed by J.K. Ewers, *W.A. Teachers' Journal*, LVI, 1966, 52; J. Gribble, *ABR*, V, 1966, 85; D. Hewett, *The Critic*, VI, 1965, 86-7; D.A.N. Jones, *London Review of Books*, VI, No. 7, 1984, 23; L.V. Kepert, *S.M.H.*, 27 November, 1965, 20; N. McPherson, *Westerly*, No. 1, 1966, 59-62; W. Noonan, *Australian*, 4 December, 1965, 10; *T.L.S.*, 8 November, 1965, 1028; E. Yeats, *Journal of Commonwealth Literature*, No. 3, 1967, 126.

The Suburbs of Hell. (Richmond, Vic.: Heinemann Australia, 1984). Simultaneously published London: Secker & Warburg.
Reviewed by J. Bedford, *National Times*, 17-23 August, 1984, 31; A. Brien, *New Statesman*, 24 May, 1985, 32; B. Clunies Ross, *Kunapipi*, VI, No. 1, 1984, 97-99; J. Davison, *Overland*, No. 97, 1984, 75; M. Dunlevy, *Canberra Times*, 25 August, 1984, 22; G. Dutton, *Bulletin*, 31 July, 1984, 59-60; L. Forsyth, *ABR*, No. 70, 1985, 18-19; A.J. Hassall, *Westerly*, XXIX, No. 4, 1984, 92-95; I. Hicks, *S.M.H.*, 30 June, 1984, 40; R. Hill, *Books & Bookmen*, No. 358, 1985, 33; D.A.N. Jones, *London Review of Books*, VI, No. 7, 1984, 23; N. Jose, *Age Monthly Review*, IV, No. 11, 1985, 6-8; F. King, *Spectator*, 7 April, 1984, 27-28; J. Mellors, *London Magazine*, N.S., XXIV, Nos. 1-2, 1984, 135-37; N.J. Richey, *World Literature*

Today, No. 59, 1985, 315-316; C. Semmler, *Courier-Mail*, 6 October, 1984, 30; H. Watson-Williams, *Westerly*, XXX, No. 2, 1985, 88-91.

To the Islands. (London: Secker & Warburg; Sydney: A.& R.). Revised edition. First edition published London: Macdonald, 1958.
Reviewed by A. Hassall, *ABR*, No. 45, 1982, 14; C. Hope, *T.L.S.*, 12 March, 1982, 277; L. Hughes-Hallett, *Spectator*, 27 February, 1982, 23-24; B. King, *Sewanee Review*, CXII, 1984, 136-39.

Tourmaline. (London: Macdonald, 1963). Reprinted London: Secker & Warburg; New York: Taplinger, 1982.
Reviewed by B. Burns, *Prospect*, VII, No. 1, 1964, 28; H.P. Heseltine, *Meanjin*, XXII, No. 4, 1963, 422-6; B. King, *Sewanee Review*, CXII, 1984, 136-39; L. Kramer, *Bulletin*, 6 July, 1963, 41; C. Semmler, *ABR*, II, 1963, 124; H.M.W., *CRNLE Reviews Journal*, No. 2, 1984, 106.

Visitants. (London: Secker & Warburg, 1979).
Reviewed by B. Clunies Ross, *Kunapipi*, II, No. 1, 1980, 184-85; G. Dutton, *Bulletin*, 22 January, 1980, 48-49; S. Edgar, *Canberra Times*, 29 March, 1980, 14; G. Goulder, *Westerly*, XXIX, No. 3, 1984, 91-93; A.J. Hassall, *ABR*, No. 19, 1980, 23; B. Hill, *National Times*, 24 February-1 March, 1980, 46; T.A.G. Hungerford, *Westerly*, XXV, No. 1, 1980, 105-07; B. King, *Sewanee Review*, LXXXIX, 1981, 461-69; F. King, *Spectator*, 1 December, 1979, 29; P. Lewis, *Stand*, XXI, No. 3, 1980, 70-71; E. Riddell, *24 Hours*, IV, No. 12, 1980, 67; N. Shrimpton, *New Statesman*, XCVIII, 1979, 902; J. Sinclair, *S.M.H.*, 1 December, 1979, 18; R. Soaba, *Overland*, No. 80, 1980, 64-66; N. Talbot, *CRNLE Reviews Journal*, No. 2, 1981, 52-53.

Poetry

A Counterfeit Silence: Selected Poems. (Sydney: A.& R., 1969).
Reviewed by R. Dunlop, *Poetry Australia*, No. 32, 1970, 50-51; R. Hall, *Australian*, 25 October, 1969, 26; F. Kellaway, *Overland*, No. 46, 1970/71, 39; *T.L.S.*, 15 January, 1970, 60; S.E. Lee, *Southerly*, XXX, 1970, 306-08; G. Lehmann, *Bulletin*, 25 October, 1969, 67-68; T. Rowse, *Union Recorder*, XLIX, No. 21, 1969, 39-40; T.W. Shapcott, *ABR*, VIII, 1969, 245; R.A. Simpson, *Age*, 25 October, 1969, 17.

Eight Songs for a Mad King. Music by Peter Maxwell Davies. (London: Boosey & Hawkes, 1971) (Recording: Unicorn RHS308).
Reviewed by J. Noble, *Gramophone*, LXIX, 1971, 1078, 1083.

Randolph Stow Reads from His Own Work. (St Lucia: U.Q.P., 1974). Poets on Record, 11. Record and booklet. Booklet includes notes by Thomas W. Shapcott and selected bibliography.
Reviewed by J. Beston, *S.M.H.*, 6 July, 1974, 15; R.M. Beston, *Makar*, X, No. 2, 1974, 47-48.

Non-Fiction

'The Southland of Antichrist: The *Batavia* Disaster of 1629'. In *Common Wealth*. Edited by Anna Rutherford (Aarhus: Akademisk Boghandel, 1971), 160-67. Papers delivered at the Conference of Commonwealth Literature, Aarhus University, 26-30 April, 1971.
'Transplantable Roots: On Being a Regional Writer in Two Countries'. *BASA Magazine*, II, No. 1, 1985, 3-8.

Critical Material

Beston, Rose Marie. 'A Randolph Stow Bibliography'. *Literary Half-Hearly*, XVI, No. 2, 1975, 137-44.
O'Brien, Patricia. *Randolph Stow: A Bibliography*. (Adelaide: Libraries Board of South Australia, 1968). Bibliographies of Australian Writers.
State Library of South Australia. Bibliographies of Australian Writers Supplements.

Index to Australian Book Reviews, IV, 1968, 267-71; V, 1969, 253-60; VI, 1970, 324-5; VII, 1971, 296-98; VIII, 1972, 252-4; IX, 1973, 154-63; X, 1974, 173-5; XI, 1975, 221-4.

Stenderup, Vibeke. 'Randolph Stow in Scandinavia'. *Kunapipi* (Aarhus), I, No. 1, 1979, 37-40. Bibliography.

Baker, Candida. 'Randolph Stow'. In her *Yacker 3* (Sydney: Picador, 1989), 284-300.

Bennett, Bruce. 'Australian Perspectives on the Near North: Hal Porter and Randolph Stow'. In *South Pacific Images*, edited by Chris Tiffin (St Lucia: SPACLALS, 1978), 124-44.

---. 'Discussions with Randolph Stow'. *Westerly*, XXVI, 1981, No. 4, 53-60.

Beston, John B. 'The Family Background and Literary Career of Randolph Stow'. *Literary Half-Yearly* (Mysore), XVI, No. 2, 1975, 125-34.

---. 'Heriot's Literary Allusions in Randolph Stow's *To The Islands*'. *Southerly*, XXXV, 1975, 168-77.

---. 'An Interview with Randolph Stow'. *WLWE*, XIV, 1975, 221-30.

---. 'The Theme of Reconciliation in Stow's *To the Islands*'. *Modern Fiction Studies*, XXVII, No. 1, 1981, 95-107.

Bhagat, Nidhi. 'The Millenarians: A Discussion of Randolph Stow's *Tourmaline*'. *Rajasthan University Studies in English*, 21-22, 1989-90, 132-44.

Blomfield, Jocelyn Dunphy. 'Understanding and Narrative: Race Relations in Australia, 1965-1994'. In *Tilting at Matilda: Literature, Aborigines, Women and the Church in Contemporary Australia*, edited by Dennis Haskell (South Fremantle, WA: Fremantle Arts Centre P., 1994), 154-73. Includes a discussion of *The Merry-Go-Round in the Sea*.

Boyce, Patrick. 'Author Planning Fresh Sorties'. *Age*, 17 November, 1979, 22.

Brady, Veronica. '"In a Critical Condition": Two Responses to John Docker: II'. *Westerly*, XXX, No. 2, 1985, 83-87. Refers to Stow's *The Suburbs of Hell* to refute an argument of Docker's.

---. 'The Struggle Against Forgetfulness: Childhood in the Novels of Randolph Stow'. In *Childhood and Society in Western Australia*, edited by Penelope Hetherington (Nedlands, W.A.: University of Western Australia Press, 1988), 60-70.

Brydon, Diana. 'Troppo Agitato: Writing and Reading Cultures'. *Ariel*, XIX, No. 1, 1988, 13-32. Discusses Stow and Canadian Rudy Wiebe. Revised as 'Writing and Reading Cultures: Randolph Stow's *Visitants* and Rudy Wiebe's *The Temptations of Big Bear*', in *Decolonising Fictions*, edited by Diana Brydon and Helen Tiffin (Sydney: Dangaroo P., 1993), 127-41.

Brydon, Diana, and Helen Tiffin. 'Resistance and Repetition: V.S. Naipaul's *Guerrillas*, Jean Rhys's *Wide Sargasso Sea* and Randolph Stow's *Visitants*'. In *Decolonising Fictions*, (Sydney: Dangaroo P., 1993), 105-25.

Burgess, O.N. 'The Novels of Randolph Stow'. *Australian Quarterly*, XXXVII, 1965, 73-81.

Clarke, Donovan. '"My Soul is a Strange Country": On Randolph Stow'. *The Bridge*, II, No. 1, 1965, 37-43.

---. 'New Aspects of the Novel'. *Australian Highway*, XLVI, No. 3, 1966, 5-8.

---. 'The Realities of Randolph Stow'. *Bridge*, II, No. 2, 1966, 37-42.

Clunies Ross, Bruce. 'The Art of Randolph Stow'. *Meridian*, VI, No. 1, 1987, 47-55.

Cole-Adams, Peter. 'The Divided Affections of a Restless Novelist'. *Age*, 12 August, 1972, 12.

Cotter, Michael. 'The Image of the Aboriginal in Three Modern Australian Novels'. *Meanjin*, XXXVI, 1977, 582-91.

Cross, Gustav. 'Australian Poetry in the 'Sixties'. *Poetry Australia*, No. 5, 1965, 33-8.

Delrez, Marc. 'Antipodean Dialogue: R. Stow and D. Malouf'. In *Crisis and Creativity in the New Literatures in English*, Cross/Cultures 1, edited by Geoffrey V.

Davis and Hena Maes-Jelinek (Amsterdam; Atlanta, Ga.: Rodopi, 1990), 291-307.
---.' From Metastasis to Metamorphosis: The House of Self in the Novels of Randolph Stow'. *Kunapipi*, 12, No. 1, 1990, 32-47.
Dommergues, Andre. 'The Confluence of Three Cultures in Randolph Stow's *To the Islands*'. *Commonwealth* (Paris), VI, No. 2, 1984, 49-55.
Drummond, Lun. 'A Place to Come to: Lyn Drummond visits the past and Randolph Stow in the English Port City of Harwich'. *Island*, 54, 1993, 48-50.
Dunlevy, Maurice. '*The Merry-Go-Round* [in the Sea] and Other Excursions of 1972'. *Canberra Times*, 23 December, 1972, 8.
Dutton, Geoffrey. 'The Search for Permanence: The Novels of Randolph Stow'. *Journal of Commonwealth Literature*, No. 1, 1965, 135-48.
Elliott, Brian, and Teo Hee Lian. 'Oh No, Here We go Again: A View of World, Blood and Australia in *The Merry-Go-Round in the Sea*, in a Perspective from Singapore'. [*Adelaide*] *A.L.S. Working Papers*, I, No. 1, 1975, 11-24.
Fiaccavento, Luisa Quartermaine. 'Il Meglio degli Altri: Australia: La Storia de un Selvaggio Ragazzo Coloniale'. *Schedario* (Florence), Nos. 130-31, 1974, 20-25. About *Midnite*.
Frizell, Helen. 'Randolph Stow Wins $11,000 [Patrick White] Literary Award'. *S.M.H.*, 17 November, 1979, 13.
Geering, R.G. *Recent Fiction*. (Melbourne: O.U.P., 1974). Australian Writers and Their Work. Reviewed by C. Hadgraft, *A.L.S.*, VI, 1974, 441-2.
Hassall, Anthony J. *Strange Country: A Study of Randolph Stow*. (St Lucia: U.Q.P., 1986). Reviewed by V. Brady, *Westerly*, XXXI, No. 2, 1986, 87-92; L. Forsyth, *ABR*, No. 85, 1986, 33-34; R. Gostand, *Social Alternatives*, VI, No. 2, 1987, 75-77; esp. 77; D. Green, *LiNQ*, XIV, No. 3, 1987, 23-33; M. Johnson, *Modern Fiction Studies*, XXXIII, 1987, 395-396; B. King, *World Literature Today*, LXI, No. 1, 1987, 154; G. Moore, *International Fiction Review*, XIV, No. 1, 1987, 48-49; P. Quartermaine, *T.L.S.*, 20 March, 1987, 302; W. Senn, *A.L.S.*, XII, No. 4, 1986, 532-34;H. Watson-Williams, *Westerly*, XXXI, No. 2, 1986, 83-87.
---. 'The Alienation of Alistair Cawdor in Randolph Stow's *Visitants*'. *A.L.S.*, IX, 1980, 449-59.
---. 'Full Circle: Randolph Stow's *The Merry-Go-Round in the Sea*'. *Meanjin*, XXXII, 1973, 58-64.
---. 'Interview with Randolph Stow'. *A.L.S.*, X, 1982, 311-25.
---. 'The Poetry of Randolph Stow'. *Southerly*, XLII, 1982, 259-76.
---. 'Randolph Stow's *The Girl Green as Elderflower*'. *LiNQ*, XI, No. 2, 1983-1984, 5-13.
Hergenhan, L.T. 'Randolph Stow's *To the Islands*'. *Southerly*, XXXV, 1975, 234-47.
---. 'War in Post-1960s Fiction: Johnston, Stow, McDonald, Malouf and Les Murray'. *A.L.S.*, XII, No. 2, 1985, 248-260.
Hewett, Dorothy. 'Silence, Exile and Cunning: The Poetry of Randolph Stow'. *Westerly*, XXXIII, No. 2, 1988, 59-66.
Higginbotham, Paul D. '"Honour the Single Soul": Randolph Stow and his Novels'. *Southerly*, XXXIX, 1979, 378-92.
Hope, A.D. 'Randolph Stow and the *Tourmaline* Affair'. In *The Australian Experience: Critical Essays on Australian Novels*, edited by W.S. Ramson (Canberra: Australian National University Press, 1974), 249-68.
---. 'Randolph Stow and the Way of Heaven'. *Hemisphere*, XVIII, No. 6, 1974, 33-35.
Keneally, Thomas. 'The Novelist's Poison'. *Australian Author*, I, No. 4, 1969, 3-6.
King, Bruce. 'Randolph Stow's Novels of Exile'. *Antipodes*, I, No. 2, 1987, 74-78.
Kramer, Leonie. 'The Novels of Randolph Stow'. *Southerly*, XXIV, No. 2, 1964, 78-91.
Kuch, Peter and Kavanagh, Paul. 'The Self-Critical Craftsman: Randolph Stow talks

to Peter Kuch and Paul Kavanagh'. *Southerly*, XLVI, No. 4, 1986, 437-43. Reprinted in *Conversations: Interviews with Australian Writers*, edited by Paul Kavanagh and Peter Kuch (North Ryde, NSW: Collins/A.& R, 1991), 231-241.

Leer, Martin. 'Mal du pays: Symbolic Geography in the Work of Randolph Stow'. *A.L.S.*, 15.1, 1991, 3-25.

Maxwell, D.E.S. 'Landscape and Theme'. In *Commonwealth Literature: Unity and Diversity in a Common Culture*, edited by John Press (London: Heinemann, 1965), 82-89. Discusses *To the Islands*.

McDougall, Russell. 'Language, Silence and the Laws of the Land: Randolph Stow's *Tourmaline*'. In *Aspects of Australian Fiction: Essays Presented to John Colmer*, edited by Alan Brissenden (Nedlands, W.A.: University of Western Australia Press, 1990), 127-147.

McDougall, Russell. 'Stow's *Tourmaline*: A Test Town for Structural Anthropology'. In *From Commonwealth to Post-Colonial*, edited by Anna Rutherford (Sydney; Aarhus: Dangaroo P, 1992), 420-27.

McLaren, John. 'Security and Violation: Randolph Stow's *The Merry-Go-Round in the Sea*'. *Westerly*, 36.4, 1991, 75-81.

Moore, Gerald. 'Islands of Ascent: The Australasian Novels of Randolph Stow'. *International Fiction Review*, XIII, No. 2, 1986, 61-68.

---. 'Randolph Stow's *Tourmaline* and *To The Islands*'. *The International Fiction Review*, 14, No. 2, 1987, 68-74.

Narasimhaiah, C.D. 'Introduction'. *Literary Criterion* (Mysore), XV, Nos. 3-4, 1980, xxiv-xxv.

Nelson, Penelope. 'Randolph Stow, the Poet'. *Drylight*, 1965, 37-8.

New, William H. 'Outsider Looking Out: The Novels of Randolph Stow'. *Critique*, IX, No. 1, 1966, 90-99.

---. 'The Island and the Madman: Recurrent Imagery in the Major Novelists of the Fifties'. *Arizona Quarterly*, XXII, 1966, 328-37.

Oppen, Alice. 'Myth and Reality in Randolph Stow'. *Southerly*, XXVII, 1967, 82-94.

Perkins, Elizabeth. 'Randolph Stow and the Dimdims'. *Quadrant*, XXVI, No. 7, 1982, 28-33.

Pons, Xavier, and Keeble, Neil. 'A Colonist with Words: An Interview with Randolph Stow'. *Commonwealth* (Rodez), II, 1976, 70-80.

Priessnitz, Horst. '"vox et praeterea nihil . . .": Randolph Stow'. In *Essays on Contemporary Post-Colonial Fiction*, edited by Hedwig Bock and Albert Wertheim (Munchen: Huber, 1986), 371-88.

Ramsey, S.A. '"The silent griefs"; Randolph Stow's *Visitants*'. *Critical Quarterly*, XXIII, No. 2, 1981, 73-81.

Riem, Antonella. 'The "Double" Character and the Growing Up Process in David Malouf's *Johnno* and Randolph Stow's *The Merry-Go-Round In the Sea*' In her *The Labyrinths of Self: A Collection of Essays on Australian and Caribbean Literature*. (Leichhardt, N.S.W.: FILEF. Italo-Australian Publications, 1987), 181-95.

---. 'The Use of Names and Colours in Randolph Stow's *Tourmaline*'. *A.L.S.*, 14, No. 4, 1990, 510-17.

---. '*Voss* and *To the Islands*: The Search for the Self - "A Country of Great Subtelty" - An Essay on Patrick White and Randolph Stow'. In her *The Labyrinths of Self: A Collection of Essays on Australian and Caribbean Literature*. (Leichhardt, N.S.W.: FILEF. Italo-Australian Publications, 1987), 13-97.

Robieson, Sinclair. 'Stow the Money'. *Weekend Australian Magazine*, 17-18 November, 1979, 14.

Rowley, Hazel. 'Becoming a Man: Mateship and Horsemanship in Randolph Stow's *The Merry-Go-Round in the Sea*'. *Southerly*, XLVII, No. 4, 1987, 410-425.

Rutherford, Anna and Boelsmand, Andreas. 'Interview with Randolph Stow'. *Commonwealth Newsletter* [1974], pp 17-20.

Senn, Werner. 'The Conradian Intertext in the Fiction of Randolph Stow: *Tourmaline* and *Lord Jim*'. *Conradian: Journal of the Joseph Conrad Society* UK., 15.1, June 1990. 12-29.

---. 'Crisis and Reconstitution of Self in Recent Australian Fiction: The Latest Novels of Patrick White and Randolph Stow'. In *Australian Papers: Yugoslavia, Europe and Australia*, edited by Mirko Jurak (Ljubljana: Edvard Cardelj University, 1983), 277-82.

Shapcott, Thomas. 'Breaking the Drought'. *London Magazine*, N.S. XX, Nos. 8-9, 1980, 70-75.

Sharrad, Paul. '*Pour Mieux Sauter*: Christopher Koch's Novels in Relation to White, Stow and the Quest for a Post-Colonial Fiction'. *WLWE*, XXIII, 1984, 208-23.

Smith, Graeme Kinross. 'Randolph Stow - A Double Nostalgia'. *This Australia*, IV, No. 4, 1985, 17-23.

Stevens, John. 'Going home...150 Years on'. *S.M.H.*, 23 December, 1984, 35. Interview.

Tanner, Godfrey. 'The Road to Jerusalem'. *Nimrod*, II, No. 1, 1964, 33-9. Contains material on *To The Islands*.

Thomas, Sue. 'Randolph Stow's Revision of *To the Islands*'. *Southerly*, XLII, 1982, 288-94.

Tiffin, Chris. 'Mates, Mum and Maui: The Theme of Maturity in Three Antipodean Novels'. In *Readings in Pacific Literature*, edited by Paul Sharrad (Wollongong, NSW: New Literatures Research Centre, U of Wollongong, 1993), 173-89. Discusses novels by Witi Ihimaera, Albert Wendt and *The Merry-Go-Round in the Sea*.

Tiffin, Helen. 'Melanesian Cargo Cults in *Tourmaline* and *Visitants*'. *Journal of Commonwealth Literature*, XVI, 1981, 109-25.

---. 'Tourmaline and the Tao Te Ching: Randolph Stow's *Tourmaline*'. In *Studies in the Recent Australian Novel*, edited by K.G. Hamilton (St Lucia: U.Q.P., 1978), 84-120.

Wallace, Richard. 'The Man Behind the Pseudonym'. *Canberra Times*, 1 June, 1985, 17.

Wightman, Jennifer. 'Waste Places, Dry Souls: The Novels of Randolph Stow'. *Meanjin*, XXVIII, 1969, 239-52.

Willbanks, Ray. *Randolph Stow*. (Boston: Twayne, 1978). Twayne's World Authors Series, 472. Reviewed by J. Croft, *A.L.S.*, IX, 1979, 129.

---. 'Randolph Stow: An Australian Angst'. In *International Literature in English: Essays on the Major Writers*, edited by Robert L. Ross (New York: Garland, 1991), 217-24.

Wright, Derek. 'The Mansren Myth in Randolph Stow's *Visitants*'. *International Fiction Review*, XIII, No. 2, 1986, 82-86

Zwicky, Fay. 'Speeches and Silences'. *Quadrant*, XXVII, No. 5, 1983, 40-46.

T

TAYLOR, ANDREW

Poetry

The Cool Change. (St Lucia: U.Q.P., 1971).
Reviewed by P. Annand, *Makar*, VII, No. 1, 1971, 37-38; C. Beck, *Sunday Review*, 18 April, 1971, 805; P. Martin, *Twentieth Century*, XXVI, 1971, 177-80; R.A. Simpson, *Age*, 24 April, 1971, 15; J. Tulip, *Bulletin*, 1 May, 1971, 48.

The Cat's Chin and Ears. (Sydney: A.& R., 1976).
Reviewed by V. Ikin, *Quadrant*, XXI, No. 9, 1977, 78-79.

The Crystal Absences, The Trout. (Sydney: Island Press, 1978).
Reviewed by J. Tranter, *National Times*, 26 August, 1978, 42; C. Vleeskens, *Semper*, 7 June, 1978, 30.

Folds in the Map. (St. Lucia: U.Q.P., 1991).
Reviewed by H. Cam, *S.M.H.*, 11 January, 1992, 29; G. Catalano, *Age*, 11 January, 1992, Saturday Extra 6; H. Horton, *Imago*, 4.1, 1992, 108-13; S.K. Kelen, *Southerly*, 52.1, 1992, 173-77; C. Wallace-Crabbe, *ABR*, 135, 1991, 34,36.

Ice Fishing. (St Lucia: U.Q.P., 1973).
Reviewed by E. Balderston, *Southerly*, XXXIV, 1974, 86-9; J. Grant, *Poetry Australia*, No. 49, 1973, 56-60; I Reid, *New Poetry*, XXI, No. 3, 1973, 63-66; P. Roberts, *S.M.H.*, 15 December, 1973, 16; C. Sansom, *Nation Review*, 1-7 February, 1974, 503.

The Invention of Fire. (St Lucia: U.Q.P., 1976).
Reviewed by A. Gould, *Nation Review*, 20-26 August, 1976, 1105; T. Harrington, *Luna*, No. 3, 1976, 54-5; K. Singh, *Quadrant*, XX, No. 10, 1976, 55-6; P. Law, *Poetry Australia*, No. 62, 1977, 67-69; J. Rodriguez, *Age*, 25 September, 1976, 24.

Parabolas. (St Lucia: Makar, 1976).
Reviewed by P. Neilsen, *Age*, 12 March, 1977, 18; J. Tranter, *Australian*, 8 January, 1977, 27.

Sandstone. (St Lucia: U.Q.P., 1995).
Reviewed by K. Brophy, *ABR*, 170, 1995, 54; M. Duwell, *Weekend Australian*, 19-20 Aug., 1995, Review 10.

Selected Poems 1960-1980. (St Lucia: U.Q.P., 1982).
Reviewed by C. Benfey, *Parnassus: Poetry in Review*, XI, No. 2, 1983/84, 236-25; D. Carter, *Age Saturday Extra*, 6 March, 1982, 14; C. Churches, *Advertiser*, 6 March, 1982, 26; G. Dutton, *Bulletin*, 4 May, 1982, 68 & 71-72; M. Duwell, *Australian*, 9 March, 1982; L.A. Murray, *S.M.H.*, 6 March, 1982, 44; G. Page, *Quadrant*, XXVI, No. 8, 1982, 76; G. Rowlands, *Overland*, No. 88, 1982, 66.

Selected Poems, 1960-1985. (St Lucia: U.Q.P., 1988). Previous edition *Selected Poems 1960-1980* (St Lucia: U.Q.P., 1982).
Reviewed by P. Salom, *ABR*, No. 102, 1988, 36-38.

Travelling. (St Lucia: U.Q.P., 1986).
Reviewed by A. Gould, *Quadrant*, XXX, No. 10, 1986, 69-74; H. Hewitt, *Canberra Times*, 10 May, 1986, B3; M. Heyward, *ABR*, No. 78, 1986, 29-30; M. Hulse, *PN Review*, XIV, No. 1, 1987, 61-62; P. Mead, *Island Magazine*, No. 29, 1986, 32-40; F. Zwicky, *Weekend Australian Magazine*, 12-13 April, 1986, 15.

Non-Fiction
Reading Australian Poetry. (St Lucia: U.Q.P., 1987).
Reviewed by K. Hart, *Phoenix Review*, No. 3, 1988, 114-16; H.P. Heseltine, *Meridian*, 8, No. 1, 1989, 66-9; M. Macleod, *A.L.S.*, 13, 1988, 396-98; L. McCredden, *ABR*, No. 94, 1987, 28-30; I. Salusinszky, *Age Saturday Extra*, 26 September, 1987, 13.

'The American Model: Penelope or Circe?'. In *The American Model: Influence and Independence in Australian Poetry*, edited by Joan Kirkby (Sydney: Hale & Iremonger, 1982), 54-68.

Critical Material
Duwell, Martin. 'Developing the Self'. *Makar*, XIII, No. 2, 1978, 4-11. Interview.
Page, Geoff. 'Andrew Taylor'. In his *A Reader's Guide To Contemporary Australian Poetry* (St. Lucia: U.Q.P., 1995), 285-289.

TAYLOR, KEN

Poetry
A Secret Australia: Selected and New Poems. (Clifton, Vic.: Rigmarole Books, 1985).
Reviewed by G. Catalano, *Age*, 29 June, 1985, 16; M. Hulse, *PN Review*, 12.5, 1986, 49, 56; M. Morgan, *ABR*, 73, 1985, 32-33; G. Page, *Island Magazine*, 30, 1987, 64-67; J. Rodriguez, *S.M.H.*, 22 February, 1986, 43.

At Valentine's: Poems 1966-1969. (Melbourne: Contempa Publications, 1975).
Reviewed by T. Harrington, *Foundation & Reality*, 3, 1977, 92-94: I. Stubbin, *Australasian Small Press Review*, 4, 1976, 22-23.

Critical Material
Catalano, Gary. 'An American Education: The Poetry of Ken Taylor'. *Overland*, 131, 1992, 74-77.

TENNANT, KYLIE

Fiction
The Battlers. (Sydney: A.& R., 1965). First published London: Gollancz, 1941.
Reviewed by J. McLaren, *ABR*, IV, 1965, 223.

The Honey Flow. Introduction by Jean Bedford. (North Ryde, NSW: A.& R., 1991). First published London: Macmillan, 1956.
Reviewed by R. Sorensen, *ABR*, 130, 1991, 41-42.

Lost Haven. (Melbourne: Macmillan, 1968). First published Melbourne: Macmillan, 1946.
Reviewed by D. Green, *Nation*, 7 December, 1968, 21-22.

Ma Jones and the Little White Cannibals. (London: Macmillan, 1967).
Reviewed by A. Ashbolt, *ABR*, VI, 1967, 136; A.R. Chisholm, *Age*, 29 July, 1967, 23; E. Corsellis, *S.M.H.*, 15 July, 1967, 14; S. Despoja, *Adelaide Advertiser*, 8 July, 1967, 18; S. Edgar, *Canberra Times*, 15 July, 1967, 10; F. Roberts, *Bulletin*, 8 July, 1967, 68.

Ride on Stranger. (Melbourne: Macmillan, 1968). First published Sydney: A.& R., 1943. Reprinted with an introduction by Kerryn Goldsworthy (North Ryde, N.S.W.: A.& R., 1990).
Reviewed by D. Green, *Nation*, 7 December, 1968, 22.

Tantavallon. (South Melbourne: Macmillan, 1983).
Reviewed by L. Clancy, *Age Saturday Extra*, 27 August, 1983, 11; M. Dunlevy, *Canberra Times*, 6 August, 1983, 16; N. Keesing, *Weekend Australian Magazine*, 2-3 July, 1983, 16; S. McKernan, *ABR*, No. 57, 1983, 12-13.

Tell Morning This. (Sydney: A.& R., 1967). Originally published as *The Joyful Condemned* (London: Macmillan, 1953).
Reviewed by A.R. Chisholm, *Age*, 11 November, 1967, 23; M. Dick, *S.M.H.*, 14 October, 1967, 24; H. James, *Australian*, 20 January, 1968, 14; J. McLaren, *Overland*, No. 40, 1968, 41; *T.L.S.*, 8 February, 1968, 141; M. Wolkowsky, *Bulletin*, 25 November, 1967, 82.

Tiburon. Introduction by the author. (Sydney: A.& R. Education, 1972). Paperback edition. First published Sydney: Bulletin, 1935.

Non-Fiction
Evatt: Politics and Justice. (Sydney: A.& R., 1970).
Reviewed by D. Aitken, *Meanjin*, XXX, 1971, 121-22; D.J. Ashenden, *Bulletin*, 14 November, 1970, 56-57; W. M. Ball, *Age*, 14 November, 1970, 17; M. Harris, *ABR*, X, 1970, 13; K. Randall, *Australian*, 5 December, 1970, 27; M. Stanley, *Nation*, 12 December, 1970, 21-22; P. Wesley-Smith, *Australian University*, IX, 1971, 72-76. See also letter to the editor by F.P. McManus, *Age*, 9 September, 1970, 9.

The Man on the Headland. (Sydney: A.& R., 1971).
Reviewed by M. Fisher, *Growing Point*, XI, 1956-57; B. Kiernan, *Australian*, 24 July, 1971, 22; C. McNamara, *Review* (Melbourne), 3 September, 1971, 1343; W.A. Murray, *ABR*, XI, 1972, 10; N. Phelan, *S.M.H.*, 14 August, 1971, 21; J.D. Pringle, *Hemisphere*, XVI, No. 5, 1972, 34-35. W.S. Ramson, *Canberra Times*, 16 October, 1971, 14; C. Tolchard, *Bulletin*, 14 August, 1971, 48-49.

The Missing Heir: The Autobiography of Kylie Tennant. (Melbourne: Macmillan, 1986).
Reviewed by E. Campion, *Bulletin*, 6 May, 1986, 94; J. Hanrahan, *Age Saturday Extra*, 19 April, 1986, 13; E. Lindsay, *S.M.H.*, 3 May, 1986, 48; H. McPhee, *ABR*, No. 82, 1986, 8-10; E. Riddell, *National Times*, 23-29 May, 1986, 34.

'I'm Going to Jail...'. *Women's Weekly*, 25 October, 1967, 4-5. Interview with Kay Keavney on personal experience behind *Tell Morning This*.
'A Moral Story'. *Australian Author*, I, No. 4, 1969, 11-13. An account of the writing of Tennant's *Australia, Her Story*.
'My Bad Old Days with Radio'. *S.M.H.*, 3 January, 1974, 10.

Critical Material
'The Bird with the Bees'. *S.M.H.*, 11 January, 1974, 10. On *The Honey Flow*. Interview.
'"Undergrowth" to Orchard: Interview with Kylie Tennant'. *Hemisphere*, XXV, No. 3, 1980, 146-53.
Cahill, Rowan. 'More Than a Footnote: A Biographical Portrait of L.C. Rodd'. *The Hummer* (Sydney), No. 27, 1990, 3-10.
Capp, Fiona. *Writers Defiled: Security Surveillance of Australian Authors and Intellectuals 1920-1960*. (Ringwood, Vic.: McPhee Gribble, 1993). Includes discussion of Prichard.
Clancy, Laurie. Fathers and Lovers: Three Australian Novels'. *A.L.S.*, X, 1982, 459-67. *Time Enough Later*.
Colmer, John. 'Autobiography and Three Women Writers: Barbara Hanrahan, Oriel Gray and Kylie Tennant'. In his *Australian Autobiography: A Personal Quest*. (Melbourne: O.U.P., 1989), 128-46.
Dick, Margaret. *The Novels of Kylie Tennant*. (Adelaide: Rigby, 1966). With a Bibliography. Reviewed by A. Brissenden, *Bulletin*, 23 July, 1966, 45-6; J.K. Ewers, *ABR*, V, 1966, 182 and *W.A. Teachers' Journal*, LVI, 1966, 258-9; D. Green,

Australian, 15 October, 1966, 10 and *A.L.S.*, II, 1966, 305-7; T.I. Moore, *Canberra Times*, 30 July, 1966, 13; R. Robinson, *S.M.H.*, 2 July, 1966, 15; P. Steele, *Twentieth Century*, XXI, 1966, 90-1.
Giuffre, Giulia. 'Kylie Tennant'. In her *A Writing Life: Interviews with Australian Women Writers*. (Sydney: Allen & Unwin, 1990), 225-39.
Hersey, April. 'Back to the Battling'. *Bulletin*, 29 April, 1967, 32.
Hillary, Gay. 'Kylie Tennant Remembers the Depression'. *Canberra Times*, 15 January, 1969, 2.
Jones, Dorothy. '"A Kingdom and a Place of Exile": Women Writers and the World of Nature'. *WLWE*, XXIV, No. 2, 1984, 257-273.
Knuckey, Marie. 'A Battler Still - Away from the Ratrace'. *S.M.H.*, 19 July, 1979, 13-14. Rptd. as 'A Pause in a Literary Life'. *Advertiser*, 1 August, 1979, 28.
Lockwood, Betty. 'And Then, There Were Women'. *Womanspeak*, II, No. 4, 1976, 20-21.
McInerney, Sally. 'Kylie Awaits Hunters Hill's Verdict'. *S.M.H.*, 11 June, 1983, 45. Interview.
Nicklin, Lenore. 'Fruitful Life of a "Lazy Old Lady"'. *Bulletin*, 23 August, 1983, 64-65.
Pons, Xavier. '*The Battlers*: Kylie Tennant and the Australian Tradition'. *A.L.S.*, VI, 1974, 364-80.
Sawer, Geoffrey. 'Alwyn Lee in Fiction'. *Nation*, 28 November, 1970, 15. Comments on letter by Vigoreux (see below).
Sayers, Stuart. 'Journalist who Writes Books'. *Age Saturday Extra*, 6 August, 1983, 10.
Smith, Graeme Kinross. 'Kylie Tennant'. *Westerly*, No. 1, 1975, 35-40.
Sunderland, Jane. 'A Form of Resistance; The Problematic Protagonist in the Novels of Kylie Tennant'. *Hecate*, V, No. 1, 1979, 87-100.
Vigoreux, L. 'Adulation of Alwyn'. *Nation*, 3 October, 1970, 16. Identifies Alwyn Lee as the basis for a character in *Ride on Stranger*.

THATCHER, CHARLES

Poetry
Charles Thatcher's Songbook: edited by Hugh Anderson. Vol.1: *When First I Landed Here*. (Melbourne: Red Rooster Press, 1980).
Reviewed by W. Fahey, *Labour History*, No. 49, 1981, 137-39.

Thatcher's Colonial Minstrel. (Adelaide: Libraries Board of South Australia, 1964). First published Melbourne: Charlwood & Son, 1864.
Reviewed by D. Hewett, *Westerly*, No. 3, 1964, 64-5; N. Keesing, *ABR*, III, 1964, 247; M. Officer, *Twentieth Century*, XIX, 1965, 368-9; D. Potts, *Dissent*, No. 14, 1965, 54-5; G.A. Wilkes, *Southerly*, XXIV, No. 4, 1964, 250.

Critical Material
Anderson, Hugh. 'Charles Thatcher: The Bard of Bendigo'. *Victorian Historical Magazine*, XLII, 1971, 554-64.

THIELE, COLIN

Fiction
The Rim of the Morning. (Adelaide: Rigby, 1966).
Reviewed by B. Eastman, *Canberra Times*, 12 November, 1966, 10; N. Keesing, *ABR*, V, 1966, 236.

Seashores and Shadows. (Glebe, N.S.W.: Walter McVitty, 1986).
Reviewed by M. Dunkle, *Age Saturday Extra*, 25 January, 1986, 11.

The Shadow On the Hills. (Adelaide: Rigby, 1977).
Reviewed by M. Jones, *Canberra Times*, 24 September, 1977, 15.

Poetry
In Charcoal and Conte. (Adelaide: Rigby, 1966).
Reviewed by B. Beaver, *S.M.H.*, 13 August, 1966, 18; T.I. Moore, *Canberra Times*, 19 November, 1966, 10; B. Nesbitt, *Australian*, 25 June, 1966, 8; R. Robinson, *Poetry Magazine*, No. 4, 1966, 25-7; T. Shapcott, *ABR*, V, 1966, 180; V. Smith, *Bulletin*, 30 July, 1966, 47; A. Taylor, *Overland*, No. 35, 1966, 55-6.
Selected Verse. (Adelaide: Rigby, 1970).
Reviewed by G. Page, *Canberra Times*, 18 July, 1970, 15; T.W. Shapcott, *ABR*, IX, 1970, 185-86; K. Slessor, *Daily Telegraph*, Sydney, 15 August, 1970, 13.
Labourers in the Vineyard. (Adelaide: Rigby, 1970).
Reviewed by R. Davies, *Age*, 19 September, 1970, 14; S. Despoja, *Advertiser*, 14 March, 1970, 18; B. Kiernan, *Australian*, 25 July, 1970, 20.

Critical Material
Brechin, Robbie. 'Success ... and the Flaws and the Pain'. *Courier-Mail*, 24 July, 1982, 25. Interview.
Carmody, Margaret. 'An Interview with Colin Thiele'. *The Lu Rees Archives*, No. 8, 1987, 6-13.
Covernton, Helen. 'The Ink of Colin Thiele's Past'. *National Times*, 18 November, 1978, 59.
Gordon, Nancy. 'A Talk with Colin Thiele'. *Issue*, V, No. 16, 1975, 59-64.

TIPPING, RICHARD KELLY

Poetry
Domestic Hardcore. (St Lucia: U.Q.P., 1975).
Reviewed by R. Adamson, *Australian*, 8 May, 1976, 30 and *New Poetry*, XXIV, No. 1, 1976, 78-81; A. Gould, *Nation Review*, 2-8 April, 1976, 621; J. Grant, *Contempa*, Series 2, No. 2, 1976, 50-51; P. Kavanagh, *Southerly*, XXXVI, 1976, 471-478; J. McLaren, *Segment*, No. 5, 1976, 53-59, esp. 57; M. Nordland, *Union Recorder*, LVI, No. 3, 1976, 27; T. Shapcott, *Age*, 17 July, 1976, 23; R. Tamplin, *T.L.S.*, 9 April, 1976, 443.
Nearer By Far. (St Lucia: U.Q.P., 1986).
Reviewed by M. Hulse, *P.N. Review*, XIV, No. 1, 1987, 61-62; V. O'Sullivan, *Meanjin*, XLVI, No. 3, 1987, 347-354; K. Russell, *Quadrant*, XXXI, No. 9, 1987, 61-66.
Soft Riots. (St Lucia: U.Q.P., 1972). Paperback Poets, No. 10.
Reviewed by *ABR*, No. 11, 1973, 67; R. Adamson, *Australian*, 12 May, 1973, 22; D. Douglas, *Overland*, No. 56, 1973, 50-52; P. Law, *Poetry Australia*, No. 47, 1973, 75-80; P. Roberts, *S.M.H.*, 7 April, 1973, 23; G. Rowlands, *Makar*, VIII, No. 3, 1972, 35-39; C. Sansom, *Nation Review*, 5-11 January, 1973, 376; R.A. Simpson, *Age*, 7 April, 1973, 13; *T.L.S.*, 12 October, 1973, 1216; J. Tulip, *Southerly*, XXXIII, 1973, 231, 240 and *Bulletin*, 13 January, 1973, 42.
The Sydney Morning Volume III. [12 silkscreen prints.] (Wangi Wangi, NSW: Thorny Devil P., 1993).
Reviewed by A. Selenitsch, *Overland*, 131, 1993, 88-89.

Non-Fiction
'Subvertising: Word Works'. *Kunapipi*, 16.2, 1994, 24-26. Discusses examples of his 'visual poetry' subsequently published 27-34.

Critical Material
McDonald, Roger and Duwell, Martin. 'Keep Moving: An Interview'. *Makar*, IX, No. 1, 1973, 1-6.
Page, Geoff. 'Richard Tipping'. In his *A Reader's Guide To Contemporary Australian Poetry* (St. Lucia: U.Q.P., 1995), 291-294.

Richardson, Pat. 'Adelaide's Top Poets'. *Ash Magazine*, No. 5, 1981, 16.
Swann, Joseph. 'What You See Must Be Other': Language and Eros in the Poetry of Richard Kelly Tipping'. *A.L.S.*, XIII, No. 3, 1988, 296-307.

TOMPSON, CHARLES

Poetry
Wild Notes, from the Lyre of a Native Minstrel. With an introduction by G.A. Wilkes and G.A. Turnbull (Sydney: Sydney University Press, 1973). Australian Literary Reprints. First published by the Government Printer, 1826.
Reviewed by M. Wilding, *Southerly*, XXXV, 1975, 95-102.

Critical Material
Proudfoot, Helen. 'Another Age, Another Place: The Camden Diaries of the Colonial Poet, Charles Tompson Junior (1848-1852)'. *The Push: A Journal of Early Australian Social History*, 29, 1991, 1-14.

TRANTER, JOHN

Poetry
The Alphabet Murders. (Sydney: A.& R., 1975). Poets of the Month.
Reviewed by J. Maiden, *New Poetry*, XXIV, No. 2, 1976, 91-93; C. Pollnitz, *Southerly*, XXXVI, 1976, 467; R.A. Simpson, *Age*, 29 May, 1976, 21.
At the Florida. (St Lucia: U.Q.P., 1993).
Reviewed by T. Austin, *Northern Perspective*, 18.1, 1995, 124-30; D. Barbour, *Australian Canadian Studies*, 12.2, 1994, 75-84; H. Cam, *S.M.H.*, 28 August, 1993, 49; M. Duwell, *Weekend Australian*, 13-14 November, 1993, Review 7; P. Kane, *Antipodes*, 8.2, 1994, 159; M. Langford, *Southerly*, 54.4, 1994-95, 171-79; L. McCredden, *ABR*, 155, 1993, 35-36; A. Riemer, *Meanjin*, 35.1, 1994, 156-64; P. Salom, *Overland*, 139, 1995, 83-85; J. Sharah, *Quadrant*, 37.12, 1993, 87-88.
The Blast Area. (Brisbane: Makar, 1974).
Reviewed by K. Bolton and J. Jenkins, *Magic Sam*, No. 2, 1976; D. Hewett, *Australian*, 12 April, 1975, 38; G. Langford, *New Poetry*, 23, No. 1, 1974, 81-2.
Crying In Early Infancy: One Hundred Sonnets. (Brisbane: Makar, 1978).
Reviewed by R. Adamson, *New Poetry*, 26, No. 1, 1978, 21-4; J. Davis, *LiNQ*, 6, No. 2, 1978, 74-6; J. Grant, *Poetry Australia*, No. 67, 1978, 70-2; C. Harrison-Ford, *S.M.H.*, 8 April, 1978, 17; C. Pollnitz, *Southerly*, 29, 1978, 344-46; G. Ryan, *Australasian Small Press Review*, Nos. 7-8, 1979, 44-47; T. Shapcott, *Australian*, 4-5 February, 1978, 9; A. Taylor, *National Times*, 27 May, 1978, 31; J. Vasudeva, *Luna*, 3, No. 1, 1978, 34-6.
Dazed in the Ladies Lounge. (Sydney: Island Press, 1979).
Reviewed by G. Harwood, *Luna*, No. 12, 1981, 35-36; G. Page, *National Times*, 4-10 May, 1980, 45; R.A. Simpson, *Age*, 5 April, 1980, 18.
The Floor of Heaven. (Pymble, NSW: A.& R., 1992).
Reviewed by C. Bird, *ABR*, 146, 1992, 42-43; C. Keneally, *ABR*, 43-44 (see also interview with Tranter, *ABR*, 146, 1992, 40-41); P. Nelson, *Quadrant*, 37.7-8, 1993, 117-19; C. Pollnitz, *Weekend Australian*, 3-4 October, 1992, Review 4; A. Riemer, *S.M.H.*, 19 September, 1992, 42; P. Steele, *Age*, 14 November, 1992, Saturday Extra 9.
Parallax. (Sydney: South Head Press, 1970).
Reviewed by R. Hall, *Australian*, 24 October, 1970, 23; M. Johnston, *Poetry Magazine*, No. 18, 1970, 41.
Red Movie. (Sydney: A.& R., 1972).
Reviewed by R. Adamson, *Australian*, 27 January, 1973, 33; M. Dransfield, *Canberra Times*, 27 January, 1973, 11; C. Harrison-Ford, *New Poetry*, 20, Nos. 5-6,

1972, 70-72; P. Roberts, *S.M.H.*, 23 December, 1972, 13; G. Rowlands, *Makar*, 8, No. 3, 1972, 38-9; T. Shapcott, *ABR*, 12, 1973, 134-6.
Selected Poems. (Sydney: Hale & Iremonger, 1982).
Reviewed by D. Carter, *Scripsi*, II, No. 4, 1984, 117-22; G. Dutton, *Bulletin*, 4 January, 1983, 74-76; M. Duwell, *Australian Weekend Magazine*, 11-12 September, 1982, 10; J. Forbes, *Meanjin*, XLII, 1983, 249-53; B. Giles, *ABR*, No. 44, 1982, 28-29; K. Goldsworthy, *Age Saturday Extra*, 11 December, 1982, 12; L. Keim, *Image*, VI, No. 3, 1983, 47-48; R. Kenny, *S.M.H.*, 13 November, 1982, 37; S. McKernan, *Canberra Times*, 18 December, 1982, 16; G. Rowlands, *Overland*, No. 91, 1983, 58-60; A. Stewart, *Island Magazine*, No. 16, 1983, 45-47.
Under Berlin: New Poems 1988. (St Lucia: U.Q.P., 1988).
Reviewed by H. Cam, *S.M.H.*, 3 September, 1988, 82; L. Dobrez, *Age Monthly Review*, 9, No. 1, 1989, 7-8; A. Gould, *Editions*, No. 4, 1989, 30-31; P. Kirkpatrick, *Antithesis*, 4, No. 1, 1990, 189-94; T. Lintermans, *Age Saturday Extra*, 12 November, 1988, 24; P. Neilsen, *Imago*, 1, No. 1, 1989, 49-50; V. O'Sullivan, *Island Magazine*, No. 40, 1989, 29-33; G. Page, *Weekend Australian*, 3-4 September, 1988, Weekend 13; C. Pollnitz, *Scripsi*, 6, No. 1, 1990, 255-66; P. Salom, *Fremantle Arts Review*, 4, No. 1, 1989, 14-15.

Non-Fiction

'Anaesthetics: Some Notes on the New Australian Poetry'. In *The American Model: Influence and Independence in Australian Poetry*, edited by Joan Kirkby (Sydney: Hale & Iremonger, 1982), 99-116.
'Australian Poet in Profile: 4'. *Southerly*, XLI, 1981, 243-49.
'Four Notes on the Practice of Revolution'. *A.L.S.*, VIII, 1977, 127-35.

Critical Material

Baker, Candida. 'John Tranter'. In her *Yacker 3* (Sydney: Picador, 1989), 302-333.
Brooks, David. 'Feral Symbolists: Robert Adamson, John Tranter, and the Response to Rimbaud'. *A.L.S.*, 16.3, 1994, 280-88.
Craft, Stephen, and Loughlin, Helen. 'An Interview with John Tranter'. *Hermes*, 7, 1991, 37-47.
Davidson, Jim. 'John Tranter'. *Meanjin*, XL, 1981, 427-41. Interview. Reprinted in his *Sideways From the Page* (Melbourne: Fontana, 1983), 324-45.
Dunlevy, Maurice. 'A Revolutionary of the Sixties Joins the Establishment'. *Canberra Times*, 19 November, 1977, 18.
Duwell, Martin. 'A Possible Contemporary Poetry'. *Makar*, XII, No. 2, 1976, 4-16. Interview. An excerpt also published in *A.L.S.*, VIII, 1977, 157-64. Reprinted with an additional interview in his *A Possible Contemporary Poetry* (St Lucia: Makar, 1982), 15-30 and 30-37.
Haskell, Dennis. 'Thoughts on Some Recent Poetry'. *A.L.S.*, VIII, 1977, 136-48.
Jones, Rae Desmond. 'The Ambiguous Modernist: Themes in the Development of the Poetry of John Tranter'. *A.L.S.*, IX, 1980, 497-501.
Keim, Laurie. 'Cultural or Logical Artefacts - an Interview with John Tranter'. *Image*, VI, No. 3, 1983, 28-32.
Lilley, Kate. 'Tranter's Plots'. *A.L.S.*, 14, No. 1, 1989, 41-50.
Morris, Ronnith. 'Interview: A Conversation with John Tranter'. *Antithesis*, 7.1, 1995, 148-59.
Page, Geoff. 'John Tranter'. In his *A Reader's Guide To Contemporary Australian Poetry* (St. Lucia: U.Q.P., 1995), 295-300.
Rowe, Noel. *Modern Australian Poets*. (Sydney: Sydney UP in association with O.U.P. Includes discussion of the poetry of Tranter.
Shapcott, Thomas. 'John Tranter and Les Murray'. *A.L.S.*, X, 1982, 381-88.
Taylor, Andrew. 'John Tranter: Absence in Flight'. *A.L.S.*, XII, No. 4, 1986, 458-70. Reprinted in his *Reading Australian Poetry* (St Lucia: U.Q.P., 1987), 156-

170.
---. 'Resisting the Mad Professor: Narrative and Metaphor in the Poetry of John Tranter'. *Journal of Narrative Technique*, 21.1, 1991, 14-23.
Travers, Erica. 'An Interview with John Tranter'. *Southerly*, 51.4, 1991, 14-28.
Urquhart, Alan. 'Hacking at the Pattern: Post-Romantic Consciousness in the Poetry of John Tranter'. *Southerly*, 53.3, 1993, 12-29.

TRITTON, H.P. (DUKE)

Non-Fiction
Time Means Tucker. (Sydney: Shakespeare Head Press, 1964).
Reviewed by M. Durack, *Age*, 8 May, 1965, 24.

Critical Material
Meredith, John. *Duke of the Outback: The Adventures of "Shearer Named Tritton"*. (Ascot Vale: Red Rooster Press, 1983). Reviewed by N. Keesing, *Weekend Australian Magazine*, 31 December, 1983-1 January, 1984, 11.

TROLLOPE, ANTHONY

Fiction
Harry Heathcote of Gangoil. With an introduction by Marcie Muir. (Melbourne: Lansdowne Press, 1963). First published London: Sampson Low, Marston, Low & Searle, 1874.
Reviewed by P.D. Edwards, *A.L.S.*, I, No. 3, 1964, 208-212.
Harry Heathcote of Gangoil: A Tale of Australian Bushlife. Edited and introduced by P.D. Edwards. (Oxford: O.U.P., 1992) First published London: Sampson Low, Marston, Low & Searle, 1874.

Non-Fiction
Australia. Edited by P.D. Edwards and R.B. Joyce. (Brisbane: U.Q.P., 1967 i.e. 1968). First published London: Chapman & Hall, 1873.
Reviewed by C. Bateson, *Australian*, 5 October, 1968, 10; C.M. Clark, *A.L.S.*, IV, 1969, 85; P. Coleman, *Bulletin*, 3 August, 1968, 74; H. Dow, *Overland*, No. 41, 1969, 43-45; M. Harris, *ABR*, VII, 1968, 178; G.F. James, *Meanjin*, XXVIII, 1969, 124-29; R. Murray, *Nation*, 12 October, 1968, 23.

Trollope's Australia. (Melbourne: Thomas Nelson, 1966). Edited with a Foreword and Introduction by Hume Dow. A Selection from the Australian passages in *Australia and New Zealand*. First published London: Chapman & Hall, 1873.
Reviewed by D. Archdall, *Australian*, 15 October, 1966, 10; M. Clark, *Age*, 12 November, 1966, 23; G. Farwell, *S.M.H.*, 12 November, 1966, 20; S. Lawson, *Canberra Times*, 15 October, 1966, 11.

Critical Material
Davidson, J.H. 'Anthony Trollope and the Colonies'. *Victorian Studies*, XII, 1969, 305-30.
Edwards, P.D. 'Anthony Trollope's "Australian" Novels'. *Southerly*, XXV, No. 3, 1965, 200-7.
Friederich, Werner P. *Australia in Western Imaginative Prose Writings 1600-1960: An Anthology and a History of Literature*. (Chapel Hill: University of North Carolina Press, 1967), 95-110.
Hamer, Clive. 'Anthony Trollope's Australian Novels'. *Biblionews*, I, No. 4, 1966, 24-9.
Harris, Max. *Australian*, 20 July, 1968, 11.
James, G.F. 'Anthony Trollope in Australia'. *Age*, 19 March, 1966, 22.
Joyce, R.B. 'Editorial Problems in Presenting Trollope's Views on Australia'. *Queensland Heritage*, No. 1, November, 1964, 5-10.
Watson-Williams, Helen. 'Land into Literature. The Western Australian Bush Seen

by some Early Writers and D.H. Lawrence'. *Westerly*, XXV, No. 1, 1980, 59-72.

TSALOUMAS, DIMITRIS

Poetry

The Barge. (St Lucia: U.Q.P., 1993).
Reviewed by M. Duwell, *Weekend Australian*, 24-25 July, 1993, Review 7; L. McCredden, *ABR*, 149, 1993, 35-36 [with portrait of the author by R. Sorensen, 33-35]; J. Owen, *Meanjin*, 52.3, 1993, 573-81; A. Riemer, *Age*, 17 July, 1993, Saturday Extra 8; G. Rowlands, *Overland*, 136, 1994, 83-84.

A Book of Epigrams. Translated by Philip Grundy, bilingual edition (St Lucia; London; New York: U.Q.P., 1985). First published in Greek only, Thessaloniki: Nea Poreia Press, 1982.
Reviewed by K. Belou, *ABR*, 71, 1985, 26-27; S. Edgar, *Island Magazine*, 24. 1985, 60-61; E. Perkins, *Outrider*, II, No. 2, 1986, 172-74.

Falcon Drinking: The English Poems. (St Lucia: U.Q.P., 1988).
Reviewed by R.F. Brissenden, *Weekend Australian*, 23-24 July, 1988, Weekend 15; H. Cam, *S.M.H.*, 1 October, 1988, 74; D. Constantine, *Meridian*, 8, No. 2, 1989, 188-89; J. Grant, *ABR*, No. 99, 1988, 25-27; E. Perkins, *LiNQ*, 16, No. 1, 1988, 13-20; J. Strauss, *Age Saturday Extra*, 28 May, 1988, 14.

The Observatory. Translated by Philip Grundy, bilingual edition (St Lucia: U.Q.P., 1983).
Reviewed by B. Beaver, *Quadrant*, XXVII, No. 12, 1983, 94-5; K. Goldsworthy, *Age Saturday Extra*, 15 October, 1983, 15; K. Hemensley, *Earth Ship*, No. 42, 1984, 59-67; A. Karakostas, *Outrider*, I, No. 1, 1984, 180-82; A. Kefala, *Scripsi*, II, No. 4, 1984, 91-4; G. Lehmann, *S.M.H.*, 16 July, 1983, 38; S. McKernan, *Canberra Times*, 18 February, 1984, 19; P. Martin, *ABR*, No. 55, 1983, 12-13; C. Miller, *PN Review*, XIV, No. 1, 1987, 62-63.

The Observatory. New and enlarged edition. (St Lucia: U.Q.P., 1991).
Reviewed by D.Porter, *Voices*, 2.1, 1992, 101-04.

Portrait of a Dog: And Other Classical Bagatelles. Illustrated by Michael Winters. (St. Lucia: U.Q.P., 1991).
Reviewed by L. Bourke, *Southerly*, 52.4, 1992, 158-64; M. Duwell, *Weekend Australian*, 31 October-1 November, 1992, Review 7; T. Shapcott, *Age*, 26 September, 1992, Saturday Extra 10.

Non-Fiction

With David J. Tacey. 'Reflections on *Falcon Drinking*'. *Meridian*, 9, No. 2, 1990, 102-110.

Critical Material

Barnes, John. 'Notes on the Poetry of Dimitris Tsaloumas'. *Meridian*, VI, No. 2, 1987, 104-106.
Castan, Con. *Dimitris Tsaloumas: Poet*. (Melbourne: Elikia books, 1990). Reviewed by K. Bellon, *Journal of Australian Studies*, No. 27, 1990, 97-100; J. Burke, *ABR*, No. 127, 1990, 18; M. Duwell, *A.L.S.*, 14, No. 4, 1990, 522-25; S. Gauntlett, *Meridian*, 9, No. 2, 1990, 158-61.
---. 'Form, Place and Structure in a Poem of Dimitris Tsaloumas'. *Outrider*, II, No. 2, 1985, 14-20.
---. 'Interview with Dimitris Tsaloumas'. *Outrider*, II, No. 2, 1986, 3-14.
Constantine, D and H. Constantine. 'Dimitris Tsaloumas'. *Poetry Review*, 76.1-2, 1986, 62-63.
Duwell, Martin. 'Notes on the Poetry of Dimitris Tsaloumas'. *Meridian*, VI, No. 2, 1987, 109-112.
Martinez, Enrique. '"The Glint and the Shadow": The Poetry of Dimitris Tsaloumas'. In *Australian Literature Today*, edited by R.K. Dhawan and David Kerr (New York:

Indian Society for Commonwealth Studies/ Advent P, 1993), 192-210.
Meraklis, M.G. 'Notes of the Poetry of Dimitris Tsaloumas'. *Meridian*, VI, No. 2, 1987, 106-109.
Morgan, W. and Sneja Gunew. 'Dimitris Tsaloumas: An Interview'. *Mattoid*, 11-12, [1982], 23-32.
Page, Geoff. 'Dmitris Tsaloumas'. In his *A Reader's Guide To Contemporary Australian Poetry* (St. Lucia: U.Q.P., 1995), 300-304.
Rodriguez, Judith. 'Dimitris Tsaloumas Observed'. *Meanjin*, 42.1, 1983, 104-09.
Shapcott, Thomas. 'Dimitris Tsaloumas'. *Outrider*, II, No. 2, 1986, 22-24.

TUCKER, JAMES

Fiction
Ralph Rashleigh. Introduced by Colin Roderick. (Pymble, NSW: Collins A.& R., 1992). First published Sydney: A.& R., 1952.

Critical Material
Argyle, Barry. '*Ralph Rashleigh*'. *Ariel* (Calgary, Alberta), II, No. 1, 1971, 5-25.
Boehm, Harold J. 'The Date of Compostion of *Ralph Rashleigh*'. *A.L.S.*, VI, 1974, 428-30.
Dixon, Robert. '*Ralph Rashleigh*: A History of Civil Society in New South Wales'. *Southerly*, XLI, 1981, 300-16.
Ellis, M.H. 'Dr Roderick's Latest'. *Bulletin*, 9 February, 1963, 40-2. Review of the reprint of *Ralph Rashleigh* (Sydney: A.& R., 1962) edited by Colin Roderick. Disputes Roderick's claim that Tucker was the author.
Healy, J.J. 'The Convict and the Aborigine: The Quest for Freedom in *Ralph Rashleigh*'. *A.L.S.*, III, 1968, 243-53.
Hergenhan, L.T. '*Ralph Rashleigh*: A Convict Dream'. *A.L.S.*, VII, 1976, 279-93. Reprinted in his *Unnatural Lives*. (St Lucia: U.Q.P., 1983), 16-30.
Middleton, Delys E.J. 'Villain or Hero? The Bushranger in *Ralph Rashleigh, Robbery Under Arms*, and *The Hero of Too*'. *Armidale and District Historical Society Journal and Proceedings*, No. 13, 1970, 27-36.

TURNER, ETHEL

Fiction
Seven Little Australians. Centennial edition. (Montville, Qld: McVitty, 1994). First published London: Ward, Lock, 1894.
Reviewed by B. Niall, *S.M.H.*, 22 October, 1994, Spectrum 12A; C. Pybus, *ABR*, 166, 1994, 27.

Non-Fiction
The Diaries of Ethel Turner. Edited by Philippa Poole. (Sydney: Ure Smith, 1979; Lansdowne, 1980). Reprinted Sydney: Collins, 1987.
Reviewed by C. Burt, *Courier-Mail*, 16 February, 1980, 20; R. Elliott, *Canberra Times*, 25 May, 1980, 8; K. England, *Advertiser*, 22 March, 1980, 25; B. Niall, *Times on Sunday*, 21 February, 1988, 33; J. Rodriguez, *A.L.S.*, IX, 1980, 413-16.

Critical Material
Gollan, Myfanwy. 'Starting a Conversation'. *Bulletin Literary Supplement*, 30 June, 1981, 24-47.
Morris, Myra. 'Ethel Turner'. In *An Overland Muster*, edited by Stephen Murray-Smith (Brisbane: Jacaranda Press, 1965), 99-100. Originally published *Overland*, No. 13, 1958, 38.
Niall, Brenda. *Seven Little Billabongs: The World of Ethel Turner and Mary Grant Bruce*. (Carlton: M.U.P., 1979). Reviewed by R. Elliott, *Canberra Times*, 30 December, 1979, 8; C. Fleming, *CRNLE Reviews Journal*, No. 2, 1980, 59-62; P. Grimshaw, *Overland*, No. 80, 1980, 58-60; H. King, *Journal of the Royal Australian*

Historical Society, LXVII, No. 1, 1981, 75-76; W. McVitty, *Age*, 23 February, 1980, 26; J. Pausacker, *ABR*, No. 17, 1979-1980, 12-13; E. Riddell, *Bulletin*, 13 November, 1979, 93-94; J. Rodriguez, *A.L.S.*, IX, 1980, 413-16; M. Saxby, *S.M.H.*, 26 January, 1980, 16.

---. 'Mythmakers of Australian Childhood'. *This Australia* (Maryborough), No. 1, 1981-82, 64-72.

Rossiter, Richard. '"Thou oughtest to be mine": Father and Lover in Ethel Turner's *Nicola Silver*'. *Westerly*, 37.3, 1992, 71-78.

Shepherd, Ron. 'Larrikinism and Ethel Turner's Fiction: The Sand-Patch and the Garde'. In *Tilting at Matilda: Literature, Aborigines, Women and the Church in Contemporary Australia*, edited by Dennis Haskell (South Fremantle, WA: Fremantle Arts Centre P., 1994), 46-59.

Yarwood, A.T. *From a Chair in the Sun: The Life of Ethel Turner*. (Ringwood, Vic.: Viking, 1994). Reviewed by E. Campion, *Bulletin*, 25 October, 1994, 97; H. Horton, *Imago*, 7.2, 1995, 101-02; P. MacIntyre, *Age*, 19 November, 1994, Saturday Extra 11; *Margin*, 35, 1995, 34; B. Niall, *S.M.H.*, 22 October, 1994, Spectrum 12A; M. Saxby, *Weekend Australian*, 29-30 October, 1994, Review 6.

TURNER, GEORGE

Fiction

Beloved Son. (London: Faber, 1978).
Reviewed by D. Broderick, *24 Hours*, III, No. 7, 1978, 61, 72; A. de Jonge, *Spectator*, 1 April, 1978, 25; S. Gunew, *Meanjin*, XLI, 1982, 279; J. Mackenzie, *Nation Review*, 1-6 July, 1978, 19; M. McAuliffe, *ABR*, No. 2, 1978, 144; W. Noonan, *S.M.H.*, 24 June, 1978, 16; T. Paulin, *New Statesman*, 26 May, 1978, 714; S. Sayers, *Age*, 1 April, 1978, 23; G. Stone, *Weekend Australian Magazine*, 5-6 August, 1978, 9.

The Cupboard Under the Stairs. (London: Cassell, 1962).
Reviewed by J.F. Burrows, *Southerly*, XXIII, No. 4, 1963, 276-80; S. Murray-Smith, *ABR*, II, 1963, 46.

Genetic Soldier. (New York: William Morrow, 1994).
Reviewed by K. Burkhouse, *Antipodes*, 9.1, 1995, 50-51.

In the Heart or in the Head: An Essay in Time Travel. (Carlton, Vic.: Norstrilia Press, 1984).
Reviewed by R. Anderson, *Courier-Mail*, 22 September, 1984, 28; J. Foyster, *ABR*, No. 76, 1985, 5-6; N. Keesing, *Overland*, No. 97, 1984, 72-73; C. Steele, *Canberra Times*, 22 September, 1984, 15.

The Lame Dog Man. (Melbourne: Cassell Australia, 1967).
Reviewed by S. Despoja, *Adelaide Advertiser*, 30 September, 1967, 22; N. Jillett, *Age*, 30 September, 1967, 23; N. Keesing, *Bulletin*, 7 October, 1967, 83; T. Keneally, *Australian*, 11 November, 1967, 13; M. Vintner, *S.M.H.*, 11 November, 1967, 19; R. Wighton, *ABR*, VI, 1967, 194-95.

A Pursuit of Miracles: Eight Stories. (North Adelaide: Aphelion, 1990).
Reviewed by C. Steele, *ABR*, No. 123, 1990, 37.

The Sea and Summer. (London: Faber, 1987).
Reviewed by J. Hanrahan, *Age Saturday Extra*, 16 January, 1988, 10; V. Ikin, *S.M.H.*, 10 September, 1988, 76.

Transit of Cassidy. (Melbourne: Nelson (Australia), 1978).
Reviewed by F. Kellaway, *ABR*, No. 8, 1979, 12-13; G. Muirden, *Southerly*, XXXIX, 1979, 227-28; R. Nicholls, *Age*, 27 January, 1979, 26; W. Noonan, *S.M.H.*, 18 November, 1978, 17; P. Ward, *Weekend Australian Magazine*, 9-10 December, 1978, 8.

Vaneglory. (London: Faber, 1981).
Reviewed by D. Broderick, *Age Saturday Extra*, 13 February, 1982, 14; J. McLaren, *Overland*, No. 89, 1982, 58-59; K. Methold, *Weekend Australian Magazine*, 30-31 January, 1982, 12; Y. Rousseau, *ABR*, No. 41, 1982, 21-22; C. Steele, *Canberra Times*, 20 March, 1982, 13; E. Williams, *S.M.H.*, 17 April, 1982, 42.

A Waste of Shame. (Melbourne: Cassell, 1965).
Reviewed by B. Byrom, *The Spectator*, 20 August, 1965, 242; L.V. Kepert, *S.M.H.*, 24 April, 1965, 17; C. Semmler, *ABR*, IV, 1965, 149; *T.L.S.*, 23 September, 1965, 834.

Yesterday's Men. (London: Faber, 1983).
Reviewed by S. Bann, *London Review of Books*, V, No. 5, 1983, 22; D. Broderick, *Age Saturday Extra*, 5 February, 1983, 11; P. Byrnes, *S.M.H.*, 30 April, 1983, 36; R. Cowper, *Foundation*, No. 28, 1983, 95-97; T. Dowling, *National Times*, 13-19 February, 1983, 31; B. Hunter, *Courier-Mail*, 19 February, 1983, 26; Y. Rousseau, *ABR*, No. 51, 1983, 14; C. Steele, *Canberra Times*, 19 March, 1983, 12.

Non-Fiction

'Not taking it all too Seriously (The Profession of Science Fiction, 27)'. *Foundation* (London), No. 24, 1982, 49-58.
Debate between Russell Blackford, Damien Broderick, David Lake and George Turner. *Science Fiction*, No. 20, 1985, 40-47.

Critical Material

Buckrich, Judith Raphael. 'George Turner: One of Australia's Best Kept Secrets'. *Overland*, 133, 1993, 24-30.
Hosking, Rick. 'The Usable Past: Australian War Fiction of the 1950s'. *A.L.S.*, XII, No. 2, 1985, 234-247.
Ikin, Van. 'George Turner: The Man, the Writer, the Critic - An Interview'. *Science Fiction* (Sydney), I, No. 3, 1978, 119-38.
Kellaway, Frank. 'Visions of Conflict: The Novels of George Turner'. *Overland*, No. 87, 1982, 9-13.
McLaren, John. 'The Image of Reality in Our Writing'. *Overland*, Nos. 27-8, 1963, 43-7. Makes specific references to Turner's novels.
Ward, Peter. 'The Novels of George Turner'. *Australian Letters*, V, No. 4, 1963, 40-4.

TURNER, W.J.

Poetry

Selected Poems. Edited with Introduction by Wayne McKenna. (Kensington, N.S.W.: New South Wales University Press, 1990)
Reviewed by John Foulcher, *Quadrant*, 35.7-8, 1991, 102-05.

Critical Material

McKenna, Wayne. *W.J. Turner: Poet and Music Critic*. (Kensington, N.S.W.: New South Wales University Press, 1990).

U

UNAIPON, DAVID

Critical Material

Hosking, Susan. 'David Unaipon: His Story'. In *Southwords: Essays on South Australian Writing*, edited by Philip Butterss (Kent Town, SA: Wakefield, 1995), 85-101.

UPFIELD, ARTHUR

Critical Material

Browne, Ray B. 'The Frontier Heroism of Arthur W. Upfield'. *Clues*, 7.1, 1986, 127-46.

Browne, Ray B. *The Spirit of Australia: The Crime Fiction of Arthur W. Upfield.* (Bowling Green, Ohio: Bowling Green State University Popular Press, 1988). Reviewed by D. Crawford, *Armchair Detective*, 21.4, 1988, 415; D. Walden, *Journal of Popular Culture*, 23.2, 1989,172-74.

Cawelti, John G. 'Murder in the Outback: Arthur W. Upfield'. *New Republic*, 177.5, 1977, 39-44.

Donaldson, Betty. 'Arthur William Upfield: September 1 1888 - February 13 1964'. *Armchair Detective*, 8, 1974, 1-11.

Donaldson, Tamsin. 'Australian Tales of Mystery and Miscegenation'. *Meanjin*, 50.2-3, 1991, 341-52.

King, Margaret J. 'Binocular Eyes: Cross-Cultural Detectives'. *Armchair Detective*, 13, 1980, 253-60.

Knight, Stephen. 'The Case of the Missing Genre: In Search of Australian Crime Fiction'. *Southerly* 48.3, 1988, 235-49.

---. 'Crime Runs Rampant'. *Australian Society* 6.7, 1977, 61-62.

McQueen, Humphrey. 'Racism and Australian Literature'. In *Racism: The Australian Experience. A Study of Race Prejudice in Australia. Volume I. Prejudice and Xenophobia*, edited by F.S. Stevens (Sydney: Australia and New Zealand Book Company, 1971), 115-22.

Martin, Murray S. 'The New Frontier in Australian Detective Fiction'. *Antipodes*, 9.2, 1995, 113-17. Includes discussion of Upfield's fiction.

Pierson, James C. 'Mystery Literature and Ethnography: Fictional Detectives as Anthropologists'. In *Literature and Anthropology*, edited by Philip A. Dennis and Wendell Aycock (Lubbock: Texas Tech University Press, 1989), 15-30.

Reilly, John ed. *Twentieth-Century Crime and Mystery Writers.* New York: St. Martin's Press, 1985. 860-61. Short biography and bibliography.

Ruskin, Pamela. 'Arthur Upfield: An Epitaph'. *Walkabout*, 30.5, 1964, 37-40.

---. 'Arthur Upfield Made Crime Pay'. *Mean Streets: A Quarterly Journal of Crime, Mystery and Detection*, 5, 1992, 24-30.

VIDAL, MARY THERESA

Fiction

Bengala or Some Time Ago. Edited and introduced by Susan McKernan. (Kensington, NSW: New South Wales UP, 1990). First published 1860.
Reviewed by S.K. Martin, *Bibliographical Society of Australia and New Zealand Bulletin*, 15.1, 1991, 40-41; E. Morrison, *Overland*, 122, 1991, 77-79; A. Smith, *Australian Studies*, 5, 1991, 148-50; S. Walker, *A.L.S.*, 15.3, 1992, 238-41; J. Waterman, *Antipodes*, 5.2, 1991, 164.

Tales for the Bush. Introduced by Susan Lever. Aust. Books on Demand 13. (Canberra: Mulini Press, 1995).

Critical Material

Lever, Susan. 'Mary Theresa Vidal and Eton'. *Notes & Furphies*, 34, 1995, 3.

WALCH, GARNET

Drama
Australia Felix, or Harlequin Laughing Jackass and the Magic Bat. Edited by Veronica Kelly. (St Lucia: U.Q.P., 1988). First published Melbourne: Azzopardi, Hildreth, 1873.
Reviewed by K. Stewart, *A.L.S.*, 14, No. 1, 1989, 122-26.

Critical Material
Kelly, Veronica. 'Melodrama, an Australian Pantomime, and the Theatrical Constructions of Colonial History'. *Journal of Australian Studies*, 38, 1993, 51-61.
Richardson, Paul. 'Garnet Walch's "Australia Felix": A Reconstruction'. *Australasian Drama Studies*, I, No. 2, 1983, 63-81.

WALKER, BRENDA

Fiction
Crush. (Fremantle, WA: Fremantle Arts Centre Press, 1991).
Reviewed by A. Bartlett, *Refractory Girl*, 41, 1991, 38-40; J. Bedford, *Voices*, 1.3, 1991, 97-100; R. Bittoun, *ABR*, 128, 1991, 13-14; S. Creane, *Australian Women's Book Review*, 3.3, 1991, 30-31; D. Davison, *Weekend Australian*, 4-5 May, 1991, Review 5; M. Day, *S.M.H.*, 30 March, 1991, 29; A. Gibbs, *Editions*, 11, 1991, 31; K. Lamb, *Age*, 23 March, 1991, Saturday Extra 7; J. Stephens, *Australian Society*, May, 1991, 43; J. Waterman, *Antipodes*, 5.2, 1991, 164.
One More River. (Fremantle, WA: Fremantle Arts Centre Press, 1993).
Reviewed by E. Abbey, *S.M.H.*, 6 March, 1993, 44; B. Brook, *Australian Women's Book Review*, 5.4, 1993, 6-7; H. Daniel, *Age*, 13 March, 1993, Saturday Extra 8; M. MacLean, *ABR*, 149, 1993, 5-6 (see also interview with Rosemary Sorensen, 7-8); J. Tanner, *Antipodes*, 7.2, 1993, 153; G, Windsor, *Weekend Australian*, 27-28 February, 1993, Review 4.

Critical Material
Evans, Christine. 'Between Love and Castration: On Brenda Walker's novel *Crush*'. *Westerly*, 40.2, 1995, 41-49.

WALKER, KATH

See Oodgeroo Noonucal.

WALLACE-CRABBE, CHRIS

Fiction
Splinters. (Adelaide: Rigby, 1981).
Reviewed by G. Catalano, *Age*, 26 September, 1981, 28; A. Hollinghurst, *T.L.S.*, 5 February, 1982, 147; T. Shapcott, *Courier-Mail*, 31 July, 1982, 26; J. Tittensor,

Overland, No. 87, 1982, 62-63.

Poetry

The Amorous Cannibal. (Oxford: O.U.P., 1985).
Reviewed by G. Ewart, *Overland*, No. 103, 1986, 58-59; M. Hulse, *PN Review*, XII, No. 5, 1986, 56; L. MacKinnon, *T.L.S.*, 18 April, 1986, 430; P. Porter, *ABR*, No. 80, 1986, 9-10; K. Russell, *Quadrant*, XXXI, Nos. 1-2, 1987, 109-115; esp. 110; J. Strauss, *Age Saturday Extra*, 8 February, 1986, 14.

Chris Wallace-Crabbe Reads from his Own Work. (St Lucia: U.Q.P., 1973). Poets on Record, 10. Record and booklet. Booklet includes notes by Chris Wallace-Crabbe and selected bibliography.

The Emotions are not Skilled Workers. (Sydney: A.& R., 1980).
Reviewed by G. Catalano, *Meanjin*, XXXIX, 1980, 358-59; B. Giles, *ABR*, No. 26, 1980, 40; R. Gray, *S.M.H.*, 15 March, 1980, 16; J. Griffin, *Advertiser*, 8 March, 1980, 27; P. Neilsen, *Age*, 30 August, 1980, 25.

The Foundations of Joy. (Sydney: A.& R., 1976). Poets of the Month, Series 2.
Reviewed by V. Ikin, *Quadrant*, XXI, No. 9, 1977, 78-79.

For Crying Out Loud. (Oxford; Melbourne: O.U.P., 1990).
Reviewed by K. Goodwin, *Voices*, 1.2, 1991, 109-11; K. Hemensley, *ABR*, 129, 1991, 30-31; J. Owen, *Quadrant*, 35.9, 1991, 84-86; P. Salom, *Westerly*, 36.4, 1991, 120-21; J. Strauss, *Age*, 13 April, 1991, Saturday Extra 7; M. Wormald, *T.L.S.*, 29 March, 1991, 20.

I'm Deadly Serious. (Oxford: O.U.P., 1988).
Reviewed by D. Byrne, *Unisa English Studies*, 27, No. 1, 1989, 57-7; H. Cam, *S.M.H.*, 30 July, 1988, 78; P. Goldsworthy, *Age Saturday Extra*, 27 August, 1988, 15; P. Mead, *Age Monthly Review*, 9, No. 5, 1989, 22; P. Porter, *Overland*, No. 113, 1988, 14-16; W. Tonetto, *Southerly*, 49, No. 4, 1989, 660-67.

In Light and Darkness. (Sydney: A.& R., 1963).
Reviewed by J.M. Couper, *Poetry Magazine*, No. 2, 1964, 34-5; P. Jeffery, *Westerly*, No. 4, 1964, 55-9; E. Jones, *Prospect*, VII, No. 2, 1964, 27-8; S.E. Lee, *Southerly*, XXIV, No. 2, 1964, 133; *T.L.S.*, 10 September, 1964, 842; P. Steele, *Meanjin*, XXIII, No. 4, 1964, 439-40.

The Rebel General. (Sydney: A.& R., 1967).
Reviewed by L.J. Clancy, *Westerly*, No. 1 1969, 62-64; R. Dunlop, *Poetry Australia*, No. 20, 1968, 40-41; R. Hall, *Australian*, 18 May, 1968, 13; H. Hewitt, *Canberra Times*, 15 June, 1968, 14; M. Irvin, *Bulletin*, 6 January, 1968, 44-45; A. King, *Meanjin*, XXVII, 1968, 179-80; S.E. Lee, *Southerly*, XXVIII, 1968, 152-53; B. Matthews, *Overland*, No. 38, 1968, 46; B. Medlin, *ABR*, VII, 1967, 41; P. Nase, *Poetry Magazine*, No. 2, 1968, 27-29.

Rungs of Time. (Oxford; New York; Melbourne: O.U.P., 1993).
Reviewed by L. Bourke, *ABR*, 155, 1993, 39-40; G. Catalano, *Overland*, 135, 1994, 75-76; M. Duwell, *Weekend Australian*, 22-23 January, 1994, Review 7; H.C. Jaffa, *Antipodes*, 8.2, 1994, 166-67; P. Porter, *Age*, 27 November, 1993, Saturday Extra 9; E. Watts, *Antipodes*, 7.2, 1994, 168-69.

Selected Poems: 1956-1994. (Oxford; Melbourne: O.U.P., 1995).
Reviewed by D. Leadbetter, *Overland*, 141, 1995, 74-75; D. McCooey, *Age*, 10 June, 1995, Saturday Extra 8; P. Porter, *ABR*, 172, 1995, 42-43.

Where the Wind Came. (Sydney: A.& R., 1971).
Reviewed by L.J. Clancy, *Age*, 1 January, 1972, 11; C. Harrison-Ford, *New Poetry*, XIX, No. 6, 1971, 35-36; E. Kynaston, *Review*, 26 February-3 March, 1972, 530; A. Pollard, *Journal of Commonwealth Literature*, X, No. 3, 1976, 75-76; P. Roberts, *S.M.H.*, 25 March, 1972, 19 (see also letter to the editor by D. Stewart, *S.M.H.*, 29 March, 1972, 6); J. Tulip, *Bulletin*, 8 January, 1972, 35.

Non-Fiction

Falling into Language. (Melbourne: O.U.P., 1990).
Reviewed by K. Goodwin, *Voices*, 1.2, 1991, 109-11; J. Hanrahan, *ABR*, 135, 1991, 19-20; P. Steele, *Age*, 2 February, 1991, Saturday Extra 8; J. Strauss, *Overland*, 123, 1991, 47-50; E. Watts, *Antipodes*, 7.2, 1993, 168-69.

Melbourne or the Bush: Essays on Australian Literature and Society. (Sydney: A.& R., 1974). Perspectives in Australian Literature.
Reviewed by J. Waten, *Age*, 26 October, 1974, 18.

'Beginning'. In *Autobiographical and Biographical Writing in the Commonwealth*, edited by D. MacDermott (Sadabell, Barcelona: Editorial AUSA, 1984), 235-240.
'Chris Wallace-Crabbe Answers R.A. Simpson'. *Poetry Magazine*, No. 3, 1966, 3-5.
'A Quaker Graveyard in Carlton'. In *The American Model: Influence and Independence in Australian Poetry*, edited by Joan Kirkby (Sydney: Hale & Iremonger, 1982), 42-53
'Self-Portrait'. *ABR*, No. 93, 1987, 7-9.

Critical Material

Carter, David. 'Shape-Changing'. *Helix*, Nos. 7-8, 1981, 101-09. Interview.
---. 'The Death of Satan and the Persistence of Romanticism'. *Literary Criterion* (Mysore), XV, Nos. 3-4, 1980, 69-72.
Colman, E.A.M. 'A Modest Radiance: The Poetry of Chris Wallace-Crabbe'. *Westerly*, No. 1, 1969, 45-51.
Kiernan, Brian. 'Poet in Public'. *Australian*, 13 November, 1971, 16.
Malouf, David. 'Some Volumes of Selected Poems of the 1970s'. *A.L.S.*, X, 1981, 13-21.
McKinlay, Brian. [Letter to the editor about 'The Numbers']. *Age*, 21 December, 1974, 12.
Page, Geoff. 'Chris Wallace-Crabbe'. In his *A Reader's Guide To Contemporary Australian Poetry* (St. Lucia: U.Q.P., 1995), 304-308.
Rama, R.P. '[Interview with] Chris Wallace-Crabbe'. In *Dialogues with Australian Poets* (Calcutta: P. Lal/Writers Workshop, 1993), 99-110.
Shapcott, Thomas. 'The Imaginative Enterprise: An Interview with Chris Wallace-Crabbe'. *Makar*, XIII, No. 3, 1978, 38-43.
Steele, Peter. 'To Move in Light: The Poetry of Chris Wallace-Crabbe'. *Meanjin*, XXIX, 1970, 149-55.
Strauss, Jennifer. 'Chris Wallace-Crabbe: An Ironist at Work "In the Gap Between Gluecklicher Dichter and Obiter Dicta"'. In her *Stop Laughing! I'm Being Serious: Three Studies in Seriousness and Wit in Contemporary Australian Poetry*. Monograph, Foundation for Australian Literary Studies 21 (Townsville, Qld.: James Cook University of North Qld, 1990), 53-74.
Williams, Barbara. 'Interview with Chris Wallace-Crabbe'. *Ariel*, 21, No. 2, 1990, 77-90.

WALWICZ, ANIA

Fiction

Boat. (North Ryde, N.S.W.: A.& R., 1989).
Reviewed by A. Gibbs, *Age Monthly Review*, 9, No. 9, 1989, 9-10; I. Indyk, *S.M.H.*, 25 November, 1989, 88; B. Matthews, *Weekend Australian*, 16-17 December, 1989, Weekend 7; R. Sorensen, *ABR*, No. 116, 34-35.

Red Roses. (St Lucia: U.Q.P., 1992).
Reviewed by A. Bartlett, *ABR*, 146: 49; F. Capp, *Age*, 20 June, 1992, Saturday Extra 9; D. Davison, *Weekend Australian*, 5-6 September, 1992, Review 4.

A Rose Is Not a Rose. (Melbourne: Rigmarole Books, 1982).
Reviewed by J. Clarke-Powell, *Earth Ship*, No. 43, 1984/85, 277-80.

Writing. (Clifton Hill, Vic.: Rigmarole Books, 1982).
Reviewed by B. Giles, *ABR*, No. 45, 1982, 20; S. Gunew, *Going Down Swinging*, No. 5, 1982, 50-52; A. Kefala, *Aspect*, No. 25, 1982, 73-78; J. Maiden, *S.M.H.*, 12 June, 1982, 37 and *Going Down Swinging*, No. 5, 1982, 37-42; G. Rowlands, *Luna*, No. 16, 1983, 30; T. Shapcott, *National Times*, 17-23 October, 1982, 17-18; E. Webby, *Meanjin*, 41, No. 1, 1983, 34-41.

Philip Hammial and Ania Walwicz. *Travel/Writing*. (North Ryde, N.S.W.: A.& R.).
Reviewed by A. Gibbs, *Age Monthly Review*, 9, No. 9, 1989, 9-10; I. Indyk, *S.M.H.*, 25 November, 1989, 88; B. Matthews, *Weekend Australian*, 16-17 December, 1989, Weekend 7.

   Critical Material
Brewster, Anne. 'Ania Walwicz's Vagrant Narration: Cosmopolitanism vs Nationalism in Australian "Migrant Writing"'. *Kunapipi*, 16.1, 1994, 181-88.
Digby, Jenny. 'The Politics of Experience: Ania Walwicz interviewed by Jenny Digby'. *Meanjin*, 51.4, 1991, 819-38.
Fitzgerald, Ursel. 'Introducing Ania Walwicz'. Supplement to *Mattoid*, 28, 1987, 1-23. Interview. Also includes poems and paintings by Walwicz, 24-57.
Gillett, Sue. 'At the Beginning: Ania Walwicz's Writing'. *Southerly*, 51.2, 1991, 239-52.
Gunew, Sneja. 'Ania Walwicz and Antigone Kefala: Varieties of Migrant Dreaming'. *Arena*, No. 76, 1986, 65-80. Reprinted in *Poetry and Gender: Statements and Essays in Australian Women's Poetry and Poetics*, edited by David Brooks and Brenda Walker (St Lucia: U.Q.P., 1989), 205-219.
----. 'Ania Walwicz: A Non-Celtic Australian Writer'. *Hecate*, XIII, No. 2, 1987/88, 69-72.
----. 'In Journeys Begin Dreams: Antigone Kefala and Ania Walwicz'. In her *Framing Marginality: Multicultural Literary Studies*. (Carlton, Vic.: MUP, 1994), 71-92.
Jacobsen, Lisa. 'Reading Ania Walwicz'. *Outrider 90*, 1990, 148-59.
Lysenko, Myron and Kevin Brophy. 'Interviewing: Ania Walwicz'. *Going Down Swinging*, No. 5, 1982, 43-49.

WARUNG, PRICE (WILLIAM ASTLEY)

   Fiction
Tales of the Convict System: Selected Stories. Edited by B.G. Andrews. (St Lucia: U.Q.P., 1975).
Reviewed by M. Dunlevy, *Canberra Times*, 25 July, 1975, 10; B. Elliott, *A.L.S.*, VII, 1976, 336-37.

   Critical Material
Andrews, Barry. 'Price Warung: Some Bibliographical Details and a Checklist of the Stories'. *A.L.S.*, III, 1968, 290-304.
----. 'Price Warung: Some Corrections and Additions'. *A.L.S.*, VII, 1975, 95-98.
Andrews, Barry. *Price Warung (William Astley)*. (Boston: Twayne, 1976). Twayne's World Authors series 383. Reviewed by L.T. Hergenhan, *A.L.S.*, VIII, 1978, 522-24.
----. '"Dynamite, Barricades, Brimstone": Price Warung's Political Themes'. *Labour History*, No. 22, 1972, 1-12.
----. 'Price Warung, the *Bulletin*, and the 1890s'. In *Individual and Community in Commonwealth Literature*, edited by Daniel Massa (Msida, Malta: Old University Press, 1979), 123-30.
Hergenhan, L.T. 'Convict Legends, Australian Legends: Price Warung and the Palmers'. *A.L.S.*, IX, 1980, 337-45. Reprinted in his *Unnatural Lives*. (St Lucia: U.Q.P., 1983), 122-29.
----. 'Price Warung and the Convicts: A View from (and of) the Nineties'. *Southerly*, XXXIX, 1979, 309-26. Reprinted in his *Unnatural Lives*. (St Lucia: U.Q.P., 1983),

62-75.
Nesbitt, Bruce. 'Price Warung's Fiction'. *A.L.S.*, V, 1972, 322.
Poole, Joan E. 'A Source for "John Price's Bar of Steel"'. *Southerly*, XXVII, 1967, 300-301.
Watts, Edward. 'William Astley and "The Mystery Which Men in Their Ignorance Label Eternity"'. *Antipodes*, 4.2, 1990, 99-104.

WATEN, JUDAH

Fiction

Alien Son. (Melbourne: Sun Books, 1966). First published Sydney: A.& R., 1952.
Reviewed by H. Brezniak, *Bridge*, II, No. 2, 1966, 57; S. Pritchard, *Weekend Australian Magazine*, 20-21 March, 1982, 11.

Alien Son. Introduction by David Carter. (North Ryde, N.S.W.: A.& R., 1990). First published Sydney: A.& R., 1952.
Reviewed by L. Clancy, *Weekend Australian*, 20-21 October, 1990, Review 5.

Distant Land. (Melbourne: F.W. Cheshire, 1965).
Reviewed by J. Bradley, *Westerly*, No. 2, 1965, 51-3; J. Ewers, *W.A. Teachers' Journal*, LV, 1965, 104; J. McLaren, *Overland*, No. 31, 1965, 48-9.

Love and Rebellion. (Melbourne: Macmillan, 1978).
Reviewed by P. Corris, *Weekend Australian Magazine*, 20-21 May, 1978, 9; B. Elliott, *Advertiser*, 17 June, 1978, 23; I. Fraser, *Tribune*, 16 August, 1978, 8; N. Keesing, *S.M.H.*, 6 May, 1978, 16, reprinted in *Survey*, IV, No. 6, 1978, 13; J. McLaren, *ABR*, No. 2, 1978, 26; R. Nicholls, *Age*, 6 May, 1978, 26; P. Rolfe, *Bulletin*, 11 July, 1978, 60; D. Rowbotham, *Courier-Mail*, 28 April, 1979, 29; C. Semmler, *24 Hours*, IV, No. 1, 1979, 55; E. Webby, *Meanjin*, XXXVIII, 1979, 124-25.

Scenes of Revolutionary Life. (Sydney: A.& R., 1982).
Reviewed by P. Botsman, *Courier-Mail*, 30 July, 1983, 26; G. Dutton, *Bulletin*, 18 January, 1983, 56-57; B. Hill, *National Times*, 3-9 October, 1982, 23; F. Kellaway, *Overland*, No. 92, 1983, 63-64; M. Lord, *ABR*, No. 46, 1982, 24-25; J. Pringle, *S.M.H.*, 16 October, 1982, 35; G. Turner, *Age Saturday Extra*, 25 September, 1982, 14.

Season of Youth. (Melbourne: Cheshire, 1966).
Reviewed by E. Castle, *Overland*, No. 36, 1967, 45; A.R. Chisholm, *Age*, 12 November, 1966, 24; R.G. Geering, *Southerly*, XXVII, 1967, 223-224; J. Laird, *Canberra Times*, 7 January, 1967, 10; M.J. McIntyre, *ABR*, VI, 1967, 55; M. Vintner, *S.M.H.*, 26 November, 1966, 21.

So Far No Further. (Mt. Eliza, Vic.: Wren, 1971).
Reviewed by A.R. Chisholm, *Age*, 4 December, 1971, 13; M. Costigan, *Review*, 5-11 February, 1972, 447; C. Harrison-Ford, *Nation*, 5 February, 1972, 21-22; N. Keesing, *Bulletin*, 15 January, 1972, 34; B. Kiernan, *Australian*, 1 January, 1972, 14; J. McLaren, *Overland*, No. 52, 1972, 53; *National Times*, 14-19 February, 1972, 21; N. Phelan, *S.M.H.*, 29 January, 1972, 18; A. Roberts, *Advertiser*, 11 December, 1971, 20; G. Wells, *Canberra Times*, 12 February, 1972, 13.

The Unbending. Introduced by David Carter. (North Ryde, NSW: A.& R., 1992).
First published Melbourne: Australasian Book Society, 1954.

Non-Fiction

From Odessa to Odessa: The Journey of an Australian Writer. (Melbourne: Cheshire, 1969).
Reviewed by L. Cantrell, *Australian Left Review*, No. 6, 1969, 74-75; A.D. Crown, *Bridge*, V, No. 1, 1970, 59-60; G. Dutton, *ABR*, IX, 1969, 20-21; R. Jones, *Bulletin*, 22 November, 1969, 67; B. Kiernan, *Australian*, 25 October, 1969, 23; K. Slessor, *Daily Telegraph*, Sydney, 14 February, 1970, 19; *T.L.S.*, 21 May, 1970, 567; C.

Turnbull, *Age*, 11 October, 1969, 13.
'Books and the Bottle-O's Son'. *S.M.H.*, 12 April, 1969, 19.
'Books that Influenced me Deeply'. *Educational Magazine*, XXXVI, No. 3, 1979, 30-32.
'A Child of Wars and Revolution: An Autobiographical Sketch'. *Southerly*, XXXIII, 1973, 411-19.
'Going Back to Odessa'. *Communist Review*, No. 288, 1966, 17-19.
[Letter to the editor about his association with Hardy and the Realists]. *Quadrant*, XIII, No. 3, 1969, 80.
'My Literary Education'. *Bulletin Literary Supplement*, 21 April, 1981, 24-28.
'My Two Literary Careers (Australian Writers in Profile, 8)'. *Southerly*, XXXI, 1971, 83-92.

Critical Material

'Judah Waten, Literary Pioneer, Dies at 74'. *Age*, 30 July, 1985, 17. For other obituaries see *ABR*, No. 74, 1985, 10-11; *Australian Jewish News*, 2 August, 1985, 39; *Australian Short Stories*, No. 11, 1985; *Bulletin*, 13 August, 1985, 22; *National Times*, 18-24 October, 1985, 29; *Notes & Furphies*, No. 15, 1985, 9; see also later entries by David Carter and Nancy Keesing.
'Racial Alienation: Common Theme in Contemporary Jewish Literature: Sydney Paper on Jewish Writers'. *Australian Jewish News*, 31 December, 1971, 14. Report of a paper by M.J. Haddock, to the 33rd AGM of the Australian Jewish Historical Society, 7 December, 1971.
Ballyn Susan. 'Judah Waten and the Jewish Immigrant Experience'. In *A Passage to Somewhere Else*. Proceedings of the Commonwealth Conference held in the University of Barcelona 30 September-2 October, 1987, edited by Doireann MacDermott and Susan Ballyn (Barcelona: Promociones y Publicaciones Universitarias, 1988), 11-18.
Bandman, Ken. 'The Terms of Achievement'. *Australian Jewish News*, 13 July, 1979, 3.
Beasley, Jack. 'Echoes of Ancestral Footsteps'. In his *Red Letter Days*. (Sydney: Australasian Book Society, 1979), 97-128.
Capp, Fiona. *Writers Defiled: Security Surveillance of Australian Authors and Intellectuals 1920-1960*. (Ringwood, Vic.: McPhee Gribble, 1993). Includes discussion of Waten.
Carter, David. 'Biography, Politics, a Novel: Reading Judah Waten'. *Southern Review*, 22, No. 1, 1989, 35-52.
---. 'Judah Waten'. *Notes and Furphies*, No. 16, 1986, 3-4. Obituary.
Ezawa, Sokushin. 'A Study on "Humour", "Pathos" and "Symbolism" in *The Unbending* by Judah Waten'. *The Journal of the Faculty of General Education* (Tottori University), 19, 1985, 115-34.
Gunew, Sneja, and Kateryna O. Longley, eds. *Striking Chords: Multicultural Literary Interpretations* (North Sydney: Allen & Unwin, 1992), 101-110.
Haddock, M.J. 'The Prose Fiction of Jewish Writers of Australia 1945 - 1969'. Part I, *Australian Jewish Historical Society Journal and Proceedings*, VII, 1974, 495-512.
Keesing, Nancy. 'Obituary'. *Australian Jewish Historical Society. Journal of Proceedings*, X, No. 8, 195, 646-47.
Kiernan, Brian. 'Memoirs of an Australian Alien Son'. *Australian*, 1 April, 1972, 14. Interview.
Larkin, John. 'Scenes from a Revolution'. *Age*, 4 October, 1982, 11.
Lipski, Sam. 'Why the Party Is Split over Moscow'. *Australian*, 25 February, 1969, 9.
Morrison, John. 'Judah Waten'. In his *The Happy Warrior*. (Fairfield, Vic.: Pascoe Publishing, 1987), 51-54. Originally published *Overland*, No. 11, 1958, 13-14.
O'Brien, Patrick. 'Zhdanov in Australia'. *Quadrant*, XVIII, No. 5, 1974, 37-55.

WATSON, E.L. GRANT

Collection
Descent of the Spirit: Writings of E.L. Grant Watson. Edited by Dorothy Green.
(Sydney: Primavera Press, 1990).
Reviewed by P. Cowan, *Westerly*, 36.1, 1991, 89-90; J. Dabbs, *ABR*, No. 119, 1990,
29; J. Larkin, *Age*, 14 April, 1990, Saturday Extra 9; S. Morgan, *Weekend
Australian*, 7-8 April, 1990, Weekend 8.

Fiction
The Nun and the Bandit. (Sydney: Primavera P., 1993). First published London:
Cresset Press, 1935.
Reviewed by G. Dutton, *Weekend Australian* 2-3 October, 1993, Review 4; A.
O'Neill, *Westerly*, 38.4, 1993, 125-27; E. Riddell, *Bulletin*, 5 October, 1993, 106-07.

Critical Material
Cowan, Peter. 'E.L. Grant Watson and Western Australia. A Concern for
Landscape'. *Westerly*, XXV, No. 1, 1980, 39-58.
Dossetor, R.F. 'Reminiscences of Kenneth Seaforth Mackenzie and E.L. Grant
Watson'. *A.L.S.*, XIII, No. 1, 1987, 99-104.
Green, Dorothy. 'The Daimon and the Fringe-Dweller: The Novels of Grant Watson'.
Meanjin, XXX, 1971, 277-93.
---. 'Vale Grant Watson'. *Meanjin*, XXXI, 1972, 84.
Healy, J.J. 'Grant Watson and the Aborigine: A Tragic Voice in an Age of
Optimism'. *A.L.S.*, VII, 1975, 24-38.

WATSON, SAM

Fiction
The Kadaitcha Sung. (Ringwood, Vic.: Penguin, 1990).
Reviewed by H. Daniel, *Weekend Australian*, 28-29 July, 1990, Review 6; J. Davis,
Age, 14 July, 1990, Saturday Extra 9; W. Dix, *ABR*, 123, 1990, 6-7; M. Fuary,
Australian Aboriginal Studies, 19.2, 1993, 113-14; M. Halligan, *National Library of
Australia News*, 1.1, 1990, 8-11; M. Harris, *Antipodes*, 6.1, 1992, 91; J. Turner
Hospital, *T.L.S.*, 20 August, 1993, 4; P. Wilson, *S.M.H.*, 11 August, 1990, 73.

Non-Fiction
'*Blast* Interview: Sam Watson'. *Blast*, 27, 1995, 4-6.
'I Say This to You: Sam Watson talks to *Meanjin*'. *Meanjin*, 53.4, 1994, 589-96.

Critical Material
Baker, Suzanne. 'Magic Realism as a Postcolonial Strategy: *The Kadaitcha Sung*'.
SPAN, 32, 1991, 55-62.
Gelder, Ken. 'The Politics of the Sacred'. *World Literature Today*, 67.3, 1993, 499-
504. Discusses Ruby Langford Ginibi and Watson.

WEARNE, ALAN

Poetry
The Nightmarkets. (Ringwood, Vic.: Penguin, 1986).
Reviewed by J. Forbes, *Scripsi*, IV, No. 3, 1987, 71-74; K. Hart, *Overland*, No.
107, 1987, 80-81; J. Hibberd, *Age Saturday Extra*, 1 November, 1986, 14; S.
McKernan, *Bulletin*, 3 February, 1987, 54-55; G. Page, *Island Magazine*, No. 30,
1987, 62-63; M. Roberts, *ABR*, No. 88, 1987, 24-25; J. Rodriguez, *S.M.H.*, 29
November, 1986, 49; K. Russell, *Quadrant*, XXXI, No. 9, 1987, 61-66, esp. 61-62;
T. Thorne, *Overland*, No. 106, 1987, 74-75; B. Tully, *Muse Communique*, No. 61,
1987, 23-24.

New Devil, New Parish. (St Lucia: U.Q.P., 1976).
Reviewed by A. Gould, *Nation Review*, 17-23 March, 1977, 524; J. Grant,

Contempa, Series 2, No. 4, 49-50; C. Pollnitz, *Southerly*, XXXVII, 1977, 455-58; L.K. Robinson, *LiNQ*, V, 1977, 74-5; J. Tranter, *Australian*, 11 June, 1977, Weekend 9.

Public Relations. (St Lucia: Makar, 1972). Gargoyle Poets 2.
Reviewed by J.E. Tranter, *New Poetry*, XXII, No. 1, 1974, 47-9; C. Wallace-Crabbe, *Poetry Australia*, No. 44, 1972, 61-2.

   Non-Fiction
'Though Not for Amateurs: Thoughts on Hubris or the Lack of It'. *Island Magazine*, No. 40, 1989, 87-90. Paper presented at Salamanca Writers Weekend, 1988, on the theme 'The Uses of the Past'.

   Critical Material
Carter, David. 'Night-thoughts on *The Nightmarkets* or "Can We Become Our Future"'. *Scripsi*, IV, No. 3, 1987, 79-83.
Craven, Peter. 'Melways to his Melbourne: Alan Wearne's *The Nightmarkets*'. *Meanjin*, XLVI, No. 3, 1987, 410-421.
Gelder, Kenneth. 'History, Politics and the (Post) modern: Receiving Australian Fiction'. *Meanjin*, XLVII, No. 3, 1988, 551-559. Discusses the work of Gerald Murnane, Alan Wearne and Peter Carey.
Leonard, John. '*The Nightmarkets*: Nothing Fated or Rarefied'. *Scripsi*, IV, No. 3, 1987, 117-121.
Liddelow, Eden. 'Nightmarketing Melbourne or How Correct-Line Can a Juggernaut Be?' *Scripsi*, IV, No. 3, 1987, 107-113.
Page, Geoff. 'Alan Wearne'. In his *A Reader's Guide To Contemporary Australian Poetry* (St. Lucia: U.Q.P., 1995), 309-312.
Pollnitz, Christopher. '"Our Ennui and Job Applications": Alan Wearne's *The Nightmarkets*'. *Scripsi*, IV, No. 3, 1987, 91-97.

WEBB, FRANCIS

   Poetry
Cap and Bells: The Poetry of Francis Webb. Edited by Michael Griffith and James McGlade. (North Ryde, NSW: Collins/A.& R., 1991).
Reviewed by P. Excell, *Antipodes*, 7.1, 1993, 63-64; K. Hart, *Overland*, 124, 1991, 94-95; L. Jacobs, *CRNLE Reviews Journal*, 1, 1992, 90-93; N. Kidd, *Imago*, 4.3, 1992, 94-96; J. Owen, *Quadrant*, 35.12, 1991, 86-88; S. Patton, *ABR*, 133, 1991, 47-48; C. Powell, *Southerly*, 52.1, 1992, 160-69; T. Shapcott, *Age*, 7 September, 1991, Saturday Extra 9; C. Wallace-Crabbe, *Weekend Australian*, 26-27 October, 1991, Review 6. See also P. Excell in *ABR*, 135, 1991, 56.

Collected Poems. With a preface by Herbert Read. (Sydney: A.& R., 1969).
Reviewed by B. Beaver, *S.M.H.*, 10 May, 1969, 22; R. Dunlop, *Poetry Australia*, XXVIII, 1969, 35-36; J. Frow, *Canberra Times*, 12 July, 1969, 15; R. Hall, *Australian*, 9 August, 1969, 19; C. Harrison-Ford, *Poetry Magazine*, No. 4, 1969, 5-11; G. Lehmann, *Bulletin*, 19 July, 1969, 49-50; T.W. Shapcott, *Poetry Magazine*, No. 5, 1969, 5-9; R.A. Simpson, *Age*, 4 October, 1969, 13; F. Zwicky, *Westerly*, No. 1, 1970, 48-49.

The Ghost of the Cock. (Sydney: A.& R., 1964).
Reviewed by A. Brissenden, *Southerly*, XXV, No. 2, 1965, 138-41; V. Buckley, *Prospect*, VII, No. 3, 1964, 28-9; B. Davies, *Nation*, 5 September, 1964, 22; R.G. Geering, *Bulletin*, 1 August, 1964, 49-50; D. Hewett, *Overland*, No. 32, 1965, 46-7; P. Mares, *ABR*, III, 1964, 208; P. Steele, *Meanjin*, XXIII, No. 4, 1964, 441.

   Critical Material
Fryer Memorial Library of Australian Literature, University of Queensland. 'Francis Webb (1925-1973) Bibliography'. *Poetry Australia*, No. 56, 1975, 87-95.

Poet and Patient. A joint seminar of the Department of English, Faculty of Military Studies, Duntroon and the School of Psychiatry, the University of New South Wales. (Duntroon, A.C.T.: University of New South Wales, Faculty of Military Studies, 1983). (Occasional Paper; Department of English, University of New South Wales, Faculty of Military Studies; No. 1).

Poetry Australia no. 56: Francis Webb commemorative issue. Individual items are listed below by author. Reviewed by J. Griffin, *Advertiser*, 6 March, 1976, 28; K. Hart, *Canberra Poetry*, 1976, 73-74; P. Porter, *T.L.S.*, 9 April, 1976, 431; T. Thorne, *Australian*, 7 February, 1976, 30.

Ashcroft, W.D. '"All Joy ... and all Pain"'. *Hemisphere*, XX, No. 8, 1976, 25-27.

---. '"The Broads of the Spirit": The Poetry of Francis Webb'. *Meanjin*, XXXIII, 1974, 7-18.

---. 'Centre of Fierceness: Francis Webb's Vision of the Artist'. *A.L.S.*, VII, 1975, 160-75.

---. 'Pain's Amalgam with Gold: Francis Webb's "Around Costessy"'. *Westerly*, No. 2, 1977, 62-72.

---. '"realer than the Real": Francis Webb's "Ward Two"'. *A.L.S.*, IX, 1979, 59-70.

---. 'The Storming of the Bastille: The Technique of Francis Webb's Poetry'. *Southerly*, XXXIV, 1974, 355-70.

---. 'Two Perspectives of Webb's Thought'. *Poetry Australia*, No. 56, 1975, 55-61.

Brissenden, R.F. 'Francis Webb's Country: The Landscape of a Mind'. *Poetry Australia*, No. 56, 1975, 44-50.

Buckley, Vincent. 'A Poetry of Harmony'. *Poetry Australia*, No. 56, 1975, 39-43.

---. 'The Poetry of Francis Webb'. *Quadrant*, XIII, No. 8 (retrospectively renumbered as XIV, No. 2), 1970, 11-15.

Campbell, David. 'Francis Webb'. In *The Literature of Australia*, edited by Geoffrey Dutton. Revised edition (Ringwood, Vic.: Penguin, 1976), 500-08.

Carter, David. 'The Death of Satan and the Persistence of Romanticism'. *Literary Criterion* (Mysore), XV, Nos. 3-4, 1980, 59-62.

Cross, Gustav. 'Australian Poetry in the 'Sixties'. *Poetry Australia*, No. 5, 1965, 33-8.

Delmonte, Rodolfo. *Piercing into the Psyche: The Poetry of Francis Webb*. (Venice: C.E.T.I.D., 1979). Reviewed by D. Carter, *Helix*, Nos. 7-8, 187-88; L. Jacobs, *CRNLE Reviews Journal*, No. 1, 1981, 51-53; E. Perkins, *LiNQ*, VIII, No. 2, 1980, 107-08.

Dobson, Rosemary. 'Francis Webb'. *Australian Author*, VI, No. 2, 1974, 41.

---. 'Francis Webb'. *A.L.S.*, VI, 1974, 227-29.

---. 'Francis Webb'. *Poetry Australia*, No. 56, 1975, 5-8.

---. 'Francis Webb: A Note on a Letter from Herbert Read about Webb's Poetry'. *Southerly*, 52.4, 1992, 144-45.

Excell, Patricia. '"Before Two Girls": A "Lost" Poem by Francis Webb'. *Southerly*, 53.3, 1993, 54-62.

---. *Dancings of the Sound: A Study of Francis Webb's 'Eyre All Alone'*. Occasional Paper 13 (Canberra: English Department, University College, Australian Defence Force Academy, n.d.). Reviewed by H. C. Jaffa, *Antipodes*, 7.1, 1993, 61-63.

---. '"Eyre All Alone": Francis Webb as Mythmaker'. *A.L.S.*, X, 1981, 101-05.

---. 'Francis Webb's *Collected Poems*'. *A.L.S.*, XII, No. 4, 1986, 527-31.

Fitz-Walter, Sister M. Francisca. 'From Word to Wonder'. *Poetry Australia*, No. 56, 1975, 73-77.

Griffith, Michael. 'Francis Webb and Norman Lindsay'. *Southerly*, 49, No. 1, 1989, 32-43.

---. 'Francis Webb - The Poet as Hero'. *Poetry Australia*, No. 56, 1975, 62-72.

---. 'Francis Webb: "The Poet of Desolation" (Two Visions of Sydney)'. *Southerly*, XLII, 1982, 189-202.

--- 'Francis Webb's Challenge to Mid-Century Mythmaking: The Case of Ludwig

Leichhardt'. *A.L.S.*, X, 1982, 448-58.

---. 'Francis Webb's Library'. *Southerly*, XL, 1980, 348-58.

---. *God's Fool: The Life and Poetry of Francis Webb*. (North Ryde, NSW: A.& R., 1991). Reviewed by M. Duwell, *A.L.S.*, 15.4, 1992, 362-64; L. Jacobs, *CRNLE Reviews Journal*, 1, 1992, 90-93; N. Kidd, *Imago*, 4.3, 1992, 94-96; E. McMahon, *S.M.H.*, 18 April, 1992, 29; C. Powell, *Southerly*, 52.1, 1992, 160-69; T. Shapcott, *Age*, 7 September, 1991, Saturday Extra 9; C. Wallace-Crabbe, *Weekend Australian*, 26-27 October, 1991, Review 6.

---. 'The Revelatory Character of Francis Webb's Poetry'. *St Mark's Review*, No. 91, 1977, 39-49.

Heseltine, H.P. 'Francis Webb, 1925 - 1973: A Tribute'. *Meanjin*, XXXIII, 1974, 5-6.

---. 'The Very Gimbals of Unease: The Poetry of Francis Webb'. *Meanjin*, XXVI, 1967, 255-274.

Hope, A.D. 'Talking to God, The Poetry of Francis Webb'. *Poetry Australia*, No. 56, 1975, 31-35.

Kemp, Geoff. 'The Presentation and Allegorical Function of the Explorer Figure in Webb's "Leichhardt in Theatre"'. *Adelaide A.L.S. Working Papers*, III, 1979, 17-26.

Lamond, David. 'Notes and Reflections on Webb's Last Poem: "Lament for St. Maria Goretti"'. *Poetry Australia*, No. 56, 1975, 78.

McGlade, J.A. 'Finder of the "Meaning Beyond Mystery"'. *Catholic Weekly*, 8 June, 1980, 32, 35.

Murphy, R.D. 'Notes and Reflections on Webb's Last Poem: "Lament for St. Maria Goretti"'. *Poetry Australia*, No. 56, 1975, 78-82.

Murray, Les. 'The Death of a Poet'. *S.M.H.*, 19 January, 1974, 15.

Paull, James. 'The Thematic History in Francis Webb's Poetry'. *New Literatures Review*, 26, 1994, 58-67.

Powell, Craig. 'Francis Webb - A Memoir'. *Poetry Australia*, No. 56, 1975, 83-86.

---. 'Francis Webb: The Poet and Schizophrenia'. *Helix*, No. 16, 1983, 39-46.

Read, Herbert. [Letter to the editor on the neglect of Francis Webb's poetry]. *London Magazine*, VII, No. 9, 1967, 116.

Rowe, Noel. 'Francis Webb and the Will of the Poem'. *Southerly*, XLVII, No. 2, 1987, 180-196.

Sellick, Robert. 'Francis Webb's "Sturt and the Vultures": A Note on Sources'. *A.L.S.*, VI, 1974, 310-14.

Smith, Graeme Kinross. 'The Gull in a Green Storm - a Profile of Francis Webb (1925-1973)'. *Westerly*, XXVI, No. 2, 1981, 49-64.

Taylor, Andrew. 'The Spilled Cruet of Innocence: Subject in Francis Webb's Poetry'. In his *Reading Australian Poetry* (St Lucia: U.Q.P., 1987), 98-111.

Tulip, James. '"Banksia" - An Australian Epiphany'. *Poetry Australia*, No. 56, 1975, 36-39.

---. 'David Malouf, Francis Webb and Australian Religious Consciousness'. In *Reconnoitres: Essays in Australian Literature in Honour of G.A. Wilkes*, edited by Margaret Harris and Elizabeth Webby (South Melbourne: O.U.P. in association with Sydney U.P., 1992), 226-37.

---. 'The Poetry of Francis Webb'. *Southerly*, XXIX, 1969, 184-91.

Wallace-Crabbe, Chris. 'Order and Turbulence'. In his *Melbourne or the Bush: Essays on Australian Literature and Society*. (Sydney: A.& R., 1974), 114-26.

---. 'Some Aspects of Early Webb'. *Poetry Australia*, No. 56, 1975, 51-54.

Wright, Judith. 'Poets of the 'Forties and 'Fifties'. In her *Preoccupations in Australian Poetry*. (Melbourne: O.U.P., 1965), 193-210.

WELLER, ARCHIE

Fiction

The Day of the Dog. (Sydney: Allen & Unwin, 1981).
Reviewed by R. Barnes, *National Times*, 2-8 August, 1981, 30; L. Clancy, *ABR*, No. 47, 1982/83, 47; H. Daniel, *Age*, 8 August, 1981, 26; G. Dutton, *Bulletin*, 15 September, 1981, 72; R. Harris, *Overland*, No. 85, 1981, 78-80; N. Keesing, *ABR*, No. 32, 1981, 20-21; J. Magnus, *Artlook*, VII, No. 9, 1981, 19-20; M. Vernon, *Weekend Australian*, 12-13 September, 1981, Weekend 14.

Going Home: Stories. (Sydney: Allen & Unwin, 1986).
Reviewed by J. Barnes, *Age Saturday Extra*, 16 August, 1986, 13; N. Keesing, *S.M.H.*, 29 March, 1986, 30; G. Windsor, *ABR*, No. 78, 1986, 24-5.

Non-Fiction

'Thoughts on Aboriginal Writing'. *Literary Criterion*, 30.1&2, 1995, 49-55.

Critical Material

Little, Janine. '"Deadly" Work: Reading the Short Fiction of Archie Weller'. *A.L.S.*, 16.2, 1993, 190-99.
---. 'An Interview with Archie Weller'. *A.L.S.*, 16.2, 1993, 200-07.
Muecke, Stephen. 'On Not Comparing'. *Age Monthly Review*, V, No. 7, 1985, 8-10.
Shoemaker, Adam. '"Fiction or Assumed Fiction": The Short Stories of Colin Johnson, Jack Davis and Archie Weller'. In *Connections: Essays on Black Literatures*, edited by Emmanuel S. Nelson (Canberra: Aboriginal Studies Press, 1989), 53-9.
Tiffin, Chris. 'Relentless Realism: Archie Weller's *Going Home*'. *Kunapipi*, 10, Nos. 1&2, 1988, 222-35.

WENTWORTH, WILLIAM CHARLES

Critical Material

Ackland, Michael. 'Nature Through Currency Lad Eyes: Wentworth, Harpur, Kendall and the Australian Landscape'. In *Mapped But Not Known: The Australian Landscape of the Imagination*, edited by P.R. Eaden and F.H. Mares (Netley, S.A.: Wakefield Press, 1986), 73-85.
Byrnes, John V. 'William Charles Wentworth and the Continuity of Australian Literature'. *Australian Letters*, V, 1963, 10-18.

WEST, MORRIS

Fiction

The Ambassador. (London: Heinemann, 1965).
Reviewed by A. Ashbolt, *ABR*, IV, 1965, 145; A.R. Chisholm, *Age*, 15 May, 1965, 21; L. Kramer, *Bulletin*, 22 May, 1965, 55; K. Thomas, *Nation*, 12 June, 1965, 23; *T.L.S.*, 6 May, 1965, 345.

Cassidy. (Sydney; London: Hodder & Stoughton, 1986).
Reviewed by M. Costigan, *Weekend Australian Magazine*, 19-20 July, 1986, 16; G. Curran, *S.M.H.*, 12 July, 1985, 49; A. Fitzgerald, *Muse*, No. 64, 1987, 25; H. Knight, *New York Times Book Review*, 9 November, 1986, 32; D. Rowbotham, *Courier-Mail: The Great Weekend*, 12 July, 1986, 6.

Harlequin. (London; Sydney: Collins; New York: William Morrow & Co., 1974).
Reviewed by M. Barber, *Books and Bookmen*, XX, No. 10, 1975, 30-31; M. Levin, *New York Times Book Review*, 27 October, 1974, 56; A. Roberts, *Advertiser*, 11 January, 1975, 20; D. Robins, *Spectator*, 5 October, 1974, 438-39; P. Straub, *New Statesman*, LXXXVIII, 1974, 477-78; M. Williams, *S.M.H.*, 7 December, 1974, 19; *T.L.S.*, 4 October, 1974, 1092.

The Heretic. (New York: Morrow, 1969; London: Heinemann, 1970).
Reviewed by L. Radic, *Age*, 14 July, 1971, 16; P. Roberts, *Stand* (Newcastle-upon-Tyne), XII, No. 2, 1971, 72-73.

Lazarus. (Richmond, Vic.: Heinemann; New York: St Martin's, 1990).
Reviewed by D. Davison, *Weekend Australian*, 10-11 March, 1990, Weekend 8; S. Geason, *S.M.H.*, 3 March, 1990, 81; A. Gurr, *Australian Studies*, No. 4, 1990, 127-29; J. Hall, *Bulletin*, 6 March, 1990, 117; H. Knight, *New York Times Book Review*, 15 April, 1990, 14.

The Lovers. (Port Melbourne: Heinemann, 1993).
Reviewed by John Hanrahan, *Age*, 13 March, 1993, Saturday Extra 8; R. Lucas, *Bulletin*, 9 March, 1993, 87; P. Pierce, *S.M.H.*, 27 February, 1993, 45; L. Trainor, *Weekend Australian*, 24-25 April, 1993, Review 5.

Masterclass. (London: Hutchinson, 1988; New York: St. Martin's, 1991).
Reviewed by S. Geason, *S.M.H.*, 5 November, 1988, 91; C. Irving, *New York Times Book Review*, 9 June, 1991, 12; P. Rolfe, *Bulletin*, 22 November, 1988, 134.

The Navigator. (London: Collins, 1976).
Reviewed by R. Nicholls, *S.M.H.*, 8 January, 1977, 15.

The Ringmaster. (Melbourne: Heinemann, 1991).
Reviewed by G. Flynn, *Weekend Australian*, 9-10 November, 1991, Review 7; S. Hughes, *S.M.H.*, 5 October, 1991, 38; P. Pierce, *Age*, 28 September, 1991, Saturday Extra 10.

The Salamander. (London: Heinemann; New York: William Morrow, 1973).
Reviewed by S. Hall, *ABR*, XI, 1973, 123-24; M. Jones, *S.M.H.*, 1 September, 1973, 24; W. Noonan, *Australian*, 15 September, 1973, 44; J. Philip, *Canberra Times*, 28 September, 1973, 13; E. Riddell, *Australian*, 11 July, 1973, 12; A. Roberts, *Advertiser*, 18 August, 1973, 26; D. Rowbotham, *Courier-Mail*, 25 August, 1973, 19; W. Schott, *New York Times Book Review*, 21 October, 1973, 46; *T.L.S.*, 3 August, 1973, 911; J. Tittensor, *Nation Review*, 28 September-4 October, 1973, 1589; R. Wade, *Contemporary Review*, CCXXIII, 1973, 213.

Summer of the Red Wolf. (London: Heinemann; New York: Morrow, 1971).
Reviewed by E. Campion, *S.M.H.*, 23 October, 1971, 21; A.R. Chisholm, *Age*, 9 October, 1971, 14; S. Forbes, *Bulletin*, 2 October, 1971, 52; J. Hepworth, *Review* (Melbourne), 17 September, 1971, 1394; B. Kiernan, *Australian*, 16 October, 1971, 18; M. Levin, *New York Times Book Review*, 19 September, 1971, 44; B. Oakley, *Sunday Australian*, 7 November, 1971, 29.

The Tower of Babel. (London: Heinemann; New York: Morrow, 1968).
Reviewed by M. Conroy, *Times*, 9 March, 1968, 21; J. Graham, *Canberra Times*, 30 March, 1968, 10; B. Jefferis, *S.M.H.*, 20 April, 1968, 21; N. Jillett, *Age*, 2 March, 1968, 9; M.L., *Twentieth Century*, XXIII, 1968, 88-89; T. Moody, *Australian Left Review*, No. 3, 1968, 79; W. Noonan, *Australian*, 2 March, 1968, 11; F. Roberts, *Bulletin*, 9 March, 1968, 66; K. Thomas, *Nation*, 2 March, 1968, 23.

The World is Made of Glass. (Hornsby: Hodder & Stoughton, 1983).
Reviewed by M. Dunlevy, *Canberra Times*, 20 August, 1983, 12; H. Hebert, *S.M.H.*, 6 August, 1983, 38; F. King, *Spectator*, 23 July, 1983, 20; H.G. Kippax, *S.M.H.*, 16 March, 1984, 11; J. McLaren, *ABR*, No. 58, 1984, 26; L. Radic, *Age*, 26 March, 1984, 14; E. Riddell, *Bulletin*, 23 August, 1983, 70-71; D. Rowbotham, *Courier-Mail*, 13 August, 1983, 26.

> Drama

The Heretic. (New York: Morrow, 1969).
Reviewed by M. Jones, *S.M.H.*, 5 December, 1970, 25.

> Non-Fiction

Morris West and Robert Francis. *Scandal in the Assembly: A Bill of Complaints and a Proposal for Reform on the Matrimonial Laws and Tribunals of the Roman Catholic Church*. (London: Heinemann in association with Pan Books, 1970).
Reviewed by J.B., *Twentieth Century*, XXV, 1970, 91-92; L. Radic, *Age*, 1 August,

1970, 18; *Time*, 6 July, 1970, 62.
'The Heretic: Morris West on the Need for Dissent'. *Blast*, 26, 1994, 4-5. From a talk given at the PEN/*Blast* Forum, 1994.
'The Struggle for Identity'. *Age*, 3 December, 1966, 21.

Critical Material
Armstrong, Madelaine. 'Saints Alive'. *Bulletin*, 29 July, 1967, 37.
Bell, Lynne. 'Right to be Wrong'. *S.M.H.*, 25 July, 1970, 20.
Brisbane, Katharine. 'Flamboyant Dancing - And the Worst of West'. *Australian*, 15 July, 1967, 8.
Brown, Anthony. 'Who Killed the Cuckoo? Morris West's Saigon'. *Bulletin*, 15 May, 1965, 27-8.
Confoy, Maryanne. *Morris West: Wandering Scholar and Restless Spirit*. (Canberra: Friends of the National Library, 1992).
Cunningham, James. 'Morris West: An Interview'. *S.M.H.*, 17 July, 1965, 13.
Elliott, Brian; O'Brien, J.A.; Rudrum, A.W.; Ward, Peter. 'A Morris West Symposium'. *ABR*, II, 1963, 142-3.
Fuller, Peter. 'Morris West and the Need for a Saving "Binding"'. *Canberra Times*, 13 August, 1983, 15.
Higham, Charles. 'The Fictionaires'. *Bulletin*, 25 February, 1967, 18.
Johns, Brian. 'Second Calling: the Formative Years of Morris West'. *Nation*, 10 August, 1963, 11-12.
Kahan, Yitshok. 'Moris Vest [Morris West]: Fun di Derfolgraykhste Shrayber'. *Unser Tzait*. XI-XII, 1975, 42-46. In Yiddish.
McCallum, Gerald. 'A Note on Morris West's First Novel'. *A.L.S.*, VI, 1974, 314-16.
Molloy, Bruce. 'Morris West: An Interview'. *Arts National*, II, No. 3, 1985, 28-32.
Pearl, Cyril. 'Aye, Aye, Mr. West'. *Nation*, 7 August, 1965, 7.
Rolfe, Patricia. 'Profit without Honor'. *Bulletin*, 24 August, 1963, 15-18.
Sayers, Stuart. 'Jung and the Restless Vision of Morris West'. *National Times*, 12-18 August, 1983, 31 & 34.
---. 'West Seeks Readers'. *Age Saturday Extra*, 20 August, 1983, 12.
Thomas, Keith. 'Theatre: Wanted - A Devil's Advocate'. *Nation*, 29 July, 1967, 18.
Tilley, Lorna. 'Morris West - Author: Against the Tyrannies of Power'. *Redoubt*, 19, 1994, 99-106. Interview.
Urban, Andrew L. 'Morris West: A "Heretic" Speaks Out'. *Weekend Australian Magazine*, 27-28 August, 1985, 9.

WHITE, PATRICK

Collection
Patrick White: Selected Writings. Edited by Alan Lawson. (St Lucia: U.Q.P., 1994).
Reviewed by C. Bliss, *Antipodes*, 9.1, 1995, 64-65; C. Lee, *Coppertales*, 1, 1995, 159-66; D. Myers, *Imago*, 7.1, 1995, 86-87; E. Riddell, *S.M.H.*, 16 July, 1994, Spectrum 9A.

Fiction
The Burnt Ones. (London: Eyre and Spottiswoode, 1964).
Reviewed by H.P. Heseltine, *Southerly*, XXV, No. 1, 1965, 69-71; H. Hossain, *Australian Quarterly*, XXXVII, 1965, 120-3; J.M. Keeley, *Westerly*, No. 1, 1965, 67-8; T.G. Rosenthal, *ABR*, IV, 1964, 6; *T.L.S.*, 25 October, 1964, 953; G. Taylor, *The Sewanee Review*, LXXIII, 1965, 736-47.

The Cockatoos: Shorter Novels and Stories. (London: Cape, New York: Viking, 1974). Reprinted Ringwood, Vic.: Penguin, 1978.
Reviewed by P. Ackroyd, *Spectator*, CCXXXII, 1975, 772; B. Allen, *Saturday Review*, 25 January, 1975, 34-35, 37; A. Broyard, *New York Times*, 14 January,

1975, 31, excerpted in *Canberra Times*, 24 January, 1975, 8; G. Fawcett, *Books and Bookmen*, XXI, No. 3, 1974, 58-59; B.H. Gelfant, *Hudson Review*, XXVIII, 1975, 316-17; D. Green, *National Times*, 22 July, 1978, 28; C. Harrison-Ford, *Australian*, Weekend section, 22 June, 1974, 6; B. Kiernan, *Meanjin*, XXXIV, 1975, 37; L. Kramer, *S.M.H.*, 22 June, 1974, 13; *T.L.S.*, 28 June, 1974, 687; J. Mellors, *Listener*, XCIII, 1975, 61-62; R. Wade, *Contemporary Review*, CCXXV, 1974, 215; W. Walsh, *Sewanee Review*, LXXXIII, 1975, lxxii-lxxiv, lxxvi; E. Welty, *New York Times Book Review*, 19 January, 1975, 4, 37.

The Eye of the Storm. (London: Jonathan Cape, 1973).
Reviewed by P. Ackroyd, *Spectator*, CCXXXI, 1973, 312-13; P. Bailey, *Observer* (London), 9 September, 1973, 37; A.F. Bellette, *Ariel* (Calgary), V, No. 3, 1974, 128-30; R.M. Beston, *Hemisphere*, XVII, No. 12, 1973, 35 and *WLWE*, XIII, 1974, 93-98; I. Bjorksten, *Bonniers Litterara Magasin*, XLII, 1973, 221-23; V. Brady, *Westerly*, No. 4, 1973, 60-70; A. Broyard, *New York Times*, 2 January, 1974, 35; G. Dutton, *ABR*, XI, 1973, 121-23; C. Flower, *Bulletin*, 20 October, 1973, 52-53; D. Green, *Meanjin*, XXXII, 1973, 395-405; C. Harrison-Ford, *Australian*, 29 September, 1973, 45; S. Hazzard, *New York Times Book Review*, 6 January, 1974, 1, 12 and 14; J. Healy, *Queen's Quarterly*, LXXXII, 1975, 135-36; L.V. Kepert, *Sun-Herald*, 23 September, 1973, 76; B. Kiernan, *Age*, 6 October, 1973, 13; L. Kramer, *Quadrant*, XVIII, No. 1, 1974, 65-68; E. Kynaston, *Nation Review*, 12-18 October, 1973, 1647; V. Lakshmi, *Literary Half-Yearly*, XVII, 1976, 115-20; A. Mitchell, *Advertiser*, 6 October, 1973, 20; T. O'Keefe, *Listener*, XC, 1973, 427; E. Perkins, *LiNQ*, III, No. 1, 1974, 23-26; M. Pettigrove, *Canberra Times*, 5 October, 1973, 11; R. Phillips, *Commonweal*, C, 1975, 269-70; M. Ratcliffe, *Times*, 6 September, 1973, 12; D. Rowbotham, *Courier-Mail*, 10 November, 1973, 16; P. Ruskin, *Sunday Telegraph*, 14 October, 1973, 53; P.M. Spacks, *Hudson Review*, XXVII, 1974, 286-87; J. Symons, *Washington Post Book World*, 20 January, 1974, 3; K. Tennant, *S.M.H.*, 6 October, 1973, 22; *T.L.S.*, 21 September, 1973, 1072; M. Thorpe, *English Studies*, LV, 1974, 549-50; W. Trevor, *Guardian Weekly*, 15 September, 1973, 21; W. Walsh, *New Statesman*, LXXXVI, 1973, 320. See also article by E.H. Gross, *Australian*, 9 August, 1975, 27.

A Fringe of Leaves. (London: Cape, New York: Viking, 1976).
Reviewed by J. Banerjee, *Journal of Commonwealth Literature*, XII, No. 1, 1977, 74-75; J. Barnes, *New Statesman*, XCII, 10 September, 1976, 348; P. Beer, *The Listener*, XCVI, 1976, 409-10; I. Bjorksten, *Svenska Dagbladet*, 9 September, 1976; J. Brunskill, *The Sunday Star Bulletin and Advertiser* (Honolulu), 6 February, 1977, C11; E. Connell, *Harper's*, CCLIV, 1977, 1521; G. Core, *Virginia Quarterly Review*, LIII, 1977, 766-72; M. Dunlevy, *Canberra Times*, 25 September, 1976, 14; S. Edgar, *Quadrant*, XXI, No. 10, 1977, 69-72, commentary on review by L. Kramer, *Quadrant*, XX, No. 11, 1976, 62-63, reply by L. Kramer, *Quadrant*, XXI, No. 11, 1977, 60; H. af Enehjelm, *Hufvudstadsbladet* (Helsinki), 1 February, 1977; K. England, *Advertiser*, 25 September, 1976, 25; D. Flower, *Hudson Review*, XXX, 1977, 308-09; D. Green, *Nation Review*, 22-28 October, 1976, 20; M. Ivens, *Books and Bookmen*, XXI, No. 1, 1976, 64; J. Leclaire, *Etudes Anglaises*, XXXI, 1978, 98-100; A. Lundkvist, *Dagens Nyheter*, 26 November, 1976, in Swedish; R.E. McDowell, *World Literature Today*, LI, 1977, 330-31; J. McLaren, *Overland*, No. 65, 1976, 71-72; H. Miller, *Antioch Review*, XXXV, 1977, 322; I. Murray, *Financial Times*, 16 September, 1976, 15; E. Perkins, *Meanjin*, XXXVI, 1977, 265-69; A.A. Phillips, *Age*, 9 October, 1977, 22; P.T. Plowman, *Bulletin*, 25 September, 1976, 62; J.D. Pringle, *S.M.H.*, 25 September, 1976, 15; R. Ross, *WLWE*, XVI, 1977, 324-25; D. Rowbotham, *Courier-Mail*, 16 October, 1976, 17; C. Rudbeck, *Sydsvenska Dagbladet Snellposten*, 15 October, 1976, in Swedish; J.S. Ryan, *Hemisphere*, XXI, No. 4, 1977, 13-14; T. Shapcott, *Australian*, 25 September, 1976, 41; G. Steiner, *New Yorker*, 23 May, 1977, 131-34; R. Stow, *T.L.S.*, 10 September, 1976, 1097,

reprinted *National Times*, 11-16 October, 1976, 25; P. Vansittart, *London Magazine*, N.S. XVI, No. 5, 1976-1977, 108-09; R. Wade, *Contemporary Review*, CCXXX, 1977, 45; J. Ward, *Critical Quarterly*, XIX, No. 3, 1977, 77-81.

The Living and the Dead. First published London: Eyre and Spottiswoode, 1962.
Reviewed by H.P. Heseltine, *Southerly*, XXIII, No. 3, 1963, 211-13; T.G. Rosenthal, *ABR*, II, 1963, 38.

Memoirs of Many in One by Alex Xenophon Demirjian Gray; edited by Patrick White. (London: Jonathan Cape; New York: Viking, 1986).
Reviewed by R. Bates, *British Book News*, July, 1986, 426; J. Baumbach, *New York Times Book Review*, 26 October, 1986, 12; V. Brady, *Westerly*, XXXI, No. 3, 1986, 71-78; A. Byatt, *T.L.S.*, 4 April, 1986, 357; L. Clancy, *Overland*, No. 104, 1986, 72; A. Clark, *Scripsi*, IV, No. 2, 1986, 1-5; B. Clunies Ross, *Politken* (Copenhagen), 21 May, 1986, Section II, 7; D. English, *Age Saturday Extra*, 5 April, 1986, 13; K. Goldsworthy, *National Times*, 4-10 April, 1986, 31; GruF, *Campaign Australia*, No. 126, 1986, 34; P. Horne, *London Review of Books*, VIII, No. 8, 1986, 15-16; L. Kramer, *Quadrant*, XXX, No. 9, 1986, 66-67; B. Maddox, *Listener*, 3 April, 1986, 28; D. Malouf, *Weekend Australian Magazine*, 5-6 April, 1986, 13; B. Martin, *Spectator*, 12 April, 1986, 32-33; S. McKernan, *Bulletin*, 15 April, 1986, 117-18; J. Neville, *London Magazine*, XXVI, Nos. 1-2, 1986, 143-45; A.P. Riemer, *Southerly*, XLVI, No. 2, 1986, 239-44; D. Rowbotham, *Courier-Mail Magazine: The Great Weekend*, 5 April, 1986, 6; V. Sen, *Canberra Times*, 12 April, 1986, B2; M. Seymour, *Books & Bookmen*, No. 366, 1986, 28; D.J. Tacey, *Meridian*, V, No. 1, 1986, 89-91; C. Wallace-Crabbe, *ABR*, No. 82, 1986, 7-8; W.L. Webb, *Guardian*, 13 April, 1986, 21; S. Whaley, *Globe & Mail* (Toronto), 25 October, 1986, E21; G. Wilce, *New Statesman*, 25 April, 1986, 26-27.

The Solid Mandala. (London: Eyre and Spottiswoode; New York: Viking Press, 1966).
Reviewed by J. Barbour, *Nation*, 28 May, 1966, 21-2; K. Dick, *Spectator*, 20 May, 1966, 639; M. Dunlevy, *Canberra Times*, 9 April, 1966, 11, and 31 December, 1966, 10; J.K. Ewers, *W.A. Teachers' Journal*, LVI, 1966, 219; H.P. Heseltine, *ABR*, V, 1966, 84-5; C. Higham, *Bulletin*, 14 May, 1966, 54-5; N. Jillett, *Age*, 28 May, 1966, 21; F. King, *Sunday Telegraph* (Sydney), 15 May, 1966, 12; H.G. Kippax, *S.M.H.*, 14 May, 1966, 15; J. McLaren, *Overland*, No. 34, 1966, 49-50; K. Miller, *New Statesman*, 27 May, 1966, 781; *Newsweek*, 14 February, 1966, 58; A.A. Phillips, *Meanjin*, XXV, 1966, 31-3; T.G. Rosenthal, *Australian*, 2 April, 1966, 10; Scrutarius, *Walkabout*, XXXII, No. 10, 1966, 47; T. Tanner, *London Magazine*, VI, No. 3, 1966, 112-17; *Time*, 11 February, 1966, 58; *T.L.S.*, 9 June, 1966, 509.

Three Uneasy Pieces. (Fairfield, Vic.: Pascoe Publishing, 1987; London: Cape, 1988).
Reviewed by D. Anderson, *S.M.H.*, 26 December, 1987, 34; C. Bliss, *Antipodes*, II, No. 1, 1988, 30; A. Burgess, *Weekend Australian. Weekend Magazine*, 20-21 February, 1988, 14; M. Dunning, *Australian Studies*, No. 3, 1989, 151-57; N. Dutton, *Overland*, No. 111, 1988, 17-18; A. Jackson, *Lot's Wife*, XXVIII, No. 1, 1988, 20; D.G. Jones, *Times on Sunday*, 10 January, 1988, 29; P. Lewis, *Stand Magazine*, 30, No. 4, 1989, 72-5; B. Reid, *Age Saturday Extra*, 26 December, 1987, 8; R.L. Ross, *WLWE*, XXVIII, No. 2, 1988, 267-268; L. Sage, *Observer*, 1988, 44.

The Twyborn Affair. (London: Cape, 1979).
Reviewed by P. Ableman, *Spectator*, 29 September, 1979, 24-25; J. Bedford, *National Times*, 24 November, 1979, 55; J.B. Beston, *WLWE*, No. 19, 1980, 200-03; D. Blamires, *Critical Quarterly*, XXII, No. 1, 1980, 77-85; V. Brady, *Kunapipi*, II, No. 1, 1980, 178-80; C.M.H. Clark, *S.M.H.*, 13 October, 1979, 20; J. Davidson, *National Times*, 24 November, 1979, 54-55; B. DeMott, *New York Times Book Review*, 27 April, 1980, 3, 32; G. Dutton, *Bulletin*, 27 November, 1979, 86, 88-99;

K. England, *Advertiser*, 3 November, 1979, 25; H. Hewitt, *Canberra Times*, 27 October, 1979, 15; B. Jefferis, *Hemisphere*, XXV, No. 1, 1980, 21; N. Jillett, *Age*, 29 September, 1979, 27; L. Kramer, *Quadrant*, XXIV, No. 7, 1980, 66-67; B. Levin, *Sunday Times*, 16 December, 1979, 44; J. McLaren, *ABR*, No. 16, 1979, 8-9; A.L. McLeod, *World Literature Today*, LV, No. 1, 1981, 173; P. Morley, *CRNLE Reviews Journal*, No. 2, 1980, 57-58; N. Mosley, *Listener*, 29 November, 1979, 761-62; A. Motion, *New Statesman*, 28 September, 1979, 470-71; T. Paulin, *Encounter*, LIV, No. 1, 1980, 58-60; P. Pierce, *Meanjin*, XXXIX, 1980, 260-63; W. Scammell, *London Magazine*, N.S., XIX, No. 12, 1980, 92-94; G. Tout-Smith, *Overland*, No. 78, 1979, 65-67; W. Walsh, *T.L.S.*, 30 November, 1979, 77; R. Wetherell, *24 Hours*, IV, No. 11, 1979, 70-71; G.A. Wilkes, *Weekend Australian Magazine*, 10-11 November, 1979, 12.

The Vivisector. (New York: Viking Press, London: Jonathan Cape, 1970). Reviewed by J. Barbour, *Nation*, 28 November, 1970, 21-22; J.B. Beston, *Makar*, VI, No. 4, 1970, 15-18, and *Westerly*, No. 4, 1970, 58-61; L. Cantrell, *Meanjin*, XXX, 1971, 125-29; R.N. Coe, *Meanjin*, XXIX, 1970, 526-29; P. Cosgrave, *Spectator*, CCXXV, 1970, 525; P. Cruttwell, *Hudson Review*, XXIV, 1971, 180-81; K. England, *Advertiser*, 24 October, 1970, 16; D. Green, *Canberra Times*, 7 November, 1970, 14; B. Kiernan, *Australian*, 17 October, 1970, 22; D. Mahon, *Listener*, LXXXIV, 1970, 635-36; P.W. McDowell, *Contemporary Literature*, XIII, 1972, 383-84; J. McLaren, *Overland*, No. 46, 1970/71, 37-38; D.J. O'Hearn, *Age*, 31 October, 1970, 16; C. Osborne, *London Magazine*, N.S., X, No. 10, 1971, 98-101; E. Perkins, *LiNQ*, I, No. 1, 1972, [9-12]; D. Pryce-Jones, *New York Times Book Review*, 8 November, 1970, 50; T.G. Rosenthal, *New Statesman*, 23 October, 1970, 536-38; C. Semmler, *ABR*, IX, 1970, 331-32 and *Hemisphere*, XV, No. 3, 1971, 38; J. Thompson, *Harper's Magazine*, CCXLI, No. 1444, 1970, 94-96; M. Thorpe, *English Studies*, LIII, 1972, 283-84; G. Turner, *Overland*, Nos. 50-51, 1972, 93-95. W. Walsh, *Encounter*, XXXVI, No. 5, 1971, 81-82; O. Webster, *Bulletin*, 31 October, 1970, 52-53; E. Williams, *S.M.H.*, 17 October, 1970, 19; *T.L.S.*, 23 October, 1970, 1213; T. Wiseman, *Sunday Australian*, 28 February, 1971, 33. See also summaries of some U.S. reviews by P. Michelmore, *S.M.H.*, 22 August, 1970, 11, and S. Lipski, *Australian*, 29 August, 1970, 8.

Voss. (London: Longmans Green, 1965). Reprinted London: Cape, 1980. Edited with an Introduction by H.P. Heseltine. Also contains a Select Bibliography and 'Issues and Problems' (extracts from criticism). First published London: Eyre & Spottiswood; New York: Viking, 1957.
Reviewed by D.J. O'Hearn, *Age*, 27 September, 1980, 25.

A Woman's Hand' (novella) *Australian Letters*, VII, No. 3, 1966, 13-41.
Reviewed by G. Lehmann, *Bulletin*, 15 October, 1966, 57.

    Drama
Big Toys. (Sydney: Currency Press, 1978).
Reviewed by P. Corris, *National Times*, 10 February, 1979, 29; F. de Groen, *CRNLE Reviews Journal*, No. 1, 1980, 102-09; G. Dutton, *Weekend Australian Magazine*, 10-11 February, 1979, 8; H. Hewitt, *Canberra Times*, 5 May, 1979, 17; J. McCallum, *Theatre-Australia*, III, No. 8, 1979, 49.

Collected Plays Vol. I. (Sydney: Currency Press, 1985).
Reviewed by E. Perkins, *LiNQ*, XIII, No. 3, 1985, 62-66.

Collected Plays. Vol. II. (Paddington, NSW: Currency Press, 1994).
Reviewed by D. Coad, *World Literature Today*, 69.2, 1995, 429; P. Fitzpatrick, *ABR*, 165, 1993, 50-51.

Four Plays. (London: Eyre & Spottiswoode, 1965). Reprinted Melbourne: Sun Books, 1967, with an introduction by H.G. Kippax.
Reviewed by R.F. Brissenden, *Australian*, 6 January, 1968, 9; R. Flantz, *Overland*,

No. 35, 1966, 53-4; K. Harrison, *The Spectator*, 24 September, 1965, 385-6; E. James, *Australian*, 15 January, 1966, 9; H.G. Kippax, *S.M.H.*, 23 October, 1965, 19; L. Kramer, *Bulletin*, 11 December, 1965, 52-3; K. Macartney, *Meanjin*, XXIV, 1965, 528-30; C. Osborne, *The London Magazine*, V, No. 6, 1965, 95-100; C. Pieterse, *Journal of Commonwealth Literature*, No. 2, 1966, 170-171; T.G. Rosenthal, *ABR*, IV, 1965, 196-7.

Netherwood. (Sydney: Currency Press, 1983).
Reviewed by M.-B. Akerholt, *Australasian Drama Studies*, III, No. 11, 1984, 144-46; B. Oakley, *S.M.H.*, 16 July, 1983, 38; E. Perkins, *LiNQ*, XI, No. 11, 1983, 89-100; L. Radic, *Age Saturday Extra*, 1 October, 1983, 18; J. Weir, *Meridan*, IV, No. 1, 1985, 94-95.

Signal Driver: A Morality Play for the Times. (Sydney: Currency Press, 1983).
Reviewed by J. McCallum, *Australasian Drama Studies*, II, No. 2, 1984, 120-22; B. Oakley, *S.M.H.*, 16 July, 1983, 38; E. Perkins, *LiNQ*, XI, No. 1, 1983, 99-100; L. Radic, *Age Saturday Extra*, 1 October, 1983, 18; J. Weir, *Meridian*, IV, No. 1, 1985, 94-95.

Non-Fiction

Flaws in the Glass: A Self-Portrait. (London: Cape, 1981). Reprinted Harmondsworth: Penguin, 1983.
Reviewed by J.B. Beston, *WLWE*, XXI, No. 1, 1982, 83-86; R. Blythe, *Listener*, CVI, 1981, 722-23; V. Brady, *Westerly*, XXVII, No. 1, 1982, 102-09; D. Carter, *Helix*, No. 15, 1983, 2-4; R. Conway, *Weekend Australian Magazine*, 24-25 October, 1981, 8; M. Davie, *Age*, 17 October, 1981, 25; D. Davin *T.L.S.*, 20 November, 1981, 1373; M. Dunlevy, *Canberra Times*, 24 October, 1981, 12; A. Field, *Age Monthly Review*, February, 1982, 3-4; J. Flanagan, *Age Saturday Extra*, 2 July, 1983, 8; D. Green, *National Times*, 8-14 November, 1981, 54, 57; J. Hay, *Courier-Mail*, 26 October, 1981, 4; D. Herkt, *Campaign*, No. 71, 1981, 39; M. Howard, *Atlantic*, March, 1982, 83-84; S.F.D. Hughes, *Modern Fiction Studies*, CXII, 1984, 140-43; K. Kellaway, *New Statesman*, 30 October, 1981, 30; B. Kiernan, *Southerly*, XLII, 1982, 165-73; F. King, *London Magazine*, N.S. XXI, No. 7, 1981, 87-90; D. Malouf, *Scripsi*, I, Nos. 3-4, 1982, 76-79; J. McLaren, *ABR*, No. 37, 1981, 16-18; C. Morehead, *Spectator*, 7 November, 1981, 34-35; H. Porter, *Age*, 24 October, 1981, 23; J.D. Pringle, *S.M.H.*, 17 October, 1981, 49; E. Riddell, *Bulletin*, 10 November, 1981, 90-92; D. Rowbotham, *Courier-Mail*, 24 October, 1981, 27; C.K. Stead, *London Review of Books*, III, No. 19, 1981, 19-20; K. Tennant, *Hemisphere*, XXVI, 1982, 375; J. Walter, *Institute of Modern Biography Newsletter*, III, No. 3, 1983, 27-28; F. Zwicky, *Island Magazine*, Nos. 9-10, 1982, 74-75.

Patrick White: Letters. Edited by David Marr. (Milsons Point, NSW: Random House Australia, 1994).
Reviewed by A. Ashbold, *Editions*, 22, 1995, 27; D. Coad, *World Literature Today*, 69.3, 1995, 642; A. Croggon, *Voices*, 4.4, 1994-95, 99-102; C. Lloyd da Silva, *Antipodes*, 9.2, 1995, 173-74; M. Davie, *S.M.H.*, 1 October, 1994, Spectrum 11A; M. Heyward, *ABR*, 166, 1994, 6-7; B. Kiernan, *Weekend Australian*, 1-2 October, 1994, Review 5; B. Matthews, *Age*, 1 October, 1994, Saturday Extra 8; A. Riemer, *Independent Monthly* (November), 1994, 72-74; C. Semmler, *Quadrant*, 39.3, 1995, 79-81; D. Tacey, *T.L.S.*, 3 March, 1995, 23 (see also letter in reply from D. Rain, *T.L.S.*, 10 March, 1995, 19; and Tacey's reply, *T.L.S.*, 24 March, 1995, 15); B. Williams, *Eureka Street*, 4.8, 1994, 30-32; T. Winton, *London Review of Books*, 17.12, 1995, 18.

Patrick White Speaks. Edited by Christine Flynn and Paul Brennan (Sydney: Primavera Press, 1989).
Reviewed by C. Bliss, *Australian and New Zealand Studies in Canada*, No. 4, 1990, 112-14; P. Carter, *ABR*, No. 114, 1989, 12-13; L. Clancy, *Age*, 17 February, 1990,

Saturday Extra, 10; J. Haines, *Weekend Australian*, 26-27 August, 1989, Weekend 7; J. McClelland, *S.M.H.*, 19 August, 1989, 80; A. Nugent, *Age Monthly Review*, 9, No. 10, 1990, 5-6; P. Pierce, *Bulletin*, 19 September, 1989, 118-9; R. Summy, *Social Alternatives*, 8, No. 3, 1989, 71-2.

'Finding the Faith to Save the World'. *Age*, 1 June, 1983, 11. Report of a speech.

'Flaws in the Glass'. *Bulletin*, 29 January, 1980, 146-54. Autobiographical.

'Libraries for Living'. *Weekend Australian Magazine*, 20-21 September, 1980, 13. Address, also reported in *Age*, 20 September, 1980, 24; *S.M.H.*, 20 September, 1980, 11.

'Patrick White: Self-Portrait of an Intensely Political Writer'. *Age*, 11 October, 1980, 28. Address, at National Book Council awards ceremony, also reported in *S.M.H.*, 11 October, 1980, 20.

'Patrick White Speaks on Factual Writing and Fiction'. *A.L.S.*, X, 1981, 99-101. Reprint of 1980 Australian National Book Council Award speech.

Critical Material

Finch, Janette H. (comp.). *Bibliography of Patrick White*. (Adelaide: Libraries Board of South Australia, 1966). Bibliographies of Australian Writers Series. Reviewed by M. Wilding, *A.L.S.*, III, 1967, 142-148.

State Library of South Australia. 'Bibliographies of Australian Writers. Supplements'. *Index of Australian Book Reviews*. I, 1965, 172-3; II, 1966, 228-30; III, 1967, 218-22; IV, 1968, 258-62; V, 1969, 261-62; 267-69; VI, 1970, 325-9; VII, 1971, 298-300; VIII, 1972, 254-7; IX, 1973, 163-69; X, 1974, 175-84; XI, 1975, 224-35.

Lawson, Alan. *Patrick White*. (Melbourne: O.U.P., 1974). Australian Bibliographies. Reviewed by L. Cantrell, *A.L.S.*, VII, 1975, 103-04; J.S. Ryan, *The Yearbook of English Studies*, VIII, 1978, 361-62.

Scheick, William J. 'A Bibliography of Writings about Patrick White, 1972-1978'. *Texas Studies in Literature and Language*, XXI, 1979, 296-303.

The award of the Nobel Prize to Patrick White was followed by many newspaper reports and articles, especially on October 19, October 20, October 27 and November, 30, 1973.

The award of Australian of the Year by Australia Day Council to Patrick White on 15 January, 1974 was followed by reports and articles: *S.M.H.*, 26 January, 1974, 1, and *Australian*, 26 January, 1974, 1, on his speech at the Australian of the Year

For reports on White's statements on conservation and political issues see for example *Australian*, 10 May, 1975, 3; *Australian*, 28 May, 1975, 1; *Courier-Mail*, 28 May, 1975, 2; *Australian*, 29 November, 1975, 5; *S.M.H*, 29 November, 1975, 1; *Bulletin*, 13 December, 1975, 39.

For letters to the newspaper by Patrick White see under the Lawson, Henry entry, at the end of reviews of Clark, Manning. *In Search of Henry Lawson*.

'Australia Abhorrent to Writer'. *Canberra Times*, 7 March, 1978, 7.

'Long-Haired Promotion'. *Nation*, 1 November, 1969, 13-14. Mentions the sale of film rights of *Voss*.

'New Order Honors for White and Sutherland'. *Australian*, 14 June, 1975, 1.

'Nocturnal Columbus: Richard Meale by Day and Night'. *Nation*, 13 April, 1968, 11-12. See letters to the editor by Patrick White, *Nation*, 11 May, 1968, 15, and William Green, 8 June, 1968, 16.

'Old Bottles For The New Wine'. *T.L.S.*, 16 September, 1965, 793-4.

'Patrick White'. *Contemporary Literary Criticism* 69. Edited by Roger Matuz (Detroit: Gale, 1992), 390-415.

'Patrick White, Australian puts his Country under the Microscope'. *Beacon*, May, 1981, 3-4.

'Patrick White Mirrors Collapse of Capitalism'. *Australian Communist*, No. 66, 1974, 58-68.

'Patrick White Bans Play to SA Students'. *Advertiser*, 17 August, 1974, 2.

'A Patrick White Chronology'. *Texas Studies in Literature and Language*, XXI, 1979, 304.

'Patrick White Hands Back OA'. *Age*, 19 June, 1976, 1, 4; see also *Australian*, 19 June, 1976, 1; *S.M.H.*, 21 June, 1976, 1; *Canberra Times*, 22 June, 1976, 8.

'Patrick White is Nobel Prize Candidate'. *Canberra Times*, 19 October, 1972, 27. See also Phillip Adams, *Australian*, 1 April, 1972, 11.

'Setting Out Blueprints for a Better Year'. *S.M.H.*, 3 January, 1974, 9. Interview.

Abraham, P.A. 'Patrick White's *Voss* and Arun Joshi's *The Strange Case of Billy Biswas*: A Comparative Note on a Journey into the Interior'. *Literary Criterion*, 27.4, 1992, 22-30.

Ahuja, Chaman. 'Modernism in Patrick White's Plays - An Exercise in Synthesis'. *The Literary Criterion* (Mysore), XI, No. 4, 1975, 53-63.

Akerholt, May-Brit. *Patrick White*. (Amsterdam: Rodopi, 1988). Australian Playwrights Monograph Series edited by Ortrun Zuber-Skerritt, No. 2. Reviewed by C. Bliss, *Antipodes*, 3.2, 1989, 152; R. Corballis, *Modern Drama*, 34.1, 1991, 163-67; P.P. Heckenberg, *ABR*, No. 103, 1988, 8-10; A. Wimmer, *Australasian Drama Studies*, No. 17, 1990, 233-36.

---. 'Female Figures in the Plays of Dorothy Hewett and Patrick White'. *Westerly*, XXIX, No. 1, 1984, 69-77.

---. 'Story into Play: The Two Versions of Patrick White's *A Cheery Soul*'. *Southerly*, XL, 1980, 460-72.

---. 'Structure and Themes in Patrick White's *Four Plays*'. In *Patrick White: A Critical Symposium*, edited by R. Shepherd and K. Singh (Adelaide: Centre for Research in the New Literatures in English, 1978), 52-61.

Anderson, Don. 'A Severed Leg: Anthropophagy and Communion in Patrick White's Fiction'. *Southerly*, XL, 1980, 399-417.

Antonini, Maria. 'Patrick White: La Terza Fase'. *Spicilego Moderno* (Pisa), V, 1976, 107-31.

Argyle, Barry. *Patrick White*. (Edinburgh: Oliver & Boyd, 1967). Writers and Critics series. Reviewed by *ABR*: VII, 1968, 145; P. Beatson, *Cambridge Review*, 31 May, 1968, 521-22; R.F. Brissenden, *A.L.S.*, IV, 1969, 84-85; B. Davies, *Wascana Review* (Regina, Saskatchewan, Canada), III, 1968, 100-101; E. Jones, *Nation*, 6 July, 1968, 22; M. Luke, *Critic*, Perth, IX, 1968, 30; J. Pilling, *Journal of Commonwealth Literature*, XII, No. 3, 1978, 89-92; *T.L.S.*, 8 February, 1968, 126.

Ashcroft, W.D. 'More Than One Horizon'. In *Patrick White: A Critical Symposium*, edited by R. Shepherd and K. Singh (Adelaide: Centre for Research in the New Literatures in English, 1978), 123-4.

Astley, Thea. 'Patrick White: *The Burnt Ones*'. In her *Three Australian Authors*. (Townsville: Townsville Foundation for Australian Literary Studies, 1979), 23-34.

Baker, Robert S. 'Romantic Onanism In Patrick White's *The Vivisector*'. *Texas Studies in Literature and Language*, XXI, 1979, 203-25.

Banerjee, Jacqueline. 'A Reassessment of Patrick White's *Riders in the Chariot*'. *Literary Half-Yearly*, XX, No. 2, 1979, 91-113.

Barbour, Judith. 'Cheery Souls and Lost Souls: The Outsiders in Patrick White's Plays'. *Southerly*, XLII, 1982, 137-48.

---. 'Privileged, Authentic, Transcendent, Arcane: Limits of Naturalism in Some Contemporary Australian Plays'. *Southerly*, XXXVII, 1977, 77-92.

Barclay, Anthony. 'Jim Sharman Directs Patrick White's most Challenging Play'. *Theatre-Australia*, III, No. 8, 1979, 15-17, 34. *A Cheery Soul*.

Barden, Garrett. 'Patrick White's *The Tree of Man*'. *Studies*, Dublin, LVII, 1968, 78-85.

Barnes, John. 'Introduction'. To *Patrick White: A Critical Symposium*, edited by R. Shepherd and K. Singh (Adelaide: Centre for Research in the New Literatures in English, 1978), 1-4.

---. 'New Tracks to Travel: The Stories of White, Porter and Cowan'. *Meanjin*,

XXV, 1966, 154-70.

---. 'A Note on Patrick White's Novels'. *Literary Criterion* (Mysore), VI, No. 3, 1964, 93-101.

Beasley, Jack. *Journal of an Era: Notes from the Red Letter Days*. (Earlwood, N.S.W.: Wedgetail Press, 1988), 97-100, 101-107.

Beatson, P.R. *The Eye in the Mandala: Patrick White: A Vision of Man and God*. (London: Elek; New York: Barnes & Noble; 1976; Sydney: Reed, 1977). Reviewed by J.F. Burrows, *Yearbook of English Studies*, XII, 1982, 361-62; L. Clancy, *Age*, 11 March, 1978, 26; J. Colmer, *Weekend Australian Magazine*, 15 April, 1978, 8 and *A.L.S.*, VIII, 1978, 371-74; K. Garebian, *Modern Fiction Studies*, XXIV, 1978, 327-28; D. Green, *Nation Review*, 11-17 August, 1977, 16; J. Leclaire, *Etudes Anglaises*, XXXI, 1978, 100-01; P. Pierce, *Meanjin*, XXXVI, 1977, 384-90; P. Quartermaine, *Notes & Queries*, N.S., XXVI, 1979, 87-88; R. Stow, *T.L.S.*, 10 September, 1976, 1097.

---. 'The Skiapod and the Eye: Patrick White's *The Eye of the Storm*'. *Southerly*, XXXIV, 1974, 219-32.

---. 'The Three Stages: Mysticism in Patrick White's *Voss*'. *Southerly*, XXX, 1970, 111-21.

Berg, Mari-Ann. *Aspects of Time, Ageing and Old Age in the Novels of Patrick White, 1939-1979*. (Goteborg, 1983). Acta Universitatis Gotheburgensis, Gothenburg Studies in English, 53. Reviewed by R. Asselineau, *Etudes Anglaises*, XXXVII, No. 3, 1985, 351; B. Kiernan, *A.L.S.*, XII, No. 3, 1986, 417-21.

Beston, John B. 'Alienation and Humanization, Damnation and Salvation in *Voss*'. *Meanjin*, XXX, 1971, 208-16.

---. 'Dreams and Visions in *The Tree of Man*'. *A.L.S.*, VI, 1973, 152-66.

---. 'The Effect of Alienation on the Themes and Characters of Patrick White and Janet Frame'. In *Individual and Community in Commonwealth Literature*, edited by Daniel Massa (Msida, Malta: Old University Press: 1979), 131-39.

---. 'The Family Background and Early Years of Patrick White'. *Descent*, VII, No. 1, 1974, 16-19.

---. 'A Giant among Australian Writers'. *Hemisphere*, XVII, No. 2, 1973, 10-12.

---. 'The Influence of John Steinbeck's *The Pastures of Heaven* on Patrick White'. *A.L.S.*, VI, 1974, 317-19.

---. 'The Influence of *Madame Bovary* on *The Tree of Man*'. *Revue de Litterature Comparee*, XLVI, 1972, 555-68.

---. 'Love and Sex in a Staid Spinster: *The Aunt's Story*'. *Quadrant*, XV, No. 5, 1971, 22-27.

---. 'Mythmaking in P. White's *Voss*: A Stylistic Approach to *Tree of Man* and *Voss*'. *Echos du Commonwealth*, No. 3, 1976, 28-41.

---. 'Patrick White: Novelist of the *Burnt Ones*'. *S.M.H.*, 27 May, 1972, 26.

---. 'Patrick White's *The Vivisector*: The Artist in Relation to His Art'. *A.L.S.*, V, 1971, 168-75.

---. 'Three Conclusions: *Buddenbrooks*, *The Aunt's Story* and *Voss*'. *Literary Half-Yearly*, XX, No. 1, 1979, 134-41.

---. 'Unattractive Saints and a Poor Devil: Ambivalence in Patrick White's *The Solid Mandala*'. *Literary Half-yearly*, XIV, 1973, 106-14.

---. 'Voss's Proposal and Laura's Acceptance Letter: The Struggle for Dominance in *Voss*'. *Quadrant*, XVI, No. 4, 1972, 24-30.

Beston, John B. and Beston, Rose Marie. 'The Black Volcanic Hills of Meroe: Fire Imagery in Patrick White's *The Aunt's Story*'. *Ariel*, III, No. 4, 1972, 33-43.

---. 'A Brief Biography of Patrick White: A Note on the Dedications of Patrick White's Works: A Patrick White Bibliography'. *WLWE*, XII, 1973, 208-29.

---. 'The Theme of Spiritual Progression in *Voss*'. *Ariel* (Calgary), V, No. 3, 1974, 99-114.

---. 'The Several Lives of Theodora Goodman: The "Jardin Exotique" Section of

Patrick White's *The Aunt's Story*. *Journal of Commonwealth Literature*, IX, No. 3, 1975, 1-13.

Beston, John and Groves, Kerry. 'The Function of Ray and Thelma Parker in *The Tree of Man*'. *Literary Half-Yearly*, XVIII, 1977, 64-75.

Beston, Rose Marie. 'More Burnt Ones: Patrick White's *The Cockatoos*'. *WLWE*, XIV, 1975, 520-24.

---. 'Patrick White after the Nobel Prize'. *WLWE*, XIII, 1974, 91-92.

Bjorksten, Ingmar. *Patrick White: A General Introduction*. Translated from the Swedish by Stanley Gerson (St Lucia: U.Q.P., 1976). Original published Stockholm: Forum, 1973. Reviewed by S. Amanuddin, *World Literature Today*, LII, 1978, 518; J. Colmer, *A.L.S.*, VIII, 1977, 95-96; L. Hergenhan, *Age*, 29 July, 1978, 22; P. Pierce, *Meanjin*, XXXVI, 1977, 384-90.

---. *Patrick White: Epikern fran Australien*. (Stockholm: Forum, 1973).

---. 'A Day with Patrick White'. Translated by John Stanley Martin, *Nation Review*, 21-27 June, 1974, 1179. First published in *Veckojournalen* (Stockholm).

Bliss, Carolyn. 'Dialectic of Many and One: City and Outback in Patrick White's Fiction'. In *From Outback to City: Changing Preoccupations in Australian Literature of the Twentieth Century*, edited by Alexandra Cromwell (New York: American Association of Australian Literary Studies, 1988), 3-13.

---. 'Introduction: A Radiant Cacophony'. *Antipodes*, 6.1, 1992, 5-8. Introduction to issue of *Antipodes* devoted to White.

---. 'Patrick White'. *Antipodes*, 4.2, 1990, 84-86. Obituary.

---. *Patrick White's Fiction: The Paradox of Fortunate Failure*. (London: Macmillan, 1986). Reviewed by V. Sen, *Canberra Times*, 13 December, 1986, B5.

---. 'Patrick White: Vision and Visions'. In *International Literature in English: Essays on the Major Writers*, edited by Robert L. Ross (New York: Garland, 1991), 505-24.

---. 'Transpositions: Patrick White's Most Recent Fiction'. *Westerly*, 34, No. 3, 1989, 77-82.

---. 'Woman as Seeker in Patrick White's Fiction'. In *Prophet from the Desert: Critical Essays on Patrick White*, edited by John McLaren (Melbourne: Red Hill Press, 1995), 38-48.

Bradbrook, M.C. 'The Australian Legend'. In her *Literature in Action: Studies in Continental and Commonwealth Society*. (London: Chatto & Windus, 1972), 116-52.

Brady, Veronica. 'Appendix: Two Critical Positions, 2'. In *Patrick White: A Critical Symposium*, edited by R. Shepherd and K. Singh (Adelaide: Centre for Research in the New Literatures in English, 1978), 137-40.

---. 'The Artist and the Savage God: Patrick White's *The Vivisector*'. *Meanjin*, XXXIII, 1974, 136-45.

---. 'Of Castles and Censorship'. *Westerly*, No. 2, 1974, 45-50. *Voss* discussed in comparison with Solzhenitsyn, *The First Circle*.

---. '"Down at the Dump" and Lacan's Mirror Stage'. *A.L.S.*, XI, 1983, 233-37.

---. '*A Fringe of Leaves*: Civilization by the Skin of Our Own Teeth'. *Southerly*, XXXVII, 1977, 123-40.

---. '"A Grandeur Too Overwhelming to Express": Patrick White's Vision of God'. *Faith and Freedom*, 2.1, 1993, 3-7.

---. 'Making Things Appear: Patrick White and the Politics of Modernism'. *Island*, 52, 1992, 32-37.

---. 'In My End is My Beginning: Laura as Heroine of *Voss*'. *Southerly*, XXXV, 1975, 16-32. Reprinted in *Caliban*, XIV, 1977, 23-38.

---. 'The Novelist and the New World: Patrick White's *Voss*'. *Texas Studies in Literature and Language*, XXI, 1979, 169-85.

---. 'The Novelist and the Reign of Necessity'. In *Patrick White: A Critical Symposium*, edited by R. Shepherd and K. Singh (Adelaide: Centre for Research in the New Literatures in English, 1978), 108-116.

---. 'Patrick White and Literary Criticism'. *ABR*, 133, 1991, 7-10.

---. 'Patrick White and The Question of Woman'. In *Who is She?*, edited by Shirley Walker (St Lucia: U.Q.P., 1983), 178-90.
---. 'Patrick White, Rediscovering Australia'. *Melbourne University Magazine*, 1974, 12-18.
---. 'A Properly Appointed Humanism: Australian Culture and the Aborigines in Patrick White's *A Fringe of Leaves*'. *Westerly*, XXVIII, No. 2, 1983, 61-68. Revised as 'A Properly Appointed Humanism?: *A Fringe of Leaves* and the Aborigines', in *Prophet from the Desert: Critical Essays on Patrick White*, edited by John McLaren (Melbourne: Red Hill Press, 1995), 49-62.
---. '"A Single Bone-Clean Button": The Achievement of Patrick White'. *Literary Criterion* (Mysore), XV, Nos. 3-4, 1980, 35-47.
---. 'To Be or Not to Be? The Verbal History of Patrick White'. *Westerly*, 37.2, 1992, 23-34.
---. 'The Utopian Impulse in Australian Literature with Special Reference to P. White and T. Keneally'. *Caliban*, XIV, 1977, 109-21.
Brainerd, Barron, and Neufeldt, Victoria. 'On Marcus' Methods for the Analysis of the Strategy of a Play'. *Poetics*, No. 10, 1974, 31-74. *The Season at Sarsaparilla* is one of the plays used as examples.
Brand, Mona. 'Another Look at Patrick White'. *Realist Writer*, No. 12, 1963, 21-2.
Brissenden, R.F. *Patrick White*. (London: Longmans, Green, 1966). Writers and their Work: No. 190. Includes a Select Bibliography. Reviewed by L. Kramer, *Bulletin*, 7 May, 1966, 52-4.
---. 'The Plays of Patrick White'. *Meanjin*, XXIII, No. 3, 1964, 243-56.
---. '*The Vivisector*: Art and Science'. In *The Australian Experience: Critical Essays on Australian Novels*, edited by W.S. Ramson (Canberra: Australian National University Press, 1974), 311-24.
Brown, Ruth. 'The Country, the City, and *The Tree of Man*'. *Modern Language Review*, 90.4, 1995, 861-69.
---. 'Patrick White and Australia as *Terra Nullius*'. In *Patrick White: Life and Writings. Five Essays*, edited by Martin Gray (U. of Stirling: Centre of Commonwealth Studies, 1991), 3-21.
---. 'White and the Wart'. *Australian Studies*, 6, 1992, 1-9.
Brydon, Diana. '"The Thematic Ancestor": Joseph Conrad, Patrick White and Margaret Atwood'. *WLWE*, XXIV, No. 2, 1984, 386-397. Revised version in Diana Brydon and Helen Tiffin, *Decolonising Fictions* (Sydney: Dangaroo P., 1993), 89-104.
Buckley, Vincent. 'The Novels of Patrick White'. In *The Literature of Australia*, edited by Geoffrey Dutton (Adelaide: Penguin Books, 1964), 413-26.
Burman, Beyla. 'The Misanthropic Painting or Settling an Account with the Almighty Mother: *The Vivisector* - Patrick White's Universal Work of Art'. *Orbis Litterarum*, XXXIX, No. 3, 1984, 266-283.
Burns, D.R. 'The Elitist Case For Equality: Patrick White's Pioneering "Visionary Monster" Novel'. *Overland*, 125, 1991, 68-75.
Burrows, John. 'Archetypes and Stereotypes: *Riders in the Chariot*. *Southerly*, XXV, No.1, 1965, 46-68. Reprinted in *Ten Essays on Patrick White*, edited by G.A. Wilkes (Sydney: A.& R., 1970), 47-71.
---. '"Jardin Exotique": The Central Phase of *The Aunt's Story*'. *Southerly*, XXVI, 1966, 152-73. Reprinted in *Ten Essays on Patrick White*, edited by G.A. Wilkes (Sydney: A.& R., 1970), 85-108.
---. 'Patrick White's Four Plays'. *A.L.S.*, II, 1966, 155-70.
---. 'The Short Stories of Patrick White'. *Southerly*, XXIV, No. 2, 1964, 116-25. Revised version reprinted in *Ten Essays on Patrick White*, edited by G.A. Wilkes (Sydney: A.& R., 1970), 163-181.
---. 'Stan Parker's *Tree of Man*'. *Southerly*, XXIX, 1969, 257-79.
---. '*Voss* and the Explorers'. *AUMLA*, No. 26, 1966, 234-40.

Cantrell, Leon. 'Patrick White's First Book'. *A.L.S.*, VI, 1974, 434-36.

Carroll, Dennis. 'Stage Convention in the Plays of Patrick White'. *Modern Drama*, XIX, 1976, 11-24.

Carruthers, Virginia Kirby-Smith. 'Patrick White's Improbable Iseult: Living Legend in *A Fringe of Leaves*'. *Antipodes*, 6.1, 1992, 37-43.

Chandra, Shalini. 'Women Protagonists of Patrick White's *Fringe of Leaves* and Thomas Hardy's *Tess of the D'Urbervilles*'. *Rajasthan University Studies in English*, 21-22, 1989-90, 118-22.

Chapman, Edgar L. 'The Mandala Design of Patrick White's *Riders in the Chariot*'. *Texas Studies in Literature and Language*, XXI, 1979, 186-202.

Chatterjee, Visvanath. 'The Achievement of Patrick White'. *Journal of Australian Literature*, 1, No. 1, 1990, 20-24.

Chellappan, K. 'Self, Space and Art in a Few Novels of Patrick White'. *Literary Half-Yearly*, XXIV, No. 1, 1983, 24-34. *Riders in the Chariot; The Vivisector; Voss*.

Chellappan, K. and N. E. Pavithra. 'The Influence of Eliot's *The Waste Land* on Patrick White's *The Living and the Dead*'. *Commonwealth Review*, 2.1-2, 1990-91, 43-52.

Chellappan, K. and N.E. Pavithra. 'The Romantic and Mystic Elements in *Voss* and *A Fringe of Leaves*'. *Journal of Australian Literature*, 1, No. 1, 1990, 35-42.

Clancy, Laurie. 'Patrick White: A Major Target for the Critics'. *Age*, 11 March, 1978, 26.

---. 'A State of Nature: Patrick White's *A Fringe of Leaves*'. *Viewpoints: H.S.C. English Literature*, 1984, 150-160.

Clancy, Patricia. 'The Actor's Dilemma: Patrick White and Henry de Montherlant'. *Meanjin*, XXXIII, 1974, 298-302.

Clark, Andrew. 'The Private Patrick White'. *New York Times Book Review*, 27 April, 1980, 32-33.

Clarke, Donovan. 'New Aspects of the Novel'. *Australian Highway*, XLVI, No. 3, 1966, 5-8.

Coad, David. 'Intertextuality in Patrick White's *The Solid Mandala*'. *Commonwealth*, 17.2, 1995, 111-16.

---. 'Patrick White: Prophet in the Wilderness'. *World Literature Today*, 67.3, 1993, 510-14.

---. 'Patrick White's Castrated Country'. *Commonwealth*, 15.1, 1992, 88-95.

---. 'Patrick White's Libidinous Eudoxical Lexis in *The Twyborn Affair*'. *Commonwealth*, 14.1, 1991, 65-69.

---. 'Platonic Return in Patrick White's *The Eye of the Storm*'. In *'Return' in Post-Colonial Writing: A Cultural Labyrinth*, edited by Vera Mihailovich-Dickman, Cross/Cultures 12 (Amsterdam; Atlanta: Rodopi, 1994), 51-55.

Coates, John. 'Byzantine References in *The Twyborn Affair*'. *A.L.S.*, XI, 1984, 508-13.

---. '*Voss* and Jacob Boehme: A Note on the Spirituality of Patrick White'. *A.L.S.*, IX, 1979, 119-22.

Collier, Gordon. *The Rocks and Sticks of Words: Style, Discourse and Narrative Structure in the Fiction of Patrick White*. Cross/Cultures 5. (Amsterdam; Atlanta: Rodopi, 1992). Reviewed by G. Träbing, *AUMLA*, 82, 1994, 123-24; R. Wallach, *Antipodes*, 7.1, 1993, 83.

Colmer, John. 'Appendix: Two Critical Positions, 1'. In *Patrick White: A Critical Symposium*, edited by R. Shepherd and K. Singh (Adelaide: Centre for Research in the New Literatures in English, 1978), 135-6.

---. 'Duality in Patrick White'. In *Patrick White: A Critical Symposium*, edited by R. Shepherd and K. Singh (Adelaide: Centre for Research in the New Literatures in English, 1978), 70-76

---. 'Flawed and Fortunate Lives: Patrick White and A.B. Facey'. In his *Australian Autobiography: A Personal Quest*. (Melbourne: O.U.P., 1989), 86-97.

---. *Patrick White*. (London; New York: Methuen, 1984). Reviewed by L. Clancy, *Age Saturday Extra*, 14 September, 1985, 14; S. Edgar, *ABR*, No. 81, 1986, 9-10; B. Kiernan, *A.L.S.*, XII, No. 3, 1986, 417-21; A. Mitchell, *Weekend Australian Magazine*, 13-14 April, 1985, 15; G. Parker, *British Book News*, April, 1985, 245-246; P. Quartermaine, *Notes and Queries*, N.S., XXXIII, No. 4, 1986, 568-56; D.J. Tacey, *Meridian*, IV, No. 1, 1985, 49-53.

---. 'Patrick White's *A Fringe of Leaves*'. *Literary Half-Yearly*, XXIII, No. 2, 1982, 85-100.

---. 'Patrick White's Quest for Truth'. In *Essays on Contemporary Post-Colonial Fiction*, edited by Hedwig Bock and Albert Wertheim (Munchen: Hueber, 1986), 355-69.

---. 'The Quest Motif in Patrick White'. *Review of National Literatures*, XI, 1982, 192-210.

---. *Riders in the Chariot, Patrick White*. (Melbourne: Edward Arnold (Australia), 1978). Studies in Australian Literature. Reviewed by F.D. Glass, *Span*, No. 7, 1978, 62-64; J. McLaren, *ABR*, No. 9, 1979, 23-24; A. Mitchell, *A.L.S.*, IX, 1979, 250; J. Waten, *Age*, 14 October, 1978, 26.

Core, George. 'A Terrible Majesty: The Novels of Patrick White'. *Hollins Critic* (Roanoke, Virginia), XI, No. 1, 1974, 1-16.

Cotter, Michael. 'Fragmentation, Reconstitution and the Colonial Experience: The Aborigine in White's Fiction'. In *South Pacific Images*, edited by Chris Tiffin (St Lucia: SPACLALS, 1978), 173-85.

---. 'The Function of Imagery in Patrick White's Novels'. In *Patrick White: A Critical Symposium*, edited by R. Shepherd and K. Singh (Adelaide: Centre for Research in the New Literatures in English, 1978), 17-27.

---. 'The Image of the Aboriginal in Three Modern Australian Novels'. *Meanjin*, XXXVI, 1977, 582-92.

Covell, Roger. 'Patrick White's Plays'. *Quadrant*, VIII, No. 1, 1964, 7-12.

Cowburn, John. 'The Metaphysics of *Voss*'. *Twentieth Century*, XVIII, 1964, 352-61.

Cowell, Lauren. *Against the Monotonous Surge: Patrick White's Metafiction*. (Ottawa: National Library of Canada, 1990).

Crick, Don. 'Critical Comment'. *Overland*, No. 38, 1968, 35-37.

Crisp, Lyndall. 'Patrick White, the Monster with a Twinkle in his Eye'. *National Times*, 17-23 May, 1985, 18, 20.

Cvetkovski, Vladimir. 'Linguistic Reconstruction of Patrick White's Graphemic Sign in Translation'. In *Australian Papers: Yugoslavia, Europe and Australia*, edited by Mirko Jurak (Ljubljana: Edvard Cardelj University, 1983), 283-86.

Da Silva, Cleo Lloyd. 'Separation and Individuation in *The Aunt's Story*', *Kunapipi*, 17.2, 1995, 42-51.

Darby, Robert. 'Patrick White and "The Dun-Coloured Offspring"'. *Notes & Furphies*, No. 18, 1988, 16-17.

Davidson, Jim. 'Beyond the Fatal Shore: The Mythologization of Mrs Fraser'. *Meanjin*, 49, No. 3, 1990, 449-61.

Dawson, Sally. '*Et in Australia Ego*: Framing the Pastoral Experience in Patrick White's *A Fringe of Leaves*'. In *Patrick White: Life and Writings. Five Essays*, edited by Martin Gray (U. of Stirling: Centre of Commonwealth Studies, 1991), 22-42.

Delbaere-Garant, Jeanne. 'Decolonising the Self in *Surfacing, Bear* and *A Fringe of Leaves*'. In *Colonisations*, edited by X. Pons and M. Rocard (Toulouse: Universite de Toulouse-Le Mirail, 1985), 67-78.

Delmonte, Rodolfo. 'Various types of Ambiguity in Patrick White's *Riders in the Chariot*'. *LiNQ*, III, Nos. 3-4, 1974, 37-52.

Dillistone, F.W. 'Meaning and Meaninglessness in Recent Literature'. In *Man, Fallen and Free: Oxford Essays on the Condition of Man*, edited by E.W. Kemp (London: Hodder & Stoughton, 1969), 59-77.

---. *Patrick White's Riders in the Chariot*. (New York: Seabury Press, 1969).

Religious Dimensions in Literature, No. 1.

Docker, John. 'Patrick White and Romanticism: *The Vivisector*'. *Southerly*, XXXIII, 1973, 44-61.

---. 'Patrick White's Australian Literary Context'. In his *Australian Cultural Elites: Intellectual Traditions in Sydney and Melbourne*. (Sydney: A.& R., 1974), 59-76. Revised from *Southerly*, 1973.

---. 'Romanticism, Modernism, Exoticism: Patrick White in Biography and Autobiography'. *Southern Review*, 26.3, 1993, 358-76.

Dolphin, Joan L. 'The Rhetoric of Painting in Patrick White's Novels'. *Ariel*, 24.3, 1993, 33-52.

Dommergues, Andre. '*A Fringe of Leaves* de Patrick White ou Le Voyage aux Antipodes'. *Commonwealth* (Toulouse), IV, 1979-1980, 27-38. In French.

Donaldson, Ian. 'Return to Abyssinia'. *Essays in Criticism*, XIV, 1964, 210-14.

Douglas, Dennis. 'Influence and Individuality: The Indebtedness of Patrick White's *The Ham Funeral* and *The Season at Sarsaparilla* to Strindberg and the German Expressionist Movement'. In *Bards, Bohemians, and Bookmen* edited by Leon Cantrell (St Lucia: U.Q.P., 1976), 266-80.

Drewe, Robert. 'The Confessions of Patrick White in a Searing Autobiography'. *Bulletin*, 20 October, 1981, 26-30.

Dreisen, C. van der. 'The Artist and Society: Jung and Patrick White'. *Commonwealth Review*, 3.2, 1991-92, 119-32. Reprinted in *Australian Literature Today*, edited by R. K. Dhawan and David Kerr (New York: Indian Society for Commonwealth Studies/Advent Press, 1993), 119-32.

---. 'The Figure of the Holy Fool in the Novels of Patrick White'. In *Patrick White: Life and Writings. Five Essays*, edited by Martin Gray (U. of Stirling: Centre of Commonwealth Studies, 1991), 60-77.

---. 'Patrick White and the "Unprofessed Factor": The Challenge Before the Contemporary Religious Novelist'. In *Patrick White: A Critical Symposium*, edited by R. Shepherd and K. Singh (Adelaide: Centre for Research in the New Literatures in English, 1978), 77-86.

Durix, Jean-Pierre. 'Masks and Travesties: *The Twyborn Affair* by Patrick White'. *Commonwealth* (Toulouse), IV, 1979-1980, 39-49.

---. 'Natural Elements in Patrick White's *Voss*'. *WLWE*, XVIII, 1979, 345-52.

Durr-Chamley, Monique. 'Vers une Etude de Voss: Quelques Jalons'. *Etudes Anglaises*, XXXIV, 1976, 561-71. In French.

Dutton, Geoffrey. 'Gentlemen vs. Lairs'. *Quadrant*, IX, No. 1, 1965, 14-20.

---. *Patrick White*. (Melbourne: O.U.P., 1971). Fourth ed. First puiblished Melbourne: Lansdowne, 1961. Australian Writers and Their Work. Reviewed by B. Kiernan, *Australian*, 6 November, 1971, 18; E. Kynaston, *Review* (Melbourne), 1 October, 1971, 1456.

---. 'A Prism's Light Shining in Flawed Glass'. *Bulletin*, 1 May, 1982, 62-64 & 66.

Dyce, J.R. *Patrick White as Playwright*. (St Lucia: U.Q.P., 1974). Reviewed by J.F. Burrows, *A.L.S.*, VII, 1975, 105-07; T. Herring, *AUMLA*, No. 42, 1975, 119-20.

Elfenbein, Andrew. 'Narrating Australia: Competing Heroisms in *A Fringe of Leaves*'. *Commonwealth Novel in English*, 6.1&2, 1993, 39-49.

E[lliott], B.R. 'Notes and Queries'. *Adelaide A.L.S. Working Papers*, III, 1979, 52-55. About *The Aunt's Story*.

Edelson, Phyllis. 'The Hatching Process: The Female's Struggle for Identity in Four Novels by Patrick White'. *WLWE*, XXV, No. 2, 1985, 229-40.

Edgar, Suzanne. 'A Woman's Life and Love'. *Quadrant*, XXI, No. 10, 1977, 69-71.

Edgecombe, Rodney S. 'Faith, Pride and Selfhood in Patrick White's *Voss*'. *English Studies in Africa*, No. 27, 1984, 133-145.

---. 'No Gift for Words: The Role of Miss Hare in Patrick White's *Riders in the Chariot*'. *WLWE*, XXV, No. 1, 1985, 52-66.

---. 'A Note on Patrick White: The Snake Episode in *Riders in the Chariot*'.

Antipodes, 7.1, 1993, 37-38.

---. 'Patrick White, Leigh Hunt and "Sweet Music"'. *Quadrant*, 39.1-2, 1995, 97-99.

---. 'Patrick White's Style - Again'. *Antipodes*, I, No. 2, 1987, 83-87.

---. 'Retrospectives in Patrick White and Margaret Atwood'. *Quadrant*, 39.7-8, 1995, 85-89.

---. *Vision and Style in Patrick White: A Study of Five Novels*. (Tuscaloosa, Ala.: University of Alabama Press, 1989). Reviewed by M. V. Kim, *Antipodes*, 3.2, 1989, 152-3.

---. 'The Weeds and Gardens in *Riders in the Chariot*'. *Antipodes*, 6.1, 1992, 25-31.

Evans, Patrick. 'Alienation and the Imagery of Death: The Novels of Janet Frame'. *Meanjin*, XXXII, 1973, 294-303. Compares novels of Frame with *The Tree of Man* and *Riders in the Chariot*.

Ewans, Michael. '*Voss*: White, Malouf, Meale'. *Meanjin*, 48, No. 3, 1989, 513-25.

Fernandes, Maria Priscilla. 'The Theme of Exploration in Patrick White's *Voss* and Conrad's *Heart of Darkness*'. In *Critical Interactions: Reading 20th Century Literary Texts*, edited by R.P. Rama (Jaipur: Pointer Publ., 1992) 23-47.

Excell, Patricia. 'Patrick White, *The Tree of Man* and *Meanjin*'. *Antipodes*, 9.2, 1995, 127-29.

Fitzpatrick, Kathleen. 'Ludwig Leichhardt'. *Victorian Historical Magazine*, XL, 1969, 190-203, esp. pp. 194-96.

Fitzpatrick, Peter. 'Patrick White'. In his *After 'The Doll'*. (Melbourne: Edward Arnold, 1979), 49-68.

Foulds, Stuart H. 'Distraction and Reconciliation: The Evolution of Interpersonal Relationships in Three Novels by Patrick White'. *Commonwealth Novel in English*, 4.2, 1991, 33-44.

Garebian, Keith. 'The Desert and the Garden: The Theme of Completeness in *Voss*'. *Modern Fiction Studies*, XXII, 1977, 557-59.

Gay, Penny. '*Flaws in the Glass*: The Confessions of St. Patrick'. *Southerly*, XLVII, No. 4, 1987, 403-408.

Ghose, Zulfikar. 'The One Comprehensive Vision'. *Texas Studies in Literature and Language*, XXI, 1979, 260-79.

---. 'On Re-reading *Riders in the Chariot*'. *Antipodes*, 6.1, 1992, 33-36.

Giffin, Michael. 'Judaism Between *Torah*, *Haskalah* and *Kabbalah*: The Revealed Imagination in the Novels of Patrick White'. *Literature & Theology*, (Oxford) 8.1, 1994, 64-79.

Gilbert, Helen M. 'The Prison and the Font: An Essay on Patrick White's *A Fringe of Leaves*'. *Kunapipi*, 11, No. 2, 1989, 17-22.

Gingell-Beckmann, Susan. 'Seven Black Swans: The Symbolic Logic of Patrick White's *The Eye of the Storm*'. *WLWE*, XXI, 1982, 315-25.

Glover, Richard. 'There's Still a Lot of Black in White'. *S.M.H. Magazine: Good Weekend*, 18 May, 1985, 26-27, 30. Interview.

Goldie, Terry. 'Contemporary Views of an Aboriginal Past: Rudy Wiebe and Patrick White' *WLWE*, XXIII, 1984, 429-39.

---. 'The Man of the Land/The Land of the Man: Patrick White and Scott Symons'. In *Postcolonial Fictions*, edited by Michèle Drouart (special issue in two volumes including SPACLALS Conference Proceedings, *SPAN*, 36, 1993), 156-63.

Gray, Martin, ed. *Patrick White: Life and Writings. Five Essays*. Occasional Papers 2. (U of Stirling: Centre of Commonwealth Studies, 1991). Articles listed under authors.

Gray, Martin. '*Flaws in the Glass*'. In *Patrick White: Life and Writings. Five Essays*, edited by Martin Gray (U. of Stirling: Centre of Commonwealth Studies, 1991), 78-89.

Green, Dorothy. 'The Edge of Error'. *Quadrant*, XVII, Nos. 5-6, 1973, 36-47. Discusses article by Leonie Kramer, 'Patrick White's *Gotterdammerung*', listed below.

---. 'An Over-Rated Invention?' *Bowyang*, No. 5, 1981, 38-45.

---. 'Patrick White's Nobel Prize'. *Overland*, No. 57, 1973/74, 23-25. See also Jean Crowcroft, 'Patrick White: A Reply to Dorothy Green', *Overland*, No. 59, 1974, 49-53.

---. '*Voss*: Stubborn Music'. In *The Australian Experience: Critical Essays on Australian Novels*, edited by W.S. Ramson (Canberra: Australian National University Press, 1974), 284-310.

Grenville, Kate, and Sue Woolfe. *Making Stories: How Ten Australian Novels Were Written*. (St Leonards, NSW: Allen & Unwin, 1993). Includes contribution on *Memoirs of Many in One*.

Gribble, Jennifer. 'Patrick White, Vivisector'. In *Reconnoitres: Essays in Australian Literature in Honour of G.A. Wilkes*, edited by Margaret Harris and Elizabeth Webby (South Melbourne: O.U.P. in association with Sydney U.P., 1992), 154-67.

Grosman, Meta. 'Patrick White's *Voss*: An Attempt at Interpretation'. In *Australian Papers: Yugoslavia, Europe and Australia*, edited by Mirko Jurak (Ljubljana: Edvard Cardelj University, 1983), 263-68.

Hadgraft, Cecil. 'The Theme of Revelation in Patrick White's Novels'. *Southerly*, XXXVII, 1977, 34-46.

Hanger, Eunice. 'The Setting in Patrick White's Two Plays: Unlocalized in *The Ham Funeral*, Australian in *Season At Sarsaparilla*'. *Proceedings of the IVth Congress of the International Comparative Literature Association* (The Hague and Paris: Mouton and Co., 1966), 644-53.

Hansson, Karin. 'The Indigenous and the Metropolitan in *A Fringe of Leaves*'. *WLWE*, XXIV, No. 1, 1984, 178-189.

---. '"The Terrible Nostalgia of the Desert Landscapes": Reflections on Patrick White's Australia from a European Point of View'. In *Australian Papers: Yugoslavia, Europe and Australia*, edited by Mirko Jurak (Ljubljana: Edvard Cardelj University, 1983), 255-62.

---. *The Warped Universe: A Study of Imagery and Structure in Seven Novels by Patrick White*. (Lund: CWK Gleerup, 1984). Reviewed by B. Kiernan, *A.L.S.*, XII, No. 3, 1986, 417-21; H. Priessnitz, *Anglia*, 108, Nos. 1-2, 1990, 264-68; G.A. Wilkes, *Southerly*, XLV, No. 2, 1985, 243.

Harries, Lyndon. 'The Peculiar Gifts of Patrick White'. *Contemporary Literature*, XIX, 1975. 459-71.

Harris, Max. 'Browsing'. *Australian*, 15 November, 1975, 11. On the publication of a Japanese translation of *Voss*. For related reports see *Canberra Times*, 6 May, 1975, 15; *Bulletin*, 27 September, 1975, 12; *Bulletin*, 8 November, 1975, 12-13.

---. 'A Brush Dipped in Vitriol'. *Weekend Australian Magazine*, 27-28 February, 1982, 4. Nolan portrait.

---. 'The Public Severity and Private Sincerity of Patrick White'. *Australian*, 5 April, 1969, 10.

Haskell, Dennis. '"A Lady Only by Adoption": Civilization in *A Fringe of Leaves*'. *Southerly*, XLVII, No. 4, 1987, 433-442.

Hasluck, Nicholas. 'Encounters with Patrick White'. *Quadrant*, 34, No. 12, 1990, 54-56.

Hassall, A.J. 'The Making of a Colonial Myth: The Mrs. Fraser Story in Patrick White's *A Fringe of Leaves* and Andre Brink's *An Instant in the Wind*'. *Ariel*, XVIII, No. 3, 1987, 3-28.

---. 'Patrick White's *The Cockatoos*'. *Southerly*, XXXV, 1975, 3-13.

Heltay, Hilary. *The Articles and the Novelist: Reference Conventions and Reader Manipulation in Patrick White's Creation of Fictional Worlds*. (Tubingen: Gunter Narr, 1983). Studies and Texts in English 4. Reviewed by B. Kiernan, *A.L.S.*, XII, No. 3, 1986, 417-21.

---. 'Patrick Whites Romanwerk'. *Akzente*, XIX, 1972, 518-39. Translated by John B. Beston and published as two articles: 'The Novels of Patrick White'. *Southerly*,

XXXIII, 1973, 92-104 and 'Patrick White in German'. *Southerly*, XXXIII, 1973, 421-27.

Herd, Jean. 'The Development of Stan and Amy Parker in *The Tree of Man*'. *The Teaching of English*, No. 24, 1973, 3-19.

Hergenhan, L.T. 'The City or the Desert: Patrick White's *A Fringe of Leaves*'. In his *Unnatural Lives: Studies in Australian Fiction about the Convicts*. (St Lucia: U.Q.P., 1983), 151-66.

---. 'The Past as "The Present Rendered Fabulous": The Confronting of European Origins in *Bring Larks and Heroes* and *A Fringe of Leaves*'. In *Australian Papers*: *Yugoslavia, Europe and Australia*, edited by Mirko Jurak (Ljubljana: Edvard Cardelj University, 1983), 269-75.

---. 'Patrick White's "Return to Abyssinia"'. *A.L.S.*, VII, 1976, 421-24.

Herring, Thelma, and Wilkes, G.A. 'A Conversation with Patrick White'. *Southerly*, XXXIII, 1973, 132-43. Interview.

Herring, Thelma. 'Maenads and Goat-Song: The Plays of Patrick White'. *Southerly*, XXV, No. 4, 1965, 219-33. Reprinted in *Ten Essays on Patrick White*, edited by G.A. Wilkes (Sydney: A.& R., 1970), 147-162.

---. 'Odyssey of a Spinster: A Study of *The Aunt's Story*'. *Southerly*, XXV, No. 1, 1965, 6-22. Reprinted in *Ten Essays on Patrick White*, edited by G.A. Wilkes (Sydney: A.& R., 1970), 3-20.

---. 'Patrick White's *The Vivisector*'. *Southerly*, XXXI, 1971, 3-16.

---. 'Self and Shadow: The Quest for Totality in *The Solid Mandala*'. *Southerly*, XXVI, 1966, 180-9. Reprinted in *Ten Essays on Patrick White*, edited by G.A. Wilkes (Sydney: A.& R., 1970), 72-82.

---. '*The Solid Mandala*: Two Notes'. *Southerly*, XXVIII, 1968, 216-22.

Heseltine, Harry 'Patrick White's Style'. *Quadrant*, VII, No. 3, 1963, 61-74.

---. '"Show me the Way to Go Home": *The Burnt Ones*'. In his *Acquainted with the Night*. (Townsville: Townsville Foundation for Australian Literary Studies, 1979), 57-82.

Hewett, Dorothy. 'The White Phenomena'. *Theatre-Australia*, II, No. 4, 1977, 18-21.

Heydon, J.D. 'Patrick White'. *Oxford Review*, I, No. 1, 1966, 33-46.

Hickey, Bernard. *Aspects of Alienation in James Joyce and Patrick White: A Study in Correspondences*. (Rome: Zampini, 1971).

---. 'Breakthrough: White and Whitlam in the Early 1970s'. In *Imagination and the Creative Impulse in the New Literatures in English*, edited by M-T Bindella and G.V. Davis, Cross/Cultures 9 (Amsterdam; Atlanta: Rodopi, 1993), 281-90.

Hill, Barry. 'White takes us Beyond the Spiritual Fringe'. *Age*, 3 May, 1983, 18.

Hooton, Joy. 'Australian Autobiography and the Question of National Identity: Patrick White, Barry Humphries, and Manning Clark'. *A-B: Auto-Biography Studies*, 9.1, 1994, 43 63.

---. 'A Patrick White Sketch'. *A.L.S.*, XII, No. 3, 1986, 410.

Hu Wenzhong. 'The Myth and the Facts: A Reconsideration of Australia's Critical Reception of Patrick White'. *A.L.S.*, 16.3, 1994, 333-41.

---. 'The White I Know'. *Voices*, 4 1, 1994, 17 53.

Johnson, Manly. '*A Fringe of Leaves*: White's Genethlicon'. *Texas Studies in Literature and Language*, XXI, 1979, 226-39.

---. 'Patrick White: The Eye of the Language'. *WLWE*, XV, 1976, 339-58.

---. 'Patrick White: "Failure" as Ontology'. *Journal of Popular Culture*, 23, No. 2, 1989, 73-80.

---. 'Patrick White: *A Fringe of Leaves*'. In *Patrick White: A Critical Symposium*, edited by R. Shepherd and K. Singh (Adelaide: Centre for Research in the New Literatures in English, 1978), 87-98.

---.'*Twyborn*: The Abbess, the Bulbul, and the Bawdy House'. *Modern Fiction Studies*, XXVII, No. 1, 1981, 159-68.

Jones, Dorothy. 'Matters of Geography and Countries of the Mind: *Voss* and

Badlands Compared'. *New Literatures Review*, 23, 1992, 73-85.

Jones, Joseph and Jones, Johanna. *Australian Fiction*. (Boston: Twayne Publishers, 1983).

Jose, Nicholas. 'The Dream of Europe: *For Love Alone, The Aunt's Story* and *The Cardboard Crown*'. *Meridian*, VI, No. 2, 1987, 113-125; esp. 119-121.

Kantor, P.P. 'Jews and Jewish Mysticism in Patrick White's *Riders in the Chariot*'. *B.B. Bulletin*, XI, March, 14-16, 1963, 20.

Joyce, Clayton, ed. *Patrick White: A Tribute*. (North Ryde, NSW: Collins/A.& R., 1991). Reviewed by D. Dunstan, *ABR*, 135, 1991, 48; P. Nelson, *Weekend Australian*, 28-29 September, 1991, Review 5; D.J. Tacey, *Age*, 7 September, 1991, Saturday Extra 9.

Karalis, Vrasidas. 'Some Observations on the Translation and Interpretation of *Voss*'. *Southerly*, 55.2, 1995, 6-22.

Keig, Carlene. 'Nietzsche's Influence on Australian Literature'. *Adelaide A.L.S. Working Papers*, I, No. 2, 1975, 56-61.

Kelly, David. 'The Structure of *The Eye of the Storm*'. In *Patrick White: A Critical Symposium*, edited by R. Shepherd and K. Singh (Adelaide: Centre for Research in the New Literatures in English, 1978), 62-9.

Kiernan, Brian. 'From the *Ham Funeral* to *Signal Driver*: Patrick White on Stage'. *S.M.H.*, 6 March, 1982, 46.

---. 'The Novels of Patrick White'. In *The Literature of Australia*, edited by Geoffrey Dutton. Revised edition (Ringwood, Vic.: Penguin, 1976), 461-84.

---. 'The Novelist and the Modern World'. In *Prophet from the Desert: Critical Essays on Patrick White*, edited by John McLaren (Melbourne: Red Hill Press, 1995), 1-23.

---. *Patrick White*. (London: Macmillan, New York: St Martin's Press, 1980). Reviewed by M. Arkin, *Comparative Literature Studies*, XXI, 1984, 244-45; J.B. Beston, *WLWE*, XX, 1981, 274-77; V. Brady, *Westerly*, XXV, No. 4, 1980, 84-86; J. Croft, *Age*, 7 March, 1981, 27 and *A.L.S.*, XI, 1983, 141-42; S.F.D. Hughes, *Modern Fiction Studies*, XXVII, No. 1, 1981, 186-88; L. Jacobs, *ABR*, No. 29, 1981, 35; J. Waten, *S.M.H.*, 6 December, 1980, 20.

---. 'Patrick White: The Novelist and the Modern World'. In *Cunning Exiles: Studies of Modern Prose Writers*, edited by Don Anderson and Stephen Knight (Sydney: A.& R., 1974), 81-103.

Kinnane, Garry. 'The Artist and Two Authors'. *Age Saturday Extra*, 10 April, 1982, 9. Interview with Sidney Nolan.

Kippax, H.G. 'Re-Enter Patrick White'. *S.M.H.*, 23 July, 1977, 16.

Kirkby, Joan. 'Fetishizing the Father: David Tacey on Patrick White'. *Meridian*, 10.1, 1991, 35-44.

Kitson, Jill. 'A Conversation with Barry Humphries on Patrick White'. *Quadrant*, 37.4, 1993, 53-57.

Knox-Shaw, Peter H. '"The Country of the Mind": Exploration as Metaphor in *Voss*'. *Commonwealth Novel in English*, I, No. 2, 1982, 202-25.

Koch-Emmery, Erwin. 'Theme and Language in Patrick White's Novels'. *Wiener Beitrage zur englischen Philologie*, LXXV, 1973, 136-46.

Koljevic, Svetozar. 'Patrick White in Serbo-Croat Literary Criticism'. In *Australian Papers*: *Yugoslavia, Europe and Australia*, edited by Mirko Jurak (Ljubljana: Edvard Cardelj University, 1983), 63-67.

Kramer, Leonie. 'Adventures of the Mind'. *Etruscan*, XVIII, No. 3, 1969, 15-17.

---. 'Home Thoughts from Abroad'. *Quadrant*, XXVI, Nos. 1-2, 1982, 57-59. Review of *Flaws in the Glass*.

---. 'Patrick White's *Gotterdammerung*'. *Quadrant*, XVII, No. 3, 1973, 8-19. See also Dorothy Green, 'The Edge of Error', above.

---. '*The Tree of Man*: An Essay in Scepticism'. In *The Australian Experience: Critical Essays on Australian Novels*, edited by W.S. Ramson (Canberra: Australian

National University Press, 1974), 269-83.

Kruse, Axel. 'Puzzles and Word-Games: Patrick White's *Night on Bald Mountain*'. *Southerly*, XXXV, 1975, 403-17.

Laidlaw, R.P. 'The Complexity of *Voss*'. *Southern Review*, IV, 1970, 3-14.

Laigle, Genevieve. 'L'œuvre "picturale" de Patrick White'. *Commonwealth* (Paris), VIII, No. 1, 1985, 107-117.

---. 'Patrick White Et Le Corps Humain'. *Etudes Anglaises*, XXXVII, No. 3, 1985, 266-276. In French.

---. 'Patrick White et l'empreinte de la mere'. *Commonwealth* (Paris), IX, No. 2, 1987, 92-98. In French.

---. 'The Reality of Illusion and the Illusion of Reality'. *Commonwealth*, 16.1, 1993, 77-88. Discusses *Memoirs of Many in One*.

---. 'La symbolique de l'arbre dans l'œuvre romanesque de Patrick White'. *Études Anglaises*, 47.3, 1994, 295-306.

Lawson, Alan. 'Bound to Dis-integrate: Narrative and Interpretation in *The Aunt's Story*'. *Antipodes*, 6.1, 1992, 9-15.

---. 'Meaning and Experience: A Review-Essay on some Recurrent Problems in Patrick White Criticism'. *Texas Studies in Literature and Language*, XXI, 1979, 280-95.

---. 'Patrick White: Australian Explorer'. *Age Saturday Extra*, 29 May, 1982, 11.

---. 'Patrick White's Critical Reception'. *Canberra Times*, 27 October, 1973, 2. See also ensuing discussion in *Canberra Times*, 30 October to 5 November, 1973.

---. 'P. White's Fan Club'. *Nation Review*, 9-15 November, 1973, 104. Letter to the editor.

---. 'Unmerciful Dingoes? The Critical Reception of Patrick White'. *Meanjin*, XXXII, 1973, 379-92.

---. 'White for White's Sake: Studies of Patrick White's Novels'. *Meanjin*, XXXII, 1973, 343-49.

Leitch, David. 'Patrick White: A Revealing Profile'. *National Times*, 27 March-1 April, 1978, 30, 32-35.

Lever, Susan. '*The Twyborn Affair*: Beyond "the Human Hierarchy of Men and Women"'. *A.L.S.*, 16.3, 1994, 289-96.

Lindman-Strafford, Kerstin. 'Patrick White'. In *Sandhogen och andra essaer* [Heap of Sand and Other Essays]. (Ekenas: Finland, 1974), Ch. 8, 67-75.

Lindsay, Jack. 'The Alienated Australian Intellectual'. *Meanjin*, XXII, No. 1, 1963, 48-59. Makes specific references to White's novels.

---. 'Patrick White: *The Burnt Ones*'. In his *Decay and Renewal*. (Sydney: Wild & Woolley, 1976), 364-69. Originally published as 'The Stories of Patrick White', *Meanjin*, XXIII, No. 4, 1964, 372-6.

Linguanti, Elsa. 'Heretical Ethics: The Female Element in Margaret Laurence's *The Stone Angel* and in Patrick White's *The Eye of the Storm*'. In *Saggi e richerche sulle culture extraeuropee*, edited by G. Bellini, C. Gorlier and S. Zoppi (Rome, Bulzoni, 1986), 25-38. Africa, America, Asia, Australia, 2.

---. 'Sequenze e Ritmi in *A Fringe of Leaves* di Patrick White'. In *Australiana*, edited by Paolo Bertinetti and Claudio Gorlier (Rome: Bulzoni, 1982), 209-21; abstract 269-70.

Liuleviciene, A. 'Nobelio Laureatas Patrick White'. *Aidai* (Franciscan Fathers, Kennebunk Port, Me), 1974, 39-42. In Lithuanian.

Loder, Elizabeth. '*The Ham Funeral*: Its Place in the Development of Patrick White'. *Southerly*, XXIII, No. 2, 1963, 78-91.

Loney, Douglas. 'Theodora Goodman and the Minds of Mortals: Patrick White's *The Aunt's Story*'. *English Studies in Canada*, VIII, 1982, 483-500.

Lyon, George W. 'The Ordinary Bread of Words: The Dissonant Unity of *Voss*'. *Australian and New Zealand Studies in Canada*, No. 4, 1990, 15-26.

Maack, Annegret. 'Shakespearean Reference as Structural Principle in Patrick White's

The Tree of Man and *The Eye of the Storm*'. Translated J.T. Swan, *Southerly*, XXXVIII, 1978, 123-40.

Macainsh, Noel. 'The Character of Voss'. *Quadrant*, XXVI, No. 5, 1982, 38-43. Reprinted in his *The Pathos of Distance* (Bern: Peter Lang, 1992), 243-253.

---. 'Nihilism, Nature and *A Fringe of Leaves*'. *Quadrant*, XXVII, No. 4, 1983, 36-41. Reprinted in his *The Pathos of Distance* (Bern: Peter Lang, 1992), 279-289.

---. 'Patrick White - A Note on the Phoenix'. *LiNQ*, V, No. 1, 1976, 15-19.

---. 'Patrick White - Fragments of a Swedish Correspondence'. *LiNQ*, IV, Nos. 1-2, 1975, 7-12.

---. 'Patrick White and the Aesthetics of Death'. *LiNQ*, XV, No. 2, 1987, 2-14. Reprinted in his *The Pathos of Distance* (Bern: Peter Lang, 1992), 290-303.

---. 'Patrick White's Aesthetic'. *LiNQ*, XII, Nos. 1-3, 1984, 55-70. Reprinted in his *The Pathos of Distance* (Bern: Peter Lang, 1992), 304-319.

---. 'Patrick White's Myth of the Artist'. *Quadrant*, XXIX, No. 11, 1985, 77-81. Reprinted in his *The Pathos of Distance* (Bern: Peter Lang, 1992), 267-278.

---. 'Patrick White's *Voss*: The Irony'. In *Lesen und Schreiben: Literatur - Kritik - Germanistik*, edited by Volker Wolf (Tübingen and Basel: Francke, 1955), 125-33.

---. 'The Poems of Patrick White'. *LiNQ*, IV, Nos. 3-4, 1975, 18-22.

---. 'A Queer Unity: Patrick White's *The Twyborn Affair*'. *Southerly*, XLIII, 1983, 143-54.

---. 'Voss and his Communications - A Structural Contrast'. *A.L.S.*, X, 1982, 437-47. Reprinted in his *The Pathos of Distance* (Bern: Peter Lang, 1992), 254-266.

Mackenzie, Manfred. 'Apocalypse in Patrick White's *The Tree of Man*'. *Meanjin*, XXV, 1966, 405-16.

---. 'The Consciousness of "Twin Consciousness": Patrick White's *The Solid Mandala*'. *Novel* (Providence, R.I.), II, 1969, 241-54.

---. 'Dark Birds of Light: *The Eye of the Storm* as Swansong'. *Southern Review*, X, 1977, 270-84.

---. 'Family Affairs/National Fictions, and *The Tree of Man*'. In *Postcolonial Fictions*, edited by Michèle Drouart (special issue in two volumes including SPACLALS Conference Proceedings, *SPAN*, 36, 1993), 164-73.

---. 'Patrick White's Later Novels: A Generic Reading'. *Southern Review*, I, No. 3, 1965, 5-18.

---. 'Tradition and Patrick White's Individual Talent'. *Texas Studies in Literature and Language*, XXI, 1979, 147-68.

Maes-Jelinek, Hena. 'Altering Boundaries: The Art of Translation in *The Angel at the Gate* and *The Twyborn Affair*'. *WLWE*, XXIII, 1984, 165-74.

---. 'Fictional Breakthrough and the Unveiling of "Unspeakable Rites" in Patrick White's *A Fringe of Leaves* and Wilson Harris's *Yurokon*'. *Kunapipi*, II, No. 2, 1980, 33-43.

---. 'Last Flight to Byzantium: Patrick White's *Memoirs of Many in One*'. In *European Perspectives: Contemporary Essays on Australian Literature*, edited by Giovanna Capone (*A.L.S.* 15.2 (special issue)/ St. Lucia: U.Q.P., 1991), 173-83.

Magee, Penelope. 'Religion, Culture and Difference: The "Uneasiness" of Patrick White'. In *Religion and Multiculturalism in Australia: Essays in Honour of Victor Hayes* edited by Norman Habel, Special Studies in Religions Series 7 (Adelaide: AASR, 1992), 159-69.

Marr, David. *Patrick White: A Life*. (Milsons Point, NSW: Random House Australia, 1991; New York: Alfred Knopf, 1992). Reviewed by D. Altman, *Journal of Australian Studies*, 32, 1992, 83-85; A. Clark, *Scripsi*, 7.3, 1992, 37-41; P. Craven, *Age*, 13 July, 1991, Saturday Extra 7; J. Docker, *Australian Historical Studies*, 99, 1992, 346-48; C. Floyd, *SPAN*, 32, 1991, 116-20; R. Gray, *T.L.S.*, 9 August, 1991, 5-6; E. Jolley, *Scripsi*, 7.3, 1992, 27-31; B. Kiernan, *Weekend Australian*, 13-14 July, 1991, Review 4; A. Lawson, *A.L.S.*, 15.4, 1992, 354-58; S. Lawson, *London Review of Books*, 13.5, 1991, 11-12; D. Malouf, *ABR*, 133, 1991, 4-6; D. Modjeska,

Australian Society, 10.8, 1991, 34-35; P. Morley, *Antipodes*, 6.1, 1992, 45-47 (Review essay); P. Pierce, *Bulletin*, 23 July, 1991, 92-93; A.P. Riemer, *S.M.H.*, 13 July, 1991, 41; N. Rowe, *Southerly*, 52.4, 1992, 146-57; T. Shapcott, *Voices*, 1.4, 1991, 94-96; P. Wolfe, *Antipodes*, 6.1, 1992, 47-50 (Review essay). Extract published in *Overland*, No. 121, 1990, 6-7. See also Tacey, David J., 'Patrick White Marred', *Quadrant*, 35.10, 1991, 7-11; Kitson, Jill, 'A Conversation with David Marr', *Quadrant*, 35.9, 1991, 21-25.

Martin, David. 'A Chariot Between Faith and Despair'. *The Bridge*, I, No. 1, 1964, 7-12.

Mather, Rodney. 'Patrick White and Lawrence: A Contrast'. *Critical Review*, No. 13, 1970, 34-50.

---. '*Voss*'. *Melbourne Critical Review*, No. 6, 1963, 93-101.

McAuley, James. 'The Gothic Splendours: Patrick White's *Voss*'. *Southerly*, XXV, No. 1, 1965, 34-44. Reprinted in *Ten Essays on Patrick White*, edited by G.A. Wilkes (Sydney: A.& R., 1970), 34-46.

McCulloch, A.M. *A Tragic Vision: The Novels of Patrick White*. (St Lucia: U.Q.P., 1983). Reviewed by J.B. Beston, *Ariel*, XVII, No. 1, 1986, 91-94; B. Elliott, *A.L.S.*, XI, 1984, 554-59; V. Sen, *Canberra Times*, 15 October, 1983, 18; D.J. Tacey, *Meridian*, IV, No. 1, 1985, 49-53.

---. 'Patrick White's Novels and Nietzsche'. *A.L.S.*, IX, 1980, 308-20.

---. 'Queen Lear Down Under: *The Eye of the Storm*'. In *Prophet from the Desert: Critical Essays on Patrick White*, edited by John McLaren (Melbourne: Red Hill Press, 1995), 92-105.

McDougall, R. *Australia Felix: Joseph Furphy and Patrick White*. (Canberra: A.N.U. Press, 1966). C.L.F. lectures.

McFarlane, Brian. 'Inhumanity in the Australian Novel: *Riders in the Chariot*'. *The Critical Review*, No. 19, 1977, 24-41.

McGregor, Craig (ed.). *In the Making*. (Melbourne: Nelson Australia, 1969), 218-22. Reprinted in *Patrick White Speaks*, edited by Christine Flynn and Paul Brennan (Sydney: Primavera Press, 1989), 19-23.

McInerney, Sally. 'Voss, the Movie, Becomes a Pawn in Nolan-White "Feud"'. *S.M.H.*, 16 July, 1983, 42.

McKernan, Susan. 'A New Kind of Novel: the Work of Patrick White'. In her *A Question of Commitment: Australian Literature in the Twenty Years After the War* (Sydney: Allen & Unwin, 1989), 166-88.

McLaren, John. 'The Image of Reality in Our Writing'. *Overland*, Nos. 27-8, 1963, 43-7.

---. 'Patrick White's Use of Imagery'. *A.L.S.*, II, 1966, 217-20.

McLeod, A.L. 'Patrick White: Nobel Prize for Literature 1973'. *Books Abroad*, XLVIII, 1974, 439-45.

McLaren, John, and Mary-Ellen Ryan, eds. *Prophet from the Desert: Critical Essays on Patrick White*. (Melbourne: Red Hill Press, 1995).

Mercer, David. 'A Film Script of *Voss*: Interview by Rodney Wetherell'. *A.L.S.*, VIII, 1978, 395-401.

Mihailovich-Dickman, Vera, ed. *'Return' in Post-Colonial Writing: A Cultural Labyrinth*. Cross/Cultures 12. (Amsterdam; Atlanta: Rodopi, 1994). Includes discussion of White.

Mishra, Vijay. 'Negotiating an Autobiography: Patrick White's *Flaws in the Glass*'. *Span*, No. 14, 1982, 25-32.

---. 'White's Poetics: Patrick White through Mikhail Bakhtin'. *Span*, No. 18, 1984, 54-75.

Mitchell, Adrian. 'Eventually, White's Language: Words and More Than Words'. In *Patrick White: A Critical Symposium*, edited by R. Shepherd and K. Singh (Adelaide: Centre for Research in the New Literatures in English, 1978), 5-16.

Moore, Susan. 'The Quest for Wholeness in *Riders in the Chariot*'. *Southerly*,

XXXV, 1975, 50-67.

Morley, Patricia A. *The Mystery of Unity: Theme and Technique in the Novels of Patrick White*. (St Lucia: U.Q.P.; Montreal: McGill-Queen's University Press, 1972). Reviewed by G. Aggeler, *Modern Fiction Studies*, XIX, 1973-74, 628-30; J. Beston, *S.M.H.*, 14 October, 1972, 24 and *AUMLA*, XXXIX, 1973, 121-23 and *Journal of Modern Literature*, IV, 1974, 475-76; V. Brady, *Westerly*, No. 4, 1972, 63-66; J. Colmer, *A.L.S.*, VI, 1973, 95-99; M. Dunlevy, *Canberra Times*, 7 April, 1973, 13; B. Kiernan, *Yearbook of English Studies*, IV, 1974, 338-40; W. Noonan, *Australian*, 25 November, 1972, 37; A.A. Phillips, *Age*, 24 February, 1973, 17; *T.L.S.*, 6 April, 1973, 401; J. Pilling, *Journal of Commonwealth Literature*, XII, No. 3, 1978, 89-92.

---. 'Doppelganger's Dilemma Artist and Man: *The Vivisector*'. *Queen's Quarterly*, LXXVIII, 1971, 407-20.

---. 'Patrick White's *A Fringe of Leaves*: Journey to Tintagel'. *WLWE*, XXI, 1982, 303-15.

---. 'Patrick White: "World of Semblance, World of Dream"'. *St. Mark's Review*, No. 86, 1976, 30-38.

Murphy, Paul. 'An Interview with Patrick White'. *Island Magazine*, No. 7, 1981, 6-7.

Myers, David. *The Peacocks and the Bourgeoisie: Ironic Vision in Patrick White's Shorter Prose Fiction*. (Adelaide: Adelaide University Union Press, 1978). Reviewed by D. Attridge, *Journal of English and Germanic Philology*, LXXIX, No. 1, 1980, 150-52; L.R. Broer, *Studies in Short Fiction*, XVII, 1980, 516-17; J.F. Burrows, *A.L.S.*, IX, 1980, 407-10; F.D. Hughes, *Modern Fiction Studies*, XXVII, No. 1, 1981, 185-86; L. Kramer, *S.M.H.*, 7 June, 1980, 21; A. Lawson, *AUMLA*, No. 54, 1980, 262-64; R.B.J. Wilson, *ABR*, No. 15, 1979, 18-19.

---. 'A Galaxy of Haloed Suns: Epiphanies and Peacocks in Patrick White's "A Woman's Hand" and Flannery O'Connor's "The Displaced Person"'. *Literatur in Wissenschaft und Unterricht*, XIV, 1981, 214-24.

Nandan, Satendra. 'Beyond Colonialism: The Artist as Healer'. In *South Pacific Images*, edited by Chris Tiffin (St Lucia: SPACLALS, 1978), 11-25.

Nedeljkovic, Maryvonne. '*Voss*, or The Uneasy Conscience'. *Commonwealth* (Paris), IX, No. 2, 1987, 84-91.

Nelson, Timothy G.A. 'Proserpina and Pluto, Ariadne and Bacchus: Myth in Patrick White's "Dead Roses"'. *A.L.S.*, X, 1981, 111-14.

Nesbitt, Bruce. 'Displacement in Patrick White and Sheila Watson: Musical and Mythic Forms'. In *Australian/Canadian Literatures in English: Comparative Perspectives*, edited by Russell McDougall and Gillian Whitlock (North Ryde, N.S.W.: Methuen Australia, 1987), 151-169.

New, William H. 'The Island and the Madman: Recurrent Imagery in the Major Novelists of the Fifties'. *Arizona Quarterly*, XXII, 1966, 328-37.

Newman, Joan. 'The Significance of Christian Myth Structures in *Voss*'. In *Prophet from the Desert: Critical Essays on Patrick White*, edited by John McLaren (Melbourne: Red Hill Press, 1995), 106-17.

Nicklin, Lenore. 'The Martin Road Folk Get Ready for a Fight'. *S.M.H.*, 17 March, 1972, 2. See also reports in *S.M.H.*, 18 March, 1972, 1; *Australian*, 8 June, 1972, 9; *S.M.H.*, 19 June, 1972, 2.

Niris, Victor. 'Parody Competition: First Winning Entry'. *Australian*, 23 January, 1971, 22.

Noble, Veena. 'A Study of the Hermaphroditic Element in Patrick White's *The Solid Mandala*'. *Commonwealth Review* 2.1-2, 1990-91, 30-35.

Nugnes, Barbara. '*King Lear* e *A Fringe of Leaves*: Influssi e Suggestioni'. In *Australiana*, edited by Paolo Bertinetti and Claudio Gorlier (Rome: Bulzoni, 1982), 223-36; abstract 270-71.

Oakley, Barry. 'White on Green'. *Quadrant*, XXIV, Nos. 1-2, 1980, 68-69. Humorous.

PATRICK WHITE 461

O'Brien, Geraldine. 'No-one realises how Frivolous Patrick White Can be'. *S.M.H.*, 10 December, 1983, 31.
O'Carrigan, Catherine. 'Patrick White and the World of Art'. *ASEA Bulletin*, V, No. 5, 1973, 11-16.
O'Carroll, John. 'Voss, the Opera: Romanticism Rewritten'. *Hermes*, II, No. 1, 1986, 29-31.
O'Grady, Desmond. 'Patrick White's *Voss* in Italy'. *Age*, 10 December, 1966, 22.
Orel, Harold. 'Is Patrick White's *Voss* the Real Leichhardt of Australia?' *Costerus: Essays in English and American Language and Literature* (Amsterdam), VI, 1972, 109-19.
Osborne, Charles. 'Literature'. In his *Australian, New Zealand and the South Pacific: A Handbook*. (London: Blond, 1970), 291-97.
Paolini, Shirley. 'Desert Metaphors and Self-Enlightenment in Patrick White's *Voss*'. *Antipodes*, 4.2, 1990, 87-91.
Patin, Claire. 'Poésie et poétique du récit sur un passage de *The Twyborn Affair* de Patrick White'. *Commonwealth* (France), 13.2, 1991, 104-08.
Petersson, Irmtraud. 'Leichhardt and Voss: The Changing Image of a German Explorer'. In *The German Presence in Queensland over the Last 150 Years*, edited by Manfred Jurgensen and Alan Corkhill (St Lucia: Department of German, University of Queensland, 1988), 313-325.
---. 'New "Light" on *Voss*: The Significance of its Title'. *WLWE*, XXVIII, No. 2, 1988, 245-259.
Phillips, A.A. 'The Dogs Have Their Day'. *Overland*, No. 25, 1963, 33-4. Review of *The Season at Sarsaparilla*.
---. 'Patrick White And The Algebraic Symbol'. *Meanjin*, XXIV, 1965, 455-61. Reprinted in his *Responses: Selected Writings*. (Kew, Vic.: Australian International Press & Publications, 1979), 124-30.
---. 'A Persuasion to Charity'. In his *Responses: Selected Writings*. (Kew, Vic.: Australian International Press & Publications, 1979), 210-12. Review of *A Fringe of Leaves* first published as 'Exploring Spiritual Issues' in the *Age*, 9 October, 1976, 22.
Pierce, Peter. '*Big Toys* and the Play-Making of Patrick White'. In *Patrick White: A Critical Symposium*, edited by R. Shepherd and K. Singh (Adelaide: Centre for Research in the New Literatures in English, 1978), 41-51.
Platz, Norbert H. 'The Western Consciousness of Novel Writing and the Image of Australia in Patrick White's *Voss*'. *WLWE*, XXIV, No. 1, 1984, 170-177.
Pons, Xavier. 'Patrick White's *Voss*: A Psychoanalytical Approach'. *Commonwealth* (Toulouse), IV, 1979-1980, 7-26.
---. 'Patrick White: *Voss* et l'Australie'. *Commonwealth* (Rodez), I, 1974-1975, 96-103.
Porteous, Alexander. 'Some Recent Australian Plays and Problems of Their Criticism'. *A.L.S.*, III, 1967, 83-97.
Porter, Peter. 'Sydneyside'. *New Statesman*, 29 January, 1965, 171. Discusses *The Season at Sarsaparilla*.
Potter, Nancy A.J. 'Allegory in Patrick White's *The Solid Mandala* [abstract]'. *WLWE Newsletter*, No. 15, 1969, 5.
---. 'Patrick White's Minor Saints'. *Review of English Literature*, XV, No. 4, 1964, 9-19.
Pounder, Nicholas. 'A Tribute to Patrick White'. *Island*, 48, 1991, 56-59.
Prerauer, Maria. 'The Wit and Wisdom of Patrick White: Dinner with the Great Australian Author'. *Sunday Telegraph*, 12 August, 1973, 71.
Raddatz, Volker. 'Interkulturelle Begegnungen: Kommunikationsformen zwischen Aborigines und Weissen am Beispiel von Patrick Whites *Voss* und Ludwig Leichhardts *Journal of an Overland Expedition in Australia from Moreton Bay to Port Essington*'. In *Australienstudien in Deutschland: Grundlagen und Perspektiven*, edited by Gerhard Stilz and Heinrich Lamping (Bern; Frankfurt a.M.; New York: Paris: Peter Lang,

1990), 147-61.

Radic, Leonard. 'That Man White'. *Age Saturday Extra*, 13 March, 1982, 1.

Raizis, M. Byron. 'The Image of the Greek in Australian Literature'. In *Australian Papers: Yugoslavia, Europe and Australia*, edited by Mirko Jurak (Ljubljana: Edvard Cardelj University, 1983), 115-32.

Ramsay, S.A. '*The Twyborn Affair*: "The Beginning in an End" or "The End of a Beginning"?' *Ariel*, XI, No. 4, 1980, 87-95.

Rao, B. Damodar. '*Riders in the Chariot*: A Note'. *ACLALS Bulletin*, Series 4, No. 4, 1976, 50-54.

Realist Writer, Editorial Board. 'The Patrick White Controversy'. *Realist Writer*, No. 12, 1963, 3-4.

Reid, Ian. 'The Landscape of Narration in *The Aunt's Story*'. In *Mapped But Not Known: The Australian Landscape of the Imagination*, edited by P.R. Eaden and F.H. Mares (Netley, S.A.: Wakefield Press, 1986), 210-218.

Richards, Jack. 'Patrick White, Australian Novelist'. *Studia Anglica Posnaniensia*, III, 1971, 113-19.

Rickard, John. 'Manning Clark and Patrick White: A Reflection'. *Australian Historical Studies*, 98, 1992, 116-22.

Riddell, Elizabeth. 'Australian of the Year'. *Australian*, 1 January, 1974, 7.

---. 'White'. *Australian*, 1 August, 1970, 15. Interview.

---. 'The Whites: Patrick, Pastoralists and Polo Ponies'. *Bulletin*, 8 January, 1986, 44-49.

Riem, Antonella. 'Autobiography or Fiction? Patrick White's *Memoirs of Many in One*'. *Westerly*, 36.3, 1991, 95-101.

---. 'The Quest Motif in David Malouf's *An Imaginary Life* and Patrick White's *The Aunt's Story*'. In her *The Labyrinths of Self: A Collection of Essays on Australian and Caribbean Literature*. (Leichhardt, N.S.W.: FILEF. Italo-Australian Publications, 1987), 99-109.

---. *L'universo terra in Voss di Patrick White*. (Verona: Edizioni Universitarie, 1986). Reviewed by A. Stewart, *A.L.S.*, 14, No. 2, 1989, 268-69.

---. '*Voss* and *To the Islands*: The Search for the Self - "A Country of Great Subtelty" - An Essay on Patrick White and Randolph Stow'. In her *The Labyrinths of Self: A Collection of Essays on Australian and Caribbean Literature*. (Leichhardt, N.S.W.: FILEF. Italo-Australian Publications, 1987), 13-97.

Riemer, A.P. 'Back to the Abyss: Patrick White's Early Novels'. *Southerly*, XLVII, No. 4, 1987, 347-369.

---. 'Death of the Author, Birth of the Classic'. *Antipodes*, 6.1, 1992, 51-59.

---. 'Eddie and the Bogomils - Some Observations on *The Twyborn Affair*'. *Southerly*, XL, 12-29.

---. 'The Eye of the Needle: Patrick White's Recent Novels'. *Southerly*, XXXIV, 1974, 248-66.

---. 'It Doesn't Pay to be Different: The Perils of Translating Patrick White'. *Southerly*, 49, No. 3, 1989, 463-77. Discusses Hungarian translation of 'Clay'.

---. 'Landscape with Figures - Images of Australia in Patrick White's Fiction'. *Southerly*, XLII, 1982, 20-38.

---. 'This World, the Next, and Australia - the Emergence of a Literary Commonplace'. *Southerly*, XLIV, 1984, 251-70.

---. 'Vision of the Mandala in *The Tree of Man*'. *Southerly*, XXVII, 1967, 3-19. Reprinted in *Ten Essays on Patrick White*, edited by G.A. Wilkes (Sydney: A.& R., 1970), 109-26.

Roberts, Alan. 'Now it's Back to White. Pointer to the Festival'. *Advertiser*, 23 January, 1982, 26.

---. 'Patrick White: The Inner Struggle'. *Advertiser*, 13 February, 1982, 21 & 26. See also *Courier-Mail*, 20 February, 1982, 25. Interview.

Robinson, Jeffrey. 'The Aboriginal Enigma: *Heart of Darkness*, *Voss* and *Palace of*

the Peacock'. Journal of Commonwealth Literature, XX, No. 1, 1985, 148-55.
Roderick, Colin. 'Four Lectures on P. White's *Voss*'. *Echos du Commonwealth*, No. 3, 1976, 15-27.
---. 'Patrick White and *Voss*: An Exegesis in Six Chapters. First Chapter: White's Life, Mind and Technique'. *C.A.R.A.: Estudios de Cultura Britanica en España* (Valladolid, Spain) 1.
Rohde, Hedwig. 'Patrick White - A German Review'. Translated by Noel Macainsh, *LiNQ*, III, Nos. 3-4, 1974, 34-36.
Ross, Robert. 'Patrick White and "Multi-Textuality"'. *Journal of Commonwealth and Post-Colonial Studies*, 1.1, 1993, 70-72.
---. 'Patrick White's *The Twyborn Affair*: A Portrait of the Artist'. *Commonwealth Novel in English*, II, No. 2, 1983, 94-105.
Rowbotham, David. 'Patrick White and the Mess we're in'. *Courier-Mail*, 13 August, 1983, 22.
Russell, D.W. '*Voss* and *La Voie Royale*: A Comparison of Patrick White and Andre, Malraux'. *WLWE*, XIX, 1980, 200-03.
Ryan, J.S. 'Cockatoos and Peacocks'. *Hemisphere*, XIX, No. 2, 1975, 26-31.
---. 'The Faith of his Fathers - Another Source for Patrick White's Mysticism'. *Notes & Furphies*, No. 5, 1980, 16-20.
---. 'Patrick White'. *Yearbook of English Studies*, XXVIII, 1978, 323-24.
---. 'Patrick White and Germany'. *Notes & Furphies*, No. 8, 1982, 9-11.
---. 'Patrick White and the Study of French Literature'. *Commonwealth* (Paris), IX, No. 2, 1987, 77-83.
---. 'The Several Fates of Eliza Fraser'. *Journal of the Royal Historical Society of Queensland*, XI, No. 4, 1983, 88-112.
Ryan, Mary-Ellen. 'The Selfish Eye: Self and Circles in *The Eye of the Storm*'. In *Prophet from the Desert: Critical Essays on Patrick White*, edited by John McLaren (Melbourne: Red Hill Press, 1995), 73-91.
Sadawarte, R. S. 'Occult Symbolism in Patrick White's *The Solid Mandala*'. *Commonwealth Review*, 2.1-2, 1990-91, 36-42.
Sampson, David. 'Black and White: *A Fringe of Leaves*'. *Meridian*, II, 1983, 109-15.
Sarkar, Subhas. 'Patrick White: The Quest for Human Values'. *Journal of Australian Literature*, 1, No. 1, 1990, 43-47.
Sayers, Stuart. 'Patrick White in Sweden'. *Age*, 28 March, 1970, 14. See also his report, *Age*, 10 October, 1970, 14.
Schaffer, Kay. 'Australian Mythologies: The Eliza Fraser Story and Constructions of the Feminine in Patrick White's *A Fringe of Leaves* and Sidney Nolan's "Eliza Fraser" Paintings'. *Kunapipi*, 11, No. 2, 1989, 1-15. Reprinted in *Us/Them: Translation Transcription and Identity in Post-Colonial Literary Cultures*, edited by Gordon Collier, Cross/Cultures 6, (Amsterdam; Atlanta, GA: Rodopi, 1992), 371-83.
---. *In the Wake of First Contact: The Eliza Fraser Stories*. (Cambridge: Cambridge UP., 1995), 157-75.
Scheick, William J. 'The Gothic Grace and Rainbow Aesthetic of Patrick White's Fiction: An Introduction'. *Texas Studies in Literature and Language*, XXI, 1979, 131-46.
Schulz, Gerhard. 'Die Herausforderung des Patrick White'. *Merian* (Hamburg), XXVII, No. 3, 1974, 92-93.
---. 'Urmythos in Australien - Zum Werk des Nobelpreistragers Patrick White'. *Neue Rundschau* (Frankfurt a.M.), LXXXV, 1974, 163-67.
Seaton, Dorothy. 'Land and History: Inter-Discursive Conflict in *Voss*'. *Australian and New Zealand Studies in Canada*, No. 4, 1-14.
Segerstrom, Henry. 'From Rowcroft to White: Australian Fiction in Sweden'. Arranged and translated by S. Gerson. *A.L.S.*, VII, 347-55.
Senn, Werner. 'Crisis and Reconstitution of Self in Recent Australian Fiction: The Latest Novels of Patrick White and Randolph Stow'. In *Australian Papers*:

Yugoslavia, Europe and Australia, edited by Mirko Jurak (Ljubljana: Edvard Cardelj University, 1983), 227-82.

---. 'Personal and Social Identity in *A Fringe of Leaves* by Patrick White'. *Commonwealth* (Paris), IX, No. 2, 1987, 71-76.

Seymour, Alan. 'Patrick White'. In *Patrick White: Life and Writings. Five Essays*, edited by Martin Gray (U. of Stirling: Centre of Commonwealth Studies, 1991), 43-59.

Shahane, V.A. 'An Approach to Patrick White's *The Solid Mandala*'. *ACLALS Bulletin*, Series 4, No. 4, 1976, 55-64.

Sharman, Jim, and Knight, Elisabeth. 'A Very Literary Luncheon'. *National Times*, 30 June, 1979, 26-27, 30-31. Interview.

Sharr, Roger. 'Old Women, Nuns and Idiots: Transcendentalism in *The Tree of Man*'. *St. Mark's Review*, No. 86, 1976, 39-43.

Sharrad, Paul. '*Pour Mieux Sauter*: Christopher Koch's Novels in Relation to White, Stow and the Quest for a Post-Colonial Fiction'. *WLWE*, XXIII, 1984, 208-23.

Shepherd, R. 'CRNLE Patrick White Seminar'. *Span*, No. 6, 1978, 9-14.

---. 'An Indian Story: "The Twitching Colonel"'. In *Patrick White: A Critical Symposium*, edited by R. Shepherd and K. Singh (Adelaide: Centre for Research in the New Literatures in English, 1978), 28-33.

Shepherd, R. and Singh, K. (eds.). *Patrick White: A Critical Symposium*. (Adelaide: Centre for Research in the New Literatures in English, 1978). Individual contributions are listed under the authors' names. Reviewed by J.F. Burrows, *A.L.S.*, IX, 407-10; D. Carter, *Pacific Moana Quarterly*, V, No. 2, 1980, 251-55; B. Elliott, *Advertiser*, 10 February, 1979, 23; A. Hassall, *ABR*, No. 12, 1979, 14; A. Heywood, *Kunapipi*, II, No. 2, 1980, 180-83.

Short, Susanna. 'Nolan Hauls Patrick White over Burning Coals'. *S.M.H.*, 29 April, 1982, 8.

Shrubb, Peter. 'Flaws'. *Quadrant*, XXV, No. 12, 1981, 28-32.

---. 'Patrick White: Chaos Accepted'. *Quadrant*, XII, No. 3, 1968, 7-19.

Simons, Margaret. 'Patrick White Finds it Hard to Forgive'. *Age Saturday Extra*, 24 September, 1983, 3.

Singh, Kirpal. 'The Fiend of Motion: Theodora Goodman in Patrick White's *The Aunt's Story*'. *Quadrant*, XIX, No. 9, 1975, 90-92.

---. 'The Nostalgia of Permanence: Stan Parker in Patrick White's *The Tree of Man*'. *ACLALS Bulletin*, Series 4, No. 4, 1976, 1-5.

---. 'Patrick White: An Outsider's View'. In *Patrick White: A Critical Symposium*, edited by R. Shepherd and K. Singh (Adelaide: Centre for Research in the New Literatures in English, 1978), 117-22.

Smith, Angela. 'Is Phallocentricity a Sin? or a Peccadillo? Comedy and Gender in Ethel Anderson's *At Parramatta* and Patrick White's *Voss*'. In *European Perspectives: Contemporary Essays on Australian Literature*, edited by Giovanna Capone (*A.L.S.* 15.2 (special issue)/ St. Lucia: U.Q.P., 1991), 149-61.

Smith, Derek. 'Patrick White's Poetical Motivations: Imagery and Colour in *Voss*'. *Adelaide A.L.S. Working Papers*, I, No. 2, 1975, 68-77.

Smith, Margaret. 'Patrick White in Perspective'. *Social Alternatives*, III, No. 1, 1982, 68-70.

Smith, Terry. 'Portrait of the Artist in Patrick White's *The Vivisector*'. *Meanjin*, XXXI, 1972, 167-77.

Souter, Gavin. 'White in the Literaries'. *S.M.H.*, 12 January, 1974, 15.

Spies, Marion. '"Affecting Godhead": Religious Language in *Voss* and *Riders in the Chariot*'. *Antipodes*, 6.1, 1992, 17-23.

Spinks, Lee. 'Austerities and Epiphanies: A Note on Fantasy and Repression in Patrick White's "Five-Twenty"'. *Westerly*, 40.1, 1995, 39-44.

Spinucci, Pietro. *Il Verme e La Rosa, La Narrativa di Patrick White*. (Rome, Bulzoni Editore, 1983). In Italian. Reviewed by D. Malouf, *A.L.S.*, XII, No. 1, 1985, 152.

---. 'Patrick White e l'Australia'. In *Australiana*, edited by Paolo Bertinetti and Claudio Gorlier (Rome: Bulzoni, 1982), 237-52; abstract 271-72.

---. 'Patrick White in Italy'. *Australian Literature Bulletin* (Venice), II, No. 1, 1979, 40-48.

St. Pierre, Paul M. 'Coterminous Beginnings'. In *Patrick White: A Critical Symposium*, edited by R. Shepherd and K. Singh (Adelaide: Centre for Research in the New Literatures in English, 1978), 99-107.

Stapleton, Eugenie. 'The Teeth of Patrick White'. *Nepean Review*, No. 3, 1977, 57-59, reprinted in *S.M.H.*, 3 June, 1978, 13. Letter from J. Leigh, *S.M.H.*, 9 June, 1978, 6.

Stein, Thomas Michael. *Illusions of Solidity: Individuum und Gesellschaft im Romanwerk Patrick Whites*. Anglistik in der Blauen Eule 11. (Essen: Verlag die Blaue Eule, 1990).

---. Thomas M. *Patrick White: 'Voss'*. (Munich: Wilhelm Fink, 1983). Reviewed by W. Sehn, *CRNLE Reviews Journal*, No. 2, 1984, 71-73.

Steven, Laurence. *Dissociation and Wholeness in Patrick White's Fiction*. (Waterloo, Ontario: Wilfred Laurier University Press, 1989). Reviewed by C. Bliss, *Antipodes*, 4.1, 1990, 76; R. Shepherd, *CRNLE Reviews Journal*, No. 2, 1989, 48-50.

Stewart, Annette. 'Art and the Australian Artist: In White, Malouf, Murnane and Bail'. *Quadrant*, XXI, No. 8, 1987, 52-59.

Stow, Randolph. 'Transfigured Histories: Recent Novels of Patrick White and Robert Drewe'. *A.L.S.*, IX, 1979, 26-38.

Strauss, Jennifer. 'Patrick White's Versions of Pastoral'. *WLWE*, XXIV, No. 2, 1984, 273-287.

Tacey, David J. 'Denying the Shadow As the Day Lengthens: Patrick White's *The Living and the Dead*'. *Southern Review*, XI, 1978, 165-79.

---. 'In the Lap of the Land: Misogyny and Earth Mother Worship in *Tree of Man*'. In *Mapped But Not Known: The Australian Landscape of the Imagination*, edited by P.R. Eaden and F.H. Mares (Netley, S.A.: Wakefield Press, 1986), 192-209. Reprinted in *Prophet from the Desert: Critical Essays on Patrick White*, edited by John McLaren (Melbourne: Red Hill Press, 1995), 118-37.

---. '"It's Happening Inside": The Individual and Changing Consciousness in White's Fiction'. In *Patrick White: A Critical Symposium*, edited by R. Shepherd and K. Singh (Adelaide: Centre for Research in the New Literatures in English, 1978), 34-40.

---. 'A Paler Shade of White'. *Age Saturday Extra*, 19 July, 1986, 13.

---. *Patrick White: Fiction and the Unconscious*. (Melbourne: O.U.P., 1988). Reviewed by V. Brady, *Age Saturday Extra*, 27 February, 1988, 12 and *ABR*, No. 98, 1988, 38-40; R.F. Brissenden, *Weekend Australian, Weekend Magazine*, 19-20 March, 1988, 18; M. Dunning, *Australian Studies*, No. 3, 1989, 151-57; L. Kramer, *Southerly*, 49, No. 2, 1989, 247-49; A.P. Riemer, *S.M.H.*, 5 March, 1988, 69; R. Shepherd, *AUMLA*, 75, 1991, 110-13.

---. 'Patrick White: Misconceptions about Jung's Influence'. *A.L.S.*, IX, 245-46.

---. 'Patrick White, 1912-1990: A Critical Appreciation'. *Quadrant*, 34, No. 11, 1990, 8-10.

---. 'Patrick White: The Great Mother and her Son'. *Journal of Analytical Psychology*, XXVIII, 1983, 165-83.

---. 'Patrick White's *Voss*: The Teller and the Tale'. *Southern Review*, XVIII, No. 3, 1985, 251-71.

---. 'A Search for a New Ethic: White's *A Fringe of Leaves*'. In *South Pacific Images*, edited by Chris Tiffin (St Lucia: SPACLALS, 1978), 186-95. Reprinted in *Prophet from the Desert: Critical Essays on Patrick White*, edited by John McLaren (Melbourne: Red Hill Press, 1995), 63-72.

---. 'The Secret of the Black Rose: Spiritual Alchemy in Patrick White's *The Aunt's Story*'. *Adelaide A.L.S. Working Papers*, II, No. 2, 1977, 36-78.

Tanner, Godfrey. 'The Road to Jerusalem'. *Nimrod*, II, No. 1, 1964, 33-9. Contains material on *The Aunt's Story*.

Tasker, John. 'Notes on *The Ham Funeral*'. *Meanjin*, XXIII, No. 3, 1964, 299-302. Discusses White's dramatic style.

Taylor, Andrew. 'Patrick White's *The Ham Funeral*'. *Meanjin*, XXXII, 1973, 270-78.

---. 'White's Short Stories'. *Overland*, No. 31, 1965, 17-19.

Teetzmann, Karin. *Patrick White und die journalistische Literaturkritik in der Bundesrepublik Deutschland im Vergleich mit Grossbritannien*. (Duisburg: Gilles & Francke, 1993).

Thomas, Daniel. 'Painting's Influence on Literature'. *S.M.H.*, 14 September, 1976, 7. Roy de Maistre and White.

Thomas, Glen. '"Am I Not a Person?": Character and Narrative in Patrick White's *The Aunt's Story*'. *Commonwealth Review* 3.2, 1991-92, 105-18. Reprinted in *Australian Literature Today*, edited by R. K. Dhawan and David Kerr (New York: Indian Society for Commonwealth Studies/Advent Press, 1993), 105-18.

---. 'Patrick White and Murray Bail: Appropriations of "The Prodigal Son"'. *A.L.S.*, 15.1, 1991, 81-86.

Thomson, A.K. 'Patrick White's *The Tree of Man*'. *Meanjin*, XXV, 1966, 21-30.

Tiffin, Helen. 'New Concepts of Person and Place in *The Twyborn Affair* and *A Bend in the River*'. In *A Sense of Place in the New Literatures in English*, edited by Peggy Nightingale (St Lucia: U.Q.P., 1986), 22-31.

---. 'Recuperative Strategies in the Post-Colonial Novel'. *Span*, No. 24, 1987, 27-45. Revised version 'Recuperative Strategies: George Lamming's *Natives of My Person* and Patrick White's *A Fringe of Leaves*' printed in Diana Brydon and Helen Tiffin, *Decolonising Fictions* (Sydney: Dangaroo P., 1993), 77-88.

Turner, George. 'Looking at a Portrait: An approach to *Flaws in the Glass*'. *Overland*, No. 87, 1982, 20-27.

Turner, Ian. 'The Parable of Voss'. In *An Overland Muster*, edited by S. Murray-Smith (Brisbane: Jacaranda Press, 1965), 71-75. Reprinted from *Overland*, No. 12, 1958, 36-7.

Wainwright, J.A. '"The Real Voss as Opposed to the Actual Leichhardt": Biography, Art, and Patrick White'. *Antipodes*, 7.2, 1993, 139-41.

Wallach, Rick. 'Allegories of Fiction in Patrick White's Early Novels'. In *Prophet from the Desert: Critical Essays on Patrick White*, edited by John McLaren (Melbourne: Red Hill Press, 1995), 138-48.

---. 'On the Limits of Archetypal Criticism'. *Antipodes*, 6.2, 1992, 133-38.

Walsh, William. 'Fiction as Metaphor: The Novels of Patrick White'. *Sewanee Review*, LXXXII, 1974, 197-211.

---. 'Patrick White'. In his *A Manifold Voice: Studies in Commowealth Literature*. (London: Chatto & Windus, 1970), 86-125.

---. *Patrick White's Fiction*. (Sydney: Allen & Unwin, 1978). Reviewed by L. Clancy, *Age*, 11 March, 1978, 26; J. Colmer, *Australian*, 15 April, 1978, 8; G. Core, *Sewanee Review*, LXXXVII, 1979, ii-iv, vi; J. Croft, *A.L.S.*, IX, 1979, 128-29; J.H. McDowell, *Modern Fiction Studies*, XXIV, 1978/79, 661; R. Munro, *ABR*, No. 2, 1978, 27.

---. *Patrick White: Voss*. (London: Edward Arnold, 1976). Studies in English Literature. Reviewed by J. Colmer, *A.L.S.*, VIII, 1978, 372-74; J. Pilling, *Journal of Commonwealth Literature*, XII, No. 3, 1978, 89-92; M. Thorpe, *English Studies*, LVIII, 1977, 556.

---. 'Patrick White: The Latest Phase'. *Echos du Commonwealth*, No. 3, 1976, 42-51.

---. 'Patrick White's Vision of Human Incompleteness'. *Journal of Commonwealth Literature*, No. 7, 1969, 127-32. Review of *The Solid Mandala*.

Walters, Margaret. 'Patrick White'. *New Left Review*, II, 1963, 37-50.

Ward, Jill. 'Patrick White's *A Fringe of Leaves*: History and Fiction'. *A.L.S.*, VIII, 1978, 402-18.

Warren, Thomas L. 'Patrick White: The Early Novels'. *Modern Fiction Studies*,

XXVII, No. 1, 1981, 121-39.
---. 'Patrick White's *The Living and the Dead* - A Struggle for Identity'. *Antipodes*, 8.1, 1994, 37-40.
Waten, Judah. 'Marxism and Australian Literature'. *Issue*, I, No. 1, 1971, 8-10.
Watson, Betty L. 'Patrick White, Some Lines of Development: *The Living and the Dead* to *The Solid Mandala*'. *A.L.S.*, V, 1971, 158-67.
Watson, Moira. 'Herbert Dyce Murphy: The Fact behind Patrick White's Fiction'. *ABR*, 137, 1991, 4-7.
Wattie, Nelson. 'Patrick White as a Dramatist'. In *Drama im Commonwealth*, edited by Gerhard Stilz (Tubingen: Gunter Narr, 1981), 41-50.
Webby, Elizabeth. *Modern Australian Plays*. Horizon Studies in Literature. (Sydney: Sydney UP in association with O.U.P., 1990). Includes discussion of *Signal Driver*.
Weigel, John A. *Patrick White*. (Boston: Twayne Publishers, 1983). Twayne's World Authors series - 711. Reviewed by T.P. Coakley, *Newsletter of the A.A.A.L.S.*, II, No. 1, 1986, 11-12; B. Kiernan, A.LS., XII, No. 3, 1986, 417-21; N.J. Richey, *World Literature Today*, No. 58, 1984, 668-669.
Whaley, Susan. 'Food for Thought in Patrick White's Fiction'. *WLWE*, XXII, 1983, 197-212.
Whitman, Robert F. 'The Dream Plays of Patrick White'. *Texas Studies in Literature and Language*, XXI, 1979, 240-59.
Wiersma, Stanley M. 'The German Poems in Patrick White's *Voss*'. *Notes and Queries*, XXXIV, No. 1, 1987, 60.
Wilding, Michael. 'Patrick White: the Politics of Modernism'. *RANAM* (Recherches Anglaises et Nord-Americaines, Strasbourg), 24, 1991, 163-70. Reprinted in *Prophet from the Desert: Critical Essays on Patrick White*, edited by John McLaren (Melbourne: Red Hill Press, 1995), 24-33.
Wilkes, G.A. 'An Approach to Patrick White's *The Solid Mandala*'. *Southerly*, XXIX, 1969, 97-110.
---. 'Patrick White's *The Tree of Man*'. *Southerly*, XXV, No. 1, 1965, 23-33. Reprinted in *Ten Essays on Patrick White*, edited by G.A. Wilkes (Sydney: A.& R., 1970), 21-33.
---. 'A Reading of Patrick White's *Voss*'. *Southerly*, XXVII, 1967, 159-173. Reprinted in *Ten Essays on Patrick White*, edited by G.A. Wilkes (Sydney: A.& R., 1970), 127-44.
Wilkes, G.A. (ed.). *Ten Essays on Patrick White, Selected from Southerly (1964-67)*. (Sydney: A.& R., 1970). Essays virtually unrevised except for J.F. Burrows, 'The Short Stories of Patrick White'. Individual essays can be found under their authors' names. Reviewed by J.B. Beston, *Makar*, VI, No. 4, 1970, 43-46; J. Colmer, *A.L.S.*, V, 1971, 110-12; J. Drury, *Library Review*, XXIII, Nos. 1-2, 1971, 60-61; M. Jones, *S.M.H.*, 12 September, 1970, 18; B. Kiernan, *Australian*, 22 August, 1970, 19; J. Pilling, *Journal of Commonwealth Literature*, XII, No. 3, 1978, 89-92; C. Semmler, *Hemisphere*, XV, No. 2, 1971, 18-19.
Willbanks, Ray. 'Patrick White at Seventy-Five'. *Antipodes*, II, No. 1, 1988, 31-32.
Williams, Mark. 'Containing Continents: the Moralized Landscapes of Conrad, Greene, White and Harris'. *Kunapipi*, VII, No. 1, 1985, 34-45.
---. 'Countries of the Mind: Patrick White's Australia, Malcolm Lowry's Canada'. *WLWE*, XXV, No. 1, 1985, 127-137.
---. 'The "English" Patrick White: The 1930's Context of *The Living and the Dead*'. *Westerly*, XXXIII, No. 1, 1988, 69-76.
---. *Patrick White*. (Basingstoke: Macmillan, 1993). Reviewed by D. Coad, *World Literature Today*, 68.2, 1994, 426.
Williamson, Kristin. 'Slashes from Patrick White'. *National Times*, 25-31 October, 1981, 24-25.
Wilson, R.B.J. 'The Rhetoric of Patrick White's "Down at the Dump"'. In *Bards, Bohemians, and Bookmen*, edited by Leon Cantrell (St Lucia: U.Q.P., 1976), 281-88.

---. '"The Splinters of a Mind Make a Whole Piece': Patrick White's *The Eye of the Storm*'. In *Studies in the Recent Australian Novel*, edited by K.G. Hamilton (St Lucia: U.Q.P., 1978), 61-83.

Wolf, Volker. 'A Note on the Reception of Patrick White's Novels in German Speaking Countries (1957-1979)'. *A.L.S.*, XI,983, 108-19.

Wolfe, Peter. *Laden Choirs: The Fiction of Patrick White*. (Lexington, Kentucky: The University Press of Kentucky, 1983). Reviewed by G. Dutton, *ABR*, No. 69, 1985, 26-27; B. Kiernan, *A.L.S.*, XII, No. 3, 1986, 417-21; B. King, *Newsletter of the A.A.A.L.S.*, II, No. 1, 1986, 11; P. Quartermaine, *Notes and Queries*, N.S., XXXIII, No. 4, 1986, 568-569; N.J. Richey, *World Literature Today*, No. 58, 1984, 668-669; W.J. Schneick, *Contemporary Literature*, XXV, 1984, 374-78; D.J. Tacey, *Meridian*, IV, No. 1, 1985, 49-53.

Wolfe, Peter, ed. *Critical Essays on Patrick White*. (Boston, Mass.: G.K. Hall, 1990). Reviewed by M. Harris, *Antipodes*, 4.2, 1990, 143.

Wood, Susan A. 'The Power and Failure of "Vision" in Patrick White's *Voss*'. *Modern Fiction Studies*, XXVII, No. 1, 1981, 141-58.

Yang, William. *Patrick White: The Late Years*. (Chippendale, NSW: Pan Macmillan, 1995). Mainly photographs.

WHITEHEAD, CHARLES

Critical Material

Turnbull, Clive. 'Mulberry Leaves: The Story of Charles Whitehead'. *Australian Lives* (Melbourne: Cheshire, 1965), 1-22.

WICKHAM, ANNA

Collection

The Writings of Anna Wickham, Free Woman and Poet. Edited by R.D. Smith (London: Virago, 1984).

Reviewed by N. Braybrooke, *Age Saturday Extra*, 21 July, 1984, 15; D. Davis, *T.L.S.*, 10 August, 1984, 900; A. Horner, *PN Review*, No. 43, 1984, 62-63; S. Walls, *Weekend Australian Magazine*, 26-27 May, 1984, 19.

WILDING, MICHAEL

Fiction

Aspects of the Dying Process. (St Lucia: U.Q.P., 1972). Paperback Prose, 1.

Reviewed by B. Bennett, *Westerly*, No. 4, 1972, 66-67; D.R. Burns, *Bulletin*, 16 Sepember, 1972, 48-50; A.R. Chisholm, *Age*, 23 Sepember, 1972, 14; G. Curtis, *Makar*, VIII, No. 3, 1972, 48-49; P. Dunn, *Nation Review*, 14-20 October, 1972, 1549; B. Jefferis, *S.M.H.*, 114 October, 1972, 23; B. Kiernan, *Australian*, 9 September, 1972, 33; W.A. Murray, *ABR*, XI, 1973, 72-73; D.J. O'Hearn, *Overland*, No. 56, 1973, 60-61; *T.L.S.*, 13 July, 1973, 797; H. Rosenbloom, *National Times*, 28 October-3 November, 1972, 64.

Book of the Reading. (Brooklyn: Paper Bark P., 1994).
Reviewed by I. Syson, *Overland*, 140, 1995, 83-85.

Great Climate. (London; Boston: Faber and Faber, 1990). Published in US as *Her Most Bizarre Sexual Experience* (New York: W.W. Norton, 1990).
Reviewed by V. Brady, *ABR*, 131: 40-41; D. Davison, *Weekend Australian*, 4-5 May, 1991, Review 5; D. Durrant, *London Magazine*, 31.1&2, 1991, 137-40; D. Graham, *Antipodes*, 6.1, 1992, 89; J. Hanrahan, *Age*, 25 May, 1991, Saturday Extra 7; I. Maver, *Westerly*, 36.3, 1991, 125-26; N. Obradovic, *World Literature Today*, 65.3, 1991, 543-44; P. Trikha, *Literary Criterion*, 30.1&2, 1995, 141-43.

Living Together. (St Lucia: U.Q.P., 1974). Paperback Prose.
Reviewed by W. Billeter, *Etymspheres*, series I, No. 2, 1975, 56-57; D. Gilbey,

Southerly, XXXVI, 1976, 450-54; C. Harrison-Ford, *Australian*, 14 September, 1975, 39 and *Stand*, XVI, No. 3, 1975, 43; E.S. Lindsay, *Issue* (Adelaide), IV, No. 14, 1974, 56-57; R. McConchie, *Overland*, No. 60, 1975, 83-85; R. Nicholls, *Age*, 23 November, 1974, 19; D. Stewart, *S.M.H.*, 19 October, 1974, 13.

The Man of Slow Feeling: Selected Short Stories. (Ringwood, Vic.: Penguin, 1985).
Reviewed by H. Hauge, *Kunapapi*, VIII, No. 3, 1986, 137-138; B. Jefferis, *Weekend Australian Magazine*, 21-22 December, 1985, 12; S. Moore, *ABR*, No. 79, 1986, 13-14; D. Myers, *Age Saturday Extra*, 15 February, 1986, 14; C.K. Stead, *S.M.H.*, 8 February, 1986, 47; G. Windsor, *Bulletin*, 14 January, 1986, 44-45.

Pacific Highway. (Sydney: Hale & Iremonger, 1982).
Reviewed by R. Barnes, *National Times*, 11-17 July, 1982, 22; M. Beresford, *Union Recorder*, LXII, No. 12, 1982, 7; V. Brady, *ABR*, No. 44, 1982, 27; G. Dutton, *Bulletin*, 6 July, 1982, 53-54; G. Turner, *Age Saturday Extra*, 7 August, 1982, 14.

The Paraguayan Experiment. (Ringwood, Vic.: Penguin, 1984).
Reviewed by G. Burns, *ABR*, No. 74, 1985, 14-15; L. Clancy, *Age Saturday Extra*, 29 June, 1985, 15; G. Dutton, *Bulletin*, 28 May, 1985, 92, 94; K. England, *Advertiser*, 18 May, 1985, 7; A. Field, *Age Monthly Review*, V, No. 5, 1985, 8; H. Hauge, *Kunapipi*, VIII, No. 3, 1986, 137-138; B. Jefferis, *Weekend Australian Magazine*, 18-19 May, 1985, 14; F. Kellaway, *Overlund*, No. 101, 1985, 103-104; P. Lewis, *Stand Magazine*, XXVII, No. 3, 1986, 57; V. Sen, *Canberra Times*, 8 June, 1985, 18; C. Traill, *Union Recorder* (Sydney), LXV, No. 7, 1985, 15; J. Williams, *Fremantle Arts Centre Broadsheet: Books*, IV, No. 5, 1985, 2.

The Phallic Forest. (Sydney: Wild & Woolley, 1978).
Reviewed by J. Bedford, *National Times*, 14 October, 1978, 38; B. Clunies Ross, *Kunapipi*, I, No. 2, 1979, 179-80; G. Dutton, *Bulletin*, 31 October, 1978, 76, 78; P. Edmonds, *Australasian Small Press Review*, Nos. 7-8, 1979, 64; N. Jillett, *Age*, 9 September, 1978, 27; P. Lewis, *Stand*, XX, No. 4, 1979, 73; M. Macdonald, *24 Hours*, III, No. 9, 1978, 71; R. McDonald, *ABR*, No. 6, 1978, 17; E. Perkins, *LiNQ*, VII, Nos. 2-3, 1979, 112-13; C. Symes, *Makar*, XIV, No. 3, 1980, 54-55; P. Ward, *Weekend Australian Magazine*, 28-29 October, 1978, 9.

Reading the Signs. (Sydney: Hale & Iremonger, 1984).
Reviewed by L. Clancy, *ABR*, No. 70, 1985, 23; A. Field, *Age Monthly Review*, V, No. 5, 1985, 8; M. Harrison, *Look & Listen*, I, No. 9, 1985, 91; F. Kellaway, *Overland*, No. 101, 1985, 103-104; P. Lewis, *Stand Magazine*, XXVII, No. 3, 1986, 57; A. Mitchell, *Weekend Australian Magazine*, 19-20 January, 1985, 12; D. Myers, *S.M.H.*, 2 February, 1985, 40.

Scenic Drive. (Sydney: Wild & Woolley, 1976).
Reviewed by S. Hall, *Australian*, 2 October, 1976, 32; B. Jefferis, *S.M.H.*, 25 September, 1976, 17; J. Maddocks, *Quadrant*, XXI, No. 2, 1977, 77-78; J. McLaren, *Overland*, No. 68, 1977, 65; R. Nicholls, *Age*, 4 December, 1976, 23.

The Short Story Embassy. (Sydney: Wild & Woolley, 1975).
Reviewed by D. Douglas, *Union Recorder*, LV, No. 13, 1975; R. Garfitt, *T.L.S.*, 9 April, 1976, 445; D. Gilbey, *Southerly*, XXXVI, 1976, 454-57; C. Harrison-Ford, *Age*, 7 June, 1975, 17; G. Hutchinson, *Makar*, XI, No. 3, 1975, 42-51; M. Macleod, *S.M.H.*, 19 April, 1975, 15; P. Rappolt, *Canberra Times*, 8 August, 1975, 10; E. Riddell, *Australian*, 7 June, 1975, 29; N. Stender, *San Francisco Review of Books*, March, 1977, 18-19; A. Summers, *Advertiser*, 5 July, 1975, 18.

This Is for You. (Sydney: A.& R., 1994).
Reviewed by L. Hard, *Voices*, 5.1, 1995, 108-12; L. Hergenhan, *Imago*, 7.2, 1995, 90-92; B. Hoogendoorn, *Redoubt*, 20, 1995, 125-27; M. Jones, *S.M.H.*, 3 December, 1994, Spectrum 10A; F. McCombie, *Notes & Queries*, March, 1995, 131-32; M. McGirr, *ABR*, 165, 1994, 24; N. Obradovic, *World Literature Today*, 69.2, 1995, 429-30; F. Parigi, *Antipodes*, 9.1, 1995, 44-45; A. Riemer, *Age*, 21 Jan., 1995, Saturday Extra 7; M. Sharkey, *Weekend Australian*, 24-25 September, 1994, Review 7; I. Syson, *Overland*, 140: 83-85; P. Trikha, *Literary Criterion*, 30.1&2, 1995, 143-44.

Under Saturn: Four Stories. (Moorebank, N.S.W.: Black Swan Australia, 1988).
Reviewed by H. Daniel, *ABR*, No. 108, 1989, 30-31; D. English, *Australian*, 28-29 January, 1989, Weekend 6; P. Fuller, *Canberra Times*, 4 March, 1989, B4; J. MacGregor, *Age Saturday Extra*, 11 February, 1989, 14. H. Zengos, *Antipodes*, 3, 1989, 145.

The West Midland Underground. (St Lucia: U.Q.P., 1975). Paperback Prose 9.
Reviewed by L. Cataldi, *Nation Review*, 12-18 December, 1975, 236; A.R. Chisholm, *Age*, 18 October, 1975, 19; S. Dawson, *Australian*, 15 November, 1975, 40; C. Harrison-Ford, *S.M.H.*, 18 October, 1975, 19; G. Hutchinson, *Makar*, XI, No. 3, 1975, 42-51; B. Kiernan, *National Times*, 2-7 August, 1976, 36-37.

Non-Fiction

Political Fictions. (London: Routledge and Kegan Paul, 1980; Sydney: Hale and Iremonger, 1984).
Reviewed by T. Eagleton, *Meanjin*, 40, 1981, 383-88; L.T. Hergenhan, *A.L.S.*, 10, 1982, 413; B. Hill, *National Times*, 19-25 October, 1980, 55; K. Goldsworthy, *Australian*, 17-18 January, 1981.

Social Visions. (Sydney: Sydney Studies in Society and Culture, 1993).
Reviewed by D. Brooks, *Literature and Aesthetics*, 4, 1994, 121-4; J. Lucas, *T.L.S.*, 25 March, 1994, 25; F. McCombie, *Notes and Queries*, March 1995, 131-2; S. Monod, *Etudes Anglaises*, 48, 1995, 75; I. Syson, *Overland*, 140, 1995, 83-5; T. Youngs, *Critical Survey*, 6, 1994, 291-3.

'Basics of a Radical Criticism'. *Island Magazine*, No. 12, 1982, 36-37.
'I Wish I'd Written That'. *S.M.H.*, 9 January, 1982, 34.
'Literary Critics and Mass Media Culture'. *Dissent*, No. 18, 1967, 4.
'Now You See It, Now You Don't'. *S.M.H.*, 19 July, 1975, 18. Series: 'An Author Speaks'.
[Statement in Response to Questionnaire]. *A.L.S.*, X, 1981, 238.

Critical Material

Albahari, David. 'Michael Wilding'. *A.L.S.*, IX, 1980, 321-27. Interview, translated from Yugoslav periodical. First published as 'Ostavljam Stvari Otvorenim' [I'm Keeping Things Open]. *Knizevna rec* (Belgrade) 25 September, 1979. See also letter from Tom Shapcott, *A.L.S.*, IX, 1980, 567-69.
Brophy, Kevin and Lysenko, Myron. 'Talking Together - an Interview with Michael Wilding'. *Going Down Swinging*, No. 3, 1981, 50-62.
Cantrell, Leon. 'The New Novel: David Ireland's *The Unknown Industrial Prisoner*, Michael Wilding's *The Short Story Embassy*, and Frank Moorhouse's *The Electrical Experience*'. In *Studies in the Recent Australian Novel*, edited by K.G. Hamilton (St Lucia: U.Q.P., 1978), 225-57.
Clunies Ross, Bruce. 'A New Version of Pastoral: Developments in Michael Wilding's Fiction'. *A.L.S.*, XI, 1983, 182-94.
---. 'Paradise, Politics and Fiction: The Writing of Michael Wilding'. *Meanjin*, XLV, No. 1, 1986, 19-27.
Gillard, G.M. 'The New Writing: Whodunnit?'. *Meanjin*, XL, 1981, 167-74.

Giuffre, Giulia. 'An Interview with Michael Wilding'. *Southerly*, XLVI, No. 3, 1986, 313-21.

Graham, Don. 'Koka Kola Kulture: Reflections Upon Things American Down Under'. *Southwest Review*, 78.2, 1993, 231-44. Includes discussion of Michael Wilding and Frank Moorhouse.

Harrison-Ford, Carl. 'The Short Stories of Wilding and Moorhouse'. *Southerly*, XXXIII, 1973, 167-78.

Krausmann, Rudi. 'A Reluctant Moralist'. *Aspect*, Spring, 1975, 21-24. Interview.

Obradovic, Nadezda. 'Interview with Michael Wilding'. *Riding Out: New Writing from around the World*. Edited by M. Jurgensen, (Brisbane: Outrider/Phoenix, 1994), 200-11. Also published, with minor changes, as 'Talking with Michael Wilding' in *Antipodes*, 8.1, 1994, 9-13.

Maver, Igor. 'O My America, My Newfoundland, Australia...'. Interview *Acta Neophilologica* (Ljubljana), 28, 1995, 75-80.

Parigi, Frank. 'Frank Moorhouse and Michael Wilding - and Internationalism'. *Antipodes*, 8.1, 1994, 15-20.

Smith, Martin. 'Author, Critic, Radical, Michael Wilding'. *Campaign*, No. 23, 1977, 23-24.

Vauthier, Simone. 'Lost and Found: The Narrative and the Descriptive in Michael Wilding's "What I Was Like, Sometimes"'. *Journal of the Short Story in English* (U. d'Angers), No. 12, 1989, 63-76.

Vauthier, Simone. 'Reading the Signs of Michael Wilding's "Knock, Knock"'. In *European Perspectives: Contemporary Essays on Australian Literature*, edited by Giovanna Capone (*A.L.S.* 15.2 (special issue)/ St. Lucia: U.Q.P., 1991), 128-39.

WILLIAMSON, DAVID

Drama

Brilliant Lies. (Sydney: Currency Press, 1993).
Reviewed by P. Fitzpatrick, *Australasian Drama Studies*, 24, 1994, 200-03.

The Club. (Sydney: Currency Press, 1978).
Reviewed by A. Godfrey-Smith, *ABR*, No. 2, 1978, 20-21; F. Kelly, *Weekend Australian Magazine*, 5-6 August, 1978, 9.

Collected Plays, Volume One. (Sydney: Currency Press, 1986).
Reviewed by B. Kiernan, *Australasian Drama Studies*, No. 8, 1986, 125-28; E. Perkins, *LiNQ*, XIII, No. 3, 1985, 62-66.

Collected Plays, Volume Two. (Sydney: Currency Press, 1993).
Reviewed by P. Fitzpatrick, *ABR*, 165, 1994, 50-51.

The Coming of Stork: Jugglers Three: What If You Died Tomorrow? (Sydney: Currency Press; London: Eyre Methuen, 1974).
Reviewed by L. Radic, *Age*, 7 September, 1974, 20.

Dead White Males. (Sydney: Currency Press, 1995).
Reviewed by J. Hibberd, *ABR*, 174, 1995, 18-19.

The Department. Introduction by Rodney Fisher. (Sydney: Currency Press; London: Eyre Methuen, 1975).
Reviewed by L. Radic, *Age*, 1 November, 1975, 20.

Don's Party. Introduction by John Clark; preface by H.G. Kippax (Sydney: Currency Press; London: Eyre Methuen, 1973). Currency Playtexts Series 2.
Reviewed by R. Cavan, *Plays and Players*, XXI, No. 11, 1974, 55; K. Jamieson, *Makar*, X, No. 1, 1974, 46-50; M. Pettigrove, *Canberra Times*, 30 August, 1974, 11; L. Radic, *Age*, 9 February, 1974, 15.

Emerald City. (Sydney: Currency Press, 1987).
Reviewed by A. Cromwell, *Antipodes*, 3.2, 1989, 149; D. Emmerson, *ABR*, 140,

1992, 25-26; J. Hall, *Bulletin*, 13 December, 1988, 20-21; S. McKernan, *Australasian Drama Studies*, Nos. 12-13, 1988, 203-206.

A Handful of Friends. Introduction Rodney Fisher (Sydney: Currency Press, 1976).
Reviewed by K. Brisbane, *24 Hours*, II, No. 4, 1977, 56.

Money and Friends. (Sydney: Currency Press, 1992).
Reviewed by D. Emmerson, *ABR*, 140, 1992, 25-26; V. Kelly, *Australasian Drama Studies*, 22, 1993, 133-38.

The Perfectionist. (Sydney: Currency Press, 1983).
Reviewed by P. Adams, *Weekend Australian Magazine*, 26-27 October, 1985, 11; K. Ferres, *LiNQ*, XI, No. 1, 1983, 76-79; H. Hewitt, *Canberra Times*, 21 May, 1983, 13; M. Lord, *ABR*, No. 54, 1983, 29; A. Sykes, *Australasian Drama Studies*, II, No. 1, 1983 126-27; A.L. Urban, *Australian*, 30 October, 1985, 12; J. Weir, *Meridian*, IV, No. 1, 1985, 94-95.

The Removalists. With notes on authority & violence past & present by Ian Turner, Frank Galbally and Kerry Milte. Further comment by Bruce Petty. Director's notes by John Bell. Edited by Sylvia Lawson (Sydney: Currency Press, 1972).
Reviewed by R. Blair, *Nation Review*, 25-30 November, 1972, 201; A. Kruse, *Southerly*, XXXIII, 1973, 243-44; A.A. Phillips, *Meanjin*, XXXII, 1973, 191-93; L. Radic, *Age*, 30 September, 1972, 14; D. Rowbotham, *Courier Mail*, 14 October, 1972, 15; R. Wissler, *Makar*, IX, No. 1, 1973, 45-48.

Sanctuary. (Sydney, Currency Press, 1994).
Reviewed by S. Clews, *ABR*, 168, 1995, 54-55.

Siren. (Sydney: Currency Press, 1991).
Reviewed by A. Cromwell, *Antipodes*, 7.1, 1993, 70-72; D. Emmerson, *ABR*, 140, 1992, 25-26; V. Kelly, *Australasian Drama Studies*, 22, 1993, 133-38.

Sons of Cain. (Sydney: Currency Press, 1985).
Reviewed by B. Kiernan, *Australasian Drama Studies*, No. 8, 1986, 125-28.

Top Silk. (Sydney: Currency Press and Festival of Sydney, 1989).
Reviewed by D. Varney, *Australasian Drama Studies*, 19, 1991, 120-24.

Travelling North. (Sydney: Currency Press, 1980).
Reviewed by M. Lord, *ABR*, No. 23, 1980, 23; J. McCallum, *Theatre Australia*, V, No. 6, 1981, 44; P. Pierce, *Tasmanian Review*, No. 5, 1980, 39; A. Sykes, *CRNLE Reviews Journal*, No. 1, 1981, 38-40.

Non-Fiction

'Failed Footballer'. *Kunapipi*, I, No. 2, 1979, 123-27. Autobiographical.
'*The Removalists*: A Conjunction of Limitations'. *Meanjin*, XXXIII, 1974, 413-17.
'Shafts from the Wings'. *National Times*, 7-12 February, 1977, 26-28. On theatre and film criticism.

Critical Material

News reports on *Evening Standard* award in *Canberra Times*, 23 January, 1974, 21, and *S.M.H.*, 23 January, 1974, 12. Details of Williamson's career in *Australian*, 10 April, 1974, 14, *S.M.H.*, 18 September, 1974, 7, *Age*, 16 November, 1974, 2.
'"As Close as I Can Get to Realism..."': An Interview with David Williamson'. *Farrago*, 23 March, 1973, 13.
'A Bit of a Saint, a Bit of a Lecher, a Barb-Witted Recorder of Wild Life in Suburbia'. *Australian Playboy*, November, 1979, 35-60.
'The Contented Playwright: David Williamson Talks about his Reasons for Staying in Australia Instead of Following the Herd Overseas'. *Australian*, 27 April, 1976,

Magazine 6, 10-11.
'David Williamson'. *Kunapipi*, I, No. 2, 1979, 127-36. Interview.
'Out of the Wasteland'. *Walkabout*, March, 1974, 61. Abridged from the *Age*.
Aiton, Douglas. 'Chills Off-Stage, Then Curtain-Up'. *Age*, 26 July, 1975, 12.
Armstrong, Madelaine. 'David Williamson's *The Club*'. *Quadrant*, XXII, No. 3, 1978, 71.
Arnold, Roslyn. 'Agressive Vernacular: Williamson, Buzo and the Australian Tradition'. *Southerly*, XXXV, 1975, 385-96.
Baker, Candida. 'David Williamson'. In her *Yacker: Australian Writers Talk About Their Work* (Sydney: Picador, 1986), 290-315.
Beresford, Bruce. 'Don's Party; From Play to Film'. *Theatre-Australia*, I, No. 5, 1976-1977, 32-33.
Beston, Rose Marie. 'Sexual Antagonisms in David Williamson's *Jugglers Three*'. *Refractory Girl*, No. 4, 1973, 42-43.
Blundell, Graeme. 'Don's Party Then and Now'. *Theatre-Australia*, I, No. 5, 1976-1977, 34-37.
Brisbane, Katharine. 'David Williamson - The Looming Giant'. *This Australia*, VI, No. 2, 1987, 33-36.
---. 'Thermodynamics to Theatre'. *Hemisphere*, XX, No. 2, 1976, 8-12.
Brooks, Geraldine. 'Williamson: "I Don't Want to End in Barry Humphries Land"'. *S.M.H.*, 1 August, 1981, 41. Interview.
Butler, Chris. '"Attacks Hard to Swallow": Interview'. *Advertiser*, 14 November, 1974, 1.
Carrick, Noel. 'Dramatist with a Critical Mirror'. *Australia Now*, XII, No. 4, 1987, 26-27.
Carroll, Dennis. 'David Williamson'. In *Post-Colonial English Drama: Commonwealth Drama since 1960*, edited by Bruce King (London: Macmillan; New York: St Martin's, 1992), 35-49.
Clavaud, Evelyne. 'An Interview with David Williamson'. *Commonwealth* (Paris), X, No. 2, 1988, 63-69.
Dare, Tim. 'Theatre Group Shelved His Prize-winning Play, but Olivier Thought It Too Good to be Ignored'. *Australian*, 18 April, 1972, 3. George Devine award for *The Removalists*. See also related reports, *Australian*, 15 June, 1972, 1; *S.M.H.*, 15 June, 1972, 12.
Davidson, Jim. 'David Williamson'. *Meanjin*, XXXVIII, 1979, 173-86. Interview. Reprinted in his *Sideways from the Page* (Melbourne: Fontana, 1983), 164-83.
Duigan, Virginia. 'David (*Don's Party*) Williamson Takes His Timely Success Easily'. *National Times*, 25-30 December, 1972, 13.
Eccles, Jeremy. 'David Williamson'. *Centre Stage*, 1, No. 5, 1987, 10-11.
Ellis, Bob. 'Veges take the Piss out of you'. *Nation Review*, 19-25 November, 1976, 107.
Evans, Michael Morton. 'Open Road to a Perfect Marriage'. *Weekend Australian Magazine*, 10 11 July, 1982, 11.
Farwagi, Peta Lyn. 'Williamson: No Place like Home'. *Weekend Australian Magazine*, 26-27 January, 1980, 10.
Fitzpatrick, Peter. *Williamson*. (North Ryde, N.S.W.: Methuen Australia, 1987). Reviewed by H. McNaughton, *Australasian Drama Studies*, 18, 1991, 220-24.
---. *David Williamson's* The Club: *A Critical Introduction*. (Sydney: Currency Press, 1980). Reviewed by G.D., *English in Australia*, No. 65, 1983, 65-66.
---. 'David Williamson'. In his *After 'The Doll'*. (Melbourne: Edward Arnold, 1979), 112-28.
Griffiths, Gareth. 'Experiments with Form in Recent Australian Drama'. *Kunapipi*, II, No. 1, 1980, 71-73.
Hall, Sandra. 'Williamson's Year'. *Bulletin*, 15 July, 1972, 39.

Hoad, Brian. 'The Theatre as Political Tool'. *Bulletin*, 18 August, 1973, 35-38.
Hogan, Christine. 'Attentive UK Audiences Pleasure for Playwright'. *S.M.H.*, 8 February, 1980, 25. Interview.
---. *'The Club* Takes Top Awgie'. *S.M.H.*, 15 July, 1978, 5. Also reported in *Canberra Times*, 15 July, 1978,3.
Jones, Dave. 'Dave Jones Talks with David Williamson'. *Cinema Papers*, (Richmond, Vic.), 1974, 6-9 and 93.
Jones, Margaret. 'Awfully Unique'. *S.M.H.*, 3 July, 1972, 7.
---. 'Writing His Way to Success: Three Plays Staged in Past Twelve Months'. *S.M.H.*, 3 January, 1973, 9.
Kavanagh, Paul and Kuch, Peter. 'What are the Shades of Grey?' *Southerly*, XLVI, No. 2, 1986, 131-41. Reprinted in Paul Kavanagh and Peter Kuch, eds. *Conversations: Interviews with Australian Writers*, (North Ryde, NSW: Collins/A.& R, 1991).
Kemp, Kevon. 'An Australian Goer, Says Harry M. Miller'. *National Times*, 7-12 August, 1972, 23.
Kiernan, Brian. 'An Australian Playwright Goes to Washington'. *Antipodes*, 3.2, 1989, 105-07.
---. 'David Williamson: Satiric Comedies'. In *International Literature in English: Essays on the Major Writers*, edited by Robert L. Ross (New York: Garland, 1991), 659-67.
---. *David Williamson: A Writer's Career*. (Richmond, Vic.: Heinemann, 1990). Reviewed by J. Davidson, *Weekend Australian*, 28-29 April, 1990, Weekend 5; R. Fotheringham, *A.L.S.*, 15.3, 1992, 241-43; M. Lord, *ABR*, No. 121, 1990, 20-21; L. Radic, *Age*, 7 April, 1990, Saturday Extra 11.
---. 'Comic-Satiric-Realism: David Williamson's Plays Since *The Department*'. *Southerly*, XLVI, No. 1, 1986, 3-18.
---. 'The Games People Play: The Development of David Williamson'. *Southerly*, XXXV, 1975, 315-29.
___. 'Satiric Comedies'. In *International Literature in English,* edited by Robert Ross (New York: Garland, 1991), 659-67.
Lewis, Peter. 'After *The Perfectionist*'. *London Magazine*, N.S. XXIII, Nos 5-6, 1983, 70-82. Interview.
Lurie, Morris. 'It's Only Play Money'. *Age Saturday Extra*, 5 June, 1982, 3.
Macainsh, Noel. 'Footy in Berlin - David Williamson's *The Club* - First German Performance'. *LiNQ*, VII, No. 1, 1979, 80-81.
McCallum, John. 'A New Map of Australia: The Plays of David Williamson'. *A.L.S.*, XI, 1984, 342-54.
McGregor, Craig. 'David Williamson: What do We do About Our Guilt?' *National Times*, 24-29 October, 1977, 39-40.
McGuinness, P.P. 'A Master of Black Humour Talks on Authoritarianism, Plays and Films: Williamson Looks for His Screenplay Role'. *National Times*, 21-26 August, 1972, 20.
Morgan, Patricia. 'David: A Question of Class'. *Courier-Mail*, 4 March, 1975, 5.
Morley, Sheridan. 'Sydney Actors Play Another Town'. *Times*, 2 September, 1974, 11.
O'Brien, Geraldine. 'After Plays, Mini-Series and Film Scripts, now David's to Be a Director'. *S.M.H.*, 3 March, 1984, 44. Interview.
Page, Robert. 'David Williamson and Frank Wilson Travelling North'. *Theatre-Australia*, IV, No. 2, 1979, 11.
Parsons, Philip. 'This World and the Next'. *London Magazine*, N.S. XX, Nos. 8-9, 1980, 121-26. *Travelling North*.
Prerauer, Maria. 'Making Power Plays on the Laws of Libel'. *Weekend Australian Magazine*, 3-4 December, 1977, 8.

Radic, Leonard. 'David Williamson Goes On Writing'. *Age*, 28 April, 1973, 19. Reprinted in *Advertiser*, 27 October, 1973, 25.

---. 'Playwright Travels North for a Change of Style'. *Age*, 28 April, 1979, 23.

Rice, Cecilia. 'David Williamson. Plays into Films'. *Cinema Papers*, No. 32, 1981, 123-27.

Roberts, Alan. 'Is this Really our Club, Mate?' *Advertiser*, 20 May, 1978, 24.

Rowbotham, David. 'State May Ban New Hit Play'. *Courier-Mail*, 2 March, 1973, 1. See also ensuing reports and correspondence, *Courier-Mail*, 3-5 March, 1973. *Don's Party*.

Seymour, Alan. 'Coming Up From Down Under'. *Plays and Players*, XX, No. 11, 1973, 24-25.

Smith, Margaret. 'The New Theatrical Consciousness'. *Nation Review*, 11-17 November, 1972, 119.

Sykes, Alrene. 'Australian Bards and British Reviewers'. *A.L.S.*, VII, 1975, 39-49.

Sykes, Jill. 'Biting the Hand that Films Him'. *Sun-Herald*, 30 November, 1980, 37.

Tarrant, Deborah. 'Williamson on the Box'. *National Times*, 29 June-5 July, 1984, 28. Interview.

Thomas, Keith. 'Williamson'. *Weekend Australian Magazine*, 5-6 May, 1979, 5. Interview.

Thomas, Mark. 'David Williamson'. In his *Australia in Mind: Thirteen Influential Australian Thinkers* (Sydney: Hale & Iremonger, 1989), 181-93.

Tobin, Meryl. 'David Williamson: Playwright - A Profile'. *Westerly*, No. 2, 1975, 39-41.

Veitch, John. 'David Williamson, Talking to John Veitch'. *Sunday Telegraph*, 1 October, 1972, 74.

Wertheim, Albert. 'Comedy of Manners in Australia: The Plays of David Williamson'. *Essays in Theatre*, 7.2, 1989, 99-109.

White, Sally. 'David is New Goliath of Australian Theatre'. *Age*, 19 July, 1972, 2.

Willbanks, Ray. *Speaking Volumes: Australian Writers and Their Work*. (Ringwood, Vic.: Penguin, 1991). Includes interview with Williamson.

Williams, Bruce. 'David Williamson: The Powerless Audience'. *Meridian*, V, No. 2, 1986, 23-32.

Williams, Graham. 'Playwright Bows Out with Attack on ABC Chiefs'. *S.M.H.*, 27 July, 1979, 3.

Yuille, Anne. 'Will Success Spoil David Williamson?'. *Cleo*, No. 10, 1973, 22-26.

Zuber-Skerrit, Ortrun ed. *David Williamson*. (Amsterdam: Rodopi, 1988). Reviewed by R. Corballis, *Modern Drama*, 34.1, 1991, 163-67; A. Cromwell, *Antipodes*, 3.2, 1989, 149; B. King, *World Literature Today*, 63.2, 1989, 363; H. McNaughton, *Australasian Drama Studies*, 18, 1991, 220-24.

WINTON, TIM

Fiction

Blood and Water: Stories. (London: Picador, 1993).
Reviewed by P. Kemp, *T.L.S.*, 3 September, 1993, 23.

Cloudstreet. (Melbourne: McPhee Gribble, 1991; St.Paul, Mn.: Greywolf, 1992).
Reviewed by M. Anthony, *Westerly*, 37.2, 1992, 91-93; L. Clancy, *Weekend Australian*, 20-21 April, 1991, Review 4; H. Daniel, *Age*, 30 March, 1991, Saturday Extra 6; C. Franklin, *Southerly*, 51.4, 1991, 152-63; M. Halligan, *ABR*, 129, 1991, 3-4; K. Jennings, *S.M.H.*, 30 March, 1991, 29; D. Myers, *LiNQ*, 19.1, 1992, 133-36; J. Olshan, *New York Times Book Review*, 23 August, 1992,

15; P. Pierce, *Bulletin*, 9 April, 1991, 104; J. Stephens, *Australian Society*, 10.6, 1991, 40; C. Thompson, *Scripsi*, 7.3, 1992, 119-24; B. Watzke, *Antipodes*, 5.2, 1991, 147.

In the Winter Dark. (Fitzroy, Vic.: McPhee Gribble, 1988).
Reviewed by D. Bird, *ABR*, No. 102, 1988, 27-28; T. Code, *Mattoid*, No. 32, 1988, 107-11; P. Craven, *Weekend Australian*, 9-10 July, 1988, Weekend 16; H. Daniel, *Age Saturday Extra*, 25 June, 1988, 14; W. Goulston, *Antipodes*, 5.1, 1991, 68; B. Hickey, *Span*, No. 26, 1988, 112-116; P. Magee, *Redoubt*, No. 3, 1988, 76-78; P. Pierce, *Bulletin*, 12 July, 1988, 110-111; A. Rombouts, *Phoenix Review*, No. 4, 1989, 11-15.

Minimum of Two. (Fitzroy, Vic.: McPhee Gribble/Penguin, 1987; New York: Atheneum, 1988).
Reviewed by E. Campion, *Fremantle Arts Review*, II, No. 6, 1987, 14; J. Carroll, *Age Saturday Extra*, 7 March, 1987, 12; D. English, *ABR*, No. 89, 1987, 10-11; S. McKernan, *Bulletin*, 31 March, 1987, 80-81; D. Parker, *Phoenix Review*, No. 2, 1987/88, 110-112; C. Peake, *Times on Sunday*, 1 March, 1987, 30; R. Sorensen, *Lot's Wife*, XXVII, No. 4, 1987, 30; T. Tate, *Westerly*, XXXII, No. 3, 1987, 93-95; R. Willbanks, *World Literature Today*, 63.1, 1989, 161.

The Riders. (Sydney: Macmillan, 1994; New York: Scribner's, 1995).
Reviewed by R. Brain, *T.L.S.*, 17 Feb., 1995, 20; D. Coad, *World Literature Today*, 69.2, 1995, 430-431; J. Coe, *London Review of Books*, 17.9, 1995, 21; M. Fraser, *S.M.H.*, 3 September, 1994, Spectrum 11A; B. Hill, *Age*, 3 September, 1994, Saturday Extra 7; N. Krauth, *ABR*, 164, 1994, 15-16; R. Lucas, *Bulletin*, 27 September, 1994, 105; D. Myers, *Quadrant*, 38.12, 1994, 79-80; M. Sharkey, *Weekend Australian*, 17-18 September, 1994, Review 6; J. Turner, *Antipodes*, 9.2, 1995, 148-49.

Scission. (Ringwood, Vic.: McPhee Gribble/Penguin, 1985).
Reviewed by R. Blaber, *CRNLE Reviews Journal*, No. 2, 1985, 32-33; K. England, *Advertiser Saturday Review*, 9 March, 1985, 7; R. Gostand and S. Cassidy, *Social Alternatives*, V, No. 4, 1986, 56-57; S. McKernan, *ABR*, No. 71, 1985, 21; A. Mitchell, *Weekend Australian Magazine*, 16-17 March, 1985, 11; V. Sen, *Canberra Times*, 10 March, 1985, 8; R. Stone, *S.M.H.*, 13 April, 1985, 40; G. Turner, *Age Saturday Extra*, 16 March, 1985, 14.

Shallows. (Sydney: Allen & Unwin, 1984; St Paul, Mn.: Graywolf, 1995).
Reviewed by P. Burgess, *S.M.H.*, 26 January, 1985, 37; M. Eldridge, *Canberra Times*, 9 March, 1985, 18; K. England, *Advertiser Saturday Review*, 8 December, 1984, 9; S. Erickson, *New York Times Book Review*, 3 August, 1986, 18; T. Forshaw, *Quadrant*, XXIX, No. 3, 1985, 77-79; H. Garner, *Helix*, Nos. 21-22, 1985, 110-111; N. Keesing, *ABR*, No. 68, 1985, 12-14 (See also letter by T. Hogan in response in *ABR*, No. 70, 1985, 42); R. Milliss, *Overland*, No. 102, 1986, 74-77; D. Myers, *Age Saturday Extra*, 1 December, 1984, 18; W. Noonan, *Weekend Australian Magazine*, 22-23 December, 1984, 11; M. Sanderson, *T.L.S.*, 10 October, 1986, 1130; R. Willbanks, *World Literature Today*, 69.1, 1995, 221; V. Wright, *Weekend Australian Magazine*, 19-20 October, 1985, 20.

That Eye The Sky. (Melbourne: McPhee Gribble; London: Weidenfeld & Nicolson, 1986).
Reviewed by J. Crace, *T.L.S.*, 13 June, 1986, 645; H. Garner, *ABR*, No. 78, 1986, 20-21; F. Kellaway, *Overland*, No. 104, 1986, 64-65; P. Kincaid, *British Book News*, April, 1986, 242-43; P. Kirk, *Margin*, No. 20, 1988, 23-25; N. Lee-Jones, *Antipodes*, I, No. 2, 1987, 115; D. Matthews, *Island Magazine*, No. 31, 1987, 75; A. Mitchell, *Australian*, 4 March, 1986, 10; E. Riddell, *National Times*, 18-24 April, 1986, 31; V. Sen, *Canberra Times*, 10 May, 1986, B2; B. Williams, *Courier-Mail Magazine: The Great Weekend*, 22 March, 1986, 6.

Non-Fiction
Land's Edge. Photographs by Trish Ainslie and Roger Garwood. (Chippendale, NSW: Pan Macmillan, 1993). Photographs of the West Australian Coast prefaced by a partly autobiographical essay.
Reviewed by R. Cassin, *Voices* 4.1, 1994, 118-22; B. Farmer, *Age*, 26 February, 1994, Saturday Extra 9; M. McGirr, *ABR*, 159, 1994, 17-18.
'Why I Write As I Do'. *Australian Literary Quarterly*, 6-7 June, 1987, 6.

Critical Material
Bennett, Bruce. 'Nostalgia for Community: Tim Winton's Essays and Stories'. In *Tilting at Matilda: Literature, Aborigines, Women and the Church in Contemporary Australia*, edited by Dennis Haskell (South Fremantle, WA: Fremantle Arts Centre P., 1994), 60-73.
Buffi, Roberta. 'Perth and Naples: Two "Corrupted" Mediterranean Cities'. *Westerly*, 39.4, 1994, 14-19. Includes discussion of the representation of Perth in works by Jolley and Winton.
Despoja, Shirley Stott. 'Good On You Tim. You're a Winner at 24'. *Advertiser*, 20 May, 1985, 2.
Edelson, Phyllis Fahrie. 'The Role of History In Three Contemporary Novels' [by Robert Drewe, Tim Winton and Nigel Krauth]. *Journal of Popular Culture*, 23, No. 2, 1989, 63-71.
Jacobs, Lyn. 'Looking into the Light: Tim Winton's *That Eye the Sky*'. In *Making Connections: Introducing Nine Texts for Senior English Students*, edited by Graham Tulloch and Annie Greet (Adelaide: CRNLE/Flinders University of South Australia and Trinity Gardens: SAETA, 1990), 49-58.
Kroll, Jeri. 'An Interview with Tim Winton'. *Southerly*, 51.2, 1991, 222-24.
Matthews, Brian. 'Burning Bright: Impressions of Tim Winton'. *Meanjin*, XLV, No. 1, 1986, 83-93.
Rossiter, Richard. 'Speaking to Adults, Speaking to Children: Tim Winton's *Cloudstreet* and *Lockie Leonard, Human Torpedo*'. *Southerly*, 53.3, 1993, 92-99.
---. and Lyn Jacobs, eds. *Reading Tim Winton*. (Pymble, NSW: A.& R., 1993). Reviewed by V. Armanno, *Imago*, 6.2, 1994, 95-96; P. Pierce, *A.L.S.*, 16.3, 1994, 352-55.
Sayers, Stuart. 'Why Hurry, When You Are a Success at 24?' *Age Saturday Extra*, 25 May, 1985, 17.
Turner, John P. 'Tim Winton's *Shallows* and the End of Whaling in Australia'. *Westerly*, 38.1, 1993, 79-85.
Watzke, Beth. 'Where Pigs Speak in Tongues and Angels Come and Go: A Conversation with Tim Winton'. *Antipodes*, 5.2, 1991, 96-98.
Willbanks, Ray. *Speaking Volumes: Australian Writers and Their Work*. (Ringwood, Vic.: Penguin, 1991). Includes interview with Winton.

WONGAR, B.
(Also writes as Sreten Bozic)
Fiction
Babaru. (Urbana: University of Illinois Press, 1982). Republished North Ryde, NSW: A.& R., 1991).
Reviewed by R. Adams, L. Kohut, E. Webber and J. Noyce, *ABR*, 130, 1991, 8-9; P. Excell, *Antipodes*, 5.2, 1991, 52; M. Jurgensen, *Outrider*, I, No. 1, 1984, 175-6; W.P. Keen, *Studies in Short Fiction*, XX, 1983, 327-28.
Gabo Djara. (South Melbourne: Macmillan, 1988). First published New York: Dodd, Mead & Co., 1987.
Reviewed by S. Amanuddin, *Antipodes*, II, No. 1, 1988, 58-59; M. Gorra, *New York Times Book Review*, 6 September, 1987, 27.

Karan: A Novel of the Australian Hinterland. (South Melbourne: Macmillan; New York: Dodd, Mead & Co., 1985).
Reviewed by S. Amanuddin, *Newsletter of the A.A.A.L.S.*, II, No. 1, 1986, 10; D. Whittingham, *LiNQ*, XV, No. 3, 1987, 95-97.

The Last Pack of Dingoes. (Pymble, NSW: A.& R., 1993).
Reviewed by L. Altomari, *Antipodes*, 7.2, 1993, 152; J. Donnelly, *ABR*, 150, 1993, 14; J. Finlayson, *Age*, 17 April, 1993, Saturday Extra 7; R. Ross, *World Literature Today*, 68.3, 1994, 633-34.

Marngit. (North Ryde, NSW: A.& R., 1992).
Reviewed by J. Hanrahan, *ABR*, 138, 1992, 15-16.

Raki. (Pymble, NSW: A.& R., 1994).
Reviewed by J. Huggins, *Imago*, 7.1, 1995, 89-90; S. Masson, *ABR*, 166, 1994, 12-13; D. Matthews, *Weekend Australian*, 31 December 1994-1 January 1995, Review 6; R. Ross, *World Literature Today*, 69.2, 1995, 431 and *Antipodes*, 9.1, 1995, 46-47. See also letter by H. Demidenko and Wongar's and Masson's replies, *ABR*, 175, 1995, 8-9.

The Track to Bralgu. (London: Cape, 1978). Republished Pymble, NSW: A.& R., 1992.
Reviewed by R. Brain, *T.L.S.*, 13 October, 1978, 1142; H. Frizell, *S.M.H.*, 30 September, 1978, 17; J. Hanrahan, *ABR*, 138, 1992, 15-16; H. Hewitt, *Canberra Times*, 16 December, 1978, 18; S. Hosking, *CRNLE Reviews Journal*, 1, 1992, 14-17; T. Keneally, *New York Times Book Review*, 25 June, 1978, 14-15; J. Larkin, *Age*, 21 October, 1978, 26.

The Trackers. (Melbourne: Outback Press, 1978).
Reviewed by P. Pierce, *National Times*, 11 November, 1978, 53-54; R. Stow, *T.L.S.*, 21 December, 1975, 150.

Walg. (New York: Dodd, Mead, 1984).
Reviewed by R. Drewe, *Weekend Australian Magazine*, 3-4 March, 1984, 13.

    Critical Material
Connor, Michael and David Matthews. 'In the Tracks of the Reader, in the Tracks of B. Wongar'. *Meanjin*, 48, No. 4, 1989, 713-21.
Dobrez, Livio. 'Wongar's Metamorphoses: *The Track to Bralgu*'. In *Aspects of Australian Fiction: Essays Presented to John Colmer*, edited by Alan Brissenden (Nedlands, W.A.: University of Western Australia Press, 1990), 161-72.
Gunew, Sneja. 'Culture, Gender and the Author-Function: "Wongar's" Walg'. *Southern Review*, XX, No. 3, 1987, 261-270. Reprinted in *Australian Cultural Studies: A Reader*, edited by John Frow and Meaghan Morris (St Leonards, NSW: Allen & Unwin, 1993), 3-14.
Prentice, Chris. 'Grounding Postcolonial Fictions: Cultural Constituencies, Cultural Credentials and Uncanny Questions of Authority'. In *Postcolonial Fictions*, edited by Michèle Drouart (special issue in two volumes including SPACLALS Conference Proceedings, *SPAN*, 36, 1993), 100-12. Discusses Wongar and Kerri Hulme.
Ross, Robert. 'The Track to Armageddon in B. Wongar's Nuclear Trilogy'. *World Literature Today*, 64.1, 1990, 34-8.
Velickovic, Dusan. 'Sreten Bozic's "Aboriginal Myths": A Specific Form of "Field-Work"'. In *Australian Papers: Yugoslavia, Europe and Australia*, edited by Mirko Jurak (Ljubljana: Edvard Cardelj University, 1983), 95-98.
Willbanks, Ray. *Speaking Volumes: Australian Writers and Their Work*. (Ringwood, Vic.: Penguin, 1991). Includes interview with Wongar.

WRIGHT, JUDITH

Fiction

The Nature of Love. (Melbourne: Sun Books, 1966).
Reviewed by B. Beaver, *S.M.H.*, 24 December, 1966, 13; L.J. Clancy, *Australian*, 1 July, 1967, 13; J. Colmer, *ABR*, VI, 1967, 44; M. Dunlevy, *Canberra Times*, 7 January, 1967, 11; N. Keesing, *Bulletin*, 21 January, 1967, 31.

The River and the Road. (Melbourne: Lansdowne Press, 1966).
Reviewed by B. Eastman, *Canberra Times*, 10 June, 1967, 12; D. Hall, *ABR*, V, 1966, 243; G. Lehmann, *Bulletin*, 10 December, 1966, 58.

Poetry

Alive: Poems 1971-72. (Sydney: A.& R., 1973).
Reviewed by R. Adamson, *Australian*, 7 July, 1973, 37 (see also letter to the editor by G. Sinclair, 25 July, 1973, 12); M. Dunlevy, *Canberra Times*, 1 September, 1973, 13; K. England, *Advertiser*, 14 July, 1973, 20; C. Ferrier, *Semper Floreat*, XLIII, No. 13, 1973, 7; K.L. Goodwin, *Makar*, IX, No. 2, 1973, 38-40; P. Porter, *Observer* (London), 7 May, 1978, 33; P. Roberts, *S.M.H.*, 14 July, 1973, 24; C. Sansom, *Nation Review*, 17-23 August, 1973, 1392 (see also letter to the editor by K. Russell, *Nation Review*, 24-30 August, 1973, 1399); R.A. Simpson, *Age*, 30 June, 1973, 18.

Birds. Second edition. (Sydney: A.& R., 1967).
Reviewed by B. Beaver, *S.M.H.*, 9 March, 1968, 16; A. Brissenden, *Adelaide Advertiser*, 14 October, 1967, 14; V. Smith, *Bulletin*, 9 December, 1967, 84.

Collected Poems, 1942-1970. (Sydney: A.& R., 1971).
Reviewed by M. Dunlevy, *Canberra Times*, 1 May, 1971, 14; R. Dunlop, *Poetry Australia*, No. 40, 1971, 52-53; C. Harrison-Ford, *Nation*, 15 May, 1971, 21; E. Irvin, *S.M.H.*, 15 May, 1971, 23; F. Kellaway, *Overland*, Nos. 50-51, 1972, 90-92; A. Pollard, *Journal of Commonwealth Literature*, X, No. 1, 1975, 71-77; C. Semmler, *Hemisphere*, XV, No. 12, 1971, 40-41; K. Slessor, *Daily Telegraph* (Sydney), 15 May, 1971, 12; D. Stewart, *Sunday Australian*, 25 April, 1971, 30; C. Wallace-Crabbe, *Age*, 3 April, 1971, 13.

Collected Poems 1942-1985. (Pymble, NSW: A.& R., 1994).
Reviewed by H. Brophy, *Australian Multicultural Book Review*, 3.1, 1995, 38-40; H. Cam, *S.M.H.*, 12 March, 1994, Spectrum 11A; G. Dutton, *ABR*, 164, 1994, 44-45; C. Pollnitz, *Weekend Australian*, 23-24 April, 1994, Review 7; J. Strauss, *Age*, 7 May, 1994, Saturday Extra 8; S. Walker, *Westerly*, 39.2, 1994, 91-93.

The Double Tree: Selected Poems 1942-1976. (Boston: Houghton Mifflin, 1978).
Reviewed by W.H. Pritchard, *New York Times Book Review*, 26 November, 1978, 62, 64.

Five Senses. (Sydney: A.& R., 1963).
Reviewed by R.F. Brissenden, *Australian Quarterly*, XXXVI, 1964, 85-91; *T.L.S.*, 10 September, 1964, 842; T. Sturm, *Landfall*, XIX, 1965, 391-3.

The Flame Tree = Aogiri no ki. With parallel translation into Japanese by Sakai Nobuo and Meredith McKinney. Introduced by Mark O'Connor. (Canberra: National Library of Australia, 1993). Reviewed by H. Cam, *S.M.H.*, 12 March, 1994, Spectrum 11A; L. Morton, *ABR*, 164, 1994, 47-48; C. Pollnitz, *Weekend Australian*, 23-24 April, 1994, Review 7; J. Strauss, *Age*, 7 May, 1994, Saturday Extra 8; S. Walker, *Westerly*, 39.2, 1994, 91-93.

Fourth Quarter. (Sydney: A.& R., 1976).
Reviewed by R. Gray, *S.M.H.*, 30 April, 1977, 19; D. Green, *Nation Review*, 16-22 June, 1977, 16; J. Griffin, *Advertiser*, 23 April, 1977, 27; [S.E. Lee], *Southerly*, XXXIX, 1979, 436-39; P. Porter, *Observer* (London), 7 May, 1978, 33; R.A. Simpson, *Age*, 5 November, 1977, 24; J. Tranter, *Weekend Australian*

Magazine, 6-7 August, 1977, 13; J. Vasudeva, *Luna*, II, No. 2, 1977, 40-43; S. Walker, *Westerly*, No. 4, 1977, 104-10.

A Human Pattern: Selected Poems. (North Ryde, N.S.W.: 1990; Manchester: Carcanet, 1993).
Reviewed by F. Adcock, *T.L.S.*, 5 February, 1993, 23; J. Bridge, *Westerly*, 37.1, 1992, 89-90; H. Cam, *S.M.H.*, 28 April, 1990, 74; W. Wynne, *ABR*, No. 122, 1990, 39-41.

Judith Wright Reads from Her Own Work. (St Lucia: U.Q.P., 1973). Poets on Record, 9. Record and booklet. Booklet includes notes by Judith Wright and selected bibliography.
Reviewed by D. Rowbotham, *Courier-Mail*, 12 January, 1974, 2.

The Other Half. (Sydney: A.& R., 1966).
Reviewed by R.F. Brissenden, *Australian*, 5 November, 1966, 8; J. Colmer, *ABR*, VI, 1966, 6; J.M. Couper, *Poetry Magazine*, No. 1, 1967, 28-30; D. Douglas, *Age*, 3 December, 1966, 23; R. Dunlop, *Poetry Australia*, No. 14, 1967, 44-46; D. Green, *Canberra Times*, 8 October, 1966, 11; A. King, *Meanjin*, XXVII, 1968, 177; S.E. Lee, *Southerly*, XXVII, 1967, 66-67; J. McAuley, *S.M.H.*, 8 October, 1966, 20; V. Smith, *Bulletin*, 22 October, 1966, 57-8; A. Taylor, *Overland*, No. 36, 1967, 43; D.M. Thomas, *London Magazine*, VII, No. 2, 1967, 70-73.

Phantom Dwelling. (North Ryde, N.S.W.; London: A.& R., 1985).
Reviewed by H. Heseltine, *Overland*, No. 105, 1986, 46-53; P. Lugg, *Canberra Times*, 3 May, 1986, B3; P. Mead, *Island Magazine*, No. 29, 1986, 32-40; R. Morse, *PN Review*, XIII, No. 5, 1987, 93-94; E. Riddell, *Bulletin*, 13 May, 1986, 105-06; J. Rodriguez, *S.M.H.*, 22 November, 1986, 46; J. Strauss, *Age Saturday Extra*, 8 February, 1986, 14.

Woman to Man. (Sydney: A.& R., 1967). First published Sydney: A.& R., 1949.
Reviewed by D. Douglas, *Age*, 16 March, 1968, 13; D. Green, *Canberra Times*, 27 April, 1968, 10.

        Non-Fiction
Born of the Conquerors: Selected Essays. (Canberra: Aboriginal Studies P., 1991).
Reviewed by V. Brady, *Overland*, 129, 1992, 78-80.

The Cry for the Dead. (Melbourne: O.U.P., 1981).
Reviewed by R. Anderson, *Courier-Mail*, 27 February, 1982, 27; P. Biskup, *ABR*, No. 44, 1982, 11; E. Campion, *Bulletin*, 15 December, 1981, 80-82; A. Clark, *S.M.H.*, 30 January, 1982, 40; P. Corris, *National Times*, 15-21 November, 1981, 38; D.J. Enright, *Listener*, 19 August, 1982, 21; J. Factor, *Arena*, No. 61, 1982, 177-81; P. Levi, *PN Review*, No. 31, 75-76; T.B. Millar, *Canberra Times*, 12 June, 1982, 18; P. Read, *Aboriginal History*, VII, 1983, 211-13; I. Richards, *Advertiser*, 9 January, 1982, 25; M. Roe, *Island Magazine*, No. 11, 1982, 3-4; C.D. Rowley, *Australian Journal of Politics and History*, XXVIII, 1982, 487; A.W. Sheppard, *Hemisphere*, XXVII, 1982, 31; R. Stow, *T.L.S.*, 15 October, 1982, 1123; D. Watson, *Meanjin*, XLI, 1982, 138-46.

The Generations of Men. (Sydney: ETT Imprint, 1995). Revised edition with new foreword by author. First published Melbourne: O.U.P., 1959.
Reviewed by A. Riemer, *S.M.H.*, 19 Aug., 1995, Spectrum 13A.

Going on Talking. (Springwood, NSW: Butterfly Books, 1991).
Reviewed by H. Horton, *Imago*, 5.2, 1993, 91-92; C. Pybus, *ABR*, 148, 1993, 12.

Preoccupations in Australian Poetry. (Melbourne: O.U.P., 1965).
Reviewed by R. Burns, *Nation*, 10 July, 1965, 22; E.A.M. Colman, *Poetry Magazine*, No. 4, 1965, 25-9; G. Cross, *S.M.H.*, 17 July, 1965, 14; D. Douglas, *Age*, 12 June, 21; D. Green, *Southern Review*, II, No. 1, 1966, 70-6; G. Johnston,

Australian, 21 August, 1965, 11; L. Kramer, *ABR*, IV, 1965, 159; P. Oettle, *Poetry Australia*, No. 7, 1965, 43-4; A. Porteous, *Bulletin*, 2 October, 1965, 53-4; V. Smith, *A.L.S.*, II, No. 2, 1965, 147-9; T. Sturm, *Landfall*, XX, 1966, 405-9; *T.L.S.*, 30 June, 1966, 574; C. Wallace-Crabbe, *Meanjin*, XXIV, 1965, 371-3.

We Call For a Treaty. (Sydney: Collins/Fontana, 1985).
Reviewed by P. Bayne, *Aboriginal History*, No. 11, Nos. 1-2, 1987, 179-83; B. Hill, *ABR*, No. 95, 1987, 4-6; J. Malone, *Imago*, 1, No. 2, 1989, 62-3; E. Riddell, *Bulletin*, 13 May, 1986, 105-06.
'Brisbane in Wartime'. *Overland*, No. 100, 1985, 64-68. A draft extract from an autobiography in progress.
'Conservation as a Concept'. *Quadrant*, XII, No. 1, 1968, 29-33.
'Critics, Reviewers and Aboriginal Writers'. *Aboriginal History*, 11, Nos. 1-2, 1987, 24-26
'Darkie Point: New England National Park'. *Notes & Furphies*, No. 12, 1984, 6-7. Poem 'Nigger's Leap'.
'I, the Writer'. *Nation Review*, 18-24 November, 1972, 154-55.
'A Letter to Peter Abotomey and Noel Macainsh'. *LiNQ*, VI, No. 2, 1978, 60-62. See 'Noel Macainsh Replies'. *LiNQ*, VI, No. 2, 1978, 63-66. Concerns articles in *LiNQ*, VI, No. 1, about her visit to James Cook University.
'Meaning, Value, and Poetry'. *Meanjin*, XXVII, 1968, 244-50.
'The Poem as Art'. *A.U.L.L.A. 19th Congress. Papers and Proceedings*, 1978, 8-13.
'The Role of Poetry in Education'. *English in Australia*, No. 2, 1966, 35-43. Refers to 'Legend'.
'The Upside-down Hut'. In *The Writer in Australia*, edited by John Barnes (Melbourne: O.U.P., 1969), 331-36. This essay first published *Australian Letters*, III, No. 4, 1961, 30-4.
'Judith Wright: Interview'. *Meanjin*, XLI, 1982, 321-38.

   Critical Material
Fryer Memorial Library, 'Bibliography'. In *Critical Essays on Judith Wright*, edited by A.K. Thomson (Brisbane: Jacaranda, 1968), 1-33.
O'Brien, P. and Robinson, E. *Judith Wright: A Bibliography*. (Adelaide: Libraries Board of South Australia, 1968). Bibliographies of Australian Writers series. Reviewed by H. Anderson, *A.L.S.*, III, 1968, 312-13.
State Library of South Australia. 'Bibliographies of Australian Writers. Supplements'. *Index of Australian Book Reviews*. IV, 1968, 258-62; V, 1969, 262-4; VI, 1970, 330-35; VII, 1971, 301-3; VIII, 1972, 257-69, IX, 1973, 170-82; X, 1974, 184-89; XI, 1975, 235-41.
Walker, Shirley. *Judith Wright*. (Melbourne: O.U.P., 1981). Australian Bibliographies. Reviewed by P. Levi, *PN Review*, No. 31, 1983, 75.

News reports, *Australian*, 12 February, 1974, 12, on her term with the National Estate Commission and *S.M.H.*, 12 October, 1974, 2, on her becoming a A.N.U. Councillor.
'A.N.U. Fellowship for Judith Wright'. *Canberra Times*, 22 June, 1973, 9. Similar report in *Australian*, 30 April, 1973, 11.
'Pirate Copies are "Starving" Poet'. *Courier-Mail*, 22 August, 1978, 9. Report on an address to A.U.L.L.A.
'Women Building a New Australia'. *S.M.H.*, Look! Section, 22 March, 1973, 3.
Abotomey, Peter. 'Class Lecture after a Recent Visit by Judith Wright'. *LiNQ*, VI, No. 1, 1978, 1-5.
Ash, Jennifer. 'Paradise and Australian Women Poets'. *Southerly*, XLVIII, No. 3, 1988, 259-273.

Bennett, Bruce. 'Judith Wright: An Ecological Vision'. In *International Literature in English: Essays on the Major Writers*, edited by Robert L. Ross (New York: Garland, 1991), 205-21.

---. 'Judith Wright, Moralist'. *Westerly*, No. 1, 1976, 76-82.

Beston, John B. 'Judith Wright's "The Surfer" and Gerard Manley Hopkins'. *Southerly*, XXXIV, 1974, 63-66.

Bhushan, Kul. 'Judith Wright's *The Generations of Men* and *The Cry for the Dead*: Two versions of the Colonial History'. In *Critical Interactions: Reading 20th Century Literary Texts*, edited by R.P. Rama (Jaipur: Pointer Publishers, 1992), 89-111.

Brennan, G.A. 'The Aborigine in the Works of Judith Wright'. *Westerly*, No. 4, 1972 46-50.

Bridge, Jenny. 'Landscape and Identity in Judith Wright's Poetry: An Introduction'. *Australian Studies*, No. 4, 1990, 1-19.

Brissenden, R.F. 'Five Senses'. In *Critical Essays on Judith Wright*, edited by A.K. Thomson (Brisbane: Jacaranda, 1968), 105-10. Originally published in *Australian Quarterly*, XXXVI, No. 1, 1964, 85.

---. 'The Poetry of Judith Wright'. In *Critical Essays on Judith Wright*, edited by A.K. Thomson (Brisbane: Jacaranda, 1968), 39-50. Originally published in *Meanjin*, XII, 1953, 255-67.

Brooks, David. 'Judith Wright and the Image'. In *Poetry and Gender: Statements and Essays in Australian Women's Poetry and Poetics*, edited by David Brooks and Brenda Walker (St Lucia: U.Q.P., 1989), 93-104.

Buckley, Vincent. 'The Poetry of Judith Wright'. In *Critical Essays on Judith Wright*, edited by A.K. Thomson (Brisbane: Jacaranda, 1968), 59-74. Originally published in his *Essays in Poetry: Mainly Australian* (Melbourne: M.U.P., 1957).

Butler, N. 'Wright Wrong'. *Nation Review*, 11-17 May, 1973, 907. Letter to the editor.

Chakravarty, Radharani. 'Time and Change in Judith Wright'. *Commonwealth Review*, 2.1-2, 1990-91, 96-112.

Cross, Gustav. 'Australian Poetry in the Sixties'. *Poetry Australia*, No. 5, 1965, 33-8.

Cross, K.G.W. and Marsh, D.R.C. *Poetry Reading and Understanding*. (Melbourne: Cheshire, 1966), 223-8. Discusses 'Bullocky'.

Davidson, Jim. 'Judith Wright'. *Meanjin*, 41, 1982, 321-338. Interview. Reprinted in his *Sideways from the Page* (Melbourne: Fontana, 1983), 391-415.

Dowling, David. 'Judith Wright's Delicate Balance'. *A.L.S.*, IX, 1980, 488-96.

Dunlevy, Maurice. 'Environmental Doom-Watcher and a Poet'. *Canberra Times*, 3 June, 1971, 8.

Ewers, John K. 'The Genius of Judith Wright'. *Westerly*, No. 1, 1968, 42-51.

Foley, Larry. 'All Eyes on the Reef'. *S.M.H.*, 31 August, 1968, 20. Interview with Judith Wright on conservation.

Foster, Susan. 'Poet's First Birthday Party in 39 Years Marks Start of Time for Calm Enjoyment'. *Australian*, 9 June, 1975, 3.

Fremd, Angelika. 'A Terrible Lie: Judith Wright Interviewed by Angelika Fremd'. *Imago*, 1, No. 2, 1989, 27-29.

Gowda, H.H. Anniah. 'Perfected Passions: The Love Poetry of Kamala Das and Judith Wright'. *Literary Half-yearly*, XX, No. 1, 1979, 116-30.

---. 'The Poetry of Judith Wright'. *ACLALS Bulletin*, Series 4, No. 4, 1976, 16-25.

Hall, Rodney. 'Themes in Judith Wright's Poetry'. In *The Literature of Australia*, edited by Geoffrey Dutton. Revised edition (Ringwood, Vic.: Penguin, 1976), 388-405.

Harris, Max. 'Judith Wright'. In *The Literature of Australia*, edited by Geoffrey

Dutton (Adelaide: Penguin Books, 1964), 353-61.

Hay, R.G. 'Judith Wright's Achievements'. In *Critical Essays on Judith Wright*, edited by A.K. Thomson (Brisbane: Jacaranda, 1968), 98-104. Originally published in *Australian Letters*, III, No. 1, 1960, 30-33.

Heseltine, H.P. 'Wrestling With the Angel: Judith Wright's Poetry in the 1950s'. *Southerly*, XXXVIII, 1978, 163-71.

Hope, A.D. *Judith Wright*. (Melbourne: O.U.P., 1975). Australian Writers and Their Work. Reviewed by T. Sturm, *A.L.S.*, VII, 1976, 340; V. Vallis, *T.L.S.*, 9 April, 1976, 432.

Irvin, Margaret. 'Judith Wright's "Dark Gift"'. *Twentieth Century*, XXIII, 1968, 131-34.

Janakiram, Alur. 'Judith Wright on Creativity and the Poetic Task'. *Rajasthan University Studies in English*, XV, 1984, 1982-1983, 69-82.

Jurgensen, Manfred. 'The Poetry of Judith Wright'. *Makar*, VII, No. 2, 1971, 18-35.

Kemeny, Peter George. *Notes and Commentary on Judith Wright's Poetry*. (Perth: Carroll's, 1972).

King, Bruce. 'A.D. Hope and Australian Poetry'. *Sewanee Review*, LXXXVII, 1979, 119-41.

Kohli, Devindra. 'The Crystal Glance of Love: Judith Wright as a Love Poet'. *Journal of Commonwealth Literature*, VI, No. 1, 1971, 42-52.

Kramer, Leonie. 'Judith Wright, Hope, McAuley'. *Literary Criterion* (Mysore), XV, Nos. 3-4, 1980, 83-92.

Lindsay, Philip. 'Poetry in Australia'. In *Critical Essays on Judith Wright*, edited by A.K. Thomson (Brisbane: Jacaranda, 1968), 35-38. Originally published in *Poetry Review*, July-August, 1950, 207-11.

Macainsh, Noel. 'Last Agonies - Some Comments on a Lecture on Judith Wright'. *LiNQ*, VI, No. 1, 1978, 6-11.

---. 'Poetry into Life, Life into Poetry: Judith Wright and the Academy'. *A.L.S.*, IX, 1979, 49-58.

Mares, F.H. 'Judith Wright and Australian Poetry'. *Opinion*, VII, No. 4, 1964, 23-33.

---. 'The Poetry of Judith Wright'. In *Critical Essays on Judith Wright*, edited by A.K. Thomson (Brisbane: Jacaranda, 1968), 88-97. Originally published in *Durham University Journal*, I, No. 2, 1958.

Masel, Carolyn, and Michael Schmidt. 'Judith Wright: A Written Interview'. *PN Review*, 19.1, 1992, 13-20. Reprinted in *Outrider*, [10.1&2], 1993, 311-30.

McAuley, James. 'Some Poems of Judith Wright'. *A.L.S.*, III, 1968, 201-13. Reprinted in *Critical Essays on Judith Wright*, edited by A.K. Thomson (Brisbane: Jacaranda, 1968), 119-30.

McDonald, Roger. 'Judith Wright: From the Ridge to the River'. In his *Gone Bush*, (Sydney: Bantam, 1990), 15-27.

McGregor, Craig (ed.). *In the Making*. (Melbourne: Nelson Australia, 1969), 52-59.

McKernan, Susan. 'The Writer and the Crisis: Judith Wright and David Campbell'. In her *A Question of Commitment: Australian Literature in the Twenty Years After the War* (Sydney: Allen & Unwin, 1989), 141-65.

McKinney, Meredith. 'Getting Wright Right'. *ABR*, 164, 1994, 46-47. On translating Wright's poems into Japanese.

Mezger, Ross. 'Changes in Direction in the Poetry of Judith Wright'. *Teaching of English*, No. 32, 1977, 24-30.

Moore, T. Inglis. 'The Quest of Judith Wright'. In *Critical Essays on Judith Wright*, edited by A.K. Thomson (Brisbane: Jacaranda, 1968), 75-87. Originally published in *Meanjin*, XVII, 1958, 237-50.

Nedeljkovic, Maryvonne. 'The Sense of Reality in Judith Wright's Poetry'. *Commonwealth* (Paris), VI, No. 2, 1986, 15-24.

Page, Geoff. 'Judith Wright'. In his *A Reader's Guide To Contemporary Australian Poetry* (St. Lucia: U.Q.P., 1995), 316-319.

Potter, Nancy. 'Setting Her Signature on the Land: The Poetry of Judith Wright'. *Antipodes*, 3.1, 1989, 37-39.

Rama, R.P. 'The Bewildering Metaphor: Towards a Post-Colonial Reading of Judith Wright's Language Poems'. *Rajasthan University Studies in English*, 21-22, 1989-90, 203-10.

Rexroth, Kenneth. 'What is There to Alienate From?' *Bulletin*, 29 April, 1967, 34. Rexroth's opinion on Hope and Wright: interview with Charles Higham.

Roberts, Greg. 'A Writer with many Causes Keeps up the Fight at 69'. *S.M.H.*, 8 December, 1984, 10-11.

Robinson, Dennis. 'Australia's "Double Aspect" in Judith Wright's *The Generations of Men*'. *Southerly*, XXXIX, 1979, 283-97.

Rowbotham, David. 'Judith Wright, Poet and Conservationist Extraordinary'. *Courier-Mail*, 6 April, 1970, 2. Other reports principally concerned with Judith Wright's work for conservation not listed here.

Rowse, A.L. 'The Voice of Australia: Judith Wright'. *Blackwood's*, CCCXXVII, 1980, 164-73.

Ryan, J.S. 'Judith Wright and the Bushranger: A Haunting'. *Westerly*, No. 4, 1972, 51-54.

---. 'Judith Wright: Those "Aunts in the Close" and the "Remittance Man"'. *Westerly*, No. 4, 1974, 65-69.

Salter, John. 'Re-reading Judith Wright'. *New Literatures Review*, No. 18, 1989, 48-59.

Schmidt, Barbara. 'Die Fruehe Lyrik Judith Wrights und ihre Rezeption'. In her *Die Verordnete Kultur: Stereotypien der australischen Literaturkritik*. (Frankfurt a.M.: Peter Lang, 1989).

Scott, Robert Ian. 'Judith Wright's World-View'. In *Critical Essays on Judith Wright*, edited by A.K. Thomson (Brisbane: Jacaranda, 1968), 51-8. Originally published in *Southerly*, XVII, 1956, 189-95.

Scott, W.N. *Focus on Judith Wright*. (Brisbane: U.Q.P., 1967). Reviewed by *ABR*, VII, 100; S. Edgar, *Canberra Times*, 13 January, 1968, 10; R. Hall, *Australian*, 25 May, 1968, 14; G. Johnston, *Nation*, 20 January, 1968, 21.

Shapcott, Thomas. 'Judith Wright - Her Year'. *Bulletin*, 14 November, 1964, 34.

Sinha, Shalini. 'Judith Wright as Literary Critic'. In *Critical Interactions: Reading 20th Century Literary Texts*, edited by R.P. Rama (Jaipur: Pointer Publishers, 1992), 48-69.

Skrzynecki, Peter. 'Ulysses in New England: A Tribute to Judith Wright'. *Southerly*, 52.3, 1992, 101-06.

Smith, Graeme Kinross. 'Judith Wright'. *Luna*, No. 2, 1976, 18-26. Interview.

Smith, Vivian. 'Australian Poetry in the '60's: Some Mid-Century Notes'. *Balcony*, No. 4, 1966, 46-51.

---. 'Emperiment and Renewal: A Missing Link in Modern Australian Poetry'. *Southerly*, XLVII, No. 1, 1987, 3-18; esp. 12-18.

Somapala, Wijetunga. 'Australia in Poetry'. *Hemisphere*, XII, No. 2, 1968, 7-8.

Strauss, Jennifer. *Judith Wright*. (Melbourne: O.U.P., 1995). Reviewed by M. Costigan, *ABR*, 173, 1995, 50-51; L. Jacobs, *Antipodes*, 9.2, 1995, 161-62; A. Taylor, *Voices*, 5.4, 1995-96, 114-18.

---. 'Modulations of High Seriousness: The Later Poetry of Judith Wright'. In her *Stop Laughing! I'm Being Serious: Three Studies in Seriousness and Wit in Contemporary Australian Poetry*. Monograph/Foundation for Australian Literary Studies 21 (Townsville, Qld.: James Cook University of North Queensland, 1990),

1-29.

---. 'The Poetry of Dobson, Harwood & Wright: "within the bounds of feminine sensibility?"' *Meanjin*, XXXVIII, 1979, 334-49. Reprinted in *Still the Frame Holds: Essays on Women Poets and Writers*, edited by Sheila Roberts and Yvonne Pacheco Tevis (San Bernadino, CA: Borgo P., 1993), 79-99.

Sturm, Terry. 'Continuity and Development in the Work of Judith Wright'. *Southerly*, XXXVI, 1976, 161-76.

Taylor, Andrew. 'Always The Other Half: The Poetry of Judith Wright'. In his *Reading Australian Poetry* (St Lucia: U.Q.P., 1987), 85-97.

Thompson, John. 'Poetry in Australia: Judith Wright'. *Southerly*, XXVII, 1967, 35-44. Transcript of an interview telecast in 1965. First published as 'John Thompson Interviews Judith Wright'. *Opinion*, IX, No. 2, 1965, 40-6. From an A.B.C. interview.

Thomson, A.K. (ed.). *Critical Essays on Judith Wright*. (Brisbane: Jacaranda, 1968). Articles are included under their authors' names. Reviewed by J. Colmer, *A.L.S.*, IV, 1969, 190-93.

---. 'Judith Wright: An Introductory Essay in Interpretation'. In *Critical Essays on Judith Wright*, edited by A.K. Thomson (Brisbane: Jacaranda, 1968), 1-33.

---. 'Judith Wright and Her Poetry'. *Opinion*, VII, 1963, 5-14.

W., D.A. Letter to the Editor. *ABR*, V, 1966, 31.

Walker, R.B. *Old New England: A History of the Northern Tablelands of New South Wales* 1818-1900. (Sydney: Sydney University Press, 1966), 84-7 and passim.

Walker, Shirley. '*The Cry for the Dead*: Judith Wright and the Aborigines'. In *The Writer's Sense of the Past: Essays on Southeast Asian and Australasian Literature*, edited by Kirpal Singh (Singapore: Singapore University Press, 1987), 152-159.

---. *Flame and Shadow: A Study of Judith Wright's Poetry*. (St. Lucia: U.Q.P., 1991). A revised version of her *The Poetry of Judith Wright: A Search for Unity*. Reviewed by J. Bridge, *Westerly*, 37.1, 1992, 89-90; R. Darling, *Antipodes*, 5.2, 1991, 156; P. Mead, *A.L.S.*, 16.2, 1993, 140-51; A. Taylor, *ABR*, 129, 1991, 28-29.

---. 'Herakleitan Elements in the Poetry of Judith Wright'. *Southerly*, XXXV, 1975, 183-91.

---. 'Judith Wright's Linguistic Philosophy - "It's the Word that's Strange"'. *A.L.S.*, VIII, 1977, 7-15.

---. 'Judith Wright's New England Poems: Early and Late'. *Rajasthan University Studies in English*, XV, 1982-1983, 26-32.

---, Judith Wright's Poetic *I Set Upon This Land My Signature*. (Sydney: English Association, Sydney Branch, 1985).

---. 'A Note on Sense-Perception in the Poetry of Judith Wright'. *Westerly*, No. 4, 1973, 56-59.

---. 'The Philosophical Basis of Judith Wright's Poetry'. In *South Pacific Images*, edited by Chris Tiffin (St Lucia: SPACLALS, 1978), 158-72.

---. *The Poetry of Judith Wright: A Search for Unity*. (Port Melbourne: Edward Arnold (Australia), 1980). Reviewed by M. Duwell, *A.L.S.*, X, 1982, 410-12; J. Grant, *Quadrant*, XXV, Nos. 1-2, 1981, 117-18; S. Kobulniczky, *Westerly*, XXV, No. 4, 1980, 82-84; J. Strauss, *ABR*, No. 19, 1981, 31.

---. *Vanishing Edens: Responses to Australia in the Works of Mary Gilmore, Judith Wright and Dorothy Hewett*. Monograph 23. (Townsville, Qld.: Foundation for Australian Literary Studies/James Cook U of North Queensland, 1992). Reviewed by S. Bennett, *Imago*, 5.3, 1993, 95-97; N. Birns, *Antipodes*, 7.2, 1993, 167-68.

Wallace-Crabbe, Chris. 'Matters of Style: Judith Wright and Elizabeth Bishop'. *Westerly*, No. 1, 1978, 53-57.

Waugh, John. 'Judith Wright - In the Wasteland'. *S.M.H.*, 21 February, 1980, 17.

Wilkes, G.A. 'The Later Poetry of Judith Wright'. *Southerly*, XXV, No. 3, 1965, 163-71. Reprinted in *Critical Essays on Judith Wright*, edited by A.K. Thomson (Brisbane: Jacaranda, 1968), 111-18.
Wilson, Richard. 'The Short Stories of Judith Wright'. *A.L.S.*, I, No. 1, 1963, 58-61.
Wright, Dorena. 'Judith Wright. "Brother and Sisters". "Old Man". "Two Old Men"'. In *Australian Poems in Perspective*, edited by P.K. Elkin (St Lucia: U.Q.P., 1978), 141-59.
Wright, Phillip A. *Memories of a Bushwhacker*. (Armidale: printed by University of New England, 1971). Judith Wright's father. Reviewed by J.S. Ryan, *University of New England Bulletin*, No. 33, 1972, 14-15.
Zwicky, Fay. 'Another Side of Paradise: A.D. Hope and Judith Wright'. *Southerly*, XLVIII, No. 1, 1988, 3-21.

WRIGHTSON, PATRICIA

Fiction

Baylet. (London: Hutchinson, 1989).
Reviewed by A. Nieuwenhuizen, *Age*, 11 November, 1989, Saturday Extra 10.

Behind the Wind. (Richmond, Vic.: Hutchinson, 1978 reprinted 1981).
Reviewed by M. Dunkle, *ABR*, 31, 1981, 34-36; M. Dunkle, *ABR*, 39, 1982, 27-29; M. McVitty, Age, 16 January, 1982, 22; D. Zeigler, S.M.H., 24 July, 1982, 38.

The Dark Bright Water. (London, Richmond, Vic.: Hutchinson, 1978).
Reviewed by M. Dugan, *Age*, 10 March, 1978, 28; M. Dunkle, *ABR*, 31, 1981, 34-36; E. Pownall, *National Times*, 14 July, 1979, 32-33; M. Saxby, *S.M.H.*, 24 April, 1979, 19.

Down to Earth. (Ringwood, Vic.: Puffin, 1981). First published London: Hutchinson, 1965.
Reviewed by K. Commins, *S.M.H.*, 30 October, 1965, 19; D. Oberg, *Words'worth*, 15.1, 1982, 49.

The Ice is Coming. (Richmond South, Vic.: Hutchinson, 1977, reprinted 1983).
Reviewed by M. Dunkle, *ABR*, 31, 1981, 34-36 and *ABR*, 54, 1983, 26; Eljayar, *Aboriginal and Islander Identity*, 8.3, 1978. 28; H. Frizell, *S.M.H.*, 10 December, 1977, 19; J. Langton, *New York Times Book Review*, 29 January, 1978, 26; M. Mcleod, *S.M.H.*, 24 December, 1977, 13; W. McVitty, *Age*, 8 July, 1978, 24; M. Saxby, *S.M.H.*, 8 July, 1978, 17; P. Young, *National Times*, 15 July, 1978, 25.

A Little Fear. (Richmond, Vic.: Hutchinson, 1984).
Reviewed by M. Dunkle, *ABR*, 61, 1984, 28-29 and *ABR*, 71, 1985, 30-31; S. McInerney, *S.M.H.*, 30 March, 1985, 46; W. McVitty, *Age*, 24 March, 1984, Saturday Extra 14; T. Thompson, *National Times*, 20-26 July, 1984, 30.

The Nargun and the Stars. (Richmond, Vic.: Hutchinson, 1973).
Reviewed by A. Bower Ingram, *S.M.H.*, 6 October, 1973, 23 and *S.M.H.*, 6 July, 1974, 13; F. King, *Australian*, 21 December, 1974, 20; *T.L.S.*, 23 November, 1973, 1434; C. Storr, *New Stateman*, 9 November, 1973, 699-70.

Night Outside. (Adelaide: Rigby, 1979, reprinted 1980).
Reviewed by M. Dunkle, *ABR*, 28, 1981, 49-50; D. Oberg, *Words'worth*, 13.1, 1980, 62.

An Older Kind of Magic. (London, Melbourne: Hutchinson; New York: Harcourt Brace Jovanovich, 1972).
Reviewed by D. Campbell, *National Times*, 16-21 July, 1973, 24; D. Dugan, *Age*, 7 July, 1973, 20 and *Age*, 13 January 1973, 16; A. Bower Ingram, *S.M.H.*, 14 October, 1972, 23 and *S.M.H.*, 7 July, 1973, 26; F. King, *Australian*, 17

December, 1973, 19; B.J.Manton, *Australian*, 7 July, 1973, 38; D. Orgel, *New York Times Book Review*, 5 November, 1972, 12; A. Read, *National Times*, 16-21 July, 1973, 24; *T.L.S.*, 3 November, 1972, 4325.

The Rocks of Honey. (Richmond South, Vic.: Hutchinson, 1960).
Reviewed by M. Dunkle, *ABR*, 31, 1981, 34-36.

    Critical Material

Dunkle, Margaret. 'Patricia Wrightson: Writer of Legends'. *Overland*, 139, 1995, 16-18.

Gough, John. 'Ice, Dark Water and Wind in Patricia Wrightson's Wirrun Trilogy'. *Idiom*, 19.1, 1984, 13-18.

Hillel, Margot. 'Patricia Wrightson Talks to Margot Hillel'. *ABR*, 167, 1994-95, 58-59.

McVitty, Walter. 'Patricia Wrightson: At the Edge of Australian Vision'. In his *Innocence and Experience: Essays on Contemporary Australian Children's Writers* (Melbourne: Thomas Nelson Australia, 1981), 99-132. Includes notes by Wrightson and bibliography.

Nieuwenhuizen, Agnes. 'Patricia Wrightson'. In her *No Kidding: Top Writers for Young People Talk About Their Work* (Chippendale, NSW: Sun/Pan Macmillan, 1991), 309-38. Interview.

FAY ZWICKY

Fiction

Hostages. (Fremantle: Fremantle Arts Centre Press, 1984).
Reviewed by C. Causley, *Westerly*, 29, No. 1, 1983, 90-91; R. Chimni, *Rajasthan University Studies in English*, No. 15, 1982/83, 109-11; J. Duffy, *Overland*, Nos. 94-95, 1984, 87-88; K. Gelder, *CRNLE Reviews Journal*, No. 1, 1984, 79-82; A. Hildyard, *Island Magazine*, Nos. 18-19, 1984, 40-44; F. Kellaway, *Overland*, No. 93, 1983, 65-66; D. Kerr, *A.B.R.*, No. 55, 1983, 22-23; L.R. Leavis and J.M. Blom, *English Studies*, No. 65, 1984, 441-44; M. Macleod, *Kunapipi*, 6, No. 1, 1984, 79-83; C.K. Stead, *S.M.H.*, 2 July, 1983, 37; E. Webby, *Meanjin*, 42, 1983, 399-400.

Poetry

Ask Me. (St Lucia, Qld.: U.Q.P., 1990).
Reviewed by M. Duwell, *Weekend Australian*, 9-10 July, 1990, Review 8; M. Freiman, *CRNLE Reviews Journal*, No. 1, 1990, 120-30; B. Giles, *Age*, 23 June, 1990, Saturday Extra 9; C.L. Innes, *Australian Studies*, No. 4, 1990, 157-59; J. Kinsella, *Westerly*, 36.3, 1991, 124-25; J. Strauss, *Australian Women's Book Review*, 2, No. 4, 1990, 4-5.

Isaac Babel's Fiddle. (Adelaide: Maximus Books, 1975).
Reviewed by A.J. Ames, *Artlook*, 1, No. 3, 1975, 4, 16; B. Beaver, *S.M.H.*, 28 June, 1975, 16; S.E. Lee, *Southerly*, 36, 1976, 331-56; K.L. Macrae, *New Poetry*, 23, No. 2, 1975, 83; J. Whitehead, *Westerly*, No. 1, 1975, 73-75.

Kaddish and Other Poems. (St Lucia, Qld.: U.Q.P., 1981).
Reviewed by B. Beaver, *S.M.H.*, 6 March, 1982, 45; R.F. Brissenden, *Westerly*, 28, No. 2, 1983, 77-79; G. Dutton, *Bulletin*, 4 May, 1982, 68; M. Duwell, *Weekend Australian*, 31 July-1 August, 1982, Weekend 10; K. Goldsworthy, *Island Magazine*, No. 16, 1983, 43-45; J. McLaren, *A.B.R.*, No. 39, 1982, 21-24; M. Macleod, *Kunapipi*, 5, No. 1, 1983, 101-5 and *Meanjin*, 41, 1982, 406-9 and *Span*, No. 14, 1982, 20-24; P. Neilsen, *Age Saturday Extra*, 4 September, 1982, 15; G. Page, *Quadrant*, 26, No. 8, 1982, 75-77; J. Rodriguez, *Overland*, No. 89, 1982, 60-62.

Poems 1970-1992. (St Lucia: U.Q.P., 1993).
Reviewed by R. Adamson, *Island*, 57, 1993, 61-63; C. Bateson, *Overland*, 134, 1994, 81-83; M. Duwell, *Weekend Australian*, 22-23 January, 1994, Review 7; K. Hart, *Age*, 25 September, 1993, Saturday Extra 8; M. Johnson, *Antipodes*, 7.2, 1993, 150-51; L. McCredden, *ABR*, 152, 1993, 39-40 (see also interview 40-42); V. Muller, *Imago*, 6.1, 1994, 100-02; S. O'Brien, *T.L.S.*, 20 August, 1993, 6; N. Stasko, *Southerly*, 54.3, 1994, 174-79.

Non-Fiction

'Democratic Repression and the Admission of Difference: The Ethnic Strain'. In *The American Model: Influence and Independence in Australian Poetry*, edited by Joan Kirkby (Sydney: Hale & Iremonger, 1982), 84-98.

'The Deracinated Writer: Another Australia'. In *Crisis and Creativity in the New Literatures in English*, edited by Geoffrey Davis and Hena Maes-Jelinek (Amsterdam; Atlanta: Rodopi, 1990), 75-87.

'Vast Spaces Quiet Voices: Chinese Connections in Australian Poetry'. *ABR*, 164, 1994, 34-42.

'A Writer's Journal'. *Southerly*, 54.3, 1994, 6-30.

Critical Material

Gordon, Nancy. 'Fay Zwicky: Interview'. *Opinion*, 5, No. 1, 1976, 11-12.

Kerr, David. 'Writing in the Eighties'. *Westerly*, 29, No. 3, 1984, 59-64. Interview.

Indyk, Ivor. 'Fay Zwicky: The Poet as Moralist'. *Southerly*, 54.3, 1994, 33-50.

Kirkby, Joan. 'Finding a Voice in "this fiercely fathered and unmothered world": The Poetry of Fay Zwicky'. In *Poetry and Gender: Statements and Essays in Australian Women's Poetry and Poetics*, edited by David Brooks and Brenda Walker (St. Lucia, Qld.: U.Q.P., 1989), 175-93.

Linguanti, Elsa. 'On the Shifting Sands of Our Experience: Fay Zwicky's Poetry'. *Southerly*, 54.3, 1994, 51-64.

Maes-Jelinek, Hena. 'An Interview with Fay Zwicky'. *Commonwealth* (France), 13.2, 1991, 115-24.

Page, Geoff. 'Fay Zwicky'. In his *A Reader's Guide To Contemporary Australian Poetry* (St. Lucia: U.Q.P., 1995), 320-324.

Sant, Andrew, ed. *Toads: Australian Writers: Other Work, Other Lives*, edited by Andrew Sant (Sydney: Allen & Unwin, 1992). Collection of autobiographical essays on writing and money. Includes Zwicky.

Willbanks, Ray. 'A Conversation with Fay Zwicky'. *Antipodes*, 3.2, 1989, 135-38.

---. *Speaking Volumes: Australian Writers and Their Work*. (Ringwood, Vic.: Penguin, 1991). Includes interview with Zwicky.

UQP STUDIES IN AUSTRALIAN LITERATURE

Black Words, White Page
Aboriginal Literature 1929-1988
Adam Shoemaker

This is the first comprehensive study of Black Australian literature in English. Combining historical and literary analysis, it attempts to come to terms with the diversity and difference of this new, exciting literature that has been gaining strength since 1929 when David Unaipon became the first published Aboriginal writer. **Winner: 1990 Walter McRae Russell Award.**

Poetry and Gender
Statements and Essays in Australian Women's Poetry and Poetics
edited by David Brooks and Brenda Walker

The exciting diversity of Australian women's poetry and poetics is explored through essays on the work of writers of the twenties and thirties, Aborigines, migrant women and other contemporary poets.

The Folly of Spring
A Study of John Shaw Neilson's Poetry
Cliff Hanna

This is the first comprehensive study of John Shaw Neilson's verse and the first chronological approach to his work. Using all of the available manuscript material, the study focuses on Neilson's lifelong battle with his Presbyterian "thunder-blue God", which eventually pushed him beyond Christianity into pagan myth. **Winner: 1991 Walter McRae Russell Award.**

Strange Country
A Study of Randolph Stow
Anthony J. Hassall

Strange Country explores the themes of alienation and the failure of love in the novels, poetry and stories of internationally acclaimed Australian writer, Randolph Stow. This new edition has an up-to-date chronology and a revised bibliography.

Imagined Lives
A Study of David Malouf
Philip Neilsen (new edition)

This first book-length study of David Malouf focuses primarily on a literary analysis of his six novels, from *Johnno* (1975) to *Remembering Babylon* (1993). It also deals with his key poems, especially as they relate to the fiction.

Parnassus Mad Ward
Michael Dransfield and the New Australian Poetry
Livio Dobrez

Avant-garde Australian poetry from the sixties to the eighties is explored here
with flair and originality. This is the first book to place in perspective the New
Australian Poetry, product of the extraordinary generation of '68. Dobrez
discusses diverse poets against the broader background of cultural developments in Australia and abroad.

Flame and Shadow
A Study of Judith Wright's Poetry
Shirley Walker (new edition)

This book provides an accessible and indispensable complete analysis of the
poetry of Judith Wright, from *The Moving Image* (1946) to *Phantom Dreaming*
(1985). Shirley Walker places the poetry of one of Australia's most celebrated
poets in social and aesthetic perspective, and against a background of twentieth
century philosophical theories.

The Life and Opinions of Tom Collins
A Study of the Works of Joseph Furphy
Julian Croft

This first comprehensive study of the work of one of Australia's most important
and enigmatic writers serves as a pilgrim's guide to the difficulties and delights
of his work. Detailed readings of *Such is Life, Rigby's Romance, The Buln-Buln
and the Brolga,* Furphy's short stories, journalism and poetry are preceded by
a short biography, a critical survey and a discussion of the variant texts.
Winner: 1992 Walter McRae Russell Award

Gender, Politics and Fiction
Twentieth Century Australian Women's Novels
edited by Carole Ferrier (new edition)

This groundbreaking collection of essays brings a range of feminist and social
perspectives to selected twentieth-century Australian novels by women. The
new edition has an updated bibliography and introduction, and new essays on
contemporary issues.

Boundary Conditions
The Poetry of Gwen Harwood
Jennifer Strauss (new edition)

This critical study of the work and career of Gwen Harwood explores the
intellectual influences of music, philosophy and theology on the poetry, and
looks also at the politics of gender in publishing. The interlocked themes of
her writing are traced from Harwood's early poems through to *Present Tense*.

Fabricating the Self
The Fictions of Jessica Anderson
Elaine Barry (new edition)

Jessica Anderson is a writer who resists any easy labelling. Her technical virtuosity, range of narrative experimentation, and recurring themes are here discussed, through examination of all of her works, from *An Ordinary Lunacy* to *One of the Wattle Birds*.

The ALS Guide to Australian Writers
A Bibliography 1963-1995
Second edition
Edited by Martin Duwell, Marianne Ehrhardt and Carol Hetherington

This is the most comprehensive published guide to recent commentary about Australian literature, ranging over critical, biographical and historical articles, reviews and interviews. The second edition draws on, integrates and updates thirty-five years of the *Australian Literary Studies* Annual Bibliographies.

Dancing on Hot Macadam
Peter Carey's Fiction
Anthony J. Hassall (new edition)

This is the first comprehensive study of one of the world's most gifted and exciting writers. Alert to recent critical debates, it provides a lucid account of Peter Carey's fiction, its international literary context and critical reception.

That Shining Band
A Study of Australian Colonial Verse Tradition
Michael Ackland

This study illuminates a vital and forgotten part of Australia's cultural heritage by exploring the tradition of colonial verse that preceded the balladists of the 1890s. Neglected talents are rediscovered, particularly among women.

Helplessly Tangled in Female Arms and Legs
Elizabeth Jolley's Fictions
Paul Salzman

Elizabeth Jolley has been hailed as a major Australian writer since the publication of her two story collections, Five Acre Virgin and The Travelling Entertainer and her first novel, Palomino. This provocative study explores the critical reception of Jolley's fiction, and the varied interpretations it attracts.

Atomic Fiction
The Novels of David Ireland
Ken Gelder

This study discusses the fiction of one of Australia's most controversial writers, from *The Chantic Bird* to *A Woman of the Future*, exploring its "atomic" structure.

Australian Melodramas
Thomas Keneally's Fictions
Peter Pierce

Thomas Keneally is the writer most attuned to the melodramatic temper and genius of Australian literary culture. This first comprehensive critical study covers his plays and nonfiction as well as his novels.

The 1890s
Australian Literature and Literary Culture
Ken Stewart (ed.)

Fifteen lively essays by historians and literary critics re-evaluate the 1890s from the perspective of the 1990s. Contributors include Ken Stewart, Geoffrey Serle, Christopher Lee, Michael Sharkey, Mark Horgan, Julian Croft, Teresa Pagliano, Peter Pierce, John Docker, Veronica Kelly, Patricia Barton, Rick Hosking, Robert Dingley, Neville Meaney and Joy Hooton.

Kenneth Slessor
Critical Essays
Philip Mead (ed.)

This comprehensive collection of critical readings includes an authoritative introduction by Philip Mead, "classic" essays by Jack Lindsay, Vincent Buckley, Adrian Mitchell, Judith Wright, A.K. Thomson, John Docker and Andrew Taylor, and new essays by Greg Badcock, Peter Kirkpatrick, Julian Croft, Dennis Haskell, Leigh Dale and Kate Lilley, with a select bibliography and illustrations from newspapers and manuscripts.